American Medical Asso[c]

Physicians dedicated to the health of Americ[a]

MW01224858

Current Procedural Terminology

cpt® 2002

Caryn A. Anderson, RHIT, CCS
Michael Beebe, MS
Joyce A. Dalton
Catherine Duffy, RHIT, BS
Desiree Evans, AD
Rejina L. Glenn

DeHandro Hayden, BS
Grace M. Kotowicz, RN, BS
Elizabeth Lumakovska, RHIT, BS
Marie L. Mindeman, RHIT
Karen E. O'Hara, BS, CCS-P
Mary R. O'Heron, RHIA, CCS-P

Dan Reyes, BA
Desiree Rozell, MPA
Lianne Stancik, RHIT
Ada Walker
Arletrice A. Watkins, RHIA
Joan Zacharias, RHIT

AMA *press*

Professional ISBN: 1-57947-221-4
ISSN: 0276-8283

For questions regarding the use of CPT codes, please contact the American Medical Association CPT
Information and Education Services at 800 634-6922.

To purchase additional CPT products, contact the American Medical Association Customer Service
at 800 621-8335.

To request a license for distribution of products containing or reprinting CPT, please see our Web site
at *www.ama-assn.org/cpt* or contact the American Medical Association CPT Intellectual Property
Services, 515 N. State Street, Chicago, Illinois 60610, 312 464-5022.

AC25:0097-01:10/01

Foreword

Current Procedural Terminology, Fourth Edition (*CPT*®) is a listing of descriptive terms and identifying codes for reporting medical services and procedures performed by physicians. The purpose of the terminology is to provide a uniform language that will accurately describe medical, surgical, and diagnostic services, and will thereby provide an effective means for reliable nationwide communication among physicians, patients, and third parties. *CPT 2002* is the most recent revision of a work that first appeared in 1966.

CPT descriptive terms and identifying codes currently serve a wide variety of important functions in the field of medical nomenclature. CPT is the most widely accepted nomenclature for the reporting of physician procedures and services under government and private health insurance programs. CPT is also useful for administrative management purposes such as claims processing and for the development of guidelines for medical care review. The uniform language is likewise applicable to medical education and research by providing a useful basis for local, regional, and national utilization comparisons.

The changes that appear in this revision have been prepared by the CPT Editorial Panel with the assistance of physicians representing all specialties of medicine, and with important contributions from many third party payors and governmental agencies.

The American Medical Association trusts that this revision will continue the usefulness of its predecessors in identifying, describing, and coding medical, surgical, and diagnostic services.

Acknowledgements

Publication of each annual *CPT* represents many challenges and opportunities. From reconciling the many differences of opinion about the best way to describe a procedure, to last details on the placement of a semicolon, many individuals and organizations devote their energies and expertise to the preparation of this revision.

The editorial staff wishes to express sincere thanks to the many national medical specialty societies, health insurance organizations and agencies, and to the many individual physicians and other health professionals who have made contributions.

Thanks are due to Robert A. Musacchio, PhD, Sr VP, American Medical Association; Claudia Bonnell, Blue Cross and Blue Shield Association; Nelly Leon-Chisen, American Hospital Association; Thomas Musco, Health Insurance Association of America; and Sue Prophet, RHIA, American Health Information Management Association, for their invaluable assistance in enhancing CPT.

And finally, our gratitude to AMA Press of the American Medical Association for their assistance in producing the books, diskettes, magnetic tapes, and CD-ROMs that contain CPT, including Rosalyn Carlton, Senior Production Coordinator, Erin Kalitowski, Marketing Manager, Pat Lee, Technical Developmental Editor, Jean Roberts, Director, Production and Manufacturing, Elise Schumacher, Senior Acquisition Editor, Ronnie Summers, Senior Print Coordinator, Boon Ai Tan, Senior Production Coordinator, and Todd Feinstein, Application Developer.

AMA CPT Editorial Panel

Chair
Tracy R. Gordy, MD*
Vice-Chair
Karen R. Borman, MD*
James Adamson, Jr, MD**
Simon Philip Cohn, MD
Lee D. Eisenberg, MD
Helene M. Fearon, PT
Laurie Feinberg, MD
Blair C. Filler, MD
Diller B. Groff, MD
Samuel Hassenbusch, MD
Lee Harold Hilborne, MD
Glenn D. Littenberg, MD
Allen J. McBride, MD*
Gerald E. Silverstein, MD*
Stanley W. Stead, MD
William T. Thorwarth, MD
James A. Zalla, MD
Secretary
Michael Beebe, MS
* Member of the CPT Executive Committee
** New Panel Member August 2001

AMA CPT Advisory Committee

Donald W. Aaronson, MD
American Academy of Allergy, Asthma and Immunology
H. Christopher Alexander III, MD
American College of Physicians-American Society of Internal Medicine
Freda Arlow, MD
American College of Gastroenterology
Michael Ashcraft, MD
The Endocrine Society
C. Robert Baisden, MD
Beverly P. Nelson, MD*
United States and Canadian Academy of Pathology
Stephen N. Bauer, MD
College of American Pathologists
David I. Berland, MD
American Academy of Child and Adolescent Psychiatry
Robert L. Bree, MD*
*Society of Radiologists in Ultrasound****
Joel Brill, MD
American Gastroenterological Association
Boyd Buser, DO
American Osteopathic Association
Neil A. Busis, MD
American Association of Electrodiagnostic Medicine
Jeffery B. Carter, MD, DMD
American Dental Association
Jean M. Colandrea, MD
David C. Hoak, MD*
American Society of Cytopathology
Mark V. Connelly, MD
American Academy of Facial Plastic and Reconstructive Surgery

John P. Crow, MD
American Pediatric Surgical Association
David O. Davis, MD
Radiology Society of North America
Robin K. Dore, MD
David A. Cooley MD*
American College of Rheumatology
Gary S. Dorfman, MD
Society of Cardiovascular and Interventional Radiology
Charles Drueck III, MD*
*American Society of General Surgeons****
Philip N. Eskew Jr, MD
American College of Obstetricians and Gynecologists
Tom Faciszewski, MD
Francis P. Lagattuta, MD*
North American Spine Society
Morton H. Field, MD
American Association of Clinical Endocrinologists
Robert H. Haralson III, MD
American Orthopaedic Association
David B. Flannery, MD
American College of Medical Genetics
P. Franco, MD
American Sleep Disorders Association
Gary F. Gates, MD
American College of Nuclear Physicians
Bob W. Gayler, MD
Association of University Radiologists
Elizabeth Genovese, MD*
American College of Occupational and Environmental Medicine
Dean Gesme, MD
American Society of Clinical Oncology
Thomas G. Goergen, MD
Jonathan Breslau, MD**
American Roentgen Ray Society
Arvind K. Goyal, MD, MPH
American Association of Public Health Physicians
Gary N. Gross, MD
American College of Allergy, Asthma and Immunology
Richard J. Hamburger, MD
Renal Physicians Association
Curtis Hawkins, MD
Society for Investigative Dermatology
Charles A. Hawtrey, MD
Jeffrey A. Dann, MD*
American Urological Association, Inc.
George A. Hill, MD
John T. Queenan, MD*
American Society for Reproductive Medicine
Raymond V. Janevicius, MD
American Society of Plastic and Reconstructive Surgeons
Blake A. Johnson, MD
Robert A. Murray, MD*
American Society of Neuroradiology

Dean L. Johnston, MD
Paul R. Weiss, MD*
American Society for Aesthetic Surgery

Christine L. Kasser, MD
American Society of Addiction Medicine

Stephen S. Lane, MD
American Society of Cataract and Refractive Surgery

James M. Levett, MD
American Association for Thoracic Surgery

Sidney Levitsky, MD
Keith S. Naunheim, MD*
Society of Thoracic Surgeons

Thomas B. Logan, MD
Harold R. Wright, Jr, MD*
American Academy of Otolaryngic Allergy

Martin A. Luchtefeld, MD
American Society of Colon and Rectal Surgeons

A. Clinton MacKinney, MD, MS
American Academy of Family Physicians

Vivek Mahendru, MD
American Academy of Pain Medicine

Robert H. Maisel, MD
Triological Society

Scott Manaker, MD
American Thoracic Society

Kenneth A. McKusick, MD
Society of Nuclear Medicine

Gregory J. Mulford, MD
American Academy of Physical Medicine and Rehabilitation

Daniel J. Nagle, MD
American Society for Surgery of the Hand

Fred T. Nobrega, MD
American College of Preventive Medicine

Marc Nuwer, MD, PhD
American Academy of Neurology, American Clinical Neurophysiology Society

Walter J. O'Donohue, Jr, MD
American College of Chest Physicians

Walter J. Pedowitz, MD
American Orthopaedic Foot and Ankle Society

Gordon S. Perlmutter, MD
American College of Radiology

Neal Persky, MD
Peter A. Hollmann, MD*
American Geriatric Society

John T. Preskitt, MD
American College of Surgeons

H. J. Przybylo, MD
American Society of Anesthesiologists

Gregory J. Przybylski, MD
R. Patrick Jacob, MD*
Congress of Neurological Surgeons

Michael X. Repka, MD
American Academy of Ophthalmology

Nigel K. Roberts, MD
American Academy of Insurance Medicine

Nicholas L. Rock, MD (In Memoriam)
Society of Medical Consultants to the Armed Forces

Allison T. Vidimos, MD
American Society for Dermatologic Surgery

Demostene Romanucci, MD
Louis F. Alfano, Jr, MD*
American Society of Abdominal Surgeons

Richard A. Roski, MD
Jeffrey W. Cozzens, MD*
American Association of Neurological Surgeons

George A. Sample, MD
Society of Critical Care Medicine

Peter L. Sawchuk, MD
American College of Emergency Physicians

Chester W. Schmidt, Jr, MD
American Psychiatric Association

Charles J. Schulte III, MD
Joel F. Bradley, Jr, MD*
American Academy of Pediatrics

Alan E. Seyfer, MD
American Society of Maxillofacial Surgeons

Anton N. Sidawy, MD
International Society for Cardiovascular Surgery

Samuel M. Silver, MD, PhD
American Society of Hematology

Charles B. Slonim, MD
Contact Lens Association of Ophthalmologists

Dennis L. Stone, MD
American Medical Directors Association

Mark S. Synovec, MD
American Society of Clinical Pathologists

Susan K. Turney, MD
American Medical Group Association

Richard W. Waguespack, MD
American Academy of Otolaryngology Head and Neck Surgery

Paul E. Wallner, DO
American Society for Therapeutic Radiology and Oncology

Thomas J. Weatherall, Jr, MD
American College of Radiation Oncology

Eric G. Weiss, MD
Society of American Gastrointestinal Endoscopic Surgeons

William N. Werner, MD, MPH
American College of Medical Quality

Maurits J. Wiersema, MD
American Society for Gastrointestinal Endoscopy

Allan S. Wirtzer, MD
American Academy of Dermatology

Richard L. Wixson, MD
American Academy of Orthopaedic Surgeons

Robert Wolfson, MD, PhD
Harvey L. Nisenbaum, MD*
American Institute of Ultrasound in Medicine

Douglas L. Wood, MD
American College of Cardiology

*New Advisor June 2001
**New Advisor October 2001
***New Specialty June 2001

AMA Health Care Professionals Advisory Committee (HCPAC)

Tracy R. Gordy, MD, Co-Chair
AMA CPT Editorial Panel

Helene Fearon, PT, Co-Chair

Linda Botten, OTR, CHT
American Occupational Therapy Association

Patrick J. Cafferty, PA-C
American Academy of Physician Assistants

Rhea Cohn, PT
American Physical Therapy Association

R. Wayne Holland, EdD
American Speech-Language Hearing Association

K. Michael Larkin, OD (In Memoriam)
American Optometric Association

Craig S. Little, DC
American Chiropractic Association

Antonio Puente, PhD
American Psychological Association

Robert D. Sowell, DPM
American Podiatric Medical Association

Nelda Spyres, ACSW, LCSW
National Association of Social Workers

Ann M. Thrailkill, RN
American Nurses Association

Jane V. White, PhD, RD, FADA*
American Dietetic Association**
*New Advisor June 2001
**New Specialty June 2001

Notes

Contents

Contents

Introduction

Current Procedural Terminology, Fourth Edition (*CPT*®) is a systematic listing and coding of procedures and services performed by physicians. Each procedure or service is identified with a five-digit code. The use of CPT codes simplifies the reporting of services. With this coding and recording system, the procedure or service rendered by the physician is accurately identified.

Inclusion of a descriptor and its associated specific five-digit identifying code number in *CPT* is generally based upon the procedure being consistent with contemporary medical practice and being performed by many physicians in clinical practice in multiple locations. Inclusion in *CPT* does not represent endorsement by the American Medical Association of any particular diagnostic or therapeutic procedure. Inclusion or exclusion of a procedure does not imply any health insurance coverage or reimbursement policy.

The main body of the material is listed in six sections. Within each section are subsections with anatomic, procedural, condition, or descriptor subheadings. The procedures and services with their identifying codes are presented in numeric order with one exception—the entire **Evaluation and Management** section (99201-99499) has been placed at the beginning of the listed procedures. These items are used by most physicians in reporting a significant portion of their services. The **Medicine** (procedures) section now follows **Pathology and Laboratory.**

Section Numbers and Their Sequences

Evaluation and Management . . . . .99201 to 99499

Anesthesiology . . . . .00100 to 01999, 99100 to 99140

Surgery . . . . .10021 to 69990

Radiology (Including Nuclear Medicine and Diagnostic Ultrasound) . . . . .70010 to 79999

Pathology and Laboratory . . . . .80048 to 89399

Medicine (except Anesthesiology) . . .90281 to 99199, 99500-99569

The first and last code numbers and the subsection name of the items appear at the top of each page (eg, "11000-11313 Surgery/Integumentary System"). The continuous pagination of *CPT* is found on the lower, outer margin of each page along with the section name.

Instructions for Use of CPT

Select the name of the procedure or service that accurately identifies the service performed. ▶Do not select a CPT code that merely approximates the service provided. If no such procedure or service exists, then report the service using the appropriate unlisted procedure or service code.◀ In surgery, it may be an operation; in medicine, a diagnostic or therapeutic procedure; in radiology, a radiograph. Other additional procedures performed or pertinent special services are also listed. When necessary, any modifying or extenuating circumstances are added. Any service or procedure should be adequately documented in the medical record.

It is important to recognize that the listing of a service or procedure and its code number in a specific section of this book does not restrict its use to a specific specialty group. Any procedure or service in any section of this book may be used to designate the services rendered by any qualified physician ▶or other qualified health care professional.◀

Format of the Terminology

CPT procedure terminology has been developed as stand-alone descriptions of medical procedures. However, some of the procedures in *CPT* are not printed in their entirety but refer back to a common portion of the procedure listed in a preceding entry. This is evident when an entry is followed by one or more indentations. This is done in an effort to conserve space.

Example

25100   Arthrotomy, wrist joint; with biopsy

25105   with synovectomy

Note that the common part of code 25100 (that part before the semicolon) should be considered part of code 25105. Therefore the full procedure represented by code 25105 should read:

25105   Arthrotomy, wrist joint; for synovectomy

Requests to Update CPT

The effectiveness of *Current Procedural Terminology* (*CPT*™) is dependent upon constant updating to reflect changes in medical practice. This can only be accomplished through the interest and timely suggestions of practicing physicians, medical specialty societies, state medical associations, and other organizations and agencies. Accordingly, the American Medical Association welcomes correspondence, inquiries, and suggestions concerning old and new procedures, as well as other matters such as codes and indices.

For suggestions concerning the introduction of new procedures, or the coding, deleting, or revising of procedures contained in *CPT 2002*, correspondence requesting an application for coding change should be directed to:

CPT Editorial Research & Development
American Medical Association
515 North State Street
Chicago, Illinois 60610

▶Coding change request forms to introduce new procedures or to delete or revise procedures already in CPT are also available at the AMA/CPT website http://www.ama-assn.org/ama/pub/article/3866-3846.html.◀

All proposed additions to, or modifications of, *CPT 2002* will be by decision of the CPT Editorial Panel after consultation with appropriate medical specialty societies.

Guidelines

Specific "Guidelines" are presented at the beginning of each of the six sections. These guidelines define items that are necessary to appropriately interpret and report the procedures and services contained in that section. For example, in the **Medicine** section, specific instructions are provided for handling unlisted services or procedures, special reports, and supplies and materials provided. Guidelines also provide explanations regarding terms that apply only to a particular section. For instance, **Surgery Guidelines** provides an explanation of the use of the star, while in **Radiology**, the unique term, "radiological supervision and interpretation" is defined.

Starred Procedures

The star "∗" is used to identify certain surgical procedures. A description of this reporting mechanism will be found in the **Surgery Guidelines**.

Modifiers

A modifier provides the means by which the reporting physician can indicate that a service or procedure that has been performed has been altered by some specific circumstance but not changed in its definition or code. The judicious application of modifiers obviates the necessity for separate procedure listings that may describe the modifying circumstance. Modifiers may be used to indicate to the recipient of a report that:

- A service or procedure has both a professional and technical component.

- A service or procedure was performed by more than one physician and/or in more than one location.

- A service or procedure has been increased or reduced.

- Only part of a service was performed.

- An adjunctive service was performed.

- A bilateral procedure was performed.

- A service or procedure was provided more than once.

- Unusual events occurred.

Example

A physician providing diagnostic or therapeutic radiology services, ultrasound or nuclear medicine services in a hospital would use either modifier '-26' or 09926 to report the professional component.

73090-26 = Professional component only for an x-ray of the forearm

or

73090 AND 09926 = Professional component only for an x-ray of the forearm

Example

Two surgeons may be required to manage a specific surgical problem. When two surgeons work together as primary surgeons performing distinct part(s) of a procedure, each surgeon should report his/her distinct operative work by adding the modifier '-62' to the procedure code ▶and any associated code(s) for that procedure as long as both surgeons continue to work together as primary surgeons◀. Each surgeon should report the co-surgery once using the same procedure code. The modifier '-62' or the alternative modifier five-digit code 09962 would be applicable. For instance, a neurological surgeon and an otolaryngologist are working as co-surgeons in performing transphenoidal excision of a pituitary neoplasm.

61548-62 = Hypophysectomy or excision of pitiutary tumor, transnasal or transseptal approach, nonstereotactic + two surgeons modifier

or

61548 AND 09962 = Hypophysectomy or excision of pituitary tumor, transnasal or transseptal approach, nonstereotactic + two surgeons modifier

AND the second surgeon would report:

61548-62 = Hypophysectomy or excision of pitiutary tumor, transnasal or transseptal approach, nonstereotactic + two surgeons modifier

or

61548 AND 09962 = Hypophysectomy or excision of pitiutary tumor, transnasal or transseptal approach, nonstereotactic + two surgeons modifier

If additional procedure(s) (including add-on procedure(s)) are performed during the same surgical session, separate code(s) may ▶also◀ be reported with the modifier '-62' added. ▶Modifier code 09962 may be used as an alternative to modifier '-62'.◀ **Note:** If a co-surgeon acts as an assistant in the performance of additional procedure(s) during the same surgical session, those services may be reported using separate procedure code(s) with the modifier '-80' or modifier '-82' added, as appropriate. A complete listing of modifiers is found in Appendix A.

Unlisted Procedure or Service

It is recognized that there may be services or procedures performed by physicians that are not found in *CPT*. Therefore, a number of specific code numbers have been designated for reporting unlisted procedures. When an unlisted procedure number is used, the service or procedure should be described. Each of these unlisted procedural code numbers (with the appropriate accompanying topical entry) relates to a specific section of the book and is presented in the Guidelines of that section.

Special Report

A service that is rarely provided, unusual, variable, or new may require a special report in determining medical appropriateness of the service. Pertinent information should include an adequate definition or description of the nature, extent, and need for the procedure; and the time, effort, and equipment necessary to provide the service. Additional items which may be included are: complexity of symptoms, final diagnosis, pertinent physical findings, diagnostic and therapeutic procedures, concurrent problems, and follow-up care.

Code Changes

A summary listing of additions, deletions, and revisions applicable to *CPT 2002* is found in Appendix B. New procedure numbers added to *CPT* are identified throughout the text with the symbol "●" placed before the code number. In instances where a code revision has resulted in a substantially altered procedure descriptor, the symbol "▲" is placed before the code number. The symbols "► ◄" are used to indicate new and revised text other than the procedure descriptors. CPT add-on codes are annotated by a "✚" symbol and are listed in **Appendix E**. The "⊘" symbol is used to identify codes that are exempt from the use of modifier '-51', but have not been designated as CPT add-on procedures/services. A list of codes exempt from modifier '-51' usage is included in **Appendix F**.

Alphabetical Reference Index

A new, expanded alphabetical index is found in the back of the book. It includes listings by procedure and anatomic site. Procedures and services commonly known by their eponyms or other designations are also included.

CPT in Electronic Formats

CPT 2002 procedure codes and descriptors are also available on magnetic computer tapes, diskettes, and CD-ROM in various formats. For more information call 800 621-8335.

Visit CPT on the AMA Website
http://www.ama-assn.org/cpt

CPT Assistant Newsletter and CPT Changes 2000, 2001, and 2002 References

In instances where a code has been referenced in either the *CPT Assistant,* the AMA's authoritative coding newsletter, or the *CPT Changes* 2000, 2001, and 2002 books, the symbol "➋" is placed before the code number. For more information on these publications, visit the AMA Press website at *www.amapress.org* or call 800 621-8335.

Illustrated Anatomical and Procedural Review

It is essential that coders have a thorough understanding of medical terminology and anatomy to code accurately. The following section reviewing the basics of vocabulary and anatomy can be used as a quick reference to help you with your coding. It is not intended as a replacement for up-to-date medical dictionaries and anatomy texts, which are essential tools for accurate coding.

Prefixes, Suffixes, and Roots

Although medical terminology may seem complex, many medical terms can be broken into component parts which makes them easier to understand. Many of these terms are derived from Latin or Greek words, but some include the names of physicians.

Prefixes are word parts that appear at the beginning of a word and modify their meaning; suffixes are found at the end of words. By learning what various prefixes and suffixes mean, it is possible to decipher the meaning of a word quickly. The following lists are a quick reference for some common prefixes and suffixes.

Numbers

Prefix	Meaning	Example
mono, uni	one	monocyte, unilateral
bi	two	bilateral
tri	three	triad
quadr	four	quadriplegia
hex, sex	six	hexose
diplo	double	diplopia

Surgical Procedures

Suffix	Meaning	Example
-centesis	puncture a cavity to remove fluid	amniocentesis
-ectomy	surgical removal (excision)	appendectomy
-ostomy	a new permanent opening	colostomy
-otomy	cutting into (incision)	tracheotomy
-orrhaphy	surgical repair/suture	herniorrhaphy
-opexy	surgical fixation	nephropexy
-oplasty	surgical repair	rhinoplasty
-otripsy	crushing, destroying	lithotripsy

Conditions

Prefix	Meaning	Example
ambi	both	ambidextrous
aniso	unequal	aniscoria
dys	bad, painful, difficult	dysphoria
eu	good, normal	euthanasia
hetero	different	heterogeneous
homo	same	homogeneous
hyper	excessive, above	hypergastric
hypo	deficient, below	hypogastric
iso	equal, same	isotonic
mal	bad, poor	malaise
megalo	large	megalocardia

Conditions (contd.)

Suffix	Meaning	Example
-algia	pain	neuralgia
-asthenia	weakness	myasthenia
-emia	blood	anemia
-iasis	condition of	amobiasis
-itis	inflammation	appendicitis
-lysis	destruction, break down	hemolysis
-lytic	destroy, break down	hemolytic
-oid	like	lipoid
-oma	tumor	carcinoma
-opathy	disease of	arthropathy
-orrhagia	hemorrhage	menorrhagia
-orrhea	flow or discharge	amenorrhea
-osis	abnormal condition of	tuberculosis
-paresis	weakness	hemiparesis
-plasia	growth	hyperplasia
-plegia	paralysis	paraplegia
-pnea	breathing	apnea

Directions/Positions

Prefix	Meaning	Example
ab	away from	abduction
ad	toward	adduction
ecto, exo	outside	ectopic, exocrine
endo	within	endoscope
epi	upon	epigastric
infra	below, under	infrastructure
ipsi	same	ipsilateral
meso	middle	mesopexy
meta	after, beyond, transformation	metastasis
peri	surrounding	pericardium
retro	behind, back	retroversion
trans	across, through	transvaginal

Word	Meaning
anterior or ventral	at or near the front surface of the body
posterior or dorsal	at or near the back surface of the body
superior	above
inferior	below
lateral	side

Directions/Positions (contd.)

Word	Meaning
distal	farthest from center
proximal	nearest to center
medial	middle
supine	face up or palm up
prone	face down or palm down
sagittal	vertical body plane, divides the body into equal right and left sides
transverse	horizontal body plane, divides the body into top and bottom sections
coronal	vertical body plane, divides the body into front and back sections

Additional References

For best coding results, you will need to use other reference materials in addition to your coding books. These references include a medical dictionary and one or more anatomy books and can be purchased from the American Medical Association by calling 800 621-8335.

Medical Dictionaries

Merriam Webster's Medical Desk Dictionary. Springfield, MA: Merriam Webster, 1998 OP941493

Stedman's Medical Dictionary. 27th ed. Baltimore, MD: Williams & Wilkins: 2000 OP982900

Anatomy Reference

Netter, FH. *Atlas of Human Anatomy.* East Hanover, NJ: Novartis, 1998 OP936798

List of Illustrations

Anatomical Illustrations

Procedural Illustrations

Procedural Illustrations

CPT Code(s)	Title
33517–33530	Coronary Artery Bypass—Combined Arterial—Venous Grafting
33517–33530	Coronary Artery Bypass—Sequential Combined Arterial-Venous Grafting
33820	Patent Ductus Arteriosus
34831	Endovascular Repair of Abdominal Aortic Aneurysm
35371–35372	Thromboendarterectomy
35473	Transluminal Balloon Angioplasty
35571	Bypass Graft, Vein
35600	Harvest of Upper Extremity Artery
36488	Placement of Central Venous Catheter
36489	Placement of Central Venous Catheter
36533	Implantable Venous Access Device
36821	Arteriovenous Anastomosis, Direct
36822	Insertion of Cannulas for Prolonged Extracorporeal Circulation Membrane Oxygenation (ECMO)
36825–36830	Arteriovenous Fistula
37700	Ligation and Division of Long Saphenous Vein
38230	Bone Marrow Harvesting for Transplantation
43260	Endoscopic Retrograde Cholangiopancreatography (ERCP)
43324	Nissen Fundoplasty
43750	Gastrostomy Tube Placement
43846	Gastric Bypass for Morbid Obesity
44140	Colectomy, Partial
44160	Colectomy with Removal of Terminal Ileum and Ileocolostomy
45378	Colonoscopy
47562	Laparoscopic Cholecystectomy
49320	Laparoscopy
50020	Drainage of Renal Abscess
50060–50075	Nephrolithotomy with Calculus Removal
50392	Introduction of Catheter into Renal Pelvis
50545	Laparoscopic Radical Nephrectomy
50546	Laparoscopic Nephrectomy
50590	Lithotripsy
50605	Indwelling Ureteral Stent
50820	Ureteroileal Conduit
50947	Laparoscopic Ureteroneocystostomy
51990	Laparoscopic Sling Suspension Urinary Incontinence
52005	Cystourethroscopy with Ureteral Catheterization
52601	Transurethral Resection of Prostate, Complete
52648	Contact Laser Vaporization of Prostate
54692	Laparoscopic Orchiopexy
57106	Vaginectomy, Partial Removal of Vaginal Wall
57111	Vaginectomy, Complete Removal of Vaginal Wall (Radical Vaginectomy)

CPT Code(s)	Title
59150	Laparoscopic Treatment of Ectopic Pregnancy
60225	Thyroid Lobectomy
60650	Laparoscopic Adrenalectomy
61862, 61885	Placement of Cranial Neurostimulator
62223	Cerebrospinal Fluid (CSF) Shunt (Ventricular Peritoneal)
62362	Intrathecal or Epidural Drug Infusion Pump Implantation
63005	Lumbar Laminectomy
63650	Percutaneous Implantation of Neurostimulator Electrodes
63655	Placement of Neurostimulator Electrodes through Laminectomy
64573, 61885	Implantation Neurostimulator Electrodes, Cranial Nerve (Vagal Nerve Stimulation)
65450	Cryotherapy of Lesion on Cornea
67027	Intravitreal Drug Delivery System
67107	Repair of Retinal Detachment
67311–67350	Extraocular Muscles of Right Eye
67311–67312	Strabismus Surgery—Horizontal Muscles
67314–67316	Strabismus Surgery—Vertical Muscles
67320	Transposition Procedure
67335	Strabismus Surgery—Adjustable Sutures
67820–67825	Trichiasis
68761	Closure of Lacrimal Punctum by Plug
68815	Probing of Nasolacrimal Duct
69433–69436	Tympanostomy
69635–69646	Tympanoplasty
69930	Cochlear Device Implantation
69990	Operating Microscope
75600–75630	Aortography
75660–75680	Angiography, Carotid Artery
75820–75822	Venography
91032	Esophageal Acid Reflux Test
91105	Gastric Intubation
92235	Fluoroscein Angiography
92978	Intravascular Ultrasound (Coronary Vessel or Graft)
92982	Percutaneous Transluminal Coronary Angioplasty (PTCA)
93312–93318	Transesophageal Echocardiography (TEE)
93501	Right Heart Catheterization
93508	Coronary Angiography without Concomitant Left Heart Catheterization
93510	Left Heart Catheterization
93571	Intravascular Distal Blood Flow Velocity

Figure 1A
Body Planes — 3/4 View

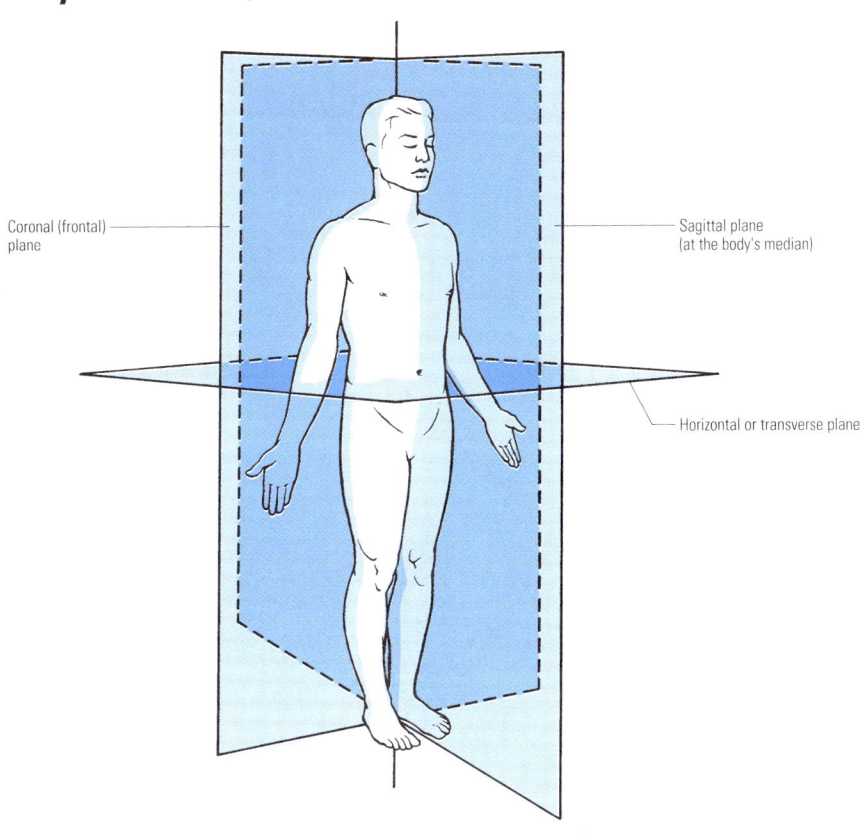

Coronal (frontal) plane

Sagittal plane (at the body's median)

Horizontal or transverse plane

Figure 1B
Body Aspects — Side View

Superior (cranial) aspect

Posterior aspect

Anterior aspect

Dorsal surface of hand

Palmar surface of hand

Dorsal surface of foot

Plantar surface of foot

Inferior aspect

Figure 1C
Body Planes — Front View

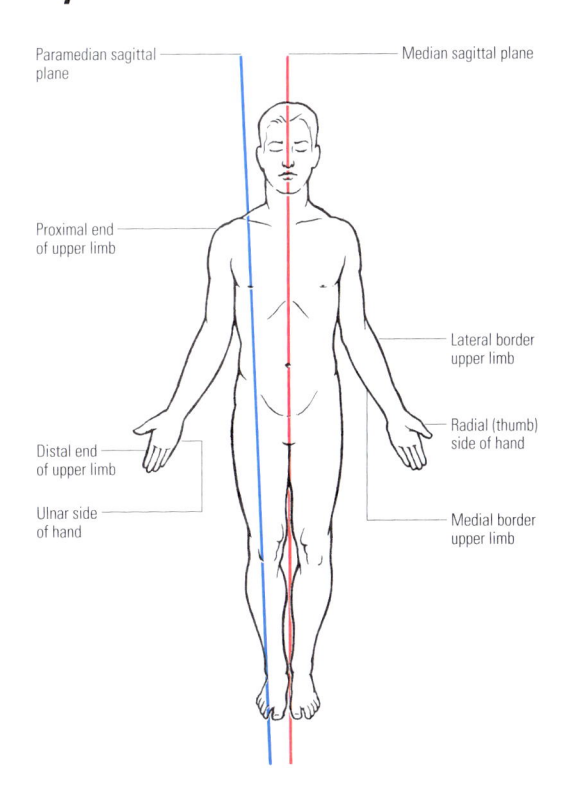

Paramedian sagittal plane

Median sagittal plane

Proximal end of upper limb

Lateral border upper limb

Radial (thumb) side of hand

Distal end of upper limb

Ulnar side of hand

Medial border upper limb

Figure 2
Structure of Skin

Hair shaft

Hair root

Epidermis

Sebaceous gland

Dermis

Nerve endings

Hair bulb

Subcutaneous tissue

Sweat gland

Cutaneous nerve

Blood vessels

Figure 3
Skeletal System

Skull

Maxilla

Mandible

Cervical vertebra

First rib

Clavicle

Scapula

Sternum

Humerus

Lumbar vertebra

Ilium

Radius

Sacrum

Ulna

Pubis

Ischium

Carpals

Metacarpals

Phalanges

Femur

Patella

Tibia

Fibula

Tarsals

Metatarsals

Phalanges

Figure 4A
Muscular System — Front

Figure 4B
Muscular System — Back

Figure 5
Respiratory System

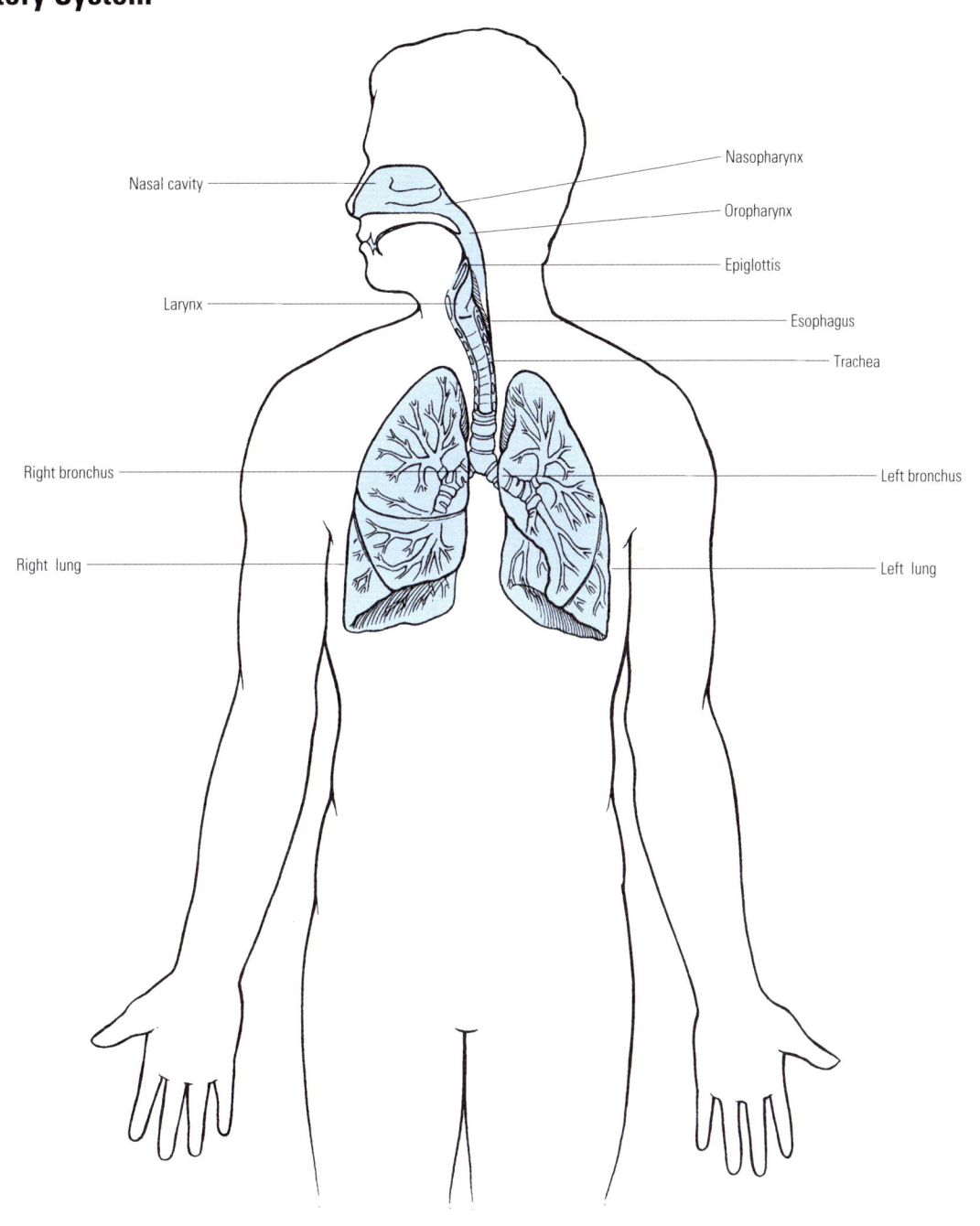

- Nasal cavity
- Nasopharynx
- Oropharynx
- Epiglottis
- Larynx
- Esophagus
- Trachea
- Right bronchus
- Left bronchus
- Right lung
- Left lung

Figure 6A
Circulatory System — Arteries

Superficial temporal a.
Posterior auricular a.
Common carotid a.
Subclavian a.
Brachiocephalic trunk
Axillary a.
Deep brachial a.
Brachial a.
Aorta
Radial a.
Interosseous a.
Ulnar a.
Deep palmar arch
Superficial palmar arch
Descending genicular a.

External carotid a.
Internal carotid a.
Vertebral a.
Aorta and arch
Pulmonary a.
Cardiac a.
Thoracic aorta
Celiac trunk
Superior mesenteric a.
Renal a.
Gonadal a.
Inferior mesenteric a.
Common iliac a.
External iliac a.
Internal iliac a.
Deep femoral a.
Femoral a.
Popliteal a.
Anterior tibial a.
Peroneal a.
Posterior tibial a.

Figure 6B
Circulatory System — Veins

Superficial temporal v.
External jugular v.
Subclavian v.
Brachiocephalic v.
Axillary v.
Brachial v.
Cephalic v.
Basilic v.
Median cubital v.
Medial antebrachial v.
Superficial venous palmar arch
Small saphenous v.

Facial v.
Internal jugular v.
Superior vena cava
Hepatic v.
Renal v.
Gonadal v.
Inferior vena cava
Common iliac v.
Internal iliac v.
External iliac v.
Deep femoral v.
Femoral v.
Great saphenous v.
Popliteal v.
Anterior tibial v.
Posterior tibial v.
Dorsal venous arch

Figure 7
Lymphatic System

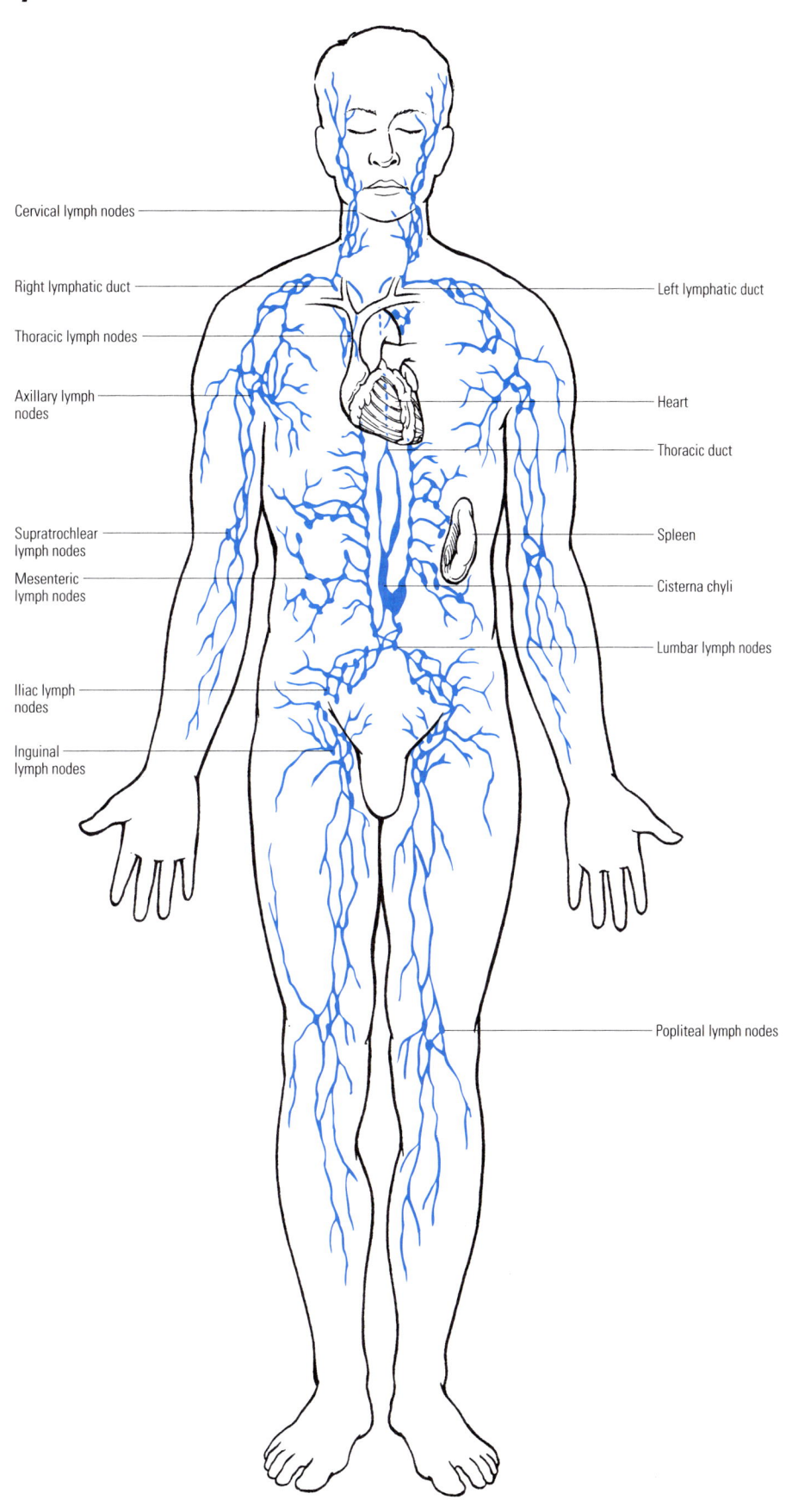

Cervical lymph nodes

Right lymphatic duct

Thoracic lymph nodes

Axillary lymph nodes

Supratrochlear lymph nodes

Mesenteric lymph nodes

Iliac lymph nodes

Inguinal lymph nodes

Left lymphatic duct

Heart

Thoracic duct

Spleen

Cisterna chyli

Lumbar lymph nodes

Popliteal lymph nodes

Figure 8
Digestive System

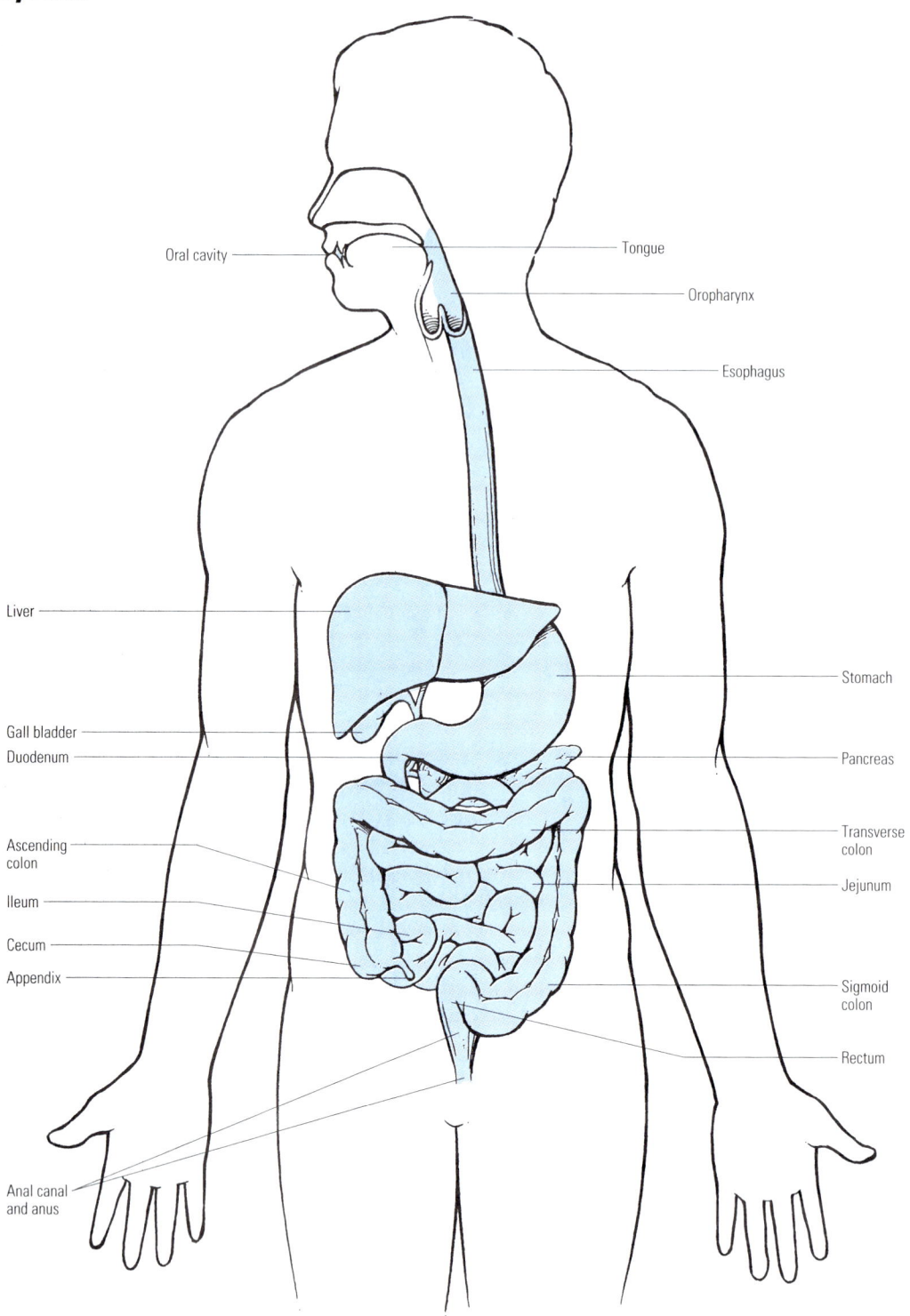

Figure 9
Urinary System

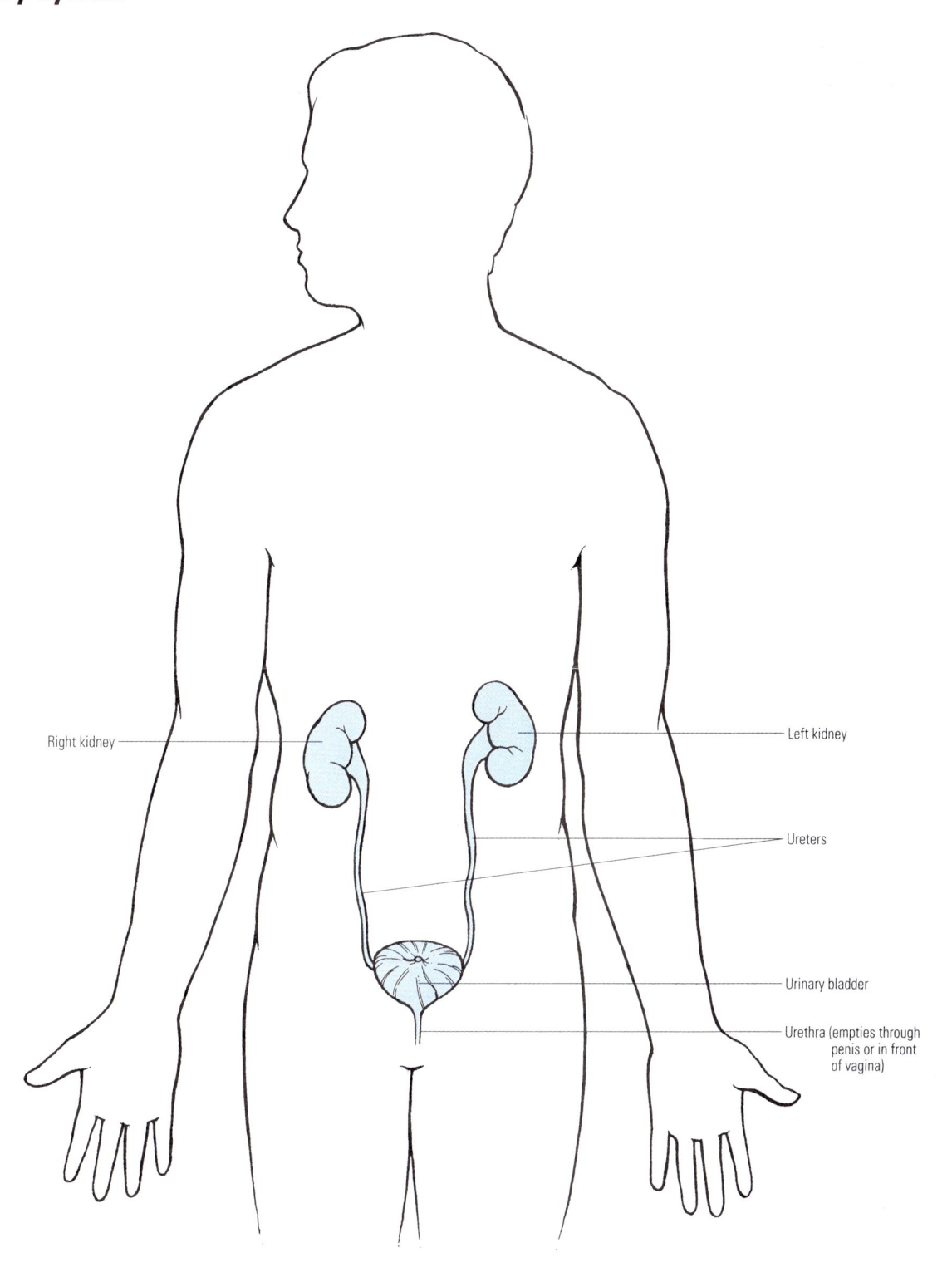

Right kidney

Left kidney

Ureters

Urinary bladder

Urethra (empties through
penis or in front
of vagina)

Figure 10
Male Genital System

Deferent duct

Urinary bladder and cavity

Corpus cavernosa

Corpus spongiosum

Penis

Glans penis

Prepuce

Seminal vesicle

Ejaculatory duct

Prostate gland

Spermatic cord and deferent duct

Epididymus

Testes

Scrotum

Figure 11
Female Genital System

Uterine tube

Ligament of ovary

Body of uterus and uterine cavity

Fundus of uterus

Ampulla

Infundibulum with fimbriae

Ovary

Cervix and cervical canal

Vagina

Figure 12
Endocrine System

Figure 13
Nervous System

Brain

Cerebellum

Spinal cord

Brachial plexus

Musculocutaneous n.

Radial n.

Intercostal nerves
(with ribs)

Subcostal nerve
(12th thoracic)

Lumbar plexus

Median n.

Iliohypogastric n.

Ilioinguinal n.

Deep branch of radial n.

Lat. femoral cutaneous n.

Genitofemoral n.

Superficial branch of radial n.

Obturator n.

Sacral plexus

Femoral n.

Pudendal n.

Sciatic n.

Ulnar n.

Muscular branches
of femoral n.

Saphenous n.

Tibial n.

Common peroneal n.

Deep peroneal n.

Superficial peroneal n.

Figure 14
Skull

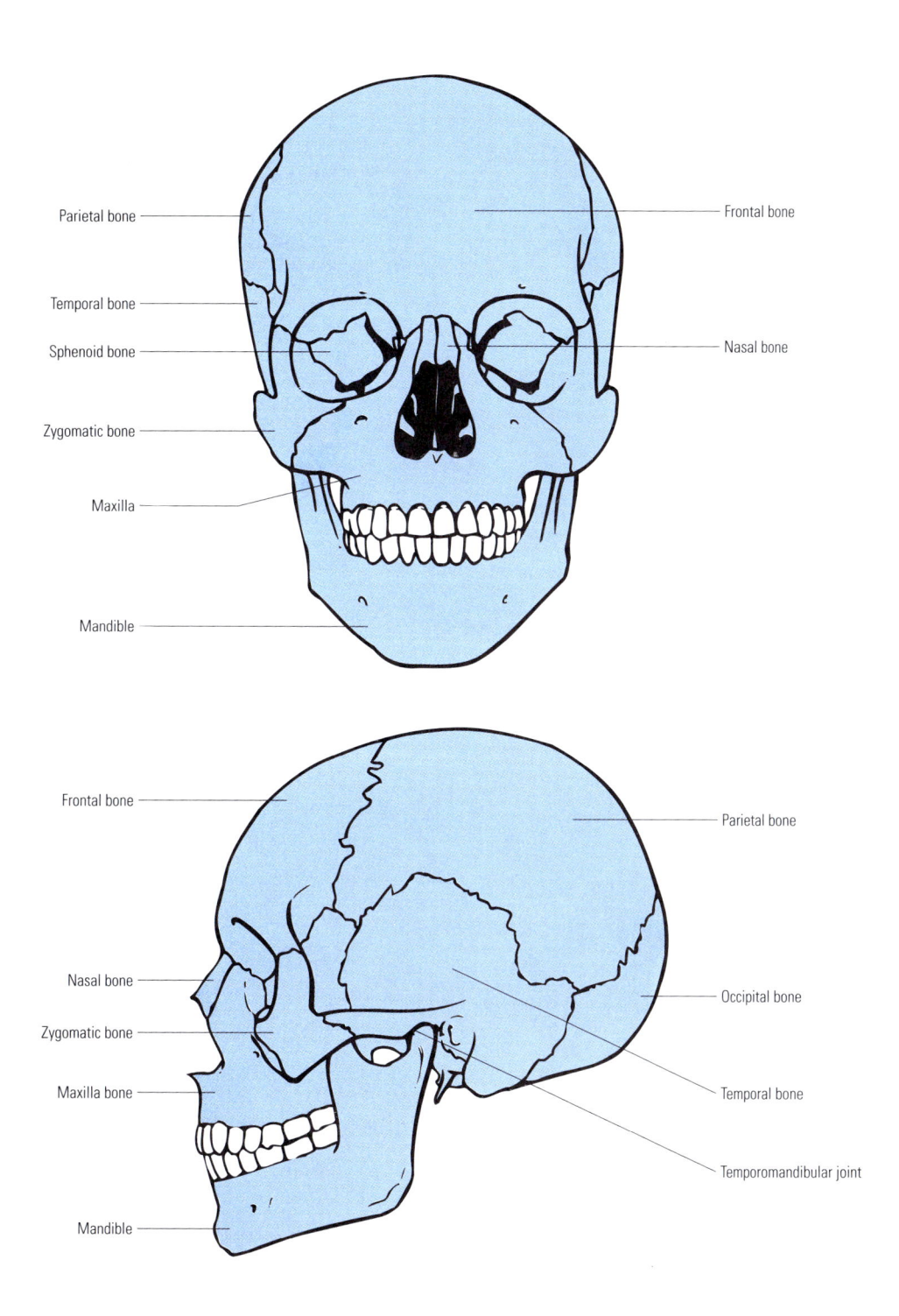

Figure 15
Bones, Muscles, and Tendons of Hand

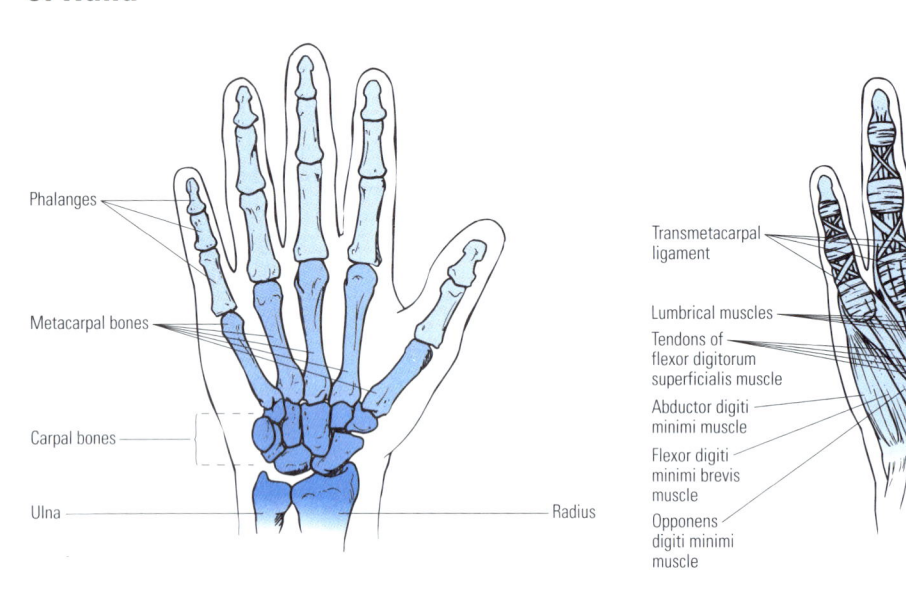

Figure 16
Bones and Muscles of Foot

Figure 17A
Brain Anatomy

Figure 17B
Saggital Section of Brain and Brain Stem

Figure 18
Eyeball

Transverse (horizontal) section of eyeball

Figure 19
Ear

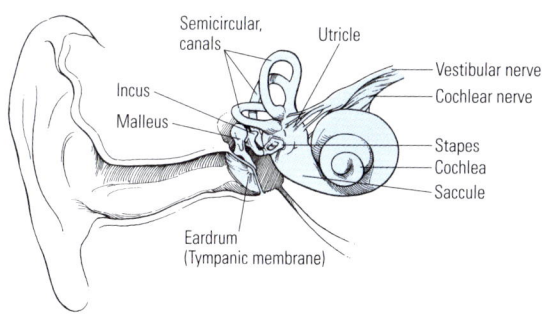

Figure 20
Paranasal Sinuses

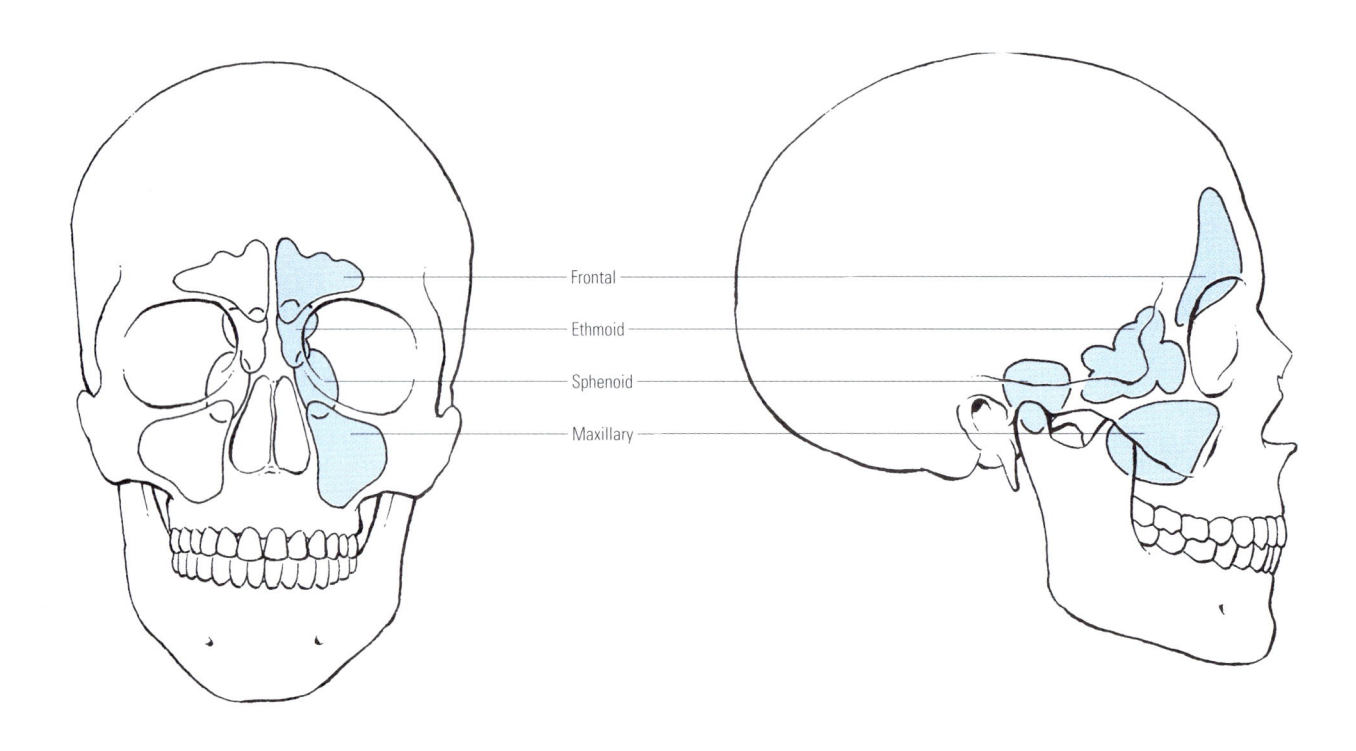

Frontal
Ethmoid
Sphenoid
Maxillary

Figure 21
Cardiac Anatomy

Superior vena cava
Right pulmonary artery
Pulmonary valve
Location of sinoatrial valve
Location of atrioventricular valve
Right atrium
Tricuspid valve
Right ventricle
Inferior vena cava

Aorta
Pulmonary artery
Left atrium
Aortic valve
Mitral valve
Left ventricle
Ventricular septum
Descending thoracic aorta

Evaluation and Management (E/M) Services Guidelines

In addition to the information presented in the **Introduction,** several other items unique to this section are defined or identified here.

Classification of Evaluation and Management (E/M) Services

The E/M section is divided into broad categories such as office visits, hospital visits, and consultations. Most of the categories are further divided into two or more subcategories of E/M services. For example, there are two subcategories of office visits (new patient and established patient) and there are two subcategories of hospital visits (initial and subsequent). The subcategories of E/M services are further classified into levels of E/M services that are identified by specific codes. This classification is important because the nature of physician work varies by type of service, place of service, and the patient's status.

The basic format of the levels of E/M services is the same for most categories. First, a unique code number is listed. Second, the place and/or type of service is specified, eg, office consultation. Third, the content of the service is defined, eg, comprehensive history and comprehensive examination. (See "Levels of E/M Services," page 2, for details on the content of E/M services.) Fourth, the nature of the presenting problem(s) usually associated with a given level is described. Fifth, the time typically required to provide the service is specified. (A detailed discussion of time is provided on page 3.)

Definitions of Commonly Used Terms

Certain key words and phrases are used throughout the E/M section. The following definitions are intended to reduce the potential for differing interpretations and to increase the consistency of reporting by physicians in differing specialties.

New and Established Patient

Solely for the purposes of distinguishing between new and established patients, **professional services** are those face-to-face services rendered by a physician and reported by a specific CPT code(s). A new patient is one who has not received any professional services from the physician or another physician of the same specialty who belongs to the same group practice, within the past three years.

An established patient is one who has received professional services from the physician or another physician of the same specialty who belongs to the same group practice, within the past three years.

In the instance where a physician is on call for or covering for another physician, the patient's encounter will be classified as it would have been by the physician who is not available.

No distinction is made between new and established patients in the emergency department. E/M services in the emergency department category may be reported for any new or established patient who presents for treatment in the emergency department.

Chief Complaint

A concise statement describing the symptom, problem, condition, diagnosis or other factor that is the reason for the encounter, usually stated in the patient's words.

Concurrent Care

Concurrent care is the provision of similar services, eg, hospital visits, to the same patient by more than one physician on the same day. When concurrent care is provided, no special reporting is required. Modifier '-75' has been deleted.

Counseling

Counseling is a discussion with a patient and/or family concerning one or more of the following areas:

- diagnostic results, impressions, and/or recommended diagnostic studies;
- prognosis;
- risks and benefits of management (treatment) options;
- instructions for management (treatment) and/or follow-up;

- importance of compliance with chosen management (treatment) options;
- risk factor reduction; and
- patient and family education.

(For psychotherapy, see 90804-90857)

Family History

A review of medical events in the patient's family that includes significant information about:

- the health status or cause of death of parents, siblings, and children;
- specific diseases related to problems identified in the Chief Complaint or History of the Present Illness, and/or System Review;
- diseases of family members which may be hereditary or place the patient at risk.

History of Present Illness

A chronological description of the development of the patient's present illness from the first sign and/or symptom to the present. This includes a description of location, quality, severity, timing, context, modifying factors and associated signs and symptoms significantly related to the presenting problem(s).

Levels of E/M Services

Within each category or subcategory of E/M service, there are three to five levels of E/M services available for reporting purposes. Levels of E/M services are **not** interchangeable among the different categories or subcategories of service. For example, the first level of E/M services in the subcategory of office visit, new patient, does not have the same definition as the first level of E/M services in the subcategory of office visit, established patient.

The levels of E/M services include examinations, evaluations, treatments, conferences with or concerning patients, preventive pediatric and adult health supervision, and similar medical services, such as the determination of the need and/or location for appropriate care. Medical screening includes the history, examination, and medical decision making required to determine the need and/or location for appropriate care and treatment of the patient (eg, office and other outpatient setting, emergency department, nursing facility, etc.). The levels of E/M services encompass the wide variations in skill, effort, time, responsibility and medical knowledge required for the prevention or diagnosis and treatment of illness or injury and the promotion of optimal health. Each level of E/M services may be used by all physicians.

The descriptors for the levels of E/M services recognize seven components, six of which are used in defining the levels of E/M services. These components are:

- history;
- examination;

- medical decision making;
- counseling;
- coordination of care;
- nature of presenting problem; and
- time.

The first three of these components (history, examination, and medical decision making) are considered the **key** components in selecting a level of E/M services. (See "Determine the Extent of History Obtained," page 5.)

The next three components (counseling, coordination of care, and the nature of the presenting problem) are considered **contributory** factors in the majority of encounters. Although the first two of these contributory factors are important E/M services, it is not required that these services be provided at every patient encounter.

Coordination of care with other providers or agencies without a patient encounter on that day is reported using the case management codes.

The final component, time, is discussed in detail (see page 3).

Any specifically identifiable procedure (ie, identified with a specific CPT code) performed on or subsequent to the date of initial or subsequent "E/M Services" should be reported separately.

The actual performance and/or interpretation of diagnostic tests/studies ordered during a patient encounter are not included in the levels of E/M services. Physician performance of diagnostic tests/studies for which specific CPT codes are available may be reported separately, in addition to the appropriate E/M code. The physician's interpretation of the results of diagnostic tests/studies (ie, professional component) with preparation of a separate distinctly identifiable signed written report may also be reported separately, using the appropriate CPT code with the modifier '-26' appended.

The physician may need to indicate that on the day a procedure or service identified by a CPT code was performed, the patient's condition required a significant separately identifiable E/M service above and beyond other services provided or beyond the usual preservice and postservice care associated with the procedure that was performed. The E/M service may be caused or prompted by the symptoms or condition for which the procedure and/or service was provided. This circumstance may be reported by adding the modifier '-25' to the appropriate level of E/M service. As such, different diagnoses are not required for reporting of the procedure and the E/M services on the same date.

Nature of Presenting Problem

A presenting problem is a disease, condition, illness, injury, symptom, sign, finding, complaint, or other reason for encounter, with or without a diagnosis being established at the time of the encounter. The E/M codes recognize five types of presenting problems that are defined as follows:

Minimal: A problem that may not require the presence of the physician, but service is provided under the physician's supervision.

Self-limited or minor: A problem that runs a definite and prescribed course, is transient in nature, and is not likely to permanently alter health status OR has a good prognosis with management/compliance.

Low severity: A problem where the risk of morbidity without treatment is low; there is little to no risk of mortality without treatment; full recovery without functional impairment is expected.

Moderate severity: A problem where the risk of morbidity without treatment is moderate; there is moderate risk of mortality without treatment; uncertain prognosis OR increased probability of prolonged functional impairment.

High severity: A problem where the risk of morbidity without treatment is high to extreme; there is a moderate to high risk of mortality without treatment OR high probability of severe, prolonged functional impairment.

Past History

A review of the patient's past experiences with illnesses, injuries, and treatments that includes significant information about:

- prior major illnesses and injuries;
- prior operations;
- prior hospitalizations;
- current medications;
- allergies (eg, drug, food);
- age appropriate immunization status;
- age appropriate feeding/dietary status.

Social History

An age appropriate review of past and current activities that includes significant information about:

- marital status and/or living arrangements;
- current employment;
- occupational history;
- use of drugs, alcohol, and tobacco;
- level of education;
- sexual history;
- other relevant social factors.

System Review (Review of Systems)

An inventory of body systems obtained through a series of questions seeking to identify signs and/or symptoms which the patient may be experiencing or has experienced. For the purposes of CPT the following elements of a system review have been identified:

- Constitutional symptoms (fever, weight loss, etc.)
- Eyes
- Ears, Nose, Mouth, Throat
- Cardiovascular
- Respiratory
- Gastrointestinal
- Genitourinary
- Musculoskeletal
- Integumentary (skin and/or breast)
- Neurological
- Psychiatric
- Endocrine
- Hematologic/Lymphatic
- Allergic/Immunologic

The review of systems helps define the problem, clarify the differential diagnosis, identify needed testing, or serves as baseline data on other systems that might be affected by any possible management options.

Time

The inclusion of time in the definitions of levels of E/M services has been implicit in prior editions of *CPT.* The inclusion of time as an explicit factor beginning in *CPT 1992* is done to assist physicians in selecting the most appropriate level of E/M services. It should be recognized that the specific times expressed in the visit code descriptors are averages, and therefore represent a range of times which may be higher or lower depending on actual clinical circumstances.

Time is **not** a descriptive component for the emergency department levels of E/M services because emergency department services are typically provided on a variable intensity basis, often involving multiple encounters with several patients over an extended period of time. Therefore, it is often difficult for physicians to provide accurate estimates of the time spent face-to-face with the patient.

Studies to establish levels of E/M services employed surveys of practicing physicians to obtain data on the amount of time and work associated with typical E/M services. Since "work" is not easily quantifiable, the codes must rely on other objective, verifiable measures that correlate with physicians' estimates of their "work". It has been demonstrated that physicians' estimations of **intraservice time** (as explained on the next page), both within and across specialties, is a variable that is predictive of the "work" of E/M services. This same research has shown there is a strong relationship between intra-service time and total time for E/M services. Intra-service time, rather than total time, was chosen for inclusion with the codes because of its relative ease of measurement and because of its direct correlation with measurements of the total amount of time and work associated with typical E/M services.

Intra-service times are defined as **face-to-face** time for office and other outpatient visits and as **unit/floor** time for hospital and other inpatient visits. This distinction is necessary because most of the work of typical office visits takes place during the face-to-face time with the patient, while most of the work of typical hospital visits takes place during the time spent on the patient's floor or unit.

Face-to-face time (office and other outpatient visits and office consultations): For coding purposes, face-to-face time for these services is defined as only that time that the physician spends face-to-face with the patient and/or family. This includes the time in which the physician performs such tasks as obtaining a history, performing an examination, and counseling the patient.

Physicians also spend time doing work before or after the face-to-face time with the patient, performing such tasks as reviewing records and tests, arranging for further services, and communicating further with other professionals and the patient through written reports and telephone contact.

This **non-face-to-face** time for office services—also called pre- and post-encounter time—is not included in the time component described in the E/M codes. However, the pre- and post-face-to-face work associated with an encounter was included in calculating the total work of typical services in physician surveys.

Thus, the face-to-face time associated with the services described by any E/M code is a valid proxy for the total work done before, during, and after the visit.

Unit/floor time (hospital observation services, inpatient hospital care, initial and follow-up hospital consultations, nursing facility): For reporting purposes, intra-service time for these services is defined as unit/floor time, which includes the time that the physician is present on the patient's hospital unit and at the bedside rendering services for that patient. This includes the time in which the physician establishes and/or reviews the patient's chart, examines the patient, writes notes and communicates with other professionals and the patient's family.

In the hospital, pre- and post-time includes time spent off the patient's floor performing such tasks as reviewing pathology and radiology findings in another part of the hospital.

This pre- and post-visit time is not included in the time component described in these codes. However, the pre- and post-work performed during the time spent off the floor or unit was included in calculating the total work of typical services in physician surveys.

Thus, the unit/floor time associated with the services described by any code is a valid proxy for the total work done before, during, and after the visit.

Unlisted Service

An E/M service may be provided that is not listed in this section of *CPT*. When reporting such a service, the appropriate "Unlisted" code may be used to indicate the service, identifying it by "Special Report", as discussed in the following paragraph. The "Unlisted Services" and accompanying codes for the E/M section are as follows:

99429   Unlisted preventive medicine service

99499   Unlisted evaluation and management service

99539   Unlisted home visit service or procedure

Special Report

An unlisted service or one that is unusual, variable, or new may require a special report demonstrating the medical appropriateness of the service. Pertinent information should include an adequate definition or description of the nature, extent, and need for the procedure; and the time, effort, and equipment necessary to provide the service. Additional items which may be included are complexity of symptoms, final diagnosis, pertinent physical findings, diagnostic and therapeutic procedures, concurrent problems, and follow-up care.

Clinical Examples

Clinical examples of the codes for E/M services are provided to assist physicians in understanding the meaning of the descriptors and selecting the correct code. The clinical examples are listed in Appendix D. Each example was developed by physicians in the specialties shown.

The same problem, when seen by physicians in different specialties, may involve different amounts of work. Therefore, the appropriate level of encounter should be reported using the descriptors rather than the examples.

The examples have been tested for validity and approved by the CPT Editorial Panel. Physicians were given the examples and asked to assign a code or assess the amount of time and work involved. Only those examples that were rated consistently have been included in Appendix D.

Table 1
Categories and Subcategories of Service

Category/Subcategory	Code Numbers	Category/Subcategory	Code Numbers
Office or Other Outpatient Services		Nursing Facility Discharge Services	99315-99316
New Patient	99201-99205	Domiciliary, Rest Home or	
Established Patient	99211-99215	Custodial Care Services	
Hospital Observation Discharge Services	99217	New Patient	99321-99323
Hospital Observation Services	99218-99220	Established Patient	99331-99333
Hospital Observation or Inpatient Care		Home Services	
Services (Including Admission and		New Patient	99341-99345
Discharge Services)	99234-99236	Established Patient	99347-99350
Hospital Inpatient Services		Prolonged Services	
Initial Hospital Care	99221-99223	With Direct Patient Contact	99354-99357
Subsequent Hospital Care	99231-99233	Without Direct Patient Contact	99358-99359
Hospital Discharge Services	99238-99239	Standby Services	99360
Consultations		Case Management Services	
Office Consultations	99241-99245	Team Conferences	99361-99362
Initial Inpatient Consultations	99251-99255	Telephone Calls	99371-99373
Follow-up Inpatient Consultations	99261-99263	Care Plan Oversight Services	99374-99380
Confirmatory Consultations	99271-99275	Preventive Medicine Services	
Emergency Department Services	99281-99288	New Patient	99381-99387
▶Patient Transport◀	99289-99290	Established Patient	99391-99397
Critical Care Services	99291-99292	Individual Counseling	99401-99404
Neonatal Intensive Care	99295-99298	Group Counseling	99411-99412
Nursing Facility Services		Other	99420-99429
Comprehensive Nursing Facility		Newborn Care	99431-99440
Assessments	99301-99303	Special E/M Services	99450-99456
Subsequent Nursing Facility Care	99311-99313	Other E/M Services	99499

Instructions for Selecting a Level of E/M Service

Identify the Category and Subcategory of Service
The categories and subcategories of codes available for reporting E/M services are shown in Table 1.

Review the Reporting Instructions for the Selected Category or Subcategory
Most of the categories and many of the subcategories of service have special guidelines or instructions unique to that category or subcategory. Where these are indicated, eg, "Inpatient Hospital Care," special instructions will be presented preceding the levels of E/M services.

Review the Level of E/M Service Descriptors and Examples in the Selected Category or Subcategory
The descriptors for the levels of E/M services recognize seven components, six of which are used in defining the levels of E/M services. These components are:

■ history;

■ examination;

■ medical decision making;

■ counseling;

■ coordination of care;

■ nature of presenting problem; and

■ time.

The first three of these components (ie, history, examination, and medical decision making) should be considered the **key** components in selecting the level of E/M services. An exception to this rule is in the case of visits which consist predominantly of counseling or coordination of care (See numbered paragraph 3, page 7.)

The nature of the presenting problem and time are provided in some levels to assist the physician in determining the appropriate level of E/M service.

Determine the Extent of History Obtained
The extent of the history is dependent upon clinical judgment and on the nature of the presenting problems(s). The levels of E/M services recognize four types of history that are defined as follows:

Problem focused: chief complaint; brief history of present illness or problem.

Expanded problem focused: chief complaint; brief history of present illness; problem pertinent system review.

Detailed: chief complaint; extended history of present illness; problem pertinent system review extended to include a review of a limited number of additional systems; **pertinent** past, family, and/or social history **directly related to the patient's problems.**

Comprehensive: chief complaint; extended history of present illness; review of systems which is directly related to the problem(s) identified in the history of the present illness plus a review of all additional body systems; **complete** past, family, and social history.

The comprehensive history obtained as part of the preventive medicine evaluation and management service is not problem-oriented and does not involve a chief complaint or present illness. It does, however, include a comprehensive system review and comprehensive or interval past, family, and social history as well as a comprehensive assessment/history of pertinent risk factors.

Determine the Extent of Examination Performed

The extent of the examination performed is dependent on clinical judgment and on the nature of the presenting problem(s). The levels of E/M services recognize four types of examination that are defined as follows:

Problem focused: a limited examination of the affected body area or organ system.

Expanded problem focused: a limited examination of the affected body area or organ system and other symptomatic or related organ system(s).

Detailed: an extended examination of the affected body area(s) and other symptomatic or related organ system(s).

Comprehensive: a general multi-system examination or a complete examination of a single organ system. **Note:** The comprehensive examination performed as part of the preventive medicine evaluation and management service is multisystem, but its extent is based on age and risk factors identified.

For the purposes of these CPT definitions, the following body areas are recognized:

- Head, including the face
- Neck
- Chest, including breasts and axilla
- Abdomen
- Genitalia, groin, buttocks
- Back
- Each extremity

For the purposes of these CPT definitions, the following organ systems are recognized:

- Eyes
- Ears, Nose, Mouth, and Throat
- Cardiovascular
- Respiratory
- Gastrointestinal
- Genitourinary
- Musculoskeletal
- Skin
- Neurologic
- Psychiatric
- Hematologic/Lymphatic/Immunologic

Determine the Complexity of Medical Decision Making

Medical decision making refers to the complexity of establishing a diagnosis and/or selecting a management option as measured by:

- the number of possible diagnoses and/or the number of management options that must be considered;
- the amount and/or complexity of medical records, diagnostic tests, and/or other information that must be obtained, reviewed, and analyzed; and
- the risk of significant complications, morbidity, and/or mortality, as well as comorbidities, associated with the patient's presenting problems(s), the diagnostic procedure(s) and/or the possible management options.

Four types of medical decision making are recognized: straightforward; low complexity; moderate complexity; and high complexity. To qualify for a given type of decision making, two of the three elements in Table 2 on the following page must be met or exceeded.

Comorbidities/underlying diseases, in and of themselves, are not considered in selecting a level of E/M services *unless* their presence significantly increases the complexity of the medical decision making.

Select the Appropriate Level of E/M Services Based on the Following

1. For the following categories/subcategories, **all of the key components,** ie, history, examination, and medical decision making, must meet or exceed the stated requirements to qualify for a particular level of E/M service: office, new patient; hospital observation services; initial hospital care; office consultations; initial inpatient consultations; confirmatory consultations; emergency department services; comprehensive nursing facility assessments; domiciliary care, new patient; and home, new patient.

2. For the following categories/subcategories, **two of the three key components** (ie, history, examination, and medical decision making) must meet or exceed the stated requirements to qualify for a particular level of E/M services: office, established patient; subsequent hospital care; follow-up inpatient consultations; subsequent nursing facility care; domiciliary care, established patient; and home, established patient.

Table 2
Complexity of Medical Decision Making

Number of Diagnoses or Management Options	Amount and/or Complexity of Data to be Reviewed	Risk of Complications and/or Morbidity or Mortality	Type of Decision Making
minimal	minimal or none	minimal	**straightforward**
limited	limited	low	**low complexity**
multiple	moderate	moderate	**moderate complexity**
extensive	extensive	high	**high complexity**

3. When counseling and/or coordination of care dominates (more than 50%) the physician/patient and/or family encounter (face-to-face time in the office or other outpatient setting or floor/unit time in the hospital or nursing facility), then **time** may be considered the key or controlling factor to qualify for a particular level of E/M services. This includes time spent with parties who have assumed responsibility for the care of the patient or decision making whether or not they are family members (eg, foster parents, person acting in locum parentis, legal guardian). The extent of counseling and/or coordination of care must be documented in the medical record.

Notes

Evaluation and Management

Office or Other Outpatient Services

The following codes are used to report evaluation and management services provided in the physician's office or in an outpatient or other ambulatory facility. A patient is considered an outpatient until inpatient admission to a health care facility occurs.

To report services provided to a patient who is admitted to a hospital or nursing facility in the course of an encounter in the office or other ambulatory facility, see the notes for initial hospital inpatient care (page 12) or comprehensive nursing facility assessments (page 23).

For services provided by physicians in the emergency department, see 99281-99285.

For observation care, see 99217-99220.

For observation or inpatient care services (including admission and discharge services), see 99234-99236.

New Patient

99201 **Office or other outpatient visit** for the evaluation and management of a new patient, which requires these three key components:

> ➔ *CPT Assistant* Winter 91:11; Spring 92:9, 24; Summer 92:1, 24; Spring 93:34; Summer 93:2; Fall 93:9; Spring 95:1; Summer 95:4; Fall 95:9; Jul 98:9; Jun 99:8; Feb 00:3, 9,11

- **a problem focused history;**
- **a problem focused examination; and**
- **straightforward medical decision making.**

Counseling and/or coordination of care with other providers or agencies are provided consistent with the nature of the problem(s) and the patient's and/or family's needs.

Usually, the presenting problems are self limited or minor. Physicians typically spend 10 minutes face-to-face with the patient and/or family.

99202 **Office or other outpatient visit** for the evaluation and management of a new patient, which requires these three key components:

> ➔ *CPT Assistant* Winter 91:11; Spring 92:9, 24; Summer 92:1, 24; Spring 93:34; Summer 93:2; Fall 93:9; Spring 95:1; Summer 95:4; Fall 95:9; Jul 98:9; Feb 00:11

- **an expanded problem focused history;**
- **an expanded problem focused examination; and**
- **straightforward medical decision making.**

Counseling and/or coordination of care with other providers or agencies are provided consistent with the nature of the problem(s) and the patient's and/or family's needs.

Usually, the presenting problem(s) are of low to moderate severity. Physicians typically spend 20 minutes face-to-face with the patient and/or family.

99203 **Office or other outpatient visit** for the evaluation and management of a new patient, which requires these three key components:

> ➔ *CPT Assistant* Winter 91:11; Spring 92:9, 24; Summer 92:1, 24; Spring 93:34; Summer 93:2; Fall 93:9; Spring 95:1; Summer 95:4; Fall 95:9; Jul 98:9; Feb 00:11

- **a detailed history;**
- **a detailed examination; and**
- **medical decision making of low complexity.**

Counseling and/or coordination of care with other providers or agencies are provided consistent with the nature of the problem(s) and the patient's and/or family's needs.

Usually, the presenting problem(s) are of moderate severity. Physicians typically spend 30 minutes face-to-face with the patient and/or family.

99204 **Office or other outpatient visit** for the evaluation and management of a new patient, which requires these three key components:

> ➔ *CPT Assistant* Winter 91:11; Spring 92:9, 24; Summer 92:1, 24; Spring 93:34; Summer 93:2; Fall 93:9; Spring 95:1; Summer 95:4; Fall 95:9; Jul 98:9; Feb 00:11

- **a comprehensive history;**
- **a comprehensive examination; and**
- **medical decision making of moderate complexity.**

Counseling and/or coordination of care with other providers or agencies are provided consistent with the nature of the problem(s) and the patient's and/or family's needs.

Usually, the presenting problem(s) are of moderate to high severity. Physicians typically spend 45 minutes face-to-face with the patient and/or family.

99205 **Office or other outpatient visit** for the evaluation and management of a new patient, which requires these three key components:

> ➔ *CPT Assistant* Winter 91:11; Spring 92:9, 24; Summer 92:1, 24; Spring 93:34; Summer 93:2; Fall 93:9; Spring 95:1; Summer 95:4; Fall 95:9; Jul 98:9; Feb 00:11

- **a comprehensive history;**
- **a comprehensive examination; and**
- **medical decision making of high complexity.**

Counseling and/or coordination of care with other providers or agencies are provided consistent with the nature of the problem(s) and the patient's and/or family's needs.

Usually, the presenting problem(s) are of moderate to high severity. Physicians typically spend 60 minutes face-to-face with the patient and/or family.

Established Patient

99211 **Office or other outpatient visit** for the evaluation and management of an established patient, that may not require the presence of a physician. Usually, the presenting problem(s) are minimal. Typically, 5 minutes are spent performing or supervising these services.

➜ *CPT Assistant* Winter 91:11; Spring 92:9, 24; Summer 92:1, 24; Spring 93:34; Summer 93:2; Fall 93:9; Spring 95:1; Summer 95:4; Fall 95:9; Oct 96:10; Feb 97:9; Jul 98:9; Oct 99:9; Feb 00:11

99212 **Office or other outpatient visit** for the evaluation and management of an established patient, which requires at least two of these three key components:

➜ *CPT Assistant* Winter 91:11; Spring 92:9, 24; Summer 92:1, 24; Spring 93:34; Summer 93:2; Fall 93:9; Spring 95:1; Summer 95:4; Fall 95:9; Jul 98:9; Feb 00:11; Jun 00:11

- **a problem focused history;**
- **a problem focused examination;**
- **straightforward medical decision making.**

Counseling and/or coordination of care with other providers or agencies are provided consistent with the nature of the problem(s) and the patient's and/or family's needs.

Usually, the presenting problem(s) are self limited or minor. Physicians typically spend 10 minutes face-to-face with the patient and/or family.

99213 **Office or other outpatient visit** for the evaluation and management of an established patient, which requires at least two of these three key components:

➜ *CPT Assistant* Winter 91:11; Spring 92:9, 24; Summer 92:1, 24; Spring 93:34; Summer 93:2; Fall 93:9; Spring 95:1; Summer 95:4; Fall 95:9; Jan 97:10; Jul 98:9

- **an expanded problem focused history;**
- **an expanded problem focused examination;**
- **medical decision making of low complexity.**

Counseling and coordination of care with other providers or agencies are provided consistent with the nature of the problem(s) and the patient's and/or family's needs.

Usually, the presenting problem(s) are of low to moderate severity. Physicians typically spend 15 minutes face-to-face with the patient and/or family.

99214 **Office or other outpatient visit** for the evaluation and management of an established patient, which requires at least two of these three key components:

➜ *CPT Assistant* Winter 91:11; Spring 92:9, 24; Summer 92:1, 24; Spring 93:34; Summer 93:2; Fall 93:9; Spring 95:1; Summer 95:4; Fall 95:9; Jul 98:9

- **a detailed history;**
- **a detailed examination;**
- **medical decision making of moderate complexity.**

Counseling and/or coordination of care with other providers or agencies are provided consistent with the nature of the problem(s) and the patient's and/or family's needs.

Usually, the presenting problem(s) are of moderate to high severity. Physicians typically spend 25 minutes face-to-face with the patient and/or family.

99215 **Office or other outpatient visit** for the evaluation and management of an established patient, which requires at least two of these three key components:

➜ *CPT Assistant* Winter 91:11; Spring 92:9, 24; Summer 92:1, 24; Spring 93:34; Summer 93:2; Fall 93:9; Spring 95:1; Summer 95:4; Fall 95:9; Jan 97:10; Jul 98:9

- **a comprehensive history;**
- **a comprehensive examination;**
- **medical decision making of high complexity.**

Counseling and/or coordination of care with other providers or agencies are provided consistent with the nature of the problem(s) and the patient's and/or family's needs.

Usually, the presenting problem(s) are of moderate to high severity. Physicians typically spend 40 minutes face-to-face with the patient and/or family.

Hospital Observation Services

The following codes are used to report evaluation and management services provided to patients designated/admitted as "observation status" in a hospital. It is not necessary that the patient be located in an observation area designated by the hospital.

If such an area does exist in a hospital (as a separate unit in the hospital, in the emergency department, etc.), these codes are to be utilized if the patient is placed in such an area.

For definitions of key components and commonly used terms, please see **Evaluation and Management Services Guidelines.**

Typical times have not yet been established for this category of services.

Observation Care Discharge Services

Observation care discharge of a patient from "observation status" includes final examination of the patient, discussion of the hospital stay, instructions for continuing care, and preparation of discharge records. For observation or inpatient hospital care including the admission and discharge of the patient on the same date, see codes 99234-99236 as appropriate.

99217   **Observation care discharge** day management (This code is to be utilized by the physician to report all services provided to a patient on discharge from "observation status" if the discharge is on other than the initial date of "observation status." To report services to a patient designated as "observation status" or "inpatient status" and discharged on the same date, use the codes for Observation or Inpatient Care Services [including Admission and Discharge Services, 99234-99236 as appropriate.])

→ *CPT Assistant* Nov 97:2; Mar 98:1; May 98:1

Initial Observation Care

New or Established Patient

The following codes are used to report the encounter(s) by the supervising physician with the patient when designated as "observation status." This refers to the initiation of observation status, supervision of the care plan for observation and performance of periodic reassessments. For observation encounters by other physicians, see Office or Other Outpatient Consultation codes (99241-99245).

To report services provided to a patient who is admitted to the hospital after receiving hospital observation care services on the same date, see the notes for initial hospital inpatient care (page 12). For a patient admitted to the hospital on a date subsequent to the date of observation status, the hospital admission would be reported with the appropriate Initial Hospital Care codes (99221-99223). For a patient admitted and discharged from observation or inpatient status on the same date, the services should be reported with codes 99234-99236 as appropriate. Do not report observation discharge (99217) in conjunction with a hospital admission.

When "observation status" is initiated in the course of an encounter in another site of service (eg, hospital emergency department, physician's office, nursing facility) all evaluation and management services provided by the supervising physician in conjunction with initiating "observation status" are considered part of the initial observation care when performed on the same date. The observation care level of service reported by the supervising physician should include the services related to initiating "observation status" provided in the other sites of service as well as in the observation setting.

Evaluation and management services on the same date provided in sites that are related to initiating "observation status" should NOT be reported separately.

These codes may not be utilized for post-operative recovery if the procedure is considered part of the surgical "package." These codes apply to all evaluation and management services that are provided on the same date of initiating "observation status."

99218   **Initial observation care,** per day, for the evaluation and management of a patient which requires these three key components:

→ *CPT Assistant* Spring 93:34; Fall 95:9; Mar 98:1

- ■ **a detailed or comprehensive history;**
- ■ **a detailed or comprehensive examination; and**
- ■ **medical decision making that is straightforward or of low complexity.**

Counseling and/or coordination of care with other providers or agencies are provided consistent with the nature of the problem(s) and the patient's and/or family's needs.

Usually, the problem(s) requiring admission to "observation status" are of low severity.

99219   **Initial observation care,** per day, for the evaluation and management of a patient, which requires these three key components:

→ *CPT Assistant* Spring 93:34; Fall 95:16; Mar 98:1

- ■ **a comprehensive history;**
- ■ **a comprehensive examination; and**
- ■ **medical decision making of moderate complexity.**

Counseling and/or coordination of care with other providers or agencies are provided consistent with the nature of the problem(s) and the patient's and/or family's needs.

Usually, the problem(s) requiring admission to "observation status" are of moderate severity.

99220   **Initial observation care,** per day, for the evaluation and management of a patient, which requires these three key components:

→ *CPT Assistant* Spring 93:34; Fall 95:16; Mar 98:1

- ■ **a comprehensive history;**
- ■ **a comprehensive examination; and**
- ■ **medical decision making of high complexity.**

Counseling and/or coordination of care with other providers or agencies are provided consistent with the nature of the problem(s) and the patient's and/or family's needs.

Usually, the problem(s) requiring admission to "observation status" are of high severity.

Hospital Inpatient Services

The following codes are used to report evaluation and management services provided to hospital inpatients. Hospital inpatient services include those services provided to patients in a "partial hospital" setting. These codes are to be used to report these partial hospitalization services. See also psychiatry notes in the full text of *CPT.*

For definitions of key components and commonly used terms, please see **Evaluation and Management Services Guidelines.** For Hospital Observation Services, see 99218-99220. For a patient admitted and discharged from observation or inpatient status on the same date, the services should be reported with codes 99234-99236 as appropriate.

Initial Hospital Care

New or Established Patient

The following codes are used to report the first hospital inpatient encounter with the patient by the admitting physician.

For initial inpatient encounters by physicians other than the admitting physician, see initial inpatient consultation codes (99251-99255) or subsequent hospital care codes (99231-99233) as appropriate.

When the patient is admitted to the hospital as an inpatient in the course of an encounter in another site of service (eg, hospital emergency department, observation status in a hospital, physician's office, nursing facility) all evaluation and management services provided by that physician in conjunction with that admission are considered part of the initial hospital care when performed on the same date as the admission. The inpatient care level of service reported by the admitting physician should include the services related to the admission he/she provided in the other sites of service as well as in the inpatient setting.

Evaluation and management services on the same date provided in sites that are related to the admission "observation status" should NOT be reported separately. For a patient admitted and discharged from observation or inpatient status on the same date, the services should be reported with codes 99234-99236 as appropriate.

99221 **Initial hospital care,** per day, for the evaluation and management of a patient which requires these three key components:

> ⮕ *CPT Assistant* Winter 91:11; Spring 92:13, 24; Summer 92:1, 24; Fall 92:1; Spring 93:34; Spring 95:1; Fall 95:9; Jul 96:11; Sep 96:10; Mar 98:1

- **a detailed or comprehensive history;**
- **a detailed or comprehensive examination; and**
- **medical decision making that is straightforward or of low complexity.**

Counseling and/or coordination of care with other providers or agencies are provided consistent with the nature of the problem(s) and the patient's and/or family's needs.

Usually, the problem(s) requiring admission are of low severity. Physicians typically spend 30 minutes at the bedside and on the patient's hospital floor or unit.

99222 **Initial hospital care,** per day, for the evaluation and management of a patient, which requires these three key components:

> ⮕ *CPT Assistant* Winter 91:11; Spring 92:13, 24; Summer 92:1, 24; Fall 92:1; Spring 93:34; Spring 95:1; Fall 95:9; Jul 96:11; Sep 96:10; Mar 98:1

- **a comprehensive history;**
- **a comprehensive examination; and**
- **medical decision making of moderate complexity.**

Counseling and/or coordination of care with other providers or agencies are provided consistent with the nature of the problem(s) and the patient's and/or family's needs.

Usually, the problem(s) requiring admission are of moderate severity. Physicians typically spend 50 minutes at the bedside and on the patient's hospital floor or unit.

99223 **Initial hospital care,** per day, for the evaluation and management of a patient, which requires these three key components:

> ⮕ *CPT Assistant* Winter 91:11; Spring 92:13, 24; Summer 92:1, 24; Fall 92:1; Spring 93:34; Spring 95:1; Fall 95:9; Jul 96:11; Sep 96:10; Mar 98:1

- **a comprehensive history;**
- **a comprehensive examination; and**
- **medical decision making of high complexity.**

Counseling and/or coordination of care with other providers or agencies are provided consistent with the nature of the problem(s) and the patient's and/or family's needs.

Usually, the problem(s) requiring admission are of high severity. Physicians typically spend 70 minutes at the bedside and on the patient's hospital floor or unit.

Subsequent Hospital Care

All levels of subsequent hospital care include reviewing the medical record and reviewing the results of diagnostic studies and changes in the patient's status, (ie, changes in history, physical condition and response to management) since the last assessment by the physician.

99231 **Subsequent hospital care,** per day, for the evaluation and management of a patient, which requires at least two of these three key components:

> ⮕ *CPT Assistant* Winter 91:11; Spring 92:13, 24; Summer 92:1, 24; Fall 92:1; Spring 93:34; Spring 95:1; Fall 95:16

- **a problem focused interval history;**
- **a problem focused examination;**
- **medical decision making that is straightforward or of low complexity.**

Counseling and/or coordination of care with other providers or agencies are provided consistent with the nature of the problem(s) and the patient's and/or family's needs.

⊘ =Modifier '-51' Exempt ▶◀=New or Revised Text ✚=Add-on Code CPT 2002

Usually, the patient is stable, recovering or improving. Physicians typically spend 15 minutes at the bedside and on the patient's hospital floor or unit.

99232   **Subsequent hospital care,** per day, for the evaluation and management of a patient, which requires at least two of these three key components:

➔ *CPT Assistant* Winter 91:11; Spring 92:13, 24; Summer 92:1, 24; Fall 92:1; Spring 93:34; Spring 95:1; Fall 95:16; Jan 00:11

- **an expanded problem focused interval history;**
- **an expanded problem focused examination;**
- **medical decision making of moderate complexity.**

Counseling and/or coordination of care with other providers or agencies are provided consistent with the nature of the problem(s) and the patient's and/or family's needs.

Usually, the patient is responding inadequately to therapy or has developed a minor complication. Physicians typically spend 25 minutes at the bedside and on the patient's hospital floor or unit.

99233   **Subsequent hospital care,** per day, for the evaluation and management of a patient, which requires at least two of these three key components:

➔ *CPT Assistant* Winter 91:11; Spring 92:13, 24; Summer 92:1, 24; Fall 92:1; Spring 93:34; Spring 95:1; Fall 95:16

- **a detailed interval history;**
- **a detailed examination;**
- **medical decision making of high complexity.**

Counseling and/or coordination of care with other providers or agencies are provided consistent with the nature of the problem(s) and the patient's and/or family's needs.

Usually, the patient is unstable or has developed a significant complication or a significant new problem. Physicians typically spend 35 minutes at the bedside and on the patient's hospital floor or unit.

Observation or Inpatient Care Services (Including Admission and Discharge Services)

The following codes are used to report observation or inpatient hospital care services provided to patients admitted and discharged on the same date of service. When a patient is admitted to the hospital from observation status on the same date, the physician should report only the initial hospital care code. The initial hospital care code reported by the admitting physician should include the services related to the observation status services he/she provided on the same date of inpatient admission.

When "observation status" is initiated in the course of an encounter in another site of service (eg, hospital emergency department, physician's office, nursing facility) all evaluation and management services provided by the supervising physician in conjunction with initiating "observation status" are considered part of the initial observation care when performed on the same date. The observation care level of service should include the services related to initiating "observation status" provided in the other sites of service as well as in the observation setting when provided by the same physician.

For patients admitted to observation or inpatient care and discharged on a different date, see codes 99218-99220 and 99217, or 99221-99223 and 99238-99239.

99234   **Observation or inpatient hospital care,** for the evaluation and management of a patient including admission and discharge on the same date which requires these three key components:

➔ *CPT Assistant* Mar 98:1; May 98:1; Jan 00:11

- **a detailed or comprehensive history;**
- **a detailed or comprehensive examination; and**
- **medical decision making that is straightforward or of low complexity.**

Counseling and/or coordination of care with other providers or agencies are provided consistent with the nature of the problem(s) and the patient's and/or family's needs.

Usually the presenting problem(s) requiring admission are of low severity.

99235   **Observation or inpatient hospital care,** for the evaluation and management of a patient including admission and discharge on the same date which requires these three key components:

➔ *CPT Assistant* Mar 98:1; May 98:1; Jan 00:11

- **a comprehensive history;**
- **a comprehensive examination; and**
- **medical decision making of moderate complexity.**

Counseling and/or coordination of care with other providers or agencies are provided consistent with the nature of the problem(s) and the patient's and/or family's needs.

Usually the presenting problem(s) requiring admission are of moderate severity.

99236   **Observation or inpatient hospital care,** for the evaluation and management of a patient including admission and discharge on the same date which requires these three key components:

➔ *CPT Assistant* Mar 98:1; May 98:1; Jan 00:11

- **a comprehensive history;**
- **a comprehensive examination; and**
- **medical decision making of high complexity.**

Counseling and/or coordination of care with other providers or agencies are provided consistent with the nature of the problem(s) and the patient's and/or family's needs.

Usually the presenting problem(s) requiring admission are of high severity.

Hospital Discharge Services

The hospital discharge day management codes are to be used to report the total duration of time spent by a physician for final hospital discharge of a patient. The codes include, as appropriate, final examination of the patient, discussion of the hospital stay, even if the time spent by the physician on that date is not continuous, instructions for continuing care to all relevant caregivers, and preparation of discharge records, prescriptions and referral forms. For a patient admitted and discharged from observation or inpatient status on the same date, the services should be reported with codes 99234-99236 as appropriate.

99238 **Hospital discharge day management;** 30 minutes or less

➔ *CPT Assistant* Fall 92:1; Spring 93:4; Nov 97:4; Mar 98:1, 11; May 98:1; Jan 99:10

99239 more than 30 minutes

➔ *CPT Assistant* Nov 97:4; Mar 98:1, 11; May 98:1; Jan 99:10

(These codes are to be utilized by the physician to report all services provided to a patient on the date of discharge, if other than the initial date of inpatient status. To report services to a patient who is admitted as an inpatient, and discharged on the same date, see codes 99234-99236 for observation or inpatient hospital care including the admission and discharge of the patient on the same date. To report concurrent care services provided by a physician(s) other than the attending physician, use subsequent hospital care codes (99231-99233) on the day of discharge.)

(For Observation Care Discharge, use 99217)

(For observation or inpatient hospital care including the admission and discharge of the patient on the same date, see 99234-99236)

(For Nursing Facility Care Discharge, see 99315, 99316)

(For discharge services provided to newborns admitted and discharged on the same date, use 99435)

Consultations

A consultation is a type of service provided by a physician whose opinion or advice regarding evaluation and/or management of a specific problem is requested by another physician or other appropriate source.

A physician consultant may initiate diagnostic and/or therapeutic services at the same or subsequent visit.

The written or verbal request for a consult may be made by a physician or other appropriate source and documented in the patient's medical record. The consultant's opinion and any services that were ordered or performed must also be documented in the patient's medical record and communicated by written report to the requesting physician or other appropriate source.

A "consultation" initiated by a patient and/or family, and not requested by a physician, is not reported using the initial consultation codes but may be reported using the codes for confirmatory consultation or office visits, as appropriate.

If a confirmatory consultation is required, eg, by a third party payor, the modifier '-32', mandated services, should also be reported.

Any specifically identifiable procedure (ie, identified with a specific CPT code) performed on or subsequent to the date of the initial consultation should be reported separately.

If subsequent to the completion of a consultation, the consultant assumes responsibility for management of a portion or all of the patient's condition(s), the follow-up consultation codes should not be used. In the hospital setting, the consulting physician should use the appropriate inpatient hospital consultation code for the initial encounter and then subsequent hospital care codes (not follow-up consultation codes). In the office setting, the appropriate established patient code should be used.

There are four subcategories of consultations: office, initial inpatient, follow-up inpatient, and confirmatory. See each subcategory for specific reporting instructions.

For definitions of key components and commonly used terms, please see **Evaluation and Management Services Guidelines**.

Office or Other Outpatient Consultations

New or Established Patient

The following codes are used to report consultations provided in the physician's office or in an outpatient or other ambulatory facility, including hospital observation services, home services, domiciliary, rest home, custodial care, or emergency department (see consultation definition, above). Follow-up visits in the consultant's office or other outpatient facility that are initiated by the physician consultant are reported using office visit codes for established patients (99211-99215). If an additional request for an opinion or advice regarding the same or a new problem is received from the attending physician and documented in the medical record, the office consultation codes may be used again.

⊘ =Modifier '-51' Exempt   ▶ ◀ =New or Revised Text   ✚ =Add-on Code   CPT 2002

99241   **Office consultation** for a new or established patient, which requires these three key components:

➔ *CPT Assistant* Winter 91:11; Spring 92:1, 13, 24; Summer 92:1; Spring 93:1, 34; Spring 95:1; Oct 97:1; Jun 99:10; Apr 00:10

- **a problem focused history;**
- **a problem focused examination; and**
- **straightforward medical decision making.**

Counseling and/or coordination of care with other providers or agencies are provided consistent with the nature of the problem(s) and the patient's and/or family's needs.

Usually, the presenting problem(s) are self limited or minor. Physicians typically spend 15 minutes face-to-face with the patient and/or family.

99242   **Office consultation** for a new or established patient, which requires these three key components:

➔ *CPT Assistant* Winter 91:11; Spring 92:1, 13, 24; Summer 92:1; Spring 93:1, 34; Spring 95:1; *CPT Changes* 2000

- **an expanded problem focused history;**
- **an expanded problem focused examination; and**
- **straightforward medical decision making.**

Counseling and/or coordination of care with other providers or agencies are provided consistent with the nature of the problem(s) and the patient's and/or family's needs.

Usually, the presenting problem(s) are of low severity. Physicians typically spend 30 minutes face-to-face with the patient and/or family.

99243   **Office consultation** for a new or established patient, which requires these three key components:

➔ *CPT Assistant* Winter 91:11; Spring 92:1, 13, 24; Summer 92:1; Spring 93:1, 34; Spring 95:1

- **a detailed history;**
- **a detailed examination; and**
- **medical decision making of low complexity.**

Counseling and/or coordination of care with other providers or agencies are provided consistent with the nature of the problem(s) and the patient's and/or family's needs.

Usually, the presenting problem(s) are of moderate severity. Physicians typically spend 40 minutes face-to-face with the patient and/or family.

99244   **Office consultation** for a new or established patient, which requires these three key components:

➔ *CPT Assistant* Winter 91:11; Spring 92:1, 13, 24; Summer 92:1; Spring 93:1, 34; Spring 95:1

- **a comprehensive history;**
- **a comprehensive examination; and**
- **medical decision making of moderate complexity.**

Counseling and/or coordination of care with other providers or agencies are provided consistent with the nature of the problem(s) and the patient's and/or family's needs.

Usually, the presenting problem(s) are of moderate to high severity. Physicians typically spend 60 minutes face-to-face with the patient and/or family.

99245   Office consultation for a new or established patient, which requires these three key components:

➔ *CPT Assistant* Winter 91:11; Spring 92:1, 13, 24; Summer 92:1; Spring 93:1, 34; Spring 95:1; Oct 97:1

- **a comprehensive history;**
- **a comprehensive examination; and**
- **medical decision making of high complexity.**

Counseling and/or coordination of care with other providers or agencies are provided consistent with the nature of the problem(s) and the patient's and/or family's needs.

Usually, the presenting problem(s) are of moderate to high severity. Physicians typically spend 80 minutes face-to-face with the patient and/or family.

Initial Inpatient Consultations

New or Established Patient

The following codes are used to report physician consultations provided to hospital inpatients, residents of nursing facilities, or patients in a partial hospital setting. Only one initial consultation should be reported by a consultant per admission.

99251   **Initial inpatient consultation** for a new or established patient, which requires these three key components:

➔ *CPT Assistant* Winter 91:11; Spring 92:1, 13, 24; Summer 92:1; Spring 93:34; Spring 95:1; Oct 97:1

- **a problem focused history;**
- **a problem focused examination; and**
- **straightforward medical decision making.**

Counseling and/or coordination of care with other providers or agencies are provided consistent with the nature of the problem(s) and the patient's and/or family's needs.

Usually, the presenting problem(s) are self limited or minor. Physicians typically spend 20 minutes at the bedside and on the patient's hospital floor or unit.

99252   **Initial inpatient consultation** for a new or established patient, which requires these three key components:

➔ *CPT Assistant* Winter 91:11; Spring 92:1, 13, 24; Summer 92:1; Summer 93:34; Spring 95:1

- **an expanded problem focused history;**
- **an expanded problem focused examination; and**
- **straightforward medical decision making.**

Counseling and/or coordination of care with other providers or agencies are provided consistent with the nature of the problem(s) and the patient's and/or family's needs.

Usually, the presenting problem(s) are of low severity. Physicians typically spend 40 minutes at the bedside and on the patient's hospital floor or unit.

99253 **Initial inpatient consultation** for a new or established patient, which requires these three key components:

→ *CPT Assistant* Winter 91:11; Spring 92:1, 13, 24; Summer 92:1; Summer 93:34; Spring 95:1

- **a detailed history;**
- **a detailed examination; and**
- **medical decision making of low complexity.**

Counseling and/or coordination of care with other providers or agencies are provided consistent with the nature of the problem(s) and the patient's and/or family's needs.

Usually, the presenting problem(s) are of moderate severity. Physicians typically spend 55 minutes at the bedside and on the patient's hospital floor or unit.

99254 **Initial inpatient consultation** for a new or established patient, which requires three key components:

→ *CPT Assistant* Winter 91:11; Spring 92:1, 13, 24; Summer 92:1; Summer 93:34; Spring 95:1

- **a comprehensive history;**
- **a comprehensive examination; and**
- **medical decision making of moderate complexity.**

Counseling and/or coordination of care with other providers or agencies are provided consistent with the nature of the problem(s) and the patient's and/or family's needs.

Usually, the presenting problem(s) are of moderate to high severity. Physicians typically spend 80 minutes at the bedside and on the patient's hospital floor or unit.

99255 **Initial inpatient consultation** for a new or established patient, which requires these three key components:

→ *CPT Assistant* Winter 91:11; Spring 92:1, 13, 24; Summer 92:1; Summer 93:34; Spring 95:1

- **a comprehensive history;**
- **a comprehensive examination; and**
- **medical decision making of high complexity.**

Counseling and/or coordination of care with other providers or agencies are provided consistent with the nature of the problem(s) and the patient's and/or family's needs.

Usually, the presenting problem(s) are of moderate to high severity. Physicians typically spend 110 minutes at the bedside and on the patient's hospital floor or unit.

Follow-Up Inpatient Consultations

Established Patient

Follow-up consultations are visits to complete the initial consultation OR subsequent consultative visits requested by the attending physician.

A follow-up consultation includes monitoring progress, recommending management modifications or advising on a new plan of care in response to changes in the patient's status.

If the physician consultant has initiated treatment at the initial consultation, and participates thereafter in the patient's management, the codes for subsequent hospital care should be used (99231-99233).

The following codes are used to report follow-up consultations provided to hospital inpatients or nursing facility residents only. For consultative services provided in other settings, the codes for office or other outpatient consultations should be reported (99241-99245).

99261 **Follow-up inpatient consultation** for an established patient, which requires at least two of these three key components:

→ *CPT Assistant* Winter 91:11; Spring 92:1, 13, 24; Summer 92:1; Spring 93:34; Spring 95:1

- **a problem focused interval history;**
- **a problem focused examination;**
- **medical decision making that is straightforward or of low complexity.**

Counseling and/or coordination of care with other providers or agencies are provided consistent with nature of the problem(s) and the patient's and/or family's needs.

Usually, the patient is stable, recovering or improving. Physicians typically spend 10 minutes at the bedside and on the patient's hospital floor or unit.

99262 **Follow-up inpatient consultation** for an established patient which requires at least two of these three key components:

→ *CPT Assistant* Winter 91:11; Spring 92:1, 13, 24; Summer 92:1; Spring 93:34; Spring 95:1

- **an expanded problem focused interval history;**
- **an expanded problem focused examination;**
- **medical decision making of moderate complexity.**

Counseling and/or coordination of care with other providers or agencies are provided consistent with the nature of the problem(s) and the patient's and/or family's needs.

Usually, the patient is responding inadequately to therapy or has developed a minor complication. Physicians typically spend 20 minutes at the bedside and on the patient's hospital floor or unit.

99263 **Follow-up inpatient consultation** for an established patient which requires at least two of these three key components:

➔ *CPT Assistant* Winter 91:11; Spring 92:1, 13, 24; Summer 92:1; Spring 93:34; Spring 95:1; Oct 97:1

- **a detailed interval history;**
- **a detailed examination;**
- **medical decision making of high complexity.**

Counseling and/or coordination of care with other providers or agencies are provided consistent with the nature of the problem(s) and the patient's and/or family's needs.

Usually, the patient is unstable or has developed a significant complication or a significant new problem. Physicians typically spend 30 minutes at the bedside and on the patient's hospital floor or unit.

Confirmatory Consultations

New or Established Patient

The following codes are used to report the evaluation and management services provided to patients when the consulting physician is aware of the confirmatory nature of the opinion sought (eg, when a second/third opinion is requested or required on the necessity or appropriateness of a previously recommended medical treatment or surgical procedure).

Confirmatory consultations may be provided in any setting.

A physician consultant providing a confirmatory consultation is expected to provide an opinion and/or advice only. Any services subsequent to the opinion are coded at the appropriate level of office visit, established patient, or subsequent hospital care. If a confirmatory consultation is required, eg, by a third party payor, the modifier '-32', mandated services, should also be reported. (See also Consultation notes, page 14.) Typical times have not yet been established for this subcategory of services.

99271 **Confirmatory consultation** for a new or established patient, which requires these three key components:

➔ *CPT Assistant* Winter 91:11; Spring 92:1, 24; Summer 92:1; Spring 93:34; Spring 95:1

- **a problem focused history;**
- **a problem focused examination; and**
- **straightforward medical decision making.**

Counseling and/or coordination of care with other providers or agencies are provided consistent with the nature of the problem(s) and the patient's and/or family's needs.

Usually, the presenting problem(s) are self limited or minor.

99272 **Confirmatory consultation** for a new or established patient, which requires these three key components:

➔ *CPT Assistant* Winter 91:11; Spring 92:1, 24; Summer 92:1; Spring 93:34; Spring 95:1

- **an expanded problem focused history;**
- **an expanded problem focused examination; and**
- **straightforward medical decision making.**

Counseling and/or coordination of care with other providers or agencies are provided consistent with the nature of the problem(s) and the patient's and/or family's needs.

Usually, the presenting problem(s) are of low severity.

99273 **Confirmatory consultation** for a new or established patient, which requires these three key components:

➔ *CPT Assistant* Spring 92:1

- **a detailed history;**
- **a detailed examination; and**
- **medical decision making of low complexity.**

Counseling and/or coordination of care with other providers or agencies are provided consistent with the nature of the problem(s) and the patient's and/or family's needs.

Usually, the presenting problem(s) are of moderate severity.

99274 **Confirmatory consultation** for a new or established patient, which requires these three key components:

➔ *CPT Assistant* Winter 91:11; Spring 92:1, 24; Summer 92:1; Spring 93:34; Spring 95:1

- **a comprehensive history;**
- **a comprehensive examination; and**
- **medical decision making of moderate complexity.**

Counseling and/or coordination of care with other providers or agencies are provided consistent with the nature of the problem(s) and the patient's and/or family's needs.

Usually, the presenting problem(s) are of moderate to high severity.

99275 **Confirmatory consultation** for a new or established patient, which requires these three key components:

➔ *CPT Assistant* Winter 91:11; Spring 92:1, 24; Summer 92:1; Spring 93:34; Spring 95:1

- **a comprehensive history;**
- **a comprehensive examination; and**
- **medical decision making of high complexity.**

Counseling and/or coordination of care with other providers or agencies are provided consistent with the nature of the problem(s) and the patient's and/or family's needs.

Usually, the presenting problem(s) are of moderate to high severity.

Emergency Department Services

New or Established Patient

The following codes are used to report evaluation and management services provided in the emergency department. No distinction is made between new and established patients in the emergency department.

An emergency department is defined as an organized hospital-based facility for the provision of unscheduled episodic services to patients who present for immediate medical attention. The facility must be available 24 hours a day.

For critical care services provided in the emergency department, see Critical Care notes and 99291, 99292.

For evaluation and management services provided to a patient in an observation area of a hospital, see 99217-99220.

For observation or inpatient care services (including admission and discharge services), see 99234-99236.

99281 **Emergency department visit** for the evaluation and management of a patient, which requires these three key components:

➔ *CPT Assistant* Winter 91:11; Spring 92:24; Summer 92:1; Spring 93:34; Spring 95:1; Jan 00:11; Feb 00:11

- **a problem focused history;**
- **a problem focused examination; and**
- **straightforward medical decision making.**

Counseling and/or coordination of care with other providers or agencies are provided consistent with the nature of the problem(s) and the patient's and/or family's needs.

Usually, the presenting problem(s) are self limited or minor.

99282 **Emergency department visit** for the evaluation and management of a patient, which requires these three key components:

➔ *CPT Assistant* Winter 91:11; Spring 92:24; Summer 92:1, 18; Spring 93:34; Spring 95:1; Summer 95:1; Jan 00:11; Feb 00:11

- **an expanded problem focused history;**
- **an expanded problem focused examination; and**
- **medical decision making of low complexity.**

Counseling and/or coordination of care with other providers or agencies are provided consistent with the nature of the problem(s) and the patient's and/or family's needs.

Usually, the presenting problem(s) are of low to moderate severity.

99283 **Emergency department visit** for the evaluation and management of a patient, which requires these three key components:

➔ *CPT Assistant* Winter 91:11; Spring 92:24; Summer 92:1, 18; Spring 93:34; Spring 95:1; Summer 95:1; Jan 00:11; Feb 00:11

- **an expanded problem focused history;**
- **an expanded problem focused examination; and**
- **medical decision making of moderate complexity.**

Counseling and/or coordination of care with other providers or agencies are provided consistent with the nature of the problem(s) and the patient's and/or family's needs.

Usually, the presenting problem(s) are of moderate severity.

99284 **Emergency department visit** for the evaluation and management of a patient, which requires these three key components:

➔ *CPT Assistant* Winter 91:11; Spring 92:24; Summer 92:1, 18; Spring 93:34; Spring 95:1; Summer 95:1; Jan 00:11; Feb 00:11

- **a detailed history;**
- **a detailed examination; and**
- **medical decision making of moderate complexity.**

Counseling and/or coordination of care with other providers or agencies are provided consistent with the nature of the problem(s) and the patient's and/or family's needs.

Usually, the presenting problem(s) are of high severity, and require urgent evaluation by the physician but do not pose an immediate significant threat to life or physiologic function.

99285 **Emergency department visit** for the evaluation and management of a patient, which requires these three key components within the constraints imposed by the urgency of the patient's clinical condition and/or mental status:

➔ *CPT Assistant* Winter 91:11; Spring 92:24; Summer 92:1, 18; Spring 93:34; Spring 95:1; Summer 95:1; Nov 99:2-3; Jan 00:11; Feb 00:11; *CPT Changes* 2000

- **a comprehensive history;**
- **a comprehensive examination; and**
- **medical decision making of high complexity.**

Counseling and/or coordination of care with other providers or agencies are provided consistent with the nature of the problem(s) and the patient's and/or family's needs.

Usually, the presenting problem(s) are of high severity and pose an immediate significant threat to life or physiologic function.

Other Emergency Services

In physician directed emergency care, advanced life support, the physician is located in a hospital emergency or critical care department, and is in two-way voice communication with ambulance or rescue personnel outside the hospital. The physician directs the performance of necessary medical procedures, including but not limited to: telemetry of cardiac rhythm; cardiac and/or pulmonary resuscitation; endotracheal or esophageal obturator airway intubation; administration of intravenous fluids and/or administration of intramuscular, intratracheal or subcutaneous drugs; and/or electrical conversion of arrhythmia.

99288   **Physician direction of** emergency medical systems (EMS) emergency care, advanced life support

→ *CPT Assistant* Summer 92:18

►Patient Transport◄

►The following codes 99289 and 99290 are used to report the physical attendance and direct face-to-face care by a physician during the interfacility transport of a critically ill or injured patient. For the purpose of reporting codes 99289 and 99290, face-to-face care begins when the physician assumes the primary responsibility of the patient at the referring hospital/facility, and ends when the receiving hospital/facility accepts responsibility for the patient's care. Only the time the physician spends in direct face-to-face contact with the patient during the transport should be reported. Patient transport services involving less than 30 minutes of face-to-face physician care should not be reported using 99289, 99290. Procedure(s) or service(s) performed by other members of the transporting team may not be reported by the supervising physician. Any procedure(s) or service(s) performed by the physician before or during transport that are identified in *CPT* may be reported separately with the exception of routine monitoring evaluations (eg, heart rate, respiratory rate, blood pressure, and pulse oximetry) and the initiation of mechanical ventilation. Routine monitoring evaluations and initiation of mechanical ventilation performed by the physician are to be included in the face-to-face time reported by codes 99289, 99290 and should not be reported separately.

The time spent by the physician performing separately reportable services or procedures should not be included in the face-to-face time reported by codes 99289, 99290.

The direction of emergency care to transporting staff by a physician located in a hospital or other facility by two-way communication is not considered direct face-to-face care and should not be reported with codes 99289, 99290. Physician directed emergency care through outside voice communication to transporting staff personnel is reported with code 99288.

The emergency department services codes (99281-99285), initial hospital care codes (99221-99223), hourly critical care codes (99291, 99292), or initial date neonatal intensive care code (99295) are only reported after the patient has been admitted to the emergency department, the inpatient floor or the critical care unit of the receiving facility.

Code 99289 is used to report the first 30-74 minutes of direct face-to-face time with the transport patient and should be reported only once on a given date. Code 99290 is used to report each additional 30 minutes provided on a given date. Face-to-face services less than 30 minutes should not be reported with these codes.◄

● **99289**   **Physician constant attention of** the critically ill or injured patient during an interfacility transport; first 30-74 minutes

→ *CPT Changes* 2002

+● **99290**   each additional 30 minutes (List separately in addition to code for primary service)

→ *CPT Changes* 2002

►(Use 99290 in conjunction with 99289)◄

►(Codes 99289, 99290 may be reported separately from any other procedure/service provided on the date of the transfer. The time spent by the physician performing separately reportable services or procedures should not be included in the face-to-face time reported by codes 99289, 99290)◄

Critical Care Services

Critical care is the direct delivery by a physician(s) of medical care for a critically ill or critically injured patient. A critical illness or injury acutely impairs one or more vital organ systems such that there is a high probability of imminent or life threatening deterioration in the patient's condition. Critical care involves high complexity decision making to assess, manipulate, and support vital system function(s) to treat single or multiple vital organ system failure and/or to prevent further life threatening deterioration of the patient's condition. Examples of vital organ system failure include, but are not limited to: central nervous system failure, circulatory failure, shock, renal, hepatic, metabolic, and/or respiratory failure. Although critical care typically requires interpretation of multiple physiologic parameters and/or application of advanced technology(s), critical care may be provided in life threatening situations when these elements are not present. Critical care may be provided on multiple days, even if no changes are made in the treatment rendered to the patient, provided that the patient's condition continues to require the level of physician attention described above.

Providing medical care to a critically ill, injured, or postoperative patient qualifies as a critical care service only if both the illness or injury and the treatment being provided meet the above requirements. Critical care is usually, but not always, given in a critical care area, such as the coronary care unit, intensive care unit, pediatric intensive care unit, respiratory care unit, or the emergency care facility.

Critical care services provided to infants older than one month of age at the time of admission to an intensive care unit are reported with critical care codes 99291 and 99292. Critical care services provided to neonates (30 days of age or less at the time of admission to an intensive care unit) are reported with the neonatal critical care codes 99295, 99296, 99297 and 99298. The neonatal critical care codes are reported as long as the neonate qualifies for critical care services during the hospital stay. The reporting of neonatal critical care services is not based on time, the type of unit (eg, pediatric or neonatal critical care unit) or the type of provider delivering the care. For additional instructions on reporting these services, see the Neonatal Intensive Care section and codes 99295-99298.

Services for a patient who is not critically ill but happens to be in a critical care unit are reported using other appropriate E/M codes.

Critical care and other E/M services may be provided to the same patient on the same date by the same physician.

The following services are included in reporting critical care when performed during the critical period by the physician(s) providing critical care: the interpretation of cardiac output measurements (93561, 93562), chest x-rays (71010, 71015, 71020), pulse oximetry (94760, 94761, 94762), blood gases, and information data stored in computers (eg, ECGs, blood pressures, hematologic data (99090)); gastric intubation (43752, 91105); temporary transcutaneous pacing (92953); ventilatory management (94656, 94657, 94660, 94662); and vascular access procedures (36000, 36410, 36415, 36540, 36600). Any services performed which are not listed above should be reported separately.

▶Codes 99291-99292 should not be reported for the physician's attendance during the transport of critically ill or injured patients to or from a facility or hospital. Physician transport services of critically ill or injured patients are separately reportable, see 99289, 99290.◀

The critical care codes 99291 and 99292 are used to report the total duration of time spent by a physician providing critical care services to a critically ill or critically injured patient, even if the time spent by the physician on that date is not continuous. For any given period of time spent providing critical care services, the physician must devote his or her full attention to the patient and, therefore, cannot provide services to any other patient during the same period of time.

Time spent with the individual patient should be recorded in the patient's record. The time that can be reported as critical care is the time spent engaged in work directly related to the individual patient's care whether that time was spent at the immediate bedside or elsewhere on the floor or unit. For example, time spent on the unit or at the nursing station on the floor reviewing test results or imaging studies, discussing the critically ill patient's care with other medical staff or documenting critical care services in the medical record would be reported as critical care, even though it does not occur at the bedside. Also, when the patient is unable or clinically incompetent to participate in discussions, time spent on the floor or unit with family members or surrogate decision makers obtaining a medical history, reviewing the patient's condition or prognosis, or discussing treatment or limitation(s) of treatment may be reported as critical care, provided that the conversation bears directly on the management of the patient.

Time spent in activities that occur outside of the unit or off the floor (eg, telephone calls, whether taken at home, in the office, or elsewhere in the hospital) may not be reported as critical care since the physician is not immediately available to the patient. Time spent in activities that do not directly contribute to the treatment of the patient may not be reported as critical care, even if they are performed in the critical care unit (eg, participation in administrative meetings or telephone calls to discuss other patients). Time spent performing separately reportable procedures or services should not be included in the time reported as critical care time.

Code 99291 is used to report the first 30-74 minutes of critical care on a given date. It should be used only once per date even if the time spent by the physician is not continuous on that date. Critical care of less than 30 minutes total duration on a given date should be reported with the appropriate E/M code.

Code 99292 is used to report ▶additional block(s) of time, of up to◀ 30 minutes ▶each◀ beyond the first 74 minutes. ▶(See table on following page.)◀

The following examples illustrate the correct reporting of critical care services:

Total Duration of Critical Care	Codes
less than 30 minutes (less than 1/2 hour)	appropriate E/M codes
30-74 minutes (1/2 hr. - 1 hr. 14 min.)	99291 X 1
75-104 minutes (1 hr. 15 min. - 1 hr. 44 min.)	99291 X 1 AND 99292 X 1
105-134 minutes (1 hr. 45 min. - 2 hr. 14 min.)	99291 X 1 AND 99292 X 2
135 - 164 minutes (2 hr. 15 min. - 2 hr. 44 min.)	99291 X 1 AND 99292 X 3
165 - 194 minutes (2 hr. 45 min. - 3 hr. 14 min.)	99291 X 1 AND 99292 X 4
▶194 minutes or longer (3 hr. 14 min. - etc.)◀	▶99291 and 99292 as appropriate (see illustrated reporting examples above)◀

99291 **Critical care, evaluation and management** of the critically ill or critically injured patient; first 30-74 minutes

➔ *CPT Assistant* Summer 92:18; Summer 93:1; Summer 95:1; Jan 96:7; Dec 98:6; Nov 99:3-5; Apr 00:6

+ 99292 each additional 30 minutes (List separately in addition to code for primary service)

➔ *CPT Assistant* Summer 92:18; Summer 93:1; Summer 95:1; Jan 96:7; Dec 98:6; Apr 00:6; Dec 00:15

(Use 99292 in conjunction with 99291)

Neonatal Intensive Care

The following codes (99295-99298) are used to report services provided by a physician directing the care of a critically ill newborn (or managing the continuing intensive care of the very low birth weight (VLBW) infant). They represent care starting with the date of admission and may be reported only once per day, per patient. Once the neonate is no longer considered to be critically ill and attains a body weight which exceeds 1500 grams, the codes for Subsequent Hospital Care (99231-99233) should be utilized.

These neonatal critical care codes are to be used in addition to codes 99360, 99436 or 99440 as appropriate, when the physician is present for the delivery and newborn resuscitation is required.

The same definitions for critical care services apply for the adult, child and neonate. The neonatal critical care codes, however, are global 24-hour codes and not reported as hourly services. Services for a patient who is not critically ill but happens to be in a critical care unit are reported using other appropriate E/M codes.

The neonatal critical care codes (99295, 99296, 99297, 99298) are applied to neonates (30 days of age or less) admitted to an intensive care unit. These codes will be applicable as long as the child qualifies for critical care services during this hospital stay. Infants admitted to an intensive care unit older than one month of age would be coded with hourly critical care codes (99291, 99292) if they qualify for critical care services. These neonatal codes are not applied based upon the type of unit (eg, pediatric or neonatal critical care unit) in which the child receives care nor the type of provider delivering the care.

Care rendered includes management, monitoring, and treatment of the patient including enteral and parenteral nutritional maintenance, metabolic and hematologic maintenance, pharmacologic control of the circulatory system, parent counseling, case management services, and personal direct supervision of the health care team in the performance of cognitive and procedural activities.

In addition to those services listed above for adult and pediatric hourly codes, the following procedures are also included in the bundled (global) neonatal codes (99295, 99296, 99297 and 99298): umbilical venous (36510) and umbilical arterial (36620) catheters, central (36488, 36490) or peripheral vessel catheterization (36000), other arterial catheters (36140, 36620), oral or nasogastric tube placement, endotracheal intubation (31500), lumbar puncture (62270), suprapubic bladder aspiration (51000), bladder catheterization (53670), initiation and management of mechanical ventilation (94656, 94657) or continuous positive airway pressure (CPAP) (94660), surfactant administration, intravascular fluid administration, transfusion of blood components (36430, 36440), vascular punctures (36420, 36600), invasive or non-invasive electronic monitoring of vital signs, bedside pulmonary function testing, and/or monitoring or interpretation of blood gases or oxygen saturation (94760-94762). Any services performed which are not listed above should be reported separately.

For additional instructions, see descriptions listed for 99295-99298.

99295 **Initial neonatal intensive care,** per day, for the evaluation and management of a critically ill neonate or infant

➔ *CPT Assistant* Summer 93:1; Nov 97:4-5; Mar 98:11; Nov 99:5-6; Dec 00:14; *CPT Changes* 2000

This code is reserved for the date of admission for neonates who are critically ill. Critically ill neonates require cardiac and/or respiratory support (including ventilator or nasal CPAP when indicated), continuous or frequent vital sign monitoring, laboratory and blood gas interpretations, follow-up physician reevaluations, and constant observation by the health care team under direct physician supervision. Immediate preoperative evaluation and stabilization of neonates with life threatening surgical or cardiac conditions are included under this code.

99296 **Subsequent neonatal intensive care,** per day, for the evaluation and management of a critically ill and unstable neonate or infant

➔ *CPT Assistant* Summer 93:1; Nov 97:4-5; Mar 98:11; Nov 99:5-6; Dec 00: 14; *CPT Changes* 2000

A critically ill and unstable neonate will require cardiac and/or respiratory support (including ventilator or nasal CPAP when indicated), continuous or frequent vital sign monitoring, laboratory and blood gas interpretations, follow-up physician re-evaluations throughout a 24-hour period, and constant observation by the health care team under direct physician supervision. In addition, most will require frequent ventilator changes, intravenous fluid alterations, and/or early initiation of parenteral nutrition. Neonates in the immediate post-operative period or those who become critically ill and unstable during the hospital stay will commonly qualify for this level of care.

This code encompasses intensive care provided on dates subsequent to the admission date.

99297 **Subsequent neonatal intensive care,** per day, for the evaluation and management of a critically ill though stable neonate or infant

➔ *CPT Assistant* Summer 93:1; Nov 97:4-5; Mar 98:11; Nov 99:5-6; Dec 00:14; *CPT Changes* 2000

Critically ill though stable neonates require cardiac and/or respiratory support (including ventilator and nasal CPAP when indicated), continuous or frequent vital sign monitoring, laboratory and blood gas interpretations, follow-up physician re-evaluations throughout a 24-hour period, and constant observation by the health care team under direct physician supervision. Neonates at this level of care would be expected to require less frequent changes in respiratory, cardiovascular and fluid and electrolyte therapy as those included under code 99296.

This code encompasses intensive care provided on dates subsequent to the admission date.

99298 **Subsequent neonatal intensive care,** per day, for the evaluation and management of the recovering very low birth weight infant (less than 1500 grams)

➔ *CPT Assistant* Nov 98:2-3; Dec 00:15; *CPT Changes* 2000

Very low birth weight neonates who are no longer critically ill continue to require intensive cardiac and respiratory monitoring, continuous and/or frequent vital sign monitoring, heat maintenance, enteral and/or parenteral nutritional adjustments, laboratory and oxygen monitoring and constant observation by the health care team under direct physician supervision. Neonates of this level of care would be expected to require infrequent changes in respiratory, cardiovascular and/or fluid and electrolyte therapy as those induced under 99296 or 99297.

This code encompasses intensive care provided on days subsequent to the admission date.

➔ *CPT Assistant* Nov 98:2-3

Nursing Facility Services

The following codes are used to report evaluation and management services to patients in Nursing Facilities (formerly called Skilled Nursing Facilities (SNFs), Intermediate Care Facilities (ICFs) or Long Term Care Facilities (LTCFs)).

These codes should also be used to report evaluation and management services provided to a patient in a psychiatric residential treatment center (a facility or a distinct part of a facility for psychiatric care, which provides a 24-hour therapeutically planned and professionally staffed group living and learning environment). If procedures such as medical psychotherapy are provided in addition to evaluation and management services, these should be reported in addition to the evaluation and management services provided.

Nursing facilities that provide convalescent, rehabilitative, or long term care are required to conduct comprehensive, accurate, standardized, and reproducible assessments of each resident's functional capacity using a Resident Assessment Instrument (RAI). All RAIs include the Minimum Data Set (MDS), Resident Assessment Protocols (RAPs) and utilization guidelines. The MDS is the primary screening and assessment tool; the RAPs trigger the identification of potential problems and provide guidelines for follow-up assessments.

Physicians have a central role in assuring that all residents receive thorough assessments and that medical plans of care are instituted or revised to enhance or maintain the residents' physical and psychosocial functioning.

Two subcategories of nursing facility services are recognized: Comprehensive Nursing Facility Assessments and Subsequent Nursing Facility Care. Both subcategories apply to new or established patients.

Comprehensive Assessments may be performed at one or more sites in the assessment process: the hospital, observation unit, office, nursing facility, domiciliary/non-nursing facility or patient's home.

For definitions of key components and commonly used terms, please see **Evaluation and Management Services Guidelines.**

Comprehensive Nursing Facility Assessments

New or Established Patient

When the patient is admitted to the nursing facility in the course of an encounter in another site of service (eg, hospital emergency department, physician's office), all evaluation and management services provided by that physician in conjunction with that admission are considered part of the initial nursing facility care when performed on the same date as the admission or readmission. The nursing facility care level of service reported by the admitting physician should include the services related to the admission he/she provided in the other sites of service as well as in the nursing facility setting.

Hospital discharge or observation discharge services performed on the same date of nursing facility admission or readmission may be reported separately. For a patient discharged from inpatient status on the same date of nursing facility admission or readmission, the hospital discharge services should be reported with codes 99238-99239 as appropriate. For a patient discharged from observation status on the same date of nursing facility admission or readmission, the observation care discharge services should be reported with code 99217. For a patient admitted and discharged from observation or inpatient status on the same date, see codes 99234-99236.

(For nursing facility care discharge, see 99315, 99316)

More than one comprehensive assessment may be necessary during an inpatient confinement.

99301   **Evaluation and management** of a new or established patient involving an annual nursing facility assessment which requires these three key components:

➔ *CPT Assistant* Winter 91:11; Spring 92:24; Summer 92:1; Fall 92:34; Winter 92:22; Spring 93:34; Spring 95:1; Nov 97:5; Mar 98:1; May 98:1

- **a detailed interval history;**
- **a comprehensive examination; and**
- **medical decision making that is straightforward or of low complexity.**

Counseling and/or coordination of care with other providers or agencies are provided consistent with the nature of the problem(s) and the patient's and/or family's needs.

Usually, the patient is stable, recovering or improving. The review and affirmation of the medical plan of care is required. Physicians typically spend 30 minutes at the bedside and on the patient's facility floor or unit.

99302   **Evaluation and management** of a new or established patient involving a nursing facility assessment which requires these three key components:

➔ *CPT Assistant* Winter 91:11; Spring 92:24; Summer 92:1; Fall 92:34; Winter 92:22; Spring 93:34; Spring 95:1; Nov 97:5; Mar 98:1; May 98:1

- **a detailed interval history;**
- **a comprehensive examination; and**
- **medical decision making of moderate to high complexity.**

Counseling and/or coordination of care with other providers or agencies are provided consistent with the nature of the problem(s) and the patient's and/or family's needs.

Usually, the patient has developed a significant complication or a significant new problem and has had a major permanent change in status.

The creation of a new medical plan of care is required. Physicians typically spend 40 minutes at the bedside and on the patient's facility floor or unit.

99303   **Evaluation and management** of a new or established patient involving a nursing facility assessment at the time of initial admission or readmission to the facility, which requires these three key components:

➔ *CPT Assistant* Winter 91:11; Spring 92:24; Summer 92:1; Fall 92:34; Winter 92:22; Spring 93:34; Spring 95:1; Nov 97:5; Mar 98:1; May 98:1

- **a comprehensive history;**
- **a comprehensive examination; and**
- **medical decision making of moderate to high complexity.**

Counseling and/or coordination of care with other providers or agencies are provided consistent with the nature of the problem(s) and the patient's and/or family's needs.

The creation of a medical plan of care is required. Physicians typically spend 50 minutes at the bedside and on the patient's facility floor or unit.

Subsequent Nursing Facility Care

New or Established Patient

The following codes are used to report the services provided to residents of nursing facilities who do not require a comprehensive assessment, and/or who have not had a major, permanent change of status.

All levels include reviewing the medical record, noting changes in the resident's status since the last visit, and reviewing and signing orders.

99311 **Subsequent nursing facility care,** per day, for the evaluation and management of a new or established patient, which requires at least two of these three key components:

➔ *CPT Assistant* Winter 91:11; Spring 92:24; Summer 92:1; Fall 92:34; Winter 92:22; Spring 93:34; Spring 95:1; May 98:1

- **a problem focused interval history;**
- **a problem focused examination;**
- **medical decision making that is straightforward or of low complexity.**

Counseling and/or coordination of care with other providers or agencies are provided consistent with the nature of the problem(s) and the patient's and/or family's needs.

Usually, the patient is stable, recovering or improving. Physicians typically spend 15 minutes at the bedside and on the patient's facility floor or unit.

99312 **Subsequent nursing facility care,** per day, for the evaluation and management of a new or established patient, which requires at least two of these three key components:

➔ *CPT Assistant* Winter 91:11; Spring 92:24; Summer 92:1; Fall 92:34; Winter 92:22; Spring 93:34; Spring 95:1; May 98:1

- **an expanded problem focused interval history;**
- **an expanded problem focused examination;**
- **medical decision making of moderate complexity.**

Counseling and/or coordination of care with other providers or agencies are provided consistent with the nature of the problem(s) and the patient's and/or family's needs.

Usually, the patient is responding inadequately to therapy or has developed a minor complication. Physicians typically spend 25 minutes at the bedside and on the patient's facility floor or unit.

99313 **Subsequent nursing facility care,** per day, for the evaluation and management of a new or established patient, which requires at least two of these three key components:

➔ *CPT Assistant* Winter 91:11; Spring 92:24; Summer 92:1; Fall 92:34; Winter 92:22; Spring 93:34; Spring 95:1; May 98:1

- **a detailed interval history;**
- **a detailed examination;**
- **medical decision making of moderate to high complexity.**

Counseling and/or coordination of care with other providers or agencies are provided consistent with the nature of the problem(s) and the patient's and/or family's needs.

Usually, the patient has developed a significant complication or a significant new problem. Physicians typically spend 35 minutes at the bedside and on the patient's facility floor or unit.

Nursing Facility Discharge Services

The nursing facility discharge day management codes are to be used to report the total duration of time spent by a physician for the final nursing facility discharge of a patient. The codes include, as appropriate, final examination of the patient, discussion of the nursing facility stay, even if the time spent by the physician on that date is not continuous. Instructions are given for continuing care to all relevant caregivers, and preparation of discharge records, prescriptions and referral forms.

99315 Nursing facility discharge day management; 30 minutes or less

➔ *CPT Assistant* Nov 97:5-6; May 98:1

99316 more than 30 minutes

➔ *CPT Assistant* Nov 97:5-6; May 98:1

Domiciliary, Rest Home (eg, Boarding Home), or Custodial Care Services

The following codes are used to report evaluation and management services in a facility which provides room, board and other personal assistance services, generally on a long-term basis. The facility's services do not include a medical component.

For definitions of key components and commonly used terms, please see **Evaluation and Management Services Guidelines.**

Typical times have not yet been established for this category of services.

New Patient

99321 **Domiciliary or rest home visit** for the evaluation and management of a new patient which requires these three key components:

➔ *CPT Assistant* Winter 91:11; Spring 92:24; Summer 92:1; Spring 93:34; Spring 95:1

- **a problem focused history;**
- **a problem focused examination; and**
- **medical decision making that is straightforward or of low complexity.**

Counseling and/or coordination of care with other providers or agencies are provided consistent with the nature of the problem(s) and the patient's and/or family's needs.

Usually, the presenting problem(s) are of low severity.

99322 **Domiciliary or rest home visit** for the evaluation and management of a new patient, which requires these three key components:

- **an expanded problem focused history;**
- **an expanded problem focused examination; and**
- **medical decision making of moderate complexity.**

Counseling and/or coordination of care with other providers or agencies are provided consistent with the nature of the problem(s) and the patient's and/or family's needs.

Usually, the presenting problem(s) are of moderate severity.

99323 **Domiciliary or rest home visit** for the evaluation and management of a new patient, which requires these three key components:

- **a detailed history;**
- **a detailed examination; and**
- **medical decision making of high complexity.**

Counseling and/or coordination of care with other providers or agencies are provided consistent with the nature of the problem(s) and the patient's and/or family's needs.

Usually, the presenting problem(s) are of high complexity.

Established Patient

99331 **Domiciliary or rest home visit** for the evaluation and management of an established patient, which requires at least two of these three key components:

➔ *CPT Assistant* Winter 91:11; Spring 92:24; Summer 92:1; Spring 93:34; Spring 95:1

- **a problem focused interval history;**
- **a problem focused examination;**
- **medical decision making that is straightforward or of low complexity.**

Counseling and/or coordination of care with other providers or agencies are provided consistent with the nature of the problem(s) and the patient's and/or family's needs.

Usually, the patient is stable, recovering or improving.

99332 **Domiciliary or rest home visit** for the evaluation and management of an established patient, which requires at least two of these three key components:

- **an expanded problem focused interval history;**
- **an expanded problem focused examination;**
- **medical decision making of moderate complexity.**

Counseling and/or coordination of care with other providers or agencies are provided consistent with the nature of the problem(s) and the patient's and/or family's needs.

Usually, the patient is responding inadequately to therapy or has developed a minor complication.

99333 **Domiciliary or rest home visit** for the evaluation and management of an established patient, which requires at least two of these three key components:

- **a detailed interval history;**
- **a detailed examination;**
- **medical decision making of high complexity.**

Counseling and/or coordination of care with other providers or agencies are provided consistent with the nature of the problem(s) and the patient's and/or family's needs.

Usually, the patient is unstable or has developed a significant complication or a significant new problem.

Home Services

The following codes are used to report evaluation and management services provided in a private residence.

For definitions of key components and commonly used terms, please see **Evaluation and Management Services Guidelines.**

New Patient

99341 **Home visit** for the evaluation and management of a new patient, which requires these three key components:

➔ *CPT Assistant* Winter 91:11; Spring 92:24; Summer 92:1; Spring 93:34; Spring 95:1; Jun 97:6; Nov 97:6-8; Oct 98:6

- **a problem focused history;**
- **a problem focused examination; and**
- **straightforward medical decision making.**

Counseling and/or coordination of care with other providers or agencies are provided consistent with the nature of the problem(s) and the patient's and/or family's needs.

Usually, the presenting problem(s) are of low severity. Physicians typically spend 20 minutes face-to-face with the patient and/or family.

99342 **Home visit** for the evaluation and management of a new patient, which requires these three key components:

➔ *CPT Assistant* Winter 91:11; Spring 92:24; Summer 92:1; Spring 93:34; Spring 95:1; Jun 97:6; Nov 97:6-8; Oct 98:6

- **an expanded problem focused history;**
- **an expanded problem focused examination; and**
- **medical decision making of low complexity.**

Counseling and/or coordination of care with other providers or agencies are provided consistent with the nature of the problem(s) and the patient's and/or family's needs.

Usually, the presenting problem(s) are of moderate severity. Physicians typically spend 30 minutes face-to-face with the patient and/or family.

99343 **Home visit** for the evaluation and management of a new patient, which requires these three key components:

➔*CPT Assistant* Winter 91:11; Spring 92:24; Summer 92:1; Spring 93:34; Spring 95:1; Jun 97:6; Nov 97:6-8; Oct 98:6

- **a detailed history;**
- **a detailed examination; and**
- **medical decision making of moderate complexity.**

Counseling and/or coordination of care with other providers or agencies are provided consistent with the nature of the problem(s) and the patient's and/or family's needs.

Usually, the presenting problem(s) are of moderate to high severity. Physicians typically spend 45 minutes face-to-face with the patient and/or family.

99344 **Home visit** for the evaluation and management of a new patient, which requires these three components:

➔*CPT Assistant* Nov 97:6-8; Oct 98:6

- **a comprehensive history;**
- **a comprehensive examination; and**
- **medical decision making of moderate complexity.**

Counseling and/or coordination of care with other providers or agencies are provided consistent with the nature of the problem(s) and the patient's and/or family's needs.

Usually, the presenting problem(s) are of high severity. Physicians typically spend 60 minutes face-to-face with the patient and/or family.

99345 **Home visit** for the evaluation and management of a new patient, which requires these three key components:

➔*CPT Assistant* Nov 97:6-8; Oct 98:6

- **a comprehensive history;**
- **a comprehensive examination; and**
- **medical decision making of high complexity.**

Counseling and/or coordination of care with other providers or agencies are provided consistent with the nature of the problem(s) and the patient's and/or family's needs.

Usually, the patient is unstable or has developed a significant new problem requiring immediate physician attention. Physicians typically spend 75 minutes face-to-face with the patient and/or family.

Established Patient

99347 **Home visit** for the evaluation and management of an established patient, which requires at least two of these three key components:

➔*CPT Assistant* Nov 97:6-8; Oct 98:6

- **a problem focused interval history;**
- **a problem focused examination;**
- **straightforward medical decision making.**

Counseling and/or coordination of care with other providers or agencies are provided consistent with the nature of the problem(s) and the patient's and/or family's needs.

Usually, the presenting problem(s) are self limited or minor. Physicians typically spend 15 minutes face-to-face with the patient and/or family.

99348 **Home visit** for the evaluation and management of an established patient, which requires at least two of these three key components:

➔*CPT Assistant* Nov 97:6-8; Oct 98:6

- **an expanded problem focused interval history;**
- **an expanded problem focused examination;**
- **medical decision making of low complexity.**

Counseling and/or coordination of care with other providers or agencies are provided consistent with the nature of the problem(s) and the patient's and/or family's needs.

Usually, the presenting problem(s) are of low to moderate severity. Physicians typically spend 25 minutes face-to-face with the patient and/or family.

99349 **Home visit** for the evaluation and management of an established patient, which requires at least two of these three key components:

➔*CPT Assistant* Nov 97:6-8; Oct 98:6

- **a detailed interval history;**
- **a detailed examination;**
- **medical decision making of moderate complexity.**

Counseling and/or coordination of care with other providers or agencies are provided consistent with the nature of the problem(s) and the patient's and/or family's needs.

Usually, the presenting problem(s) are moderate to high severity. Physicians typically spend 40 minutes face-to-face with the patient and/or family.

99350 **Home visit** for the evaluation and management of an established patient, which requires at least two of these three key components:

➔*CPT Assistant* Nov 97:6-8; Oct 98:6

- **a comprehensive interval history;**
- **a comprehensive examination;**
- **medical decision making of moderate to high complexity.**

Counseling and/or coordination of care with other providers or agencies are provided consistent with the nature of the problem(s) and the patient's and/or family's needs.

Usually, the presenting problem(s) are of moderate to high severity. The patient may be unstable or may have developed a significant new problem requiring immediate physician attention. Physicians typically spend 60 minutes face-to-face with the patient and/or family.

(99351 has been deleted. To report, use 99347)

(99352 has been deleted. To report, use 99348)

(99353 has been deleted. To report, use 99349)

Prolonged Services

Prolonged Physician Service With Direct (Face-To-Face) Patient Contact

Codes 99354-99357 are used when a physician provides prolonged service involving direct (face-to-face) patient contact that is beyond the usual service in either the inpatient or outpatient setting. This service is reported in addition to other physician service, including evaluation and management services at any level. Appropriate codes should be selected for supplies provided or procedures performed in the care of the patient during this period.

Codes 99354-99357 are used to report the total duration of face-to-face time spent by a physician on a given date providing prolonged service, even if the time spent by the physician on that date is not continuous.

Code 99354 or 99356 is used to report the first hour of prolonged service on a given date, depending on the place of service.

Either code also may be used to report a total duration of prolonged service of 30-60 minutes on a given date. Either code should be used only once per date, even if the time spent by the physician is not continuous on that date. Prolonged service of less than 30 minutes total duration on a given date is not separately reported because the work involved is included in the total work of the evaluation and management codes.

Code 99355 or 99357 is used to report each additional 30 minutes beyond the first hour, depending on the place of service. Either code may also be used to report the final 15-30 minutes of prolonged service on a given date. Prolonged service of less than 15 minutes beyond the first

hour or less than 15 minutes beyond the final 30 minutes is not reported separately.

The following examples illustrate the correct reporting of prolonged physician service with direct patient contact in the office setting:

Total Duration of Prolonged Services	Code(s)
less than 30 minutes (less than 1/2 hour)	Not reported separately
30-74 minutes (1/2 hr. - 1 hr. 14 min.)	99354 X 1
75-104 minutes (1 hr. 15 min. - 1 hr. 44 min.)	99354 X 1 AND 99355 X 1
105-134 minutes (1 hr. 45 min. - 2 hr. 14 min.)	99354 X 1 AND 99355 X 2
135-164 minutes (2 hr. 15 min. - 2 hr. 44 min.)	99354 X 1 AND 99355 X 3
165-194 minutes (2 hr. 45 min. - 3 hr. 14 min.)	99354 X 1 AND 99355 X 4

+ **99354**   Prolonged physician service in the office or other outpatient setting requiring direct (face-to-face) patient contact beyond the usual service (eg, prolonged care and treatment of an acute asthmatic patient in an outpatient setting); first hour (List separately in addition to code for office or other outpatient Evaluation and Management service)

➔ *CPT Assistant* Spring 94:30, 32; Sep 00:1

(Use 99354 in conjunction with codes 99201-99215, 99241-99245, 99301-99350)

+ **99355**   each additional 30 minutes (List separately in addition to code for prolonged physician service)

➔ *CPT Assistant* Spring 94:30, 32; Sep 00:1

(Use 99355 in conjunction with codes 99354)

+ **99356**   Prolonged physician service in the inpatient setting, requiring direct (face-to-face) patient contact beyond the usual service (eg, maternal fetal monitoring for high risk delivery or other physiological monitoring, prolonged care of an acutely ill inpatient); first hour (List separately in addition to code for inpatient Evaluation and Management service)

➔ *CPT Assistant* Spring 94:30, 32

(Use 99356 in conjunction with codes 99221-99233, 99251-99255, 99261-99263)

+ **99357**   each additional 30 minutes (List separately in addition to code for prolonged physician service)

(Use 99357 in conjunction with code 99356)

Prolonged Physician Service Without Direct (Face-To-Face) Patient Contact

Codes 99358 and 99359 are used when a physician provides prolonged service not involving direct (face-to-face) care that is beyond the usual service in either the inpatient or outpatient setting.

This service is to be reported in addition to other physician service, including evaluation and management services at any level.

Codes 99358 and 99359 are used to report the total duration of non-face-to-face time spent by a physician on a given date providing prolonged service, even if the time spent by the physician on that date is not continuous. Code 99358 is used to report the first hour of prolonged service on a given date regardless of the place of service.

It may also be used to report a total duration of prolonged service of 30-60 minutes on a given date. It should be used only once per date even if the time spent by the physician is not continuous on that date.

Prolonged service of less than 30 minutes total duration on a given date is not separately reported.

Code 99359 is used to report each additional 30 minutes beyond the first hour regardless of the place of service. It may also be used to report the final 15-30 minutes of prolonged service on a given date.

Prolonged service of less than 15 minutes beyond the first hour or less than 15 minutes beyond the final 30 minutes is not reported separately.

+ 99358 **Prolonged evaluation and management service** before and/or after direct (face-to-face) patient care (eg, review of extensive records and tests, communication with other professionals and/or the patient/family); first hour (List separately in addition to code(s) for other physician service(s) and/or inpatient or outpatient Evaluation and Management service)

➔ *CPT Assistant* Spring 94:32; Nov 98:3

+ 99359 each additional 30 minutes (List separately in addition to code for prolonged physician service)

(Use 99359 in conjunction with code 99358)

(To report telephone calls, see 99371-99373)

Physician Standby Services

Code 99360 is used to report physician standby service that is requested by another physician and that involves prolonged physician attendance without direct (face-to-face) patient contact. The physician may not be providing care or services to other patients during this period. This code is not used to report time spent proctoring another physician. It is also not used if the period of standby ends with the performance of a procedure subject to a "surgical" package by the physician who was on standby.

Code 99360 is used to report the total duration of time spent by a physician on a given date on standby. Standby service of less than 30 minutes total duration on a given date is not reported separately.

Second and subsequent periods of standby beyond the first 30 minutes may be reported only if a full 30 minutes of standby was provided for each unit of service reported.

99360 **Physician standby service,** requiring prolonged physician attendance, each 30 minutes (eg, operative standby, standby for frozen section, for cesarean/high risk delivery, for monitoring EEG)

➔ *CPT Assistant* Spring 94:32; Apr 97:10; Aug 97:18; Nov 97:8

(99360 may be reported in addition to 99431, 99440 as appropriate)

(99360 may not be reported in addition to 99436)

Case Management Services

Physician case management is a process in which a physician is responsible for direct care of a patient, and for coordinating and controlling access to or initiating and/or supervising other health care services needed by the patient.

Team Conferences

99361 **Medical conference** by a physician with interdisciplinary team of health professionals or representatives of community agencies to coordinate activities of patient care (patient not present); approximately 30 minutes

99362 approximately 60 minutes

Telephone Calls

99371 **Telephone call** by a physician to patient or for consultation or medical management or for coordinating medical management with other health care professionals (eg, nurses, therapists, social workers, nutritionists, physicians, pharmacists); simple or brief (eg, to report on tests and/or laboratory results, to clarify or alter previous instructions, to integrate new information from other health professionals into the medical treatment plan, or to adjust therapy)

➔ *CPT Assistant* May 00:11

99372 intermediate (eg, to provide advice to an established patient on a new problem, to initiate therapy that can be handled by telephone, to discuss test results in detail, to coordinate medical management of a new problem in an established patient, to discuss and evaluate new information and details, or to initiate new plan of care)

➔ *CPT Assistant* May 00:11

99373   complex or lengthy (eg, lengthy counseling session with anxious or distraught patient, detailed or prolonged discussion with family members regarding seriously ill patient, lengthy communication necessary to coordinate complex services of several different health professionals working on different aspects of the total patient care plan)

➔ *CPT Assistant* May 00:11

Care Plan Oversight Services

Care Plan Oversight Services are reported separately from codes for office/outpatient, hospital, home, nursing facility or domiciliary services. The complexity and approximate physician time of the care plan oversight services provided within a 30-day period determine code selection. Only one physician may report services for a given period of time, to reflect that physician's sole or predominant supervisory role with a particular patient. These codes should not be reported for supervision of patients in nursing facilities or under the care of home health agencies unless they require recurrent supervision of therapy.

The work involved in providing very low intensity or infrequent supervision services is included in the pre- and post-encounter work for home, office/outpatient and nursing facility or domiciliary visit codes.

▲ **99374**   **Physician supervision** of a patient under care of home health agency (patient not present) in home, domiciliary or equivalent environment (eg, Alzheimer's facility) requiring complex and multidisciplinary care modalities involving regular physician development and/or revision of care plans, review of subsequent reports of patient status, review of related laboratory and other studies, communication (including telephone calls) for purposes of assessment or care decisions with health care professional(s), family member(s), surrogate decision maker(s) (eg, legal guardian) and/or key caregiver(s) involved in patient's care, integration of new information into the medical treatment plan and/or adjustment of medical therapy, within a calendar month; 15-29 minutes

➔ *CPT Assistant* Summer 94:9; Nov 97:8-9; *CPT Changes* 2002

99375   30 minutes or more

➔ *CPT Assistant* Summer 94:9; Nov 97:8-9

(99376 has been deleted. To report, see 99375, 99378, 99380)

▲ **99377**   **Physician supervision** of a hospice patient (patient not present) requiring complex and multidisciplinary care modalities involving regular physician development and/or revision of care plans, review of subsequent reports of patient status, review of related laboratory and other studies, communication (including telephone calls) for purposes of assessment or care decisions with health care professional(s), family member(s), surrogate decision maker(s) (eg, legal guardian) and/or key caregiver(s) involved in patient's care, integration of new information into the medical treatment plan and/or adjustment of medical therapy, within a calendar month; 15-29 minutes

➔ *CPT Assistant* Nov 97:8-9; *CPT Changes* 2001; 2002

99378   30 minutes or more

➔ *CPT Assistant* Nov 97:8-9

▲ **99379**   **Physician supervision** of a nursing facility patient (patient not present) requiring complex and multidisciplinary care modalities involving regular physician development and/or revision of care plans, review of subsequent reports of patient status, review of related laboratory and other studies, communication (including telephone calls) for purposes of assessment or care decisions with health care professional(s), family member(s), surrogate decision maker(s) (eg, legal guardian) and/or key caregiver(s) involved in patient's care, integration of new information into the medical treatment plan and/or adjustment of medical therapy, within a calendar month; 15-29 minutes

➔ *CPT Changes* 2002

99380   30 minutes or more

➔ *CPT Assistant* Nov 97: 8-9

Preventive Medicine Services

The following codes are used to report the preventive medicine evaluation and management of infants, children, adolescents and adults.

The extent and focus of the services will largely depend on the age of the patient.

If an abnormality/ies is encountered or a preexisting problem is addressed in the process of performing this preventive medicine evaluation and management service, and if the problem/abnormality is significant enough to require additional work to perform the key components of a problem-oriented E/M service, then the appropriate Office/Outpatient code 99201-99215 should also be reported. Modifier '-25' should be added to the Office/Outpatient code to indicate that a significant, separately identifiable Evaluation and Management service was provided by the same physician on the same day as the preventive medicine service. The appropriate preventive medicine service is additionally reported.

An insignificant or trivial problem/abnormality that is encountered in the process of performing the preventive medicine evaluation and management service and which does not require additional work and the performance of the key components of a problem-oriented E/M service should not be reported.

The "comprehensive" ►nature◄ of the Preventive Medicine Services codes 99381-99397 ►reflects an age and gender appropriate history/exam and◄ is NOT synonymous with the "comprehensive" examination required in Evaluation and Management codes 99201-99350.

Codes 99381-99397 include counseling/anticipatory guidance/risk factor reduction interventions which are provided at the time of the initial or periodic comprehensive preventive medicine examination. (Refer to codes 99401-99412 for reporting those counseling/anticipatory guidance/risk factor reduction interventions that are provided at an encounter separate from the preventive medicine examination.)

Immunizations and ancillary studies involving laboratory, radiology, other procedures, or screening tests identified with a specific CPT code are reported separately. For immunizations, see 90471-90474 and 90476-90749.

New Patient

▲**99381** **Initial comprehensive preventive medicine**
evaluation and management of an individual including an age and gender appropriate history, examination, counseling/anticipatory guidance/risk factor reduction interventions, and the ordering of appropriate immunization(s), laboratory/diagnostic procedures, new patient; infant (age under 1 year)
➔*CPT Assistant* Winter 91:11; Spring 92:24; Summer 92:1; Spring 93:14, 34; Spring 95:1; Aug 97:1; Jul 98:9; Nov 98:3-4; *CPT Changes* 2002

99382 early childhood (age 1 through 4 years)
➔*CPT Assistant* Winter 91:11; Spring 92:24; Summer 92:1; Spring 93:14, 34; Spring 95:1; Aug 97:1; Jul 98:9; Nov 98:3-4

99383 late childhood (age 5 through 11 years)
➔*CPT Assistant* Winter 91:11; Spring 92:24; Summer 92:1; Spring 93:14, 34; Spring 95:1; Aug 97:1; Jul 98:9; Nov 98:3-4

99384 adolescent (age 12 through 17 years)
➔*CPT Assistant* Winter 91:11; Spring 92:24; Summer 92:1; Spring 93:14, 34; Spring 95:1; Aug 97:1; Jul 98:9; Nov 98:3-4

99385 18-39 years
➔*CPT Assistant* Winter 91:11; Spring 92:24; Summer 92:1; Spring 93:14, 34; Spring 95:1; Aug 97:1; Jul 98:9; Nov 98:3-4

99386 40-64 years
➔*CPT Assistant* Winter 91:11; Spring 92:24; Summer 92:1; Spring 93:14, 34; Spring 95:1; Aug 97:1; Jul 98:9; Nov 98:3-4

99387 65 years and over
➔*CPT Assistant* Winter 91:11; Spring 92:24; Summer 92:1; Spring 93:14, 34; Spring 95:1; Aug 97:1; Jul 98:9; Nov 98:3-4

Established Patient

▲**99391** **Periodic comprehensive preventive medicine**
reevaluation and management of an individual including an age and gender appropriate history, examination, counseling/anticipatory guidance/risk factor reduction interventions, and the ordering of appropriate immunization(s), laboratory/diagnostic procedures, established patient; infant (age under 1 year)
➔*CPT Assistant* Winter 91:11; Spring 92:24; Summer 92:1; Spring 93:14, 34; Spring 95:1; Aug 97:1; Jul 98:9; Nov 98:3-4; *CPT Changes* 2002

99392 early childhood (age 1 through 4 years)
➔*CPT Assistant* Winter 91:11; Spring 92:24; Summer 92:1; Spring 93:14, 34; Spring 95:1; Aug 97:1; Jul 98:9; Nov 98:3-4

99393 late childhood (age 5 through 11 years)
➔*CPT Assistant* Winter 91:11; Spring 92:24; Summer 92:1; Spring 93:14, 34; Spring 95:1; Aug 97:1; Jul 98:9; Nov 98:3-4

99394 adolescent (age 12 through 17 years)
➔*CPT Assistant* Winter 91:11; Spring 92:24; Summer 92:1; Spring 93:14, 34; Spring 95:1; Aug 97:1; Jul 98:9; Nov 98:3-4

99395 18-39 years
➔*CPT Assistant* Winter 91:11; Spring 92:24; Summer 92:1; Spring 93:14, 34; Spring 95:1; Aug 97:1; Jul 98:9; Nov 98:3-4

99396 40-64 years
➔*CPT Assistant* Winter 91:11; Spring 92:24; Summer 92:1; Spring 93:14, 34; Spring 95:1; Aug 97:1; Jul 98:9; Nov 98:3-4

99397 65 years and over
➔*CPT Assistant* Winter 91:11; Spring 92:24; Summer 92:1; Spring 93:14, 34; Spring 95:1; Aug 97:1; Jul 98:9; Nov 98:3-4

Counseling and/or Risk Factor Reduction Intervention

New or Established Patient

These codes are used to report services provided to individuals at a separate encounter for the purpose of promoting health and preventing illness or injury.

Preventive medicine counseling and risk factor reduction interventions provided as a separate encounter will vary with age and should address such issues as family problems, diet and exercise, substance abuse, sexual practices, injury prevention, dental health, and diagnostic and laboratory test results available at the time of the encounter.

These codes are not to be used to report counseling and risk factor reduction interventions provided to patients with symptoms or established illness. For counseling individual patients with symptoms or established illness, use the appropriate office, hospital or consultation or other evaluation and management codes. For counseling groups of patients with symptoms or established illness, use 99078.

Preventive Medicine, Individual Counseling

99401   **Preventive medicine counseling** and/or risk factor reduction intervention(s) provided to an individual (separate procedure); approximately 15 minutes
> *CPT Assistant* Aug 97:1; Jan 98:12

99402   approximately 30 minutes
> *CPT Assistant* Aug 97:1

99403   approximately 45 minutes
> *CPT Assistant* Aug 97:1

99404   approximately 60 minutes
> *CPT Assistant* Aug 97:1

Preventive Medicine, Group Counseling

99411   **Preventive medicine counseling** and/or risk factor reduction intervention(s) provided to individuals in a group setting (separate procedure); approximately 30 minutes
> *CPT Assistant* Aug 97:1

99412   approximately 60 minutes
> *CPT Assistant* Aug 97:1; Jan 98:12

Other Preventive Medicine Services

99420   **Administration and interpretation** of health risk assessment instrument (eg, health hazard appraisal)

99429   **Unlisted preventive** medicine service

Newborn Care

The following codes are used to report the services provided to newborns in several different settings.

For newborn hospital discharge services provided on a date subsequent to the admission date of the newborn, use 99238.

For discharge services provided to newborns admitted and discharged on the same date, use 99435.

99431   **History and examination** of the normal newborn infant, initiation of diagnostic and treatment programs and preparation of hospital records. (This code should also be used for birthing room deliveries.)
> *CPT Assistant* Apr 97:10

99432   **Normal newborn care** in other than hospital or birthing room setting, including physical examination of baby and conference(s) with parent(s)
> *CPT Assistant* May 99:11

99433   **Subsequent hospital care,** for the evaluation and management of a normal newborn, per day

99435   **History and examination** of the normal newborn infant, including the preparation of medical records. (This code should only be used for newborns assessed and discharged from the hospital or birthing room on the same date.)

99436   **Attendance** at delivery (when requested by delivering physician) and initial stabilization of newborn
> *CPT Assistant* Nov 97:9-10

(99436 may be reported in addition to 99431)

(99436 may not be reported in addition to 99440)

(99438 has been deleted)

99440   **Newborn resuscitation:** provision of positive pressure ventilation and/or chest compressions in the presence of acute inadequate ventilation and/or cardiac output
> *CPT Assistant* Summer 93:1; Mar 96:10

Special Evaluation and Management Services

The following codes are used to report evaluations performed to establish baseline information prior to life or disability insurance certificates being issued. This service is performed in the office or other setting, and applies to both new and established patients. When using these codes, no active management of the problem(s) is undertaken during the encounter.

If other evaluation and management services and/or procedures are performed on the same date, the appropriate E/M or procedure code(s) should be reported in addition to these codes.

Basic Life and/or Disability Evaluation Services

99450   **Basic life** and/or disability examination that includes:
> *CPT Assistant* Summer 95:14

- **measurement of height, weight and blood pressure;**
- **completion of a medical history following a life insurance pro forma;**
- **collection of blood sample and/or urinalysis complying with "chain of custody" protocols; and**
- **completion of necessary documentation/certificates.**

Work Related or Medical Disability Evaluation Services

99455 **Work related** or medical disability examination by the treating physician that includes:

➔ *CPT Assistant* Summer 95:14

- **completion of a medical history commensurate with the patient's condition;**
- **performance of an examination commensurate with the patient's condition;**
- **formulation of a diagnosis, assessment of capabilities and stability, and calculation of impairment;**
- **development of future medical treatment plan; and**
- **completion of necessary documentation/certificates and report.**

99456 **Work related** or medical disability examination by other than the treating physician that includes:

➔ *CPT Assistant* Summer 95:14

- **completion of a medical history commensurate with the patient's condition;**
- **performance of an examination commensurate with the patient's condition;**
- **formulation of a diagnosis, assessment of capabilities and stability, and calculation of impairment;**
- **development of future medical treatment plan; and**
- **completion of necessary documentation/certificates and report.**

Other Evaluation and Management Services

99499 **Unlisted evaluation and management** service

➔ *CPT Assistant* Apr 96:10

◯ =Modifier '-51' Exempt ▶ ◀=New or Revised Text ✚=Add-on Code CPT 2002

Anesthesia Guidelines

Services involving administration of anesthesia are reported by the use of the anesthesia five digit procedure code (00100-01999) plus modifier codes (defined under "Anesthesia Modifiers" later in these Guidelines).

The reporting of anesthesia services is appropriate by or under the responsible supervision of a physician. These services may include but are not limited to general, regional, supplementation of local anesthesia, or other supportive services in order to afford the patient the anesthesia care deemed optimal by the anesthesiologist during any procedure. These services include the usual preoperative and postoperative visits, the anesthesia care during the procedure, the administration of fluids and/or blood and the usual monitoring services (eg, ECG, temperature, blood pressure, oximetry, capnography, and mass spectrometry). Unusual forms of monitoring (eg, intra-arterial, central venous, and Swan-Ganz) are not included.

Items used by all physicians in reporting their services are presented in the **Introduction.** Some of the commonalities are repeated here for the convenience of those physicians referring to this section on **Anesthesia.** Other definitions and items unique to anesthesia are also listed.

To report sedation with or without analgesia (conscious sedation) provided by a physician also performing the service for which conscious sedation is being provided, see codes 99141, 99142.

To report regional or general anesthesia provided by a physician also performing the services for which the anesthesia is being provided, see modifier '-47,' Anesthesia by Surgeon, in Appendix A.

Time Reporting

Time for anesthesia procedures may be reported as is customary in the local area. Anesthesia time begins when the anesthesiologist begins to prepare the patient for the induction of anesthesia in the operating room or in an equivalent area and ends when the anesthesiologist is no longer in personal attendance, that is, when the patient may be safely placed under postoperative supervision.

Physician's Services

Physician's services rendered in the office, home, or hospital, consultation, and other medical services are listed in the section entitled **Evaluation and Management Services** (99200 series) found in the front of the book, beginning on page 1. "Special Services and Reporting" (99000 series) are presented in the **Medicine** section.

Materials Supplied by Physician

Supplies and materials provided by the physician (eg, sterile trays, drugs) over and above those usually included with the office visit or other services rendered may be listed separately. List drugs, tray supplies, and materials provided. Identify as 99070.

Separate or Multiple Procedures

It is appropriate to designate multiple procedures that are rendered on the same date by separate entries. This can be reported by using the multiple procedure modifier '-51'. See "Anesthesia Modifiers" for modifier definitions.

Special Report

A service that is rarely provided, unusual, variable, or new may require a special report in determining medical appropriateness of the service. Pertinent information should include an adequate definition or description of the nature, extent, and need for the procedure; and the time, effort, and equipment necessary to provide the service. Additional items which may be included are:

- complexity of symptoms;
- final diagnosis;
- pertinent physical findings;
- diagnostic and therapeutic procedures;
- concurrent problems;
- follow-up care.

Anesthesia Modifiers

All anesthesia services are reported by use of the anesthesia five digit procedure code (00100-01999) plus the addition of a physical status modifier. The use of other optional modifiers may be appropriate.

Physical Status Modifiers

Physical Status modifiers are represented by the initial letter 'P' followed by a single digit from 1 to 6 defined below.

P1-A normal healthy patient.

P2-A patient with mild systemic disease.

P3-A patient with severe systemic disease.

P4-A patient with severe systemic disease that is a constant threat to life.

P5-A moribund patient who is not expected to survive without the operation.

P6-A declared brain-dead patient whose organs are being removed for donor purposes.

The above six levels are consistent with the American Society of Anesthesiologists (ASA) ranking of patient physical status. Physical status is included in CPT to distinguish among various levels of complexity of the anesthesia service provided.

Example: 00100-P1

Qualifying Circumstances

More than one may be selected.

Many anesthesia services are provided under particularly difficult circumstances, depending on factors such as extraordinary condition of patient, notable operative conditions, and/or unusual risk factors. This section includes a list of important qualifying circumstances that significantly impact on the character of the anesthesia service provided. These procedures would not be reported alone but would be reported as additional procedure numbers qualifying an anesthesia procedure or service.

+ **99100** Anesthesia for patient of extreme age, under one year and over seventy (List separately in addition to code for primary anesthesia procedure)

+ **99116** Anesthesia complicated by utilization of total body hypothermia (List separately in addition to code for primary anesthesia procedure)

+ **99135** Anesthesia complicated by utilization of controlled hypotension (List separately in addition to code for primary anesthesia procedure)

+ **99140** Anesthesia complicated by emergency conditions (specify) (List separately in addition to code for primary anesthesia procedure)

(An emergency is defined as existing when delay in treatment of the patient would lead to a significant increase in the threat to life or body part.)

Anesthesia

Head

00100 Anesthesia for procedures on salivary glands, including biopsy
➡ *CPT Assistant* Feb 97:4; Nov 99:6

00102 Anesthesia for procedures on plastic repair of cleft lip
➡ *CPT Assistant* Nov 99:6; *CPT Changes* 2000

00103 Anesthesia for reconstructive procedures of eyelid (eg, blepharoplasty, ptosis surgery)
➡ *CPT Assistant* Nov 99:6; *CPT Changes* 2000

00104 Anesthesia for electroconvulsive therapy

00120 Anesthesia for procedures on external, middle, and inner ear including biopsy; not otherwise specified

(00122 has been deleted. To report, use 00120)

00124 otoscopy
➡ *CPT Assistant* Nov 99:7

00126 tympanotomy

00140 Anesthesia for procedures on eye; not otherwise specified

00142 lens surgery

00144 corneal transplant

00145 vitreoretinal surgery
➡ *CPT Changes* 2001

(00146 has been deleted. To report, use 00140)

00147 iridectomy

00148 ophthalmoscopy

00160 Anesthesia for procedures on nose and accessory sinuses; not otherwise specified

00162 radical surgery

00164 biopsy, soft tissue

00170 Anesthesia for intraoral procedures, including biopsy; not otherwise specified

00172 repair of cleft palate

00174 excision of retropharyngeal tumor

00176 radical surgery

00190 Anesthesia for procedures on facial bones or skull; not otherwise specified
➡ *CPT Changes* 2001

00192 radical surgery (including prognathism)

00210 Anesthesia for intracranial procedures; not otherwise specified

00212 subdural taps

00214 burr holes, including ventriculography
➡ *CPT Assistant* Nov 99:7; *CPT Changes* 2000

00215 cranioplasty or elevation of depressed skull fracture, extradural (simple or compound)
➡ *CPT Changes* 2001

00216 vascular procedures

00218 procedures in sitting position

▲ **00220** cerebrospinal fluid shunting procedures

00222 electrocoagulation of intracranial nerve

Neck

00300 Anesthesia for all procedures on the integumentary system, muscles and nerves of head, neck, and posterior trunk, not otherwise specified
➡ *CPT Assistant* Nov 99:7

00320 Anesthesia for all procedures on esophagus, thyroid, larynx, trachea and lymphatic system of neck; not otherwise specified

00322 needle biopsy of thyroid

(For procedures on cervical spine and cord, see 00600, 00604, 00670)

00350 Anesthesia for procedures on major vessels of neck; not otherwise specified

00352 simple ligation

(For arteriography, use 01916)

Thorax (Chest Wall and Shoulder Girdle)

00400 Anesthesia for procedures on the integumentary system on the extremities, anterior trunk and perineum; not otherwise specified

00402 reconstructive procedures on breast (eg, reduction or augmentation mammoplasty, muscle flaps)

00404 radical or modified radical procedures on breast

00406 radical or modified radical procedures on breast with internal mammary node dissection

00410 electrical conversion of arrhythmias

(00420 has been deleted. To report, use 00300)

00450 Anesthesia for procedures on clavicle and scapula; not otherwise specified

00452 radical surgery

00454   biopsy of clavicle

00470   Anesthesia for partial rib resection; not otherwise specified

00472   thoracoplasty (any type)

00474   radical procedures (eg, pectus excavatum)

(00476 has been deleted. To report, use 00470)

Intrathoracic

00500   Anesthesia for all procedures on esophagus

00520   Anesthesia for closed chest procedures; (including bronchoscopy) not otherwise specified
➔ *CPT Assistant* Nov 99:7; *CPT Changes* 2000

00522   needle biopsy of pleura

00524   pneumocentesis

(00526 has been deleted. To report, use 00520)

00528   mediastinoscopy and diagnostic thoracoscopy
➔ *CPT Assistant* Nov 99:7; *CPT Changes* 2000

00530   Anesthesia for permanent transvenous pacemaker insertion
➔ *CPT Changes* 2001

00532   Anesthesia for access to central venous circulation

00534   Anesthesia for transvenous insertion or replacement of pacing cardioverter-defibrillator
➔ *CPT Changes* 2001

(For transthoracic approach, use 00560)

00537   Anesthesia for cardiac electrophysiologic procedures including radiofrequency ablation
➔ *CPT Changes* 2001

00540   Anesthesia for thoracotomy procedures involving lungs, pleura, diaphragm, and mediastinum (including surgical thoracoscopy); not otherwise specified

00542   decortication

00544   pleurectomy

00546   pulmonary resection with thoracoplasty

00548   intrathoracic procedures on the trachea and bronchi
➔ *CPT Assistant* Nov 97:10

00550   Anesthesia for sternal debridement
➔ *CPT Changes* 2001

▲ **00560**   Anesthesia for procedures on heart, pericardial sac, and great vessels of chest; without pump oxygenator
➔ *CPT Changes* 2002

00562   with pump oxygenator

00563   with pump oxygenator with hypothermic circulatory arrest
➔ *CPT Changes* 2001

00566   Anesthesia for direct coronary artery bypass grafting without pump oxygenator
➔ *CPT Changes* 2001

00580   Anesthesia for heart transplant or heart/lung transplant

Spine and Spinal Cord

00600   Anesthesia for procedures on cervical spine and cord; not otherwise specified

(For myelography and diskography, see radiological procedures ▶01905◀)

00604   procedures with patient in the sitting position
➔ *CPT Changes* 2001

00620   Anesthesia for procedures on thoracic spine and cord; not otherwise specified

00622   thoracolumbar sympathectomy

00630   Anesthesia for procedures in lumbar region; not otherwise specified

00632   lumbar sympathectomy

00634   chemonucleolysis

(00650 has been deleted. To report, use 00220)

00635   diagnostic or therapeutic lumbar puncture
➔ *CPT Changes* 2001

00670   Anesthesia for extensive spine and spinal cord procedures (eg, spinal instrumentation or vascular procedures)
➔ *CPT Changes* 2001

Upper Abdomen

00700   Anesthesia for procedures on upper anterior abdominal wall; not otherwise specified

00702   percutaneous liver biopsy

00730   Anesthesia for procedures on upper posterior abdominal wall

00740   Anesthesia for upper gastrointestinal endoscopic procedures, endoscope introduced proximal to duodenum
➔ *CPT Assistant* Nov 99:7; *CPT Changes* 2000

00750   Anesthesia for hernia repairs in upper abdomen; not otherwise specified

00752   lumbar and ventral (incisional) hernias and/or wound dehiscence

00754   omphalocele

00756   transabdominal repair of diaphragmatic hernia

00770   Anesthesia for all procedures on major abdominal blood vessels

00790 Anesthesia for intraperitoneal procedures in upper abdomen including laparoscopy; not otherwise specified

00792 partial hepatectomy or management of liver hemorrhage (excluding liver biopsy)
➲ *CPT Changes* 2001

00794 pancreatectomy, partial or total (eg, Whipple procedure)

00796 liver transplant (recipient)

(For harvesting of liver, use 01990)

● **00797** gastric restrictive procedure for morbid obesity
➲ *CPT Changes* 2002

Lower Abdomen

00800 Anesthesia for procedures on lower anterior abdominal wall; not otherwise specified

00802 panniculectomy

(00806 has been deleted. To report, see 00790, 00840)

00810 Anesthesia for lower intestinal endoscopic procedures, endoscope introduced distal to duodenum
➲ *CPT Assistant* Nov 99:7; *CPT Changes* 2000

00820 Anesthesia for procedures on lower posterior abdominal wall

00830 Anesthesia for hernia repairs in lower abdomen; not otherwise specified

00832 ventral and incisional hernias

00840 Anesthesia for intraperitoneal procedures in lower abdomen including laparoscopy; not otherwise specified

00842 amniocentesis

00844 abdominoperineal resection

00846 radical hysterectomy

00848 pelvic exenteration

▶(00850 has been deleted. To report, use 01961)◀

● **00851** tubal ligation/transection
➲ *CPT Changes* 2002

▶(00855 has been deleted. To report, use 01963)◀

▶(00857 has been deleted. To report, use 01968, 01969)◀

00860 Anesthesia for extraperitoneal procedures in lower abdomen, including urinary tract; not otherwise specified

00862 renal procedures, including upper 1/3 of ureter, or donor nephrectomy

00864 total cystectomy

00865 radical prostatectomy (suprapubic, retropubic)

00866 adrenalectomy

00868 renal transplant (recipient)

(For donor nephrectomy, use 00862)

(For harvesting kidney from brain-dead patient, use 01990)

● **00869** vasectomy, unilateral/bilateral
➲ *CPT Changes* 2002

00870 cystolithotomy

00872 Anesthesia for lithotripsy, extracorporeal shock wave; with water bath

00873 without water bath

00880 Anesthesia for procedures on major lower abdominal vessels; not otherwise specified

00882 inferior vena cava ligation

▶(00884 has been deleted. To report, use 01930)◀

Perineum

(00900 has been deleted. To report, see 00300, 00400)

00902 Anesthesia for; anorectal procedure
➲ *CPT Changes* 2001

00904 radical perineal procedure

00906 vulvectomy

00908 perineal prostatectomy

00910 Anesthesia for transurethral procedures (including urethrocystoscopy); not otherwise specified

00912 transurethral resection of bladder tumor(s)

00914 transurethral resection of prostate

00916 post-transurethral resection bleeding

00918 with fragmentation, manipulation and/or removal of ureteral calculus
➲ *CPT Assistant* Nov 99:8; *CPT Changes* 2000

00920 Anesthesia for procedures on male genitalia (including open urethral procedures); not otherwise specified
➲ *CPT Changes* 2001

00922 seminal vesicles

00924 undescended testis, unilateral or bilateral

00926 radical orchiectomy, inguinal

00928 radical orchiectomy, abdominal

00930 orchiopexy, unilateral or bilateral

00932 complete amputation of penis

00934 radical amputation of penis with bilateral inguinal lymphadenectomy

00936 radical amputation of penis with bilateral inguinal and iliac lymphadenectomy

00938 insertion of penile prosthesis (perineal approach)

00940 Anesthesia for vaginal procedures (including biopsy of labia, vagina, cervix or endometrium); not otherwise specified

▲ **00942** colpotomy, vaginectomy, colporrhaphy, and open urethral procedures
➔ *CPT Changes* 2001, 2002

00944 vaginal hysterectomy

►(00946 has been deleted. To report, use 01960)◄

00948 cervical cerclage

00950 culdoscopy

00952 hysteroscopy and/or hysterosalpingography
➔ *CPT Assistant* Nov 99:8; *CPT Changes* 2000

►(00955 has been deleted. To report, use 01967)◄

Pelvis (Except Hip)

(01000 has been deleted. To report, use 00400)

(01110 has been deleted. To report, use 00300)

01112 Anesthesia for bone marrow aspiration and/or biopsy, anterior or posterior iliac crest
➔ *CPT Changes* 2001

01120 Anesthesia for procedures on bony pelvis

(01122 has been deleted. To report, use 01120)

01130 Anesthesia for body cast application or revision

01140 Anesthesia for interpelviabdominal (hindquarter) amputation

01150 Anesthesia for radical procedures for tumor of pelvis, except hindquarter amputation

01160 Anesthesia for closed procedures involving symphysis pubis or sacroiliac joint

01170 Anesthesia for open procedures involving symphysis pubis or sacroiliac joint

01180 Anesthesia for obturator neurectomy; extrapelvic

01190 intrapelvic

Upper Leg (Except Knee)

01200 Anesthesia for all closed procedures involving hip joint

01202 Anesthesia for arthroscopic procedures of hip joint

01210 Anesthesia for open procedures involving hip joint; not otherwise specified

01212 hip disarticulation

▲ **01214** total hip arthroplasty
➔ *CPT Changes* 2001; 2002

01215 revision of total hip arthroplasty
➔ *CPT Changes* 2001; 2002

01220 Anesthesia for all closed procedures involving upper 2/3 of femur

01230 Anesthesia for open procedures involving upper 2/3 of femur; not otherwise specified

01232 amputation

01234 radical resection

(01240 has been deleted. To report, use 00400)

01250 Anesthesia for all procedures on nerves, muscles, tendons, fascia, and bursae of upper leg

01260 Anesthesia for all procedures involving veins of upper leg, including exploration

01270 Anesthesia for procedures involving arteries of upper leg, including bypass graft; not otherwise specified

01272 femoral artery ligation

01274 femoral artery embolectomy

(01276 has been deleted. To report, use 00880)

Knee and Popliteal Area

(01300 has been deleted. To report, use 00400)

01320 Anesthesia for all procedures on nerves, muscles, tendons, fascia, and bursae of knee and/or popliteal area

01340 Anesthesia for all closed procedures on lower 1/3 of femur

01360 Anesthesia for all open procedures on lower 1/3 of femur

01380 Anesthesia for all closed procedures on knee joint

01382 Anesthesia for arthroscopic procedures of knee joint

01390 Anesthesia for all closed procedures on upper ends of tibia, fibula, and/or patella

01392 Anesthesia for all open procedures on upper ends of tibia, fibula, and/or patella

01400 Anesthesia for open procedures on knee joint; not otherwise specified

▲ **01402** total knee arthroplasty
➔ *CPT Changes* 2002

01404 disarticulation at knee

01420 Anesthesia for all cast applications, removal, or repair involving knee joint

01430 Anesthesia for procedures on veins of knee and popliteal area; not otherwise specified

01432 arteriovenous fistula

01440 Anesthesia for procedures on arteries of knee and popliteal area; not otherwise specified

01442 popliteal thromboendarterectomy, with or without patch graft

01444 popliteal excision and graft or repair for occlusion or aneurysm

⊘ =Modifier '-51' Exempt   ►◄ =New or Revised Text   ✚ =Add-on Code   CPT 2002

Lower Leg (Below Knee, Includes Ankle and Foot)

(01460 has been deleted. To report, use 00400)

01462 Anesthesia for all closed procedures on lower leg, ankle, and foot

01464 Anesthesia for arthroscopic procedures of ankle joint

01470 Anesthesia for procedures on nerves, muscles, tendons, and fascia of lower leg, ankle, and foot; not otherwise specified

01472   repair of ruptured Achilles tendon, with or without graft

01474   gastrocnemius recession (eg, Strayer procedure)

01480 Anesthesia for open procedures on bones of lower leg, ankle, and foot; not otherwise specified

01482   radical resection (including below knee amputation)
    ➔ *CPT Changes* 2001

01484   osteotomy or osteoplasty of tibia and/or fibula

01486   total ankle replacement

01490 Anesthesia for lower leg cast application, removal, or repair

01500 Anesthesia for procedures on arteries of lower leg, including bypass graft; not otherwise specified

01502   embolectomy, direct or with catheter

01520 Anesthesia for procedures on veins of lower leg; not otherwise specified

01522   venous thrombectomy, direct or with catheter

Shoulder and Axilla

Includes humeral head and neck, sternoclavicular joint, acromioclavicular joint, and shoulder joint.

(01600 has been deleted. To report, use 00400)

01610 Anesthesia for all procedures on nerves, muscles, tendons, fascia, and bursae of shoulder and axilla

01620 Anesthesia for all closed procedures on humeral head and neck, sternoclavicular joint, acromioclavicular joint, and shoulder joint

01622 Anesthesia for arthroscopic procedures of shoulder joint

01630 Anesthesia for open procedures on humeral head and neck, sternoclavicular joint, acromioclavicular joint, and shoulder joint; not otherwise specified

01632   radical resection

01634   shoulder disarticulation

01636   interthoracoscapular (forequarter) amputation

01638   total shoulder replacement

01650 Anesthesia for procedures on arteries of shoulder and axilla; not otherwise specified

01652   axillary-brachial aneurysm

01654   bypass graft

01656   axillary-femoral bypass graft

01670 Anesthesia for all procedures on veins of shoulder and axilla

01680 Anesthesia for shoulder cast application, removal or repair; not otherwise specified

01682   shoulder spica

Upper Arm and Elbow

(01700 has been deleted. To report, use 00400)

01710 Anesthesia for procedures on nerves, muscles, tendons, fascia, and bursae of upper arm and elbow; not otherwise specified

01712   tenotomy, elbow to shoulder, open

01714   tenoplasty, elbow to shoulder

01716   tenodesis, rupture of long tendon of biceps

01730 Anesthesia for all closed procedures on humerus and elbow

01732 Anesthesia for arthroscopic procedures of elbow joint

01740 Anesthesia for open procedures on humerus and elbow; not otherwise specified

01742   osteotomy of humerus

01744   repair of nonunion or malunion of humerus

01756   radical procedures

01758   excision of cyst or tumor of humerus

01760   total elbow replacement

01770 Anesthesia for procedures on arteries of upper arm and elbow; not otherwise specified

01772   embolectomy

01780 Anesthesia for procedures on veins of upper arm and elbow; not otherwise specified

01782   phleborrhaphy

(01784 has been deleted. To report, see 01770, 01780)

Forearm, Wrist, and Hand

(01800 has been deleted. To report, use 00400)

01810   Anesthesia for all procedures on nerves, muscles, tendons, fascia, and bursae of forearm, wrist, and hand

01820   Anesthesia for all closed procedures on radius, ulna, wrist, or hand bones

01830   Anesthesia for open procedures on radius, ulna, wrist, or hand bones; not otherwise specified

01832   total wrist replacement

01840   Anesthesia for procedures on arteries of forearm, wrist, and hand; not otherwise specified

01842   embolectomy

01844   Anesthesia for vascular shunt, or shunt revision, any type (eg, dialysis)

01850   Anesthesia for procedures on veins of forearm, wrist, and hand; not otherwise specified

01852   phleborrhaphy

01860   Anesthesia for forearm, wrist, or hand cast application, removal, or repair

Radiological Procedures

(01900 has been deleted. To report, use 00952)

(01902 has been deleted. To report, use 00214)

►(01904 has been deleted. To report, use 01905)◄

● **01905**   Anesthesia for myelography, diskography, vertebroplasty
      ➔ *CPT Changes* 2002

►(01906 has been deleted. To report, use 01905)◄

►(01908 has been deleted. To report, use 01905)◄

►(01910 has been deleted. To report, use 01905)◄

►(01912 has been deleted. To report, use 01905)◄

►(01914 has been deleted. To report, use 01905)◄

▲ **01916**   Anesthesia for diagnostic arteriography/venography
      ➔ *CPT Changes* 2002

►(Do not report 01916 in conjunction with therapeutic codes 01924-01926, 01930-01933)◄

►(01918 has been deleted. To report, use 01916)◄

▲ **01920**   Anesthesia for cardiac catheterization including coronary angiography and ventriculography (not to include Swan-Ganz catheter)

►(01921 has been deleted. To report, see 01924-01926)◄

01922   Anesthesia for non-invasive imaging or radiation therapy

● **01924**   Anesthesia for therapeutic interventional radiologic procedures involving the arterial system; not otherwise specified
      ➔ *CPT Changes* 2002

● **01925**   carotid or coronary
      ➔ *CPT Changes* 2002

● **01926**   intracranial, intracardiac, or aortic
      ➔ *CPT Changes* 2002

● **01930**   Anesthesia for therapeutic interventional radiologic procedures involving the venous/lymphatic system (not to include access to the central circulation); not otherwise specified
      ➔ *CPT Changes* 2002

● **01931**   intrahepatic or portal circulation (eg, transcutaneous porto-caval shunt (TIPS))
      ➔ *CPT Changes* 2002

● **01932**   intrathoracic or jugular
      ➔ *CPT Changes* 2002

● **01933**   intracranial
      ➔ *CPT Changes* 2002

Burn Excisions or Debridement

▲ **01951**   Anesthesia for second and third degree burn excision or debridement with or without skin grafting, any site, for total body surface area (TBSA) treated during anesthesia and surgery; less than four percent total body surface area
      ➔ *CPT Changes* 2001; 2002

▲ **01952**   between four and nine percent of total body surface area
      ➔ *CPT Changes* 2001; 2002

➕ **01953**   each additional nine percent total body surface area or part thereof (List separately in addition to code for primary procedure)
      ➔ *CPT Changes* 2001

(Use 01953 in conjunction with code 01952)

►Obstetric◄

● **01960**   Anesthesia for; vaginal delivery only
      ➔ *CPT Changes* 2002

● **01961**   cesarean delivery only
      ➔ *CPT Changes* 2002

● **01962**   urgent hysterectomy following delivery
   ➲ *CPT Changes* 2002

● **01963**   cesarean hysterectomy without any labor
   analgesia/anesthesia care
   ➲ *CPT Changes* 2002

● **01964**   abortion procedures
   ➲ *CPT Changes* 2002

● **01967**   Neuraxial labor analgesia/anesthesia for planned vaginal
   delivery (this includes any repeat subarachnoid needle
   placement and drug injection and/or any necessary
   replacement of an epidural catheter during labor)
   ➲ *CPT Changes* 2002

+ ● **01968**   Cesarean delivery following neuraxial labor
   analgesia/anesthesia (List separately in addition to code
   for primary procedure)
   ➲ *CPT Changes* 2002

   ▶(Use 01968 in conjunction with code 01967)◀

+ ● **01969**   Cesarean hysterectomy following neuraxial labor
   analgesia/anesthesia (List separately in addition to code
   for primary procedure)
   ➲ *CPT Changes* 2002

   ▶(Use 01969 in conjunction with code 01967)◀

Other Procedures

01990   Physiological support for harvesting of organ(s) from
   brain-dead patient

▲ **01995**   Regional intravenous administration of local anesthetic
   agent or other medication (upper or lower extremity)
   ➲ *CPT Changes* 2002

   (For intra-arterial or intravenous therapy for pain
   management, see 90783, 90784)

01996   Daily management of epidural or subarachnoid drug
   administration
   ➲ *CPT Assistant* Nov 97:10

01999   Unlisted anesthesia procedure(s)
   ➲ *CPT Assistant* Feb 97:4

Notes

Surgery Guidelines

Items used by all physicians in reporting their services are presented in the **Introduction.** Some of the commonalities are repeated here for the convenience of those physicians referring to this section on **Surgery.** Other definitions and items unique to Surgery are also listed.

Physicians' Services

Physicians' services rendered in the office, home, or hospital, consultations, and other medical services are listed in the section entitled **Evaluation and Management Services** (99200 series) found in the front of the book, beginning on page 9. "Special Services and Reports" (99000 series) is presented in the **Medicine** section.

►CPT Surgical Package Definition◄

►The services provided by the physician to any patient by their very nature are variable. The CPT codes that represent a readily identifiable surgical procedure thereby include, on a procedure-by-procedure basis, a variety of services. In defining the specific services "included" in a given CPT surgical code, the following services are always included in addition to the operation per se:

- local infiltration, metacarpal/metatarsal/digital block or topical anesthesia;
- subsequent to the decision for surgery, one related E/M encounter on the date immediately prior to or on the date of procedure (including history and physical);
- immediate postoperative care, including dictating operative notes, talking with the family and other physicians;
- writing orders;
- evaluating the patient in the postanesthesia recovery area;
- typical postoperative follow-up care.◄

Follow-Up Care for Diagnostic Procedures

Follow-up care for diagnostic procedures (eg, endoscopy, arthroscopy, injection procedures for radiography) includes only that care related to recovery from the diagnostic procedure itself. Care of the condition for which the diagnostic procedure was performed or of other concomitant conditions is not included and may be listed separately.

Follow-Up Care for Therapeutic Surgical Procedures

Follow-up care for therapeutic surgical procedures includes only that care which is usually a part of the surgical service. Complications, exacerbations, recurrence, or the presence of other diseases or injuries requiring additional services should be ►separately◄ reported.

Materials Supplied by Physician

Supplies and materials provided by the physician (eg, sterile trays/drugs), over and above those usually included with the ►procedure(s)◄ rendered ►are reported◄ separately. List drugs, trays, supplies, and materials provided. Identify as 99070 ►or specific supply code.◄

Reporting More Than One Procedure/Service

When a physician performs more than one procedure/service on the same date, same session or during a post-operative period (subject to the "surgical package" concept), several CPT modifiers may apply. (See Appendix A for definition.)

►-27 Multiple Outpatient Hospital E/M Encounters on the Same Date◄

►For hospital outpatient reporting purposes, utilization of hospital resources related to separate and distinct E/M encounters performed in multiple outpatient hospital settings on the same date may be reported by adding the modifier '-27' to each appropriate level outpatient and/or emergency department E/M code(s). This modifier provides a means of reporting circumstances involving evaluation and management services provided by physician(s) in more than one (multiple) outpatient hospital setting(s) (eg, hospital emergency department, clinic). **Note:** This modifier is not to be used for physician reporting of multiple E/M services performed by the same physician on the same date. For physician reporting of all outpatient evaluation and management services provided by the same physician on the same date and performed in multiple outpatient setting(s) (eg, hospital emergency department, clinic), see **Evaluation and Management, Emergency Department,** or **Preventive Medicine Services** codes.◄

-51 Multiple Procedures

When multiple procedures/services (other than evaluation and management) are performed at the same session, report the most significant procedure first, with all other procedures listed with the '-51' modifier appended. For a list of procedures exempt from the use of the '-51' modifier, see Appendices E and F.

-58 Staged or Related Procedure or Service by the Same Physician During the Postoperative Period

When a procedure(s) is prospectively planned as a staged procedure, or when the secondary and subsequent procedure(s) is more extensive, or to indicate therapy following a diagnostic surgical procedure, use the '-58' modifier with the staged procedure(s).

-59 Distinct Procedural Service

For procedure(s)/service(s) not ordinarily performed or encountered on the same day by the same physician, but appropriate under certain circumstances (eg, different site or organ system, separate excision or lesion), use the '-59' modifier.

-76 Repeat Procedure by Same Physician

When a procedure or service is repeated by the same physician subsequent to the original service, use the '-76' modifier.

-77 Repeat Procedure by Another Physician

When a procedure is repeated by another physician subsequent to the original service, use the '-77' modifier.

-78 Return to the Operating Room for a Related Procedure During the Postoperative Period

When a procedure, related to the initial procedure, requires a return to the operating room during the postoperative period of that initial procedure, use the '-78' modifier.

-79 Unrelated Procedure or Service by the Same Physician During the Postoperative Period

When a procedure, unrelated to the initial procedure, is performed by the same physician during the postoperative period of the initial procedure, use the '-79' modifier.

►-91 Repeat Clinical Diagnostic Laboratory Test◄

►In the course of treatment of the patient, it may be necessary to repeat the same laboratory test on the same day to obtain subsequent (multiple) test results. Under these circumstances, the laboratory test performed can be identified by its usual procedure number and the addition of the modifier '-91'. **Note:** This modifier may not be used when tests are rerun to confirm initial results; due to testing problems with specimens or equipment; or for any other reason when a normal, one-time, reportable result is all that is required. This modifier may not be used when other code(s) describe a series of test results (eg, glucose tolerance tests, evocative/suppression testing). This modifier may only be used for laboratory test(s) performed more than once on the same day on the same patient.◄

Add-on Codes

Some of the listed procedures are commonly carried out in addition to the primary procedure performed. These additional or supplemental procedures are designated as "add-on" codes with a "✦" symbol, and are listed in Appendix E of *CPT*. Add-on codes in *CPT* can be readily identified by specific descriptor nomenclature which includes phrases such as "each additional" or "(List separately in addition to primary procedure)".

The "add-on" code concept in *CPT* applies only to add-on procedures/services performed by the same physician. Add-on codes describe additional intra-service work associated with the primary procedure (eg, additional digit(s), lesion(s), neurorrhaphy(s), vertebral segment(s), tendon(s), joint(s)).

Add-on codes are always performed in addition to the primary service/procedure, and must never be reported as a stand-alone code. All add-on codes found in *CPT* are exempt from the multiple procedure concept (see modifier '-51' definition of Surgery Guidelines).

Separate Procedure

Some of the procedures or services listed in *CPT* that are commonly carried out as an integral component of a total service or procedure have been identified by the inclusion of the term "separate procedure." The codes designated as "separate procedure" should not be reported in addition to the code for the total procedure or service of which it is considered an integral component.

However, when a procedure or service that is designated as a "separate procedure" is carried out independently or considered to be unrelated or distinct from other procedures/services provided at that time, it may be reported by itself, or in addition to other procedures/services by appending the modifier '-59' to the specific "separate procedure" code to indicate that the procedure is not considered to be a component of another procedure, but is a distinct, independent procedure. This may represent a different session or patient encounter, different procedure or surgery, different site or organ system, separate incision/excision, separate lesion, or separate injury (or area of injury in extensive injuries).

Subsection Information

Several of the subheadings or subsections have special needs or instructions unique to that section. Where these are indicated (eg, "Maternity Care and Delivery"), special **"Notes"** will be presented preceding those procedural terminology listings, referring to that subsection specifically. If there is an "Unlisted Procedure" code number (see below) for the individual subsection, it will also be shown. Those subsections within the **Surgery** section that have **"Notes"** are as follows:

Removal of Skin Tags	11200-11201
Shaving of Lesions	11300-11313
Excision—Benign Lesions	11400-11471
Excision—Malignant Lesions	11600-11646
Repair (Closure)	12001-13160
Adjacent Tissue Transfer or Rearrangement	14000-14350
Free Skin Grafts	15000-15400
Flaps (Skin and/or Deep Tissue)	15570-15999
Burns, Local Treatment	16000-16042
Destruction, Benign Lesions	17000-17250
Destruction, Malignant Lesions	17260-17286
Mohs Micrographic Surgery	17304-17310
Musculoskeletal	20000-29909
Wound Exploration—Trauma	20100-20103
Grafts (or Implants)	20900-20999
Spine: Excision	22100-22116
Spine: Osteotomy	22210-22226
Spine: Fracture/Dislocation	22305-22328
Spine: Arthrodesis	22548-22812

Spinal Instrumentation	22840-22855
Casting and Strapping	29000-29750
Cardiovascular System	33010-37799
Pacing Cardioverter-Pacemaker or Defibrillator	33200-33249
Venous—CABG	33510-33516
Arterial—Venous—CABG	33517-33530
Arterial—CABG	33533-33545
▶Endovascular Repair of Abdominal Aortic Aneurysm	34800-34826◀
Transluminal Angioplasty	35450-35476
Transluminal Atherectomy	35480-35495
Composite Grafts	35681-35683
Arteries and Veins	34001-35907
Vascular Injection Procedures:	
Intravenous	36000-36015
▶Intra-Arterial/Intra-Aortic	36100-36299◀
Endoscopy	31505-31579, 32601-32665, 43200-43272, 44360-▶44397◀, 45300-▶45387◀, 46600-46615, ▶47370-47371◀, 47550-47556
Herniotomy	▶49491◀-49611
Urodynamics	51725-51797
Endoscopy	
▶Urinary◀	▶50945-50980, 51990-52400◀
▶Testis◀	▶54690-54699◀
▶Female Genital◀	▶58550-58579,◀ ▶58660-58679◀
▶Endocrine◀	▶60650-60659◀
Ureter and Pelvis	52320-52339
Maternity Care and Delivery	59000-59899
Surgery of Skull Base	61580-61619
Neurostimulators (Intracranial)	61850-61888
Neurostimulators (Spinal)	63650-63688
Neurostimulators (Peripheral Nerve)	64553-64595
Secondary Implants(s)	65125-65175
Removal Cataract	66830-66999
Prophylaxis	67141-67145
Operating Microscope	69990

Unlisted Service or Procedure

A service or procedure may be provided that is not listed in this edition of *CPT*. When reporting such a service, the appropriate "Unlisted Procedure" code may be used to indicate the service, identifying it by "Special Report" as discussed in the section below. The "Unlisted Procedures" and accompanying codes for **Surgery** are as follows:

15999	Unlisted procedure, excision pressure ulcer
17999	Unlisted procedure, skin, mucous membrane and subcutaneous tissue
19499	Unlisted procedure, breast
20999	Unlisted procedure, musculoskeletal system, general
21089	Unlisted maxillofacial prosthetic procedure

21299	Unlisted craniofacial and maxillofacial procedure
21499	Unlisted musculoskeletal procedure, head
21899	Unlisted procedure, neck or thorax
22899	Unlisted procedure, spine
22999	Unlisted procedure, abdomen, musculoskeletal system
23929	Unlisted procedure, shoulder
24999	Unlisted procedure, humerus or elbow
25999	Unlisted procedure, forearm or wrist
26989	Unlisted procedure, hands or fingers
27299	Unlisted procedure, pelvis or hip joint
27599	Unlisted procedure, femur or knee
27899	Unlisted procedure, leg or ankle
28899	Unlisted procedure, foot or toes
29799	Unlisted procedure, casting or strapping
▶ **29999**	Unlisted procedure, arthroscopy ◀
30999	Unlisted procedure, nose
31299	Unlisted procedure, accessory sinuses
31599	Unlisted procedure, larynx
31899	Unlisted procedure, trachea, bronchi
32999	Unlisted procedure, lungs and pleura
33999	Unlisted procedure, cardiac surgery
36299	Unlisted procedure, vascular injection
37799	Unlisted procedure, vascular surgery
38129	Unlisted laparoscopy procedure, spleen
38589	Unlisted laparoscopy procedure, lymphatic system
38999	Unlisted procedure, hemic or lymphatic system
39499	Unlisted procedure, mediastinum
39599	Unlisted procedure, diaphragm
40799	Unlisted procedure, lips
40899	Unlisted procedure, vestibule of mouth
41599	Unlisted procedure, tongue, floor of mouth
41899	Unlisted procedure, dentoalveolar structures
42299	Unlisted procedure, palate, uvula
42699	Unlisted procedure, salivary glands or ducts
42999	Unlisted procedure, pharynx, adenoids, or tonsils
43289	Unlisted laparoscopy procedure, esophagus
43499	Unlisted procedure, esophagus
43659	Unlisted laparoscopy procedure, stomach
43999	Unlisted procedure, stomach
44209	Unlisted laparoscopy procedure, intestine (except rectum)
44799	Unlisted procedure, intestine
44899	Unlisted procedure, Meckels diverticulum and the mesentery
44979	Unlisted laparoscopy procedure, appendix
45999	Unlisted procedure, rectum
46999	Unlisted procedure, anus
47379	Unlisted laparoscopic procedure, liver
47399	Unlisted procedure, liver
47579	Unlisted laparoscopy procedure, biliary tract
47999	Unlisted procedure, biliary tract

48999	Unlisted procedure, pancreas
49329	Unlisted laparoscopy procedure, abdomen, peritoneum and omentum
49659	Unlisted laparoscopy procedure, hernioplasty, herniorrhaphy, herniotomy
49999	Unlisted procedure, abdomen, peritoneum and omentum
50549	Unlisted laparoscopy procedure, renal
50949	Unlisted laparoscopy procedure, ureter
53899	Unlisted procedure, urinary system
54699	Unlisted laparoscopy procedure, testis
55559	Unlisted laparoscopy procedure, spermatic cord
55899	Unlisted procedure, male genital system
58578	Unlisted laparoscopy procedure, uterus
58579	Unlisted hysteroscopy procedure, uterus
58679	Unlisted laparoscopy procedure, oviduct, ovary
58999	Unlisted procedure, female genital system (nonobstetrical)
59898	Unlisted laparoscopy procedure, maternity care and delivery
59899	Unlisted procedure, maternity care and delivery
60659	Unlisted laparoscopy procedure, endocrine system
60699	Unlisted procedure, endocrine system
64999	Unlisted procedure, nervous system
66999	Unlisted procedure, anterior segment of eye
67299	Unlisted procedure, posterior segment
67399	Unlisted procedure, ocular muscle
67599	Unlisted procedure, orbit
67999	Unlisted procedure, eyelids
68399	Unlisted procedure, conjunctiva
68899	Unlisted procedure, lacrimal system
69399	Unlisted procedure, external ear
69799	Unlisted procedure, middle ear
69949	Unlisted procedure, inner ear
69979	Unlisted procedure, temporal bone, middle fossa approach

Special Report

A service that is rarely provided, unusual, variable, or new may require a special report in determining medical appropriateness of the service. Pertinent information should include an adequate definition or description of the nature, extent, and need for the procedure, and the time, effort, and equipment necessary to provide the service. Additional items which may be included are:

- complexity of symptoms;
- final diagnosis;
- pertinent physical findings (such as size, locations, and number of lesion(s), if appropriate);

- diagnostic and therapeutic procedures (including major and supplementary surgical procedures, if appropriate);
- concurrent problems;
- follow-up care.

Starred (*) Procedures or Items

Certain relatively small surgical services involve a readily identifiable surgical procedure but include variable preoperative and postoperative services (eg, incision and drainage of an abscess, injection of a tendon sheath, manipulation of a joint under anesthesia, dilation of the urethra). Because of the indefinite pre- and postoperative services the usual "package" concept for surgical services (see above) cannot be applied. Such procedures are identified by a star (*) following the procedure code number.

When a star (*) follows a surgical procedure code number, the following rules apply:

1. *The service as listed includes the surgical procedure only.* Associated pre- and postoperative services are not included in the service as listed.

2. *Preoperative services are considered as one of the following:*

- When the starred (*) procedure is carried out at the time of an initial visit (new patient) and this procedure constitutes the major service at that visit, procedure number 99025 is listed in lieu of the usual initial visit as an additional service.

- When the starred (*) procedure is carried out at the time of an initial or established patient visit involving significant identifiable services, the appropriate visit is listed with the modifier '-25' appended in addition to the starred (*) procedure and its follow-up care.

- When the starred (*) procedure requires hospitalization, an appropriate hospital visit is listed in addition to the starred (*) procedure and its follow-up care.

3. *All postoperative care is added on a service-by-service basis (eg, office or hospital visit, cast change).*

4. *Complications are added on a service-by-service basis (as with all surgical procedures).*

Surgical Destruction

Surgical destruction is a part of a surgical procedure and different methods of destruction are not ordinarily listed separately unless the technique substantially alters the standard management of a problem or condition. Exceptions under special circumstances are provided for by separate code numbers.

Notes

Surgery

►General◄

(10000-10020 have been deleted. To report see 10060, 10061)

● **10021** Fine needle aspiration; without imaging guidance
⊃ *CPT Changes* 2002

● **10022** with imaging guidance
⊃ *CPT Changes* 2002

►(For radiological supervision and interpretation, see 76003, 76360, 76942)◄

►(For percutaneous needle biopsy, see 32405 for lung, 47000, 47001 for liver, 48102 for pancreas, 49180 for abdominal or retroperitoneal mass)◄

►(For evaluation of fine needle aspirate, see 88172, 88173)◄

Integumentary System

Skin, Subcutaneous and Accessory Structures

Incision and Drainage

(For excision, see 11400, et seq)

10040 * Acne surgery (eg, marsupialization, opening or removal of multiple milia, comedones, cysts, pustules)
⊃ *CPT Assistant* Fall 92:10

Measuring and Coding the Removal of a Lesion

Measuring lesion removal.
A. Example: excision, malignant lesion of the back, 0.3 centimeters. Code 11600.

Measuring and Coding (continued)

B. Example: excision of benign lesion of the neck, 1.0 centimeter by 2.0 centimeters. Code 11422.

C. Example: excision, malignant lesion of the nose, 1.0 centimeters with skin margins of 2.1 centimeters. Code 11641.

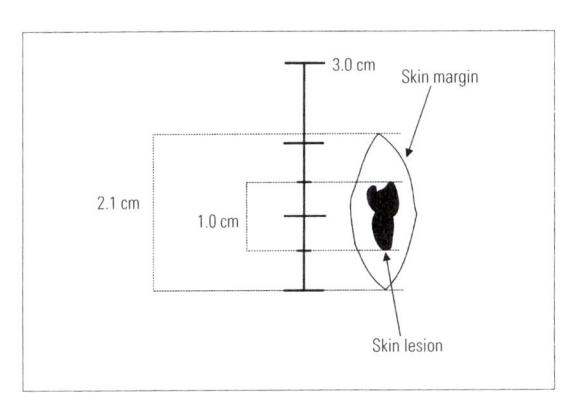

10060 * Incision and drainage of abscess (eg, carbuncle, suppurative hidradenitis, cutaneous or subcutaneous abscess, cyst, furuncle, or paronychia); simple or single

10061 complicated or multiple

10080 * Incision and drainage of pilonidal cyst; simple

10081 complicated

(For excision of pilonidal cyst, see 11770-11772)

(10100, 10101 have been deleted. To report, see 10060, 10061)

10120 * Incision and removal of foreign body, subcutaneous tissues; simple

10121 complicated

(To report wound exploration due to penetrating trauma without laparotomy or thoracotomy, see 20100-20103, as appropriate)

(To report debridement associated with open fracture(s) and/or dislocation(s), use 11010-11012, as appropriate)

10140 * Incision and drainage of hematoma, seroma or fluid collection
> *CPT Changes* 2002

▶(If imaging guidance is performed, see 76360, 76393, 76942)◀

(10141 has been deleted. To report, use 10140)

10160 * Puncture aspiration of abscess, hematoma, bulla, or cyst
> *CPT Changes* 2002

▶(If imaging guidance is performed, see 76360, 76393, 76942)◀

10180 Incision and drainage, complex, postoperative wound infection

(For secondary closure of surgical wound, see 12020, 12021, 13160)

Excision—Debridement

(For dermabrasions, see 15780-15783)

(For nail debridement, see 11720-11721)

(For burn(s), see 16000-16035)

11000 * Debridement of extensive eczematous or infected skin; up to 10% of body surface

+ 11001 each additional 10% of the body surface (List separately in addition to code for primary procedure)

(Use 11001 in conjunction with code 11000)

11010 Debridement including removal of foreign material associated with open fracture(s) and/or dislocation(s); skin and subcutaneous tissues
> *CPT Assistant* Mar 97:1; Apr 97:10; Aug 97:6

11011 skin, subcutaneous tissue, muscle fascia, and muscle
> *CPT Assistant* Mar 97:1; Apr 97:10; Aug 97:6

11012 skin, subcutaneous tissue, muscle fascia, muscle, and bone
> *CPT Assistant* Mar 97:1; Apr 97:10; Aug 97:6

11040 Debridement; skin, partial thickness
> *CPT Assistant* Fall 93:21; May 96:6; Feb 97:7; Aug 97:6

11041 skin, full thickness
> *CPT Assistant* Fall 93:21; May 96:6; Feb 97:7; Aug 97:6

11042 skin, and subcutaneous tissue
> *CPT Assistant* Winter 92:10; May 96:6; Feb 97:7; Aug 97:6

11043 skin, subcutaneous tissue, and muscle
> *CPT Assistant* May 96:6; Feb 97:7; Apr 97:11; Aug 97:6; Dec 99:10

11044 skin, subcutaneous tissue, muscle, and bone
> *CPT Assistant* Fall 93:21; Mar 96:10; May 96:6; Feb 97:7; Apr 97:11; Aug 97:6

(Do not report 11040-11044 in addition to 97601, 97602)

Paring or Cutting

(11050-11052 have been deleted. To report paring, see 11055-11057, or to report destruction, see 17000-17004)

11055 Paring or cutting of benign hyperkeratotic lesion (eg, corn or callus); single lesion
> *CPT Assistant* Nov 97:11; Jan 99:11

11056 two to four lesions
> *CPT Assistant* Nov 97:11; Jan 99:11

11057 more than four lesions
> *CPT Assistant* Nov 97:11; Jan 99:11

(11060-11062 have been deleted. To report, see 11300-11313)

Biopsy

11100 Biopsy of skin, subcutaneous tissue and/or mucous membrane (including simple closure), unless otherwise listed (separate procedure); single lesion
> *CPT Assistant* Fall 94:18; Mar 97:4; Jun 97:5

+ 11101 each separate/additional lesion (List separately in addition to code for primary procedure)
> *CPT Assistant* Fall 94:18; Apr 00:6

(Use 11101 in conjunction with code 11100)

(For biopsy of conjunctiva, use 68100; eyelid, use 67810)

Removal of Skin Tags

Removal by scissoring or any sharp method, ligature strangulation, electrosurgical destruction or combination of treatment modalities including chemical or electrocauterization of wound, with or without local anesthesia.

11200 * Removal of skin tags, multiple fibrocutaneous tags, any area; up to and including 15 lesions
> *CPT Assistant* Nov 97:11-12

+ 11201 each additional ten lesions (List separately in addition to code for primary procedure)
> *CPT Assistant* Nov 97:11-12

(Use 11201 in conjunction with code 11200)

Shaving of Epidermal or Dermal Lesions

Shaving is the sharp removal by transverse incision or horizontal slicing to remove epidermal and dermal lesions without a full-thickness dermal excision. This includes local anesthesia, chemical or electrocauterization of the wound. The wound does not require suture closure.

11300 * Shaving of epidermal or dermal lesion, single lesion, trunk, arms or legs; lesion diameter 0.5 cm or less
> *CPT Assistant* Feb 00:11

11301 lesion diameter 0.6 to 1.0 cm
> *CPT Assistant* Feb 00:11

11302   lesion diameter 1.1 to 2.0 cm
➔ *CPT Assistant* Feb 00:10

11303   lesion diameter over 2.0 cm
➔ *CPT Assistant* Feb 00:10

11305* Shaving of epidermal or dermal lesion, single lesion, scalp, neck, hands, feet, genitalia; lesion diameter 0.5 cm or less
➔ *CPT Assistant* Feb 00:10

11306   lesion diameter 0.6 to 1.0 cm
➔ *CPT Assistant* Feb 00:10

11307   lesion diameter 1.1 to 2.0 cm
➔ *CPT Assistant* Feb 00:10

11308   lesion diameter over 2.0 cm
➔ *CPT Assistant* Feb 00:10

11310* Shaving of epidermal or dermal lesion, single lesion, face, ears, eyelids, nose, lips, mucous membrane; lesion diameter 0.5 cm or less
➔ *CPT Assistant* Feb 00:10

11311   lesion diameter 0.6 to 1.0 cm
➔ *CPT Assistant* Feb 00:10

11312   lesion diameter 1.1 to 2.0 cm
➔ *CPT Assistant* Feb 00:10

11313   lesion diameter over 2.0 cm
➔ *CPT Assistant* Feb 00:10

Excision—Benign Lesions

Excision (including simple closure) of benign lesions of skin or subcutaneous tissues (eg, cicatricial, fibrous, inflammatory, congenital, cystic lesions), including local anesthesia. See appropriate size and area below.

Excision is defined as full-thickness (through the dermis) removal of the following lesions and includes simple (non-layered) closure. The closure of defects created by incision, excision, or trauma may require intermediate or complex closure. Repair by intermediate or complex closure should be reported separately. See page 53 for definition of intermediate or complex closure.

(For excision of benign lesions requiring more than simple closure, ie, requiring intermediate or complex closure, report 11400-11446 in addition to appropriate intermediate (12031-12057) or complex closure (13100-13153) codes. For reconstructive closure, see 14000-14300, 15000-15261, 15570-15770)

(For electrosurgical and other methods, see 17000 et seq)

11400 Excision, benign lesion, except skin tag (unless listed elsewhere), trunk, arms or legs; lesion diameter 0.5 cm or less
➔ *CPT Assistant* Fall 93:7; Fall 95:3; May 96:11

11401   lesion diameter 0.6 to 1.0 cm
➔ *CPT Assistant* Fall 93:7; Fall 95:3; May 96:11

11402   lesion diameter 1.1 to 2.0 cm
➔ *CPT Assistant* Fall 93:7; Fall 95:3; May 96:11

11403   lesion diameter 2.1 to 3.0 cm
➔ *CPT Assistant* Fall 93:7; Fall 95:3; May 96:11

11404   lesion diameter 3.1 to 4.0 cm
➔ *CPT Assistant* Fall 93:7; Fall 95:3; May 96:11

11406   lesion diameter over 4.0 cm
➔ *CPT Assistant* Fall 93:7; Fall 95:3; May 96:11

(For unusual or complicated excision, add modifier '-22')

11420 Excision, benign lesion, except skin tag (unless listed elsewhere), scalp, neck, hands, feet, genitalia; lesion diameter 0.5 cm or less
➔ *CPT Assistant* Fall 95:3

11421   lesion diameter 0.6 to 1.0 cm
➔ *CPT Assistant* Fall 95:3; May 96:11

11422   lesion diameter 1.1 to 2.0 cm
➔ *CPT Assistant* Fall 95:3; May 96:11; Aug 00:5

11423   lesion diameter 2.1 to 3.0 cm
➔ *CPT Assistant* Fall 95:3; May 96:11

11424   lesion diameter 3.1 to 4.0 cm
➔ *CPT Assistant* Fall 95:3; May 96:11

11426   lesion diameter over 4.0 cm
➔ *CPT Assistant* Fall 95:3; May 96:11

(For unusual or complicated excision, add modifier '-22')

11440 Excision, other benign lesion (unless listed elsewhere), face, ears, eyelids, nose, lips, mucous membrane; lesion diameter 0.5 cm or less
➔ *CPT Assistant* Fall 95:3; May 96:11

11441   lesion diameter 0.6 to 1.0 cm
➔ *CPT Assistant* Fall 95:3; May 96:11

11442   lesion diameter 1.1 to 2.0 cm
➔ *CPT Assistant* Fall 95:3; May 96:11; Aug 00:5

11443   lesion diameter 2.1 to 3.0 cm
➔ *CPT Assistant* Fall 95:3; May 96:11

11444   lesion diameter 3.1 to 4.0 cm
➔ *CPT Assistant* Fall 95:3; May 96:11

11446   lesion diameter over 4.0 cm
➔ *CPT Assistant* Fall 95:3; May 96:11

(For unusual or complicated excision, add modifier '-22')

(For eyelids involving more than skin, see also 67800 et seq)

11450 Excision of skin and subcutaneous tissue for hidradenitis, axillary; with simple or intermediate repair

11451   with complex repair

11462 Excision of skin and subcutaneous tissue for hidradenitis, inguinal; with simple or intermediate repair

11463   with complex repair

11470 Excision of skin and subcutaneous tissue for hidradenitis, perianal, perineal, or umbilical; with simple or intermediate repair

11471 with complex repair

(When skin graft or flap is used for closure, use appropriate procedure code in addition)

(For bilateral procedure, add modifier '-50')

Excision—Malignant Lesions

Excision (including simple closure) of malignant lesion of skin or subcutaneous tissues including local anesthesia, each lesion. For removal of malignant lesions of skin by any method other than excision, as defined above, see destruction codes 17000-17999.

Excision is defined as full-thickness (through the dermis) removal of the following lesions and includes simple (non-layered) closure. The closure of defects created by incision, excision, or trauma may require intermediate or complex closure. Repair by intermediate or complex closure should be reported separately. See page 53 for definition of intermediate or complex closure.

(For excision of malignant lesions requiring more than simple closure, ie, requiring intermediate or complex closure, report 11600-11646 in addition to appropriate intermediate (12031-12057) or complex closure (13100-13153) codes. For reconstructive closure, see 14000-14300, 15000-15261, 15570-15770)

11600 Excision, malignant lesion, trunk, arms, or legs; lesion diameter 0.5 cm or less
➔ *CPT Assistant* Fall 95:3; May 96:11

11601 lesion diameter 0.6 to 1.0 cm
➔ *CPT Assistant* Fall 95:3; May 96:11

11602 lesion diameter 1.1 to 2.0 cm
➔ *CPT Assistant* Fall 95:3; May 96:11

11603 lesion diameter 2.1 to 3.0 cm
➔ *CPT Assistant* Fall 95:3; May 96:11

11604 lesion diameter 3.1 to 4.0 cm
➔ *CPT Assistant* Fall 95:3; May 96:11

11606 lesion diameter over 4.0 cm
➔ *CPT Assistant* Fall 91:6; Fall 95:3; May 96:11

11620 Excision, malignant lesion, scalp, neck, hands, feet, genitalia; lesion diameter 0.5 cm or less
➔ *CPT Assistant* Fall 95:3

11621 lesion diameter 0.6 to 1.0 cm
➔ *CPT Assistant* Fall 95:3; May 96:11

11622 lesion diameter 1.1 to 2.0 cm
➔ *CPT Assistant* Fall 95:3; May 96:11

11623 lesion diameter 2.1 to 3.0 cm
➔ *CPT Assistant* Fall 95:3; May 96:11

11624 lesion diameter 3.1 to 4.0 cm
➔ *CPT Assistant* Fall 95:3; May 96:11

11626 lesion diameter over 4.0 cm
➔ *CPT Assistant* Fall 95:3; May 96:11

11640 Excision, malignant lesion, face, ears, eyelids, nose, lips; lesion diameter 0.5 cm or less
➔ *CPT Assistant* Fall 95:3; May 96:11

11641 lesion diameter 0.6 to 1.0 cm
➔ *CPT Assistant* Fall 95:3; May 96:11

11642 lesion diameter 1.1 to 2.0 cm
➔ *CPT Assistant* Fall 95:3; May 96:11

11643 lesion diameter 2.1 to 3.0 cm
➔ *CPT Assistant* Fall 95:3; May 96:11

11644 lesion diameter 3.1 to 4.0 cm
➔ *CPT Assistant* Fall 95:3; May 96:11

11646 lesion diameter over 4.0 cm
➔ *CPT Assistant* Fall 95:3; May 96:11

(For eyelids involving more than skin, see also 67800 et seq)

Nails

(For drainage of paronychia or onychia, see 10060, 10061)

(11700, 11701 have been deleted. To report, use 11720, 11721)

(11710, 11711 have been deleted. To report, use 11720, 11721)

11719 Trimming of nondystrophic nails, any number
➔ *CPT Assistant* Nov 97:12

11720 Debridement of nail(s) by any method(s); one to five

11721 six or more

11730 ✱ Avulsion of nail plate, partial or complete, simple; single
➔ *CPT Assistant* Mar 96:10

(11731 has been deleted. To report, use 11732)

+ 11732 each additional nail plate (List separately in addition to code for primary procedure)

(Use 11732 in conjunction with code 11730)

11740 Evacuation of subungual hematoma

11750 Excision of nail and nail matrix, partial or complete, (eg, ingrown or deformed nail) for permanent removal;

11752 with amputation of tuft of distal phalanx

(For skin graft, if used, use 15050)

▲ 11755 Biopsy of nail unit (eg, plate, bed, matrix, hyponychium, proximal and lateral nail folds) (separate procedure)
➔ *CPT Assistant* Mar 96:11; *CPT Changes* 2002

11760 Repair of nail bed

11762 Reconstruction of nail bed with graft

11765 Wedge excision of skin of nail fold (eg, for ingrown toenail)

(For incision of pilonidal cyst, see 10080, 10081)

⊘ =Modifier '-51' Exempt   ▶ ◀=New or Revised Text   ✚ =Add-on Code   CPT 2002

11770   Excision of pilonidal cyst or sinus; simple

11771   extensive

11772   complicated

Introduction

11900*   Injection, intralesional; up to and including seven lesions
   ➔ *CPT Assistant* Sep 96:5; May 98:10; Feb 00:11

11901*   more than seven lesions
   ➔ *CPT Assistant* Sep 96:5; May 98:10; Feb 00:11

   (11900, 11901 are not to be used for preoperative local anesthetic injection)

   (For veins, see 36470, 36471)

   (For intralesional chemotherapy administration, see 96405, 96406)

11920   Tattooing, intradermal introduction of insoluble opaque pigments to correct color defects of skin, including micropigmentation; 6.0 sq cm or less

11921   6.1 to 20.0 sq cm

+ 11922   each additional 20.0 sq cm (List separately in addition to code for primary procedure)

   (Use 11922 in conjunction with code 11921)

11950   Subcutaneous injection of filling material (eg, collagen); 1 cc or less

11951   1.1 to 5.0 cc

11952   5.1 to 10.0 cc

11954   over 10.0 cc

11960   Insertion of tissue expander(s) for other than breast, including subsequent expansion

   (For breast reconstruction with tissue expander(s), use 19357)

11970   Replacement of tissue expander with permanent prosthesis

11971   Removal of tissue expander(s) without insertion of prosthesis

11975   Insertion, implantable contraceptive capsules

11976   Removal, implantable contraceptive capsules

11977   Removal with reinsertion, implantable contraceptive capsules

11980   Subcutaneous hormone pellet implantation (implantation of estradiol and/or testosterone pellets beneath the skin)
   ➔ *CPT Assistant* Nov 99:8; *CPT Changes* 2000

● **11981**   Insertion, non-biodegradable drug delivery implant
   ➔ *CPT Changes* 2002

● **11982**   Removal, non-biodegradable drug delivery implant
   ➔ *CPT Changes* 2002

● **11983**   Removal with reinsertion, non-biodegradable drug delivery implant
   ➔ *CPT Changes* 2002

Repair (Closure)

Use the codes in this section to designate wound closure utilizing sutures, staples, or tissue adhesives (eg, 2-cyanoacrylate), either singly or in combination with each other, or in combination with adhesive strips. Wound closure utilizing adhesive strips as the sole repair material should be coded using the appropriate E/M code.

Definitions

The repair of wounds may be classified as Simple, Intermediate, or Complex.

Simple repair is used when the wound is superficial; eg, involving primarily epidermis or dermis, or subcutaneous tissues without significant involvement of deeper structures, and requires simple one layer closure. This includes local anesthesia and chemical or electrocauterization of wounds not closed.

Intermediate repair includes the repair of wounds that, in addition to the above, require layered closure of one or more of the deeper layers of subcutaneous tissue and superficial (non-muscle) fascia, in addition to the skin (epidermal and dermal) closure. Single-layer closure of heavily contaminated wounds that have required extensive cleaning or removal of particulate matter also constitutes intermediate repair.

Complex repair includes the repair of wounds requiring more than layered closure, viz., scar revision, debridement, (eg, traumatic lacerations or avulsions), extensive undermining, stents or retention sutures. Necessary preparation includes creation of a defect for repairs (eg, excision of a scar requiring a complex repair) or the debridement of complicated lacerations or avulsions. Complex repair does not include excision of benign (11400-11446) or malignant (11600-11646) lesions.

Instructions for listing services at time of wound repair:

1. The repaired wound(s) should be measured and recorded in centimeters, whether curved, angular, or stellate.

2. When multiple wounds are repaired, add together the lengths of those in the same classification (see above) and from all anatomic sites that are grouped together into the same code descriptor. For example, add together the lengths of intermediate repairs to the trunk and extremities. Do not add lengths of repairs from different groupings of anatomic sites (eg, face and extremities). Also, do not add together lengths of different classifications (eg, intermediate and complex repairs).

When more than one classification of wounds is repaired, list the more complicated as the primary procedure and the less complicated as the secondary procedure, using modifier '-51'.

3. Decontamination and/or debridement: Debridement is considered a separate procedure only when gross contamination requires prolonged cleansing, when appreciable amounts of devitalized or contaminated tissue are removed, or when debridement is carried out separately without immediate primary closure. (For extensive debridement of soft tissue and/or bone, see 11040-11044.)

(For extensive debridement of soft tissue and/or bone, not associated with open fracture(s) and/or dislocation(s) resulting from penetrating and/or blunt trauma, see 11040-11044.)

(For extensive debridement of subcutaneous tissue, muscle fascia, muscle, and/or bone associated with open fracture(s) and/or dislocation(s), see 11010-11012.)

4. Involvement of nerves, blood vessels and tendons: Report under appropriate system (Nervous, Cardiovascular, Musculoskeletal) for repair of these structures. The repair of these associated wounds is included in the primary procedure unless it qualifies as a complex wound, in which case modifier '-51' applies.

Simple ligation of vessels in an open wound is considered as part of any wound closure.

Simple "exploration" of nerves, blood vessels or tendons exposed in an open wound is also considered part of the essential treatment of the wound and is not a separate procedure unless appreciable dissection is required. If the wound requires enlargement, extension of dissection (to determine penetration), debridement, removal of foreign body(s), ligation or coagulation of minor subcutaneous and/or muscular blood vessel(s) of the subcutaneous tissue, muscle fascia, and/or muscle, not requiring thoracotomy or laparotomy, use codes 20100-20103, as appropriate.

Repair—Simple

Sum of lengths of repairs for each group of anatomic sites.

12001 * Simple repair of superficial wounds of scalp, neck, axillae, external genitalia, trunk and/or extremities (including hands and feet); 2.5 cm or less
→ *CPT Assistant* Jun 96:7; Feb 98:11; Jan 00:11; Apr 00:8; Jul 00:10

12002 * 2.6 cm to 7.5 cm

12004 * 7.6 cm to 12.5 cm

12005 12.6 cm to 20.0 cm

12006 20.1 cm to 30.0 cm
→ *CPT Assistant* Feb 98:11

12007 over 30.0 cm

12011 * Simple repair of superficial wounds of face, ears, eyelids, nose, lips and/or mucous membranes; 2.5 cm or less
→ *CPT Assistant* May 00:8

12013 * 2.6 cm to 5.0 cm

12014 5.1 cm to 7.5 cm

12015 7.6 cm to 12.5 cm

12016 12.6 cm to 20.0 cm

12017 20.1 cm to 30.0 cm

12018 over 30.0 cm

12020 Treatment of superficial wound dehiscence; simple closure

12021 with packing

(For extensive or complicated secondary wound closure, use 13160)

Repair—Intermediate

Sum of lengths of repairs for each group of anatomic sites.

12031 * Layer closure of wounds of scalp, axillae, trunk and/or extremities (excluding hands and feet); 2.5 cm or less
→ *CPT Assistant* Sep 97:11; Apr 00:8

12032 * 2.6 cm to 7.5 cm
→ *CPT Assistant* Jun 96:8

12034 7.6 cm to 12.5 cm
→ *CPT Assistant* Fall 91:6

12035 12.6 cm to 20.0 cm

12036 20.1 cm to 30.0 cm

12037 over 30.0 cm

12041 * Layer closure of wounds of neck, hands, feet and/or external genitalia; 2.5 cm or less
→ *CPT Assistant* Sep 97:11; Apr 00:8

12042 2.6 cm to 7.5 cm

12044 7.6 cm to 12.5 cm

12045 12.6 cm to 20.0 cm

12046 20.1 cm to 30.0 cm

12047 over 30.0 cm

12051 * Layer closure of wounds of face, ears, eyelids, nose, lips and/or mucous membranes; 2.5 cm or less
→ *CPT Assistant* Sep 97:11; Apr 00:8

12052 2.6 cm to 5.0 cm

12053 5.1 cm to 7.5 cm

12054 7.6 cm to 12.5 cm

12055 12.6 cm to 20.0 cm

12056 20.1 cm to 30.0 cm

12057 over 30.0 cm

Repair—Complex

Reconstructive procedures, complicated wound closure.

Sum of lengths of repairs for each group of anatomic sites.

(For full thickness repair of lip or eyelid, see respective anatomical subsections)

13100 Repair, complex, trunk; 1.1 cm to 2.5 cm
➔ *CPT Assistant* Sep 97:11; Dec 98:5; Nov 99:9-10; Apr 00:8

(For 1.0 cm or less, see simple or intermediate repairs)

13101 2.6 cm to 7.5 cm
➔ *CPT Assistant* Dec 98:5; Nov 99:9-10

+ 13102 each additional 5 cm or less (List separately in addition to code for primary procedure)
➔ *CPT Assistant* Nov 99:9-10; *CPT Changes* 2000

(Use 13102 in conjunction with code 13101)

13120 Repair, complex, scalp, arms, and/or legs; 1.1 cm to 2.5 cm
➔ *CPT Assistant* Sep 97:11; Apr 99:11; Nov 99:9-10, Apr 00:8

(For 1.0 cm or less, see simple or intermediate repairs)

13121 2.6 cm to 7.5 cm
➔ *CPT Assistant* Dec 98:5; Nov 99:9-10; Feb 00:10

+ 13122 each additional 5 cm or less (List separately in addition to code for primary procedure)
➔ *CPT Assistant* Nov 99:10; *CPT Changes* 2000

(Use 13122 in conjunction with code 13121)

13131 Repair, complex, forehead, cheeks, chin, mouth, neck, axillae, genitalia, hands and/or feet; 1.1 cm to 2.5 cm
➔ *CPT Assistant* Fall 93:7; Sep 97:11; Dec 98:5; Nov 99:10; Apr 00:8

(For 1.0 cm or less, see simple or intermediate repairs)

13132 2.6 cm to 7.5 cm
➔ *CPT Assistant* Fall 93:7; Dec 98:5; Nov 99:10; Dec 99:10

+ 13133 each additional 5 cm or less (List separately in addition to code for primary procedure)
➔ *CPT Assistant* Fall Nov 98:10; *CPT Changes* 2000

(Use 13133 in conjunction with code 13132)

13150 Repair, complex, eyelids, nose, ears and/or lips; 1.0 cm or less
➔ *CPT Assistant* Sep 97:11; Dec 98:5; Nov 99:10; Apr 00:8

(See also 40650-40654, 67961-67975)

13151 1.1 cm to 2.5 cm
➔ *CPT Assistant* Dec 98:5; Nov 99:10

13152 2.6 cm to 7.5 cm
➔ *CPT Assistant* Dec 98:5; Nov 99:10

+ 13153 each additional 5 cm or less (List separately in addition to code for primary procedure)
➔ *CPT Assistant* Nov 99:10; *CPT Changes* 2000

(Use 13153 in conjunction with code 13152)

13160 Secondary closure of surgical wound or dehiscence, extensive or complicated
➔ *CPT Assistant* Sep 97:11; Dec 98:5; Apr 00:8

(For packing or simple secondary wound closure, see 12020, 12021)

(13300 has been deleted. To report, see 13102, 13122, 13133 and 13153)

Adjacent Tissue Transfer or Rearrangement

For full thickness repair of lip or eyelid, see respective anatomical subsections.

Excision (including lesion) and/or repair by adjacent tissue transfer or rearrangement (eg, Z-plasty, W-plasty, V-Y plasty, rotation flap, advancement flap, double pedicle flap). When applied in repairing lacerations, the procedures listed must be developed by the surgeon to accomplish the repair. They do not apply when direct closure or rearrangement of traumatic wounds incidentally result in these configurations.

Skin graft necessary to close secondary defect is considered an additional procedure.

14000 Adjacent tissue transfer or rearrangement, trunk; defect 10 sq cm or less
➔ *CPT Assistant* Sep 96:11; Jul 99:3; Jul 00:10

14001 defect 10.1 sq cm to 30.0 sq cm
➔ *CPT Assistant* Jul 99:3

14020 Adjacent tissue transfer or rearrangement, scalp, arms and/or legs; defect 10 sq cm or less
➔ *CPT Assistant* Jul 99:3

14021 defect 10.1 sq cm to 30.0 sq cm
➔ *CPT Assistant* Jul 99:3

14040 Adjacent tissue transfer or rearrangement, forehead, cheeks, chin, mouth, neck, axillae, genitalia, hands and/or feet; defect 10 sq cm or less
➔ *CPT Assistant* Jul 99:3; Jul 00:10

14041 defect 10.1 sq cm to 30.0 sq cm
➔ *CPT Assistant* Jul 99:3

14060 Adjacent tissue transfer or rearrangement, eyelids, nose, ears and/or lips; defect 10 sq cm or less
➔ *CPT Assistant* Fall 93:7; Jul 99:3; Dec 99:10

14061 defect 10.1 sq cm to 30.0 sq cm
➔ *CPT Assistant* Jul 99:3

(For eyelid, full thickness, see 67961 et seq)

14300 Adjacent tissue transfer or rearrangement, more than 30 sq cm, unusual or complicated, any area
➔ *CPT Assistant* Sep 96:11

14350 Filleted finger or toe flap, including preparation of recipient site

Free Skin Grafts

Identify by size and location of the defect (recipient area) and the type of graft; includes simple debridement of granulations or recent avulsion.

When a primary procedure such as orbitectomy, radical mastectomy, or deep tumor removal requires skin graft for definitive closure, see appropriate anatomical subsection for primary procedure and this section for skin graft.

▶Use 15000 for initial wound preparation.◀

▶Use 15100-15261 for autogenous skin grafts. For autogenous tissue-cultured skin grafts, use 15100-15121. These codes include harvesting of keratinocytes and their subsequent application. Procedures are coded by recipient site. Use codes 15342 and 15343 for application of skin substitute/neodermis. Use modifier '-58' for staged application procedure(s).◀

Repair of donor site requiring skin graft or local flaps is to be added as an additional procedure.

Codes 15000, 15001, 15350, 15351, 15400, 15401 describe burn and wound preparation and management procedures. The following definition should be applied to codes 15000, 15001, 15100, 15101, 15120, 15121 when determining the involvement of body size. The measurement of 100 sq cm is applicable to adults and children age 10 and over, percentages apply to infants and children under the age of 10.

(For microvascular flaps, see 15756-15758)

15000 Surgical preparation or creation of recipient site by excision of open wounds, burn eschar, or scar (including subcutaneous tissues); first 100 sq cm or one percent of body area of infants and children

→ *CPT Assistant* Fall 93:7; April 97:4; Aug 96:7; Sep 97:1; Nov 98:5; Jan 99:4, 10; April 99:10; May 99:10; *CPT Changes* 2001

(For appropriate skin grafts, see 15050-15261; list the free graft separately by its procedure number when the graft, immediate or delayed, is applied)

+ 15001 each additional 100 sq cm or each additional one percent of body area of infants and children (List separately in addition to code for primary procedure)

→ *CPT Assistant* Nov 98:5-6; Jan 99:4; May 99:10

(Use code 15001 in conjunction with code 15000)

(For excision of benign lesions, see 11400-11471)

(For excision of malignant lesions, see 11600-11646)

(For excision with alloplastic dressing, use 15000 only)

(For excision with immediate skin grafting use 15050-15261 in addition to 15000)

(For excision with immediate allograft placement use 15350 in addition to 15000)

(For excision with immediate xenograft placement use 15400 in addition to 15000)

15050 Pinch graft, single or multiple, to cover small ulcer, tip of digit, or other minimal open area (except on face), up to defect size 2 cm diameter

→ *CPT Assistant* April 97:4; Sep 97:1; Nov 98:6

15100 Split graft, trunk, arms, legs; first 100 sq cm or less, or one percent of body area of infants and children (except 15050)

→ *CPT Assistant* Fall 93:7; April 97:4; Aug 97:6; Sep 97:1; Nov 98:6; *CPT Changes* 2002

+ 15101 each additional 100 sq cm, or each additional one percent of body area of infants and children, or part thereof (List separately in addition to code for primary procedure)

→ *CPT Assistant* April 97:4; Nov 98:6; *CPT Changes* 2002

(Use 15101 in conjunction with code 15100)

15120 Split graft, face, scalp, eyelids, mouth, neck, ears, orbits, genitalia, hands, feet and/or multiple digits; first 100 sq cm or less, or one percent of body area of infants and children (except 15050)

→ *CPT Assistant* April 97:4; Aug 97:6; Sep 97:1; Nov 98:6; Jan 99:4; *CPT Changes* 2002

+ 15121 each additional 100 sq cm, or each additional one percent of body area of infants and children, or part thereof (List separately in addition to code for primary procedure)

→ *CPT Assistant* April 97:4; Aug 97:6; Sep 97:1; Nov 98:6; Jan 99:4; *CPT Changes* 2002

(Use 15121 in conjunction with code 15120)

(For eyelids, see also 67961 et seq)

15200 Full thickness graft, free, including direct closure of donor site, trunk; 20 sq cm or less

→ *CPT Assistant* Aug 96:11; Aug 97:6; Sep 97:1; *CPT Changes* 2002

+ 15201 each additional 20 sq cm (List separately in addition to code for primary procedure)

→ *CPT Assistant* April 97:4; Aug 97:6; Sep 97:1; *CPT Changes* 2002

(Use 15201 in conjunction with code 15200)

15220 Full thickness graft, free, including direct closure of donor site, scalp, arms, and/or legs; 20 sq cm or less

→ *CPT Assistant* April 97:4; Aug 97:6; Sep 97:1; *CPT Changes* 2002

+ 15221 each additional 20 sq cm (List separately in addition to code for primary procedure)

→ *CPT Assistant* April 97:4; Aug 97:6; Sep 97:1; *CPT Changes* 2002

(Use 15221 in conjunction with code 15220)

15240 Full thickness graft, free, including direct closure of donor site, forehead, cheeks, chin, mouth, neck, axillae, genitalia, hands, and/or feet; 20 sq cm or less

→ *CPT Assistant* April 97:4; Aug 97:6; Sep 97:1; Nov 00:10; *CPT Changes* 2002

(For finger tip graft, use 15050)

(For repair of syndactyly, fingers, see 26560-26562)

+ 15241 each additional 20 sq cm (List separately in addition to code for primary procedure)

→ *CPT Assistant* April 97:4; Aug 97:6; Sep 97:1; *CPT Changes* 2002

(Use 15241 in conjunction with code 15240)

15260 Full thickness graft, free, including direct closure of donor site, nose, ears, eyelids, and/or lips; 20 sq cm or less

→ *CPT Assistant* Fall 93:7; Fall 91:7; April 97:4; Aug 97:6; Sep 97:1; Jul 99:3; *CPT Changes* 2002

+ 15261 each additional 20 sq cm (List separately in addition to code for primary procedure)

→ *CPT Assistant* Fall 91:7; April 97:4; Aug 97:6; Sep 97:1; *CPT Changes* 2002

(Use 15261 in conjunction with code 15260)

(For eyelids, see also 67961 et seq)

(Repair of donor site requiring skin graft or local flaps, to be added as additional separate procedure)

15342 Application of bilaminate skin substitute/neodermis; 25 sq cm

+ 15343 each additional 25 sq cm (List separately in addition to code for primary procedure)

(Use 15343 in conjunction with code 15342)

15350 Application of allograft, skin; 100 sq cm or less

→ *CPT Assistant* April 97:4; Sep 97:1; Nov 97:12; Nov 98:6; Jan 99:4

Allograft, Skin
15350

Application of an alloplastic graft (homograft) from healthy donor (cadaver) skin is applied to a part of the patient's body to resurface an area damaged by burns, traumatic injury or surgery.

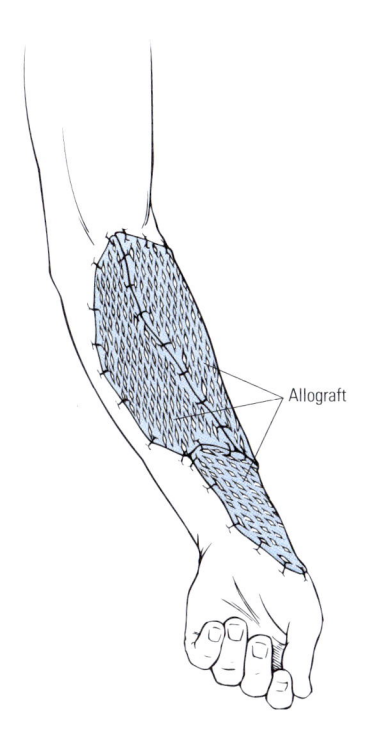

Allograft

(For staged tissue graft implantation, use modifier '-58')

+ 15351 each additional 100 sq cm (List separately in addition to code for primary procedure)

→ *CPT Assistant* Jan 99:4

(Use 15351 in conjunction with code 15350)

15400 Application of xenograft, skin; 100 sq cm or less

→ *CPT Assistant* April 97:4; Sep 97:1; Nov 98:6; Jan 99:4

Xenograft, Skin
15400

Application of a biologic wound dressing, thin meshed skin, or porcine graft following excision of the burn wound and/or surgical preparation of the site.

Xenograft

(15410-15416 have been deleted. To report, see 15756-15758)

+ 15401 each additional 100 sq cm (List separately in addition to code for primary procedure)

→ *CPT Assistant* Nov 98:6; Jan 99:4

(Use 15401 in conjunction with code 15400)

Flaps (Skin and/or Deep Tissues)

Regions listed refer to recipient area (not donor site) when flap is being attached in transfer or to final site.

Regions listed refer to donor site when tube is formed for later or when "delay" of flap is prior to transfer.

Procedures 15570-15738 do not include extensive immobilization (eg, large plaster casts and other immobilizing devices are considered additional separate procedures).

Repair of donor site requiring skin graft or local flaps is considered an additional separate procedure.

(For microvascular flaps, see 15756-15758)

(15500-15515 have been deleted. To report, use 15000)

(15540-15555 have been deleted. To report, see 15570-15576)

15570 Formation of direct or tubed pedicle, with or without transfer; trunk

15572 scalp, arms, or legs

15574 forehead, cheeks, chin, mouth, neck, axillae, genitalia, hands or feet

15576 eyelids, nose, ears, lips, or intraoral

(15580 has been deleted. To report, use 15574)

15600 Delay of flap or sectioning of flap (division and inset); at trunk
➔ *CPT Assistant* Nov 99:10

15610 at scalp, arms, or legs

15620 at forehead, cheeks, chin, neck, axillae, genitalia, hands, or feet

(15625 has been deleted. To report, use 15620)

15630 at eyelids, nose, ears, or lips

15650 Transfer, intermediate, of any pedicle flap (eg, abdomen to wrist, Walking tube), any location

(15700-15730 have been deleted. To report, see 15570-15576)

(For eyelids, nose, ears, or lips, see also anatomical area)

(For revision, defatting or rearranging of transferred pedicle flap or skin graft, see 13100-14300)

(Procedures 15732-15738 are described by donor site of the muscle, myocutaneous, or fasciocutaneous flap)

▲ **15732** Muscle, myocutaneous, or fasciocutaneous flap; head and neck (eg, temporalis, masseter muscle, sternocleidomastoid, levator scapulae)
➔ *CPT Changes* 2002

15734 trunk

15736 upper extremity

15738 lower extremity

Other Flaps and Grafts

Repair of donor site requiring skin graft or local flaps should be reported as an additional procedure.

15740 Flap; island pedicle

(15745 has been deleted. To report, see 15732-15738)

15750 neurovascular pedicle

(15755 has been deleted. To report, see 15756-15758)

15756 Free muscle flap with or without skin with microvascular anastomosis
➔ *CPT Assistant* Apr 97:5; Nov 97:12; Nov 98:6

(Do not report code 69990 in addition to code 15756)

15757 Free skin flap with microvascular anastomosis
➔ *CPT Assistant* Apr 97:5; Nov 98:6

(Do not report code 69990 in addition to code 15757)

15758 Free fascial flap with microvascular anastomosis
➔ *CPT Assistant* Apr 97:5; Nov 98:6

(Do not report code 69990 in addition to code 15758)

15760 Graft; composite (eg, full thickness of external ear or nasal ala), including primary closure, donor area
➔ *CPT Assistant* Sep 97:1

15770 derma-fat-fascia
➔ *CPT Assistant* Sep 97:1

15775 Punch graft for hair transplant; 1 to 15 punch grafts
➔ *CPT Assistant* Sep 97:1

15776 more than 15 punch grafts
➔ *CPT Assistant* Sep 97:1

(For strip transplant, use 15220)

Other Procedures

15780 Dermabrasion; total face (eg, for acne scarring, fine wrinkling, rhytids, general keratosis)

15781 segmental, face

15782 regional, other than face

15783 superficial, any site, (eg, tattoo removal)

(15785 has been deleted. To report, see 15781, 15782)

15786 * Abrasion; single lesion (eg, keratosis, scar)

+ **15787** each additional four lesions or less (List separately in addition to code for primary procedure)

(Use 15787 in conjunction with code 15786)

15788 Chemical peel, facial; epidermal

15789 dermal

(15790, 15791 have been deleted. To report, see 15788-15793)

15792 Chemical peel, nonfacial; epidermal

15793 dermal

(15800 has been deleted)

15810 Salabrasion; 20 sq cm or less

15811 over 20 sq cm

15819 Cervicoplasty

15820 Blepharoplasty, lower eyelid;

15821 with extensive herniated fat pad

⊘ =Modifier '-51' Exempt ▶ ◀=New or Revised Text ✚ =Add-on Code CPT 2002

15822 Blepharoplasty, upper eyelid;

15823   with excessive skin weighting down lid
> *CPT Assistant* Sep 00:7

(For bilateral blepharoplasty, add modifier '-50')

(See also 67916, 67917, 67923, 67924)

15824 Rhytidectomy; forehead

(For repair of brow ptosis, use 67900)

15825   neck with platysmal tightening (platysmal flap, P-flap)

15826   glabellar frown lines

(15827 has been deleted. To report, use 15838)

15828   cheek, chin, and neck

15829   superficial musculoaponeurotic system (SMAS) flap

(For bilateral rhytidectomy, add modifier '-50')

15831 Excision, excessive skin and subcutaneous tissue (including lipectomy); abdomen (abdominoplasty)

15832   thigh

15833   leg

15834   hip

15835   buttock

15836   arm

15837   forearm or hand

15838   submental fat pad

15839   other area

(For bilateral procedure, add modifier '-50')

15840 Graft for facial nerve paralysis; free fascia graft (including obtaining fascia)

(For bilateral procedure, add modifier '-50')

15841   free muscle graft (including obtaining graft)

15842   free muscle flap by microsurgical technique
> *CPT Changes* 2001

(Do not report code 69990 in addition to code 15842)

15845   regional muscle transfer

(For intravenous fluorescein examination of blood flow in graft or flap, use 15860)

(For nerve transfers, decompression, or repair, see 64831-64876, 64905, 64907, 69720, 69725, 69740, 69745, 69955)

15850 Removal of sutures under anesthesia (other than local), same surgeon
> *CPT Assistant* Spring 93:34

15851 Removal of sutures under anesthesia (other than local), other surgeon
> *CPT Assistant* Spring 93:34

15852 Dressing change (for other than burns) under anesthesia (other than local)

▲ **15860** Intravenous injection of agent (eg, fluorescein) to test vascular flow in flap or graft
> *CPT Changes* 2002

(15875 has been deleted. To report, see 15876-15879)

15876 Suction assisted lipectomy; head and neck

15877   trunk
> *CPT Assistant* Oct 99:10

15878   upper extremity

15879   lower extremity

Pressure Ulcers (Decubitus Ulcers)

15920 Excision, coccygeal pressure ulcer, with coccygectomy; with primary suture

15922   with flap closure

(15930 has been deleted. To report, use 15934)

15931 Excision, sacral pressure ulcer, with primary suture;

(15932 has been deleted)

15933   with ostectomy

15934 Excision, sacral pressure ulcer, with skin flap closure;

15935   with ostectomy

15936 Excision, sacral pressure ulcer, in preparation for muscle or myocutaneous flap or skin graft closure;
> *CPT Assistant* Nov 98:6-7

15937   with ostectomy

(For repair of defect using muscle or myocutaneous flap, use code(s) 15734 and/or 15738 in addition to 15936, 15937. For repair of defect using split skin graft, use codes 15100 and/or 15101 in addition to 15936, 15937)

15940 Excision, ischial pressure ulcer, with primary suture;

15941   with ostectomy (ischiectomy)

(15942, 15943 have been deleted. To report, see 15944-15946)

15944 Excision, ischial pressure ulcer, with skin flap closure;

15945   with ostectomy

15946 Excision, ischial pressure ulcer, with ostectomy, in preparation for muscle or myocutaneous flap or skin graft closure
> *CPT Assistant* Nov 98:6-7

(For repair of defect using muscle or myocutaneous flap, use code(s) 15734 and/or 15738 in addition to 15946. For repair of defect using split skin graft, use codes 15100 and/or 15101 in addition to 15946)

15950 Excision, trochanteric pressure ulcer, with primary suture;

15951   with ostectomy

15952 Excision, trochanteric pressure ulcer, with skin flap closure;

15953 with ostectomy

(15954 and 15955 have been deleted. To report, use appropriate debridement, closure or flap codes)

15956 Excision, trochanteric pressure ulcer, in preparation for muscle or myocutaneous flap or skin graft closure;

➔ *CPT Assistant* Nov 98:6-7

15958 with ostectomy

➔ *CPT Assistant* Nov 98:6-7

(For repair of defect using muscle or myocutaneous flap, use code(s) 15734 and/or 15738 in addition to 15956, 15958. For repair of defect using split skin graft, use codes 15100 and/or 15101 in addition to 15956, 15958)

(15960-15983 have been deleted. To report, use appropriate debridement, closure or flap codes)

15999 Unlisted procedure, excision pressure ulcer

(For free skin graft to close ulcer or donor site, see 15000 et seq)

Burns, Local Treatment

Procedures 16000-16036 refer to local treatment of burned surface only.

List percentage of body surface involved and depth of burn.

For necessary related medical services (eg, hospital visits, detention) in management of burned patients, see appropriate services in **Evaluation and Management** and **Medicine** sections.

(For skin graft, see 15100-15650)

16000 Initial treatment, first degree burn, when no more than local treatment is required

➔ *CPT Assistant* Aug 97:6

Rule of Nines
16000

The "rule of nines" is used to calculate the percentage of a body burned by dividing the total body surface area into nine percent or multiples of nine percent segments. In the infant or child, the "rule" deviates because of the large surface area of the child's head.

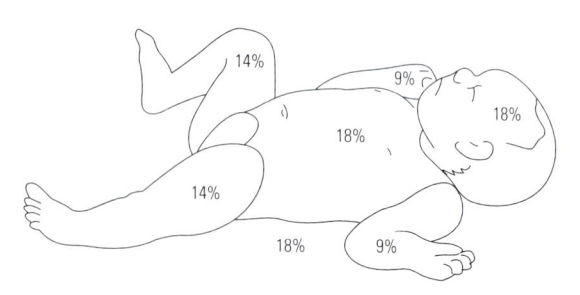

Rule of Nines (continued)

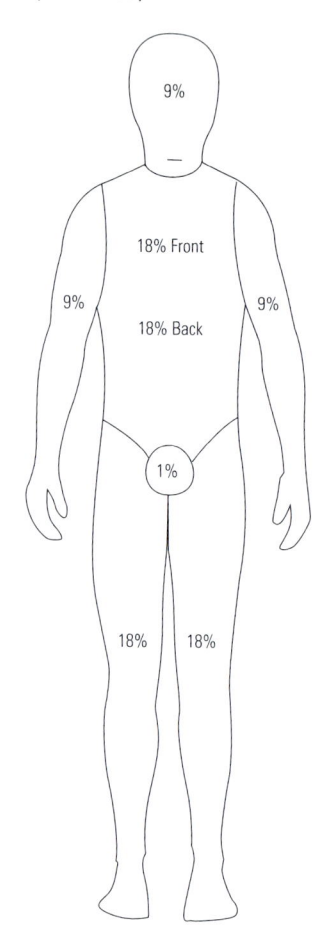

16010 Dressings and/or debridement, initial or subsequent; under anesthesia, small

➔ *CPT Assistant* Aug 97:6

16015 under anesthesia, medium or large, or with major debridement

➔ *CPT Assistant* Aug 97:6

16020 ✳ without anesthesia, office or hospital, small

➔ *CPT Assistant* Aug 97:6

16025 ✳ without anesthesia, medium (eg, whole face or whole extremity)

➔ *CPT Assistant* Aug 97:6

16030 without anesthesia, large (eg, more than one extremity)

➔ *CPT Assistant* Aug 97:6

16035 Escharotomy; initial incision

➔ *CPT Assistant* Aug 97:6; *CPT Changes* 2001

+ 16036 each additional incision (List separately in addition to code for primary procedure)

➔ *CPT Changes* 2001

(Use 16036 in conjunction with code 16035)

(For debridement, curettement of burn wound, see 16010-16030)

(16040-16042 have been deleted. To report, use 15000)

Destruction

Destruction means the ablation of benign, premalignant or malignant tissues by any method, with or without curettement, including local anesthesia, and not usually requiring closure.

Any method includes electrosurgery, cryosurgery, laser and chemical treatment. Lesions include condylomata, papillomata, molluscum contagiosum, herpetic lesions, warts (ie, common, plantar, flat), milia, or other benign, premalignant (eg, actinic keratoses), or malignant lesions.

(For destruction of lesion(s) in specific anatomic sites, see 40820, 46900-46917, 46924, 54050-54057, 54065, 56501, 56515, 57061, 57065, 67850, 68135)

(For paring or cutting of benign hyperkeratotic lesions (eg, corns or calluses), see 11055-11057)

(For sharp removal or electrosurgical destruction of skin tags and fibrocutaneous tags, see 11200, 11201)

(For cryotherapy of acne, use 17340)

(For initiation or follow-up care of topical chemotherapy (eg, 5-FU or similar agents), see appropriate office visits)

(For shaving of epidermal or dermal lesions, see 11300-11313)

Destruction, Benign or Premalignant Lesions

▲ **17000*** Destruction (eg, laser surgery, electrosurgery, cryosurgery, chemosurgery, surgical curettement), all benign or premalignant lesions (eg, actinic keratoses) other than skin tags or cutaneous vascular proliferative lesions; first lesion
➔ *CPT Assistant* Nov 97:12; Jun 99:10; *CPT Changes* 2002

(17001, 17002 have been deleted. To report, see 17003, 17004)

+ **17003** second through 14 lesions, each (List separately in addition to code for first lesion)
➔ *CPT Assistant* Nov 97:12; Jun 99:10

(Use 17003 in conjunction with code 17000)

⊘ ▲ **17004** Destruction (eg, laser surgery, electrosurgery, cryosurgery, chemosurgery, surgical curettement), all benign or premalignant lesions (eg, actinic keratoses) other than skin tags or cutaneous vascular proliferative lesions; 15 or more lesions
➔ *CPT Assistant* Nov 97:12; Nov 98:7; Jun 99:10; *CPT Changes* 2002

(Do not report 17004 in conjunction with codes 17000-17003)

(17010 has been deleted. To report, see specific anatomic site code)

(17100-17105 have been deleted. To report, see 17000, 17003, 17004)
➔ *CPT Assistant* Dec 96:11; Feb 97:11; Nov 97:12

17106 Destruction of cutaneous vascular proliferative lesions (eg, laser technique); less than 10 sq cm

17107 10.0 - 50.0 sq cm

17108 over 50.0 sq cm

▲ **17110*** Destruction (eg, laser surgery, electrosurgery, cryosurgery, chemosurgery, surgical curettement), of flat warts, molluscum contagiosum, or milia; up to 14 lesions
➔ *CPT Assistant* Nov 97:13; *CPT Changes* 2002

17111 15 or more lesions
➔ *CPT Assistant* Nov 97:13

(For destruction of common or plantar warts, see 17000, 17003, 17004)

(17200, 17201 have been deleted. To report, see 11200, 11201)

17250* Chemical cauterization of granulation tissue (proud flesh, sinus or fistula)
➔ *CPT Assistant* Nov 97:14

(17250 is not to be used with removal or excision codes for the same lesion)
➔ *CPT Assistant* Nov 97:14

Destruction, Malignant Lesions, Any Method

▲ **17260*** Destruction, malignant lesion (eg, laser surgery, electrosurgery, cryosurgery, chemosurgery, surgical curettement), trunk, arms or legs; lesion diameter 0.5 cm or less
➔ *CPT Changes* 2002

17261 lesion diameter 0.6 to 1.0 cm

17262 lesion diameter 1.1 to 2.0 cm

17263 lesion diameter 2.1 to 3.0 cm

17264 lesion diameter 3.1 to 4.0 cm

17266 lesion diameter over 4.0 cm

▲ **17270*** Destruction, malignant lesion (eg, laser surgery, electrosurgery, cryosurgery, chemosurgery, surgical curettement), scalp, neck, hands, feet, genitalia; lesion diameter 0.5 cm or less
➔ *CPT Changes* 2002

17271 lesion diameter 0.6 to 1.0 cm

17272 lesion diameter 1.1 to 2.0 cm

17273 lesion diameter 2.1 to 3.0 cm

17274 lesion diameter 3.1 to 4.0 cm

17276 lesion diameter over 4.0 cm

▲ **17280*** Destruction, malignant lesion (eg, laser surgery, electrosurgery, cryosurgery, chemosurgery, surgical curettement), face, ears, eyelids, nose, lips, mucous membrane; lesion diameter 0.5 cm or less
➔ *CPT Changes* 2002

17281 lesion diameter 0.6 to 1.0 cm

17282	lesion diameter 1.1 to 2.0 cm
17283	lesion diameter 2.1 to 3.0 cm
17284	lesion diameter 3.1 to 4.0 cm
17286	lesion diameter over 4.0 cm

Mohs Micrographic Surgery

Mohs micrographic surgery, for the removal of complex or ill-defined skin cancer, requires a single physician to act in two integrated, but separate and distinct capacities: surgeon and pathologist. If either of these responsibilities are delegated to another physician who reports his services separately, these codes are not appropriate. If repair is performed, use separate repair, flap, or graft codes.

(17300-17302 have been deleted. To report, use 17304-17310)

(17303 has been deleted)

⊘ **17304** Chemosurgery (Mohs micrographic technique), including removal of all gross tumor, surgical excision of tissue specimens, mapping, color coding of specimens, microscopic examination of specimens by the surgeon, and complete histopathologic preparation; first stage, fresh tissue technique, up to 5 specimens
➔ *CPT Assistant* Winter 94:19; Mar 99:11; Jun 99:10

⊘ **17305** second stage, fixed or fresh tissue, up to 5 specimens
➔ *CPT Assistant* Winter 94:19; Mar 99:11; Jun 99:10

⊘ **17306** third stage, fixed or fresh tissue, up to 5 specimens
➔ *CPT Assistant* Winter 94:19; Mar 99:11; Jun 99:10

⊘ **17307** additional stage(s), up to 5 specimens, each stage
➔ *CPT Assistant* Winter 94:19; Mar 99:11; Jun 99:10

⊘ **17310** more than 5 specimens, fixed or fresh tissue, any stage
➔ *CPT Assistant* Winter 94:19; Mar 99:11; Jun 99:10

Other Procedures

17340 ✱ Cryotherapy (CO_2 slush, liquid N_2) for acne

17360 ✱ Chemical exfoliation for acne (eg, acne paste, acid)

17380 ✱ Electrolysis epilation, each 1/2 hour

(For actinotherapy, use 96900)

17999 Unlisted procedure, skin, mucous membrane and subcutaneous tissue
➔ *CPT Assistant* Dec 98:9

Breast

Incision

19000 ✱ Puncture aspiration of cyst of breast;
➔ *CPT Assistant* Fall 94:18

+ 19001 each additional cyst (List separately in addition to code for primary procedure)
➔ *CPT Assistant* Fall 94:18

(Use 19001 in conjunction with code 19000)

▶(If imaging guidance is performed, see 76095, 76096, 76393, 76942)◀

19020 Mastotomy with exploration or drainage of abscess, deep

19030 Injection procedure only for mammary ductogram or galactogram

(For radiological supervision and interpretation, see 76086, 76088)

Excision

(All codes for bilateral procedures have been deleted. To report, add modifier '-50')

19100 ✱ Biopsy of breast; percutaneous, needle core, not using imaging guidance (separate procedure)
➔ *CPT Assistant* Fall 94:18; Apr 96:8; Mar 97:4; Nov 98:7; Jan 01:8; *CPT Changes* 2001

(For fine needle aspiration, use ▶10021)◀

(For image guided breast biopsy, see 19102, 19103, ▶10022)◀

19101 open, incisional
➔ *CPT Assistant* Fall 94:19; Jan 01:8; *CPT Changes* 2001

19102 percutaneous, needle core, using imaging guidance
➔ *CPT Assistant* Jan 01:8; *CPT Changes* 2001

(For placement of percutaneous localization clip, use 19295)

19103 percutaneous, automated vacuum assisted or rotating biopsy device, using imaging guidance
➔ *CPT Assistant* Jan 01:8; *CPT Changes* 2001

(For imaging guidance performed in conjunction with 19102, 19103, see 76095, ▶76096,◀ 76360, 76393, 76942)

▶(For placement of percutaneous localization clip, use 19295)◀

19110 Nipple exploration, with or without excision of a solitary lactiferous duct or a papilloma lactiferous duct

19112 Excision of lactiferous duct fistula

19120 Excision of cyst, fibroadenoma, or other benign or malignant tumor, aberrant breast tissue, duct lesion, nipple or areolar lesion (except 19140), open, male or female, one or more lesions
➔ *CPT Assistant* Feb 96:9; Nov 97:14; Jan 01:8; *CPT Changes* 2001

19125 Excision of breast lesion identified by preoperative placement of radiological marker, open; single lesion
➔ *CPT Assistant* Fall 94:18; Mar 98:10; Jan 01:8; *CPT Changes* 2001

⊘ = Modifier '-51' Exempt   ▶ ◀ = New or Revised Text   ✚ = Add-on Code   CPT 2002

+ 19126 each additional lesion separately identified by a preoperative radiological marker (List separately in addition to code for primary procedure)
→ *CPT Assistant* Fall 94:18; Mar 98:10; Jan 01:8; *CPT Changes* 2001

(Use 19126 in conjunction with code 19125)

19140 Mastectomy for gynecomastia
→ *CPT Assistant* Feb 96:9

19160 Mastectomy, partial;

19162 with axillary lymphadenectomy
→ *CPT Assistant* Jun 00:11

19180 Mastectomy, simple, complete

(For immediate or delayed insertion of implant, use 19340 or 19342)

(For gynecomastia, use 19140)

19182 Mastectomy, subcutaneous

(19184-19187 have been deleted. To report, use 19182 with 19340 or 19342)

19200 Mastectomy, radical, including pectoral muscles, axillary lymph nodes

(19211-19216 have been deleted. To report, use 19200 with 19340 or 19342)

19220 Mastectomy, radical, including pectoral muscles, axillary and internal mammary lymph nodes (Urban type operation)

(19224-19229 have been deleted. To report, use 19220 with 19340 or 19342)

19240 Mastectomy, modified radical, including axillary lymph nodes, with or without pectoralis minor muscle, but excluding pectoralis major muscle

(19250-19255 have been deleted. To report, use 19240 with 19340 or 19342)

19260 Excision of chest wall tumor including ribs

19271 Excision of chest wall tumor involving ribs, with plastic reconstruction; without mediastinal lymphadenectomy

19272 with mediastinal lymphadenectomy

Introduction

19290 Preoperative placement of needle localization wire, breast;
→ *CPT Assistant* Fall 94:19

+ 19291 each additional lesion (List separately in addition to code for primary procedure)
→ *CPT Assistant* Fall 94:19

(Use 19291 in conjunction with code 19290)

(For radiological supervision and interpretation, see ▶76095, 76096, 76942)◄

+ 19295 Image guided placement, metallic localization clip, percutaneous, during breast biopsy (List separately in addition to code for primary procedure)
→ *CPT Assistant* Jan 01:8; *CPT Changes* 2001

(Use 19295 in conjunction with codes 19102, ▶19103)◄

Repair and/or Reconstruction

(19300-19304 have been deleted. To report, see 19316, 19318)

(19310, 19311 have been deleted. To report, use 19325)

(All codes for bilateral procedures have been deleted. To report, add modifier '-50')

19316 Mastopexy

19318 Reduction mammaplasty

19324 Mammaplasty, augmentation; without prosthetic implant

19325 with prosthetic implant

(For flap or graft, use also appropriate number)

19328 Removal of intact mammary implant

19330 Removal of mammary implant material

19340 Immediate insertion of breast prosthesis following mastopexy, mastectomy or in reconstruction
→ *CPT Assistant* Aug 96:8

19342 Delayed insertion of breast prosthesis following mastopexy, mastectomy or in reconstruction
→ *CPT Assistant* Aug 96:8

(For supply of implant, use 99070)

(For preparation of custom breast implant, use 19396)

19350 Nipple/areola reconstruction
→ *CPT Assistant* Aug 96:11

19355 Correction of inverted nipples

19357 Breast reconstruction, immediate or delayed, with tissue expander, including subsequent expansion

(19360 has been deleted)

19361 Breast reconstruction with latissimus dorsi flap, with or without prosthetic implant

(19362 has been deleted. To report, see 19367-19369)

19364 Breast reconstruction with free flap
→ *CPT Assistant* Aug 96:8; Nov 98:7

(Do not report code 69990 in addition to code 19364)

(19364 includes harvesting of the flap, microvascular transfer, closure of the donor site, and inset shaping the flap into a breast)

19366 Breast reconstruction with other technique
→ *CPT Assistant* Aug 96:8; Nov 98:7

(For operating microscope, use 69990)

(For insertion of prosthesis, use also 19340 or 19342)

19367 Breast reconstruction with transverse rectus abdominis myocutaneous flap (TRAM), single pedicle, including closure of donor site;
➔ *CPT Assistant* Nov 98:7

19368 with microvascular anastomosis (supercharging)
➔ *CPT Assistant* Nov 98:7

(Do not report code 69990 in addition to code 19368)

19369 Breast reconstruction with transverse rectus abdominis myocutaneous flap (TRAM), double pedicle, including closure of donor site
➔ *CPT Assistant* Oct 00:1

19370 Open periprosthetic capsulotomy, breast
➔ *CPT Assistant* Aug 96:8

19371 Periprosthetic capsulectomy, breast
➔ *CPT Assistant* Aug 96:8

19380 Revision of reconstructed breast

19396 Preparation of moulage for custom breast implant

Other Procedures

19499 Unlisted procedure, breast

⃠ =Modifier '-51' Exempt   ▶ ◀=New or Revised Text   ✚ =Add-on Code

Musculoskeletal System

Cast and strapping procedures appear at the end of this section.

The services listed below include the application and removal of the first cast or traction device only. Subsequent replacement of cast and/or traction device may require an additional listing.

Definitions

The terms "closed treatment," "open treatment," and "percutaneous skeletal fixation" have been carefully chosen to accurately reflect current orthopaedic procedural treatments.

Closed treatment specifically means that the fracture site is not surgically opened (exposed to the external environment and directly visualized). This terminology is used to describe procedures that treat fractures by three methods: 1) without manipulation 2) with manipulation 3) with or without traction.

Open treatment is used when the fracture is surgically opened (exposed to the external environment). In this instance, the fracture (bone ends) is visualized and internal fixation may be used.

Percutaneous skeletal fixation describes fracture treatment which is neither open nor closed. In this procedure, the fracture fragments are not visualized, but fixation (eg, pins) is placed across the fracture site, usually under x-ray imaging.

The type of fracture (eg, open, compound, closed) does not have any coding correlation with the type of treatment (eg, closed, open, or percutaneous) provided.

The codes for treatment of fractures and joint injuries (dislocations) are categorized by the type of manipulation (reduction) and stabilization (fixation or immobilization). These codes can apply to either open (compound) or closed fractures or joint injuries.

Skeletal traction is the application of a force (distracting or traction force) to a limb segment through a wire, pin, screw, or clamp that is attached (eg, penetrates) to bone.

Skin traction is the application of a force (longitudinal) to a limb using felt or strapping applied directly to skin only.

External fixation is the usage of skeletal pins plus an attaching mechanism/device used for temporary or definitive treatment of acute or chronic bony deformity.

Codes for obtaining autogenous bone grafts, cartilage, tendon, fascia lata grafts or other tissues through separate incisions are to be used only when the graft is not already listed as part of the basic procedure.

Re-reduction of a fracture and/or dislocation performed by the primary physician may be identified by the addition of the modifier '-76' to the usual procedure number to indicate "Repeat Procedure by Same Physician." (See guidelines.)

Codes for external fixation are to be used only when external fixation is not already listed as part of the basic procedure.

All codes for suction irrigation have been deleted. To report, list only the primary surgical procedure performed (eg, sequestrectomy, deep incision).

Manipulation is used throughout the musculoskeletal fracture and dislocation subsections to specifically mean the attempted reduction or restoration of a fracture or joint dislocation to its normal anatomic alignment by the application of manually applied forces.

General

Incision

20000 * Incision of soft tissue abscess (eg, secondary to osteomyelitis); superficial

20005   deep or complicated

(20010 has been deleted)

Wound Exploration—Trauma (eg, Penetrating Gunshot, Stab Wound)

20100-20103 relate to wound(s) resulting from penetrating trauma. These codes describe surgical exploration and enlargement of the wound, extension of dissection (to determine penetration), debridement, removal of foreign body(s), ligation or coagulation of minor subcutaneous and/or muscular blood vessel(s), of the subcutaneous tissue, muscle fascia, and/or muscle, not requiring thoracotomy or laparotomy. If a repair is done to major structure(s) or major blood vessel(s) requiring thoracotomy or laparotomy, then those specific code(s) would supersede the use of codes 20100-20103. To report Simple, Intermediate, or Complex repair of wound(s) that do not require enlargement of the wound, extension of dissection, etc., as stated above, use specific Repair code(s) in the Integumentary System section.

20100   Exploration of penetrating wound (separate procedure); neck
➲ *CPT Assistant* Jun 96:7; Aug 96:10

20101   chest
➲ *CPT Assistant* Jun 96:7

20102   abdomen/flank/back
➲ *CPT Assistant* Jun 96:7

20103   extremity
➲ *CPT Assistant* Jun 96:7; Aug 96:10

Excision

20150 Excision of epiphyseal bar, with or without autogenous soft tissue graft obtained through same fascial incision

(For aspiration of bone marrow, use ►38220)◄

20200 Biopsy, muscle; superficial

20205 deep

20206* Biopsy, muscle, percutaneous needle

►(If imaging guidance is performed,◄ see 76360, ►76393,◄ 76942)

►(For fine needle aspiration, use 10021 or 10022)◄

►(For evaulation of fine needle aspirate, see 88172-88173)◄

(For excision of muscle tumor, deep, see specific anatomic section)

20220 Biopsy, bone, trocar, or needle; superficial (eg, ilium, sternum, spinous process, ribs)
➔ *CPT Assistant* Winter 92:17; Jul 98:4

▲**20225** deep (eg, vertebral body, femur)
➔ *CPT Assistant* Winter 92:17; Jul 98:4; *CPT Changes* 2002

(For bone marrow biopsy, use ►38221◄)

►(For radiologic supervision and interpretation, see 76003, 76360, 76393)◄

20240 Biopsy, bone, excisional; superficial (eg, ilium, sternum, spinous process, ribs, trochanter of femur)
➔ *CPT Assistant* Winter 92:17; Jul 98:4

20245 deep (eg, humerus, ischium, femur)
➔ *CPT Assistant* Winter 92:17; Jul 98:4

20250 Biopsy, vertebral body, open; thoracic
➔ *CPT Assistant* Winter 92:17; Jul 98:4

20251 lumbar or cervical
➔ *CPT Assistant* Winter 92:17; Jul 98:4

(For sequestrectomy, osteomyelitis or drainage of bone abscess, see anatomical area)

Introduction or Removal

(For injection procedure for arthrography, see anatomical area)

20500* Injection of sinus tract; therapeutic (separate procedure)

20501* diagnostic (sinogram)

(For radiological supervision and interpretation, use 76080)

20520* Removal of foreign body in muscle or tendon sheath; simple

20525 deep or complicated

●**20526** Injection, therapeutic (eg, local anesthetic; corticosteroid), carpal tunnel
➔ *CPT Changes* 2002

▲**20550*** Injection; tendon sheath, ligament, ganglion cyst
➔ *CPT Assistant* Jan 96:7; Jun 98:10; *CPT Changes* 2002

►(If imaging guidance is performed, see 76003, 76393, 76942)◄

●**20551** tendon origin/insertion
➔ *CPT Changes* 2002

●**20552** single or multiple trigger point(s), one or two muscle group(s)
➔ *CPT Changes* 2002

●**20553** single or multiple trigger point(s), three or more muscle groups
➔ *CPT Changes* 2002

20600* Arthrocentesis, aspiration and/or injection; small joint, bursa or ganglion cyst (eg, fingers, toes)

20605* intermediate joint, bursa or ganglion cyst (eg, temporomandibular, acromioclavicular, wrist, elbow or ankle, olecranon bursa)

20610* major joint or bursa (eg, shoulder, hip, knee joint, subacromial bursa)
➔ *CPT Assistant* Spring 92:8

►(If imaging guidance is performed, see 76003, 76360, 76393, 76942)◄

20615 Aspiration and injection for treatment of bone cyst

20650* Insertion of wire or pin with application of skeletal traction, including removal (separate procedure)

⊘**20660** Application of cranial tongs, caliper, or stereotactic frame, including removal (separate procedure)
➔ *CPT Assistant* Jun 96:10; Nov 97:14

20661 Application of halo, including removal; cranial

20662 pelvic

20663 femoral

20664 Application of halo, including removal, cranial, 6 or more pins placed, for thin skull osteology (eg, pediatric patients, hydrocephalus, osteogenesis imperfecta), requiring general anesthesia

⊘ =Modifier '-51' Exempt   ► ◄=New or Revised Text   ✦=Add-on Code   CPT 2002

Halo Application for Thin Skull Osteology
20664

A cranial halo is placed on the head of a child whose skull is unusually thin due to congenital or developmental problems.

Uniplane External Fixation System
20690

Examples of types of stabilization devices. Codes 20690 and 20692 describe the placement of types of external fixation devices. The method of stabilization depends upon fracture grade (degree of soft tissue injury/skin integrity disruption), type (eg, comminuted, spiral, impacted), and location (eg, extremity, pelvis).

External fixation system

Fracture

External fixation system

20665*   Removal of tongs or halo applied by another physician

20670*   Removal of implant; superficial, (eg, buried wire, pin or rod) (separate procedure)

20680   deep (eg, buried wire, pin, screw, metal band, nail, rod or plate)
> ➔ *CPT Assistant* Spring 92:11

⊘ **20690**   Application of a uniplane (pins or wires in one plane), unilateral, external fixation system
> ➔ *CPT Assistant* Fall 93:21; Oct 99:4

(20691 has been deleted. To report, use 20690)

⊘ **20692** Application of a multiplane (pins or wires in more than one plane), unilateral, external fixation system (eg, Ilizarov, Monticelli type)

➔ *CPT Assistant* Fall 93:21; Oct 99:4; Jul 00:11

Multiplane External Fixation System
20692

An example of a type of multiplane stabilization device. Codes 20690 and 20692 describe the placement of types of external fixation devices. The method of stabilization depends upon fracture grade (degree of soft tissue injury/skin integrity disruption), type (eg, comminuted, spiral, impacted), and location (eg, extremity, pelvis).

Defect

External fixation system

20693 Adjustment or revision of external fixation system requiring anesthesia (eg, new pin(s) or wire(s) and/or new ring(s) or bar(s))

➔ *CPT Assistant* Fall 93:21; Oct 99:4; Jul 00:11

20694 Removal, under anesthesia, of external fixation system

➔ *CPT Assistant* Winter 92:10; Fall 93:21; Oct 99:4; Jul 00:11

Replantation

20802 Replantation, arm (includes surgical neck of humerus through elbow joint), complete amputation

(20804 has been deleted. To report, see specific code(s) for repair of bone(s), ligament(s), tendon(s), nerve(s), or blood vessel(s) with modifier '-52')

20805 Replantation, forearm (includes radius and ulna to radial carpal joint), complete amputation

(20806 has been deleted. To report, see specific code(s) for repair of bone(s), ligament(s), tendon(s), nerve(s), or blood vessel(s) with modifier '-52')

20808 Replantation, hand (includes hand through metacarpophalangeal joints), complete amputation

(20812 has been deleted. To report, see specific code(s) for repair of bone(s), ligament(s), tendon(s), nerve(s), or blood vessel(s) with modifier '-52')

20816 Replantation, digit, excluding thumb (includes metacarpophalangeal joint to insertion of flexor sublimis tendon), complete amputation

➔ *CPT Assistant* Oct 96:11

(20820 has been deleted. To report, see specific code(s) for repair of bone(s), ligament(s), tendon(s), nerve(s), or blood vessel(s) with modifier '-52')

20822 Replantation, digit, excluding thumb (includes distal tip to sublimis tendon insertion), complete amputation

(20823 has been deleted. To report, see specific code(s) for repair of bone(s), ligament(s), tendon(s), nerve(s), or blood vessel(s) with modifier '-52')

20824 Replantation, thumb (includes carpometacarpal joint to MP joint), complete amputation

(20826 has been deleted. To report, see specific code(s) for repair of bone(s), ligament(s), tendon(s), nerve(s), or blood vessel(s) with modifier '-52')

20827 Replantation, thumb (includes distal tip to MP joint), complete amputation

(20828 has been deleted. To report, see specific code(s) for repair of bone(s), ligament(s), tendon(s), nerve(s), or blood vessel(s) with modifier '-52')

(20832 has been deleted. To report, see specific code(s) for repair of bone(s), ligament(s), tendon(s), nerve(s), or blood vessel(s) with modifier '-52')

(20834 has been deleted. To report, see specific code(s) for repair of bone(s), ligament(s), tendon(s), nerve(s), or blood vessel(s) with modifier '-52')

20838 Replantation, foot, complete amputation

(20840 has been deleted. To report, see specific code(s) for repair of bone(s), ligament(s), tendon(s), nerve(s), or blood vessel(s) with modifier '-52')

Grafts (or Implants)

Codes for obtaining autogenous bone, cartilage, tendon, fascia lata grafts, or other tissues through separate incisions are to be used only when graft is not already listed as part of basic procedure.

►Do not append modifier '-62' to bone graft codes 20900-20938.◄

(For spinal surgery bone graft(s) see codes 20930-20938)

⊘ **20900** Bone graft, any donor area; minor or small (eg, dowel or button)

➔ *CPT Assistant* Dec 00:15

⊘ **20902** major or large

➔ *CPT Assistant* Dec 00:15

⊘ =Modifier '-51' Exempt   ► ◄=New or Revised Text   ✚=Add-on Code   CPT 2002

⊘ **20910** Cartilage graft; costochondral

⊘ **20912** nasal septum

(For ear cartilage, use 21235)

⊘ **20920** Fascia lata graft; by stripper
➔ *CPT Assistant* Aug 99:5

⊘ **20922** by incision and area exposure, complex or sheet

⊘ **20924** Tendon graft, from a distance (eg, palmaris, toe extensor, plantaris)

⊘ **20926** Tissue grafts, other (eg, paratenon, fat, dermis)
➔ *CPT Assistant* Summer 91:12; Aug 99:5; Nov 99:10

(Codes 20930-20938 are reported in addition to codes for the definitive procedure(s) without modifier '-51')

⊘ **20930** Allograft for spine surgery only; morselized
➔ *CPT Assistant* Feb 96:6; Mar 96:4; Sep 97:8; Nov 99:10

⊘ **20931** structural
➔ *CPT Assistant* Feb 96:6

⊘ **20936** Autograft for spine surgery only (includes harvesting the graft); local (eg, ribs, spinous process, or laminar fragments) obtained from same incision
➔ *CPT Assistant* Feb 96:6; Sep 97:8

⊘ **20937** morselized (through separate skin or fascial incision)
➔ *CPT Assistant* Feb 96:6; Sep 97:8; Dec 99:2

⊘ **20938** structural, bicortical or tricortical (through separate skin or fascial incision)
➔ *CPT Assistant* Feb 96:6; Mar 96:5; Sep 97:8

(For needle aspiration of bone marrow for the purpose of bone grafting, use ▶38220)◀

Other Procedures

20950 Monitoring of interstitial fluid pressure (includes insertion of device, eg, wick catheter technique, needle manometer technique) in detection of muscle compartment syndrome

20955 Bone graft with microvascular anastomosis; fibula
➔ *CPT Assistant* Apr 97:4

20956 iliac crest
➔ *CPT Assistant* Apr 97:4

20957 metatarsal
➔ *CPT Assistant* Apr 97:4

(20960 has been deleted. To report, use 20962)

20962 other than fibula, iliac crest, or metatarsal
➔ *CPT Assistant* Apr 97:4

(Do not report code 69990 in addition to codes 20955-20962)

20969 Free osteocutaneous flap with microvascular anastomosis; other than iliac crest, metatarsal, or great toe
➔ *CPT Assistant* Apr 97:4

20970 iliac crest
➔ *CPT Assistant* Apr 97:4

(20971 has been deleted. To report, use 20969)

20972 metatarsal
➔ *CPT Assistant* Apr 97:4

20973 great toe with web space
➔ *CPT Assistant* Apr 97:4

(Do not report code 69990 in addition to codes 20969-20973)

(For great toe, wrap-around procedure, use 26551)

⊘ **20974** Electrical stimulation to aid bone healing; noninvasive (nonoperative)
➔ *CPT Assistant* Sep 96:11

⊘ **20975** invasive (operative)

(20976 has been deleted)

20979 Low intensity ultrasound stimulation to aid bone healing, noninvasive (nonoperative)
➔ *CPT Assistant* Nov 99:10; Nov 00:8; *CPT Changes* 2000

20999 Unlisted procedure, musculoskeletal system, general

Head

Skull, facial bones and temporomandibular joint.

Incision

(For drainage of superficial abscess and hematoma, use 20000)

(For removal of embedded foreign body from dentoalveolar structure, see 41805, 41806)

21010 Arthrotomy, temporomandibular joint

(21011 has been deleted. To report, use 21010 with modifier '-50')

Excision

(For biopsy, see 20220, 20240)

21015 Radical resection of tumor (eg, malignant neoplasm), soft tissue of face or scalp

(21020 has been deleted. To report, use 61501)

21025 Excision of bone (eg, for osteomyelitis or bone abscess); mandible

21026 facial bone(s)

21029 Removal by contouring of benign tumor of facial bone (eg, fibrous dysplasia)

21030 Excision of benign tumor or cyst of facial bone other than mandible

21031 Excision of torus mandibularis

21032 Excision of maxillary torus palatinus

21034 Excision of malignant tumor of facial bone other than mandible

21040 Excision of benign cyst or tumor of mandible; simple

21041 complex

21044 Excision of malignant tumor of mandible;

21045 radical resection

(For bone graft, use 21215)

21050 Condylectomy, temporomandibular joint (separate procedure)

(21051 has been deleted. To report, use 21050 with modifier '-50')

21060 Meniscectomy, partial or complete, temporomandibular joint (separate procedure)

(21061 has been deleted. To report, use 21060 with modifier '-50')

21070 Coronoidectomy (separate procedure)

(21071 has been deleted. To report, use 21070 with modifier '-50')

Introduction or Removal

(For application or removal of caliper or tongs, see 20660, 20665.) Codes 21076-21089 describe professional services for the rehabilitation of patients with oral, facial or other anatomical deficiencies by means of prostheses such as an artificial eye, ear, or nose or intraoral obturator to close a cleft. Codes 21076-21089 should only be used when the physician actually designs and prepares the prosthesis (ie, not prepared by an outside laboratory).

21076 Impression and custom preparation; surgical obturator prosthesis

21077 orbital prosthesis

21079 interim obturator prosthesis

21080 definitive obturator prosthesis

21081 mandibular resection prosthesis

21082 palatal augmentation prosthesis

21083 palatal lift prosthesis

21084 speech aid prosthesis

21085 oral surgical splint

21086 auricular prosthesis

21087 nasal prosthesis

21088 facial prosthesis

21089 Unlisted maxillofacial prosthetic procedure

21100* Application of halo type appliance for maxillofacial fixation, includes removal (separate procedure)

21110 Application of interdental fixation device for conditions other than fracture or dislocation, includes removal
➔ *CPT Assistant* Mar 97:10

(For removal of interdental fixation by another physician, see 20670-20680)

21116 Injection procedure for temporomandibular joint arthrography

(For radiological supervision and interpretation, use 70332. ▶Do not report 76003 in addition to 70332)◀

Repair, Revision, and/or Reconstruction

(For cranioplasty, see 21179, 21180 and 62116, 62120, 62140-62147)

21120 Genioplasty; augmentation (autograft, allograft, prosthetic material)

21121 sliding osteotomy, single piece

21122 sliding osteotomies, two or more osteotomies (eg, wedge excision or bone wedge reversal for asymmetrical chin)

21123 sliding, augmentation with interpositional bone grafts (includes obtaining autografts)

21125 Augmentation, mandibular body or angle; prosthetic material

21127 with bone graft, onlay or interpositional (includes obtaining autograft)

21137 Reduction forehead; contouring only

21138 contouring and application of prosthetic material or bone graft (includes obtaining autograft)

21139 contouring and setback of anterior frontal sinus wall

21141 Reconstruction midface, LeFort I; single piece, segment movement in any direction (eg, for Long Face Syndrome), without bone graft

21142 two pieces, segment movement in any direction, without bone graft

21143 three or more pieces, segment movement in any direction, without bone graft

(21144 has been deleted. To report, use 21141)

21145 single piece, segment movement in any direction, requiring bone grafts (includes obtaining autografts)

21146 two pieces, segment movement in any direction, requiring bone grafts (includes obtaining autografts) (eg, ungrafted unilateral alveolar cleft)

21147 three or more pieces, segment movement in any direction, requiring bone grafts (includes obtaining autografts) (eg, ungrafted bilateral alveolar cleft or multiple osteotomies)

21150   Reconstruction midface, LeFort II; anterior intrusion (eg, Treacher-Collins Syndrome)

21151   any direction, requiring bone grafts (includes obtaining autografts)

21154   Reconstruction midface, LeFort III (extracranial), any type, requiring bone grafts (includes obtaining autografts); without LeFort I

21155   with LeFort I

21159   Reconstruction midface, LeFort III (extra and intracranial) with forehead advancement (eg, mono bloc), requiring bone grafts (includes obtaining autografts); without LeFort I

21160   with LeFort I

21172   Reconstruction superior-lateral orbital rim and lower forehead, advancement or alteration, with or without grafts (includes obtaining autografts)

(For frontal or parietal craniotomy performed for craniosynostosis, use 61556)

21175   Reconstruction, bifrontal, superior-lateral orbital rims and lower forehead, advancement or alteration (eg, plagiocephaly, trigonocephaly, brachycephaly), with or without grafts (includes obtaining autografts)

(For bifrontal craniotomy performed for craniosynostosis, use 61557)

21179   Reconstruction, entire or majority of forehead and/or supraorbital rims; with grafts (allograft or prosthetic material)

21180   with autograft (includes obtaining grafts)

(For extensive craniectomy for multiple suture craniosynostosis, use only 61558 or 61559)

21181   Reconstruction by contouring of benign tumor of cranial bones (eg, fibrous dysplasia), extracranial

▲ **21182**   Reconstruction of orbital walls, rims, forehead, nasoethmoid complex following intra- and extracranial excision of benign tumor of cranial bone (eg, fibrous dysplasia), with multiple autografts (includes obtaining grafts); total area of bone grafting less than 40 sq cm

▲ **21183**   total area of bone grafting greater than 40 sq cm but less than 80 sq cm
➔ *CPT Changes* 2002

▲ **21184**   total area of bone grafting greater than 80 sq cm
➔ *CPT Changes* 2002

(For excision of benign tumor of cranial bones, see 61563, 61564)

21188   Reconstruction midface, osteotomies (other than LeFort type) and bone grafts (includes obtaining autografts)

21193   Reconstruction of mandibular rami, horizontal, vertical, C, or L osteotomy; without bone graft
➔ *CPT Assistant* Apr 96:11

21194   with bone graft (includes obtaining graft)
➔ *CPT Assistant* Apr 96:11

21195   Reconstruction of mandibular rami and/or body, sagittal split; without internal rigid fixation
➔ *CPT Assistant* Apr 96:11

21196   with internal rigid fixation
➔ *CPT Assistant* Apr 96:11; Mar 97:11

Reconstruction of Mandibular Rami
21196

The mandibular ramus is reconstructed to lengthen, set back, or rotate the mandible.

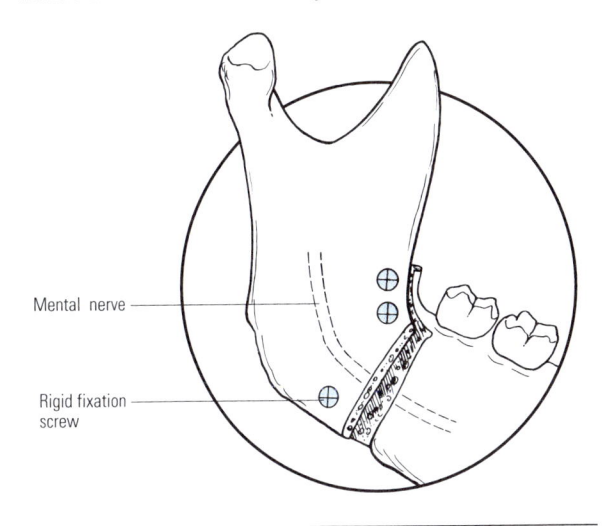

Mental nerve

Rigid fixation screw

21198   Osteotomy, mandible, segmental;
➔ *CPT Changes* 2001

21199   with genioglossus advancement
➔ *CPT Changes* 2001

(21200, 21202, 21203 have been deleted. To report, see 21193-21198)

(21204 has been deleted. To report, see 21141-21160)

21206   Osteotomy, maxilla, segmental (eg, Wassmund or Schuchard)

(21207 has been deleted. To report, use 21209)

21208   Osteoplasty, facial bones; augmentation (autograft, allograft, or prosthetic implant)

21209   reduction

21210   Graft, bone; nasal, maxillary or malar areas (includes obtaining graft)

(For cleft palate repair, see 42200-42225)

21215   mandible (includes obtaining graft)

21230   Graft; rib cartilage, autogenous, to face, chin, nose or ear (includes obtaining graft)

21235   ear cartilage, autogenous, to nose or ear (includes obtaining graft)

(21239 has been deleted. To report, use 21208)

21240 Arthroplasty, temporomandibular joint, with or without autograft (includes obtaining graft)

(21241 has been deleted. To report, use 21240)

21242 Arthroplasty, temporomandibular joint, with allograft

21243 Arthroplasty, temporomandibular joint, with prosthetic joint replacement

21244 Reconstruction of mandible, extraoral, with transosteal bone plate (eg, mandibular staple bone plate)

21245 Reconstruction of mandible or maxilla, subperiosteal implant; partial

21246 complete

21247 Reconstruction of mandibular condyle with bone and cartilage autografts (includes obtaining grafts) (eg, for hemifacial microsomia)

21248 Reconstruction of mandible or maxilla, endosteal implant (eg, blade, cylinder); partial

21249 complete

(21250, 21254 have been deleted. To report, see 21141-21160)

21255 Reconstruction of zygomatic arch and glenoid fossa with bone and cartilage (includes obtaining autografts)

21256 Reconstruction of orbit with osteotomies (extracranial) and with bone grafts (includes obtaining autografts) (eg, micro-ophthalmia)

21260 Periorbital osteotomies for orbital hypertelorism, with bone grafts; extracranial approach

21261 combined intra- and extracranial approach

21263 with forehead advancement

21267 Orbital repositioning, periorbital osteotomies, unilateral, with bone grafts; extracranial approach

21268 combined intra- and extracranial approach

21270 Malar augmentation, prosthetic material

(For malar augmentation with bone graft, use 21210)

21275 Secondary revision of orbitocraniofacial reconstruction

21280 Medial canthopexy (separate procedure)

(For medial canthoplasty, use 67950)

21282 Lateral canthopexy

21295 Reduction of masseter muscle and bone (eg, for treatment of benign masseteric hypertrophy); extraoral approach

21296 intraoral approach

Other Procedures

21299 Unlisted craniofacial and maxillofacial procedure

Fracture and/or Dislocation

21300 Closed treatment of skull fracture without operation

(For operative repair, see 62000-62010)

21310 Closed treatment of nasal bone fracture without manipulation

21315* Closed treatment of nasal bone fracture; without stabilization

21320 with stabilization

21325 Open treatment of nasal fracture; uncomplicated

21330 complicated, with internal and/or external skeletal fixation

21335 with concomitant open treatment of fractured septum

21336 Open treatment of nasal septal fracture, with or without stabilization

21337 Closed treatment of nasal septal fracture, with or without stabilization

21338 Open treatment of nasoethmoid fracture; without external fixation

21339 with external fixation

21340 Percutaneous treatment of nasoethmoid complex fracture, with splint, wire or headcap fixation, including repair of canthal ligaments and/or the nasolacrimal apparatus

21343 Open treatment of depressed frontal sinus fracture

21344 Open treatment of complicated (eg, comminuted or involving posterior wall) frontal sinus fracture, via coronal or multiple approaches

21345 Closed treatment of nasomaxillary complex fracture (LeFort II type), with interdental wire fixation or fixation of denture or splint

21346 Open treatment of nasomaxillary complex fracture (LeFort II type); with wiring and/or local fixation

21347 requiring multiple open approaches

21348 with bone grafting (includes obtaining graft)

(21350 has been deleted. If necessary to report, use appropriate Evaluation and Management code)

21355* Percutaneous treatment of fracture of malar area, including zygomatic arch and malar tripod, with manipulation

21356 Open treatment of depressed zygomatic arch fracture (eg, Gillies approach)

21360 Open treatment of depressed malar fracture, including zygomatic arch and malar tripod

21365 Open treatment of complicated (eg, comminuted or involving cranial nerve foramina) fracture(s) of malar area, including zygomatic arch and malar tripod; with internal fixation and multiple surgical approaches

$\bigcirc$ =Modifier '-51' Exempt   ▶ ◀ =New or Revised Text   ✚ =Add-on Code   CPT 2002

21366	with bone grafting (includes obtaining graft)

(21380 has been deleted. If necessary to report, use appropriate Evaluation and Management code)

21385 Open treatment of orbital floor blowout fracture; transantral approach (Caldwell-Luc type operation)

21386 periorbital approach

21387 combined approach

21390 periorbital approach, with alloplastic or other implant

21395 periorbital approach with bone graft (includes obtaining graft)

21400 Closed treatment of fracture of orbit, except blowout; without manipulation

21401 with manipulation

21406 Open treatment of fracture of orbit, except blowout; without implant

21407 with implant

21408 with bone grafting (includes obtaining graft)

(21420 has been deleted. If necessary to report, use appropriate Evaluation and Management code)

21421 Closed treatment of palatal or maxillary fracture (LeFort I type), with interdental wire fixation or fixation of denture or splint

21422 Open treatment of palatal or maxillary fracture (LeFort I type);

21423 complicated (comminuted or involving cranial nerve foramina), multiple approaches

21431 Closed treatment of craniofacial separation (LeFort III type) using interdental wire fixation of denture or splint

21432 Open treatment of craniofacial separation (LeFort III type); with wiring and/or internal fixation

21433 complicated (eg, comminuted or involving cranial nerve foramina), multiple surgical approaches

21435 complicated, utilizing internal and/or external fixation techniques (eg, head cap, halo device, and/or intermaxillary fixation)

(For removal of internal or external fixation device, use 20670)

21436 complicated, multiple surgical approaches, internal fixation, with bone grafting (includes obtaining graft)

21440 Closed treatment of mandibular or maxillary alveolar ridge fracture (separate procedure)

21445 Open treatment of mandibular or maxillary alveolar ridge fracture (separate procedure)

21450 Closed treatment of mandibular fracture; without manipulation

21451 with manipulation

21452 Percutaneous treatment of mandibular fracture, with external fixation

21453 Closed treatment of mandibular fracture with interdental fixation

21454 Open treatment of mandibular fracture with external fixation

(21455 has been deleted. To report, use 21453)

21461 Open treatment of mandibular fracture; without interdental fixation

21462 with interdental fixation

21465 Open treatment of mandibular condylar fracture

21470 Open treatment of complicated mandibular fracture by multiple surgical approaches including internal fixation, interdental fixation, and/or wiring of dentures or splints

21480 Closed treatment of temporomandibular dislocation; initial or subsequent

21485 complicated (eg, recurrent requiring intermaxillary fixation or splinting), initial or subsequent

21490 Open treatment of temporomandibular dislocation

(For interdental wire fixation, use 21497)

21493 Closed treatment of hyoid fracture; without manipulation

21494 with manipulation

21495 Open treatment of hyoid fracture

(For treatment of fracture of larynx, see 31584-31586)

21497 Interdental wiring, for condition other than fracture
⮕ *CPT Assistant* Mar 97:10

Other Procedures

21499 Unlisted musculoskeletal procedure, head

(For unlisted craniofacial or maxillofacial procedure, use 21299)

Neck (Soft Tissues) and Thorax

(For cervical spine and back, see 21920 et seq)

(For injection of fracture site or trigger point, use 20550)

Incision

(For incision and drainage of abscess or hematoma, superficial, see 10060, 10140)

21501 Incision and drainage, deep abscess or hematoma, soft tissues of neck or thorax;

21502 with partial rib ostectomy

21510 Incision, deep, with opening of bone cortex (eg, for osteomyelitis or bone abscess), thorax

(21511 has been deleted)

Excision

(For bone biopsy, see 20220-20251)

21550 Biopsy, soft tissue of neck or thorax

(For needle biopsy of soft tissue, use 20206)

21555 Excision tumor, soft tissue of neck or thorax; subcutaneous

21556 deep, subfascial, intramuscular

21557 Radical resection of tumor (eg, malignant neoplasm), soft tissue of neck or thorax

21600 Excision of rib, partial

(For radical resection of chest wall and rib cage for tumor, use 19260)

(For radical debridement of chest wall and rib cage for injury, see 11040-11044)

21610 Costotransversectomy (separate procedure)

21615 Excision first and/or cervical rib;

21616 with sympathectomy

21620 Ostectomy of sternum, partial

21627 Sternal debridement

(For debridement and closure, use 21750)

21630 Radical resection of sternum;

21632 with mediastinal lymphadenectomy

(21633 has been deleted. To report, use 21630)

Repair, Revision, and/or Reconstruction

(For superficial wound, see **Integumentary System** section under Repair—Simple)

21700 Division of scalenus anticus; without resection of cervical rib

21705 with resection of cervical rib

21720 Division of sternocleidomastoid for torticollis, open operation; without cast application

(For transection of spinal accessory and cervical nerves, see 63191, 64722)

21725 with cast application

21740 Reconstructive repair of pectus excavatum or carinatum

(21741 has been deleted. To report, use 21899)

▲ **21750** Closure of median sternotomy separation with or without debridement (separate procedure)

➲ *CPT Changes* 2002

Fracture and/or Dislocation

21800 Closed treatment of rib fracture, uncomplicated, each

21805 Open treatment of rib fracture without fixation, each

21810 Treatment of rib fracture requiring external fixation (flail chest)

21820 Closed treatment of sternum fracture

21825 Open treatment of sternum fracture with or without skeletal fixation

(For sternoclavicular dislocation, see 23520-23532)

Other Procedures

21899 Unlisted procedure, neck or thorax

Back and Flank

Excision

21920 Biopsy, soft tissue of back or flank; superficial

21925 deep

(For needle biopsy of soft tissue, use 20206)

21930 Excision, tumor, soft tissue of back or flank

21935 Radical resection of tumor (eg, malignant neoplasm), soft tissue of back or flank

Spine (Vertebral Column)

Cervical, thoracic, and lumbar spine.

Within the SPINE section, bone grafting procedures are reported separately and in addition to arthrodesis. For bone grafts in other Musculoskeletal sections, see specific code(s) descriptor(s) and/or accompanying guidelines.

To report bone grafts performed after arthrodesis, see codes 20930-20938. Bone graft codes are reported without modifier '-51' (multiple procedure). ▶Do not append modifier '-62' to bone graft codes 20900-20938.◀

Example:

Posterior arthrodesis of L5-S1 for degenerative disc disease utilizing morselized autogenous iliac bone graft harvested through a separate fascial incision.

Report as 22612 and 20937.

Within the SPINE section, instrumentation is reported separately and in addition to arthrodesis. To report instrumentation procedures performed with definitive vertebral procedure(s), see codes 22840-22855. Instrumentation procedure codes 22840-22848 and 22851 are reported in addition to the definitive

⊘ =Modifier '-51' Exempt   ▶ ◀=New or Revised Text   ✚ =Add-on Code

procedure(s) without modifier '-51'. ▶The modifier '-62' may not be appended to the definitive or add-on spinal instrumentation procedure code(s) 22840-22855.◀

Example:

Posterior arthrodesis of L4-S1, utilizing morselized autogenous iliac bone graft harvested through separate fascial incision, and pedicle screw fixation.

Report as 22612, 22614, 22842, and 20937.

Vertebral procedures are sometimes followed by arthrodesis and in addition may include bone grafts and instrumentation.

When arthrodesis is performed in addition to another procedure, the arthrodesis should be reported in addition to the original procedure with a modifier '-51' (multiple procedures). Examples are after osteotomy, fracture care, vertebral corpectomy and laminectomy. Since bone grafts and instrumentation are never performed without arthrodesis, modifier '-51' (multiple procedures) is not used.

Arthrodesis, however, may be performed in the absence of other procedures and therefore when it is combined with another definitive procedure, modifier '-51' (multiple procedure) is appropriate.

Example:

Treatment of a burst fracture of L2 by corpectomy followed by arthrodesis of L1-L3, utilizing anterior instrumentation L1-L3 and structural allograft.

Report as 63090, 22558-51, 22585, 22845, and 20931.

When two surgeons work together as primary surgeons performing distinct part(s) of a single reportable procedure, each surgeon should report his/her distinct operative work by appending the modifier '-62' to the single definitive procedure code. If additional procedure(s) (including add-on procedure(s)) are performed during the same surgical session, separate code(s) may be reported by each co-surgeon, without the modifier '-62' appended (see Appendix A).

Example:

A 42-year-old male with a history of posttraumatic degenerative disc disease at L3-4 and L4-5 (internal disc disruption) underwent surgical repair. Surgeon A performed an anterior exposure of the spine with mobilization of the great vessels. Surgeon B performed anterior (minimal) diskectomy and fusion at L3-4 and L4-5 using anterior interbody technique.

Report surgeon A: 22558-62, ▶22585-62◀
Report surgeon B: 22558-62, ▶22585-62◀, 20931

▶(Do not append modifier -62 to bone graft code 20931)◀

(For injection procedure for myelography, use 62284)

(For injection procedure for diskography, see 62290, 62291)

(For injection procedure, chemonucleolysis, single or multiple levels, use 62292)

(For injection procedure for facet joints, see 64470-64476, 64622-64627)

(For needle or trocar biopsy, see 20220-20225)

Excision

▶For the following codes, when two surgeons work together as primary surgeons performing distinct part(s) of partial vertebral body excision, each surgeon should report his/her distinct operative work by appending the modifier '-62' to the procedure code. In this situation, the modifier '-62' may be appended to the procedure code(s) 22100-22102, 22110-22114 and, as appropriate, to the associated additional vertebral segment add-on code(s) 22103, 22116 as long as both surgeons continue to work together as primary surgeons.◀

(For bone biopsy, see 20220-20251)

(22010 has been deleted. To report, use 21920)

(22011 has been deleted. To report, use 21925)

(22012 has been deleted. To report, use 20206)

(22030-22033 have been deleted. To report, use 21930)

22100   Partial excision of posterior vertebral component (eg, spinous process, lamina or facet) for intrinsic bony lesion, single vertebral segment; cervical

22101   thoracic

22102   lumbar

+ 22103   each additional segment (List separately in addition to code for primary procedure)

(Use 22103 in conjunction with codes 22100, 22101, 22102)

(22105 has been deleted. To report, use 22100)

(22106 has been deleted. To report, use 22101)

(22107 has been deleted. To report, use 22102)

22110   Partial excision of vertebral body, for intrinsic bony lesion, without decompression of spinal cord or nerve root(s), single vertebral segment; cervical

(22111 has been deleted)

22112   thoracic

(22113 has been deleted)

22114   lumbar

(22115 has been deleted)

+ 22116   each additional vertebral segment (List separately in addition to code for primary procedure)

(Use 22116 in conjunction with codes 22110, 22112, 22114)

(22120-22130 have been deleted. For complete or near complete resection of vertebral body, see vertebral corpectomy, 63081-63091)

(22140 has been deleted. To report, use 63081 and 22554 and 20931 or 20938)

(22141 has been deleted. To report, use 63085 or 63087 and 22556 and 20931 or 20938)

(22142 has been deleted. To report, use 63087 or 63090 and 22558 and 20931 or 20938)

(22145 has been deleted. To report, use 63082 or 63086 or 63088 or 63091, and 22585)

(22148 has been deleted. To report, see 20931 or 20938)

(22150 has been deleted. To report, use 63081 and 22554 and 20931 or 20938 and 22851)

(22151 has been deleted. To report, use 63085 or 63087 and 22556 and 20931 or 20938 and 22851)

(22152 has been deleted. To report, use 63087 or 63090 and 22558, and 20931 or 20938 and 22851)

(22200-22207 have been deleted. For osteotomy of spine, see 22210-22226)

Osteotomy

To report arthrodesis, see codes 22590-22632. (Report in addition to code(s) for the definitive procedure with modifier '-51'.)

To report instrumentation procedures, see codes 22840-22855. (Report in addition to code(s) for the definitive procedure(s) without modifier '-51'.) ▶Do not append modifier '-62' to spinal instrumentation codes 22840-22855.◀

To report bone graft procedures, see codes 20930-20938. (Report in addition to code(s) for the definitive procedure(s) without modifier '-51'.) ▶Do not append modifier '-62' to bone graft codes 20900-20938.◀

▶For the following codes, when two surgeons work together as primary surgeons performing distinct part(s) of an anterior spine osteotomy, each surgeon should report his/her distinct operative work by appending the modifier '-62' to the procedure code. In this situation, the modifier '-62' may be appended to the procedure code(s) 22210-22214, 22220-22224 and, as appropriate, to associated additional segment add-on code(s) 22216,

22226 as long as both surgeons continue to work together as primary surgeons.◀

22210   Osteotomy of spine, posterior or posterolateral approach, one vertebral segment; cervical

22212   thoracic

22214   lumbar

+ 22216   each additional vertebral segment (List separately in addition to primary procedure)

(Use 22216 in conjunction with codes 22210, 22212, 22214)

22220   Osteotomy of spine, including diskectomy, anterior approach, single vertebral segment; cervical

22222   thoracic

22224   lumbar

+ 22226   each additional vertebral segment (List separately in addition to code for primary procedure)

(Use 22226 in conjunction with codes 22220, 22222, 22224)

(22230 has been deleted. To report, use 22216 or 22226)

(22250, 22251 have been deleted. For vertebral corpectomy, see 63081-63091)

Fracture and/or Dislocation

To report arthrodesis, see codes 22590-22632. (Report in addition to code(s) for the definitive procedure with modifier '-51'.)

To report instrumentation procedures, see codes 22840-22855. (Report in addition to code(s) for the definitive procedure(s) without modifier '-51'.) ▶Do not append modifier '-62' to spinal instrumentation codes 22840-22855.◀

To report bone graft procedures, see codes 20930-20938. (Report in addition to code(s) for the definitive procedure(s) without modifier '-51'.) ▶Do not append modifier '-62' to bone graft codes 20900-20938.◀

▶For the following codes, when two surgeons work together as primary surgeons performing distinct part(s) of open fracture and/or dislocation procedure(s), each surgeon should report his/her distinct operative work by appending the modifier '-62' to the procedure code. In this situation, the modifier '-62' may be appended to the procedure code(s) 22318-22327 and, as appropriate, the associated additional fracture vertebrae or dislocated segment add-on code 22328 as long as both surgeons continue to work together as primary surgeons.◀

22305   Closed treatment of vertebral process fracture(s)

22310   Closed treatment of vertebral body fracture(s), without manipulation, requiring and including casting or bracing

22315   Closed treatment of vertebral fracture(s) and/or dislocation(s) requiring casting or bracing, with and including casting and/or bracing, with or without anesthesia, by manipulation or traction

(For spinal subluxation, use 97140)

22318   Open treatment and/or reduction of odontoid fracture(s) and or dislocation(s) (including os odontoideum), anterior approach, including placement of internal fixation; without grafting

➔ *CPT Assistant* Nov 99:11; *CPT Changes* 2000

22319   with grafting

➔ *CPT Assistant* Nov 99:11; *CPT Changes* 2000

22325   Open treatment and/or reduction of vertebral fracture(s) and/or dislocation(s), posterior approach, one fractured vertebrae or dislocated segment; lumbar

➔ *CPT Assistant* Sep 97:8

22326   cervical

➔ *CPT Assistant* Sep 97:8

22327   thoracic

➔ *CPT Assistant* Sep 97:8

+ 22328   each additional fractured vertebrae or dislocated segment (List separately in addition to code for primary procedure)

(Use 22328 in conjunction with codes 22325, 22326, 22327)

(For treatment of vertebral fracture by the anterior approach, see corpectomy 63081-63091, and appropriate arthrodesis, bone graft and instrument codes)

(22330-22379 have been deleted. For decompression of spine following fracture, see 63001-63091; for arthrodesis of spine following fracture, see 22548-22632)

Manipulation

(22500 has been deleted. To report, use 97140)

22505   Manipulation of spine requiring anesthesia, any region

➔ *CPT Assistant* Mar 97:11; Jan 99:11

Vertebral Body, Embolization or Injection

22520   Percutaneous vertebroplasty, one vertebral body, unilateral or bilateral injection; thoracic

➔ *CPT Changes* 2001

22521   lumbar

➔ *CPT Changes* 2001

+ 22522   each additional thoracic or lumbar vertebral body (List separately in addition to code for primary procedure)

➔ *CPT Changes* 2001

(Use 22522 in conjunction with codes 22520, 22521 as appropriate)

(For radiological supervision and interpretation, see 76012, 76013)

Percutaneous Vertebroplasty
22520

Augmentation of a vertebral fracture is achieved by percutaneous injections of polymethylmethacrylate under fluoroscopic guidance.

Spinal canal (vertebral foramen)

Fractured vertebral body

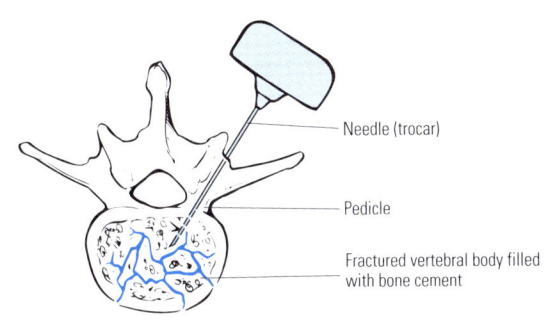

Needle (trocar)

Pedicle

Fractured vertebral body filled with bone cement

Arthrodesis

Arthrodesis may be performed in the absence of other procedures and therefore when it is combined with another definitive procedure (eg, osteotomy, fracture care, vertebral corpectomy or laminectomy), modifier '-51' is appropriate. However, arthrodesis codes 22585, 22614, and 22632 are considered add-on procedure codes and should not be used with modifier '-51'.

To report instrumentation procedures, see codes 22840-22855. (Report in addition to code(s) for the definitive procedure(s) without modifier '-51'.) ▶Do not append modifier '-62' to spinal instrumentation codes 22840-22855.◀

To report bone graft procedures, see codes 20930-20938. (Report in addition to code(s) for the definitive procedure(s) without modifier '-51'.) ▶Do not append modifier '-62' to bone graft codes 20900-20938.◀

Anterior or Anterolateral Approach Technique

Procedure codes 22554-22558 are for SINGLE interspace; for additional interspaces, use 22585. A vertebral interspace is the non-bony compartment between two adjacent vertebral bodies, which contains the intervertebral disk, and includes the nucleus pulposus, annulus fibrosus, and two cartilagenous endplates.

▶For the following codes, when two surgeons work together as primary surgeons performing distinct part(s) of an anterior interbody arthrodesis, each surgeon should report his/her distinct operative work by appending the modifier '-62' to the procedure code. In this situation, the modifier '-62' may be appended to the procedure code(s) 22548-22558 and, as appropriate, to the associated additional interspace add-on code 22585 as long as both surgeons continue to work together as primary surgeons.◄

22548 Arthrodesis, anterior transoral or extraoral technique, clivus-C1-C2 (atlas-axis), with or without excision of odontoid process

> *CPT Assistant* Spring 93:36; Feb 96:7 Sep 97:8; Sep 00:10

Arthrodesis (Anterior Transoral Technique)
22548

Anterior transoral technique.

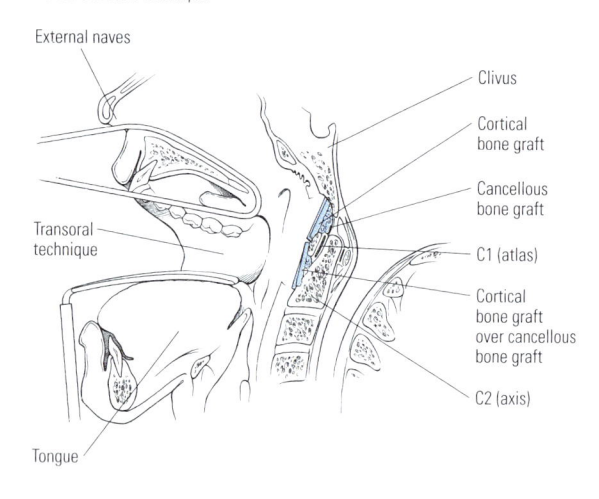

(22550, 22552, 22555, 22560, 22561, 22565 have been deleted. For intervertebral disk excision by laminotomy or laminectomy, see 63020-63042. For arthrodesis, see 22548-22632)

22554 Arthrodesis, anterior interbody technique, including minimal diskectomy to prepare interspace (other than for decompression); cervical below C2

> *CPT Assistant* Spring 93:36; Sep 97:8; Sep 00:10; Jan 01:12

22556 thoracic

> *CPT Assistant* Spring 93:36; Jul 96:7; Sep 97:8; Sep 00:10

Anterior Approach for Cervical Fusion
22554

An example of an exposure technique used to reach anterior cervical vertebrae for spinal procedures (eg, diskectomy, arthrodesis, spinal instrumentation).

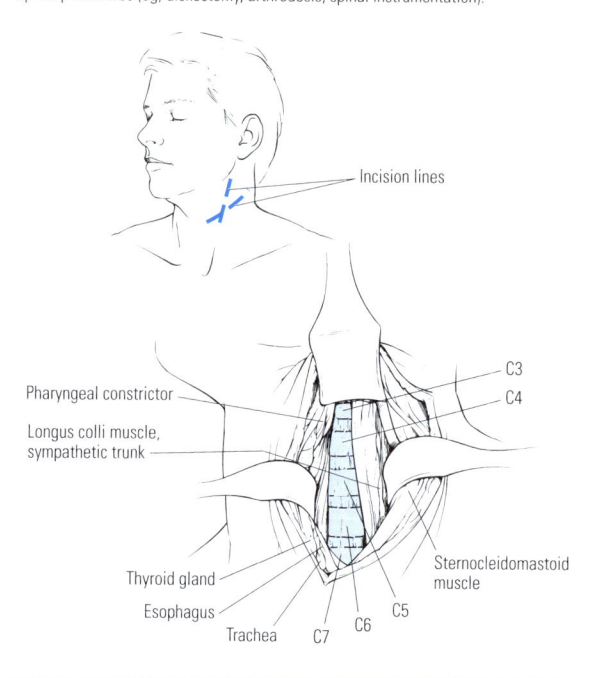

22558 lumbar

> *CPT Assistant* Spring 93:36; Mar 96:6; Jul 96:7; Sep 97:8; Sep 00:10

Anterior Approach for Lumbar Fusion (Anterior Retroperitoneal Exposure)
22558

An example of an exposure technique used to reach anterior lumbar vertebrae for spinal procedures (eg, diskectomy, arthrodesis, spinal instrumentation).

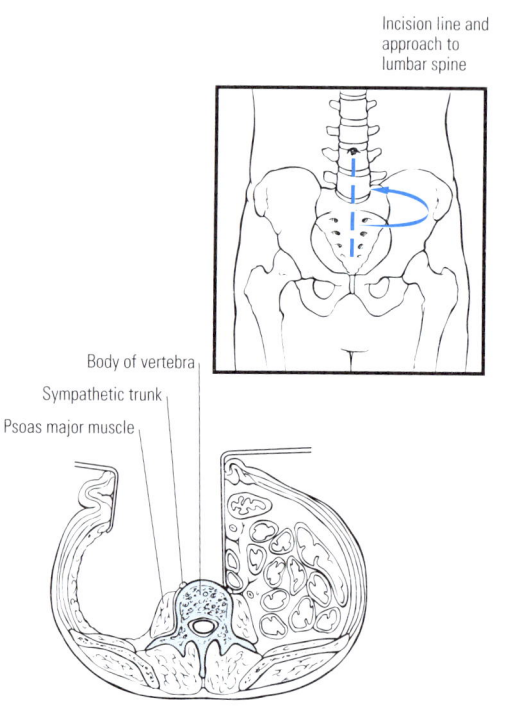

+ 22585   each additional interspace (List separately in addition to code for primary procedure)

⮕ *CPT Assistant* Spring 93:36; Mar 96:6; Sep 97:8; Sep 00:10

(Use 22585 in conjunction with codes 22554, 22556, 22558)

Posterior, Posterolateral or Lateral Transverse Process Technique

To report instrumentation procedures, see codes 22840-22855. (Report in addition to code(s) for the definitive procedure(s) without modifier '-51'.) ▶Do not append modifier '-62' to spinal instrumentation codes 22840-22855.◀

To report bone graft procedures, see codes 20930-20938. (Report in addition to code(s) for the definitive procedure(s) without modifier '-51'.) ▶Do not append modifier '-62' to bone graft codes 20900-20938.◀

A vertebral segment describes the basic constituent part into which the spine may be divided. It represents a single complete vertebral bone with its associated articular processes and laminae. A vertebral interspace is the non-bony compartment between two adjacent vertebral bodies which contains the intervertebral disk, and includes the nucleus pulposus, annulus fibrosus, and two cartilagenous endplates.

22590   Arthrodesis, posterior technique, craniocervical (occiput-C2)

⮕ *CPT Assistant* Spring 93:36; Sep 97:8

22595   Arthrodesis, posterior technique, atlas-axis (C1-C2)

⮕ *CPT Assistant* Spring 93:36; Sep 97:8

22600   Arthrodesis, posterior or posterolateral technique, single level; cervical below C2 segment

⮕ *CPT Assistant* Spring 93:36; Sep 97:8

(22605 has been deleted. To report, use 22600)

22610   thoracic (with or without lateral transverse technique)

⮕ *CPT Assistant* Spring 93:36; Sep 97:8

22612   lumbar (with or without lateral transverse technique)

⮕ *CPT Assistant* Spring 93:36; Mar 96:7; Sep 97:8;11

+ 22614   each additional vertebral segment (List separately in addition to code for primary procedure)

⮕ *CPT Assistant* Mar 96:7

(Use 22614 in conjunction with codes 22600, 22610, 22612)

(22615 has been deleted. To report, use 22554 and 20930-20938)

(22617 has been deleted. To report, use 22548 and 20930-20938)

(22620 has been deleted. To report, use 22590 and 20930-20938)

(22625 has been deleted. To report, use 22612 and 22840-22855, and 20930-20938)

22630   Arthrodesis, posterior interbody technique, including laminectomy and/or diskectomy to prepare interspace (other than for decompression), single interspace; lumbar

⮕ *CPT Assistant* Spring 93:36; Sep 97:8; Nov 99:11; Dec 99:2; Jan 01:12; *CPT Changes* 2000

+ 22632   each additional interspace (List separately in addition to code for primary procedure)

⮕ *CPT Assistant* Sep 97:8; Dec 99:2

(Use 22632 in conjunction with code 22630)

(22640-22645 have been deleted. To report, see 22610, 22612, and 20930-20938)

(22650 has been deleted. To report, use 22614)

(22655 has been deleted. To report, see 22630, 22632 and 20930-20938)

(22670 has been deleted. To report, see 22610 or 22612 and 22840-22855, and 20930-20938)

(22680 has been deleted. To report, see 22556-22585 and 20930-20938)

(22700 has been deleted. To report, see 22558 and 20930-20938)

(22720 has been deleted. To report, see 22612 and 20930-20938)

(22730 has been deleted. To report, see 22585, 22614)

(22735 has been deleted. To report, see 22585, 22614)

Spine Deformity (eg, Scoliosis, Kyphosis)

To report instrumentation procedures, see codes 22840-22855. (Report in addition to code(s) for the definitive procedure(s) without modifier '-51'.) ▶Do not append modifier '-62' to spinal instrumentation codes 22840-22855.◀

To report bone graft procedures, see codes 20930-20938. (Report in addition to code(s) for the definitive procedure(s) without modifier '-51'.) ▶Do not append modifier '-62' to bone graft codes 20900-20938.◀

A vertebral segment describes the basic constituent part into which the spine may be divided. It represents a single complete vertebral bone with its associated articular processes and laminae.

▶For the following codes, when two surgeons work together as primary surgeons performing distinct part(s) of an arthrodesis for spinal deformity, each surgeon should report his/her distinct operative work by appending the modifier '-62' to the procedure code. In this situation, the modifier '-62' may be appended to the procedure code(s) 22800-22819 as long as both surgeons continue to work together as primary surgeons.◀

22800 Arthrodesis, posterior, for spinal deformity, with or without cast; up to 6 vertebral segments

(22801 has been deleted. To report, use 22800)

22802 7 to 12 vertebral segments
> *CPT Assistant* Mar 96:10

(22803 has been deleted. To report, use 22802)

22804 13 or more vertebral segments

22808 Arthrodesis, anterior, for spinal deformity, with or without cast; 2 to 3 vertebral segments

22810 4 to 7 vertebral segments
> *CPT Assistant* Mar 96:10; Sep 97:8

22812 8 or more vertebral segments

22818 Kyphectomy, circumferential exposure of spine and resection of vertebral segment(s) (including body and posterior elements); single or 2 segments
> *CPT Assistant* Nov 97:14

22819 3 or more segments
> *CPT Assistant* Nov 97:14

(To report arthrodesis, see 22800-22804 and add modifier '-51')

Exploration

(22820 has been deleted. To report, see 20930-20938)

22830 Exploration of spinal fusion
> *CPT Assistant* Sep 97:11

Spinal Instrumentation

Segmental instrumentation is defined as fixation at each end of the construct and at least one additional interposed bony attachment.

Non-segmental instrumentation is defined as fixation at each end of the construct and may span several vertebral segments without attachment to the intervening segments.

Insertion of spinal instrumentation is reported separately and in addition to arthrodesis. Instrumentation procedure codes 22840-22848, 22851 are reported in addition to the definitive procedure(s) without modifier '-51'. ▶Do not append modifier '-62' to spinal instrumentation codes 22840-22855.◀

To report bone graft procedures, see codes 20930-20938. (Report in addition to code(s) for definitive procedure(s) without modifier '-51'.) ▶Do not append modifier '-62' to bone graft codes 20900-20938.◀

A vertebral segment describes the basic constituent part into which the spine may be divided. It represents a single complete vertebral bone with its associated articular

processes and laminae. A vertebral interspace is the non-bony compartment between two adjacent vertebral bodies, which contains the intervertebral disk, and includes the nucleus pulposus, annulus fibrosus, and two cartilagenous endplates.

(List codes 22840-22848, 22851 separately, in addition to code for fracture, dislocation, or arthrodesis of the spine, 22325, 22326, 22327, 22548-22812)

⊘ **22840** Posterior non-segmental instrumentation (eg, Harrington rod technique, pedicle fixation across one interspace, atlantoaxial transarticular screw fixation, sublaminar wiring at C1, facet screw fixation)
> *CPT Assistant* Feb 96:6; Jul 96:10; Sep 97:8; Nov 99:12; *CPT Changes* 2000

Non-Segmental Spinal Instrumentation
22840

Fixation at each end of the construct.

⊘ **22841** Internal spinal fixation by wiring of spinous processes
> *CPT Assistant* Feb 96:6; Sep 97:8

⊘ **22842** Posterior segmental instrumentation (eg, pedicle fixation, dual rods with multiple hooks and sublaminar wires); 3 to 6 vertebral segments
> *CPT Assistant* Feb 96:6; Mar 96:7; Sep 97:8

⊘ **22843** 7 to 12 vertebral segments
> *CPT Assistant* Feb 96:6; Sep 97:8

⊘ **22844**   13 or more vertebral segments

➔ *CPT Assistant* Feb 96:6; Sep 97:8

Segmental Spinal Instrumentation
22842-22844

Fixation at each end of the construct and at least one additional interposed bony attachment.

⊘ **22845**   Anterior instrumentation; 2 to 3 vertebral segments

➔ *CPT Assistant* Feb 96:6; Mar 96:10; Jul 96:7, 10; Sep 97:8

⊘ **22846**   4 to 7 vertebral segments

➔ *CPT Assistant* Feb 96:6; Sep 97:8

⊘ **22847**   8 or more vertebral segments

➔ *CPT Assistant* Feb 96:6; Sep 97:8

⊘ **22848**   Pelvic fixation (attachment of caudal end of instrumentation to pelvic bony structures) other than sacrum

➔ *CPT Assistant* Feb 96:6; Sep 97:8

22849   Reinsertion of spinal fixation device

➔ *CPT Assistant* Feb 96:6; Sep 97:8

22850   Removal of posterior nonsegmental instrumentation (eg, Harrington rod)

➔ *CPT Assistant* Feb 96:6; Sep 97:8

⊘ **22851**   Application of intervertebral biomechanical device(s) (eg, synthetic cage(s), threaded bone dowel(s), methylmethacrylate) to vertebral defect or interspace

➔ *CPT Assistant* Feb 96:6; Sep 97:8; Nov 99:12; Dec 99:2; May 00:11; *CPT Changes* 2000

Spinal Prosthetic Devices
22851

Application of prosthetic device.

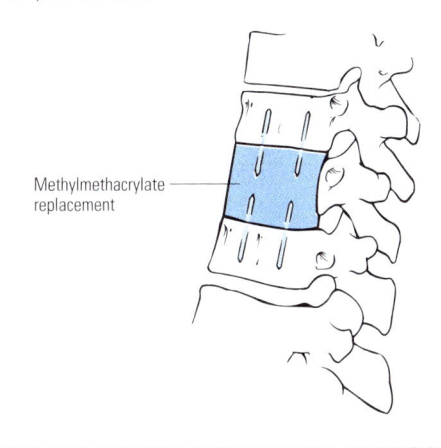

22852   Removal of posterior segmental instrumentation

➔ *CPT Assistant* Feb 96:6; Sep 97:8

22855   Removal of anterior instrumentation

➔ *CPT Assistant* Feb 96:6; Sep 97:8

Other Procedures

22899   Unlisted procedure, spine

➔ *CPT Assistant* May 00:11; Sep 00:10

Abdomen

Excision

22900   Excision, abdominal wall tumor, subfascial (eg, desmoid)

(22910 has been deleted. To report, use 22999)

Other Procedures

22999   Unlisted procedure, abdomen, musculoskeletal system

Shoulder

Clavicle, scapula, humerus head and neck, sterno-clavicular joint, acromioclavicular joint and shoulder joint.

Incision

▲ **23000**   Removal of subdeltoid calcareous deposits, open

➔ *CPT Changes* 2002

23020   Capsular contracture release (eg, Sever type procedure)

(For incision and drainage procedures, superficial, see 10040-10160)

23030 Incision and drainage, shoulder area; deep abscess or hematoma

23031   infected bursa

23035 Incision, bone cortex (eg, osteomyelitis or bone abscess), shoulder area

(23036 has been deleted)

23040 Arthrotomy, glenohumeral joint, including exploration, drainage, or removal of foreign body
> *CPT Assistant* Nov 98:8

(23042 has been deleted)

23044 Arthrotomy, acromioclavicular, sternoclavicular joint, including exploration, drainage, or removal of foreign body
> *CPT Assistant* Nov 98:8

Excision

23065 Biopsy, soft tissue of shoulder area; superficial

23066   deep

(For needle biopsy of soft tissue, use 20206)

23075 Excision, soft tissue tumor, shoulder area; subcutaneous
> *CPT Assistant* Summer 92:22; Nov 98:8

23076   deep, subfascial, or intramuscular
> *CPT Assistant* Summer 92:22

23077 Radical resection of tumor (eg, malignant neoplasm), soft tissue of shoulder area

23100 Arthrotomy, glenohumeral joint, including biopsy
> *CPT Assistant* Nov 98:8

23101 Arthrotomy, acromioclavicular joint or sternoclavicular joint, including biopsy and/or excision of torn cartilage
> *CPT Assistant* Nov 98:8

23105 Arthrotomy; glenohumeral joint, with synovectomy, with or without biopsy
> *CPT Assistant* Nov 98:8

23106   sternoclavicular joint, with synovectomy, with or without biopsy

23107 Arthrotomy, glenohumeral joint, with joint exploration, with or without removal of loose or foreign body

(23110 has been deleted. To report, use 23929)

23120 Claviculectomy; partial
> ▶(For arthroscopic procedure, use 29824)◀

23125   total

23130 Acromioplasty or acromionectomy, partial, with or without coracoacromial ligament release

23140 Excision or curettage of bone cyst or benign tumor of clavicle or scapula;

23145   with autograft (includes obtaining graft;

23146   with allograft

23150 Excision or curettage of bone cyst or benign tumor of proximal humerus;

23155   with autograft (includes obtaining graft)

23156   with allograft

23170 Sequestrectomy (eg, for osteomyelitis or bone abscess), clavicle

(23171 has been deleted)

23172 Sequestrectomy (eg, for osteomyelitis or bone abscess), scapula

(23173 has been deleted)

23174 Sequestrectomy (eg, for osteomyelitis or bone abscess), humeral head to surgical neck

(23175 has been deleted)

23180 Partial excision (craterization, saucerization, or diaphysectomy) bone (eg, osteomyelitis), clavicle
> *CPT Assistant* Nov 98:9

(23181 has been deleted)

23182 Partial excision (craterization, saucerization, or diaphysectomy) bone (eg, osteomyelitis), scapula
> *CPT Assistant* Nov 98:9

(23183 has been deleted)

23184 Partial excision (craterization, saucerization, or diaphysectomy) bone (eg, osteomyelitis), proximal humerus
> *CPT Assistant* Nov 98:9

(23185 has been deleted)

23190 Ostectomy of scapula, partial (eg, superior medial angle)

23195 Resection, humeral head

(For replacement with implant, use 23470)

23200 Radical resection for tumor; clavicle

23210   scapula

23220 Radical resection of bone tumor, proximal humerus;
> *CPT Assistant* Nov 98:8

23221   with autograft (includes obtaining graft)

23222   with prosthetic replacement

Introduction or Removal

(For arthrocentesis or needling of bursa, use 20610)

(For K-wire or pin insertion or removal, see 20650, 20670, 20680)

23330 Removal of foreign body, shoulder; subcutaneous
> *CPT Assistant* Aug 99:3

23331   deep (eg, Neer hemiarthroplasty removal)
> *CPT Assistant* Aug 99:3

23332   complicated (eg, total shoulder)
> *CPT Assistant* Jun 96:10; Nov 98:8; Aug 99:3

▲ **23350**   Injection procedure for shoulder arthrography or enhanced CT/MRI shoulder arthrography

→ *CPT Changes* 2002

(For radiological supervision and interpretation for arthrography, use 73040)

►(For radiographic arthrography, radiological supervision and interpretation, use 73040. Fluoroscopy (76003) is inclusive of radiographic arthrography)◄

►(When fluoroscopic guided injection is performed for enhanced CT arthrography, use codes 23350, 76003, and 73201 or 73202)◄

►(When fluoroscopic guided injection is performed for enhanced MR arthrography, use codes 23350, 76003, and 73222 or 73223)◄

►(For enhanced CT or enhanced MRI arthrography, use 76003 and either 73201, 73202, 73222 or 73223)◄

(23355-23358 have been deleted. To report, see ►29805◄-29826)

Repair, Revision, and/or Reconstruction

23395   Muscle transfer, any type, shoulder or upper arm; single

23397   multiple

23400   Scapulopexy (eg, Sprengels deformity or for paralysis)

23405   Tenotomy, shoulder area; single tendon

→ *CPT Assistant* Nov 98:8

23406   multiple tendons through same incision

→ *CPT Assistant* Nov 98:8

23410   Repair of ruptured musculotendinous cuff (eg, rotator cuff); acute

23412   chronic

23415   Coracoacromial ligament release, with or without acromioplasty

►(For arthroscopic procedure, use 29826)◄

23420   Reconstruction of complete shoulder (rotator) cuff avulsion, chronic (includes acromioplasty)

23430   Tenodesis of long tendon of biceps

23440   Resection or transplantation of long tendon of biceps

23450   Capsulorrhaphy, anterior; Putti-Platt procedure or Magnuson type operation

►(To report arthroscopic thermal capsulorrhaphy, use 29999)◄

23455   with labral repair (eg, Bankart procedure)

→ *CPT Assistant* Nov 98:8

►(For arthroscopic procedure, use 29807)◄

23460   Capsulorrhaphy, anterior, any type; with bone block

23462   with coracoid process transfer

►(To report open thermal capsulorrhaphy, use 23929)◄

23465   Capsulorrhaphy, glenohumeral joint, posterior, with or without bone block

→ *CPT Assistant* Nov 98:8

(For sternoclavicular and acromioclavicular reconstruction, see 23530, 23550)

23466   Capsulorrhaphy, glenohumeral joint, any type multi-directional instability

→ *CPT Assistant* Nov 98:8

23470   Arthroplasty, glenohumeral joint; hemiarthroplasty

→ *CPT Assistant* Nov 98:8

23472   total shoulder (glenoid and proximal humeral replacement (eg, total shoulder))

→ *CPT Assistant* Jun 96:10; Nov 98:8

(For removal of total shoulder implants, see 23331, 23332)

(For osteotomy, proximal humerus, use 24400)

23480   Osteotomy, clavicle, with or without internal fixation;

23485   with bone graft for nonunion or malunion (includes obtaining graft and/or necessary fixation)

23490   Prophylactic treatment (nailing, pinning, plating or wiring) with or without methylmethacrylate; clavicle

23491   proximal humerus

→ *CPT Assistant* Nov 98:8

Fracture and/or Dislocation

23500   Closed treatment of clavicular fracture; without manipulation

23505   with manipulation

(23510 has been deleted. To report, see 23500, 23505, 23515)

23515   Open treatment of clavicular fracture, with or without internal or external fixation

23520   Closed treatment of sternoclavicular dislocation; without manipulation

23525   with manipulation

23530   Open treatment of sternoclavicular dislocation, acute or chronic;

23532   with fascial graft (includes obtaining graft)

23540   Closed treatment of acromioclavicular dislocation; without manipulation

23545   with manipulation

23550   Open treatment of acromioclavicular dislocation, acute or chronic;

23552   with fascial graft (includes obtaining graft)

23570 Closed treatment of scapular fracture; without manipulation

23575 with manipulation, with or without skeletal traction (with or without shoulder joint involvement)

(23580 has been deleted. To report, see 23570, 23575, 23585)

23585 Open treatment of scapular fracture (body, glenoid or acromion) with or without internal fixation

23600 Closed treatment of proximal humeral (surgical or anatomical neck) fracture; without manipulation

23605 with manipulation, with or without skeletal traction

(23610 has been deleted. To report, see 23600, 23605, 23615)

23615 Open treatment of proximal humeral (surgical or anatomical neck) fracture, with or without internal or external fixation, with or without repair of tuberosity(s);

23616 with proximal humeral prosthetic replacement

23620 Closed treatment of greater humeral tuberosity fracture; without manipulation
> *CPT Assistant* Nov 98:8

23625 with manipulation

23630 Open treatment of greater humeral tuberosity fracture, with or without internal or external fixation
> *CPT Assistant* Nov 98:8

23650 Closed treatment of shoulder dislocation, with manipulation; without anesthesia

23655 requiring anesthesia

(23658 has been deleted. To report, see 23650, 23655, 23660, 23665, 23670)

23660 Open treatment of acute shoulder dislocation
> *CPT Assistant* Feb 96:5

(Repairs for recurrent dislocations, see 23450-23466)

23665 Closed treatment of shoulder dislocation, with fracture of greater humeral tuberosity, with manipulation
> *CPT Assistant* Nov 98:8

23670 Open treatment of shoulder dislocation, with fracture of greater humeral tuberosity, with or without internal or external fixation
> *CPT Assistant* Nov 98:8

23675 Closed treatment of shoulder dislocation, with surgical or anatomical neck fracture, with manipulation

23680 Open treatment of shoulder dislocation, with surgical or anatomical neck fracture, with or without internal or external fixation

Manipulation

23700✳ Manipulation under anesthesia, shoulder joint, including application of fixation apparatus (dislocation excluded)
> *CPT Assistant* Jan 99:1

Arthrodesis

23800 Arthrodesis, glenohumeral joint;
> *CPT Assistant* Nov 98:8

23802 with autogenous graft (includes obtaining graft)

Amputation

23900 Interthoracoscapular amputation (forequarter)

23920 Disarticulation of shoulder;

23921 secondary closure or scar revision

Other Procedures

23929 Unlisted procedure, shoulder

Humerus (Upper Arm) and Elbow

Elbow area includes head and neck of radius and olecranon process.

Incision

(For incision and drainage procedures, superficial, see 10040-10160)

23930 Incision and drainage, upper arm or elbow area; deep abscess or hematoma

23931 bursa
> *CPT Assistant* Nov 98:8

23935 Incision, deep, with opening of bone cortex (eg, for osteomyelitis or bone abscess), humerus or elbow

(23936 has been deleted)

24000 Arthrotomy, elbow, including exploration, drainage, or removal of foreign body
> *CPT Assistant* Nov 98:8-9

(24001 has been deleted)

24006 Arthrotomy of the elbow, with capsular excision for capsular release (separate procedure)

Excision

24065 Biopsy, soft tissue of upper arm or elbow area; superficial

24066 deep (subfascial or intramuscular)

(For needle biopsy of soft tissue, use 20206)

⊘ = Modifier '-51' Exempt   ▶ ◀ = New or Revised Text   ✚ = Add-on Code   CPT 2002

▲ **24075**   Excision, tumor, soft tissue of upper arm or elbow area; subcutaneous
➔ *CPT Changes* 2002

24076   deep (subfascial or intramuscular)

24077   Radical resection of tumor (eg, malignant neoplasm), soft tissue of upper arm or elbow area

24100   Arthrotomy, elbow; with synovial biopsy only

24101   with joint exploration, with or without biopsy, with or without removal of loose or foreign body

24102   with synovectomy

24105   Excision, olecranon bursa

24110   Excision or curettage of bone cyst or benign tumor, humerus;

24115   with autograft (includes obtaining graft)

24116   with allograft

24120   Excision or curettage of bone cyst or benign tumor of head or neck of radius or olecranon process;

24125   with autograft (includes obtaining graft)

24126   with allograft

24130   Excision, radial head

(For replacement with implant, use 24366)

24134   Sequestrectomy (eg, for osteomyelitis or bone abscess), shaft or distal humerus

(24135 has been deleted)

24136   Sequestrectomy (eg, for osteomyelitis or bone abscess), radial head or neck

(24137 has been deleted)

24138   Sequestrectomy (eg, for osteomyelitis or bone abscess), olecranon process

(24139 has been deleted)

24140   Partial excision (craterization, saucerization, or diaphysectomy) bone (eg, osteomyelitis), humerus
➔ *CPT Assistant* Nov 98:9

(24144 has been deleted)

24145   Partial excision (craterization, saucerization, or diaphysectomy) bone (eg, osteomyelitis), radial head or neck
➔ *CPT Assistant* Nov 98:9

(24146 has been deleted)

24147   Partial excision (craterization, saucerization, or diaphysectomy) bone (eg, osteomyelitis), olecranon process
➔ *CPT Assistant* Nov 98:9

(24148 has been deleted)

24149   Radical resection of capsule, soft tissue, and heterotopic bone, elbow, with contracture release (separate procedure)

(For capsular and soft tissue release only, use 24006)

24150   Radical resection for tumor, shaft or distal humerus;

24151   with autograft (includes obtaining graft)

24152   Radical resection for tumor, radial head or neck;

24153   with autograft (includes obtaining graft)

24155   Resection of elbow joint (arthrectomy)

Introduction or Removal

(For K-wire or pin insertion or removal, see 20650, 20670, 20680)

(For arthrocentesis or needling of bursa or joint, use 20605)

24160   Implant removal; elbow joint

24164   radial head

24200   Removal of foreign body, upper arm or elbow area; subcutaneous

24201   deep (subfascial or intramuscular)
➔ *CPT Assistant* Nov 98:8

24220   Injection procedure for elbow arthrography

(For radiological supervision and interpretation, use 73085. ▶Do not report 76003 in addition to 73085)◀

(For injection of tennis elbow, use 20550)

Repair, Revision, and/or Reconstruction

● **24300**   Manipulation, elbow, under anesthesia
➔ *CPT Changes* 2002

▶(For application of external fixation, see 20690 or 20692)◀

24301   Muscle or tendon transfer, any type, upper arm or elbow, single (excluding 24320-24331)

24305   Tendon lengthening, upper arm or elbow, each tendon
➔ *CPT Assistant* Nov 98:8

24310   Tenotomy, open, elbow to shoulder, each tendon
➔ *CPT Assistant* Nov 98:8

24320   Tenoplasty, with muscle transfer, with or without free graft, elbow to shoulder, single (Seddon-Brookes type procedure)

24330   Flexor-plasty, elbow (eg, Steindler type advancement);

24331   with extensor advancement

● **24332**   Tenolysis, triceps
➔ *CPT Changes* 2002

24340   Tenodesis of biceps tendon at elbow (separate procedure)

24341   Repair, tendon or muscle, upper arm or elbow, each tendon or muscle, primary or secondary (excludes rotator cuff)

24342   Reinsertion of ruptured biceps or triceps tendon, distal, with or without tendon graft

● **24343**   Repair lateral collateral ligament, elbow, with local tissue
> *CPT Changes* 2002

● **24344**   Reconstruction lateral collateral ligament, elbow, with tendon graft (includes harvesting of graft)
> *CPT Changes* 2002

● **24345**   Repair medial collateral ligament, elbow, with local tissue
> *CPT Changes* 2002

● **24346**   Reconstruction medial collateral ligament, elbow, with tendon graft (includes harvesting of graft)
> *CPT Changes* 2002

24350   Fasciotomy, lateral or medial (eg, tennis elbow or epicondylitis);

24351   with extensor origin detachment

24352   with annular ligament resection

24354   with stripping

24356   with partial ostectomy

24360   Arthroplasty, elbow; with membrane (eg, fascial)
> *CPT Assistant* Nov 98:8

24361   with distal humeral prosthetic replacement

24362   with implant and fascia lata ligament reconstruction

24363   with distal humerus and proximal ulnar prosthetic replacement (eg, total elbow)

24365   Arthroplasty, radial head;

24366   with implant

24400   Osteotomy, humerus, with or without internal fixation

24410   Multiple osteotomies with realignment on intramedullary rod, humeral shaft (Sofield type procedure)

24420   Osteoplasty, humerus (eg, shortening or lengthening) (excluding 64876)

24430   Repair of nonunion or malunion, humerus; without graft (eg, compression technique)

24435   with iliac or other autograft (includes obtaining graft)

(For proximal radius and/or ulna, see 25400-25420)

24470   Hemiepiphyseal arrest (eg, cubitus varus or valgus, distal humerus)

24495   Decompression fasciotomy, forearm, with brachial artery exploration

24498   Prophylactic treatment (nailing, pinning, plating or wiring), with or without methylmethacrylate, humeral shaft
> *CPT Assistant* Nov 98:8

Fracture and/or Dislocation

24500   Closed treatment of humeral shaft fracture; without manipulation

24505   with manipulation, with or without skeletal traction

(24506 has been deleted. To report, use 24516)

(24510 has been deleted. To report, see 24500, 24505, 24515, 24516)

24515   Open treatment of humeral shaft fracture with plate/screws, with or without cerclage

24516   Open treatment of humeral shaft fracture, with insertion of intramedullary implant, with or without cerclage and/or locking screws
> *CPT Assistant* Feb 96:4

24530   Closed treatment of supracondylar or transcondylar humeral fracture, with or without intercondylar extension; without manipulation

(24531 has been deleted. To report, use 24535)

24535   with manipulation, with or without skin or skeletal traction

(24536 has been deleted. To report, use 24535)

24538   Percutaneous skeletal fixation of supracondylar or transcondylar humeral fracture, with or without intercondylar extension
> *CPT Assistant* Winter 92:10

(24540 and 24542 have been deleted. To report, see 24530, 24535, 24538, 24545, 24546)

24545   Open treatment of humeral supracondylar or transcondylar fracture, with or without internal or external fixation; without intercondylar extension

24546   with intercondylar extension

24560   Closed treatment of humeral epicondylar fracture, medial or lateral; without manipulation

24565   with manipulation

24566   Percutaneous skeletal fixation of humeral epicondylar fracture, medial or lateral, with manipulation

(24570 has been deleted. To report, see 24560, 24565, 24575)

24575   Open treatment of humeral epicondylar fracture, medial or lateral, with or without internal or external fixation

24576   Closed treatment of humeral condylar fracture, medial or lateral; without manipulation

24577   with manipulation

(24578 has been deleted. To report, see 24576, 24577, 24579)

⊘ =Modifier '-51' Exempt   ▶ ◀ =New or Revised Text   ✛ =Add-on Code   CPT 2002

24579 Open treatment of humeral condylar fracture, medial or lateral, with or without internal or external fixation

(24580 has been deleted. To report, see 24530, 24560, 24576, 24650, 24670)

(24581 has been deleted. To report, see 24535, 24565, 24577, 24675)

24582 Percutaneous skeletal fixation of humeral condylar fracture, medial or lateral, with manipulation

(24583 has been deleted. To report, see 24535, 24538, 24545, 24560, 24565, 24577)

(24585 has been deleted. To report, see 24538, 24545, 24575, 24579, 24665, 24666, 24685)

24586 Open treatment of periarticular fracture and/or dislocation of the elbow (fracture distal humerus and proximal ulna and/ or proximal radius);

24587 with implant arthroplasty

(See also 24361)

(24588 has been deleted. To report, see 24586, 24587)

24600 Treatment of closed elbow dislocation; without anesthesia

24605 requiring anesthesia

(24610 has been deleted. To report, see 24586, 24600, 24605, 24615)

24615 Open treatment of acute or chronic elbow dislocation

24620 Closed treatment of Monteggia type of fracture dislocation at elbow (fracture proximal end of ulna with dislocation of radial head), with manipulation

(24625 has been deleted. To report, see 24620, 24635)

24635 Open treatment of Monteggia type of fracture dislocation at elbow (fracture proximal end of ulna with dislocation of radial head), with or without internal or external fixation

24640* Closed treatment of radial head subluxation in child, nursemaid elbow, with manipulation

24650 Closed treatment of radial head or neck fracture; without manipulation

24655 with manipulation

(24660 has been deleted. To report, see 24650, 24655, 24665, 24666)

24665 Open treatment of radial head or neck fracture, with or without internal fixation or radial head excision;

24666 with radial head prosthetic replacement

24670 Closed treatment of ulnar fracture, proximal end (olecranon process); without manipulation

24675 with manipulation

(24680 has been deleted. To report, see 24670, 24675, 24685)

24685 Open treatment of ulnar fracture proximal end (olecranon process), with or without internal or external fixation

(24700 has been deleted. To report, use 24999)

Arthrodesis

24800 Arthrodesis, elbow joint; local

24802 with autogenous graft (includes obtaining graft)

Amputation

24900 Amputation, arm through humerus; with primary closure

24920 open, circular (guillotine)

24925 secondary closure or scar revision

24930 re-amputation

24931 with implant

24935 Stump elongation, upper extremity

24940 Cineplasty, upper extremity, complete procedure

Other Procedures

24999 Unlisted procedure, humerus or elbow

Forearm and Wrist

Radius, ulna, carpal bones and joints.

Incision

25000 Incision, extensor tendon sheath, wrist (eg, deQuervains disease)

➲ *CPT Assistant* Nov 98:8

(For decompression median nerve or for carpal tunnel syndrome, use 64721)

(25005 has been deleted. To report, use 25000)

● **25001** Incision, flexor tendon sheath, wrist (eg, flexor carpi radialis)

➲ *CPT Changes* 2002

▲ **25020** Decompression fasciotomy, forearm and/or wrist, flexor OR extensor compartment; without debridement of nonviable muscle and/or nerve

➲ *CPT Changes* 2002

25023 with debridement of nonviable muscle and/or nerve

(For decompression fasciotomy with brachial artery exploration, use 24495)

(For incision and drainage procedures, superficial, see 10040-10160)

(For debridement, see also 11000-11044)

● **25024** Decompression fasciotomy, forearm and/or wrist, flexor AND extensor compartment; without debridement of nonviable muscle and/or nerve
→ *CPT Changes* 2002

● **25025** with debridement of nonviable muscle and/or nerve
→ *CPT Changes* 2002

25028 Incision and drainage, forearm and/or wrist; deep abscess or hematoma

25031 bursa
→ *CPT Assistant* Nov 98:9

25035 Incision, deep, bone cortex, forearm and/or wrist (eg, osteomyelitis or bone abscess)

(25036 has been deleted)

25040 Arthrotomy, radiocarpal or midcarpal joint, with exploration, drainage, or removal of foreign body

(25041 has been deleted)

Excision

25065 Biopsy, soft tissue of forearm and/or wrist; superficial

25066 deep (subfascial or intramuscular)
→ *CPT Assistant* Nov 98:8

(For needle biopsy of soft tissue, use 20206)

▲ **25075** Excision, tumor, soft tissue of forearm and/or wrist area; subcutaneous
→ *CPT Changes* 2002

25076 deep (subfascial or intramuscular)

25077 Radical resection of tumor (eg, malignant neoplasm), soft tissue of forearm and/or wrist area

25085 Capsulotomy, wrist (eg, contracture)

25100 Arthrotomy, wrist joint; with biopsy

25101 with joint exploration, with or without biopsy, with or without removal of loose or foreign body

25105 with synovectomy

25107 Arthrotomy, distal radioulnar joint including repair of triangular cartilage, complex

25110 Excision, lesion of tendon sheath, forearm and/or wrist

25111 Excision of ganglion, wrist (dorsal or volar); primary

25112 recurrent

(For hand or finger, use 26160)

25115 Radical excision of bursa, synovia of wrist, or forearm tendon sheaths (eg, tenosynovitis, fungus, Tbc, or other granulomas, rheumatoid arthritis); flexors

25116 extensors, with or without transposition of dorsal retinaculum

(For finger synovectomies, use 26145)

25118 Synovectomy, extensor tendon sheath, wrist, single compartment;

25119 with resection of distal ulna

25120 Excision or curettage of bone cyst or benign tumor of radius or ulna (excluding head or neck of radius and olecranon process);

(For head or neck of radius or olecranon process, see 24120-24126)

25125 with autograft (includes obtaining graft)

25126 with allograft

25130 Excision or curettage of bone cyst or benign tumor of carpal bones;

25135 with autograft (includes obtaining graft)

25136 with allograft

25145 Sequestrectomy (eg, for osteomyelitis or bone abscess), forearm and/or wrist

(25146 has been deleted)

25150 Partial excision (craterization, saucerization, or diaphysectomy) of bone (eg, for osteomyelitis); ulna

25151 radius

(25153 has been deleted)

(For head or neck of radius or olecranon process, see 24145, 24147)

25170 Radical resection for tumor, radius or ulna

25210 Carpectomy; one bone

(For carpectomy with implant, see 25441-25445)

25215 all bones of proximal row

25230 Radial styloidectomy (separate procedure)

25240 Excision distal ulna partial or complete (eg, Darrach type or matched resection)

(For implant replacement, distal ulna, use 25442)

(For obtaining fascia for interposition, see 20920, 20922)

Introduction or Removal

(For K-wire, pin or rod insertion or removal, see 20650, 20670, 20680)

25246 Injection procedure for wrist arthrography

(For radiological supervision and interpretation, use 73115. ►Do not report 76003 in addition to 73115)◄

(For foreign body removal, superficial use 20520)

25248 Exploration with removal of deep foreign body, forearm or wrist

25250	Removal of wrist prosthesis; (separate procedure)
25251	complicated, including total wrist
● 25259	Manipulation, wrist, under anesthesia

➲ *CPT Changes* 2002

▶(For application of external fixation, see 20690 or 20692)◀

Repair, Revision, and/or Reconstruction

25260	Repair, tendon or muscle, flexor, forearm and/or wrist; primary, single, each tendon or muscle
25263	secondary, single, each tendon or muscle
25265	secondary, with free graft (includes obtaining graft), each tendon or muscle
25270	Repair, tendon or muscle, extensor, forearm and/or wrist; primary, single, each tendon or muscle
25272	secondary, single, each tendon or muscle
▲ 25274	secondary, with free graft (includes obtaining graft), each tendon or muscle

➲ *CPT Changes* 2002

● 25275	Repair, tendon sheath, extensor, forearm and/or wrist, with free graft (includes obtaining graft) (eg, for extensor carpi ulnaris subluxation)

➲ *CPT Changes* 2002

25280	Lengthening or shortening of flexor or extensor tendon, forearm and/or wrist, single, each tendon
25290	Tenotomy, open, flexor or extensor tendon, forearm and/or wrist, single, each tendon
25295	Tenolysis, flexor or extensor tendon, forearm and/or wrist, single, each tendon

➲ *CPT Assistant* Apr 97:11; Aug 98:10

25300	Tenodesis at wrist; flexors of fingers
25301	extensors of fingers
25310	Tendon transplantation or transfer, flexor or extensor, forearm and/or wrist, single; each tendon
25312	with tendon graft(s) (includes obtaining graft), each tendon
25315	Flexor origin slide (eg, for cerebral palsy, Volkmann contracture), forearm and/or wrist;
25316	with tendon(s) transfer

(25317, 25318 have been deleted. To report, see 25315, 25316)

25320	Capsulorrhaphy or reconstruction, wrist, any method (eg, capsulodesis, ligament repair, tendon transfer or graft) (includes synovectomy, capsulotomy and open reduction) for carpal instability

(25330, 25331 have been deleted. To report, see 25332 and 25441-25446)

25332	Arthroplasty, wrist, with or without interposition, with or without external or internal fixation

(For obtaining fascia for interposition, see 20920, 20922)

(For prosthetic replacement arthroplasty, see 25441-25446)

25335	Centralization of wrist on ulna (eg, radial club hand)
25337	Reconstruction for stabilization of unstable distal ulna or distal radioulnar joint, secondary by soft tissue stabilization (eg, tendon transfer, tendon graft or weave, or tenodesis) with or without open reduction of distal radioulnar joint

(For harvesting of fascia lata graft, see 20920, 20922)

25350	Osteotomy, radius; distal third
25355	middle or proximal third
25360	Osteotomy; ulna
25365	radius AND ulna
25370	Multiple osteotomies, with realignment on intramedullary rod (Sofield type procedure); radius OR ulna
25375	radius AND ulna
25390	Osteoplasty, radius OR ulna; shortening
25391	lengthening with autograft
25392	Osteoplasty, radius AND ulna; shortening (excluding 64876)
25393	lengthening with autograft
● 25394	Osteoplasty, carpal bone, shortening

➲ *CPT Changes* 2002

25400	Repair of nonunion or malunion, radius OR ulna; without graft (eg, compression technique)
▲ 25405	with autograft (includes obtaining graft)

➲ *CPT Changes* 2002

25415	Repair of nonunion or malunion, radius AND ulna; without graft (eg, compression technique)
▲ 25420	with autograft (includes obtaining graft)

➲ *CPT Changes* 2002

25425	Repair of defect with autograft; radius OR ulna
25426	radius AND ulna
● 25430	Insertion of vascular pedicle into carpal bone (eg, Harii procedure)

➲ *CPT Changes* 2002

● 25431	Repair of nonunion of carpal bone (excluding carpal scaphoid (navicular)) (includes obtaining graft and necessary fixation), each bone

➲ *CPT Changes* 2002

▲25440 Repair of nonunion, scaphoid carpal (navicular) bone, with or without radial styloidectomy (includes obtaining graft and necessary fixation)
➜ *CPT Changes* 2002

25441 Arthroplasty with prosthetic replacement; distal radius

25442 distal ulna

▲25443 scaphoid carpal (navicular)
➜ *CPT Changes* 2002

25444 lunate

25445 trapezium

25446 distal radius and partial or entire carpus (total wrist)

25447 Arthroplasty, interposition, intercarpal or carpometacarpal joints
➜ *CPT Assistant* Nov 98:8

(For wrist arthroplasty, use 25332)

25449 Revision of arthroplasty, including removal of implant, wrist joint

25450 Epiphyseal arrest by epiphysiodesis or stapling; distal radius OR ulna

25455 distal radius AND ulna

25490 Prophylactic treatment (nailing, pinning, plating or wiring) with or without methylmethacrylate; radius

25491 ulna

25492 radius AND ulna

Fracture and/or Dislocation

25500 Closed treatment of radial shaft fracture; without manipulation

25505 with manipulation

(25510 has been deleted. To report, see 25500, 25505, 25515)

25515 Open treatment of radial shaft fracture, with or without internal or external fixation

▲25520 Closed treatment of radial shaft fracture and closed treatment of dislocation of distal radioulnar joint (Galeazzi fracture/dislocation)
➜ *CPT Changes* 2002

25525 Open treatment of radial shaft fracture, with internal and/ or external fixation and closed treatment of dislocation of distal radioulnar joint (Galeazzi fracture/dislocation), with or without percutaneous skeletal fixation

▲25526 Open treatment of radial shaft fracture, with internal and/or external fixation and open treatment, with or without internal or external fixation of distal radioulnar joint (Galeazzi fracture/dislocation), includes repair of triangular fibrocartilage complex
➜ *CPT Changes* 2002

25530 Closed treatment of ulnar shaft fracture; without manipulation

25535 with manipulation

(25540 has been deleted. To report, see 25530, 25535, 25545)

25545 Open treatment of ulnar shaft fracture, with or without internal or external fixation
➜ *CPT Assistant* Fall 93:23; Oct 99:4

25560 Closed treatment of radial and ulnar shaft fractures; without manipulation

25565 with manipulation

(25570 has been deleted. To report, see 25560, 25565, 25574, 25575)

25574 Open treatment of radial AND ulnar shaft fractures, with internal or external fixation; of radius OR ulna
➜ *CPT Assistant* Fall 93:23; Oct 99:4

25575 of radius AND ulna

25600 Closed treatment of distal radial fracture (eg, Colles or Smith type) or epiphyseal separation, with or without fracture of ulnar styloid; without manipulation

25605 with manipulation

(25610 has been deleted. To report, use 25605)

25611 Percutaneous skeletal fixation of distal radial fracture (eg, Colles or Smith type) or epiphyseal separation, with or without fracture of ulnar styloid, requiring manipulation, with or without external fixation
➜ *CPT Assistant* Fall 93:23; Oct 99:4

(25615 has been deleted. To report, see 25600, 25605, 25611, 25620)

25620 Open treatment of distal radial fracture (eg, Colles or Smith type) or epiphyseal separation, with or without fracture of ulnar styloid, with or without internal or external fixation

25622 Closed treatment of carpal scaphoid (navicular) fracture; without manipulation

25624 with manipulation

(25626 has been deleted. To report, see 25622, 25624, 25628)

25628 Open treatment of carpal scaphoid (navicular) fracture, with or without internal or external fixation

25630 Closed treatment of carpal bone fracture (excluding carpal scaphoid (navicular)); without manipulation, each bone

25635 with manipulation, each bone

(25640 has been deleted. To report, see 25630, 25635, 25645)

▲25645 Open treatment of carpal bone fracture (other than carpal scaphoid (navicular)), each bone
➜ *CPT Changes* 2002

25650	Closed treatment of ulnar styloid fracture
● **25651**	Percutaneous skeletal fixation of ulnar styloid fracture
	➔ *CPT Changes* 2002
● **25652**	Open treatment of ulnar styloid fracture
	➔ *CPT Changes* 2002
25660	Closed treatment of radiocarpal or intercarpal dislocation, one or more bones, with manipulation
	(25665 has been deleted. To report, see 25650, 25660, 25670)
25670	Open treatment of radiocarpal or intercarpal dislocation, one or more bones
● **25671**	Percutaneous skeletal fixation of distal radioulnar dislocation
	➔ *CPT Changes* 2002
25675	Closed treatment of distal radioulnar dislocation with manipulation
25676	Open treatment of distal radioulnar dislocation, acute or chronic
25680	Closed treatment of trans-scaphoperilunar type of fracture dislocation, with manipulation
25685	Open treatment of trans-scaphoperilunar type of fracture dislocation
25690	Closed treatment of lunate dislocation, with manipulation
25695	Open treatment of lunate dislocation
	(25700 has been deleted. To report, use 25999)

Arthrodesis

25800	Arthrodesis, wrist; complete, without bone graft (includes radiocarpal and/or intercarpal and/or carpometacarpal joints)
	➔ *CPT Assistant* Nov 98:8
25805	with sliding graft
25810	with iliac or other autograft (includes obtaining graft)
	(25815 has been deleted. To report, see 25820, 25825)
25820	Arthrodesis, wrist; limited, without bone graft (eg, intercarpal or radiocarpal)
	➔ *CPT Assistant* Nov 98:8
25825	with autograft (includes obtaining graft)
25830	Arthrodesis, distal radioulnar joint with segmental resection of ulna, with or without bone graft (eg, Sauve-Kapandji procedure)
	➔ *CPT Assistant* Nov 98:8

Amputation

25900	Amputation, forearm, through radius and ulna;
25905	open, circular (guillotine)
25907	secondary closure or scar revision
25909	re-amputation
25915	Krukenberg procedure
25920	Disarticulation through wrist;
25922	secondary closure or scar revision
25924	re-amputation
25927	Transmetacarpal amputation;
25929	secondary closure or scar revision
25931	re-amputation

Other Procedures

25999	Unlisted procedure, forearm or wrist

Hand and Fingers

Incision

26010*	Drainage of finger abscess; simple
26011*	complicated (eg, felon)
26020	Drainage of tendon sheath, digit and/or palm, each
26025	Drainage of palmar bursa; single, bursa
	➔ *CPT Assistant* Nov 98:8
26030	multiple bursa
	➔ *CPT Assistant* Nov 98:8
	(26032 has been deleted)
26034	Incision, bone cortex, hand or finger (eg, osteomyelitis or bone abscess)
	➔ *CPT Assistant* Nov 98:8
26035	Decompression fingers and/or hand, injection injury (eg, grease gun)
26037	Decompressive fasciotomy, hand (excludes 26035)
	(For injection injury, use 26035)
26040	Fasciotomy, palmar (eg, Dupuytren's contracture); percutaneous
	➔ *CPT Assistant* Nov 98:8
26045	open, partial
	(For fasciectomy, see 26121-26125)
26055	Tendon sheath incision (eg, for trigger finger)
26060	Tenotomy, percutaneous, single, each digit
26070	Arthrotomy, with exploration, drainage, or removal of loose or foreign body; carpometacarpal joint
	➔ *CPT Assistant* Nov 98:10
26075	metacarpophalangeal joint, each
26080	interphalangeal joint, each

▲ = Revised Code   ● = New Code   ✳ = Service Includes Surgical Procedure Only

Excision

26100 Arthrotomy with biopsy; carpometacarpal joint, each

26105 metacarpophalangeal joint, each

26110 interphalangeal joint, each

▲**26115** Excision, tumor or vascular malformation, soft tissue of hand or finger; subcutaneous
→ *CPT Changes* 2002

▲**26116** deep (subfascial or intramuscular)
→ *CPT Changes* 2002

26117 Radical resection of tumor (eg, malignant neoplasm), soft tissue of hand or finger

(26120 has been deleted. To report, see 26121-26125)

26121 Fasciectomy, palm only, with or without Z-plasty, other local tissue rearrangement, or skin grafting (includes obtaining graft)

(26122 has been deleted. To report, use 26121-26125)

26123 Fasciectomy, partial palmar with release of single digit including proximal interphalangeal joint, with or without Z-plasty, other local tissue rearrangement, or skin grafting (includes obtaining graft);

(26124 has been deleted. To report, use 26121-26125)

+ **26125** each additional digit (List separately in addition to code for primary procedure)

(Use 26125 in conjunction with code 26123)

(26126, 26128 have been deleted. To report, use 26121-26125)

(For fasciotomy, see 26040, 26045)

26130 Synovectomy, carpometacarpal joint

26135 Synovectomy, metacarpophalangeal joint including intrinsic release and extensor hood reconstruction, each digit

26140 Synovectomy, proximal interphalangeal joint, including extensor reconstruction, each interphalangeal joint

26145 Synovectomy, tendon sheath, radical (tenosynovectomy), flexor tendon, palm and/or finger, each tendon
→ *CPT Assistant* Nov 98:8

(For tendon sheath synovectomies at wrist, see 25115, 25116)

▲**26160** Excision of lesion of tendon sheath or joint capsule (eg, cyst, mucous cyst, or ganglion), hand or finger
→ *CPT Changes* 2002

(For wrist ganglion, see 25111, 25112)

(For trigger digit, use 26055)

26170 Excision of tendon, palm, flexor, single (separate procedure), each

26180 Excision of tendon, finger, flexor (separate procedure), each tendon
→ *CPT Assistant* Nov 98:8

26185 Sesamoidectomy, thumb or finger (separate procedure)

26200 Excision or curettage of bone cyst or benign tumor of metacarpal;

26205 with autograft (includes obtaining graft)

(26206 has been deleted. To report, use 26989)

26210 Excision or curettage of bone cyst or benign tumor of proximal, middle, or distal phalanx of finger;

26215 with autograft (includes obtaining graft)

(26216 has been deleted. To report, use 26989)

26230 Partial excision (craterization, saucerization, or diaphysectomy) bone (eg, osteomyelitis); metacarpal

26235 proximal or middle phalanx of finger

26236 distal phalanx of finger

26250 Radical resection, metacarpal (eg, tumor);
→ *CPT Assistant* Nov 98:8

26255 with autograft (includes obtaining graft)

26260 Radical resection, proximal or middle phalanx of finger (eg, tumor);
→ *CPT Assistant* Nov 98:8

26261 with autograft (includes obtaining graft)

26262 Radical resection, distal phalanx of finger (eg, tumor)
→ *CPT Assistant* Nov 98:8

Introduction or Removal

26320 Removal of implant from finger or hand

(For removal of foreign body in hand or finger, see 20520, 20525)

Repair, Revision, and/or Reconstruction

● **26340** Manipulation, finger joint, under anesthesia, each joint
→ *CPT Changes* 2002

▶(For application of external fixation, see 20690 or 20692)◀

▲**26350** Repair or advancement, flexor tendon, not in zone 2 digital flexor tendon sheath (eg, no man's land); primary or secondary without free graft, each tendon
→ *CPT Assistant* Nov 98:8; *CPT Changes* 2002

26352 secondary with free graft (includes obtaining graft), each tendon

▲**26356** Repair or advancement, flexor tendon, in zone 2 digital flexor tendon sheath (eg, no man's land); primary or secondary without free graft, each tendon
→ *CPT Assistant* Nov 98:8; Dec 98:9; *CPT Changes* 2002

26357 secondary, each tendon

26358 secondary with free graft (includes obtaining graft), each tendon

26370   Repair or advancement of profundus tendon, with intact superficialis tendon; primary, each tendon
 ➲ *CPT Assistant* Nov 98:8

26372   secondary with free graft (includes obtaining graft), each tendon
 ➲ *CPT Assistant* Nov 98:8

26373   secondary without free graft, each tendon
 ➲ *CPT Assistant* Nov 98:8

▲ **26390**   Excision flexor tendon, with implantation of synthetic rod for delayed tendon graft, hand or finger, each rod
 ➲ *CPT Assistant* Nov 98:8; *CPT Changes* 2002

▲ **26392**   Removal of synthetic rod and insertion of flexor tendon graft, hand or finger (includes obtaining graft), each rod
 ➲ *CPT Assistant* Nov 98:8; *CPT Changes* 2002

26410   Repair, extensor tendon, hand, primary or secondary; without free graft, each tendon
 ➲ *CPT Assistant* Nov 98:8

26412   with free graft (includes obtaining graft), each tendon
 ➲ *CPT Assistant* Nov 98:8

▲ **26415**   Excision of extensor tendon, with implantation of synthetic rod for delayed tendon graft, hand or finger, each rod
 ➲ *CPT Assistant* Nov 98:8; *CPT Changes* 2002

▲ **26416**   Removal of synthetic rod and insertion of extensor tendon graft (includes obtaining graft), hand or finger, each rod
 ➲ *CPT Assistant* Nov 99:12; *CPT Changes* 2000; 2002

26418   Repair, extensor tendon, finger, primary or secondary; without free graft, each tendon
 ➲ *CPT Assistant* Nov 98:8; Dec 99:10; Dec 00:14

26420   with free graft (includes obtaining graft) each tendon

▲ **26426**   Repair of extensor tendon, central slip, secondary (eg, boutonniere deformity); using local tissue(s), including lateral band(s), each finger
 ➲ *CPT Assistant* Nov 98:8; *CPT Changes* 2002

▲ **26428**   with free graft (includes obtaining graft), each finger
 ➲ *CPT Changes* 2002

26432   Closed treatment of distal extensor tendon insertion, with or without percutaneous pinning (eg, mallet finger)
 ➲ *CPT Assistant* Nov 98:8

26433   Repair of extensor tendon, distal insertion, primary or secondary; without graft (eg, mallet finger)
 ➲ *CPT Assistant* Nov 98:8

26434   with free graft (includes obtaining graft)

      (For tenovaginotomy for trigger finger, use 26055)

26437   Realignment of extensor tendon, hand, each tendon
 ➲ *CPT Assistant* Nov 98:8

26440   Tenolysis, flexor tendon; palm OR finger; each tendon

26442   palm AND finger, each tendon

▲ **26445**   Tenolysis, extensor tendon, hand OR finger; each tendon
 ➲ *CPT Assistant* Nov 98:8; *CPT Changes* 2002

26449   Tenolysis, complex, extensor tendon, finger, including forearm, each tendon
 ➲ *CPT Assistant* Nov 98:8

26450   Tenotomy, flexor, palm, open, each tendon
 ➲ *CPT Assistant* Nov 98:8

26455   Tenotomy, flexor, finger, open, each tendon
 ➲ *CPT Assistant* Nov 98:8

26460   Tenotomy, extensor, hand or finger, open, each tendon
 ➲ *CPT Assistant* Nov 98:8

26471   Tenodesis; of proximal interphalangeal joint, each joint
 ➲ *CPT Assistant* Nov 98:8

26474   of distal joint, each joint
 ➲ *CPT Assistant* Nov 98:8

26476   Lengthening of tendon, extensor, hand or finger, each tendon
 ➲ *CPT Assistant* Nov 98:8

26477   Shortening of tendon, extensor, hand or finger, each tendon
 ➲ *CPT Assistant* Nov 98:8

26478   Lengthening of tendon, flexor, hand or finger, each tendon
 ➲ *CPT Assistant* Nov 98:8

26479   Shortening of tendon, flexor, hand or finger, each tendon
 ➲ *CPT Assistant* Nov 98:8

26480   Transfer or transplant of tendon, carpometacarpal area or dorsum of hand; without free graft, each tendon
 ➲ *CPT Assistant* Nov 98:8

26483   with free tendon graft (includes obtaining graft), each tendon

26485   Transfer or transplant of tendon, palmar; without free tendon graft, each tendon
 ➲ *CPT Assistant* Nov 98:8

26489   with free tendon graft (includes obtaining graft), each tendon

26490   Opponensplasty; superficialis tendon transfer type, each tendon

26492   tendon transfer with graft (includes obtaining graft), each tendon

26494   hypothenar muscle transfer

26496   other methods

      (For thumb fusion in opposition, use 26820)

26497   Transfer of tendon to restore intrinsic function; ring and small finger
 ➲ *CPT Assistant* Nov 98:8

26498   all four fingers

26499   Correction claw finger, other methods

26500 Reconstruction of tendon pulley, each tendon; with local tissues (separate procedure)
➲ *CPT Assistant* Nov 98:8

26502 with tendon or fascial graft (includes obtaining graft) (separate procedure)

26504 with tendon prosthesis (separate procedure)

26508 Release of thenar muscle(s) (eg, thumb contracture)
➲ *CPT Assistant* Nov 98:8

▲ **26510** Cross intrinsic transfer, each tendon
➲ *CPT Changes* 2002

26516 Capsulodesis, metacarpophalangeal joint; single digit
➲ *CPT Assistant* Nov 98:8

26517 two digits

26518 three or four digits

26520 Capsulectomy or capsulotomy; metacarpophalangeal joint, each joint
➲ *CPT Assistant* Nov 98:8

26525 interphalangeal joint, each joint
➲ *CPT Assistant* Nov 98:8

(26527 has been deleted. To report, use 25447)

26530 Arthroplasty, metacarpophalangeal joint; each joint
➲ *CPT Assistant* Nov 98:8

26531 with prosthetic implant, each joint
➲ *CPT Assistant* Nov 98:8

26535 Arthroplasty, interphalangeal joint; each joint
➲ *CPT Assistant* Nov 98:8

26536 with prosthetic implant, each joint
➲ *CPT Assistant* Nov 98:8

26540 Repair of collateral ligament, metacarpophalangeal or interphalangeal joint

26541 Reconstruction, collateral ligament, metacarpophalangeal joint, single; with tendon or fascial graft (includes obtaining graft)
➲ *CPT Assistant* Jan 97:3

26542 with local tissue (eg, adductor advancement)
➲ *CPT Assistant* Jan 97:3

26545 Reconstruction, collateral ligament, interphalangeal joint, single, including graft, each joint

26546 Repair non-union, metacarpal or phalanx, (includes obtaining bone graft with or without external or internal fixation)

26548 Repair and reconstruction, finger, volar plate, interphalangeal joint

26550 Pollicization of a digit

26551 Transfer, toe-to-hand with microvascular anastomosis; great toe wrap-around with bone graft
➲ *CPT Assistant* Apr 97:7; Jun 97:9; Nov 98:8, 10-11

(For great toe with web space, use 20973)

(26552 has been deleted. To report, see 20973 or 26551, 26553, 26554)

26553 other than great toe, single
➲ *CPT Assistant* Apr 97:7; Jun 97:9; Nov 98:8, 10-11

26554 other than great toe, double
➲ *CPT Assistant* Apr 97:7; Jun 97:9; Nov 98:8, 10-11

(Do not report code 69990 in addition to codes 26551-26554)

26555 Transfer, finger to another position without microvascular anastomosis
➲ *CPT Assistant* Nov 98:8, 10-11

26556 Transfer, free toe joint, with microvascular anastomosis
➲ *CPT Assistant* Apr 97:7; Jun 97:9; Nov 98:8

(Do not report code 69990 in addition to code 26556)

(26557-26559 have been deleted. To report, see 20973 or 26551, 26553, 26554)

26560 Repair of syndactyly (web finger) each web space; with skin flaps

26561 with skin flaps and grafts

26562 complex (eg, involving bone, nails)

26565 Osteotomy; metacarpal, each
➲ *CPT Assistant* Nov 98:9

26567 phalanx of finger, each

26568 Osteoplasty, lengthening, metacarpal or phalanx

(26570, 26574 have been deleted. To report, use 26989)

26580 Repair cleft hand

▶(26585 has been deleted. To report, use 26587)◀

▲ **26587** Reconstruction of polydactylous digit, soft tissue and bone
➲ *CPT Changes* 2002

▶(For excision of polydactylous digit, soft tissue only, use 11200)◀

▲ **26590** Repair macrodactylia, each digit
➲ *CPT Changes* 2002

26591 Repair, intrinsic muscles of hand, each muscle
➲ *CPT Assistant* May 98:11; Jul 98:11; Nov 98:8, 11

26593 Release, intrinsic muscles of hand, each muscle
➲ *CPT Assistant* Nov 98:8, 11

26596 Excision of constricting ring of finger, with multiple Z-plasties

▶(26597 has been deleted. To report, see 11041-11042, 14040-14041, or 15120, 15240)◀

Fracture and/or Dislocation

26600 Closed treatment of metacarpal fracture, single; without manipulation, each bone

26605 with manipulation, each bone

▲ **26607** Closed treatment of metacarpal fracture, with manipulation, with external fixation, each bone
➲ *CPT Changes* 2002

26608 Percutaneous skeletal fixation of metacarpal fracture, each bone

(26610 has been deleted. To report, see 26605, 26607, 26608)

26615 Open treatment of metacarpal fracture, single, with or without internal or external fixation, each bone

26641 Closed treatment of carpometacarpal dislocation, thumb, with manipulation

26645 Closed treatment of carpometacarpal fracture dislocation, thumb (Bennett fracture), with manipulation

26650 Percutaneous skeletal fixation of carpometacarpal fracture dislocation, thumb (Bennett fracture), with manipulation, with or without external fixation

(26655 has been deleted. To report, see 26645, 26650, 26665)

(26660 has been deleted. To report, see 26650, 26665)

26665 Open treatment of carpometacarpal fracture dislocation, thumb (Bennett fracture), with or without internal or external fixation

▲ **26670** Closed treatment of carpometacarpal dislocation, other than thumb, with manipulation, each joint; without anesthesia
➔ *CPT Changes* 2002

26675 requiring anesthesia

▲ **26676** Percutaneous skeletal fixation of carpometacarpal dislocation, other than thumb, with manipulation, each joint
➔ *CPT Changes* 2002

(26680 has been deleted. To report, see 26670, 26675, 26676, 26685)

▲ **26685** Open treatment of carpometacarpal dislocation, other than thumb; with or without internal or external fixation, each joint
➔ *CPT Changes* 2002

26686 complex, multiple or delayed reduction

26700 Closed treatment of metacarpophalangeal dislocation, single, with manipulation; without anesthesia

26705 requiring anesthesia

26706 Percutaneous skeletal fixation of metacarpophalangeal dislocation, single, with manipulation

(26710 has been deleted. To report, see 26700, 26705, 26706, 26715)

26715 Open treatment of metacarpophalangeal dislocation, single, with or without internal or external fixation

26720 Closed treatment of phalangeal shaft fracture, proximal or middle phalanx, finger or thumb; without manipulation, each

26725 with manipulation, with or without skin or skeletal traction, each

26727 Percutaneous skeletal fixation of unstable phalangeal shaft fracture, proximal or middle phalanx, finger or thumb, with manipulation, each

(26730 has been deleted. To report, see 26720, 26725, 26727, 26735)

26735 Open treatment of phalangeal shaft fracture, proximal or middle phalanx, finger or thumb, with or without internal or external fixation, each

26740 Closed treatment of articular fracture, involving metacarpophalangeal or interphalangeal joint; without manipulation, each

26742 with manipulation, each

(26743 has been deleted. To report, use 26989)

(26744 has been deleted. To report, see 26740, 26742, 26746)

26746 Open treatment of articular fracture, involving metacarpophalangeal or interphalangeal joint, with or without internal or external fixation, each

26750 Closed treatment of distal phalangeal fracture, finger or thumb; without manipulation, each

26755 with manipulation, each

26756 Percutaneous skeletal fixation of distal phalangeal fracture, finger or thumb, each

(26760 has been deleted. To report, see 26750, 26755, 26756, 26765)

26765 Open treatment of distal phalangeal fracture, finger or thumb, with or without internal or external fixation, each

26770 Closed treatment of interphalangeal joint dislocation, single, with manipulation; without anesthesia

26775 requiring anesthesia

26776 Percutaneous skeletal fixation of interphalangeal joint dislocation, single, with manipulation

(26780 has been deleted. To report, see 26770, 26775, 26776, 26785)

26785 Open treatment of interphalangeal joint dislocation, with or without internal or external fixation, single

Arthrodesis

26820 Fusion in opposition, thumb, with autogenous graft (includes obtaining graft)

26841 Arthrodesis, carpometacarpal joint, thumb, with or without internal fixation;

26842 with autograft (includes obtaining graft)

▲ **26843** Arthrodesis, carpometacarpal joint, digit, other than thumb, each;
➔ *CPT Changes* 2002

26844 with autograft (includes obtaining graft)

26850 Arthrodesis, metacarpophalangeal joint, with or without internal fixation;

26852 with autograft (includes obtaining graft)

26860 Arthrodesis, interphalangeal joint, with or without internal fixation;

+ 26861 each additional interphalangeal joint (List separately in addition to code for primary procedure)

(Use 26861 in conjunction with code 26860)

26862 with autograft (includes obtaining graft)

+ 26863 with autograft (includes obtaining graft), each additional joint (List separately in addition to code for primary procedure)

(Use 26863 in conjunction with code 26862)

Amputation

(For hand through metacarpal bones, use 25927)

26910 Amputation, metacarpal, with finger or thumb (ray amputation), single, with or without interosseous transfer

(For repositioning, see 26550, 26555)

26951 Amputation, finger or thumb, primary or secondary, any joint or phalanx, single, including neurectomies; with direct closure

26952 with local advancement flaps (V-Y, hood)

(For repair of soft tissue defect requiring split or full thickness graft or other pedicle flaps, see 15050-15758)

Other Procedures

26989 Unlisted procedure, hands or fingers

Pelvis and Hip Joint

Including head and neck of femur.

Incision

(For incision and drainage procedures, superficial, see 10040-10160)

26990 Incision and drainage, pelvis or hip joint area; deep abscess or hematoma

26991 infected bursa

26992 Incision, bone cortex, pelvis and/or hip joint (eg, osteomyelitis or bone abscess)

(26995 has been deleted)

27000 Tenotomy, adductor of hip, percutaneous (separate procedure)

27001 Tenotomy, adductor of hip, open

(27002 has been deleted. To report, use 27001 with modifier '-50')

27003 Tenotomy, adductor, subcutaneous, open, with obturator neurectomy

(27004 has been deleted. To report, use 27003 with modifier '-50')

27005 Tenotomy, hip flexor(s), open (separate procedure)

27006 Tenotomy, abductors and/or extensor(s) of hip, open (separate procedure)

(27010, 27015 have been deleted. To report, use 27025)

27025 Fasciotomy, hip or thigh, any type

(27026 has been deleted. To report, use 27025 with modifier '-50')

27030 Arthrotomy, hip, with drainage (eg, infection)
 CPT Assistant Nov 98:8

(27031 has been deleted)

27033 Arthrotomy, hip, including exploration or removal of loose or foreign body
 CPT Assistant Spring 92:11

27035 Denervation, hip joint, intrapelvic or extrapelvic intra-articular branches of sciatic, femoral, or obturator nerves
 CPT Assistant Nov 98:8

(For obturator neurectomy, see 64763, 64766)

27036 Capsulectomy or capsulotomy, hip, with or without excision of heterotopic bone, with release of hip flexor muscles (ie, gluteus medius, gluteus minimus, tensor fascia latae, rectus femoris, sartorius, iliopsoas)

Excision

27040 Biopsy, soft tissue of pelvis and hip area; superficial

27041 deep, subfascial or intramuscular
 CPT Assistant Nov 98:8

(For needle biopsy of soft tissue, use 20206)

27047 Excision, tumor, pelvis and hip area; subcutaneous tissue
 CPT Assistant Nov 98:8

27048 deep, subfascial, intramuscular

27049 Radical resection of tumor, soft tissue of pelvis and hip area (eg, malignant neoplasm)
 CPT Assistant Nov 98:8

27050 Arthrotomy, with biopsy; sacroiliac joint

27052 hip joint

27054 Arthrotomy with synovectomy, hip joint

27060 Excision; ischial bursa

27062 trochanteric bursa or calcification

(For arthrocentesis or needling of bursa, use 20610)

$\bigcirc$ =Modifier '-51' Exempt   ▶ ◀=New or Revised Text   ✚=Add-on Code   CPT 2002

27065 Excision of bone cyst or benign tumor; superficial (wing of ilium, symphysis pubis, or greater trochanter of femur) with or without autograft

27066 deep, with or without autograft

27067 with autograft requiring separate incision

27070 Partial excision (craterization, saucerization) (eg, osteomyelitis or bone abscess); superficial (eg, wing of ilium, symphysis pubis, or greater trochanter of femur)

27071 deep (subfascial or intramuscular)

27075 Radical resection of tumor or infection; wing of ilium, one pubic or ischial ramus or symphysis pubis

27076 ilium, including acetabulum, both pubic rami, or ischium and acetabulum

27077 innominate bone, total

27078 ischial tuberosity and greater trochanter of femur

27079 ischial tuberosity and greater trochanter of femur, with skin flaps

27080 Coccygectomy, primary

(For pressure (decubitus) ulcer, see 15920, 15922 and 15931-15958)

Introduction or Removal

27086 * Removal of foreign body, pelvis or hip; subcutaneous tissue
  CPT Assistant Jul 98:8

27087 deep (subfascial or intramuscular)
➲ *CPT Assistant* Nov 98:8

(27088 has been deleted. To report, use 27087)

27090 Removal of hip prosthesis; (separate procedure)

27091 complicated, including total hip prosthesis, methylmethacrylate with or without insertion of spacer

27093 Injection procedure for hip arthrography; without anesthesia

(For radiological supervision and interpretation, use 73525. ►Do not report 76003 in addition to 73525)◄

27095 with anesthesia

(For radiological supervision and interpretation, use 73525. ►Do not report 76003 in addition to 73525)◄

27096 Injection procedure for sacroiliac joint, arthrography and/or anesthetic/steroid
➲ *CPT Assistant* Nov 99:12; *CPT Changes* 2000

►(27096 is to be used only with imaging confirmation of intra-articular needle positioning)◄

►(For radiological supervision and interpretation of sacroiliac joint arthrography, use 73542)◄

►(For fluoroscopic guidance without formal arthrography, use 76005)◄

►(Code 27096 is a unilateral procedure. For bilateral procedure, use modifier '-50')◄

Repair, Revision, and/or Reconstruction

27097 Release or recession, hamstring, proximal
➲ *CPT Assistant* Nov 98:8

27098 Transfer, adductor to ischium
➲ *CPT Assistant* Nov 98:8

27100 Transfer external oblique muscle to greater trochanter including fascial or tendon extension (graft)

27105 Transfer paraspinal muscle to hip (includes fascial or tendon extension graft)

▲**27110** Transfer iliopsoas; to greater trochanter of femur
➲ *CPT Changes* 2002

27111 to femoral neck

(27115 has been deleted. To report, use 27299)

27120 Acetabuloplasty; (eg, Whitman, Colonna, Haygroves, or cup type)

27122 resection, femoral head (eg, Girdlestone procedure)

27125 Hemiarthroplasty, hip, partial (eg, femoral stem prosthesis, bipolar arthroplasty)
➲ *CPT Assistant* Spring 92:8; Feb 98:11; Nov 98:8

(For prosthetic replacement following fracture of the hip, use 27236)

(27126, 27127 have been deleted. To report, use 27120)

Partial Hip Replacement with or without Bipolar Prosthesis
27125

The femoral neck is excised so the physician can measure and then replace the femoral stem.

Bipolar prosthesis (Acetabular cup)

▲**27130** Arthroplasty, acetabular and proximal femoral prosthetic replacement (total hip arthroplasty), with or without autograft or allograft

➔ *CPT Assistant* Spring 92:8; *CPT Changes* 2002

Total Hip Replacement
27130

The femoral head is excised, osteophytes are removed, and acetabulum is reamed out before replacement is inserted in the femoral shaft.

Acetabular component

Femoral component

Femoral shaft

(27131 has been deleted. To report, use 27132)

▲**27132** Conversion of previous hip surgery to total hip arthroplasty, with or without autograft or allograft

➔ *CPT Assistant* Spring 92:11; *CPT Changes* 2002

27134 Revision of total hip arthroplasty; both components, with or without autograft or allograft

(27135 has been deleted. To report, see 27134, 27137, 27138)

27137 acetabular component only, with or without autograft or allograft

27138 femoral component only, with or without allograft

▲**27140** Osteotomy and transfer of greater trochanter of femur (separate procedure)

➔ *CPT Changes* 2002

27146 Osteotomy, iliac, acetabular or innominate bone;

➔ *CPT Assistant* Feb 99:10

27147 with open reduction of hip

27151 with femoral osteotomy

27156 with femoral osteotomy and with open reduction of hip

(27157 has been deleted)

27158 Osteotomy, pelvis, bilateral (eg, congenital malformation)

27161 Osteotomy, femoral neck (separate procedure)

27165 Osteotomy, intertrochanteric or subtrochanteric including internal or external fixation and/or cast

➔ *CPT Assistant* Spring 92:11

27170 Bone graft, femoral head, neck, intertrochanteric or subtrochanteric area (includes obtaining bone graft)

➔ *CPT Assistant* Spring 92:11

27175 Treatment of slipped femoral epiphysis; by traction, without reduction

27176 by single or multiple pinning, in situ

27177 Open treatment of slipped femoral epiphysis; single or multiple pinning or bone graft (includes obtaining graft)

27178 closed manipulation with single or multiple pinning

27179 osteoplasty of femoral neck (Heyman type procedure)

27181 osteotomy and internal fixation

▲**27185** Epiphyseal arrest by epiphysiodesis or stapling, greater trochanter of femur

➔ *CPT Changes* 2002

27187 Prophylactic treatment (nailing, pinning, plating or wiring) with or without methylmethacrylate, femoral neck and proximal femur

Fracture and/or Dislocation

(27190, 27191 have been deleted. To report, see 27193, 27194)

(27192 has been deleted. To report, see 27215, 27216)

27193 Closed treatment of pelvic ring fracture, dislocation, diastasis or subluxation; without manipulation

27194 with manipulation, requiring more than local anesthesia

(27195 has been deleted. To report, use 27193)

(27196 has been deleted. To report, use 27194)

27200 Closed treatment of coccygeal fracture

(27201 has been deleted. To report, see 27200, 27202)

27202 Open treatment of coccygeal fracture

(27210, 27211, 27212 have been deleted. To report, see 27193, 27194, 27215, 27216, 27217, 27218)

(27214 has been deleted. To report, see 27215, 27216, 27217, 27218)

27215 Open treatment of iliac spine(s), tuberosity avulsion, or iliac wing fracture(s) (eg, pelvic fracture(s) which do not disrupt the pelvic ring), with internal fixation

27216 Percutaneous skeletal fixation of posterior pelvic ring fracture and/or dislocation (includes ilium, sacroiliac joint and/or sacrum)

⊘ =Modifier '-51' Exempt ▶ ◀=New or Revised Text ✚ =Add-on Code CPT 2002

27217 Open treatment of anterior ring fracture and/or dislocation with internal fixation (includes pubic symphysis and/or rami)

27218 Open treatment of posterior ring fracture and/or dislocation with internal fixation (includes ilium, sacroiliac joint and/or sacrum)

27220 Closed treatment of acetabulum (hip socket) fracture(s); without manipulation

27222 with manipulation, with or without skeletal traction

(27224 has been deleted. To report, see 27226, 27227)

(27225 has been deleted. To report, see 27227, 27228)

27226 Open treatment of posterior or anterior acetabular wall fracture, with internal fixation

27227 Open treatment of acetabular fracture(s) involving anterior or posterior (one) column, or a fracture running transversely across the acetabulum, with internal fixation

27228 Open treatment of acetabular fracture(s) involving anterior and posterior (two) columns, includes T-fracture and both column fracture with complete articular detachment, or single column or transverse fracture with associated acetabular wall fracture, with internal fixation

27230 Closed treatment of femoral fracture, proximal end, neck; without manipulation

27232 with manipulation, with or without skeletal traction

(27234 has been deleted. To report, see 27230, 27232, 27235, 27236)

27235 Percutaneous skeletal fixation of femoral fracture, proximal end, neck, undisplaced, mildly displaced, or impacted fracture

Percutaneous Treatment of Femoral Fracture
27235

Femoral fracture treatment without fracture exposure.

27236 Open treatment of femoral fracture, proximal end, neck, internal fixation or prosthetic replacement

➔ *CPT Assistant* Spring 92:10; Feb 98:11; *CPT Changes* 2001

Open Treatment of Femoral Fracture
27236

A. Femoral fracture treatment by internal fixation device (with fracture exposure).

B. Femoral fracture treatment by prosthetic replacement.

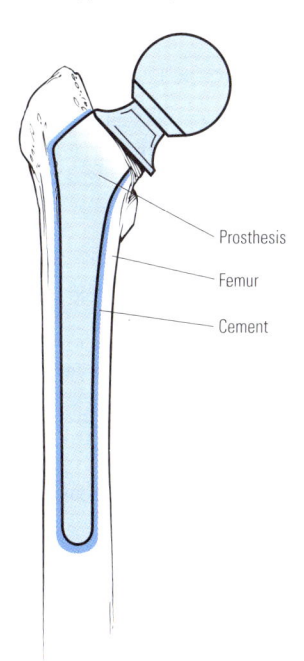

27238 Closed treatment of intertrochanteric, pertrochanteric, or subtrochanteric femoral fracture; without manipulation

27240 with manipulation, with or without skin or skeletal traction

(27242 has been deleted. To report, see 27238, 27240, 27244, 27245)

27244 Open treatment of intertrochanteric, pertrochanteric, or subtrochanteric femoral fracture; with plate/screw type implant, with or without cerclage

27245 with intramedullary implant, with or without interlocking screws and/or cerclage

27246 Closed treatment of greater trochanteric fracture, without manipulation

27248 Open treatment of greater trochanteric fracture, with or without internal or external fixation

27250 Closed treatment of hip dislocation, traumatic; without anesthesia

27252 requiring anesthesia

27253 Open treatment of hip dislocation, traumatic, without internal fixation

27254 Open treatment of hip dislocation, traumatic, with acetabular wall and femoral head fracture, with or without internal or external fixation

(27255 has been deleted. To report, see 27226, 27227, 27253, 27254)

27256* Treatment of spontaneous hip dislocation (developmental, including congenital or pathological), by abduction, splint or traction; without anesthesia, without manipulation

27257* with manipulation, requiring anesthesia

27258 Open treatment of spontaneous hip dislocation (developmental, including congenital or pathological), replacement of femoral head in acetabulum (including tenotomy, etc);

27259 with femoral shaft shortening

27265 Closed treatment of post hip arthroplasty dislocation; without anesthesia

27266 requiring regional or general anesthesia

Manipulation

27275* Manipulation, hip joint, requiring general anesthesia

Arthrodesis

27280 Arthrodesis, sacroiliac joint (including obtaining graft)

(27281 has been deleted. To report, use 27280 with modifier '-50')

27282 Arthrodesis, symphysis pubis (including obtaining graft)

27284 Arthrodesis, hip joint (including obtaining graft);

27286 with subtrochanteric osteotomy

Amputation

27290 Interpelviabdominal amputation (hindquarter amputation)

27295 Disarticulation of hip

Other Procedures

27299 Unlisted procedure, pelvis or hip joint

Femur (Thigh Region) and Knee Joint

Including tibial plateaus.

Incision

(For incision and drainage of abscess or hematoma, superficial, see 10040-10160)

27301 Incision and drainage, deep abscess, bursa, or hematoma, thigh or knee region
→ *CPT Assistant* Nov 98:9

27303 Incision, deep, with opening of bone cortex, femur or knee (eg, osteomyelitis or bone abscess)
→ *CPT Assistant* Nov 98:8

(27304 has been deleted)

27305 Fasciotomy, iliotibial (tenotomy), open

(For combined Ober-Yount fasciotomy, use 27025)

27306 Tenotomy, percutaneous, adductor or hamstring; single tendon (separate procedure)
→ *CPT Assistant* Nov 98:8

27307 multiple tendons
→ *CPT Assistant* Nov 98:8

27310 Arthrotomy, knee, with exploration, drainage, or removal of foreign body (eg, infection)
→ *CPT Assistant* Nov 98:8

(27311 has been deleted)

27315 Neurectomy, hamstring muscle

27320 Neurectomy, popliteal (gastrocnemius)

Excision

27323 Biopsy, soft tissue of thigh or knee area; superficial
→ *CPT Assistant* Jun 97:12

27324 deep (subfascial or intramuscular)
→ *CPT Assistant* Mar 97:4; Nov 98:8

(For needle biopsy of soft tissue, use 20206)

27327 Excision, tumor, thigh or knee area; subcutaneous

27328 deep, subfascial, or intramuscular

27329 Radical resection of tumor (eg, malignant neoplasm), soft tissue of thigh or knee area

⊘ =Modifier '-51' Exempt   ▶ ◀=New or Revised Text   ✚ =Add-on Code

27330 Arthrotomy, knee; with synovial biopsy only

27331 including joint exploration, biopsy, or removal of loose or foreign bodies
➔ *CPT Assistant* Nov 98:8

27332 Arthrotomy, with excision of semilunar cartilage (meniscectomy) knee; medial OR lateral
➔ *CPT Assistant* Nov 98:8

27333 medial AND lateral

27334 Arthrotomy, with synovectomy, knee; anterior OR posterior
➔ *CPT Assistant* Nov 98:8

27335 anterior AND posterior including popliteal area

27340 Excision, prepatellar bursa

27345 Excision of synovial cyst of popliteal space (eg, Baker's cyst)

27347 Excision of lesion of meniscus or capsule (eg, cyst, ganglion), knee
➔ *CPT Assistant* Nov 98:11

27350 Patellectomy or hemipatellectomy

27355 Excision or curettage of bone cyst or benign tumor of femur;

27356 with allograft

27357 with autograft (includes obtaining graft)

+ 27358 with internal fixation (List in addition to code for primary procedure)

(Use 27358 in conjunction with codes 27355, 27356, or 27357)

27360 Partial excision (craterization, saucerization, or diaphysectomy) bone, femur, proximal tibia and/or fibula (eg, osteomyelitis or bone abscess)
➔ *CPT Assistant* Nov 98:8

(27361 has been deleted)

27365 Radical resection of tumor, bone, femur or knee

(For radical resection of tumor, soft tissue, use 27329)

Introduction or Removal

27370 Injection procedure for knee arthrography

(For radiological supervision and interpretation, use 73580. ▶Do not report 76003 in addition to 73580)◀

27372 Removal of foreign body, deep, thigh region or knee area

(For removal of knee prosthesis including "total knee," use 27488)

(27373-27379 have been deleted. To report, see 29870-29887)

Repair, Revision, and/or Reconstruction

27380 Suture of infrapatellar tendon; primary

27381 secondary reconstruction, including fascial or tendon graft

27385 Suture of quadriceps or hamstring muscle rupture; primary

27386 secondary reconstruction, including fascial or tendon graft

27390 Tenotomy, open, hamstring, knee to hip; single tendon
➔ *CPT Assistant* Nov 98:8

27391 multiple tendons, one leg
➔ *CPT Assistant* Nov 98:8

27392 multiple tendons, bilateral
➔ *CPT Assistant* Nov 98:8

27393 Lengthening of hamstring tendon; single tendon
➔ *CPT Assistant* Nov 98:8

27394 multiple tendons, one leg
➔ *CPT Assistant* Nov 98:8

27395 multiple tendons, bilateral
➔ *CPT Assistant* Nov 98:8

27396 Transplant, hamstring tendon to patella; single tendon
➔ *CPT Assistant* Nov 98:8

27397 multiple tendons
➔ *CPT Assistant* Nov 98:8

27400 Transfer, tendon or muscle, hamstrings to femur (eg, Egger's type procedure)
➔ *CPT Assistant* Nov 98:8

27403 Arthrotomy with meniscus repair, knee
➔ *CPT Assistant* Nov 98:8

(For arthroscopic repair, use 29882)

27405 Repair, primary, torn ligament and/or capsule, knee; collateral

27407 cruciate

(27408 has been deleted. To report, use 27427)

27409 collateral and cruciate ligaments

(27410-27416 have been deleted. To report, see 27427-27429)

27418 Anterior tibial tubercleplasty (eg, Maquet type procedure)

27420 Reconstruction of dislocating patella; (eg, Hauser type procedure)

27422 with extensor realignment and/or muscle advancement or release (eg, Campbell, Goldwaite type procedure)

27424 with patellectomy

27425 Lateral retinacular release (any method)
➔ *CPT Assistant* Nov 00:11; *CPT Changes* 2002

27427 Ligamentous reconstruction (augmentation), knee; extra-articular

→ *CPT Assistant* Nov 99:13; *CPT Changes* 2000

27428 intra-articular (open)

→ *CPT Assistant* Nov 99:13; *CPT Changes* 2000

27429 intra-articular (open) and extra-articular

→ *CPT Assistant* Nov 99:13; *CPT Changes* 2000

(For primary repair of ligament(s) performed in addition to reconstruction, report 27405, 27407 or 27409 in addition to code 27427, 27428 or 27429)

27430 Quadricepsplasty (eg, Bennett or Thompson type)

27435 Capsulotomy, posterior capsular release, knee

→ *CPT Assistant* Nov 98:8

(27436 has been deleted. To report, use 29887)

27437 Arthroplasty, patella; without prosthesis

27438 with prosthesis

27440 Arthroplasty, knee, tibial plateau;

27441 with debridement and partial synovectomy

27442 Arthroplasty, femoral condyles or tibial plateau(s), knee;

→ *CPT Assistant* Nov 99:13

27443 with debridement and partial synovectomy

(27444 has been deleted. To report, see 27445-27447)

27445 Arthroplasty, knee, hinge prosthesis (eg, Walldius type)

→ *CPT Assistant* Nov 98:8

27446 Arthroplasty, knee, condyle and plateau; medial OR lateral compartment

▲ **27447** medial AND lateral compartments with or without patella resurfacing (total knee arthroplasty)

→ *CPT Changes* 2002

(For revision of total knee arthroplasty, use 27487)

(For removal of total knee prosthesis, use 27488)

27448 Osteotomy, femur, shaft or supracondylar; without fixation

(27449 has been deleted. To report, use 27448 with modifier '-50')

27450 with fixation

(27452 has been deleted. To report, use 27450 with modifier '-50')

27454 Osteotomy, multiple, with realignment on intramedullary rod, femoral shaft (eg, Sofield type procedure)

→ *CPT Assistant* Nov 98:8

27455 Osteotomy, proximal tibia, including fibular excision or osteotomy (includes correction of genu varus (bowleg) or genu valgus (knock-knee)); before epiphyseal closure

27457 after epiphyseal closure

(27460 has been deleted. To report, use 27455 with modifier '-50')

(27462 has been deleted. To report, use 27457 with modifier '-50')

27465 Osteoplasty, femur; shortening (excluding 64876)

27466 lengthening

27468 combined, lengthening and shortening with femoral segment transfer

27470 Repair, nonunion or malunion, femur, distal to head and neck; without graft (eg, compression technique)

27472 with iliac or other autogenous bone graft (includes obtaining graft)

27475 Arrest, epiphyseal, any method (eg, epiphysiodesis); distal femur

→ *CPT Assistant* Nov 98:8

27477 tibia and fibula, proximal

27479 combined distal femur, proximal tibia and fibula

27485 Arrest, hemiepiphyseal, distal femur or proximal tibia or fibula (eg, genu varus or valgus)

→ *CPT Assistant* Nov 98:8

27486 Revision of total knee arthroplasty, with or without allograft; one component

27487 femoral and entire tibial component

→ *CPT Assistant* Nov 98:8

27488 Removal of prosthesis, including total knee prosthesis, methylmethacrylate with or without insertion of spacer, knee

→ *CPT Assistant* Nov 98:8

(27490 has been deleted. To report, use 29882)

27495 Prophylactic treatment (nailing, pinning, plating or wiring) with or without methylmethacrylate, femur

27496 Decompression fasciotomy, thigh and/or knee, one compartment (flexor or extensor or adductor);

27497 with debridement of nonviable muscle and/or nerve

27498 Decompression fasciotomy, thigh and/or knee, multiple compartments;

27499 with debridement of nonviable muscle and/or nerve

Fracture and/or Dislocation

(For arthroscopic treatment of intercondylar spine(s) and tuberosity fracture(s) of the knee, see 29850, 29851)

(For arthroscopic treatment of tibial fracture, see 29855, 29856)

27500 Closed treatment of femoral shaft fracture, without manipulation

27501 Closed treatment of supracondylar or transcondylar femoral fracture with or without intercondylar extension, without manipulation

⊘ = Modifier '-51' Exempt   ▶ ◀ = New or Revised Text   ✚ = Add-on Code   CPT 2002

27502 Closed treatment of femoral shaft fracture, with manipulation, with or without skin or skeletal traction
➔ *CPT Assistant* Fall 93:22; Oct 99:4

27503 Closed treatment of supracondylar or transcondylar femoral fracture with or without intercondylar extension, with manipulation, with or without skin or skeletal traction

(27504 has been deleted. To report, see 27500, 27501, 27502, 27503, 27506, 27507, 27509, 27511, 27513)

27506 Open treatment of femoral shaft fracture, with or without external fixation, with insertion of intramedullary implant, with or without cerclage and/or locking screws
➔ *CPT Assistant* Winter 92:10

27507 Open treatment of femoral shaft fracture with plate/screws, with or without cerclage

27508 Closed treatment of femoral fracture, distal end, medial or lateral condyle, without manipulation

27509 Percutaneous skeletal fixation of femoral fracture, distal end, medial or lateral condyle, or supracondylar or transcondylar, with or without intercondylar extension, or distal femoral epiphyseal separation

27510 Closed treatment of femoral fracture, distal end, medial or lateral condyle, with manipulation

27511 Open treatment of femoral supracondylar or transcondylar fracture without intercondylar extension, with or without internal or external fixation

(27512 has been deleted. To report, see 27508, 27510, 27514)

27513 Open treatment of femoral supracondylar or transcondylar fracture with intercondylar extension, with or without internal or external fixation

27514 Open treatment of femoral fracture, distal end, medial or lateral condyle, with or without internal or external fixation

27516 Closed treatment of distal femoral epiphyseal separation; without manipulation

27517 with manipulation, with or without skin or skeletal traction

(27518 has been deleted. To report, see 27516, 27517, 27519)

27519 Open treatment of distal femoral epiphyseal separation, with or without internal or external fixation

27520 Closed treatment of patellar fracture, without manipulation

(27522 has been deleted. To report, see 27520, 27524)

27524 Open treatment of patellar fracture, with internal fixation and/or partial or complete patellectomy and soft tissue repair

27530 Closed treatment of tibial fracture, proximal (plateau); without manipulation

27532 with or without manipulation, with skeletal traction

(27534 has been deleted. To report, see 27530, 27532, 27535, 27536)

(For arthroscopic treatment, see 29855, 29856)

27535 Open treatment of tibial fracture, proximal (plateau); unicondylar, with or without internal or external fixation

27536 bicondylar, with or without internal fixation

(For arthroscopic treatment, see 29855, 29856)

(27537 has been deleted. To report, see 27535, 27536)

27538 Closed treatment of intercondylar spine(s) and/or tuberosity fracture(s) of knee, with or without manipulation

(For arthroscopic treatment, see 29850, 29851)

27540 Open treatment of intercondylar spine(s) and/or tuberosity fracture(s) of the knee, with or without internal or external fixation

27550 Closed treatment of knee dislocation; without anesthesia

27552 requiring anesthesia

(27554 has been deleted. To report, see 27550, 27552, 27556, 27557, 27558)

27556 Open treatment of knee dislocation, with or without internal or external fixation; without primary ligamentous repair or augmentation/reconstruction

27557 with primary ligamentous repair

27558 with primary ligamentous repair, with augmentation/reconstruction

27560 Closed treatment of patellar dislocation; without anesthesia

(For recurrent dislocation, see 27420-27424)

27562 requiring anesthesia

(27564 has been deleted. To report, see 27560, 27562, 27566)

27566 Open treatment of patellar dislocation, with or without partial or total patellectomy

Manipulation

27570✱ Manipulation of knee joint under general anesthesia (includes application of traction or other fixation devices)

Arthrodesis

27580 Arthrodesis, knee, any technique

Amputation

27590 Amputation, thigh, through femur, any level;

27591 immediate fitting technique including first cast

27592 open, circular (guillotine)

27594 secondary closure or scar revision

27596 re-amputation

27598 Disarticulation at knee

Other Procedures

27599 Unlisted procedure, femur or knee

Leg (Tibia and Fibula) and Ankle Joint

Incision

27600 Decompression fasciotomy, leg; anterior and/or lateral compartments only

27601 posterior compartment(s) only

27602 anterior and/or lateral, and posterior compartment(s)

(For incision and drainage procedures, superficial, see 10040-10160)

(For decompression fasciotomy with debridement, see 27892-27894)

27603 Incision and drainage, leg or ankle; deep abscess or hematoma

27604 infected bursa

27605* Tenotomy, percutaneous, Achilles tendon (separate procedure); local anesthesia

27606 general anesthesia

27607 Incision (eg, osteomyelitis or bone abscess), leg or ankle

(27608 has been deleted)

27610 Arthrotomy, ankle, including exploration, drainage, or removal of foreign body
➔ *CPT Assistant* Nov 98:9

(27611 has been deleted)

27612 Arthrotomy, posterior capsular release, ankle, with or without Achilles tendon lengthening
➔ *CPT Assistant* Nov 98:8

(See also 27685)

Excision

27613 Biopsy, soft tissue of leg or ankle area; superficial

27614 deep (subfascial or intramuscular)
➔ *CPT Assistant* Nov 98:8

(For needle biopsy of soft tissue, use 20206)

27615 Radical resection of tumor (eg, malignant neoplasm), soft tissue of leg or ankle area

27618 Excision, tumor, leg or ankle area; subcutaneous tissue

27619 deep (subfascial or intramuscular)

27620 Arthrotomy, ankle, with joint exploration, with or without biopsy, with or without removal of loose or foreign body

27625 Arthrotomy, with synovectomy, ankle;
➔ *CPT Assistant* Nov 98:8

27626 including tenosynovectomy

27630 Excision of lesion of tendon sheath or capsule (eg, cyst or ganglion), leg and/or ankle

27635 Excision or curettage of bone cyst or benign tumor, tibia or fibula;

27637 with autograft (includes obtaining graft)

27638 with allograft

27640 Partial excision (craterization, saucerization, or diaphysectomy) bone (eg, osteomyelitis or exostosis); tibia

27641 fibula

27645 Radical resection of tumor, bone; tibia

27646 fibula

27647 talus or calcaneus

Introduction or Removal

27648 Injection procedure for ankle arthrography

(For radiological supervision and interpretation, use 73615. ►Do not report 76003 in addition to 73615)◄

(For ankle arthroscopy, see 29894-29898)

Repair, Revision, and/or Reconstruction

27650 Repair, primary, open or percutaneous, ruptured Achilles tendon;

27652 with graft (includes obtaining graft)

27654 Repair, secondary, Achilles tendon, with or without graft

27656 Repair, fascial defect of leg

27658 Repair, flexor tendon, leg; primary, without graft, each tendon
➔ *CPT Assistant* Nov 98:8

27659 secondary, with or without graft, each tendon

○ =Modifier '-51' Exempt   ► ◄=New or Revised Text   ✚ =Add-on Code

27664 Repair, extensor tendon, leg; primary, without graft, each tendon
> *CPT Assistant* Nov 98:8

27665 secondary, with or without graft, each tendon
> *CPT Assistant* Nov 98:8

27675 Repair, dislocating peroneal tendons; without fibular osteotomy

27676 with fibular osteotomy

27680 Tenolysis, flexor or extensor tendon, leg and/or ankle; single, each tendon
> *CPT Assistant* Nov 98:8

27681 multiple tendons (through separate incision(s))
> *CPT Assistant* Nov 98:8

27685 Lengthening or shortening of tendon, leg or ankle; single tendon (separate procedure)
> *CPT Assistant* Nov 98:8

27686 multiple tendons (through same incision), each
> *CPT Assistant* Nov 98:8

27687 Gastrocnemius recession (eg, Strayer procedure)

(Toe extensors are considered as a group to be a single tendon when transplanted into midfoot)

27690 Transfer or transplant of single tendon (with muscle redirection or rerouting); superficial (eg, anterior tibial extensors into midfoot)

27691 deep (eg, anterior tibial or posterior tibial through interosseous space, flexor digitorum longus, flexor hallucis longus, or peroneal tendon to midfoot or hindfoot)

+ 27692 each additional tendon (List separately in addition to code for primary procedure)

(Use 27692 in conjunction with codes 27690, 27691)

27695 Repair, primary, disrupted ligament, ankle; collateral

27696 both collateral ligaments

27698 Repair, secondary, disrupted ligament, ankle, collateral (eg, Watson-Jones procedure)

27700 Arthroplasty, ankle;

27702 with implant (total ankle)

27703 revision, total ankle

27704 Removal of ankle implant

27705 Osteotomy; tibia

27707 fibula

27709 tibia and fibula

27712 multiple, with realignment on intramedullary rod (eg, Sofield type procedure)

(For osteotomy to correct genu varus (bowleg) or genu valgus (knock-knee), see 27455-27457)

27715 Osteoplasty, tibia and fibula, lengthening or shortening

27720 Repair of nonunion or malunion, tibia; without graft, (eg, compression technique)

27722 with sliding graft

27724 with iliac or other autograft (includes obtaining graft)

27725 by synostosis, with fibula, any method

27727 Repair of congenital pseudarthrosis, tibia

27730 Arrest, epiphyseal (epiphysiodesis), any method; distal tibia
> *CPT Assistant* Nov 98:8

27732 distal fibula

27734 distal tibia and fibula

27740 Arrest, epiphyseal (epiphysiodesis), any method, combined, proximal and distal tibia and fibula;
> *CPT Assistant* Nov 98:8

27742 and distal femur

(For epiphyseal arrest of proximal tibia and fibula, use 27477)

27745 Prophylactic treatment (nailing, pinning, plating or wiring) with or without methylmethacrylate, tibia

Fracture and/or Dislocation

27750 Closed treatment of tibial shaft fracture (with or without fibular fracture); without manipulation
> *CPT Assistant* Winter 92:10; Fall 93:21; Mar 96:10

27752 with manipulation, with or without skeletal traction
> *CPT Assistant* Winter 92:10; Fall 93:21; Feb 96:3; Mar 96:10

(27754 has been deleted. To report, see 27750, 27752, 27756, 27758)

27756 Percutaneous skeletal fixation of tibial shaft fracture (with or without fibular fracture) (eg, pins or screws)
> *CPT Assistant* Winter 92:10

27758 Open treatment of tibial shaft fracture, (with or without fibular fracture) with plate/screws, with or without cerclage
> *CPT Assistant* Winter 92:10; Mar 00:11

27759 Open treatment of tibial shaft fracture (with or without fibular fracture) by intramedullary implant, with or without interlocking screws and/or cerclage
> *CPT Assistant* Winter 92:10

27760 Closed treatment of medial malleolus fracture; without manipulation

27762 with manipulation, with or without skin or skeletal traction

(27764 has been deleted. To report, see 27762, 27766)

27766 Open treatment of medial malleolus fracture, with or without internal or external fixation

27780 Closed treatment of proximal fibula or shaft fracture; without manipulation
➲ *CPT Assistant* Winter 92:11

27781 with manipulation

(27782 has been deleted. To report, see 27780, 27781, 27784)

27784 Open treatment of proximal fibula or shaft fracture, with or without internal or external fixation
➲ *CPT Assistant* Mar 00:11

27786 Closed treatment of distal fibular fracture (lateral malleolus); without manipulation

27788 with manipulation

(27790 has been deleted. To report, see 27786, 27788, 27792)

27792 Open treatment of distal fibular fracture (lateral malleolus), with or without internal or external fixation

(27800 has been deleted. To report, use 27750)

(27802 has been deleted. To report, use 27752)

(27804 has been deleted. To report, see 27750, 27752, 27756, 27758, 27759)

(27806 has been deleted. To report, see 27756, 27758, 27759)

27808 Closed treatment of bimalleolar ankle fracture, (including Potts); without manipulation

27810 with manipulation

(27812 has been deleted. To report, see 27808, 27810, 27814)

27814 Open treatment of bimalleolar ankle fracture, with or without internal or external fixation

27816 Closed treatment of trimalleolar ankle fracture; without manipulation

27818 with manipulation

(27820 has been deleted. To report, see 27816, 27818, 27822, 27823)

27822 Open treatment of trimalleolar ankle fracture, with or without internal or external fixation, medial and/or lateral malleolus; without fixation of posterior lip

27823 with fixation of posterior lip

27824 Closed treatment of fracture of weight bearing articular portion of distal tibia (eg, pilon or tibial plafond), with or without anesthesia; without manipulation

27825 with skeletal traction and/or requiring manipulation

27826 Open treatment of fracture of weight bearing articular surface/portion of distal tibia (eg, pilon or tibial plafond), with internal or external fixation; of fibula only

27827 of tibia only

27828 of both tibia and fibula

27829 Open treatment of distal tibiofibular joint (syndesmosis) disruption, with or without internal or external fixation
➲ *CPT Assistant* Winter 92:11

27830 Closed treatment of proximal tibiofibular joint dislocation; without anesthesia

27831 requiring anesthesia

27832 Open treatment of proximal tibiofibular joint dislocation, with or without internal or external fixation, or with excision of proximal fibula

27840 Closed treatment of ankle dislocation; without anesthesia

27842 requiring anesthesia, with or without percutaneous skeletal fixation

(27844 has been deleted. To report, see 27840, 27842, 27846, 27848)

27846 Open treatment of ankle dislocation, with or without percutaneous skeletal fixation; without repair or internal fixation

27848 with repair or internal or external fixation

(27850-27853 have been deleted. To report, see 29894-29898)

Manipulation

27860* Manipulation of ankle under general anesthesia (includes application of traction or other fixation apparatus)

Arthrodesis

27870 Arthrodesis, ankle, any method

27871 Arthrodesis, tibiofibular joint, proximal or distal

Amputation

27880 Amputation, leg, through tibia and fibula;

27881 with immediate fitting technique including application of first cast

27882 open, circular (guillotine)

27884 secondary closure or scar revision

27886 re-amputation

27888 Amputation, ankle, through malleoli of tibia and fibula (eg, Syme, Pirogoff type procedures), with plastic closure and resection of nerves

27889 Ankle disarticulation

Other Procedures

27892 Decompression fasciotomy, leg; anterior and/or lateral compartments only, with debridement of nonviable muscle and/or nerve

(For decompression fasciotomy of the leg without debridement, use 27600)

27893 posterior compartment(s) only, with debridement of nonviable muscle and/or nerve

(For decompression fasciotomy of the leg without debridement, use 27601)

27894 anterior and/or lateral, and posterior compartment(s), with debridement of nonviable muscle and/or nerve

(For decompression fasciotomy of the leg without debridement, use 27602)

27899 Unlisted procedure, leg or ankle
➲ *CPT Assistant* Aug 00:11

Foot and Toes

Incision

(For incision and drainage procedures, superficial, see 10040-10160)

28001✳ Incision and drainage, bursa, foot
➲ *CPT Assistant* Nov 98:9

28002✳ Incision and drainage below fascia, with or without tendon sheath involvement, foot; single bursal space
➲ *CPT Assistant* Nov 98:8

28003 multiple areas
➲ *CPT Assistant* Nov 98:9

(28004 has been deleted)

28005 Incision, bone cortex (eg, osteomyelitis or bone abscess), foot
➲ *CPT Assistant* Nov 98:9

(28006 has been deleted)

28008 Fasciotomy, foot and/or toe

(See also 28060, 28062, 28250)

28010 Tenotomy, percutaneous, toe; single tendon
➲ *CPT Assistant* Nov 98:8

28011 multiple tendons
➲ *CPT Assistant* Nov 98:8

(For open tenotomy, see 28230-28234)

28020 Arthrotomy, including exploration, drainage, or removal of loose or foreign body; intertarsal or tarsometatarsal joint

28022 metatarsophalangeal joint

28024 interphalangeal joint

28030 Neurectomy, intrinsic musculature of foot

28035 Release, tarsal tunnel (posterior tibial nerve decompression)
➲ *CPT Assistant* Nov 98:8

(For other nerve entrapments, see 64704, 64722)

Excision

28043 Excision, tumor, foot; subcutaneous tissue

28045 deep, subfascial, intramuscular

28046 Radical resection of tumor (eg, malignant neoplasm), soft tissue of foot

28050 Arthrotomy with biopsy; intertarsal or tarsometatarsal joint

28052 metatarsophalangeal joint

28054 interphalangeal joint

28060 Fasciectomy, plantar fascia; partial (separate procedure)

28062 radical (separate procedure)

(For plantar fasciotomy, see 28008, 28250)

28070 Synovectomy; intertarsal or tarsometatarsal joint, each

28072 metatarsophalangeal joint, each

28080 Excision, interdigital (Morton) neuroma, single, each

28086 Synovectomy, tendon sheath, foot; flexor

28088 extensor

28090 Excision of lesion, tendon, tendon sheath, or capsule (including synovectomy) (eg, cyst or ganglion); foot
➲ *CPT Assistant* Nov 98:8

28092 toe(s), each

28100 Excision or curettage of bone cyst or benign tumor, talus or calcaneus;

28102 with iliac or other autograft (includes obtaining graft)

28103 with allograft

▲ **28104** Excision or curettage of bone cyst or benign tumor, tarsal or metatarsal, except talus or calcaneus;
➲ *CPT Changes* 2002

28106 with iliac or other autograft (includes obtaining graft)

28107 with allograft

28108 Excision or curettage of bone cyst or benign tumor, phalanges of foot

(For ostectomy, partial (eg, hallux valgus, Silver type procedure), use 28290)

(28109 has been deleted. To report, use 28899)

28110 Ostectomy, partial excision, fifth metatarsal head (bunionette) (separate procedure)
➲ *CPT Assistant* Oct 98:10; Sep 00:9

28111 Ostectomy, complete excision; first metatarsal head

28112 other metatarsal head (second, third or fourth)

28113   fifth metatarsal head

28114   all metatarsal heads, with partial proximal phalangectomy, excluding first metatarsal (eg, Clayton type procedure)

28116 Ostectomy, excision of tarsal coalition

28118 Ostectomy, calcaneus;

28119   for spur, with or without plantar fascial release

28120 Partial excision (craterization, saucerization, sequestrectomy, or diaphysectomy) bone (eg, osteomyelitis or bossing); talus or calcaneus

(28121 has been deleted)

28122   tarsal or metatarsal bone, except talus or calcaneus
➔ *CPT Assistant* Nov 98:11

(For partial excision of talus or calcaneus, use 28120)

(For cheilectomy for hallux rigidus, use 28289)

(28123 has been deleted)

28124   phalanx of toe

28126 Resection, partial or complete, phalangeal base, each toe
➔ *CPT Assistant* Nov 98:8

28130 Talectomy (astragalectomy)

(28135 has been deleted. To report, use 28118)

28140 Metatarsectomy

28150 Phalangectomy, toe, each toe
➔ *CPT Assistant* Nov 98:8

28153 Resection, condyle(s), distal end of phalanx, each toe
➔ *CPT Assistant* Nov 98:8

28160 Hemiphalangectomy or interphalangeal joint excision, toe, proximal end of phalanx, each
➔ *CPT Assistant* Nov 98:8

28171 Radical resection of tumor, bone; tarsal (except talus or calcaneus)

28173   metatarsal

28175   phalanx of toe

(For talus or calcaneus, use 27647)

Introduction or Removal

28190* Removal of foreign body, foot; subcutaneous

28192   deep

28193   complicated

Repair, Revision, and/or Reconstruction

28200 Repair, tendon, flexor, foot; primary or secondary, without free graft, each tendon
➔ *CPT Assistant* Nov 98:8

28202   secondary with free graft, each tendon (includes obtaining graft)

28208 Repair, tendon, extensor, foot; primary or secondary, each tendon
➔ *CPT Assistant* Nov 98:8

28210   secondary with free graft, each tendon (includes obtaining graft)

28220 Tenolysis, flexor, foot; single tendon
➔ *CPT Assistant* Nov 98:8

28222   multiple tendons
➔ *CPT Assistant* Nov 98:8

28225 Tenolysis, extensor, foot; single tendon
➔ *CPT Assistant* Nov 98:8

28226   multiple tendons
➔ *CPT Assistant* Nov 98:8

28230 Tenotomy, open, tendon flexor; foot, single or multiple tendon(s) (separate procedure)
➔ *CPT Assistant* Nov 98:8

28232   toe, single tendon (separate procedure)
➔ *CPT Assistant* Nov 98:8

28234 Tenotomy, open, extensor, foot or toe, each tendon
➔ *CPT Assistant* Nov 98:8

(28236 has been deleted. To report, see 27690, 27691)

▲ **28238** Reconstruction (advancement), posterior tibial tendon with excision of accessory tarsal navicular bone (eg, Kidner type procedure)
➔ *CPT Changes* 2002

(For subcutaneous tenotomy, see 28010, 28011)

(For transfer or transplant of tendon with muscle redirection or rerouting, see 27690-27692)

(For extensor hallucis longus transfer with great toe IP fusion (Jones procedure), use 28760)

28240 Tenotomy, lengthening, or release, abductor hallucis muscle

28250 Division of plantar fascia and muscle (eg, Steindler stripping) (separate procedure)

28260 Capsulotomy, midfoot; medial release only (separate procedure)

28261   with tendon lengthening

28262   extensive, including posterior talotibial capsulotomy and tendon(s) lengthening (eg, resistant clubfoot deformity)

28264 Capsulotomy, midtarsal (eg, Heyman type procedure)

28270   Capsulotomy; metatarsophalangeal joint, with or without tenorrhaphy, each joint (separate procedure)

28272   interphalangeal joint, each joint (separate procedure)

28280   Syndactylization, toes (eg, webbing or Kelikian type procedure)
➔ *CPT Assistant* Nov 98:8

28285   Correction, hammertoe (eg, interphalangeal fusion, partial or total phalangectomy)
➔ *CPT Assistant* Nov 98:8

28286   Correction, cock-up fifth toe, with plastic skin closure (eg, Ruiz-Mora type procedure)
➔ *CPT Assistant* Nov 98:8

28288   Ostectomy, partial, exostectomy or condylectomy, metatarsal head, each metatarsal head

28289   Hallux rigidus correction with cheilectomy, debridement and capsular release of the first metatarsophalangeal joint
➔ *CPT Assistant* Nov 98:11

28290   Correction, hallux valgus (bunion), with or without sesamoidectomy; simple exostectomy (eg, Silver type procedure)
➔ *CPT Assistant* Dec 96:5; Nov 98:8

Hallux Valgus Correction
28290

Simple resection of the medial eminence (Silver-type procedure).

28292   Keller, McBride, or Mayo type procedure
➔ *CPT Assistant* Dec 96:5; Sep 00:9

Keller-Type Procedure
28292

Simple resection of the base of the proximal phalanx with removal of the medial eminence. A hemi implant is optional.

28293   resection of joint with implant
➔ *CPT Assistant* Dec 96:6

Keller-Mayo Procedure with Implant
28293

A total double stem implant is usually used.

28294 with tendon transplants (eg, Joplin type procedure)
→ *CPT Assistant* Dec 96:6

Joplin Procedure
28294

Tendon transplant is an important part of procedure.

Extensor tendon of great toe

Medial eminence of metatarsal bone

Before

Fusion of proximal phalanx and metatarsal bone

Extensor tendon transplanted to head of metatarsal bone

After

28296 with metatarsal osteotomy (eg, Mitchell, Chevron, or concentric type procedures)
→ *CPT Assistant* Dec 96:6; Jan 97:10

Mitchell Procedure
28296

A complex, biplanar, double step-cut osteotomy through the neck of the first metatarsal. Also called Mitchell Chevron (Austin) procedure.

Medial eminence of metatarsal bone

Osteotomy

Before

Wirelink

After

28297 Lapidus type procedure
→ *CPT Assistant* Dec 96:6

Lapidus-Type Procedure
28297

A metatarsocuneiform fusion of bones and a distal bunion repair to correct valgus deformity.

Medial eminence of metatarsal bone

Before

Tenotomy

Arthrodesis of the first metatarsal±first cuneiform joint and the first and second metatarsal bases

After

28298 by phalanx osteotomy
→ *CPT Assistant* Dec 96:7

Phalanx Osteotomy
28298

The Akin procedure involves removal of a bony wedge from the base of the proximal phalanx to reorient the axis.

Proximal phalanx

Medial eminence of metatarsal bone

Before

Kirschner wire

After

▲ **28299** by double osteotomy

➔ *CPT Assistant* Dec 96:7; *CPT Changes* 2002

Double Osteotomy
28299

A. This technique depicts a medial resection of the first metatarsal, osteotomy of the distal first metatarsal with correction of the hallux valgus, followed by an osteotomy of the proximal phalanx to correct additional angular deformity, with placement of appropriate internal fixation (eg, wire(s), pin(s), screw(s)).

PRE-OP   POST-OP

Angular deformity of proximal phalanx

Medial eminence of metatarsal bone

Osteotomy proximal phalanx

Osteotomy distal first metatarsal

*Note:Internal fixation is not depicted, but would include screw(s), pin(s), wire(s), as needed.

B. This technique depicts hallux valgus correction (without the medial resection of the base of the proximal phalanx) with double osteotomy of the first metatarsal and placement of appropriate internal fixation (eg, wire(s), pin(s), screw(s)).

PRE-OP   POST-OP

Medial eminence of metatarsal bone

Double osteotomy of the metatarsal with internal fixation (eg, wire(s), pin(s), screw(s)

*Note:Internal fixation depicted is for illustrative purpose only and does not suggest to limit choice of fixation options required.

28300 Osteotomy; calcaneus (eg, Dwyer or Chambers type procedure), with or without internal fixation

28302 talus

28304 Osteotomy, tarsal bones, other than calcaneus or talus;

➔ *CPT Assistant* Nov 98:8

28305 with autograft (includes obtaining graft) (eg, Fowler type)

28306 Osteotomy, with or without lengthening, shortening or angular correction, metatarsal; first metatarsal

➔ *CPT Assistant* Nov 98:8; Dec 99:7

28307 first metatarsal with autograft (other than first toe)

➔ *CPT Assistant* Nov 98:9

28308 other than first metatarsal, each

28309 multiple (eg, Swanson type cavus foot procedure)

➔ *CPT Assistant* Nov 98:8; Dec 99:7

28310 Osteotomy, shortening, angular or rotational correction; proximal phalanx, first toe (separate procedure)

28312 other phalanges, any toe

28313 Reconstruction, angular deformity of toe, soft tissue procedures only (eg, overlapping second toe, fifth toe, curly toes)

➔ *CPT Assistant* Nov 98:8

28315 Sesamoidectomy, first toe (separate procedure)

28320 Repair, nonunion or malunion; tarsal bones

➔ *CPT Assistant* Nov 98:9

28322 metatarsal, with or without bone graft (includes obtaining graft)

28340 Reconstruction, toe, macrodactyly; soft tissue resection

28341 requiring bone resection

28344 Reconstruction, toe(s); polydactyly

28345 syndactyly, with or without skin graft(s), each web

28360 Reconstruction, cleft foot

Fracture and/or Dislocation

28400 Closed treatment of calcaneal fracture; without manipulation

28405 with manipulation

28406 Percutaneous skeletal fixation of calcaneal fracture, with manipulation

(28410 has been deleted. To report, see 28400, 28405, 28406, 28415, 28420)

28415 Open treatment of calcaneal fracture, with or without internal or external fixation;

28420 with primary iliac or other autogenous bone graft (includes obtaining graft)

28430 Closed treatment of talus fracture; without manipulation

28435 with manipulation

28436 Percutaneous skeletal fixation of talus fracture, with manipulation

(28440 has been deleted. To report, see 28430, 28435, 28436, 28445)

28445 Open treatment of talus fracture, with or without internal or external fixation

28450 Treatment of tarsal bone fracture (except talus and calcaneus); without manipulation, each

28455 with manipulation, each

28456 Percutaneous skeletal fixation of tarsal bone fracture (except talus and calcaneus), with manipulation, each

(28460 has been deleted. To report, see 28450, 28455, 28456, 28465)

28465 Open treatment of tarsal bone fracture (except talus and calcaneus), with or without internal or external fixation, each

28470 Closed treatment of metatarsal fracture; without manipulation, each

28475 with manipulation, each

28476 Percutaneous skeletal fixation of metatarsal fracture, with manipulation, each

(28480 has been deleted. To report, see 28470, 28475, 28476, 28485)

28485 Open treatment of metatarsal fracture, with or without internal or external fixation, each

28490 Closed treatment of fracture great toe, phalanx or phalanges; without manipulation

28495 with manipulation

28496 Percutaneous skeletal fixation of fracture great toe, phalanx or phalanges, with manipulation

(28500 has been deleted. To report, see 28490, 28495, 28496, 28505)

28505 Open treatment of fracture great toe, phalanx or phalanges, with or without internal or external fixation

28510 Closed treatment of fracture, phalanx or phalanges, other than great toe; without manipulation, each

28515 with manipulation, each

(28520 has been deleted. To report, see 28510, 28515, 28525)

28525 Open treatment of fracture, phalanx or phalanges, other than great toe, with or without internal or external fixation, each

28530 Closed treatment of sesamoid fracture

28531 Open treatment of sesamoid fracture, with or without internal fixation

28540 Closed treatment of tarsal bone dislocation, other than talotarsal; without anesthesia

28545 requiring anesthesia

28546 Percutaneous skeletal fixation of tarsal bone dislocation, other than talotarsal, with manipulation

(28550 has been deleted. To report, see 28540, 28545, 28546, 28555)

28555 Open treatment of tarsal bone dislocation, with or without internal or external fixation

28570 Closed treatment of talotarsal joint dislocation; without anesthesia

28575 requiring anesthesia

28576 Percutaneous skeletal fixation of talotarsal joint dislocation, with manipulation

(28580 has been deleted. To report, see 28570, 28575, 28576, 28585)

28585 Open treatment of talotarsal joint dislocation, with or without internal or external fixation

28600 Closed treatment of tarsometatarsal joint dislocation; without anesthesia

28605 requiring anesthesia

28606 Percutaneous skeletal fixation of tarsometatarsal joint dislocation, with manipulation

(28610 has been deleted. To report, see 28600, 28605, 28606, 28615)

28615 Open treatment of tarsometatarsal joint dislocation, with or without internal or external fixation

28630* Closed treatment of metatarsophalangeal joint dislocation; without anesthesia

28635* requiring anesthesia

28636 Percutaneous skeletal fixation of metatarsophalangeal joint dislocation, with manipulation

(28640 has been deleted. To report, see 28630, 28635, 28636, 28645)

28645 Open treatment of metatarsophalangeal joint dislocation, with or without internal or external fixation

28660* Closed treatment of interphalangeal joint dislocation; without anesthesia

28665* requiring anesthesia

28666 Percutaneous skeletal fixation of interphalangeal joint dislocation, with manipulation

(28670 has been deleted. To report, see 28660, 28665, 28666, 28675)

28675 Open treatment of interphalangeal joint dislocation, with or without internal or external fixation

Arthrodesis

28705 Arthrodesis; pantalar

28715 triple

28725 subtalar

28730 Arthrodesis, midtarsal or tarsometatarsal, multiple or transverse;

28735 with osteotomy (eg, flatfoot correction)

▲ **28737** Arthrodesis, with tendon lengthening and advancement, midtarsal, tarsal navicular-cuneiform (eg, Miller type procedure)
➔ *CPT Changes* 2002

28740 Arthrodesis, midtarsal or tarsometatarsal, single joint

28750 Arthrodesis, great toe; metatarsophalangeal joint
➔ *CPT Assistant* Dec 96:7

28755 interphalangeal joint

28760 Arthrodesis, with extensor hallucis longus transfer to first metatarsal neck, great toe, interphalangeal joint (eg, Jones type procedure)
➔ *CPT Assistant* Nov 98:8

(For hammertoe operation or interphalangeal fusion, use 28285)

Amputation

28800   Amputation, foot; midtarsal (eg, Chopart type procedure)

28805   transmetatarsal

28810   Amputation, metatarsal, with toe, single

28820   Amputation, toe; metatarsophalangeal joint

28825   interphalangeal joint

        (For amputation of tuft of distal phalanx, use 11752)

Other Procedures

        ▶(For extracorporeal shock wave therapy involving musculoskeletal system, or plantar fascia, see Category III codes 0019T, 0020T)◀

28899   Unlisted procedure, foot or toes

Application of Casts and Strapping

The listed procedures apply when the cast application or strapping is a replacement procedure used during or after the period of follow-up care, or when the cast application or strapping is an initial service performed without a restorative treatment or procedure(s) to stabilize or protect a fracture, injury, or dislocation and/or to afford comfort to a patient. Restorative treatment or procedure(s) rendered by another physician following the application of the initial cast/splint/strap may be reported with a treatment of fracture and/or dislocation code.

A physician who applies the initial cast, strap or splint and also assumes all of the subsequent fracture, dislocation, or injury care cannot use the application of casts and strapping codes as an initial service, since the first cast/splint or strap application is included in the treatment of fracture and/or dislocation codes. (See notes under Musculoskeletal System, page 65). A temporary cast/splint/strap is not considered to be part of the preoperative care, and the use of the modifier '-56' is not applicable. Additional evaluation and management services are reportable only if significant identifiable further services are provided at the time of the cast application or strapping.

If cast application or strapping is provided as an initial service (eg, casting of a sprained ankle or knee) in which no other procedure or treatment (eg, surgical repair, reduction of a fracture or joint dislocation) is performed or is expected to be performed by a physician rendering the initial care only, use the casting, strapping and/or supply code (99070) in addition to an evaluation and management code as appropriate.

Listed procedures include removal of cast or strapping.

        (For orthotics fitting and training, use 97504)

Body and Upper Extremity

Casts

29000   Application of halo type body cast (see 20661-20663 for insertion)
        ➔ *CPT Assistant* Feb 96:3, 5

29010   Application of Risser jacket, localizer, body; only
        ➔ *CPT Assistant* Feb 96:3

29015   including head
            ➔ *CPT Assistant* Feb 96:3

29020   Application of turnbuckle jacket, body; only
        ➔ *CPT Assistant* Feb 96:3

29025   including head
            ➔ *CPT Assistant* Feb 96:3

29035   Application of body cast, shoulder to hips;
        ➔ *CPT Assistant* Feb 96:3

29040   including head, Minerva type
            ➔ *CPT Assistant* Feb 96:3

29044   including one thigh
            ➔ *CPT Assistant* Feb 96:3

29046   including both thighs
            ➔ *CPT Assistant* Feb 96:3

▲ **29049**   Application, cast; figure-of-eight
        ➔ *CPT Assistant* Feb 96:3; *CPT Changes* 2002

29055   shoulder spica
            ➔ *CPT Assistant* Feb 96:3

29058   plaster Velpeau
            ➔ *CPT Assistant* Feb 96:3

29065   shoulder to hand (long arm)
            ➔ *CPT Assistant* Feb 96:3

29075   elbow to finger (short arm)
            ➔ *CPT Assistant* Feb 96:3, 4

29085   hand and lower forearm (gauntlet)
            ➔ *CPT Assistant* Feb 96:3

● **29086**   finger (eg, contracture)
            ➔ *CPT Changes* 2002

Splints

29105   Application of long arm splint (shoulder to hand)
        ➔ *CPT Assistant* Feb 96:3

29125   Application of short arm splint (forearm to hand); static
        ➔ *CPT Assistant* Feb 96:3, 4

29126   dynamic
            ➔ *CPT Assistant* Feb 96:3

29130 Application of finger splint; static
→ *CPT Assistant* Feb 96:3

29131 dynamic
→ *CPT Assistant* Feb 96:3

Strapping—Any Age

29200 Strapping; thorax
→ *CPT Assistant* Feb 96:3

29220 low back
→ *CPT Assistant* Feb 96:3

29240 shoulder (eg, Velpeau)
→ *CPT Assistant* Feb 96:3

29260 elbow or wrist
→ *CPT Assistant* Feb 96:3

29280 hand or finger
→ *CPT Assistant* Feb 96:3

Lower Extremity

Casts

29305 Application of hip spica cast; one leg
→ *CPT Assistant* Feb 96:3

29325 one and one-half spica or both legs
→ *CPT Assistant* Feb 96:3

(For hip spica (body) cast, including thighs only, use 29046)

29345 Application of long leg cast (thigh to toes);
→ *CPT Assistant* Feb 96:3

29355 walker or ambulatory type
→ *CPT Assistant* Feb 96:3

29358 Application of long leg cast brace
→ *CPT Assistant* Feb 96:3

29365 Application of cylinder cast (thigh to ankle)
→ *CPT Assistant* Feb 96:3

29405 Application of short leg cast (below knee to toes);
→ *CPT Assistant* Feb 96:3

29425 walking or ambulatory type
→ *CPT Assistant* Feb 96:3

29435 Application of patellar tendon bearing (PTB) cast
→ *CPT Assistant* Feb 96:3

29440 Adding walker to previously applied cast
→ *CPT Assistant* Feb 96:3

29445 Application of rigid total contact leg cast
→ *CPT Assistant* Feb 96:3

29450 Application of clubfoot cast with molding or manipulation, long or short leg
→ *CPT Assistant* Feb 96:3

(29455 has been deleted. To report, use 29450 with modifier '-50')

Splints

29505 Application of long leg splint (thigh to ankle or toes)
→ *CPT Assistant* Feb 96:3

29515 Application of short leg splint (calf to foot)
→ *CPT Assistant* Feb 96:3

Strapping—Any Age

29520 Strapping; hip
→ *CPT Assistant* Feb 96:3

29530 knee
→ *CPT Assistant* Feb 96:3

29540 ankle
→ *CPT Assistant* Feb 96:3

29550 toes
→ *CPT Assistant* Feb 96:3

29580 Unna boot
→ *CPT Assistant* Feb 96:3; Jul 99:10

29590 Denis-Browne splint strapping
→ *CPT Assistant* Feb 96:3

Removal or Repair

Codes for cast removals should be employed only for casts applied by another physician.

29700 Removal or bivalving; gauntlet, boot or body cast

29705 full arm or full leg cast

29710 shoulder or hip spica, Minerva, or Risser jacket, etc.

29715 turnbuckle jacket

29720 Repair of spica, body cast or jacket

29730 Windowing of cast

29740 Wedging of cast (except clubfoot casts)

29750 Wedging of clubfoot cast

(29751 has been deleted. To report, use 29750 with modifier '-50')

Other Procedures

29799 Unlisted procedure, casting or strapping

⊘ =Modifier '-51' Exempt ▶ ◀=New or Revised Text ✚ =Add-on Code CPT 2002

Endoscopy/Arthroscopy

▶Surgical endoscopy/arthroscopy always includes a diagnostic endoscopy/arthroscopy.◀

When arthroscopy is performed in conjunction with arthrotomy, add modifier '-51'.

29800   Arthroscopy, temporomandibular joint, diagnostic, with or without synovial biopsy (separate procedure)

29804   Arthroscopy, temporomandibular joint, surgical

▶(For open procedure, use 21010)◀

● **29805**   Arthroscopy, shoulder, diagnostic, with or without synovial biopsy (separate procedure)
➔ *CPT Changes* 2002

▶(For open procedure, see 23065-23066, 23100-23101)◀

● **29806**   Arthroscopy, shoulder, surgical; capsulorrhaphy
➔ *CPT Changes* 2002

▶(For open procedure, see 23450-23466)◀

▶(To report thermal capsulorrhaphy, use 29999)◀

● **29807**   repair of slap lesion
➔ *CPT Changes* 2002

▶(29815 has been deleted. To report, use 29805)◀

29819   with removal of loose body or foreign body
➔ *CPT Changes* 2002

▶(For open procedure, see 23040-23044, 23107)◀

29820   synovectomy, partial

▶(For open procedure, see 23105)◀

29821   synovectomy, complete

▶(For open procedure, see 23105)◀

29822   debridement, limited

▶(For open procedure, see specific open shoulder procedure performed)◀

29823   debridement, extensive

▶(For open procedure, see specific open shoulder procedure performed)◀

● **29824**   distal claviculectomy including distal articular surface (Mumford procedure)
➔ *CPT Changes* 2002

▶(For open procedure, use 23120)◀

29825   with lysis and resection of adhesions, with or without manipulation

▶(For open procedure, see specific open shoulder procedure performed)◀

29826   decompression of subacromial space with partial acromioplasty, with or without coracoacromial release

▶(For open procedure, use 23130 or 23415)◀

29830   Arthroscopy, elbow, diagnostic, with or without synovial biopsy (separate procedure)

29834   Arthroscopy, elbow, surgical; with removal of loose body or foreign body

29835   synovectomy, partial

29836   synovectomy, complete

29837   debridement, limited

29838   debridement, extensive

29840   Arthroscopy, wrist, diagnostic, with or without synovial biopsy (separate procedure)

29843   Arthroscopy, wrist, surgical; for infection, lavage and drainage

29844   synovectomy, partial

29845   synovectomy, complete

29846   excision and/or repair of triangular fibrocartilage and/or joint debridement

29847   internal fixation for fracture or instability

29848   Endoscopy, wrist, surgical, with release of transverse carpal ligament
➔ *CPT Assistant* Dec 99:7

(For open procedure, use 64721)

29850   Arthroscopically aided treatment of intercondylar spine(s) and/or tuberosity fracture(s) of the knee, with or without manipulation; without internal or external fixation (includes arthroscopy)

29851   with internal or external fixation (includes arthroscopy)

(For bone graft, use 20900, 20902)

29855   Arthroscopically aided treatment of tibial fracture, proximal (plateau); unicondylar, with or without internal or external fixation (includes arthroscopy)

29856   bicondylar, with or without internal or external fixation (includes arthroscopy)

(For bone graft, use 20900, 20902)

29860   Arthroscopy, hip, diagnostic with or without synovial biopsy (separate procedure)
➔ *CPT Assistant* Nov 97:15; Jul 98:8

29861   Arthroscopy, hip, surgical; with removal of loose body or foreign body
➔ *CPT Assistant* Nov 97:15; Jul 98:8

29862   with debridement/shaving of articular cartilage (chondroplasty), abrasion arthroplasty, and/or resection of labrum
➔ *CPT Assistant* Nov 97:15; Jul 98:8

29863   with synovectomy
➔ *CPT Assistant* Nov 97:15; Jul 98:8

29870 Arthroscopy, knee, diagnostic, with or without synovial biopsy (separate procedure)

►(For surgical arthroscopy of the knee with implantation of osteochondral graft for treatment of articular surface defect, see Category III codes 0012T, 0013T)◄

Arthroscopy of the Knee
29870-29887

Portal incisions are made on either side of the patellar tendon and compartments of the knee are examined using the arthroscope and a probe. Additional treatment is performed as needed.

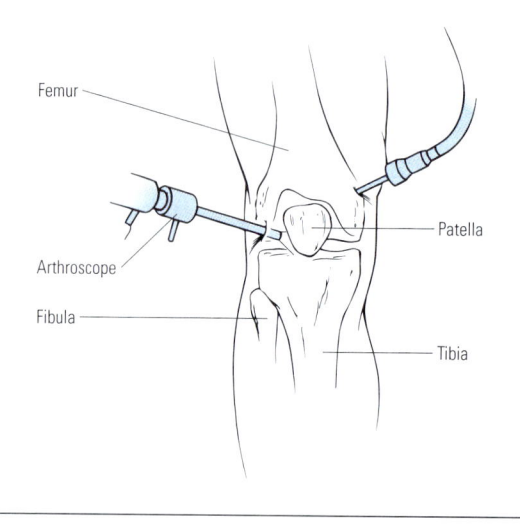

Femur
Arthroscope
Fibula
Patella
Tibia

►(For meniscal transplantation, medial or lateral, knee, use Category III code 0014T)◄

29871 Arthroscopy, knee, surgical; for infection, lavage and drainage

(29872 has been deleted)

29874 for removal of loose body or foreign body (eg, osteochondritis dissecans fragmentation, chondral fragmentation)

29875 synovectomy, limited (eg, plica or shelf resection) (separate procedure)

29876 synovectomy, major, two or more compartments (eg, medial or lateral)

29877 debridement/shaving of articular cartilage (chondroplasty)
➔ *CPT Assistant* Feb 96:9; Jun 99:11

29879 abrasion arthroplasty (includes chondroplasty where necessary) or multiple drilling or microfracture
➔ *CPT Assistant* Nov 99:13; *CPT Changes* 2000

29880 with meniscectomy (medial AND lateral, including any meniscal shaving)
➔ *CPT Assistant* Jun 99:11

29881 with meniscectomy (medial OR lateral, including any meniscal shaving)
➔ *CPT Assistant* Feb 96:9; Jun 99:11

29882 with meniscus repair (medial OR lateral)

29883 with meniscus repair (medial AND lateral)

29884 with lysis of adhesions, with or without manipulation (separate procedure)

29885 drilling for osteochondritis dissecans with bone grafting, with or without internal fixation (including debridement of base of lesion)

29886 drilling for intact osteochondritis dissecans lesion

29887 drilling for intact osteochondritis dissecans lesion with internal fixation

29888 Arthroscopically aided anterior cruciate ligament repair/augmentation or reconstruction

29889 Arthroscopically aided posterior cruciate ligament repair/augmentation or reconstruction
➔ *CPT Assistant* Sep 96:9; Oct 98:11

(Procedures 29888 and 29889 should not be used with reconstruction procedures 27427-27429)

(29890 has been deleted)

29891 Arthroscopy, ankle, surgical; excision of osteochondral defect of talus and/or tibia, including drilling of the defect

29892 Arthroscopically aided repair of large osteochondritis dissecans lesion, talar dome fracture, or tibial plafond fracture, with or without internal fixation (includes arthroscopy)
➔ *CPT Assistant* Nov 97:15

29893 Endoscopic plantar fasciotomy
➔ *CPT Assistant* Nov 97:15

29894 Arthroscopy, ankle (tibiotalar and fibulotalar joints), surgical; with removal of loose body or foreign body

Arthroscopy of the Ankle
29894-29898

Incisions are made allowing the ankle to be examined using the arthroscope and a probe. Additional treatment is performed as needed.

Tibia
Arthroscope
Fibula
Talus

29895 synovectomy, partial

(29896 has been deleted)

⊘ = Modifier '-51' Exempt   ► ◄ = New or Revised Text   ✚ = Add-on Code   CPT 2002

29897   debridement, limited

29898   debridement, extensive

● **29900**   Arthroscopy, metacarpophalangeal joint, diagnostic, includes synovial biopsy

   ➔ *CPT Changes* 2002

   ▶(Do not report 29900 with 29901, 29902)◀

● **29901**   Arthroscopy, metacarpophalangeal joint, surgical; with debridement

   ➔ *CPT Changes* 2002

● **29902**   with reduction of displaced ulnar collateral ligament (eg, Stenar lesion)

   ➔ *CPT Changes* 2002

   ▶(29909 has been deleted. To report, use 29999)◀

● **29999**   Unlisted procedure, arthroscopy

   ➔ *CPT Changes* 2002

Notes

Respiratory System

Nose

Incision

30000* Drainage abscess or hematoma, nasal, internal approach

(For external approach, see 10060, 10140)

30020* Drainage abscess or hematoma, nasal septum

(For lateral rhinotomy, see specific application (eg, 30118, 30320))

Excision

30100 Biopsy, intranasal

(For biopsy skin of nose, see 11100, 11101)

30110 Excision, nasal polyp(s), simple

(30110 would normally be completed in an office setting)

(30111 has been deleted. To report, use 30110 with modifier '-50')

30115 Excision, nasal polyp(s), extensive

(30115 would normally require the facilities available in a hospital setting)

(30116 has been deleted. To report, use 30115 with modifier '-50')

▲ **30117** Excision or destruction (eg, laser), intranasal lesion; internal approach
➲ CPT Changes 2002

30118 external approach (lateral rhinotomy)
➲ CPT Changes 2002

30120 Excision or surgical planing of skin of nose for rhinophyma

30124 Excision dermoid cyst, nose; simple, skin, subcutaneous

30125 complex, under bone or cartilage

30130 Excision turbinate, partial or complete, any method
➲ CPT Assistant Feb 98:11; Nov 98:11

30140 Submucous resection turbinate, partial or complete, any method
➲ CPT Assistant Nov 98:11

(For submucous resection of nasal septum, use 30520)

(For reduction of turbinates, use 30140 with modifier '-52')

30150 Rhinectomy; partial

30160 total

(For closure and/or reconstruction, primary or delayed, see **Integumentary System,** 13150-13160, 14060-14300, 15120, 15121, 15260, 15261, 15760, 20900-20912)

Introduction

30200* Injection into turbinate(s), therapeutic

30210* Displacement therapy (Proetz type)

30220 Insertion, nasal septal prosthesis (button)

Removal of Foreign Body

30300* Removal foreign body, intranasal; office type procedure

30310 requiring general anesthesia

30320 by lateral rhinotomy

Repair

(For obtaining tissues for graft, see 20900-20926, 21210)

30400 Rhinoplasty, primary; lateral and alar cartilages and/or elevation of nasal tip

(For columellar reconstruction, see 13150 et seq)

30410 complete, external parts including bony pyramid, lateral and alar cartilages, and/or elevation of nasal tip

30420 including major septal repair

30430 Rhinoplasty, secondary; minor revision (small amount of nasal tip work)

30435 intermediate revision (bony work with osteotomies)

30450 major revision (nasal tip work and osteotomies)

30460 Rhinoplasty for nasal deformity secondary to congenital cleft lip and/or palate, including columellar lengthening; tip only

30462 tip, septum, osteotomies

(30500 has been deleted. To report, use 30520)

Resp 30000

30465   Repair of nasal vestibular stenosis (eg, spreader grafting, lateral nasal wall reconstruction)

➔ *CPT Changes* 2001

(30465 excludes obtaining graft. For graft procedure, see 20900-20926, 21210)

(30465 is used to report a bilateral procedure. For unilateral procedure, use modifier '-52')

Surgical Repair of Vestibular Stenosis
30465

An incision is made in the upper lateral cartilage and continued as an osteotomy of the medial aspect of the nasal bones. The spreader graft is placed to widen the nasal vestibule.

Nasal bone
Osteotomy site
Lateral nasal cartilage
Incision line
Greater alar cartilage
Spreader graft providing separation of upper lateral cartilage from septum

30520   Septoplasty or submucous resection, with or without cartilage scoring, contouring or replacement with graft

➔ *CPT Assistant* Oct 97:11

(For submucous resection of turbinates, use 30140)

30540   Repair choanal atresia; intranasal

30545   transpalatine

30560 *   Lysis intranasal synechia

30580   Repair fistula; oromaxillary (combine with 31030 if antrotomy is included)

30600   oronasal

30620   Septal or other intranasal dermatoplasty (does not include obtaining graft)

30630   Repair nasal septal perforations

Destruction

(30800 has been deleted. To report, see 30801 and 30802)

▲ **30801** *   Cautery and/or ablation, mucosa of turbinates, unilateral or bilateral, any method, (separate procedure); superficial

➔ *CPT Changes* 2002

30802   intramural

(30805, 30820 have been deleted. To report, see 30801 and 30802)

Other Procedures

(30900 has been deleted. To report, see 30901, 30903)

30901 *   Control nasal hemorrhage, anterior, simple (limited cautery and/or packing) any method

(30902 has been deleted. To report, use 30901 with modifier '-50')

30903 *   Control nasal hemorrhage, anterior, complex (extensive cautery and/or packing) any method

(30904 has been deleted. To report, use 30903 with modifier '-50')

▲ **30905** *   Control nasal hemorrhage, posterior, with posterior nasal packs and/or cautery, any method; initial

➔ *CPT Changes* 2002

30906 *   subsequent

30915   Ligation arteries; ethmoidal

30920   internal maxillary artery, transantral

(For ligation external carotid artery, use 37600)

30930   Fracture nasal turbinate(s), therapeutic

30999   Unlisted procedure, nose

Accessory Sinuses

Incision

31000 *   Lavage by cannulation; maxillary sinus (antrum puncture or natural ostium)

(31001 has been deleted. To report, use 31000 with modifier '-50')

31002 *   sphenoid sinus

31020   Sinusotomy, maxillary (antrotomy); intranasal

(31021 has been deleted. To report, use 31020 with modifier '-50')

31030   radical (Caldwell-Luc) without removal of antrochoanal polyps

(31031 has been deleted. To report, use 31030 with modifier '-50')

31032   radical (Caldwell-Luc) with removal of antrochoanal polyps

(31033 has been deleted. To report, use 31032 with modifier '-50')

31040   Pterygomaxillary fossa surgery, any approach

(For transantral ligation of internal maxillary artery, use 30920)

31050   Sinusotomy, sphenoid, with or without biopsy;

31051   with mucosal stripping or removal of polyp(s)

31070   Sinusotomy frontal; external, simple (trephine operation)

Sinusotomy, Frontal
31070

A trephine is used to access the frontal sinus.

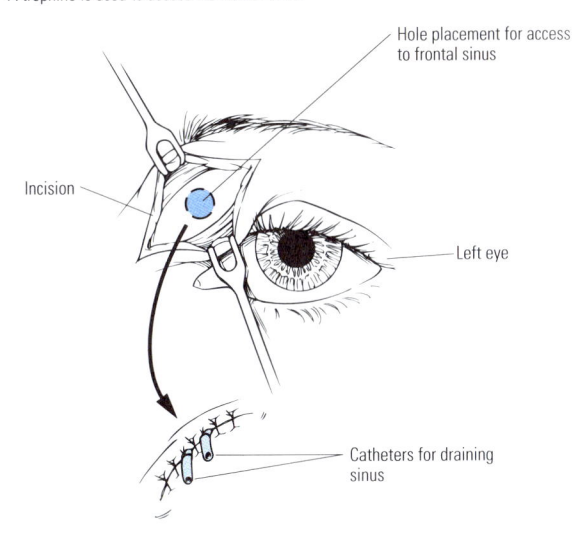

Hole placement for access to frontal sinus

Incision

Left eye

Catheters for draining sinus

(31071 has been deleted. To report, use 31276)

31075   transorbital, unilateral (for mucocele or osteoma, Lynch type)

31080   obliterative without osteoplastic flap, brow incision (includes ablation)

31081   obliterative, without osteoplastic flap, coronal incision (includes ablation)

31084   obliterative, with osteoplastic flap, brow incision

31085   obliterative, with osteoplastic flap, coronal incision

31086   nonobliterative, with osteoplastic flap, brow incision

31087   nonobliterative, with osteoplastic flap, coronal incision

31090   Sinusotomy, unilateral, three or more paranasal sinuses (frontal, maxillary, ethmoid, sphenoid)
> *CPT Assistant* Nov 97:15; Nov 98:11

Excision

31200   Ethmoidectomy; intranasal, anterior

31201   intranasal, total

31205   extranasal, total

31225   Maxillectomy; without orbital exenteration

31230   with orbital exenteration (en bloc)

(For orbital exenteration only, see 65110 et seq)

(For skin grafts, see 15120 et seq)

Endoscopy

A surgical sinus endoscopy includes a sinusotomy (when appropriate) and diagnostic endoscopy.

Codes 31231-31294 are used to report unilateral procedures unless otherwise specified.

The codes 31231-31235 for diagnostic evaluation refer to employing a nasal/sinus endoscope to inspect the interior of the nasal cavity and the middle and superior meatus, the turbinates, and the spheno-ethmoid recess. Any time a diagnostic evaluation is performed all these areas would be inspected and a separate code is not reported for each area.

Sinus Endoscopy
31231-31294

The physician uses an endoscope for visualizing and magnifying the internal structure of the sinuses.

Nasal septum

Right ethmoidal air cells or sinuses

Left ethmoidal air cells or sinuses

Left maxillary sinus

Right maxillary sinus

Superior turbinates (concha)

Middle turbinates (concha)

Right nasal cavity

Interior turbinates (concha)

Left nasal cavity

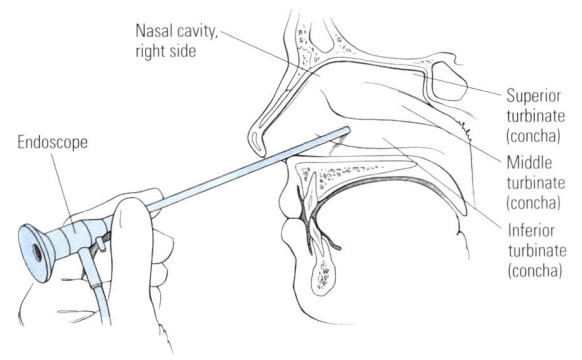

Nasal cavity, right side

Endoscope

Superior turbinate (concha)

Middle turbinate (concha)

Inferior turbinate (concha)

31231 Nasal endoscopy, diagnostic, unilateral or bilateral (separate procedure)
➔ *CPT Assistant* Jan 97:4

31233 Nasal/sinus endoscopy, diagnostic with maxillary sinusoscopy (via inferior meatus or canine fossa puncture)
➔ *CPT Assistant* Jan 97:4

31235 Nasal/sinus endoscopy, diagnostic with sphenoid sinusoscopy (via puncture of sphenoidal face or cannulation of ostium)
➔ *CPT Assistant* Jan 97:4

31237 Nasal/sinus endoscopy, surgical; with biopsy, polypectomy or debridement (separate procedure)
➔ *CPT Assistant* Jan 97:4

▲**31238** with control of nasal hemorrhage
➔ *CPT Assistant* Jan 97:4; *CPT Changes* 2002

31239 with dacryocystorhinostomy
➔ *CPT Assistant* Jan 97:4

31240 with concha bullosa resection
➔ *CPT Assistant* Jan 97:4

(31245 has been deleted. To report, use 31254)

(31246 has been deleted. To report, use 31254 and 31256)

(31247 has been deleted. To report, use 31254 and 31267)

(31248 has been deleted. To report, use 31254 and 31276)

(31249 has been deleted. To report, use 31254, 31256, and 31276)

(31250 has been deleted. To report, see 31231-31235)

(31251 has been deleted. To report, use 31254, 31267, and 31276)

(31252 has been deleted. To report, use 31237)

31254 Nasal/sinus endoscopy, surgical; with ethmoidectomy, partial (anterior)
➔ *CPT Assistant* Jan 97:4; Sep 97:10; Oct 97:5

31255 with ethmoidectomy, total (anterior and posterior)
➔ *CPT Assistant* Jan 97:4

31256 Nasal/sinus endoscopy, surgical, with maxillary antrostomy;
➔ *CPT Assistant* Jan 97:4

(31258 has been deleted. To report, use 31237)

(31260 has been deleted. To report, use 31233)

(31261 has been deleted. To report, use 31255)

(31262 has been deleted. To report, use 31255 and 31256)

(31263 has been deleted. To report, use 31267)

(31264 has been deleted. To report, use 31255 and 31267)

(31265 has been deleted. To report, use 31267)

(31266 has been deleted. To report, use 31255 and 31276)

31267 with removal of tissue from maxillary sinus
➔ *CPT Assistant* Jan 97:4

(31268 has been deleted. To report, use 31267)

(31269 has been deleted. To report, use 31255, 31256, and 31276)

(31270 has been deleted. To report, use 31235)

(31271 has been deleted. To report, use 31255, 31267, and 31276)

(31275 has been deleted. To report, use 31287)

31276 Nasal/sinus endoscopy, surgical with frontal sinus exploration, with or without removal of tissue from frontal sinus
➔ *CPT Assistant* Jan 97:4

(31277 has been deleted. To report, use 31288)

(31280 has been deleted. To report, use 31255, and 31287 or 31288)

(31281 has been deleted. To report, use 31255, 31256, and 31287 or 31288)

(31282 has been deleted. To report, use 31255, 31267, and 31287 or 31288)

(31283 has been deleted. To report, use 31255, 31287 or 31288, and 31276)

(31284 has been deleted. To report, use 31255, 31256, 31287 or 31288, and 31276)

(31285 has been deleted. To report, see 31231-31235)

(31286 has been deleted. To report, use 31255, 31267, 31287 or 31288, and 31276)

31287 Nasal/sinus endoscopy, surgical, with sphenoidotomy;
➔ *CPT Assistant* Jan 97:4

31288 with removal of tissue from the sphenoid sinus
➔ *CPT Assistant* Jan 97:4

31290 Nasal/sinus endoscopy, surgical, with repair of cerebrospinal fluid leak; ethmoid region
➔ *CPT Assistant* Jan 97:4

31291 sphenoid region
➔ *CPT Assistant* Jan 97:4

31292 Nasal/sinus endoscopy, surgical; with medial or inferior orbital wall decompression
➔ *CPT Assistant* Jan 97:4

31293 with medial orbital wall and inferior orbital wall decompression
➔ *CPT Assistant* Jan 97:4

31294 with optic nerve decompression
➔ *CPT Assistant* Jan 97:4

Other Procedures

(For hypophysectomy, transantral or transeptal approach, use 61548)

(For transcranial hypophysectomy, use 61546)

31299 Unlisted procedure, accessory sinuses

Larynx

Excision

31300 Laryngotomy (thyrotomy, laryngofissure); with removal of tumor or laryngocele, cordectomy

31320 diagnostic

31360 Laryngectomy; total, without radical neck dissection

31365 total, with radical neck dissection

31367 subtotal supraglottic, without radical neck dissection

31368 subtotal supraglottic, with radical neck dissection

31370 Partial laryngectomy (hemilaryngectomy); horizontal

31375 laterovertical

31380 anterovertical

31382 antero-latero-vertical

31390 Pharyngolaryngectomy, with radical neck dissection; without reconstruction

31395 with reconstruction

31400 Arytenoidectomy or arytenoidopexy, external approach

(For endoscopic arytenoidectomy, use 31560)

31420 Epiglottidectomy

Introduction

⊘ **31500** Intubation, endotracheal, emergency procedure

(For injection procedure for bronchography, see 31656, 31708, 31710)

31502 Tracheotomy tube change prior to establishment of fistula tract

Endoscopy

For endoscopic procedures, code appropriate endoscopy of each anatomic site examined.

31505 Laryngoscopy, indirect; diagnostic (separate procedure)
> *CPT Assistant* Nov 99:13; *CPT Changes* 2000

31510 with biopsy
> *CPT Assistant* Nov 99:13

31511 with removal of foreign body
> *CPT Assistant* Nov 99:13

31512 with removal of lesion
> *CPT Assistant* Nov 99:13

31513 with vocal cord injection
> *CPT Assistant* Nov 99:13

31515 Laryngoscopy direct, with or without tracheoscopy; for aspiration

31520 diagnostic, newborn

31525 diagnostic, except newborn

31526 diagnostic, with operating microscope
> *CPT Assistant* Nov 98:11-12

(Do not report code 69990 in addition to code 31526)

31527 with insertion of obturator

▲ **31528** with dilation, initial
> *CPT Changes* 2002

▲ **31529** with dilation, subsequent
> *CPT Changes* 2002

31530 Laryngoscopy, direct, operative, with foreign body removal;

31531 with operating microscope
> *CPT Assistant* Nov 98:11-12

(Do not report code 69990 in addition to code 31531)

31535 Laryngoscopy, direct, operative, with biopsy;

31536 with operating microscope
> *CPT Assistant* Nov 98:11-12

(Do not report code 69990 in addition to code 31536)

31540 Laryngoscopy, direct, operative, with excision of tumor and/or stripping of vocal cords or epiglottis;

31541 with operating microscope
> *CPT Assistant* Nov 98:11-12

(Do not report code 69990 in addition to code 31541)

31560 Laryngoscopy, direct, operative, with arytenoidectomy;

31561 with operating microscope
> *CPT Assistant* Nov 98:11-12

(Do not report code 69990 in addition to code 31561)

31570 Laryngoscopy, direct, with injection into vocal cord(s), therapeutic;

31571 with operating microscope
> *CPT Assistant* Nov 98:11-12

(Do not report code 69990 in addition to code 31571)

31575 Laryngoscopy, flexible fiberoptic; diagnostic

31576 with biopsy

31577 with removal of foreign body

31578 with removal of lesion

31579 Laryngoscopy, flexible or rigid fiberoptic, with stroboscopy

Repair

31580 Laryngoplasty; for laryngeal web, two stage, with keel insertion and removal

31582 for laryngeal stenosis, with graft or core mold, including tracheotomy

31584 with open reduction of fracture

31585 Treatment of closed laryngeal fracture; without manipulation

31586 with closed manipulative reduction

31587 Laryngoplasty, cricoid split

31588 Laryngoplasty, not otherwise specified (eg, for burns, reconstruction after partial laryngectomy)

31590 Laryngeal reinnervation by neuromuscular pedicle

Destruction

31595 Section recurrent laryngeal nerve, therapeutic (separate procedure), unilateral

Other Procedures

31599 Unlisted procedure, larynx

Trachea and Bronchi

Incision

31600 Tracheostomy, planned (separate procedure);

31601 under two years

31603 Tracheostomy, emergency procedure; transtracheal

31605 cricothyroid membrane

31610 Tracheostomy, fenestration procedure with skin flaps

(For endotracheal intubation, use 31500)

(For tracheal aspiration under direct vision, use 31515)

31611 Construction of tracheoesophageal fistula and subsequent insertion of an alaryngeal speech prosthesis (eg, voice button, Blom-Singer prosthesis)

31612 Tracheal puncture, percutaneous with transtracheal aspiration and/or injection

31613 Tracheostoma revision; simple, without flap rotation

31614 complex, with flap rotation

Endoscopy

For endoscopy procedures, code appropriate endoscopy of each anatomic site examined. Surgical bronchoscopy always includes diagnostic bronchoscopy when performed by the same physician. Codes 31622-31646 include fluoroscopic guidance, when performed.

(For tracheoscopy, see laryngoscopy codes 31515-31578)

31615 Tracheobronchoscopy through established tracheostomy incision

(31620, 31621 have been deleted. To report, use 31622)

31622 Bronchoscopy (rigid or flexible); diagnostic, with or without cell washing (separate procedure)
➲ *CPT Assistant* Jul 96:11; Nov 98:12; Dec 98:8; Mar 99:3; Nov 99:13; Apr 00:10

31623 with brushing or protected brushings
➲ *CPT Assistant* Nov 98:12; Mar 99:3; Nov 99:13

31624 with bronchial alveolar lavage
➲ *CPT Assistant* Nov 98:12; Feb 99:9; Mar 99:3, 11; April 99:11; Nov 99:13

31625 with biopsy
➲ *CPT Assistant* Spring 91:2

Bronchoscopy
31622–31656

A rigid or flexible bronchoscope is inserted through the oropharynx, vocal cords and beyond the trachea into the right/left bronchi.

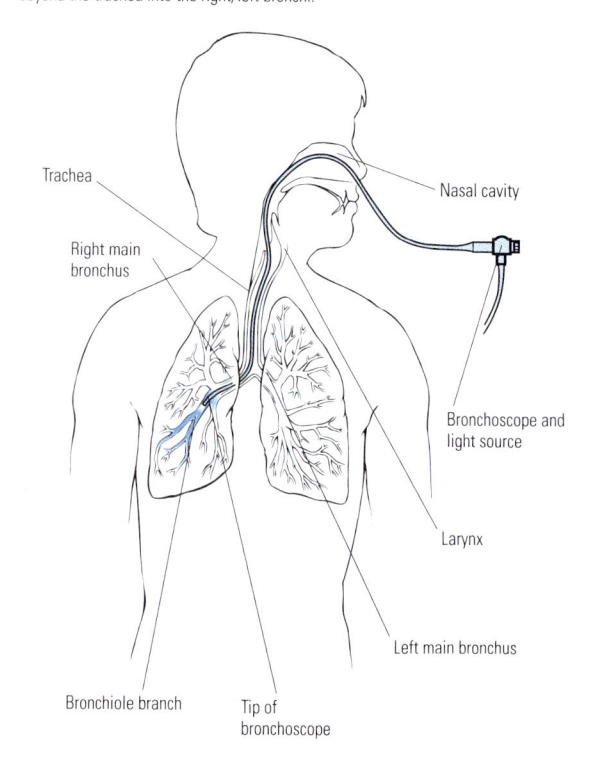

Trachea

Nasal cavity

Right main bronchus

Bronchoscope and light source

Larynx

Left main bronchus

Bronchiole branch

Tip of bronchoscope

(31626 has been deleted. To report, use 31625)

(31627 has been deleted. To report, use 31622)

31628   with transbronchial lung biopsy, with or without fluoroscopic guidance

31629   with transbronchial needle aspiration biopsy
→ *CPT Assistant* Apr 00:10

31630   with tracheal or bronchial dilation or closed reduction of fracture

31631   with tracheal dilation and placement of tracheal stent

31635   with removal of foreign body

31640   with excision of tumor

▲**31641**   Bronchoscopy, (rigid or flexible); with destruction of tumor or relief of stenosis by any method other than excision (eg, laser therapy, cryotherapy)
→ *CPT Assistant* Nov 99:13; Sep 00:5; *CPT Changes* 2002

(For bronchoscopic photodynamic therapy, report 31641 in addition to 96570, 96571 as appropriate)

31643   with placement of catheter(s) for intracavitary radioelement application
→ *CPT Assistant* Nov 98:12; Mar 99:3

(For intracavitary radioelement application, see 77761-77763, 77781-77784)

31645   with therapeutic aspiration of tracheobronchial tree, initial (eg, drainage of lung abscess)

31646   with therapeutic aspiration of tracheobronchial tree, subsequent

(For catheter aspiration of tracheobronchial tree at bedside, use 31725)

(31650, 31651 have been deleted. To report, see 31645, 31646)

31656   with injection of contrast material for segmental bronchography (fiberscope only)

(For radiological supervision and interpretation, see 71040, 71060)

(31659 has been deleted)

Introduction

(For endotracheal intubation, use 31500)

(For tracheal aspiration under direct vision, see 31515)

31700   Catheterization, transglottic (separate procedure)
→ *CPT Assistant* Feb 01:11

31708   Instillation of contrast material for laryngography or bronchography, without catheterization

(For radiological supervision and interpretation, see 70373, 71040, 71060)

31710   Catheterization for bronchography, with or without instillation of contrast material

(For bronchoscopic catheterization for bronchography, fiberscope only, use 31656)

(For radiological supervision and interpretation, see 71040, 71060)

31715   Transtracheal injection for bronchography

(For radiological supervision and interpretation, see 71040, 71060)

(For prolonged services, see 99354-99360)

31717   Catheterization with bronchial brush biopsy
→ *CPT Assistant* Feb 01:11

(31719 has been deleted. To report, use 31730)

31720   Catheter aspiration (separate procedure); nasotracheal

31725   tracheobronchial with fiberscope, bedside

31730   Transtracheal (percutaneous) introduction of needle wire dilator/stent or indwelling tube for oxygen therapy

Repair

31750   Tracheoplasty; cervical

31755   tracheopharyngeal fistulization, each stage

31760   intrathoracic

31766   Carinal reconstruction

31770   Bronchoplasty; graft repair

31775   excision stenosis and anastomosis

(For lobectomy and bronchoplasty, use 32501)

31780   Excision tracheal stenosis and anastomosis; cervical

31781   cervicothoracic

31785   Excision of tracheal tumor or carcinoma; cervical

31786   thoracic

31800   Suture of tracheal wound or injury; cervical

31805   intrathoracic

31820   Surgical closure tracheostomy or fistula; without plastic repair

31825   with plastic repair

(For repair tracheoesophageal fistula, see 43305, 43312)

31830   Revision of tracheostomy scar

Other Procedures

31899   Unlisted procedure, trachea, bronchi

Lungs and Pleura

Incision

⊘ **32000** * Thoracentesis, puncture of pleural cavity for aspiration, initial or subsequent

➔ *CPT Assistant* Spring 91:4

(▶If imaging guidance is performed,◀ see 76003, 76360, ▶76942◀)

Thoracentesis
32000-32002

Accumulated fluid or air is removed from the pleural space by puncturing space between the ribs. In 32002, a tube is inserted and a syringe attached to the catheter for the removal of fluid and/or air.

(32001 has been deleted. To report, use 32997)

⊘ **32002** Thoracentesis with insertion of tube with or without water seal (eg, for pneumothorax) (separate procedure)

▶(If imaging guidance is performed, see 76003, 76360, 76942)◀

32005 Chemical pleurodesis (eg, for recurrent or persistent pneumothorax)

⊘ **32020** Tube thoracostomy with or without water seal (eg, for abscess, hemothorax, empyema) (separate procedure)

(If imaging guidance is performed, use 75989)

Insertion of Chest Tube
32020

A trocar is used to puncture through the space between the ribs into the pleural cavity for the insertion of a chest tube via a thoracic drainage system to drain air and/or fluid from the pleural space, promoting lung re-expansion.

32035 Thoracostomy; with rib resection for empyema

32036 with open flap drainage for empyema

32095 Thoracotomy, limited, for biopsy of lung or pleura

(To report wound exploration due to penetrating trauma without thoractomy, use 20102)

32100 Thoracotomy, major; with exploration and biopsy

32110 with control of traumatic hemorrhage and/or repair of lung tear

32120 for postoperative complications

32124 with open intrapleural pneumonolysis

32140 with cyst(s) removal, with or without a pleural procedure

32141 with excision-plication of bullae, with or without any pleural procedure

(For lung volume reduction, use 32491)

32150 with removal of intrapleural foreign body or fibrin deposit

32151 with removal of intrapulmonary foreign body

32160 with cardiac massage

(For segmental or other resections of lung, see 32480-32525)

⊘ =Modifier '-51' Exempt ▶ ◀=New or Revised Text ✚=Add-on Code CPT 2002

32200 Pneumonostomy; with open drainage of abscess or cyst

32201 with percutaneous drainage of abscess or cyst
➔ *CPT Assistant* Nov 97:15-16; Mar 98:8

(For radiological supervision and interpretation, use 75989)

32215 Pleural scarification for repeat pneumothorax

32220 Decortication, pulmonary (separate procedure); total

32225 partial

Excision

32310 Pleurectomy, parietal (separate procedure)

(32315 has been deleted. To report, use 32310)

32320 Decortication and parietal pleurectomy

32400✱ Biopsy, pleura; percutaneous needle
➔ *CPT Assistant* Fall 94:1, 2

▶(If imaging guidance is performed, see 76003, 76360, 76393, 76942)◀

▶(For fine needle aspiration, use 10021 or 10022)◀

▶(For evaluation of fine needle aspirate, see 88172, 88173)◀

32402 open
➔ *CPT Assistant* Fall 94:1, 2

32405 Biopsy, lung or mediastinum, percutaneous needle
➔ *CPT Assistant* Fall 94:1, 2; Mar 97:4

(For radiological supervision and interpretation, see ▶76003, 76360, 76393, 76942◀)

(For fine needle aspiration, use ▶10022◀)

▶(For evaluation of fine needle aspirate, see 88172, 88173)◀

▲ **32420**✱ Pneumocentesis, puncture of lung for aspiration
➔ *CPT Assistant* Fall 94:1, 2; *CPT Changes* 2002

32440 Removal of lung, total pneumonectomy;
➔ *CPT Assistant* Fall 94:1

32442 with resection of segment of trachea followed by broncho-tracheal anastomosis (sleeve pneumonectomy)
➔ *CPT Assistant* Fall 94:1, 3

32445 extrapleural
➔ *CPT Assistant* Fall 94:1, 3

(32450 has been deleted. To report, use 32445 and 32540)

32480 Removal of lung, other than total pneumonectomy; single lobe (lobectomy)
➔ *CPT Assistant* Spring 91:5; Fall 94:1, 4

32482 two lobes (bilobectomy)
➔ *CPT Assistant* Fall 94:1, 4

32484 single segment (segmentectomy)
➔ *CPT Assistant* Fall 94:1, 4

(32485 has been deleted. To report, use 32501)

32486 with circumferential resection of segment of bronchus followed by broncho-bronchial anastomosis (sleeve lobectomy)
➔ *CPT Assistant* Fall 94:1, 4

32488 all remaining lung following previous removal of a portion of lung (completion pneumonectomy)
➔ *CPT Assistant* Fall 94:1, 4

(32490 has been deleted. To report, use 32320 and the appropriate removal of lung code)

32491 excision-plication of emphysematous lung(s) (bullous or non-bullous) for lung volume reduction, sternal split or transthoracic approach, with or without any pleural procedure

32500 wedge resection, single or multiple
➔ *CPT Assistant* Fall 94:1, 5; Mar 97:4

+ **32501** Resection and repair of portion of bronchus (bronchoplasty) when performed at time of lobectomy or segmentectomy (List separately in addition to code for primary procedure)

(Use 32501 in conjunction with codes 32480, 32482, 32484)

(32501 is to be used when a portion of the bronchus to preserved lung is removed and requires plastic closure to preserve function of that preserved lung. It is not to be used for closure for the proximal end of a resected bronchus.)

32520 Resection of lung; with resection of chest wall

32522 with reconstruction of chest wall, without prosthesis

32525 with major reconstruction of chest wall, with prosthesis

32540 Extrapleural enucleation of empyema (empyemectomy)

(32545 has been deleted. To report, use 32540 and the appropriate removal of lung code)

Endoscopy

Surgical thoracoscopy always includes diagnostic thoracoscopy.

For endoscopic procedures, code appropriate endoscopy of each anatomic site examined.

Thoracoscopy
32601-32665

The inside of the chest cavity is examined through a fiberoptic endoscope.

Placement of endoscope

Endoscope

Pleural cavity

Lung

Heart

Schematic transverse section of thoracic region

32601 Thoracoscopy, diagnostic (separate procedure); lungs and pleural space, without biopsy
➔ *CPT Assistant* Fall 94:1, 4

32602 lungs and pleural space, with biopsy
➔ *CPT Assistant* Fall 94:1, 4 Jun 97:5

32603 pericardial sac, without biopsy
➔ *CPT Assistant* Fall 94:1, 4

32604 pericardial sac, with biopsy
➔ *CPT Assistant* Fall 94:1, 4

32605 mediastinal space, without biopsy
➔ *CPT Assistant* Fall 94:1, 4

32606 mediastinal space, with biopsy
➔ *CPT Assistant* Fall 94:1, 5

(Surgical thoracoscopy always includes diagnostic thoracoscopy)

▲**32650** Thoracoscopy, surgical; with pleurodesis (eg, mechanical or chemical)
➔ *CPT Assistant* Fall 94:1, 6; *CPT Changes* 2002

32651 with partial pulmonary decortication
➔ *CPT Assistant* Fall 94:1, 6

32652 with total pulmonary decortication, including intrapleural pneumonolysis
➔ *CPT Assistant* Fall 94:1, 6

32653 with removal of intrapleural foreign body or fibrin deposit
➔ *CPT Assistant* Fall 94:1, 6

32654 with control of traumatic hemorrhage
➔ *CPT Assistant* Fall 94:1, 6

32655 with excision-plication of bullae, including any pleural procedure
➔ *CPT Assistant* Fall 94:1, 6

32656 with parietal pleurectomy
➔ *CPT Assistant* Fall 94:1, 6

32657 with wedge resection of lung, single or multiple
➔ *CPT Assistant* Fall 94:1, 6

32658 with removal of clot or foreign body from pericardial sac
➔ *CPT Assistant* Fall 94:1, 6

32659 with creation of pericardial window or partial resection of pericardial sac for drainage
➔ *CPT Assistant* Fall 94:1, 6

32660 with total pericardiectomy
➔ *CPT Assistant* Fall 94:1, 6

32661 with excision of pericardial cyst, tumor, or mass
➔ *CPT Assistant* Fall 94:1, 6

32662 with excision of mediastinal cyst, tumor, or mass
➔ *CPT Assistant* Fall 94:1, 6

32663 with lobectomy, total or segmental
➔ *CPT Assistant* Fall 94:1, 6

32664 with thoracic sympathectomy
➔ *CPT Assistant* Fall 94:1; Oct 99:10

32665 with esophagomyotomy (Heller type)
➔ *CPT Assistant* Fall 94:1, 6

(32700 and 32705 have been deleted. To report, see 32601-32606)

Repair

32800 Repair lung hernia through chest wall

32810 Closure of chest wall following open flap drainage for empyema (Clagett type procedure)

32815 Open closure of major bronchial fistula

32820 Major reconstruction, chest wall (posttraumatic)

Lung Transplantation

32850   Donor pneumonectomy(ies) with preparation and maintenance of allograft (cadaver)

32851   Lung transplant, single; without cardiopulmonary bypass

32852   with cardiopulmonary bypass

32853   Lung transplant, double (bilateral sequential or en bloc); without cardiopulmonary bypass

32854   with cardiopulmonary bypass

Surgical Collapse Therapy; Thoracoplasty

(See also 32520-32525)

32900   Resection of ribs, extrapleural, all stages

32905   Thoracoplasty, Schede type or extrapleural (all stages);

32906   with closure of bronchopleural fistula

(For open closure of major bronchial fistula, use 32815)

(For resection of first rib for thoracic outlet compression, see 21615, 21616)

32940   Pneumonolysis, extraperiosteal, including filling or packing procedures

32960*   Pneumothorax, therapeutic, intrapleural injection of air

Other Procedures

32997   Total lung lavage (unilateral)
➔ *CPT Assistant* Nov 98:13; Nov 99:14; *CPT Changes* 2000; 2002

(For bronchoscopic bronchial alveolar lavage, use 31624)

32999   Unlisted procedure, lungs and pleura

Notes

⊘ =Modifier '-51' Exempt   ▶◀=New or Revised Text   ✚=Add-on Code   CPT 2002

Cardiovascular System

Selective vascular catheterizations should be coded to include introduction and all lesser order selective catheterizations used in the approach (eg, the description for a selective right middle cerebral artery catheterization includes the introduction and placement catheterization of the right common and internal carotid arteries).

Additional second and/or third order arterial catheterizations within the same family of arteries supplied by a single first order artery should be expressed by 36218 or 36248. Additional first order or higher catheterizations in vascular families supplied by a first order vessel different from a previously selected and coded family should be separately coded using the conventions described above.

> (For monitoring, operation of pump and other nonsurgical services, see 99190-99192, 99291, 99292, 99354-99360)
>
> (For other medical or laboratory related services, see appropriate section)
>
> (For radiological supervision and interpretation, see 75600-75978)

Heart and Pericardium

Pericardium

33010✳ Pericardiocentesis; initial

> (For radiological supervision and interpretation, use 76930)

33011✳ subsequent

> (For radiological supervision and interpretation, use 76930)

33015 Tube pericardiostomy

33020 Pericardiotomy for removal of clot or foreign body (primary procedure)

33025 Creation of pericardial window or partial resection for drainage

33030 Pericardiectomy, subtotal or complete; without cardiopulmonary bypass

33031 with cardiopulmonary bypass

> (33035 has been deleted. To report, use 33031)

33050 Excision of pericardial cyst or tumor

> (33100 has been deleted. To report, see 33030, 33031)

Cardiac Tumor

33120 Excision of intracardiac tumor, resection with cardiopulmonary bypass

33130 Resection of external cardiac tumor

Transmyocardial Revascularization

33140 Transmyocardial laser revascularization, by thoracotomy; (separate procedure)
> ➔ *CPT Assistant* Nov 99:14; Nov 00:5,; *CPT Changes* 2000; 2001; 2002

+ 33141 performed at the time of other open cardiac procedure(s) (List separately in addition to code for primary procedure)
> ➔ *CPT Changes* 2001

> (Use 33141 in conjunction with codes ▶33400-33496,◀ 33510-33536)

Pacemaker or Pacing Cardioverter-Defibrillator

A pacemaker system includes a pulse generator containing electronics and a battery, and one or more electrodes (leads). Pulse generators are placed in a subcutaneous "pocket" created in either a subclavicular site or underneath the abdominal muscles just below the ribcage. Electrodes may be inserted through a vein (transvenous) or they may be placed on the surface of the heart (epicardial). The epicardial location of electrodes requires a thoracotomy for electrode insertion.

A single chamber pacemaker system includes a pulse generator and one electrode inserted in either the atrium or ventricle. A dual chamber pacemaker system includes a pulse generator and one electrode inserted in the atrium and one electrode inserted in the ventricle.

Like a pacemaker system, a pacing cardioverter-defibrillator system includes a pulse generator and electrodes, although pacing cardioverter-defibrillators may require multiple leads, even when only a single chamber is being paced. A pacing cardioverter-defibrillator system may be inserted in a single chamber (pacing in the ventricle) or in dual chambers (pacing in atrium and ventricle). These devices use a combination of antitachycardia pacing, low energy cardioversion or defibrillating shocks to treat ventricular tachycardia or ventricular fibrillation.

Pacing cardioverter-defibrillator pulse generators may be implanted in a subcutaneous infraclavicular pocket or in an abdominal pocket. Removal of a pacing cardioverter-

Cardio 33010

defibrillator pulse generator requires opening of the existing subcutaneous pocket and disconnection of the pulse generator from its electrode(s). A thoracotomy (or laparotomy in the case of abdominally placed pulse generators) is not required to remove the pulse generator.

The electrodes (leads) of a pacing cardioverter-defibrillator system are positioned in the heart via the venous system (transvenously), in most circumstances. Electrode positioning on the epicardial surface of the heart requires a thoracotomy (codes 33245-33246). Removal of electrode(s) may first be attempted by transvenous extraction (code 33244). However, if transvenous extraction is unsuccessful, a thoracotomy may be required to remove the electrodes (code 33243).

When the "battery" of a pacemaker or pacing cardioverter-defibrillator is changed, it is actually the pulse generator that is changed. Replacement of a pulse generator should be reported with a code for removal of the pulse generator and another code for insertion of a pulse generator.

These procedures include repositioning or replacement in the first 14 days after the insertion (or replacement) of the device.

Modifiers '-76' and '-77' are not reported with pacemaker or pacing cardioverter-defibrillator codes after 14 days as these are considered new, not repeat, services.

> (For electronic, telephonic analysis of internal pacemaker system, see 93731-93736)

> (For radiological supervision and interpretation with insertion of pacemaker, use 71090)

33200 Insertion of permanent pacemaker with epicardial electrode(s); by thoracotomy
> ➜ *CPT Assistant* Summer 94:10, 17; Jun 00:5

33201 by xiphoid approach
> ➜ *CPT Assistant* Summer 94:10, 17

> (33205 has been deleted. To report, see 33206-33208)

33206 Insertion or replacement of permanent pacemaker with transvenous electrode(s); atrial
> ➜ *CPT Assistant* Summer 94:10, 17; Oct 96:9; Nov 99:15

33207 ventricular
> ➜ *CPT Assistant* Summer 94:10, 17; Oct 96:9; Nov 99:15

33208 atrial and ventricular
> ➜ *CPT Assistant* Summer 94:10, 17; Jul 96:10; Nov 99:15

> (Codes 33206-33208 include subcutaneous insertion of the pulse generator and transvenous placement of electrode(s))

33210 Insertion or replacement of temporary transvenous single chamber cardiac electrode or pacemaker catheter (separate procedure)
> ➜ *CPT Assistant* Summer 94:10, 17

Temporary Pacemaker
33210

The pacemaker pulse generator with the electrodes transvenously placed.

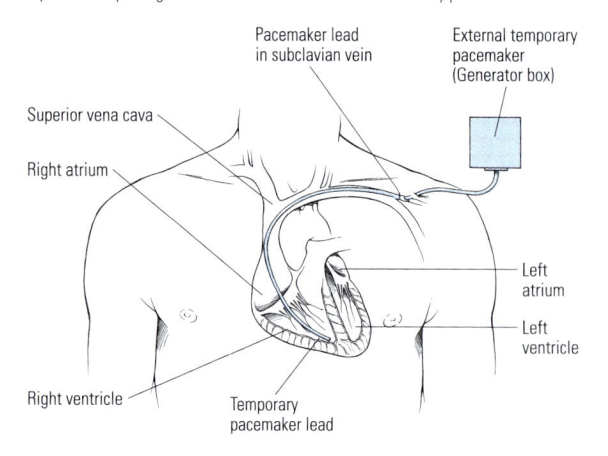

33211 Insertion or replacement of temporary transvenous dual chamber pacing electrodes (separate procedure)
> ➜ *CPT Assistant* Summer 94:10, 17

33212 Insertion or replacement of pacemaker pulse generator only; single chamber, atrial or ventricular
> ➜ *CPT Assistant* Summer 94:10, 18; Fall 94:24

33213 dual chamber
> ➜ *CPT Assistant* Summer 94:10, 18; Oct 96:10; Feb 98:11

Implanted Pacemaker
33212-33214

A. In 33212, a pacemaker pulse generator is inserted or replaced in a single chamber.

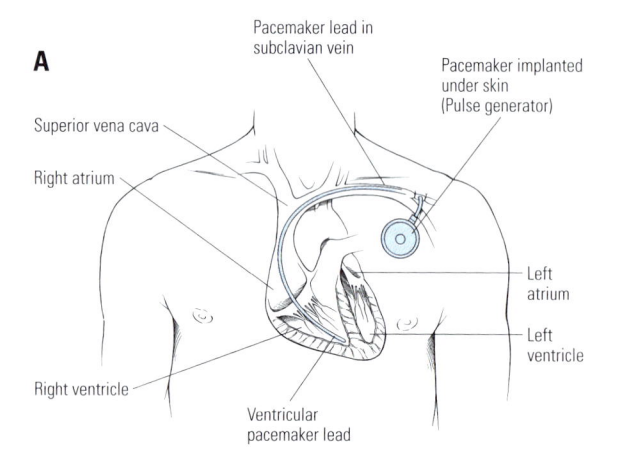

B. In 33213, it is inserted or replaced in two chambers. In 33214, an upgrade to an existing pacemaker system is done.

B

Pacemaker leads in subclavian vein

Pacemaker implanted under skin (Pulse generator)

Superior vena cava

Atrial pacemaker lead

Right atrium

Left atrium

Left ventricle

Right ventricle

Ventricular pacemaker lead

33214 Upgrade of implanted pacemaker system, conversion of single chamber system to dual chamber system (includes removal of previously placed pulse generator, testing of existing lead, insertion of new lead, insertion of new pulse generator)

➔ *CPT Assistant* Summer 94:10, 18; Fall 94:24

33216 Insertion or repositioning of a transvenous electrode (15 days or more after initial insertion); single chamber (one electrode) permanent pacemaker or single chamber pacing cardioverter-defibrillator

➔ *CPT Assistant* Summer 94:10, 18; Jul 96:10; Nov 99:15-16; Jun 00:5; *CPT Changes* 2000

33217 dual chamber (two electrodes) permanent pacemaker or dual chamber pacing cardioverter-defibrillator

➔ *CPT Assistant* Summer 94:10, 18; Jul 96:10; Nov 99:15-16; Jul 00:5; *CPT Changes* 2000

(Do not report 33216-33217 in conjunction with code 33214)

33218 Repair of single transvenous electrode for a single chamber, permanent pacemaker or single chamber pacing cardioverter-defibrillator

➔ *CPT Assistant* Summer 94:10, 19; Oct 96:1, 9; Nov 99:15-16; *CPT Changes* 2000

(33219 has been deleted. To report, see 33212 or 33213 and 33218 or 33220)

33220 Repair of two transvenous electrodes for a dual chamber permanent pacemaker or dual chamber pacing cardioverter-defibrillator

➔ *CPT Assistant* Summer 94:10, 19; Oct 96:9; Nov 99:15-16; *CPT Changes* 2000

33222 Revision or relocation of skin pocket for pacemaker

➔ *CPT Assistant* Spring 94:30; Summer 94:10; Nov 99:15-16; *CPT Changes* 2000

33223 Revision of skin pocket for single or dual chamber pacing cardioverter-defibrillator

➔ *CPT Assistant* Summer 94:10, 19; Nov 99:15-16; *CPT Changes* 2000

(33232 has been deleted. To report, see 33233, 33234, 33236)

33233 Removal of permanent pacemaker pulse generator

➔ *CPT Assistant* Summer 94:10, 19; Fall 94:24; Oct 96:10; Nov 99:16; *CPT Changes* 2000

33234 Removal of transvenous pacemaker electrode(s); single lead system, atrial or ventricular

➔ *CPT Assistant* Summer 94:10, 19; Nov 99:16; *CPT Changes* 2000

33235 dual lead system

➔ *CPT Assistant* Summer 94:10, 19; Nov 99:16; *CPT Changes* 2000

33236 Removal of permanent epicardial pacemaker and electrodes by thoracotomy; single lead system, atrial or ventricular

➔ *CPT Assistant* Summer 94:10, 19; Nov 99:16; *CPT Changes* 2000

33237 dual lead system

➔ *CPT Assistant* Summer 94:10, 19; Nov 99:16; *CPT Changes* 2000

33238 Removal of permanent transvenous electrode(s) by thoracotomy

➔ *CPT Assistant* Summer 94:10, 19; Nov 99:16; *CPT Changes* 2000

33240 Insertion of single or dual chamber pacing cardioverter-defibrillator pulse generator

➔ *CPT Assistant* Summer 94:40; Jun 96:10; Nov 99:16-17; Jul 00:5; *CPT Changes* 2000

33241 Subcutaneous removal of single or dual chamber pacing cardioverter-defibrillator pulse generator

➔ *CPT Assistant* Summer 94:40; Nov 99:16-17; *CPT Changes* 2000

(For removal of electrode(s) by thoracotomy, use 33243 in conjunction with code 33241)

(For removal of electrode(s) by transvenous extraction, use 33244 in conjunction with code 33241)

(For removal and reinsertion of a pacing cardioverter-defibrillator system (pulse generator and electrodes), report 33241 and 33243 or 33244 and 33249)

(33242 has been deleted. To report, see 33218, 33220)

33243 Removal of single or dual chamber pacing cardioverter-defibrillator electrode(s); by thoracotomy

➔ *CPT Assistant* Summer 94:40; Nov 99:16-17; *CPT Changes* 2000

33244 by transvenous extraction

➔ *CPT Assistant* Summer 94:40; Nov 99:16-17; Jul 00:5; *CPT Changes* 2000

(For subcutaneous removal of the pulse generator, use 33241 in conjunction with code 33243 or 33244)

33245 Insertion of epicardial single or dual chamber pacing cardioverter-defibrillator electrodes by thoracotomy;

➔ *CPT Assistant* Summer 94:21; Nov 99:16-17; *CPT Changes* 2000

33246 with insertion of pulse generator

➔ *CPT Assistant* Summer 94:21; Nov 99:16-17; *CPT Changes* 2000

(33247 has been deleted. To report, use 33216)

(33248 has been deleted. To report, see 33242, 33243, 33244)

33249 Insertion or repositioning of electrode lead(s) for single or dual chamber pacing cardioverter-defibrillator and insertion of pulse generator

➲ *CPT Assistant* Summer 94:21; Nov 99:16-17; *CPT Changes* 2000

(For removal and reinsertion of a pacing cardioverter-defibrillator system (pulse generator and electrodes), report 33241 and 33243 or 33244 and 33249)

Electrophysiologic Operative Procedures

▲ **33250** Operative ablation of supraventricular arrhythmogenic focus or pathway (eg, Wolff-Parkinson-White, atrioventricular node re-entry), tract(s) and/or focus (foci); without cardiopulmonary bypass

➲ *CPT Assistant* Summer 94:16; Nov 99:17-18; *CPT Changes* 2000; 2002

33251 with cardiopulmonary bypass

➲ *CPT Assistant* Summer 94:16; Nov 99:17-18; *CPT Changes* 2000

33253 Operative incisions and reconstruction of atria for treatment of atrial fibrillation or atrial flutter (eg, maze procedure)

(33260 has been deleted. To report, use 33261)

33261 Operative ablation of ventricular arrhythmogenic focus with cardiopulmonary bypass

➲ *CPT Assistant* Summer 94:16

Patient-Activated Event Recorder

33282 Implantation of patient-activated cardiac event recorder

➲ *CPT Assistant* Nov 99:17-18; Jul 00:5; *CPT Changes* 2000

(Initial implantation includes programming. For subsequent electronic analysis and/or reprogramming, use 93727)

33284 Removal of an implantable, patient-activated cardiac event recorder

➲ *CPT Assistant* Nov 99:17-18; Jul 00:5; *CPT Changes* 2000

Wounds of the Heart and Great Vessels

33300 Repair of cardiac wound; without bypass

33305 with cardiopulmonary bypass

33310 Cardiotomy, exploratory (includes removal of foreign body); without bypass

33315 with cardiopulmonary bypass

33320 Suture repair of aorta or great vessels; without shunt or cardiopulmonary bypass

33321 with shunt bypass

33322 with cardiopulmonary bypass

33330 Insertion of graft, aorta or great vessels; without shunt, or cardiopulmonary bypass

33332 with shunt bypass

33335 with cardiopulmonary bypass

(33350 has been deleted)

Cardiac Valves

Aortic Valve

33400 Valvuloplasty, aortic valve; open, with cardiopulmonary bypass

33401 open, with inflow occlusion

33403 using transventricular dilation, with cardiopulmonary bypass

33404 Construction of apical-aortic conduit

33405 Replacement, aortic valve, with cardiopulmonary bypass; with prosthetic valve other than homograft or stentless valve

➲ *CPT Assistant* Nov 99:18; *CPT Changes* 2000

▲ **33406** with allograft valve (freehand)

➲ *CPT Assistant* Nov 99:18; *CPT Changes* 2002

(33407 has been deleted. To report, use 33403)

(33408 has been deleted. To report, use 33401)

33410 with stentless tissue valve

➲ *CPT Assistant* Nov 99:18; *CPT Changes* 2000

33411 Replacement, aortic valve; with aortic annulus enlargement, noncoronary cusp

33412 with transventricular aortic annulus enlargement (Konno procedure)

▲ **33413** by translocation of autologous pulmonary valve with allograft replacement of pulmonary valve (Ross procedure)

➲ *CPT Changes* 2002

33414 Repair of left ventricular outflow tract obstruction by patch enlargement of the outflow tract

33415 Resection or incision of subvalvular tissue for discrete subvalvular aortic stenosis

33416 Ventriculomyotomy (-myectomy) for idiopathic hypertrophic subaortic stenosis (eg, asymmetric septal hypertrophy)

33417 Aortoplasty (gusset) for supravalvular stenosis

Mitral Valve

33420 Valvotomy, mitral valve; closed heart

33422 open heart, with cardiopulmonary bypass

33425 Valvuloplasty, mitral valve, with cardiopulmonary bypass;

33426 with prosthetic ring

33427 radical reconstruction, with or without ring

33430 Replacement, mitral valve, with cardiopulmonary bypass

Tricuspid Valve

(33450 has been deleted. To report, see 33463, 33464)

(33452 has been deleted. To report, see 33463, 33464)

33460   Valvectomy, tricuspid valve, with cardiopulmonary bypass

33463   Valvuloplasty, tricuspid valve; without ring insertion

33464   with ring insertion

33465   Replacement, tricuspid valve, with cardiopulmonary bypass

33468   Tricuspid valve repositioning and plication for Ebstein anomaly

Pulmonary Valve

33470   Valvotomy, pulmonary valve, closed heart; transventricular

33471   via pulmonary artery

(To report percutaneous valvuloplasty of pulmonary valve, use 92990)

33472   Valvotomy, pulmonary valve, open heart; with inflow occlusion

33474   with cardiopulmonary bypass

33475   Replacement, pulmonary valve

33476   Right ventricular resection for infundibular stenosis, with or without commissurotomy

33478   Outflow tract augmentation (gusset), with or without commissurotomy or infundibular resection

(33480-33492 have been deleted. To report, see 33400-33478 and add modifier '-51' to the secondary valve procedure code when multiple valve procedures are performed.)

Other Valvular Procedures

33496   Repair of non-structural prosthetic valve dysfunction with cardiopulmonary bypass (separate procedure)
→ *CPT Assistant* Nov 97:16

(For reoperation, use 33530 in addition to 33496)

Coronary Artery Anomalies

Basic procedures include endarterectomy or angioplasty.

33500   Repair of coronary arteriovenous or arteriocardiac chamber fistula; with cardiopulmonary bypass

33501   without cardiopulmonary bypass

33502   Repair of anomalous coronary artery; by ligation

33503   by graft, without cardiopulmonary bypass

33504   by graft, with cardiopulmonary bypass

33505   with construction of intrapulmonary artery tunnel (Takeuchi procedure)

33506   by translocation from pulmonary artery to aorta

Venous Grafting Only for Coronary Artery Bypass

The following codes are used to report coronary artery bypass procedures using venous grafts only. These codes should NOT be used to report the performance of coronary artery bypass procedures using arterial grafts and venous grafts during the same procedure. See 33517-33523 and 33533-33536 for reporting combined arterial-venous grafts.

Procurement of the saphenous vein graft is included in the description of the work for 33510-33516 and should not be reported as a separate service or co-surgery. When graft procurement is performed by surgical assistant, add modifier '-80' to 33510-33516.

33510   Coronary artery bypass, vein only; single coronary venous graft
→ *CPT Assistant* Fall 91:5; Winter 92:12; Jul 99:11

Coronary Artery Bypass—Venous Grafting Only
33510-33516

A. Use 33510 to report a single coronary venous graft.

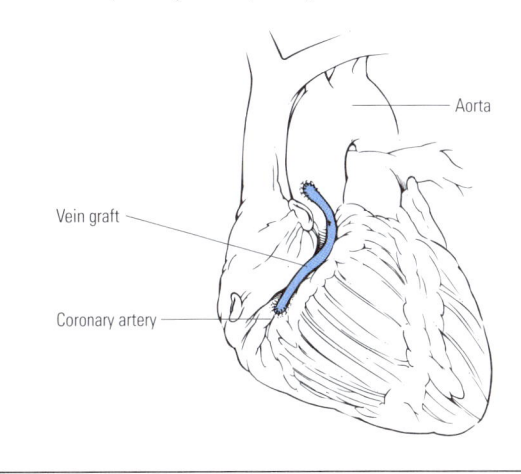

33511   two coronary venous grafts
→ *CPT Assistant* Fall 91:5; Winter 92:12; Jul 99:11

33512 three coronary venous grafts
→ *CPT Assistant* Fall 91:5; Winter 92:12

Coronary Artery Bypass—Venous Grafting Only
(continued)

B. Report 33512 when three coronary venous grafts are performed.

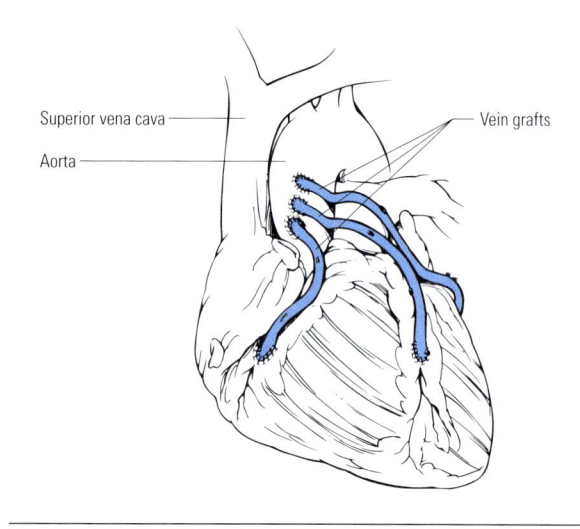

Superior vena cava

Aorta

Vein grafts

33513 four coronary venous grafts
→ *CPT Assistant* Fall 91:5; Winter 92:12

33514 five coronary venous grafts
→ *CPT Assistant* Fall 91:5; Winter 92:12

33516 six or more coronary venous grafts
→ *CPT Assistant* Fall 91:5; Winter 92:12; Jul 99:11

Combined Arterial-Venous Grafting for Coronary Bypass

The following codes are used to report coronary artery bypass procedures using venous grafts and arterial grafts during the same procedure. These codes may NOT be used alone.

To report combined arterial-venous grafts it is necessary to report two codes: 1) the appropriate combined arterial-venous graft code (33517-33523); and 2) the appropriate arterial graft code (33533-33536).

Procurement of the saphenous vein graft is included in the description of the work for 33517-33523 and should not be reported as a separate service or co-surgery. Procurement of the artery for grafting is included in the description of the work for 33533-33536 and should not be reported as a separate service or co-surgery, except when an upper extremity artery (eg, radial artery) is procured. To report harvesting of an upper extremity artery, use 35600 in addition to the bypass procedure(s). When arterial and/or venous graft procurement is performed by surgical assistant, add modifier '-80' to 33517-33523, 33533-33536, as appropriate.

⊘ **33517** Coronary artery bypass, using venous graft(s) and arterial graft(s); single vein graft (List separately in addition to code for arterial graft)
→ *CPT Assistant* Fall 91:5; Winter 92:13; Nov 99:18; *CPT Changes* 2000

Coronary Artery Bypass—Combined Arterial-Venous Grafting
33517-33530

Both venous and arterial grafts are used in these bypass procedures. The appropriate arterial graft codes (33533-33536) must also be reported in conjunction with codes 33517-33523.

Left subclavian artery

Arterial graft—left internal mammary artery

Aorta

Vein graft

Coronary Artery Bypass—Sequential Combined Arterial-Venous Grafting
33517-33530

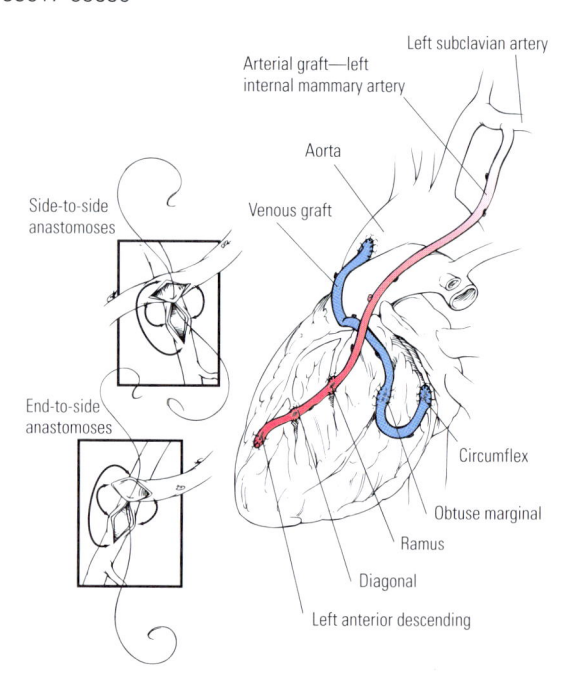

Left subclavian artery

Arterial graft—left internal mammary artery

Aorta

Side-to-side anastomoses

Venous graft

End-to-side anastomoses

Circumflex

Obtuse marginal

Ramus

Diagonal

Left anterior descending

Note: To determine the number of bypass grafts in a coronary artery bypass (CABG), count the number of distal anastomoses (contact point(s)) where the bypass graft artery or vein is sutured to the diseased coronary artery(s).

⊘ **33518**   two venous grafts (List separately in addition to code for arterial graft)

→ *CPT Assistant* Fall 91:5; Winter 92:13

⊘ **33519**   three venous grafts (List separately in addition to code for arterial graft)

→ *CPT Assistant* Fall 91:5; Winter 92:13

(33520 has been deleted)

⊘ **33521**   four venous grafts (List separately in addition to code for arterial graft)

→ *CPT Assistant* Fall 91:5; Winter 92:13

⊘ **33522**   five venous grafts (List separately in addition to code for arterial graft)

→ *CPT Assistant* Fall 91:5; Winter 92:13

⊘ **33523**   six or more venous grafts (List separately in addition to code for arterial graft)

→ *CPT Assistant* Fall 91:5; Winter 92:13

(33525, 33528 have been deleted)

+ **33530**   Reoperation, coronary artery bypass procedure or valve procedure, more than one month after original operation (List separately in addition to code for primary procedure)

→ *CPT Assistant* Fall 91:5; Winter 92:13

(Use 33530 in conjunction with codes 33400-33496; 33510-33536, 33863)

(33532 has been deleted. To report, use 33999)

Arterial Grafting for Coronary Artery Bypass

The following codes are used to report coronary artery bypass procedures using either arterial grafts only or a combination of arterial-venous grafts. The codes include the use of the internal mammary artery, gastroepiploic artery, epigastric artery, radial artery, and arterial conduits procured from other sites.

To report combined arterial-venous grafts it is necessary to report two codes: 1) the appropriate arterial graft code (33533-33536); and 2) the appropriate combined arterial-venous graft code (33517-33523).

Procurement of the artery for grafting is included in the description of the work for 33533-33536 and should not be reported as a separate service or co-surgery, except when an upper extremity artery (eg, radial artery) is procured. To report harvesting of an upper extremity artery, use 35600 in addition to the bypass procedure. Procurement of the saphenous vein graft is included in the description of the work for 33517-33523 and should not be reported as a separate service or co-surgery. When arterial and/or venous graft procurement is performed by surgical assistant, add modifier '-80' to 33517-33523, 33533-33536, as appropriate.

33533   Coronary artery bypass, using arterial graft(s); single arterial graft

→ *CPT Assistant* Winter 92:12; Nov 99:18; *CPT Changes* 2000

33534   two coronary arterial grafts

→ *CPT Assistant* Winter 92:12

33535   three coronary arterial grafts

→ *CPT Assistant* Winter 92:12

33536   four or more coronary arterial grafts

→ *CPT Assistant* Winter 92:12

33542   Myocardial resection (eg, ventricular aneurysmectomy)

33545   Repair of postinfarction ventricular septal defect, with or without myocardial resection

(33560 has been deleted)

Coronary Endarterectomy

(33570 has been deleted. To report, see 33510-33536 and 33572)

+ **33572**   Coronary endarterectomy, open, any method, of left anterior descending, circumflex, or right coronary artery performed in conjunction with coronary artery bypass graft procedure, each vessel (List separately in addition to primary procedure)

(Use 33572 in conjunction with 33510-33516, 33533-33536)

(33575 has been deleted. To report, see 33510-33536 and 33572)

Single Ventricle and Other Complex Cardiac Anomalies

33600   Closure of atrioventricular valve (mitral or tricuspid) by suture or patch

33602   Closure of semilunar valve (aortic or pulmonary) by suture or patch

33606   Anastomosis of pulmonary artery to aorta (Damus-Kaye-Stansel procedure)

33608   Repair of complex cardiac anomaly other than pulmonary atresia with ventricular septal defect by construction or replacement of conduit from right or left ventricle to pulmonary artery

(For repair of pulmonary atresia with ventricular septal defect, see 33918, 33919, 33920)

▲ **33610**   Repair of complex cardiac anomalies (eg, single ventricle with subaortic obstruction) by surgical enlargement of ventricular septal defect

→ *CPT Changes* 2002

33611   Repair of double outlet right ventricle with intraventricular tunnel repair;

33612   with repair of right ventricular outflow tract obstruction

33615 Repair of complex cardiac anomalies (eg, tricuspid atresia) by closure of atrial septal defect and anastomosis of atria or vena cava to pulmonary artery (simple Fontan procedure)

33617 Repair of complex cardiac anomalies (eg, single ventricle) by modified Fontan procedure

33619 Repair of single ventricle with aortic outflow obstruction and aortic arch hypoplasia (hypoplastic left heart syndrome) (eg, Norwood procedure)

Septal Defect

(33640 has been deleted. To report, use 33641)

33641 Repair atrial septal defect, secundum, with cardiopulmonary bypass, with or without patch

(33643 has been deleted. To report, use 33641)

33645 Direct or patch closure, sinus venosus, with or without anomalous pulmonary venous drainage

33647 Repair of atrial septal defect and ventricular septal defect, with direct or patch closure

(33649 has been deleted. To report, use 33615)

33660 Repair of incomplete or partial atrioventricular canal (ostium primum atrial septal defect), with or without atrioventricular valve repair

33665 Repair of intermediate or transitional atrioventricular canal, with or without atrioventricular valve repair

33670 Repair of complete atrioventricular canal, with or without prosthetic valve

33681 Closure of ventricular septal defect, with or without patch;

(33682 has been deleted. To report, use 33681)

33684 with pulmonary valvotomy or infundibular resection (acyanotic)

33688 with removal of pulmonary artery band, with or without gusset

33690 Banding of pulmonary artery

33692 Complete repair tetralogy of Fallot without pulmonary atresia;

33694 with transannular patch

(33696 has been deleted. To report, use 33924)

33697 Complete repair tetralogy of Fallot with pulmonary atresia including construction of conduit from right ventricle to pulmonary artery and closure of ventricular septal defect

(33698 has been deleted. To report, use 33924)

Sinus of Valsalva

33702 Repair sinus of Valsalva fistula, with cardiopulmonary bypass;

33710 with repair of ventricular septal defect

33720 Repair sinus of Valsalva aneurysm, with cardiopulmonary bypass

33722 Closure of aortico-left ventricular tunnel

Total Anomalous Pulmonary Venous Drainage

33730 Complete repair of anomalous venous return (supracardiac, intracardiac, or infracardiac types)

(For partial anomalous return, see atrial septal defect)

33732 Repair of cor triatriatum or supravalvular mitral ring by resection of left atrial membrane

Shunting Procedures

33735 Atrial septectomy or septostomy; closed heart (Blalock-Hanlon type operation)

33736 open heart with cardiopulmonary bypass

33737 open heart, with inflow occlusion

(33738 has been deleted. To report, use 92992)

(33739 has been deleted. To report, use 92993)

33750 Shunt; subclavian to pulmonary artery (Blalock-Taussig type operation)

33755 ascending aorta to pulmonary artery (Waterston type operation)

33762 descending aorta to pulmonary artery (Potts-Smith type operation)

33764 central, with prosthetic graft

33766 superior vena cava to pulmonary artery for flow to one lung (classical Glenn procedure)

33767 superior vena cava to pulmonary artery for flow to both lungs (bidirectional Glenn procedure)

Transposition of the Great Vessels

33770 Repair of transposition of the great arteries with ventricular septal defect and subpulmonary stenosis; without surgical enlargement of ventricular septal defect

33771 with surgical enlargement of ventricular septal defect

33774 Repair of transposition of the great arteries, atrial baffle procedure (eg, Mustard or Senning type) with cardiopulmonary bypass;

33775 with removal of pulmonary band

33776 with closure of ventricular septal defect

33777 with repair of subpulmonic obstruction

33778 Repair of transposition of the great arteries, aortic pulmonary artery reconstruction (eg, Jatene type);

33779 with removal of pulmonary band

33780 with closure of ventricular septal defect

33781 with repair of subpulmonic obstruction

(33782, 33783, 33784, 33785 have been deleted. To report, see 33774-33781)

Truncus Arteriosus

33786 Total repair, truncus arteriosus (Rastelli type operation)

33788 Reimplantation of an anomalous pulmonary artery

(For pulmonary artery band, use 33690)

Aortic Anomalies

33800 Aortic suspension (aortopexy) for tracheal decompression (eg, for tracheomalacia) (separate procedure)

33802 Division of aberrant vessel (vascular ring);

33803 with reanastomosis

(33810, 33812 have been deleted)

33813 Obliteration of aortopulmonary septal defect; without cardiopulmonary bypass

33814 with cardiopulmonary bypass

33820 Repair of patent ductus arteriosus; by ligation

Patent Ductus Arteriosus
33820

The tissues surrounding the ductus are dissected away and then several heavy ligatures are passed around the ductus and tied off on both ends.

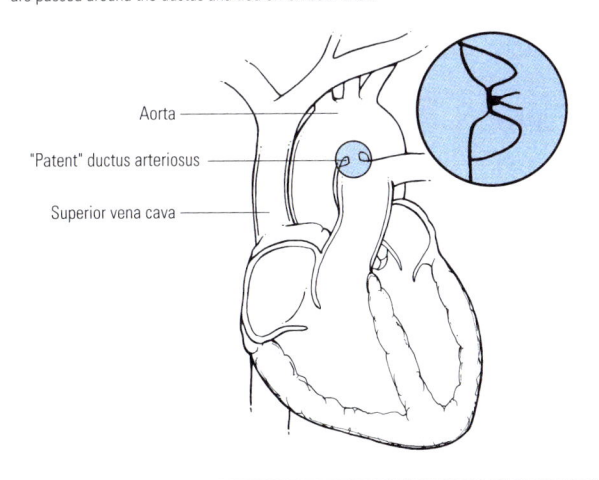

Aorta

"Patent" ductus arteriosus

Superior vena cava

33822 by division, under 18 years

33824 by division, 18 years and older

(33830 has been deleted. To report, see 33820-33824)

33840 Excision of coarctation of aorta, with or without associated patent ductus arteriosus; with direct anastomosis

33845 with graft

(33850 has been deleted. To report, use 33999)

33851 repair using either left subclavian artery or prosthetic material as gusset for enlargement

33852 Repair of hypoplastic or interrupted aortic arch using autogenous or prosthetic material; without cardiopulmonary bypass

33853 with cardiopulmonary bypass

(33855 has been deleted. To report, use 33619)

Thoracic Aortic Aneurysm

33860 Ascending aorta graft, with cardiopulmonary bypass, with or without valve suspension;

33861 with coronary reconstruction

33863 with aortic root replacement using composite prosthesis and coronary reconstruction

(33865 has been deleted. To report, see 33860 or 33861 and 33405 or 33406)

33870 Transverse arch graft, with cardiopulmonary bypass

33875 Descending thoracic aorta graft, with or without bypass

33877 Repair of thoracoabdominal aortic aneurysm with graft, with or without cardiopulmonary bypass

Pulmonary Artery

33910 Pulmonary artery embolectomy; with cardiopulmonary bypass

33915 without cardiopulmonary bypass

33916 Pulmonary endarterectomy, with or without embolectomy, with cardiopulmonary bypass

33917 Repair of pulmonary artery stenosis by reconstruction with patch or graft

33918 Repair of pulmonary atresia with ventricular septal defect, by unifocalization of pulmonary arteries; without cardiopulmonary bypass

33919 with cardiopulmonary bypass

33920 Repair of pulmonary atresia with ventricular septal defect, by construction or replacement of conduit from right or left ventricle to pulmonary artery

(For repair of other complex cardiac anomalies by construction or replacement of right or left ventricle to pulmonary artery conduit, use 33608)

33922 Transection of pulmonary artery with cardiopulmonary bypass

+ 33924 Ligation and takedown of a systemic-to-pulmonary artery shunt, performed in conjunction with a congenital heart procedure (List separately in addition to code for primary procedure)

(Use 33924 in conjunction with 33470-33475, 33600-33619, 33684-33688, 33692-33697, 33735-33767, 33770-33781, 33786, 33918-33922)

Heart/Lung Transplantation

33930 Donor cardiectomy-pneumonectomy, with preparation and maintenance of allograft

33935 Heart-lung transplant with recipient cardiectomy-pneumonectomy

33940 Donor cardiectomy, with preparation and maintenance of allograft

33945 Heart transplant, with or without recipient cardiectomy

(33950 has been deleted. To report, see 33940, 33945)

Cardiac Assist

33960 Prolonged extracorporeal circulation for cardiopulmonary insufficiency; initial 24 hours

+ 33961 each additional 24 hours (List separately in addition to code for primary procedure)

(Use 33961 in conjunction with code 33960)

(For insertion of cannula for prolonged extracorporeal circulation, use 36822)

● 33967 Insertion of intra-aortic balloon assist device, percutaneous
➔ *CPT Changes* 2002

33968 Removal of intra-aortic balloon assist device, percutaneous
➔ *CPT Assistant* Nov 99:19; Jan 00:10; *CPT Changes* 2000

33970 Insertion of intra-aortic balloon assist device through the femoral artery, open approach
➔ *CPT Assistant* Nov 99:19; *CPT Changes* 2000

33971 Removal of intra-aortic balloon assist device including repair of femoral artery, with or without graft

(33972 has been deleted. To report, use appropriate E/M code)

33973 Insertion of intra-aortic balloon assist device through the ascending aorta

33974 Removal of intra-aortic balloon assist device from the ascending aorta, including repair of the ascending aorta, with or without graft

▲ 33975 Insertion of ventricular assist device; extracorporeal, single ventricle
➔ *CPT Changes* 2002

▲ 33976 extracorporeal, biventricular
➔ *CPT Changes* 2002

▲ 33977 Removal of ventricular assist device; extracorporeal, single ventricle
➔ *CPT Changes* 2002

▲ 33978 extracorporeal, biventricular
➔ *CPT Changes* 2002

● 33979 Insertion of ventricular assist device, implantable intracorporeal, single ventricle
➔ *CPT Changes* 2002

● 33980 Removal of ventricular assist device, implantable intracorporeal, single ventricle
➔ *CPT Changes* 2002

Other Procedures

33999 Unlisted procedure, cardiac surgery
➔ *CPT Assistant* Oct 99:11

Arteries and Veins

Primary vascular procedure listings include establishing both inflow and outflow by whatever procedures necessary. Also included is that portion of the operative arteriogram performed by the surgeon, as indicated. Sympathectomy, when done, is included in the listed aortic procedures. For unlisted vascular procedure, use 37799.

Embolectomy/Thrombectomy

Arterial, With or Without Catheter

34001 Embolectomy or thrombectomy, with or without catheter; carotid, subclavian or innominate artery, by neck incision

34051 innominate, subclavian artery, by thoracic incision

34101 axillary, brachial, innominate, subclavian artery, by arm incision

34111 radial or ulnar artery, by arm incision

34151 renal, celiac, mesentery, aortoiliac artery, by abdominal incision

34201 femoropopliteal, aortoiliac artery, by leg incision

34203 popliteal-tibio-peroneal artery, by leg incision

Venous, Direct or With Catheter

34401 Thrombectomy, direct or with catheter; vena cava, iliac vein, by abdominal incision

34421 vena cava, iliac, femoropopliteal vein, by leg incision
➔ *CPT Assistant* Spring 94:30

34451 vena cava, iliac, femoropopliteal vein, by abdominal and leg incision

34471 subclavian vein, by neck incision

34490 axillary and subclavian vein, by arm incision

⊘ =Modifier '-51' Exempt   ►◄=New or Revised Text   ✦=Add-on Code   CPT 2002

Venous Reconstruction

34501 Valvuloplasty, femoral vein

34502 Reconstruction of vena cava, any method

34510 Venous valve transposition, any vein donor

34520 Cross-over vein graft to venous system

34530 Saphenopopliteal vein anastomosis

Endovascular Repair of Abdominal Aortic Aneurysm

Codes 34800-34826 ▶represent a family of component procedures to report◀ placement of an endovascular graft for abdominal aortic aneurysm repair. ▶These codes describe open femoral or iliac artery exposure, device manipulation and deployment, and closure of the arteriotomy sites. Balloon angioplasty and/or stent deployment within the target treatment zone for the endoprosthesis, either before or after endograft deployment, are not separately reportable. Introduction of guidewires and catheters should be reported separately (eg, 36200, 36245-36248, 36140).◀ Extensive repair or replacement of an artery should be additionally reported (eg, 35226 or 35286).

For fluoroscopic guidance in conjunction with endovascular aneurysm repair, see code 75952 or 75953, as appropriate. Code 75952 includes angiography of the aorta and its branches for diagnostic imaging prior to deployment of the endovascular device (including all routine components of modular devices), fluoroscopic guidance in the delivery of the endovascular components, and intraprocedural arterial angiography (eg, confirm position, detect endoleak, evaluate runoff). Code 75953 includes the analogous services for placement of additional extension prostheses (not for routine components of modular devices).

Other interventional procedures performed at the time of endovascular abdominal aortic aneurysm repair should be additionally reported (eg, renal transluminal angioplasty, arterial embolization, intravascular ultrasound, balloon angioplasty or stenting of native artery(s) outside the ▶endoprosthesis target zone, when done◀ before ▶or after◀ deployment of graft).

34800 Endovascular repair of infrarenal abdominal aortic aneurysm or dissection; using aorto-aortic tube prosthesis
→ *CPT Assistant* Dec 00:1; *CPT Changes* 2001

34802 using modular bifurcated prosthesis (one docking limb)
→ *CPT Assistant* Dec 00:1; *CPT Changes* 2001

▶(For endovascular repair of infrarenal abdominal aortic aneurysm or dissection using a modular bifurcated prosthesis (two docking limbs), use Category III code 0001T)◀

34804 using unibody bifurcated prosthesis
→ *CPT Assistant* Dec 00:1; *CPT Changes* 2001

▶(For endovascular repair of infrarenal abdominal aortic aneurysm or dissection using an aorto-uniiliac or aorto-unifemoral prosthesis, use Category III code 0002T)◀

+ 34808 Endovascular placement of iliac artery occlusion device (List separately in addition to code for primary procedure)
→ *CPT Assistant* Dec 00:1; *CPT Changes* 2001

(Use 34808 in conjunction with codes 34800, 34813, 34825, 34826)

(For radiological supervision and interpretation, use 75952 in conjunction with 34800, 34802, 34804, 34808)

(For open approach, report codes 34812-34820 in addition to codes 34800, 34802, 34804, 34808 as appropriate)

34812 Open femoral artery exposure for delivery of aortic endovascular prosthesis, by groin incision, unilateral
→ *CPT Assistant* Dec 00:1; *CPT Changes* 2001

(For bilateral procedure, use modifier '-50')

+ 34813 Placement of femoral-femoral prosthetic graft during endovascular aortic aneurysm repair (List separately in addition to code for primary procedure)
→ *CPT Assistant* Dec 00:1; *CPT Changes* 2001

(Use 34813 in conjunction with code 34812)

(For femoral artery grafting, see 35521, 35533, 35546, 35551-35558, 35566, 35621, 35646, 35651-35661, 35666, 35700)

34820 Open iliac artery exposure for delivery of endovascular prosthesis or iliac occlusion during endovascular therapy, by abdominal or retroperitoneal incision, unilateral
→ *CPT Assistant* Dec 00:1; *CPT Changes* 2001

(For bilateral procedure, use modifier '-50')

34825 Placement of proximal or distal extension prosthesis for endovascular repair of infrarenal abdominal aortic aneurysm; initial vessel
→ *CPT Assistant* Dec 00:1; *CPT Changes* 2001

+ 34826 each additional vessel (List separately in addition to code for primary procedure)
→ *CPT Assistant* Dec 00:1; *CPT Changes* 2001

(Use 34826 in conjunction with code 34825)

(Use 34825, 34826 in addition to codes 34800-34808, as appropriate)

(For staged procedure, use modifier '-58')

(For radiological supervision and interpretation, use 75953)

34830 Open repair of infrarenal aortic aneurysm or dissection, plus repair of associated arterial trauma, following unsuccessful endovascular repair; tube prosthesis
→ *CPT Assistant* Dec 00:1; *CPT Changes* 2001

34831 aorto-bi-iliac prosthesis
→ *CPT Assistant* Dec 00:1; *CPT Changes* 2001

34832 aorto-bifemoral prosthesis

➔ *CPT Assistant* Dec 00:1; *CPT Changes* 2001

Endovascular Repair of Abdominal Aortic Aneurysm
34831

Using fluoroscopic guidance, a "compressed" prosthesis is introduced through arteries in the groin and advanced into position with the aneurysm. Once in the aorta, the prosthesis is expanded.

Renal arteries

Bifurcated stent-graft

Abdominal aortic aneurysm

Common iliac arteries

Direct Repair of Aneurysm or Excision (Partial or Total) and Graft Insertion for Aneurysm, False Aneurysm, Ruptured Aneurysm, and Associated Occlusive Disease

Procedures 35001-35162 include preparation of artery for anastomosis including endarterectomy.

(For direct repairs associated with occlusive disease only, see 35201-35286)

(For intracranial aneurysm, see 61700 et seq)

(For thoracic aortic aneurysm, see 33860-33875)

▲ **35001** Direct repair of aneurysm, pseudoaneurysm, or excision (partial or total) and graft insertion, with or without patch graft; for aneurysm and associated occlusive disease, carotid, subclavian artery, by neck incision

➔ *CPT Changes* 2002

35002 for ruptured aneurysm, carotid, subclavian artery, by neck incision

▲ **35005** for aneurysm, pseudoaneurysm, and associated occlusive disease, vertebral artery

➔ *CPT Changes* 2002

35011 for aneurysm and associated occlusive disease, axillary-brachial artery, by arm incision

35013 for ruptured aneurysm, axillary-brachial artery, by arm incision

▲ **35021** for aneurysm, pseudoaneurysm, and associated occlusive disease, innominate, subclavian artery, by thoracic incision

➔ *CPT Changes* 2002

35022 for ruptured aneurysm, innominate, subclavian artery, by thoracic incision

▲ **35045** for aneurysm, pseudoaneurysm, and associated occlusive disease, radial or ulnar artery

➔ *CPT Changes* 2002

▲ **35081** for aneurysm, pseudoaneurysm, and associated occlusive disease, abdominal aorta

➔ *CPT Assistant* Dec 00:1; *CPT Changes* 2002

35082 for ruptured aneurysm, abdominal aorta

▲ **35091** for aneurysm, pseudoaneurysm, and associated occlusive disease, abdominal aorta involving visceral vessels (mesenteric, celiac, renal)

➔ *CPT Assistant* Dec 00:1; *CPT Changes* 2002

35092 for ruptured aneurysm, abdominal aorta involving visceral vessels (mesenteric, celiac, renal)

▲ **35102** for aneurysm, pseudoaneurysm, and associated occlusive disease, abdominal aorta involving iliac vessels (common, hypogastric, external)

➔ *CPT Changes* 2002

35103 for ruptured aneurysm, abdominal aorta involving iliac vessels (common, hypogastric, external)

▲ **35111** for aneurysm, pseudoaneurysm, and associated occlusive disease, splenic artery

➔ *CPT Changes* 2002

35112 for ruptured aneurysm, splenic artery

▲ **35121** for aneurysm, pseudoaneurysm, and associated occlusive disease, hepatic, celiac, renal, or mesenteric artery

➔ *CPT Changes* 2002

35122 for ruptured aneurysm, hepatic, celiac, renal, or mesenteric artery

▲ **35131** for aneurysm, pseudoaneurysm, and associated occlusive disease, iliac artery (common, hypogastric, external)

➔ *CPT Changes* 2002

35132 for ruptured aneurysm, iliac artery (common, hypogastric, external)

▲ **35141** for aneurysm, pseudoaneurysm, and associated occlusive disease, common femoral artery (profunda femoris, superficial femoral)

➔ *CPT Changes* 2002

35142 for ruptured aneurysm, common femoral artery (profunda femoris, superficial femoral)

▲ **35151** for aneurysm, pseudoaneurysm, and associated occlusive disease, popliteal artery
➔ *CPT Changes* 2002

35152 for ruptured aneurysm, popliteal artery

▲ **35161** for aneurysm, pseudoaneurysm, and associated occlusive disease, other arteries
➔ *CPT Changes* 2002

35162 for ruptured aneurysm, other arteries

Repair Arteriovenous Fistula

35180 Repair, congenital arteriovenous fistula; head and neck

35182 thorax and abdomen

35184 extremities

35188 Repair, acquired or traumatic arteriovenous fistula; head and neck

35189 thorax and abdomen

35190 extremities

Repair Blood Vessel Other Than for Fistula, With or Without Patch Angioplasty

(For AV fistula repair, see 35180-35190)

35201 Repair blood vessel, direct; neck

35206 upper extremity
➔ *CPT Assistant* Oct 00:1

35207 hand, finger

35211 intrathoracic, with bypass

35216 intrathoracic, without bypass

35221 intra-abdominal

35226 lower extremity

35231 Repair blood vessel with vein graft; neck

35236 upper extremity

35241 intrathoracic, with bypass

35246 intrathoracic, without bypass

35251 intra-abdominal

35256 lower extremity

35261 Repair blood vessel with graft other than vein; neck

35266 upper extremity

35271 intrathoracic, with bypass

35276 intrathoracic, without bypass

35281 intra-abdominal

35286 lower extremity

Thromboendarterectomy

(For coronary artery, see 33510-33536 and 33572)

35301 Thromboendarterectomy, with or without patch graft; carotid, vertebral, subclavian, by neck incision

35311 subclavian, innominate, by thoracic incision

35321 axillary-brachial

35331 abdominal aorta

35341 mesenteric, celiac, or renal

35351 iliac

35355 iliofemoral

35361 combined aortoiliac

35363 combined aortoiliofemoral

35371 common femoral

35372 deep (profunda) femoral

35381 femoral and/or popliteal, and/or tibioperoneal

+ **35390** Reoperation, carotid, thromboendarterectomy, more than one month after original operation (List separately in addition to code for primary procedure)

(Use 35390 in conjunction with code 35301)
➔ *CPT Assistant* Nov 97:16

Thromboendarterectomy
35371-35372

The common femoral artery (35371) or the deep (profunda) femoral artery (35372) is incised and the plaque and lining are removed, enlarging the diameter of the artery.

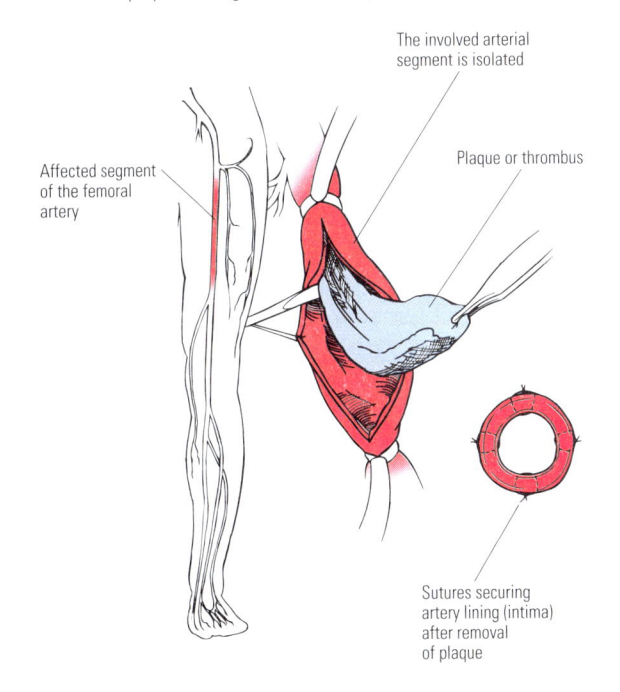

The involved arterial segment is isolated

Plaque or thrombus

Affected segment of the femoral artery

Sutures securing artery lining (intima) after removal of plaque

Angioscopy

✛ 35400 Angioscopy (non-coronary vessels or grafts) during therapeutic intervention (List separately in addition to code for primary procedure)

Transluminal Angioplasty

If done as part of another operation, use modifier '-51' or use modifier '-52'.

(For radiological supervision and interpretation, see 75962-75968 and 75978)

Open

35450 Transluminal balloon angioplasty, open; renal or other visceral artery
➔ *CPT Assistant* Feb 97:2, 3; Dec 00:1

35452 aortic
➔ *CPT Assistant* Feb 97:2, 3

35454 iliac
➔ *CPT Assistant* Feb 97:2, 3; Dec 00:1

35456 femoral-popliteal
➔ *CPT Assistant* Feb 97:2, 3

35458 brachiocephalic trunk or branches, each vessel
➔ *CPT Assistant* Feb 97:2, 3

35459 tibioperoneal trunk and branches
➔ *CPT Assistant* Feb 97:2, 3

35460 venous
➔ *CPT Assistant* Feb 97:2, 3

Percutaneous

►Codes for catheter placement and the radiologic supervision and interpretation should also be reported, in addition to the code(s) for the therapeutic aspect of the procedure.◄

35470 Transluminal balloon angioplasty, percutaneous; tibioperoneal trunk or branches, each vessel
➔ *CPT Assistant* Aug 96:3; Feb 97:2, 3

35471 renal or visceral artery
➔ *CPT Assistant* Aug 96:3; Feb 97:2, 3

35472 aortic
➔ *CPT Assistant* Aug 96:3; Feb 97:2, 3

35473 iliac
➔ *CPT Assistant* Fall 93:11; Aug 96:3; Feb 97:2, 3

Transluminal Balloon Angioplasty
35473

A balloon catheter is passed into the iliac artery and inflated to stretch the blood vessel to a larger diameter.

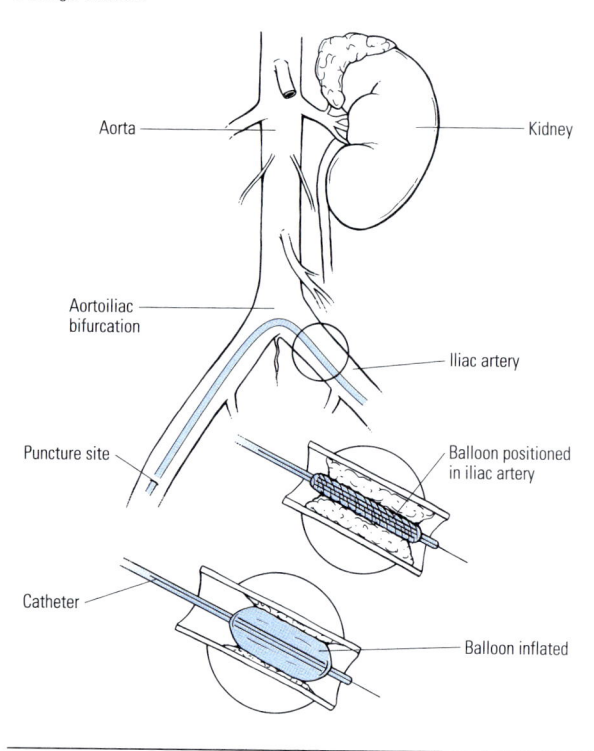

35474 femoral-popliteal
➔ *CPT Assistant* Aug 96:3; Feb 97:2, 3

35475 brachiocephalic trunk or branches, each vessel
➔ *CPT Assistant* Aug 96:3; Feb 97:2, 3

35476 venous
➔ *CPT Assistant* Aug 96:3; Feb 97:2, 3

(For radiological supervision and interpretation, use 75978)

Transluminal Atherectomy

If done as part of another operation, use modifier '-51' or use modifier '-52'.

(For radiological supervision and interpretation, see 75992-75996)

Open

35480 Transluminal peripheral atherectomy, open; renal or other visceral artery
➔ *CPT Assistant* Feb 97:2, 3

35481 aortic
➔ *CPT Assistant* Feb 97:2

⊘ =Modifier '-51' Exempt ►◄=New or Revised Text ✛=Add-on Code CPT 2002

35482	iliac	**35508**	carotid-vertebral
	CPT Assistant Feb 97:2	**35509**	carotid-carotid
35483	femoral-popliteal	**35511**	subclavian-subclavian
	CPT Assistant Feb 97:2	**35515**	subclavian-vertebral
35484	brachiocephalic trunk or branches, each vessel	**35516**	subclavian-axillary
	CPT Assistant Feb 97:2	**35518**	axillary-axillary
35485	tibioperoneal trunk and branches	**35521**	axillary-femoral

35482 iliac
> *CPT Assistant* Feb 97:2

35483 femoral-popliteal
> *CPT Assistant* Feb 97:2

35484 brachiocephalic trunk or branches, each vessel
> *CPT Assistant* Feb 97:2

35485 tibioperoneal trunk and branches
> *CPT Assistant* Feb 97:2

Percutaneous

►Codes for catheter placement and the radiologic supervision and interpretation should also be reported, in addition to the code(s) for the therapeutic aspect of the procedure.◄

35490 Transluminal peripheral atherectomy, percutaneous; renal or other visceral artery
> *CPT Assistant* Feb 97:2

35491 aortic
> *CPT Assistant* Feb 97:2

35492 iliac
> *CPT Assistant* Feb 97:2

35493 femoral-popliteal
> *CPT Assistant* Feb 97:2

35494 brachiocephalic trunk or branches, each vessel
> *CPT Assistant* Feb 97:2

35495 tibioperoneal trunk and branches
> *CPT Assistant* Feb 97:2

Bypass Graft

Vein

+ 35500 Harvest of upper extremity vein, one segment, for lower extremity or coronary artery bypass procedure (List separately in addition to code for primary procedure)
> *CPT Assistant* Nov 98:13; Mar 99:6; Nov 99:19; *CPT Changes* 2000

> ►(Use 35500 in conjunction with codes 33510-33536, 35556, 35566, 35571, 35583-35587)◄

(For harvest of more than one vein segment, see 35682, 35683)

35501 Bypass graft, with vein; carotid
> *CPT Assistant* April 99:11

35506 carotid-subclavian

35507 subclavian-carotid

35508 carotid-vertebral

35509 carotid-carotid

35511 subclavian-subclavian

35515 subclavian-vertebral

35516 subclavian-axillary

35518 axillary-axillary

35521 axillary-femoral

(For bypass graft performed with synthetic graft, use 35621)

35526 aortosubclavian or carotid

(For bypass graft performed with synthetic graft, use 35626)

35531 aortoceliac or aortomesenteric

35533 axillary-femoral-femoral

(For bypass graft performed with synthetic graft, use 35654)

35536 splenorenal
> *CPT Assistant* Jun 99:10

35541 aortoiliac or bi-iliac

(For bypass graft performed with synthetic graft, use 35641)

35546 aortofemoral or bifemoral

(For bypass graft performed with synthetic graft, use 35646)

35548 aortoiliofemoral, unilateral

(For bypass graft performed with synthetic graft, use 37799)

35549 aortoiliofemoral, bilateral

(For bypass graft performed with synthetic graft, use 37799)

35551 aortofemoral-popliteal

35556 femoral-popliteal

35558 femoral-femoral

35560 aortorenal
> *CPT Assistant* Jun 99:10

35563 ilioiliac

35565 iliofemoral

35566 femoral-anterior tibial, posterior tibial, peroneal artery or other distal vessels

35571   popliteal-tibial, -peroneal artery or other distal vessels

Bypass Graft, Vein
35571

The physician creates a bypass around the popliteal artery, using a harvested vein that is sutured to the tibial artery.

Affected arterial segment is isolated during operation

Popliteal artery

Affected arterial segment

Obstruction

Graft from patient or donor

Anterior tibial artery

Posterior tibial artery

Peroneal artery

In-Situ Vein

35582   In-situ vein bypass; aortofemoral-popliteal (only femoral-popliteal portion in-situ)

35583   femoral-popliteal

35585   femoral-anterior tibial, posterior tibial, or peroneal artery

35587   popliteal-tibial, peroneal
         → *CPT Assistant* April 99:11

Other Than Vein

⊘ **35600**   Harvest of upper extremity artery, one segment, for coronary artery bypass procedure
     → *CPT Changes* 2001

Harvest of Upper Extremity Artery
35600

Open procurement of a radial artery to secure conduit for construction of a coronary artery bypass graft.

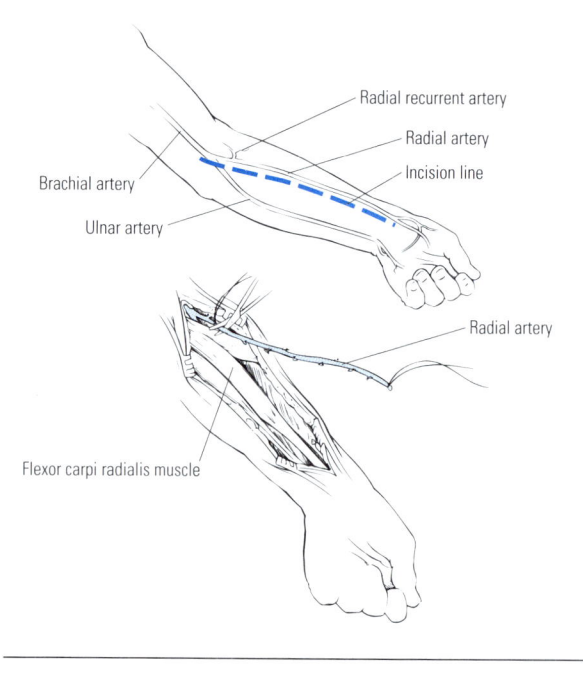

Radial recurrent artery

Radial artery

Incision line

Brachial artery

Ulnar artery

Radial artery

Flexor carpi radialis muscle

35601   Bypass graft, with other than vein; carotid

35606   carotid-subclavian

35612   subclavian-subclavian

35616   subclavian-axillary

35621   axillary-femoral

35623   axillary-popliteal or -tibial

35626   aortosubclavian or carotid

35631   aortoceliac, aortomesenteric, aortorenal

35636   splenorenal (splenic to renal arterial anastomosis)

         (35637 has been deleted. To report, use 35691)

         (35638 has been deleted. To report, use 35693)

35641   aortoiliac or bi-iliac

35642   carotid-vertebral

35645   subclavian-vertebral

▲ **35646**   aortobifemoral
    ● *CPT Changes* 2002

● **35647**   aortofemoral
    ● *CPT Changes* 2002

35650   axillary-axillary

35651   aortofemoral-popliteal

35654   axillary-femoral-femoral

35656   femoral-popliteal

35661   femoral-femoral

35663   ilioiliac

35665   iliofemoral

35666   femoral-anterior tibial, posterior tibial, or peroneal artery

35671   popliteal-tibial or -peroneal artery

Composite Grafts

Codes 35682-35683 are used to report harvest and anastomosis of multiple vein segments from distant sites for use as arterial bypass graft conduits. These codes are intended for use when the two or more vein segments are harvested from a limb other than that undergoing bypass. ►Add-on codes 35682 and 35683 may be reported in addition to codes 35556, 35566, 35571, 35583-35587, as appropriate.◄

+ **35681**   Bypass graft; composite, prosthetic and vein (List separately in addition to code for primary procedure)
    ● *CPT Assistant* Nov 98:13-14; Mar 99:6; April 99:11

    (Do not report 35681 in addition to 35682, 35683)

+ **35682**   autogenous composite, two segments of veins from two locations (List separately in addition to code for primary procedure)
    ● *CPT Assistant* Nov 98:13-14; Mar 99:6; April 99:11

    (Do not report 35682 in addition to 35681, 35683)

+ **35683**   autogenous composite, three or more segments of vein from two or more locations (List separately in addition to code for primary procedure)
    ● *CPT Assistant* Nov 98:13-14; Mar 99:6; April 99:11

    (Do not report 35683 in addition to 35681, 35682)

►Adjuvant Techniques◄

►Adjuvant (additional) technique(s) may be required at the time a bypass graft is created to improve patency of the lower extremity autogenous or synthetic bypass graft (eg, femoral-popliteal, femoral-tibial, or popliteal-tibial arteries). Code 35685 should be reported in addition to the primary synthetic bypass graft procedure, when an interposition of venous tissue (vein patch or cuff) is placed at the anastomosis between the synthetic bypass conduit and the involved artery (includes harvest).◄

►Code 35686 should be reported in addition to the primary bypass graft procedure, when autogenous vein is used to create a fistula between the tibial or peroneal artery and vein at or beyond the distal bypass anastomosis site of the involved artery.◄

►(For composite graft(s), see 35681-35683)◄

+ ● **35685**   Placement of vein patch or cuff at distal anastomosis of bypass graft, synthetic conduit (List separately in addition to code for primary procedure)
    ● *CPT Changes* 2002

    ►(Use 35685 in conjunction with codes 35656, 35666, or 35671)◄

+ ● **35686**   Creation of distal arteriovenous fistula during lower extremity bypass surgery (non-hemodialysis) (List separately in addition to code for primary procedure)
    ● *CPT Changes* 2002

    ►(Use 35686 in conjunction with codes 35556, 35566, 35571, 35583-35587, 35623, 35656, 35666, 35671)◄

Arterial Transposition

35691   Transposition and/or reimplantation; vertebral to carotid artery

35693   vertebral to subclavian artery

35694   subclavian to carotid artery

35695   carotid to subclavian artery

Exploration/Revision

+ **35700**   Reoperation, femoral-popliteal or femoral (popliteal)-anterior tibial, posterior tibial, peroneal artery or other distal vessels, more than one month after original operation (List separately in addition to code for primary procedure)

    (Use 35700 in conjunction with codes 35556, 35566, 35571, 35583, 35585, 35587, 35656, 35666, 35671)

35701   Exploration (not followed by surgical repair), with or without lysis of artery; carotid artery

35721   femoral artery
    ● *CPT Assistant* Jun 96:8

35741   popliteal artery

35761   other vessels

35800   Exploration for postoperative hemorrhage, thrombosis or infection; neck

35820   chest

35840   abdomen

35860   extremity

35870   Repair of graft-enteric fistula

35875 Thrombectomy of arterial or venous graft (other than hemodialysis graft or fistula);

➔ *CPT Assistant* Nov 98:14; Feb 99:6; Mar 99:6; Apr 00:10

35876 with revision of arterial or venous graft

➔ *CPT Assistant* Nov 98:14

(For thrombectomy of hemodialysis graft or fistula, see 36831, 36833)

(35880 has been deleted. To report, use 35875)

(35900 has been deleted. To report, see 35901-35907 and appropriate revascularization code)

Codes 35879 and 35881 describe open revision of graft-threatening stenoses of lower extremity arterial bypass graft(s) (previously constructed with autogenous vein conduit) using vein patch angioplasty or segmental vein interposition techniques. For thrombectomy with revision of any non-coronary arterial or venous graft, including those of the lower extremity, (other than hemodialysis graft or fistula), use 35876. For direct repair (other than for fistula) of a lower extremity blood vessel (with or without patch angioplasty), use 35226. For repair (other than for fistula) of a lower extremity blood vessel using a vein graft, use 35256.

35879 Revision, lower extremity arterial bypass, without thrombectomy, open; with vein patch angioplasty

➔ *CPT Assistant* Nov 99:19; *CPT Changes* 2000

35881 with segmental vein interposition

➔ *CPT Assistant* Nov 99:19; *CPT Changes* 2000

35901 Excision of infected graft; neck

35903 extremity

35905 thorax

35907 abdomen

(35910 has been deleted. To report, see 35901-35907 and appropriate revascularization code)

Vascular Injection Procedures

Listed services for injection procedures include necessary local anesthesia, introduction of needles or catheter, injection of contrast media with or without automatic power injection, and/or necessary pre- and postinjection care specifically related to the injection procedure.

Catheters, drugs, and contrast media are not included in the listed service for the injection procedures.

Selective vascular catheterization should be coded to include introduction and all lesser order selective catheterization used in the approach (eg, the description for a selective right middle cerebral artery catheterization includes the introduction and placement catheterization of the right common and internal carotid arteries).

Additional second and/or third order arterial catheterization within the same family of arteries or veins supplied by a single first order vessel should be expressed by 36012, 36218 or 36248.

Additional first order or higher catheterization in vascular families supplied by a first order vessel different from a previously selected and coded family should be separately coded using the conventions described above.

(For radiological supervision and interpretation, see **Radiology**)

(For injection procedures in conjunction with cardiac catheterization, see 93541-93545)

(For chemotherapy of malignant disease, see 96400-96549)

Intravenous

An intracatheter is a sheathed combination of needle and short catheter.

36000＊ Introduction of needle or intracatheter, vein

➔ *CPT Assistant* Apr 98:1, 3, 7; Jul 98:1

(36001 has been deleted. To report, use 36000 with modifier '-50')

● **36002** Injection procedures (eg, thrombin) for percutaneous treatment of extremity pseudoaneurysm

➔ *CPT Changes* 2002

▶(For imaging guidance, see 76003, 76360, 76393, or 76942)◀

▶(For ultrasound guided compression repair of pseudoaneurysms, use 76936)◀

▶(Do not report 36002 for vascular sealant of an arteriotomy site)◀

▲ **36005** Injection procedure for extremity venography (including introduction of needle or intracatheter)

➔ *CPT Changes* 2002

(For radiological supervision and interpretation, see 75820, 75822)

36010 Introduction of catheter, superior or inferior vena cava

➔ *CPT Assistant* Aug 96:2; Apr 98:1; Sep 00:11

36011 Selective catheter placement, venous system; first order branch (eg, renal vein, jugular vein)

➔ *CPT Assistant* Aug 96:11; Apr 98:1

36012 second order, or more selective, branch (eg, left adrenal vein, petrosal sinus)

➔ *CPT Assistant* Aug 96:11

36013 Introduction of catheter, right heart or main pulmonary artery

➔ *CPT Assistant* Aug 96:11

36014   Selective catheter placement, left or right pulmonary artery
➔ *CPT Assistant* Aug 96:11; Apr 98:1

36015   Selective catheter placement, segmental or subsegmental pulmonary artery
➔ *CPT Assistant* Aug 96:11; Sep 00:11

(For insertion of flow directed catheter (eg, Swan-Ganz), use 93503)

(For venous catheterization for selective organ blood sampling, use 36500)

Intra-Arterial—Intra-Aortic

(For radiological supervision and interpretation, see **Radiology**)

36100   Introduction of needle or intracatheter, carotid or vertebral artery
➔ *CPT Assistant* Aug 96:11

(36101 has been deleted. To report, use 36100 with modifier '-50')

36120   Introduction of needle or intracatheter; retrograde brachial artery
➔ *CPT Assistant* Fall 93:16; Aug 96:3

36140   extremity artery
➔ *CPT Assistant* Fall 93:16; Aug 96:3

36145   arteriovenous shunt created for dialysis (cannula, fistula, or graft)
➔ *CPT Assistant* Aug 96:3; Feb 97:2

(For insertion of arteriovenous cannula, see 36810-36821)

36160   Introduction of needle or intracatheter, aortic, translumbar
➔ *CPT Assistant* Aug 96:3

36200   Introduction of catheter, aorta
➔ *CPT Assistant* Fall 93:16; Aug 96:3

(36210 has been deleted. To report, see 36215-36218)

36215   Selective catheter placement, arterial system; each first order thoracic or brachiocephalic branch, within a vascular family
➔ *CPT Assistant* Fall 93:15; Aug 96:3; Nov 97:16; Apr 98:1; Sep 00:11; Oct 00:4

(For catheter placement for coronary angiography, use 93508)

36216   initial second order thoracic or brachiocephalic branch, within a vascular family
➔ *CPT Assistant* Fall 93:15; Aug 96:3; Oct 00:4

36217   initial third order or more selective thoracic or brachiocephalic branch, within a vascular family
➔ *CPT Assistant* Fall 93:15; Aug 96:3; Oct 00:4

+ 36218   additional second order, third order, and beyond, thoracic or brachiocephalic branch, within a vascular family (List in addition to code for initial second or third order vessel as appropriate)
➔ *CPT Assistant* Fall 93:15; Aug 96:3; Oct 00:4

(Use 36218 in conjunction with codes 36216, 36217)

(For angiography, see 75600-75790)

(For angioplasty, see 35470-35475)

(For transcatheter therapies, see 37200-37208, 61624, 61626)

(36220 has been deleted. To report, see 36215-36218)

(36230 has been deleted. When coronary artery, arterial conduit (eg, internal mammary, inferior epigastric or free radial artery) or venous bypass graft angiography is performed in conjunction with cardiac catheterization, see the appropriate cardiac catheterization code(s) (93501-93556) in the **Medicine** section of *CPT*. When coronary artery, arterial coronary conduit or venous bypass graft angiography is performed without concomitant left heart cardiac catheterization, use 93508. When internal mammary artery angiography only is performed without a concomitant left heart cardiac catheterization, use 36216 or 36217 as appropriate.)

(36240 has been deleted. To report, use 36248)

36245   Selective catheter placement, arterial system; each first order abdominal, pelvic, or lower extremity artery branch, within a vascular family
➔ *CPT Assistant* Fall 93:15; Aug 96:3

36246   initial second order abdominal, pelvic, or lower extremity artery branch, within a vascular family
➔ *CPT Assistant* Fall 93:15; Aug 96:3

36247   initial third order or more selective abdominal, pelvic, or lower extremity artery branch, within a vascular family
➔ *CPT Assistant* Fall 93:15; Aug 96:3

+ 36248   additional second order, third order, and beyond, abdominal, pelvic, or lower extremity artery branch, within a vascular family (List in addition to code for initial second or third order vessel as appropriate)
➔ *CPT Assistant* Fall 93:15; Aug 96:3; Apr 98:1, 7

(Use 36248 in conjunction with codes 36246, 36247)

(36250 has been deleted. To report, use 36248)

36260   Insertion of implantable intra-arterial infusion pump (eg, for chemotherapy of liver)
➔ *CPT Assistant* Fall 95:5

36261   Revision of implanted intra-arterial infusion pump

36262   Removal of implanted intra-arterial infusion pump

36299   Unlisted procedure, vascular injection

Venous

Venipuncture, needle or catheter for diagnostic study or intravenous therapy, percutaneous.

▲**36400**   Venipuncture, under age 3 years; femoral or jugular
  ➲ *CPT Changes* 2002

36405✳   scalp vein

36406   other vein

36410✳   Venipuncture, child over age 3 years or adult, necessitating physician's skill (separate procedure), for diagnostic or therapeutic purposes. Not to be used for routine venipuncture.

36415✳   Routine venipuncture or finger/heel/ear stick for collection of specimen(s)
  ➲ *CPT Assistant* Jun 96:10; Feb 97:9; Mar 98:10; Oct 99:11

36420   Venipuncture, cutdown; under age 1 year

36425   age 1 or over

36430   Transfusion, blood or blood components
  ➲ *CPT Assistant* Aug 97:18

  (36431 has been deleted)

36440✳   Push transfusion, blood, 2 years or under

36450   Exchange transfusion, blood; newborn

36455   other than newborn

36460   Transfusion, intrauterine, fetal

  (For radiological supervision and interpretation, use 76941)

36468   Single or multiple injections of sclerosing solutions, spider veins (telangiectasia); limb or trunk

36469   face

36470✳   Injection of sclerosing solution; single vein

36471✳   multiple veins, same leg

  (36480 has been deleted. To report, use 36488 or 36489)

36481   Percutaneous portal vein catheterization by any method
  ➲ *CPT Assistant* Oct 96:1

  (For radiological supervision and interpretation, see 75885, 75887)

  (36485 has been deleted. To report, use 36490 or 36491)

⊘**36488**✳   Placement of central venous catheter (subclavian, jugular, or other vein) (eg, for central venous pressure, hyperalimentation, hemodialysis, or chemotherapy); percutaneous, age 2 years or under
  ➲ *CPT Assistant* Spring 93:12; Fall 95:5; Oct 97:10; Oct 98:10; Feb 99:1; Jul 99:10

⊘**36489**✳   percutaneous, over age 2
  ➲ *CPT Assistant* Spring 93:12; Fall 95:5; Oct 97:10; Feb 99:1; Jul 99:10; May 00:11

  ►(If imaging guidance is performed, see 76000, 76003, 76942)◄

Placement of Central Venous Catheter
36488

During placement of a central venous catheter, a short tract is developed as the catheter is advanced from the skin entry site to the point of venous cannulation. The catheter must terminate in either the subclavian, brachiocephalic, innominate or iliac veins or at the junction of one or more of these veins and the superior or inferior vena cavae.

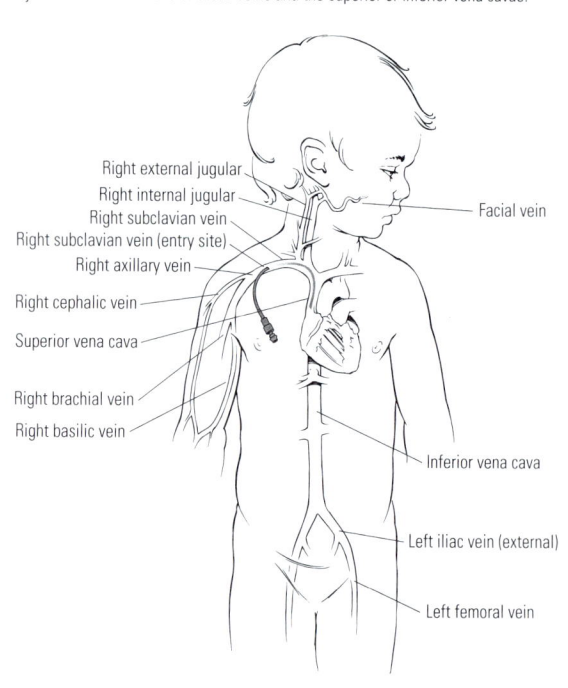

Placement of Central Venous Catheter
36489

During placement of a central venous catheter, a short tract is developed as the catheter is advanced from the skin entry site to the point of venous cannulation. The catheter must terminate in either the subclavian, brachiocephalic, innominate or iliac veins or at the junction of one or more of these veins and the superior or inferior vena cavae.

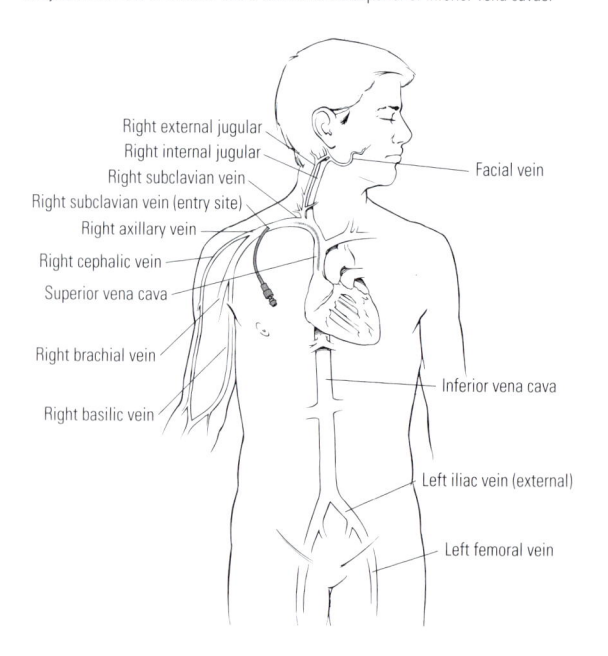

⊘ **36490***   cutdown, age 2 years or under
→ *CPT Assistant* Spring 93:12; Fall 95:5; Oct 97:10; Feb 99:1; Jul 99:10; May 00:11

⊘ **36491***   cutdown, over age 2
→ *CPT Assistant* Spring 91:10; Spring 93:12; Fall 95:5; Oct 97:10; Feb 99:1; Jul 99:10; May 00:11

(For examination of patient and instruction to patient, review of prescription of fluids for long-term or permanent hyperalimentation, use **Evaluation and Management** codes for office or hospital inpatient category or follow-up inpatient consultation codes as appropriate)

36493   Repositioning of previously placed central venous catheter under fluoroscopic guidance
→ *CPT Assistant* Spring 93:12

(For fluoroscopic guidance use 76000)

(36495-36497 have been deleted. To report, see 36530-36535)

36500   Venous catheterization for selective organ blood sampling

(For catheterization in superior or inferior vena cava, use 36010)

(For radiological supervision and interpretation, use 75893)

36510*   Catheterization of umbilical vein for diagnosis or therapy, newborn

36520   Therapeutic apheresis; plasma and/or cell exchange
→ *CPT Assistant* Apr 96:1; Jul 00:11

36521   with extracorporeal affinity column adsorption and plasma reinfusion
→ *CPT Assistant* Nov 99:19; Jul 00:11; *CPT Changes* 2000

36522   Photopheresis, extracorporeal
→ *CPT Assistant* Fall 93:25

36530   Insertion of implantable intravenous infusion pump
→ *CPT Assistant* Fall 95:9

▶(If imaging guidance is performed, see 76000, 76003, 76942)◀

36531   Revision of implantable intravenous infusion pump

36532   Removal of implantable intravenous infusion pump

▶(If imaging guidance is performed, use 76000)◀

36533   Insertion of implantable venous access device, with or without subcutaneous reservoir
→ *CPT Assistant* Spring 93:12; Fall 95:9; Oct 97:10; Feb 99:1; Nov 99:19-20; *CPT Changes* 2000

(For removal, use 36535)

▶(If imaging guidance is performed, see 76000, 76003, 76942)◀

(For refilling and maintenance of an implantable venous access device reservoir, use 96530)

Implantable Venous Access Device
36533

Implantable venous access device

Noncoring needle
Venous access port
Central vein

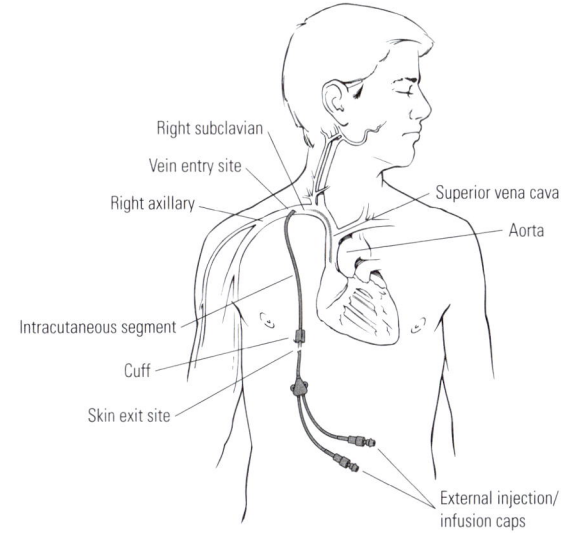

Right subclavian
Vein entry site
Right axillary
Superior vena cava
Aorta
Intracutaneous segment
Cuff
Skin exit site
External injection/infusion caps

36534 Revision of implantable venous access device, and/or subcutaneous reservoir

➔ *CPT Assistant* Nov 99:19-20; Jan 01:11; *CPT Changes* 2000

(For removal, use 36535)

36535 Removal of implantable venous access device, and/or subcutaneous reservoir

➔ *CPT Assistant* Spring 93:12; Feb 99:1; Nov 99:19-20; *CPT Changes* 2000

(Use 36535 in conjunction with codes 36533, 36534, as appropriate)

(Do not use 36535 in conjunction with codes 36488-36491)

▶(If imaging guidance is performed, use 76000)◀

36540 Collection of blood specimen from a partially or completely implantable venous access device

➔ *CPT Changes* 2001

36550 Declotting by thrombolytic agent of implanted vascular access device or catheter

➔ *CPT Assistant* Nov 99:20; *CPT Changes* 2000

Arterial

36600 * Arterial puncture, withdrawal of blood for diagnosis

➔ *CPT Assistant* Fall 95:7

⊘ **36620** Arterial catheterization or cannulation for sampling, monitoring or transfusion (separate procedure); percutaneous

➔ *CPT Assistant* Fall 95:7; Apr 98:3

36625 cutdown

➔ *CPT Assistant* Fall 95:7

36640 Arterial catheterization for prolonged infusion therapy (chemotherapy), cutdown

➔ *CPT Assistant* Fall 95:7

(See also 96420-96425)

(For arterial catheterization for occlusion therapy, see 75894)

⊘ **36660** * Catheterization, umbilical artery, newborn, for diagnosis or therapy

➔ *CPT Assistant* Fall 95:8

Intraosseous

36680 Placement of needle for intraosseous infusion

▶Hemodialysis Access, Intervascular Cannulation for Extracorporeal Circulation, or Shunt Insertion◀

36800 Insertion of cannula for hemodialysis, other purpose (separate procedure); vein to vein

➔ *CPT Assistant* Fall 93:3

36810 arteriovenous, external (Scribner type)

➔ *CPT Assistant* Fall 93:3

36815 arteriovenous, external revision, or closure

➔ *CPT Assistant* Fall 93:3

(36820 has been deleted. To report, use 36821)

▲ **36819** Arteriovenous anastomosis, open; by upper arm basilic vein transposition

➔ *CPT Assistant* Nov 99:20; *CPT Changes* 2000; 2002

● **36820** by forearm vein transposition

➔ *CPT Changes* 2002

36821 direct, any site (eg, Cimino type) (separate procedure)

➔ *CPT Assistant* Fall 93:3; Feb 97:2; Nov 99:20; *CPT Changes* 2000

Arteriovenous Anastomosis, Direct
36821

A section of artery and a neighboring vein are joined, allowing blood to flow down the artery and into the vein for the purpose of increasing blood flow, usually in hemodialysis.

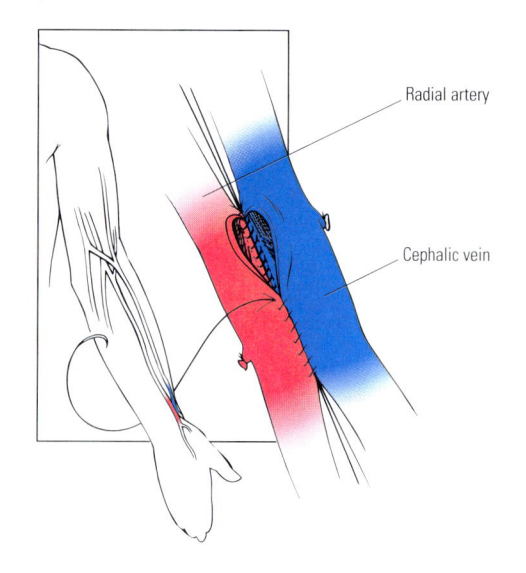

Radial artery

Cephalic vein

36822 Insertion of cannula(s) for prolonged extracorporeal circulation for cardiopulmonary insufficiency (ECMO) (separate procedure)

➔ *CPT Assistant* Fall 93:3; Feb 97:11

Insertion of Cannulas for Prolonged Extracorporeal Circulation Membrane Oxygenation (ECMO)
36822

The patient's venous blood is shunted and oxygenated outside of the body, bypassing the lungs. The treated blood is returned to body tissues through the femoral artery.

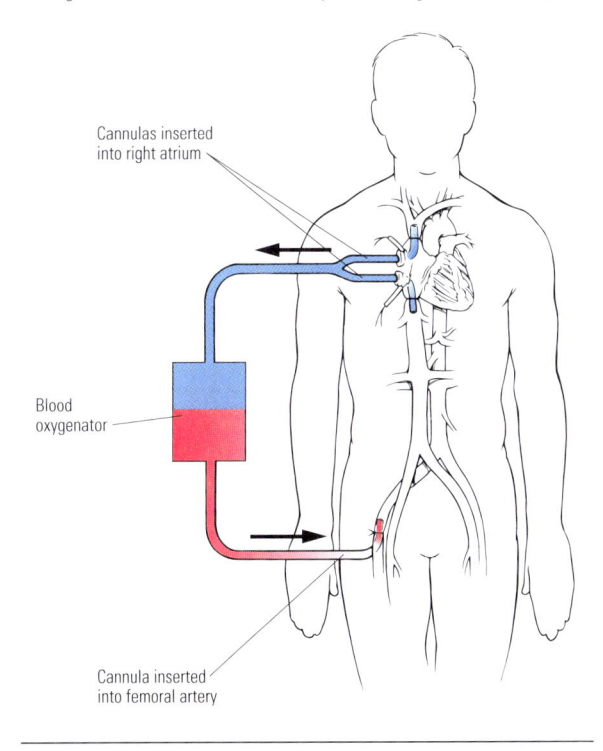

(For maintenance of prolonged extracorporeal circulation, use 33960)

▲ **36823** Insertion of arterial and venous cannula(s) for isolated extracorporeal circulation including regional chemotherapy perfusion to an extremity, with or without hyperthermia, with removal of cannula(s) and repair of arteriotomy and venotomy sites

➔ *CPT Assistant* Nov 98:14-15; *CPT Changes* 2002

▶(36823 includes chemotherapy perfusion supported by a membrane oxygenator/perfusion pump. Do not report 96408-96425 in conjunction with 36823)◀

36825 Creation of arteriovenous fistula by other than direct arteriovenous anastomosis (separate procedure); autogenous graft

➔ *CPT Assistant* Fall 93:3; Feb 97:1

(For direct arteriovenous anastomosis, use 36821)

36830 nonautogenous graft

➔ *CPT Assistant* Fall 93:3; Feb 97:1

Arteriovenous Fistula
36825-36830

A donor's vein (36825) or a synthetic vein (36830) is used to connect an artery and vein.

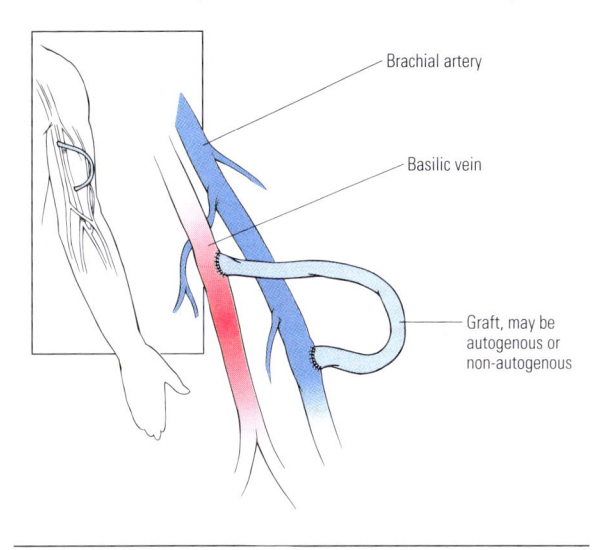

(For direct arteriovenous anastomosis, use 36821)

36831 Thrombectomy, open, arteriovenous fistula without revision, autogenous or nonautogenous dialysis graft (separate procedure)

➔ *CPT Assistant* Nov 98:14-15; Feb 99:6; Mar 99:6; Apr 99:11; *CPT Changes* 2001

36832 Revision, open, arteriovenous fistula; without thrombectomy, autogenous or nonautogenous dialysis graft (separate procedure)

➔ *CPT Assistant* Fall 93:3; Feb 97:2; Nov 98:15; Feb 99:6; Mar 99:6; Apr 99:11; Nov 99; *CPT Changes* 2000; 2001

36833 with thrombectomy, autogenous or nonautogenous dialysis graft (separate procedure)

➔ *CPT Assistant* Nov 98:15; Feb 99:6; Apr 99:11

36834 Plastic repair of arteriovenous aneurysm (separate procedure)

➔ *CPT Assistant* Fall 93:3

36835 Insertion of Thomas shunt (separate procedure)

(36840 has been deleted)

(36845 has been deleted)

36860 External cannula declotting (separate procedure); without balloon catheter

➔ *CPT Assistant* Fall 93:3; Feb 97:2; Nov 98:15; Feb 99:6

36861 with balloon catheter

> *CPT Assistant* Fall 93:3; Feb 97:2

▶(If imaging guidance is performed, use 76000)◀

36870 Thrombectomy, percutaneous, arteriovenous fistula, autogenous or nonautogenous graft (includes mechanical thrombus extraction and intra-graft thrombolysis)

> *CPT Changes* 2001

(Do not report 36550 in conjunction with code 36870)

(For catheterization, use 36145)

(For radiological supervision and interpretation, use 75790)

Portal Decompression Procedures

37140 Venous anastomosis; portocaval

(For peritoneal-venous shunt, use 49425)

37145 renoportal

37160 caval-mesenteric

37180 splenorenal, proximal

37181 splenorenal, distal (selective decompression of esophagogastric varices, any technique)

(37190 has been deleted. To report, use 36834)

Transcatheter Procedures

▶Codes for catheter placement and the radiologic supervision and interpretation should also be reported, in addition to the code(s) for the therapeutic aspect of the procedure.◀

37195 Thrombolysis, cerebral, by intravenous infusion

> *CPT Assistant* Nov 97:16

37200 Transcatheter biopsy

(For radiological supervision and interpretation, use 75970)

37201 Transcatheter therapy, infusion for thrombolysis other than coronary

> *CPT Assistant* Feb 97:2; Feb 01:10

(For radiological supervision and interpretation, use 75896)

37202 Transcatheter therapy, infusion other than for thrombolysis, any type (eg, spasmolytic, vasoconstrictive)

> *CPT Assistant* Oct 96:11; Jan 98:11; Apr 98:3, 9

(For thrombolysis of coronary vessels, see 92975, 92977)

(For radiological supervision and interpretation, use 75896)

37203 Transcatheter retrieval, percutaneous, of intravascular foreign body (eg, fractured venous or arterial catheter)

(For radiological supervision and interpretation, use 75961)

37204 Transcatheter occlusion or embolization (eg, for tumor destruction, to achieve hemostasis, to occlude a vascular malformation), percutaneous, any method, non-central nervous system, non-head or neck

> *CPT Assistant* Sep 98:7; Oct 98:10

(See also 61624, 61626)

(For radiological supervision and interpretation, use 75894)

37205 Transcatheter placement of an intravascular stent(s), (non-coronary vessel), percutaneous; initial vessel

> *CPT Assistant* Fall 93:18

(For radiological supervision and interpretation, use 75960)

+ 37206 each additional vessel (List separately in addition to code for primary procedure)

> *CPT Assistant* Fall 93:18

(Use 37206 in conjunction with code 37205)

▶(For transcatheter placement of extracranial cerebrovascular artery stent(s), see Category III codes 0005T, 0006T)◀

(For radiological supervision and interpretation, use 75960)

37207 Transcatheter placement of an intravascular stent(s), (non-coronary vessel), open; initial vessel

+ 37208 each additional vessel (List separately in addition to code for primary procedure)

(Use 37208 in conjunction with code 37207)

(For radiological supervision and interpretation, use 75960)

(For catheterizations, see 36215-36248)

(For transcatheter placement of intracoronary stent(s), see 92980, 92981)

37209 Exchange of a previously placed arterial catheter during thrombolytic therapy

(For radiological supervision and interpretation, use 75900)

Intravascular Ultrasound Services

Intravascular ultrasound services include all transducer manipulations and repositioning within the specific vessel being examined, both before and after therapeutic intervention (eg, stent placement).

Vascular access for intravascular ultrasound performed during a therapeutic intervention is not reported separately.

+ 37250   Intravascular ultrasound (non-coronary vessel) during diagnostic evaluation and/or therapeutic intervention; initial vessel (List separately in addition to code for primary procedure)

➲ *CPT Assistant* Nov 97:17; Nov 99:20; *CPT Changes* 2000

+ 37251   each additional vessel (List separately in addition to code for primary procedure)

➲ *CPT Assistant* Nov 97:17; Nov 99:20; *CPT Changes* 2000

(Use 37251 in conjunction with code 37250)

(For catheterizations, see 36215-36248)

(For transcatheter therapies, see 37200-37208, 61624, 61626)

(For radiological supervision and interpretation see 75945, 75946)

Ligation and Other Procedures

(37400-37560 have been deleted. To report, see 35201-35286)

37565   Ligation, internal jugular vein

37600   Ligation; external carotid artery

37605   internal or common carotid artery

37606   internal or common carotid artery, with gradual occlusion, as with Selverstone or Crutchfield clamp

(For ligation treatment of intracranial aneurysm, use 61703)

37607   Ligation or banding of angioaccess arteriovenous fistula

37609   Ligation or biopsy, temporal artery

37615   Ligation, major artery (eg, post-traumatic, rupture); neck

37616   chest

37617   abdomen

37618   extremity

37620   Interruption, partial or complete, of inferior vena cava by suture, ligation, plication, clip, extravascular, intravascular (umbrella device)

➲ *CPT Assistant* Nov 00:10

(For radiological supervision and interpretation, use 75940)

37650   Ligation of femoral vein

(37651 has been deleted. To report, use 37650 with modifier '-50')

37660   Ligation of common iliac vein

37700   Ligation and division of long saphenous vein at saphenofemoral junction, or distal interruptions

➲ *CPT Assistant* Aug 96:10

Ligation and Division of Long Saphenous Vein
37700

The physician ligates sections of the saphenous vein along the leg.

Femoral vein

Great saphenous vein

Isolating vein

Ligating branches

(37701 has been deleted. To report, use 37700 with modifier '-50')

37720 Ligation and division and complete stripping of long or short saphenous veins
➔ *CPT Assistant* Aug 96:10

(37721 has been deleted. To report, use 37720 with modifier '-50')

37730 Ligation and division and complete stripping of long and short saphenous veins
➔ *CPT Assistant* Aug 96:10

(37731 has been deleted. To report, use 37730 with modifier '-50')

37735 Ligation and division and complete stripping of long or short saphenous veins with radical excision of ulcer and skin graft and/or interruption of communicating veins of lower leg, with excision of deep fascia

(37737 has been deleted. To report, use 37735 with modifier '-50')

37760 Ligation of perforators, subfascial, radical (Linton type), with or without skin graft

37780 Ligation and division of short saphenous vein at saphenopopliteal junction (separate procedure)
➔ *CPT Assistant* Aug 96:10

(37781 has been deleted. To report, use 37780 with modifier '-50')

37785 Ligation, division, and/or excision of recurrent or secondary varicose veins (clusters), one leg

(37787 has been deleted. To report, use 37785 with modifier '-50')

37788 Penile revascularization, artery, with or without vein graft

37790 Penile venous occlusive procedure

37799 Unlisted procedure, vascular surgery
➔ *CPT Assistant* Spring 93:12; Fall 93:3; Feb 97:10; Sep 97:10

Hemic and Lymphatic Systems

Spleen

Excision

(38090 has been deleted. To report, use 38999)

38100 Splenectomy; total (separate procedure)

38101 partial (separate procedure)

+ 38102 total, en bloc for extensive disease, in conjunction with other procedure (List in addition to code for primary procedure)

Repair

38115 Repair of ruptured spleen (splenorrhaphy) with or without partial splenectomy

Laparoscopy

Surgical laparoscopy always includes diagnostic laparoscopy. To report a diagnostic laparoscopy (peritoneoscopy) (separate procedure), use 49320.

38120 Laparoscopy, surgical, splenectomy
➔ *CPT Assistant* Nov 99:20-21; Mar 00:5; *CPT Changes* 2000

38129 Unlisted laparoscopy procedure, spleen
➔ *CPT Assistant* Nov 99:20-21; Mar 00:5; *CPT Changes* 2000

Introduction

38200 Injection procedure for splenoportography

(For radiological supervision and interpretation, use 75810)

▶General◀

Bone Marrow or Stem Cell Services/▶Procedures◀

● **38220** Bone marrow aspiration
➔ *CPT Changes* 2002

● **38221** Bone marrow biopsy, needle or trocar
➔ *CPT Changes* 2002

▶(For bone marrow biopsy interpretation, use 88305)◀

38230 Bone marrow harvesting for transplantation

Bone Marrow Harvesting for Transplantation
38230

A biopsy needle is inserted into the marrow cavity of the iliac crest and bone marrow is removed from the donor.

Placement of biopsy needle — Posterior iliac spine

Biopsy needle — Bone marrow

38231 Blood-derived peripheral stem cell harvesting for transplantation, per collection
→ *CPT Assistant* Apr 96:1; Jul 00:11

38240 Bone marrow or blood-derived peripheral stem cell transplantation; allogenic
→ *CPT Assistant* Apr 96:1; Nov 98:15; Nov 99:21; *CPT Changes* 2000

38241 autologous
→ *CPT Assistant* Apr 96:1; Nov 98:15; Nov 99:21; *CPT Changes* 2000

(For bone marrow aspiration, use ▶38220◀)

(For modification, treatment, and processing of bone marrow or blood-derived stem cell specimens for transplantation, use 86915)

(For cryopreservation, freezing and storage of blood-derived stem cells for transplantation, use 88240)

(For thawing and expansion of blood-derived stem cells for transplantation, use 88241)

(For compatibility studies, see 86812-86822)

Lymph Nodes and Lymphatic Channels

Incision

38300* Drainage of lymph node abscess or lymphadenitis; simple

38305   extensive

38308 Lymphangiotomy or other operations on lymphatic channels

38380 Suture and/or ligation of thoracic duct; cervical approach

38381   thoracic approach

38382   abdominal approach

Excision

(For injection for sentinel node identification, use 38792)

38500 Biopsy or excision of lymph node(s); open, superficial
→ *CPT Assistant* Jun 97:5; Jul 99:6; *CPT Changes* 2001

(Do not report 38500 with 38700-38780)

38505   by needle, superficial (eg, cervical, inguinal, axillary)

▶(If imaging guidance is performed, see 76360, 76393, 76942)◀

(For fine needle aspiration, use ▶10021 or 10022◀)

▶(For evaluation of fine needle aspirate, see 88172, 88173)◀

38510   open, deep cervical node(s)
→ *CPT Assistant* May 98:10; *CPT Changes* 2001

38520   open, deep cervical node(s) with excision scalene fat pad
→ *CPT Assistant* May 98:10; *CPT Changes* 2001

38525   open, deep axillary node(s)
→ *CPT Assistant* May 98:10; Jul 99:6; *CPT Changes* 2001

38530   open, internal mammary node(s)
→ *CPT Assistant* May 98:10; *CPT Changes* 2001

(Do not report 38530 with 38720-38746)

(For percutaneous needle biopsy, retroperitoneal lymph node or mass, use 49180. For fine needle aspiration, use ▶10022)◀

(38540 has been deleted. To report, see 38510, 38520)

38542 Dissection, deep jugular node(s)
→ *CPT Assistant* Jul 99:6

(For radical cervical neck dissection, use 38720)

38550 Excision of cystic hygroma, axillary or cervical; without deep neurovascular dissection

38555   with deep neurovascular dissection

Limited Lymphadenectomy for Staging

38562 Limited lymphadenectomy for staging (separate procedure); pelvic and para-aortic

(When combined with prostatectomy, use 55812 or 55842)

(When combined with insertion of radioactive substance into prostate, use 55862)

38564 retroperitoneal (aortic and/or splenic)

Laparoscopy

Surgical laparoscopy always includes diagnostic laparoscopy. To report a diagnostic laparoscopy (peritoneoscopy) (separate procedure), use 49320.

38570 Laparoscopy, surgical; with retroperitoneal lymph node sampling (biopsy), single or multiple
> *CPT Assistant* Nov 99:21; Mar 00:5; *CPT Changes* 2000

38571 with bilateral total pelvic lymphadenectomy
> *CPT Assistant* Nov 99:21; Mar 00:5; *CPT Changes* 2000

38572 with bilateral total pelvic lymphadenectomy and peri-aortic lymph node sampling (biopsy), single or multiple
> *CPT Assistant* Nov 99:21; *CPT Changes* 2000

(For drainage of lymphocele to peritoneal cavity, use 49323)

38589 Unlisted laparoscopy procedure, lymphatic system
> *CPT Assistant* Nov 99:21; Mar 00:5; *CPT Changes* 2000

Radical Lymphadenectomy (Radical Resection of Lymph Nodes)

(For limited pelvic and retroperitoneal lymphadenectomies, see 38562, 38564)

38700 Suprahyoid lymphadenectomy

(38701 has been deleted. To report, use 38700 with modifier '-50')

38720 Cervical lymphadenectomy (complete)

(38721 has been deleted. To report, use 38720 with modifier '-50')

38724 Cervical lymphadenectomy (modified radical neck dissection)
> *CPT Assistant* Jan 01:13

38740 Axillary lymphadenectomy; superficial

38745 complete

+ 38746 Thoracic lymphadenectomy, regional, including mediastinal and peritracheal nodes (List separately in addition to code for primary procedure)

+ 38747 Abdominal lymphadenectomy, regional, including celiac, gastric, portal, peripancreatic, with or without para-aortic and vena caval nodes (List separately in addition to code for primary procedure)
> *CPT Assistant* Nov 98:15

38760 Inguinofemoral lymphadenectomy, superficial, including Cloquets node (separate procedure)

(38761 has been deleted. To report, use 38760 with modifier '-50')

38765 Inguinofemoral lymphadenectomy, superficial, in continuity with pelvic lymphadenectomy, including external iliac, hypogastric, and obturator nodes (separate procedure)

(38766 has been deleted. To report, use 38765 with modifier '-50')

38770 Pelvic lymphadenectomy, including external iliac, hypogastric, and obturator nodes (separate procedure)

(38771 has been deleted. To report, use 38770 with modifier '-50')

38780 Retroperitoneal transabdominal lymphadenectomy, extensive, including pelvic, aortic, and renal nodes (separate procedure)

(For excision and repair of lymphedematous skin and subcutaneous tissue, see 15000, 15570-15650)

Introduction

38790 Injection procedure; lymphangiography

(For radiological supervision and interpretation, see 75801-75807)

(38791 has been deleted. To report, use 38790 with modifier '-50')

⊘ **38792** for identification of sentinel node
> *CPT Assistant* Nov 98:15; Jul 99:6

(For excision of sentinel node, see 38500-38542)

(For nuclear medicine lymphatics and lymph gland imaging, use 78195)

38794 Cannulation, thoracic duct

Other Procedures

38999 Unlisted procedure, hemic or lymphatic system
> *CPT Assistant* May 98:10

Mediastinum and Diaphragm

Mediastinum

Incision

39000   Mediastinotomy with exploration, drainage, removal of foreign body, or biopsy; cervical approach

39010   transthoracic approach, including either transthoracic or median sternotomy

(39020 has been deleted. To report, use 39010)

(39050-39070 have been deleted. To report, see 39000-39010)

Excision

39200   Excision of mediastinal cyst

39220   Excision of mediastinal tumor

(For substernal thyroidectomy, use 60270)

(For thymectomy, use 60520)

Endoscopy

39400   Mediastinoscopy, with or without biopsy

Other Procedures

39499   Unlisted procedure, mediastinum

Diaphragm

Repair

(39500 has been deleted. To report, see 43324, 43325)

39501   Repair, laceration of diaphragm, any approach
➔ *CPT Assistant* Nov 00:3

39502   Repair, paraesophageal hiatus hernia, transabdominal, with or without fundoplasty, vagotomy, and/or pyloroplasty, except neonatal

39503   Repair, neonatal diaphragmatic hernia, with or without chest tube insertion and with or without creation of ventral hernia

(39510 has been deleted. To report, see 43324, 43325)

39520   Repair, diaphragmatic hernia (esophageal hiatal); transthoracic

39530   combined, thoracoabdominal

39531   combined, thoracoabdominal, with dilation of stricture (with or without gastroplasty)

39540   Repair, diaphragmatic hernia (other than neonatal), traumatic; acute
➔ *CPT Assistant* Nov:00 3

39541   chronic

39545   Imbrication of diaphragm for eventration, transthoracic or transabdominal, paralytic or nonparalytic
➔ *CPT Assistant* Nov 00:3

(39547 has been deleted. To report, use 39545)

39560   Resection, diaphragm; with simple repair (eg, primary suture)
➔ *CPT Assistant* Nov 99:21; Nov 00:3; *CPT Changes* 2000

39561   with complex repair (eg, prosthetic material, local muscle flap)
➔ *CPT Assistant* Nov 99:21; Nov 00:3; *CPT Changes* 2000

Other Procedures

39599   Unlisted procedure, diaphragm

Notes

⊘ =Modifier '-51' Exempt   ► ◄=New or Revised Text   ✚=Add-on Code   CPT 2002

Digestive System

Lips

(For procedures on skin of lips, see 10040 et seq)

Excision

40490 Biopsy of lip

40500 Vermilionectomy (lip shave), with mucosal advancement

40510 Excision of lip; transverse wedge excision with primary closure

40520 V-excision with primary direct linear closure

(For excision of mucous lesions, see 40810-40816)

40525 full thickness, reconstruction with local flap (eg, Estlander or fan)

40527 full thickness, reconstruction with cross lip flap (Abbe-Estlander)

40530 Resection of lip, more than one-fourth, without reconstruction

(For reconstruction, see 13131 et seq)

Repair (Cheiloplasty)

40650 Repair lip, full thickness; vermilion only
➜ *CPT Assistant* Jul 00:10

40652 up to half vertical height
➜ *CPT Assistant* Jul 00:10

40654 over one-half vertical height, or complex

40700 Plastic repair of cleft lip/nasal deformity; primary, partial or complete, unilateral

40701 primary bilateral, one stage procedure

40702 primary bilateral, one of two stages

40720 secondary, by recreation of defect and reclosure

(To report rhinoplasty only for nasal deformity secondary to congenital cleft lip, see 30460, 30462)

(40740 has been deleted. To report, use 40720 with modifier '-50')

(40760 has been deleted. To report, use 40527)

40761 with cross lip pedicle flap (Abbe-Estlander type), including sectioning and inserting of pedicle

(For repair cleft palate, see 42200 et seq)

(For other reconstructive procedures, see 14060, 14061, 15120-15261, 15574, 15576, 15630)

Other Procedures

40799 Unlisted procedure, lips

Vestibule of Mouth

The vestibule is the part of the oral cavity outside the dentoalveolar structures; it includes the mucosal and submucosal tissue of lips and cheeks.

Incision

40800* Drainage of abscess, cyst, hematoma, vestibule of mouth; simple

40801 complicated

40804* Removal of embedded foreign body, vestibule of mouth; simple

40805 complicated

40806 Incision of labial frenum (frenotomy)

Excision, Destruction

40808 Biopsy, vestibule of mouth

40810 Excision of lesion of mucosa and submucosa, vestibule of mouth; without repair

40812 with simple repair

40814 with complex repair

40816 complex, with excision of underlying muscle

40818 Excision of mucosa of vestibule of mouth as donor graft

40819 Excision of frenum, labial or buccal (frenumectomy, frenulectomy, frenectomy)

40820 Destruction of lesion or scar of vestibule of mouth by physical methods (eg, laser, thermal, cryo, chemical)

Repair

40830 Closure of laceration, vestibule of mouth; 2.5 cm or less

40831 over 2.5 cm or complex

40840 Vestibuloplasty; anterior

40842 posterior, unilateral

40843 posterior, bilateral

40844 entire arch

40845 complex (including ridge extension, muscle repositioning)

(For skin grafts, see 15000 et seq)

Other Procedures

40899 Unlisted procedure, vestibule of mouth

Digest 40490

Tongue and Floor of Mouth

Incision

41000* Intraoral incision and drainage of abscess, cyst, or hematoma of tongue or floor of mouth; lingual

41005* sublingual, superficial

41006 sublingual, deep, supramylohyoid

41007 submental space

41008 submandibular space

41009 masticator space

41010 Incision of lingual frenum (frenotomy)

41015 Extraoral incision and drainage of abscess, cyst, or hematoma of floor of mouth; sublingual

41016 submental

41017 submandibular

41018 masticator space

(For frenoplasty, use 41520)

Excision

41100 Biopsy of tongue; anterior two-thirds

41105 posterior one-third

41108 Biopsy of floor of mouth

41110 Excision of lesion of tongue without closure

41112 Excision of lesion of tongue with closure; anterior two-thirds

41113 posterior one-third

41114 with local tongue flap

(List 41114 in addition to code 41112 or 41113)

41115 Excision of lingual frenum (frenectomy)

41116 Excision, lesion of floor of mouth

41120 Glossectomy; less than one-half tongue

41130 hemiglossectomy

41135 partial, with unilateral radical neck dissection

41140 complete or total, with or without tracheostomy, without radical neck dissection

41145 complete or total, with or without tracheostomy, with unilateral radical neck dissection

41150 composite procedure with resection floor of mouth and mandibular resection, without radical neck dissection

41153 composite procedure with resection floor of mouth, with suprahyoid neck dissection

41155 composite procedure with resection floor of mouth, mandibular resection, and radical neck dissection (Commando type)
➔ *CPT Assistant* Jan 01:13

Repair

41250* Repair of laceration 2.5 cm or less; floor of mouth and/or anterior two-thirds of tongue

41251* posterior one-third of tongue

41252* Repair of laceration of tongue, floor of mouth, over 2.6 cm or complex

Other Procedures

41500 Fixation of tongue, mechanical, other than suture (eg, K-wire)

41510 Suture of tongue to lip for micrognathia (Douglas type procedure)

41520 Frenoplasty (surgical revision of frenum, eg, with Z-plasty)

(For frenotomy, see 40806, 41010)

41599 Unlisted procedure, tongue, floor of mouth
➔ *CPT Assistant* Dec 00:14

Dentoalveolar Structures

Incision

41800* Drainage of abscess, cyst, hematoma from dentoalveolar structures

41805 Removal of embedded foreign body from dentoalveolar structures; soft tissues

41806 bone

Excision, Destruction

41820 Gingivectomy, excision gingiva, each quadrant

41821 Operculectomy, excision pericoronal tissues

41822 Excision of fibrous tuberosities, dentoalveolar structures

41823 Excision of osseous tuberosities, dentoalveolar structures

41825 Excision of lesion or tumor (except listed above), dentoalveolar structures; without repair

41826 with simple repair

41827 with complex repair

(For nonexcisional destruction, use 41850)

41828 Excision of hyperplastic alveolar mucosa, each quadrant (specify)

41830 Alveolectomy, including curettage of osteitis or sequestrectomy

41850 Destruction of lesion (except excision), dentoalveolar structures

⊘ =Modifier '-51' Exempt   ▶ ◀=New or Revised Text   ✛ =Add-on Code

Other Procedures

41870 Periodontal mucosal grafting

41872 Gingivoplasty, each quadrant (specify)

41874 Alveoloplasty, each quadrant (specify)

(For closure of lacerations, see 40830, 40831)

(For segmental osteotomy, use 21206)

(For reduction of fractures, see 21421-21490)

41899 Unlisted procedure, dentoalveolar structures

Palate and Uvula

Incision

42000* Drainage of abscess of palate, uvula

Excision, Destruction

42100 Biopsy of palate, uvula

42104 Excision, lesion of palate, uvula; without closure

42106 with simple primary closure

42107 with local flap closure

(For skin graft, see 14040-14300)

(For mucosal graft, use 40818)

42120 Resection of palate or extensive resection of lesion

(For reconstruction of palate with extraoral tissue, see 14040-14300, 15050, 15120, 15240, 15576)

42140 Uvulectomy, excision of uvula

42145 Palatopharyngoplasty (eg, uvulopalatopharyngoplasty, uvulopharyngoplasty)

(42150 has been deleted. To report, see 21031, 21032)

42160 Destruction of lesion, palate or uvula (thermal, cryo or chemical)

Repair

42180 Repair, laceration of palate; up to 2 cm

42182 over 2 cm or complex

42200 Palatoplasty for cleft palate, soft and/or hard palate only

42205 Palatoplasty for cleft palate, with closure of alveolar ridge; soft tissue only

42210 with bone graft to alveolar ridge (includes obtaining graft)

42215 Palatoplasty for cleft palate; major revision

42220 secondary lengthening procedure

42225 attachment pharyngeal flap
➲ *CPT Assistant* Aug 97:18

42226 Lengthening of palate, and pharyngeal flap

42227 Lengthening of palate, with island flap

42235 Repair of anterior palate, including vomer flap

(42250 has been deleted. To report, use 30600)

42260 Repair of nasolabial fistula

(For repair of cleft lip, see 40700 et seq)

42280 Maxillary impression for palatal prosthesis

42281 Insertion of pin-retained palatal prosthesis

Other Procedures

42299 Unlisted procedure, palate, uvula

Salivary Gland and Ducts

Incision

42300* Drainage of abscess; parotid, simple

42305 parotid, complicated

42310* Drainage of abscess; submaxillary or sublingual, intraoral

42320* submaxillary, external

42325 Fistulization of sublingual salivary cyst (ranula);

42326 with prosthesis

42330 Sialolithotomy; submandibular (submaxillary), sublingual or parotid, uncomplicated, intraoral

42335 submandibular (submaxillary), complicated, intraoral

42340 parotid, extraoral or complicated intraoral

Excision

42400* Biopsy of salivary gland; needle

42405 incisional

▶(If imaging guidance is performed, see 76003, 76360, 76393, 76942)◀

42408 Excision of sublingual salivary cyst (ranula)

42409 Marsupialization of sublingual salivary cyst (ranula)

(For fistulization of sublingual salivary cyst, use 42325)

42410 Excision of parotid tumor or parotid gland; lateral lobe, without nerve dissection

42415 lateral lobe, with dissection and preservation of facial nerve

42420 total, with dissection and preservation of facial nerve

42425 total, en bloc removal with sacrifice of facial nerve

42426 total, with unilateral radical neck dissection

(For suture or grafting of facial nerve, see 64864, 64865, 69740, 69745)

42440 Excision of submandibular (submaxillary) gland

42450 Excision of sublingual gland

Repair

42500 Plastic repair of salivary duct, sialodochoplasty; primary or simple

42505 secondary or complicated

42507 Parotid duct diversion, bilateral (Wilke type procedure);

42508 with excision of one submandibular gland

42509 with excision of both submandibular glands

42510 with ligation of both submandibular (Wharton's) ducts

Other Procedures

42550 Injection procedure for sialography

(For radiological supervision and interpretation, use 70390)

42600 Closure salivary fistula

42650* Dilation salivary duct

42660* Dilation and catheterization of salivary duct, with or without injection

42665 Ligation salivary duct, intraoral

42699 Unlisted procedure, salivary glands or ducts

Pharynx, Adenoids, and Tonsils

Incision

42700* Incision and drainage abscess; peritonsillar

42720 retropharyngeal or parapharyngeal, intraoral approach

42725 retropharyngeal or parapharyngeal, external approach

Excision, Destruction

42800 Biopsy; oropharynx

42802 hypopharynx

42804 nasopharynx, visible lesion, simple

42806 nasopharynx, survey for unknown primary lesion

(For laryngoscopic biopsy, see 31510, 31535, 31536)

42808 Excision or destruction of lesion of pharynx, any method

42809 Removal of foreign body from pharynx

42810 Excision branchial cleft cyst or vestige, confined to skin and subcutaneous tissues

42815 Excision branchial cleft cyst, vestige, or fistula, extending beneath subcutaneous tissues and/or into pharynx

42820 Tonsillectomy and adenoidectomy; under age 12
➜ *CPT Assistant* Aug 97:18; Feb 98:11

42821 age 12 or over
➜ *CPT Assistant* Aug 97:18

42825 Tonsillectomy, primary or secondary; under age 12
➜ *CPT Assistant* Aug 97:18

42826 age 12 or over
➜ *CPT Assistant* Aug 97:18

42830 Adenoidectomy, primary; under age 12

42831 age 12 or over

42835 Adenoidectomy, secondary; under age 12

42836 age 12 or over
➜ *CPT Assistant* Feb 98:11

42842 Radical resection of tonsil, tonsillar pillars, and/or retromolar trigone; without closure

42844 closure with local flap (eg, tongue, buccal)

42845 closure with other flap

(For closure with other flap(s), use appropriate number for flap(s))

(When combined with radical neck dissection, use also 38720)

42860 Excision of tonsil tags

42870 Excision or destruction lingual tonsil, any method (separate procedure)

(42880 has been deleted. For resection of the nasopharynx (eg, juvenile angiofibroma) by bicoronal and/or transzygomatic approach, see 61586 and 61600)

42890 Limited pharyngectomy

42892 Resection of lateral pharyngeal wall or pyriform sinus, direct closure by advancement of lateral and posterior pharyngeal walls

(When combined with radical neck dissection, use also 38720)

42894 Resection of pharyngeal wall requiring closure with myocutaneous flap

(When combined with radical neck dissection, use also 38720)

(42895 has been deleted. To report, use 38720 with 42890)

Repair

42900 Suture pharynx for wound or injury

42950 Pharyngoplasty (plastic or reconstructive operation on pharynx)

(For pharyngeal flap, use 42225)

42953 Pharyngoesophageal repair

(For closure with myocutaneous or other flap, use appropriate number in addition)

Other Procedures

42955   Pharyngostomy (fistulization of pharynx, external for feeding)

42960   Control oropharyngeal hemorrhage, primary or secondary (eg, post-tonsillectomy); simple

42961   complicated, requiring hospitalization

42962   with secondary surgical intervention

▲ **42970**   Control of nasopharyngeal hemorrhage, primary or secondary (eg, postadenoidectomy); simple, with posterior nasal packs, with or without anterior packs and/or cautery
➲ *CPT Changes* 2002

42971   complicated, requiring hospitalization

42972   with secondary surgical intervention

42999   Unlisted procedure, pharynx, adenoids, or tonsils

Esophagus

Incision

(For esophageal intubation with laparotomy, use 43510)

(43000 has been deleted)

43020   Esophagotomy, cervical approach, with removal of foreign body

43030   Cricopharyngeal myotomy

(43040 has been deleted)

43045   Esophagotomy, thoracic approach, with removal of foreign body

Excision

(For gastrointestinal reconstruction for previous esophagectomy, see 43360, 43361)

43100   Excision of lesion, esophagus, with primary repair; cervical approach

43101   thoracic or abdominal approach

(43105 has been deleted. To report, see 43107, 43116, 43124, and 31360)

(43106 has been deleted. To report, see 43107, 43116, 43124, and 31365)

43107   Total or near total esophagectomy, without thoracotomy; with pharyngogastrostomy or cervical esophagogastrostomy, with or without pyloroplasty (transhiatal)

▲ **43108**   with colon interposition or small intestine reconstruction, including intestine mobilization, preparation and anastomosis(es)
➲ *CPT Changes* 2002

(43110 has been deleted. To report, see 43107-43113)

(43111 has been deleted. To report, see 43107-43113)

43112   Total or near total esophagectomy, with thoracotomy; with pharyngogastrostomy or cervical esophagogastrostomy, with or without pyloroplasty

▲ **43113**   with colon interposition or small intestine reconstruction, including intestine mobilization, preparation, and anastomosis(es)
➲ *CPT Changes* 2002

(43115 has been deleted. To report, see 43116-43118)

43116   Partial esophagectomy, cervical, with free intestinal graft, including microvascular anastomosis, obtaining the graft and intestinal reconstruction
➲ *CPT Assistant* Nov 97:17; Nov 98:16

(Do not report code 69990 in addition to code 43116)

(Report 43116 with the modifier '-52' appended if intestinal or free jejunal graft with microvascular anastomosis is performed by another physician)

(For free jejunal graft with microvascular anastomosis performed by another physician, use 43496)

43117   Partial esophagectomy, distal two-thirds, with thoracotomy and separate abdominal incision, with or without proximal gastrectomy; with thoracic esophagogastrostomy, with or without pyloroplasty (Ivor Lewis)

▲ **43118**   with colon interposition or small intestine reconstruction, including intestine mobilization, preparation, and anastomosis(es)
➲ *CPT Changes* 2002

(43119 has been deleted. To report, see 43107, 43124)

(43120 has been deleted. To report, use 43122)

43121   Partial esophagectomy, distal two-thirds, with thoracotomy only, with or without proximal gastrectomy, with thoracic esophagogastrostomy, with or without pyloroplasty

43122   Partial esophagectomy, thoracoabdominal or abdominal approach, with or without proximal gastrectomy; with esophagogastrostomy, with or without pyloroplasty

▲ **43123**   with colon interposition or small intestine reconstruction, including intestine mobilization, preparation, and anastomosis(es)
➲ *CPT Changes* 2002

43124   Total or partial esophagectomy, without reconstruction (any approach), with cervical esophagostomy

43130   Diverticulectomy of hypopharynx or esophagus, with or without myotomy; cervical approach

43135   thoracic approach

(43136 has been deleted. To report, use 43499)

Endoscopy

For endoscopic procedures, code appropriate endoscopy of each anatomic site examined.

Surgical endoscopy always includes diagnostic endoscopy.

43200 Esophagoscopy, rigid or flexible; diagnostic, with or without collection of specimen(s) by brushing or washing (separate procedure)
→ *CPT Assistant* Spring 94:1; Jun 98:10; Nov 99:21; *CPT Changes* 2000

43202 with biopsy, single or multiple
→ *CPT Assistant* Spring 94:1

43204 with injection sclerosis of esophageal varices
→ *CPT Assistant* Spring 94:1

43205 with band ligation of esophageal varices
→ *CPT Assistant* Spring 94:1

43215 with removal of foreign body
→ *CPT Assistant* Spring 94:1

(For radiological supervision and interpretation, use 74235)

43216 with removal of tumor(s), polyp(s), or other lesion(s) by hot biopsy forceps or bipolar cautery
→ *CPT Assistant* Spring 94:1

43217 with removal of tumor(s), polyp(s), or other lesion(s) by snare technique
→ *CPT Assistant* Spring 94:1

(43218 has been deleted. To report, use 43499)

43219 with insertion of plastic tube or stent
→ *CPT Assistant* Spring 94:2

43220 with balloon dilation (less than 30 mm diameter)
→ *CPT Assistant* Spring 94:2; Jan 97:10

(If imaging guidance is performed, use 74360)

(For endoscopic dilation with balloon 30 mm diameter or larger, use 43458)

(For dilation without visualization, see 43450-43453)

(43221 has been deleted. To report, use 43200 or 43235)

(43222 has been deleted. To report, use 43200, 43202, 43235, or 43239)

(43223 has been deleted. To report, use 43215 or 43247)

(43224 has been deleted. To report, use 43217 or 43251)

(43225 has been deleted. To report, use 43499)

43226 with insertion of guide wire followed by dilation over guide wire
→ *CPT Assistant* Spring 94:2

(For radiological supervision and interpretation, use 74360)

▲ **43227** with control of bleeding (eg, injection, bipolar cautery, unipolar cautery, laser, heater probe, stapler, plasma coagulator)
→ *CPT Assistant* Spring 94:2; *CPT Changes* 2002

43228 with ablation of tumor(s), polyp(s), or other lesion(s), not amenable to removal by hot biopsy forceps, bipolar cautery or snare technique
→ *CPT Assistant* Spring 94:2; Nov 98:21

(For esophagoscopic photodynamic therapy, report 43228 in addition to 96570, 96571 as appropriate)

43231 with endoscopic ultrasound examination
→ *CPT Changes* 2001

43232 with transendoscopic ultrasound-guided intramural or transmural fine needle aspiration/biopsy(s)
→ *CPT Changes* 2001

(Do not report 76975 in conjunction with 43231, 43232)

(For interpretation of specimen, see 88172-88173)

43234 Upper gastrointestinal endoscopy, simple primary examination (eg, with small diameter flexible endoscope) (separate procedure)

43235 Upper gastrointestinal endoscopy including esophagus, stomach, and either the duodenum and/or jejunum as appropriate; diagnostic, with or without collection of specimen(s) by brushing or washing (separate procedure)
→ *CPT Assistant* Spring 94:4; Dec 97:11

43239 with biopsy, single or multiple
→ *CPT Assistant* Spring 94:4; Apr 98:14; Feb 99:11

▶(For upper gastrointestinal endoscopy with suturing of the esophagogastric junction, use Category III code 0008T)◀

43240 with transmural drainage of pseudocyst
→ *CPT Changes* 2001

43241 with transendoscopic intraluminal tube or catheter placement
→ *CPT Assistant* Spring 94:4; *CPT Changes* 2001

43242 with transendoscopic ultrasound-guided intramural or transmural fine needle aspiration/biopsy(s)
→ *CPT Changes* 2001

(Do not report 76975 in conjunction with 43242)

(For interpretation of specimen, see 88172-88173)

43243 with injection sclerosis of esophageal and/or gastric varices
→ *CPT Assistant* Spring 94:4

43244   with band ligation of esophageal and/or gastric varices

> *CPT Assistant* Spring 94:4

▲ **43245**   with dilation of gastric outlet for obstruction (eg, balloon, guide wire, bougie)

> *CPT Assistant* Spring 94:4; *CPT Changes* 2002

43246   with directed placement of percutaneous gastrostomy tube

> *CPT Assistant* Spring 94:4; Feb 97:10

(For radiological supervision and interpretation, use 74350)

43247   with removal of foreign body

> *CPT Assistant* Spring 94:4

(For radiological supervision and interpretation, use 74235)

43248   with insertion of guide wire followed by dilation of esophagus over guide wire

> *CPT Assistant* Spring 94:4; Dec 97:11

43249   with balloon dilation of esophagus (less than 30 mm diameter)

43250   with removal of tumor(s), polyp(s), or other lesion(s) by hot biopsy forceps or bipolar cautery

> *CPT Assistant* Spring 94:4; Feb 99:11

43251   with removal of tumor(s), polyp(s), or other lesion(s) by snare technique

> *CPT Assistant* Spring 94:4

43255   with control of bleeding, any method

> *CPT Assistant* Spring 94:4

43256   with transendoscopic stent placement (includes predilation)

> *CPT Changes* 2001

43258   with ablation of tumor(s), polyp(s), or other lesion(s) not amenable to removal by hot biopsy forceps, bipolar cautery or snare technique

> *CPT Assistant* Spring 94:4

(For injection sclerosis of esophageal varices, use 43204 or 43243)

43259   with endoscopic ultrasound examination

> *CPT Assistant* Spring 94:4

(For radiological supervision and interpretation, use 76975)

43260   Endoscopic retrograde cholangiopancreatography (ERCP); diagnostic, with or without collection of specimen(s) by brushing or washing (separate procedure)

> *CPT Assistant* Spring 94:5

Endoscopic Retrograde Cholangiopancreatography (ERCP)
43260

Examination of the hepatobiliary system (pancreatic ducts, hepatic ducts, common bile ducts, duodenal papilla (ampulla of Vater) and gallbladder (if present) performed through a side-viewing flexible fiberoptic endoscope.

(For radiological supervision and interpretation, see 74328, 74329, 74330)

43261   with biopsy, single or multiple

> *CPT Assistant* Spring 94:5

43262   with sphincterotomy/papillotomy

> *CPT Assistant* Spring 94:5

(For radiological supervision and interpretation, see 74328, 74329, 74330)

43263   with pressure measurement of sphincter of Oddi (pancreatic duct or common bile duct)

> *CPT Assistant* Spring 94:5

(For radiological supervision and interpretation, see 74328, 74329, 74330)

▲ **43264**   with endoscopic retrograde removal of calculus/calculi from biliary and/or pancreatic ducts

> *CPT Assistant* Spring 94:5; *CPT Changes* 2002

(When done with sphincterotomy, also use 43262)

(For radiological supervision and interpretation, see 74328, 74329, 74330)

▲ **43265**   with endoscopic retrograde destruction, lithotripsy of calculus/calculi, any method

> *CPT Assistant* Spring 94:5; *CPT Changes* 2002

(When done with sphincterotomy, also use 43262)

(For radiological supervision and interpretation, see 74328, 74329, 74330)

43267   with endoscopic retrograde insertion of nasobiliary or nasopancreatic drainage tube

> *CPT Assistant* Spring 94:6

(When done with sphincterotomy, also use 43262)

(For radiological supervision and interpretation, see 74328, 74329, 74330)

43268   with endoscopic retrograde insertion of tube or stent into bile or pancreatic duct

> *CPT Assistant* Spring 94:6

(When done with sphincterotomy, also use 43262)

(For radiological supervision and interpretation, see 74328, 74329, 74330)

43269   with endoscopic retrograde removal of foreign body and/or change of tube or stent

> *CPT Assistant* Spring 94:6

(When done with sphincterotomy, also use 43262)

(For radiological supervision and interpretation, see 74328, 74329, 74330)

43271   with endoscopic retrograde balloon dilation of ampulla, biliary and/or pancreatic duct(s)

> *CPT Assistant* Spring 94:6

(When done with sphincterotomy, also use 43262)

(For radiological supervision and interpretation, see 74328, 74329, 74330)

43272   with ablation of tumor(s), polyp(s), or other lesion(s) not amenable to removal by hot biopsy forceps, bipolar cautery or snare technique

(For radiological supervision and interpretation, see 74328, 74329, 74330)

Laparoscopy

Surgical laparoscopy always includes diagnostic laparoscopy. To report a diagnostic laparoscopy (peritoneoscopy) (separate procedure), use 49320.

43280   Laparoscopy, surgical, esophagogastric fundoplasty (eg, Nissen, Toupet procedures)

> *CPT Assistant* Nov 99:22; Mar 00:5; *CPT Changes* 2000

(For open approach, use 43324)

43289   Unlisted laparoscopy procedure, esophagus

> *CPT Assistant* Nov 99:22; Mar 00:5; *CPT Changes* 2000

Repair

43300   Esophagoplasty, (plastic repair or reconstruction), cervical approach; without repair of tracheoesophageal fistula

43305   with repair of tracheoesophageal fistula

43310   Esophagoplasty, (plastic repair or reconstruction), thoracic approach; without repair of tracheoesophageal fistula

43312   with repair of tracheoesophageal fistula

● **43313**   Esophagoplasty for congenital defect, (plastic repair or reconstruction), thoracic approach; without repair of congenital tracheoesophageal fistula

> *CPT Changes* 2002

● **43314**   with repair of congenital tracheoesophageal fistula

> *CPT Changes* 2002

43320   Esophagogastrostomy (cardioplasty), with or without vagotomy and pyloroplasty, transabdominal or transthoracic approach

(43321 has been deleted. To report, use 43320)

43324   Esophagogastric fundoplasty (eg, Nissen, Belsey IV, Hill procedures)

> *CPT Assistant* Sep 96:10; Nov 99:22; *CPT Changes* 2000

(For laparoscopic procedure, use 43280)

Nissen Fundoplasty
43324

The lower esophagus is accessed through an upper abdominal or lower thoracic incision. The fundus of the stomach is mobilized and wrapped around the lower esophageal sphincter, and the wrap is sutured into place.

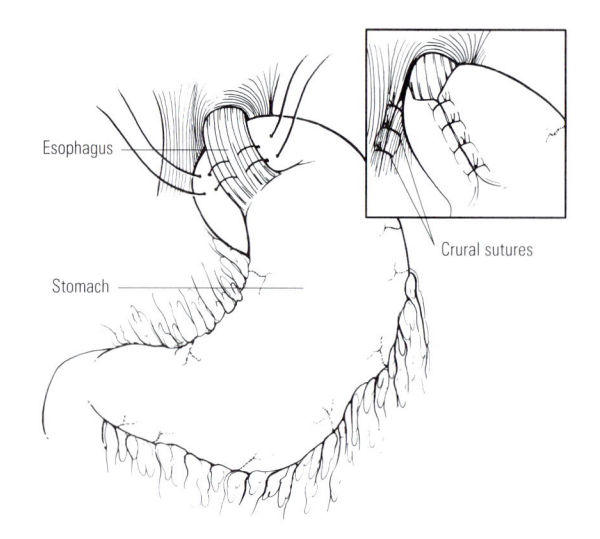

Esophagus

Crural sutures

Stomach

43325   Esophagogastric fundoplasty; with fundic patch (Thal-Nissen procedure)

(For cricopharyngeal myotomy, use 43030)

43326   with gastroplasty (eg, Collis)

43330 Esophagomyotomy (Heller type); abdominal approach
➲ CPT Assistant Nov 99:22; CPT Changes 2000

43331 thoracic approach
➲ CPT Assistant Nov 99:22; CPT Changes 2000

(For thoracoscopic esophagomyotomy, use 32665)

43340 Esophagojejunostomy (without total gastrectomy); abdominal approach

43341 thoracic approach

43350 Esophagostomy, fistulization of esophagus, external; abdominal approach

43351 thoracic approach

43352 cervical approach

43360 Gastrointestinal reconstruction for previous esophagectomy, for obstructing esophageal lesion or fistula, or for previous esophageal exclusion; with stomach, with or without pyloroplasty

▲ **43361** with colon interposition or small intestine reconstruction, including intestine mobilization, preparation, and anastomosis(es)
➲ CPT Changes 2002

43400 Ligation, direct, esophageal varices

43401 Transection of esophagus with repair, for esophageal varices

43405 Ligation or stapling at gastroesophageal junction for pre-existing esophageal perforation

43410 Suture of esophageal wound or injury; cervical approach
➲ CPT Assistant Jun 96:7

43415 transthoracic or transabdominal approach

43420 Closure of esophagostomy or fistula; cervical approach

43425 transthoracic or transabdominal approach

(For repair of esophageal hiatal hernia, see 39520 et seq)

Manipulation

(For associated esophagogram, use 74220)

43450＊ Dilation of esophagus, by unguided sound or bougie, single or multiple passes
➲ CPT Assistant Spring 94:1; Jan 97:10; Apr 98:14; Jun 98:10

(43451 has been deleted. To report, use 43450)

43453 Dilation of esophagus, over guide wire
➲ CPT Assistant Spring 94:1; Jan 97:10; Dec 97:11

(For dilation with direct visualization, use 43220)

(43455 has been deleted. To report, see 43220, 43458, 74360)

43456 Dilation of esophagus, by balloon or dilator, retrograde
➲ CPT Assistant Spring 94:3; Jan 97:10

43458 Dilation of esophagus with balloon (30 mm diameter or larger) for achalasia
➲ CPT Assistant Spring 94:3; Jan 97:10

(For dilation with balloon less than 30 mm diameter, use 43220)

(For radiological supervision and interpretation, use 74360)

43460 Esophagogastric tamponade, with balloon (Sengstaaken type)

(For removal of esophageal foreign body by balloon catheter, see 43215, 43247, 74235)

Other Procedures

43496 Free jejunum transfer with microvascular anastomosis
➲ CPT Assistant Apr 97:4; Jun 97:10; Nov 97:17; Nov 98:16

(Do not report code 69990 in addition to code 43496)

43499 Unlisted procedure, esophagus

Stomach

Incision

43500 Gastrotomy; with exploration or foreign body removal

43501 with suture repair of bleeding ulcer

43502 with suture repair of pre-existing esophagogastric laceration (eg, Mallory-Weiss)

43510 with esophageal dilation and insertion of permanent intraluminal tube (eg, Celestin or Mousseaux-Barbin)

43520 Pyloromyotomy, cutting of pyloric muscle (Fredet-Ramstedt type operation)

Excision

43600 Biopsy of stomach; by capsule, tube, peroral (one or more specimens)

43605 by laparotomy

43610 Excision, local; ulcer or benign tumor of stomach

43611 malignant tumor of stomach

43620 Gastrectomy, total; with esophagoenterostomy

43621 with Roux-en-Y reconstruction

43622 with formation of intestinal pouch, any type

(43625 has been deleted. To report, use 43622)

(43630 has been deleted. To report, see 43631-43634)

43631 Gastrectomy, partial, distal; with gastroduodenostomy

43632 with gastrojejunostomy

43633 with Roux-en-Y reconstruction

43634 with formation of intestinal pouch

+ 43635 Vagotomy when performed with partial distal gastrectomy (List separately in addition to code(s) for primary procedure)
→ *CPT Assistant* Nov 97:17

(Use 43635 in conjunction with codes 43631, 43632, 43633, 43634)

43638 Gastrectomy, partial, proximal, thoracic or abdominal approach including esophagogastrostomy, with vagotomy;

43639 with pyloroplasty or pyloromyotomy

(For regional thoracic lymphadenectomy, use 38746)

(For regional abdominal lymphadenectomy, use 38747)

43640 Vagotomy including pyloroplasty, with or without gastrostomy; truncal or selective

(For pyloroplasty, use 43800)

(For vagotomy, see 64752-64760)

43641 parietal cell (highly selective)

(For upper gastrointestinal endoscopy, see 43234-43259)

(43700 has been deleted. To report, use 43235)

(43702 has been deleted. To report, use 43239)

(43709 has been deleted. To report, use 43247)

(43711 has been deleted. To report, use 43251)

(43712 has been deleted. To report, use 43255)

(43714 has been deleted. To report, use 43258)

Laparoscopy

Surgical laparoscopy always includes diagnostic laparoscopy. To report a diagnostic laparoscopy (peritoneoscopy) (separate procedure), use 49320.

43651 Laparoscopy, surgical; transection of vagus nerves, truncal
→ *CPT Assistant* Nov 99:22; Mar 00:5; *CPT Changes* 2000

43652 transection of vagus nerves, selective or highly selective
→ *CPT Assistant* Nov 99:22; Mar 00:5; *CPT Changes* 2000

43653 gastrostomy, without construction of gastric tube (eg, Stamm procedure) (separate procedure)
→ *CPT Assistant* Nov 99:22; Mar 00:5; *CPT Changes* 2000

43659 Unlisted laparoscopy procedure, stomach
→ *CPT Assistant* Nov 99:22; Mar 00:5; *CPT Changes* 2000

Introduction

43750 Percutaneous placement of gastrostomy tube
→ *CPT Assistant* Spring 94:1

Gastrostomy Tube Placement
43750

A needle with a suture attached is passed through an incision into the stomach. The needle is snared and removed via the mouth. The gastrostomy tube is connected to the suture and passed through the mouth into the stomach and out the abdominal wall.

Gastrostomy tube is passed through mouth and esophagus

Needle trocar

Gastrostomy tube in place inside stomach

Sutured to skin

(For radiological supervision and interpretation, use 74350)

43752 Naso- or oro-gastric tube placement, necessitating physician's skill
→ *CPT Changes* 2001

(If imaging guidance is performed, use 76000)

(For enteric tube placement, see 44500, 74340)

(Do not report 43752 in conjunction with critical care codes 99291-99292, or neonatal intensive care codes, 99295-99298)

43760✱ Change of gastrostomy tube

(For endoscopic placement of gastrostomy tube, use 43246)

(For radiological supervision and interpretation, use 75984)

43761 Repositioning of the gastric feeding tube, any method, through the duodenum for enteric nutrition
⊃ *CPT Assistant* Oct 96:9; Nov 99:22; *CPT Changes* 2000

▶(If imaging guidance is performed, use 75984)◀

(43765 has been deleted. To report, use 43760)

Other Procedures

43800 Pyloroplasty

(For pyloroplasty and vagotomy, use 43640)

43810 Gastroduodenostomy

43820 Gastrojejunostomy; without vagotomy

43825   with vagotomy, any type

43830 Gastrostomy, open; without construction of gastric tube (eg, Stamm procedure) (separate procedure)
⊃ *CPT Assistant* Nov 99:22; *CPT Changes* 2000

43831   neonatal, for feeding
⊃ *CPT Assistant* Nov 99:22; *CPT Changes* 2000

(For change of gastrostomy tube, use 43760)

43832   with construction of gastric tube (eg, Janeway procedure)
⊃ *CPT Assistant* Nov 99:22; *CPT Changes* 2000

(43834 has been deleted. To report, use 43246)

43840 Gastrorrhaphy, suture of perforated duodenal or gastric ulcer, wound, or injury

43842 Gastric restrictive procedure, without gastric bypass, for morbid obesity; vertical-banded gastroplasty
⊃ *CPT Assistant* May 98:5

43843   other than vertical-banded gastroplasty
⊃ *CPT Assistant* May 98:5

(43844 has been deleted. To report, use 43847)

(43845 has been deleted. To report, see 43842, 43843)

43846 Gastric restrictive procedure, with gastric bypass for morbid obesity; with short limb (less than 100 cm) Roux-en-Y gastroenterostomy
⊃ *CPT Assistant* May 98:5

Gastric Bypass for Morbid Obesity
43846

The stomach is partitioned with a staple line on the lesser curvature (no band, no gastric transection). A short limb of small bowel (less than 100 cm) is divided and anastomosed to the small upper stomach pouch.

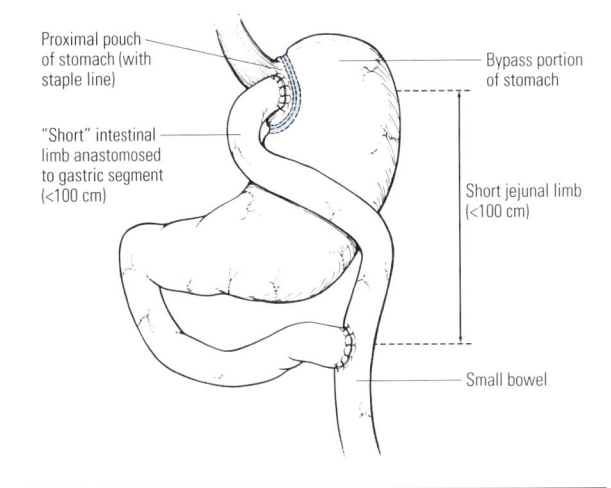

▲ 43847   with small intestine reconstruction to limit absorption
⊃ *CPT Assistant* May 98:5; *CPT Changes* 2002

43848 Revision of gastric restrictive procedure for morbid obesity (separate procedure)
⊃ *CPT Assistant* May 98:5

43850 Revision of gastroduodenal anastomosis (gastroduodenostomy) with reconstruction; without vagotomy

43855   with vagotomy

▲ 43860 Revision of gastrojejunal anastomosis (gastrojejunostomy) with reconstruction, with or without partial gastrectomy or intestine resection; without vagotomy
⊃ *CPT Changes* 2002

43865   with vagotomy

43870 Closure of gastrostomy, surgical

43880 Closure of gastrocolic fistula

(43885 has been deleted)

43999 Unlisted procedure, stomach

Intestines (Except Rectum)

Incision

(44000 has been deleted)

44005 Enterolysis (freeing of intestinal adhesion) (separate procedure)

→ *CPT Assistant* Nov 97:17; Nov 99:23; Jan 00:11; Apr 00:10; *CPT Changes* 2000

►(Do not report 44005 in addition to 45136)◄

(For laparoscopic approach, use 44200)

44010 Duodenotomy, for exploration, biopsy(s), or foreign body removal

+ 44015 Tube or needle catheter jejunostomy for enteral alimentation, intraoperative, any method (List separately in addition to primary procedure)

▲ 44020 Enterotomy, small intestine, other than duodenum; for exploration, biopsy(s), or foreign body removal

→ *CPT Changes* 2002

44021 for decompression (eg, Baker tube)

44025 Colotomy, for exploration, biopsy(s), or foreign body removal

(44040 has been deleted. To report, see 44602-44605)

44050 Reduction of volvulus, intussusception, internal hernia, by laparotomy

44055 Correction of malrotation by lysis of duodenal bands and/or reduction of midgut volvulus (eg, Ladd procedure)

(44060 has been deleted. To report, use 44799)

Excision

44100 Biopsy of intestine by capsule, tube, peroral (one or more specimens)

▲ 44110 Excision of one or more lesions of small or large intestine not requiring anastomosis, exteriorization, or fistulization; single enterotomy

→ *CPT Changes* 2002

44111 multiple enterotomies

(44115 has been deleted. To report, use 44799)

44120 Enterectomy, resection of small intestine; single resection and anastomosis

►(Do not report 44120 in addition to 45136)◄

+ 44121 each additional resection and anastomosis (List separately in addition to code for primary procedure)

(Use 44121 in conjunction with code 44120)

44125 with enterostomy

● 44126 Enterectomy, resection of small intestine for congenital atresia, single resection and anastomosis of proximal segment of intestine; without tapering

→ *CPT Changes* 2002

● 44127 with tapering

→ *CPT Changes* 2002

+ ● 44128 each additional resection and anastomosis (List separately in addition to code for primary procedure)

→ *CPT Changes* 2002

►(Use 44128 in conjunction with codes 44126, 44127)◄

44130 Enteroenterostomy, anastomosis of intestine, with or without cutaneous enterostomy (separate procedure)

(44131 has been deleted)

44132 Donor enterectomy, open, with preparation and maintenance of allograft; from cadaver donor

→ *CPT Changes* 2001

44133 partial, from living donor

→ *CPT Changes* 2001

44135 Intestinal allotransplantation; from cadaver donor

→ *CPT Changes* 2001

44136 from living donor

→ *CPT Changes* 2001

+ 44139 Mobilization (take-down) of splenic flexure performed in conjunction with partial colectomy (List separately in addition to primary procedure)

(Use 44139 in conjunction with codes 44140-44147)

44140 Colectomy, partial; with anastomosis

►(For laparoscopic procedure, use 44204)◄

Colectomy, Partial
44140

A segment of the colon is resected and an anastomosis is performed between the remaining ends of the colon.

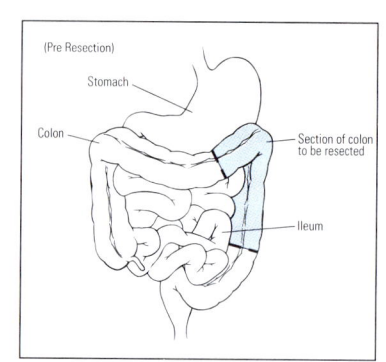

⊘ =Modifier '-51' Exempt ► ◄=New or Revised Text + =Add-on Code CPT 2002

44141	with skin level cecostomy or colostomy
44143	with end colostomy and closure of distal segment (Hartmann type procedure)
44144	with resection, with colostomy or ileostomy and creation of mucofistula
44145	with coloproctostomy (low pelvic anastomosis)
44146	with coloproctostomy (low pelvic anastomosis), with colostomy
44147	abdominal and transanal approach
44150	Colectomy, total, abdominal, without proctectomy; with ileostomy or ileoproctostomy
44151	with continent ileostomy
44152	with rectal mucosectomy, ileoanal anastomosis, with or without loop ileostomy
44153	with rectal mucosectomy, ileoanal anastomosis, creation of ileal reservoir (S or J), with or without loop ileostomy
44155	Colectomy, total, abdominal, with proctectomy; with ileostomy
44156	with continent ileostomy
▲ **44160**	Colectomy, partial, with removal of terminal ileum with ileocolostomy

> ⮕ *CPT Changes* 2002

Colectomy with Removal of Terminal Ileum and Ileocolostomy
44160

A segment of the colon and terminal ileum is removed and an anastomosis is performed between the remaining ileum and colon.

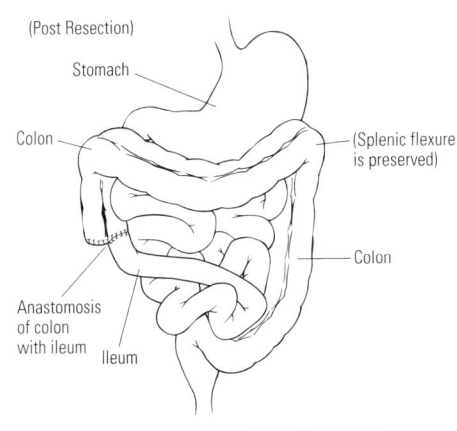

(Post Resection)

Stomach

Colon

(Splenic flexure is preserved)

Colon

Anastomosis of colon with ileum

Ileum

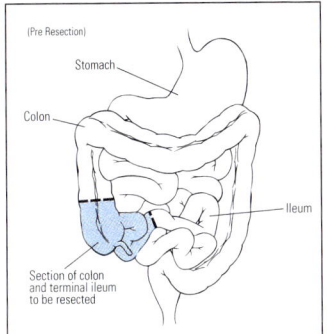

(Pre Resection)

Stomach

Colon

Ileum

Section of colon and terminal ileum to be resected

▶(For laparoscopic procedure, use 44205)◀

Laparoscopy

Surgical laparoscopy always includes diagnostic laparoscopy. To report a diagnostic laparoscopy (peritoneoscopy) (separate procedure), use 49320.

44200	Laparoscopy, surgical; enterolysis (freeing of intestinal adhesion) (separate procedure)

> ⮕ *CPT Assistant* Nov 99:23; Mar 00:5; *CPT Changes* 2000

(For laparoscopy with salpingolysis, ovariolysis, use 58660)

44201	jejunostomy (eg, for decompression or feeding)

> ⮕ *CPT Assistant* Nov 99:23; Mar 00:5; *CPT Changes* 2000

▲ **44202**	enterectomy, resection of small intestine, single resection and anastomosis

> ⮕ *CPT Assistant* Nov 99:23; Mar 00:5; *CPT Changes* 2000; 2002

+ ● **44203**	each additional small intestine resection and anastomosis (List separately in addition to code for primary procedure)

> ⮕ *CPT Changes* 2002

▶(Use 44203 in conjunction with code 44202)◀

▶(For open procedure, see 44120, 44121)◀

● **44204**	colectomy, partial, with anastomosis

> ⮕ *CPT Changes* 2002

▶(For open procedure, use 44140)◀

● **44205**	colectomy, partial, with removal of terminal ileum with ileocolostomy

> ⮕ *CPT Changes* 2002

▶(For open procedure, use 44160)◀

44209	Unlisted laparoscopy procedure, intestine (except rectum)

> ⮕ *CPT Assistant* Nov 99:23; Mar 00:5; *CPT Changes* 2000

Enterostomy—External Fistulization of Intestines

44300	Enterostomy or cecostomy, tube (eg, for decompression or feeding) (separate procedure)

(44305 has been deleted)

(44308 has been deleted. To report, use 44799)

44310	Ileostomy or jejunostomy, non-tube (separate procedure)

▶(Do not report 44310 in addition to 45136)◀

44312	Revision of ileostomy; simple (release of superficial scar) (separate procedure)
44314	complicated (reconstruction in-depth) (separate procedure)
44316	Continent ileostomy (Kock procedure) (separate procedure)

(For fiberoptic evaluation, use 44385)

44320	Colostomy or skin level cecostomy; (separate procedure)
▲ **44322**	with multiple biopsies (eg, for congenital megacolon) (separate procedure)
	➔ *CPT Changes* 2002
44340	Revision of colostomy; simple (release of superficial scar) (separate procedure)
44345	complicated (reconstruction in-depth) (separate procedure)
44346	with repair of paracolostomy hernia (separate procedure)

Endoscopy, Small ▸Intestine◂ and Stomal

Surgical endoscopy always includes diagnostic endoscopy.

(For upper gastrointestinal endoscopy, see 43234-43258)

44360	Small intestinal endoscopy, enteroscopy beyond second portion of duodenum, not including ileum; diagnostic, with or without collection of specimen(s) by brushing or washing (separate procedure)
	➔ *CPT Assistant* Spring 94:7
44361	with biopsy, single or multiple
44363	with removal of foreign body
44364	with removal of tumor(s), polyp(s), or other lesion(s) by snare technique
44365	with removal of tumor(s), polyp(s), or other lesion(s) by hot biopsy forceps or bipolar cautery
▲ **44366**	with control of bleeding (eg, injection, bipolar cautery, unipolar cautery, laser, heater probe, stapler, plasma coagulator)
	➔ *CPT Changes* 2002
44369	with ablation of tumor(s), polyp(s), or other lesion(s) not amenable to removal by hot biopsy forceps, bipolar cautery or snare technique
44370	with transendoscopic stent placement (includes predilation)
	➔ *CPT Changes* 2001
44372	with placement of percutaneous jejunostomy tube
	➔ *CPT Assistant* Spring 94:7
44373	with conversion of percutaneous gastrostomy tube to percutaneous jejunostomy tube
	➔ *CPT Assistant* Spring 94:7

(44375 has been deleted. To report, use 43235)

44376	Small intestinal endoscopy, enteroscopy beyond second portion of duodenum, including ileum; diagnostic, with or without collection of specimen(s) by brushing or washing (separate procedure)
	➔ *CPT Assistant* Spring 94:7
44377	with biopsy, single or multiple
	➔ *CPT Assistant* Spring 94:7
▲ **44378**	with control of bleeding (eg, injection, bipolar cautery, unipolar cautery, laser, heater probe, stapler, plasma coagulator)
	➔ *CPT Assistant* Spring 94:7; *CPT Changes* 2002
44379	with transendoscopic stent placement (includes predilation)
	➔ *CPT Changes* 2001
44380	Ileoscopy, through stoma; diagnostic, with or without collection of specimen(s) by brushing or washing (separate procedure)
44382	with biopsy, single or multiple
44383	with transendoscopic stent placement (includes predilation)
	➔ *CPT Changes* 2001
44385	Endoscopic evaluation of small intestinal (abdominal or pelvic) pouch; diagnostic, with or without collection of specimen(s) by brushing or washing (separate procedure)
44386	with biopsy, single or multiple
44388	Colonoscopy through stoma; diagnostic, with or without collection of specimen(s) by brushing or washing (separate procedure)
44389	with biopsy, single or multiple
44390	with removal of foreign body
▲ **44391**	with control of bleeding (eg, injection, bipolar cautery, unipolar cautery, laser, heater probe, stapler, plasma coagulator)
	➔ *CPT Changes* 2002
44392	with removal of tumor(s), polyp(s), or other lesion(s) by hot biopsy forceps or bipolar cautery
44393	with ablation of tumor(s), polyp(s), or other lesion(s) not amenable to removal by hot biopsy forceps, bipolar cautery or snare technique
44394	with removal of tumor(s), polyp(s), or other lesion(s) by snare technique

(For colonoscopy per rectum, see 45330-45385)

(44400, 44405 have been deleted. To report, use 44799)

44397	with transendoscopic stent placement (includes predilation)
	➔ *CPT Changes* 2001

Introduction

⊘ **44500**	Introduction of long gastrointestinal tube (eg, Miller-Abbott) (separate procedure)

(For radiological supervision and interpretation, use 74340)

(For naso- or oro-gastric tube placement, use 43752)

Repair

(44600 has been deleted. To report, see 44602, 44604)

44602 Suture of small intestine (enterorrhaphy) for perforated ulcer, diverticulum, wound, injury or rupture; single perforation

44603   multiple perforations

44604 Suture of large intestine (colorrhaphy) for perforated ulcer, diverticulum, wound, injury or rupture (single or multiple perforations); without colostomy

44605   with colostomy

(44610 has been deleted. To report, see 44603, 44604)

44615 Intestinal stricturoplasty (enterotomy and enterorrhaphy) with or without dilation, for intestinal obstruction

44620 Closure of enterostomy, large or small intestine;
➜ *CPT Assistant* Nov 97:17

44625   with resection and anastomosis other than colorectal
➜ *CPT Assistant* Nov 97:17

44626   with resection and colorectal anastomosis (eg, closure of Hartmann type procedure)
➜ *CPT Assistant* Nov 97:17

44640 Closure of intestinal cutaneous fistula

44650 Closure of enteroenteric or enterocolic fistula

44660 Closure of enterovesical fistula; without intestinal or bladder resection

▲ **44661**   with intestine and/or bladder resection
➜ *CPT Changes* 2002

(For closure of renocolic fistula, see 50525, 50526)

(For closure of gastrocolic fistula, use 43880)

(For closure of rectovesical fistula, see 45800, 45805)

44680 Intestinal plication (separate procedure)

Other Procedures

▲ **44700** Exclusion of small intestine from pelvis by mesh or other prosthesis, or native tissue (eg, bladder or omentum)
➜ *CPT Assistant* Nov 97:18; *CPT Changes* 2002

(For therapeutic radiation clinical treatment, see **Radiation Oncology** section)

44799 Unlisted procedure, intestine
➜ *CPT Assistant* Dec 00:14

Meckel's Diverticulum and the Mesentery

Excision

44800 Excision of Meckel's diverticulum (diverticulectomy) or omphalomesenteric duct

44820 Excision of lesion of mesentery (separate procedure)

(With intestine resection, see 44120 or 44140 et seq)

Suture

44850 Suture of mesentery (separate procedure)

(For reduction and repair of internal hernia, use 44050)

Other Procedures

44899 Unlisted procedure, Meckels diverticulum and the mesentery

Appendix

Incision

44900 Incision and drainage of appendiceal abscess; open
➜ *CPT Assistant* Nov 97:18

44901   percutaneous
➜ *CPT Assistant* Nov 97:18; Mar 98:8

(For radiological supervision and interpretation, use 75989)

Excision

44950 Appendectomy;
➜ *CPT Assistant* Sep 96:4

(Incidental appendectomy during intra-abdominal surgery does not usually warrant a separate identification. If necessary to report, add modifier '-52')

+ **44955**   when done for indicated purpose at time of other major procedure (not as separate procedure) (List separately in addition to code for primary procedure)
➜ *CPT Assistant* Sep 96:4

44960   for ruptured appendix with abscess or generalized peritonitis

Laparoscopy

Surgical laparoscopy always includes diagnostic laparoscopy. To report a diagnostic laparoscopy (peritoneoscopy) (separate procedure), use 49320.

44970 Laparoscopy, surgical, appendectomy
➜ *CPT Assistant* Nov 99:23; Mar 00:5; *CPT Changes* 2000

44979 Unlisted laparoscopy procedure, appendix
➜ *CPT Assistant* Nov 99:23; Mar 00:5; *CPT Changes* 2000

Rectum

Incision

45000 Transrectal drainage of pelvic abscess

45005 Incision and drainage of submucosal abscess, rectum

45020 Incision and drainage of deep supralevator, pelvirectal, or retrorectal abscess

(See also 46050, 46060)

Excision

45100 Biopsy of anorectal wall, anal approach (eg, congenital megacolon)

(45105 has been deleted. To report, use 45100)

(For endoscopic biopsy, use 45305)

45108 Anorectal myomectomy

45110 Proctectomy; complete, combined abdominoperineal, with colostomy

45111 partial resection of rectum, transabdominal approach

45112 Proctectomy, combined abdominoperineal, pull-through procedure (eg, colo-anal anastomosis)
➔ *CPT Assistant* Nov 97:18

(For colo-anal anastomosis with colonic reservoir or pouch, use 45119)

45113 Proctectomy, partial, with rectal mucosectomy, ileoanal anastomosis, creation of ileal reservoir (S or J), with or without loop ileostomy

45114 Proctectomy, partial, with anastomosis; abdominal and transsacral approach

45116 transsacral approach only (Kraske type)

45119 Proctectomy, combined abdominoperineal pull-through procedure (eg, colo-anal anastomosis), with creation of colonic reservoir (eg, J-pouch), with or without proximal diverting ostomy
➔ *CPT Assistant* Nov 97:18

45120 Proctectomy, complete (for congenital megacolon), abdominal and perineal approach; with pull-through procedure and anastomosis (eg, Swenson, Duhamel, or Soave type operation)

45121 with subtotal or total colectomy, with multiple biopsies

45123 Proctectomy, partial, without anastomosis, perineal approach

45126 Pelvic exenteration for colorectal malignancy, with proctectomy (with or without colostomy), with removal of bladder and ureteral transplantations, and/or hysterectomy, or cervicectomy, with or without removal of tube(s), with or without removal of ovary(s), or any combination thereof
➔ *CPT Assistant* Nov 98:16

45130 Excision of rectal procidentia, with anastomosis; perineal approach

45135 abdominal and perineal approach

● **45136** Excision of ileoanal reservoir with ileostomy
➔ *CPT Changes* 2002

▶(Do not report 45136 in addition to 44005, 44120, 44310)◀

45150 Division of stricture of rectum

45160 Excision of rectal tumor by proctotomy, transsacral or transcoccygeal approach

45170 Excision of rectal tumor, transanal approach

(45180, 45181 have been deleted. To report, see 45170, 45190)

Destruction

▲**45190** Destruction of rectal tumor (eg, electrodessication, electrosurgery, laser ablation, laser resection, cryosurgery) transanal approach
➔ *CPT Changes* 2002

Endoscopy

Definitions

Proctosigmoidoscopy is the examination of the rectum and sigmoid colon.

Sigmoidoscopy is the examination of the entire rectum, sigmoid colon and may include examination of a portion of the descending colon.

Colonoscopy is the examination of the entire colon, from the rectum to the cecum, and may include the examination of the terminal ileum.

For an incomplete colonoscopy, with full preparation for a colonoscopy, use a colonoscopy code with the modifier '-52' and provide documentation.

Surgical endoscopy always includes diagnostic endoscopy.

45300 Proctosigmoidoscopy, rigid; diagnostic, with or without collection of specimen(s) by brushing or washing (separate procedure)
➔ *CPT Assistant* Spring 94:8; Oct 97:6

(45302 has been deleted. To report, use 45300)

▲**45303** with dilation (eg, balloon, guide wire, bougie)
➔ *CPT Assistant* Spring 94:8; Oct 97:6; *CPT Changes* 2002

(For radiological supervision and interpretation, use 74360)

45305 with biopsy, single or multiple
➔ *CPT Assistant* Oct 97:6

45307 with removal of foreign body
➔ *CPT Assistant* Spring 94:8; Oct 97:6

45308 with removal of single tumor, polyp, or other lesion by hot biopsy forceps or bipolar cautery
➔ *CPT Assistant* Spring 94:8; Oct 97:6

45309 with removal of single tumor, polyp, or other lesion by snare technique
➔ *CPT Assistant* Spring 94:8; Oct 97:6

(45310 has been deleted. To report, see 45308, 45309)

◯ =Modifier '-51' Exempt   ▶ ◀=New or Revised Text   ✚=Add-on Code   CPT 2002

45315   with removal of multiple tumors, polyps, or other lesions by hot biopsy forceps, bipolar cautery or snare technique

> ➲ *CPT Assistant* Spring 94:8; Oct 97:6

▲ **45317**   with control of bleeding (eg, injection, bipolar cautery, unipolar cautery, laser, heater probe, stapler, plasma coagulator)

> ➲ *CPT Assistant* Spring 94:8; Oct 97:6; *CPT Changes* 2002

(45319 has been deleted. To report, use 45999)

45320   with ablation of tumor(s), polyp(s), or other lesion(s) not amenable to removal by hot biopsy forceps, bipolar cautery or snare technique (eg, laser)

> ➲ *CPT Assistant* Spring 94:8; Oct 97:6

45321   with decompression of volvulus

> ➲ *CPT Assistant* Spring 94:8; Oct 97:6

(45325 colonoscopy has been renumbered 45355 without change in terminology)

45327   with transendoscopic stent placement (includes predilation)

> ➲ *CPT Changes* 2001

45330   Sigmoidoscopy, flexible; diagnostic, with or without collection of specimen(s) by brushing or washing (separate procedure)

> ➲ *CPT Assistant* Spring 94:9

45331   with biopsy, single or multiple

> ➲ *CPT Assistant* Spring 94:9; Sep 96:6

45332   with removal of foreign body

> ➲ *CPT Assistant* Spring 94:9

45333   with removal of tumor(s), polyp(s), or other lesion(s) by hot biopsy forceps or bipolar cautery

> ➲ *CPT Assistant* Spring 94:9

▲ **45334**   with control of bleeding (eg, injection, bipolar cautery, unipolar cautery, laser, heater probe, stapler, plasma coagulator)

> ➲ *CPT Assistant* Spring 94:9; Sep 96:6; *CPT Changes* 2002

(45336 has been deleted. To report, use 45339)

45337   with decompression of volvulus, any method

> ➲ *CPT Assistant* Spring 94:9

45338   with removal of tumor(s), polyp(s), or other lesion(s) by snare technique

> ➲ *CPT Assistant* Spring 94:9

45339   with ablation of tumor(s), polyp(s), or other lesion(s) not amenable to removal by hot biopsy forceps, bipolar cautery or snare technique

> ➲ *CPT Assistant* Spring 94:9

45341   with endoscopic ultrasound examination

> ➲ *CPT Changes* 2001

45342   with transendoscopic ultrasound guided intramural or transmural fine needle aspiration/biopsy(s)

> ➲ *CPT Changes* 2001

(Do not report 76975 in conjunction with codes 45341, 45342)

(For interpretation of specimen, see 88172-88173)

(For transrectal ultrasound utilizing rigid probe device, use 76872)

45345   with transendoscopic stent placement (includes predilation)

> ➲ *CPT Changes* 2001

45355   Colonoscopy, rigid or flexible, transabdominal via colotomy, single or multiple

(45360-45372 have been deleted. To report, see 45330-45337)

45378   Colonoscopy, flexible, proximal to splenic flexure; diagnostic, with or without collection of specimen(s) by brushing or washing, with or without colon decompression (separate procedure)

> ➲ *CPT Assistant* Spring 94:9; Aug 99:3

Colonoscopy
45378

A colonoscope is inserted in the anus and moved through the colon past the splenic flexure in order to visualize the lumen of the rectum and colon.

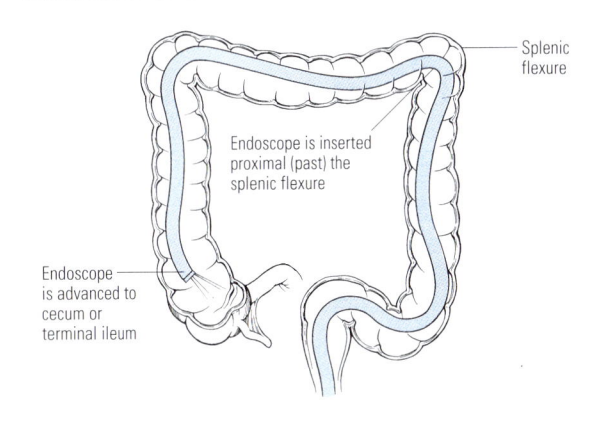

Splenic flexure

Endoscope is inserted proximal (past) the splenic flexure

Endoscope is advanced to cecum or terminal ileum

45379   with removal of foreign body

> ➲ *CPT Assistant* Spring 94:9; Aug 99:3

45380   with biopsy, single or multiple

> ➲ *CPT Assistant* Spring 94:9; Jan 96:7; Feb 99:11; Aug 99:3

▲ **45382**   with control of bleeding (eg, injection, bipolar cautery, unipolar cautery, laser, heater probe, stapler, plasma coagulator)

> ➲ *CPT Assistant* Spring 94:9; Aug 99:3; *CPT Changes* 2002

45383   with ablation of tumor(s), polyp(s), or other lesion(s) not amenable to removal by hot biopsy forceps, bipolar cautery or snare technique

> ➲ *CPT Assistant* Spring 94:9; Aug 99:3

45384   with removal of tumor(s), polyp(s), or other lesion(s) by hot biopsy forceps or bipolar cautery

> ➲ *CPT Assistant* Spring 94:9; Jul 98:10; Feb 99:11; Aug 99:3

45385   with removal of tumor(s), polyp(s), or other lesion(s) by snare technique

> ➲ *CPT Assistant* Spring 94:9; Jan 96:7; Jul 98:10; Aug 99:3

(45386 has been deleted. To report, use 44799)

(For small ▶intestine◀ and stomal endoscopy, see 44360-44393)

45387 with transendoscopic stent placement (includes predilation)
➔ *CPT Changes* 2001

Repair

45500 Proctoplasty; for stenosis

45505 for prolapse of mucous membrane

45520 Perirectal injection of sclerosing solution for prolapse

(45521 has been deleted)

45540 Proctopexy for prolapse; abdominal approach

45541 perineal approach

45550 Proctopexy combined with sigmoid resection, abdominal approach

45560 Repair of rectocele (separate procedure)

(For repair of rectocele with posterior colporrhaphy, use 57250)

45562 Exploration, repair, and presacral drainage for rectal injury;

45563 with colostomy

45800 Closure of rectovesical fistula;

45805 with colostomy

45820 Closure of rectourethral fistula;

45825 with colostomy

(For rectovaginal fistula closure, see 57300-57308)

Manipulation

45900* Reduction of procidentia (separate procedure) under anesthesia

45905* Dilation of anal sphincter (separate procedure) under anesthesia other than local

45910 Dilation of rectal stricture (separate procedure) under anesthesia other than local

45915* Removal of fecal impaction or foreign body (separate procedure) under anesthesia

Other Procedures

45999 Unlisted procedure, rectum

● **46020** Placement of seton
➔ *CPT Changes* 2002

▶(Do not report 46020 in addition to 46060, 46280, 46600)◀

Anus

Incision

(46000 has been deleted. To report, use 46270)

46030* Removal of anal seton, other marker

(46032 has been deleted. To report, use 46999)

46040 Incision and drainage of ischiorectal and/or perirectal abscess (separate procedure)

46045 Incision and drainage of intramural, intramuscular, or submucosal abscess, transanal, under anesthesia

46050* Incision and drainage, perianal abscess, superficial

(See also 45020, 46060)

46060 Incision and drainage of ischiorectal or intramural abscess, with fistulectomy or fistulotomy, submuscular, with or without placement of seton

▶(Do not report 46060 in addition to 46020)◀

(See also 45020)

46070 Incision, anal septum (infant)

(For anoplasty, see 46700-46705)

46080* Sphincterotomy, anal, division of sphincter (separate procedure)

46083 Incision of thrombosed hemorrhoid, external
➔ *CPT Assistant* Jun 97:10

Excision

46200 Fissurectomy, with or without sphincterotomy

46210 Cryptectomy; single

46211 multiple (separate procedure)

46220 Papillectomy or excision of single tag, anus (separate procedure)

46221 Hemorrhoidectomy, by simple ligature (eg, rubber band)
➔ *CPT Assistant* Oct 97:6

46230 Excision of external hemorrhoid tags and/or multiple papillae

46250 Hemorrhoidectomy, external, complete

46255 Hemorrhoidectomy, internal and external, simple;

46257 with fissurectomy

46258 with fistulectomy, with or without fissurectomy

46260 Hemorrhoidectomy, internal and external, complex or extensive;

46261 with fissurectomy

46262 with fistulectomy, with or without fissurectomy

46270 Surgical treatment of anal fistula (fistulectomy/fistulotomy); subcutaneous

46275 submuscular

46280	complex or multiple, with or without placement of seton

▶(Do not report 46280 in addition to 46020)◀

(46281 has been renumbered to 46288 without change in terminology)

46285	second stage
46288	Closure of anal fistula with rectal advancement flap
46320✲	Enucleation or excision of external thrombotic hemorrhoid

Introduction

46500✲ Injection of sclerosing solution, hemorrhoids

(46510, 46530 have been deleted. To report, use 46999)

Endoscopy

Surgical endoscopy always includes diagnostic endoscopy.

46600 Anoscopy; diagnostic, with or without collection of specimen(s) by brushing or washing (separate procedure)
➲ *CPT Assistant* Spring 94:9; Oct 97:6

▶(Do not report 46600 in addition to 46020)◀

(46602 has been deleted. To report, use 46600)

▲ 46604 with dilation (eg, balloon, guide wire, bougie)
➲ *CPT Assistant* Spring 94:9; Oct 97:6; *CPT Changes* 2002

46606 with biopsy, single or multiple
➲ *CPT Assistant* Spring 94:9; Oct 97:6

46608 with removal of foreign body
➲ *CPT Assistant* Spring 94:9; Oct 97:6

46610 with removal of single tumor, polyp, or other lesion by hot biopsy forceps or bipolar cautery
➲ *CPT Assistant* Spring 94:10; Oct 97:6

46611 with removal of single tumor, polyp, or other lesion by snare technique
➲ *CPT Assistant* Spring 94:10; Oct 97:6

46612 with removal of multiple tumors, polyps, or other lesions by hot biopsy forceps, bipolar cautery or snare technique
➲ *CPT Assistant* Spring 94:10; Oct 97:6

▲ 46614 with control of bleeding (eg, injection, bipolar cautery, unipolar cautery, laser, heater probe, stapler, plasma coagulator)
➲ *CPT Assistant* Spring 94:10; Oct 97:6; *CPT Changes* 2002

46615 with ablation of tumor(s), polyp(s), or other lesion(s) not amenable to removal by hot biopsy forceps, bipolar cautery or snare technique
➲ *CPT Assistant* Spring 94:10; Oct 97:6

Repair

46700 Anoplasty, plastic operation for stricture; adult

46705 infant

(For simple incision of anal septum, use 46070)

46715 Repair of low imperforate anus; with anoperineal fistula (cut-back procedure)

46716 with transposition of anoperineal or anovestibular fistula

46730 Repair of high imperforate anus without fistula; perineal or sacroperineal approach

46735 combined transabdominal and sacroperineal approaches

46740 Repair of high imperforate anus with rectourethral or rectovaginal fistula; perineal or sacroperineal approach

46742 combined transabdominal and sacroperineal approaches

46744 Repair of cloacal anomaly by anorectovaginoplasty and urethroplasty, sacroperineal approach

46746 Repair of cloacal anomaly by anorectovaginoplasty and urethroplasty, combined abdominal and sacroperineal approach;

46748 with vaginal lengthening by intestinal graft or pedicle flaps

46750 Sphincteroplasty, anal, for incontinence or prolapse; adult

46751 child

46753 Graft (Thiersch operation) for rectal incontinence and/or prolapse

46754 Removal of Thiersch wire or suture, anal canal

46760 Sphincteroplasty, anal, for incontinence, adult; muscle transplant

46761 levator muscle imbrication (Park posterior anal repair)

46762 implantation artificial sphincter

Destruction

46900✲ Destruction of lesion(s), anus (eg, condyloma, papilloma, molluscum contagiosum, herpetic vesicle), simple; chemical

46910✲ electrodesiccation

46916 cryosurgery

46917 laser surgery

(46920 has been deleted. To report, use 46922)

46922 surgical excision

▲**46924** Destruction of lesion(s), anus (eg, condyloma, papilloma, molluscum contagiosum, herpetic vesicle), extensive (eg, laser surgery, electrosurgery, cryosurgery, chemosurgery)
➜ *CPT Changes* 2002

(46930 has been deleted. To report, use 46924)

(46932 has been deleted. To report, use 46916)

(46933 has been deleted. To report, use 46924)

46934 Destruction of hemorrhoids, any method; internal

46935 external

46936 internal and external

46937 Cryosurgery of rectal tumor; benign

46938 malignant

▲**46940** Curettage or cautery of anal fissure, including dilation of anal sphincter (separate procedure); initial
➜ *CPT Changes* 2002

46942 subsequent

Suture

46945 Ligation of internal hemorrhoids; single procedure

46946 multiple procedures

Other Procedures

46999 Unlisted procedure, anus
➜ *CPT Assistant* Oct 97:6

Liver

Incision

47000＊ Biopsy of liver, needle; percutaneous
➜ *CPT Assistant* Fall 93:12

▶(If imaging guidance is performed,◀ see 76003, 76360, ▶76393,◀ 76942)

＋**47001** when done for indicated purpose at time of other major procedure (List separately in addition to code for primary procedure)

▶(If imaging guidance is performed,◀ see 76003, 76942)

▶(For fine needle aspiration in conjunction with 47000, 47001, see 10021, 10022)◀

▶(For evaluation of fine needle aspirate in conjunction with 47000, 47001, see 88172, 88173)◀

47010 Hepatotomy; for open drainage of abscess or cyst, one or two stages
➜ *CPT Assistant* Nov 97:18

47011 for percutaneous drainage of abscess or cyst, one or two stages
➜ *CPT Assistant* Nov 97:18; Mar 98:8

(For radiological supervision and interpretation, use 75989)

47015 Laparotomy, with aspiration and/or injection of hepatic parasitic (eg, amoebic or echinococcal) cyst(s) or abscess(es)

Excision

47100 Biopsy of liver, wedge

47120 Hepatectomy, resection of liver; partial lobectomy
➜ *CPT Assistant* May 98:10

47122 trisegmentectomy

47125 total left lobectomy

47130 total right lobectomy

47133 Donor hepatectomy, with preparation and maintenance of allograft; from cadaver donor

47134 partial, from living donor

47135 Liver allotransplantation; orthotopic, partial or whole, from cadaver or living donor, any age

47136 heterotopic, partial or whole, from cadaver or living donor, any age

Repair

47300 Marsupialization of cyst or abscess of liver

47350 Management of liver hemorrhage; simple suture of liver wound or injury

(47355 has been deleted)

47360 complex suture of liver wound or injury, with or without hepatic artery ligation

47361 exploration of hepatic wound, extensive debridement, coagulation and/or suture, with or without packing of liver

47362 re-exploration of hepatic wound for removal of packing

▶Laparoscopy◀

▶Surgical laparoscopy always includes diagnostic laparoscopy. To report a diagnostic laparoscopy (peritoneoscopy) (separate procedure), use 49320◀

●**47370** Laparoscopy, surgical, ablation of one or more liver tumor(s); radiofrequency
➜ *CPT Changes* 2002

▶(For imaging guidance, use 76490)◀

●**47371** cryosurgical
➜ *CPT Changes* 2002

▶(For imaging guidance, use 76490)◀

47379 Unlisted laparoscopic procedure, liver
➜ *CPT Changes* 2001

Other Procedures

🔴 **47380** Ablation, open, of one or more liver tumor(s); radiofrequency
➔ *CPT Changes* 2002

►(For imaging guidance, use 76490)◄

🔴 **47381** cryosurgical
➔ *CPT Changes* 2002

►(For imaging guidance, use 76490)◄

🔴 **47382** Ablation, one or more liver tumor(s), percutaneous, radiofrequency
➔ *CPT Changes* 2002

►(For imaging guidance and monitoring, see code 76362, 76394, or 76490)◄

47399 Unlisted procedure, liver

Biliary Tract

Incision

47400 Hepaticotomy or hepaticostomy with exploration, drainage, or removal of calculus

47420 Choledochotomy or choledochostomy with exploration, drainage, or removal of calculus, with or without cholecystotomy; without transduodenal sphincterotomy or sphincteroplasty

47425 with transduodenal sphincterotomy or sphincteroplasty

(47440 has been deleted)

47460 Transduodenal sphincterotomy or sphincteroplasty, with or without transduodenal extraction of calculus (separate procedure)

47480 Cholecystotomy or cholecystostomy with exploration, drainage, or removal of calculus (separate procedure)

47490 Percutaneous cholecystostomy

(For radiological supervision and interpretation, use 75989)

Introduction

47500 Injection procedure for percutaneous transhepatic cholangiography

(For radiological supervision and interpretation, use 74320)

47505 Injection procedure for cholangiography through an existing catheter (eg, percutaneous transhepatic or T-tube)

(For radiological supervision and interpretation, use 74305)

47510 Introduction of percutaneous transhepatic catheter for biliary drainage

(For radiological supervision and interpretation, use 75980)

47511 Introduction of percutaneous transhepatic stent for internal and external biliary drainage

(For radiological supervision and interpretation, use 75982)

47525 Change of percutaneous biliary drainage catheter

(For radiological supervision and interpretation, use 75984)

47530 Revision and/or reinsertion of transhepatic tube

(For radiological supervision and interpretation, use 75984)

Endoscopy

Surgical endoscopy always includes diagnostic endoscopy.

+ **47550** Biliary endoscopy, intraoperative (choledochoscopy) (List separately in addition to code for primary procedure)

47552 Biliary endoscopy, percutaneous via T-tube or other tract; diagnostic, with or without collection of specimen(s) by brushing and/or washing (separate procedure)

47553 with biopsy, single or multiple

▲ **47554** with removal of calculus/calculi
➔ *CPT Changes* 2002

47555 with dilation of biliary duct stricture(s) without stent

(For ERCP, see 43260-43272, 74363)

(If imaging guidance is performed, see 74363, 75982)

47556 with dilation of biliary duct stricture(s) with stent

(If imaging guidance is performed, see 74363, 75982)

Laparoscopy

Surgical laparoscopy always includes diagnostic laparoscopy. To report a diagnostic laparoscopy (peritoneoscopy) (separate procedure), use 49320.

47560 Laparoscopy, surgical; with guided transhepatic cholangiography, without biopsy
➔ *CPT Assistant* Nov 99:23; Mar 00:5; *CPT Changes* 2000

47561 with guided transhepatic cholangiography with biopsy
➔ *CPT Assistant* Nov 99:23; Mar 00:5; *CPT Changes* 2000

47562   cholecystectomy
CPT Assistant Nov 99:23; Mar 00:5; *CPT Changes* 2000

Laparoscopic Cholecystectomy
47562

The gallbladder is dissected and removed from the liver bed under laparoscopic guidance.

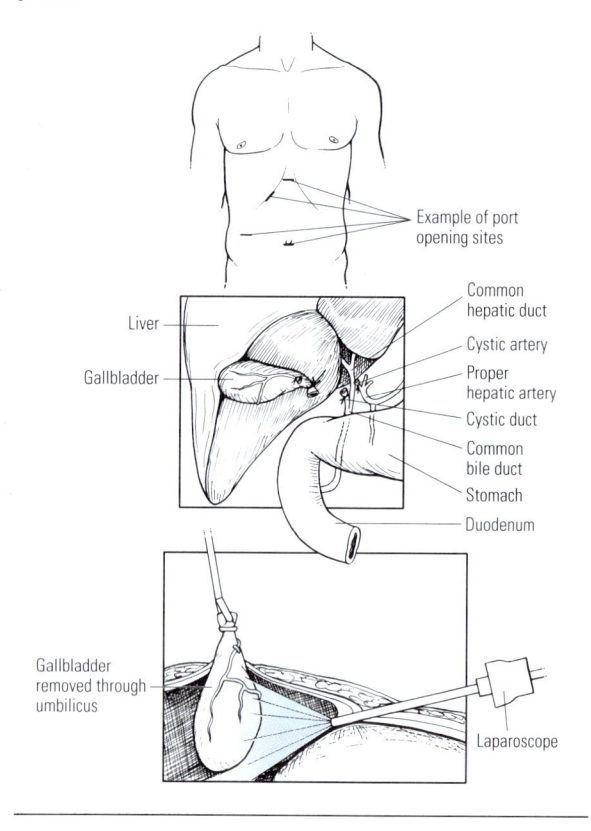

Example of port opening sites

Liver
Gallbladder

Common hepatic duct
Cystic artery
Proper hepatic artery
Cystic duct
Common bile duct
Stomach
Duodenum

Gallbladder removed through umbilicus

Laparoscope

47563   cholecystectomy with cholangiography
CPT Assistant Nov 99:23; Mar 00:5; Dec 00:14; *CPT Changes* 2000

47564   cholecystectomy with exploration of common duct
CPT Assistant Nov 99:23; Mar 00:5; *CPT Changes* 2000

47570   cholecystoenterostomy
CPT Assistant Nov 99:23; Mar 00:5; *CPT Changes* 2000

47579   Unlisted laparoscopy procedure, biliary tract
CPT Assistant Nov 99:23; Mar 00:5; *CPT Changes* 2000

Excision

47600   Cholecystectomy;
CPT Assistant Nov 99:24; *CPT Changes* 2000

47605   with cholangiography
CPT Assistant Nov 99:24; *CPT Changes* 2000

(For laparoscopic approach, see 47562-47564)

47610   Cholecystectomy with exploration of common duct;

(47611 has been deleted. To report, use 47610 and 47550)

47612   with choledochoenterostomy

47620   with transduodenal sphincterotomy or sphincteroplasty, with or without cholangiography

47630   Biliary duct stone extraction, percutaneous via T-tube tract, basket, or snare (eg, Burhenne technique)
CPT Assistant Jun 98:10

(For radiological supervision and interpretation, use 74327)

47700   Exploration for congenital atresia of bile ducts, without repair, with or without liver biopsy, with or without cholangiography

47701   Portoenterostomy (eg, Kasai procedure)

(47710 has been deleted. To report, see 47711, 47712)

47711   Excision of bile duct tumor, with or without primary repair of bile duct; extrahepatic

47712   intrahepatic

(For anastomosis, see 47760-47800)

47715   Excision of choledochal cyst

47716   Anastomosis, choledochal cyst, without excision

Repair

47720   Cholecystoenterostomy; direct
CPT Assistant Nov 99:24; *CPT Changes* 2000

(For laparoscopic approach, use 47570)

47721   with gastroenterostomy

47740   Roux-en-Y

47741   Roux-en-Y with gastroenterostomy

47760   Anastomosis, of extrahepatic biliary ducts and gastrointestinal tract

47765   Anastomosis, of intrahepatic ducts and gastrointestinal tract

47780   Anastomosis, Roux-en-Y, of extrahepatic biliary ducts and gastrointestinal tract

47785   Anastomosis, Roux-en-Y, of intrahepatic biliary ducts and gastrointestinal tract

47800   Reconstruction, plastic, of extrahepatic biliary ducts with end-to-end anastomosis

47801   Placement of choledochal stent

47802   U-tube hepaticoenterostomy

(47810 has been deleted. To report, use 47999)

(47850, 47855 have been deleted. To report, use 47999)

47900   Suture of extrahepatic biliary duct for pre-existing injury (separate procedure)

Other Procedures

47999   Unlisted procedure, biliary tract

Pancreas

(For peroral pancreatic endoscopic procedures, see 43260-43272)

Incision

48000 Placement of drains, peripancreatic, for acute pancreatitis;

48001   with cholecystostomy, gastrostomy, and jejunostomy

48005 Resection or debridement of pancreas and peripancreatic tissue for acute necrotizing pancreatitis

48020 Removal of pancreatic calculus

Excision

▲ **48100** Biopsy of pancreas, open (eg, fine needle aspiration, needle core biopsy, wedge biopsy)
  ➔ *CPT Changes* 2002

48102 ✱ Biopsy of pancreas, percutaneous needle

(For radiological supervision and interpretation, see 76003, 76360, ▶76393,◀ 76942)

▶(For fine needle aspiration, use 10022)◀

▶(For evaluation of fine needle aspirate, see 88172, 88173)◀

48120 Excision of lesion of pancreas (eg, cyst, adenoma)

48140 Pancreatectomy, distal subtotal, with or without splenectomy; without pancreaticojejunostomy

48145   with pancreaticojejunostomy

48146 Pancreatectomy, distal, near-total with preservation of duodenum (Child-type procedure)

48148 Excision of ampulla of Vater

48150 Pancreatectomy, proximal subtotal with total duodenectomy, partial gastrectomy, choledochoenterostomy and gastrojejunostomy (Whipple-type procedure); with pancreatojejunostomy

(48151 has been deleted. To report, use 48146)

48152   without pancreatojejunostomy

48153 Pancreatectomy, proximal subtotal with near-total duodenectomy, choledochoenterostomy and duodenojejunostomy (pylorus-sparing, Whipple-type procedure); with pancreatojejunostomy

48154   without pancreatojejunostomy

48155 Pancreatectomy, total

▲ **48160** Pancreatectomy, total or subtotal, with autologous transplantation of pancreas or pancreatic islet cells
  ➔ *CPT Changes* 2002

48180 Pancreaticojejunostomy, side-to-side anastomosis (Puestow-type operation)

Introduction

➕ **48400** Injection procedure for intraoperative pancreatography (List separately in addition to code for primary procedure)

(For radiological supervision and interpretation, see 74300-74305)

Repair

▲ **48500** Marsupialization of pancreatic cyst
  ➔ *CPT Changes* 2002

48510 External drainage, pseudocyst of pancreas; open
  ➔ *CPT Assistant* Nov 97:18

48511   percutaneous
      ➔ *CPT Assistant* Nov 97:18; Mar 98:8

(For radiological supervision and interpretation, use 75989)

48520 Internal anastomosis of pancreatic cyst to gastrointestinal tract; direct

48540   Roux-en-Y

▲ **48545** Pancreatorrhaphy for injury
  ➔ *CPT Changes* 2002

▲ **48547** Duodenal exclusion with gastrojejunostomy for pancreatic injury
  ➔ *CPT Changes* 2002

Pancreas Transplantation

48550 Donor pancreatectomy, with preparation and maintenance of allograft from cadaver donor, with or without duodenal segment for transplantation

48554 Transplantation of pancreatic allograft

48556 Removal of transplanted pancreatic allograft

Other Procedures

48999 Unlisted procedure, pancreas

Abdomen, Peritoneum, and Omentum

Incision

49000 Exploratory laparotomy, exploratory celiotomy with or without biopsy(s) (separate procedure)

(To report wound exploration due to penetrating trauma without laparotomy, use 20102)

49002 Reopening of recent laparotomy

(To report re-exploration of hepatic wound for removal of packing, use 47362)

49010 Exploration, retroperitoneal area with or without biopsy(s) (separate procedure)

(To report wound exploration due to penetrating trauma without laparotomy, use 20102)

49020 Drainage of peritoneal abscess or localized peritonitis, exclusive of appendiceal abscess; open

(For appendiceal abscess, use 44900)

49021 percutaneous

(For radiological supervision and interpretation, use 75989)

49040 Drainage of subdiaphragmatic or subphrenic abscess; open
  ➲ *CPT Assistant* Nov 97:18

49041 percutaneous
  ➲ *CPT Assistant* Nov 97:18; Mar 98:8

(For radiological supervision and interpretation, use 75989)

49060 Drainage of retroperitoneal abscess; open
  ➲ *CPT Assistant* Nov 97:18; Nov 99:24; *CPT Changes* 2000

49061 percutaneous
  ➲ *CPT Assistant* Nov 97:18; Mar 98:8; Nov 99:24; *CPT Changes* 2000

(For laparoscopic drainage, use 49323)

(For radiological supervision and interpretation, use 75989)

49062 Drainage of extraperitoneal lymphocele to peritoneal cavity, open
  ➲ *CPT Assistant* Nov 97:19

49080 * Peritoneocentesis, abdominal paracentesis, or peritoneal lavage (diagnostic or therapeutic); initial

49081 * subsequent

  ►(If imaging guidance is performed, see 76360, 76942)◄

49085 Removal of peritoneal foreign body from peritoneal cavity

(For lysis of intestinal adhesions, use 44005)

Excision, Destruction

49180 * Biopsy, abdominal or retroperitoneal mass, percutaneous needle
  ➲ *CPT Assistant* Fall 93:11

  ►(If imaging guidance is performed,◄ see 76003, 76360, ►76393,◄ 76942)

  ►(For fine needle aspiration, use 10021 or 10022)◄

  ►(For evaluation of fine needle aspirate, see 88172, 88173)◄

49200 Excision or destruction by any method of intra-abdominal or retroperitoneal tumors or cysts or endometriomas;

49201 extensive

49215 Excision of presacral or sacrococcygeal tumor

▲ **49220** Staging laparotomy for Hodgkins disease or lymphoma (includes splenectomy, needle or open biopsies of both liver lobes, possibly also removal of abdominal nodes, abdominal node and/or bone marrow biopsies, ovarian repositioning)
  ➲ *CPT Changes* 2002

49250 Umbilectomy, omphalectomy, excision of umbilicus (separate procedure)

49255 Omentectomy, epiploectomy, resection of omentum (separate procedure)
  ➲ *CPT Assistant* Nov 99:24; *CPT Changes* 2000

(49300 has been deleted. To report, use 49320)

(49301 has been deleted. To report, use 49321)

(49302 has been deleted. To report, use 47560)

(49303 has been deleted. To report, use 47561)

(49310 has been deleted. To report, use 47562)

(49311 has been deleted. To report, use 47563)

(49315 has been deleted. To report, use 44970)

Laparoscopy

Surgical laparoscopy always includes diagnostic laparoscopy. To report a diagnostic laparoscopy (peritoneoscopy), (separate procedure), use 49320.

For laparoscopic fulguration or excision of lesions of the ovary, pelvic viscera, or peritoneal surface use 58662.

49320 Laparoscopy, abdomen, peritoneum, and omentum, diagnostic, with or without collection of specimen(s) by brushing or washing (separate procedure)
  ➲ *CPT Assistant* Nov 99:24; Mar 00:5; *CPT Changes* 2000, 2001

Laparoscopy
49320

The physician inserts a fiberoptic laparoscope to observe the necessary organs in these procedures.

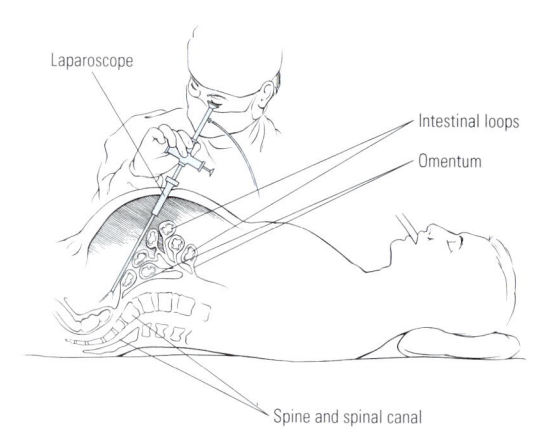

Laparoscope

Intestinal loops

Omentum

Spine and spinal canal

49321	Laparoscopy, surgical; with biopsy (single or multiple)
	→ *CPT Assistant* Nov 99:24; Mar 00:5; *CPT Changes* 2000, 2001
49322	with aspiration of cavity or cyst (eg, ovarian cyst) (single or multiple)
	→ *CPT Assistant* Nov 99:24; Mar 00:5; *CPT Changes* 2000
49323	with drainage of lymphocele to peritoneal cavity
	→ *CPT Assistant* Nov 99:24; Mar 00:5; May 00:4; *CPT Changes* 2000

(For percutaneous or open drainage, see 49060, 49061)

49329 Unlisted laparoscopy procedure, abdomen, peritoneum and omentum

→ *CPT Assistant* Nov 99:24; Mar 00:5; *CPT Changes* 2000

Introduction, Revision, and/or Removal

49400* Injection of air or contrast into peritoneal cavity (separate procedure)

(For radiological supervision and interpretation, use 74190)

(49401 has been deleted. To report, use 49400)

49420* Insertion of intraperitoneal cannula or catheter for drainage or dialysis; temporary

→ *CPT Assistant* Fall 93:2

49421 permanent

→ *CPT Assistant* Fall 93:2

49422 Removal of permanent intraperitoneal cannula or catheter

(For removal of a temporary catheter/cannula, use appropriate E/M code)

49423 Exchange of previously placed abscess or cyst drainage catheter under radiological guidance (separate procedure)

→ *CPT Assistant* Nov 97:19; Mar 98:8

(For radiological supervision and interpretation, use 75984)

▲ **49424** Contrast injection for assessment of abscess or cyst via previously placed drainage catheter or tube (separate procedure)

→ *CPT Assistant* Nov 97:19; Mar 98:8; *CPT Changes* 2002

(For radiological supervision and interpretation, use 76080)

49425 Insertion of peritoneal-venous shunt

49426 Revision of peritoneal-venous shunt

(For shunt patency test, use 78291)

49427 Injection procedure (eg, contrast media) for evaluation of previously placed peritoneal-venous shunt

(For radiological supervision and interpretation, see 75809, 78291)

49428 Ligation of peritoneal-venous shunt

49429 Removal of peritoneal-venous shunt

(49430, 49440 have been deleted. To report, use 49999)

Repair

Hernioplasty, Herniorrhaphy, Herniotomy

The hernia repair codes in this section are categorized primarily by the type of hernia (inguinal, femoral, incisional, etc.).

Some types of hernias are further categorized as "initial" or "recurrent" based on whether or not the hernia has required previous repair(s).

Additional variables accounted for by some of the codes include patient age and clinical presentation (reducible vs. incarcerated or strangulated).

With the exception of the incisional hernia repairs (see 49560-49566) the use of mesh or other prostheses is not separately reported.

The excision/repair of strangulated organs or structures such as testicle(s), intestine, ovaries are reported by using the appropriate code for the excision/repair (eg, 44120, 54520, and 58940) in addition to the appropriate code for the repair of the strangulated hernia.

(For reduction and repair of intra-abdominal hernia, use 44050)

(For debridement of abdominal wall, see 11042, 11043)

(All codes for bilateral procedures in hernia repair have been deleted. To report, add modifier '-50')

● **49491** Repair, initial inguinal hernia, preterm infant (less than 37 weeks gestation at birth), performed from birth up to 50 weeks post-conceptual age, with or without hydrocelectomy; reducible

→ *CPT Changes* 2002

● **49492** incarcerated or strangulated

→ *CPT Changes* 2002

▶(Post-conceptual age equals gestational age at birth plus age of infant in weeks at the time of the hernia repair. Initial inguinal hernia repairs that are performed on preterm infants who are over 50 weeks postconceptual age and under age 6 months at the time of surgery, should be reported using codes 49495, 49496)◀

▲ **49495** Repair, initial inguinal hernia, full term infant under age 6 months, or preterm infant over 50 weeks postconceptual age and under age 6 months at the time of surgery, with or without hydrocelectomy; reducible

→ *CPT Assistant* Winter 93:6; Winter 94:13; *CPT Changes* 2002

49496 incarcerated or strangulated
CPT Assistant Winter 93:6; Winter 94:13

►(Post-conceptual age equals gestational age at birth plus age in weeks at the time of the hernia repair. Initial inguinal hernia repairs that are performed on preterm infants who are under or up to 50 weeks postconceptual age but under 6 months of age since birth, should be reported using codes 49491, 49492. Inguinal hernia repairs on infants age 6 months to under 5 years should be reported using codes 49500-49501)◄

49500 Repair initial inguinal hernia, age 6 months to under 5 years, with or without hydrocelectomy; reducible
CPT Assistant Winter 94:13; *CPT Changes* 2002

49501 incarcerated or strangulated
CPT Assistant Winter 94:13; *CPT Changes* 2002

49505 Repair initial inguinal hernia, age 5 years or over; reducible
CPT Assistant Winter 94:13; Sep 00:10

49507 incarcerated or strangulated
CPT Assistant Winter 94:13

(49510 has been deleted. To report, see 49505 or 49507 and 54520)

(49515 has been deleted. To report, see 49505 or 49507 and 54840 or 55040)

49520 Repair recurrent inguinal hernia, any age; reducible
CPT Assistant Winter 94:13

49521 incarcerated or strangulated
CPT Assistant Winter 94:13

49525 Repair inguinal hernia, sliding, any age
CPT Assistant Winter 94:14

(49530 has been deleted. To report, see 49496, 49501, 49507, 49521)

(49535 has been deleted. To report, see 49496, 49501, 49507, 49521)

49540 Repair lumbar hernia
CPT Assistant Winter 94:14

49550 Repair initial femoral hernia, any age; reducible
CPT Assistant Winter 94:14

(49552 has been deleted. To report, see 49550 or 49553)

49553 incarcerated or strangulated
CPT Assistant Winter 94:14

49555 Repair recurrent femoral hernia; reducible
CPT Assistant Winter 94:14

49557 incarcerated or strangulated
CPT Assistant Winter 94:14

49560 Repair initial incisional or ventral hernia; reducible
CPT Assistant Winter 93:6; Winter 94:14; Nov 97:19

49561 incarcerated or strangulated
CPT Assistant Winter 94:14

49565 Repair recurrent incisional or ventral hernia; reducible
CPT Assistant Winter 94:14; Nov 97:19

49566 incarcerated or strangulated
CPT Assistant Winter 94:14

+ 49568 Implantation of mesh or other prosthesis for incisional or ventral hernia repair (List separately in addition to code for the incisional or ventral hernia repair)
CPT Assistant Winter 94:14; Nov 97:19

49570 Repair epigastric hernia (eg, preperitoneal fat); reducible (separate procedure)
CPT Assistant Winter 94:15

49572 incarcerated or strangulated
CPT Assistant Winter 94:15

(49575 has been deleted. To report, use 49572)

49580 Repair umbilical hernia, under age 5 years; reducible
CPT Assistant Winter 94:15

(49581 has been deleted. To report, see 49585 or 49587)

49582 incarcerated or strangulated
CPT Assistant Winter 94:15

49585 Repair umbilical hernia, age 5 years or over; reducible
CPT Assistant Winter 94:15

49587 incarcerated or strangulated
CPT Assistant Winter 94:15

49590 Repair spigelian hernia
CPT Assistant Winter 94:15

49600 Repair of small omphalocele, with primary closure
CPT Assistant Winter 94:15

49605 Repair of large omphalocele or gastroschisis; with or without prosthesis
CPT Assistant Winter 94:15

49606 with removal of prosthesis, final reduction and closure, in operating room
CPT Assistant Winter 94:15

49610 Repair of omphalocele (Gross type operation); first stage
CPT Assistant Winter 94:15

49611 second stage
CPT Assistant Winter 94:15

(For diaphragmatic or hiatal hernia repair, see 39502-39541)

(49630-49640 have been deleted. For surgical repair of omentum, use 49999)

 ⊘ =Modifier '-51' Exempt ► ◄=New or Revised Text ✚ =Add-on Code CPT 2002

Laparoscopy

Surgical laparoscopy always includes diagnostic laparoscopy. To report a diagnostic laparoscopy (peritoneoscopy) (separate procedure), use 49320.

49650   Laparoscopy, surgical; repair initial inguinal hernia
  ➔ *CPT Assistant* Nov 99:24; Mar 00:5; *CPT Changes* 2000

49651   repair recurrent inguinal hernia
  ➔ *CPT Assistant* Nov 99:24; Mar 00:5; *CPT Changes* 2000

49659   Unlisted laparoscopy procedure, hernioplasty, herniorrhaphy, herniotomy
  ➔ *CPT Assistant* Nov 99:25; Mar 00:5; *CPT Changes* 2000

Suture

49900   Suture, secondary, of abdominal wall for evisceration or dehiscence

  (For suture of ruptured diaphragm, see 39540, 39541)

  (For debridement of abdominal wall, see 11042, 11043)

Other Procedures

+ 49905   Omental flap (eg, for reconstruction of sternal and chest wall defects) (List separately in addition to code for primary procedure)
  ➔ *CPT Assistant* Nov 00:11

  (49910 has been deleted. To report, use 49999)

49906   Free omental flap with microvascular anastomosis
  ➔ *CPT Assistant* Apr 97:8, Nov 98:16

  (Do not report code 69990 in addition to code 49906)

49999   Unlisted procedure, abdomen, peritoneum and omentum

Notes

Urinary System

(For provision of chemotherapeutic agents, use 96545 in addition to code for primary procedure)

Kidney

Incision

(For retroperitoneal exploration, abscess, tumor, or cyst, see 49010, 49060, 49200, 49201)

50010   Renal exploration, not necessitating other specific procedures

50020   Drainage of perirenal or renal abscess; open
➔ *CPT Assistant* Nov 97:19

Drainage of Renal Abscess
50020

An incision is made to the abscess cavity and the site is irrigated and drained.

50021   percutaneous
➔ *CPT Assistant* Nov 97:19; Mar 98:8

(For radiological supervision and interpretation, use 75989)

50040   Nephrostomy, nephrotomy with drainage

50045   Nephrotomy, with exploration

(For renal endoscopy performed in conjunction with this procedure, see 50570-50580)

50060   Nephrolithotomy; removal of calculus

Nephrolithotomy with Calculus Removal
50060-50075

A kidney stone (calculus) is removed by an incision in the kidney. Use 50070 if complicated by a congenital kidney abnormality.

50065   secondary surgical operation for calculus

50070   complicated by congenital kidney abnormality

50075   removal of large staghorn calculus filling renal pelvis and calyces (including anatrophic pyelolithotomy)

50080   Percutaneous nephrostolithotomy or pyelostolithotomy, with or without dilation, endoscopy, lithotripsy, stenting, or basket extraction; up to 2 cm

50081   over 2 cm

(For establishment of nephrostomy without nephrostolithotomy, see 50040, 50395, 52334)

(For fluoroscopic guidance, see 76000, 76001)

50100   Transection or repositioning of aberrant renal vessels (separate procedure)

50120   Pyelotomy; with exploration

(For renal endoscopy performed in conjunction with this procedure, see 50570-50580)

50125   with drainage, pyelostomy

50130   with removal of calculus (pyelolithotomy, pelviolithotomy, including coagulum pyelolithotomy)

50135   complicated (eg, secondary operation, congenital kidney abnormality)

(For supply of anticarcinogenic agents, use 99070 in addition to code for primary procedure)

Excision

(For excision of retroperitoneal tumor or cyst, see 49200, 49201)

50200* Renal biopsy; percutaneous, by trocar or needle

(For radiological supervision and interpretation, see 76003, 76360, ▶76393,◀ 76942)

▶(For fine needle aspiration, use 10022)◀

▶(For evaluation of fine needle aspirate, see 88172, 88173)◀

50205 by surgical exposure of kidney

▲**50220** Nephrectomy, including partial ureterectomy, any open approach including rib resection;
→ *CPT Changes* 2002

50225 complicated because of previous surgery on same kidney

50230 radical, with regional lymphadenectomy and/or vena caval thrombectomy

(When vena caval resection with reconstruction is necessary, use 37799)

50234 Nephrectomy with total ureterectomy and bladder cuff; through same incision

50236 through separate incision

50240 Nephrectomy, partial

50280 Excision or unroofing of cyst(s) of kidney
→ *CPT Assistant* Nov 99:25; *CPT Changes* 2000

(For laparoscopic ablation of renal cysts, use 50541)

50290 Excision of perinephric cyst

Renal Transplantation

(For dialysis, see 90935-90999)

(For laparoscopic donor nephrectomy, use 50547)

(For laparoscopic drainage of lymphocele to peritoneal cavity, use 49323)

50300 Donor nephrectomy, with preparation and maintenance of allograft, from cadaver donor, unilateral or bilateral
→ *CPT Assistant* Nov 99:25; *CPT Changes* 2000

50320 Donor nephrectomy, open from living donor (excluding preparation and maintenance of allograft)
→ *CPT Assistant* Nov 99:25; May 00:4; *CPT Changes* 2000

50340 Recipient nephrectomy (separate procedure)

(50341 has been deleted. To report, use 50340 with modifier '-50')

50360 Renal allotransplantation, implantation of graft; excluding donor and recipient nephrectomy

50365 with recipient nephrectomy

(50366 has been deleted. To report, use 50365 with modifier '-50')

50370 Removal of transplanted renal allograft

50380 Renal autotransplantation, reimplantation of kidney

(For extra-corporeal "bench" surgery, use autotransplantation as the primary procedure and add the secondary procedure (eg, partial nephrectomy, nephrolithotomy), and use the modifier '-51')

Introduction

50390* Aspiration and/or injection of renal cyst or pelvis by needle, percutaneous
→ *CPT Assistant* Fall 93:14; Dec 97:7

▶(For radiological supervision and interpretation, see 74425, 74470, 76003, 76360, ▶76393, 76942◀)

▶(For evaluation of fine needle aspirate, see 88172, 88173)◀

50392 Introduction of intracatheter or catheter into renal pelvis for drainage and/or injection, percutaneous
→ *CPT Assistant* Dec 97:7

Introduction of Catheter into Renal Pelvis
50392

The physician inserts a catheter into the renal pelvis in order to drain urine and/or give an injection.

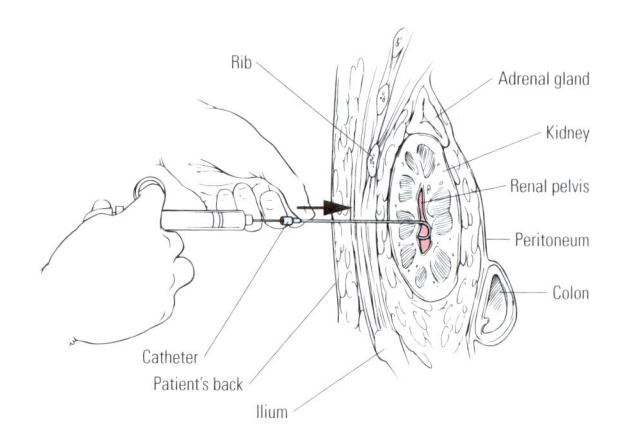

(For radiological supervision and interpretation, see 74475, 76360, ▶76942◀)

50393 Introduction of ureteral catheter or stent into ureter through renal pelvis for drainage and/or injection, percutaneous
→ *CPT Assistant* Fall 93:14

(For radiological supervision and interpretation, see 74480, 76003, 76360, ▶76942◀)

⊘ =Modifier '-51' Exempt ▶ ◀=New or Revised Text ✚ =Add-on Code CPT 2002

50394   Injection procedure for pyelography (as nephrostogram, pyelostogram, antegrade pyeloureterograms) through nephrostomy or pyelostomy tube, or indwelling ureteral catheter

➔ *CPT Assistant* Fall 93:15; Dec 97:7

(For radiological supervision and interpretation, use 74425)

50395   Introduction of guide into renal pelvis and/or ureter with dilation to establish nephrostomy tract, percutaneous

(For radiological supervision and interpretation, see 74475, 74480, 74485)

(For nephrostolithotomy, see 50080, 50081)

(For retrograde percutaneous nephrostomy, use 52334)

(For endoscopic surgery, see 50551-50561)

50396   Manometric studies through nephrostomy or pyelostomy tube, or indwelling ureteral catheter

➔ *CPT Assistant* Fall 93:16; Dec 97:7

(For radiological supervision and interpretation, see 74425, 74475, 74480)

50398*   Change of nephrostomy or pyelostomy tube

(For radiological supervision and interpretation, use 75984)

Repair

50400   Pyeloplasty (Foley Y-pyeloplasty), plastic operation on renal pelvis, with or without plastic operation on ureter, nephropexy, nephrostomy, pyelostomy, or ureteral splinting; simple

➔ *CPT Assistant* Nov 99:25; May 00:4; *CPT Changes* 2000

50405   complicated (congenital kidney abnormality, secondary pyeloplasty, solitary kidney, calycoplasty)

➔ *CPT Assistant* Nov 99:25; May 00:4; *CPT Changes* 2000

(For laparoscopic approach, use 50544)

(50420 has been deleted)

50500   Nephrorrhaphy, suture of kidney wound or injury

50520   Closure of nephrocutaneous or pyelocutaneous fistula

50525   Closure of nephrovisceral fistula (eg, renocolic), including visceral repair; abdominal approach

50526   thoracic approach

50540   Symphysiotomy for horseshoe kidney with or without pyeloplasty and/or other plastic procedure, unilateral or bilateral (one operation)

Laparoscopy

Surgical laparoscopy always includes diagnostic laparoscopy. To report a diagnostic laparoscopy (peritoneoscopy) (separate procedure), use 49320.

50541   Laparoscopy, surgical; ablation of renal cysts

➔ *CPT Assistant* Nov 99:25; May 00:4; *CPT Changes* 2000

50544   pyeloplasty

➔ *CPT Assistant* Nov 99:25; May 00:4; *CPT Changes* 2000

50545   radical nephrectomy (includes removal of Gerota's fascia and surrounding fatty tissue, removal of regional lymph nodes, and adrenalectomy)

➔ *CPT Changes* 2001

(For open procedure, use 50230)

Laparoscopic Radical Nephrectomy
50545

Radical nephrectomy (includes removal of Gerota's fascia and surrounding fatty tissue, removal of regional lymph nodes, and adrenalectomy).

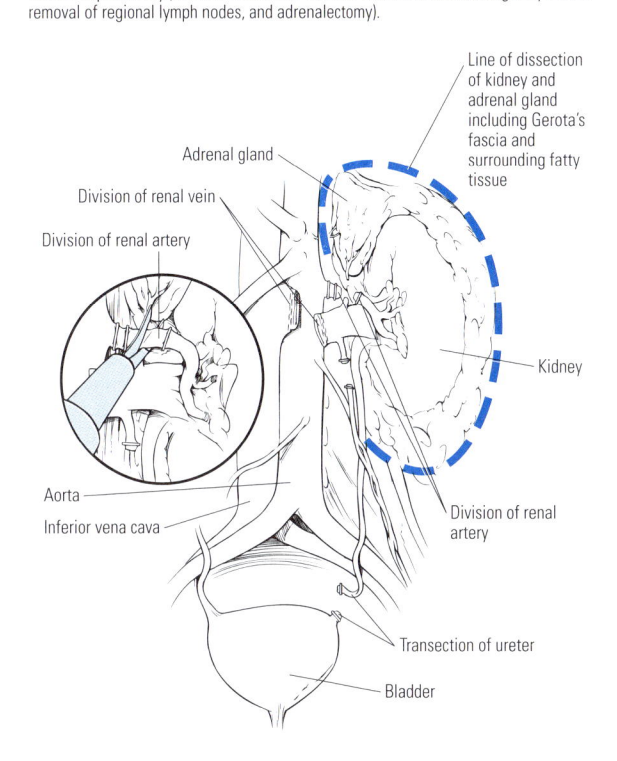

50546 nephrectomy, including partial ureterectomy

➔ *CPT Assistant* Nov 99:25; May 00:4; *CPT Changes* 2000, 2001

Laparoscopic Nephrectomy
50546

A kidney is dissected and removed under laparoscopic guidance.

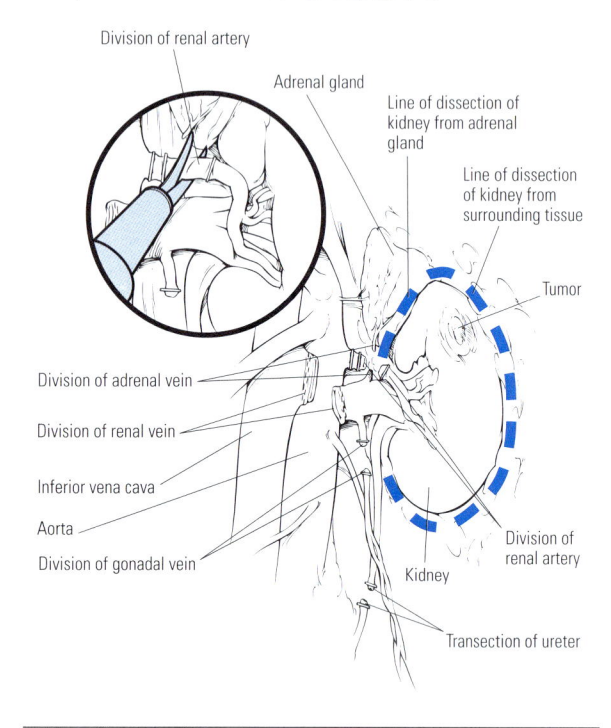

50547 donor nephrectomy from living donor (excluding preparation and maintenance of allograft)

➔ *CPT Assistant* Nov 99:25; May 00:4; *CPT Changes* 2000

(For open procedure, use 50320)

50548 nephrectomy with total ureterectomy

➔ *CPT Assistant* Nov 99:25; May 00:4; *CPT Changes* 2000, 2001

(For open procedure, see 50234, 50236)

50549 Unlisted laparoscopy procedure, renal

➔ *CPT Assistant* Nov 99:25; Mar 00:5; May 00:4; *CPT Changes* 2000

(For laparoscopic drainage of lymphocele to peritoneal cavity, use 49323)

Endoscopy

(For supplies and materials, use 99070)

(References to office and hospital have been deleted)

50551 Renal endoscopy through established nephrostomy or pyelostomy, with or without irrigation, instillation, or ureteropyelography, exclusive of radiologic service;

50553 with ureteral catheterization, with or without dilation of ureter

50555 with biopsy

50557 with fulguration and/or incision, with or without biopsy

50559 with insertion of radioactive substance with or without biopsy and/or fulguration

50561 with removal of foreign body or calculus

(When procedures 50570-50580 provide a significant identifiable service, they may be added to 50045 and 50120)

50570 Renal endoscopy through nephrotomy or pyelotomy, with or without irrigation, instillation, or ureteropyelography, exclusive of radiologic service;

(For nephrotomy, use 50045)

(For pyelotomy, use 50120)

50572 with ureteral catheterization, with or without dilation of ureter

50574 with biopsy

50575 with endopyelotomy (includes cystoscopy, ureteroscopy, dilation of ureter and ureteral pelvic junction, incision of ureteral pelvic junction and insertion of endopyelotomy stent)

50576 with fulguration and/or incision, with or without biopsy

50578 with insertion of radioactive substance, with or without biopsy and/or fulguration

50580 with removal of foreign body or calculus

Other Procedures

50590 Lithotripsy, extracorporeal shock wave

Lithotripsy
50590

The physician breaks up a kidney stone(s) (calculus) by directing shock waves through a liquid surrounding the patient.

⊘ =Modifier '-51' Exempt   ▶ ◀ =New or Revised Text   ✚ =Add-on Code   CPT 2002

Ureter

Incision

50600 Ureterotomy with exploration or drainage (separate procedure)

(For ureteral endoscopy performed in conjunction with this procedure, see 50970-50980)

50605 Ureterotomy for insertion of indwelling stent, all types

Indwelling Ureteral Stent
50605

The physician makes an incision in the ureter (ureterotomy) and inserts a stent. For placement using cystourethroscopic technique, use 52332.

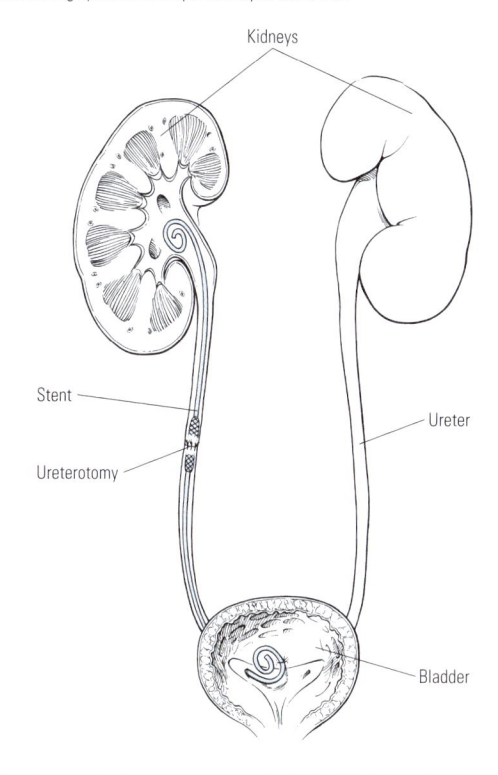

Kidneys

Stent

Ureterotomy

Ureter

Bladder

50610 Ureterolithotomy; upper one-third of ureter

➔ *CPT Assistant* Nov 99:26; *CPT Changes* 2000

50620 middle one-third of ureter

➔ *CPT Assistant* Nov 99:26; *CPT Changes* 2000

50630 lower one-third of ureter

➔ *CPT Assistant* Nov 99:26; *CPT Changes* 2000

(For laparoscopic approach, use 50945)

(For transvesical ureterolithotomy, use 51060)

(For cystotomy with stone basket extraction of ureteral calculus, use 51065)

(For endoscopic extraction or manipulation of ureteral calculus, see 50080, 50081, 50561, 50961, 50980, 52320-52330, 52352, 52353)

Excision

(For ureterocele, see 51535, 52300)

50650 Ureterectomy, with bladder cuff (separate procedure)

50660 Ureterectomy, total, ectopic ureter, combination abdominal, vaginal and/or perineal approach

Introduction

50684 Injection procedure for ureterography or ureteropyelography through ureterostomy or indwelling ureteral catheter

(For radiological supervision and interpretation, use 74425)

50686 Manometric studies through ureterostomy or indwelling ureteral catheter

50688✻ Change of ureterostomy tube

(If imaging guidance is performed, use 75984)

50690 Injection procedure for visualization of ileal conduit and/or ureteropyelography, exclusive of radiologic service

(For radiological supervision and interpretation, use 74425)

Repair

50700 Ureteroplasty, plastic operation on ureter (eg, stricture)

50715 Ureterolysis, with or without repositioning of ureter for retroperitoneal fibrosis

(50716 has been deleted. To report, use 50715 with modifier '-50')

50722 Ureterolysis for ovarian vein syndrome

50725 Ureterolysis for retrocaval ureter, with reanastomosis of upper urinary tract or vena cava

50727 Revision of urinary-cutaneous anastomosis (any type urostomy);

50728   with repair of fascial defect and hernia

50740 Ureteropyelostomy, anastomosis of ureter and renal pelvis

50750 Ureterocalycostomy, anastomosis of ureter to renal calyx

50760 Ureteroureterostomy

50770 Transureteroureterostomy, anastomosis of ureter to contralateral ureter

(Codes 50780-50785 include minor procedures to prevent vesicoureteral reflux)

50780 Ureteroneocystostomy; anastomosis of single ureter to bladder

(50781 has been deleted. To report, use 50780 with modifier '-50')

(When combined with cystourethroplasty or vesical neck revision, use 51820)

50782   anastomosis of duplicated ureter to bladder

50783   with extensive ureteral tailoring

50785   with vesico-psoas hitch or bladder flap

(50786 has been deleted. To report, use 50785 with modifier '-50')

50800   Ureteroenterostomy, direct anastomosis of ureter to intestine

(50801 has been deleted. To report, use 50800 with modifier '-50')

▲**50810**   Ureterosigmoidostomy, with creation of sigmoid bladder and establishment of abdominal or perineal colostomy, including intestine anastomosis

➜ *CPT Changes* 2002

▲**50815**   Ureterocolon conduit, including intestine anastomosis

(50816 has been deleted. To report, use 50815 with modifier '-50')

➜ *CPT Changes* 2002

▲**50820**   Ureteroileal conduit (ileal bladder), including intestine anastomosis (Bricker operation)

➜ *CPT Changes* 2002

Ureteroileal Conduit
50820

The ureters are connected to a segment of intestine to divert urine flow through an opening in the skin.

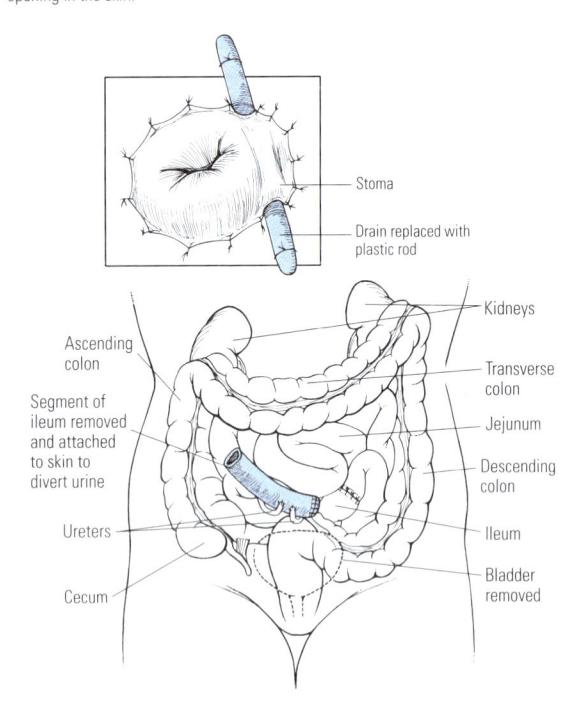

Stoma

Drain replaced with plastic rod

Kidneys

Ascending colon

Transverse colon

Segment of ileum removed and attached to skin to divert urine

Jejunum

Descending colon

Ureters

Ileum

Cecum

Bladder removed

(50821 has been deleted. To report, use 50820 with modifier '-50')

(For combination of 50800-50820 with cystectomy, see 51580-51595)

▲**50825**   Continent diversion, including intestine anastomosis using any segment of small and/or large intestine (Kock pouch or Camey enterocystoplasty)

➜ *CPT Changes* 2002

50830   Urinary undiversion (eg, taking down of ureteroileal conduit, ureterosigmoidostomy or ureteroenterostomy with ureteroureterostomy or ureteroneocystostomy)

▲**50840**   Replacement of all or part of ureter by intestine segment, including intestine anastomosis

➜ *CPT Changes* 2002

(50841 has been deleted. To report, use 50840 with modifier '-50')

50845   Cutaneous appendico-vesicostomy

50860   Ureterostomy, transplantation of ureter to skin

(50861 has been deleted. To report, use 50860 with modifier '-50')

50900   Ureterorrhaphy, suture of ureter (separate procedure)

50920   Closure of ureterocutaneous fistula

50930   Closure of ureterovisceral fistula (including visceral repair)

50940   Deligation of ureter

(For ureteroplasty, ureterolysis, see 50700-50860)

Laparoscopy

Surgical laparoscopy always includes diagnostic laparoscopy. To report a diagnostic laparoscopy (peritoneoscopy) (separate procedure), use 49320.

50945   Laparoscopy, surgical; ureterolithotomy

➜ *CPT Assistant* Nov 99:26; May 00:4; *CPT Changes* 2000

50947   ureteroneocystostomy with cystoscopy and ureteral stent placement

➜ *CPT Changes* 2001

Laparoscopic Ureteroneocystostomy
50947

Ureteroneocystostomy with cystoscopy and ureteral stent placement.

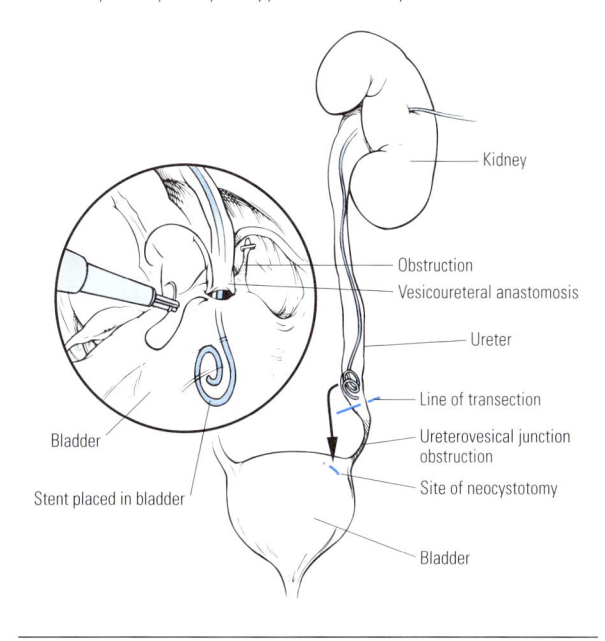

Kidney

Obstruction
Vesicoureteral anastomosis

Ureter

Line of transection

Ureterovesical junction
obstruction

Site of neocystotomy

Bladder

Bladder

Stent placed in bladder

50948   ureteroneocystostomy without cystoscopy and ureteral stent placement
➲ *CPT Changes* 2001

(For open ureteroneocystostomy, see 50780-50785)

50949   Unlisted laparoscopy procedure, ureter
➲ *CPT Changes* 2001

Endoscopy

(References to office and hospital have been deleted)

50951   Ureteral endoscopy through established ureterostomy, with or without irrigation, instillation, or ureteropyelography, exclusive of radiologic service;

50953   with ureteral catheterization, with or without dilation of ureter

50955   with biopsy

50957   with fulguration and/or incision, with or without biopsy

50959   with insertion of radioactive substance, with or without biopsy and/or fulguration (not including provision of material)

50961   with removal of foreign body or calculus

(When procedures 50970-50980 provide a significant identifiable service, they may be added to 50600)

50970   Ureteral endoscopy through ureterotomy, with or without irrigation, instillation, or ureteropyelography, exclusive of radiologic service;

(For ureterotomy, use 50600)

50972   with ureteral catheterization, with or without dilation of ureter

50974   with biopsy

50976   with fulguration and/or incision, with or without biopsy

50978   with insertion of radioactive substance, with or without biopsy and/or fulguration (not including provision of material)

50980   with removal of foreign body or calculus

Bladder

Incision

51000＊   Aspiration of bladder by needle

51005＊   Aspiration of bladder; by trocar or intracatheter

51010   with insertion of suprapubic catheter

▶(If imaging guidance is performed, see 76003, 76360, 76942)◀

51020   Cystotomy or cystostomy; with fulguration and/or insertion of radioactive material

51030   with cryosurgical destruction of intravesical lesion

51040   Cystostomy, cystotomy with drainage

51045   Cystotomy, with insertion of ureteral catheter or stent (separate procedure)

51050   Cystolithotomy, cystotomy with removal of calculus, without vesical neck resection

51060   Transvesical ureterolithotomy

▲**51065**   Cystotomy, with calculus basket extraction and/or ultrasonic or electrohydraulic fragmentation of ureteral calculus
➲ *CPT Changes* 2002

51080   Drainage of perivesical or prevesical space abscess

Excision

51500   Excision of urachal cyst or sinus, with or without umbilical hernia repair

51520   Cystotomy; for simple excision of vesical neck (separate procedure)

51525   for excision of bladder diverticulum, single or multiple (separate procedure)

51530   for excision of bladder tumor

(For transurethral resection, see 52234-52240, 52305)

51535 Cystotomy for excision, incision, or repair of ureterocele

(For transurethral excision, use 52300)

(51536 has been deleted. To report, use 51535 with modifier '-50')

51550 Cystectomy, partial; simple

51555 complicated (eg, postradiation, previous surgery, difficult location)

51565 Cystectomy, partial, with reimplantation of ureter(s) into bladder (ureteroneocystostomy)

51570 Cystectomy, complete; (separate procedure)

51575 with bilateral pelvic lymphadenectomy, including external iliac, hypogastric, and obturator nodes

51580 Cystectomy, complete, with ureterosigmoidostomy or ureterocutaneous transplantations;

51585 with bilateral pelvic lymphadenectomy, including external iliac, hypogastric, and obturator nodes

▲ **51590** Cystectomy, complete, with ureteroileal conduit or sigmoid bladder, including intestine anastomosis;
→ *CPT Changes* 2002

51595 with bilateral pelvic lymphadenectomy, including external iliac, hypogastric, and obturator nodes

▲ **51596** Cystectomy, complete, with continent diversion, any open technique, using any segment of small and/or large intestine to construct neobladder
→ *CPT Changes* 2002

51597 Pelvic exenteration, complete, for vesical, prostatic or urethral malignancy, with removal of bladder and ureteral transplantations, with or without hysterectomy and/or abdominoperineal resection of rectum and colon and colostomy, or any combination thereof

(For pelvic exenteration for gynecologic malignancy, use 58240)

Introduction

(For bladder catheterization, see 53670, 53675)

51600* Injection procedure for cystography or voiding urethrocystography

(For radiological supervision and interpretation, see 74430, 74455)

51605 Injection procedure and placement of chain for contrast and/or chain urethrocystography

(For radiological supervision and interpretation, use 74430)

51610 Injection procedure for retrograde urethrocystography

(For radiological supervision and interpretation, use 74450)

51700* Bladder irrigation, simple, lavage and/or instillation

51705* Change of cystostomy tube; simple

51710* complicated

(If imaging guidance is performed, use 75984)

51715 Endoscopic injection of implant material into the submucosal tissues of the urethra and/or bladder neck

51720 Bladder instillation of anticarcinogenic agent (including detention time)

Urodynamics

The following section (51725-51797) lists procedures that may be used separately or in many and varied combinations.

When multiple procedures are performed in the same investigative session, modifier '-51' should be employed.

All procedures in this section imply that these services are performed by, or are under the direct supervision of, a physician and that all instruments, equipment, fluids, gases, probes, catheters, technician's fees, medications, gloves, trays, tubing and other sterile supplies be provided by the physician. When the physician only interprets the results and/or operates the equipment, a professional component, modifier '-26', should be used to identify physicians' services.

51725 Simple cystometrogram (CMG) (eg, spinal manometer)

51726 Complex cystometrogram (eg, calibrated electronic equipment)

(51727-51733 have been deleted. To report, use 51726)

51736 Simple uroflowmetry (UFR) (eg, stop-watch flow rate, mechanical uroflowmeter)

(51737, 51738 have been deleted. To report, use 51736)

(51739 has been deleted)

51741 Complex uroflowmetry (eg, calibrated electronic equipment)

(51742-51749 have been deleted. To report, use 51741)

(51751-51769 have been deleted. To report, use 53899)

51772 Urethral pressure profile studies (UPP) (urethral closure pressure profile), any technique

(51773-51783 have been deleted. To report, use 51772)

⊘ =Modifier '-51' Exempt ▶ ◀ =New or Revised Text ✚ =Add-on Code

51784 Electromyography studies (EMG) of anal or urethral sphincter, other than needle, any technique

51785 Needle electromyography studies (EMG) of anal or urethral sphincter, any technique

(51786-51791 have been deleted. To report, use 51785)

51792 Stimulus evoked response (eg, measurement of bulbocavernosus reflex latency time)

51795 Voiding pressure studies (VP); bladder voiding pressure, any technique

(51796 has been deleted. To report, use 51795)

51797 intra-abdominal voiding pressure (AP) (rectal, gastric, intraperitoneal)

Repair

51800 Cystoplasty or cystourethroplasty, plastic operation on bladder and/or vesical neck (anterior Y-plasty, vesical fundus resection), any procedure, with or without wedge resection of posterior vesical neck

51820 Cystourethroplasty with unilateral or bilateral ureteroneocystostomy

51840 Anterior vesicourethropexy, or urethropexy (eg, Marshall-Marchetti-Krantz, Burch); simple
→ *CPT Assistant* Jan 97:1; Nov 97:19; Apr 98:15

51841 complicated (eg, secondary repair)
→ *CPT Assistant* Jan 97:1

(For urethropexy (Pereyra type), use 57289)

51845 Abdomino-vaginal vesical neck suspension, with or without endoscopic control (eg, Stamey, Raz, modified Pereyra)
→ *CPT Assistant* Jan 97:3

51860 Cystorrhaphy, suture of bladder wound, injury or rupture; simple

51865 complicated

51880 Closure of cystostomy (separate procedure)

51900 Closure of vesicovaginal fistula, abdominal approach

(For vaginal approach, see 57320-57330)

51920 Closure of vesicouterine fistula;

51925 with hysterectomy

(For closure of vesicoenteric fistula, see 44660, 44661)

(For closure of rectovesical fistula, see 45800-45805)

▲ **51940** Closure, exstrophy of bladder
→ *CPT Changes* 2002

(See also 54390)

▲ **51960** Enterocystoplasty, including intestinal anastomosis
→ *CPT Changes* 2002

51980 Cutaneous vesicostomy

Laparoscopy

Surgical laparoscopy always includes diagnostic laparoscopy. To report a diagnostic laparoscopy (peritoneoscopy) (separate procedure), use 49320.

51990 Laparoscopy, surgical; urethral suspension for stress incontinence
→ *CPT Assistant* Nov 99:26; May 00:4; *CPT Changes* 2000

51992 sling operation for stress incontinence (eg, fascia or synthetic)
→ *CPT Assistant* Nov 99:26; May 00:4; *CPT Changes* 2000

(For open sling operation for stress incontinence, use 57288)

(For reversal or removal of sling operation for stress incontinence, use 57287)

Laparoscopic Sling Suspension Urinary Incontinence
51990

Laparoscopic placement of nonabsorbable sutures are placed into the endopelvic fascia at the bladder neck region on each side and secured to the ipsilateral pectineal ligament. The sutures are tied using extra vaginal-urethral knots so as to create a hammock type suspension of the bladder neck, without urethral occlusion.

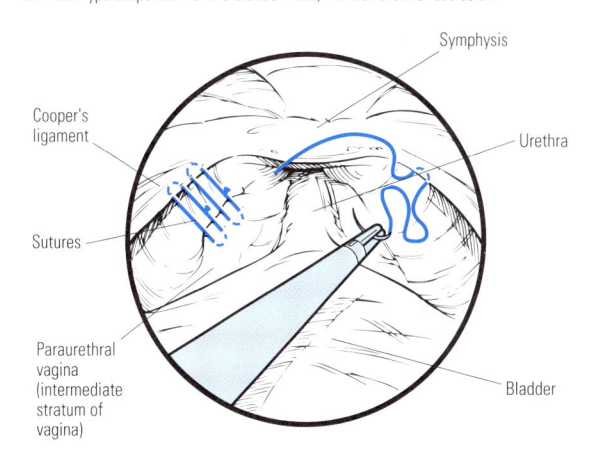

Endoscopy—Cystoscopy, Urethroscopy, Cystourethroscopy

Endoscopic descriptions are listed so that the main procedure can be identified without having to list all the minor related functions performed at the same time. For example: meatotomy, urethral calibration and/or dilation, urethro-scopy, and cystoscopy prior to a transurethral resection of prostate; ureteral catheterization following extraction of ureteral calculus; internal urethrotomy and bladder neck fulguration when performing a cystourethroscopy for the female urethral syndrome. When the secondary procedure requires significant additional time and effort, it may be identified by the addition of modifier '-22'.

For example: urethrotomy performed for a documented pre-existing stricture or bladder neck contracture.

(References to office and hospital have been deleted)

52000 Cystourethroscopy (separate procedure)
➲ *CPT Assistant* Oct 00:7

● **52001** Cystourethroscopy with irrigation and evacuation of clots
➲ *CPT Changes* 2002

▶(Do not report 52001 in addition to 52000)◀

52005 Cystourethroscopy, with ureteral catheterization, with or without irrigation, instillation, or ureteropyelography, exclusive of radiologic service;
➲ *CPT Assistant* Sep 00:11

Cystourethroscopy with Ureteral Catheterization
52005

A cystourethroscope is passed through the urethra and bladder in order to view the urinary collecting system.

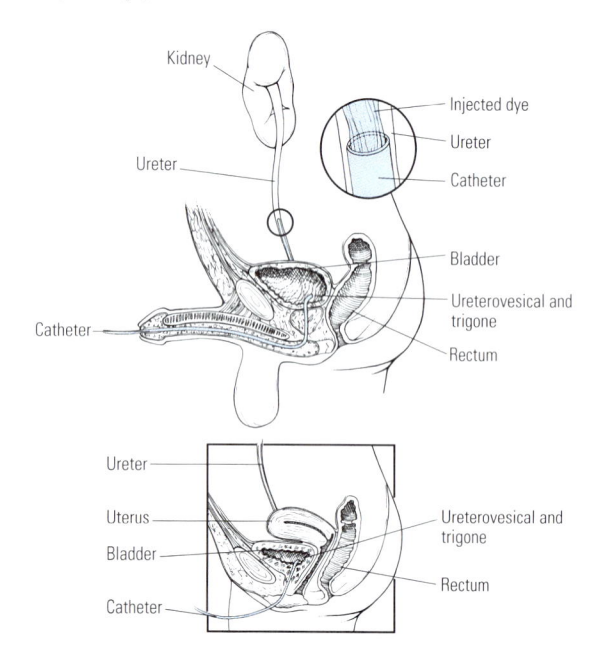

Kidney · Injected dye · Ureter · Catheter · Ureter · Bladder · Ureterovesical and trigone · Rectum · Catheter

Ureter · Uterus · Bladder · Catheter · Ureterovesical and trigone · Rectum

---

52007 with brush biopsy of ureter and/or renal pelvis

52010 Cystourethroscopy, with ejaculatory duct catheterization, with or without irrigation, instillation, or duct radiography, exclusive of radiologic service

(For radiological supervision and interpretation, use 74440)

(52190 has been deleted)

Transurethral Surgery

Urethra and Bladder

(References to office and hospital have been deleted)

52204 Cystourethroscopy, with biopsy

52214 Cystourethroscopy, with fulguration (including cryosurgery or laser surgery) of trigone, bladder neck, prostatic fossa, urethra, or periurethral glands

52224 Cystourethroscopy, with fulguration (including cryosurgery or laser surgery) or treatment of MINOR (less than 0.5 cm) lesion(s) with or without biopsy

52234 Cystourethroscopy, with fulguration (including cryosurgery or laser surgery) and/or resection of; SMALL bladder tumor(s) (0.5 to 2.0 cm)

52235   MEDIUM bladder tumor(s) (2.0 to 5.0 cm)

52240   LARGE bladder tumor(s)

52250 Cystourethroscopy with insertion of radioactive substance, with or without biopsy or fulguration

52260 Cystourethroscopy, with dilation of bladder for interstitial cystitis; general or conduction (spinal) anesthesia

52265   local anesthesia

52270 Cystourethroscopy, with internal urethrotomy; female

52275   male

52276 Cystourethroscopy with direct vision internal urethrotomy

52277 Cystourethroscopy, with resection of external sphincter (sphincterotomy)

52281 Cystourethroscopy, with calibration and/or dilation of urethral stricture or stenosis, with or without meatotomy, with or without injection procedure for cystography, male or female
➲ *CPT Assistant* Nov 97:20

52282 Cystourethroscopy, with insertion of urethral stent
➲ *CPT Assistant* Nov 97:20

52283 Cystourethroscopy, with steroid injection into stricture

52285 Cystourethroscopy for treatment of the female urethral syndrome with any or all of the following: urethral meatotomy, urethral dilation, internal urethrotomy, lysis of urethrovaginal septal fibrosis, lateral incisions of the bladder neck, and fulguration of polyp(s) of urethra, bladder neck, and/or trigone

52290 Cystourethroscopy; with ureteral meatotomy, unilateral or bilateral

52300 with resection or fulguration of orthotopic ureterocele(s), unilateral or bilateral

52301 with resection or fulguration of ectopic ureterocele(s), unilateral or bilateral

52305 with incision or resection of orifice of bladder diverticulum, single or multiple

52310 Cystourethroscopy, with removal of foreign body, calculus, or ureteral stent from urethra or bladder (separate procedure); simple

52315 complicated

52317 Litholapaxy: crushing or fragmentation of calculus by any means in bladder and removal of fragments; simple or small (less than 2.5 cm)

52318 complicated or large (over 2.5 cm)

Ureter and Pelvis

Surgical cystourethroscopy always includes diagnostic cystourethroscopy. To report a diagnostic cystourethroscopy, use 52351.

Do not report 52351 in conjunction with 52341-52346, 52352-52355.

The insertion and removal of a temporary stent during diagnostic or therapeutic cystourethroscopic intervention(s) is included in 52320-52355 and should not be reported separately.

To report insertion of a self-retaining, indwelling stent performed during cystourethroscopic diagnostic or therapeutic intervention(s), use code 52332, in addition to primary procedure(s) performed, and append the modifier '-51'. Code 52332 is used to report a unilateral procedure unless otherwise specified.

For bilateral insertion of self-retaining, indwelling ureteral stents, use code 52332, and append the modifier '-50'.

To report cystourethroscopic removal of a self-retaining, indwelling ureteral stent, see codes 52310, 52315, and append the modifier '-58'.

52320 Cystourethroscopy (including ureteral catheterization); with removal of ureteral calculus
➔ *CPT Assistant* Mar 96:1; May 96:11

52325 with fragmentation of ureteral calculus (eg, ultrasonic or electro-hydraulic technique)
➔ *CPT Assistant* Mar 96:1; May 96:11

52327 with subureteric injection of implant material
➔ *CPT Assistant* Mar 96:1; May 96:11

52330 with manipulation, without removal of ureteral calculus
➔ *CPT Assistant* Mar 96:1; May 96:11; Sep 00:11

52332 Cystourethroscopy, with insertion of indwelling ureteral stent (eg, Gibbons or double-J type)
➔ *CPT Assistant* Mar 96:1; May 96:11

52334 Cystourethroscopy with insertion of ureteral guide wire through kidney to establish a percutaneous nephrostomy, retrograde
➔ *CPT Assistant* Mar 96:11; May 96:11

(For percutaneous nephrostolithotomy, see 50080, 50081; for establishment of nephrostomy tract only, use 50395)

(52335 has been deleted. To report, use 52351)

(52336 has been deleted. To report, use 52352)

(52337 has been deleted. To report, use 52353)

(52338 has been deleted. To report, use 52354)

(52339 has been deleted. To report, use 52355)

(52340 has been deleted. To report, use 52400)

52341 Cystourethroscopy; with treatment of ureteral stricture (eg, balloon dilation, laser, electrocautery, and incision)
➔ *CPT Changes* 2001

52342 with treatment of ureteropelvic junction stricture (eg, balloon dilation, laser, electrocautery, and incision)
➔ *CPT Changes* 2001

52343 with treatment of intra-renal stricture (eg, balloon dilation, laser, electrocautery, and incision)
➔ *CPT Changes* 2001

52344 Cystourethroscopy with ureteroscopy; with treatment of ureteral stricture (eg, balloon dilation, laser, electrocautery, and incision)
➔ *CPT Changes* 2001

52345 with treatment of ureteropelvic junction stricture (eg, balloon dilation, laser, electrocautery, and incision)
➔ *CPT Changes* 2001

52346 with treatment of intra-renal stricture (eg, balloon dilation, laser, electrocautery, and incision)
➔ *CPT Changes* 2001

●**52347** Cystourethroscopy with transurethral resection or incision of ejaculatory ducts
➔ *CPT Changes* 2002

52351 Cystourethroscopy, with ureteroscopy and/or pyeloscopy; diagnostic
➔ *CPT Changes* 2001

(For radiological supervision and interpretation, use 74485)

(Do not report 52351 in conjunction with 52341-52346, 52352-52355)

52352 with removal or manipulation of calculus (ureteral catheterization is included)
➔ *CPT Changes* 2001

52353 with lithotripsy (ureteral catheterization is included)
➔ *CPT Changes* 2001

52354 with biopsy and/or fulguration of lesion
➡ *CPT Changes* 2001

52355 with resection of tumor
➡ *CPT Changes* 2001

Vesical Neck and Prostate

52400 Cystourethroscopy with incision, fulguration, or resection of congenital posterior urethral valves, or congenital obstructive hypertrophic mucosal folds
➡ *CPT Changes* 2001

52450 Transurethral incision of prostate

52500 Transurethral resection of bladder neck (separate procedure)

▲ **52510** Transurethral balloon dilation of the prostatic urethra
➡ *CPT Changes* 2002

52601 Transurethral electrosurgical resection of prostate, including control of postoperative bleeding, complete (vasectomy, meatotomy, cystourethroscopy, urethral calibration and/or dilation, and internal urethrotomy are included)

Transurethral Resection of Prostate, Complete
52601

The physician removes the prostate gland using an electrocautery knife.

(For other approaches, see 55801-55845)

(52605 has been deleted. To report, use 52606)

52606 Transurethral fulguration for postoperative bleeding occurring after the usual follow-up time

52612 Transurethral resection of prostate; first stage of two-stage resection (partial resection)

52614 second stage of two-stage resection (resection completed)

52620 Transurethral resection; of residual obstructive tissue after 90 days postoperative

52630 of regrowth of obstructive tissue longer than one year postoperative

52640 of postoperative bladder neck contracture

52647 Non-contact laser coagulation of prostate, including control of postoperative bleeding, complete (vasectomy, meatotomy, cystourethroscopy, urethral calibration and/or dilation, and internal urethrotomy are included)
➡ *CPT Assistant* Mar 98:11

52648 Contact laser vaporization with or without transurethral resection of prostate, including control of postoperative bleeding, complete (vasectomy, meatotomy, cystourethroscopy, urethral calibration and/or dilation, and internal urethrotomy are included)
➡ *CPT Assistant* Mar 98:11

Contact Laser Vaporization of Prostate
52648

A laser is used to vaporize the prostate.

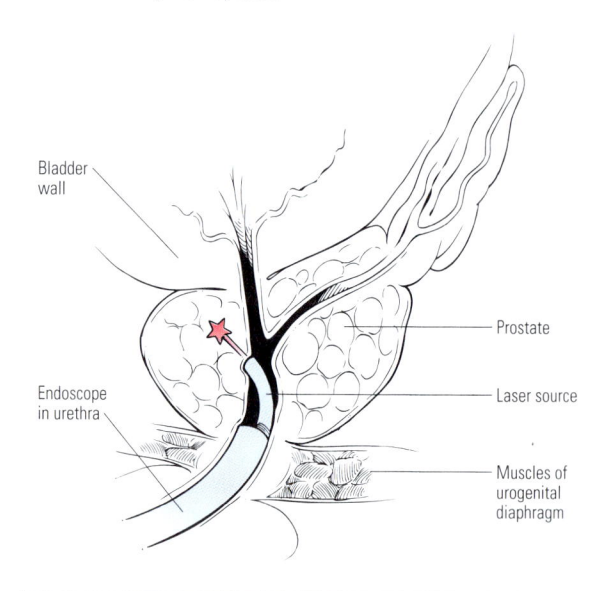

(52650 has been deleted)

52700 Transurethral drainage of prostatic abscess

(52800, 52805 have been deleted. To report, see 52317, 52318)

⊘ =Modifier '-51' Exempt   ▶ ◀ =New or Revised Text   ✚ =Add-on Code   CPT 2002

Urethra

(For endoscopy, see cystoscopy, urethroscopy, cystourethroscopy, 52000-52700)

(For injection procedure for urethrocystography, see 51600-51610)

Incision

53000 Urethrotomy or urethrostomy, external (separate procedure); pendulous urethra

53010   perineal urethra, external

53020 Meatotomy, cutting of meatus (separate procedure); except infant

(53021 has been deleted. To report, use 53020)

53025   infant

53040 Drainage of deep periurethral abscess

(For subcutaneous abscess, see 10060, 10061)

53060 Drainage of Skene's gland abscess or cyst

53080 Drainage of perineal urinary extravasation; uncomplicated (separate procedure)

53085   complicated

Excision

53200 Biopsy of urethra

53210 Urethrectomy, total, including cystostomy; female

53215   male

53220 Excision or fulguration of carcinoma of urethra

53230 Excision of urethral diverticulum (separate procedure); female

53235   male

53240 Marsupialization of urethral diverticulum, male or female

53250 Excision of bulbourethral gland (Cowper's gland)

53260 Excision or fulguration; urethral polyp(s), distal urethra

(For endoscopic approach, see 52214, 52224)

53265   urethral caruncle

53270   Skene's glands

53275   urethral prolapse

Repair

(For hypospadias, see 54300-54352)

53400 Urethroplasty; first stage, for fistula, diverticulum, or stricture (eg, Johannsen type)

53405   second stage (formation of urethra), including urinary diversion

53410 Urethroplasty, one-stage reconstruction of male anterior urethra

53415 Urethroplasty, transpubic or perineal, one stage, for reconstruction or repair of prostatic or membranous urethra

53420 Urethroplasty, two-stage reconstruction or repair of prostatic or membranous urethra; first stage

53425   second stage

53430 Urethroplasty, reconstruction of female urethra

● **53431** Urethroplasty with tubularization of posterior urethra and/or lower bladder for incontinence (eg, Tenago, Leadbetter procedure)
→ *CPT Changes* 2002

53440 Operation for correction of male urinary incontinence, with or without introduction of prosthesis

53442 Removal of perineal prosthesis introduced for continence

▶(53443 has been deleted. To report, use 53431)◀

● **53444** Insertion of tandem cuff (dual cuff)
→ *CPT Changes* 2002

▲ **53445** Insertion of inflatable urethral/bladder neck sphincter, including placement of pump, reservoir, and cuff
→ *CPT Changes* 2002

● **53446** Removal of inflatable urethral/bladder neck sphincter, including pump, reservoir, and cuff
→ *CPT Changes* 2002

▲ **53447** Removal and replacement of inflatable urethral/bladder neck sphincter including pump, reservoir, and cuff at the same operative session
→ *CPT Changes* 2002

● **53448** Removal and replacement of inflatable urethral/bladder neck sphincter including pump, reservoir, and cuff through an infected field at the same operative session including irrigation and debridement of infected tissue
→ *CPT Changes* 2002

▶(Do not report 11040-11043 in addition to 53448)◀

▲ **53449** Repair of inflatable urethral/bladder neck sphincter, including pump, reservoir, and cuff
→ *CPT Changes* 2002

53450 Urethromeatoplasty, with mucosal advancement

(For meatotomy, see 53020, 53025)

53460 Urethromeatoplasty, with partial excision of distal urethral segment (Richardson type procedure)

53502 Urethrorrhaphy, suture of urethral wound or injury, female

53505 Urethrorrhaphy, suture of urethral wound or injury; penile

53510   perineal

53515   prostatomembranous

53520   Closure of urethrostomy or urethrocutaneous fistula, male (separate procedure)

(For closure of urethrovaginal fistula, use 57310)

(For closure of urethrorectal fistula, see 45820, 45825)

Manipulation

(For radiological supervision and interpretation, use 74485)

53600*   Dilation of urethral stricture by passage of sound or urethral dilator, male; initial

53601*   subsequent

53605   Dilation of urethral stricture or vesical neck by passage of sound or urethral dilator, male, general or conduction (spinal) anesthesia

53620*   Dilation of urethral stricture by passage of filiform and follower, male; initial

53621*   subsequent

(53640 has been deleted. To report, use 53620)

53660*   Dilation of female urethra including suppository and/or instillation; initial

53661*   subsequent

53665   Dilation of female urethra, general or conduction (spinal) anesthesia

53670*   Catheterization, urethra; simple

53675*   complicated (may include difficult removal of balloon catheter)

Other Procedures

(53800 has been deleted. To report, use 81020)

53850   Transurethral destruction of prostate tissue; by microwave thermotherapy
   ➔ *CPT Assistant* Nov 97:20

53852   by radiofrequency thermotherapy
   ➔ *CPT Assistant* Nov 97:20

● **53853**   by water-induced thermotherapy
   ➔ *CPT Changes* 2002

53899   Unlisted procedure, urinary system

Male Genital System

Penis

Incision

54000   Slitting of prepuce, dorsal or lateral (separate procedure); newborn

54001   except newborn

54015   Incision and drainage of penis, deep

(For skin and subcutaneous abscess, see 10060-10160)

Destruction

54050 ✳   Destruction of lesion(s), penis (eg, condyloma, papilloma, molluscum contagiosum, herpetic vesicle), simple; chemical

54055 ✳   electrodesiccation

54056   cryosurgery

54057   laser surgery

54060   surgical excision

▲ **54065**   Destruction of lesion(s), penis (eg, condyloma, papilloma, molluscum contagiosum, herpetic vesicle), extensive (eg, laser surgery, electrosurgery, cryosurgery, chemosurgery)
➔ *CPT Changes* 2002

(For destruction or excision of other lesions, see **Integumentary System**)

Excision

54100   Biopsy of penis; (separate procedure)
➔ *CPT Assistant* Nov 99:26; *CPT Changes* 2000

54105   deep structures

54110   Excision of penile plaque (Peyronie disease);

54111   with graft to 5 cm in length
➔ *CPT Assistant* Aug 99:5

54112   with graft greater than 5 cm in length

54115   Removal foreign body from deep penile tissue (eg, plastic implant)

54120   Amputation of penis; partial

54125   complete

54130   Amputation of penis, radical; with bilateral inguinofemoral lymphadenectomy

54135   in continuity with bilateral pelvic lymphadenectomy, including external iliac, hypogastric and obturator nodes

(For lymphadenectomy (separate procedure), see 38760-38770)

54150   Circumcision, using clamp or other device; newborn
➔ *CPT Assistant* Sep 96:11; May 98:11

54152   except newborn
➔ *CPT Assistant* Sep 96:11; Dec 96:10; May 98:11

(54154 has been deleted. To report, use 54152)

54160   Circumcision, surgical excision other than clamp, device or dorsal slit; newborn
➔ *CPT Assistant* Sep 96:11; May 98:11

54161   except newborn
➔ *CPT Assistant* Sep 96:11; Dec 96:10; May 98:11

● **54162**   Lysis or excision of penile post-circumcision adhesions
➔ *CPT Changes* 2002

● **54163**   Repair incomplete circumcision
➔ *CPT Changes* 2002

● **54164**   Frenulotomy of penis
➔ *CPT Changes* 2002

►(Do not report with circumcision codes 54150-54161, 54162, 54163)◄

Introduction

54200 ✳   Injection procedure for Peyronie disease;

54205   with surgical exposure of plaque

54220   Irrigation of corpora cavernosa for priapism

54230   Injection procedure for corpora cavernosography

(For radiological supervision and interpretation, use 74445)

54231   Dynamic cavernosometry, including intracavernosal injection of vasoactive drugs (eg, papaverine, phentolamine)

54235   Injection of corpora cavernosa with pharmacologic agent(s) (eg, papaverine, phentolamine)
➔ *CPT Assistant* Sep 96:10

54240   Penile plethysmography

54250   Nocturnal penile tumescence and/or rigidity test

Repair

(For other urethroplasties, see 53400-53430)

(For penile revascularization, use 37788)

54300   Plastic operation of penis for straightening of chordee (eg, hypospadias), with or without mobilization of urethra

54304   Plastic operation on penis for correction of chordee or for first stage hypospadias repair with or without transplantation of prepuce and/or skin flaps

(54305 has been deleted. To report, see 54304 et seq)

54308   Urethroplasty for second stage hypospadias repair (including urinary diversion); less than 3 cm

54312   greater than 3 cm

54316 Urethroplasty for second stage hypospadias repair (including urinary diversion) with free skin graft obtained from site other than genitalia

54318 Urethroplasty for third stage hypospadias repair to release penis from scrotum (eg, third stage Cecil repair)

(54320 has been deleted. To report, see 54308 et seq)

54322 One stage distal hypospadias repair (with or without chordee or circumcision); with simple meatal advancement (eg, Magpi, V-flap)

54324 with urethroplasty by local skin flaps (eg, flip-flap, prepucial flap)

(54325 has been deleted. To report, see 54308 et seq)

54326 with urethroplasty by local skin flaps and mobilization of urethra

54328 with extensive dissection to correct chordee and urethroplasty with local skin flaps, skin graft patch, and/or island flap

(54330 has been deleted. To report, use 54308)

54332 One stage proximal penile or penoscrotal hypospadias repair requiring extensive dissection to correct chordee and urethroplasty by use of skin graft tube and/or island flap

54336 One stage perineal hypospadias repair requiring extensive dissection to correct chordee and urethroplasty by use of skin graft tube and/or island flap

54340 Repair of hypospadias complications (ie, fistula, stricture, diverticula); by closure, incision, or excision, simple

54344 requiring mobilization of skin flaps and urethroplasty with flap or patch graft

54348 requiring extensive dissection and urethroplasty with flap, patch or tubed graft (includes urinary diversion)

54352 Repair of hypospadias cripple requiring extensive dissection and excision of previously constructed structures including re-release of chordee and reconstruction of urethra and penis by use of local skin as grafts and island flaps and skin brought in as flaps or grafts

54360 Plastic operation on penis to correct angulation

54380 Plastic operation on penis for epispadias distal to external sphincter;

54385 with incontinence

54390 with exstrophy of bladder

54400 Insertion of penile prosthesis; non-inflatable (semi-rigid)

54401 inflatable (self-contained)

▶(54402 has been deleted. To report, see 54415, 54416)◀

▲**54405** Insertion of multi-component, inflatable penile prosthesis, including placement of pump, cylinders, and reservoir
➔ *CPT Changes* 2002

▶(For reduced services, report 54405 with modifier '-52')◀

●**54406** Removal of all components of a multi-component, inflatable penile prosthesis without replacement of prosthesis
➔ *CPT Changes* 2002

▶(For reduced services, report 54406 with modifier '-52')◀

▶(54407 has been deleted. To report, see 54406, 54408, 54410)◀

●**54408** Repair of component(s) of a multi-component, inflatable penile prosthesis
➔ *CPT Changes* 2002

▶(54409 has been deleted. To report, use 54408)◀

●**54410** Removal and replacement of all component(s) of a multi-component, inflatable penile prosthesis at the same operative session
➔ *CPT Changes* 2002

●**54411** Removal and replacement of all components of a multi-component inflatable penile prosthesis through an infected field at the same operative session, including irrigation and debridement of infected tissue
➔ *CPT Changes* 2002

▶(For reduced services, report 54411 with modifier '-52')◀

▶(Do not report 11040-11043 in addition to 54411)◀

●**54415** Removal of non-inflatable (semi-rigid) or inflatable (self-contained) penile prosthesis, without replacement of prosthesis
➔ *CPT Changes* 2002

●**54416** Removal and replacement of non-inflatable (semi-rigid) or inflatable (self-contained) penile prosthesis at the same operative session
➔ *CPT Changes* 2002

●**54417** Removal and replacement of non-inflatable (semi-rigid) or inflatable (self-contained) penile prosthesis through an infected field at the same operative session, including irrigation and debridement of infected tissue
➔ *CPT Changes* 2002

▶(Do not report 11040-11043 in addition to 54417)◀

54420 Corpora cavernosa-saphenous vein shunt (priapism operation), unilateral or bilateral

54430 Corpora cavernosa-corpus spongiosum shunt (priapism operation), unilateral or bilateral

54435 Corpora cavernosa-glans penis fistulization (eg, biopsy needle, Winter procedure, rongeur, or punch) for priapism

54440 Plastic operation of penis for injury

⊘ =Modifier '-51' Exempt ▶ ◀=New or Revised Text ✚ =Add-on Code CPT 2002

Manipulation

54450   Foreskin manipulation including lysis of preputial adhesions and stretching

Testis

Excision

54500   Biopsy of testis, needle (separate procedure)

▶(For fine needle aspiration, see 10021, 10022)◀

▶(For evaluation of fine needle aspirate, see 88172, 88173)◀

54505   Biopsy of testis, incisional (separate procedure)

(When combined with vasogram, seminal vesiculogram, or epididymogram, use 55300)

(54506 has been deleted. To report, use 54505 with modifier '-50')

▶(54510 has been deleted. To report, use 54512)◀

54512   Excision of extraparenchymal lesion of testis
➔ *CPT Changes* 2001

54520   Orchiectomy, simple (including subcapsular), with or without testicular prosthesis, scrotal or inguinal approach

(54521 has been deleted. To report, use 54520 with modifier '-50')

54522   Orchiectomy, partial
➔ *CPT Changes* 2001

54530   Orchiectomy, radical, for tumor; inguinal approach

54535   with abdominal exploration

(For orchiectomy with repair of hernia, see 49505 or 49507 and 54520)

(For radical retroperitoneal lymphadenectomy, use 38780)

54550   Exploration for undescended testis (inguinal or scrotal area)

(54555 has been deleted. To report, use 54550 with modifier '-50')

54560   Exploration for undescended testis with abdominal exploration

(54565 has been deleted. To report, use 54560 with modifier '-50')

Repair

54600   Reduction of torsion of testis, surgical, with or without fixation of contralateral testis

54620   Fixation of contralateral testis (separate procedure)

54640   Orchiopexy, inguinal approach, with or without hernia repair

(For inguinal hernia repair performed in conjunction with inguinal orchiopexy, see 49495-49525)

(54641 has been deleted. To report, use 54640 with modifier '-50')

(54645 has been deleted)

54650   Orchiopexy, abdominal approach, for intra-abdominal testis (eg, Fowler-Stephens)
➔ *CPT Assistant* Nov 99:26; May 00:4; *CPT Changes* 2000

(For laparoscopic approach, use 54692)

54660   Insertion of testicular prosthesis (separate procedure)

(54661 has been deleted. To report, use 54660 with modifier '-50')

54670   Suture or repair of testicular injury

54680   Transplantation of testis(es) to thigh (because of scrotal destruction)

Laparoscopy

Surgical laparoscopy always includes diagnostic laparoscopy. To report a diagnostic laparoscopy (peritoneoscopy) (separate procedure), use 49320.

54690   Laparoscopy, surgical; orchiectomy
➔ *CPT Assistant* Nov 99:26; Mar 00:5; *CPT Changes* 2000

54692   orchiopexy for intra-abdominal testis
➔ *CPT Assistant* Nov 99:27; May 00:4; *CPT Changes* 2000

Laparoscopic Orchiopexy
54692

Surgical fixation of an undescended testis in the scrotum under laparoscopic guidance.

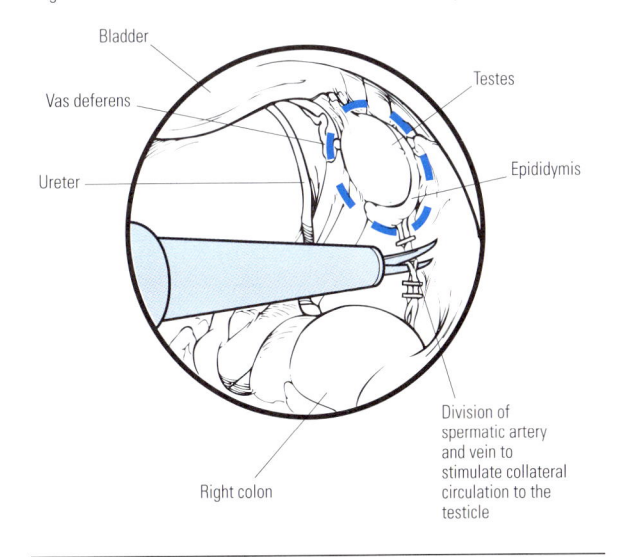

Bladder

Vas deferens

Ureter

Testes

Epididymis

Right colon

Division of spermatic artery and vein to stimulate collateral circulation to the testicle

54699   Unlisted laparoscopy procedure, testis
➔ *CPT Assistant* Nov 99:27; Mar 00:5; *CPT Changes* 2000

Epididymis

Incision

54700 Incision and drainage of epididymis, testis and/or scrotal space (eg, abscess or hematoma)

Excision

54800 Biopsy of epididymis, needle

►(For fine needle aspiration, see 10021, 10022)◄

►(For evaluation of fine needle aspirate, see 88172, 88173)◄

54820 Exploration of epididymis, with or without biopsy

54830 Excision of local lesion of epididymis

54840 Excision of spermatocele, with or without epididymectomy

54860 Epididymectomy; unilateral

54861   bilateral

Repair

54900 Epididymovasostomy, anastomosis of epididymis to vas deferens; unilateral
➔ *CPT Assistant* Nov 98:16

54901   bilateral
➔ *CPT Assistant* Nov 98:16

(For operating microscope, use 69990)

Tunica Vaginalis

Incision

55000* Puncture aspiration of hydrocele, tunica vaginalis, with or without injection of medication

Excision

55040 Excision of hydrocele; unilateral

55041   bilateral

(With hernia repair, see 49495-49501)

Repair

55060 Repair of tunica vaginalis hydrocele (Bottle type)

Scrotum

Incision

55100* Drainage of scrotal wall abscess

(See also 54700)

55110 Scrotal exploration

55120 Removal of foreign body in scrotum

Excision

(For excision of local lesion of skin of scrotum, see **Integumentary System**)

55150 Resection of scrotum

Repair

(55170 has been deleted. To report, see 55175, 55180)

55175 Scrotoplasty; simple

55180   complicated

Vas Deferens

Incision

55200 Vasotomy, cannulization with or without incision of vas, unilateral or bilateral (separate procedure)

Excision

55250 Vasectomy, unilateral or bilateral (separate procedure), including postoperative semen examination(s)
➔ *CPT Assistant* Jun 98:10; Jul 98:10

Introduction

55300 Vasotomy for vasograms, seminal vesiculograms, or epididymograms, unilateral or bilateral

(For radiological supervision and interpretation, use 74440)

(When combined with biopsy of testis, see 54505 and use modifier '-51')

Repair

55400 Vasovasostomy, vasovasorrhaphy
➔ *CPT Assistant* Nov 98:16

(For operating microscope, use 69990)

(55401 has been deleted. To report, use 55400 with modifier '-50')

⊘=Modifier '-51' Exempt   ►◄=New or Revised Text   ✦=Add-on Code   CPT 2002

Suture

55450   Ligation (percutaneous) of vas deferens, unilateral or bilateral (separate procedure)

Spermatic Cord

Excision

55500   Excision of hydrocele of spermatic cord, unilateral (separate procedure)

55520   Excision of lesion of spermatic cord (separate procedure)
   CPT Assistant Sep 00:10

55530   Excision of varicocele or ligation of spermatic veins for varicocele; (separate procedure)

55535   abdominal approach

55540   with hernia repair

Laparoscopy

Surgical laparoscopy always includes diagnostic laparoscopy. To report a diagnostic laparoscopy (peritoneoscopy) (separate procedure), use 49320.

55550   Laparoscopy, surgical, with ligation of spermatic veins for varicocele
   CPT Assistant Nov 99:27; Mar 00:5; *CPT Changes* 2000

55559   Unlisted laparoscopy procedure, spermatic cord
   CPT Assistant Nov 99:27; Mar 00:5; *CPT Changes* 2000

Seminal Vesicles

Incision

55600   Vesiculotomy;

   (55601 has been deleted. To report, use 55600 with modifier '-50')

55605   complicated

Excision

55650   Vesiculectomy, any approach

   (55651 has been deleted. To report, use 55650 with modifier '-50')

55680   Excision of Mullerian duct cyst

   (For injection procedure, see 52010, 55300)

Prostate

Incision

55700   Biopsy, prostate; needle or punch, single or multiple, any approach
   CPT Assistant May 96:3

   ►(If imaging guidance is performed, use 76942)◄

   ►(For fine needle aspiration, see 10021, 10022)◄

   ►(For evaluation of fine needle aspirate, see 88172, 88173)◄

55705   incisional, any approach

55720   Prostatotomy, external drainage of prostatic abscess, any approach; simple

55725   complicated

   (For transurethral drainage, use 52700)

   (55740 has been deleted. To report, use 55899)

Excision

   (For transurethral removal of prostate, see 52601-52640)

   (For transurethral destruction of prostate, see 53850-53852)

   (For limited pelvic lymphadenectomy for staging (separate procedure), use 38562)

   (For independent node dissection, see 38770-38780)

55801   Prostatectomy, perineal, subtotal (including control of postoperative bleeding, vasectomy, meatotomy, urethral calibration and/or dilation, and internal urethrotomy)

55810   Prostatectomy, perineal radical;

55812   with lymph node biopsy(s) (limited pelvic lymphadenectomy)

55815   with bilateral pelvic lymphadenectomy, including external iliac, hypogastric and obturator nodes

   (If 55815 is carried out on separate days, use 38770 with modifier '-50' and 55810)

55821   Prostatectomy (including control of postoperative bleeding, vasectomy, meatotomy, urethral calibration and/or dilation, and internal urethrotomy); suprapubic, subtotal, one or two stages

55831   retropubic, subtotal

55840   Prostatectomy, retropubic radical, with or without nerve sparing;

55842   with lymph node biopsy(s) (limited pelvic lymphadenectomy)

55845   with bilateral pelvic lymphadenectomy, including external iliac, hypogastric, and obturator nodes

   (If 55845 is carried out on separate days, use 38770 with modifier '-50' and 55840)

55859 Transperineal placement of needles or catheters into prostate for interstitial radioelement application, with or without cystoscopy

(For interstitial radioelement application, see 77776-77778)

(For ultrasonic guidance for interstitial radioelement application, use 76965)

55860 Exposure of prostate, any approach, for insertion of radioactive substance;

(For application of interstitial radioelement, see 77776-77778)

55862 with lymph node biopsy(s) (limited pelvic lymphadenectomy)

55865 with bilateral pelvic lymphadenectomy, including external iliac, hypogastric and obturator nodes

Other Procedures

(For artificial insemination, see 58321, 58322)

55870 Electroejaculation

55873 Cryosurgical ablation of the prostate (includes ultrasonic guidance for interstitial cryosurgical probe placement)
➲ *CPT Changes* 2001

55899 Unlisted procedure, male genital system

Intersex Surgery

55970 Intersex surgery; male to female

55980 female to male

(56300 has been deleted. To report, use 49320)

(56301 has been deleted. To report, use 58670)

(56302 has been deleted. To report, use 58671)

(56303 has been deleted. To report, use 58662)

(56304 has been deleted. To report, use 58660)

(56305 has been deleted. To report, use 49321)

(56306 has been deleted. To report, use 49322)

(56307 has been deleted. To report, use 58661)

(56308 has been deleted. To report, use 58550)

(56309 has been deleted. To report, use 58551)

(56310 has been deleted. To report, use 44200)

(56311 has been deleted. To report, use 38570)

(56312 has been deleted. To report, use 38571)

(56313 has been deleted. To report, use 38572)

(56314 has been deleted. To report, use 49323)

(56315 has been deleted. To report, use 44970)

(56316 has been deleted. To report, use 49650)

(56317 has been deleted. To report, use 49651)

(56318 has been deleted. To report, use 54690)

(56320 has been deleted. To report, use 55550)

(56321 has been deleted. To report, use 60650)

(56322 has been deleted. To report, use 43651)

(56323 has been deleted. To report, use 43652)

(56324 has been deleted. To report, use 47570)

(56340 has been deleted. To report, use 47562)

(56341 has been deleted. To report, use 47563)

(56342 has been deleted. To report, use 47564)

(56343 has been deleted. To report, use 58673)

(56344 has been deleted. To report, use 58672)

(56345 has been deleted. To report, use 38120)

(56346 has been deleted. To report, use 43653)

(56347 has been deleted. To report, use 44201)

(56348 has been deleted. To report, use 44202)

(56349 has been deleted. To report, use 43280)

(56350 has been deleted. To report, use 58555)

(56351 has been deleted. To report, use 58558)

(56352 has been deleted. To report, use 58559)

(56353 has been deleted. To report, use 58560)

(56354 has been deleted. To report, use 58561)

(56355 has been deleted. To report, use 58562)

(56356 has been deleted. To report, use 58563)

(56360 has been deleted. To report, use 49320)

(56361 has been deleted. To report, use 49321)

(56362 has been deleted. To report, use 47560)

(56363 has been deleted. To report, use 47561)

(56399 has been deleted. To report, see site-specific unlisted laparoscopy/hysteroscopy procedure codes)

Female Genital System

(For pelvic laparotomy, use 49000)

(For excision or destruction of endometriomas, open method, see 49200, 49201)

(For paracentesis, see 49080, 49081)

(For secondary closure of abdominal wall evisceration or disruption, use 49900)

(For fulguration or excision of lesions, laparoscopic approach, use 58662)

(For chemotherapy, see 96400-96549)

(56000 has been deleted. To report, use 56405)

(56100 has been deleted. To report, use 56605)

(56200 has been deleted. To report, use 56810)

Vulva, Perineum and Introitus

Definitions

The following definitions apply to the vulvectomy codes (56620-56640).

A *simple* procedure is the removal of skin and superficial subcutaneous tissues.

A *radical* procedure is the removal of skin and deep subcutaneous tissue.

A *partial* procedure is the removal of less than 80% of the vulvar area.

A *complete* procedure is the removal of greater than 80% of the vulvar area.

Incision

(For incision and drainage of sebaceous cyst, furuncle, or abscess, see 10040, 10060, 10061)

(56400 has been deleted. To report, use 56405)

56405* Incision and drainage of vulva or perineal abscess

56420* Incision and drainage of Bartholin's gland abscess

(For incision and drainage of Skene's gland abscess or cyst, use 53060)

56440 Marsupialization of Bartholin's gland cyst

56441 Lysis of labial adhesions

Destruction

(56500 has been deleted. To report, use 56501)

▲ **56501** Destruction of lesion(s), vulva; simple (eg, laser surgery, electrosurgery, cryosurgery, chemosurgery)
> *CPT Changes* 2002

(56505-56507, 56510 have been deleted. To report, use 56501)

▲ **56515** extensive (eg, laser surgery, electrosurgery, cryosurgery, chemosurgery)
> *CPT Changes* 2002

(56520, 56521 have been deleted. To report, use 56501 or 56515)

(For destruction of Skene's gland cyst or abscess, use 53270)

(For cautery destruction of urethral caruncle, use 53265)

Excision

(56600 has been deleted. To report, use 56605)

56605* Biopsy of vulva or perineum (separate procedure); one lesion
> *CPT Assistant* Sep 00:9

+ **56606*** each separate additional lesion (List separately in addition to code for primary procedure)

(Use 56606 in conjunction with code 56605)

(For excision of local lesion, see 11420-11426, 11620-11626)

56620 Vulvectomy simple; partial

56625 complete

(For skin graft, see 15000 et seq)

56630 Vulvectomy, radical, partial;

(For skin graft, if used, see 15000, 15120, 15121, 15240, 15241)

56631 with unilateral inguinofemoral lymphadenectomy

56632 with bilateral inguinofemoral lymphadenectomy

56633 Vulvectomy, radical, complete;

56634 with unilateral inguinofemoral lymphadenectomy

(56635 has been deleted. To report, see 56634, 56637)

(56636 has been deleted. To report, see 56634, 56637)

56637 with bilateral inguinofemoral lymphadenectomy

56640 Vulvectomy, radical, complete, with inguinofemoral, iliac, and pelvic lymphadenectomy

(56641 has been deleted. To report, use 56640 with modifier '-50')

(For lymphadenectomy, see 38760-38780)

(56680, 56685 have been deleted)

56700 Partial hymenectomy or revision of hymenal ring

(56710 has been deleted. To report, use 56700)

56720* Hymenotomy, simple incision

56740 Excision of Bartholin's gland or cyst

(For excision of Skene's gland, use 53270)

(For excision of urethral caruncle, use 53265)

(For excision or fulguration of urethral carcinoma, use 53220)

(For excision or marsupialization of urethral diverticulum, see 53230, 53240)

Repair

(For repair of urethra for mucosal prolapse, use 53275)

56800 Plastic repair of introitus

56805 Clitoroplasty for intersex state

56810 Perineoplasty, repair of perineum, nonobstetrical (separate procedure)

(See also 56800)

(For repair of wounds to genitalia, see 12001-12007, 12041-12047, 13131-13133)

(For repair of recent injury of vagina and perineum, nonobstetrical, use 57210)

(For anal sphincteroplasty, see 46750, 46751)

(For episiorrhaphy, episioperineorrhaphy for recent injury of vulva and/or perineum, nonobstetrical, use 57210)

Vagina

Incision

57000 Colpotomy; with exploration

57010   with drainage of pelvic abscess

57020* Colpocentesis (separate procedure)

▲**57022** Incision and drainage of vaginal hematoma; obstetrical/postpartum
> *CPT Changes* 2001; 2002

57023   non-obstetrical (eg, post-trauma, spontaneous bleeding)
> *CPT Changes* 2001

Destruction

(57050, 57057, 57060 have been deleted. To report, use 57061 or 57065)

▲**57061** Destruction of vaginal lesion(s); simple (eg, laser surgery, electrosurgery, cryosurgery, chemosurgery)
> *CPT Assistant* Apr 96:11; *CPT Changes* 2002

(57063 has been deleted. To report, use 57061 or 57065)

▲**57065**   extensive (eg, laser surgery, electrosurgery, cryosurgery, chemosurgery)
> *CPT Assistant* Apr 96:11; *CPT Changes* 2002

Excision

57100* Biopsy of vaginal mucosa; simple (separate procedure)

57105   extensive, requiring suture (including cysts)

57106 Vaginectomy, partial removal of vaginal wall;
> *CPT Assistant* Nov 98:17; Oct 99:4

Vaginectomy, Partial Removal of Vaginal Wall
57106

A specific portion of the upper or lower vaginal wall is excised.

57107   with removal of paravaginal tissue (radical vaginectomy)
> *CPT Assistant* Nov 98:17; Oct 99:4

(57108 has been deleted. To report, use 57106)

57109   with removal of paravaginal tissue (radical vaginectomy) with bilateral total pelvic lymphadenectomy and para-aortic lymph node sampling (biopsy)
> *CPT Assistant* Nov 98:17; Oct 99:4

57110 Vaginectomy, complete removal of vaginal wall;
> *CPT Assistant* Nov 98:17; Oct 99:4

57111   with removal of paravaginal tissue (radical vaginectomy)
> *CPT Assistant* Nov 98:17; Oct 99:4

Vaginectomy, Complete Removal of Vaginal Wall (Radical Vaginectomy)
57111

Removal of all of the vaginal wall and removal of paravaginal tissue (the highly vascular supporting connective tissue next to the vagina).

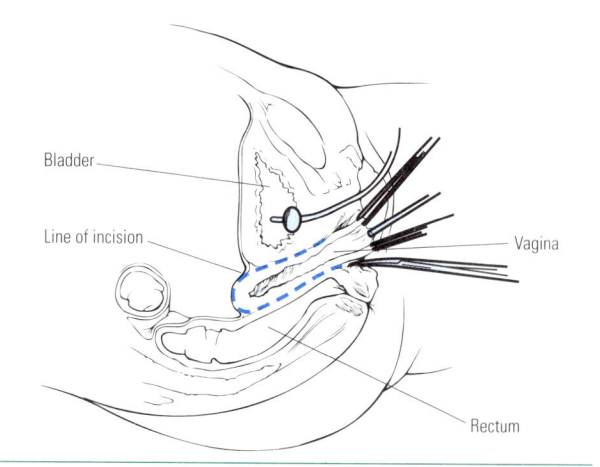

⊘ =Modifier '-51' Exempt   ▶ ◀=New or Revised Text   ✦=Add-on Code   CPT 2002

57112	with removal of paravaginal tissue (radical vaginectomy) with bilateral total pelvic lymphadenectomy and para-aortic lymph node sampling (biopsy)

➔ *CPT Assistant* Nov 98:17; Oct 99:4

57120 Colpocleisis (Le Fort type)

57130 Excision of vaginal septum

57135 Excision of vaginal cyst or tumor

Introduction

57150* Irrigation of vagina and/or application of medicament for treatment of bacterial, parasitic, or fungoid disease

● **57155** Insertion of uterine tandems and/or vaginal ovoids for clinical brachytherapy

➔ *CPT Changes* 2002

▶(For insertion of radioelement sources or ribbons, see 77761-77763, 77781-77784)◄

57160* Fitting and insertion of pessary or other intravaginal support device

➔ *CPT Assistant* Oct 98:11; Jun 00:11

57170 Diaphragm or cervical cap fitting with instructions

57180 Introduction of any hemostatic agent or pack for spontaneous or traumatic nonobstetrical vaginal hemorrhage (separate procedure)

Repair

(For urethral suspension, Marshall-Marchetti-Krantz type, abdominal approach, see 51840, 51841)

(For laparoscopic suspension, use 51990)

57200 Colporrhaphy, suture of injury of vagina (nonobstetrical)

57210 Colpoperineorrhaphy, suture of injury of vagina and/or perineum (nonobstetrical)

57220 Plastic operation on urethral sphincter, vaginal approach (eg, Kelly urethral plication)

57230 Plastic repair of urethrocele

57240 Anterior colporrhaphy, repair of cystocele with or without repair of urethrocele

➔ *CPT Assistant* Jan 97:3

57250 Posterior colporrhaphy, repair of rectocele with or without perineorrhaphy

(For repair of rectocele (separate procedure) without posterior colporrhaphy, use 45560)

57260 Combined anteroposterior colporrhaphy;

57265 with enterocele repair

57268 Repair of enterocele, vaginal approach (separate procedure)

57270 Repair of enterocele, abdominal approach (separate procedure)

57280 Colpopexy, abdominal approach

➔ *CPT Assistant* Jan 97:1

57282 Sacrospinous ligament fixation for prolapse of vagina

➔ *CPT Assistant* Jan 97:1

57284 Paravaginal defect repair (including repair of cystocele, stress urinary incontinence, and/or incomplete vaginal prolapse)

➔ *CPT Assistant* Jan 97:1

57287 Removal or revision of sling for stress incontinence (eg, fascia or synthetic)

➔ *CPT Changes* 2001

57288 Sling operation for stress incontinence (eg, fascia or synthetic)

➔ *CPT Assistant* Nov 99:28; May 00:4; Oct 00:7; *CPT Changes* 2000

(For laparoscopic approach, use 51992)

57289 Pereyra procedure, including anterior colporrhaphy

➔ *CPT Assistant* Jan 97:3

(57290 has been deleted. To report, use 57291 or 57292)

57291 Construction of artificial vagina; without graft

57292 with graft

57300 Closure of rectovaginal fistula; vaginal or transanal approach

➔ *CPT Assistant* Nov 97:21

57305 abdominal approach

➔ *CPT Assistant* Nov 97:21

57307 abdominal approach, with concomitant colostomy

➔ *CPT Assistant* Nov 97:21

57308 transperineal approach, with perineal body reconstruction, with or without levator plication

➔ *CPT Assistant* Nov 97:21

57310 Closure of urethrovaginal fistula;

57311 with bulbocavernosus transplant

57320 Closure of vesicovaginal fistula; vaginal approach

(For concomitant cystostomy, see 51005-51040)

57330 transvesical and vaginal approach

(For abdominal approach, use 51900)

57335 Vaginoplasty for intersex state

Manipulation

57400* Dilation of vagina under anesthesia

57410* Pelvic examination under anesthesia

➔ *CPT Assistant* Spring 93:34

57415 Removal of impacted vaginal foreign body (separate procedure) under anesthesia

(For removal without anesthesia of an impacted vaginal foreign body, use the appropriate E/M code)

Endoscopy

(57450, 57451 have been deleted)

57452 * Colposcopy (vaginoscopy); (separate procedure)
➔ *CPT Assistant* Apr 00:5

57454 * with biopsy(s) of the cervix and/or endocervical curettage
➔ *CPT Assistant* Apr 00:5

57460 with loop electrode excision procedure of the cervix
➔ *CPT Assistant* Apr 00:5

Cervix Uteri

Excision

(For radical surgical procedures, see 58200-58240)

57500 * Biopsy, single or multiple, or local excision of lesion, with or without fulguration (separate procedure)

57505 Endocervical curettage (not done as part of a dilation and curettage)

▲**57510** Cautery of cervix; electro or thermal
➔ *CPT Changes* 2002

57511 * cryocautery, initial or repeat

57513 laser ablation

57520 Conization of cervix, with or without fulguration, with or without dilation and curettage, with or without repair; cold knife or laser
➔ *CPT Assistant* Apr 00:5

(See also 58120)

57522 loop electrode excision
➔ *CPT Assistant* Apr 00:5

57530 Trachelectomy (cervicectomy), amputation of cervix (separate procedure)

57531 Radical trachelectomy, with bilateral total pelvic lymphadenectomy and para-aortic lymph node sampling biopsy, with or without removal of tube(s), with or without removal of ovary(s)
➔ *CPT Assistant* Nov 97:21

(For radical abdominal hysterectomy, use 58210)

57540 Excision of cervical stump, abdominal approach;

57545 with pelvic floor repair

57550 Excision of cervical stump, vaginal approach;

57555 with anterior and/or posterior repair

57556 with repair of enterocele

(For insertion of intrauterine device, use 58300)

(57600-57620 have been deleted. For insertion of any hemostatic agent or pack for control of spontaneous non-obstetrical hemorrhage, use 57180)

Repair

57700 Cerclage of uterine cervix, nonobstetrical

57720 Trachelorrhaphy, plastic repair of uterine cervix, vaginal approach

Manipulation

57800 * Dilation of cervical canal, instrumental (separate procedure)

57820 Dilation and curettage of cervical stump

Corpus Uteri

Excision

58100 * Endometrial sampling (biopsy) with or without endocervical sampling (biopsy), without cervical dilation, any method (separate procedure)

(For endocervical curettage only, use 57505)

(58101, 58102, 58103 have been deleted)

58120 Dilation and curettage, diagnostic and/or therapeutic (nonobstetrical)
➔ *CPT Assistant* Fall 95:16; Nov 97:21

(For postpartum hemorrhage, use 59160)

▲**58140** Myomectomy, excision of leiomyomata of uterus, single or multiple (separate procedure); abdominal approach
➔ *CPT Changes* 2002

58145 vaginal approach

58150 Total abdominal hysterectomy (corpus and cervix), with or without removal of tube(s), with or without removal of ovary(s);
➔ *CPT Assistant* Dec 96:10; Apr 97:3; Nov 97:21; Sep 00:9

58152 with colpo-urethrocystopexy (eg, Marshall-Marchetti-Krantz, Burch)
➔ *CPT Assistant* Jan 97:1; Nov 97:22

(For urethrocystopexy without hysterectomy, see 51840, 51841)

58180 Supracervical abdominal hysterectomy (subtotal hysterectomy), with or without removal of tube(s), with or without removal of ovary(s)

58200 Total abdominal hysterectomy, including partial vaginectomy, with para-aortic and pelvic lymph node sampling, with or without removal of tube(s), with or without removal of ovary(s)

(58205 has been deleted. For hysterectomy with pelvic lymphadenectomy, use 58210)

58210 Radical abdominal hysterectomy, with bilateral total pelvic lymphadenectomy and para-aortic lymph node sampling (biopsy), with or without removal of tube(s), with or without removal of ovary(s)

(For radical hysterectomy with ovarian transposition, use also 58825)

⊘ =Modifier '-51' Exempt   ▶ ◀=New or Revised Text   ✚ =Add-on Code   CPT 2002

58240 Pelvic exenteration for gynecologic malignancy, with total abdominal hysterectomy or cervicectomy, with or without removal of tube(s), with or without removal of ovary(s), with removal of bladder and ureteral transplantations, and/or abdominoperineal resection of rectum and colon and colostomy, or any combination thereof

(For pelvic exenteration for lower urinary tract or male genital malignancy, use 51597)

58260 Vaginal hysterectomy;

58262 with removal of tube(s), and/or ovary(s)

58263 with removal of tube(s), and/or ovary(s), with repair of enterocele

(58265 has been deleted. To report, see 57240, 57250, 57260, 57265)

58267 with colpo-urethrocystopexy (Marshall-Marchetti-Krantz type, Pereyra type, with or without endoscopic control)

58270 with repair of enterocele

(For repair of enterocele with removal of tubes and/or ovaries, use 58263)

▲**58275** Vaginal hysterectomy, with total or partial vaginectomy;
> *CPT Changes* 2002

58280 with repair of enterocele

58285 Vaginal hysterectomy, radical (Schauta type operation)

Introduction

(For insertion/removal of implantable contraceptive capsules, see 11975, 11976, 11977)

58300* Insertion of intrauterine device (IUD)
> *CPT Assistant* Apr 98:14

58301 Removal of intrauterine device (IUD)
> *CPT Assistant* Apr 98:14

(58310 has been deleted. To report, see 58321, 58322)

(58311 has been deleted. To report, use 58323)

(58320 has been deleted)

58321 Artificial insemination; intra-cervical

58322 intra-uterine

58323 Sperm washing for artificial insemination
> *CPT Assistant* Jan 98:6

58340* Catheterization and introduction of saline or contrast material for hysterosonography or hysterosalpingography
> *CPT Assistant* Nov 97:22; Jul 99:8

(For radiological supervision and interpretation of hysterosonography, use 76831)

(For radiological supervision and interpretation of hysterosalpingography, use 74740)

▶(For endometrial cryoablation with ultrasonic guidance, use Category III code 0009T)◄

58345 Transcervical introduction of fallopian tube catheter for diagnosis and/or re-establishing patency (any method), with or without hysterosalpingography
> *CPT Assistant* Nov 97:22

(For radiological supervision and interpretation, use 74742)

●**58346** Insertion of Heyman capsules for clinical brachytherapy
> *CPT Changes* 2002

▶(For insertion of radioelement sources or ribbons, see 77761-77763, 77781-77784)◄

58350* Chromotubation of oviduct, including materials

(For materials supplied by physician, use 99070)

58353 Endometrial ablation, thermal, without hysteroscopic guidance
> *CPT Changes* 2001

(For hysteroscopic procedure, use 58563)

Repair

58400 Uterine suspension, with or without shortening of round ligaments, with or without shortening of sacrouterine ligaments; (separate procedure)

58410 with presacral sympathectomy

(58430 has been deleted. To report, use 58999)

(58500 has been deleted. To report, use 58752)

58520 Hysterorrhaphy, repair of ruptured uterus (nonobstetrical)

58540 Hysteroplasty, repair of uterine anomaly (Strassman type)

(For closure of vesicouterine fistula, use 51920)

Laparoscopy/Hysteroscopy

Surgical laparoscopy always includes diagnostic laparoscopy. To report a diagnostic laparoscopy (peritoneoscopy) (separate procedure), use 49320. To report a diagnostic hysteroscopy (separate procedure), use 58555.

58550 Laparoscopy, surgical; with vaginal hysterectomy with or without removal of tube(s), with or without removal of ovary(s) (laparoscopic assisted vaginal hysterectomy)
> *CPT Assistant* Nov 99:28; Mar 00:5; *CPT Changes* 2000

58551 with removal of leiomyomata (single or multiple)
> *CPT Assistant* Nov 99:28; Mar 00:5; *CPT Changes* 2000

58555 Hysteroscopy, diagnostic (separate procedure)
> *CPT Assistant* Nov 99:28; Mar 00:5; *CPT Changes* 2000

58558 Hysteroscopy, surgical; with sampling (biopsy) of endometrium and/or polypectomy, with or without D & C
> *CPT Assistant* Nov 99:28; Mar 00:5; *CPT Changes* 2000

58559 with lysis of intrauterine adhesions (any method)
> *CPT Assistant* Nov 99:28; Mar 00:5; *CPT Changes* 2000

58560 with division or resection of intrauterine septum (any method)

> *CPT Assistant* Nov 99:28; Mar 00:5; *CPT Changes* 2000

58561 with removal of leiomyomata

> *CPT Assistant* Nov 99:28; Mar 00:5; *CPT Changes* 2000

58562 with removal of impacted foreign body

> *CPT Assistant* Nov 99:28; Mar 00:5; *CPT Changes* 2000

▲ **58563** with endometrial ablation (eg, endometrial resection, electrosurgical ablation, thermoablation)

> *CPT Assistant* Nov 99:28; Mar 00:5; *CPT Changes* 2000; 2002

58578 Unlisted laparoscopy procedure, uterus

> *CPT Assistant* Nov 99:28; Mar 00:5; *CPT Changes* 2000

58579 Unlisted hysteroscopy procedure, uterus

> *CPT Assistant* Nov 99:28; Mar 00:5; *CPT Changes* 2000

Oviduct/Ovary

Incision

58600 Ligation or transection of fallopian tube(s), abdominal or vaginal approach, unilateral or bilateral

> *CPT Assistant* Nov 99:28; *CPT Changes* 2000

58605 Ligation or transection of fallopian tube(s), abdominal or vaginal approach, postpartum, unilateral or bilateral, during same hospitalization (separate procedure)

> *CPT Assistant* Nov 99:28; *CPT Changes* 2000

(For laparoscopic procedures, use 58670, 58671)

(58610 has been deleted. To report, see 58600-58611)

+ ▲ **58611** Ligation or transection of fallopian tube(s) when done at the time of cesarean delivery or intra-abdominal surgery (not a separate procedure) (List separately in addition to code for primary procedure)

> *CPT Changes* 2002

58615 Occlusion of fallopian tube(s) by device (eg, band, clip, Falope ring) vaginal or suprapubic approach

> *CPT Assistant* Nov 99:28; *CPT Changes* 2000

(For laparoscopic approach, use 58671)

(58618 has been deleted. To report, use 58740)

Laparoscopy

Surgical laparoscopy always includes diagnostic laparoscopy. To report a diagnostic laparoscopy (peritoneoscopy) (separate procedure), use 49320.

(For laparoscopic biopsy of the ovary or fallopian tube, use 49321)

58660 Laparoscopy, surgical; with lysis of adhesions (salpingolysis, ovariolysis) (separate procedure)

> *CPT Assistant* Nov 99:28; Mar 00:5; *CPT Changes* 2000

58661 with removal of adnexal structures (partial or total oophorectomy and/or salpingectomy)

> *CPT Assistant* Nov 99:28; Mar 00:5; *CPT Changes* 2000

58662 with fulguration or excision of lesions of the ovary, pelvic viscera, or peritoneal surface by any method

> *CPT Assistant* Nov 99:28; Mar 00:5; *CPT Changes* 2000

58670 with fulguration of oviducts (with or without transection)

> *CPT Assistant* Nov 99:29; Mar 00:5; *CPT Changes* 2000

58671 with occlusion of oviducts by device (eg, band, clip, or Falope ring)

> *CPT Assistant* Nov 99:29; Mar 00:5; *CPT Changes* 2000

58672 with fimbrioplasty

> *CPT Assistant* Nov 99:29; Mar 00:5; *CPT Changes* 2000

58673 with salpingostomy (salpingoneostomy)

> *CPT Assistant* Nov 99:29; Mar 00:5; *CPT Changes* 2000

(Codes 58672 and 58673 are used to report unilateral procedures. For bilateral procedure, use modifier '-50')

58679 Unlisted laparoscopy procedure, oviduct, ovary

> *CPT Assistant* Nov 99:29; Mar 00:5; *CPT Changes* 2000

Excision

58700 Salpingectomy, complete or partial, unilateral or bilateral (separate procedure)

58720 Salpingo-oophorectomy, complete or partial, unilateral or bilateral (separate procedure)

> *CPT Assistant* Sep 00:9

Repair

58740 Lysis of adhesions (salpingolysis, ovariolysis)

> *CPT Assistant* Sep 96:9; Nov 99:29; *CPT Changes* 2000

(For laparoscopic approach, use 58660)

(For excision or destruction of endometriomas, open method, see 49200, 49201)

(For fulguration or excision of lesions, laparoscopic approach, use 58662)

58750 Tubotubal anastomosis

58752 Tubouterine implantation

58760 Fimbrioplasty

> *CPT Assistant* Nov 99:29; *CPT Changes* 2000

(For laparoscopic approach, use 58672)

58770 Salpingostomy (salpingoneostomy)

> *CPT Assistant* Nov 99:29; *CPT Changes* 2000

(For laparoscopic approach, use 58673)

Ovary

Incision

58800 Drainage of ovarian cyst(s), unilateral or bilateral, (separate procedure); vaginal approach

58805 abdominal approach

⊘ =Modifier '-51' Exempt   ▶ ◀=New or Revised Text   ✚ =Add-on Code   CPT 2002

58820   Drainage of ovarian abscess; vaginal approach, open
　➔ *CPT Assistant* Nov 97:22

58822   abdominal approach
　➔ *CPT Assistant* Nov 97:22

58823   Drainage of pelvic abscess, transvaginal or transrectal approach, percutaneous (eg, ovarian, pericolic)
　➔ *CPT Assistant* Nov 97:22; Mar 98:8

　(For radiological supervision and interpretation, use 75989)

58825   Transposition, ovary(s)

Excision

58900   Biopsy of ovary, unilateral or bilateral (separate procedure)
　➔ *CPT Assistant* Nov 99:29; *CPT Changes* 2000

　(For laparoscopic biopsy of the ovary or fallopian tube, use 49321)

58920   Wedge resection or bisection of ovary, unilateral or bilateral

58925   Ovarian cystectomy, unilateral or bilateral

58940   Oophorectomy, partial or total, unilateral or bilateral;

　(58942 has been deleted. To report, use 58952)

58943   for ovarian, tubal or primary peritoneal malignancy, with para-aortic and pelvic lymph node biopsies, peritoneal washings, peritoneal biopsies, diaphragmatic assessments, with or without salpingectomy(s), with or without omentectomy
　➔ *CPT Changes* 2001

　(58945 has been deleted. To report, use 58950)

58950   Resection of ovarian, tubal or primary peritoneal malignancy with bilateral salpingo-oophorectomy and omentectomy;
　➔ *CPT Changes* 2001

58951   with total abdominal hysterectomy, pelvic and limited para-aortic lymphadenectomy

58952   with radical dissection for debulking (ie, radical excision or destruction, intra-abdominal or retroperitoneal tumors)
　➔ *CPT Assistant* Dec 96:10; *CPT Changes* 2001

● **58953**   Bilateral salpingo-oophorectomy with omentectomy, total abdominal hysterectomy and radical dissection for debulking;
　➔ *CPT Changes* 2002

● **58954**   with pelvic lymphadenectomy and limited para-aortic lymphadenectomy
　➔ *CPT Changes* 2002

58960   Laparotomy, for staging or restaging of ovarian, tubal or primary peritoneal malignancy (second look), with or without omentectomy, peritoneal washing, biopsy of abdominal and pelvic peritoneum, diaphragmatic assessment with pelvic and limited para-aortic lymphadenectomy
　➔ *CPT Changes* 2001

In Vitro Fertilization

58970   Follicle puncture for oocyte retrieval, any method

　(For radiological supervision and interpretation, use 76948)

　(58972 has been deleted. To report, use 89250)

58974   Embryo transfer, intrauterine

58976   Gamete, zygote, or embryo intrafallopian transfer, any method
　➔ *CPT Assistant* Nov 99:29; *CPT Changes* 2000

　(58980 has been deleted. To report, use 49320)

　(58982 has been deleted. To report, use 58670)

　(58983 has been deleted. To report, use 58671)

　(58984 has been deleted. To report, use 58662)

　(58985 has been deleted. To report, use 58660)

　(58986 has been deleted. To report, use 49321)

　(58987 has been deleted. To report, use 49322)

　(58988 has been deleted. To report, use 58661)

　(58990 has been deleted. To report, use 58555)

　(58992 has been deleted. To report, see 58559, 58560)

　(58994 has been deleted. To report, use 58561)

　(58995 has been deleted. To report, see 58559, 58561, 58563)

　(58996 has been deleted. To report, use 58563)

Other Procedures

58999   Unlisted procedure, female genital system (nonobstetrical)

Maternity Care and Delivery

The services normally provided in uncomplicated maternity cases include antepartum care, delivery, and postpartum care.

Antepartum care includes the initial and subsequent history, physical examinations, recording of weight, blood pressures, fetal heart tones, routine chemical urinalysis, and monthly visits up to 28 weeks gestation, biweekly visits to 36 weeks gestation, and weekly visits until delivery. Any other visits or services within this time period should be coded separately.

Delivery services include admission to the hospital, the admission history and physical examination, management of uncomplicated labor, vaginal delivery (with or without episiotomy, with or without forceps), or cesarean delivery. Medical problems complicating labor and delivery management may require additional resources and should be identified by utilizing the codes in the **Medicine** and **Evaluation and Management Services** section in addition to codes for maternity care.

Postpartum care includes hospital and office visits following vaginal or cesarean section delivery.

For medical complications of pregnancy (eg, cardiac problems, neurological problems, diabetes, hypertension, toxemia, hyperemesis, pre-term labor, premature rupture of membranes), see services in the **Medicine** and **Evaluation and Management Services** section.

For surgical complications of pregnancy (eg, appendectomy, hernia, ovarian cyst, Bartholin cyst), see services in the **Surgery** section.

If a physician provides all or part of the antepartum and/or postpartum patient care but does not perform delivery due to termination of pregnancy by abortion or referral to another physician for delivery, see the antepartum and postpartum care codes 59425-59426 and 59430.

(For circumcision of newborn, see 54150, 54160)

Antepartum Services

▶(For insertion of transcervical or transvaginal fetal oximetry sensor, use Category III code 0021T)◀

▲**59000** * Amniocentesis; diagnostic
→ *CPT Assistant* Apr 97:2; *CPT Changes* 2002

(For radiological supervision and interpretation, use 76946)

●**59001**   therapeutic amniotic fluid reduction (includes ultrasound guidance)
→ *CPT Changes* 2002

(59010, 59011 have been deleted)

59012 Cordocentesis (intrauterine), any method

(For radiological supervision and interpretation, use 76941)

59015 Chorionic villus sampling, any method
→ *CPT Assistant* Apr 97:2

(For radiological supervision and interpretation, use 76945)

59020 * Fetal contraction stress test
→ *CPT Assistant* Apr 97:2

59025 Fetal non-stress test
→ *CPT Assistant* May 98:10

59030 * Fetal scalp blood sampling

(59031 has been deleted. To report, use 59030 and see modifiers '-76' and '-77')

59050 Fetal monitoring during labor by consulting physician (ie, non-attending physician) with written report; supervision and interpretation
→ *CPT Assistant* Nov 97:22

59051   interpretation only
→ *CPT Assistant* Nov 97:22

Excision

59100 Hysterotomy, abdominal (eg, for hydatidiform mole, abortion)

(When tubal ligation is performed at the same time as hysterotomy, use 58611 in addition to 59100)

(59101, 59105, 59106 have been deleted. To report, see 59100, 58611)

59120 Surgical treatment of ectopic pregnancy; tubal or ovarian, requiring salpingectomy and/or oophorectomy, abdominal or vaginal approach

59121   tubal or ovarian, without salpingectomy and/or oophorectomy

(59125, 59126 have been deleted. To report, see 59120, 59121)

59130   abdominal pregnancy

59135   interstitial, uterine pregnancy requiring total hysterectomy

59136   interstitial, uterine pregnancy with partial resection of uterus

59140   cervical, with evacuation

59150 Laparoscopic treatment of ectopic pregnancy; without salpingectomy and/or oophorectomy
→ *CPT Assistant* Sep 96:9

Laparoscopic Treatment of Ectopic Pregnancy
59150

The site of gestation is located with a laparoscope and a small incision is made above the site. The ectopic pregnancy is then removed.

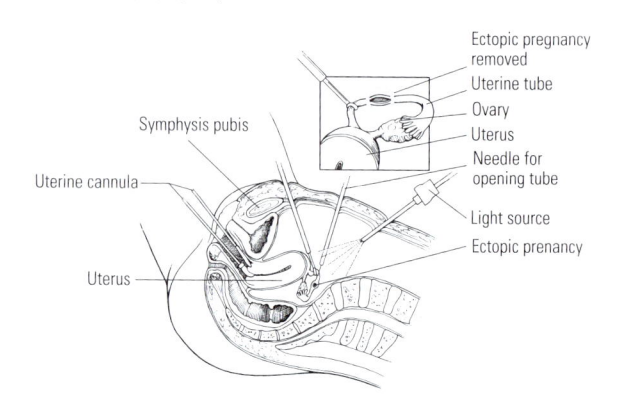

Ectopic pregnancy removed
Uterine tube
Ovary
Uterus
Needle for opening tube
Light source
Ectopic prenancy
Symphysis pubis
Uterine cannula
Uterus

⊘ =Modifier '-51' Exempt   ▶ ◀=New or Revised Text   ✛ =Add-on Code   CPT 2002

59151   with salpingectomy and/or oophorectomy

59160   Curettage, postpartum
➔ *CPT Assistant* Nov 97:22

Introduction

(For intrauterine fetal transfusion, use 36460)

(For introduction of hypertonic solution and/or prostaglandins to initiate labor, see 59850-59857)

59200   Insertion of cervical dilator (eg, laminaria, prostaglandin) (separate procedure)
➔ *CPT Assistant* Fall 93:9; Apr 97:3

Repair

(For tracheloplasty, use 57700)

59300   Episiotomy or vaginal repair, by other than attending physician

(59305 has been deleted)

59320   Cerclage of cervix, during pregnancy; vaginal

59325   abdominal

59350   Hysterorrhaphy of ruptured uterus

(59351 has been deleted)

Vaginal Delivery, Antepartum and Postpartum Care

▶(For insertion of transcervical or transvaginal fetal oximetry sensor, use Category III code 0021T)◀

59400   Routine obstetric care including antepartum care, vaginal delivery (with or without episiotomy, and/or forceps) and postpartum care
➔ *CPT Assistant* Mar 96:11; Feb 97:11; Apr 97:3; Apr 98:15; Jun 98:10

59409   Vaginal delivery only (with or without episiotomy and/or forceps);
➔ *CPT Assistant* Mar 96:11; Jul 96:11; Sep 96:4; Feb 97:11; Apr 97:1

59410   including postpartum care

59412   External cephalic version, with or without tocolysis

(Use 59412 in addition to code(s) for delivery)

59414   Delivery of placenta (separate procedure)
➔ *CPT Assistant* Jun 96:10; Jun 98:10

(59420 has been deleted. To report, see 59425, 59426 or appropriate E/M code(s))

(For 1-3 antepartum care visits, see appropriate E/M code(s))

59425   Antepartum care only; 4-6 visits
➔ *CPT Assistant* Fall 94:21; Apr 97:11

59426   7 or more visits
➔ *CPT Assistant* Fall 94:21; Apr 97:11

59430   Postpartum care only (separate procedure)
➔ *CPT Assistant* Jun 96:10

Cesarean Delivery

(For standby attendance for infant, use 99360)

▶(For insertion of transcervical or transvaginal fetal oximetry sensor, use Category III code 0021T)◀

(59500, 59501 have been deleted. To report, see 59510, 59515, 59525)

59510   Routine obstetric care including antepartum care, cesarean delivery, and postpartum care
➔ *CPT Assistant* Jul 96:11; Sep 96:4; Oct 96:10; Feb 97:11; Apr 97:2

59514   Cesarean delivery only;
➔ *CPT Assistant* Oct 96:10; Feb 97:11

59515   including postpartum care

(59520, 59521 have been deleted. To report, see 59510, 59515, 59525)

+ 59525   Subtotal or total hysterectomy after cesarean delivery (List separately in addition to code for primary procedure)

(Use 59525 in conjunction with codes 59510, 59514, 59515, 59618, 59620, 59622)

(59540, 59541, 59560, 59561, 59580, 59581 have been deleted. To report, see 59510, 59515, 59525)

Delivery After Previous Cesarean Delivery

Patients who have had a previous cesarean delivery and now present with the expectation of a vaginal delivery are coded using codes 59610-59622. If the patient has a successful vaginal delivery after a previous cesarean delivery (VBAC), use codes 59610-59614. If the attempt is unsuccessful and another cesarean delivery is carried out, use codes 59618-59622. To report elective cesarean deliveries use code 59510, 59514 or 59515.

▶(For insertion of transcervical or transvaginal fetal oximetry sensor, use Category III code 0021T)◀

59610   Routine obstetric care including antepartum care, vaginal delivery (with or without episiotomy, and/or forceps) and postpartum care, after previous cesarean delivery
➔ *CPT Assistant* Feb 96:2; Apr 97:3

59612   Vaginal delivery only, after previous cesarean delivery (with or without episiotomy and/or forceps);
➔ *CPT Assistant* Feb 96:2

59614   including postpartum care
➔ *CPT Assistant* Feb 96:2

59618 Routine obstetric care including antepartum care, cesarean delivery, and postpartum care, following attempted vaginal delivery after previous cesarean delivery
➔ *CPT Assistant* Feb 96:2

59620 Cesarean delivery only, following attempted vaginal delivery after previous cesarean delivery;
➔ *CPT Assistant* Feb 96:2

59622 including postpartum care
➔ *CPT Assistant* Feb 96:2

Abortion

(For medical treatment of spontaneous complete abortion, any trimester, use E/M codes 99201-99233)

(59800, 59810 have been deleted. To report, see 99201-99233)

(59801, 59811 have been deleted. To report, use 59812)

59812 Treatment of incomplete abortion, any trimester, completed surgically
➔ *CPT Assistant* Fall 93:9; Fall 95:16

59820 Treatment of missed abortion, completed surgically; first trimester
➔ *CPT Assistant* Fall 93:9; Fall 95:16; Feb 99:10

59821 second trimester
➔ *CPT Assistant* Fall 93:9; Fall 95:16

59830 Treatment of septic abortion, completed surgically
➔ *CPT Assistant* Fall 93:9

59840 Induced abortion, by dilation and curettage
➔ *CPT Assistant* Fall 93:9

59841 Induced abortion, by dilation and evacuation
➔ *CPT Assistant* Fall 93:9

59850 Induced abortion, by one or more intra-amniotic injections (amniocentesis-injections), including hospital admission and visits, delivery of fetus and secundines;
➔ *CPT Assistant* Fall 93:10

59851 with dilation and curettage and/or evacuation
➔ *CPT Assistant* Fall 93:10

59852 with hysterotomy (failed intra-amniotic injection)
➔ *CPT Assistant* Fall 93:10

(For insertion of cervical dilator, use 59200)

59855 Induced abortion, by one or more vaginal suppositories (eg, prostaglandin) with or without cervical dilation (eg, laminaria), including hospital admission and visits, delivery of fetus and secundines;

59856 with dilation and curettage and/or evacuation

59857 with hysterotomy (failed medical evacuation)

Other Procedures

59866 Multifetal pregnancy reduction(s) (MPR)

59870 Uterine evacuation and curettage for hydatidiform mole
➔ *CPT Assistant* Feb 99:10

59871 Removal of cerclage suture under anesthesia (other than local)
➔ *CPT Assistant* Nov 97:22

59898 Unlisted laparoscopy procedure, maternity care and delivery
➔ *CPT Assistant* Nov 99:29; Mar 00:5; *CPT Changes* 2000

59899 Unlisted procedure, maternity care and delivery
➔ *CPT Assistant* Jun 97:10

Endocrine System

(For pituitary and pineal surgery, see **Nervous System**)

Thyroid Gland

Incision

▲**60000*** Incision and drainage of thyroglossal duct cyst, infected
➔ *CPT Changes* 2002

Excision

60001 Aspiration and/or injection, thyroid cyst

(For fine needle aspiration, see ▶10021, 10022◀)

▶(If imaging guidance is performed, see 76360, 76942)◀

60100* Biopsy thyroid, percutaneous core needle
➔ *CPT Assistant* Jun 97:5

▶(If imaging guidance is performed,◀ see ▶76003◀, 76360, ▶76393◀, 76942)

▶(For fine needle aspiration, use 10021 or 10022)◀

▶(For evaluation of fine needle aspirate, see 88172, 88173)◀

60200 Excision of cyst or adenoma of thyroid, or transection of isthmus

60210 Partial thyroid lobectomy, unilateral; with or without isthmusectomy

60212 with contralateral subtotal lobectomy, including isthmusectomy

60220   Total thyroid lobectomy, unilateral; with or without isthmusectomy

60225   with contralateral subtotal lobectomy, including isthmusectomy

Thyroid Lobectomy
60225

The thyroid is exposed via a transverse cervical incision. The superior and inferior thyroid vessels serving the lobe are ligated, the isthmus is severed, and the entire thyroid lobe is resected.

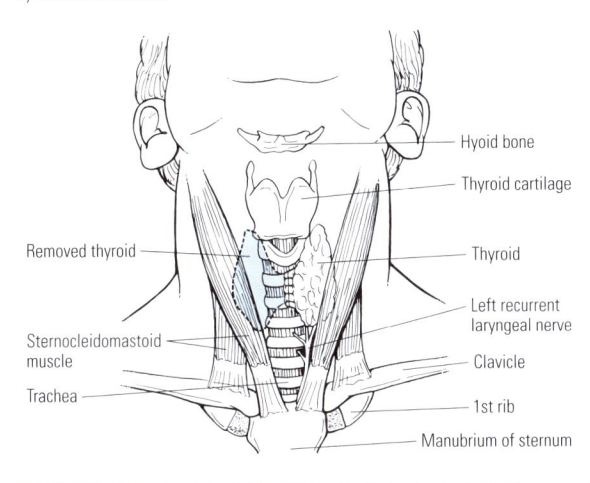

60240   Thyroidectomy, total or complete

(60242 has been deleted. To report, see 60210-60225)

(60245 has been deleted. To report, see 60210-60225)

(60246 has been deleted. To report, use 60271)

60252   Thyroidectomy, total or subtotal for malignancy; with limited neck dissection
➔ *CPT Assistant* Nov 00:10

60254   with radical neck dissection
➔ *CPT Assistant* Nov 00:10

60260   Thyroidectomy, removal of all remaining thyroid tissue following previous removal of a portion of thyroid

(60261 has been deleted. To report, use 60260 with modifier '-50')

▲**60270**   Thyroidectomy, including substernal thyroid; sternal split or transthoracic approach
➔ *CPT Changes* 2002

60271   cervical approach

60280   Excision of thyroglossal duct cyst or sinus;

60281   recurrent

(For thyroid ultrasonography, use 76536)

Parathyroid, Thymus, Adrenal Glands, and Carotid Body

Excision

(For pituitary and pineal surgery, see **Nervous System**)

60500   Parathyroidectomy or exploration of parathyroid(s);

60502   re-exploration

60505   with mediastinal exploration, sternal split or transthoracic approach

(60510 has been deleted)

+ **60512**   Parathyroid autotransplantation (List separately in addition to code for primary procedure)

(Use 60512 in conjunction with codes 60500, 60502, 60505, 60212, 60225, 60240, 60252, 60254, 60260, 60270, 60271)

60520   Thymectomy, partial or total; transcervical approach (separate procedure)

60521   sternal split or transthoracic approach, without radical mediastinal dissection (separate procedure)

60522   sternal split or transthoracic approach, with radical mediastinal dissection (separate procedure)

60540   Adrenalectomy, partial or complete, or exploration of adrenal gland with or without biopsy, transabdominal, lumbar or dorsal (separate procedure);
➔ *CPT Assistant* Nov 98:17

60545   with excision of adjacent retroperitoneal tumor
➔ *CPT Assistant* Nov 98:17

(For excision of remote or disseminated pheochromocytoma, see 49200, 49201)

(For laparoscopic approach, use 56321)

(60550, 60555 have been deleted. To report, use 60540 with modifier '-50')

60600   Excision of carotid body tumor; without excision of carotid artery

60605   with excision of carotid artery

Laparoscopy

Surgical laparoscopy always includes diagnostic laparoscopy. To report a diagnostic laparoscopy (peritoneoscopy) (separate procedure), use 49320.

60650 Laparoscopy, surgical, with adrenalectomy, partial or complete, or exploration of adrenal gland with or without biopsy, transabdominal, lumbar or dorsal

➔ *CPT Assistant* Nov 99:30; Mar 00:5; *CPT Changes* 2000

Laparoscopic Adrenalectomy
60650

An adrenal gland is dissected and removed under laparoscopic guidance. Multiple small blood vessels from the vena cava and the aorta do not follow standard anatomic pattern, requiring intricate dissection.

60659 Unlisted laparoscopy procedure, endocrine system

➔ *CPT Assistant* Nov 99:30; Mar 00:5; *CPT Changes* 2000

Other Procedures

60699 Unlisted procedure, endocrine system

⊘ =Modifier '-51' Exempt   ▶ ◀ =New or Revised Text   ✚ =Add-on Code   CPT 2002

Nervous System

Skull, Meninges, and Brain

(For injection procedure for cerebral angiography, see 36100-36218)

(For injection procedure for ventriculography, see 61026, 61120, 61130)

(For injection procedure for pneumoencephalography, use 61055)

Injection, Drainage, or Aspiration

61000* Subdural tap through fontanelle, or suture, infant, unilateral or bilateral; initial

61001*   subsequent taps

61020* Ventricular puncture through previous burr hole, fontanelle, suture, or implanted ventricular catheter/reservoir; without injection

(61025 has been deleted. To report, use 61026)

▲ **61026***   with injection of medication or other substance for diagnosis or treatment
➔ *CPT Changes* 2002

(61030, 61045 have been deleted. To report, use 61026)

61050* Cisternal or lateral cervical (C1-C2) puncture; without injection (separate procedure)

(61051, 61052, 61053 have been deleted. To report, use 61055)

▲ **61055***   with injection of medication or other substance for diagnosis or treatment (eg, C1-C2)
➔ *CPT Changes* 2002

(For radiological supervision and interpretation, see **Radiology**)

61070* Puncture of shunt tubing or reservoir for aspiration or injection procedure

(For radiological supervision and interpretation, use 75809)

Twist Drill, Burr Hole(s), or Trephine

61105* Twist drill hole for subdural or ventricular puncture;

(61106 has been deleted)

⊘ **61107***   for implanting ventricular catheter or pressure recording device

61108   for evacuation and/or drainage of subdural hematoma

61120 Burr hole(s) for ventricular puncture (including injection of gas, contrast media, dye, or radioactive material)

(61130 has been deleted)

61140 Burr hole(s) or trephine; with biopsy of brain or intracranial lesion

61150   with drainage of brain abscess or cyst

61151   with subsequent tapping (aspiration) of intracranial abscess or cyst

61154 Burr hole(s) with evacuation and/or drainage of hematoma, extradural or subdural

(61155 has been deleted. To report, use 61154 with modifier '-50')

61156 Burr hole(s); with aspiration of hematoma or cyst, intracerebral

⊘ **61210***   for implanting ventricular catheter, reservoir, EEG electrode(s) or pressure recording device (separate procedure)

61215 Insertion of subcutaneous reservoir, pump or continuous infusion system for connection to ventricular catheter
➔ *CPT Assistant* Spring 93:13

(For chemotherapy, use 96450)

61250 Burr hole(s) or trephine, supratentorial, exploratory, not followed by other surgery

(61251 has been deleted. To report, use 61250 with modifier '-50')

61253 Burr hole(s) or trephine, infratentorial, unilateral or bilateral

(If burr hole(s) or trephine are followed by craniotomy at same operative session, use 61304-61321; do not use 61250 or 61253)

Craniectomy or Craniotomy

61304 Craniectomy or craniotomy, exploratory; supratentorial

61305   infratentorial (posterior fossa)

(61310, 61311 have been deleted. To report, see 61312-61315)

61312 Craniectomy or craniotomy for evacuation of hematoma, supratentorial; extradural or subdural

61313   intracerebral

61314 Craniectomy or craniotomy for evacuation of hematoma, infratentorial; extradural or subdural

61315   intracerebellar

61320 Craniectomy or craniotomy, drainage of intracranial abscess; supratentorial

61321   infratentorial

61330 Decompression of orbit only, transcranial approach

(61331 has been deleted. To report, use 61330 with modifier '-50')

61332 Exploration of orbit (transcranial approach); with biopsy

61333   with removal of lesion

61334   with removal of foreign body

Nervous
61000

61340 Other cranial decompression (eg, subtemporal), supratentorial

(61341 has been deleted. To report, use 61340 with modifier '-50')

61343 Craniectomy, suboccipital with cervical laminectomy for decompression of medulla and spinal cord, with or without dural graft (eg, Arnold-Chiari malformation)

61345 Other cranial decompression, posterior fossa

(For orbital decompression by lateral wall approach, Kroenlein type, use 67445)

61440 Craniotomy for section of tentorium cerebelli (separate procedure)

61450 Craniectomy, subtemporal, for section, compression, or decompression of sensory root of gasserian ganglion

61458 Craniectomy, suboccipital; for exploration or decompression of cranial nerves

61460   for section of one or more cranial nerves

61470   for medullary tractotomy

61480   for mesencephalic tractotomy or pedunculotomy

61490 Craniotomy for lobotomy, including cingulotomy

(61491 has been deleted. To report, use 61490 with modifier '-50')

61500 Craniectomy; with excision of tumor or other bone lesion of skull

61501   for osteomyelitis

61510 Craniectomy, trephination, bone flap craniotomy; for excision of brain tumor, supratentorial, except meningioma

61512   for excision of meningioma, supratentorial

61514   for excision of brain abscess, supratentorial

61516   for excision or fenestration of cyst, supratentorial

(For excision of pituitary tumor or craniopharyngioma, see 61545, 61546, 61548)

61518 Craniectomy for excision of brain tumor, infratentorial or posterior fossa; except meningioma, cerebellopontine angle tumor, or midline tumor at base of skull

61519   meningioma

61520   cerebellopontine angle tumor

61521   midline tumor at base of skull

61522 Craniectomy, infratentorial or posterior fossa; for excision of brain abscess

61524   for excision or fenestration of cyst

61526 Craniectomy, bone flap craniotomy, transtemporal (mastoid) for excision of cerebellopontine angle tumor;
➲ *CPT Assistant* Summer 91:8

61530   combined with middle/posterior fossa craniotomy/craniectomy

61531 Subdural implantation of strip electrodes through one or more burr or trephine hole(s) for long term seizure monitoring

(For stereotactic implantation of electrodes, use 61760)

(61532 has been deleted. To report, see 61680-61692)

61533 Craniotomy with elevation of bone flap; for subdural implantation of an electrode array, for long term seizure monitoring

(For continuous EEG monitoring, see 95950-95954)

61534   for excision of epileptogenic focus without electrocorticography during surgery

61535   for removal of epidural or subdural electrode array, without excision of cerebral tissue (separate procedure)

61536   for excision of cerebral epileptogenic focus, with electrocorticography during surgery (includes removal of electrode array)

61538   for lobectomy with electrocorticography during surgery, temporal lobe

61539   for lobectomy with electrocorticography during surgery, other than temporal lobe, partial or total

61541   for transection of corpus callosum

61542   for total hemispherectomy

61543   for partial or subtotal hemispherectomy

61544   for excision or coagulation of choroid plexus

61545   for excision of craniopharyngioma

61546 Craniotomy for hypophysectomy or excision of pituitary tumor, intracranial approach

61548 Hypophysectomy or excision of pituitary tumor, transnasal or transseptal approach, nonstereotactic
➲ *CPT Assistant* Nov 98:17

(Do not report code 69990 in addition to code 61548)

61550 Craniectomy for craniosynostosis; single cranial suture

61552   multiple cranial sutures

(61553 has been deleted. To report, see 61552, 61558, 61559)

(61555 has been deleted. To report, see 21172-21180, 61552, 61558, 61559)

(For cranial reconstruction for orbital hypertelorism, see 21260-21263)

61556 Craniotomy for craniosynostosis; frontal or parietal bone flap

61557   bifrontal bone flap

61558 Extensive craniectomy for multiple cranial suture craniosynostosis (eg, cloverleaf skull); not requiring bone grafts

61559   recontouring with multiple osteotomies and bone autografts (eg, barrel-stave procedure) (includes obtaining grafts)

(61561 has been deleted. To report, see 21172-21180)

61563 Excision, intra and extracranial, benign tumor of cranial bone (eg, fibrous dysplasia); without optic nerve decompression

61564 with optic nerve decompression

(For reconstruction, see 21181-21183)

61570 Craniectomy or craniotomy; with excision of foreign body from brain

61571 with treatment of penetrating wound of brain

(For sequestrectomy for osteomyelitis, use 61501)

61575 Transoral approach to skull base, brain stem or upper spinal cord for biopsy, decompression or excision of lesion;

61576 requiring splitting of tongue and/or mandible (including tracheostomy)

(For arthrodesis, use 22548)

Surgery of Skull Base

The surgical management of lesions involving the skull base (base of anterior, middle, and posterior cranial fossae) often requires the skills of several surgeons of different surgical specialties working together or in tandem during the operative session. These operations are usually not staged because of the need for definitive closure of dura, subcutaneous tissues, and skin to avoid serious infections such as osteomyelitis and/or meningitis.

The procedures are categorized according to: 1) *approach procedure* necessary to obtain adequate exposure to the lesion (pathologic entity), 2) *definitive procedure(s)* necessary to biopsy, excise or otherwise treat the lesion, and 3) *repair/reconstruction* of the defect present following the definitive procedure(s).

The *approach procedure* is described according to anatomical area involved, ie, anterior cranial fossa, middle cranial fossa, posterior cranial fossa, and brain stem or upper spinal cord.

The *definitive procedure(s)* describes the repair, biopsy, resection, or excision of various lesions of the skull base and, when appropriate, primary closure of the dura, mucous membranes, and skin.

The *repair/reconstruction procedure(s)* is reported separately if extensive dural grafting, cranioplasty, local or regional myocutaneous pedicle flaps, or extensive skin grafts are required.

For primary closure, see the appropriate codes, ie, 15732, 15755.

When one surgeon performs the approach procedure, another surgeon performs the definitive procedure, and another surgeon performs the repair/reconstruction procedure, each surgeon reports only the code for the specific procedure performed.

If one surgeon performs more than one procedure (ie, approach procedure and definitive procedure), then both codes are reported, adding modifier '-51' to the secondary, additional procedure(s).

Approach Procedures

Anterior Cranial Fossa

61580 Craniofacial approach to anterior cranial fossa; extradural, including lateral rhinotomy, ethmoidectomy, sphenoidectomy, without maxillectomy or orbital exenteration
➔ *CPT Assistant* Spring 94:11

61581 extradural, including lateral rhinotomy, orbital exenteration, ethmoidectomy, sphenoidectomy and/or maxillectomy
➔ *CPT Assistant* Spring 94:11

61582 extradural, including unilateral or bifrontal craniotomy, elevation of frontal lobe(s), osteotomy of base of anterior cranial fossa
➔ *CPT Assistant* Spring 94:11

61583 intradural, including unilateral or bifrontal craniotomy, elevation or resection of frontal lobe, osteotomy of base of anterior cranial fossa
➔ *CPT Assistant* Spring 94:11

61584 Orbitocranial approach to anterior cranial fossa, extradural, including supraorbital ridge osteotomy and elevation of frontal and/or temporal lobe(s); without orbital exenteration

61585 with orbital exenteration

61586 Bicoronal, transzygomatic and/or LeFort I osteotomy approach to anterior cranial fossa with or without internal fixation, without bone graft

Middle Cranial Fossa

61590 Infratemporal pre-auricular approach to middle cranial fossa (parapharyngeal space, infratemporal and midline skull base, nasopharynx), with or without disarticulation of the mandible, including parotidectomy, craniotomy, decompression and/or mobilization of the facial nerve and/or petrous carotid artery

61591 Infratemporal post-auricular approach to middle cranial fossa (internal auditory meatus, petrous apex, tentorium, cavernous sinus, parasellar area, infratemporal fossa) including mastoidectomy, resection of sigmoid sinus, with or without decompression and/or mobilization of contents of auditory canal or petrous carotid artery

61592 Orbitocranial zygomatic approach to middle cranial fossa (cavernous sinus and carotid artery, clivus, basilar artery or petrous apex) including osteotomy of zygoma, craniotomy, extra- or intradural elevation of temporal lobe

Posterior Cranial Fossa

61595 Transtemporal approach to posterior cranial fossa, jugular foramen or midline skull base, including mastoidectomy, decompression of sigmoid sinus and/or facial nerve, with or without mobilization

61596 Transcochlear approach to posterior cranial fossa, jugular foramen or midline skull base, including labyrinthectomy, decompression, with or without mobilization of facial nerve and/or petrous carotid artery

61597 Transcondylar (far lateral) approach to posterior cranial fossa, jugular foramen or midline skull base, including occipital condylectomy, mastoidectomy, resection of C1-C3 vertebral body(s), decompression of vertebral artery, with or without mobilization

61598 Transpetrosal approach to posterior cranial fossa, clivus or foramen magnum, including ligation of superior petrosal sinus and/or sigmoid sinus

Definitive Procedures

Base of Anterior Cranial Fossa

61600 Resection or excision of neoplastic, vascular or infectious lesion of base of anterior cranial fossa; extradural
➔ *CPT Assistant* Spring 94:12

61601 intradural, including dural repair, with or without graft
➔ *CPT Assistant* Spring 94:12

Base of Middle Cranial Fossa

61605 Resection or excision of neoplastic, vascular or infectious lesion of infratemporal fossa, parapharyngeal space, petrous apex; extradural

61606 intradural, including dural repair, with or without graft

61607 Resection or excision of neoplastic, vascular or infectious lesion of parasellar area, cavernous sinus, clivus or midline skull base; extradural

61608 intradural, including dural repair, with or without graft

Codes 61609-61612 are reported in addition to code(s) for primary procedure(s) 61605-61608. Report only one transection or ligation of carotid artery code per operative session.

+ 61609 Transection or ligation, carotid artery in cavernous sinus; without repair (List separately in addition to code for primary procedure)

+ 61610 with repair by anastomosis or graft (List separately in addition to code for primary procedure)

+ 61611 Transection or ligation, carotid artery in petrous canal; without repair (List separately in addition to code for primary procedure)

+ 61612 with repair by anastomosis or graft (List separately in addition to code for primary procedure)

61613 Obliteration of carotid aneurysm, arteriovenous malformation, or carotid-cavernous fistula by dissection within cavernous sinus

Base of Posterior Cranial Fossa

61615 Resection or excision of neoplastic, vascular or infectious lesion of base of posterior cranial fossa, jugular foramen, foramen magnum, or C1-C3 vertebral bodies; extradural

61616 intradural, including dural repair, with or without graft

Repair and/or Reconstruction of Surgical Defects of Skull Base

▲**61618** Secondary repair of dura for cerebrospinal fluid leak, anterior, middle or posterior cranial fossa following surgery of the skull base; by free tissue graft (eg, pericranium, fascia, tensor fascia lata, adipose tissue, homologous or synthetic grafts)
➔ *CPT Assistant* Spring 94:19; Mar 00:11; *CPT Changes* 2002

61619 by local or regionalized vascularized pedicle flap or myocutaneous flap (including galea, temporalis, frontalis or occipitalis muscle)
➔ *CPT Assistant* Spring 94:19; Mar 00:11

Endovascular Therapy

61624 Transcatheter occlusion or embolization (eg, for tumor destruction, to achieve hemostasis, to occlude a vascular malformation), percutaneous, any method; central nervous system (intracranial, spinal cord)
➔ *CPT Assistant* Jun 99:10

(See also 37204)

(For radiological supervision and interpretation, use 75894)

61626 non-central nervous system, head or neck (extracranial, brachiocephalic branch)

(See also 37204)

(For radiological supervision and interpretation, use 75894)

Surgery for Aneurysm, Arteriovenous Malformation or Vascular Disease

Includes craniotomy when appropriate for procedure.

61680 Surgery of intracranial arteriovenous malformation; supratentorial, simple

61682 supratentorial, complex

61684 infratentorial, simple

61686 infratentorial, complex

⊘ =Modifier '-51' Exempt   ▶ ◀=New or Revised Text   ✚=Add-on Code

61690   dural, simple

61692   dural, complex

61697   Surgery of complex intracranial aneurysm, intracranial approach; carotid circulation
➲ *CPT Changes* 2001

61698   vertebrobasilar circulation
➲ *CPT Changes* 2001

(61697, 61698 involve aneurysms that are larger than 15 mm or with calcification of the aneurysm neck, or with incorporation of normal vessels into the aneurysm neck, or a procedure requiring temporary vessel occlusion, trapping or cardiopulmonary bypass to successfully treat the aneurysm)

61700   Surgery of simple intracranial aneurysm, intracranial approach; carotid circulation
➲ *CPT Assistant* Jun 99:11; Jul 99:10; *CPT Changes* 2001

61702   vertebrobasilar circulation
➲ *CPT Changes* 2001

61703   Surgery of intracranial aneurysm, cervical approach by application of occluding clamp to cervical carotid artery (Selverstone-Crutchfield type)

(For cervical approach for direct ligation of carotid artery, see 37600-37606)

61705   Surgery of aneurysm, vascular malformation or carotid-cavernous fistula; by intracranial and cervical occlusion of carotid artery

61708   by intracranial electrothrombosis

(For ligation or gradual occlusion of internal/common carotid artery, see 37605, 37606)

61710   by intra-arterial embolization, injection procedure, or balloon catheter

61711   Anastomosis, arterial, extracranial-intracranial (eg, middle cerebral/cortical) arteries

(For carotid or vertebral thromboendarterectomy, use 35301)

(61712 has been deleted. Use 69990 when the surgical microscope is employed for the microsurgical procedure. Do not use 69990 for visualization with magnifying loupes or corrected vision.)

Stereotaxis

61720   Creation of lesion by stereotactic method, including burr hole(s) and localizing and recording techniques, single or multiple stages; globus pallidus or thalamus

61735   subcortical structure(s) other than globus pallidus or thalamus

61750   Stereotactic biopsy, aspiration, or excision, including burr hole(s), for intracranial lesion;
➲ *CPT Assistant* Nov 99:30; *CPT Changes* 2000

61751   with computerized axial tomography and/or magnetic resonance guidance
➲ *CPT Assistant* Jun 96:10; Nov 99:30; *CPT Changes* 2000

(For radiological supervision and interpretation of computerized tomography, see 70450, 70460, or 70470 as appropriate)

(For radiological supervision and interpretation of magnetic resonance imaging, see 70551, 70552, or 70553 as appropriate)

61760   Stereotactic implantation of depth electrodes into the cerebrum for long term seizure monitoring

61770   Stereotactic localization, including burr hole(s), with insertion of catheter(s) or probe(s) for placement of radiation source
➲ *CPT Changes* 2001

(61780 has been deleted. To report, use 61760)

61790   Creation of lesion by stereotactic method, percutaneous, by neurolytic agent (eg, alcohol, thermal, electrical, radiofrequency); gasserian ganglion

61791   trigeminal medullary tract

61793   Stereotactic radiosurgery (particle beam, gamma ray or linear accelerator), one or more sessions
➲ *CPT Assistant* Nov 97:23

▶(For intensity modulated beam delivery plan and treatment, see 77301, 77418)◀

+ 61795 Stereotactic computer assisted volumetric (navigational) procedure, intracranial, extracranial, or spinal (List separately in addition to code for primary procedure)
➲ *CPT Assistant* Nov 99:30; *CPT Changes* 2000

Neurostimulators (Intracranial)

Codes 61850-61888 apply to both simple and complex neurostimulators. For initial or subsequent electronic analysis and programming of neurostimulator pulse generators, see codes 95970-95975.

61850   Twist drill or burr hole(s) for implantation of neurostimulator electrodes, cortical
➲ *CPT Assistant* Nov 99:30; *CPT Changes* 2000

(61855 has been deleted. To report, use 61862)

61860 Craniectomy or craniotomy for implantation of neurostimulator electrodes, cerebral, cortical

→ *CPT Assistant* Nov 99:30; *CPT Changes* 2000

Placement of Cranial Neurostimulator
61862, 61885

Placement of subcortical (eg, thalamic) neurostimulator electrode via burr hole (61862) with connection of the electrode to an implanted programmable pulse generator (61885) in the infraclavicular area.

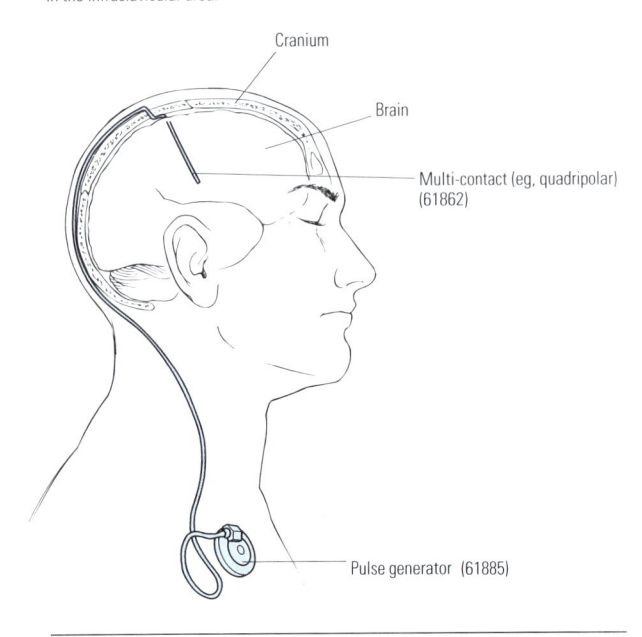

61862 Twist drill, burr hole, craniotomy, or craniectomy for stereotactic implantation of one neurostimulator array in subcortical site (eg, thalamus, globus pallidus, subthalamic nucleus, periventricular, periaqueductal gray)

→ *CPT Assistant* Nov 99:30; Jun 00:3; *CPT Changes* 2000

(61865 has been deleted. To report, use 61862)

61870 Craniectomy for implantation of neurostimulator electrodes, cerebellar; cortical

61875   subcortical

61880 Revision or removal of intracranial neurostimulator electrodes

61885 Incision and subcutaneous placement of cranial neurostimulator pulse generator or receiver, direct or inductive coupling; with connection to a single electrode array

→ *CPT Assistant* Nov 99:30; Jun 00:3; *CPT Changes* 2000

61886   with connection to two or more electrode arrays

→ *CPT Assistant* Nov 99:30; Jun 00:3; *CPT Changes* 2000

(For open placement of cranial nerve (eg, vagal, trigeminal) neurostimulator electrode(s), use 64573)

(For percutaneous placement of cranial nerve (eg, vagal, trigeminal) neurostimulator electrode(s), use 64553)

(For revision or removal of cranial nerve (eg, vagal, trigeminal) neurostimulator electrode(s), use 64585)

61888 Revision or removal of cranial neurostimulator pulse generator or receiver

Repair

62000 Elevation of depressed skull fracture; simple, extradural

62005   compound or comminuted, extradural

62010   with repair of dura and/or debridement of brain

▲ **62100** Craniotomy for repair of dural/cerebrospinal fluid leak, including surgery for rhinorrhea/otorrhea

→ *CPT Changes* 2002

(For repair of spinal dural/CSF leak, see 63707, 63709)

62115 Reduction of craniomegalic skull (eg, treated hydrocephalus); not requiring bone grafts or cranioplasty

62116   with simple cranioplasty

62117   requiring craniotomy and reconstruction with or without bone graft (includes obtaining grafts)

62120 Repair of encephalocele, skull vault, including cranioplasty

62121 Craniotomy for repair of encephalocele, skull base

62140 Cranioplasty for skull defect; up to 5 cm diameter

62141   larger than 5 cm diameter

62142 Removal of bone flap or prosthetic plate of skull

62143 Replacement of bone flap or prosthetic plate of skull

62145 Cranioplasty for skull defect with reparative brain surgery

62146 Cranioplasty with autograft (includes obtaining bone grafts); up to 5 cm diameter

62147   larger than 5 cm diameter

Cerebrospinal Fluid (CSF) Shunt

62180 Ventriculocisternostomy (Torkildsen type operation)

62190 Creation of shunt; subarachnoid/subdural-atrial, -jugular, -auricular

62192   subarachnoid/subdural-peritoneal, -pleural, other terminus

62194 Replacement or irrigation, subarachnoid/subdural catheter

62200 Ventriculocisternostomy, third ventricle;

62201   stereotactic method

62220 Creation of shunt; ventriculo-atrial, -jugular, -auricular

⊘ =Modifier '-51' Exempt ▶ ◀=New or Revised Text ✚ =Add-on Code CPT 2002

62223 ventriculo-peritoneal, -pleural, other terminus

Cerebrospinal Fluid (CSF) Shunt (Ventricular Peritoneal)
62223

A ventriculostomy is performed to drain CSF into the peritoneal cavity.

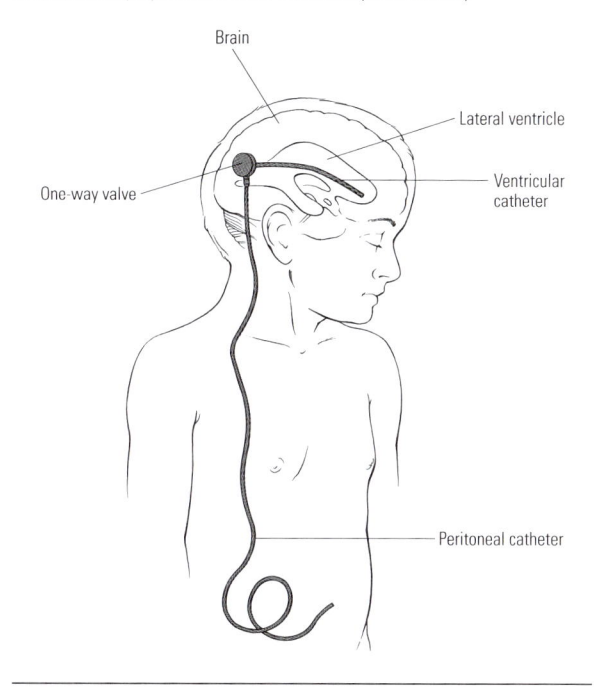

62225 Replacement or irrigation, ventricular catheter

▲ **62230** Replacement or revision of cerebrospinal fluid shunt, obstructed valve, or distal catheter in shunt system
➲ *CPT Changes* 2002

▲ **62252** Reprogramming of programmable cerebrospinal shunt
➲ *CPT Changes* 2001; 2002

▲ **62256** Removal of complete cerebrospinal fluid shunt system; without replacement
➲ *CPT Changes* 2002

62258 with replacement by similar or other shunt at same operation

(For percutaneous irrigation or aspiration of shunt reservoir, use 61070)

(For reprogramming of programmable CSF shunt, use 62252)

Spine and Spinal Cord

(For application of caliper or tongs, use 20660)

(For treatment of fracture or dislocation of spine, see 22305-22327)

Injection, Drainage, or Aspiration

Injection of contrast during fluoroscopic guidance and localization is an inclusive component of codes 62270-62273, 62280-62282, 62310-62319. Fluoroscopic guidance and localization is reported by code 76005, ° unless a formal contrast study (myelography, epidurography, or arthrography) is performed, in which case the use of fluoroscopy is included in the supervision and interpretation codes.

For radiologic supervision and interpretation of epidurography, use 72275. Code 72275 is only to be used when an epidurogram is performed, recorded, and a formal radiologic report is issued.

For codes 62318 and 62319, use code 01996 for subsequent daily management of epidural or subarachnoid catheter drug administration.

62263 Percutaneous lysis of epidural adhesions using solution injection (eg, hypertonic saline, enzyme) or mechanical means (eg, spring-wound catheter) including radiologic localization (includes contrast when administered)
➲ *CPT Assistant* Nov 99:33; *CPT Changes* 2000

62268 * Percutaneous aspiration, spinal cord cyst or syrinx

(For radiological supervision and interpretation, see 76003, 76360, ▶76942◀)

62269 * Biopsy of spinal cord, percutaneous needle

(For radiological supervision and interpretation, see 76003, 76360, 76942)

62270 * Spinal puncture, lumbar, diagnostic
➲ *CPT Assistant* Nov 99:32-33; *CPT Changes* 2000; 2002

▲ **62272** * Spinal puncture, therapeutic, for drainage of cerebrospinal fluid (by needle or catheter)
➲ *CPT Assistant* Nov 99:32-33; *CPT Changes* 2000

62273 * Injection, epidural, of blood or clot patch
➲ *CPT Assistant* Nov 99:32-34; *CPT Changes* 2000

(62274 has been deleted. To report, see 62310, 62311)

(62275 has been deleted. To report, use 62310)

(62276 has been deleted. To report, see 62318, 62319)

(62277 has been deleted. To report, see 62318, 62319)

(62278 has been deleted. To report, use 62311)

(62279 has been deleted. To report, use 62319)

62280* Injection/infusion of neurolytic substance (eg, alcohol, phenol, iced saline solutions), with or without other therapeutic substance; subarachnoid

➔ *CPT Assistant* Nov 99:32-34; Jan 00:1; *CPT Changes* 2000

62281* epidural, cervical or thoracic

➔ *CPT Assistant* Apr 96:10; Nov 99:32-34; Jan 00:1; *CPT Changes* 2000

62282* epidural, lumbar, sacral (caudal)

➔ *CPT Assistant* Apr 96:10; Nov 99:32-34; Jan 00:1; *CPT Changes* 2000

⊘ **62284*** Injection procedure for myelography and/or computerized axial tomography, spinal (other than C1-C2 and posterior fossa)

➔ *CPT Assistant* Fall 93:13

(For injection procedure at C1-C2, use 61055)

(For radiological supervision and interpretation, see **Radiology**)

(62286 has been deleted. To report, use 64999)

62287 Aspiration or decompression procedure, percutaneous, of nucleus pulposus of intervertebral disk, any method, single or multiple levels, lumbar (eg, manual or automated percutaneous diskectomy, percutaneous laser diskectomy)

➔ *CPT Assistant* Nov 99:34; *CPT Changes* 2000

(For fluoroscopic guidance, use 76003)

(62288 has been deleted. To report, see 62310, 62311)

(62289 has been deleted. To report, use 62311)

62290* Injection procedure for diskography, each level; lumbar

➔ *CPT Assistant* Nov 99:35; *CPT Changes* 2000

62291* cervical or thoracic

➔ *CPT Assistant* Nov 99:35; *CPT Changes* 2000

(For radiological supervision and interpretation, see 72285, 72295)

62292 Injection procedure for chemonucleolysis, including diskography, intervertebral disk, single or multiple levels, lumbar

➔ *CPT Assistant* Oct 99:10

(62293 has been deleted)

62294 Injection procedure, arterial, for occlusion of arteriovenous malformation, spinal

(62295-62297 have been deleted. To report, see 63001-63017)

(62298 has been deleted. To report, use 62310)

62310 Injection, single (not via indwelling catheter), not including neurolytic substances, with or without contrast (for either localization or epidurography), of diagnostic or therapeutic substance(s) (including anesthetic, antispasmodic, opioid, steroid, other solution), epidural or subarachnoid; cervical or thoracic

➔ *CPT Assistant* Nov 99:32-35; Jan 00:1; Dec 00:15; *CPT Changes* 2000

62311 lumbar, sacral (caudal)

➔ *CPT Assistant* Nov 99:32-35; Jan 00:1; Dec 00:15; *CPT Changes* 2000

62318 Injection, including catheter placement, continuous infusion or intermittent bolus, not including neurolytic substances, with or without contrast (for either localization or epidurography), of diagnostic or therapeutic substance(s) (including anesthetic, antispasmodic, opioid, steroid, other solution), epidural or subarachnoid; cervical or thoracic

➔ *CPT Assistant* Nov 99:32-35; Jan 00:1; Dec 00:15; *CPT Changes* 2000

62319 lumbar, sacral (caudal)

➔ *CPT Assistant* Nov 99:32-35; Jan 00:1; Dec 00:15; *CPT Changes* 2000

(For transforaminal epidural injection, see 64479-64484)

Catheter Implantation

(For percutaneous placement of intrathecal or epidural catheter, see codes 62270-62273, 62280-62284, 62310-62319)

(62301-62303 have been deleted. To report, see 63001-63017)

62350 Implantation, revision or repositioning of tunneled intrathecal or epidural catheter, for long-term medication administration via an external pump or implantable reservoir/infusion pump; without laminectomy

➔ *CPT Assistant* Nov 99:36; *CPT Changes* 2000; 2001

62351 with laminectomy

➔ *CPT Assistant* Nov 99:36; *CPT Changes* 2000

(For refilling and maintenance of an implantable reservoir or infusion pump, use 96530)

62355 Removal of previously implanted intrathecal or epidural catheter

Reservoir/Pump Implantation

62360   Implantation or replacement of device for intrathecal or epidural drug infusion; subcutaneous reservoir

62361   non-programmable pump

62362   programmable pump, including preparation of pump, with or without programming
→ *CPT Assistant* Mar 97:11

Intrathecal or Epidural Drug Infusion Pump Implantation
62362

The reservoir is placed in the subcutaneous tissues and attached to a previously placed catheter for intrathecal or epidural drug infusion.

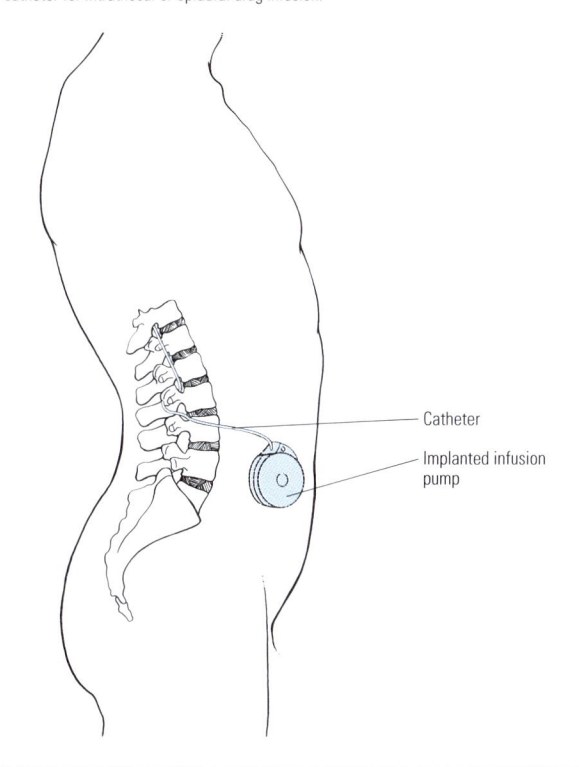

Catheter

Implanted infusion pump

62365   Removal of subcutaneous reservoir or pump, previously implanted for intrathecal or epidural infusion

62367   Electronic analysis of programmable, implanted pump for intrathecal or epidural drug infusion (includes evaluation of reservoir status, alarm status, drug prescription status); without reprogramming

62368   with reprogramming

(To report implantable pump or reservoir refill, use 96530)

Posterior Extradural Laminotomy or Laminectomy for Exploration/ Decompression of Neural Elements or Excision of Herniated Intervertebral Disks

(When 63001-63048 are followed by arthrodesis, see 22590-22614)

63001   Laminectomy with exploration and/or decompression of spinal cord and/or cauda equina, without facetectomy, foraminotomy or diskectomy, (eg, spinal stenosis), one or two vertebral segments; cervical
→ *CPT Assistant* Jan 01:12

63003   thoracic
→ *CPT Assistant* Jan 01:12

63005   lumbar, except for spondylolisthesis
→ *CPT Assistant* Jan 01:12

(63010 has been deleted. To report, use 63012)

Lumbar Laminectomy
63005

With the patient prone and under general anesthesia, the laminae and underlying ligamentum flavum are removed.

Cauda equina

Dura

Nerve root

5th lumbar vertebra

63011   sacral
→ *CPT Assistant* Jan 01:12

63012   Laminectomy with removal of abnormal facets and/or pars inter-articularis with decompression of cauda equina and nerve roots for spondylolisthesis, lumbar (Gill type procedure)
→ *CPT Assistant* Jan 01:12

63015   Laminectomy with exploration and/or decompression of spinal cord and/or cauda equina, without facetectomy, foraminotomy or diskectomy, (eg, spinal stenosis), more than 2 vertebral segments; cervical
→ *CPT Assistant* Jan 01:12

63016   thoracic
→ *CPT Assistant* Jan 01:12

63017   lumbar
> *CPT Assistant* Jan 01:12

63020   Laminotomy (hemilaminectomy), with decompression of nerve root(s), including partial facetectomy, foraminotomy and/or excision of herniated intervertebral disk; one interspace, cervical
> *CPT Assistant* Nov 99:36; Jan 01:12; *CPT Changes* 2000

(63021 has been deleted. To report, use 63020 with modifier '-50')

63030   one interspace, lumbar (including open or endoscopically-assisted approach)
> *CPT Assistant* Mar 96:7; Nov 99:36; Jan 01:12; Feb 01:10; *CPT Changes* 2000

(63031 has been deleted. To report, use 63030 with modifier '-50')

+ 63035   each additional interspace, cervical or lumbar (List separately in addition to code for primary procedure)
> *CPT Assistant* Mar 96:7; Nov 99:36; Jan 01:12; Feb 01:10; *CPT Changes* 2000

(Use 63035 in conjunction with codes 63020-63030)

63040   Laminotomy (hemilaminectomy), with decompression of nerve root(s), including partial facetectomy, foraminotomy and/or excision of herniated intervertebral disk, reexploration, single interspace; cervical
> *CPT Assistant* Jan 99:11; Jan 01:12; *CPT Changes* 2001

(63041 has been deleted)

63042   lumbar
> *CPT Assistant* Jan 99:11; Jan 01:12

(Codes 63040-▶63044◀ are unilateral procedures. For bilateral procedures, use modifier '-50')

+ 63043   each additional cervical interspace (List separately in addition to code for primary procedure)
> *CPT Changes* 2001

(Use 63043 in conjunction with code 63040)

+ 63044   each additional lumbar interspace (List separately in addition to code for primary procedure)
> *CPT Changes* 2001

(Use 63044 in conjunction with code 63042)

63045   Laminectomy, facetectomy and foraminotomy (unilateral or bilateral with decompression of spinal cord, cauda equina and/or nerve root(s), (eg, spinal or lateral recess stenosis)), single vertebral segment; cervical
> *CPT Assistant* Jan 01:12

63046   thoracic
> *CPT Assistant* Jan 99:11; Jan 01:12

63047   lumbar
> *CPT Assistant* Jan 99:11; Jan 01:12; Feb 01:10

+ 63048   each additional segment, cervical, thoracic, or lumbar (List separately in addition to code for primary procedure)
> *CPT Assistant* Jan 99:11; Jan 01:12

(Use 63048 in conjunction with codes 63045-63047)

Transpedicular or Costovertebral Approach for Posterolateral Extradural Exploration/Decompression

63055   Transpedicular approach with decompression of spinal cord, equina and/or nerve root(s) (eg, herniated intervertebral disk), single segment; thoracic
> *CPT Assistant* Nov 99:36; *CPT Changes* 2000

63056   lumbar (including transfacet, or lateral extraforaminal approach) (eg, far lateral herniated intervertebral disk)
> *CPT Assistant* Nov 99:36; *CPT Changes* 2000

+ 63057   each additional segment, thoracic or lumbar (List separately in addition to code for primary procedure)
> *CPT Assistant* Nov 99:36; *CPT Changes* 2000

(Use 63057 in conjunction with codes 63055, 63056)

(63060 has been deleted)

63064   Costovertebral approach with decompression of spinal cord or nerve root(s), (eg, herniated intervertebral disk), thoracic; single segment

(63065 has been deleted)

+ 63066   each additional segment (List separately in addition to code for primary procedure)

(Use 63066 in conjunction with code 63064)

(For excision of thoracic intraspinal lesions by laminectomy, see 63266, 63271, 63276, 63281, 63286)

Anterior or Anterolateral Approach for Extradural Exploration/Decompression

▶For the following codes, when two surgeons work together as primary surgeons performing distinct part(s) of spinal cord exploration/decompression operation, each surgeon should report his/her distinct operative work by appending the modifier '-62' to the procedure code (and any associated add-on codes for that procedure code as long as both surgeons continue to work together as primary surgeons). In this situation, the modifier '-62' may be appended to the definitive procedure code(s) 63075, 63077, 63081, 63085, 63087, 63090 and, as appropriate, to associated additional interspace add-on code(s) 63076, 63078 or additional segment add-on code(s) 63082, 63086, 63088, 63091 as long as both surgeons continue to work together as primary surgeons.◀

63075   Diskectomy, anterior, with decompression of spinal cord and/or nerve root(s), including osteophytectomy; cervical, single interspace
> *CPT Assistant* Nov 98:18; Jan 01:12; *CPT Changes* 2002

+ 63076   cervical, each additional interspace (List separately in addition to code for primary procedure)
> *CPT Assistant* Nov 98:18; Jan 01:12; *CPT Changes* 2002

(Use 63076 in conjunction with code 63075)

⊘ = Modifier '-51' Exempt   ▶ ◀ = New or Revised Text   ✚ = Add-on Code   CPT 2002

63077 thoracic, single interspace
➔ *CPT Assistant* Nov 98:18; Jan 01:12; *CPT Changes* 2002

+ 63078 thoracic, each additional interspace (List separately in addition to code for primary procedure)
➔ *CPT Assistant* Nov 98:18; Jan 01:12; *CPT Changes* 2002

(Use 63078 in conjunction with code 63077)

(Do not report code 69990 in addition to codes 63075-63078)

63081 Vertebral corpectomy (vertebral body resection), partial or complete, anterior approach with decompression of spinal cord and/or nerve root(s); cervical, single segment
➔ *CPT Assistant* Spring 93:37; *CPT Changes* 2002

+ 63082 cervical, each additional segment (List separately in addition to code for primary procedure)
➔ *CPT Assistant* Spring 93:37; *CPT Changes* 2002

(Use 63082 in conjunction with code 63081)

(For transoral approach, see 61575, 61576)

63085 Vertebral corpectomy (vertebral body resection), partial or complete, transthoracic approach with decompression of spinal cord and/or nerve root(s); thoracic, single segment
➔ *CPT Assistant* Spring 93:37; *CPT Changes* 2002

+ 63086 thoracic, each additional segment (List separately in addition to code for primary procedure)
➔ *CPT Assistant* Spring 93:37; *CPT Changes* 2002

(Use 63086 in conjunction with code 63085)

63087 Vertebral corpectomy (vertebral body resection), partial or complete, combined thoracolumbar approach with decompression of spinal cord, cauda equina or nerve root(s), lower thoracic or lumbar; single segment
➔ *CPT Assistant* Spring 93:37; *CPT Changes* 2002

+ 63088 each additional segment (List separately in addition to code for primary procedure)
➔ *CPT Assistant* Spring 93:37; *CPT Changes* 2002

(Use 63088 in conjunction with code 63087)

63090 Vertebral corpectomy (vertebral body resection), partial or complete, transperitoneal or retroperitoneal approach with decompression of spinal cord, cauda equina or nerve root(s), lower thoracic, lumbar, or sacral; single segment
➔ *CPT Assistant* Spring 93:37; Mar 96:6; *CPT Changes* 2002

+ 63091 each additional segment (List separately in addition to code for primary procedure)
➔ *CPT Assistant* Spring 93:37; Mar 96:6; *CPT Changes* 2002

(Use 63091 in conjunction with code 63090)

(Procedures 63081-63091 include diskectomy above and/or below vertebral segment)

(If followed by arthrodesis, see 22548-22812)

(For reconstruction of spine, use appropriate vertebral corpectomy codes 63081-63091, bone graft codes 20930-20938, arthrodesis codes 22548-22812, and spinal instrumentation codes 22840-22855)

Incision

63170 Laminectomy with myelotomy (eg, Bischof or DREZ type), cervical, thoracic, or thoracolumbar

63172 Laminectomy with drainage of intramedullary cyst/syrinx; to subarachnoid space

63173 to peritoneal space

63180 Laminectomy and section of dentate ligaments, with or without dural graft, cervical; one or two segments

63182 more than two segments

63185 Laminectomy with rhizotomy; one or two segments

63190 more than two segments

63191 Laminectomy with section of spinal accessory nerve

(63192 has been deleted. To report, use 63191 with modifier '-50')

(For resection of sternocleidomastoid muscle, use 21720)

63194 Laminectomy with cordotomy, with section of one spinothalamic tract, one stage; cervical

63195 thoracic

63196 Laminectomy with cordotomy, with section of both spinothalamic tracts, one stage; cervical

63197 thoracic

63198 Laminectomy with cordotomy with section of both spinothalamic tracts, two stages within 14 days; cervical

63199 thoracic

63200 Laminectomy, with release of tethered spinal cord, lumbar

Excision by Laminectomy of Lesion Other Than Herniated Disk

(63210-63242 have been deleted. To report, see 63265-63290)

63250 Laminectomy for excision or occlusion of arteriovenous malformation of spinal cord; cervical

63251 thoracic

63252 thoracolumbar

63265 Laminectomy for excision or evacuation of intraspinal lesion other than neoplasm, extradural; cervical

63266 thoracic

63267 lumbar

63268 sacral

63270 Laminectomy for excision of intraspinal lesion other than neoplasm, intradural; cervical

63271 thoracic

63272 lumbar

63273 sacral

63275 Laminectomy for biopsy/excision of intraspinal neoplasm; extradural, cervical

63276 extradural, thoracic

63277 extradural, lumbar

63278 extradural, sacral

63280 intradural, extramedullary, cervical

63281 intradural, extramedullary, thoracic

63282 intradural, extramedullary, lumbar

63283 intradural, sacral

63285 intradural, intramedullary, cervical

63286 intradural, intramedullary, thoracic

63287 intradural, intramedullary, thoracolumbar

63290 combined extradural-intradural lesion, any level

(For drainage of intramedullary cyst/syrinx, use 63172, 63173)

Excision, Anterior or Anterolateral Approach, Intraspinal Lesion

▶For the following codes, when two surgeons work together as primary surgeons performing distinct part(s) of an anterior approach for an intraspinal excision, each surgeon should report his/her distinct operative work by appending the modifier '-62' to the single definitive procedure code. In this situation, the modifier '-62' may be appended to the definitive procedure code(s) 63300-63307 and, as appropriate, to the associated additional segment add-on code 63308 as long as both surgeons continue to work together as primary surgeons.◀

(For arthrodesis, see 22548-22585)

(For reconstruction of spine, see 20930-20938)

63300 Vertebral corpectomy (vertebral body resection), partial or complete, for excision of intraspinal lesion, single segment; extradural, cervical

63301 extradural, thoracic by transthoracic approach

63302 extradural, thoracic by thoracolumbar approach

63303 extradural, lumbar or sacral by transperitoneal or retroperitoneal approach

63304 intradural, cervical

63305 intradural, thoracic by transthoracic approach

63306 intradural, thoracic by thoracolumbar approach

63307 intradural, lumbar or sacral by transperitoneal or retroperitoneal approach

+ 63308 each additional segment (List separately in addition to codes for single segment)

(Use 63308 in conjunction with codes 63300-63307)

Stereotaxis

63600 Creation of lesion of spinal cord by stereotactic method, percutaneous, any modality (including stimulation and/or recording)

63610 Stereotactic stimulation of spinal cord, percutaneous, separate procedure not followed by other surgery

63615 Stereotactic biopsy, aspiration, or excision of lesion, spinal cord

Neurostimulators (Spinal)

Codes 63650-63688 apply to both simple and complex neurostimulators. For initial or subsequent electronic analysis and programming of neurostimulator pulse generators, see codes 95970-95975.

Codes 63650, 63655, and 63660 describe the operative placement, revision, or removal of the spinal neurostimulator system components to provide spinal electrical stimulation. A neurostimulator system includes an implanted neurostimulator, external controller, extension, and collection of contacts. Multiple contacts or electrodes (4 or more) provide the actual electrical stimulation in the epidural space.

For percutaneously placed neurostimulator systems (63650, 63660), the contacts are on a catheter-like lead. An array defines the collection of contacts that are on one catheter.

For systems placed via an open surgical exposure (63655, 63660), the contacts are on a plate or paddle-shaped surface.

⊘ =Modifier '-51' Exempt   ▶◀=New or Revised Text   ✚=Add-on Code

63650   Percutaneous implantation of neurostimulator electrode array, epidural

→ *CPT Assistant* Jun 98:1; Nov 98:18; Mar 99:11; Apr 99:10; Sep 99:1

(63652 has been deleted)

Percutaneous Implantation of Neurostimulator Electrodes
63650

Single or dual catheter electrode array(s) is inserted percutaneously into the epidural space. A simple or complex receiver is subcutaneously implanted.

63655   Laminectomy for implantation of neurostimulator electrodes, plate/paddle, epidural

→ *CPT Assistant* Jun 98:1; Nov 98:18; Sep 99:1

Placement of Neurostimulator Electrodes through Laminectomy
63655

The electrode plate or paddle is placed in the epidural space via open exposure through large laminotomy or small laminectomy. The simple or complex receiver is subcutaneously implanted.

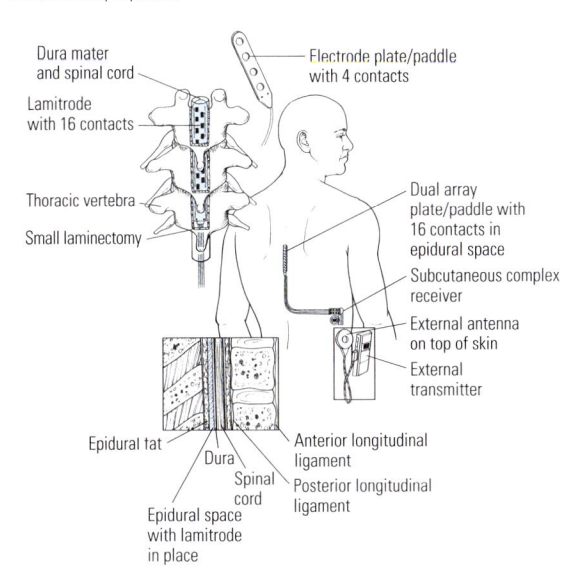

(63656 has been deleted)

(63657 and 63658 have been deleted)

63660   Revision or removal of spinal neurostimulator electrode percutaneous array(s) or plate/paddle(s)

→ *CPT Assistant* Jun 98:1; Nov 98:18

63685   Incision and subcutaneous placement of spinal neurostimulator pulse generator or receiver, direct or inductive coupling

→ *CPT Assistant* Jun 98:1

63688   Revision or removal of implanted spinal neurostimulator pulse generator or receiver

→ *CPT Assistant* Jun 98:1

(63690, 63691 have been deleted. To report, see 95970-95975)

Repair

63700   Repair of meningocele; less than 5 cm diameter

63702   larger than 5 cm diameter

63704   Repair of myelomeningocele; less than 5 cm diameter

63706   larger than 5 cm diameter

(For complex skin closure, see **Integumentary System**)

▲ **63707**   Repair of dural/cerebrospinal fluid leak, not requiring laminectomy

→ *CPT Changes* 2002

(63708 has been deleted. To report, see 63707, 63709)

▲ **63709**   Repair of dural/cerebrospinal fluid leak or pseudomeningocele, with laminectomy

→ *CPT Changes* 2002

63710   Dural graft, spinal

(For laminectomy and section of dentate ligaments, with or without dural graft, cervical, see 63180, 63182)

Shunt, Spinal CSF

63740   Creation of shunt, lumbar, subarachnoid-peritoneal, -pleural, or other; including laminectomy

63741   percutaneous, not requiring laminectomy

63744   Replacement, irrigation or revision of lumbosubarachnoid shunt

63746   Removal of entire lumbosubarachnoid shunt system without replacement

(63750 has been deleted. To report, see 62351 and 62360, 62361 or 62362)

(63780 has been deleted. To report, see 62350 and 62360, 62361 or 62362)

Extracranial Nerves, Peripheral Nerves, and Autonomic Nervous System

(For intracranial surgery on cranial nerves, see 61450, 61460, 61790)

Introduction/Injection of Anesthetic Agent (Nerve Block), Diagnostic or Therapeutic

Somatic Nerves

64400* Injection, anesthetic agent; trigeminal nerve, any division or branch
➔ *CPT Assistant* Jul 98:10; May 99:8; Nov 99:36; *CPT Changes* 2000

64402* facial nerve
➔ *CPT Assistant* Jul 98:10

64405* greater occipital nerve
➔ *CPT Assistant* Jul 98:10

64408* vagus nerve
➔ *CPT Assistant* Jul 98:10

64410* phrenic nerve
➔ *CPT Assistant* Jul 98:10

64412* spinal accessory nerve
➔ *CPT Assistant* Jul 98:10

64413* cervical plexus
➔ *CPT Assistant* Jul 98:10

64415* brachial plexus
➔ *CPT Assistant* Jul 98:10; May 99:8

64417* axillary nerve
➔ *CPT Assistant* Jul 98:10

64418* suprascapular nerve
➔ *CPT Assistant* Jul 98:10

64420* intercostal nerve, single
➔ *CPT Assistant* Jul 98:10

64421* intercostal nerves, multiple, regional block
➔ *CPT Assistant* Jul 98:10

64425* ilioinguinal, iliohypogastric nerves
➔ *CPT Assistant* Jul 98:10

64430* pudendal nerve
➔ *CPT Assistant* Jul 98:10

64435* paracervical (uterine) nerve
➔ *CPT Assistant* Jul 98:10

(64440 has been deleted. To report, see 64479, 64483)

(64441 has been deleted. To report, see 64480, 64484)

(64442 has been deleted. To report, use 64475)

(64443 has been deleted. To report, use 64476)

64445* sciatic nerve
➔ *CPT Assistant* Jul 98:10; May 99:8

64450* other peripheral nerve or branch
➔ *CPT Assistant* Jul 98:10; Nov 99:37; Dec 99:7; *CPT Changes* 2000

(For phenol destruction, see 64622-64627)

(For subarachnoid or subdural injection, see 62280, 62310-62319)

(For epidural or caudal injection, see 62273, 62281-62282, 62310-62319)

(Codes 64470-64484 are unilateral procedures. For bilateral procedures, use modifier '-50')

(For fluoroscopic guidance and localization for needle placement and injection in conjunction with codes 64470-64484, use code 76005)

64470 Injection, anesthetic agent and/or steroid, paravertebral facet joint or facet joint nerve; cervical or thoracic, single level
➔ *CPT Assistant* Nov 99:33, 37; Feb 00:4; *CPT Changes* 2000

+ 64472 cervical or thoracic, each additional level (List separately in addition to code for primary procedure)
➔ *CPT Assistant* Nov 99:33, 37; Feb 00:4; *CPT Changes* 2000

(Use code 64472 in conjunction with code 64470)

64475 lumbar or sacral, single level
➔ *CPT Assistant* Nov 99:33, 37; Feb 00:4; *CPT Changes* 2000

+ 64476 lumbar or sacral, each additional level (List separately in addition to code for primary procedure)
➔ *CPT Assistant* Nov 99:33, 37; Feb 00:4; *CPT Changes* 2000

(Use code 64476 in conjunction with code 64475)

64479 Injection, anesthetic agent and/or steroid, transforaminal epidural; cervical or thoracic, single level
➔ *CPT Assistant* Nov 99:33, 37; Feb 00:4; *CPT Changes* 2000

+ 64480 cervical or thoracic, each additional level (List separately in addition to code for primary procedure)
➔ *CPT Assistant* Nov 99:33, 37; Feb 00:4; *CPT Changes* 2000

(Use code 64480 in conjunction with code 64479)

64483 lumbar or sacral, single level
➔ *CPT Assistant* Nov 99:33, 37; Feb 00:4; *CPT Changes* 2000

+ 64484 lumbar or sacral, each additional level (List separately in addition to code for primary procedure)
➔ *CPT Assistant* Nov 99:33, 37; Feb 00:4; *CPT Changes* 2000

(Use code 64484 in conjunction with code 64483)

Sympathetic Nerves

64505* Injection, anesthetic agent; sphenopalatine ganglion
➔ *CPT Assistant* Jul 98:10

64508* carotid sinus (separate procedure)
➔ *CPT Assistant* Jul 98:10

64510* stellate ganglion (cervical sympathetic)
➔ *CPT Assistant* Jul 98:10

64520 * lumbar or thoracic (paravertebral sympathetic)

→ *CPT Assistant* Jul 98:10

64530 * celiac plexus, with or without radiologic monitoring

→ *CPT Assistant* Jul 98:10

Neurostimulators (Peripheral Nerve)

Codes 64553-64595 apply to both simple and complex neurostimulators. For initial or subsequent electronic analysis and programming of neurostimulator pulse generators, see codes 95970-95975.

64550 Application of surface (transcutaneous) neurostimulator

64553 Percutaneous implantation of neurostimulator electrodes; cranial nerve

→ *CPT Assistant* Nov 99:38; *CPT Changes* 2000

(For open placement of cranial nerve (eg, vagal, trigeminal) neurostimulator pulse generator or receiver, see 61885, 61886, as appropriate)

▲ **64555** peripheral nerve (excludes sacral nerve)

→ *CPT Changes* 2002

64560 autonomic nerve

● **64561** sacral nerve (transforaminal placement)

→ *CPT Changes* 2002

64565 neuromuscular

→ *CPT Assistant* Jul 00:11

64573 Incision for implantation of neurostimulator electrodes; cranial nerve

→ *CPT Assistant* Sep 99:1; Nov 99:38; *CPT Changes* 2000

Implantation Neurostimulator Electrodes, Cranial Nerve (Vagal Nerve Stimulation)
61885, 64573

Open incision for implantation of a neurostimulator electrode (64573) on the vagus nerve (a cranial nerve) with connection of the electrode to an implanted programmable pulse generator (61885) in the infraclavicular area.

(For open placement of cranial nerve (eg, vagal, trigeminal) neurostimulator pulse generator or receiver, see 61885, 61886, as appropriate)

(For revision or removal of cranial nerve (eg, vagal, trigeminal) neurostimulator pulse generator or receiver, use 61888)

▲ **64575** peripheral nerve (excludes sacral nerve)

→ *CPT Changes* 2002

64577 autonomic nerve

64580 neuromuscular

● **64581** sacral nerve (transforaminal placement)

→ *CPT Changes* 2002

64585 Revision or removal of peripheral neurostimulator electrodes

64590 Incision and subcutaneous placement of peripheral neurostimulator pulse generator or receiver, direct or inductive coupling

→ *CPT Assistant* Sep 99:1; *CPT Changes* 2002

64595 Revision or removal of peripheral neurostimulator pulse generator or receiver

Destruction by Neurolytic Agent (eg, Chemical, Thermal, Electrical, Radiofrequency or Chemodenervation)

Somatic Nerves

64600 Destruction by neurolytic agent, trigeminal nerve; supraorbital, infraorbital, mental, or inferior alveolar branch

64605 second and third division branches at foramen ovale

64610 second and third division branches at foramen ovale under radiologic monitoring

64612 Chemodenervation of muscle(s); muscle(s) innervated by facial nerve (eg, for blepharospasm, hemifacial spasm)

→ *CPT Assistant* Oct 98:10; *CPT Changes* 2000; 2001

64613 cervical spinal muscle(s) (eg, for spasmodic torticollis)

→ *CPT Assistant* Sep 00:10; *CPT Changes* 2001

64614 extremity(s) and/or trunk muscle(s) (eg, for dystonia, cerebral palsy, multiple sclerosis)

→ *CPT Changes* 2001

(For chemodenervation for strabismus involving the extraocular muscles, use 67345)

64620 Destruction by neurolytic agent, intercostal nerve

→ *CPT Assistant* Nov 99:38; *CPT Changes* 2000

(Codes 64622-64627 are unilateral procedures. For bilateral procedures, use modifier '-50')

(For fluoroscopic guidance and localization for needle placement and neurolysis in conjunction with codes 64622-64627, use 76005)

64622 Destruction by neurolytic agent, paravertebral facet joint nerve; lumbar or sacral, single level
> *CPT Assistant* Nov 99:33, 39; Dec 99:7; Mar 00:4; *CPT Changes* 2000

+ 64623 lumbar or sacral, each additional level (List separately in addition to code for primary procedure)
> *CPT Assistant* Nov 99:33, 39; Mar 00:4; *CPT Changes* 2000

(Use 64623 in conjunction with code 64622)

64626 cervical or thoracic, single level
> *CPT Assistant* Nov 99:33, 39; Mar 00:4; *CPT Changes* 2000

+ 64627 cervical or thoracic, each additional level (List separately in addition to code for primary procedure)
> *CPT Assistant* Nov 99:33, 39; Mar 00:4; *CPT Changes* 2000

(Use 64627 in conjunction with code 64626)

64630 Destruction by neurolytic agent; pudendal nerve
> *CPT Changes* 2001

64640 other peripheral nerve or branch

Sympathetic Nerves

64680 Destruction by neurolytic agent, celiac plexus, with or without radiologic monitoring
> *CPT Assistant* Feb 99:10

Neuroplasty (Exploration, Neurolysis or Nerve Decompression)

Neuroplasty is the decompression or freeing of intact nerve from scar tissue, including external neurolysis and/or transposition.

(For internal neurolysis requiring use of operating microscope, use 64727)

(For facial nerve decompression, use 69720)

64702 Neuroplasty; digital, one or both, same digit

64704 nerve of hand or foot

64708 Neuroplasty, major peripheral nerve, arm or leg; other than specified

64712 sciatic nerve

64713 brachial plexus

64714 lumbar plexus
> *CPT Assistant* Jun 97:11

64716 Neuroplasty and/or transposition; cranial nerve (specify)

64718 ulnar nerve at elbow

64719 ulnar nerve at wrist

64721 median nerve at carpal tunnel
> *CPT Assistant* Sep 97:10

(For arthroscopic procedure, use 29848)

64722 Decompression; unspecified nerve(s) (specify)
> *CPT Assistant* May 99:11

64726 plantar digital nerve

+ 64727 Internal neurolysis, requiring use of operating microscope (List separately in addition to code for neuroplasty) (Neuroplasty includes external neurolysis)
> *CPT Assistant* Nov 98:19

(Do not report code 69990 in addition to code 64727)

Transection or Avulsion

(For stereotactic lesion of gasserian ganglion, use 61790)

64732 Transection or avulsion of; supraorbital nerve
> *CPT Assistant* Nov 99:39; *CPT Changes* 2000

64734 infraorbital nerve

64736 mental nerve

64738 inferior alveolar nerve by osteotomy

64740 lingual nerve

64742 facial nerve, differential or complete

64744 greater occipital nerve

64746 phrenic nerve

(For section of recurrent laryngeal nerve, use 31595)

64752 vagus nerve (vagotomy), transthoracic

▲ 64755 vagus nerves limited to proximal stomach (selective proximal vagotomy, proximal gastric vagotomy, parietal cell vagotomy, supra- or highly selective vagotomy)
> *CPT Assistant* Nov 99:39; *CPT Changes* 2000; 2002

(For laparoscopic approach, use 43652)

64760 vagus nerve (vagotomy), abdominal
> *CPT Assistant* Nov 99:39; *CPT Changes* 2000

(For laparoscopic approach, use 43651)

64761 pudendal nerve

(64762 has been deleted. To report, use 64761 with modifier '-50')

64763 Transection or avulsion of obturator nerve, extrapelvic, with or without adductor tenotomy

(64764 has been deleted. To report, use 64763 with modifier '-50')

64766 Transection or avulsion of obturator nerve, intrapelvic, with or without adductor tenotomy

(64768 has been deleted. To report, use 64766 with modifier '-50')

64771 Transection or avulsion of other cranial nerve, extradural

64772 Transection or avulsion of other spinal nerve, extradural

(For excision of tender scar, skin and subcutaneous tissue, with or without tiny neuroma, see 11400-11446, 13100-13153)

Excision

Somatic Nerves

(For Morton neurectomy, use 28080)

64774 Excision of neuroma; cutaneous nerve, surgically identifiable

64776 digital nerve, one or both, same digit

+ 64778 digital nerve, each additional digit (List separately in addition to code for primary procedure)

(Use 64778 in conjunction with code 64776)

64782 hand or foot, except digital nerve

+ 64783 hand or foot, each additional nerve, except same digit (List separately in addition to code for primary procedure)

(Use 64783 in conjunction with code 64782)

64784 major peripheral nerve, except sciatic

64786 sciatic nerve

+ 64787 Implantation of nerve end into bone or muscle (List separately in addition to neuroma excision)

(Use 64787 in conjunction with codes 64774-64786)

64788 Excision of neurofibroma or neurolemmoma; cutaneous nerve

64790 major peripheral nerve

64792 extensive (including malignant type)

64795 Biopsy of nerve

Sympathetic Nerves

64802 Sympathectomy, cervical

(64803 has been deleted. To report, use 64802 with modifier '-50')

64804 Sympathectomy, cervicothoracic

(64806 has been deleted. To report, use 64804 with modifier '-50')

64809 Sympathectomy, thoracolumbar

(64811 has been deleted. To report, use 64809 with modifier '-50')

(64814 has been deleted. To report, use 64999)

64818 Sympathectomy, lumbar

(64819 has been deleted. To report, use 64818 with modifier '-50')

▲ 64820 Sympathectomy; digital arteries, each digit
    ➔ *CPT Changes* 2002

▶(Do not report 69990 in addition to code 64820)◀

(64824 has been deleted. To report, use 64999)

● 64821 radial artery
    ➔ *CPT Changes* 2002

▶(Do not report 69990 in addition to code 64821)◀

● 64822 ulnar artery
    ➔ *CPT Changes* 2002

▶(Do not report 69990 in addition to code 64822)◀

● 64823 superficial palmar arch
    ➔ *CPT Changes* 2002

▶(Do not report 69990 in addition to code 64823)◀

Neurorrhaphy

(64830 has been deleted. Use 69990 when the surgical microscope is employed for the microsurgical procedure. Do not use 69990 for visualization with magnifying loupes or corrected vision)

64831 Suture of digital nerve, hand or foot; one nerve

+ 64832 each additional digital nerve (List separately in addition to code for primary procedure)
    ➔ *CPT Assistant* Apr 00:6

(Use 64832 in conjunction with code 64831)

64834 Suture of one nerve, hand or foot; common sensory nerve

64835 median motor thenar

64836 ulnar motor

+ 64837 Suture of each additional nerve, hand or foot (List separately in addition to code for primary procedure)

(Use 64837 in conjunction with codes 64834-64836)

64840 Suture of posterior tibial nerve

64856 Suture of major peripheral nerve, arm or leg, except sciatic; including transposition

64857 without transposition

64858 Suture of sciatic nerve

+ 64859 Suture of each additional major peripheral nerve (List separately in addition to code for primary procedure)

(Use 64859 in conjunction with codes 64856, 64857)

64861 Suture of; brachial plexus

64862 lumbar plexus

64864 Suture of facial nerve; extracranial

64865 infratemporal, with or without grafting

64866 Anastomosis; facial-spinal accessory

64868 facial-hypoglossal

64870 facial-phrenic

+ 64872 Suture of nerve; requiring secondary or delayed suture (List separately in addition to code for primary neurorrhaphy)

(Use 64872 in conjunction with codes 64831-64865)

+ 64874 requiring extensive mobilization, or transposition of nerve (List separately in addition to code for nerve suture)

(Use 64874 in conjunction with codes 64831-64865)

+ 64876 requiring shortening of bone of extremity (List separately in addition to code for nerve suture)

(Use 64876 in conjunction with codes 64831-64865)

Neurorrhaphy With Nerve Graft

64885 Nerve graft (includes obtaining graft), head or neck; up to 4 cm in length
> *CPT Assistant* Nov 00:11

64886 more than 4 cm length
> *CPT Assistant* Nov 00:11

64890 Nerve graft (includes obtaining graft), single strand, hand or foot; up to 4 cm length

64891 more than 4 cm length

64892 Nerve graft (includes obtaining graft), single strand, arm or leg; up to 4 cm length

64893 more than 4 cm length

64895 Nerve graft (includes obtaining graft), multiple strands (cable), hand or foot; up to 4 cm length
> *CPT Assistant* Nov 00:11

64896 more than 4 cm length
> *CPT Assistant* Nov 00:11

64897 Nerve graft (includes obtaining graft), multiple strands (cable), arm or leg; up to 4 cm length
> *CPT Assistant* Nov 00:11

64898 more than 4 cm length
> *CPT Assistant* Nov 00:11

+ 64901 Nerve graft, each additional nerve; single strand (List separately in addition to code for primary procedure)
> *CPT Assistant* Nov 00:11

(Use 64901 in conjunction with codes 64885-64893)

+ 64902 multiple strands (cable) (List separately in addition to code for primary procedure)
> *CPT Assistant* Nov 00:11

(Use 64902 in conjunction with codes 64885, 64886, 64895-64898)

64905 Nerve pedicle transfer; first stage

64907 second stage

Other Procedures

64999 Unlisted procedure, nervous system
> *CPT Assistant* Apr 96:10; Sep 98:16; Oct 98:10; Jan 00:10; Aug 00:7; Sep 00:10

Eye and Ocular Adnexa

(For diagnostic and treatment ophthalmological services, see **Medicine, Ophthalmology,** and 92002 et seq)

(Do not report code 69990 in addition to codes 65091-68850)

Eyeball

Removal of Eye

65091   Evisceration of ocular contents; without implant

65093   with implant

65101   Enucleation of eye; without implant

65103   with implant, muscles not attached to implant

65105   with implant, muscles attached to implant

(For conjunctivoplasty after enucleation, see 68320 et seq)

65110   Exenteration of orbit (does not include skin graft), removal of orbital contents; only

65112   with therapeutic removal of bone

65114   with muscle or myocutaneous flap

(For skin graft to orbit (split skin), see 15120, 15121; free, full thickness, see 15260, 15261)

(For eyelid repair involving more than skin, see 67930 et seq)

Secondary Implant(s) Procedures

An ocular implant is an implant inside muscular cone; an orbital implant is an implant outside muscular cone.

65125   Modification of ocular implant with placement or replacement of pegs (eg, drilling receptacle for prosthesis appendage) (separate procedure)

65130   Insertion of ocular implant secondary; after evisceration, in scleral shell

65135   after enucleation, muscles not attached to implant

65140   after enucleation, muscles attached to implant

65150   Reinsertion of ocular implant; with or without conjunctival graft

65155   with use of foreign material for reinforcement and/or attachment of muscles to implant

65175   Removal of ocular implant

(For orbital implant (implant outside muscle cone) insertion, use 67550; removal, use 67560)

Removal of Foreign Body

(For removal of implanted material: ocular implant, use 65175; anterior segment implant, use 65920; posterior segment implant, use 67120; orbital implant, use 67560)

(For diagnostic x-ray for foreign body, use 70030)

(For diagnostic echography for foreign body, use 76529)

(For removal of foreign body from orbit: frontal approach, use 67413; lateral approach, use 67430; transcranial approach, use 61334)

(For removal of foreign body from eyelid, embedded, use 67938)

(For removal of foreign body from lacrimal system, use 68530)

65205✳ Removal of foreign body, external eye; conjunctival superficial

65210✳   conjunctival embedded (includes concretions), subconjunctival, or scleral nonperforating

65220✳   corneal, without slit lamp

65222✳   corneal, with slit lamp

(For repair of corneal laceration with foreign body, use 65275)

(65230 has been deleted. To report, use 65235)

▲**65235**   Removal of foreign body, intraocular; from anterior chamber of eye or lens

   ➔ *CPT Changes* 2002

(65240, 65245 have been deleted. To report, use 65235)

(For removal of implanted material from anterior segment, use 65920)

65260   from posterior segment, magnetic extraction, anterior or posterior route

65265   from posterior segment, nonmagnetic extraction

(For removal of implanted material from posterior segment, use 67120)

Repair of Laceration

(For fracture of orbit, see 21385 et seq)

(For repair of wound of eyelid, skin, linear, simple, see 12011-12018; intermediate, layered closure, see 12051-12057; linear, complex, see 13150-13160; other, see 67930, 67935)

(For repair of wound of lacrimal system, use 68700)

(For repair of operative wound, use 66250)

Oc/Aud 65091

65270* Repair of laceration; conjunctiva, with or without nonperforating laceration sclera, direct closure

65272 conjunctiva, by mobilization and rearrangement, without hospitalization

65273 conjunctiva, by mobilization and rearrangement, with hospitalization

65275 cornea, nonperforating, with or without removal foreign body

65280 cornea and/or sclera, perforating, not involving uveal tissue

65285 cornea and/or sclera, perforating, with reposition or resection of uveal tissue

65286 application of tissue glue, wounds of cornea and/or sclera

(Repair of laceration includes use of conjunctival flap and restoration of anterior chamber, by air or saline injection when indicated)

(For repair of iris or ciliary body, use 66680)

65290 Repair of wound, extraocular muscle, tendon and/or Tenon's capsule

Anterior Segment

Cornea

Excision

(65300 has been deleted)

65400 Excision of lesion, cornea (keratectomy, lamellar, partial), except pterygium

65410* Biopsy of cornea

65420 Excision or transposition of pterygium; without graft

65426 with graft

Removal or Destruction

65430* Scraping of cornea, diagnostic, for smear and/or culture

65435* Removal of corneal epithelium; with or without chemocauterization (abrasion, curettage)

65436 with application of chelating agent (eg, EDTA)

(65445 has been deleted. To report, use 65450)

65450 Destruction of lesion of cornea by cryotherapy, photocoagulation or thermocauterization

Cryotherapy of Lesion on Cornea
65450

A freezing probe is applied directly to the corneal defect to destroy it.

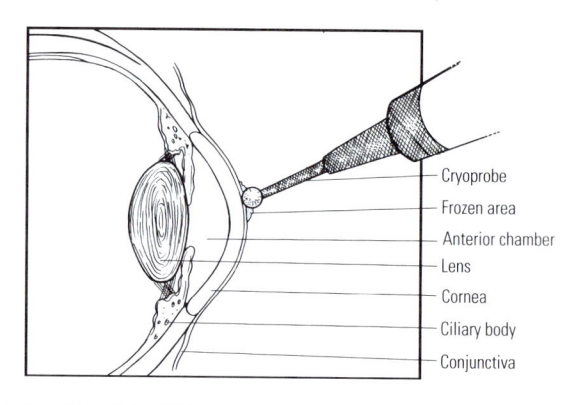

Cryoprobe
Frozen area
Anterior chamber
Lens
Cornea
Ciliary body
Conjunctiva

(65455 has been deleted. To report, use 65450)

65600 Multiple punctures of anterior cornea (eg, for corneal erosion, tattoo)

Keratoplasty

Corneal transplant includes use of fresh or preserved grafts, and preparation of donor material.

(Keratoplasty excludes refractive keratoplasty procedures, 65760, 65765, and 65767)

65710 Keratoplasty (corneal transplant); lamellar

(65720, 65725 have been deleted. To report, use 65710)

65730 penetrating (except in aphakia)

(65740, 65745 have been deleted. To report, use 65730)

65750 penetrating (in aphakia)

65755 penetrating (in pseudophakia)

Other Procedures

65760 Keratomileusis

65765 Keratophakia

65767 Epikeratoplasty

65770 Keratoprosthesis

65771 Radial keratotomy

65772 Corneal relaxing incision for correction of surgically induced astigmatism

65775 Corneal wedge resection for correction of surgically induced astigmatism

(For fitting of contact lens for treatment of disease, use 92070)

(For unlisted procedures on cornea, use 66999)

Anterior Chamber

Incision

65800* Paracentesis of anterior chamber of eye (separate procedure); with diagnostic aspiration of aqueous

65805*   with therapeutic release of aqueous

65810   with removal of vitreous and/or discission of anterior hyaloid membrane, with or without air injection

65815   with removal of blood, with or without irrigation and/or air injection

(For injection, see 66020-66030)

(For removal of blood clot, use 65930)

65820 Goniotomy

(65825, 65830 have been deleted)

65850 Trabeculotomy ab externo

65855 Trabeculoplasty by laser surgery, one or more sessions (defined treatment series)
> *CPT Assistant* Mar 98:7

(If re-treatment is necessary after several months because of disease progression, a new treatment or treatment series should be reported with a modifier, if necessary, to indicate lesser or greater complexity)

(For trabeculectomy, use 66170)

65860 Severing adhesions of anterior segment, laser technique (separate procedure)

Other Procedures

65865 Severing adhesions of anterior segment of eye, incisional technique (with or without injection of air or liquid) (separate procedure); goniosynechiae

(For trabeculoplasty by laser surgery, use 65855)

65870   anterior synechiae, except goniosynechiae

65875   posterior synechiae

65880   corneovitreal adhesions

(For laser surgery, use 66821)

▲ **65900** Removal of epithelial downgrowth, anterior chamber of eye
> *CPT Changes* 2002

▲ **65920** Removal of implanted material, anterior segment of eye
> *CPT Changes* 2002

▲ **65930** Removal of blood clot, anterior segment of eye
> *CPT Changes* 2002

▲ **66020** Injection, anterior chamber of eye (separate procedure); air or liquid
> *CPT Changes* 2002

66030*   medication

(For unlisted procedures on anterior segment, use 66999)

Anterior Sclera

Excision

(For removal of intraocular foreign body, use 65235)

(For operations on posterior sclera, use 67250, 67255)

66130 Excision of lesion, sclera

66150 Fistulization of sclera for glaucoma; trephination with iridectomy

66155   thermocauterization with iridectomy

66160   sclerectomy with punch or scissors, with iridectomy

66165   iridencleisis or iridotasis

66170   trabeculectomy ab externo in absence of previous surgery

(For trabeculotomy ab externo, use 65850)

(For repair of operative wound, use 66250)

66172   trabeculectomy ab externo with scarring from previous ocular surgery or trauma (includes injection of antifibrotic agents)

66180 Aqueous shunt to extraocular reservoir (eg, Molteno, Schocket, Denver-Krupin)

66185 Revision of aqueous shunt to extraocular reservoir

(For removal of implanted shunt, use 67120)

Repair or Revision

(For scleral procedures in retinal surgery, see 67101 et seq)

66220 Repair of scleral staphyloma; without graft

66225   with graft

(For scleral reinforcement, see 67250, 67255)

66250 Revision or repair of operative wound of anterior segment, any type, early or late, major or minor procedure

(For unlisted procedures on anterior sclera, use 66999)

Iris, Ciliary Body

Incision

66500 Iridotomy by stab incision (separate procedure); except transfixion

66505   with transfixion as for iris bombe

(For iridotomy by photocoagulation, use 66761)

Excision

66600   Iridectomy, with corneoscleral or corneal section; for removal of lesion

66605   with cyclectomy

66625   peripheral for glaucoma (separate procedure)

66630   sector for glaucoma (separate procedure)

66635   optical (separate procedure)

(For coreoplasty by photocoagulation, use 66762)

Repair

66680   Repair of iris, ciliary body (as for iridodialysis)

(For reposition or resection of uveal tissue with perforating wound of cornea or sclera, use 65285)

66682   Suture of iris, ciliary body (separate procedure) with retrieval of suture through small incision (eg, McCannel suture)

Destruction

66700   Ciliary body destruction; diathermy

(66701, 66702 have been deleted. To report, see 66700, 66710, 66720, 66740)

66710   cyclophotocoagulation

66720   cryotherapy

(66721 has been deleted. To report, see 66700, 66710, 66720, 66740)

66740   cyclodialysis

(66741 has been deleted. To report, see 66700, 66710, 66720, 66740)

66761   Iridotomy/iridectomy by laser surgery (eg, for glaucoma) (one or more sessions)
→ *CPT Assistant* Mar 98:7

66762   Iridoplasty by photocoagulation (one or more sessions) (eg, for improvement of vision, for widening of anterior chamber angle)
→ *CPT Assistant* Mar 98:7

66770   Destruction of cyst or lesion iris or ciliary body (nonexcisional procedure)

(For excision lesion iris, ciliary body, see 66600, 66605; for removal of epithelial downgrowth, use 65900)

(For unlisted procedures on iris, ciliary body, use 66999)

Lens

Incision

(66800, 66801 have been deleted. To report, use 66999)

(66802 has been deleted)

66820   Discission of secondary membranous cataract (opacified posterior lens capsule and/or anterior hyaloid); stab incision technique (Ziegler or Wheeler knife)

66821   laser surgery (eg, YAG laser) (one or more stages)

66825   Repositioning of intraocular lens prosthesis, requiring an incision (separate procedure)

Removal Cataract

Lateral canthotomy, iridectomy, iridotomy, anterior capsulotomy, posterior capsulotomy, the use of viscoelastic agents, enzymatic zonulysis, use of other pharmacologic agents, and subconjunctival or sub-tenon injections are included as part of the code for the extraction of lens.

66830   Removal of secondary membranous cataract (opacified posterior lens capsule and/or anterior hyaloid) with corneo-scleral section, with or without iridectomy (iridocapsulotomy, iridocapsulectomy)

66840   Removal of lens material; aspiration technique, one or more stages
→ *CPT Assistant* Fall 92:4

66850   phacofragmentation technique (mechanical or ultrasonic) (eg, phacoemulsification), with aspiration
→ *CPT Assistant* Fall 92:6

66852   pars plana approach, with or without vitrectomy
→ *CPT Assistant* Fall 92:8

(66915 has been deleted)

66920   intracapsular
→ *CPT Assistant* Fall 92:8

66930   intracapsular, for dislocated lens
→ *CPT Assistant* Fall 92:8

66940   extracapsular (other than 66840, 66850, 66852)
→ *CPT Assistant* Fall 92:4

(66945 has been deleted. To report, see 66920-66940)

(For removal of intralenticular foreign body without lens extraction, use 65235)

(For repair of operative wound, use 66250)

(66980 has been deleted. To report, see 66983, 66984)

▲**66982** Extracapsular cataract removal with insertion of intraocular lens prosthesis (one stage procedure), manual or mechanical technique (eg, irrigation and aspiration or phacoemulsification), complex, requiring devices or techniques not generally used in routine cataract surgery (eg, iris expansion device, suture support for intraocular lens, or primary posterior capsulorrhexis) or performed on patients in the amblyogenic developmental stage

➔ *CPT Assistant* Feb 01:7; *CPT Changes* 2001; 2002

66983 Intracapsular cataract extraction with insertion of intraocular lens prosthesis (one stage procedure)

➔ *CPT Assistant* Fall 92:5, 8

66984 Extracapsular cataract removal with insertion of intraocular lens prosthesis (one stage procedure), manual or mechanical technique (eg, irrigation and aspiration or phacoemulsification)

➔ *CPT Assistant* Fall 92:5, 8; Feb 01:7

(For complex extracapsular cataract removal, use 66982)

66985 Insertion of intraocular lens prosthesis (secondary implant), not associated with concurrent cataract removal

(To code implant at time of concurrent cataract surgery, see 66982, 66983, 66984)

(For intraocular lens prosthesis supplied by physician, use 99070)

(For ultrasonic determination of intraocular lens power, use 76519)

(For removal of implanted material from anterior segment, use 65920)

(For secondary fixation (separate procedure), use 66682)

66986 Exchange of intraocular lens

Other Procedures

66999 Unlisted procedure, anterior segment of eye

Posterior Segment

Vitreous

67005 Removal of vitreous, anterior approach (open sky technique or limbal incision); partial removal

➔ *CPT Assistant* Fall 92:4

67010 subtotal removal with mechanical vitrectomy

➔ *CPT Assistant* Fall 92:4

(For removal of vitreous by paracentesis of anterior chamber, use 65810)

(For removal of corneovitreal adhesions, use 65880)

67015 Aspiration or release of vitreous, subretinal or choroidal fluid, pars plana approach (posterior sclerotomy)

67025 Injection of vitreous substitute, pars plana or limbal approach, (fluid-gas exchange), with or without aspiration (separate procedure)

67027 Implantation of intravitreal drug delivery system (eg, ganciclovir implant), includes concomitant removal of vitreous

➔ *CPT Assistant* Nov 97:23; Nov 98:19

Intravitreal Drug Delivery System
67027

A drug delivery system that releases medication into the vitreous is implanted into the vitreous by pars plana incision.

(For removal, use 67121)

67028 Intravitreal injection of a pharmacologic agent (separate procedure)

67030 Discission of vitreous strands (without removal), pars plana approach

67031 Severing of vitreous strands, vitreous face adhesions, sheets, membranes or opacities, laser surgery (one or more stages)

(67035 has been deleted. To report, use 67036)

67036 Vitrectomy, mechanical, pars plana approach;

➔ *CPT Assistant* Fall 92:6

67038 with epiretinal membrane stripping

67039 with focal endolaser photocoagulation

67040 with endolaser panretinal photocoagulation

(For associated lensectomy, use 66850)

(For use of vitrectomy in retinal detachment surgery, use 67108)

(For associated removal of foreign body, see 65260, 65265)

(For unlisted procedures on vitreous, use 67299)

Retina or Choroid

Repair

(If diathermy, cryotherapy and/or photocoagulation are combined, report under principal modality used)

67101   Repair of retinal detachment, one or more sessions; cryotherapy or diathermy, with or without drainage of subretinal fluid
➜ *CPT Assistant* Mar 98:7

(67102, 67103 have been deleted. To report, use 67101)

(67104 has been deleted. To report, use 67105)

67105   photocoagulation, with or without drainage of subretinal fluid
➜ *CPT Assistant* Mar 98:7

(67106 has been deleted. To report, use 67105)

67107   Repair of retinal detachment; scleral buckling (such as lamellar scleral dissection, imbrication or encircling procedure), with or without implant, with or without cryotherapy, photocoagulation, and drainage of subretinal fluid

Repair of Retinal Detachment
67107

The retinal tear is treated externally by placing a hot or cold probe over the scleral and then depressing it. The burn seals the choroid to the retina at the site of the tear. The healing scar is supported by the encircling band which buckles the eye.

Clove hitch suture securing ends of buckle

Silicone sponge

Encircling silicone exoplant

67108   with vitrectomy, any method, with or without air or gas tamponade, focal endolaser photocoagulation, cryotherapy, drainage of subretinal fluid, scleral buckling, and/or removal of lens by same technique

(67109 has been deleted. To report, use 67299)

67110   by injection of air or other gas (eg, pneumatic retinopexy)

67112   by scleral buckling or vitrectomy, on patient having previous ipsilateral retinal detachment repair(s) using scleral buckling or vitrectomy techniques

(For aspiration or drainage of subretinal or subchoroidal fluid, use 67015)

67115   Release of encircling material (posterior segment)

67120   Removal of implanted material, posterior segment; extraocular

67121   intraocular
➜ *CPT Assistant* Nov 97:23; Nov 98:19

(For removal from anterior segment, use 65920)

(For removal of foreign body, see 65260, 65265)

Prophylaxis

Repetitive services. The services listed below are often performed in multiple sessions or groups of sessions. The methods of reporting vary.

The following descriptors are intended to include all sessions in a defined treatment period.

67141   Prophylaxis of retinal detachment (eg, retinal break, lattice degeneration) without drainage, one or more sessions; cryotherapy, diathermy
➜ *CPT Assistant* Mar 98:7

(67142, 67143 have been deleted. To report, use 67141)

(67144 has been deleted. To report, use 67145)

67145   photocoagulation (laser or xenon arc)
➜ *CPT Assistant* Fall 92:4; Mar 98:7

(67146 has been deleted. To report, use 67145)

Destruction

67208   Destruction of localized lesion of retina (eg, macular edema, tumors), one or more sessions; cryotherapy, diathermy
➜ *CPT Assistant* Mar 98:7; Nov 98:19

67210   photocoagulation
➜ *CPT Assistant* Mar 98:7; Nov 98:19

(67212, 67213 have been deleted. To report, use 67208)

(67214, 67216 have been deleted. To report, use 67210)

67218   radiation by implantation of source (includes removal of source)
➜ *CPT Assistant* Mar 98:7

67220   Destruction of localized lesion of choroid (eg, choroidal neovascularization); photocoagulation (eg, laser), one or more sessions
➜ *CPT Assistant* Nov 98:19; Nov 99:39; Feb 01:7; *CPT Changes* 2000; 2001

▶(For destruction of macular drusen, photocoagulation, use Category III code 0017T)◀

►(For destruction of localized lesion of choroid by transpupillary thermotherapy, use Category III code 0016T)◄

67221   photodynamic therapy (includes intravenous infusion)
   → *CPT Changes* 2001

(67222, 67223 have been deleted. To report, use 67227)

►(67224 has been deleted. To report, use 67228)◄

+ ● 67225   photodynamic therapy, second eye, at single session (List separately in addition to code for primary eye treatment)
   → *CPT Changes* 2002

►(Use 67225 in conjunction with code 67221)◄

►(67226 has been deleted. To report, use 67228)◄

67227   Destruction of extensive or progressive retinopathy (eg, diabetic retinopathy), one or more sessions; cryotherapy, diathermy
   → *CPT Assistant* Mar 98:7

67228   photocoagulation (laser or xenon arc)
   → *CPT Assistant* Mar 98:7

(For unlisted procedures on retina, use 67299)

Sclera

Repair

(For excision lesion sclera, use 66130)

67250   Scleral reinforcement (separate procedure); without graft

67255   with graft

(For repair scleral staphyloma, see 66220, 66225)

Other Procedures

67299   Unlisted procedure, posterior segment

Ocular Adnexa

Extraocular Muscles of Right Eye

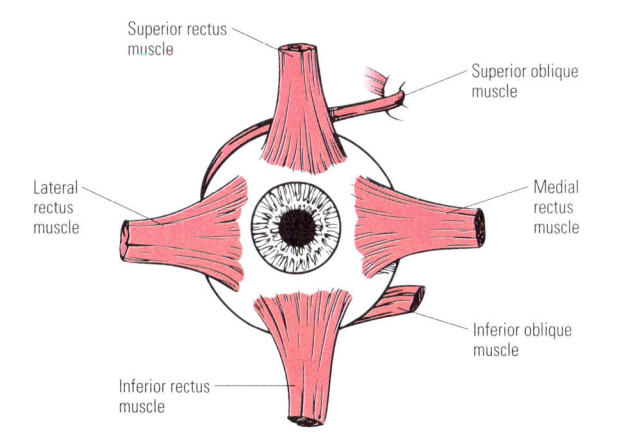

Extraocular Muscles

67311   Strabismus surgery, recession or resection procedure; one horizontal muscle
   → *CPT Assistant* Summer 93:20; Mar 97:5; Nov 98:19

Strabismus Surgery—Horizontal Muscles
67311–67312

In Figure A, the medial or lateral rectus muscle is made weaker by recession (retroplacement of the muscle attachment). In Figure B, it is made stronger by resection (removal of a segment). Use 67311 for one horizontal muscle and 67312 for two muscles of the same eye.

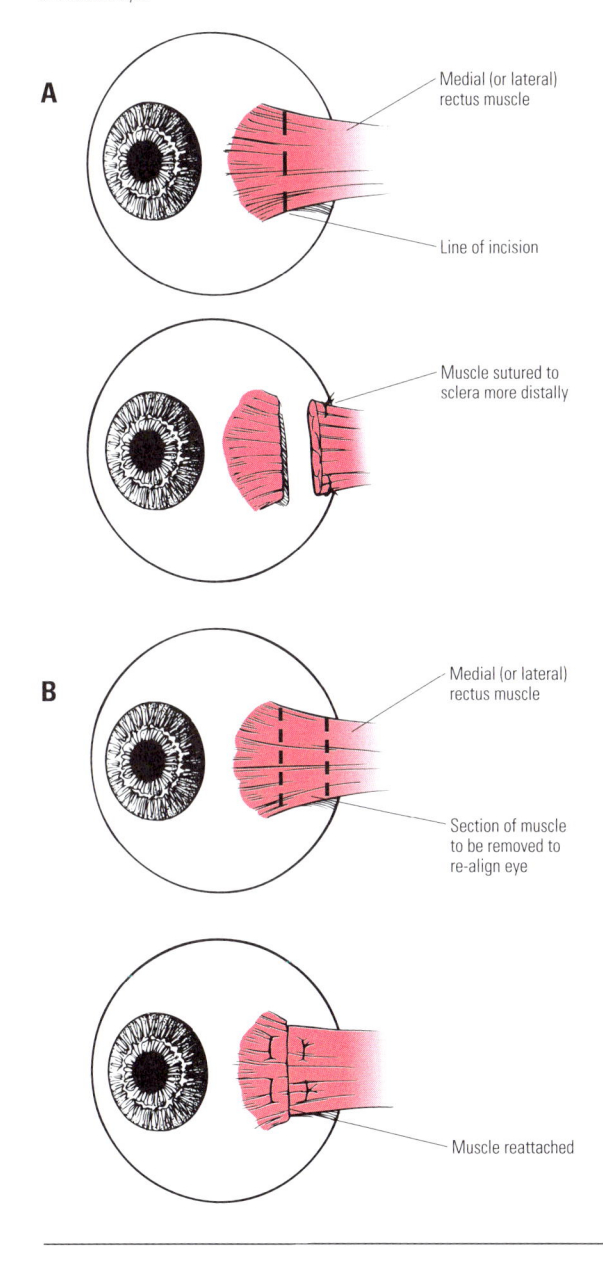

67312   two horizontal muscles
   → *CPT Assistant* Summer 93:20; Mar 97:5

(67313 has been deleted)

67314   one vertical muscle (excluding superior oblique)

→ *CPT Assistant* Summer 93:20; Mar 97:5

Strabismus Surgery—Vertical Muscles
67314-67316

Either the superior or inferior rectus muscle is strengthened or weakened. Use 67316 for two muscles of the same eye.

Inferior (or superior) rectus muscle

67316   two or more vertical muscles (excluding superior oblique)

→ *CPT Assistant* Summer 93:20; Mar 97:5

(For adjustable sutures, use 67335 in addition to codes 67311-67334 for primary procedure reflecting number of muscles operated on)

67318   Strabismus surgery, any procedure, superior oblique muscle

→ *CPT Assistant* Summer 93:20; Mar 97:5; Nov 98:19

+ 67320   Transposition procedure (eg, for paretic extraocular muscle), any extraocular muscle (specify) (List separately in addition to code for primary procedure)

→ *CPT Assistant* Summer 93:20; Mar 97:5

Transposition Procedure
67320

The extraocular muscles are transposed.

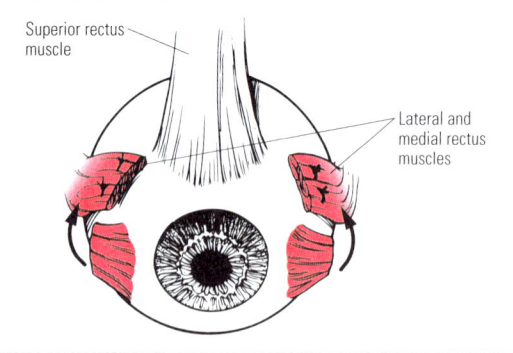

Superior rectus muscle

Lateral and medial rectus muscles

(Use 67320 in conjunction with codes 67311-67318)

+ 67331   Strabismus surgery on patient with previous eye surgery or injury that did not involve the extraocular muscles (List separately in addition to code for primary procedure)

→ *CPT Assistant* Summer 93:20; Mar 97:5

(Use 67331 in conjunction with codes 67311-67318)

+ 67332   Strabismus surgery on patient with scarring of extraocular muscles (eg, prior ocular injury, strabismus or retinal detachment surgery) or restrictive myopathy (eg, dysthyroid ophthalmopathy) (List separately in addition to code for primary procedure)

→ *CPT Assistant* Summer 93:20; Mar 97:5

(Use 67332 in conjunction with codes 67311-67318)

+ 67334   Strabismus surgery by posterior fixation suture technique, with or without muscle recession (List separately in addition to code for primary procedure)

→ *CPT Assistant* Summer 93:20; Mar 97:5

(Use 67334 in conjunction with codes 67311-67318)

+ 67335   Placement of adjustable suture(s) during strabismus surgery, including postoperative adjustment(s) of suture(s) (List separately in addition to code for specific strabismus surgery)

→ *CPT Assistant* Summer 93:20; Mar 97:5

(Use 67335 in conjunction with codes 67311-67334)

Strabismus Surgery—Adjustable Sutures
67335

Sutures are tied in such a way as to allow the tension on the muscle to be adjusted after the anesthetic is not affecting the position of the globe.

Superior rectus muscle

Adjustable suture

+ 67340   Strabismus surgery involving exploration and/or repair of detached extraocular muscle(s) (List separately in addition to code for primary procedure)

→ *CPT Assistant* Summer 93:20; Mar 97:5

(Use 67340 in conjunction with codes 67311-67334)

67343   Release of extensive scar tissue without detaching extraocular muscle (separate procedure)

→ *CPT Assistant* Summer 93:20; Mar 97:5

(Use 67343 in conjunction with codes 67311-67340, when such procedures are performed other than on the affected muscle)

67345   Chemodenervation of extraocular muscle

→ *CPT Assistant* Summer 93:20; Mar 97:5

(For chemodenervation for blepharospasm and other neurological disorders, see 64612 and 64613)

Other Procedures

67350 Biopsy of extraocular muscle

(For repair of wound, extraocular muscle, tendon or Tenon's capsule, use 65290)

67399 Unlisted procedure, ocular muscle

Orbit

Exploration, Excision, Decompression

67400 Orbitotomy without bone flap (frontal or transconjunctival approach); for exploration, with or without biopsy

67405 with drainage only

67412 with removal of lesion

67413 with removal of foreign body

67414 with removal of bone for decompression
➔ *CPT Assistant* Jul 99:10

67415 Fine needle aspiration of orbital contents

(For exenteration, enucleation, and repair, see 65101 et seq; for optic nerve decompression, use 67570)

67420 Orbitotomy with bone flap or window, lateral approach (eg, Kroenlein); with removal of lesion

67430 with removal of foreign body

67440 with drainage

67445 with removal of bone for decompression

(For optic nerve sheath decompression, use 67570)

67450 for exploration, with or without biopsy

(For orbitotomy, transcranial approach, see 61330-61334)

(For orbital implant, see 67550, 67560)

(For removal of eyeball or for repair after removal, see 65091-65175)

Other Procedures

67500* Retrobulbar injection; medication (separate procedure, does not include supply of medication)

67505 alcohol

(67510 has been deleted. To report, use 67599)

▲ **67515*** Injection of medication or other substance into Tenon's capsule
➔ *CPT Changes* 2002

(For subconjunctival injection, use 68200)

67550 Orbital implant (implant outside muscle cone); insertion

67560 removal or revision

(For ocular implant (implant inside muscle cone), see 65093-65105, 65130-65175)

(For treatment of fractures of malar area, orbit, see 21355 et seq)

67570 Optic nerve decompression (eg, incision or fenestration of optic nerve sheath)

67599 Unlisted procedure, orbit

Eyelids

Incision

67700* Blepharotomy, drainage of abscess, eyelid

67710* Severing of tarsorrhaphy

67715* Canthotomy (separate procedure)

(For canthoplasty, use 67950)

(For division of symblepharon, use 68340)

Excision

Codes for removal of lesion include more than skin (ie, involving lid margin, tarsus, and/or palpebral conjunctiva).

(For removal of lesion, involving mainly skin of eyelid, see 11310-11313; 11440-11446, 11640-11646; 17000-17004)

(For repair of wounds, blepharoplasty, grafts, reconstructive surgery, see 67930-67975)

67800 Excision of chalazion; single
➔ *CPT Assistant* Sept 99:10

67801 multiple, same lid

67805 multiple, different lids
➔ *CPT Assistant* Sep 99:10

67808 under general anesthesia and/or requiring hospitalization, single or multiple

67810* Biopsy of eyelid

67820* Correction of trichiasis; epilation, by forceps only
➔ *CPT Assistant* Jul 98:10

Trichiasis
67820-67825

When the eyelashes are ingrown or misdirected (trichiasis), the physician uses a biomicroscope and forceps to remove the offending eyelashes. Report 67825 when cryosurgery or electrosurgery is used to destroy the follicles.

Forceps

Ingrown or misdirected eyelashes

67825 *   epilation by other than forceps (eg, by electrosurgery, cryotherapy, laser surgery)
➔ *CPT Assistant* Jul 98:10

67830   incision of lid margin

67835   incision of lid margin, with free mucous membrane graft

67840 *   Excision of lesion of eyelid (except chalazion) without closure or with simple direct closure

(For excision and repair of eyelid by reconstructive surgery, see 67961, 67966)

67850 *   Destruction of lesion of lid margin (up to 1 cm)

(For Mohs micrographic surgery, see 17304-17310)

(For initiation or follow-up care of topical chemotherapy (eg, 5-FU or similar agents), see appropriate office visits)

Tarsorrhaphy

67875   Temporary closure of eyelids by suture (eg, Frost suture)

67880   Construction of intermarginal adhesions, median tarsorrhaphy, or canthorrhaphy;

67882   with transposition of tarsal plate

(For severing of tarsorrhaphy, use 67710)

(For canthoplasty, reconstruction canthus, use 67950)

(For canthotomy, use 67715)

Repair (Brow Ptosis, Blepharoptosis, Lid Retraction, Ectropion, Entropion)

67900   Repair of brow ptosis (supraciliary, mid-forehead or coronal approach)

(For forehead rhytidectomy, use 15824)

67901   Repair of blepharoptosis; frontalis muscle technique with suture or other material
➔ *CPT Assistant* Sep 00:7

67902   frontalis muscle technique with fascial sling (includes obtaining fascia)
➔ *CPT Assistant* Sep 00:7

67903   (tarso) levator resection or advancement, internal approach
➔ *CPT Assistant* Sep 00:7

67904   (tarso) levator resection or advancement, external approach
➔ *CPT Assistant* Sep 00:7

67906   superior rectus technique with fascial sling (includes obtaining fascia)
➔ *CPT Assistant* Sep 00:7

(67907 has been deleted. To report, use 67999)

67908   conjunctivo-tarso-Muller's muscle-levator resection (eg, Fasanella-Servat type)
➔ *CPT Assistant* Sep 00:7

67909   Reduction of overcorrection of ptosis

67911   Correction of lid retraction

(For obtaining autogenous graft materials, see 20920, 20922 or 20926)

(For correction of trichiasis by mucous membrane graft, use 67835)

67914   Repair of ectropion; suture

67915   thermocauterization

67916   blepharoplasty, excision tarsal wedge

67917   blepharoplasty, extensive (eg, Kuhnt-Szymanowski or tarsal strip operations)

(For correction of everted punctum, use 68705)

67921   Repair of entropion; suture

67922   thermocauterization

67923   blepharoplasty, excision tarsal wedge

67924   blepharoplasty, extensive (eg, Wheeler operation)

(For repair of cicatricial ectropion or entropion requiring scar excision or skin graft, see also 67961 et seq)

Reconstruction

Codes for blepharoplasty involve more than skin (ie, involving lid margin, tarsus, and/or palpebral conjunctiva).

67930   Suture of recent wound, eyelid, involving lid margin, tarsus, and/or palpebral conjunctiva direct closure; partial thickness

67935   full thickness

67938   Removal of embedded foreign body, eyelid

(For repair of skin of eyelid, see 12011-12018; 12051-12057; 13150-13153)

(For tarsorrhaphy, canthorrhaphy, see 67880, 67882)

(For repair of blepharoptosis and lid retraction, see 67901-67911)

(For blepharoplasty for entropion, ectropion, see 67916, 67917, 67923, 67924)

(For correction of blepharochalasis (blepharorhytidectomy), see 15820-15823)

(For repair of skin of eyelid, adjacent tissue transfer, see 14060, 14061; preparation for graft, use 15000; free graft, see 15120, 15121, 15260, 15261)

(For excision of lesion of eyelid, use 67800 et seq)

(For repair of lacrimal canaliculi, use 68700)

67950   Canthoplasty (reconstruction of canthus)

67961   Excision and repair of eyelid, involving lid margin, tarsus, conjunctiva, canthus, or full thickness, may include preparation for skin graft or pedicle flap with adjacent tissue transfer or rearrangement; up to one-fourth of lid margin

67966	over one-fourth of lid margin		**68330**	Repair of symblepharon; conjunctivoplasty, without graft

67966 over one-fourth of lid margin

(For canthoplasty, use 67950)

(For free skin grafts, see 15120, 15121, 15260, 15261)

(For tubed pedicle flap preparation, use 15576; for delay, use 15630; for attachment, use 15650)

67971 Reconstruction of eyelid, full thickness by transfer of tarsoconjunctival flap from opposing eyelid; up to two-thirds of eyelid, one stage or first stage

67973 total eyelid, lower, one stage or first stage

67974 total eyelid, upper, one stage or first stage

67975 second stage

Other Procedures

67999 Unlisted procedure, eyelids

Conjunctiva

(For removal of foreign body, see 65205 et seq)

Incision and Drainage

68020 Incision of conjunctiva, drainage of cyst

68040 Expression of conjunctival follicles (eg, for trachoma)

Excision and/or Destruction

68100 Biopsy of conjunctiva

68110 Excision of lesion, conjunctiva; up to 1 cm

68115 over 1 cm

68130 with adjacent sclera

68135✳ Destruction of lesion, conjunctiva

Injection

(For injection into Tenon's capsule or retrobulbar injection, see 67500-67515)

68200✳ Subconjunctival injection

Conjunctivoplasty

(For wound repair, see 65270-65273)

68320 Conjunctivoplasty; with conjunctival graft or extensive rearrangement

68325 with buccal mucous membrane graft (includes obtaining graft)

68326 Conjunctivoplasty, reconstruction cul-de-sac; with conjunctival graft or extensive rearrangement

68328 with buccal mucous membrane graft (includes obtaining graft)

68330 Repair of symblepharon; conjunctivoplasty, without graft

68335 with free graft conjunctiva or buccal mucous membrane (includes obtaining graft)

68340 division of symblepharon, with or without insertion of conformer or contact lens

Other Procedures

68360 Conjunctival flap; bridge or partial (separate procedure)

68362 total (such as Gunderson thin flap or purse string flap)

(For conjunctival flap for perforating injury, see 65280, 65285)

(For repair of operative wound, use 66250)

(For removal of conjunctival foreign body, see 65205, 65210)

68399 Unlisted procedure, conjunctiva

Lacrimal System

Incision

68400 Incision, drainage of lacrimal gland

68420 Incision, drainage of lacrimal sac (dacryocystotomy or dacryocystostomy)

68440✳ Snip incision of lacrimal punctum

Excision

68500 Excision of lacrimal gland (dacryoadenectomy), except for tumor; total

68505 partial

68510 Biopsy of lacrimal gland

68520 Excision of lacrimal sac (dacryocystectomy)

68525 Biopsy of lacrimal sac

68530 Removal of foreign body or dacryolith, lacrimal passages

68540 Excision of lacrimal gland tumor; frontal approach

68550 involving osteotomy

Repair

68700 Plastic repair of canaliculi

68705 Correction of everted punctum, cautery

68720 Dacryocystorhinostomy (fistulization of lacrimal sac to nasal cavity)

68745 Conjunctivorhinostomy (fistulization of conjunctiva to nasal cavity); without tube

68750 with insertion of tube or stent

68760   Closure of the lacrimal punctum; by thermocauterization, ligation, or laser surgery

68761   by plug, each
> *CPT Assistant* Jun 96:10

Closure of Lacrimal Punctum by Plug
68761

The physician inserts a lacrimal duct implant into a lacrimal punctum.

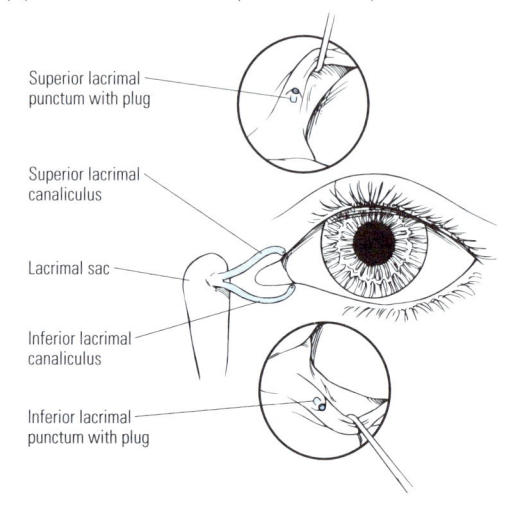

68770   Closure of lacrimal fistula (separate procedure)

Probing and/or Related Procedures

(68800 has been deleted. To report, use 68801)

68801 *   Dilation of lacrimal punctum, with or without irrigation

(To report a bilateral procedure, use 68801 with modifier '-50')

68810 *   Probing of nasolacrimal duct, with or without irrigation;

68811   requiring general anesthesia

68815   with insertion of tube or stent

(See also 92018)

(To report a bilateral procedure, use 68810, 68811, or 68815 with modifier '-50')

(68820, 68825, 68830 have been deleted. To report, see 68810, 68811, or 68815)

Probing of Nasolacrimal Duct
68815

A balloon catheter is in the nasolacrimal duct.

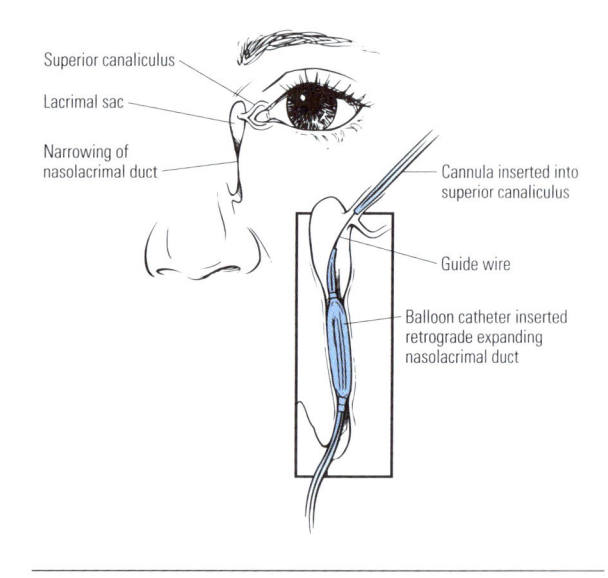

68840 *   Probing of lacrimal canaliculi, with or without irrigation

68850 *   Injection of contrast medium for dacryocystography
> *CPT Assistant* Feb 01:7

(For radiological supervision and interpretation, see 70170, 78660)

Other Procedures

68899   Unlisted procedure, lacrimal system

⊘ =Modifier '-51' Exempt   ▶ ◀=New or Revised Text   ✚=Add-on Code   CPT 2002

Auditory System

(For diagnostic services (eg, audiometry, vestibular tests), see 92502 et seq)

External Ear

Incision

69000* Drainage external ear, abscess or hematoma; simple
→ *CPT Assistant* Oct 97:11; Oct 99:10

69005 complicated

69020* Drainage external auditory canal, abscess
→ *CPT Assistant* Oct 97:11

69090 Ear piercing

Excision

69100 Biopsy external ear

69105 Biopsy external auditory canal

69110 Excision external ear; partial, simple repair

69120 complete amputation

(For reconstruction of ear, see 15120 et seq)

69140 Excision exostosis(es), external auditory canal

69145 Excision soft tissue lesion, external auditory canal

69150 Radical excision external auditory canal lesion; without neck dissection

69155 with neck dissection

(For resection of temporal bone, use 69535)

(For skin grafting, see 15000-15261)

Removal of Foreign Body

69200 Removal foreign body from external auditory canal; without general anesthesia

69205 with general anesthesia

69210 Removal impacted cerumen (separate procedure), one or both ears

69220 Debridement, mastoidectomy cavity, simple (eg, routine cleaning)

(69221 has been deleted. To report, use 69220 with modifier '-50')

69222 Debridement, mastoidectomy cavity, complex (eg, with anesthesia or more than routine cleaning)

(69223 has been deleted. To report, use 69222 with modifier '-50')

Repair

(For suture of wound or injury of external ear, see 12011-14300)

69300 Otoplasty, protruding ear, with or without size reduction

(69301 has been deleted. To report, use 69300 with modifier '-50')

▲ **69310** Reconstruction of external auditory canal (meatoplasty) (eg, for stenosis due to injury, infection) (separate procedure)
→ *CPT Changes* 2002

69320 Reconstruction external auditory canal for congenital atresia, single stage

(For combination with middle ear reconstruction, see 69631, 69641)

(For other reconstructive procedures with grafts (eg, skin, cartilage, bone), see 13150-15760, 21230-21235)

Other Procedures

(For otoscopy under general anesthesia, use 92502)

69399 Unlisted procedure, external ear

Middle Ear

Introduction

69400 Eustachian tube inflation, transnasal; with catheterization

69401 without catheterization

69405 Eustachian tube catheterization, transtympanic

69410 Focal application of phase control substance, middle ear (baffle technique)

Incision

69420* Myringotomy including aspiration and/or eustachian tube inflation

69421* Myringotomy including aspiration and/or eustachian tube inflation requiring general anesthesia

69424 Ventilating tube removal when originally inserted by another physician

(69425 has been deleted. To report, use 69424 with modifier '-50')

(Tympanostomy 69431-69435 has been revised as 69433, 69436)

69433 * Tympanostomy (requiring insertion of ventilating tube), local or topical anesthesia

Tympanostomy
69433-69436

A ventilating tube is inserted into the opening of the tympanum.

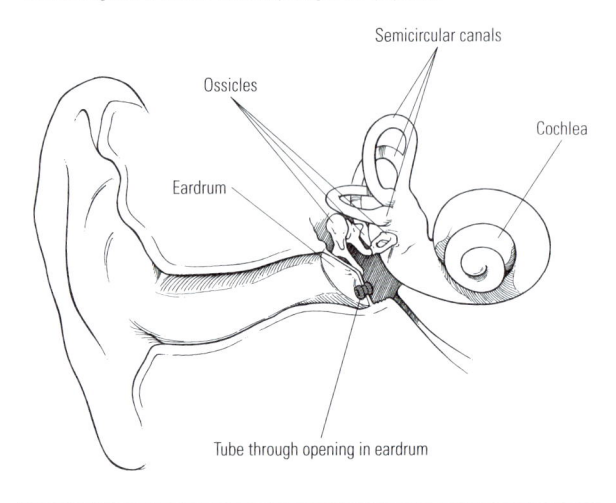

Semicircular canals
Ossicles
Cochlea
Eardrum
Tube through opening in eardrum

(69434 has been deleted. To report, use 69433 with modifier '-50')

69436 Tympanostomy (requiring insertion of ventilating tube), general anesthesia

(69437 has been deleted. To report, use 69436 with modifier '-50')

69440 Middle ear exploration through postauricular or ear canal incision

(For atticotomy, see 69601 et seq)

69450 Tympanolysis, transcanal

Excision

69501 Transmastoid antrotomy (simple mastoidectomy)

69502 Mastoidectomy; complete

69505 modified radical

69511 radical

(For skin graft, see 15000 et seq)

(For mastoidectomy cavity debridement, see 69220, 69222)

69530 Petrous apicectomy including radical mastoidectomy

69535 Resection temporal bone, external approach

(For middle fossa approach, see 69950-69970)

69540 Excision aural polyp

69550 Excision aural glomus tumor; transcanal

69552 transmastoid

69554 extended (extratemporal)

Repair

69601 Revision mastoidectomy; resulting in complete mastoidectomy

69602 resulting in modified radical mastoidectomy

69603 resulting in radical mastoidectomy

69604 resulting in tympanoplasty

(For planned secondary tympanoplasty after mastoidectomy, see 69631, 69632)

69605 with apicectomy

(For skin graft, see 15120, 15121, 15260, 15261)

69610 Tympanic membrane repair, with or without site preparation or perforation for closure, with or without patch

(69611 has been deleted. To report, use 69610)

69620 Myringoplasty (surgery confined to drumhead and donor area)

69631 Tympanoplasty without mastoidectomy (including canalplasty, atticotomy and/or middle ear surgery), initial or revision; without ossicular chain reconstruction
➔ *CPT Assistant* Jul 98:11

69632 with ossicular chain reconstruction (eg, postfenestration)

69633 with ossicular chain reconstruction and synthetic prosthesis (eg, partial ossicular replacement prosthesis (PORP), total ossicular replacement prosthesis (TORP))

69635 Tympanoplasty with antrotomy or mastoidotomy (including canalplasty, atticotomy, middle ear surgery, and/or tympanic membrane repair); without ossicular chain reconstruction

69636 with ossicular chain reconstruction

Tympanoplasty
69635-69646

A graft is used to repair the tympanic membrane perforation.

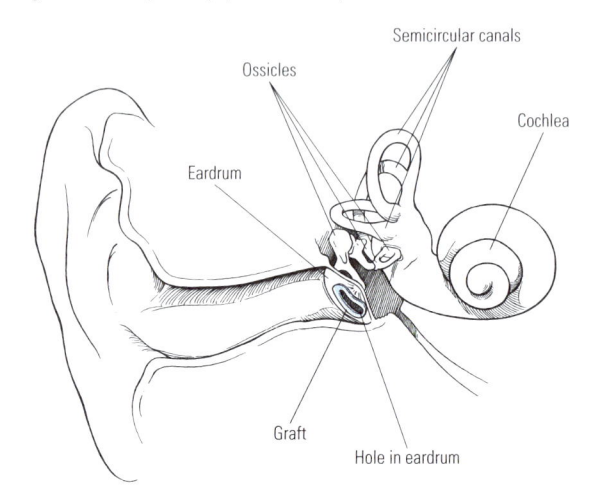

Semicircular canals
Ossicles
Cochlea
Eardrum
Graft
Hole in eardrum

69637   with ossicular chain reconstruction and synthetic prosthesis (eg, partial ossicular replacement prosthesis (PORP), total ossicular replacement prosthesis (TORP))

69641   Tympanoplasty with mastoidectomy (including canalplasty, middle ear surgery, tympanic membrane repair); without ossicular chain reconstruction

69642   with ossicular chain reconstruction

69643   with intact or reconstructed wall, without ossicular chain reconstruction

69644   with intact or reconstructed canal wall, with ossicular chain reconstruction

69645   radical or complete, without ossicular chain reconstruction

69646   radical or complete, with ossicular chain reconstruction

69650   Stapes mobilization

69660   Stapedectomy or stapedotomy with reestablishment of ossicular continuity, with or without use of foreign material;

69661   with footplate drill out

69662   Revision of stapedectomy or stapedotomy

69666   Repair oval window fistula

69667   Repair round window fistula

69670   Mastoid obliteration (separate procedure)

(69675 Tympanic neurectomy has been revised as 69676)

69676   Tympanic neurectomy

(69677 has been deleted. To report, use 69676 with modifier '-50')

Other Procedures

69700   Closure postauricular fistula, mastoid (separate procedure)

69710   Implantation or replacement of electromagnetic bone conduction hearing device in temporal bone

(Replacement procedure includes removal of old device)

69711   Removal or repair of electromagnetic bone conduction hearing device in temporal bone

69714   Implantation, osseointegrated implant, temporal bone, with percutaneous attachment to external speech processor/cochlear stimulator; without mastoidectomy
➔ *CPT Changes* 2001

69715   with mastoidectomy
➔ *CPT Changes* 2001

69717   Replacement (including removal of existing device), osseointegrated implant, temporal bone, with percutaneous attachment to external speech processor/cochlear stimulator; without mastoidectomy
➔ *CPT Changes* 2001

69718   with mastoidectomy
➔ *CPT Changes* 2001

69720   Decompression facial nerve, intratemporal; lateral to geniculate ganglion

69725   including medial to geniculate ganglion

69740   Suture facial nerve, intratemporal, with or without graft or decompression; lateral to geniculate ganglion

69745   including medial to geniculate ganglion

(For extracranial suture of facial nerve, use 64864)

69799   Unlisted procedure, middle ear
➔ *CPT Assistant* Oct 99:10

Inner Ear

Incision and/or Destruction

69801   Labyrinthotomy, with or without cryosurgery including other nonexcisional destructive procedures or perfusion of vestibuloactive drugs (single or multiple perfusions); transcanal

(69801 includes all required infusions performed on initial and subsequent days of treatment)

69802   with mastoidectomy

69805   Endolymphatic sac operation; without shunt

69806   with shunt

69820   Fenestration semicircular canal

69840   Revision fenestration operation

Excision

69905   Labyrinthectomy; transcanal

69910   with mastoidectomy

69915   Vestibular nerve section, translabyrinthine approach

(For transcranial approach, use 69950)

Introduction

69930 Cochlear device implantation, with or without mastoidectomy

Cochlear Device Implantation
69930

An internal coil is attached to the temporal bone and the ground wire attached to the internal coil is connected to the temporalis muscle.

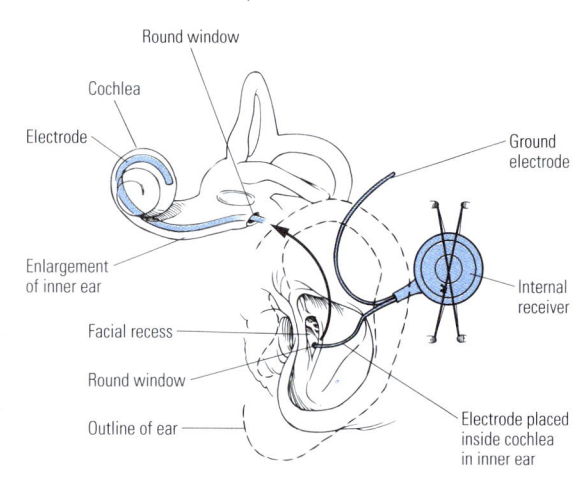

Other Procedures

69949 Unlisted procedure, inner ear

Temporal Bone, Middle Fossa Approach

(For external approach, use 69535)

69950 Vestibular nerve section, transcranial approach

69955 Total facial nerve decompression and/or repair (may include graft)

69960 Decompression internal auditory canal

(69965 has been deleted. To report, use 69979)

69970 Removal of tumor, temporal bone

Other Procedures

69979 Unlisted procedure, temporal bone, middle fossa approach

Operating Microscope

The surgical microscope is employed when the surgical services are performed using the techniques of microsurgery. Code 69990 should be reported (without the modifier '-51' appended) in addition to the code for the primary procedure performed. Do not use 69990 for visualization with magnifying loupes or corrected vision. Do not report code 69990 in addition to procedures where use of the operating microscope is an inclusive component (15756-15758, 15842, 19364, 19368, 20955-20962, 20969-20973, 26551-26554, 26556, 31526, 31531, 31536, 31541, 31561, 31571, 43116, 43496, 49906, 61548, 63075-63078, 64727, ▶64820–64823◀, 65091-68850).

✚ ▲ 69990 Microsurgical techniques, requiring use of operating microscope (List separately in addition to code for primary procedure)

➔ *CPT Assistant* Nov 98:20; Apr 99:11; Jun 99:11; Jul 99:11; Oct 99:10; *CPT Changes* 2002

Operating Microscope
69990

Surgical operating microscope used to obtain good visualization of fine structures in the operating field. The lens system may be operated by hand or foot controls to adjust to working distance, with interchangeable oculars providing magnification as needed.

Radiology Guidelines (Including Nuclear Medicine and Diagnostic Ultrasound)

Items used by all physicians in reporting their services are presented in the **Introduction.** Some of the commonalities are repeated here for the convenience of those physicians referring to this section on **Radiology (Including Nuclear Medicine and Diagnostic Ultrasound).** Other definitions and items unique to Radiology are also listed.

Subject Listings

Subject listings apply when radiological services are performed by or under the responsible supervision of a physician.

Multiple Procedures

It is appropriate to designate multiple procedures that are rendered on the same date by separate entries. This can be reported by using the multiple procedure modifier '-51'. See Appendix A for modifier definitions.

Separate Procedures

Some of the procedures or services listed in *CPT* that are commonly carried out as an integral component of a total service or procedure have been identified by the inclusion of the term "separate procedure." The codes designated as "separate procedure" should not be reported in addition to the code for the total procedure or service of which it is considered an integral component.

However, when a procedure or service that is designated as a "separate procedure" is carried out independently or considered to be unrelated or distinct from other procedures/services provided at that time, it may be reported by itself, or in addition to other procedures/ services by appending the modifier '-59' to the specific "separate procedure" code to indicate that the procedure is not considered to be a component of another procedure, but is a distinct, independent procedure. This may represent a different session or patient encounter, different procedure or surgery, different site or organ system, separate incision/excision, separate lesion, or separate injury (or area of injury in extensive injuries).

Subsection Information

Several of the subheadings or subsections have special needs or instructions unique to that section. Where these are indicated (eg, "Radiation Oncology") special **"Notes"** will be presented preceding those procedural terminology listings, referring to that subsection specifically. If there is an "Unlisted Procedure" code number (see section below) for the individual subsection, it will be shown. Those subsections with **"Notes"** are as follows:

Diagnostic Radiology (Diagnostic Imaging)	70010-76499
Aorta and Arteries	75600-75790
Diagnostic Ultrasound	76506-76999
Radiation Oncology	77261-77799
Clinical Treatment Planning	77261-77299
Radiation Treatment Management	77427-77499
Proton Beam Treatment Delivery	77520-77523
Hyperthermia	77600-77620
Clinical Brachytherapy	77750-77799
Nuclear Medicine	78000-78299
Musculoskeletal System	78300-78399
Cardiovascular System	78414-78499

Unlisted Service or Procedure

A service or procedure may be provided that is not listed in this edition of *CPT*. When reporting such a service, the appropriate "Unlisted Procedure" code may be used to indicate the service, identifying it by "Special Report" as discussed below. The "Unlisted Procedures" and accompanying codes for **Radiology (Including Nuclear Medicine and Diagnostic Ultrasound)** are as follows:

76499	Unlisted diagnostic radiologic procedure
76999	Unlisted ultrasound procedure
77299	Unlisted procedure, therapeutic radiology clinical treatment planning
77399	Unlisted procedure, medical radiation physics, dosimetry and treatment devices, and special services
77499	Unlisted procedure, therapeutic radiology treatment management

77799	Unlisted procedure, clinical brachytherapy
78099	Unlisted endocrine procedure, diagnostic nuclear medicine
78199	Unlisted hematopoietic, reticuloendothelial and lymphatic procedure, diagnostic nuclear medicine
78299	Unlisted gastrointestinal procedure, diagnostic nuclear medicine
78399	Unlisted musculoskeletal procedure, diagnostic nuclear medicine
78499	Unlisted cardiovascular procedure, diagnostic nuclear medicine
78599	Unlisted respiratory procedure, diagnostic nuclear medicine
78699	Unlisted nervous system procedure, diagnostic nuclear medicine
78799	Unlisted genitourinary procedure, diagnostic nuclear medicine
78999	Unlisted miscellaneous procedure, diagnostic nuclear medicine
79999	Unlisted radiopharmaceutical therapeutic procedure

Special Report

A service that is rarely provided, unusual, variable, or new may require a special report in determining medical appropriateness of the service. Pertinent information should include an adequate definition or description of the nature, extent, and need for the procedure; and the time, effort, and equipment necessary to provide the service. Additional items which may be included are:

- complexity of symptoms;
- final diagnosis;
- pertinent physical findings;
- diagnostic and therapeutic procedures;
- concurrent problems;
- follow-up care.

Supervision and Interpretation

When a procedure is performed by two physicians, the radiologic portion of the procedure is designated as "radiological supervision and interpretation." When a physician performs both the procedure and provides imaging supervision and interpretation, a combination of procedure codes outside the 70000 series and imaging supervision and interpretation codes are to be used.

(The Radiological Supervision and Interpretation codes are not applicable to the Radiation Oncology subsection.)

Administration of Contrast Material(s)

Some of the listed procedures are commonly carried out without the use of contrast material for imaging enhancement. For those codes that may or may not be performed using contrast material for imaging enhancement, the phrase "with contrast" represents contrast material administered intravascularly or intra-articularly (for intra-articular injection use appropriate joint injection code and, if used, appropriate imaging guidance code).

For spine examinations using computerized tomography, magnetic resonance imaging, magnetic resonance angiography, "with contrast" includes intrathecal or intravascular injection. For intrathecal injection, use also 61055 or 62284.

Injection of contrast material is part of the "with contrast" CT, MRI, MRA procedure.

Oral and /or rectal contrast administration alone does not qualify as a study "with contrast."

Written Report(s)

A written report, signed by the interpreting physician, should be considered an integral part of a radiologic procedure or interpretation.

Radiology

Diagnostic Radiology (Diagnostic Imaging)

Head and Neck

(70002, 70003 have been deleted. To report, use 76499)

70010 Myelography, posterior fossa, radiological supervision and interpretation

(70011 (complete procedure) has been deleted, see 61055, 62284, 70010)

70015 Cisternography, positive contrast, radiological supervision and interpretation

(70016 (complete procedure) has been deleted, see 61055, 62284, 70015)

(70020, 70021 have been deleted. To report, use 76499)

(70022 has been deleted. To report CT guidance for stereotactic localization, use 76355)

70030 Radiologic examination, eye, for detection of foreign body

(70040, 70050 have been deleted)

70100 Radiologic examination, mandible; partial, less than four views

70110 complete, minimum of four views

70120 Radiologic examination, mastoids; less than three views per side

70130 complete, minimum of three views per side

70134 Radiologic examination, internal auditory meati, complete

70140 Radiologic examination, facial bones; less than three views

70150 complete, minimum of three views

70160 Radiologic examination, nasal bones, complete, minimum of three views

70170 Dacryocystography, nasolacrimal duct, radiological supervision and interpretation

(70171 (complete procedure) has been deleted, see 68850, 70170)

70190 Radiologic examination; optic foramina

70200 orbits, complete, minimum of four views

70210 Radiologic examination, sinuses, paranasal, less than three views

70220 Radiologic examination, sinuses, paranasal, complete, minimum of three views

(70230, 70231 have been deleted. To report, use 76499)

70240 Radiologic examination, sella turcica

70250 Radiologic examination, skull; less than four views, with or without stereo

70260 complete, minimum of four views, with or without stereo

70300 Radiologic examination, teeth; single view

70310 partial examination, less than full mouth

70320 complete, full mouth

70328 Radiologic examination, temporomandibular joint, open and closed mouth; unilateral

70330 bilateral

70332 Temporomandibular joint arthrography, radiological supervision and interpretation

►(Do not report 76003 in addition to 70332)◄

(70333 (complete procedure) has been deleted, see 21116, 70332)

70336 Magnetic resonance (eg, proton) imaging, temporomandibular joint(s)
➔ *CPT Assistant* Jul 99:11; *CPT Changes* 2001

70350 Cephalogram, orthodontic

70355 Orthopantogram

70360 Radiologic examination; neck, soft tissue

70370 pharynx or larynx, including fluoroscopy and/or magnification technique

70371 Complex dynamic pharyngeal and speech evaluation by cine or video recording

70373 Laryngography, contrast, radiological supervision and interpretation

(70374 (complete procedure) has been deleted, see 31708, 70373)

70380 Radiologic examination, salivary gland for calculus

70390 Sialography, radiological supervision and interpretation

(70391 (complete procedure) has been deleted, see 42550, 70390)

(70400, 70401 have been deleted. To report, use 76499)

70450 Computerized axial tomography, head or brain; without contrast material
➔ *CPT Assistant* Apr 96:11

70460 with contrast material(s)
➔ *CPT Assistant* Apr 96:11

70470 without contrast material, followed by contrast material(s) and further sections
➔ *CPT Assistant* Apr 96:11

(For coronal, sagittal, and/or oblique sections, use 76375)

Rad 70010

70480   Computerized axial tomography, orbit, sella, or posterior fossa or outer, middle, or inner ear; without contrast material

70481   with contrast material(s)

70482   without contrast material, followed by contrast material(s) and further sections

(For coronal, sagittal, and/or oblique sections, use 76375)

70486   Computerized axial tomography, maxillofacial area; without contrast material

70487   with contrast material(s)

70488   without contrast material, followed by contrast material(s) and further sections

(For coronal, sagittal, and/or oblique sections, use 76375)

70490   Computerized axial tomography, soft tissue neck; without contrast material

70491   with contrast material(s)

70492   without contrast material followed by contrast material(s) and further sections

(For coronal, sagittal, and/or oblique sections, use 76375)

(For cervical spine, see 72125, 72126)

70496   Computed tomographic angiography, head, without contrast material(s), followed by contrast material(s) and further sections, including image post-processing
➔ *CPT Changes* 2001

70498   Computed tomographic angiography, neck, without contrast material(s), followed by contrast material(s) and further sections, including image post-processing
➔ *CPT Changes* 2001

70540   Magnetic resonance (eg, proton) imaging, orbit, face, and neck; without contrast material(s)
➔ *CPT Changes* 2001

(70541 has been deleted. To report head or neck magnetic resonance angiography studies, see 70544-70546, 70547-70549)

70542   with contrast material(s)
➔ *CPT Changes* 2001

70543   without contrast material(s), followed by contrast material(s) and further sequences
➔ *CPT Changes* 2001

70544   Magnetic resonance angiography, head; without contrast material(s)
➔ *CPT Changes* 2001

70545   with contrast material(s)
➔ *CPT Changes* 2001

70546   without contrast material(s), followed by contrast material(s) and further sequences
➔ *CPT Changes* 2001

70547   Magnetic resonance angiography, neck; without contrast material(s)
➔ *CPT Changes* 2001

70548   with contrast material(s)
➔ *CPT Changes* 2001

70549   without contrast material(s), followed by contrast material(s) and further sequences
➔ *CPT Changes* 2001

(70550 has been deleted. To report, use 70551)

70551   Magnetic resonance (eg, proton) imaging, brain (including brain stem); without contrast material
➔ *CPT Assistant* May 98:10

70552   with contrast material(s)

70553   without contrast material, followed by contrast material(s) and further sequences
➔ *CPT Assistant* Nov 97:24

(For magnetic spectroscopy, use 76390)

Chest

(71000 has been deleted)

71010   Radiologic examination, chest; single view, frontal

71015   stereo, frontal

71020   Radiologic examination, chest, two views, frontal and lateral;

71021   with apical lordotic procedure

71022   with oblique projections

71023   with fluoroscopy

71030   Radiologic examination, chest, complete, minimum of four views;

71034   with fluoroscopy

(For separate chest fluoroscopy, use 76000)

71035   Radiologic examination, chest, special views (eg, lateral decubitus, Bucky studies)

(71036 has been deleted. To report, use 76003)

(71037 (complete procedure) has been deleted, see 32400, 32405, 76003)

(71038 has been deleted. To report, use 31628)

71040   Bronchography, unilateral, radiological supervision and interpretation

(71041 (complete procedure) has been deleted, see 31656, 31708, 31710, 31715, 71040)

71060   Bronchography, bilateral, radiological supervision and interpretation

(71061 (complete procedure) has been deleted, see 31656, 31708, 31710, 31715, 71060)

71090   Insertion pacemaker, fluoroscopy and radiography, radiological supervision and interpretation

▶(For procedure, see appropriate organ or site)◀

71100   Radiologic examination, ribs, unilateral; two views

71101   including posteroanterior chest, minimum of three views

⊘ =Modifier '-51' Exempt   ▶ ◀=New or Revised Text   ✚ =Add-on Code

71110 Radiologic examination, ribs, bilateral; three views

71111 including posteroanterior chest, minimum of four views

71120 Radiologic examination; sternum, minimum of two views

71130 sternoclavicular joint or joints, minimum of three views

71250 Computerized axial tomography, thorax; without contrast material

71260 with contrast material(s)

71270 without contrast material, followed by contrast material(s) and further sections

(For coronal, sagittal, and/or oblique sections, use 76375)

71275 Computed tomographic angiography, chest, without contrast material(s), followed by contrast material(s) and further sections, including image post-processing
➔ *CPT Changes* 2001

71550 Magnetic resonance (eg, proton) imaging, chest (eg, for evaluation of hilar and mediastinal lymphadenopathy); without contrast material(s)
➔ *CPT Changes* 2001

71551 with contrast material(s)
➔ *CPT Changes* 2001

71552 without contrast material(s), followed by contrast material(s) and further sequences
➔ *CPT Changes* 2001

(For breast MRI, see 76093 and 76094)

71555 Magnetic resonance angiography, chest (excluding myocardium), with or without contrast material(s)
➔ *CPT Assistant* Fall 95:2

Spine and Pelvis

72010 Radiologic examination, spine, entire, survey study, anteroposterior and lateral

72020 Radiologic examination, spine, single view, specify level

72040 Radiologic examination, spine, cervical; two or three views
➔ *CPT Changes* 2001

72050 minimum of four views

72052 complete, including oblique and flexion and/or extension studies .

72069 Radiologic examination, spine, thoracolumbar, standing (scoliosis)

72070 Radiologic examination, spine; thoracic, two views
➔ *CPT Changes* 2001

72072 thoracic, three views
➔ *CPT Changes* 2001

72074 thoracic, minimum of four views
➔ *CPT Changes* 2001

72080 thoracolumbar, two views
➔ *CPT Changes* 2001

72090 scoliosis study, including supine and erect studies

72100 Radiologic examination, spine, lumbosacral; two or three views
➔ *CPT Changes* 2001

72110 minimum of four views
➔ *CPT Changes* 2001

72114 complete, including bending views

72120 Radiologic examination, spine, lumbosacral, bending views only, minimum of four views

(Contrast material in CT of spine is either by intrathecal or intravenous injection. For intrathecal injection, use also 61055 or 62284. IV injection of contrast material is part of the CT procedure)

72125 Computerized axial tomography, cervical spine; without contrast material

72126 with contrast material

72127 without contrast material, followed by contrast material(s) and further sections

(For intrathecal injection procedure, see 61055, 62284)

72128 Computerized axial tomography, thoracic spine; without contrast material

72129 with contrast material

(For intrathecal injection procedure, see 61055, 62284)

72130 without contrast material, followed by contrast material(s) and further sections

(For intrathecal injection procedure, see 61055, 62284)

72131 Computerized axial tomography, lumbar spine; without contrast material

72132 with contrast material
➔ *CPT Assistant* Fall 93:13

72133 without contrast material, followed by contrast material(s) and further sections

(For intrathecal injection procedure, see 61055, 62284)

(For coronal, sagittal, and/or oblique sections, use 76375)

(72140 has been deleted. To report, see 72141-72149)

72141 Magnetic resonance (eg, proton) imaging, spinal canal and contents, cervical; without contrast material

72142 with contrast material(s)

(For cervical spinal canal imaging without contrast material followed by contrast material, use 72156)

(72143 has been deleted. To report, see 72146, 72147)

(72144 has been deleted. To report, see 72148, 72149)

(72145 has been deleted. To report, see 72125-72133)

72146 Magnetic resonance (eg, proton) imaging, spinal canal and contents, thoracic; without contrast material
➔ *CPT Assistant* May 99:10

72147 with contrast material(s)
➔ *CPT Assistant* May 99:10

(For thoracic spinal canal imaging without contrast material followed by contrast material, use 72157)

72148 Magnetic resonance (eg, proton) imaging, spinal canal and contents, lumbar; without contrast material

72149 with contrast material(s)

(For lumbar spinal canal imaging without contrast material followed by contrast material, use 72158)

72156 Magnetic resonance (eg, proton) imaging, spinal canal and contents, without contrast material, followed by contrast material(s) and further sequences; cervical

72157 thoracic

72158 lumbar

72159 Magnetic resonance angiography, spinal canal and contents, with or without contrast material(s)

72170 Radiologic examination, pelvis; one or two views
➔ *CPT Changes* 2001

(72180 has been deleted. To report, use 72170)

72190 complete, minimum of three views

(For pelvimetry, use 74710)

72191 Computed tomographic angiography, pelvis, without contrast material(s), followed by contrast material(s) and further sections, including image post-processing
➔ *CPT Changes* 2001

(For CTA aorto-iliofemoral runoff, use 75635)

72192 Computerized axial tomography, pelvis; without contrast material

72193 with contrast material(s)

72194 without contrast material, followed by contrast material(s) and further sections

(For coronal, sagittal, and/or oblique sections, use 76375)

72195 Magnetic resonance (eg, proton) imaging, pelvis; without contrast material(s)
➔ *CPT Changes* 2001

72196 with contrast material(s)
➔ *CPT Changes* 2001

72197 without contrast material(s), followed by contrast material(s) and further sequences
➔ *CPT Changes* 2001

72198 Magnetic resonance angiography, pelvis, with or without contrast material(s)

72200 Radiologic examination, sacroiliac joints; less than three views

72202 three or more views

72220 Radiologic examination, sacrum and coccyx, minimum of two views

72240 Myelography, cervical, radiological supervision and interpretation
➔ *CPT Assistant* Fall 93:13

(72241 (complete procedure) has been deleted, see 61055, 62284, 72240)

72255 Myelography, thoracic, radiological supervision and interpretation

(72256 (complete procedure) has been deleted, see 61055, 62284, 72255)

72265 Myelography, lumbosacral, radiological supervision and interpretation
➔ *CPT Assistant* Fall 93:13; Aug 00:7

(72266 (complete procedure) has been deleted, see 61055, 62284, 72265)

72270 Myelography, entire spinal canal, radiological supervision and interpretation

(72271 (complete procedure) has been deleted, see 61055, 62284, 72270)

72275 Epidurography, radiological supervision and interpretation
➔ *CPT Assistant* Nov 99:40; Jan 00:1; Aug 00:7; *CPT Changes* 2000

(For injection procedure, see 62280-62282, 62310-62319, 64479-64484)

72285 Diskography, cervical or thoracic, radiological supervision and interpretation
➔ *CPT Assistant* Nov 99:35, 40; *CPT Changes* 2000

(72286 (complete procedure) has been deleted, see 62291, 72285)

72295 Diskography, lumbar, radiological supervision and interpretation

(72296 (complete procedure) has been deleted, see 62290, 72295)

Upper Extremities

(For stress views, any joint, use 76006)

73000 Radiologic examination; clavicle, complete

73010 scapula, complete

73020 Radiologic examination, shoulder; one view

73030 complete, minimum of two views

73040 Radiologic examination, shoulder, arthrography, radiological supervision and interpretation

▶(Do not report 76003 in addition to 73040)◀

(73041 (complete procedure) has been deleted, see 23350, 73040)

73050 Radiologic examination; acromioclavicular joints, bilateral, with or without weighted distraction

73060 humerus, minimum of two views

⊘ =Modifier '-51' Exempt   ▶ ◀=New or Revised Text   ✛ =Add-on Code   CPT 2002

73070 Radiologic examination, elbow; two views
➔ *CPT Changes* 2001

73080 complete, minimum of three views

73085 Radiologic examination, elbow, arthrography, radiological supervision and interpretation

▶(Do not report 76003 in addition to 73085)◀

(73086 (complete procedure) has been deleted, see 24220, 73085)

73090 Radiologic examination; forearm, two views
➔ *CPT Changes* 2001

73092 upper extremity, infant, minimum of two views

73100 Radiologic examination, wrist; two views
➔ *CPT Changes* 2001

73110 complete, minimum of three views
➔ *CPT Assistant* Mar 97:10

73115 Radiologic examination, wrist, arthrography, radiological supervision and interpretation

▶(Do not report 76003 in addition to 73115)◀

(73116 (complete procedure) has been deleted, see 25246, 73115)

73120 Radiologic examination, hand; two views

73130 minimum of three views

73140 Radiologic examination, finger(s), minimum of two views

73200 Computerized axial tomography, upper extremity; without contrast material

73201 with contrast material(s)

73202 without contrast material, followed by contrast material(s) and further sections

(For coronal, sagittal, and/or oblique sections, use 76375)

73206 Computed tomographic angiography, upper extremity, without contrast material(s), followed by contrast material(s) and further sections, including image post-processing
➔ *CPT Changes* 2001

73218 Magnetic resonance (eg, proton) imaging, upper extremity, other than joint; without contrast material(s)
➔ *CPT Changes* 2001

73219 with contrast material(s)
➔ *CPT Changes* 2001

73220 without contrast material(s), followed by contrast material(s) and further sequences
➔ *CPT Changes* 2001

73221 Magnetic resonance (eg, proton) imaging, any joint of upper extremity; without contrast material(s)
➔ *CPT Changes* 2001

73222 with contrast material(s)
➔ *CPT Changes* 2001

73223 without contrast material(s), followed by contrast material(s) and further sequences
➔ *CPT Changes* 2001

73225 Magnetic resonance angiography, upper extremity, with or without contrast material(s)

Lower Extremities

(For stress views, any joint, use 76006)

73500 Radiologic examination, hip, unilateral; one view

73510 complete, minimum of two views
➔ *CPT Assistant* Spring 92:9; May 99:10

73520 Radiologic examination, hips, bilateral, minimum of two views of each hip, including anteroposterior view of pelvis

73525 Radiologic examination, hip, arthrography, radiological supervision and interpretation

▶(Do not report 76003 in addition to 73525)◀

(73526 (complete procedure) has been deleted, see 27093, 27095, 73525)

73530 Radiologic examination, hip, during operative procedure

(73531 has been deleted. To report, use 73530)

73540 Radiologic examination, pelvis and hips, infant or child, minimum of two views

73542 Radiological examination, sacroiliac joint arthrography, radiological supervision and interpretation
➔ *CPT Assistant* Nov 99:40-41; *CPT Changes* 2000

▶(Do not report 76003 in addition to 73542)◀

(For procedure, use 27096. If formal arthrography is not performed, recorded, and a formal radiologic report is not issued, use 76005 for fluoroscopic guidance for sacroiliac joint injections)

73550 Radiologic examination, femur, two views
➔ *CPT Changes* 2001

73560 Radiologic examination, knee; one or two views

73562 three views

73564 complete, four or more views
➔ *CPT Assistant* Jun 98:11; Nov 98:21

73565 both knees, standing, anteroposterior

(73570 has been deleted. To report, see 73562, 73564)

73580 Radiologic examination, knee, arthrography, radiological supervision and interpretation

▶(Do not report 76003 in addition to 73580)◀

(73581 (complete procedure) has been deleted, see 27370, 73580)

73590 Radiologic examination; tibia and fibula, two views
➔ *CPT Changes* 2001

73592 lower extremity, infant, minimum of two views

73600 Radiologic examination, ankle; two views
> *CPT Changes* 2001

73610 complete, minimum of three views

73615 Radiologic examination, ankle, arthrography, radiological supervision and interpretation

▶(Do not report 76003 in addition to 73615)◀

(73616 (complete procedure) has been deleted, see 27648, 73615)

73620 Radiologic examination, foot; two views
> *CPT Changes* 2001

73630 complete, minimum of three views

73650 Radiologic examination; calcaneus, minimum of two views

73660 toe(s), minimum of two views

73700 Computerized axial tomography, lower extremity; without contrast material

73701 with contrast material(s)

73702 without contrast material, followed by contrast material(s) and further sections

(For coronal, sagittal, and/or oblique sections, use 76375)

73706 Computed tomographic angiography, lower extremity, without contrast material(s), followed by contrast material(s) and further sections, including image post-processing
> *CPT Changes* 2001

(For CTA aorto-iliofemoral runoff, use 75635)

73718 Magnetic resonance (eg, proton) imaging, lower extremity other than joint; without contrast material(s)
> *CPT Changes* 2001

73719 with contrast material(s)
> *CPT Changes* 2001

73720 without contrast material(s), followed by contrast material(s) and further sequences
> *CPT Changes* 2001

73721 Magnetic resonance (eg, proton) imaging, any joint of lower extremity; without contrast material
> *CPT Changes* 2001

73722 with contrast material(s)
> *CPT Changes* 2001

73723 without contrast material(s), followed by contrast material(s) and further sequences
> *CPT Changes* 2001

73725 Magnetic resonance angiography, lower extremity, with or without contrast material(s)

Abdomen

74000 Radiologic examination, abdomen; single anteroposterior view
> *CPT Assistant* Nov 98:21

74010 anteroposterior and additional oblique and cone views

74020 complete, including decubitus and/or erect views

74022 complete acute abdomen series, including supine, erect, and/or decubitus views, upright PA chest

74150 Computerized axial tomography, abdomen; without contrast material

74160 with contrast material(s)

74170 without contrast material, followed by contrast material(s) and further sections

(For coronal, sagittal, and/or oblique sections, use 76375)

74175 Computed tomographic angiography, abdomen, without contrast material(s), followed by contrast material(s) and further sections, including image post-processing
> *CPT Changes* 2001

(For CTA aorto-iliofemoral runoff, use 75635)

74181 Magnetic resonance (eg, proton) imaging, abdomen; without contrast material(s)
> *CPT Changes* 2001

74182 with contrast material(s)
> *CPT Changes* 2001

74183 without contrast material(s), followed by with contrast material(s) and further sequences
> *CPT Changes* 2001

74185 Magnetic resonance angiography, abdomen, with or without contrast material(s)

74190 Peritoneogram (eg, after injection of air or contrast), radiological supervision and interpretation

(For procedure, use 49400)

(For computerized axial tomography, see 72192 or 74150)

Gastrointestinal Tract

(For percutaneous placement of gastrostomy tube, use 43750)

74210 Radiologic examination; pharynx and/or cervical esophagus

74220 esophagus

▲ **74230** Swallowing function, with cineradiography/videoradiography
> *CPT Changes* 2002

74235 Removal of foreign body(s), esophageal, with use of balloon catheter, radiological supervision and interpretation

(For procedure, see 43215, 43247)

74240 Radiologic examination, gastrointestinal tract, upper; with or without delayed films, without KUB

74241 with or without delayed films, with KUB

▲ **74245** with small intestine, includes multiple serial films
> *CPT Changes* 2002

⊘ =Modifier '-51' Exempt ▶ ◀=New or Revised Text ✚=Add-on Code CPT 2002

74246 Radiological examination, gastrointestinal tract, upper, air contrast, with specific high density barium, effervescent agent, with or without glucagon; with or without delayed films, without KUB

74247 with or without delayed films, with KUB

▲ **74249** with small intestine follow-through
➔ *CPT Changes* 2002

▲ **74250** Radiologic examination, small intestine, includes multiple serial films;
➔ *CPT Changes* 2002

74251 via enteroclysis tube

74260 Duodenography, hypotonic

74270 Radiologic examination, colon; barium enema, with or without KUB

(74275 has been deleted. To report, use 76499)

74280 air contrast with specific high density barium, with or without glucagon

74283 Therapeutic enema, contrast or air, for reduction of intussusception or other intraluminal obstruction (eg, meconium ileus)
➔ *CPT Assistant* Nov 97:24

(74285 has been deleted. To report, see 74270, 74280)

74290 Cholecystography, oral contrast;

74291 additional or repeat examination or multiple day examination

74300 Cholangiography and/or pancreatography; intraoperative, radiological supervision and interpretation
➔ *CPT Assistant* Nov 99:41; Dec 00:14; *CPT Changes* 2000

+ **74301** additional set intraoperative, radiological supervision and interpretation (List separately in addition to code for primary procedure)

(Use 74301 in conjunction with code 74300)

▲ **74305** through existing catheter, radiological supervision and interpretation
➔ *CPT Assistant* Nov 99:41; *CPT Changes* 2000, 2002

(For procedure, see 47505, 48400, 47560-47561, 47563)

(For biliary duct stone extraction, percutaneous, see 47630, 74327)

(74310, 74315 have been deleted. To report, use 76499)

74320 Cholangiography, percutaneous, transhepatic, radiological supervision and interpretation

(74321 (complete procedure) has been deleted, see 47500, 74320)

(74325, 74326 have been deleted. To report, use 76499)

▲ **74327** Postoperative biliary duct calculus removal, percutaneous via T-tube tract, basket, or snare (eg, Burhenne technique), radiological supervision and interpretation
➔ *CPT Changes* 2002

(For procedure, use 47630)

74328 Endoscopic catheterization of the biliary ductal system, radiological supervision and interpretation

(For procedure, see 43260-43272 as appropriate)

74329 Endoscopic catheterization of the pancreatic ductal system, radiological supervision and interpretation

(For procedure, see 43260-43272 as appropriate)

74330 Combined endoscopic catheterization of the biliary and pancreatic ductal systems, radiological supervision and interpretation

(For procedure, see 43260-43272 as appropriate)

(74331 has been deleted. To report, use 43262)

74340 Introduction of long gastrointestinal tube (eg, Miller-Abbott), including multiple fluoroscopies and films, radiological supervision and interpretation

(For tube placement, use 44500)

74350 Percutaneous placement of gastrostomy tube, radiological supervision and interpretation

74355 Percutaneous placement of enteroclysis tube, radiological supervision and interpretation

(74356 (complete procedure) has been deleted, see 44015, 74355)

74360 Intraluminal dilation of strictures and/or obstructions (eg, esophagus), radiological supervision and interpretation
➔ *CPT Assistant* Spring 94:3

(74361 (complete procedure) has been deleted, see 43220, 43458, 74360)

▲ **74363** Percutaneous transhepatic dilation of biliary duct stricture with or without placement of stent, radiological supervision and interpretation
➔ *CPT Changes* 2002

(For procedure, see 47510, 47511, 47555, 47556)

Urinary Tract

74400 Urography (pyelography), intravenous, with or without KUB, with or without tomography

(74405 has been deleted. To report, see 74400, 74410 or 74415)

74410 Urography, infusion, drip technique and/or bolus technique;

74415 with nephrotomography

74420 Urography, retrograde, with or without KUB
➔ *CPT Assistant* Sep 00:11

74425 Urography, antegrade, (pyelostogram, nephrostogram, loopogram), radiological supervision and interpretation
➔ *CPT Assistant* Fall 93:14; Dec 97:7

(74426 (complete procedure) has been deleted, see 50394, 50684, 50690, 74425)

74430 Cystography, minimum of three views, radiological supervision and interpretation

(74431 (complete procedure) has been deleted, see 51600, 51605, 74430)

74440 Vasography, vesiculography, or epididymography, radiological supervision and interpretation

(74441 (complete procedure) has been deleted, see 52010, 55300, 74440)

74445 Corpora cavernosography, radiological supervision and interpretation

(74446 (complete procedure) has been deleted, see 54230, 74445)

74450 Urethrocystography, retrograde, radiological supervision and interpretation

(74451 (complete procedure) has been deleted, see 51610, 74450)

74455 Urethrocystography, voiding, radiological supervision and interpretation

(74456 (complete procedure) has been deleted, see 51600, 74455)

(74460, 74461 have been deleted. To report, use 76499)

74470 Radiologic examination, renal cyst study, translumbar, contrast visualization, radiological supervision and interpretation

(74471 (complete procedure) has been deleted, see 50390, 74470)

74475 Introduction of intracatheter or catheter into renal pelvis for drainage and/or injection, percutaneous, radiological supervision and interpretation
➔ *CPT Assistant* Dec 97:7

(74476 (complete procedure) has been deleted, see 50392-50398, 74475)

74480 Introduction of ureteral catheter or stent into ureter through renal pelvis for drainage and/or injection, percutaneous, radiological supervision and interpretation
➔ *CPT Assistant* Fall 93:14

(74481 (complete procedure) has been deleted, see 50392-50398, 74480)

(For transurethral surgery (ureter and pelvis), see 52320-52355)

74485 Dilation of nephrostomy, ureters, or urethra, radiological supervision and interpretation

(74486 (complete procedure) has been deleted, see 50395, 53600-53621, 74485)

(For dilation of ureter without radiologic guidance, use ▶52341, 52344◀)

(For change of nephrostomy or pyelostomy tube, use 50398)

Gynecological and Obstetrical

(For abdomen and pelvis, see 72170-72190, 74000-74170)

74710 Pelvimetry, with or without placental localization

(74720, 74725 have been deleted. To report, use 74000)

(74730, 74731 have been deleted. To report, use 76499)

74740 Hysterosalpingography, radiological supervision and interpretation
➔ *CPT Assistant* Nov 97:24; Jul 99:8

(For introduction of saline or contrast for hysterosalpingography, see 58340)

(74741 (complete procedure) has been deleted, see 58340, 74740)

74742 Transcervical catheterization of fallopian tube, radiological supervision and interpretation

(For procedure, use 58345)

(74760, 74761, 74770, 74771 have been deleted. To report, use 76499)

74775 Perineogram (eg, vaginogram, for sex determination or extent of anomalies)

Heart

(For separate injection procedures for vascular radiology, see **Surgery** section, 36000-36299)

(For cardiac catheterization procedures, see 93501-93556)

(75500 has been deleted. To report, use 93555)

(75501 (complete procedure) has been deleted, see 93501-▶93533◀, 93542, 93543, 93555)

(75505 has been deleted. To report, use 93555)

(75506 (complete procedure) has been deleted, see 36400-36425 for intravenous procedure, 36100-36248 for intra-arterial procedure and 93501-▶93533◀, 93542, 93543, 93555)

(75507 has been deleted. To report, use 93555)

(75509 (complete procedure) has been deleted. To report, see 36400-36425 for intravenous procedure, 36100-36248 for intra-arterial procedure and 93501-▶93533◀, 93542, 93543)

(75510, 75511 have been deleted. To report, use 76499)

(75519 has been deleted. To report, use 93555)

(75520 (complete procedure) has been deleted, see 36400-36425 for intravenous procedure, 36100-36248 for intra-arterial procedure, and 93501, 93542)

(75523 has been deleted. To report, use 93555)

(75524 has been deleted, see 36400-36425 for intravenous procedure, 36100-36248 for intra-arterial procedure, and 93510-93514, 93524, 93543)

(75527 has been deleted. To report, use 93555)

⊘ =Modifier '-51' Exempt   ▶ ◀=New or Revised Text   ✚ =Add-on Code   CPT 2002

(75528 has been deleted, see 36400-36425 for intravenous procedure, 36100-36248 for intra-arterial procedure, and 93526-93529, 93543, and 93555)

75552 Cardiac magnetic resonance imaging for morphology; without contrast material
→ *CPT Assistant* Fall 95:1

75553 with contrast material
→ *CPT Assistant* Fall 95:1

75554 Cardiac magnetic resonance imaging for function, with or without morphology; complete study
→ *CPT Assistant* Fall 95:2

75555 limited study
→ *CPT Assistant* Fall 95:2

75556 Cardiac magnetic resonance imaging for velocity flow mapping
→ *CPT Assistant* Fall 95:2

Aorta and Arteries

Selective vascular catheterizations should be coded to include introduction and all lesser order selective catheterizations used in the approach (eg, the description for a selective right middle cerebral artery catheterization includes the introduction and placement catheterization of the right common and internal carotid arteries).

Additional second and/or third order arterial catheterizations within the same family of arteries supplied by a single first order artery should be expressed by 36218 or 36248. Additional first order or higher catheterizations in vascular families supplied by a first order vessel different from a previously selected and coded family should be separately coded using the conventions described above.

(For intravenous procedure, see 36000-36013, 36400-36425 and 36100-36248 for intra-arterial procedure)

(For radiological supervision and interpretation, see 75600-75978)

75600 Aortography, thoracic, without serialography, radiological supervision and interpretation

(For injection procedure, use 93544)

(75601 (complete procedure) has been deleted, see 36000-36013, 36400-36425 for intravenous procedure, and 36100-36200 for intra-arterial procedure and 75600)

75605 Aortography, thoracic, by serialography, radiological supervision and interpretation
→ *CPT Assistant* Spring 94:29; Dec 98:9

(For injection procedure, use 93544)

(75606 (complete procedure) has been deleted, see 36000-36013, 36400-36425 for intravenous procedure, and 36100-36200 for intra-arterial procedure and 75605)

(75620, 75621, 75622, 75623 have been deleted. To report, use 76499)

Aortography
75600-75630

A radiographic contrast study is performed on the abdominal or thoracic aorta.

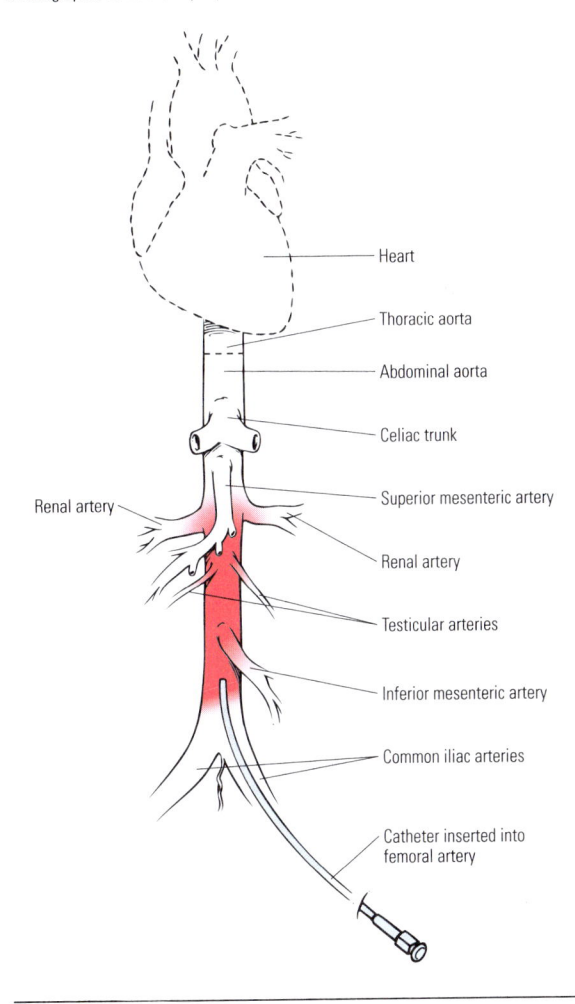

75625 Aortography, abdominal, by serialography, radiological supervision and interpretation
→ *CPT Assistant* Fall 93:16

(For injection procedure, use 93544)

(75626, 75627 and 75628 have been deleted, see 36000-36013, 36400-36425 for intravenous procedure, and 36100-36200 for intra-arterial procedure and 75625)

75630 Aortography, abdominal plus bilateral iliofemoral lower extremity, catheter, by serialography, radiological supervision and interpretation
→ *CPT Assistant* Fall 93:16

(75631 (complete procedure) has been deleted, see 36000-36013, 36400-36425 for intravenous procedure, and 36100-36200 and 36245-36248 for intra-arterial procedure and 75630)

75635 Computed tomographic angiography, abdominal aorta and bilateral iliofemoral lower extremity runoff, radiological supervision and interpretation, without contrast material(s), followed by contrast material(s) and further sections, including image post-processing
➔ *CPT Changes* 2001

75650 Angiography, cervicocerebral, catheter, including vessel origin, radiological supervision and interpretation
➔ *CPT Assistant* Spring 94:29; Apr 98:3; Oct 00:4

(75651-75657 (complete procedure) have been deleted, see 36000-36013, 36400-36425 for intravenous procedure, and 36100-36218 for intra-arterial procedure and 75650, 75660-75685 as appropriate)

75658 Angiography, brachial, retrograde, radiological supervision and interpretation

(75659 (complete procedure) has been deleted, see 36000-36013, 36400-36425 for intravenous procedure, and 36100-36218 for intra-arterial procedure and 75658)

75660 Angiography, external carotid, unilateral, selective, radiological supervision and interpretation

(75661 (complete procedure) has been deleted, see 36000-36013, 36400-36425 for intravenous procedure, and 36100-36218 and 75660)

Angiography, Carotid Artery
75660-75680

A radiographic contrast study is performed on the carotid artery vascular family.

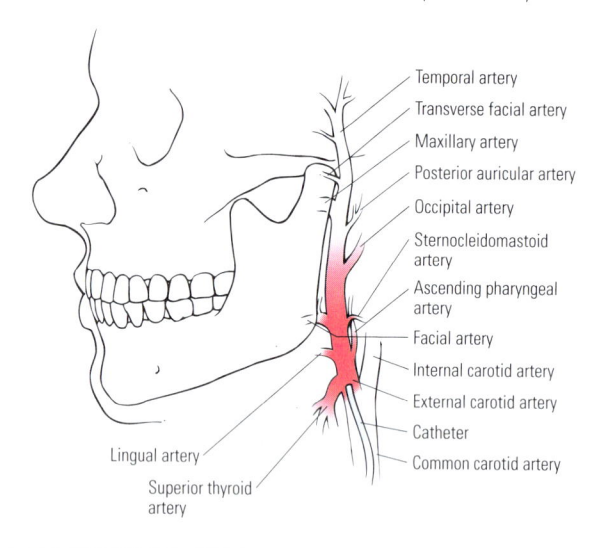

- Temporal artery
- Transverse facial artery
- Maxillary artery
- Posterior auricular artery
- Occipital artery
- Sternocleidomastoid artery
- Ascending pharyngeal artery
- Facial artery
- Internal carotid artery
- External carotid artery
- Catheter
- Common carotid artery
- Lingual artery
- Superior thyroid artery

75662 Angiography, external carotid, bilateral, selective, radiological supervision and interpretation

(75663 (complete procedure) has been deleted, see 36000-36013, 36400-36425 for intravenous procedure, and 36100-36218 for intra-arterial procedure and 75662)

75665 Angiography, carotid, cerebral, unilateral, radiological supervision and interpretation

(75667, 75669 (complete procedure) have been deleted, see 36000-36013, 36400-36425 for intravenous procedure, and 36100-36218 for intra-arterial procedure and 75665)

75671 Angiography, carotid, cerebral, bilateral, radiological supervision and interpretation
➔ *CPT Assistant* Oct 00:4

(75672, 75673 (complete procedure) have been deleted, see 36000-36013, 36400-36425 for intravenous procedure, and 36100-36218 for intra-arterial procedure and 75671)

75676 Angiography, carotid, cervical, unilateral, radiological supervision and interpretation

(75677, 75678 (complete procedure) have been deleted, see 36000-36013, 36400-36425 for intravenous procedure, and 36100-36218 for intra-arterial procedure and 75676)

75680 Angiography, carotid, cervical, bilateral, radiological supervision and interpretation
➔ *CPT Assistant* Oct 00:4

(75681, 75682 (complete procedure) have been deleted, see 36000-36013, 36400-36425 for intravenous procedure, and 36100-36218 for intra-arterial procedure and 75680)

75685 Angiography, vertebral, cervical, and/or intracranial, radiological supervision and interpretation
➔ *CPT Assistant* Oct 00:4

(75686 has been deleted)

(75687 (complete procedure) has been deleted, see 36000-36013, 36400-36425 for intravenous procedure, and 36100-36218 for intra-arterial procedure and 75685)

(75690 (complete procedure) has been deleted, see 36000-36013, 36400-36425 for intravenous procedure, and 36100-36218 for intra-arterial procedure and 75685)

(75691 has been deleted)

(75692 (complete procedure) has been deleted, see 36000-36013, 36400-36425 for intravenous procedure, and 36100-36218 for intra-arterial procedure and 75685)

(75695 (complete procedure) has been deleted, see 36000-36013, 36400-36425 for intravenous procedure, and 36100-36218 for intra-arterial procedure and 75685)

(75696 has been deleted)

(75697 (complete procedure) has been deleted, see 36000-36013, 36400-36425 for intravenous procedure, and 36100-36218 for intra-arterial procedure and 75685)

75705 Angiography, spinal, selective, radiological supervision and interpretation

(75706 (complete procedure) has been deleted, see 36000-36013, 36400-36425 for intravenous procedure, and 36100-36248 for intra-arterial procedure and 75705)

75710 Angiography, extremity, unilateral, radiological supervision and interpretation
➲ *CPT Assistant* Apr 99:11

(75711, 75712 (complete procedure) have been deleted, see 36000-36013, 36400-36425 for intravenous procedure, and 36100-36248 for intra-arterial procedure and 75710)

75716 Angiography, extremity, bilateral, radiological supervision and interpretation
➲ *CPT Assistant* Fall 93:16

(75717, 75718 (complete procedure) have been deleted, see 36000-36013, 36400-36425 for intravenous procedure, and 36100-36248 for intra-arterial procedure and 75716)

75722 Angiography, renal, unilateral, selective (including flush aortogram), radiological supervision and interpretation

(75723 (complete procedure) has been deleted, see 36000-36013, 36400-36425 for intravenous procedure, and 36100-36200 and 36245-36248 for intra-arterial procedure and 75722)

75724 Angiography, renal, bilateral, selective (including flush aortogram), radiological supervision and interpretation

(75725 (complete procedure) has been deleted, see 36000-36013, 36400-36425 for intravenous procedure, and 36100-36200 and 36245-36248 for intra-arterial procedure and 75724)

75726 Angiography, visceral, selective or supraselective, (with or without flush aortogram), radiological supervision and interpretation

(For selective angiography, each additional visceral vessel studied after basic examination, use 75774)

(75727, 75728 (complete procedure) have been deleted, see 36000-36013, 36400-36425 for intravenous procedure, and 36100-36248 for intra-arterial procedure and 75726)

75731 Angiography, adrenal, unilateral, selective, radiological supervision and interpretation

(75732 (complete procedure) has been deleted, see 36000-36013, 36400-36425 for intravenous procedure, and 36100-36200 and 36245-36248 for intra-arterial procedure and 75731)

75733 Angiography, adrenal, bilateral, selective, radiological supervision and interpretation

(75734 (complete procedure) has been deleted, see 36000-36013, 36400-36425 for intravenous procedure, and 36100-36200 and 36245-36248 for intra-arterial procedure and 75733)

75736 Angiography, pelvic, selective or supraselective, radiological supervision and interpretation

(75737, 75738 (complete procedure) have been deleted, see 36000-36013, 36400-36425 for intravenous procedure, and 36100-36200 and 36245-36248 for intra-arterial procedure and 75736)

75741 Angiography, pulmonary, unilateral, selective, radiological supervision and interpretation

(For injection procedure, use 93541)

(75742 (complete procedure) has been deleted, see 36000-36015, 36400-36425 for intravenous procedure and 75741)

75743 Angiography, pulmonary, bilateral, selective, radiological supervision and interpretation
➲ *CPT Assistant* Spring 94:29; Apr 98:3

(For injection procedure, use 93541)

(75744 (complete procedure) has been deleted, see 36000-36015, 36400-36425 for intravenous procedure and 75743)

75746 Angiography, pulmonary, by nonselective catheter or venous injection, radiological supervision and interpretation

(75747, 75748 (complete procedure) have been deleted, see 36000-36013, 36400-36425 for intravenous procedure, and 36100-36200 for intra-arterial procedure and 75746)

(For injection procedure, use 93541)

(75750 has been deleted. To report, use 93556)

(75751 (complete procedure) has been deleted, see 36000-36013, 36400-36425 for intravenous procedure, and 36100-36200 for intra-arterial procedure and 93556)

(For introduction of catheter, injection procedure, see 93501-▶93533◀, 93539, 93540, 93545, 93556)

(75752 has been deleted. To report, use 93556)

(75753 (complete procedure) has been deleted, see 36100-36218 for intra-arterial procedure and 93556)

(For introduction of catheter, injection procedure, see 93501-▶93533◀, 93545, 93556)

(75754 has been deleted. To report, use 93556)

(75755 (complete procedure) has been deleted, see 36100-36218 for intra-arterial procedure and 93556)

(For introduction of catheter, injection procedure, see 93501-▶93533◀, 93539, 93540, 93545, 93556)

75756 Angiography, internal mammary, radiological supervision and interpretation

(For introduction of catheter, injection procedure, see 93501-▶93533◀, 93545, 93556)

(75757 (complete procedure) has been deleted, see 36000-36013, 36400-36425 for intravenous procedure, and 36100-36218 for intra-arterial procedure and 93556)

(75762 has been deleted. To report, use 93556)

(75764 (complete procedure) has been deleted, see 36000-36013, 36400-36425 for intravenous procedure, and 36100-36218 for intra-arterial procedure and 93556)

(75766 has been deleted. To report, use 93556)

(75767 has been deleted. To report, see 36000-36013, 36400-36425 for intravenous procedure, and 36100-36218 for intra-arterial procedure and 93556)

(75772, 75773 have been deleted. To report, use 75774)

+ 75774 Angiography, selective, each additional vessel studied after basic examination, radiological supervision and interpretation (List separately in addition to code for primary procedure)

→ *CPT Assistant* Fall 93:17; Spring 94:29

(Use 75774 in addition to code for specific initial vessel studied)

(For angiography, see codes 75600-75790)

(For catheterizations, see codes 36215-36248)

(For introduction of catheter, injection procedure, see 93501-►93533◄, 93545, 93555, 93556)

(75775 (complete procedure) has been deleted, see 36000-36015, 36400-36425 for intravenous procedure, and 36100-36248 for intra-arterial procedure and 75774)

75790 Angiography, arteriovenous shunt (eg, dialysis patient), radiological supervision and interpretation

(For introduction of catheter, use 36140, 36145, 36215-36217, 36245-36247)

Veins and Lymphatics

(For injection procedure for venous system, see 36000-36015, 36400-36510)

(For injection procedure for lymphatic system, use 38790)

75801 Lymphangiography, extremity only, unilateral, radiological supervision and interpretation

(75802 (complete procedure) has been deleted, see 38790, 75801)

75803 Lymphangiography, extremity only, bilateral, radiological supervision and interpretation

(75804 (complete procedure) has been deleted, see 38790, 75803)

75805 Lymphangiography, pelvic/abdominal, unilateral, radiological supervision and interpretation

(75806 (complete procedure) has been deleted, see 38790, 75805)

75807 Lymphangiography, pelvic/abdominal, bilateral, radiological supervision and interpretation

(75808 (complete procedure) has been deleted, see 38790, 75807)

75809 Shuntogram for investigation of previously placed indwelling nonvascular shunt (eg, LeVeen shunt, ventriculoperitoneal shunt, indwelling infusion pump), radiological supervision and interpretation

→ *CPT Changes* 2001

(For procedure, see 49427 or 61070)

75810 Splenoportography, radiological supervision and interpretation

(75811 (complete procedure) has been deleted, see 38200, 75810)

75820 Venography, extremity, unilateral, radiological supervision and interpretation

→ *CPT Assistant* Oct 97:10

Venography
75820-75822

A radiographic contrast study is performed on the veins of the lower extremities.

Inferior vena cava
Common iliac
Percutaneous catheter
Deep femoral vein
Femoral vein
Great saphenous vein
Popliteal vein
Anterior tibial vein
Small saphenous vein
Posterior tibial vein
Peroneal vein
Venous arch on dorsum of foot

(75821 (complete procedure) has been deleted, see 36000, 36005, 36406, 36410, 36420, 36425, 75820)

75822 Venography, extremity, bilateral, radiological supervision and interpretation

(75823 (complete procedure) has been deleted, see 36000, 36005, 36406, 36410, 36420, 36425, 75822)

75825 Venography, caval, inferior, with serialography, radiological supervision and interpretation

(75826 (complete procedure) has been deleted, see 36010, 75825)

⊘ =Modifier '-51' Exempt ▶ ◀=New or Revised Text ✚=Add-on Code CPT 2002

75827   Venography, caval, superior, with serialography, radiological supervision and interpretation
> *CPT Assistant* Apr 98:3

(75828 (complete procedure) has been deleted, see 36010, 75827)

75831   Venography, renal, unilateral, selective, radiological supervision and interpretation

(75832 (complete procedure) has been deleted, see 36000-36012, 75831)

75833   Venography, renal, bilateral, selective, radiological supervision and interpretation

(75834 (complete procedure) has been deleted, see 36000-36012, 75833)

75840   Venography, adrenal, unilateral, selective, radiological supervision and interpretation

(75841 (complete procedure) has been deleted, see 36000-36012, 75840)

75842   Venography, adrenal, bilateral, selective, radiological supervision and interpretation

(75843 (complete procedure) has been deleted, see 36000-36012, 75842)

(75845, 75846, 75847, 75850, 75851 have been deleted)

75860   Venography, sinus or jugular, catheter, radiological supervision and interpretation

(75861 (complete procedure) has been deleted, see 36000-36012 for intravenous procedure and 36100-36218 for intra-arterial procedure, 75860)

75870   Venography, superior sagittal sinus, radiological supervision and interpretation

(75871 (complete procedure) has been deleted, see 36000-36012 for intravenous procedure and 36100-36218 for intra-arterial procedure, 75870)

75872   Venography, epidural, radiological supervision and interpretation

(75873 (complete procedure) has been deleted, see 36000-36012 for intravenous procedure and 36100-36218 for intra-arterial procedure, 75872)

75880   Venography, orbital, radiological supervision and interpretation

(75881 (complete procedure) has been deleted, see 36000-36012 for intravenous procedure and 36100-36218 for intra-arterial procedure, 75880)

75885   Percutaneous transhepatic portography with hemodynamic evaluation, radiological supervision and interpretation
> *CPT Assistant* Oct 96:4

(75886 (complete procedure) has been deleted, see 36011, 36012, 36481, 75885)

75887   Percutaneous transhepatic portography without hemodynamic evaluation, radiological supervision and interpretation

(75888 (complete procedure) has been deleted, see 36011, 36012, 36481, 75887)

75889   Hepatic venography, wedged or free, with hemodynamic evaluation, radiological supervision and interpretation

(75890 (complete procedure) has been deleted, see 36000-36012, 75889)

75891   Hepatic venography, wedged or free, without hemodynamic evaluation, radiological supervision and interpretation

(75892 (complete procedure) has been deleted, see 36000-36012, 75891)

75893   Venous sampling through catheter, with or without angiography (eg, for parathyroid hormone, renin), radiological supervision and interpretation

(For procedure, use 36500)

Transcatheter Procedures

75894   Transcatheter therapy, embolization, any method, radiological supervision and interpretation
> *CPT Assistant* Sep 98:7

(75895 (complete procedure) has been deleted, see 37204, 61624, 61626, 75894)

75896   Transcatheter therapy, infusion, any method (eg, thrombolysis other than coronary), radiological supervision and interpretation

(75897 (complete procedure) has been deleted, see 37201, 37202, 75896)

(For infusion for coronary disease, see 92975, 92977)

▲ **75898**   Angiography through existing catheter for follow-up study for transcatheter therapy, embolization or infusion
> *CPT Changes* 2002

75900   Exchange of a previously placed arterial catheter during thrombolytic therapy with contrast monitoring, radiological supervision and interpretation

(For procedure, use 37209)

75940   Percutaneous placement of IVC filter, radiological supervision and interpretation
> *CPT Assistant* Nov 00:11

(75941 (complete procedure) has been deleted, see 37620, 75940)

75945   Intravascular ultrasound (non-coronary vessel), radiological supervision and interpretation; initial vessel

+ 75946   each additional non-coronary vessel (List separately in addition to code for primary procedure)

(Use 75946 in conjunction with code 75945)

(For catheterizations, see codes 36215-36248)

(For transcatheter therapies, see codes 37200-37208, 61624, 61626)

(For procedure, see 37250, 37251)

(75950, 75951, 75955, 75956 (complete procedure) have been deleted, see 37204, 61624, 61626, 75894)

75952 Endovascular repair of infrarenal abdominal aortic aneurysm or dissection, radiological supervision and interpretation
→ *CPT Changes* 2001

(For implantation of endovascular grafts, see 34800-34808)

75953 Placement of proximal or distal extension prosthesis for endovascular repair of infrarenal abdominal aortic aneurysm, radiological supervision and interpretation
→ *CPT Changes* 2001

(For implantation of endovascular extension prostheses, see 34825, 34826)

75960 Transcatheter introduction of intravascular stent(s), (non-coronary vessel), percutaneous and/or open, radiological supervision and interpretation, each vessel
→ *CPT Assistant* Fall 93:18; Oct 96:2

(For procedure, see 37205-37208)

►(For radiologic supervision and interpretation for transcatheter placement of extracranial cerebrovascular artery stent(s), use Category III code 0007T)◄

75961 Transcatheter retrieval, percutaneous, of intravascular foreign body (eg, fractured venous or arterial catheter), radiological supervision and interpretation

(For procedure, use 37203)

75962 Transluminal balloon angioplasty, peripheral artery, radiological supervision and interpretation
→ *CPT Assistant* Fall 93:18

(75963 (complete procedure) has been deleted, see 35450-35460 or 35470-35476 and 75962)

+ 75964 Transluminal balloon angioplasty, each additional peripheral artery, radiological supervision and interpretation (List separately in addition to code for primary procedure)

(Use 75964 in conjunction with code 75962)

(75965 (complete procedure) has been deleted, see 35450-35460 or 35470-35476 and 75964)

75966 Transluminal balloon angioplasty, renal or other visceral artery, radiological supervision and interpretation

(75967 (complete procedure) has been deleted, see 35450-35460 or 35470-35476 and 75966)

+ 75968 Transluminal balloon angioplasty, each additional visceral artery, radiological supervision and interpretation (List separately in addition to code for primary procedure)

(Use 75968 in conjunction with code 75966)

(75969 (complete procedure) has been deleted, see 35450-35460 or 35470-35476 and 75968)

(For percutaneous transluminal coronary angioplasty, see 92982-92984)

75970 Transcatheter biopsy, radiological supervision and interpretation

(For injection procedure only for transcatheter therapy or biopsy, see 36100-36299)

(For transcatheter renal and ureteral biopsy, use 52007)

(For percutaneous needle biopsy of pancreas, use 48102; of retroperitoneal lymph node or mass, use 49180)

(75971 (complete procedure) has been deleted, see 37200, 75970)

(75972-75977 have been deleted. To report, see 75962-75968)

75978 Transluminal balloon angioplasty, venous (eg, subclavian stenosis), radiological supervision and interpretation
→ *CPT Assistant* Oct 96:4

(75979 (complete procedure) has been deleted, see 35460, 35476, 75978)

75980 Percutaneous transhepatic biliary drainage with contrast monitoring, radiological supervision and interpretation

(75981 (complete procedure) has been deleted, see 47510, 75980)

75982 Percutaneous placement of drainage catheter for combined internal and external biliary drainage or of a drainage stent for internal biliary drainage in patients with an inoperable mechanical biliary obstruction, radiological supervision and interpretation

(75983 (complete procedure) has been deleted, see 47511, 47556, 75982)

75984 Change of percutaneous tube or drainage catheter with contrast monitoring (eg, gastrointestinal system, genitourinary system, abscess), radiological supervision and interpretation

(75985 (complete procedure) has been deleted, see 43760, 47525, 47530, 50398, 50688, 51705, 51710, 75984)

(For change of nephrostomy or pyelostomy tube only, use 50398)

(For introduction procedure only for percutaneous biliary drainage, see 47510, 47511)

(For percutaneous cholecystostomy, use 47490)

(For change of percutaneous biliary drainage catheter only, use 47525)

(For percutaneous nephrostolithotomy or pyelostolithotomy, see 50080, 50081)

▲ **75989** Radiological guidance for percutaneous drainage of abscess, or specimen collection (ie, fluoroscopy, ultrasound, or computed axial tomography), with placement of indwelling catheter, radiological supervision and interpretation

➔ *CPT Assistant* Nov 97:24; Mar 98:8; *CPT Changes* 2001; 2002

(75990 (complete procedure) has been deleted, see appropriate organ or site and 75989)

Transluminal Atherectomy

75992 Transluminal atherectomy, peripheral artery, radiological supervision and interpretation

(For procedure, see 35481-35485, 35491-35495)

+ **75993** Transluminal atherectomy, each additional peripheral artery, radiological supervision and interpretation (List separately in addition to code for primary procedure)

(Use 75993 in conjunction with code 75992)

(For procedure, see 35481-35485, 35491-35495)

75994 Transluminal atherectomy, renal, radiological supervision and interpretation

(For procedure, see 35480, 35490)

75995 Transluminal atherectomy, visceral, radiological supervision and interpretation

(For procedure, see 35480, 35490)

+ **75996** Transluminal atherectomy, each additional visceral artery, radiological supervision and interpretation (List separately in addition to code for primary procedure)

(Use 75996 in conjunction with code 75995)

(For procedure, see 35480, 35490)

Other Procedures

(For arthrography of shoulder, use 73040; elbow, use 73085; wrist, use 73115; hip, use 73525; knee, use 73580; ankle, use 73615)

76000 Fluoroscopy (separate procedure), up to one hour physician time, other than 71023 or 71034 (eg, cardiac fluoroscopy)

➔ *CPT Assistant* Apr 96:10; Nov 99:32; Dec 00:14; *CPT Changes* 2000

76001 Fluoroscopy, physician time more than one hour, assisting a non-radiologic physician (eg, nephrostolithotomy, ERCP, bronchoscopy, transbronchial biopsy)

76003 Fluoroscopic guidance for needle placement (eg, biopsy, aspiration, injection, localization device)

➔ *CPT Assistant* Fall 93:14; *CPT Changes* 2001

▶(See appropriate surgical code for procedure and anatomic location)◀

▶(Fluoroscopy 76003 is considered inclusive of all radiographic arthrography with the exception of supervision and interpretation for CT and MR arthrography)◀

▶Do not report 76003 in addition to 70332, 73040, 73085, 73115, 73525, 73580, 73615)◀

▶(Fluoroscopy 76003 is considered inclusive of organ/anatomic specific radiological supervision and interpretation procedures 74320, 74350, 74355, 74445, 74470, 74475, 75809, 75810, 75885, 75887, 75980, 75982, 75989)◀

76005 Fluoroscopic guidance and localization of needle or catheter tip for spine or paraspinous diagnostic or therapeutic injection procedures (epidural, transforaminal epidural, subarachnoid, paravertebral facet joint, paravertebral facet joint nerve or sacroiliac joint), including neurolytic agent destruction

➔ *CPT Assistant* Nov 99: 32, 34, 41; Jan 00:1; Feb 00:4; Aug 00:7; *CPT Changes* 2000

(Injection of contrast during fluoroscopic guidance and localization is an inclusive component of codes 62270-62273, 62280-62282, 62310-62319)

(Fluoroscopic guidance for subarachnoid puncture for diagnostic radiographic myelography is included in supervision and interpretation codes 72240, 72255, 72265, 72270)

(For epidural or subarachnoid needle or catheter placement and injection, see codes 62270-62273, 62280-62282, 62310-62319)

(For sacroiliac joint arthrography, see 27096, 73542. If formal arthrography is not performed, recorded, and a formal radiographic report is not issued, use 76005 for fluoroscopic guidance for sacroiliac joint injections)

(For paravertebral facet joint injection, see 64470-64476. For transforaminal epidural needle placement and injection, see 64479-64484)

(For destruction by neurolytic agent, see 64600-64680)

76006 Radiologic examination, stress view(s), any joint, stress applied by a physician (includes comparison views)

➔ *CPT Assistant* Nov 98:21

76010 Radiologic examination from nose to rectum for foreign body, single view, child

➔ *CPT Changes* 2001

76012 Radiological supervision and interpretation, percutaneous vertebroplasty, per vertebral body; under fluoroscopic guidance

➔ *CPT Changes* 2001

76013 under CT guidance

➔ *CPT Changes* 2001

(For procedure, see 22520-22522)

76020 Bone age studies

76040 Bone length studies (orthoroentgenogram, scanogram)

(76060 has been deleted. See 76061, 76062)

76061 Radiologic examination, osseous survey; limited (eg, for metastases)

76062 complete (axial and appendicular skeleton)

76065 Radiologic examination, osseous survey, infant

▲ **76066** Joint survey, single view, two or more joints (specify)
➜ *CPT Changes* 2002

▲ **76070** Computerized axial tomography bone density study, one or more sites
➜ *CPT Changes* 2002

76075 Dual energy x-ray absorptiometry (DEXA), bone density study, one or more sites; axial skeleton (eg, hips, pelvis, spine)
➜ *CPT Assistant* Nov 97:24

76076 appendicular skeleton (peripheral) (eg, radius, wrist, heel)
➜ *CPT Assistant* Nov 97:24

▲ **76078** Radiographic absorptiometry (eg, photodensitometry, radiogrammetry), one or more sites
➜ *CPT Assistant* Nov 97:24; *CPT Changes* 2002

76080 Radiologic examination, abscess, fistula or sinus tract study, radiological supervision and interpretation
➜ *CPT Assistant* Nov 97:24; Mar 98:8

(76081 (complete procedure) has been deleted, see 20501, 49424, 76080)

+ ● **76085** Digitization of film radiographic images with computer analysis for lesion detection and further physician review for interpretation, screening mammography (List separately in addition to code for primary procedure)

▶(Use 76085 in conjunction with code 76092)◀

76086 Mammary ductogram or galactogram, single duct, radiological supervision and interpretation

(76087 (complete procedure) has been deleted, see 19030, 76086)

76088 Mammary ductogram or galactogram, multiple ducts, radiological supervision and interpretation

(76089 (complete procedure) has been deleted, see 19030, 76088)

76090 Mammography; unilateral
➜ *CPT Assistant* Jul 96:6; Jun 99:10

76091 bilateral
➜ *CPT Assistant* Jul 96:6

76092 Screening mammography, bilateral (two view film study of each breast)
➜ *CPT Assistant* Jul 96:6; Jun 99:10

▶(For computer aided detection applied to a screening mammogram, use 76085)◀

76093 Magnetic resonance imaging, breast, without and/or with contrast material(s); unilateral

76094 bilateral

76095 Stereotactic localization guidance for breast biopsy or needle placement (eg, for wire localization or for injection), each lesion, radiological supervision and interpretation
➜ *CPT Assistant* Apr 96:9; Nov 97:24; *CPT Changes* 2001

(For procedure, see ▶10022, 19000, 19001,◀ 19102, 19103, ▶19290, 19291◀)

(For injection for sentinel node localization without lymphoscintigraphy, use 38792)

76096 Mammographic guidance for needle placement, breast (eg, for wire localization or for injection), each lesion, radiological supervision and interpretation
➜ *CPT Assistant* Jan 01:8; *CPT Changes* 2001

(For procedure, see ▶10022,◀ 19000, 19102, 19103, ▶19290, 19291◀)

(For injection for sentinel node localization without lymphoscintigraphy, use 38792)

(76097 has been deleted. To report, see 19291, 76096)

76098 Radiological examination, surgical specimen

76100 Radiologic examination, single plane body section (eg, tomography), other than with urography

76101 Radiologic examination, complex motion (ie, hypercycloidal) body section (eg, mastoid polytomography), other than with urography; unilateral

76102 bilateral

(For nephrotomography, use 74415)

▲ **76120** Cineradiography/videoradiography, except where specifically included
➜ *CPT Assistant* Sep 00:4; *CPT Changes* 2002

+ ▲ **76125** Cineradiography/videoradiography to complement routine examination (List separately in addition to code for primary procedure)
➜ *CPT Assistant* Sep 00:4; *CPT Changes* 2002

(76127 has been deleted. The use of photographic media is not reported separately but is considered to be a component of the basic procedure)

(76130-76137 have been deleted. To report, use code for specific radiologic examination)

76140 Consultation on x-ray examination made elsewhere, written report
➜ *CPT Assistant* Summer 91:13

76150 Xeroradiography

(76150 is to be used for non-mammographic studies only)

(76300 has been deleted. To report, use 76499)

76350 Subtraction in conjunction with contrast studies

▲ **76355** Computerized axial tomographic guidance for stereotactic localization
➜ *CPT Changes* 2002

▲ **76360** Computerized axial tomographic guidance for needle biopsy, radiological supervision and interpretation
➜ *CPT Assistant* Fall 93:12; Jan 01:8; *CPT Changes* 2001; 2002

(76361 (complete procedure) has been deleted, see appropriate organ or site and 76360)

● **76362** Computerized axial tomographic guidance for, and monitoring of, tissue ablation
➔ *CPT Changes* 2002

►(For percutaneous radiofrequency ablation, use 47382)◄

(76365 has been deleted. For computed tomographic guidance for cyst aspiration, see appropriate organ or site and 76360)

(76366 (complete procedure) has been deleted, see appropriate organ or site and 76360)

▲ **76370** Computerized axial tomographic guidance for placement of radiation therapy fields
➔ *CPT Assistant* Fall 91:12; *CPT Changes* 2002

▲ **76375** Coronal, sagittal, multiplanar, oblique, 3-dimensional and/or holographic reconstruction of computerized axial tomography, magnetic resonance imaging, or other tomographic modality
➔ *CPT Assistant* Apr 96:11; Nov 97:25; *CPT Changes* 2002

(Use 76375 in addition to code for imaging procedure)

▲ **76380** Computerized axial tomography, limited or localized follow-up study
➔ *CPT Changes* 2002

76390 Magnetic resonance spectroscopy

(For magnetic resonance imaging, use appropriate MRI body site code)
➔ *CPT Assistant* Nov 97:25

76393 Magnetic resonance guidance for needle placement (eg, for biopsy, needle aspiration, injection, or placement of localization device) radiological supervision and interpretation
➔ *CPT Assistant* Jan 01:8; *CPT Changes* 2001; 2002

►(For procedure see appropriate organ or site)◄

● **76394** Magnetic resonance guidance for, and monitoring of, tissue ablation
➔ *CPT Changes* 2002

►(For percutaneous radiofrequency ablation, use 47382)◄

76400 Magnetic resonance (eg, proton) imaging, bone marrow blood supply

● **76490** Ultrasound guidance for, and monitoring of, tissue ablation
➔ *CPT Changes* 2002

►(Do not report 76490 in addition to 76986)◄

►(For ablation, see codes 47370-47382)◄

76499 Unlisted diagnostic radiologic procedure
➔ *CPT Assistant* Jul 99:10; Sep 00:4

Diagnostic Ultrasound

Definitions

A-mode implies a one-dimensional ultrasonic measurement procedure.

M-mode implies a one-dimensional ultrasonic measurement procedure with movement of the trace to record amplitude and velocity of moving echo-producing structures.

B-scan implies a two-dimensional ultrasonic scanning procedure with a two-dimensional display.

Real-time scan implies a two-dimensional ultrasonic scanning procedure with display of both two-dimensional structure and motion with time.

Head and Neck

►(For determination of corneal thickness (eg, pachymetry) with interpretation and report, bilateral, use Category III code 0025T)◄

(76500, 76505 have been deleted. To report, use 76999)

76506 Echoencephalography, B-scan and/or real time with image documentation (gray scale) (for determination of ventricular size, delineation of cerebral contents and detection of fluid masses or other intracranial abnormalities), including A-mode encephalography as secondary component where indicated

76511 Ophthalmic ultrasound, echography, diagnostic; A-scan only, with amplitude quantification
➔ *CPT Assistant* Oct 96:9; Nov 99:42

76512   contact B-scan (with or without simultaneous A-scan)
➔ *CPT Assistant* Oct 96:9

76513   anterior segment ultrasound, immersion (water bath) B-scan or high resolution biomicroscopy
➔ *CPT Assistant* Nov 99:42; *CPT Changes* 2000

(76515 has been deleted. To report, use 76999)

76516 Ophthalmic biometry by ultrasound echography, A-scan;

(76517 has been deleted. To report, use 76999)

76519   with intraocular lens power calculation

►(For partial coherence interferometry, use 92136)◄

76529 Ophthalmic ultrasonic foreign body localization

(76530 has been deleted. To report, use 76999)

(76535 has been deleted. To report, use 76536)

▲ **76536** Ultrasound, soft tissues of head and neck (eg, thyroid, parathyroid, parotid), B-scan and/or real time with image documentation
➔ *CPT Changes* 2002

(76550 has been deleted. To report, see 93880-93888)

Chest

(76601 has been deleted. To report, use 76999)

▲**76604** Ultrasound, chest, B-scan (includes mediastinum) and/or real time with image documentation
➔ *CPT Changes* 2002

(76620, 76625 have been deleted)

(76627, 76628 have been deleted. To report, see 93307, 93308)

(76629 has been deleted)

(76632 has been deleted. To report, see 93320, 93321)

(76640 has been deleted. To report, use 76999)

▲**76645** Ultrasound, breast(s) (unilateral or bilateral), B-scan and/or real time with image documentation
➔ *CPT Changes* 2002

Abdomen and Retroperitoneum

▲**76700** Ultrasound, abdominal, B-scan and/or real time with image documentation; complete
➔ *CPT Assistant* Fall 93:13; *CPT Changes* 2002

76705 limited (eg, single organ, quadrant, follow-up)
➔ *CPT Assistant* Fall 93:13

▲**76770** Ultrasound, retroperitoneal (eg, renal, aorta, nodes), B-scan and/or real time with image documentation; complete
➔ *CPT Assistant* May 99:10; Jun 99:10; *CPT Changes* 2002

76775 limited
➔ *CPT Assistant* May 99:10; Jun 99:10

▲**76778** Ultrasound, transplanted kidney, B-scan and/or real time with image documentation, with or without duplex Doppler study
➔ *CPT Changes* 2002

Spinal Canal

▲**76800** Ultrasound, spinal canal and contents
➔ *CPT Assistant* Apr 98:15; *CPT Changes* 2002

Pelvis

▲**76805** Ultrasound, pregnant uterus, B-scan and/or real time with image documentation; complete (complete fetal and maternal evaluation)
➔ *CPT Assistant* Apr 97:2; Nov 97:25; *CPT Changes* 2002

76810 complete (complete fetal and maternal evaluation), multiple gestation, after the first trimester
➔ *CPT Assistant* Apr 97:2

76815 limited (fetal size, heart beat, placental location, fetal position, or emergency in the delivery room)
➔ *CPT Assistant* Apr 97:2; Nov 97:25

76816 follow-up or repeat
➔ *CPT Assistant* Apr 97:2

76818 Fetal biophysical profile; with non-stress testing
➔ *CPT Assistant* Apr 97:2; May 98:10; *CPT Changes* 2001

▲**76819** without non-stress testing
➔ *CPT Changes* 2001; 2002

►(Fetal biophysical profile assessments for the second and any additional fetuses, should be reported separately by code 76818 or 76819 with the modifier '-51' appended)◄

(For amniotic fluid index without non-stress test, use 76815)

76825 Echocardiography, fetal, cardiovascular system, real time with image documentation (2D), with or without M-mode recording;
➔ *CPT Assistant* Apr 97:2

76826 follow-up or repeat study
➔ *CPT Assistant* Apr 97:2

76827 Doppler echocardiography, fetal, cardiovascular system, pulsed wave and/or continuous wave with spectral display; complete
➔ *CPT Assistant* Apr 97:2

76828 follow-up or repeat study
➔ *CPT Assistant* Apr 97:2

(To report the use of color mapping, use 93325)

▲**76830** Ultrasound, transvaginal
➔ *CPT Assistant* Aug 96:10; Jul 99:8; *CPT Changes* 2002

76831 Hysterosonography, with or without color flow Doppler
➔ *CPT Assistant* Nov 97:25; Jul 99:8

(For introduction of saline or contrast for hysterosonography, use 58340)

(76855 has been deleted. To report, see 93975-93979)

▲**76856** Ultrasound, pelvic (nonobstetric), B-scan and/or real time with image documentation; complete
➔ *CPT Changes* 2002

76857 limited or follow-up (eg, for follicles)
➔ *CPT Assistant* Jun 97:10

Genitalia

▲**76870** Ultrasound, scrotum and contents
➔ *CPT Changes* 2002

76872 Echography, transrectal;
➔ *CPT Assistant* May 96:3; Nov 99:42; *CPT Changes* 2000

76873 prostate volume study for brachytherapy treatment planning (separate procedure)
➔ *CPT Assistant* Nov 99:42; *CPT Changes* 2000

Extremities

▲**76880** Ultrasound, extremity, non-vascular, B-scan and/or real time with image documentation
➔ *CPT Changes* 2002

▲ **76885**   Ultrasound, infant hips, real time with imaging documentation; dynamic (requiring physician manipulation)
➔ *CPT Assistant* Nov 97:25; *CPT Changes* 2002

▲ **76886**   limited, static (not requiring physician manipulation)
➔ *CPT Assistant* Nov 97:25; *CPT Changes* 2002

Vascular Studies

(76900-76920 have been deleted. To report, see 93922-93971; for cerebrovascular studies, see 93875-93888)

(76925 has been deleted. To report, see 93922-93931 or 93965-93971)

(76926 has been deleted. To report, see 93875-93888 or 93975-93979)

Ultrasonic Guidance Procedures

76930   Ultrasonic guidance for pericardiocentesis, imaging supervision and interpretation
➔ *CPT Changes* 2001

(76931 (complete procedure) has been deleted, see 33010, 33011, 76930)

76932   Ultrasonic guidance for endomyocardial biopsy, imaging supervision and interpretation
➔ *CPT Changes* 2001

(76933 (complete procedure) has been deleted, see 93505, 76932)

(76934 has been deleted. For ultrasound guidance for thoracentesis or abdominal paracentesis, see 32000 and 76942)

(76935 (complete procedure) has been deleted, see 32000, 76942)

76936   Ultrasound guided compression repair of arterial pseudoaneurysm or arteriovenous fistulae (includes diagnostic ultrasound evaluation, compression of lesion and imaging)

(76938 has been deleted. For ultrasound guidance for cyst or renal pelvis aspiration, see appropriate organ or site and 76942)

(76939 (complete procedure) has been deleted, see appropriate organ or site and 76942)

76941   Ultrasonic guidance for intrauterine fetal transfusion or cordocentesis, imaging supervision and interpretation
➔ *CPT Changes* 2001

(For procedure, see 36460, 59012)

76942   Ultrasonic guidance for needle placement (eg, biopsy, aspiration, injection, localization device), imaging supervision and interpretation
➔ *CPT Assistant* Fall 93:12; May 96:3; Jun 97:5; *CPT Changes* 2001

(76943 (complete procedure) has been deleted, see appropriate organ or site and 76942)

(76944 has been deleted. To report, use 75989)

76945   Ultrasonic guidance for chorionic villus sampling, imaging supervision and interpretation
➔ *CPT Changes* 2001

(For procedure, use 59015)

76946   Ultrasonic guidance for amniocentesis, imaging supervision and interpretation
➔ *CPT Changes* 2001

(76947 (complete procedure) has been deleted, see 59000, 76946)

76948   Ultrasonic guidance for aspiration of ova, imaging supervision and interpretation
➔ *CPT Changes* 2001

(76949 (complete procedure) has been deleted, see 58970, 76948)

76950   Ultrasonic guidance for placement of radiation therapy fields
➔ *CPT Changes* 2001

(76960 has been deleted. To report, use 76950)

76965   Ultrasonic guidance for interstitial radioelement application

Other Procedures

76970   Ultrasound study follow-up (specify)

76975   Gastrointestinal endoscopic ultrasound, supervision and interpretation
➔ *CPT Assistant* Spring 94:5; *CPT Changes* 2001

(For procedure, use 43259)

(Do not report 76975 in conjunction with 43231, 43232, 43242, 45341, 45342)

76977   Ultrasound bone density measurement and interpretation, peripheral site(s), any method
➔ *CPT Assistant* Nov 98:21

(76980 has been deleted. To report, use code for specific ultrasound examination)

(76985 has been deleted. To report, use 76986)

76986   Ultrasonic guidance, intraoperative
➔ *CPT Changes* 2001

▶(Do not report 76986 in addition to 47370-47382)◀

▶(For ultrasound guidance for open and laparoscopic radiofrequency tissue ablation, use 76490)◀

(76990 has been deleted. To report, use 76999)

(76991 has been deleted. To report, see 76830, 76872)

76999   Unlisted ultrasound procedure

Radiation Oncology

Listings for Radiation Oncology provide for teletherapy and brachytherapy to include initial consultation, clinical treatment planning, simulation, medical radiation physics, dosimetry, treatment devices, special services, and clinical treatment management procedures. They include normal follow-up care during course of treatment and for three months following its completion.

When a service or procedure is provided that is not listed in this edition of *CPT* it should be identified by a Special Report (see page 256) and one of the unlisted procedure codes listed below:

77299 Unlisted procedure, therapeutic radiology clinical treatment planning
77399 Unlisted procedure, medical radiation physics, dosimetry and treatment devices, and special services
77499 Unlisted procedure, therapeutic radiology treatment management
77799 Unlisted procedure, clinical brachytherapy

For treatment by injectable or ingestible isotopes, see subsection **Nuclear Medicine**.

Consultation: Clinical Management

Preliminary consultation, evaluation of patient prior to decision to treat, or full medical care (in addition to treatment management) when provided by the therapeutic radiologist may be identified by the appropriate procedure codes from **Evaluation and Management, Medicine,** or **Surgery** sections.

Clinical Treatment Planning (External and Internal Sources)

The clinical treatment planning process is a complex service including interpretation of special testing, tumor localization, treatment volume determination, treatment time/dosage determination, choice of treatment modality, determination of number and size of treatment ports, selection of appropriate treatment devices, and other procedures.

Definitions

Simple planning requires a single treatment area of interest encompassed in a single port or simple parallel opposed ports with simple or no blocking.

Intermediate planning requires three or more converging ports, two separate treatment areas, multiple blocks, or special time dose constraints.

Complex planning requires highly complex blocking, custom shielding blocks, tangential ports, special wedges or compensators, three or more separate treatment areas, rotational or special beam considerations, combination of therapeutic modalities.

(77260, 77265, 77270, 77275 have been deleted. To report, see 77261-77263)

77261 Therapeutic radiology treatment planning; simple
➔ *CPT Assistant* Oct 97:1

77262 intermediate
➔ *CPT Assistant* Oct 97:1

77263 complex
➔ *CPT Assistant* Fall 91:12; Oct 97:1

Definitions

Simple simulation of a single treatment area with either a single port or parallel opposed ports. Simple or no blocking.

Intermediate simulation of three or more converging ports, two separate treatment areas, multiple blocks.

Complex simulation of tangential portals, three or more treatment areas, rotation or arc therapy, complex blocking, custom shielding blocks, brachytherapy source verification, hyperthermia probe verification, any use of contrast materials.

Three-dimensional computer-generated three dimensional reconstruction of tumor volume and surrounding critical normal tissue structures from direct CT scans and/or MRI data in preparation for non-coplanar or coplanar therapy. The simulation utilizes documented three-dimensional beam's eye view volume-dose displays of multiple or moving beams. Documentation with three-dimensional volume reconstruction and dose distribution is required.

Simulation may be carried out on a dedicated simulator, a radiation therapy treatment unit, or diagnostic x-ray machine.

77280 Therapeutic radiology simulation-aided field setting; simple
➔ *CPT Assistant* Oct 97:1; Nov 97:26

77285 intermediate
➔ *CPT Assistant* Oct 97:1

77290 complex
➔ *CPT Assistant* Fall 91:12; Oct 97:1

77295 three-dimensional
➔ *CPT Assistant* Oct 97:1; Nov 97:26

77299 Unlisted procedure, therapeutic radiology clinical treatment planning

Medical Radiation Physics, Dosimetry, Treatment Devices, and Special Services

▲**77300** Basic radiation dosimetry calculation, central axis depth dose calculation, TDF, NSD, gap calculation, off axis factor, tissue inhomogeneity factors, calculation of non-ionizing radiation surface and depth dose, as required during course of treatment, only when prescribed by the treating physician
➔ *CPT Assistant* Fall 91:13; Oct 97:1; *CPT Changes* 2002

⊘ =Modifier '-51' Exempt   ▶ ◀ =New or Revised Text   ✦ =Add-on Code   CPT 2002

● **77301** Intensity modulated radiotherapy plan, including dose-volume histograms for target and critical structure partial tolerance specifications

➲ CPT Changes 2002

▶(Dose plan is optimized using inverse or forward planning technique for modulated beam delivery (eg, binary, dynamic MLC) to create highly conformal dose distribution. Computer plan distribution must be verified for positional accuracy based on dosimetric verification of the intensity map with verification of treatment set up and interpretation of verification methodology)◀

77305 Teletherapy, isodose plan (whether hand or computer calculated); simple (one or two parallel opposed unmodified ports directed to a single area of interest)

➲ CPT Assistant Oct 97:1

77310 intermediate (three or more treatment ports directed to a single area of interest)

➲ CPT Assistant Oct 97:1

77315 complex (mantle or inverted Y, tangential ports, the use of wedges, compensators, complex blocking, rotational beam, or special beam considerations)

➲ CPT Assistant Fall 91:13; Oct 97:1

(Only one teletherapy isodose plan may be reported for a given course of therapy to a specific treatment area)

(77320 has been deleted. To report, see 77300-77399)

77321 Special teletherapy port plan, particles, hemibody, total body

➲ CPT Assistant Fall 91:14; Oct 97:1

(77325 has been deleted. To report, see 77300-77399)

77326 Brachytherapy isodose calculation; simple (calculation made from single plane, one to four sources/ribbon application, remote afterloading brachytherapy, 1 to 8 sources)

➲ CPT Assistant Winter 91:17

(For definition of source/ribbon, see page 279)

77327 intermediate (multiplane dosage calculations, application involving 5 to 10 sources/ribbons, remote afterloading brachytherapy, 9 to 12 sources)

➲ CPT Assistant Winter 91:17

77328 complex (multiplane isodose plan, volume implant calculations, over 10 sources/ribbons used, special spatial reconstruction, remote afterloading brachytherapy, over 12 sources)

➲ CPT Assistant Winter 91:17

(77330 has been deleted. To report, see 77300-77399)

77331 Special dosimetry (eg, TLD, microdosimetry) (specify), only when prescribed by the treating physician

➲ CPT Assistant Fall 91:13; Oct 97:1

77332 Treatment devices, design and construction; simple (simple block, simple bolus)

➲ CPT Assistant Oct 97:1

77333 intermediate (multiple blocks, stents, bite blocks, special bolus)

➲ CPT Assistant Oct 97:1

77334 complex (irregular blocks, special shields, compensators, wedges, molds or casts)

➲ CPT Assistant Fall 91:13; Oct 97:1

(77335 has been deleted. To report, see 77300-77399)

77336 Continuing medical physics consultation, including assessment of treatment parameters, quality assurance of dose delivery, and review of patient treatment documentation in support of the radiation oncologist, reported per week of therapy

➲ CPT Assistant Fall 91:15; Oct 97:1; Nov 98:21

(77340 has been deleted. To report, see 77300-77399)

(77345-77360 have been deleted. To report, see 77300-77399)

77370 Special medical radiation physics consultation

➲ CPT Assistant Fall 91:14; Oct 97:1

(77380 has been deleted. To report, use 77520)

(77381 has been deleted. To report, use 77523)

77399 Unlisted procedure, medical radiation physics, dosimetry and treatment devices, and special services

➲ CPT Assistant Nov 98:21

Radiation Treatment Delivery

(Radiation treatment delivery (77401-77416) recognizes the technical component and the various energy levels.)

(77400 has been deleted)

77401 Radiation treatment delivery, superficial and/or ortho voltage

77402 Radiation treatment delivery, single treatment area, single port or parallel opposed ports, simple blocks or no blocks; up to 5 MeV

77403 6-10 MeV

77404 11-19 MeV

(77405 has been deleted)

77406 20 MeV or greater

77407 Radiation treatment delivery, two separate treatment areas, three or more ports on a single treatment area, use of multiple blocks; up to 5 MeV

77408 6-10 MeV

77409 11-19 MeV

(77410 has been deleted)

77411 20 MeV or greater

77412 Radiation treatment delivery, three or more separate treatment areas, custom blocking, tangential ports, wedges, rotational beam, compensators, special particle beam (eg, electron or neutrons); up to 5 MeV

77413 6-10 MeV

➲ CPT Assistant Fall 91:14

77414   11-19 MeV

(77415 has been deleted. To report, use 77417)

77416   20 MeV or greater

77417   Therapeutic radiology port film(s)
→ *CPT Assistant* Fall 91:14; Dec 97:11

●**77418**   Intensity modulated treatment delivery, single or multiple fields/arcs, via narrow spatially and temporally modulated beams (eg, binary, dynamic MLC), per treatment session
→ *CPT Changes* 2002

▶(For intensity modulated treatment planning, use 77301)◀

Radiation Treatment Management

Radiation treatment management is reported in units of five fractions or treatment sessions, regardless of the actual time period in which the services are furnished. The services need not be furnished on consecutive days. Multiple fractions representing two or more treatment sessions furnished on the same day may be counted separately as long as there has been a distinct break in therapy sessions, and the fractions are of the character usually furnished on different days. Code 77427 is also reported if there are three or four fractions beyond a multiple of five at the end of a course of treatment; one or two fractions beyond a multiple of five at the end of a course of treatment are not reported separately. The professional services furnished during treatment management typically consists of:

- Review of port films;

- Review of dosimetry, dose delivery, and treatment parameters;

- Review of patient treatment set-up;

- Examination of patient for medical evaluation and management (eg, assessment of the patient's response to treatment, coordination of care and treatment, review of imaging and/or lab test results).

(77419, 77420, 77425, and 77430 have been deleted. To report radiation treatment management, use 77427)

77427   Radiation treatment management, five treatments
→ *CPT Assistant* Nov 99:42; Feb 00:7; *CPT Changes* 2000

77431   Radiation therapy management with complete course of therapy consisting of one or two fractions only
→ *CPT Assistant* Oct 97:1

(77431 is not to be used to fill in the last week of a long course of therapy)

77432   Stereotactic radiation treatment management of cerebral lesion(s) (complete course of treatment consisting of one session)
→ *CPT Assistant* Oct 97:1

(77435-77460 have been deleted. To report, see 77401-77499)

(77465 has been deleted)

77470   Special treatment procedure (eg, total body irradiation, hemibody radiation, per oral, endocavitary or intraoperative cone irradiation)
→ *CPT Assistant* Winter 91:22; Oct 97:1; *CPT Changes* 2001

(77470 assumes that the procedure is performed one or more times during the course of therapy, in addition to daily or weekly patient management)

77499   Unlisted procedure, therapeutic radiology treatment management
→ *CPT Assistant* Nov 99:42; Feb 00:7; *CPT Changes* 2000

Proton Beam Treatment Delivery

Definitions

Simple proton treatment delivery to a single treatment area utilizing a single non-tangential/oblique port, custom block with compensation (77522) and without compensation (77520).

Intermediate proton treatment delivery to one or more treatment areas utilizing two or more ports or one or more tangential/oblique ports, with custom blocks and compensators.

Complex proton treatment delivery to one or more treatment areas utilizing two or more ports per treatment area with matching or patching fields and/or multiple isocenters, with custom blocks and compensators.

77520   Proton treatment delivery; simple, without compensation
→ *CPT Assistant* Nov 99:43; *CPT Changes* 2000; 2001

77522   simple, with compensation
→ *CPT Changes* 2001

77523   intermediate
→ *CPT Assistant* Nov 99:43; *CPT Changes* 2000; 2001

77525   complex
→ *CPT Changes* 2001

Hyperthermia

Hyperthermia treatments as listed in this section include external (superficial and deep), interstitial, and intracavitary.

Radiation therapy when given concurrently is listed separately.

Hyperthermia is used only as an adjunct to radiation therapy or chemotherapy. It may be induced by a variety of sources (eg, microwave, ultrasound, low energy radio-frequency conduction, or by probes).

The listed treatments include management during the course of therapy and follow-up care for three months after completion.

Preliminary consultation is not included (see **Medicine** 99241-99263).

Physics planning and interstitial insertion of temperature sensors, and use of external or interstitial heat generating sources are included.

The following descriptors are included in the treatment schedule:

77600 Hyperthermia, externally generated; superficial (ie, heating to a depth of 4 cm or less)
➔ *CPT Assistant* Winter 91:22

77605 deep (ie, heating to depths greater than 4 cm)
➔ *CPT Assistant* Winter 91:22

77610 Hyperthermia generated by interstitial probe(s); 5 or fewer interstitial applicators
➔ *CPT Assistant* Winter 91:22

77615 more than 5 interstitial applicators
➔ *CPT Assistant* Winter 91:22

Clinical Intracavitary Hyperthermia

77620 Hyperthermia generated by intracavitary probe(s)
➔ *CPT Assistant* Winter 91:22

Clinical Brachytherapy

Clinical brachytherapy requires the use of either natural or man-made radioelements applied into or around a treatment field of interest. The supervision of radioelements and dose interpretation are performed solely by the therapeutic radiologist.

Services 77750-77799 include admission to the hospital and daily visits.

►For insertion of ovoids and tandems, use 57155.◄

►For insertion of Heyman capsules, use 58346.◄

Definitions

(Sources refer to intracavitary placement or permanent interstitial placement; ribbons refer to temporary interstitial placement)

A simple application has one to four sources/ribbons.

An intermediate application has five to ten sources/ribbons.

A complex application has greater than ten sources/ribbons.

(77700-77749 have been deleted. To report, see 77761-77799)

77750 Infusion or instillation of radioelement solution

(77755, 77760 have been deleted. To report, see 77761-77799)

77761 Intracavitary radiation source application; simple
➔ *CPT Assistant* Winter 91:23; Jan 96:7; Mar 99:3; *CPT Changes* 2001

77762 intermediate
➔ *CPT Assistant* Winter 91:23

77763 complex
➔ *CPT Assistant* Winter 91:23; Mar 99:3

(77765, 77770, 77775 have been deleted. To report, see 77761-77799)

77776 Interstitial radiation source application; simple
➔ *CPT Assistant* Winter 91:23; *CPT Changes* 2001

77777 intermediate
➔ *CPT Assistant* Winter 91:23

77778 complex
➔ *CPT Assistant* Winter 91:23

(77780 has been deleted. To report, see 77761-77799)

77781 Remote afterloading high intensity brachytherapy; 1-4 source positions or catheters
➔ *CPT Assistant* Winter 91:23; Mar 99:3

77782 5-8 source positions or catheters
➔ *CPT Assistant* Winter 91:23; Mar 99:3

77783 9-12 source positions or catheters
➔ *CPT Assistant* Winter 91:23; Mar 99:3

77784 over 12 source positions or catheters
➔ *CPT Assistant* Winter 91:23; Mar 99:3

(77785 has been deleted. To report, see 77761-77799)

77789 Surface application of radiation source
➔ *CPT Changes* 2001

77790 Supervision, handling, loading of radiation source
➔ *CPT Changes* 2001

77799 Unlisted procedure, clinical brachytherapy

(77800 has been deleted. To report, use 77331)

(77805-77810 have been deleted. To report, see 77305-77321 or 77326-77328)

(77850 has been deleted. To report, see 77300, 77336, 77370)

(77860 has been deleted. To report, use 77336)

(77999 has been deleted. To report, use 77399)

Nuclear Medicine

Listed procedures may be performed independently or in the course of overall medical care. If the physician providing these services is also responsible for diagnostic work-up and/or follow-up care of patient, see appropriate sections also.

Radioimmunoassay tests are found in the **Clinical Pathology** section (codes 82000-84999). These codes can be appropriately used by any specialist performing such tests in a laboratory licensed and/or certified for radioimmunoassays. The reporting of these tests is not confined to clinical pathology laboratories alone.

The services listed do not include the provision of radium or other radioelements. Those materials supplied by the physician should be listed separately and identified by the code 78990 for diagnostic radiopharmaceutical and 79900 for therapeutic radiopharmaceutical.

Diagnostic

Endocrine System

78000 Thyroid uptake; single determination

78001 multiple determinations

78003 stimulation, suppression or discharge (not including initial uptake studies)

78006 Thyroid imaging, with uptake; single determination

78007 multiple determinations

78010 Thyroid imaging; only

78011 with vascular flow

78015 Thyroid carcinoma metastases imaging; limited area (eg, neck and chest only)
> *CPT Assistant* Nov 98:21

78016 with additional studies (eg, urinary recovery)

(78017 has been deleted. To report, use 78018)

78018 whole body
> *CPT Assistant* Apr 99:4

(For calcitonin, use 82308)

(For triiodothyronine (true TT-3), use 84480)

(For triiodothyronine, free (FT-3), (unbound T-3 only), use 84481)

(For TT-4 thyroxine, use 84436)

(For T-4 thyroxine, neonatal, use 84437)

(For FT-4 thyroxine, free, (unbound T-4 only), use 84439)

+ 78020 Thyroid carcinoma metastases uptake (List separately in addition to code for primary procedure)
> *CPT Assistant* Nov 98:21; Apr 99:4

(Use 78020 in conjunction with code 78018 only)

78070 Parathyroid imaging

(For parathormone (parathyroid hormone), use 83970)

78075 Adrenal imaging, cortex and/or medulla

(For cortisol, plasma, use 82533)

(For cortisol, urine, use 82533)

(For aldosterone, double isotope technique, use 82088)

(For aldosterone, blood, use 82088)

(For aldosterone, urine, use 82088)

(For 17-ketosteroids, use 83586)

(For 17-OH ketosteroids, use 83586)

(For 17-hydroxycorticosteroids, use 83491)

(For insulin, use 83525)

(For insulin antibodies, use 86337)

(For proinsulin, use 84206)

(For glucagon, use 82943)

(For adrenocorticotropic hormone (ACTH), use 82024)

(For human growth hormone (HGH), (somatotropin), use 83003)

(For human growth antibody, use 86277)

(For thyroglobulin antibody, use 86800)

(For thyroid microsomal antibody, use 86376)

(For thyroid stimulating hormone (TSH), use 84443)

(For thyrotropin releasing factor, see 80438, 80439)

(For plus long-acting thyroid stimulator (LATS), use 84445)

(For follicle stimulating hormone (FSH component of pituitary gonadotropin), use 83001)

(For luteinizing hormone (LH component of pituitary gonadotropin), (ICSH), use 83002)

(For luteinizing releasing factor (LRH), use 83727)

(For prolactin level (mammotropin), use 84146)

(For vasopressin level (antidiuretic hormone), use 84588)

(For estradiol, use 82670)

(For progesterone, use 84144)

(For testosterone, blood, use 84403)

(For testosterone, urine, use 84403)

(For etiocholanolone, use 82696)

78099 Unlisted endocrine procedure, diagnostic nuclear medicine

(For chemical analysis, see **Chemistry** section)

Hematopoietic, Reticuloendothelial and Lymphatic System

78102 Bone marrow imaging; limited area

78103 multiple areas

78104 whole body

78110 Plasma volume, radiopharmaceutical volume-dilution technique (separate procedure); single sampling

78111 multiple samplings

78120 Red cell volume determination (separate procedure); single sampling

78121 multiple samplings

78122 Whole blood volume determination, including separate measurement of plasma volume and red cell volume (radiopharmaceutical volume-dilution technique)

78130 Red cell survival study;

78135 differential organ/tissue kinetics, (eg, splenic and/or hepatic sequestration)

78140 Labeled red cell sequestration, differential organ/tissue, (eg, splenic and/or hepatic)

78160 Plasma radioiron disappearance (turnover) rate

○ =Modifier '-51' Exempt ▶ ◀=New or Revised Text ✚=Add-on Code CPT 2002

78162	Radioiron oral absorption
78170	Radioiron red cell utilization
78172	Chelatable iron for estimation of total body iron

(78180 has been deleted. To report, use 78199)

(For hemosiderin, use 83071)

(For intrinsic factor antibodies, use 86340)

(For cyanocobalamin (vitamin B-12), use 82607)

(For folic acid (folate) serum, use 82746)

(For hepatitis B antigen, see 87340, 87350)

(For hepatitis A antibody (HAAb), see 86708, 86709)

(For hepatitis B core antibody (HBcAb), see 86704, 86705)

(For hepatitis B surface antigen (HBsAb), use 87340)

(For hepatitis B surface antibody (HBsAb), use 86706)

(For hepatitis Be antigen (HBeAg), use 87350)

(For hepatitis Be antibody (HBeAb), use 86707)

78185   Spleen imaging only, with or without vascular flow

(If combined with liver study, use procedures 78215 and 78216)

(78186 has been deleted)

78190   Kinetics, study of platelet survival, with or without differential organ/tissue localization

78191   Platelet survival study

(78192 has been deleted. To report, use 78805)

(78193 has been deleted. To report, use 78806)

▲**78195**   Lymphatics and lymph nodes imaging
  ➔ *CPT Assistant* Nov 98:22; Nov 99:43; Dec 99:8; *CPT Changes* 2000; 2002

(For sentinel node identification without scintigraphy imaging, use 38792)

(For sentinal node excision, see 38500-38542)

78199   Unlisted hematopoietic, reticuloendothelial and lymphatic procedure, diagnostic nuclear medicine

(For chemical analysis, see **Chemistry** section)

Gastrointestinal System

78201   Liver imaging; static only

78202   with vascular flow

(For spleen imaging only, use 78185)

78205   Liver imaging (SPECT);
  ➔ *CPT Assistant* Nov 98:22

78206   with vascular flow
  ➔ *CPT Assistant* Nov 98:22

78215   Liver and spleen imaging; static only

78216   with vascular flow

78220   Liver function study with hepatobiliary agents, with serial images

(78221 has been deleted. To report, use 78299)

78223   Hepatobiliary ductal system imaging, including gallbladder, with or without pharmacologic intervention, with or without quantitative measurement of gallbladder function

(78225 has been deleted)

78230   Salivary gland imaging;

78231   with serial images

78232   Salivary gland function study

(78240 has been deleted. To report pancreas imaging, use 78299)

78258   Esophageal motility

78261   Gastric mucosa imaging

78262   Gastroesophageal reflux study

78264   Gastric emptying study

78267   Urea breath test, C-14; acquisition for analysis
  ➔ *CPT Assistant* Nov 99:43; *CPT Changes* 2000

78268   analysis
  ➔ *CPT Assistant* Nov 99:43; *CPT Changes* 2000

78270   Vitamin B-12 absorption study (eg, Schilling test); without intrinsic factor

78271   with intrinsic factor

78272   Vitamin B-12 absorption studies combined, with and without intrinsic factor

(78276 has been deleted)

78278   Acute gastrointestinal blood loss imaging

(78280 has been deleted)

78282   Gastrointestinal protein loss

(78285, 78286 have been deleted. To report, use 78299)

(For gastrin, use 82941)

(For intrinsic factor level, use 83528)

(For carcinoembryonic antigen level (CEA), use 82378)

▲**78290**   Intestine imaging (eg, ectopic gastric mucosa, Meckels localization, volvulus)
  ➔ *CPT Changes* 2002

78291   Peritoneal-venous shunt patency test (eg, for LeVeen, Denver shunt)

(For injection procedure, use 49427)

78299   Unlisted gastrointestinal procedure, diagnostic nuclear medicine

(For chemical analysis, see **Chemistry** section)

Musculoskeletal System

Bone and joint imaging can be used in the diagnosis of a variety of inflammatory processes (eg, osteomyelitis), as well as for localization of primary and/or metastatic neoplasms.

78300 Bone and/or joint imaging; limited area
➔ *CPT Assistant* Mar 97:11

78305 multiple areas
➔ *CPT Assistant* Mar 97:11

78306 whole body
➔ *CPT Assistant* Mar 97:11

(78310 has been deleted. To report, use 78445)

78315 three phase study

78320 tomographic (SPECT)
➔ *CPT Assistant* Mar 97:11

78350 Bone density (bone mineral content) study, one or more sites; single photon absorptiometry
➔ *CPT Assistant* Nov 97:26

78351 dual photon absorptiometry, one or more sites
➔ *CPT Assistant* Nov 97:26

(78380, 78381 have been deleted. To report, see 78300, 78305)

(For radiographic bone density (photodensitometry), use 76078)

78399 Unlisted musculoskeletal procedure, diagnostic nuclear medicine

Cardiovascular System

Myocardial perfusion and cardiac blood pool imaging studies may be performed at rest and/or during stress. When performed during exercise and/or pharmacologic stress, the appropriate stress testing code from the 93015-93018 series should be reported in addition to code(s) 78460-78465, 78472, 78473, 78478, 78480, 78481, 78483, 78491, and 78492.

(78401-78412 have been deleted. To report, see 78472-78483)

78414 Determination of central c-v hemodynamics (non-imaging) (eg, ejection fraction with probe technique) with or without pharmacologic intervention or exercise, single or multiple determinations

(78415 has been deleted. To report, use 78472)

(78418-78424 have been deleted. To report, see 78460-78469)

(78425 has been deleted. To report, use 78472)

78428 Cardiac shunt detection

(78435 has been deleted. To report, use 78481)

78445 Non-cardiac vascular flow imaging (ie, angiography, venography)

78455 Venous thrombosis study (eg, radioactive fibrinogen)

78456 Acute venous thrombosis imaging, peptide
➔ *CPT Assistant* Nov 99:43; *CPT Changes* 2000

78457 Venous thrombosis imaging, venogram; unilateral
➔ *CPT Assistant* Nov 99:43; *CPT Changes* 2000

78458 bilateral
➔ *CPT Assistant* Nov 99:43; *CPT Changes* 2000

78459 Myocardial imaging, positron emission tomography (PET), metabolic evaluation
➔ *CPT Assistant* Jun 96:5; Nov 97:26

(For myocardial perfusion study, see 78491-78492)

78460 Myocardial perfusion imaging; (planar) single study, at rest or stress (exercise and/or pharmacologic), with or without quantification
➔ *CPT Assistant* Mar 99:10; Apr 00:1

78461 multiple studies, (planar) at rest and/or stress (exercise and/or pharmacologic), and redistribution and/or rest injection, with or without quantification
➔ *CPT Assistant* Mar 99:10

(78462, 78463 have been deleted. To report, see 78460, 78461)

78464 tomographic (SPECT), single study at rest or stress (exercise and/or pharmacologic), with or without quantification
➔ *CPT Assistant* Mar 99:10

78465 tomographic (SPECT), multiple studies, at rest and/or stress (exercise and/or pharmacologic) and redistribution and/or rest injection, with or without quantification
➔ *CPT Assistant* Aug 98:11; Mar 99:10

78466 Myocardial imaging, infarct avid, planar; qualitative or quantitative

(78467 has been deleted. To report, use 78466)

78468 with ejection fraction by first pass technique

78469 tomographic SPECT with or without quantification

(78470 has been deleted. To report, see 78472, 78473, or 78481)

(78471 has been deleted. To report, use 78472)

78472 Cardiac blood pool imaging, gated equilibrium; planar, single study at rest or stress (exercise and/or pharmacologic), wall motion study plus ejection fraction, with or without additional quantitative processing
➔ *CPT Assistant* Nov 98:22; Jun 99:8; Nov 99:44; *CPT Changes* 2000

(For assessment of cardiac function by first pass technique, use 78496)

⊘ =Modifier '-51' Exempt ▶ ◀=New or Revised Text ✚=Add-on Code CPT 2002

78473 multiple studies, wall motion study plus ejection fraction, at rest and stress (exercise and/or pharmacologic), with or without additional quantification
➔ *CPT Assistant* Jun 99:11

(78474 has been deleted. To report, use 78472)

(78475-78477 have been deleted. To report, use 78473)

+ 78478 Myocardial perfusion study with wall motion, qualitative or quantitative study (List separately in addition to code for primary procedure)
➔ *CPT Assistant* Mar 99:10

(Use 78478 in conjunction with codes 78460, 78461, 78464, 78465)

(78479 has been deleted)

+ 78480 Myocardial perfusion study with ejection fraction (List separately in addition to code for primary procedure)
➔ *CPT Assistant* Mar 97:10

(Use 78480 in conjunction with codes 78460, 78461, 78464, 78465)

78481 Cardiac blood pool imaging, (planar), first pass technique; single study, at rest or with stress (exercise and/or pharmacologic), wall motion study plus ejection fraction, with or without quantification

78483 multiple studies, at rest and with stress (exercise and/ or pharmacologic), wall motion study plus ejection fraction, with or without quantification

(78484 has been deleted. To report, use 78481)

(78485, 78486 have been deleted. To report, use 78483)

(78487 and 78489 have been deleted. To report, use 78483)

(78490 has been deleted. To report, use 78499)

(For digoxin, use 80162)

(For cerebral blood flow study, use 78615)

78491 Myocardial imaging, positron emission tomography (PET), perfusion; single study at rest or stress
➔ *CPT Assistant* Nov 97:27

78492 multiple studies at rest and/or stress
➔ *CPT Assistant* Nov 97:27

78494 Cardiac blood pool imaging, gated equilibrium, SPECT, at rest, wall motion study plus ejection fraction, with or without quantitative processing
➔ *CPT Assistant* Nov 98:22; Jun 99:3

+ 78496 Cardiac blood pool imaging, gated equilibrium, single study, at rest, with right ventricular ejection fraction by first pass technique (List separately in addition to code for primary procedure)
➔ *CPT Assistant* Nov 98:22; Jun 99:3, 11

(Use 78496 in conjunction with code 78472)

78499 Unlisted cardiovascular procedure, diagnostic nuclear medicine

(For chemical analysis, see **Chemistry** section)

Respiratory System

78580 Pulmonary perfusion imaging, particulate
➔ *CPT Assistant* Mar 99:4

(78581 and 78582 have been deleted)

78584 Pulmonary perfusion imaging, particulate, with ventilation; single breath
➔ *CPT Assistant* Mar 99:4

78585 rebreathing and washout, with or without single breath
➔ *CPT Assistant* Mar 99:4

78586 Pulmonary ventilation imaging, aerosol; single projection
➔ *CPT Assistant* Mar 99:4

78587 multiple projections (eg, anterior, posterior, lateral views)
➔ *CPT Assistant* Mar 99:4

78588 Pulmonary perfusion imaging, particulate, with ventilation imaging, aerosol, one or multiple projections
➔ *CPT Assistant* Nov 98:22; Mar 99:4

78591 Pulmonary ventilation imaging, gaseous, single breath, single projection
➔ *CPT Assistant* Mar 99:4

78593 Pulmonary ventilation imaging, gaseous, with rebreathing and washout with or without single breath; single projection
➔ *CPT Assistant* Mar 99:4

78594 multiple projections (eg, anterior, posterior, lateral views)

78596 Pulmonary quantitative differential function (ventilation/perfusion) study

78599 Unlisted respiratory procedure, diagnostic nuclear medicine

Nervous System

78600 Brain imaging, limited procedure; static

78601 with vascular flow

78605 Brain imaging, complete study; static

78606 with vascular flow

78607 tomographic (SPECT)

78608 Brain imaging, positron emission tomography (PET); metabolic evaluation

78609 perfusion evaluation

78610 Brain imaging, vascular flow only

▲ 78615 Cerebral vascular flow
➔ *CPT Changes* 2002

78630	Cerebrospinal fluid flow, imaging (not including introduction of material); cisternography
	(For injection procedure, see 61000-61070, 62270-62319)
78635	ventriculography
	(For injection procedure, see 61000-61070, 62270-62294)
	(78640 has been deleted. To report, use 78699)
78645	shunt evaluation
	(For injection procedure, see 61000-61070, 62270-62294)
78647	tomographic (SPECT)
▲**78650**	Cerebrospinal fluid leakage detection and localization

➔ *CPT Changes* 2002

(For injection procedure, see 61000-61070, 62270-62294)

(For myelin basic protein, CSF, use 83873)

(78652 has been deleted. To report, use 78647)

(78655 has been deleted. To report, use 78800)

78660	Radiopharmaceutical dacryocystography
78699	Unlisted nervous system procedure, diagnostic nuclear medicine

Genitourinary System

78700	Kidney imaging; static only
78701	with vascular flow
78704	with function study (ie, imaging renogram)
78707	Kidney imaging with vascular flow and function; single study without pharmacological intervention

➔ *CPT Assistant* Nov 97:27

78708	single study, with pharmacological intervention (eg, angiotensin converting enzyme inhibitor and/or diuretic)

➔ *CPT Assistant* Nov 97:27

78709	multiple studies, with and without pharmacological intervention (eg, angiotensin converting enzyme inhibitor and/or diuretic)

➔ *CPT Assistant* Nov 97:27

(For introduction of radioactive substance in association with renal endoscopy, see 50559, 50578)

78710	Kidney imaging, tomographic (SPECT)

➔ *CPT Assistant* Nov 97:27

78715	Kidney vascular flow only

(78720 has been deleted. To report, use 78704)

78725	Kidney function study, non-imaging radioisotopic study

➔ *CPT Assistant* Nov 98:22

(78726 has been deleted. To report, use 78799)

(78727 has been deleted. To report, see 78700-78707)

(For renin (angiotensin I), use 84244)

(For angiotensin II, use 82163)

(For beta-2 microglobulin, use 82232)

78730	Urinary bladder residual study
	(For introduction of radioactive substance in association with cystotomy or cystostomy, use 51020; in association with cystourethroscopy, use 52250)
78740	Ureteral reflux study (radiopharmaceutical voiding cystogram)
	(For catheterization, see 53670, 53675)
	(For estradiol, use 82670)
	(For estriol, use 82677)
	(For progesterone, use 84144)
	(For prostatic acid phosphatase, use 84066)
78760	Testicular imaging;
78761	with vascular flow
	(For testosterone, blood or urine, use 84403)
	(For introduction of radioactive substance in association with ureteral endoscopy, see 50959, 50978)
	(For lactogen, human placental (HPL) chorionic somatomammotropin, use 83632)
	(For chorionic gonadotropin, beta subunit, see 84702, 84703)
	(For pregnanediol, use 84135)
	(For pregnanetriol, use 84138)
	(78770, 78775 have been deleted. To report, use 78799)
78799	Unlisted genitourinary procedure, diagnostic nuclear medicine
	(For chemical analysis, see **Chemistry** section)

Other Procedures

(For specific organ, see appropriate heading)

(For radiophosphorus tumor identification, ocular, see 78800)

78800	Radiopharmaceutical localization of tumor; limited area
	(For specific organ, see appropriate heading)
78801	multiple areas
78802	whole body
78803	tomographic (SPECT)
78805	Radiopharmaceutical localization of inflammatory process; limited area

➔ *CPT Assistant* Nov 99:44; *CPT Changes* 2001

78806	whole body

➔ *CPT Assistant* Nov 99:44; *CPT Changes* 2000

⊘ =Modifier '-51' Exempt ► ◄=New or Revised Text ✚=Add-on Code

78807 tomographic (SPECT)

(For imaging bone infectious or inflammatory disease with a bone imaging radiopharmaceutical, see 78300, 78305, 78306)

(For RAST, see 82785, 83518, 86003, 86005)

(For gamma-E immunoglobulin, use 82785)

(For gamma-G immunoglobulin, use 82784)

(For alpha-1 antitrypsin, see 82103, 82104)

(For alpha-1 fetoprotein, see 82105, 82106)

(For amikacin, use 80150)

(For aminophylline, use 80198)

(For amitriptyline, use 80152)

(For amphetamine, chemical quantitative, use 82145)

(For chlordiazepoxide, see code for specific method)

(For chlorpromazine, see phenothiazine, urine 84022)

(For clonazepam, use 80154)

(For cocaine, quantitative, use 82520)

(For diazepam, use 80154)

(For dihydromorphinone, quantitative, use 82649)

(For diphenylhydantoin, use 80185)

(For flucytosine, see code for specific method)

(For gentamicin, use 80170)

(For lactic dehydrogenase, use 83615)

(For lysergic acid diethylamide (LSD), see 80100-80103, 80299)

(For morphine (heroin), see 80100-80103, 83925)

(For phencyclidine (PCP), see 80100-80103, 83992)

(For phenobarbital, see barbiturates 80100-80103, 82205)

(For phenytoin (diphenylthydantoin), use 80185)

(For tobramycin, use 80200)

78810 Tumor imaging, positron emission tomography (PET), metabolic evaluation
➔ *CPT Assistant* Jun 96:5

78890 Generation of automated data: interactive process involving nuclear physician and/or allied health professional personnel; simple manipulations and interpretation, not to exceed 30 minutes

78891 complex manipulations and interpretation, exceeding 30 minutes

(Use 78890 or 78891 in addition to primary procedure)

(78895 has been deleted)

78990 Provision of diagnostic radiopharmaceutical(s)
➔ *CPT Assistant* Apr 99:4

78999 Unlisted miscellaneous procedure, diagnostic nuclear medicine

Therapeutic

79000 Radiopharmaceutical therapy, hyper-thyroidism; initial, including evaluation of patient
➔ *CPT Assistant* Apr 99:4

79001 subsequent, each therapy

(For follow-up visit, see 99211-99215)

79020 Radiopharmaceutical therapy, thyroid suppression (euthyroid cardiac disease), including evaluation of patient

79030 Radiopharmaceutical ablation of gland for thyroid carcinoma

79035 Radiopharmaceutical therapy for metastases of thyroid carcinoma

79100 Radiopharmaceutical therapy, polycythemia vera, chronic leukemia, each treatment

79200 Intracavitary radioactive colloid therapy

79300 Interstitial radioactive colloid therapy

79400 Radiopharmaceutical therapy, nonthyroid, nonhematologic

79420 Intravascular radiopharmaceutical therapy, particulate

79440 Intra-articular radiopharmaceutical therapy

79900 Provision of therapeutic radiopharmaceutical(s)
➔ *CPT Assistant* Apr 99:4

79999 Unlisted radiopharmaceutical therapeutic procedure

Notes

Pathology and Laboratory Guidelines

Items used by all physicians in reporting their services are presented in the **Introduction.** Some of the commonalities are repeated here for the convenience of those physicians referring to this section on **Pathology and Laboratory.** Other definitions and items unique to Pathology and Laboratory are also listed.

Services in Pathology and Laboratory

Services in Pathology and Laboratory are provided by a physician or by technologists under responsible supervision of a physician.

Separate or Multiple Procedures

It is appropriate to designate multiple procedures that are rendered on the same date by separate entries.

Subsection Information

Several of the subheadings or subsections have special needs or instructions unique to that section. Where these are indicated, (eg, "Panel Tests"), special **"Notes"** will be presented preceding those procedural terminology listings referring to that subsection specifically. If there is an "Unlisted Procedure" code number (see section below) for the individual subsection, it will be shown. Those subsections with **"Notes"** are as follows:

Organ or Disease Panels 80048-80090
Drug Testing .80100-80103
Therapeutic Drug Assays 80150-80299
Evocative/Suppression Testing 80400-80440
Consultations
   (Clinical Pathology) 80500-80502
Urinalysis 81000-81099
Chemistry 82000-84999
Molecular Diagnostics 83890-83912
   ▶Infectious Agent Detection◀ . .▶87470-87999◀
Infectious Agent Antibodies 86602-86804
Microbiology . . . .▶87001-87254◀
   ▶Infectious Agent Detection◀ . .▶87260-87999◀
Anatomic Pathology 88000-88099
Cytopathology . . . .▶88104-88199◀
Surgical Pathology 88300-88399

Unlisted Service or Procedure

A service or procedure may be provided that is not listed in this edition of *CPT.* When reporting such a service, the appropriate "Unlisted Procedure" code may be used to indicate the service, identifying it by "Special Report" as discussed below. The "Unlisted Procedures" and accompanying codes for **Pathology and Laboratory** are as follows:

81099	Unlisted urinalysis procedure
84999	Unlisted chemistry procedure
85999	Unlisted hematology and coagulation procedure
86586	Unlisted antigen, each
86849	Unlisted immunology procedure
86999	Unlisted transfusion medicine procedure
87999	Unlisted microbiology procedure
88099	Unlisted necropsy (autopsy) procedure
88199	Unlisted cytopathology procedure
88299	Unlisted cytogenetic study
88399	Unlisted surgical pathology procedure
89399	Unlisted miscellaneous pathology test

Special Report

A service that is rarely provided, unusual, variable, or new may require a special report in determining medical appropriateness of the service. Pertinent information should include an adequate definition or description of the nature, extent, and need for the procedure; and the time, effort, and equipment necessary to provide the service. Additional items which may be included are:

- complexity of symptoms;
- final diagnosis;
- pertinent physical findings;
- diagnostic and therapeutic procedures;
- concurrent problems;
- follow-up care.

Notes

Pathology and Laboratory

(80002-80019 have been deleted. To report, see codes under Organ or Disease Oriented Panels)

(80031-80034 have been deleted. To report, see Therapeutic Drug Assays)

(80040 has been deleted. To report, see 80150-80299)

(80042 has been deleted. For serum cidal level, see 87197)

Organ or Disease Oriented Panels

These panels were developed for coding purposes only and should not be interpreted as clinical parameters. The tests listed with each panel identify the defined components of that panel.

These panel components are not intended to limit the performance of other tests. If one performs tests in addition to those specifically indicated for a particular panel, those tests should be reported separately in addition to the panel code.

80048 Basic metabolic panel

→ *CPT Assistant* Jan 98:6; Nov 99:44; Jan 00:7; *CPT Changes* 2000

This panel must include the following:

Calcium (82310)

Carbon dioxide (82374)

Chloride (82435)

Creatinine (82565)

Glucose (82947)

Potassium (84132)

Sodium (84295)

Urea Nitrogen (BUN) (84520)

(Do not use 80048 in addition to 80053)

(80049 has been deleted. To report, use 80048)

80050 General health panel

→ *CPT Assistant* Winter 92:14; Summer 93:14; Jun 97:10; Nov 97:28; Jan 98:6; *CPT Changes* 2001

This panel must include the following:

Comprehensive metabolic panel (80053)

Hemogram, automated, and manual differential WBC count (CBC) (85022) OR

Hemogram and platelet count, automated, and automated complete differential WBC count (CBC) (85025)

Thyroid stimulating hormone (TSH) (84443)

80051 Electrolyte panel

→ *CPT Assistant* Nov 97:28; Jan 98:6

This panel must include the following:

Carbon dioxide (82374)

Chloride (82435)

Potassium (84132)

Sodium (84295)

(80052 has been deleted. To report, see codes for specific tests)

80053 Comprehensive metabolic panel

→ *CPT Assistant* Jan 98:6; Nov 98:23; Nov 99:44; Dec 99:1; Jan 00:7; May 00:11; *CPT Changes* 2000

This panel must include the following:

Albumin (82040)

Bilirubin, total (82247)

Calcium (82310)

Carbon dioxide (bicarbonate) (82374)

Chloride (82435)

Creatinine (82565)

Glucose (82947)

Phosphatase, alkaline (84075)

Potassium (84132)

Protein, total (84155)

Sodium (84295)

Transferase, alanine amino (ALT) (SGPT) (84460)

Transferase, aspartate amino (AST) (SGOT) (84450)

Urea Nitrogen (BUN) (84520)

(Do not use 80053 in addition to 80048, 80076)

(80054 has been deleted. To report, use 80053)

80055 Obstetric panel

→ *CPT Assistant* Winter 92:14; Summer 93:14; Jun 97:10

This panel must include the following:

Hemogram, automated, and manual differential WBC count (CBC) (85022) OR

Hemogram and platelet count, automated, and automated complete differential WBC count (CBC) (85025)

Hepatitis B surface antigen (HBsAg) (87340)

Antibody, rubella (86762)

Syphilis test, qualitative (eg, VDRL, RPR, ART) (86592)

Path/Lab 80048

Antibody screen, RBC, each serum technique (86850)

Blood typing, ABO (86900) AND

Blood typing, Rh (D) (86901)

(80056 has been deleted. To report, see codes for specific tests)

(80057 has been deleted. To report, see codes for specific tests)

(80058 has been deleted. To report, use 80076)

(80059 has been deleted. To report, use 80074)

(80060 has been deleted. To report, see codes for specific tests)

80061 Lipid panel

➔ *CPT Assistant* Winter 92:14; Summer 93:14; Jun 97:10; Mar 00:11

This panel must include the following:

Cholesterol, serum, total (82465)

Lipoprotein, direct measurement, high density cholesterol (HDL cholesterol) (83718)

Triglycerides (84478)

(80062 has been deleted. To report, see 80061 and/or codes for specific tests)

(80063 has been deleted. To report, see codes for specific tests)

(80064 has been deleted. To report, see codes for specific tests)

(80065 has been deleted. To report, see codes for specific tests)

(80066 has been deleted. To report, see codes for specific tests)

(80067 has been deleted. To report, see codes for specific tests)

(80068 has been deleted. To report, see codes for specific tests)

80069 Renal function panel

➔ *CPT Assistant* Nov 99:44; Jan 00:7; *CPT Changes* 2000

This panel must include the following:

Albumin (82040)

Calcium (82310)

Carbon dioxide (bicarbonate) (82374)

Chloride (82435)

Creatinine (82565)

Glucose (82947)

Phosphorus inorganic (phosphate) (84100)

Potassium (84132)

Sodium (84295)

Urea nitrogen (BUN) (84520)

(80070 has been deleted. To report, use 80091)

(80071 has been deleted. To report, see codes for specific tests)

▶(80072 has been deleted. To report, see 84550, 85651, 86255, 86430)◀

(80073 has been deleted. To report, see codes for specific tests)

80074 Acute hepatitis panel

➔ *CPT Assistant* Nov 99:45; Jan 00:7; *CPT Changes* 2000

This panel must include the following:

Hepatitis A antibody (HAAb), IgM antibody (86709)

Hepatitis B core antibody (HbcAb), IgM antibody (86705)

Hepatitis B surface antigen (HbsAg) (87340)

Hepatitis C antibody (86803)

(80075 has been deleted. To report, see codes for specific tests)

80076 Hepatic function panel

➔ *CPT Assistant* Winter 92:14; Summer 93:14; Jun 97:10; Jan 98:6; Apr 99:6; Nov 99:45; Jan 00:7; *CPT Changes* 2000

This panel must include the following:

Albumin (82040)

Bilirubin, total (82247)

Bilirubin, direct (82248)

Phosphatase, alkaline (84075)

Protein, total (84155)

Transferase, alanine amino (ALT) (SGPT) (84460)

Transferase, aspartate amino (AST) (SGOT) (84450)

(Do not use 80076 in addition to 80053)

(80080 has been deleted. To report PSA, use 84153)

(80082 has been deleted. To report, see codes for specific tests)

(80084 has been deleted. To report, see codes for specific tests)

(80085 has been deleted. To report, see codes for specific tests)

(80086 has been deleted. To report, see codes for specific tests)

(80088 has been deleted. To report, see codes for specific tests)

(80089 has been deleted. To report, see codes for specific tests)

80090 TORCH antibody panel

➔ *CPT Assistant* Winter 92:14; Summer 93:14; Jun 97:10

This panel must include the following tests:

Antibody, cytomegalovirus (CMV) (86644)

Antibody, herpes simplex, non-specific type test (86694)

Antibody, rubella (86762)

Antibody, toxoplasma (86777)

(80091 has been deleted. To report, see codes for specific tests)

(80092 has been deleted. To report, see codes for specific test)

(80099 has been deleted. To report, see codes for specific tests)

Drug Testing

The following list contains examples of drugs or classes of drugs that are commonly assayed by qualitative screen, followed by confirmation with a second method.

Alcohols

Amphetamines

Barbiturates

Benzodiazepines

Cocaine and Metabolites

Methadones

Methaqualones

Opiates

Phencyclidines

Phenothiazines

Propoxyphenes

Tetrahydrocannabinoids

Tricyclic Antidepressants

Confirmed drugs may also be quantitated.

Use 80100 for each multiple drug class chromatographic procedure. Use 80102 for each procedure necessary for confirmation. For chromatography, each combination of stationary and mobile phase is to be counted as one procedure. For example, if detection of three drugs by chromatography requires one stationary phase with three mobile phases, use 80100 three (3) times. However, if multiple drugs can be detected using a single analysis (eg, one stationary phase with one mobile phase), use 80100 only once.

For quantitation of drugs screened, use appropriate code in **Chemistry** section (82000-84999) or **Therapeutic Drug Assay** section (80150-80299).

80100 Drug screen, qualitative; multiple drug classes chromatographic method, each procedure
➲ *CPT Assistant* Fall 93:26; Mar 00:1; *CPT Changes* 2001

80101 single drug class method (eg, immunoassay, enzyme assay), each drug class
➲ *CPT Assistant* Fall 93:26; Mar 00:1; *CPT Changes* 2001

80102 Drug confirmation, each procedure
➲ *CPT Assistant* Fall 93:26; Mar 00:1; *CPT Changes* 2001

80103 Tissue preparation for drug analysis
➲ *CPT Assistant* Mar 00:1

Therapeutic Drug Assays

The material for examination may be from any source. Examination is quantitative. For nonquantitative testing, see Drug Testing (80100-80103).
➲ *CPT Assistant* (80150-80299) Winter 92:14; Fall 93:26; Mar 00:1

80150 Amikacin

80152 Amitriptyline

80154 Benzodiazepines

80156 Carbamazepine; total
➲ *CPT Changes* 2001

80157   free
➲ *CPT Changes* 2001

80158 Cyclosporine

80160 Desipramine

80162 Digoxin

80164 Dipropylacetic acid (valproic acid)

80166 Doxepin

80168 Ethosuximide

80170 Gentamicin

80172 Gold

80173 Haloperidol
➲ *CPT Changes* 2001

80174 Imipramine

80176 Lidocaine

80178 Lithium

80182 Nortriptyline

80184 Phenobarbital

80185 Phenytoin; total

80186   free

80188 Primidone

80190 Procainamide;

80192   with metabolites (eg, n-acetyl procainamide)

80194 Quinidine

80196 Salicylate

80197	Tacrolimus
80198	Theophylline
80200	Tobramycin
80201	Topiramate
80202	Vancomycin
80299	Quantitation of drug, not elsewhere specified
	→ *CPT Assistant* Mar 00:3

Evocative/Suppression Testing

The following test panels involve the administration of evocative or suppressive agents, and the baseline and subsequent measurement of their effects on chemical constituents. These codes are to be used for the reporting of the laboratory component of the overall testing protocol. For the physician's administration of the evocative or suppressive agents, see 90780-90784; for the supplies and drugs, see 99070. To report physician attendance and monitoring during the testing, use the appropriate evaluation and management code, including the prolonged physician care codes if required. Prolonged physician care codes are not separately reported when evocative/suppression testing involves prolonged infusions reported with 90780 and 90781. In the code descriptors where reference is made to a particular analyte (eg, Cortisol (82533 x 2)) the "x 2" refers to the number of times the test for that particular analyte is performed.

80400 ACTH stimulation panel; for adrenal insufficiency

This panel must include the following:

Cortisol (82533 x 2)
→ *CPT Assistant* Summer 94:1

80402 for 21 hydroxylase deficiency

This panel must include the following:

Cortisol (82533 x 2)

17 hydroxyprogesterone (83498 x 2)
→ *CPT Assistant* Summer 94:1

80406 for 3 beta-hydroxydehydrogenase deficiency

This panel must include the following:

Cortisol (82533 x 2)

17 hydroxypregnenolone (84143 x 2)
→ *CPT Assistant* Summer 94:1

80408 Aldosterone suppression evaluation panel (eg, saline infusion)

This panel must include the following:

Aldosterone (82088 x 2)

Renin (84244 x 2)
→ *CPT Assistant* Summer 94:1

80410 Calcitonin stimulation panel (eg, calcium, pentagastrin)

This panel must include the following:

Calcitonin (82308 x 3)
→ *CPT Assistant* Summer 94:1

80412 Corticotropic releasing hormone (CRH) stimulation panel

This panel must include the following:

Cortisol (82533 x 6)

Adrenocorticotropic hormone (ACTH) (82024 x 6)
→ *CPT Assistant* Summer 94:1

80414 Chorionic gonadotropin stimulation panel; testosterone response

This panel must include the following:

Testosterone (84403 x 2 on three pooled blood samples)
→ *CPT Assistant* Summer 94:1

80415 estradiol response

This panel must include the following:

Estradiol (82670 x 2 on three pooled blood samples)
→ *CPT Assistant* Summer 94:1

80416 Renal vein renin stimulation panel (eg, captopril)

This panel must include the following:

Renin (84244 x 6)
→ *CPT Assistant* Summer 94:1

80417 Peripheral vein renin stimulation panel (eg, captopril)

This panel must include the following:

Renin (84244 x 2)

80418 Combined rapid anterior pituitary evaluation panel

This panel must include the following:

Adrenocorticotropic hormone (ACTH) (82024 x 4)

Luteinizing hormone (LH) (83002 x 4)

Follicle stimulating hormone (FSH) (83001 x 4)

Prolactin (84146 x 4)

Human growth hormone (HGH) (83003 x 4)

Cortisol (82533 x 4)

Thyroid stimulating hormone (TSH) (84443 x 4)
→ *CPT Assistant* Summer 94:1

80420 Dexamethasone suppression panel, 48 hour

This panel must include the following:

Free cortisol, urine (82530 x 2)

Cortisol (82533 x 2)

Volume measurement for timed collection (81050 x 2)

(For single dose dexamethasone, use 82533)
→ *CPT Assistant* Summer 94:1

80422   Glucagon tolerance panel; for insulinoma

This panel must include the following:

Glucose (82947 x 3)

Insulin (83525 x 3)
➔ *CPT Assistant* Summer 94:1

80424   for pheochromocytoma

This panel must include the following:

Catecholamines, fractionated (82384 x 2)
➔ *CPT Assistant* Summer 94:1

80426   Gonadotropin releasing hormone stimulation panel

This panel must include the following:

Follicle stimulating hormone (FSH) (83001 x 4)

Luteinizing hormone (LH) (83002 x 4)
➔ *CPT Assistant* Summer 94:1

80428   Growth hormone stimulation panel (eg, arginine infusion, l-dopa administration)

This panel must include the following:

Human growth hormone (HGH) (83003 x 4)
➔ *CPT Assistant* Summer 94:1

80430   Growth hormone suppression panel (glucose administration)

This panel must include the following:

Glucose (82947 x 3)

Human growth hormone (HGH) (83003 x 4)
➔ *CPT Assistant* Summer 94:1

80432   Insulin-induced C-peptide suppression panel

This panel must include the following:

Insulin (83525)

C-peptide (84681 x 5)

Glucose (82947 x 5)
➔ *CPT Assistant* Summer 94:1

80434   Insulin tolerance panel; for ACTH insufficiency

This panel must include the following:

Cortisol (82533 x 5)

Glucose (82947 x 5)
➔ *CPT Assistant* Summer 94:1

80435   for growth hormone deficiency

This panel must include the following:

Glucose (82947 x 5)

Human growth hormone (HGH) (83003 x 5)
➔ *CPT Assistant* Summer 94:1

80436   Metyrapone panel

This panel must include the following:

Cortisol (82533 x 2)

11 deoxycortisol (82634 x 2)
➔ *CPT Assistant* Summer 94:1

80438   Thyrotropin releasing hormone (TRH) stimulation panel; one hour

This panel must include the following:

Thyroid stimulating hormone (TSH) (84443 x 3)
➔ *CPT Assistant* Summer 94:1

80439   two hour

This panel must include the following:

Thyroid stimulating hormone (TSH) (84443 x 4)
➔ *CPT Assistant* Summer 94:1

80440   for hyperprolactinemia

This panel must include the following:

Prolactin (84146 x 3)
➔ *CPT Assistant* Summer 94:1

Consultations (Clinical Pathology)

A clinical pathology consultation is a service, including a written report, rendered by the pathologist in response to a request from an attending physician in relation to a test result(s) requiring additional medical interpretive judgment.

Reporting of a test result(s) without medical interpretive judgment is not considered a clinical pathology consultation.

80500   Clinical pathology consultation; limited, without review of patient's history and medical records
➔ *CPT Assistant* Apr 97:9

80502   comprehensive, for a complex diagnostic problem, with review of patient's history and medical records
➔ *CPT Assistant* Apr 97:9

(These codes may also be used for pharmacokinetic consultations)

(For consultations involving the examination and evaluation of the patient, see 99241-99275)

Urinalysis

For specific analyses, see appropriate section.

81000 Urinalysis, by dip stick or tablet reagent for bilirubin, glucose, hemoglobin, ketones, leukocytes, nitrite, pH, protein, specific gravity, urobilinogen, any number of these constituents; non-automated, with microscopy
➔ *CPT Assistant* Winter 90-91:10; Fall 93:25

81001 automated, with microscopy

81002 non-automated, without microscopy
➔ *CPT Assistant* Mar 98:3

81003 automated, without microscopy

(81004 has been deleted. To report, use 81000)

81005 Urinalysis; qualitative or semiquantitative, except immunoassays
➔ *CPT Assistant* Winter 90-91:10; Fall 93:25

(For non-immunoassay reagent strip urinalysis, see 81000, 81002)

(For immunoassay, qualitative or semiquantitative, use 83518)

(81006 has been deleted. To report, use 81099)

(For microalbumin, see 82043, 82044)

81007 bacteriuria screen, except by culture or dipstick
➔ *CPT Changes* 2001

(For culture, see 87086-87088)

(For dipstick, use 81000 or 81002)

(81010, 81011, and 81012 have been deleted)

81015 microscopic only

81020 two or three glass test
➔ *CPT Assistant* Winter 90-91:10

81025 Urine pregnancy test, by visual color comparison methods
➔ *CPT Assistant* Mar 98:3

(81030 has been deleted)

81050 Volume measurement for timed collection, each

81099 Unlisted urinalysis procedure

Chemistry

The material for examination may be from any source unless otherwise specified in the code descriptor. When an analyte is measured in multiple specimens from different sources, or in specimens that are obtained at different times, the analyte is reported separately for each source and for each specimen. The examination is quantitative unless specified. To report an organ or disease oriented panel, see codes 80048-80090.

When a code describes a method where measurement of multiple analytes may require one or several procedures, each procedure is coded separately (eg, 82491-82492, 82541-82544). For example, if two (2) analytes are measured using column chromatography using a single stationary or mobile phase, use 82492. If the same two analytes are measured using different stationary or mobile phase conditions, 82491 would be used twice. If a total of four (4) analytes are measured where two (2) analytes are measured with a single stationary and mobile phase, and the other two (2) analytes are measured using a different stationary and mobile phase, use 82492 twice. If a total of three (3) analytes are measured where two (2) analytes are measured using a single stationary or mobile phase condition, and the third analyte is measured separately using a different stationary or mobile phase procedure, use 82492 once for the (2) analytes measured under the same condition, and use 82491 once for the third analyte measured separately.

Clinical information derived from the results of laboratory data that is mathematically calculated (eg, free thyroxine index (T7)) is considered part of the test procedure and therefore is not a separately reportable service.

82000 Acetaldehyde, blood
➔ *CPT Assistant* Mar 00:1

82003 Acetaminophen

(82005 has been deleted)

82009 Acetone or other ketone bodies, serum; qualitative

82010 quantitative

(82011 has been deleted. To report, use 80196)

(82012 has been deleted)

82013 Acetylcholinesterase

(Acid, gastric, see gastric acid, 82926, 82928)

(Acid phosphatase, see 84060-84066)

(82015 has been deleted)

82016 Acylcarnitines; qualitative, each specimen
➔ *CPT Assistant* Nov 98:23

82017 quantitative, each specimen
➔ *CPT Assistant* Nov 98:23; *CPT Changes* 2000

(For carnitine, use 82379)

82024 Adrenocorticotropic hormone (ACTH)

82030 Adenosine, 5-monophosphate, cyclic (cyclic AMP)

(82035 has been deleted)

82040 Albumin; serum
➔ *CPT Assistant* Dec 99:2

82042 urine or other source, quantitative, each specimen
➔ *CPT Changes* 2001

82043 urine, microalbumin, quantitative
➔ *CPT Assistant* Summer 94:2

82044   urine, microalbumin, semiquantitative (eg, reagent strip assay)

➔ *CPT Assistant* Summer 94:2; Mar 98:3

(For prealbumin, use 84134)

82055   Alcohol (ethanol); any specimen except breath

(For other volatiles, alcohol, use 84600)

(82060, 82065, 82070 have been deleted. To report, use 82055)

(82072 has been deleted)

82075   breath

(82076, 82078 have been deleted. For ethanol, use 82055; for volatiles, use 84600)

82085   Aldolase

(82086 has been deleted. To report, use 82085)

(82087 has been deleted. To report, use 82088)

82088   Aldosterone

(82089 has been deleted. To report, use 82088)

(82091 has been deleted. To report, use 80408)

(82095 has been deleted. To report, see 80100, 80101, and 80103)

(82096 has been deleted. To report, use code for specific drug and 80103)

(82100 has been deleted. To report, use 80100 and 80101)

(Alkaline phosphatase, see 84075, 84080)

82101   Alkaloids, urine, quantitative

(Alphaketoglutarate, see 82009, 82010)

(Alpha tocopherol (Vitamin E), use 84446)

82103   Alpha-1-antitrypsin; total

82104   phenotype

82105   Alpha-fetoprotein; serum

82106   amniotic fluid

82108   Aluminum

(82112 has been deleted. To report, use 80150)

82120   Amines, vaginal fluid, qualitative

➔ *CPT Assistant* Nov 99:45; *CPT Changes* 2000

(For combined pH and amines test for vaginitis, use 82120 and 83986)

(82126 has been deleted)

82127   Amino acids; single, qualitative, each specimen

➔ *CPT Assistant* Nov 98:24

82128   multiple, qualitative, each specimen

➔ *CPT Assistant* Nov 98:24

(82130 has been deleted. To report, see 82131, 82136, 82139)

82131   single, quantitative, each specimen

➔ *CPT Assistant* May 98:11; Nov 98:24

(82134 has been deleted)

82135   Aminolevulinic acid, delta (ALA)

82136   Amino acids, 2 to 5 amino acids, quantitative, each specimen

➔ *CPT Assistant* Nov 98:24

(82137 has been deleted. To report, use 80198)

(82138 has been deleted. To report, use 80152)

82139   Amino acids, 6 or more amino acids, quantitative, each specimen

➔ *CPT Assistant* Nov 98:24

82140   Ammonia

(82141 has been deleted. To report, use 82140)

(82142 has been deleted)

82143   Amniotic fluid scan (spectrophotometric)

(For L/S ratio, use 83661)

(Amobarbital, see 80100-80103 for qualitative analysis, 82205 for quantitative analysis)

82145   Amphetamine or methamphetamine

(For qualitative analysis, see 80100-80103)

82150   Amylase

82154   Androstanediol glucuronide

➔ *CPT Assistant* Summer 94:5

(82155 has been deleted)

(82156 has been deleted. To report, use 82150)

82157   Androstenedione

(82159 has been deleted. To report, use 82160)

82160   Androsterone

82163   Angiotensin II

82164   Angiotensin I - converting enzyme (ACE)

(82165 has been deleted)

(Antidiuretic hormone (ADH), use 84588)

(82168 has been deleted. For antihistamines, see code for specific method)

(82170 has been deleted. To report, see 83015, 83018)

(Antimony, use 83015)

(Antitrypsin, alpha-1-, see 82103, 82104)

82172   Apolipoprotein, each

(82173 has been deleted. To report, use 80428)

82175   Arsenic

(For heavy metal screening, use 83015)

82180 Ascorbic acid (Vitamin C), blood

(Aspirin, see acetylsalicylic acid, 80196)

(Atherogenic index, blood, ultracentrifugation, quantitative, use 83717)

82190 Atomic absorption spectroscopy, each analyte

82205 Barbiturates, not elsewhere specified

(For qualitative analysis, see 80100-80103)

(82210 has been deleted. To report, see 80100-80103, 82205)

(82225, 82230 have been deleted. To report, see 83015, 83018)

(82231 has been deleted. To report, use 82232)

82232 Beta-2 microglobulin

(82235, 82236 have been deleted)

(Bicarbonate, use 82374)

82239 Bile acids; total

82240 cholylglycine

(For bile pigments, urine, see 81000-81005)

(82245 has been deleted. To report, see 81000, 81002, 81005)

82247 Bilirubin; total
➔ *CPT Assistant* Nov 98:24; Apr 99:6; Dec 99:1; Jan 00:7

82248 direct
➔ *CPT Assistant* Nov 98:24; Apr 99:6; Dec 99:1

(82250 has been deleted. To report, see 82247, 82248 as appropriate)

(82251 has been deleted. To report, use 82247 and 82248)

82252 feces, qualitative

(82260 has been deleted. To report, see 81000-81003, 82247, 82248, 82251)

82261 Biotinidase, each specimen
➔ *CPT Assistant* Nov 98:24

(82265 has been deleted. To report spectrophotometric scan, use 82143)

(82268 has been deleted. To report, see 83015, 83018)

▲ **82270** Blood, occult, by peroxidase activity (eg, guaiac), qualitative; feces, 1-3 simultaneous determinations
➔ *CPT Changes* 2002

▲ **82273** other sources
➔ *CPT Changes* 2002

(Blood urea nitrogen (BUN), see 84520, 84525)

(82280, 82285 have been deleted. To report, see code for specific method)

● **82274** Blood, occult, by fecal hemoglobin determination by immunoassay, qualitative, feces, 1-3 simultaneous determinations
➔ *CPT Changes* 2002

82286 Bradykinin

(82290, 82291 have been deleted. To report, use 84311)

82300 Cadmium

(82305 has been deleted. To report, see 82486, 82491)

82306 Calcifediol (25-OH Vitamin D-3)

82307 Calciferol (Vitamin D)

(For 1,25-Dihydroxyvitamin D, use 82652)

82308 Calcitonin

82310 Calcium; total
➔ *CPT Assistant* Dec 99:1

(82315, 82320, 82325 have been deleted. To report, use 82310)

82330 ionized

82331 after calcium infusion test

(82335 has been deleted)

82340 urine quantitative, timed specimen

(82345 has been deleted)

▲ **82355** Calculus; qualitative analysis
➔ *CPT Changes* 2002

82360 quantitative analysis, chemical

82365 infrared spectroscopy

82370 x-ray diffraction
➔ *CPT Changes* 2001

(82372 has been deleted. To report, use 80156)

(Carbamates, see individual listings)

82373 Carbohydrate deficient transferrin
➔ *CPT Changes* 2001

82374 Carbon dioxide (bicarbonate)
➔ *CPT Assistant* Dec 99:1

(See also 82803)

82375 Carbon monoxide, (carboxyhemoglobin); quantitative

82376 qualitative

82378 Carcinoembryonic antigen (CEA)
➔ *CPT Assistant* Fall 93:25; Aug 96:11

82379 Carnitine (total and free), quantitative, each specimen
➔ *CPT Assistant* Nov 98:24

(For acylcarnitine, see 82016, 82017)

82380 Carotene

82382   Catecholamines; total urine

82383   blood

82384   fractionated

(For urine metabolites, see 83835, 84585)

82387   Cathepsin-D

82390   Ceruloplasmin

82397   Chemiluminescent assay
→ *CPT Assistant* Fall 93:25

(82400 has been deleted. To report, see code for specific method)

(82405 has been deleted)

82415   Chloramphenicol

(82418, 82420, 82425 have been deleted. To report, see code for specific method)

82435   Chloride; blood
→ *CPT Assistant* Dec 99:1

82436   urine

(82437 has been deleted)

82438   other source

(For sweat collection by iontophoresis, use 89360)

82441   Chlorinated hydrocarbons, screen

(82443 has been deleted. To report, see code for specific method)

(Chlorpromazine, use 84022)

(Cholecalciferol (Vitamin D), use 82307)

82465   Cholesterol, serum or whole blood, total
→ *CPT Assistant* Dec 99:1; Mar 00:1; *CPT Changes* 2001

(For high density lipoprotein (HDL), use 83718)

(82470 has been deleted)

82480   Cholinesterase; serum

82482   RBC

(82484 has been deleted. To report, use 82480 and 82482)

82485   Chondroitin B sulfate, quantitative

(Chorionic gonadotropin, see gonadotropin, 84702, 84703)

82486   Chromatography, qualitative; column (eg, gas liquid or HPLC), analyte not elsewhere specified
→ *CPT Assistant* Nov 98:24-25

82487   paper, 1-dimensional, analyte not elsewhere specified

82488   paper, 2-dimensional, analyte not elsewhere specified

82489   thin layer, analyte not elsewhere specified

(82490 has been deleted)

82491   Chromatography, quantitative, column (eg, gas liquid or HPLC); single analyte not elsewhere specified, single stationary and mobile phase
→ *CPT Assistant* Fall 93:25; Nov 98:24-25; Mar 00:1

82492   multiple analytes, single stationary and mobile phase
→ *CPT Assistant* Nov 98:24-25; Mar 00:1

82495   Chromium

(82505 has been deleted)

82507   Citrate

(82512 has been deleted. To report, use 80154)

82520   Cocaine or metabolite

(Cocaine, qualitative analysis, see 80100-80103)

(Codeine, qualitative analysis, see 80100-80103)

(Codeine, quantitative analysis, see 82101)

(Complement, see 86160-86162)

82523   Collagen cross links, any method

82525   Copper

(82526 has been deleted. To report, use 82525)

(Coproporphyrin, see 84119, 84120)

(Corticosteroids, use 83491)

82528   Corticosterone

(82529 has been deleted. To report, use 82533)

82530   Cortisol; free
→ *CPT Assistant* Summer 94:3

(82531, 82532 have been deleted)

82533   total
→ *CPT Assistant* Summer 94:3

(82534 has been deleted. To report, use 82533)

(82536 has been deleted. To report, see 80400-80406)

(82537 has been deleted. To report, see 80400-80406)

(82538 has been deleted. To report, use 80436)

(82539 has been deleted. To report, use 80420)

(C-peptide, use 84681)

82540   Creatine

82541   Column chromatography/mass spectrometry (eg, GC/MS, or HPLC/MS), analyte not elsewhere specified; qualitative, single stationary and mobile phase
→ *CPT Assistant* Nov 98:24-25

82542   quantitative, single stationary and mobile phase
→ *CPT Assistant* Nov 98:24-25

82543   stable isotope dilution, single analyte, quantitative, single stationary and mobile phase
→ *CPT Assistant* Nov 98:24-25

82544 stable isotope dilution, multiple analytes, quantitative, single stationary and mobile phase
➔ *CPT Assistant* Nov 98:24-25; Dec 99:7

(82545 has been deleted. To report, use 82540)

(82546 has been deleted. To report, see 82540, 82565)

82550 Creatine kinase (CK), (CPK); total
➔ *CPT Assistant* Feb 98:1; Dec 99:1

82552 isoenzymes
➔ *CPT Assistant* Feb 98:1

82553 MB fraction only
➔ *CPT Assistant* Feb 98:1

82554 isoforms
➔ *CPT Assistant* Feb 98:1

(82555 has been deleted)

82565 Creatinine; blood
➔ *CPT Assistant* Dec 99:1

82570 other source

82575 clearance

82585 Cryofibrinogen

82595 Cryoglobulin, qualitative or semi-quantitative (eg, cryocrit)
➔ *CPT Changes* 2001

(For quantitative, cryoglobulin, see 82784, 82785)

(Crystals, pyrophosphate vs. urate, use 89060)

82600 Cyanide

(82601 has been deleted. To report, see 80103, 82600)

(82606 has been deleted)

82607 Cyanocobalamin (Vitamin B-12);

82608 unsaturated binding capacity

(Cyclic AMP, use 82030)

(Cyclic GMP, use 83008)

(Cyclosporine, use 80158)

(82610, 82614 have been deleted)

82615 Cystine and homocystine, urine, qualitative

(82620 has been deleted. For cystine and homocystine, quantitative, use 82130)

(82624 has been deleted)

82626 Dehydroepiandrosterone (DHEA)
➔ *CPT Assistant* Summer 94:4

82627 Dehydroepiandrosterone-sulfate (DHEA-S)
➔ *CPT Assistant* Summer 94:4

(82628 has been deleted. To report, see 80100-80103 for qualitative analysis; see 80160 for quantitative analysis)

(Delta-aminolevulinic acid (ALA), use 82135)

82633 Desoxycorticosterone, 11-

82634 Deoxycortisol, 11-

(Dexamethasone suppression test, use 80420)

(82635 has been deleted)

(Diastase, urine, use 82150)

(82636 has been deleted. To report, see 80100-80103, 80154)

82638 Dibucaine number

(82639 has been deleted. To report, use code for specific method)

(Dichloroethane, use 84600)

(Dichloromethane, use 84600)

(Diethylether, use 84600)

(82640, 82641 have been deleted)

(82643 has been deleted. To report, use 80162)

82646 Dihydrocodeinone

(For qualitative analysis, see 80100-80103)

82649 Dihydromorphinone

(For qualitative analysis, see 80100-80103)

82651 Dihydrotestosterone (DHT)

82652 Dihydroxyvitamin D, 1,25-

82654 Dimethadione

(For qualitative analysis, see 80100-80103)

(Diphenylhydantoin, use 80185)

(Dipropylacetic acid, use 80164)

(Dopamine, see 82382-82384)

(82656 has been deleted. To report, use 80166)

(Duodenal contents, see individual enzymes; for intubation and collection, use 89100)

82657 Enzyme activity in blood cells, cultured cells, or tissue, not elsewhere specified; nonradioactive substrate, each specimen
➔ *CPT Assistant* Nov 98:25

82658 radioactive substrate, each specimen
➔ *CPT Assistant* Nov 98:25

(82660 has been deleted. To report, see 80100, 80101)

(82662 has been deleted. To report, see 80100-80103)

82664 Electrophoretic technique, not elsewhere specified

(Endocrine receptor assays, see 84233-84235)

82666 Epiandrosterone

(Epinephrine, see 82382-82384)

82668 Erythropoietin

82670 Estradiol

82671	Estrogens; fractionated
82672	total

(82673, 82674, 82676 have been deleted. To report, use 82677)

(Estrogen receptor assay, use 84233)

82677 Estriol

(82678 has been deleted. To report, use 82679)

82679 Estrone

(Ethanol, see 82055 and 82075)

82690 Ethchlorvynol

(82691 has been deleted. To report, use 82690)

(82692 has been deleted. To report, use 80168)

(Ethyl alcohol, see 82055 and 82075)

82693 Ethylene glycol

(82694 has been deleted. To report, use 82696)

82696 Etiocholanolone

(For fractionation of ketosteroids, use 83593)

82705 Fat or lipids, feces; qualitative

82710   quantitative

82715 Fat differential, feces, quantitative

(82720 has been deleted)

82725 Fatty acids, nonesterified

82726 Very long chain fatty acids
➜ *CPT Assistant* Nov 98:25

(82727 has been deleted. To report ferric chloride test, urine, use 81005)

82728 Ferritin

(Fetal hemoglobin, see hemoglobin 83030, 83033, and 85460)

(Fetoprotein, alpha-1, see 82105, 82106)

(82730 has been deleted. To report fibrinogen, see 85384, 85385)

82731 Fetal fibronectin, cervicovaginal secretions, semi-quantitative
➜ *CPT Assistant* Nov 98:25

82735 Fluoride

(82740 has been deleted. To report, use 82735)

(82741 has been deleted. To report, see code for specific method)

82742 Flurazepam

(For qualitative analysis, see 80100-80103)

(Foam stability test, use 83662)

(82745 has been deleted)

82746 Folic acid; serum

82747   RBC

(Follicle stimulating hormone (FSH), use 83001)

(82750 has been deleted. To report, see code for specific method)

(82755, 82756 have been deleted)

82757 Fructose, semen

(Fructosamine, use 82985)

(Fructose, TLC screen, use 84375)

82759 Galactokinase, RBC

82760 Galactose

(82763 has been deleted. To report, use 82760 and codes for administration)

(82765 has been deleted. To report, use 82760)

82775 Galactose-1-phosphate uridyl transferase; quantitative

82776   screen

(82780 has been deleted. To report gallium, see code for specific method)

82784 Gammaglobulin; IgA, IgD, IgG, IgM, each
➜ *CPT Assistant* Spring 94:31; Aug 00:11

82785   IgE
➜ *CPT Assistant* Spring 94:31

(For allergen specific IgE, see 86003, 86005)

(82786 has been deleted)

82787   immunoglobulin subclasses, (IgG1, 2, 3, or 4), each
➜ *CPT Changes* 2001

(Gamma-glutamyltransferase (GGT), use 82977)

(82790, 82791 have been deleted)

(82792 has been deleted. To report, see 82805, 82810)

(82793, 82795 have been deleted)

82800 Gases, blood, pH only

(82801, 82802 have been deleted. To report, use 82803)

82803 Gases, blood, any combination of pH, pCO_2, pO_2, CO_2, HCO_3 (including calculated O_2 saturation);

(Use 82803 for two or more of the above listed analytes)

(82804 has been deleted. To report, use 82803)

82805   with O_2 saturation, by direct measurement, except pulse oximetry

82810 Gases, blood, O_2 saturation only, by direct measurement, except pulse oximetry

(For pulse oximetry, use 94760)

(82812 has been deleted. To report, use 82803)

(82817 has been deleted. To report, use 82803)

82820 Hemoglobin-oxygen affinity (pO_2 for 50% hemoglobin saturation with oxygen)

82926 Gastric acid, free and total, each specimen

(82927 has been deleted. To report, use 82926)

82928 Gastric acid, free or total; each specimen

(82929, 82931, and 82932 have been deleted. To report, use 82928)

82938 Gastrin after secretin stimulation

82941 Gastrin

(Gentamicin, use 80170)

(GGT, use 82977)

(GLC, gas liquid chromatography, use 82486)

(82942 has been deleted)

82943 Glucagon

(82944 has been deleted)

82945 Glucose, body fluid, other than blood
➔ *CPT Changes* 2001

82946 Glucagon tolerance test

82947 Glucose; quantitative, blood (except reagent strip)
➔ *CPT Assistant* Summer 93:14; Summer 94:5; Sep 99:10; Dec 99:1; *CPT Changes* 2001

82948 blood, reagent strip
➔ *CPT Assistant* Summer 94:5; Jan 99:10

(82949 has been deleted)

82950 post glucose dose (includes glucose)
➔ *CPT Assistant* Sep 99:10

82951 tolerance test (GTT), three specimens (includes glucose)
➔ *CPT Assistant* Feb 01:10

82952 tolerance test, each additional beyond three specimens
➔ *CPT Assistant* Feb 01:10

82953 tolbutamide tolerance test

(For insulin tolerance test, see 80434, 80435)

(For leucine tolerance test, use 80428)

(For semiquantitative urine glucose, see 81000, 81002, 81005, 81099)

(82954 has been deleted. To report, use 82947)

82955 Glucose-6-phosphate dehydrogenase (G6PD); quantitative

82960 screen

(82961 has been deleted)

(For glucose tolerance test with medication, use 90784 in addition)

82962 Glucose, blood by glucose monitoring device(s) cleared by the FDA specifically for home use
➔ *CPT Assistant* Summer 94:4; Jan 99:10

82963 Glucosidase, beta

82965 Glutamate dehydrogenase

82975 Glutamine (glutamic acid amide)

82977 Glutamyltransferase, gamma (GGT)
➔ *CPT Assistant* Dec 99:1

82978 Glutathione

82979 Glutathione reductase, RBC

82980 Glutethimide

(Glycohemoglobin, use 83036)

82985 Glycated protein
➔ *CPT Assistant* Summer 94:2

(82995 has been deleted. To report, use 80172)

(82996-82998 have been deleted. To report, see 84702, 84703)

(Gonadotropin, chorionic, see 84702, 84703)

(83000 has been deleted)

83001 Gonadotropin; follicle stimulating hormone (FSH)

83002 luteinizing hormone (LH)

(For luteinizing releasing factor (LRH), use 83727)

83003 Growth hormone, human (HGH) (somatotropin)

(83004 has been deleted. To report, use 80430)

(For antibody to human growth hormone, use 86277)

(83005 has been deleted)

83008 Guanosine monophosphate (GMP), cyclic

83010 Haptoglobin; quantitative

(83011 has been deleted. To report, use 83010)

83012 phenotypes

▲ **83013** Helicobacter pylori; analysis for urease activity, non-radioactive isotope
➔ *CPT Assistant* Nov 98:25; Feb 99:8; Nov 99:45; *CPT Changes* 2001; 2002

83014 drug administration and sample collection
➔ *CPT Assistant* Nov 98:25; Feb 99:8; Nov 99:45

(For H. pylori, stool, use 87338. For H. pylori, liquid scintillation counter, see 78267, 78268. For H. pylori, enzyme immunoassay, use 87339)

83015 Heavy metal (arsenic, barium, beryllium, bismuth, antimony, mercury); screen

83018 quantitative, each

(83019 has been deleted. To report, see 83013, 83014)

83020 Hemoglobin fractionation and quantitation; electrophoresis (eg, A2, S, C, and/or F)
➔ *CPT Assistant* Nov 98:25

83021 chromatography (eg, A2, S, C, and/or F)
➔ *CPT Assistant* Nov 98:25; Dec 99:7

83026 Hemoglobin; by copper sulfate method, non-automated

83030 F (fetal), chemical

⊘ =Modifier '-51' Exempt ▶ ◀ =New or Revised Text ✚ =Add-on Code CPT 2002

83033 F (fetal), qualitative
➜ *CPT Changes* 2001

83036 glycated
➜ *CPT Assistant* Summer 94:2

(For fecal hemoglobin detection by immunoassay, use
▶82274)◀

(83040 has been deleted. To report, use 83050)

83045 methemoglobin, qualitative

83050 methemoglobin, quantitative

83051 plasma

(83052, 83053 have been deleted. To report, use 85660)

83055 sulfhemoglobin, qualitative

83060 sulfhemoglobin, quantitative

83065 thermolabile

83068 unstable, screen

83069 urine

83070 Hemosiderin; qualitative

83071 quantitative

(Heroin, see 80100-80103)

(HIAA, use 83497)

(High performance liquid chromatography (HPLC), use
82486)

83080 b-Hexosaminidase, each assay
➜ *CPT Assistant* Nov 98:25

(83086, 83087 have been deleted. To report, use 82128)

83088 Histamine

(Hollander test, use 91052)

83090 Homocystine
➜ *CPT Changes* 2001

(83093, 83095 have been deleted. For homogentisic acid,
qualitative urine screen, see 81005. For quantitative
assay, see code for specific method)

83150 Homovanillic acid (HVA)

(Hormones, see individual alphabetic listings in
Chemistry section)

(Hydrogen breath test, use 91065)

(83485, 83486 have been deleted)

83491 Hydroxycorticosteroids, 17- (17-OHCS)

(For cortisol, see 82530, 82533. For deoxycortisol, use
82634)

(83492 has been deleted. To report, use 83491)

(83493 has been deleted)

(83494-83496 have been deleted. To report, use 83491)

83497 Hydroxyindolacetic acid, 5-(HIAA)

(For urine qualitative test, use 81005)

(5-Hydroxytryptamine, use 84260)

83498 Hydroxyprogesterone, 17-d

83499 Hydroxyprogesterone, 20-

83500 Hydroxyproline; free

83505 total

(83510 has been deleted. To report, use 83500 and
83505)

83516 Immunoassay for analyte other than infectious agent
antibody or infectious agent antigen, qualitative or
semiquantitative; multiple step method
➜ *CPT Assistant* Nov 98:25

83518 single step method (eg, reagent strip)
➜ *CPT Assistant* Fall 93:26

83519 Immunoassay, analyte, quantitative; by
radiopharmaceutical technique (eg, RIA)
➜ *CPT Assistant* Fall 93:26; Summer 94:2

83520 not otherwise specified
➜ *CPT Assistant* Fall 93:26

(83523 has been deleted. To report, use 80174)

(For immunoassays for antibodies to infectious agent
antigens, see analyte and method specific codes in the
Immunology section)

(For immunoassay of tumor antigen not elsewhere
specified, use 86316)

(Immunoglobulins, see 82784, 82785)

(83524 has been deleted)

83525 Insulin; total

(For proinsulin, use 84206)

(83526 has been deleted. To report, see 80434, 80435)

83527 free
➜ *CPT Assistant* Summer 94:5

83528 Intrinsic factor

(For intrinsic factor antibodies, use 86340)

(83530 has been deleted)

(83533, 83534 have been deleted. To report, use 84999)

83540 Iron
➜ *CPT Assistant* Fall 93:25

(83545, 83546 have been deleted. To report, use 83540)

83550 Iron binding capacity

(83555, 83565 have been deleted. To report, use 83550)

83570 Isocitric dehydrogenase (IDH)

(Isonicotinic acid hydrazide, INH, see code for specific
method)

(Isopropyl alcohol, use 84600)

(83571 has been deleted. To report, use 83570)

(83576 has been deleted. To report, see code for specific method)

(83578 has been deleted)

83582 Ketogenic steroids, fractionation

(83583, 83584 have been deleted)

(Ketone bodies, for serum, see 82009, 82010; for urine, see 81000-81003)

83586 Ketosteroids, 17- (17-KS); total

(83587 has been deleted. To report, use 83593)

(83588, 83589 have been deleted. To report, use 83586)

(83590 has been deleted)

83593 fractionation

(83596 has been deleted)

(83597 has been deleted)

(83599 has been deleted. To report, use 83586)

(83600 has been deleted. To report, see code for specific method)

83605 Lactate (lactic acid)

(83610 has been deleted. To report, use 83615)

83615 Lactate dehydrogenase (LD), (LDH);
→ *CPT Assistant* Fall 93:25; Feb 98:1; Dec 99:1

(83620 has been deleted. To report, use 83615)

(83624 has been deleted)

83625 isoenzymes, separation and quantitation
→ *CPT Assistant* Fall 93:25; Feb 98:1

(83626 has been deleted)

(83628 has been deleted. To report, use 83625)

(83629, 83631 have been deleted. To report, use 83615)

83632 Lactogen, human placental (HPL) human chorionic somatomammotropin

83633 Lactose, urine; qualitative

83634 quantitative

(For tolerance, see 82951, 82952)

(For breath hydrogen test for lactase deficiency, use 91065)

(83645 has been deleted. To report, see quantitative code or screening for toxicity)

(83650 has been deleted)

83655 Lead

(83660 has been deleted. To report, use 83655)

83661 Fetal lung maturity assessment; lecithin sphingomyelin (L/S) ratio
→ *CPT Changes* 2001

83662 foam stability test

83663 fluorescence polarization
→ *CPT Changes* 2001

83664 lamellar body density
→ *CPT Changes* 2001

(For phosphatidylglycerol, use 84081)

83670 Leucine aminopeptidase (LAP)

(83675, 83680 have been deleted. To report, use 83670)

(83681 has been deleted. To report, use 80428)

(83685 has been deleted. To report, use 80176)

83690 Lipase

(83700, 83705 have been deleted. For cholesterol, see 82465, 83718-83721. For triglycerides, use 84478)

83715 Lipoprotein, blood; electrophoretic separation and quantitation
→ *CPT Assistant* Nov 98:25; Oct 99:11

83716 high resolution fractionation and quantitation of lipoprotein cholesterols (eg, electrophoresis, nuclear magnetic resonance, ultracentrifugation)
→ *CPT Assistant* Nov 98:25; Oct 99:11; Mar 00:11

(83717 has been deleted. To report, use 83716)

83718 Lipoprotein, direct measurement; high density cholesterol (HDL cholesterol)
→ *CPT Assistant* Oct 99:11

83719 direct measurement, VLDL cholesterol
→ *CPT Assistant* Oct 99:11

(83720 has been deleted)

83721 direct measurement, LDL cholesterol
→ *CPT Assistant* Nov 98:25; Oct 99:11

(For fractionation by nuclear magnetic resonance or high resolution electrophoresis, use 83716)

►(To report direct measurement, intermediate density lipoproteins (remnant lipoproteins), use Category III code 0026T)◄

(Luteinizing hormone (LH), use 83002)

(83725 has been deleted. To report, use 80178)

83727 Luteinizing releasing factor (LRH)

(83728 has been deleted. To report, see 80100-80103, 80299)

(83730 has been deleted)

(For qualitative analysis, see 80100-80103)

(Macroglobulins, alpha-2, use 86329)

83735 Magnesium

(83740, 83750, 83755, 83760, 83765 have been deleted. To report, use 83735)

83775 Malate dehydrogenase

(Maltose tolerance, see 82951, 82952)

(Mammotropin, use 84146)

83785 Manganese

(83790 has been deleted)

(Marijuana, see 80100-80103)

(83795 has been deleted)

(83799 has been deleted. To report, use 83925)

83788 Mass spectrometry and tandem mass spectrometry (MS, MS/MS), analyte not elsewhere specified; qualitative, each specimen

➲ *CPT Assistant* Nov 98:26

83789 quantitative, each specimen

➲ *CPT Assistant* Nov 98:26

83805 Meprobamate

(For qualitative analysis, see 80100-80103)

83825 Mercury, quantitative

(83830 has been deleted. To report, use 83825)

(Mercury screen, use 83015)

83835 Metanephrines

(For catecholamines, see 82382-82384)

83840 Methadone

(For methadone qualitative analysis, see 80100-80103)

(Methamphetamine, see 80100-80103, 82145)

(Methanol, use 84600)

(83842 has been deleted. To report, see code for specific method)

(83845 has been deleted. To report, see 80101-80103)

83857 Methemalbumin

(Methemoglobin, see hemoglobin 83045, 83050)

83858 Methsuximide

(Methyl alcohol, use 84600)

(Microalbumin, see 82043 for quantitative, see 82044 for semiquantitative)

(Microglobulin, beta-2, use 82232)

(83859 has been deleted)

(83860-83862 have been deleted. To report, see 80100-80103 for qualitative analysis, 83925 for quantitative analysis)

83864 Mucopolysaccharides, acid; quantitative

(83865 has been deleted. To report, use 83864)

83866 screen

(83870 has been deleted. To report, use 84999)

83872 Mucin, synovial fluid (Ropes test)

▲ **83873** Myelin basic protein, cerebrospinal fluid

➲ *CPT Changes* 2002

(For oligoclonal bands, use 83916)

83874 Myoglobin

➲ *CPT Assistant* Feb 98:1

(83875 has been deleted)

(83880 has been deleted. To report, use 83925)

83883 Nephelometry, each analyte not elsewhere specified

83885 Nickel

83887 Nicotine

Codes 83890-83912 are intended for use with molecular diagnostic techniques for analysis of nucleic acids.

Codes 83890-83912 are coded by procedure rather than analyte.

Code separately for each procedure used in an analysis. For example, a procedure requiring isolation of DNA, restriction endonuclease digestion, electrophoresis, and nucleic acid probe amplification would be coded 83890, 83892, 83894, and 83898.

(For microbial identification, see 87797, 87798)

83890 Molecular diagnostics; molecular isolation or extraction

➲ *CPT Assistant* Fall 93:26; Nov 98:26

83891 isolation or extraction of highly purified nucleic acid

➲ *CPT Assistant* Nov 98:26

83892 enzymatic digestion

➲ *CPT Assistant* Fall 93:26

83893 dot/slot blot production

➲ *CPT Assistant* Nov 98:26

83894 separation by gel electrophoresis (eg, agarose, polyacrylamide)

➲ *CPT Assistant* Fall 93:25; Nov 98:26

(83895 has been deleted)

83896 nucleic acid probe, each

➲ *CPT Assistant* Fall 93:26

83897 nucleic acid transfer (eg, Southern, Northern)

➲ *CPT Assistant* Nov 98:26

83898 amplification of patient nucleic acid (eg, PCR, LCR), single primer pair, each primer pair

➲ *CPT Assistant* Fall 93:26; Nov 98:26; *CPT Changes* 2001

(83900 has been deleted)

83901 amplification of patient nucleic acid, multiplex, each multiplex reaction

➲ *CPT Assistant* Nov 98:26

83902 reverse transcription

➲ *CPT Changes* 2001

83903 mutation scanning, by physical properties (eg, single strand conformational polymorphisms (SSCP), heteroduplex, denaturing gradient gel electrophoresis (DGGE), RNA'ase A), single segment, each

➲ *CPT Assistant* Nov 98:26

83904 mutation identification by sequencing, single segment, each segment

➲ *CPT Assistant* Nov 98:26

83905	mutation identification by allele specific transcription, single segment, each segment
	➲ *CPT Assistant* Nov 98:26
83906	mutation identification by allele specific translation, single segment, each segment
	➲ *CPT Assistant* Nov 98:26
	(83910 has been deleted)
83912	interpretation and report
	(83913 has been deleted. To report, use 83898)
83915	Nucleotidase 5-
▲ 83916	Oligoclonal immune (oligoclonal bands)
	➲ *CPT Changes* 2002
	(83917 has been deleted)
83918	Organic acids; total, quantitative, each specimen
	➲ *CPT Assistant* Mar 96:11; Nov 98:26; *CPT Changes* 2001
83919	qualitative, each specimen
	➲ *CPT Assistant* Nov 98:26
	(83920 has been deleted. To report, use code for specific method)
83921	Organic acid, single, quantitative
	➲ *CPT Changes* 2001
83925	Opiates, (eg, morphine, meperidine)
83930	Osmolality; blood
83935	urine
83937	Osteocalcin (bone g1a protein)
	➲ *CPT Assistant* Summer 94:5
	(83938 has been deleted)
83945	Oxalate
	(83946 has been deleted. To report, use 80154)
	(83947 has been deleted. To report, see 82009, 82010)
	(83948 has been deleted. To report, see 80100-80103, 83925)
	(83949 has been deleted)
	(83965 has been deleted. To report, see code for specific method)
● 83950	Oncoprotein, HER-2/neu
	➲ *CPT Changes* 2002
	▶(For tissue, see 88342, 88365)◀
83970	Parathormone (parathyroid hormone)
	(83971, 83972 have been deleted. To report, see code for specific method)
	(83973 has been deleted. To report, use 84375)
	(83974 has been deleted)
	(83975, 83985 have been deleted. To report, see code for specific method)
	(Pesticide, quantitative, see code for specific method. For screen for chlorinated hydrocarbons, use 82441)

83986	pH, body fluid, except blood
	(For blood pH, see 82800, 82803)
83992	Phencyclidine (PCP)
	(For qualitative analysis, see 80100-80103)
	(Phenobarbital, use 80184)
	(83995 has been deleted. To report, see code for specific method)
	(84005 has been deleted)
	(84021 has been deleted. To report, see 80100, 80101, 84022)
84022	Phenothiazine
	(For qualitative analysis, see 80100, 80101)
84030	Phenylalanine (PKU), blood
	(Phenylalanine-tyrosine ratio, see 84030, 84510)
	(84031 has been deleted)
	(84033 has been deleted. To report, see code for specific method)
84035	Phenylketones, qualitative
	(84037 has been deleted. To report, use 84035)
	(84038 has been deleted. To report, see code for specific method)
	(84039, 84040 have been deleted)
	(84045 has been deleted. To report, see 80185, 80186)
84060	Phosphatase, acid; total
84061	forensic examination
	(84065 has been deleted. To report, use 84066)
84066	prostatic
84075	Phosphatase, alkaline;
	➲ *CPT Assistant* Dec 99:1
84078	heat stable (total not included)
84080	isoenzymes
84081	Phosphatidylglycerol
	(84082 has been deleted)
	(Phosphates inorganic, use 84100)
	(Phosphates, organic, see code for specific method. For cholinesterase, see 82480, 82482)
	(84083 has been deleted)
84085	Phosphogluconate, 6-, dehydrogenase, RBC
84087	Phosphohexose isomerase
	(84090 has been deleted)
84100	Phosphorus inorganic (phosphate);
	➲ *CPT Assistant* Dec 99:1

84105	urine

(Pituitary gonadotropins, see 83001-83002)

(PKU, see 84030, 84035)

84106 Porphobilinogen, urine; qualitative

84110 quantitative

(84118 has been deleted. To report, use 84120)

84119 Porphyrins, urine; qualitative

84120 quantitation and fractionation

(84121 has been deleted. To report, use 84120)

84126 Porphyrins, feces; quantitative

84127 qualitative

(84128 has been deleted)

(Porphyrin precursors, see 82135, 84106, 84110)

(For protoporphyrin, RBC, see 84202, 84203)

84132 Potassium; serum
→ *CPT Assistant* Dec 99:1

84133 urine

84134 Prealbumin

(For microalbumin, see 82043, 82044)

84135 Pregnanediol

(84136 has been deleted. To report, use 84135)

84138 Pregnanetriol

(84139 has been deleted. To report, use 84138)

84140 Pregnenolone
→ *CPT Assistant* Summer 94:6

(84141 has been deleted. To report, use 80188)

(84142 has been deleted. To report, see 80190, 80192)

84143 17-hydroxypregnenolone
→ *CPT Assistant* Summer 94:6

84144 Progesterone

(Progesterone receptor assay, use 84234)

(For proinsulin, use 84206)

84146 Prolactin

(84147 has been deleted. To report, see 80100-80103)

(84149 has been deleted)

84150 Prostaglandin, each

84152 Prostate specific antigen (PSA); complexed (direct measurement)
→ *CPT Changes* 2001

84153 total
→ *CPT Assistant* Fall 93:26; May 96:10; Aug 96:10; Jan 97:10; Nov 98:26; Aug 99:5; Dec 99:10

84154 free
→ *CPT Assistant* Nov 98:26; Aug 99:5; Dec 99:10

84155 Protein; total, except refractometry
→ *CPT Assistant* Dec 99:1; Jan 00:7

84160 refractometric

84165 electrophoretic fractionation and quantitation

(84170 has been deleted)

(84175 has been deleted. To report, use 84165)

(84176 has been deleted)

(84180 has been deleted. To report, use 81050 and 84155)

84181 Western Blot, with interpretation and report, blood or other body fluid

84182 Western Blot, with interpretation and report, blood or other body fluid, immunological probe for band identification, each

(For Western Blot tissue analysis, use 88371)

(84185 has been deleted)

(84190 has been deleted. To report, use 84165)

(84195 has been deleted)

(84200 has been deleted. To report, use 84165)

(84201 has been deleted. To report, see 80438, 80439)

84202 Protoporphyrin, RBC; quantitative

84203 screen

(84205 has been deleted. To report, use code for specific method)

84206 Proinsulin

(Pseudocholinesterase, use 82480)

84207 Pyridoxal phosphate (Vitamin B-6)

(84208 has been deleted. To report, use 89060)

84210 Pyruvate

84220 Pyruvate kinase

84228 Quinine

(84230 has been deleted. To report, use 80194)

(84231 has been deleted. To report radioimmunoassay not elsewhere specified, use 83519)

(84232 has been deleted)

84233 Receptor assay; estrogen

84234 progesterone

84235 endocrine, other than estrogen or progesterone (specify hormone)

(84236 has been deleted. To report, use 84233 and 84234)

84238 non-endocrine (eg, acetylcholine) (specify receptor)

84244 Renin

(84246 has been deleted)

(84250, 84251 have been deleted. To report, use 84479)

84252	Riboflavin (Vitamin B-2)

(Salicylates, use 80196)

(Secretin test, see 99070, 89100 and appropriate analyses)

84255 Selenium

84260 Serotonin

(For urine metabolites (HIAA), use 83497)

84270 Sex hormone binding globulin (SHBG)
➲ *CPT Assistant* Summer 94:4

84275 Sialic acid

(Sickle hemoglobin, use 85660)

84285 Silica

84295 Sodium; serum
➲ *CPT Assistant* Dec 99:1

84300 urine

(Somatomammotropin, use 83632)

(Somatotropin, use 83003)

84305 Somatomedin
➲ *CPT Assistant* Summer 94:4

84307 Somatostatin
➲ *CPT Assistant* Summer 94:4

(84310 has been deleted)

84311 Spectrophotometry, analyte not elsewhere specified

84315 Specific gravity (except urine)

(For specific gravity, urine, see 81000-81003)

(84317 has been deleted)

(84318 has been deleted)

(Stone analysis, see 82355-82370)

(84324 has been deleted. To report, see code for specific method)

84375 Sugars, chromatographic, TLC or paper chromatography

84376 Sugars (mono-, di-, and oligosaccharides); single qualitative, each specimen
➲ *CPT Assistant* Nov 98:26-27; Dec 99:7

84377 multiple quantitative, each specimen
➲ *CPT Assistant* Nov 98:26-27

84378 single quantitative, each specimen
➲ *CPT Assistant* Nov 98:26-27

84379 multiple quantitative, each specimen
➲ *CPT Assistant* Nov 98:26-27; Dec 99:7

(84382 has been deleted)

84392 Sulfate, urine

(Sulfhemoglobin, see hemoglobin, 83055, 83060)

(84395 has been deleted)

(84397 has been deleted)

(T-3, see 84479-84481)

(T-4, see 84436-84439)

(84401 has been deleted)

84402 Testosterone; free

84403 total

(84404 has been deleted)

(84405 has been deleted. To report, use 84403)

(84406 has been deleted. For testosterone binding protein, use sex hormone binding globulin, 84270)

(84407 has been deleted. To report, see code for specific method)

(84408 has been deleted. To report, see 80100-80103, 80299)

(84409, 84410 have been deleted. To report, see code for specific method)

(84420 has been deleted. To report, use 80198)

84425 Thiamine (Vitamin B-1)

84430 Thiocyanate

84432 Thyroglobulin
➲ *CPT Assistant* Summer 94:2

(Thyroglobulin, antibody, use 86800)

(84434 has been deleted. To report, use 84022)

(Thyrotropin releasing hormone (TRH) test, see 80438, 80439)

(84435 has been deleted. To report, use 84436)

84436 Thyroxine; total
➲ *CPT Assistant* Fall 93:25; Summer 94:3

84437 requiring elution (eg, neonatal)

84439 free

(84441 has been deleted. To report, see 84436-84439)

84442 Thyroxine binding globulin (TBG)

84443 Thyroid stimulating hormone (TSH)
➲ *CPT Assistant* Summer 94:3

(84444 has been deleted. To report, see 80438, 80439)

▲ **84445** Thyroid stimulating immune globulins (TSI)
➲ *CPT Assistant* Summer 94:3; *CPT Changes* 2002

(Tobramycin, use 80200)

84446 Tocopherol alpha (Vitamin E)

(Tolbutamide tolerance, use 82953)

(84447, 84448 have been deleted. To report, see 80100-80103)

84449 Transcortin (cortisol binding globulin)
➲ *CPT Assistant* Summer 94:6

⊘ =Modifier '-51' Exempt ▶ ◀ =New or Revised Text ✚ =Add-on Code CPT 2002

84450   Transferase; aspartate amino (AST) (SGOT)
> *CPT Assistant* Dec 99:1

(84455 has been deleted. To report, use 84450)

84460   alanine amino (ALT) (SGPT)
> *CPT Assistant* Dec 99:1

(84465 has been deleted. To report, use 84460)

84466   Transferrin
> *CPT Assistant* Summer 94:4

(Iron binding capacity, use 83550)

(84472 has been deleted. To report, see code for specific method)

(84474 has been deleted. To report, see code for specific method)

(84476 has been deleted. To report, use 84022)

84478   Triglycerides
> *CPT Assistant* Dec 99:1; Mar 00:11

84479   Thyroid hormone (T3 or T4) uptake or thyroid hormone binding ratio (THBR)
> *CPT Assistant* Fall 93:25; Summer 94:3

84480   Triiodothyronine T3; total (TT-3)

84481   free

84482   reverse
> *CPT Assistant* Summer 94:2

(84483 has been deleted. To report, see 80100-80103, 80299)

84484   Troponin, quantitative
> *CPT Assistant* Nov 97:29; Jan 98:6; Feb 98:1

(For Troponin, qualitative assay, use 84512)

84485   Trypsin; duodenal fluid

84488   feces, qualitative

84490   feces, quantitative, 24-hour collection

84510   Tyrosine

(Urate crystal identification, use 89060)

84512   Troponin, qualitative
> *CPT Assistant* Nov 97:29; Jan 98:6; Feb 98:1

(For Troponin, quantitative assay, use 84484)

84520   Urea nitrogen; quantitative
> *CPT Assistant* Dec 99:1

84525   semiquantitative (eg, reagent strip test)
> *CPT Assistant* Mar 98:3

84540   Urea nitrogen, urine

84545   Urea nitrogen, clearance

84550   Uric acid; blood
> *CPT Assistant* Dec 99:1

(84555 has been deleted. To report, use 84550)

84560   other source

(84565, 84570, 84575 have been deleted)

84577   Urobilinogen, feces, quantitative

84578   Urobilinogen, urine; qualitative

84580   quantitative, timed specimen

84583   semiquantitative

(84584 has been deleted)

(Uroporphyrins, use 84120)

(Valproic acid (dipropylacetic acid), use 80164)

84585   Vanillylmandelic acid (VMA), urine

84586   Vasoactive intestinal peptide (VIP)
> *CPT Assistant* Summer 94:6

84588   Vasopressin (antidiuretic hormone, ADH)

(84589 has been deleted. To report, use 85810)

84590   Vitamin A

(84595 has been deleted. To report, use 82380 and 84590)

(Vitamin B-1, use 84425)

(Vitamin B-2, use 84252)

(Vitamin B-6, use 84207)

(Vitamin B-12, use 82607)

(Vitamin B-12, absorption (Schilling), see 78270, 78271)

(Vitamin C, use 82180)

(Vitamin D, see 82306, 82307, 82652)

(Vitamin E, use 84446)

84591   Vitamin, not otherwise specified
> *CPT Changes* 2001

84597   Vitamin K

(VMA, use 84585)

84600   Volatiles (eg, acetic anhydride, carbon tetrachloride, dichloroethane, dichloromethane, diethylether, isopropyl alcohol, methanol)

(For acetaldehyde, use 82000)

(84605 has been deleted)

(84610 has been deleted)

(Volume, blood, RISA or Cr-51, see 78110, 78111)

(84613 has been deleted)

(84615 has been deleted. To report, see code for specific method)

84620   Xylose absorption test, blood and/or urine

(For administration, use 99070)

84630 Zinc

(84635 has been deleted. To report, use 84630)

(84645 has been deleted)

(84680 has been deleted. To report, use 82677)

84681 C-peptide

(84695 has been deleted. To report, use 80170)

(84701 has been deleted. To report, see 84702-84703)

84702 Gonadotropin, chorionic (hCG); quantitative

84703   qualitative

(For urine pregnancy test by visual color comparison, use 81025)

(84800 has been deleted. To report, use 84443)

(84810 has been deleted. To report, use 80200)

84830 Ovulation tests, by visual color comparison methods for human luteinizing hormone

84999 Unlisted chemistry procedure
→ *CPT Assistant* Oct 00:7

Hematology and Coagulation

(For blood banking procedures, see **Transfusion Medicine**)

(Agglutinins, see **Immunology**)

(Antiplasmin, use 85410)

(Antithrombin III, see 85300, 85301)

(85000 has been deleted. To report, use 85002)

85002 Bleeding time

(85003 has been deleted. To report, use 85999)

(85005 has been deleted)

85007 Blood count; manual differential WBC count (includes RBC morphology and platelet estimation)

85008   manual blood smear examination without differential parameters

(See also 85585)

(For other fluids (eg, CSF), see 89050, 89051)

85009   differential WBC count, buffy coat

(85012 has been deleted)

(Eosinophils, nasal smear, use 89190)

85013   spun microhematocrit

85014   other than spun hematocrit

85018   hemoglobin

(For other hemoglobin determination, see 83020-83069)

(For immunoassay, hemoglobin, fecal, use 86683)

85021 hemogram, automated (RBC, WBC, Hgb, Hct and indices only)

85022 hemogram, automated, and manual differential WBC count (CBC)

85023 hemogram and platelet count, automated, and manual differential WBC count (CBC)

85024 hemogram and platelet count, automated, and automated partial differential WBC count (CBC)
→ *CPT Assistant* Jul 00:11

85025 hemogram and platelet count, automated, and automated complete differential WBC count (CBC)
→ *CPT Assistant* Jul 00:11

85027 hemogram and platelet count, automated

(85028 has been deleted. To report, see 85023-85025)

(85029, 85030 have been deleted. To report, see 85021-85027)

85031 Blood count; hemogram, manual, complete CBC (RBC, WBC, Hgb, Hct, differential and indices)
→ *CPT Assistant* Nov 98:27

85041   red blood cell (RBC) only

(See also 85021-85031, 89050)

85044   reticulocyte count, manual

85045   reticulocyte count, flow cytometry

85046   reticulocytes, hemoglobin concentration
→ *CPT Assistant* Nov 98:27

85048   white blood cell (WBC)

(See also 85021-85031)

85060 Blood smear, peripheral, interpretation by physician with written report

▶(85095 has been deleted. To report, use 38220)◀

(85096 has been deleted. For interpretation of smear, use 85097; for cell block interpretation, use 88305)

▲ **85097** Bone marrow, smear interpretation
→ *CPT Assistant* Winter 92:17; Jul 98:4; *CPT Changes* 2002

(85100 has been deleted. To report, use ▶38220◀ and 85097)

(85101 has been deleted. For aspiration, use ▶38220)◀

(For special stains, see 85540, 88312, 88313)

▶(85102 has been deleted. To report, use 38221)◀

(For bone biopsy, see 20220, 20225, 20240, 20245, 20250, 20251)

(85103, 85105 have been deleted. For bone marrow biopsy interpretation, use 88305)

(85109 has been deleted)

(85120 has been deleted. To report, see 85230-85240)

⊘ =Modifier '-51' Exempt   ▶ ◀=New or Revised Text   ✛ =Add-on Code   CPT 2002

85130	Chromogenic substrate assay
	(85150, 85160, 85165 have been deleted)
	(Circulating anti-coagulant screen (mixing studies), see 85611, 85732)
85170	Clot retraction
	(85171, 85172 have been deleted)
85175	Clot lysis time, whole blood dilution
	(Clotting factor I (fibrinogen), see 85384, 85385)
85210	Clotting; factor II, prothrombin, specific
	(See also 85610-85613)
85220	factor V (AcG or proaccelerin), labile factor
85230	factor VII (proconvertin, stable factor)
85240	factor VIII (AHG), one stage
	(85242 has been deleted)
85244	factor VIII related antigen
85245	factor VIII, VW factor, ristocetin cofactor
85246	factor VIII, VW factor antigen
85247	factor VIII, von Willebrand factor, multimetric analysis
85250	factor IX (PTC or Christmas)
85260	factor X (Stuart-Prower)
85270	factor XI (PTA)
85280	factor XII (Hageman)
85290	factor XIII (fibrin stabilizing)
85291	factor XIII (fibrin stabilizing), screen solubility
85292	prekallikrein assay (Fletcher factor assay)
85293	high molecular weight kininogen assay (Fitzgerald factor assay)
85300	Clotting inhibitors or anticoagulants; antithrombin III, activity
85301	antithrombin III, antigen assay
85302	protein C, antigen
85303	protein C, activity
85305	protein S, total
85306	protein S, free
85307	Activated Protein C (APC) resistance assay
	➲ *CPT Changes* 2001
	(85310, 85311 have been deleted)
	(85320 has been deleted)
	(85330 has been deleted. To report, use 85335)
85335	Factor inhibitor test
85337	Thrombomodulin
	(For mixing studies for inhibitors, use 85732)
	(85340, 85341 have been deleted)

85345	Coagulation time; Lee and White
85347	activated
85348	other methods
	(Differential count, see 85007 et seq)
	(Duke bleeding time, use 85002)
	(Eosinophils, nasal smear, use 89190)
85360	Euglobulin lysis
	(Fetal hemoglobin, see 83030, 83033, 85460)
85362	Fibrin(ogen) degradation (split) products (FDP)(FSP); agglutination slide, semiquantitative
	(85363, 85364 have been deleted)
	(85365 has been deleted. To report, use 86320)
	(Immunoelectrophoresis, use 86320)
85366	paracoagulation
	(85367 has been deleted)
	(85368 has been deleted. To report, use 85366)
	(85369 has been deleted)
85370	quantitative
	(85371 has been deleted. To report, see 85384, 85385)
	(85372 has been deleted)
	(85376, 85377 have been deleted. To report, see 85384, 85385)
85378	Fibrin degradation products, D-dimer; semiquantitative
85379	quantitative
85384	Fibrinogen; activity
85385	antigen
85390	Fibrinolysins or coagulopathy screen, interpretation and report
	(85392 has been deleted)
	(85395 has been deleted)
	(85398 has been deleted)
85400	Fibrinolytic factors and inhibitors; plasmin
85410	alpha-2 antiplasmin
85415	plasminogen activator
85420	plasminogen, except antigenic assay
85421	plasminogen, antigenic assay
	(85426 has been deleted. For von Willebrand factor assay, see 85245-85247)
	(Fragility, red blood cell, see 85547, 85555-85557)
85441	Heinz bodies; direct
85445	induced, acetyl phenylhydrazine
	(Hematocrit (PCV), see 85014, 85021-85031)
	(Hemoglobin, see 83020-83068, 85018-85031)

85460 Hemoglobin or RBCs, fetal, for fetomaternal hemorrhage; differential lysis (Kleihauer-Betke)

➲ *CPT Assistant* Fall 93:25

(See also 83030, 83033)

(Hemogram, see 85021-85031)

(Hemolysins, see 86940, 86941)

85461 rosette

85475 Hemolysin, acid

(See also 86940, 86941)

85520 Heparin assay

85525 Heparin neutralization

85530 Heparin-protamine tolerance test

▶(85535 has been deleted. To report use 85536)◀

85536 Iron stain, peripheral blood

➲ *CPT Changes* 2001

(For iron stains on bone marrow or other tissues with physician evaluation, use 88313)

(85538 has been deleted. For leder stain, esterase, blood or bone marrow, use 88319)

85540 Leukocyte alkaline phosphatase with count

(85544 has been deleted)

85547 Mechanical fragility, RBC

(85548 has been deleted. To report, use 85008)

85549 Muramidase

(Nitroblue tetrazolium dye test, use 86384)

85555 Osmotic fragility, RBC; unincubated

(85556 has been deleted)

85557 incubated

(Packed cell volume, use 85013)

(Partial thromboplastin time, see 85730, 85732)

(Parasites, blood (eg, malaria smears), use 87207)

(Plasmin, use 85400)

(Plasminogen, use 85420)

(Plasminogen activator, use 85415)

(85560 has been deleted. For peroxidase stain, WBC, use 88319)

(85575 has been deleted)

85576 Platelet; aggregation (in vitro), each agent

➲ *CPT Assistant* Jul 96:10

(85577 has been deleted)

(85580 has been deleted. To report, use 85590)

85585 estimation on smear, only

(See also 85008)

85590 manual count

85595 automated count

85597 Platelet neutralization

85610 Prothrombin time;

85611 substitution, plasma fractions, each

85612 Russell viper venom time (includes venom); undiluted

85613 diluted

(85614 has been deleted)

(85615 has been deleted)

(85618 has been deleted)

(Red blood cell count, see 85021, 85031, 85041)

(85630 has been deleted. To report, see 85021- 85027)

(85632 has been deleted)

85635 Reptilase test

(Reticulocyte count, see 85044, 85045)

(85650 has been deleted)

85651 Sedimentation rate, erythrocyte; non-automated

85652 automated

85660 Sickling of RBC, reduction

(Hemoglobin electrophoresis, use 83020)

(Smears (eg, for parasites, malaria), use 87207)

(85665 has been deleted. For plasminogen activator, use 85415)

(85667 has been deleted)

85670 Thrombin time; plasma

85675 titer

(85700 has been deleted)

85705 Thromboplastin inhibition; tissue

(85710, 85711 have been deleted)

(85720 has been deleted)

(For individual clotting factors, see 85245-85247)

85730 Thromboplastin time, partial (PTT); plasma or whole blood

85732 substitution, plasma fractions, each

85810 Viscosity

(85820 has been deleted. To report, use 85810)

(von Willebrand factor assay, see 85245-85247)

(WBC count, see 85021-85031, 85048, 89050)

85999 Unlisted hematology and coagulation procedure

Immunology

(Acetylcholine receptor antibody, see 86255, 86256)

(Actinomyces, antibodies to, use 86602)

(Adrenal cortex antibodies, see 86255, 86256)

▶(For tuberculosis test, cell mediated immunity measurement of gamma interferon antigen response, use Category III code 0010T)◀

86000   Agglutinins, febrile (eg, Brucella, Francisella, Murine typhus, Q fever, Rocky Mountain spotted fever, scrub typhus), each antigen

(For antibodies to infectious agents, see 86602-86804)

86001   Allergen specific IgG quantitative or semiquantitative, each allergen

➔ *CPT Changes* 2001

(86002 has been deleted)

(Agglutinins and autohemolysins, see 86940, 86941)

86003   Allergen specific IgE; quantitative or semiquantitative, each allergen

➔ *CPT Assistant* Spring 94:31

(For total quantitative IgE, use 82785)

(86004 has been deleted. To report, see 86940, 86941)

86005   qualitative, multiallergen screen (dipstick, paddle or disk)

➔ *CPT Assistant* Spring 94:31

(For total qualitative IgE, use 83518)

(Alpha-1 antitrypsin, see 82103, 82104)

(Alpha-1 feto-protein, see 82105, 82106)

(Anti-AChR (acetylcholine receptor) antibody titer, see 86255, 86256)

(86006 has been deleted. To report, see 83519, 86318, 86403)

(86007, 86008, 86009 have been deleted)

(86011 has been deleted. To report, use 86021)

(86012 has been deleted. To report, use 86978)

(86013 has been deleted)

(86014 has been deleted. To report, use 86022)

(86016 has been deleted. To report, use 86850)

(86017 has been deleted. To report, see 86850 and 86901)

(86018 has been deleted)

(86019 has been deleted. To report, use 86860)

(Anticardiolipin antibody, use 86147)

(Anti-DNA, use 86225)

(Anti-deoxyribonuclease titer, use 86215)

86021   Antibody identification; leukocyte antibodies

86022   platelet antibodies

86023   platelet associated immunoglobulin assay

(86024 has been deleted. For RBC antibodies, use 86870)

(86026, 86028 have been deleted)

(86031 has been deleted. To report, use 86880)

(86032 has been deleted. To report, use 86885)

(86033 has been deleted. To report, use 86886)

(86034 has been deleted. To report, see 86880-86886 and 86971)

(86035 has been deleted. To report, use 86970)

86038   Antinuclear antibodies (ANA);

86039   titer

(86045 has been deleted)

(Antistreptococcal antibody, ie, anti-DNAse, use 86215)

(Antistreptokinase titer, use 86590)

86060   Antistreptolysin O; titer

(For antibodies to infectious agents, see 86602-86804)

86063   screen

(For antibodies to infectious agents, see 86602-86804)

(86064 has been deleted. For antitrypsin, alpha-1 use 82103, for phenotyping use 82104)

(86066 has been deleted. To report, use 82104)

(86067 has been deleted. To report, use 82103)

(86068 has been deleted. For blood compatibility test, see 86920-86922)

(Blastomyces, antibodies to, use 86612)

(86069 has been deleted)

(86070 has been deleted. To report, use 86920)

(86072 has been deleted)

(86073 has been deleted. To report, see 86156, 86157, 86904)

(86074 has been deleted)

(86075, 86076 have been deleted)

86077   Blood bank physician services; difficult cross match and/or evaluation of irregular antibody(s), interpretation and written report

86078   investigation of transfusion reaction including suspicion of transmissible disease, interpretation and written report

86079 authorization for deviation from standard blood banking procedures (eg, use of outdated blood, transfusion of Rh incompatible units), with written report

(86080 has been deleted. For blood typing, see 86900-86910)

(86082 has been deleted. To report, see 86900, 86901)

(86083 has been deleted. To report, use 86850 and 86900 or 86901)

(86084 has been deleted. To report, use 86903)

(86085 has been deleted. To report, use 86904)

(86090 has been deleted)

(86095 has been deleted. To report, use 86905)

(86096 has been deleted)

(86100 has been deleted. To report, use 86901)

(86105 has been deleted. To report, use 86906)

(86115 has been deleted)

(86120 has been deleted. To report, use 86905)

(86128 has been deleted. To report, use 86890)

(86129 has been deleted)

(86130 has been deleted. To report, use 86891)

(86131, 86134, 86138 and 86139 have been deleted)

(Brucella, antibodies to, use 86622)

(Candida, antibodies to, use 86628. For skin testing, use 86485)

86140 C-reactive protein;
➲ *CPT Changes* 2002

(Candidiasis, use 86628)

●**86141** high sensitivity (hsCRP)
➲ *CPT Changes* 2002

86146 Beta 2 Glycoprotein I antibody, each
➲ *CPT Changes* 2001

86147 Cardiolipin (phospholipid) antibody, each Ig class
➲ *CPT Changes* 2001

86148 Anti-phosphatidylserine (phospholipid) antibody
➲ *CPT Assistant* Nov 97:30

(86149 has been deleted. To report, use 82378)

(86151 has been deleted. To report, use 82378)

86155 Chemotaxis assay, specify method

(Clostridium difficile toxin, use 87230)

(Coccidioides, antibodies to, see 86635. For skin testing, use 86490)

86156 Cold agglutinin; screen

86157 titer

(86158 has been deleted)

(86159 has been deleted. To report, see 86160 and 86161)

86160 Complement; antigen, each component

86161 functional activity, each component

86162 total hemolytic (CH50)

(86163, 86164 have been deleted. To report, see 86160 and 86161)

86171 Complement fixation tests, each antigen

(Coombs test, see 86880-86886)

86185 Counterimmunoelectrophoresis, each antigen

(86201, 86202 have been deleted)

(Cryptococcus, antibodies to, use 86641)

(86209 has been deleted. To report, use 86999)

86215 Deoxyribonuclease, antibody

86225 Deoxyribonucleic acid (DNA) antibody; native or double stranded

(Echinococcus, antibodies to, see code for specific method)

(For HIV antibody tests, see 86701-86703)

86226 single stranded

(Anti D.S., DNA, IFA, eg, using C.Lucilae, see 86255 and 86256)

(86227, 86228 have been deleted. To report, use 86317)

(86229 has been deleted)

86235 Extractable nuclear antigen, antibody to, any method (eg, nRNP, SS-A, SS-B, Sm, RNP, Sc170, J01), each antibody

(86240, 86241 have been deleted)

86243 Fc receptor

(86244 has been deleted. To report fetoprotein, alpha-1, see 82105, 82106)

(86245 has been deleted)

(Filaria, antibodies to, see code for specific method)

86255 Fluorescent noninfectious agent antibody; screen, each antibody
➲ *CPT Assistant* Nov 98:27

86256 titer, each antibody

(Fluorescent technique for antigen identification in tissue, use 88346; for indirect fluorescence, use 88347)

(86265 has been deleted. To report, use 86930)

(86266 has been deleted. To report, use 86931)

(FTA, see 86781)

(86267 has been deleted. To report, use 86932)

(Gel (agar) diffusion tests, use 86331)

(86272, 86273 have been deleted)

(86274 has been deleted. To report, use 90742)

86277 Growth hormone, human (HGH), antibody

86280 Hemagglutination inhibition test (HAI)

(For rubella, use 86762)

(86281 has been deleted. To report, use 85475)

(86282 has been deleted. To report, use 86940)

(86283 has been deleted. To report, use 86941)

(86285, 86286 have been deleted)

(86287 has been deleted. To report, use 87340)

(86289 has been deleted. To report, use 86704)

(For antibodies to infectious agents, see 86602-86804)

(86290 has been deleted. To report, use 86705)

(86291 has been deleted. To report, use 86706)

(86293 has been deleted. To report, use 87350)

86294 Immunoassay for tumor antigen, qualitative or semiquantitative (eg, bladder tumor antigen)
➲ *CPT Changes* 2001

(86295 has been deleted. To report, use 86707)

(86296 has been deleted. To report, use 86708)

(86297 has been deleted. To report, use 86708)

(86299 has been deleted. To report, use 86709)

86300 Immunoassay for tumor antigen, quantitative; CA 15-3 (27.29)
➲ *CPT Changes* 2001

86301 CA 19-9
➲ *CPT Changes* 2001

(86302 has been deleted. To report, use 86803)

(86303 has been deleted. To report, use 86804)

86304 CA 125
➲ *CPT Changes* 2001

▶(For measurement of serum HER-2/neu oncoprotein, see 83950)◀

(86306 has been deleted. To report, use 87380)

(For hepatitis delta agent, antibody, use 86692)

86308 Heterophile antibodies; screening

(For antibodies to infectious agents, see 86602-86804)

86309 titer

(For antibodies to infectious agents, see 86602-86804)

86310 titers after absorption with beef cells and guinea pig kidney

(Histoplasma, antibodies to, use 86698. For skin testing, use 86510)

(For antibodies to infectious agents, see 86602-86804)

(86311 has been deleted. To report, see 87390, 87391)
➲ *CPT Assistant* Fall 93:26

(86312 has been deleted. To report, see 86701-86703)

(86313 has been deleted. To report, use 87449)

(86314 has been deleted. To report, use 86689)

(86315 has been deleted. To report, use 87450)

(Human growth hormone antibody, use 86277)

86316 Immunoassay for tumor antigen; other antigen, quantitative (eg, CA 50, 72-4, 549), each
➲ *CPT Assistant* May 96:11; Aug 96:11; Apr 98:15; Aug 99:5; Dec 99.10 *CPT Changes* 2001

86317 Immunoassay for infectious agent antibody, quantitative, not otherwise specified
➲ *CPT Assistant* Nov 97:30-31

(For immunoassay techniques for antigens, see 83516, 83518, 83519, 83520, 87301-87450, 87810-87899)

(For particle agglutination procedures, use 86403)

86318 Immunoassay for infectious agent antibody, qualitative or semiquantitative, single step method (eg, reagent strip)

(86319 has been deleted. To report immunoassays for drugs, see 80100-80103)

86320 Immunoelectrophoresis; serum

▲ **86325** other fluids (eg, urine, cerebrospinal fluid) with concentration
➲ *CPT Changes* 2002

86327 crossed (2-dimensional assay)

86329 Immunodiffusion; not elsewhere specified
➲ *CPT Assistant* Aug 00:11

86331 gel diffusion, qualitative (Ouchterlony), each antigen or antibody

86332 Immune complex assay

(86333 has been deleted. To report, use 86332)

86334 Immunofixation electrophoresis

(86335 has been deleted)

● **86336** Inhibin A
➲ *CPT Changes* 2002

86337 Insulin antibodies

(86338 has been deleted. To report, use 86337)

86340 Intrinsic factor antibodies

(Leptospira, antibodies to, use 86720)

(Leukoagglutinins, use 86021)

86341 Islet cell antibody
➲ *CPT Assistant* Summer 94:6

(86342 has been deleted. To report, use 86945)

86343 Leukocyte histamine release test (LHR)

86344 Leukocyte phagocytosis

(86345, 86346, 86347 have been deleted)

(86349 has been deleted. To report, use 86950)

(86351 has been deleted)

86353 Lymphocyte transformation, mitogen (phytomitogen) or antigen induced blastogenesis

(Lymphocytes immunophenotyping, use 88180 for cytometry; see 88342, 88346 for microscopic techniques)

(86357 has been deleted. To report, see 88180, 88342, 88346)

(86358 has been deleted. To report, see 88180, 88342, 88346)

(Malaria antibodies, use 86750)

86359 T cells; total count
➔ *CPT Assistant* Nov 97:30

86360 absolute CD4 and CD8 count, including ratio
➔ *CPT Assistant* Nov 97:30

86361 absolute CD4 count
➔ *CPT Assistant* Nov 97:30

(86365 has been deleted)

86376 Microsomal antibodies (eg, thyroid or liver-kidney), each

(86377 has been deleted. To report, use 86376)

86378 Migration inhibitory factor test (MIF)

(Mitochondrial antibody, liver, see 86255, 86256)

(Mononucleosis, see 86308-86310)

86382 Neutralization test, viral

86384 Nitroblue tetrazolium dye test (NTD)

(Ouchterlony diffusion, use 86331)

(86385, 86386 have been deleted. To report, see 86910, 86911)

(86388, 86389, 86391 have been deleted)

(Platelet antibodies, see 86022, 86023)

(86392, 86393, 86398 have been deleted)

(86402 has been deleted)

86403 Particle agglutination; screen, each antibody

(86404 has been deleted. To report, use 86965)

(86405 has been deleted)

86406 titer, each antibody

(Pregnancy test, see 84702, 84703)

(86410 has been deleted. To report, use 86970)

(86411 has been deleted. To report, use 86971)

(86412 has been deleted. To report, use 86972)

(86415, 86416 have been deleted)

(86417 has been deleted. To report, use 86975)

(86418 has been deleted. To report, use 86976)

(86419 has been deleted. To report, use 86977)

(86420 has been deleted. To report, use 86978)

(86421-86423 have been deleted. To report, see 82785, 83518, 86003, 86005)

(86424, 86425, 86427 have been deleted)

(Rapid plasma reagin test (RPR), see 86592, 86593)

86430 Rheumatoid factor; qualitative

86431 quantitative

(Serologic test for syphilis, see 86592, 86593)

(86450 has been deleted)

(86455 has been deleted. To report, use 86586)

(86460, 86470, 86480 have been deleted)

86485 Skin test; candida

(For antibody, candida, use 86628)

86490 coccidioidomycosis

(86495, 86500 have been deleted)

86510 histoplasmosis

(For histoplasma, antibody, use 86698)

(86520, 86530 have been deleted)

(86540 has been deleted. For mumps antibody, use 86735)

(86550, 86565, 86570 have been deleted)

86580 tuberculosis, intradermal

86585 tuberculosis, tine test

▶(For tuberculosis test, cell mediated immunity measurement of gamma interferon antigen response, use Category III code 0010T)◀

(For skin tests for allergy, see 95010-95199)

(Smooth muscle antibody, see 86255, 86256)

(Sporothrix, antibodies to, see code for specific method)

86586 unlisted antigen, each
➔ *CPT Assistant* Jul 98:11; *CPT Changes* 2000

(86587 has been deleted. To report, use 86985)

(86588 has been deleted. To report, see 86403, 87081, 87430, or 87880)

86590 Streptokinase, antibody

(For antibodies to infectious agents, see 86602-86804)

(Streptolysin O antibody, see antistreptolysin O, 86060, 86063)

86592 Syphilis test; qualitative (eg, VDRL, RPR, ART)

(For antibodies to infectious agents, see 86602-86804)

86593   quantitative

(For antibodies to infectious agents, see 86602-86804)

(Tetanus antibody, use 86774)

(Thyroglobulin antibody, use 86800)

(Thyroglobulin, use 84432)

(Thyroid microsomal antibody, use 86376)

(86594 has been deleted. To report, see 86376 and 86800)

(86595 has been deleted)

(86597 has been deleted. To report see 86812-86822)

(86600 has been deleted)

(For toxoplasma antibody, see 86777-86778)

The following codes (86602-86804) are qualitative or semiquantitative immunoassays performed by multiple step methods for the detection of antibodies to infectious agents. For immunoassays by single step method (eg, reagent strips), use code 86318. Procedures for the identification of antibodies should be coded as precisely as possible. For example, an antibody to a virus could be coded with increasing specificity for virus, family, genus, species, or type. In some cases, further precision may be added to codes by specifying the class of immunoglobulin being detected. When multiple tests are done to detect antibodies to organisms classified more precisely than the specificity allowed by available codes, it is appropriate to code each as a separate service. For example, a test for antibody to an enterovirus is coded as 86658. Coxsackie viruses are enteroviruses, but there are no codes for the individual species of enterovirus. If assays are performed for antibodies to coxsackie A and B species, each assay should be separately coded. Similarly, if multiple assays are performed for antibodies of different immunoglobulin classes, each assay should be coded separately.

> For the detection of antibodies other than those to infectious agents, see specific antibody (eg, 86021, 86022, 86023, 86376, 86800, 86850-86870) or specific method (eg, 83516, 86255, 86256).

> (For infectious agent/antigen detection, see 87260-87899)
> ➜ *CPT Assistant* Fall 93:26

86602   Antibody; actinomyces

86603   adenovirus

86606   Aspergillus

86609   bacterium, not elsewhere specified

86611   Bartonella
            ➜ *CPT Changes* 2001

86612   Blastomyces

86615   Bordetella

86617   Borrelia burgdorferi (Lyme disease) confirmatory test (eg, Western blot or immunoblot)

86618   Borrelia burgdorferi (Lyme disease)

86619   Borrelia (relapsing fever)

86622   Brucella

86625   Campylobacter

86628   Candida

(For skin test, candida, use 86485)

(86630 has been deleted)

86631   Chlamydia

86632   Chlamydia, IgM
            ➜ *CPT Assistant* Nov 97:31

(For chlamydia antigen, see 87270, 87320. For fluorescent antibody technique, see 86255, 86256)

86635   Coccidioides

86638   Coxiella Brunetii (Q fever)

86641   Cryptococcus

86644   cytomegalovirus (CMV)

(For TORCH panel, use 80090)

86645   cytomegalovirus (CMV), IgM

86648   Diphtheria

(86650 has been deleted. To report, use 86781)

86651   encephalitis, California (La Crosse)

86652   encephalitis, Eastern equine

86653   encephalitis, St. Louis

86654   encephalitis, Western equine

86658   enterovirus (eg, coxsackie, echo, polio)

(86662 has been deleted. To report, use 86781)

(Trichinella, antibodies to, use 86784)

(Trypanosoma, antibodies to, see code for specific method)

(Tuberculosis, use 86580 for skin testing)

(Viral antibodies, see code for specific method)

86663   Epstein-Barr (EB) virus, early antigen (EA)

86664   Epstein-Barr (EB) virus, nuclear antigen (EBNA)

86665   Epstein-Barr (EB) virus, viral capsid (VCA)

86666   Ehrlichia
            ➜ *CPT Changes* 2001

86668   Francisella Tularensis

86671   fungus, not elsewhere specified

86674   Giardia Lamblia

86677   Helicobacter pylori

(86681 has been deleted. To report, see 86255, 86256)

86682   helminth, not elsewhere specified

▶(86683 has been deleted. To report, use 82274)◀

86684	Hemophilus influenza

(86685 has been deleted. To report, see 86255, 86256)

86687	HTLV-I
86688	HTLV-II
86689	HTLV or HIV antibody, confirmatory test (eg, Western Blot)
86692	hepatitis, delta agent

➲ *CPT Assistant* Nov 97:31

(For hepatitis delta agent, antigen, use 87380)

86694	herpes simplex, non-specific type test

(For TORCH panel, use 80090)

86695	herpes simplex, type 1
86696	herpes simplex, type 2

➲ *CPT Changes* 2001

86698	histoplasma
86701	HIV-1
86702	HIV-2
86703	HIV-1 and HIV-2, single assay

➲ *CPT Assistant* Nov 97:31

(For HIV-1 antigen, use 87390)

(For HIV-2 antigen, use 87391)

(For confirmatory test for HIV antibody (eg, Western Blot), use 86689)

86704	Hepatitis B core antibody (HBcAb); total

➲ *CPT Assistant* Nov 97:31-32; *CPT Changes* 2001

86705	IgM antibody

➲ *CPT Assistant* Nov 97:31-32

86706	Hepatitis B surface antibody (HBsAb)

➲ *CPT Assistant* Nov 97:31-32

86707	Hepatitis Be antibody (HBeAb)

➲ *CPT Assistant* Nov 97:31-32

86708	Hepatitis A antibody (HAAb); total

➲ *CPT Assistant* Nov 97:31-32; Jun 00:11; *CPT Changes* 2001

86709	IgM antibody

➲ *CPT Assistant* Nov 97:31-32; Jun 00:11

86710	Antibody; influenza virus
86713	Legionella
86717	Leishmania
86720	Leptospira
86723	Listeria monocytogenes
86727	lymphocytic choriomeningitis
86729	Lymphogranuloma Venereum
86732	mucormycosis
86735	mumps

86738	Mycoplasma
86741	Neisseria meningitidis
86744	Nocardia
86747	parvovirus
86750	Plasmodium (malaria)
86753	protozoa, not elsewhere specified
86756	respiratory syncytial virus
86757	Rickettsia

➲ *CPT Changes* 2001

86759	rotavirus
86762	rubella
86765	rubeola
86768	Salmonella
86771	Shigella
86774	tetanus
86777	Toxoplasma
86778	Toxoplasma, IgM
86781	Treponema Pallidum, confirmatory test (eg, FTA-abs)
86784	trichinella
86787	varicella-zoster
86790	virus, not elsewhere specified
86793	Yersinia
86800	Thyroglobulin antibody

(For thyroglobulin, use 84432)

86803	Hepatitis C antibody;

➲ *CPT Assistant* Nov 97:31-32

86804	confirmatory test (eg, immunoblot)

➲ *CPT Assistant* Nov 97:31-32

Tissue Typing

(For pretransplant cross-match, see appropriate code or codes)

86805	Lymphocytotoxicity assay, visual crossmatch; with titration
86806	without titration
86807	Serum screening for cytotoxic percent reactive antibody (PRA); standard method
86808	quick method

(86810 has been deleted)

86812	HLA typing; A, B, or C (eg, A10, B7, B27), single antigen
86813	A, B, or C, multiple antigens
86816	DR/DQ, single antigen
86817	DR/DQ, multiple antigens

86821	lymphocyte culture, mixed (MLC)
86822	lymphocyte culture, primed (PLC)
86849	Unlisted immunology procedure

➲ *CPT Assistant* Mar 98:10

Transfusion Medicine

(For apheresis, use 36520)

(For therapeutic phlebotomy, use 99195)

86850 Antibody screen, RBC, each serum technique
➲ *CPT Assistant* Fall 93:25

86860 Antibody elution (RBC), each elution

86870 Antibody identification, RBC antibodies, each panel for each serum technique
➲ *CPT Assistant* Fall 93:25

86880 Antihuman globulin test (Coombs test); direct, each antiserum

86885 indirect, qualitative, each antiserum

86886 indirect, titer, each antiserum

86890 Autologous blood or component, collection processing and storage; predeposited
➲ *CPT Assistant* Apr 96:2

86891 intra- or postoperative salvage

(For physician services to autologous donors, see 99201-99204)

86900 Blood typing; ABO

86901 Rh (D)
➲ *CPT Assistant* Fall 93:25

86903 antigen screening for compatible blood unit using reagent serum, per unit screened

86904 antigen screening for compatible unit using patient serum, per unit screened

86905 RBC antigens, other than ABO or Rh (D), each

86906 Rh phenotyping, complete

86910 Blood typing, for paternity testing, per individual; ABO, Rh and MN

86911 each additional antigen system

86915 Bone marrow or peripheral stem cell harvest, modification or treatment to eliminate cell type(s) (eg, T-cells, metastatic carcinoma)
➲ *CPT Assistant* Apr 96:2; Nov 99:46; *CPT Changes* 2000

86920 Compatibility test each unit; immediate spin technique

86921 incubation technique

86922 antiglobulin technique

86927 Fresh frozen plasma, thawing, each unit

86930 Frozen blood, preparation for freezing, each unit;
➲ *CPT Assistant* Apr 96:2

86931 with thawing

86932 with freezing and thawing

86940 Hemolysins and agglutinins; auto, screen, each

86941 incubated

86945 Irradiation of blood product, each unit

86950 Leukocyte transfusion

(For leukapheresis, use 36520)

86965 Pooling of platelets or other blood products

86970 Pretreatment of RBCs for use in RBC antibody detection, identification, and/or compatibility testing; incubation with chemical agents or drugs, each

86971 incubation with enzymes, each

86972 by density gradient separation

86975 Pretreatment of serum for use in RBC antibody identification; incubation with drugs, each

86976 by dilution

86977 incubation with inhibitors, each

86978 by differential red cell absorption using patient RBCs or RBCs of known phenotype, each absorption

86985 Splitting of blood or blood products, each unit
➲ *CPT Assistant* Apr 96:2

86999 Unlisted transfusion medicine procedure

Microbiology

Includes bacteriology, mycology, parasitology, and virology.

Presumptive identification of microorganisms is defined as identification by colony morphology, growth on selective media, Gram stains, or up to three tests (eg, catalase, oxidase, indole, urease). Definitive identification of microorganisms is defined as an identification to the genus or species level that requires additional tests (eg, biochemical panels, slide cultures). If additional studies involve molecular probes, chromatography, or immunologic techniques, these should be separately coded in addition to definitive identification codes (87140-87158). For multiple specimens/sites use modifier '-59'. For repeat laboratory tests performed on the same day, use modifier '-91'.

87001 Animal inoculation, small animal; with observation

87003 with observation and dissection

87015 Concentration (any type), for infectious agents
➲ *CPT Changes* 2001

(Do not report 87015 in conjunction with 87177)

87040 Culture, bacterial; blood, with isolation and presumptive identification of isolates (includes anaerobic culture, if appropriate)
> *CPT Assistant* Aug 97:18; *CPT Changes* 2001

▲ **87045** feces, with isolation and preliminary examination (eg, KIA, LIA), Salmonella and Shigella species
> *CPT Changes* 2001; 2002

87046 stool, additional pathogens, isolation and preliminary examination (eg, Campylobacter, Yersinia, Vibrio, E. coli 0157), each plate
> *CPT Changes* 2001; 2002

(87060 has been deleted. To report, use 87070 or 87081)

87070 any other source except urine, blood or stool, with isolation and presumptive identification of isolates
> *CPT Assistant* Aug 97:18; *CPT Changes* 2001

(For urine, use 87088)

87071 quantitative, aerobic with isolation and presumptive identification of isolates, any source except urine, blood or stool
> *CPT Changes* 2001

(For urine, use 87088)

(87072 has been deleted. To report, use 87076 or 87077)

87073 quantitative, anaerobic with isolation and presumptive identification of isolates, any source except urine, blood or stool
> *CPT Changes* 2001

(For definitive identification of isolates, use 87076 or 87077. For typing of isolates see 87140-87158)

87075 any source, anaerobic with isolation and presumptive identification of isolates
> *CPT Changes* 2001

87076 anaerobic isolate, additional methods required for definitive identification, each isolate
> *CPT Changes* 2001

(For gas liquid chromatography (GLC) or high pressure liquid chromatography (HPLC), use 87143)

87077 aerobic isolate, additional methods required for definitive identification, each isolate
> *CPT Changes* 2001

(For gas liquid chromatography (GLC) or high pressure liquid chromatography (HPLC), use 87143)

87081 Culture, presumptive, pathogenic organisms, screening only;
> *CPT Changes* 2001

(87082 and 87083 have been deleted. To report, use 87081)

87084 with colony estimation from density chart

(87085 has been deleted. To report, use 87086)

87086 Culture, bacterial; quantitative colony count, urine
> *CPT Changes* 2001

(87087 has been deleted. To report, use 87088)

87088 with isolation and presumptive identification of isolates, urine
> *CPT Changes* 2001

87101 Culture, fungi (mold or yeast) isolation, with presumptive identification of isolates; skin, hair, or nail
> *CPT Assistant* Sep 99:10; *CPT Changes* 2001

87102 other source (except blood)

87103 blood

87106 Culture, fungi, definitive identification, each organism; yeast
> *CPT Changes* 2001

(Use 87106 in addition to codes 87101, 87102, or 87103 when appropriate)

87107 mold
> *CPT Changes* 2001

87109 Culture, mycoplasma, any source

87110 Culture, chlamydia, any source
> *CPT Changes* 2001

(For immunofluorescence staining of shell vials, use 87140)

87116 Culture, tubercle or other acid-fast bacilli (eg, TB, AFB, mycobacteria) any source, with isolation and presumptive identification of isolates
> *CPT Changes* 2001

(87117 has been deleted. For concentration, use 87015)

87118 Culture, mycobacterial, definitive identification, each isolate
> *CPT Changes* 2001

(For nucleic acid probe identification, use 87149)

(For GLC or HPLC identification, use 87143)

87140 Culture, typing; immunofluorescent method, each antiserum
> *CPT Changes* 2001

87143 gas liquid chromatography (GLC) or high pressure liquid chromatography (HPLC) method
> *CPT Changes* 2001

(87145 has been deleted)

87147 immunologic method, other than immunofluoresence (eg, agglutination grouping), per antiserum
> *CPT Changes* 2001

87149 identification by nucleic acid probe
> *CPT Changes* 2001

(87151 has been deleted. To report, use 87147)

87152 identification by pulse field gel typing
> *CPT Changes* 2001

(87155 has been deleted. To report, use 87147)

⊘ =Modifier '-51' Exempt   ▶ ◀ =New or Revised Text   ✚ =Add-on Code   CPT 2002

87158   other methods

(87163 has been deleted. To report, use 87076 or 87077)

87164   Dark field examination, any source (eg, penile, vaginal, oral, skin); includes specimen collection

87166   without collection

87168   Macroscopic examination; arthropod
➔ *CPT Changes* 2001

87169   parasite
➔ *CPT Changes* 2001

87172   Pinworm exam (eg, cellophane tape prep)
➔ *CPT Changes* 2001

(87173 has been deleted)

(87174 has been deleted)

(87175 has been deleted)

87176   Homogenization, tissue, for culture
➔ *CPT Changes* 2001

87177   Ova and parasites, direct smears, concentration and identification

(Do not report 87177 in conjunction with 87015)

(For coccidia or microsporidia exam, use 87207)

(For trichrome, iron hemotoxylin and other special stains, use ▶88313◀)

(For nucleic acid probes in cytologic material, use 88365)

(For molecular diagnostics, see 83890-83898, 87470-87799)

(87178 has been deleted. To report, use 87797)

(87179 has been deleted. To report, use 87798)

87181   Susceptibility studies, antimicrobial agent; agar dilution method, per agent (eg, antibiotic gradient strip)
➔ *CPT Changes* 2001

87184   disk method, per plate (12 or fewer agents)
➔ *CPT Changes* 2001

87185   enzyme detection (eg, beta lactamase), per enzyme
➔ *CPT Changes* 2001

87186   microdilution or agar dilution (minimum inhibitory concentration (MIC) or breakpoint), each multi-antimicrobial, per plate
➔ *CPT Changes* 2001

+ 87187   microdilution or agar dilution, minimum lethal concentration (MLC), each plate (List separately in addition to code for primary procedure)
➔ *CPT Changes* 2001

(Use 87187 in conjuction with 87186 or 87188)

87188   macrobroth dilution method, each agent
➔ *CPT Changes* 2001

87190   mycobacteria, proportion method, each agent
➔ *CPT Changes* 2001

(For other mycobacterial susceptibility studies, see 87181, 87184, 87186, or 87188)

(87192 has been deleted. For fungal susceptibility studies, see 87181, 87184, 87186, 87187, or 87188)

87197   Serum bactericidal titer (Schlicter test)

● **87198**   Cytomegalovirus, direct fluorescent antibody (DFA)
➔ *CPT Changes* 2002

● **87199**   Enterovirus, direct fluorescent antibody (DFA)
➔ *CPT Changes* 2002

87205   Smear, primary source with interpretation; Gram or Giemsa stain for bacteria, fungi, or cell types
➔ *CPT Changes* 2001

87206   fluorescent and/or acid fast stain for bacteria, fungi, parasites, viruses or cell types
➔ *CPT Changes* 2001

87207   special stain for inclusion bodies or intracellular parasites (eg, malaria, coccidia, microsporidia, cytomegalovirus, herpes viruses)
➔ *CPT Changes* 2001

(87208 has been deleted)

(For thick smear preparation, use 87015)

(For complex special stains, see 88312, 88313)

(For fat, meat, fibers, nasal eosinophils, and starch, see miscellaneous section)

87210   wet mount for infectious agents (eg, saline, India ink, KOH preps)
➔ *CPT Changes* 2001

(For KOH examination of skin, hair or nails, see 87220)

(87211 has been deleted. To report, use 87177)

87220   Tissue examination by KOH slide of samples from skin, hair, or nails for fungi or ectoparasite ova or mites (eg, scabies)
➔ *CPT Changes* 2001

87230   Toxin or antitoxin assay, tissue culture (eg, Clostridium difficile toxin)

87250   Virus isolation; inoculation of embryonated eggs, or small animal, includes observation and dissection
➔ *CPT Changes* 2001

87252   tissue culture inoculation, observation, and presumptive identification by cytopathic effect
➔ *CPT Changes* 2001

87253   tissue culture, additional studies or definitive identification (eg, hemabsorption, neutralization, immunofluoresence stain), each isolate
➔ *CPT Changes* 2001

(Electron microscopy, use 88348)

(Inclusion bodies in tissue sections, see 88304-88309; in smears, see 87207-87210; in fluids, use 88106)

87254	shell vial, includes identification with immunofluorescence stain, each virus
	→ *CPT Changes* 2001

(Report 87254 in addition to 87252 as appropriate)

These codes are intended for primary source only. For similar studies on culture material, refer to codes 87140-87158. Infectious agents by antigen detection, immunofluorescence microscopy, or nucleic acid probe techniques should be reported as precisely as possible. The most specific code possible should be reported. If there is no specific agent code, the general methodology code (eg, 87299, 87449, 87450, 87797, 87798, 87799, 87899) should be used. For identification of antibodies to many of the listed infectious agents, see 86602-86804. ►When separate assays are performed for different species or strain(s) of organisms, each assay should be reported separately.◄

87260	Infectious agent antigen detection by immunofluorescent technique; adenovirus
	→ *CPT Changes* 2001
87265	Bordetella pertussis/parapertussis
	→ *CPT Assistant* Nov 97:32
87270	Chlamydia trachomatis
	→ *CPT Assistant* Nov 97:32
87272	cryptosporidium/giardia
	→ *CPT Assistant* Nov 97:32
87273	Herpes simplex virus type 2
	→ *CPT Changes* 2001
87274	Herpes simplex virus type 1
	→ *CPT Assistant* Nov 97:32; *CPT Changes* 2001
87275	Influenza B virus
	→ *CPT Changes* 2001
87276	influenza A virus
	→ *CPT Assistant* Nov 97:32
87277	Legionella micdadei
	→ *CPT Changes* 2001
87278	Legionella pneumophila
	→ *CPT Assistant* Nov 97:32
87279	Parainfluenza virus, each type
	→ *CPT Changes* 2001
87280	respiratory syncytial virus
	→ *CPT Assistant* Nov 97:32
87281	Pneumocystis carinii
	→ *CPT Changes* 2001
87283	Rubeola
	→ *CPT Changes* 2001
87285	Treponema pallidum
	→ *CPT Assistant* Nov 97:32
87290	Varicella zoster virus
	→ *CPT Assistant* Nov 97:32

87299	not otherwise specified, each organism
	→ *CPT Assistant* Nov 97:32; *CPT Changes* 2001
87300	Infectious agent antigen detection by immunofluorescent technique, polyvalent for multiple organisms, each polyvalent antiserum
	→ *CPT Changes* 2001

(For physician evaluation of infectious disease agents by immunofluorescence, use 88346)

87301	Infectious agent antigen detection by enzyme immunoassay technique, qualitative or semiquantitative, multiple step method; adenovirus enteric types 40/41
	→ *CPT Assistant* Nov 97:32; Nov 99:46
87320	Chlamydia trachomatis
	→ *CPT Assistant* Nov 97:32
87324	Clostridium difficile toxin(s)
	→ *CPT Assistant* Nov 97:32; *CPT Changes* 2001
87327	Cryptococcus neoformans
	→ *CPT Changes* 2001

(For Cryptococcus latex agglutination, use 86403)

87328	cryptosporidium/giardia
	→ *CPT Assistant* Nov 97:32
87332	cytomegalovirus
	→ *CPT Assistant* Nov 97:32
87335	Escherichia coli 0157
	→ *CPT Assistant* Nov 97:32

(For giardia antigen, use 87328)

87336	Entamoeba histolytica dispar group
	→ *CPT Changes* 2001
87337	Entamoeba histolytica group
	→ *CPT Changes* 2001
87338	Helicobacter pylori, stool
	→ *CPT Assistant* Nov 99:46; *CPT Changes* 2000
87339	Helicobacter pylori
	→ *CPT Changes* 2001

(For H. pylori, stool, use 87338. For H. pylori, breath and blood by mass spectrometry, see 83013, 83014. For H. pylori, liquid scintillation counter, see 78267, 78268)

87340	hepatitis B surface antigen (HBsAg)
	→ *CPT Assistant* Nov 97:32; Jan 00:11
87341	hepatitis B surface antigen (HBsAg) neutralization
	→ *CPT Changes* 2001
87350	hepatitis Be antigen (HBeAg)
	→ *CPT Assistant* Nov 97:32
87380	hepatitis, delta agent
	→ *CPT Assistant* Nov 97:32
87385	Histoplasma capsulatum
	→ *CPT Assistant* Nov 97:32
87390	HIV-1
	→ *CPT Assistant* Nov 97:32

⊘ =Modifier '-51' Exempt   ► ◄=New or Revised Text   ✚ =Add-on Code   CPT 2002

87391	HIV-2	**87512**	Gardnerella vaginalis, quantification
	➔ *CPT Assistant* Nov 97:32	**87515**	hepatitis B virus, direct probe technique
87400	Influenza, A or B, each	**87516**	hepatitis B virus, amplified probe technique
	➔ *CPT Changes* 2001	**87517**	hepatitis B virus, quantification
87420	respiratory syncytial virus	**87520**	hepatitis C, direct probe technique
	➔ *CPT Assistant* Nov 97:32	**87521**	hepatitis C, amplified probe technique
87425	rotavirus	**87522**	hepatitis C, quantification
	➔ *CPT Assistant* Nov 97:32	**87525**	hepatitis G, direct probe technique
87427	Shiga-like toxin	**87526**	hepatitis G, amplified probe technique
	➔ *CPT Changes* 2001	**87527**	hepatitis G, quantification
87430	Streptococcus, group A	**87528**	Herpes simplex virus, direct probe technique
	➔ *CPT Assistant* Nov 97:32	**87529**	Herpes simplex virus, amplified probe technique

87449	Infectious agent antigen detection by enzyme immunoassay technique qualitative or semiquantitative; multiple step method, not otherwise specified, each organism
	➔ *CPT Assistant* Nov 97:32; Jan 00:11; *CPT Changes* 2001
87450	single step method, not otherwise specified, each organism
	➔ *CPT Assistant* Nov 97:33; *CPT Changes* 2001
87451	multiple step method, polyvalent for multiple organisms, each polyvalent antiserum
	➔ *CPT Changes* 2001
87470	Infectious agent detection by nucleic acid (DNA or RNA); Bartonella henselae and Bartonella quintana, direct probe technique
	➔ *CPT Assistant* Nov 97:33-34
87471	Bartonella henselae and Bartonella quintana, amplified probe technique
87472	Bartonella henselae and Bartonella quintana, quantification
87475	Borrelia burgdorferi, direct probe technique
87476	Borrelia burgdorferi, amplified probe technique
87477	Borrelia burgdorferi, quantification
87480	Candida species, direct probe technique
87481	Candida species, amplified probe technique
87482	Candida species, quantification
87485	Chlamydia pneumoniae, direct probe technique
87486	Chlamydia pneumoniae, amplified probe technique
87487	Chlamydia pneumoniae, quantification
87490	Chlamydia trachomatis, direct probe technique
87491	Chlamydia trachomatis, amplified probe technique
87492	Chlamydia trachomatis, quantification
87495	cytomegalovirus, direct probe technique
87496	cytomegalovirus, amplified probe technique
87497	cytomegalovirus, quantification
87510	Gardnerella vaginalis, direct probe technique
87511	Gardnerella vaginalis, amplified probe technique

87530	Herpes simplex virus, quantification
87531	Herpes virus-6, direct probe technique
87532	Herpes virus-6, amplified probe technique
87533	Herpes virus-6, quantification
87534	HIV-1, direct probe technique
87535	HIV-1, amplified probe technique
87536	HIV-1, quantification
87537	HIV-2, direct probe technique
87538	HIV-2, amplified probe technique
87539	HIV-2, quantification
87540	Legionella pneumophila, direct probe technique
87541	Legionella pneumophila, amplified probe technique
87542	Legionella pneumophila, quantification
87550	Mycobacteria species, direct probe technique
87551	Mycobacteria species, amplified probe technique
87552	Mycobacteria species, quantification
87555	Mycobacteria tuberculosis, direct probe technique
87556	Mycobacteria tuberculosis, amplified probe technique
87557	Mycobacteria tuberculosis, quantification
87560	Mycobacteria avium-intracellulare, direct probe technique
87561	Mycobacteria avium-intracellulare, amplified probe technique
87562	Mycobacteria avium-intracellulare, quantification
87580	Mycoplasma pneumoniae, direct probe technique
87581	Mycoplasma pneumoniae, amplified probe technique
87582	Mycoplasma pneumoniae, quantification
87590	Neisseria gonorrhoeae, direct probe technique
87591	Neisseria gonorrhoeae, amplified probe technique
87592	Neisseria gonorrhoeae, quantification

87620	papillomavirus, human, direct probe technique
87621	papillomavirus, human, amplified probe technique
87622	papillomavirus, human, quantification
87650	Streptococcus, group A, direct probe technique
87651	Streptococcus, group A, amplified probe technique
87652	Streptococcus, group A, quantification

87797 Infectious agent detection by nucleic acid (DNA or RNA), not otherwise specified; direct probe technique, each organism
> *CPT Assistant* Nov 97:34; *CPT Changes* 2001

87798 amplified probe technique, each organism
> *CPT Assistant* Nov 97:34; *CPT Changes* 2001

87799 quantification, each organism
> *CPT Assistant* Nov 97:34; *CPT Changes* 2001

87800 Infectious agent detection by nucleic acid (DNA or RNA), multiple organisms; direct probe(s) technique
> *CPT Changes* 2001

87801 amplified probe(s) technique
> *CPT Changes* 2001

● **87802** Infectious agent antigen detection by immunoassay with direct optical observation; Streptococcus, group B
> *CPT Changes* 2002

● **87803** Clostridium difficile toxin A
> *CPT Changes* 2002

● **87804** Influenza
> *CPT Changes* 2002

87810 Infectious agent detection by immunoassay with direct optical observation; Chlamydia trachomatis
> *CPT Assistant* Nov 97:34; Jan 98:6

87850 Neisseria gonorrhoeae
> *CPT Assistant* Nov 97:34; Jan 98:6

87880 Streptococcus, group A
> *CPT Assistant* Nov 97:34; Jan 98:6; Dec 98:8

87899 not otherwise specified

87901 Infectious agent genotype analysis by nucleic acid (DNA or RNA); HIV 1, reverse transcriptase and protease
> *CPT Changes* 2001; 2002

▶(For infectious agent drug susceptibility phenotype prediction for HIV-1, use Category III code 0023T)◀

● **87902** Hepatitis C virus
> *CPT Changes* 2002

▲ **87903** Infectious agent phenotype analysis by nucleic acid (DNA or RNA) with drug resistance tissue culture analysis, HIV 1; first through 10 drugs tested
> *CPT Changes* 2001; 2002

+ ▲ **87904** each additional 1 through 5 drugs tested (List separately in addition to code for primary procedure)
> *CPT Changes* 2001; 2002

(Use 87904 in conjunction with code 87903)

87999 Unlisted microbiology procedure

Anatomic Pathology

Postmortem Examination

Procedures 88000 through 88099 represent physician services only. Use modifier '-90' or 09990 for outside laboratory services.
> *CPT Assistant* Fall 93:26

88000	Necropsy (autopsy), gross examination only; without CNS
88005	with brain
88007	with brain and spinal cord
88012	infant with brain
88014	stillborn or newborn with brain
88016	macerated stillborn
88020	Necropsy (autopsy), gross and microscopic; without CNS
88025	with brain
88027	with brain and spinal cord
88028	infant with brain
88029	stillborn or newborn with brain
88036	Necropsy (autopsy), limited, gross and/or microscopic; regional
88037	single organ
88040	Necropsy (autopsy); forensic examination
88045	coroner's call
88099	Unlisted necropsy (autopsy) procedure

Cytopathology

88104 Cytopathology, fluids, washings or brushings, except cervical or vaginal; smears with interpretation
> *CPT Assistant* Spring 91:6; Fall 94:3

88106 filter method only with interpretation
> *CPT Assistant* Fall 94:3

88107 smears and filter preparation with interpretation
> *CPT Assistant* Fall 94:3

88108 Cytopathology, concentration technique, smears and interpretation (eg, Saccomanno technique)
> *CPT Assistant* Fall 94:3; Nov 97:34; Jan 98:6

(88109 has been deleted. For interpretation of smear, use 88104; for cell block interpretation, use 88305)

(For cervical or vaginal smears, see 88150-88155)

(For gastric intubation with lavage, see 89130-89141, 91055)

(For x-ray localization, use 74340)

88125 Cytopathology, forensic (eg, sperm)

⊘ =Modifier '-51' Exempt ▶ ◀=New or Revised Text ✚ =Add-on Code CPT 2002

88130 Sex chromatin identification; Barr bodies

88140 peripheral blood smear, polymorphonuclear drumsticks

→ *CPT Assistant* Nov 98:27-28

(For Guard stain, use 88313)

Codes 88141-88155, 88164-88167 are used to report cervical or vaginal screening by various methods and to report physician interpretation services. Use codes 88150-88154 to report Pap smears that are examined using non-Bethesda reporting. Use codes 88164-88167 to report Pap smears that are examined using the Bethesda System of reporting. Use codes 88142-88145 to report specimens collected in fluid medium with automated thin layer preparation that are examined using any system of reporting (Bethesda or non-Bethesda). Within each of these three code families choose the one code that describes the screening method(s) used. Codes 88141 and 88155 should be reported in addition to the screening code chosen when the additional services are provided.

+ 88141 Cytopathology, cervical or vaginal (any reporting system); requiring interpretation by physician (List separately in addition to code for technical service)

→ *CPT Assistant* Nov 97:35; Jan 98:6; Jan 99:11; May 99:6; Nov 99:46

(Use 88141 in conjunction with codes 88142-88154, 88164-88167)

88142 Cytopathology, cervical or vaginal (any reporting system), collected in preservative fluid, automated thin layer preparation; manual screening under physician supervision

→ *CPT Assistant* Nov 97:34-35; Jan 98:6; Nov 98:28; May 99:6

88143 with manual screening and rescreening under physician supervision

→ *CPT Assistant* Nov 97:34-35; Nov 98:28; May 99:6

88144 with manual screening and computer-assisted rescreening under physician supervision

→ *CPT Assistant* Nov 97:34-35; Nov 98:28; May 99:6

88145 with manual screening and computer-assisted rescreening using cell selection and review under physician supervision

→ *CPT Assistant* Nov 97:34-35; Nov 98:28; May 99:6

88147 Cytopathology smears, cervical or vaginal; screening by automated system under physician supervision

→ *CPT Assistant* Nov 97:35; Nov 98:28; Nov 99:46; Jan 99:1; May 99:6

88148 screening by automated system with manual rescreening under physician supervision

→ *CPT Assistant* Jan 99:1; May 99:6; Nov 99:46; *CPT Changes* 2000

88150 Cytopathology, slides, cervical or vaginal; manual screening under physician supervision

→ *CPT Assistant* Winter 91:19; Nov 97:34-35; Nov 98:28; May 99:6

(88151 has been deleted. To report, use 88141)

88152 with manual screening and computer-assisted rescreening under physician supervision

→ *CPT Assistant* Nov 97:35; Jan 98:6; May 99:6

88153 with manual screening and rescreening under physician supervision

→ *CPT Assistant* Nov 97:34-35; Nov 98:28; May 99:6

88154 with manual screening and computer-assisted rescreening using cell selection and review under physician supervision

→ *CPT Assistant* Nov 97:34-35; Nov 98:28; May 99:6

+ 88155 Cytopathology, slides, cervical or vaginal, definitive hormonal evaluation (eg, maturation index, karyopyknotic index, estrogenic index) (List separately in addition to code(s) for other technical and interpretation services)

→ *CPT Assistant* Nov 97:35; Nov 98:28; May 99:6; Nov 99:46

(Use 88155 in conjunction with 88142-88154, 88164-88167)

(88156 has been deleted. To report, use 88164)

(88157 has been deleted. To report, use 88141)

(88158 has been deleted. To report, use 88166)

88160 Cytopathology, smears, any other source; screening and interpretation

88161 preparation, screening and interpretation

→ *CPT Assistant* Aug 97:18

88162 extended study involving over 5 slides and/or multiple stains

(For obtaining specimen, see percutaneous needle biopsy under individual organ in **Surgery**)

(For aerosol collection of sputum, use 89350)

(For special stains, see 88312-88314)

88164 Cytopathology, slides, cervical or vaginal (the Bethesda System); manual screening under physician supervision

→ *CPT Assistant* Nov 98:28; May 99:6

88165 with manual screening and rescreening under physician supervision

→ *CPT Assistant* Nov 98:28; May 99:6

88166 with manual screening and computer-assisted rescreening under physician supervision

→ *CPT Assistant* Nov 98:28; May 99:6

88167 with manual screening and computer-assisted rescreening using cell selection and review under physician supervision

→ *CPT Assistant* Nov 98:28; May 99:6

▶(88170 has been deleted. To report, use 10021)◀

▶(88171 has been deleted. To report, use 10022)◀

88172 Cytopathology, evaluation of fine needle aspirate; immediate cytohistologic study to determine adequacy of specimen(s)

→ *CPT Assistant* Fall 93:26; Fall 94:2; Dec 98:8; *CPT Changes* 2001

88173 interpretation and report

→ *CPT Assistant* Fall 93:26; Fall 94:2; Dec 98:8

88180 Flow cytometry; each cell surface, cytoplasmic or nuclear marker

> *CPT Changes* 2001

88182 cell cycle or DNA analysis

(For tumor morphometry and DNA and ploidy analysis by imaging techniques, use 88358)

88199 Unlisted cytopathology procedure

(For electron microscopy, see 88348, 88349)

Cytogenetic Studies

(For acetylcholinesterase, use 82013)

(For alpha-fetoprotein, serum or amniotic fluid, see 82105, 82106)

▶(For laser microdissection of cells from tissue sample, see 88380)◀

88230 Tissue culture for non-neoplastic disorders; lymphocyte

> *CPT Assistant* Nov 98:29; Oct 99:1

88233 skin or other solid tissue biopsy

> *CPT Assistant* Nov 98:29; Oct 99:1

88235 amniotic fluid or chorionic villus cells

> *CPT Assistant* Nov 98:29; Oct 99:1

88237 Tissue culture for neoplastic disorders; bone marrow, blood cells

> *CPT Assistant* Nov 98:29; Oct 99:1

88239 solid tumor

> *CPT Assistant* Nov 98:29; Oct 99:1

88240 Cryopreservation, freezing and storage of cells, each cell line

> *CPT Assistant* Nov 98:29; Oct 99:1

88241 Thawing and expansion of frozen cells, each aliquot

> *CPT Assistant* Nov 98:29; Oct 99:1

88245 Chromosome analysis for breakage syndromes; baseline Sister Chromatid Exchange (SCE), 20-25 cells

> *CPT Assistant* Nov 98:29; Oct 99:1

88248 baseline breakage, score 50-100 cells, count 20 cells, 2 karyotypes (eg, for ataxia telangiectasia, Fanconi anemia, fragile X)

> *CPT Assistant* Nov 98:29; Oct 99:1

88249 score 100 cells, clastogen stress (eg, diepoxybutane, mitomycin C, ionizing radiation, UV radiation)

> *CPT Assistant* Nov 98:29; Oct 99:1

(88250 has been deleted. To report, use 88248)

(88260 has been deleted. To report, use 88261)

88261 Chromosome analysis; count 5 cells, 1 karyotype, with banding

> *CPT Assistant* Nov 98:29; Oct 99:1

88262 count 15-20 cells, 2 karyotypes, with banding

> *CPT Assistant* Nov 98:29; Oct 99:1

88263 count 45 cells for mosaicism, 2 karyotypes, with banding

> *CPT Assistant* Nov 98:29; Oct 99:1

88264 analyze 20-25 cells

> *CPT Assistant* Nov 98:29; Oct 99:1

(88265 has been deleted. To report, use 88262)

88267 Chromosome analysis, amniotic fluid or chorionic villus, count 15 cells, 1 karyotype, with banding

(88268 has been deleted. To report, use 88261)

88269 Chromosome analysis, in situ for amniotic fluid cells, count cells from 6-12 colonies, 1 karyotype, with banding

(88270 has been deleted. To report, use 88261)

88271 Molecular cytogenetics; DNA probe, each (eg, FISH)

> *CPT Assistant* Nov 98:29; Mar 99:10; Oct 99:1

88272 chromosomal in situ hybridization, analyze 3-5 cells (eg, for derivatives and markers)

> *CPT Assistant* Nov 98:29; Mar 99:10; Oct 99:1

88273 chromosomal in situ hybridization, analyze 10-30 cells (eg, for microdeletions)

> *CPT Assistant* Nov 98:29; Mar 99:10; Oct 99:1

88274 interphase in situ hybridization, analyze 25-99 cells

> *CPT Assistant* Nov 98:29; Mar 99:10; Oct 99:1

88275 interphase in situ hybridization, analyze 100-300 cells

> *CPT Assistant* Nov 98:29; Mar 99:10; Oct 99:1

88280 Chromosome analysis; additional karyotypes, each study

88283 additional specialized banding technique (eg, NOR, C-banding)

88285 additional cells counted, each study

88289 additional high resolution study

> *CPT Assistant* Oct 99:1

88291 Cytogenetics and molecular cytogenetics, interpretation and report

> *CPT Assistant* Nov 98:29; Oct 99:1

88299 Unlisted cytogenetic study

Surgical Pathology

Services 88300 through 88309 include accession, examination, and reporting. They do not include the services designated in codes 88311 through 88365 and 88399, which are coded in addition when provided.

The unit of service for codes 88300 through 88309 is the specimen.

A specimen is defined as tissue or tissues that is (are) submitted for individual and separate attention, requiring individual examination and pathologic diagnosis. Two or more such specimens from the same patient (eg, separately identified endoscopic biopsies, skin lesions, etc.) are each appropriately assigned an individual code reflective of its proper level of service.

Service code 88300 is used for any specimen that in the opinion of the examining pathologist can be accurately diagnosed without microscopic examination. Service code 88302 is used when gross and microscopic examination is performed on a specimen to confirm identification and the absence of disease. Service codes 88304 through 88309 describe all other specimens requiring gross and microscopic examination, and represent additional ascending levels of physician work. Levels 88302 through 88309 are specifically defined by the assigned specimens.

Any unlisted specimen should be assigned to the code which most closely reflects the physician work involved when compared to other specimens assigned to that code.

88300   **Level I** - Surgical pathology, gross examination only
➲ *CPT Assistant* Winter 91:18; Sep 00:10

88302   **Level II** - Surgical pathology, gross and microscopic examination
➲ *CPT Assistant* Winter 91:18; Sep 00:10

Appendix, Incidental

Fallopian Tube, Sterilization

Fingers/Toes, Amputation, Traumatic

Foreskin, Newborn

Hernia Sac, Any Location

Hydrocele Sac

Nerve

Skin, Plastic Repair

Sympathetic Ganglion

Testis, Castration

Vaginal Mucosa, Incidental

Vas Deferens, Sterilization

▲ **88304**   **Level III** - Surgical pathology, gross and microscopic examination
➲ *CPT Assistant* Spring 91:2; Winter 91:18; Aug 97:18; Sep 00:10; *CPT Changes* 2002

Abortion, Induced

Abscess

Aneurysm - Arterial/Ventricular

Anus, Tag

Appendix, Other than Incidental

Artery, Atheromatous Plaque

Bartholin's Gland Cyst

Bone Fragment(s), Other than Pathologic Fracture

Bursa/Synovial Cyst

Carpal Tunnel Tissue

Cartilage, Shavings

Cholesteatoma

Colon, Colostomy Stoma

Conjunctiva - Biopsy/Pterygium

Cornea

Diverticulum - Esophagus/Small Intestine

Dupuytren's Contracture Tissue

Femoral Head, Other than Fracture

Fissure/Fistula

Foreskin, Other than Newborn

Gallbladder

Ganglion Cyst

Hematoma

Hemorrhoids

Hydatid of Morgagni

Intervertebral Disc

Joint, Loose Body

Meniscus

Mucocele, Salivary

Neuroma - Morton's/Traumatic

Pilonidal Cyst/Sinus

Polyps, Inflammatory - Nasal/Sinusoidal

Skin - Cyst/Tag/Debridement

Soft Tissue, Debridement

Soft Tissue, Lipoma

Spermatocele

Tendon/Tendon Sheath

Testicular Appendage

Thrombus or Embolus

Tonsil and/or Adenoids

Varicocele

Vas Deferens, Other than Sterilization

Vein, Varicosity

▲ **88305**   **Level IV** - Surgical pathology, gross and microscopic examination
➲ *CPT Assistant* Spring 91:6; Winter 91:18; Winter 92:17; Aug 97:18; Jul 98:4; Nov 98:29-30; Jul 00:4; Sep 00:10; Dec 00:15; *CPT Changes* 2002

Abortion - Spontaneous/Missed

Artery, Biopsy

Bone Marrow, Biopsy

Bone Exostosis

Brain/Meninges, Other than for Tumor Resection

Breast, Biopsy, Not Requiring Microscopic Evaluation of Surgical Margins

Breast, Reduction Mammoplasty

Bronchus, Biopsy

Cell Block, Any Source

Cervix, Biopsy

Colon, Biopsy

Duodenum, Biopsy

Endocervix, Curettings/Biopsy

Endometrium, Curettings/Biopsy

Esophagus, Biopsy

Extremity, Amputation, Traumatic

Fallopian Tube, Biopsy

Fallopian Tube, Ectopic Pregnancy

Femoral Head, Fracture

Fingers/Toes, Amputation, Non-traumatic

Gingiva/Oral Mucosa, Biopsy

Heart Valve

Joint, Resection

Kidney, Biopsy

Larynx, Biopsy

Leiomyoma(s), Uterine Myomectomy - without Uterus

Lip, Biopsy/Wedge Resection

Lung, Transbronchial Biopsy

Lymph Node, Biopsy

Muscle, Biopsy

Nasal Mucosa, Biopsy

Nasopharynx/Oropharynx, Biopsy

Nerve, Biopsy

Odontogenic/Dental Cyst

Omentum, Biopsy

Ovary with or without Tube, Non-neoplastic

Ovary, Biopsy/Wedge Resection

Parathyroid Gland

Peritoneum, Biopsy

Pituitary Tumor

Placenta, Other than Third Trimester

Pleura/Pericardium - Biopsy/Tissue

Polyp, Cervical/Endometrial

Polyp, Colorectal

Polyp, Stomach/Small Intestine

Prostate, Needle Biopsy

Prostate, TUR

Salivary Gland, Biopsy

Sinus, Paranasal Biopsy

Skin, Other than Cyst/Tag/Debridement/Plastic Repair

Small Intestine, Biopsy

Soft Tissue, Other than Tumor/Mass/Lipoma/ Debridement

Spleen

Stomach, Biopsy

Synovium

Testis, Other than Tumor/Biopsy/Castration

Thyroglossal Duct/Brachial Cleft Cyst

Tongue, Biopsy

Tonsil, Biopsy

Trachea, Biopsy

Ureter, Biopsy

Urethra, Biopsy

Urinary Bladder, Biopsy

Uterus, with or without Tubes and Ovaries, for Prolapse

Vagina, Biopsy

Vulva/Labia, Biopsy

88307 **Level V** - Surgical pathology, gross and microscopic examination

➔ *CPT Assistant* Winter 91:18; Winter 92:18; Jul 98:4; Nov 98:29-30; Jul 99:10; Jul 00:4; Sep 00:10; Dec 00:15; *CPT Changes* 2001

Adrenal, Resection

Bone - Biopsy/Curettings

Bone Fragment(s), Pathologic Fracture

Brain, Biopsy

Brain/Meninges, Tumor Resection

Breast, Excision of Lesion, Requiring Microscopic Evaluation of Surgical Margins

Breast, Mastectomy - Partial/Simple

Cervix, Conization

Colon, Segmental Resection, Other than for Tumor

Extremity, Amputation, Non-traumatic

Eye, Enucleation

Kidney, Partial/Total Nephrectomy

Larynx, Partial/Total Resection

Liver, Biopsy - Needle/Wedge

Liver, Partial Resection

Lung, Wedge Biopsy

Lymph Nodes, Regional Resection

Mediastinum, Mass

Myocardium, Biopsy

Odontogenic Tumor

Ovary with or without Tube, Neoplastic

Pancreas, Biopsy

Placenta, Third Trimester

Prostate, Except Radical Resection

Salivary Gland

Sentinel Lymph Node

Small Intestine, Resection, Other than for Tumor

Soft Tissue Mass (except Lipoma) - Biopsy/Simple Excision

Stomach - Subtotal/Total Resection, Other than for Tumor

Testis, Biopsy

Thymus, Tumor

Thyroid, Total/Lobe

Ureter, Resection

Urinary Bladder, TUR

Uterus, with or without Tubes and Ovaries, Other than Neoplastic/Prolapse

88309 **Level VI** - Surgical pathology, gross and microscopic examination
> *CPT Assistant* Spring 91:2; Winter 91:18; Fall 93:2, 26; Jul 00:4; Sep 00:10

Bone Resection

Breast, Mastectomy - with Regional Lymph Nodes

Colon, Segmental Resection for Tumor

Colon, Total Resection

Esophagus, Partial/Total Resection

Extremity, Disarticulation

Fetus, with Dissection

Larynx, Partial/Total Resection - with Regional Lymph Nodes

Lung - Total/Lobe/Segment Resection

Pancreas, Total/Subtotal Resection

Prostate, Radical Resection

Small Intestine, Resection for Tumor

Soft Tissue Tumor, Extensive Resection

Stomach - Subtotal/Total Resection for Tumor

Testis, Tumor

Tongue/Tonsil - Resection for Tumor

Urinary Bladder, Partial/Total Resection

Uterus, with or without Tubes and Ovaries, Neoplastic

Vulva, Total/Subtotal Resection

▶(For fine needle aspiration, see 10021, 10022)◀

▶(For evaluation of fine needle aspirate, see 88172-88173)◀

+ 88311 Decalcification procedure (List separately in addition to code for surgical pathology examination)
> *CPT Assistant* Winter 92:18; Jul 98:4

+ 88312 Special stains (List separately in addition to code for surgical pathology examination); Group I for microorganisms (eg, Gridley, acid fast, methenamine silver), each

+ 88313 Group II, all other, (eg, iron, trichrome), except immunocytochemistry and immunoperoxidase stains, each

(For immunocytochemistry and immunoperoxidase tissue studies, use 88342)

+ 88314 histochemical staining with frozen section(s)

(88316 has been deleted. To report, use 99070)

(88317 has been deleted)

88318 Determinative histochemistry to identify chemical components (eg, copper, zinc)

88319 Determinative histochemistry or cytochemistry to identify enzyme constituents, each

88321 Consultation and report on referred slides prepared elsewhere
> *CPT Assistant* Winter 91:19; Apr 97:9; Oct 00:7

88323 Consultation and report on referred material requiring preparation of slides
> *CPT Assistant* Winter 91:19; Apr 97:9; Oct 00:7

88325 Consultation, comprehensive, with review of records and specimens, with report on referred material
> *CPT Assistant* Winter 91:19; Apr 97:9

88329 Pathology consultation during surgery;
> *CPT Assistant* Winter 91:19; Apr 97:12; Aug 97:18

88331 first tissue block, with frozen section(s), single specimen
> *CPT Assistant* Spring 91:2; Winter 91:19; Apr 97:12; Aug 97:18; Jul 00:4; *CPT Changes* 2001

88332 each additional tissue block with frozen section(s)
> *CPT Assistant* Winter 91:19; Apr 97:12; Aug 97:18; Jul 00:4

88342 Immunocytochemistry (including tissue immunoperoxidase), each antibody
> *CPT Assistant* Jul 00:10

(88345 has been deleted. To report, use 88346)

88346 Immunofluorescent study, each antibody; direct method

88347 indirect method

88348 Electron microscopy; diagnostic

88349 scanning

88355   Morphometric analysis; skeletal muscle

88356   nerve

88358   tumor
➔ *CPT Assistant* Jul 98:4; Jul 99:11

(When semi-thin plastic-embedded sections are performed in conjunction with morphometric analysis, only the morphometric analysis should be coded; if performed as an independent procedure, see codes 88300-88309 for surgical pathology.)

(88360 has been deleted. To report, use 88399)

88362   Nerve teasing preparations

(For physician interpretation of peripheral blood smear, use 85060)

88365   Tissue in situ hybridization, interpretation and report

(88370 has been deleted. To report, use 88342)

88371   Protein analysis of tissue by Western Blot, with interpretation and report;

88372   immunological probe for band identification, each

● **88380**   Microdissection (eg, mechanical, laser capture)
➔ *CPT Changes* 2002

88399   Unlisted surgical pathology procedure

Transcutaneous Procedures

88400   Bilirubin, total, transcutaneous

Other Procedures

(Basal metabolic rate has been deleted. If necessary to report, use 89399)

(89005-89007 have been deleted)

▲ **89050**   Cell count, miscellaneous body fluids (eg, cerebrospinal fluid, joint fluid), except blood;
➔ *CPT Changes* 2002

89051   with differential count

89060   Crystal identification by light microscopy with or without polarizing lens analysis, any body fluid (except urine)

(89070, 89080 have been deleted)

89100   Duodenal intubation and aspiration; single specimen (eg, simple bile study or afferent loop culture) plus appropriate test procedure

89105   collection of multiple fractional specimens with pancreatic or gallbladder stimulation, single or double lumen tube

(For radiological localization, use 74340)

(For chemical analyses, see **Chemistry,** this section)

(Electrocardiogram, see 93000-93268)

(Esophagus acid perfusion test (Bernstein), see 91030)

89125   Fat stain, feces, urine, or respiratory secretions
➔ *CPT Changes* 2001

89130   Gastric intubation and aspiration, diagnostic, each specimen, for chemical analyses or cytopathology;

89132   after stimulation

89135   Gastric intubation, aspiration, and fractional collections (eg, gastric secretory study); one hour

89136   two hours

89140   two hours including gastric stimulation (eg, histalog, pentagastrin)

89141   three hours, including gastric stimulation

(For gastric lavage, therapeutic, use 91105)

(For radiologic localization of gastric tube, use 74340)

(For chemical analyses, see 82926, 82928)

(Joint fluid chemistry, see **Chemistry,** this section)

89160   Meat fibers, feces

(89180 has been deleted. To report, use 89190)

89190   Nasal smear for eosinophils

(89205 has been deleted. To report, use 82273)

(Occult blood, feces, use 82270)

(Paternity tests, use 86910)

(89210 has been deleted)

89250   Culture and fertilization of oocyte(s);
➔ *CPT Assistant* Nov 97:35-36; Jan 98:6; Oct 98:1

89251   with co-culture of embryos
➔ *CPT Assistant* Nov 97:35-36; Jan 98:6; Oct 98:1

89252   Assisted oocyte fertilization, microtechnique (any method)
➔ *CPT Assistant* Nov 97:35-36; Jan 98:6; Oct 98:1

89253   Assisted embryo hatching, microtechniques (any method)
➔ *CPT Assistant* Nov 97:35-36; Jan 98:6; Oct 98:1

89254   Oocyte identification from follicular fluid
➔ *CPT Assistant* Nov 97:35-36; Jan 98:6; Oct 98:1

89255   Preparation of embryo for transfer (any method)
➔ *CPT Assistant* Nov 97:35-36; Jan 98:6; Oct 98:1

89256   Preparation of cryopreserved embryos for transfer (includes thaw)
➔ *CPT Assistant* Nov 97:35-36; Jan 98:6; Oct 98:1

89257   Sperm identification from aspiration (other than seminal fluid)
➔ *CPT Assistant* Nov 97:35-36; Jan 98:6; Oct 98:1; Nov 98:30

(For semen analysis, see 89300-89320)

(For sperm identification from testis tissue, use 89264)

89258   Cryopreservation; embryo
➲ *CPT Assistant* Nov 97:36; Jan 98:6; Oct 98:1

89259   sperm
➲ *CPT Assistant* Nov 97:36; Jan 98:6; Oct 98:1

89260   Sperm isolation; simple prep (eg, sperm wash and swim-up) for insemination or diagnosis with semen analysis
➲ *CPT Assistant* Nov 97:36; Jan 98:6; Oct 98:1

89261   complex prep (eg, Percoll gradient, albumin gradient) for insemination or diagnosis with semen analysis
➲ *CPT Assistant* Nov 97:36; Jan 98:6; Oct 98:1

(For semen analysis without sperm wash or swim-up, use 89320)

89264   Sperm identification from testis tissue, fresh or cryopreserved
➲ *CPT Assistant* Nov 98:30

(For biopsy of testis, see 54500, 54505)

(For sperm identification from aspiration, use 89257)

(For semen analysis, see 89300-89320)

89300   Semen analysis; presence and/or motility of sperm including Huhner test (post coital)
➲ *CPT Assistant* Nov 97:36; Jul 98:10; Oct 98:1

89310   motility and count

89320   complete (volume, count, motility, and differential)

(Skin tests, see 86485-86585 and 95010-95199)

89321   Semen analysis, presence and/or motility of sperm
➲ *CPT Changes* 2001

(89323 has been deleted. To report, use 89325)

89325   Sperm antibodies

(For medicolegal identification of sperm, use 88125)

89329   Sperm evaluation; hamster penetration test

89330   cervical mucus penetration test, with or without spinnbarkeit test

(89345 has been deleted)

89350   Sputum, obtaining specimen, aerosol induced technique (separate procedure)

89355   Starch granules, feces

89360   Sweat collection by iontophoresis

(For chloride and sodium analysis, use 84295)

89365   Water load test

89399   Unlisted miscellaneous pathology test

Notes

⊘ =Modifier '-51' Exempt ▶ ◀=New or Revised Text ✦ =Add-on Code

Medicine Guidelines

In addition to the definitions and commonly used terms presented in the **Introduction,** several other items unique to this section on **Medicine** are defined or identified here.

Multiple Procedures

It is appropriate to designate multiple procedures that are rendered on the same date by separate entries. For example: If individual medical psychotherapy (90841) is rendered in addition to subsequent hospital care (eg, 99231), the psychotherapy would be reported separately from the hospital visit. In this instance, both 99231 and 90841 would be reported.

Add-on Codes

Some of the listed procedures are commonly carried out in addition to the primary procedure performed. All add-on codes found in *CPT* are exempt from the multiple procedure concept. They are exempt from the use of the modifier '-51', as these procedures are not reported as stand-alone codes. These additional or supplemental procedures are designated as "add-on" codes. Add-on codes in *CPT* can be readily identified by specific descriptor nomenclature which includes phrases such as "each additional" or "(List separately in addition to primary procedure)."

Separate Procedures

Some of the procedures or services listed in *CPT* that are commonly carried out as an integral component of a total service or procedure have been identified by the inclusion of the term "separate procedure." The codes designated as "separate procedure" should not be reported in addition to the code for the total procedure or service of which it is considered an integral component.

However, when a procedure or service that is designated as a "separate procedure" is carried out independently or considered to be unrelated or distinct from other procedures/services provided at that time, it may be reported by itself, or in addition to other procedures/services by appending the modifier '-59' to the specific "separate procedure" code to indicate that the procedure is not considered to be a component of another procedure, but is a distinct, independent procedure. This may represent a different session or patient encounter, different procedure or surgery,

different site or organ system, separate incision/excision, separate lesion, or separate injury (or area of injury in extensive injuries).

Subsection Information

Several of the subheadings or subsections have special instructions unique to that section. These special instructions will be presented preceding those procedural terminology listings, referring to that subsection specifically. If there is an "Unlisted Procedure" code number (see section below) for the individual subsection, it will also be shown. Those subsections within the **Medicine** section that have special instructions are as follows:

Immune Globulins 90281-90399
Immunization Administration for
    Vaccines/Toxoids 90471-90474
Vaccines, Toxoids 90476-90749
Therapeutic or Diagnostic
    Infusions .90780-90781
Psychiatry 90801-90899
Dialysis 90918-90999
Ophthalmology 92002-92499
Otorhinolaryngology 92502-92599
Echocardiography 93303-93350
Cardiac Catheterization 93501-93556
►**Intracardiac Electrophysiological**
    Procedures/Studies . . . . .93600-93662◄
Peripheral Arterial Disease
    Rehabilitation .93668
Non-Invasive Vascular
    Diagnostic Studies 93875-93990
Pulmonary 94010-94799
Allergy and Clinical Immunology . . .95004-95199
Neurology and Neuromuscular 95805-95999
Neurostimulators,
    Analysis-Programming 95970-95975
►**Motion Analysis** . . . . .96000-96004◄
Central Nervous System
    Assessments/Tests 96100-96117
►**Health and Behavior**
    Assessment/Intervention . . . . .96150-96155◄
Chemotherapy Administration 96400-96549
Dermatological Procedures 96900-96999
Physical Medicine and Rehabilitation
    Modalities 97010-97028
    Constant Attendance 97032-97039
    Therapeutic Procedures 97110-97546
    Active Wound
       Care Management 97601-97602
Osteopathic Manipulative
    Treatment 98925-98929

time, effort, and equipment necessary to provide the service. Additional items which may be included are:

- complexity of symptoms;
- final diagnosis;
- pertinent physical findings;
- diagnostic and therapeutic procedures;
- concurrent problems;
- follow-up care.

Unlisted Service or Procedure

A service or procedure may be provided that is not listed in this edition of *CPT*. When reporting such a service, the appropriate "Unlisted Procedure" code may be used to indicate the service, identifying it by "Special Report" as discussed on this page. The "Unlisted Procedures" and accompanying codes for **Medicine** are as follows:

90399 Unlisted immune globulin

90749 Unlisted vaccine/toxoid

90799 Unlisted therapeutic, prophylactic or diagnostic injection

90899 Unlisted psychiatric service or procedure

90999 Unlisted dialysis procedure, inpatient or outpatient

91299 Unlisted diagnostic gastroenterology procedure

92499 Unlisted ophthalmological service or procedure

92599 Unlisted otorhinolaryngological service or procedure

93799 Unlisted cardiovascular service or procedure

94799 Unlisted pulmonary service or procedure

95199 Unlisted allergy/clinical immunologic service or procedure

95999 Unlisted neurological or neuromuscular diagnostic procedure

96549 Unlisted chemotherapy procedure

96999 Unlisted special dermatological service or procedure

97039 Unlisted modality (specify type and time if constant attendance)

97139 Unlisted therapeutic procedure (specify)

97799 Unlisted physical medicine/rehabilitation service or procedure

99199 Unlisted special service, procedure or report

▶ **99539** Unlisted home visit service or procedure◀

Materials Supplied by Physician

Supplies and materials provided by the physician (eg, sterile trays/drugs), over and above those usually included with the ▶procedure(s)◀ rendered ▶are reported◀ separately. List drugs, trays, supplies, and materials provided. Identify as 99070 ▶or specific supply code.◀

Special Report

A service that is rarely provided, unusual, variable, or new may require a special report in determining medical appropriateness of the service. Pertinent information should include an adequate definition or description of the nature, extent, and need for the procedure; and the

Medicine

(90000-90080 have been deleted. To report, see 99201-99215)

(90100-90170 have been deleted. To report, see 99341-99350)

(90200-90220 have been deleted. To report, see 99221-99223)

(90225 has been deleted. To report, use 99431)

(90240-90280 have been deleted. To report, see 99231-99233)

(90282 has been deleted. To report, use 99433)

(90292 has been deleted. To report, use 99238)

(90300-90370 have been deleted. To report, see 99301-99313)

(90400-90470 have been deleted. To report, see 99321-99333)

(90500-90580 have been deleted. To report, see 99281-99288)

(90590 has been deleted. To report, use 99288)

(90600-90630 have been deleted. To report, see 99241-99255)

(90640-90643 have been deleted. To report, see 99241-99245 or 99261-99263)

(90650-90654 have been deleted. To report, see 99271-99275)

(90699 has been deleted. To report, use 99499)

Immune Globulins

Codes 90281-90399 identify the immune globulin product only and must be reported in addition to the administration codes 90780-90784 as appropriate. Immune globulin products listed here include broad-spectrum and anti-infective immune globulins, antitoxins, and various isoantibodies.

⊘ **90281**   Immune globulin (Ig), human, for intramuscular use
➔ *CPT Assistant* Nov 98:30; Jan 99:1; Sep 99:10

⊘ **90283**   Immune globulin (IgIV), human, for intravenous use
➔ *CPT Assistant* Nov 98:30; Jan 99:1

⊘ **90287**   Botulinum antitoxin, equine, any route
➔ *CPT Assistant* Nov 98:30; Jan 99:1

⊘ **90288**   Botulism immune globulin, human, for intravenous use
➔ *CPT Assistant* Nov 98:30; Jan 99:1

⊘ **90291**   Cytomegalovirus immune globulin (CMV-IgIV), human, for intravenous use
➔ *CPT Assistant* Nov 98:30; Jan 99:1

⊘ **90296**   Diphtheria antitoxin, equine, any route
➔ *CPT Assistant* Nov 98:30; Jan 99:1

⊘ **90371**   Hepatitis B immune globulin (HBIg), human, for intramuscular use
➔ *CPT Assistant* Nov 98:30; Jan 99:1

⊘ **90375**   Rabies immune globulin (RIg), human, for intramuscular and/or subcutaneous use
➔ *CPT Assistant* Nov 98:30; Jan 99:1

⊘ **90376**   Rabies immune globulin, heat-treated (RIg-HT), human, for intramuscular and/or subcutaneous use
➔ *CPT Assistant* Nov 98:30; Jan 99:1

⊘ **90378**   Respiratory syncytial virus immune globulin (RSV-IgIM), for intramuscular use, 50 mg, each
➔ *CPT Assistant* Nov 99:47; Jun 00:10; *CPT Changes* 2000; 2001

⊘ **90379**   Respiratory syncytial virus immune globulin (RSV-IgIV), human, for intravenous use
➔ *CPT Assistant* Nov 98:30; Jan 99:1

⊘ **90384**   Rho(D) immune globulin (RhIg), human, full-dose, for intramuscular use
➔ *CPT Assistant* Nov 98:30; Jan 99:1

⊘ **90385**   Rho(D) immune globulin (RhIg), human, mini-dose, for intramuscular use
➔ *CPT Assistant* Nov 98:30; Jan 99:1

⊘ **90386**   Rho(D) immune globulin (RhIgIV), human, for intravenous use
➔ *CPT Assistant* Nov 98:30; Jan 99:1

⊘ **90389**   Tetanus immune globulin (TIg), human, for intramuscular use
➔ *CPT Assistant* Nov 98:30; Jan 99:1

⊘ **90393**   Vaccinia immune globulin, human, for intramuscular use
➔ *CPT Assistant* Nov 98:30; Jan 99:1

⊘ **90396**   Varicella-zoster immune globulin, human, for intramuscular use
➔ *CPT Assistant* Nov 98:30; Jan 99:1

⊘ **90399**   Unlisted immune globulin
➔ *CPT Assistant* Nov 98:30; Jan 99:1; Feb 99:11; Sep 99:10

Immunization Administration for Vaccines/Toxoids

Codes 90471-90474 must be reported in addition to the vaccine and toxoid code(s) 90476-90749.

If a significant separately identifiable Evaluation and Management service (eg, office or other outpatient services, preventive medicine services) is performed, the appropriate E/M service code should be reported in addition to the vaccine and toxoid administration codes.

(For allergy testing, see 95004 et seq)

(For skin testing of bacterial, viral, fungal extracts, see 86485-86586)

(For therapeutic or diagnostic injections, see 90782-90799)

▲ **90471** Immunization administration (includes percutaneous, intradermal, subcutaneous, intramuscular and jet injections); one vaccine (single or combination vaccine/toxoid)

➔ *CPT Assistant* Nov 98:31; Jan 99:1; Apr 99:10; Nov 99:47-48; Nov 00:10; Feb 01:4; *CPT Changes* 2002

+ **90472** each additional vaccine (single or combination vaccine/toxoid) (List separately in addition to code for primary procedure)

➔ *CPT Assistant* Nov 98:31; Jan 99:1; Apr 99:10; Nov 99:47-48; Nov 00:10; Feb 01:4; *CPT Changes* 2000

(Use 90472 in conjunction with code 90471)

(For administration of immune globulins, use 90780-90784, and see 90281-90399)

(For intravesical administration of BCG vaccine, use 51720, and see 90586)

● **90473** Immunization administration by intranasal or oral route; one vaccine (single or combination vaccine/toxoid)

➔ *CPT Changes* 2002

+ ● **90474** each additional vaccine (single or combination vaccine/toxoid) (List separately in addition to code for primary procedure)

➔ *CPT Changes* 2002

►(Use 90474 in conjunction with code 90473)◄

Vaccines, Toxoids

Codes 90476-90748 identify the vaccine product **only.** To report the administration of a vaccine/toxoid, the vaccine/toxoid product codes 90476-90749 must be used in addition to an immunization administration code(s) 90471, 90472. Do not append the modifier '-51' to the vaccine/toxoid product codes 90476-90749.

If a significantly separately identifiable Evaluation and Management service (eg, office or other outpatient services, preventive medicine services) is performed, the appropriate E/M service code should be reported in addition to the vaccine and toxoid administration codes.

To meet the reporting requirements of immunization registries, vaccine distribution programs, and reporting systems (eg, Vaccine Adverse Event Reporting System) the exact vaccine product administered needs to be reported. Multiple codes for a particular vaccine are provided in *CPT* when the schedule (number of doses or

timing) differs for two or more products of the same vaccine type (eg, hepatitis A, Hib) or the vaccine product is available in more than one chemical formulation, dosage, or route of administration.

Separate codes are available for combination vaccines (eg, DTP-Hib, DtaP-Hib, HepB-Hib). It is inappropriate to code each component of a combination vaccine separately. If a specific vaccine code is not available, the unlisted procedure code should be reported, until a new code becomes available.

(For immune globulins, see codes 90281-90399, and 90780-90784 for administration of immune globulins)

➔ *CPT Assistant* Nov 99:48

⊘ **90476** Adenovirus vaccine, type 4, live, for oral use

➔ *CPT Assistant* Nov 98:31-33; Jan 99:1; Sep 99:10

⊘ **90477** Adenovirus vaccine, type 7, live, for oral use

➔ *CPT Assistant* Nov 98:31-33; Jan 99:1

⊘ **90581** Anthrax vaccine, for subcutaneous use

➔ *CPT Assistant* Nov 98:31-33; Jan 99:1

⊘ **90585** Bacillus Calmette-Guerin vaccine (BCG) for tuberculosis, live, for percutaneous use

➔ *CPT Assistant* Nov 98:31-33; Jan 99:1

⊘ **90586** Bacillus Calmette-Guerin vaccine (BCG) for bladder cancer, live, for intravesical use

➔ *CPT Assistant* Nov 98:31-33; Jan 99:1

(90592 has been deleted)

⊘ **90632** Hepatitis A vaccine, adult dosage, for intramuscular use

➔ *CPT Assistant* Nov 98:31-33; Jan 99:1

⊘ **90633** Hepatitis A vaccine, pediatric/adolescent dosage-2 dose schedule, for intramuscular use

➔ *CPT Assistant* Nov 98:31-33; Jan 99:1

⊘ **90634** Hepatitis A vaccine, pediatric/adolescent dosage-3 dose schedule, for intramuscular use

➔ *CPT Assistant* Nov 98:31-33; Jan 99:1

⊘ **90636** Hepatitis A and hepatitis B vaccine (HepA-HepB), adult dosage, for intramuscular use

➔ *CPT Assistant* Nov 98:31-33; Jan 99:1

⊘ **90645** Hemophilus influenza b vaccine (Hib), HbOC conjugate (4 dose schedule), for intramuscular use

➔ *CPT Assistant* Nov 98:31-33; Jan 99:1

⊘ **90646** Hemophilus influenza b vaccine (Hib), PRP-D conjugate, for booster use only, intramuscular use

➔ *CPT Assistant* Nov 98:31-33; Jan 99:1

⊘ **90647** Hemophilus influenza b vaccine (Hib), PRP-OMP conjugate (3 dose schedule), for intramuscular use

➔ *CPT Assistant* Nov 98:31-33; Jan 99:1

⊘ **90648** Hemophilus influenza b vaccine (Hib), PRP-T conjugate (4 dose schedule), for intramuscular use

➔ *CPT Assistant* Nov 98:31-33; Jan 99:1

⊘ **90657** Influenza virus vaccine, split virus, 6-35 months dosage, for intramuscular or jet injection use

➔ *CPT Assistant* Nov 98:31-33; Jan 99:1

⊘ **90658** Influenza virus vaccine, split virus, 3 years and above dosage, for intramuscular or jet injection use
➔ *CPT Assistant* Nov 98:31-33; Jan 99:1

⊘ **90659** Influenza virus vaccine, whole virus, for intramuscular or jet injection use
➔ *CPT Assistant* Nov 98:31-33; Jan 99:1

⊘ **90660** Influenza virus vaccine, live, for intranasal use
➔ *CPT Assistant* Nov 98:31-33; Jan 99:1

⊘ **90665** Lyme disease vaccine, adult dosage, for intramuscular use
➔ *CPT Assistant* Nov 98:31-33; Jan 99:1

⊘ **90669** Pneumococcal conjugate vaccine, polyvalent, for children under five years, for intramuscular use
➔ *CPT Assistant* Nov 98:31-33; Jan 99:1; Jun 00:10; *CPT Changes* 2001

⊘ **90675** Rabies vaccine, for intramuscular use
➔ *CPT Assistant* Nov 98:31-33; Jan 99:1

⊘ **90676** Rabies vaccine, for intradermal use
➔ *CPT Assistant* Nov 98:31-33; Jan 99:1

⊘ **90680** Rotavirus vaccine, tetravalent, live, for oral use
➔ *CPT Assistant* Nov 98:31-33; Jan 99:1

⊘ **90690** Typhoid vaccine, live, oral
➔ *CPT Assistant* Nov 98:31-33; Jan 99:1

⊘ **90691** Typhoid vaccine, Vi capsular polysaccharide (ViCPs), for intramuscular use
➔ *CPT Assistant* Nov 98:31-33; Jan 99:1

⊘ **90692** Typhoid vaccine, heat- and phenol-inactivated (H-P), for subcutaneous or intradermal use
➔ *CPT Assistant* Nov 98:31-33; Jan 99:1

⊘ **90693** Typhoid vaccine, acetone-killed, dried (AKD), for subcutaneous or jet injection use (U.S. military)
➔ *CPT Assistant* Nov 98:31-33; Jan 99:1

⊘ **90700** Diphtheria, tetanus toxoids, and acellular pertussis vaccine (DTaP), for intramuscular use
➔ *CPT Assistant* Jan 96:5; Feb 97:9; Nov 98:31-33; Jan 99:1

⊘ **90701** Diphtheria, tetanus toxoids, and whole cell pertussis vaccine (DTP), for intramuscular use
➔ *CPT Assistant* Jan 96:6; Nov 98:31-33; Jan 99:1

⊘ **90702** Diphtheria and tetanus toxoids (DT) adsorbed for use in individuals younger than seven years, for intramuscular use
➔ *CPT Assistant* Jan 96:6; Nov 98:31-33; Jan 99:1; Sep 99:10; Jun 00:10; *CPT Changes* 2001

⊘ **90703** Tetanus toxoid adsorbed, for intramuscular or jet injection use
➔ *CPT Assistant* Jan 96:6; Nov 98:31-33; Jan 99:1; Sep 99:10

⊘ **90704** Mumps virus vaccine, live, for subcutaneous or jet injection use
➔ *CPT Assistant* Nov 98:31-33; Jan 99:1

⊘ **90705** Measles virus vaccine, live, for subcutaneous or jet injection use
➔ *CPT Assistant* Nov 98:31-33; Jan 99:1

⊘ **90706** Rubella virus vaccine, live, for subcutaneous or jet injection use
➔ *CPT Assistant* Nov 98:31-33; Jan 99:1

⊘ **90707** Measles, mumps and rubella virus vaccine (MMR), live, for subcutaneous or jet injection use
➔ *CPT Assistant* Jan 96:6; May 96:10; Apr 97:10; Nov 98:31-33; Jan 99:1

⊘ **90708** Measles and rubella virus vaccine, live, for subcutaneous or jet injection use
➔ *CPT Assistant* Nov 98:31-33; Jan 99:1

⊘ **90709** Rubella and mumps virus vaccine, live, for subcutaneous use
➔ *CPT Assistant* Nov 98:31-33; Jan 99:1

⊘ **90710** Measles, mumps, rubella, and varicella vaccine (MMRV), live, for subcutaneous use
➔ *CPT Assistant* May 96:10; Apr 97:10; Nov 98:31-33; Jan 99:1

(90711 has been deleted)

⊘ **90712** Poliovirus vaccine, (any type(s)) (OPV), live, for oral use
➔ *CPT Assistant* Jan 96:6; Nov 98:31-33; Jan 99:1

⊘ **90713** Poliovirus vaccine, inactivated, (IPV), for subcutaneous use
➔ *CPT Assistant* Nov 98:31-33; Jan 99:1

(90714 has been deleted. To report, see 90690-90693)

⊘ **90716** Varicella virus vaccine, live, for subcutaneous use
➔ *CPT Assistant* Jan 96:6; May 96:10; Apr 97:10; Nov 98:31-33; Jan 99:1

⊘ **90717** Yellow fever vaccine, live, for subcutaneous use
➔ *CPT Assistant* Nov 98:31-33; Jan 99:1

⊘ **90718** Tetanus and diphtheria toxoids (Td) adsorbed for use in individuals seven years or older, for intramuscular or jet injection
➔ *CPT Assistant* Aug 96:10; Nov 98:31-33; Jan 99:1; Jun 00:10; *CPT Changes* 2001

⊘ **90719** Diphtheria toxoid, for intramuscular use
➔ *CPT Assistant* Nov 98:31-33; Jan 99:1; Sep 99:10

⊘ **90720** Diphtheria, tetanus toxoids, and whole cell pertussis vaccine and Hemophilus influenza B vaccine (DTP-Hib), for intramuscular use
➔ *CPT Assistant* Jan 96:5; Nov 98:31-33; Jan 99:1

⊘ **90721** Diphtheria, tetanus toxoids, and acellular pertussis vaccine and Hemophilus influenza B vaccine (DtaP-Hib), for intramuscular use
➔ *CPT Assistant* Jan 96:5; Nov 98:31-33; Jan 99:1; *CPT Changes* 2000

(90724 has been deleted. To report, see 90657-90660)

⊘ **90723** Diphtheria, tetanus toxoids, acellular pertussis vaccine, Hepatitis B, and poliovirus vaccine, inactivated (DtaP-HepB-IPV), for intramuscular use
➔ *CPT Changes* 2001

⊘ **90725** Cholera vaccine for injectable use
➔ *CPT Assistant* Nov 98:31-33; Jan 99:1

(For oral cholera, use 90592)

(90726 has been deleted. To report, see 90675, 90676)

⊘ **90727**   Plague vaccine, for intramuscular or jet injection use
> *CPT Assistant* Nov 98:31-33; Jan 99:1

(90728 has been deleted. To report, see 90585, 90586)

(90730 has been deleted. To report, see 90632-90634)

(90731 has been deleted. To report, see 90744-90747)

⊘ ▲ **90732**   Pneumococcal polysaccharide vaccine, 23-valent, adult or immunosuppressed patient dosage, for use in individuals 2 years or older, for subcutaneous or intramuscular use
> *CPT Assistant* Nov 98:31-33; Jan 99:1; *CPT Changes* 2002

⊘ **90733**   Meningococcal polysaccharide vaccine (any group(s)), for subcutaneous or jet injection use
> *CPT Assistant* Nov 98:31-33; Jan 99:1; Dec 99:7; *CPT Changes* 2001

⊘ **90735**   Japanese encephalitis virus vaccine, for subcutaneous use
> *CPT Assistant* Nov 98:31-33; Jan 99:1

(90737 has been deleted. To report, see 90645-90648)

(90741 has been deleted. To report, see 90281-90283)

(90742 has been deleted. To report, see 90287-90399)

⊘ **90740**   Hepatitis B vaccine, dialysis or immunosuppressed patient dosage (3 dose schedule), for intramuscular use
> *CPT Changes* 2001

⊘ **90743**   Hepatitis B vaccine, adolescent (2 dose schedule), for intramuscular use
> *CPT Changes* 2001

⊘ **90744**   Hepatitis B vaccine, pediatric/adolescent dosage (3 dose schedule), for intramuscular use
> *CPT Assistant* Jan 96:5; Jun 97:10; Nov 98:31-33; Jan 99:1; Nov 99:48-49; Jun 00:10; *CPT Changes* 2000; 2001

(90745 has been deleted)

⊘ **90746**   Hepatitis B vaccine, adult dosage, for intramuscular use
> *CPT Assistant* Jan 96:5; Nov 98:31-33; Jan 99:1

⊘ **90747**   Hepatitis B vaccine, dialysis or immunosuppressed patient dosage (4 dose schedule), for intramuscular use
> *CPT Assistant* Jan 96:5; Jun 97:10; Nov 98:31-33; Jan 99:1; Jun 00:10; *CPT Changes* 2001

⊘ **90748**   Hepatitis B and Hemophilus influenza b vaccine (HepB-Hib), for intramuscular use
> *CPT Assistant* Nov 97:37; Nov 98:31-33; Jan 99:1; Sep 99:10

⊘ **90749**   Unlisted vaccine/toxoid
> *CPT Assistant* Jan 96:6; Feb 97:9; Nov 98:31-33; Jan 99:1

(90750-90754 have been deleted. To report, see 99381-99387)

(90755 has been deleted)

(90757 has been deleted. To report, use 99432)

(90760-90764 have been deleted. To report, see 99391-99397)

(90774 has been deleted. To report, use 96110)

(90778 has been deleted. To report, use 94772)

Therapeutic or Diagnostic Infusions (Excludes Chemotherapy)

These procedures encompass prolonged intravenous injections.

These codes require the presence of the physician during the infusion. These codes are not to be used for intradermal, subcutaneous or intramuscular or routine IV drug injections. For these services, see 90782-90788.

These codes may not be used in addition to prolonged services codes.

▲ **90780**   Intravenous infusion for therapy/diagnosis, administered by physician or under direct supervision of physician; up to one hour
> *CPT Assistant* Sep 99:10; Oct 00:7; Feb 01:10; *CPT Changes* 2002

+ **90781**   each additional hour, up to eight (8) hours (List separately in addition to code for primary procedure)
> *CPT Assistant* Feb 01:10

(Use 90781 in conjunction with code 90780)

Therapeutic, Prophylactic or Diagnostic Injections

90782   Therapeutic, prophylactic or diagnostic injection (specify material injected); subcutaneous or intramuscular
> *CPT Assistant* Nov 99:49

(For administration of vaccines/toxoids, see 90471-90472)

90783   intra-arterial

90784   intravenous
> *CPT Assistant* Sep 99:10; Sep 00:5

(90782-90784 do not include injections for allergen immunotherapy. For allergen immunotherapy injections, see 95115-95117)

90788   Intramuscular injection of antibiotic (specify)

(90790-90796 have been deleted. To report, see 96408-96414, 96420-96425, 96440, 96450, 96530, 96545, 96549)

(90798 has been deleted. To report, see 90780, 90781, 90784)

90799   Unlisted therapeutic, prophylactic or diagnostic injection
> *CPT Assistant* Nov 99:49; *CPT Changes* 2000

(For allergy immunizations, see 95004 et seq)

⊘ =Modifier '-51' Exempt   ▶ ◀=New or Revised Text   + =Add-on Code   CPT 2002

Psychiatry

▶(For repetitive transcranial magnetic stimulation for treatment of clinical depression, use Category III code 0018T)◀

Hospital care by the attending physician in treating a psychiatric inpatient or partial hospitalization may be initial or subsequent in nature (see 99221-99233) and may include exchanges with nursing and ancillary personnel. Hospital care services involve a variety of responsibilities unique to the medical management of inpatients, such as physician hospital orders, interpretation of laboratory or other medical diagnostic studies and observations.

Some patients receive hospital evaluation and management services only and others receive evaluation and management services and other procedures. If other procedures such as electroconvulsive therapy or psychotherapy are rendered in addition to hospital evaluation and management services, these should be listed separately (ie, hospital care service plus electroconvulsive therapy or when psychotherapy is done, an appropriate code defining psychotherapy with medical evaluation and management services). The modifier '-22' may be used to indicate a more extensive service. The modifier '-52' may be used to signify a service that is reduced or less extensive than the usual procedure.

Other evaluation and management services, such as office medical service or other patient encounters, may be described as listed in the section on **Evaluation and Management,** if appropriate.

The evaluation and management services should not be reported separately, when reporting codes 90805, 90807, 90809, 90811, 90813, 90815, 90817, 90819, 90822, 90824, 90827, 90829.

Consultation for psychiatric evaluation of a patient includes examination of a patient and exchange of information with the primary physician and other informants such as nurses or family members, and preparation of a report. These consultation services (99241-99263) are limited to initial or follow-up evaluation and do not involve psychiatric treatment.

➔ *CPT Assistant* Nov 97:37

Psychiatric Diagnostic or Evaluative Interview Procedures

Psychiatric diagnostic interview examination includes a history, mental status, and a disposition, and may include communication with family or other sources, ordering and medical interpretation of laboratory or other medical diagnostic studies. In certain circumstances other informants will be seen in lieu of the patient.

Interactive psychiatric diagnostic interview examination is typically furnished to children. It involves the use of physical aids and non-verbal communication to overcome barriers to therapeutic interaction between the clinician and a patient who has not yet developed, or has lost, either the expressive language communication skills to explain his/her symptoms and response to treatment, or the receptive communication skills to understand the clinician if he/she were to use ordinary adult language for communication.

➔ *CPT Assistant* Nov 97:37-38

90801 Psychiatric diagnostic interview examination
➔ *CPT Assistant* Summer 92:12

90802 Interactive psychiatric diagnostic interview examination using play equipment, physical devices, language interpreter, or other mechanisms of communication

Psychiatric Therapeutic Procedures

Psychotherapy is the treatment for mental illness and behavioral disturbances in which the clinician establishes a professional contract with the patient and, through definitive therapeutic communication, attempts to alleviate the emotional disturbances, reverse or change maladaptive patterns of behavior, and encourage personality growth and development. The codes for reporting psychotherapy are divided into two broad categories: Interactive Psychotherapy; and Insight Oriented, Behavior Modifying and/or Supportive Psychotherapy.

Interactive psychotherapy is typically furnished to children. It involves the use of physical aids and non-verbal communication to overcome barriers to therapeutic interaction between the clinician and a patient who has not yet developed, or has lost, either the expressive language communication skills to explain his/her symptoms and response to treatment, or the receptive communication skills to understand the clinician if he/she were to use ordinary adult language for communication.

Insight oriented, behavior modifying and/or supportive psychotherapy refers to the development of insight or affective understanding, the use of behavior modification techniques, the use of supportive interactions, the use of cognitive discussion of reality, or any combination of the above to provide therapeutic change.

Some patients receive psychotherapy only and others receive psychotherapy and medical evaluation and management services. These evaluation and management services involve a variety of responsibilities unique to the medical management of psychiatric patients, such as medical diagnostic evaluation (eg, evaluation of comorbid medical conditions, drug interactions, and physical examinations), drug management when indicated, physician orders, interpretation of laboratory or other medical diagnostic studies and observations.

In reporting psychotherapy, the appropriate code is chosen on the basis of the type of psychotherapy (interactive using non-verbal techniques versus insight oriented, behavior modifying and/or supportive using verbal techniques), the place of service (office versus inpatient), the face-to-face time spent with the patient during psychotherapy, and whether evaluation and management services are furnished on the same date of service as psychotherapy.

To report medical evaluation and management services furnished on a day when psychotherapy is not provided, select the appropriate code from the **Evaluation and Management Services Guidelines.**

➔ *CPT Assistant* Nov 97:38

Office or Other Outpatient Facility

Insight Oriented, Behavior Modifying and/or Supportive Psychotherapy

90804 Individual psychotherapy, insight oriented, behavior modifying and/or supportive, in an office or outpatient facility, approximately 20 to 30 minutes face-to-face with the patient;
➔ *CPT Assistant* Nov 97:39; Jul 99:10

90805 with medical evaluation and management services
➔ *CPT Assistant* Nov 97:39; Jul 99:10

90806 Individual psychotherapy, insight oriented, behavior modifying and/or supportive, in an office or outpatient facility, approximately 45 to 50 minutes face-to-face with the patient;
➔ *CPT Assistant* Nov 97:39; Jul 99:10

90807 with medical evaluation and management services
➔ *CPT Assistant* Nov 97:39; Jul 99:10

90808 Individual psychotherapy, insight oriented, behavior modifying and/or supportive, in an office or outpatient facility, approximately 75 to 80 minutes face-to-face with the patient;
➔ *CPT Assistant* Nov 97:39; Jul 99:10

90809 with medical evaluation and management services
➔ *CPT Assistant* Nov 97:39; Jul 99:10

Interactive Psychotherapy

90810 Individual psychotherapy, interactive, using play equipment, physical devices, language interpreter, or other mechanisms of non-verbal communication, in an office or outpatient facility, approximately 20 to 30 minutes face-to-face with the patient;
➔ *CPT Assistant* Nov 97:39

90811 with medical evaluation and management services

90812 Individual psychotherapy, interactive, using play equipment, physical devices, language interpreter, or other mechanisms of non-verbal communication, in an office or outpatient facility, approximately 45 to 50 minutes face-to-face with the patient;
➔ *CPT Assistant* Nov 97:39

90813 with medical evaluation and management services
➔ *CPT Assistant* Nov 97:39

90814 Individual psychotherapy, interactive, using play equipment, physical devices, language interpreter, or other mechanisms of non-verbal communication, in an office or outpatient facility, approximately 75 to 80 minutes face-to-face with the patient;
➔ *CPT Assistant* Nov 97:39

90815 with medical evaluation and management services
➔ *CPT Assistant* Nov 97:39

Inpatient Hospital, Partial Hospital or Residential Care Facility

Insight Oriented, Behavior Modifying and/or Supportive Psychotherapy

90816 Individual psychotherapy, insight oriented, behavior modifying and/or supportive, in an inpatient hospital, partial hospital or residential care setting, approximately 20 to 30 minutes face-to-face with the patient;
➔ *CPT Assistant* Nov 97:39-40

90817 with medical evaluation and management services
➔ *CPT Assistant* Nov 97:39-40

90818 Individual psychotherapy, insight oriented, behavior modifying and/or supportive, in an inpatient hospital, partial hospital or residential care setting, approximately 45 to 50 minutes face-to-face with the patient;
➔ *CPT Assistant* Nov 97:39-40

90819 with medical evaluation and management services

(90820 has been deleted. To report, use 90802)
➔ *CPT Assistant* Summer 92:24; Nov 97:39-40

90821 Individual psychotherapy, insight oriented, behavior modifying and/or supportive, in an inpatient hospital, partial hospital or residential care setting, approximately 75 to 80 minutes face-to-face with the patient;
➔ *CPT Assistant* Nov 97:39-40

90822 with medical evaluation and management services
➔ *CPT Assistant* Nov 97:39-40

Interactive Psychotherapy

90823 Individual psychotherapy, interactive, using play equipment, physical devices, language interpreter, or other mechanisms of non-verbal communication, in an inpatient hospital, partial hospital or residential care setting, approximately 20 to 30 minutes face-to-face with the patient;
➔ *CPT Assistant* Nov 97:40

90824 with medical evaluation and management services

(90825 has been deleted. To report, use 90885)
➔ *CPT Assistant* Summer 92:13; Nov 97:40

⊘ =Modifier '-51' Exempt ▶ ◀=New or Revised Text ✚ =Add-on Code CPT 2002

90826   Individual psychotherapy, interactive, using play equipment, physical devices, language interpreter, or other mechanisms of non-verbal communication, in an inpatient hospital, partial hospital or residential care setting, approximately 45 to 50 minutes face-to-face with the patient;
➔ *CPT Assistant* Nov 97:40

90827   with medical evaluation and management services
➔ *CPT Assistant* Nov 97:40

90828   Individual psychotherapy, interactive, using play equipment, physical devices, language interpreter, or other mechanisms of non-verbal communication, in an inpatient hospital, partial hospital or residential care setting, approximately 75 to 80 minutes face-to-face with the patient;
➔ *CPT Assistant* Nov 97:40

90829   with medical evaluation and management services
➔ *CPT Assistant* Nov 97:40

(90830 has been deleted. To report, use 96100)
➔ *CPT Assistant* Summer 92:13

(90831 has been deleted. To report, see 99371-99373)
➔ *CPT Assistant* Summer 92:13

(90835 has been deleted. To report, use 90865)
➔ *CPT Assistant* Summer 92:14

(90841 has been deleted)
➔ *CPT Assistant* Summer 92:14

(90842 has been deleted. To report, see 90808, 90809, 90821, 90822)
➔ *CPT Assistant* Summer 92:15

(90843 has been deleted. To report, see 90804, 90805, 90816, 90817)
➔ *CPT Assistant* Summer 92:14

(90844 has been deleted. To report, see 90806, 90807, 90818, 90819)
➔ *CPT Assistant* Summer 92:14

Other Psychotherapy

90845   Psychoanalysis
➔ *CPT Assistant* Summer 92:15; Nov 97:40-41

90846   Family psychotherapy (without the patient present)
➔ *CPT Assistant* Summer 92:15; Nov 97:40-41

90847   Family psychotherapy (conjoint psychotherapy) (with patient present)
➔ *CPT Assistant* Summer 92:15; Nov 97:40-41

(90848 has been deleted. To report, use 90847)

90849   Multiple-family group psychotherapy
➔ *CPT Assistant* Summer 92:15; Nov 97:40-41

90853   Group psychotherapy (other than of a multiple-family group)
➔ *CPT Assistant* Summer 92:15; Nov 97:40-41

(90855 has been deleted. To report, see 90810-90815, and 90823-90829)
➔ *CPT Assistant* Summer 92:9; Nov 97:40-41

90857   Interactive group psychotherapy
➔ *CPT Assistant* Summer 92:15; Nov 97:40-41

Other Psychiatric Services or Procedures

90862   Pharmacologic management, including prescription, use, and review of medication with no more than minimal medical psychotherapy
➔ *CPT Assistant* Summer 92:16; Nov 97:40-41

90865   Narcosynthesis for psychiatric diagnostic and therapeutic purposes (eg, sodium amobarbital (Amytal) interview)
➔ *CPT Assistant* Nov 97:41

90870   Electroconvulsive therapy (includes necessary monitoring); single seizure
➔ *CPT Assistant* Summer 92:16

90871   multiple seizures, per day
➔ *CPT Assistant* Summer 92:16

(90872 has been deleted. To report, use 90899)

90875   Individual psychophysiological therapy incorporating biofeedback training by any modality (face-to-face with the patient), with psychotherapy (eg, insight oriented, behavior modifying or supportive psychotherapy); approximately 20-30 minutes
➔ *CPT Assistant* Sep 97:11; Nov 97:41; Apr 98:14; Jun 99:5

90876   approximately 45-50 minutes
➔ *CPT Assistant* Sep 97:11; Nov 97:41; Jun 99:5

90880   Hypnotherapy
➔ *CPT Assistant* Summer 92:16; Nov 97:41

90882   Environmental intervention for medical management purposes on a psychiatric patient's behalf with agencies, employers, or institutions
➔ *CPT Assistant* Summer 92:16

90885   Psychiatric evaluation of hospital records, other psychiatric reports, psychometric and/or projective tests, and other accumulated data for medical diagnostic purposes
➔ *CPT Assistant* Nov 97:41

90887   Interpretation or explanation of results of psychiatric, other medical examinations and procedures, or other accumulated data to family or other responsible persons, or advising them how to assist patient
➔ *CPT Assistant* Summer 92:17

90889   Preparation of report of patient's psychiatric status, history, treatment, or progress (other than for legal or consultative purposes) for other physicians, agencies, or insurance carriers
➔ *CPT Assistant* Summer 92:17

90899   Unlisted psychiatric service or procedure

Biofeedback

(For psychophysiological therapy incorporating biofeedback training, see 90875, 90876)

(90900 has been deleted. To report, use 90901)

90901 Biofeedback training by any modality
➲ *CPT Assistant* Sep 97:11; Apr 98:14; Jun 98:10; Jun 99:5

(90902, 90904, 90906, 90908, 90910 have been deleted. To report, use 90901)

90911 Biofeedback training, perineal muscles, anorectal or urethral sphincter, including EMG and/or manometry
➲ *CPT Assistant* Sep 97:11; Nov 97:41; Jun 98:10; Jun 99:5

(90915 has been deleted. To report, use 90901)

Dialysis

Codes 90918-90921 are reported ONCE per month to distinguish age-specific services related to the patient's end-stage renal disease (ESRD) performed in an outpatient setting. ESRD related physician services include establishment of a dialyzing cycle, outpatient evaluation and management of the dialysis visits, telephone calls, and patient management during the dialysis, provided during a full month. These codes are not used if a hospitalization occurred during the month.

Codes 90918-90921 do not include the dialysis treatment (90935, 90937, 90945, 90947) or any non-ESRD related services or other patient care services rendered outside of the dialysis setting during that month.

Evaluation and management services unrelated to ESRD services that cannot be performed during the dialysis session may be reported separately.

Codes 90922-90925 are reported when outpatient ESRD related services are not performed consecutively during an entire full month. Codes 90922-90925 are used to report ESRD related services on a per day basis for the remaining days of that month, preceding and/or following the period of hospitalization.

Example:

A four-year old receiving continuous peritoneal dialysis has sixteen days of daily outpatient care, preceding or following a period of hospitalization.

Report 90923 for each date outpatient care was performed.

For ESRD related services and dialysis procedure(s) performed during period of hospitalization: Report appropriate inpatient Evaluation and Management Service code(s) for the hospitalized period if service(s) is unrelated to ESRD services. Report 90945 or 90947 for each inpatient dialysis procedure.

End Stage Renal Disease Services

90918 End stage renal disease (ESRD) related services per full month; for patients under two years of age to include monitoring for the adequacy of nutrition, assessment of growth and development, and counseling of parents
➲ *CPT Assistant* Fall 93:5; May 96:4

90919 for patients between two and eleven years of age to include monitoring for the adequacy of nutrition, assessment of growth and development, and counseling of parents
➲ *CPT Assistant* Fall 93:5; May 96:5

90920 for patients between twelve and nineteen years of age to include monitoring for the adequacy of nutrition, assessment of growth and development, and counseling of parents
➲ *CPT Assistant* Fall 93:5; May 96:5

90921 for patients twenty years of age and over
➲ *CPT Assistant* Fall 93:5; May 96:5

90922 End stage renal disease (ESRD) related services (less than full month), per day; for patients under two years of age
➲ *CPT Assistant* Fall 93:5; May 96:5

90923 for patients between two and eleven years of age
➲ *CPT Assistant* May 96:5

90924 for patients between twelve and nineteen years of age
➲ *CPT Assistant* May 96:5

90925 for patients twenty years of age and over
➲ *CPT Assistant* May 96:5

Hemodialysis

Codes 90935, 90937 are reported to describe the hemodialysis procedure with all evaluation and management services related to the patient's renal disease on the day of the hemodialysis procedure. These codes are used for inpatient ESRD and non-ESRD procedures or for outpatient non-ESRD dialysis services. Code 90935 is reported if only one evaluation of the patient is required related to that hemodialysis procedure. Code 90937 is reported when patient re-evaluation(s) is required during a hemodialysis procedure. Utilize the modifier '-25' with Evaluation and Management codes for ▶separately identifiable◄ services unrelated to the dialysis procedure or renal failure ►which◄ cannot be rendered during the dialysis session.

►(For home visit hemodialysis services performed by a non-physician health care professional, use 99512)◄

(For cannula declotting, see 36831, 36833, 36860, 36861)

(For declotting of implanted vascular access device or catheter by thrombolytic agent, use 36550)
➔ *CPT Assistant* Nov 99:49

(For collection of blood specimen from a partially or completely implantable venous access device, use 36540)

(For prolonged physician attendance, see 99354-99360)

90935   Hemodialysis procedure with single physician evaluation
➔ *CPT Assistant* Fall 93:2

90937   Hemodialysis procedure requiring repeated evaluation(s) with or without substantial revision of dialysis prescription
➔ *CPT Assistant* Fall 93:2

● **90939**   Hemodialysis access flow study to determine blood flow in grafts and arteriovenous fistulae by an indicator dilution method, hook-up; transcutaneous measurement and disconnection
➔ *CPT Changes* 2002

90940   measurement and disconnection
➔ *CPT Changes* 2001

(For duplex scan of hemodialysis access, use 93990)

(90941-90944 have been deleted. To report, see 90935-90937)

Miscellaneous Dialysis Procedures

Codes 90945, 90947 describe dialysis procedures other than hemodialysis (eg, peritoneal dialysis, hemofiltration or continuous renal replacement therapies), and all evaluation and management services related to the patient's renal disease on the day of the procedure. Code 90945 is reported if only one evaluation of the patient is required related to that procedure. Code 90947 is reported when patient re-evaluation(s) is required during a procedure. Utilize the modifier '-25' with Evaluation and Management codes for ►separately identifiable◄ services unrelated to the procedure or the renal failure ►which◄ cannot be rendered during the dialysis session.

(For insertion of intraperitoneal cannula or catheter, see 49420, 49421)

(For prolonged physician attendance, see 99354-99360)

90945   Dialysis procedure other than hemodialysis (eg, peritoneal dialysis, hemofiltration, or other continuous renal replacement therapies), with single physician evaluation
➔ *CPT Assistant* Fall 93:2; Nov 97:41; Jul 98:10; *CPT Changes* 2001

►(For home infusion of peritoneal dialysis, use 99559)◄

90947   Dialysis procedure other than hemodialysis (eg, peritoneal dialysis, hemofiltration, or other continuous renal replacement therapies) requiring repeated physician evaluations, with or without substantial revision of dialysis prescription
➔ *CPT Assistant* Fall 93:2; Nov 97:41; Jul 98:10; *CPT Changes* 2001

(90951-90958 have been deleted. To report, see 90935, 90937)

(90966-90985 have been deleted. To report, see 90945, 90947)

(90988, 90991 and 90994 have been deleted. To report, see 90918-90921)

90989   Dialysis training, patient, including helper where applicable, any mode, completed course
➔ *CPT Assistant* Fall 93:5

(90990, 90992 have been deleted. To report, see 90989 and 90993)

90993   Dialysis training, patient, including helper where applicable, any mode, course not completed, per training session
➔ *CPT Assistant* Fall 93:5

(90995 has been deleted. To report, see 90918-90921)

90997   Hemoperfusion (eg, with activated charcoal or resin)

(90998 has been deleted. To report, use 90922)

90999   Unlisted dialysis procedure, inpatient or outpatient

Gastroenterology

(For duodenal intubation and aspiration, see 89100-89105)

(For gastrointestinal radiologic procedures, see 74210-74363)

(For esophagoscopy procedures, see 43200-43228; upper GI endoscopy 43234-43259; endoscopy, small intestine and stomal 44360-44393; proctosigmoidoscopy 45300-45321; sigmoidoscopy 45330-45339; colonoscopy 45355-45385; anoscopy 46600-46615)

91000   Esophageal intubation and collection of washings for cytology, including preparation of specimens (separate procedure)

91010   Esophageal motility (manometric study of the esophagus and/or gastroesophageal junction) study;
➔ *CPT Assistant* Nov 97:42

91011   with mecholyl or similar stimulant

91012   with acid perfusion studies

91020   Gastric motility (manometric) studies
➔ *CPT Assistant* Nov 97:42

91030   Esophagus, acid perfusion (Bernstein) test for esophagitis

91032   Esophagus, acid reflux test, with intraluminal pH electrode for detection of gastroesophageal reflux;

Esophageal Acid Reflux Test
91032

The patient is asked to swallow a catheter with a pH electrode (attached to a manometric catheter) to evaluate competency of the lower esophageal sphincter by measuring intraesophageal pH (an indicator of gastric reflux).

Catheter

Catheter

Cross-section of esophagus

Esophageal lumen

Diaphragm

Stomach lumen

Perfusion parts (direct or indirect)

Esophageal-gastric junction

91033   prolonged recording

91052   Gastric analysis test with injection of stimulant of gastric secretion (eg, histamine, insulin, pentagastrin, calcium and secretin)

(For gastric biopsy by capsule, peroral, via tube, one or more specimens, use 43600)

(For gastric laboratory procedures, see also 89130-89141)

91055   Gastric intubation, washings, and preparing slides for cytology (separate procedure)

(For gastric lavage, therapeutic, use 91105)

91060   Gastric saline load test

(For biopsy by capsule, small intestine, per oral, via tube (one or more specimens), use 44100)

91065   Breath hydrogen test (eg, for detection of lactase deficiency)

(91090 has been deleted)

91100   Intestinal bleeding tube, passage, positioning and monitoring

91105   Gastric intubation, and aspiration or lavage for treatment (eg, for ingested poisons)
➔ *CPT Assistant* Spring 93:34; Sep 96:10; Nov 99:49

Gastric Intubation
91105

A large-bore gastric lavage tube is inserted orally through the esophagus into the stomach for expedient lavage and evacuation of stomach contents (eg, poisonings, hemorrhage).

Nasal cavity

Oral cavity

Syringe to sample gastric secretions

Esophagus

Catheter

Mercury weighted bag

Stomach

(For cholangiography, see 47500, 74320)

(For abdominal paracentesis, see 49080, 49081; with instillation of medication, see 96440, 96445)

(For peritoneoscopy, use 49320; with biopsy, use 49321)

(For peritoneoscopy and guided transhepatic cholangiography, use 47560; with biopsy, use 47561)

(For splenoportography, see 38200, 75810)

91122   Anorectal manometry

● **91123**   Pulsed irrigation of fecal impaction
➔ *CPT Changes* 2002

Gastric Physiology

91132   Electrogastrography, diagnostic, transcutaneous;
➔ *CPT Changes* 2001

91133   with provocative testing
➔ *CPT Changes* 2001

Other Procedures

91299   Unlisted diagnostic gastroenterology procedure

⊘ =Modifier '-51' Exempt   ▶ ◀=New or Revised Text   ✚ =Add-on Code   CPT 2002

Ophthalmology

(For surgical procedures, see **Surgery,** Eye and Ocular Adnexa, 65091 et seq)

Definitions

Intermediate ophthalmological services describes an evaluation of a new or existing condition complicated with a new diagnostic or management problem not necessarily relating to the primary diagnosis, including history, general medical observation, external ocular and adnexal examination and other diagnostic procedures as indicated; may include the use of mydriasis for ophthalmoscopy.

For example:

a. Review of history, external examination, ophthalmoscopy, biomicroscopy for an acute complicated condition (eg, iritis) not requiring comprehensive ophthalmological services.

b. Review of interval history, external examination, ophthalmoscopy, biomicroscopy and tonometry in established patient with known cataract not requiring comprehensive ophthalmological services.

Comprehensive ophthalmological services describes a general evaluation of the complete visual system. The comprehensive services constitute a single service entity but need not be performed at one session. The service includes history, general medical observation, external and ophthalmoscopic examinations, gross visual fields and basic sensorimotor examination. It often includes, as indicated: biomicroscopy, examination with cycloplegia or mydriasis and tonometry. It always includes initiation of diagnostic and treatment programs.

Intermediate and comprehensive ophthalmological services constitute integrated services in which medical decision making cannot be separated from the examining techniques used. Itemization of service components, such as slit lamp examination, keratometry, routine ophthalmoscopy, retinoscopy, tonometry, or motor evaluation is not applicable.

For example:

The comprehensive services required for diagnosis and treatment of a patient with symptoms indicating possible disease of the visual system, such as glaucoma, cataract or retinal disease, or to rule out disease of the visual system, new or established patient.

Initiation of diagnostic and treatment program includes the prescription of medication, and arranging for special ophthalmological diagnostic or treatment services, consultations, laboratory procedures and radiological services.

Special ophthalmological services describes services in which a special evaluation of part of the visual system is made, which goes beyond the services included under general ophthalmological services, or in which special treatment is given. Special ophthalmological services may be reported in addition to the general ophthalmological services or evaluation and management services.

For example:

Fluorescein angioscopy, quantitative visual field examination, refraction or extended color vision examination (such as Nagel's anomaloscope) should be separately reported.

Prescription of lenses, when required, is included in 92015 Determination of refractive state. It includes specification of lens type (monofocal, bifocal, other), lens power, axis, prism, absorptive factor, impact resistance, and other factors.

Interpretation and report by the physician is an integral part of special ophthalmological services where indicated. Technical procedures (which may or may not be performed by the physician personally) are often part of the service, but should not be mistaken to constitute the service itself.

➔ *CPT Assistant* Nov 97:42-43

General Ophthalmological Services

New Patient

▶Solely for the purposes of distinguishing between new and established patients, **professional services** are those face-to-face services rendered by a physician and reported by a specific CPT code(s).◀ A new patient is one who has not received any professional services from the physician or another physician of the same specialty who belongs to the same group practice within the past three years.

92002 Ophthalmological services: medical examination and evaluation with initiation of diagnostic and treatment program; intermediate, new patient
➔ *CPT Assistant* Feb 97:6; Aug 98:1

92004 comprehensive, new patient, one or more visits
➔ *CPT Assistant* Feb 97:6; Aug 98:1

Established Patient

▶Solely for the purposes of distinguishing between new and established patients, **professional services** are those face-to-face services rendered by a physician and reported by a specific CPT code(s).◀ An established patient is one who has received professional services from the physician or another physician of the same specialty who belongs to the same group practice within the past three years.

92012 Ophthalmological services: medical examination and evaluation, with initiation or continuation of diagnostic and treatment program; intermediate, established patient

➔ *CPT Assistant* Feb 97:6; Aug 98:1

92014 comprehensive, established patient, one or more visits

➔ *CPT Assistant* Feb 97:6; Aug 98:1; Dec 99:10

(For surgical procedures, see **Surgery,** Eye and Ocular Adnexa, 65091 et seq)

Special Ophthalmological Services

92015 Determination of refractive state

➔ *CPT Assistant* Mar 96:11; Feb 97:6; Aug 98:1

92018 Ophthalmological examination and evaluation, under general anesthesia, with or without manipulation of globe for passive range of motion or other manipulation to facilitate diagnostic examination; complete

➔ *CPT Assistant* Feb 97:6

92019 limited

➔ *CPT Assistant* Feb 97:6

92020 Gonioscopy (separate procedure)

➔ *CPT Assistant* Feb 97:6

(For gonioscopy under general anesthesia, use 92018)

92060 Sensorimotor examination with multiple measurements of ocular deviation (eg, restrictive or paretic muscle with diplopia) with interpretation and report (separate procedure)

➔ *CPT Assistant* Feb 97:6

92065 Orthoptic and/or pleoptic training, with continuing medical direction and evaluation

➔ *CPT Assistant* Feb 97:6; Jun 98:10

92070 Fitting of contact lens for treatment of disease, including supply of lens

➔ *CPT Assistant* Feb 97:6

92081 Visual field examination, unilateral or bilateral, with interpretation and report; limited examination (eg, tangent screen, Autoplot, arc perimeter, or single stimulus level automated test, such as Octopus 3 or 7 equivalent)

➔ *CPT Assistant* Feb 97:6

92082 intermediate examination (eg, at least 2 isopters on Goldmann perimeter, or semiquantitative, automated suprathreshold screening program, Humphrey suprathreshold automatic diagnostic test, Octopus program 33)

➔ *CPT Assistant* Feb 97:6

92083 extended examination (eg, Goldmann visual fields with at least 3 isopters plotted and static determination within the central 30°, or quantitative, automated threshold perimetry, Octopus program G-1, 32 or 42, Humphrey visual field analyzer full threshold programs 30-2, 24-2, or 30/60-2)

➔ *CPT Assistant* Feb 97:6

(Gross visual field testing (eg, confrontation testing) is a part of general ophthalmological services and is not reported separately)

92100 Serial tonometry (separate procedure) with multiple measurements of intraocular pressure over an extended time period with interpretation and report, same day (eg, diurnal curve or medical treatment of acute elevation of intraocular pressure)

➔ *CPT Assistant* Feb 97:6; Jun 98:10

92120 Tonography with interpretation and report, recording indentation tonometer method or perilimbal suction method

➔ *CPT Assistant* Feb 97:6

92130 Tonography with water provocation

➔ *CPT Assistant* Feb 97:6

92135 Scanning computerized ophthalmic diagnostic imaging (eg, scanning laser) with interpretation and report, unilateral

➔ *CPT Assistant* Nov 98:33; Mar 99:10; Apr 99:10

●**92136** Ophthalmic biometry by partial coherence interferometry with intraocular lens power calculation

➔ *CPT Changes* 2002

92140 Provocative tests for glaucoma, with interpretation and report, without tonography

➔ *CPT Assistant* Feb 97:6; Aug 98:1

Ophthalmoscopy

Routine ophthalmoscopy is part of general and special ophthalmologic services whenever indicated. It is a nonitemized service and is not reported separately.

92225 Ophthalmoscopy, extended, with retinal drawing (eg, for retinal detachment, melanoma), with interpretation and report; initial

➔ *CPT Assistant* Feb 97:6; Aug 98:1; Dec 99:10

92226 subsequent

➔ *CPT Assistant* Feb 97:6; Aug 98:1

92230 Fluorescein angioscopy with interpretation and report

➔ *CPT Assistant* Feb 97:6

⊘ =Modifier '-51' Exempt   ▶ ◀ =New or Revised Text   ✚ =Add-on Code   CPT 2002

92235   Fluorescein angiography (includes multiframe imaging) with interpretation and report
➔ *CPT Assistant* Feb 97:6

Fluorescein Angiography
92235

Fluorescein dye is injected in a peripheral vein to enhance imaging. Serial multiframe angiography is performed to evaluate choroidal and retinal circulation. In this illustration, arteries display an even fluorescence, while veins appear striped from the laminar dye flow.

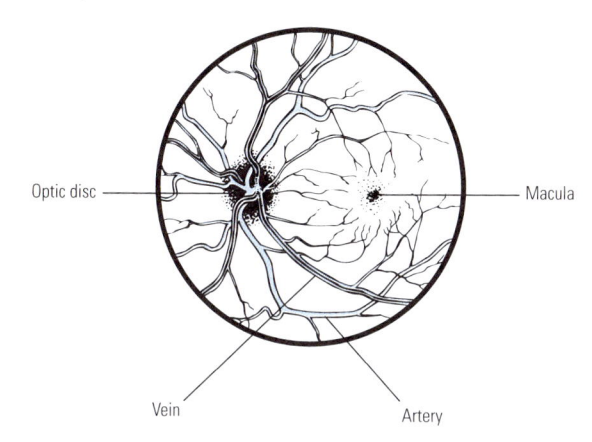

Optic disc —   — Macula

Vein   Artery

92240   Indocyanine-green angiography (includes multiframe imaging) with interpretation and report

92250   Fundus photography with interpretation and report
➔ *CPT Assistant* Feb 97:6; Apr 99:10

92260   Ophthalmodynamometry
➔ *CPT Assistant* Feb 97:6

(For ophthalmoscopy under general anesthesia, use 92018)

Other Specialized Services

92265   Needle oculoelectromyography, one or more extraocular muscles, one or both eyes, with interpretation and report
➔ *CPT Assistant* Feb 97:6

92270   Electro-oculography with interpretation and report
➔ *CPT Assistant* Feb 97:6

92275   Electroretinography with interpretation and report
➔ *CPT Assistant* Feb 97:6

(92280 has been deleted. To report visual evoked potential testing of the central nervous system, use 95930)

(For electronystagmography for vestibular function studies, see 92541 et seq)

(For ophthalmic echography (diagnostic ultrasound), see 76511-76529)

92283   Color vision examination, extended, eg, anomaloscope or equivalent
➔ *CPT Assistant* Feb 97:6

(Color vision testing with pseudoisochromatic plates (such as HRR or Ishihara) is not reported separately. It is included in the appropriate general or ophthalmological service, or 99172)

92284   Dark adaptation examination with interpretation and report
➔ *CPT Assistant* Feb 97:6

92285   External ocular photography with interpretation and report for documentation of medical progress (eg, close-up photography, slit lamp photography, goniophotography, stereo-photography)
➔ *CPT Assistant* Sep 97:10; Feb 97:6

92286   Special anterior segment photography with interpretation and report; with specular endothelial microscopy and cell count
➔ *CPT Assistant* Feb 97:6

92287   with fluorescein angiography
➔ *CPT Assistant* Feb 97:6

Contact Lens Services

The prescription of contact lens includes specification of optical and physical characteristics (such as power, size, curvature, flexibility, gas-permeability). It is NOT a part of the general ophthalmological services.

The fitting of contact lens includes instruction and training of the wearer and incidental revision of the lens during the training period.

Follow-up of successfully fitted extended wear lenses is reported as part of a general ophthalmological service (92012 et seq).

The supply of contact lenses may be reported as part of the service of fitting. It may also be reported separately by using 92391 or 92396 and modifier '-26' for the service of fitting without supply.

(For therapeutic or surgical use of contact lens, see 68340, 92070)

92310   Prescription of optical and physical characteristics of and fitting of contact lens, with medical supervision of adaptation; corneal lens, both eyes, except for aphakia
➔ *CPT Assistant* Feb 97:6

(For prescription and fitting of one eye, add modifier '-52')

92311   corneal lens for aphakia, one eye
➔ *CPT Assistant* Feb 97:6

92312   corneal lens for aphakia, both eyes
➔ *CPT Assistant* Feb 97:6

92313   corneoscleral lens
➔ *CPT Assistant* Feb 97:7

92314   Prescription of optical and physical characteristics of contact lens, with medical supervision of adaptation and direction of fitting by independent technician; corneal lens, both eyes except for aphakia
➔ *CPT Assistant* Feb 97:7

(For prescription and fitting of one eye, add modifier '-52')

92315 corneal lens for aphakia, one eye
➜ *CPT Assistant* Feb 97:7

92316 corneal lens for aphakia, both eyes
➜ *CPT Assistant* Feb 97:7

92317 corneoscleral lens
➜ *CPT Assistant* Feb 97:7

92325 Modification of contact lens (separate procedure), with medical supervision of adaptation
➜ *CPT Assistant* Feb 97:7

92326 Replacement of contact lens
➜ *CPT Assistant* Feb 97:7

Ocular Prosthetics, Artificial Eye

92330 Prescription, fitting, and supply of ocular prosthesis (artificial eye), with medical supervision of adaptation
➜ *CPT Assistant* Feb 97:7

(If supply is not included, use modifier '-26'; to report supply separately, use 92393)

92335 Prescription of ocular prosthesis (artificial eye) and direction of fitting and supply by independent technician, with medical supervision of adaptation
➜ *CPT Assistant* Feb 97:7

Spectacle Services (Including Prosthesis for Aphakia)

Prescription of lenses, when required, is included in 92015 Determination of refractive state. It includes specification of lens type (monofocal, bifocal, other), lens power, axis, prism, absorptive factor, impact resistance, and other factors.

Fitting of spectacles is a separate service; when provided by the physician, it is reported as indicated by 92340-92371.

Fitting includes measurement of anatomical facial characteristics, the writing of laboratory specifications, and the final adjustment of the spectacles to the visual axes and anatomical topography. Presence of physician is not required.

Supply of materials is a separate service component; it is not part of the service of fitting spectacles.
➜ *CPT Assistant* Nov 97:43

92340 Fitting of spectacles, except for aphakia; monofocal
➜ *CPT Assistant* Feb 97:7; Aug 98:1

92341 bifocal
➜ *CPT Assistant* Feb 97:7

92342 multifocal, other than bifocal
➜ *CPT Assistant* Feb 97:7

92352 Fitting of spectacle prosthesis for aphakia; monofocal
➜ *CPT Assistant* Feb 97:7

92353 multifocal
➜ *CPT Assistant* Feb 97:7

92354 Fitting of spectacle mounted low vision aid; single element system
➜ *CPT Assistant* Feb 97:7

92355 telescopic or other compound lens system
➜ *CPT Assistant* Feb 97:7

92358 Prosthesis service for aphakia, temporary (disposable or loan, including materials)
➜ *CPT Assistant* Feb 97:7

92370 Repair and refitting spectacles; except for aphakia
➜ *CPT Assistant* Feb 97:7

92371 spectacle prosthesis for aphakia
➜ *CPT Assistant* Feb 97:7; Aug 98:1

Supply of Materials

92390 Supply of spectacles, except prosthesis for aphakia and low vision aids
➜ *CPT Assistant* Feb 97:7

92391 Supply of contact lenses, except prosthesis for aphakia
➜ *CPT Assistant* Feb 97:7; Aug 98:1

(For supply of contact lenses reported as part of the service of fitting, see 92310-92313)

(For replacement of contact lens, use 92326)

92392 Supply of low vision aids (A low vision aid is any lens or device used to aid or improve visual function in a person whose vision cannot be normalized by conventional spectacle correction. Includes reading additions up to 4D.)
➜ *CPT Assistant* Feb 97:7

92393 Supply of ocular prosthesis (artificial eye)
➜ *CPT Assistant* Feb 97:7

(For supply reported as part of the service of fitting, use 92330)

92395 Supply of permanent prosthesis for aphakia; spectacles
➜ *CPT Assistant* Feb 97:7

(For temporary spectacle correction, use 92358)

92396 contact lenses
➜ *CPT Assistant* Feb 97:7; Aug 98:1

(For supply reported as part of the service of fitting, see 92311, 92312)

(Use 99070 for the supply of other materials, drugs, trays, etc.)

Other Procedures

92499 Unlisted ophthalmological service or procedure
➜ *CPT Assistant* Feb 97:7

Special Otorhinolaryngologic Services

Diagnostic or treatment procedures usually included in a comprehensive otorhinolaryngologic evaluation or office visit, are reported as an integrated medical service, using appropriate descriptors from the 99201 series. Itemization of component procedures (eg, otoscopy, rhinoscopy, tuning fork test) does not apply.

Special otorhinolaryngologic services are those diagnostic and treatment services not usually included in a comprehensive otorhinolaryngologic evaluation or office visit. These services are reported separately, using descriptors from the 92500 series.

All services include medical diagnostic evaluation. Technical procedures (which may or may not be performed by the physician personally) are often part of the service, but should not be mistaken to constitute the service itself.

(For laryngoscopy with stroboscopy, use 31579)

92502   Otolaryngologic examination under general anesthesia

92504   Binocular microscopy (separate diagnostic procedure)

92506   Evaluation of speech, language, voice, communication, auditory processing, and/or aural rehabilitation status

92507   Treatment of speech, language, voice, communication, and/or auditory processing disorder (includes aural rehabilitation); individual

92508   group, two or more individuals

92510   Aural rehabilitation following cochlear implant (includes evaluation of aural rehabilitation status and hearing, therapeutic services) with or without speech processor programming
➲ *CPT Assistant* May 96:10

92511   Nasopharyngoscopy with endoscope (separate procedure)

92512   Nasal function studies (eg, rhinomanometry)

92516   Facial nerve function studies (eg, electroneuronography)

92520   Laryngeal function studies

92525   Evaluation of swallowing and oral function for feeding

92526   Treatment of swallowing dysfunction and/or oral function for feeding

Vestibular Function Tests, With Observation and Evaluation by Physician, Without Electrical Recording

92531   Spontaneous nystagmus, including gaze

▲ **92532**   Positional nystagmus test
➲ *CPT Changes* 2002

92533   Caloric vestibular test, each irrigation (binaural, bithermal stimulation constitutes four tests)
➲ *CPT Assistant* May 96:5

▲ **92534**   Optokinetic nystagmus test
➲ *CPT Changes* 2002

Vestibular Function Tests, With Recording (eg, ENG, PENG), and Medical Diagnostic Evaluation

92541   Spontaneous nystagmus test, including gaze and fixation nystagmus, with recording

92542   Positional nystagmus test, minimum of 4 positions, with recording

92543   Caloric vestibular test, each irrigation (binaural, bithermal stimulation constitutes four tests), with recording
➲ *CPT Assistant* May 96:5

92544   Optokinetic nystagmus test, bidirectional, foveal or peripheral stimulation, with recording

92545   Oscillating tracking test, with recording

92546   Sinusoidal vertical axis rotational testing

+ 92547   Use of vertical electrodes (List separately in addition to code for primary procedure)

(Use 92547 in conjunction with codes 92541-92546)

(For unlisted vestibular tests, use 92599)

92548   Computerized dynamic posturography

Audiologic Function Tests With Medical Diagnostic Evaluation

The audiometric tests listed below imply the use of calibrated electronic equipment. Other hearing tests (such as whispered voice, tuning fork) are considered part of the general otorhinolaryngologic services and are not reported separately. All descriptors refer to testing both ears. Use the modifier '-52' if a test is applied to one ear instead of to two ears. All descriptors (except 92559) apply to testing of individuals; for testing of groups, use 92559 and specify test(s) used.

(For evaluation of speech, language and/or hearing problems through observation and assessment of performance, use 92506)

92551   Screening test, pure tone, air only

92552   Pure tone audiometry (threshold); air only

92553   air and bone

92555   Speech audiometry threshold;

92556   with speech recognition

92557   Comprehensive audiometry threshold evaluation and speech recognition (92553 and 92556 combined)

(For hearing aid evaluation and selection, see 92590-92595)

92559 Audiometric testing of groups

92560 Bekesy audiometry; screening

92561   diagnostic

92562 Loudness balance test, alternate binaural or monaural

92563 Tone decay test

92564 Short increment sensitivity index (SISI)
➲ *CPT Assistant* Oct 96:9

92565 Stenger test, pure tone

(92566 has been deleted. To report, use 92567)

92567 Tympanometry (impedance testing)

92568 Acoustic reflex testing

92569 Acoustic reflex decay test

92571 Filtered speech test

92572 Staggered spondaic word test

92573 Lombard test

(92574 has been deleted)

92575 Sensorineural acuity level test

92576 Synthetic sentence identification test

92577 Stenger test, speech

(92578 has been deleted)

92579 Visual reinforcement audiometry (VRA)

(92580 has been deleted)

(92581 has been deleted. To report, use 92585)

92582 Conditioning play audiometry

92583 Select picture audiometry

92584 Electrocochleography

92585 Auditory evoked potentials for evoked response audiometry and/or testing of the central nervous system; comprehensive
➲ *CPT Changes* 2001

92586   limited
➲ *CPT Changes* 2001

92587 Evoked otoacoustic emissions; limited (single stimulus level, either transient or distortion products)

92588   comprehensive or diagnostic evaluation (comparison of transient and/or distortion product otoacoustic emissions at multiple levels and frequencies)

92589 Central auditory function test(s) (specify)

92590 Hearing aid examination and selection; monaural

92591   binaural

92592 Hearing aid check; monaural

92593   binaural

92594 Electroacoustic evaluation for hearing aid; monaural

92595   binaural

92596 Ear protector attenuation measurements

92597 Evaluation for use and/or fitting of voice prosthetic or augmentative/alternative communication device to supplement oral speech

92598 Modification of voice prosthetic or augmentative/alternative communication device to supplement oral speech

Other Procedures

92599 Unlisted otorhinolaryngological service or procedure

Cardiovascular

Therapeutic Services

▶(For non-surgical septal reduction therapy (eg, alcohol ablation), use Category III code 0024T)◀

92950 Cardiopulmonary resuscitation (eg, in cardiac arrest)
➲ *CPT Assistant* Jan 96:7

(See also critical care services, 99291, 99292)

92953 Temporary transcutaneous pacing

(For physician direction of ambulance or rescue personnel outside the hospital, use 99288)

92960 Cardioversion, elective, electrical conversion of arrhythmia; external
➲ *CPT Assistant* Summer 93:13; Nov 99:49; Jun 00:5; Nov 00:9; *CPT Changes* 2000

92961   internal (separate procedure)
➲ *CPT Assistant* Summer 93:13; Nov 99:49; Jun 00:5; Jul 00:5; Nov 00:9; *CPT Changes* 2000

(Do not report 92961 in addition to codes 93662, 93618-93624, 93631, 93640-93642, 93650-93652, 93741-93744)

92970 Cardioassist-method of circulatory assist; internal

92971   external

(For balloon atrial-septostomy, use 92992)

(For placement of catheters for use in circulatory assist devices such as intra-aortic balloon pump, use 33970)

+ ●92973 Percutaneous transluminal coronary thrombectomy (List separately in addition to code for primary procedure)
➲ *CPT Changes* 2002

▶(Use 92973 in conjunction with codes 92980, 92982)◀

+ ●92974 Transcatheter placement of radiation delivery device for subsequent coronary intravascular brachytherapy (List separately in addition to code for primary procedure)
➲ *CPT Changes* 2002

▶(Use 92974 in conjunction with codes 92980, 92982, 93508)◀

▶(For intravascular radioelement application, see 77781 - 77784)◀

92975   Thrombolysis, coronary; by intracoronary infusion, including selective coronary angiography

92977   by intravenous infusion

(For thrombolysis of vessels other than coronary, see 37201, 75896)

(For cerebral thrombolysis, use 37195)

+ 92978   Intravascular ultrasound (coronary vessel or graft) during diagnostic evaluation and/or therapeutic intervention including imaging supervision, interpretation and report; initial vessel (List separately in addition to code for primary procedure)

➔ CPT Assistant Nov 97:43-44; Nov 99:49; CPT Changes 2000

Intravascular Ultrasound (Coronary Vessel or Graft)
92978

A catheter with a transducer at its tip is inserted and threaded through a selected coronary artery(s) or coronary bypass graft.

+ 92979   each additional vessel (List separately in addition to code for primary procedure)

➔ CPT Assistant Nov 97:43-44; Nov 99:49; CPT Changes 2000

(Use 92979 in conjunction with code 92978)

(Intravascular ultrasound services include all transducer manipulations and repositioning within the specific vessel being examined, both before and after therapeutic intervention (eg, stent placement))

92980   Transcatheter placement of an intracoronary stent(s), percutaneous, with or without other therapeutic intervention, any method; single vessel

➔ CPT Assistant Aug 96:2; Dec 96:11; Apr 98:9; Aug 98:3; Aug 00:11

+ 92981   each additional vessel (List separately in addition to code for primary procedure)

(Use 92981 in conjunction with code 92980)

(To report additional vessels treated by angioplasty or atherectomy only during the same session, see 92984, 92996)

▶(To report transcatheter placement of radiation delivery device for coronary intravascular brachytherapy, use 92974)◀

▶(For intravascular radioelement application, see 77781-77784)◀

92982   Percutaneous transluminal coronary balloon angioplasty; single vessel

➔ CPT Assistant Winter 92:15; Aug 96:2; Apr 97:10

Percutaneous Transluminal Coronary Angioplasty (PTCA)
92982

PTCA of a single coronary vessel.

+ 92984   each additional vessel (List separately in addition to code for primary procedure)

➔ CPT Assistant Winter 92:15; Aug 96:2; Dec 96:11; Apr 97:10

(Use 92984 in conjunction with codes 92980, 92982, 92995)

(For stent placement following completion of angioplasty or atherectomy, see 92980, 92981)

▶(To report transcatheter placement of radiation delivery device for coronary intravascular brachytherapy, use 92974)◀

▶(For intravascular radioelement application, see 77781-77784)◀

92986 Percutaneous balloon valvuloplasty; aortic valve

92987   mitral valve

92990   pulmonary valve

92992 Atrial septectomy or septostomy; transvenous method, balloon (eg, Rashkind type) (includes cardiac catheterization)
> *CPT Assistant* Nov 97:44; Apr 98:3, 10

92993   blade method (Park septostomy) (includes cardiac catheterization)
> *CPT Assistant* Apr 98:10

92995 Percutaneous transluminal coronary atherectomy, by mechanical or other method, with or without balloon angioplasty; single vessel
> *CPT Assistant* Winter 92:15

+ 92996   each additional vessel (List separately in addition to code for primary procedure)
> *CPT Assistant* Winter 92:15; Apr 98:3

(Use 92996 in conjunction with code(s) 92980, 92982, 92995)

(For stent placement following completion of angioplasty or atherectomy, see 92980, 92981)

(To report additional vessels treated by angioplasty only during the same session, use 92984)

92997 Percutaneous transluminal pulmonary artery balloon angioplasty; single vessel
> *CPT Assistant* Nov 97:44

+ 92998   each additional vessel (List separately in addition to code for primary procedure)
> *CPT Assistant* Nov 97:44

(Use 92998 in conjunction with code 92997)

Cardiography

(For echocardiography, see 93303-93350)

93000 Electrocardiogram, routine ECG with at least 12 leads; with interpretation and report
> *CPT Assistant* Aug 97:9

93005   tracing only, without interpretation and report
> *CPT Assistant* Aug 97:9

93010   interpretation and report only
> *CPT Assistant* Aug 97:9

(For ECG monitoring, see 99354-99360)

93012 Telephonic transmission of post-symptom electrocardiogram rhythm strip(s), per 30 day period of time; tracing only
> *CPT Assistant* Jun 96:2

93014   physician review with interpretation and report only
> *CPT Assistant* Jun 96:2

93015 Cardiovascular stress test using maximal or submaximal treadmill or bicycle exercise, continuous electrocardiographic monitoring, and/or pharmacological stress; with physician supervision, with interpretation and report
> *CPT Assistant* Apr 96:11; Jun 96:10

93016   physician supervision only, without interpretation and report
> *CPT Assistant* Apr 96:11

93017   tracing only, without interpretation and report

93018   interpretation and report only
> *CPT Assistant* Apr 96:11; Jun 96:10

93024 Ergonovine provocation test

● **93025** Microvolt T-wave alternans for assessment of ventricular arrhythmias
> *CPT Changes* 2002

93040 Rhythm ECG, one to three leads; with interpretation and report

93041   tracing only without interpretation and report

93042   interpretation and report only

(93045 has been deleted. To report, use 93615)

(93201, 93202, 93204, 93205, 93208, 93209 and 93210 have been deleted. To report, use 93799)

(93220, 93221, 93222 have been deleted. To report, use 93799)

93224 Electrocardiographic monitoring for 24 hours by continuous original ECG waveform recording and storage, with visual superimposition scanning; includes recording, scanning analysis with report, physician review and interpretation

93225   recording (includes hook-up, recording, and disconnection)

93226   scanning analysis with report

93227   physician review and interpretation

93230 Electrocardiographic monitoring for 24 hours by continuous original ECG waveform recording and storage without superimposition scanning utilizing a device capable of producing a full miniaturized printout; includes recording, microprocessor-based analysis with report, physician review and interpretation

93231   recording (includes hook-up, recording, and disconnection)

93232   microprocessor-based analysis with report

93233   physician review and interpretation

93235 Electrocardiographic monitoring for 24 hours by continuous computerized monitoring and non-continuous recording, and real-time data analysis utilizing a device capable of producing intermittent full-sized waveform tracings, possibly patient activated; includes monitoring and real-time data analysis with report, physician review and interpretation

93236   monitoring and real-time data analysis with report

93237   physician review and interpretation

(93255 has been deleted)

(93258, 93259, 93262, 93263, 93266 have been deleted. To report, see 93224-93237)

93268   Patient demand single or multiple event recording with presymptom memory loop, per 30 day period of time; includes transmission, physician review and interpretation

→ *CPT Assistant* Jun 96:2; Nov 99:49-50

(93269 has been deleted. To report, use 93268)

93270   recording (includes hook-up, recording, and disconnection)

→ *CPT Assistant* Jun 96:2

93271   monitoring, receipt of transmissions, and analysis

→ *CPT Assistant* Jun 96:2

93272   physician review and interpretation only

→ *CPT Assistant* Jun 96:2; Apr 98:14; Nov 99:49-50

(For postsymptom recording, see 93012, 93014)

(For implanted patient activated cardiac event recording, see 33282, 93727)

(93273-93277 have been deleted. To report, see 93224-93237)

93278   Signal-averaged electrocardiography (SAECG), with or without ECG

(For interpretation and report only, use 93278 with modifier '-26')

(For unlisted cardiographic procedure, use 93799)

(93280 has been deleted. To report, use 76000)

Echocardiography

Echocardiography includes obtaining ultrasonic signals from the heart and great arteries, with two-dimensional image and/or Doppler ultrasonic signal documentation, and interpretation and report. When interpretation is performed separately use modifier '-26'.

(For fetal echocardiography, see 76825-76828)

(93300 has been deleted)

93303   Transthoracic echocardiography for congenital cardiac anomalies; complete

→ *CPT Assistant* Nov 97:44; Dec 97:5

93304   follow-up or limited study

→ *CPT Assistant* Nov 97:44; Dec 97:5

(93305 has been deleted)

93307   Echocardiography, transthoracic, real-time with image documentation (2D) with or without M-mode recording; complete

→ *CPT Assistant* Dec 97:5; Apr 00:1

93308   follow-up or limited study

→ *CPT Assistant* Dec 97:5

(93309 has been deleted. To report, see 93307, 93308)

93312   Echocardiography, transesophageal, real time with image documentation (2D) (with or without M-mode recording); including probe placement, image acquisition, interpretation and report

→ *CPT Assistant* Dec 97:5; Jan 00:10

Transesophageal Echocardiography (TEE)
93312-93318

An endoscopic ultrasound transducer is passed through the mouth into the esophagus and two-dimensional images are obtained from the posterior aspect of the heart.

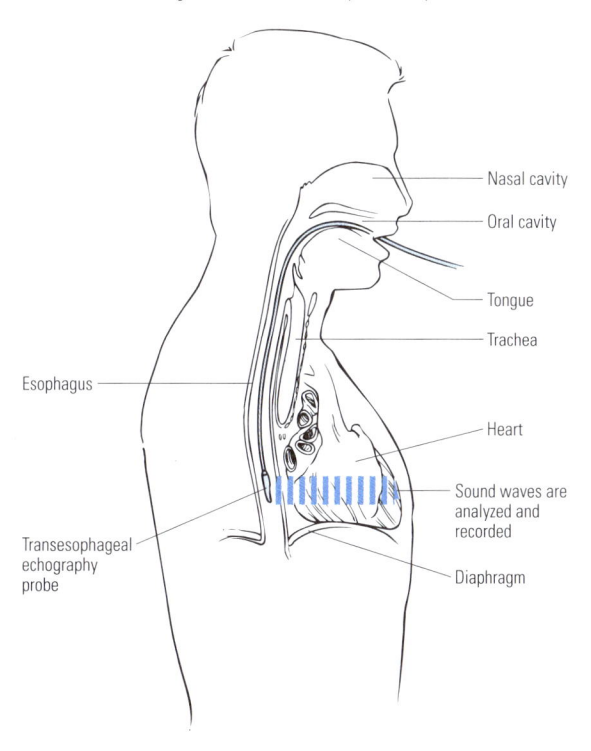

Nasal cavity

Oral cavity

Tongue

Trachea

Esophagus

Heart

Sound waves are analyzed and recorded

Transesophageal echography probe

Diaphragm

93313   placement of transesophageal probe only

→ *CPT Assistant* Dec 97:5

93314   image acquisition, interpretation and report only

→ *CPT Assistant* Dec 97:5; Jan 00:10

93315   Transesophageal echocardiography for congenital cardiac anomalies; including probe placement, image acquisition, interpretation and report

→ *CPT Assistant* Nov 97:44; Dec 97:5

93316   placement of transesophageal probe only

→ *CPT Assistant* Nov 97:44; Dec 97:5

93317   image acquisition, interpretation and report only

→ *CPT Assistant* Nov 97:44; Dec 97:5

93318 Echocardiography, transesophageal (TEE) for monitoring purposes, including probe placement, real time 2-dimensional image acquisition and interpretation leading to ongoing (continuous) assessment of (dynamically changing) cardiac pumping function and to therapeutic measures on an immediate time basis

➲ *CPT Changes* 2001

+ 93320 Doppler echocardiography, pulsed wave and/or continuous wave with spectral display (List separately in addition to codes for echocardiographic imaging); complete

➲ *CPT Assistant* Nov 97:44; Dec 97:5

(Use 93320 in conjunction with codes 93303, 93304, 93307, 93308, 93312, 93314, 93315, 93317, 93350)

+ 93321 follow-up or limited study (List separately in addition to codes for echocardiographic imaging)

➲ *CPT Assistant* Nov 97:44; Dec 97:5

(Use 93321 in conjunction with codes 93303, 93304, 93307, 93308, 93312, 93314, 93315, 93317, 93950)

+ 93325 Doppler echocardiography color flow velocity mapping (List separately in addition to codes for echocardiography)

➲ *CPT Assistant* Nov 97:44; Dec 97:5

(Use 93325 in conjunction with codes 76825, 76826, 76827, 76828, 93303, 93304, 93307, 93308, 93312, 93314, 93315, 93317, 93320, 93321, 93350)

93350 Echocardiography, transthoracic, real-time with image documentation (2D), with or without M-mode recording, during rest and cardiovascular stress test using treadmill, bicycle exercise and/or pharmacologically induced stress, with interpretation and report

(The appropriate stress testing code from the 93015-93018 series should be reported in addition to 93350 to capture the exercise stress portion of the study)

Cardiac Catheterization

Cardiac catheterization is a diagnostic medical procedure which includes introduction, positioning and repositioning of catheter(s), when necessary, recording of intracardiac and intravascular pressure, obtaining blood samples for measurement of blood gases or dilution curves and cardiac output measurements (Fick or other method, with or without rest and exercise and/or studies) with or without electrode catheter placement, final evaluation and report of procedure. When selective injection procedures are performed without a preceding cardiac catheterization, these services should be reported using codes in the Vascular Injection Procedures section, 36011-36015 and 36215-36218.

When coronary artery, arterial coronary conduit or venous bypass graft angiography is performed without concomitant left heart cardiac catheterization, use 93508. Injection procedures 93539, 93540, 93544, and 93545 represent separate identifiable services and may be coded in conjunction with one another in addition to code 93508, as appropriate. To report imaging supervision,

interpretation and report in conjunction with code 93508, use code 93556.

Modifier '-51' should not be appended to codes 93501-93533, 93539-93556.

➲ *CPT Assistant* Nov 98:33

⊘ **93501** Right heart catheterization

➲ *CPT Assistant* Spring 94:24; Apr 98:1; Apr 00:10

Right Heart Catheterization
93501

The physician introduces a cardiac catheter into the venous system. The catheter then is directed into the right atrium, right ventricle, and pulmonary artery.

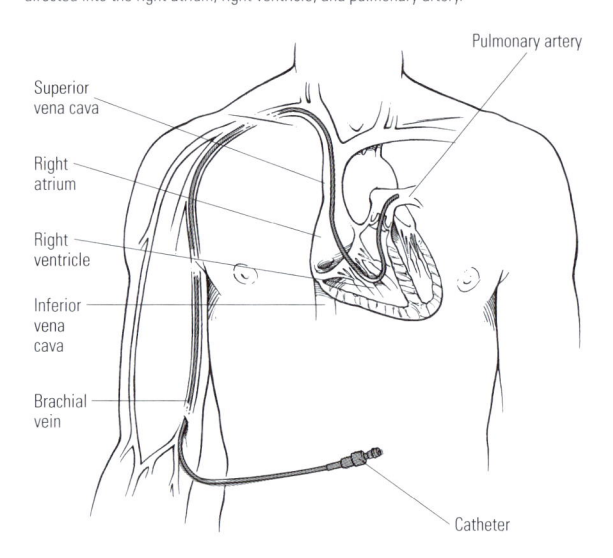

Catheter is advanced retrograde through the arterial system to the ascending aorta; pressures are measured in the aortic root; the catheter is then manipulated using fluoroscopic guidance into the ostium of a coronary artery, arterial bypass conduit, or venous coronary bypass graft.

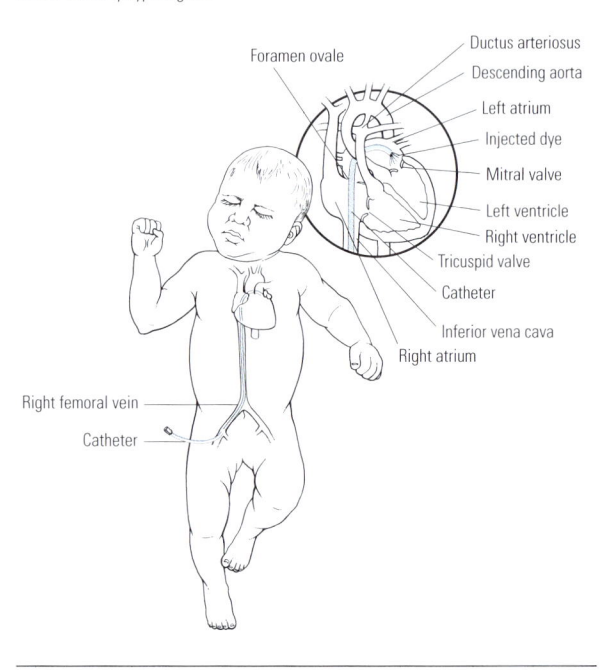

(For bundle of His recording, use 93600)

⊘ **93503** Insertion and placement of flow directed catheter (eg, Swan-Ganz) for monitoring purposes

➔ *CPT Assistant* Fall 95:8; Apr 98:1

(For subsequent monitoring, see 99356-99357)

⊘ **93505** Endomyocardial biopsy

➔ *CPT Assistant* Apr 98:1; Apr 00:10

⊘ **93508** Catheter placement in coronary artery(s), arterial coronary conduit(s), and/or venous coronary bypass graft(s) for coronary angiography without concomitant left heart catheterization

➔ *CPT Assistant* Nov 97:44-45; Apr 98:1; Apr 00:10; Aug 00:11

(93508 is to be used only when left heart catheterization 93510, 93511, 93524, 93526 is not performed)

(93508 is to be used only once per procedure)

Coronary Angiography without Concomitant Left Heart Catheterization
93508

Cardiac catheterization procedure performed wherein the catheter does not cross the aortic valve into the left ventricle (left heart catheterization).

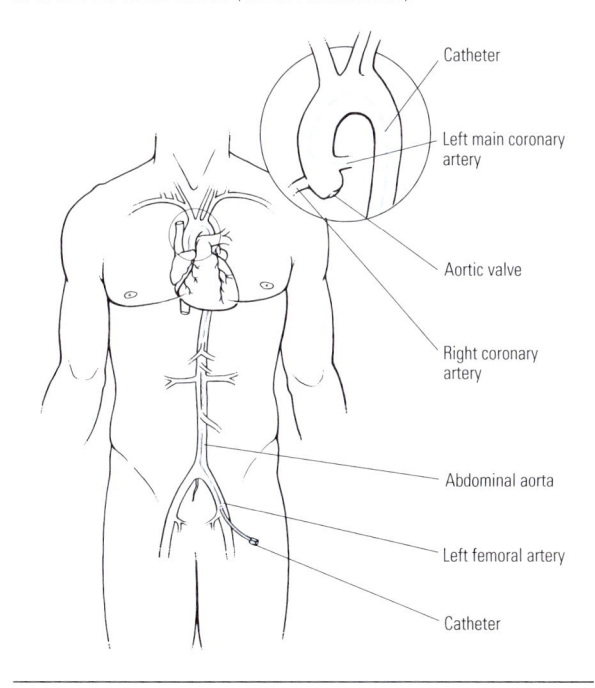

▶(To report transcatheter placement of radiation delivery device for coronary intravascular brachytherapy, use 92974)◀

▶(For intravascular radioelement application, see 77781-77784)◀

⊘ **93510** Left heart catheterization, retrograde, from the brachial artery, axillary artery or femoral artery; percutaneous

➔ *CPT Assistant* Spring 94:26; Nov 97:44-45; Apr 98:1

Left Heart Catheterization
93510

A catheter is inserted into the arterial system and then into the left ventricle.

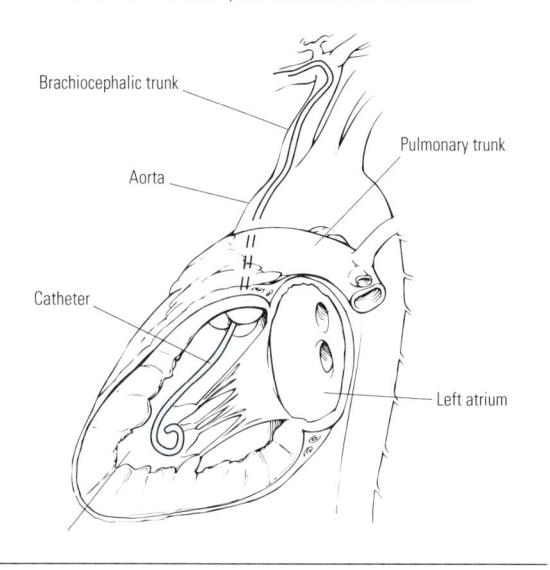

⊘ **93511** by cutdown

➔ *CPT Assistant* Spring 94:24; Nov 97:44-45; Apr 98:1

⊘ **93514** Left heart catheterization by left ventricular puncture

➔ *CPT Assistant* Spring 94:24; Apr 98:1

(93515 has been deleted. To report, use 93524)

⊘ **93524** Combined transseptal and retrograde left heart catheterization

➔ *CPT Assistant* Spring 94:24; Nov 97:44-45; Apr 98:1

⊘ **93526** Combined right heart catheterization and retrograde left heart catheterization

➔ *CPT Assistant* Spring 94:28; Nov 97:44-45; Apr 98:1

⊘ **93527** Combined right heart catheterization and transseptal left heart catheterization through intact septum (with or without retrograde left heart catheterization)

➔ *CPT Assistant* Apr 98:1

⊘ **93528** Combined right heart catheterization with left ventricular puncture (with or without retrograde left heart catheterization)

➔ *CPT Assistant* Apr 98:1

⊘ **93529** Combined right heart catheterization and left heart catheterization through existing septal opening (with or without retrograde left heart catheterization)

➔ *CPT Assistant* Apr 98:1

⊘ **93530** Right heart catheterization, for congenital cardiac anomalies

➔ *CPT Assistant* Nov 97:45; Mar 98:11; Apr 98:3, 6-7

⊘ **93531** Combined right heart catheterization and retrograde left heart catheterization, for congenital cardiac anomalies
➔ *CPT Assistant* Nov 97:45; Mar 98:11; Apr 98:8, 10, 11

⊘ **93532** Combined right heart catheterization and transseptal left heart catheterization through intact septum with or without retrograde left heart catheterization, for congenital cardiac anomalies
➔ *CPT Assistant* Nov 97:45; Mar 98:11; Apr 98:10, 11

⊘ **93533** Combined right heart catheterization and transseptal left heart catheterization through existing septal opening, with or without retrograde left heart catheterization, for congenital cardiac anomalies
➔ *CPT Assistant* Nov 97:45; Mar 98:11; Apr 98:12, 13

(93535 has been deleted. To report, see 33971)

▶(93536 has been deleted. To report, use 33967)◀

(When injection procedures are performed in conjunction with cardiac catheterization, these services do not include introduction of catheters but do include repositioning of catheters when necessary and use of automatic power injectors. Injection procedures 93539-93545 represent separate identifiable services and may be coded in conjunction with one another when appropriate. The technical details of angiography, supervision of filming and processing, interpretation and report are not included. To report imaging supervision, interpretation and report, use 93555 and/or 93556. Modifier '-51' should not be appended to 93539-93556.)

⊘ **93539** Injection procedure during cardiac catheterization; for selective opacification of arterial conduits (eg, internal mammary), whether native or used for bypass
➔ *CPT Assistant* Spring 94:27; Nov 97:44-45; Apr 98:3

⊘ **93540** for selective opacification of aortocoronary venous bypass grafts, one or more coronary arteries
➔ *CPT Assistant* Spring 94:27; Nov 97:44-45; Apr 98:3

⊘ **93541** for pulmonary angiography
➔ *CPT Assistant* Spring 94:28; Nov 97:44-45; Apr 98:3

⊘ **93542** for selective right ventricular or right atrial angiography
➔ *CPT Assistant* Spring 94:24; Nov 97:44-45; Apr 98:3

⊘ **93543** for selective left ventricular or left atrial angiography
➔ *CPT Assistant* Spring 94:28; Nov 97:44-45; Apr 98:3

⊘ **93544** for aortography
➔ *CPT Assistant* Spring 94:28; Nov 97:44-45; Apr 98:3

⊘ **93545** for selective coronary angiography (injection of radiopaque material may be by hand)
➔ *CPT Assistant* Spring 94:28; Nov 97:44-45; Apr 98:3

(93546 has been deleted. To report, use 93510 and 93543)

(To report imaging supervision and interpretation, use 93555)

(93547 has been deleted. To report, use 93510, 93543, and 93545)

(To report imaging supervision and interpretation, use 93555 and 93556)

(93548 has been deleted. To report, use 93510, 93543, 93544, 93545)

(To report imaging supervision and interpretation, use 93555 and 93556)

(93549 has been deleted. To report, use 93526, 93527 or 93528; 93543, 93545)

(To report imaging supervision and interpretation, use 93555 and 93556)

(93550 has been deleted. To report, use 93526 or 93527 or 93528; 93540, 93543; and 93545)

(To report imaging supervision and interpretation, use 93555 and 93556)

(93551 has been deleted. To report, use 93539 or 93540)

(93552 has been deleted. To report, use 93510; 93539 or 93540; 93543 and 93545)

(To report imaging supervision and interpretation, use 93555 and 93556)

(93553 has been deleted. To report, use 93510; 93539 or 93540; 93543, 93544, 93545)

(To report imaging supervision and interpretation, use 93555 and 93556)

⊘ **93555** Imaging supervision, interpretation and report for injection procedure(s) during cardiac catheterization; ventricular and/or atrial angiography
➔ *CPT Assistant* Spring 94:28; Oct 97:10 ; Nov 97:44-45; Apr 98:3, 11, 12

⊘ **93556** pulmonary angiography, aortography, and/or selective coronary angiography including venous bypass grafts and arterial conduits (whether native or used in bypass)
➔ *CPT Assistant* Spring 94:28;Oct 97:10; Nov 97:44-45; Apr 98:3, 11, 12

(Codes 93561 and 93562 are not to be used with cardiac catheterization codes)

93561 Indicator dilution studies such as dye or thermal dilution, including arterial and/or venous catheterization; with cardiac output measurement (separate procedure)
➔ *CPT Assistant* Winter 91:25

93562 subsequent measurement of cardiac output
➔ *CPT Assistant* Winter 91:25

(For radioisotope method of cardiac output, see 78472, 78473, or 78481)

(93570 has been deleted. To report, use 92982)

+ 93571 Intravascular doppler velocity and/or pressure derived coronary flow reserve measurement (coronary vessel or graft) during coronary angiography including pharmacologically induced stress; initial vessel (List separately in addition to code for primary procedure)

➔ *CPT Assistant* Nov 98:33; Apr 00:1

Intravascular Distal Blood Flow Velocity
93571

A Doppler guide wire is positioned in a proximal coronary artery with the transducer beam parallel to blood flow to measure blood flow velocity.

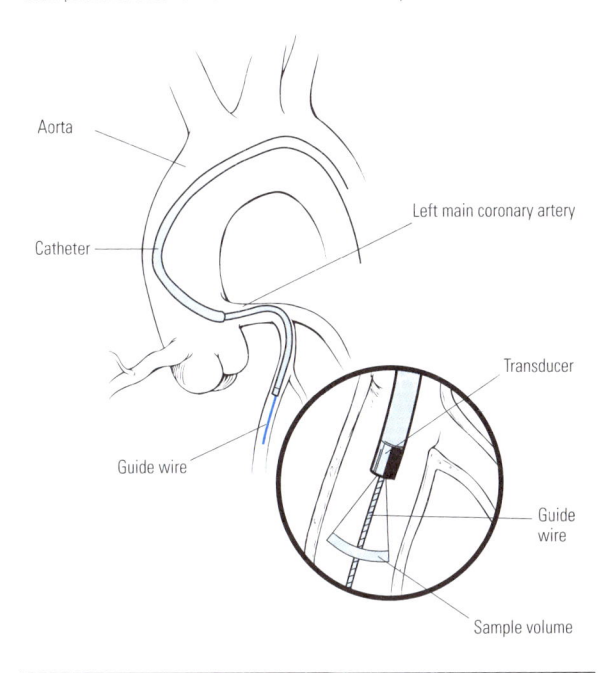

Aorta

Left main coronary artery

Catheter

Transducer

Guide wire

Guide wire

Sample volume

+ 93572 each additional vessel (List separately in addition to code for primary procedure)

➔ *CPT Assistant* Nov 98:34; Apr 00:1

(Intravascular distal coronary blood flow velocity measurements include all Doppler transducer manipulations and repositioning within the specific vessel being examined, during coronary angiography or therapeutic intervention (eg, angioplasty))

(For unlisted cardiac catheterization procedure, use 93799)

Intracardiac Electrophysiological Procedures▸/Studies◂

▸Intracardiac electrophysiologic studies (EPS) are an invasive diagnostic medical procedure which include the insertion and repositioning of electrode catheters, recording of electrograms before and during pacing or programmed stimulation of multiple locations in the heart, analysis of recorded information, and report of the procedure. Electrophysiologic studies are most often performed with two or more electrode catheters. In many circumstances, patients with arrhythmias are evaluated and treated at the same encounter. In this situation, a diagnostic *electrophysiologic study* is performed, induced

tachycardia(s) are *mapped*, and on the basis of the diagnostic and mapping information, the tissue is *ablated*. Electrophysiologic study(ies), mapping, and ablation represent distinctly different procedures, requiring individual reporting whether performed on the same or subsequent dates.◂

Definitions

▸*Arrhythmia Induction*: In most electrophysiologic studies, an attempt is made to induce arrhythmia(s) from single or multiple sites within the heart. Arrhythmia induction is achieved by performing pacing at different rates, programmed stimulation (introduction of critically timed electrical impulses), and other techniques. Because arrhythmia induction occurs via the same catheter(s) inserted for the electrophysiologic study(ies), catheter insertion and temporary pacemaker codes are not additionally reported. Codes 93600-93603, 93610-93612 and 93618 are used to describe unusual situations where there may be recording, pacing or an attempt at arrhythmia induction from only one site in the heart. Code 93619 describes only evaluation of the sinus node, atrioventricular node and His-Purkinje conduction system, without arrhythmia induction. Codes 93620-93624 and 93640-93642 all include recording, pacing and attempted arrhythmia induction from one or more site(s) in the heart.◂

▸*Mapping*: Mapping is a distinct procedure performed in addition to a diagnostic electrophysiologic procedure and should be separately reported using code 93609 or 93613.When a tachycardia is induced, the site of tachycardia origination or its electrical path through the heart is often defined by mapping. Mapping creates a multidimensional depiction of a tachycardia by recording multiple electrograms obtained sequentially or simultaneously from multiple catheter sites in the heart. Depending upon the technique, certain types of mapping catheters may be repositioned from point-to-point within the heart, allowing sequential recording from the various sites to construct maps. Other types of mapping catheters allow mapping without a point-to-point technique by allowing simultaneous recording from many electrodes on the same catheter and computer-assisted three dimensional reconstruction of the tachycardia activation sequence.◂

▸*Ablation*: Once the part of the heart involved in the tachycardia is localized, the tachycardia may be treated by ablation (the delivery of a radiofrequency energy to the area to selectively destroy cardiac tissue). Ablation procedures (93651-93652) may be performed: independently on a date subsequent to a diagnostic electrophysiologic study and mapping; or, at the time a diagnostic electrophysiologic study, tachycardia(s) induction and mapping is performed. When an electrophysiologic study, mapping, and ablation are performed on the same date, each procedure should be separately reported. In reporting catheter ablation, code 93651 and/or 93652 should be reported once to describe ablation of cardiac arrhythmias, regardless of the number of arrhythmias ablated.◄

Modifier '-51' should not be appended to 93600-93660.

⊘ **93600** Bundle of His recording
  → *CPT Assistant* Summer 94:12; Aug 97:9

⊘ **93602** Intra-atrial recording
  → *CPT Assistant* Summer 94:12; Aug 97:9

⊘ **93603** Right ventricular recording
  → *CPT Assistant* Summer 94:12; Aug 97:9

(93604, 93606 have been deleted. To report, see 93603, 93609, and ►93622◄ as appropriate)

(93605 has been deleted. To report, use 93609)

►(93607 has been deleted. To report, use 93622)◄

(93608 has been deleted. To report, use 93609)

+ ▲ **93609** Intraventricular and/or intra-atrial mapping of tachycardia site(s) with catheter manipulation to record from multiple sites to identify origin of tachycardia (List separately in addition to code for primary procedure)
  → *CPT Assistant* Summer 94:12; Aug 97:9; *CPT Changes* 2002

►(Use 93609 in conjunction with codes 93620, 93651, 93652)◄

⊘ **93610** Intra-atrial pacing
  → *CPT Assistant* Summe 94:12; Aug 97:9; Aug 97:9

⊘ **93612** Intraventricular pacing
  → *CPT Assistant* Summer 94:12; Aug 97:9

►(Do not report 93612 in conjunction with codes 93620-93622)◄

+ ● **93613** Intracardiac electrophysiologic 3-dimensional mapping (List separately in addition to code for primary procedure)
  → *CPT Changes* 2002

►(Use 93613 in conjunction with codes 93620, 93651, 93652)◄

(93614 has been deleted)

⊘ **93615** Esophageal recording of atrial electrogram with or without ventricular electrogram(s);
  → *CPT Assistant* Summer 94:12; Aug 97:9

⊘ **93616** with pacing
  → *CPT Assistant* Summer 94:12; Aug 97:9

⊘ **93618** Induction of arrhythmia by electrical pacing
  → *CPT Assistant* Summer 94:12; Aug 97:9; Apr 99:10; Jun 00:5

(For intracardiac phonocardiogram, use 93799)

⊘ ▲ **93619** Comprehensive electrophysiologic evaluation with right atrial pacing and recording, right ventricular pacing and recording, His bundle recording, including insertion and repositioning of multiple electrode catheters, without induction or attempted induction of arrhythmia
  → *CPT Assistant* Aug 97:9; *CPT Changes* 2002

►(Do not report 93619 in conjunction with codes 93600, 93602, 93610, 93612, 93618, or 93620-93622)◄

⊘ ▲ **93620** Comprehensive electrophysiologic evaluation with right atrial pacing and recording, right ventricular pacing and recording, His bundle recording, including insertion and repositioning of multiple electrode catheters with induction or attempted induction of arrhythmia;
  → *CPT Assistant* Summer 94:12; Aug 97:9; Oct 97:10; Jul 98:10; *CPT Changes* 2002

►(Do not report 93620 in conjunction with codes 93600, 93602, 93610, 93612, 93618 or 93619)◄

+ ▲ **93621** with left atrial pacing and recording from coronary sinus or left atrium (List separately in addition to code for primary procedure)
  → *CPT Assistant* Summer 94:12; Aug 97:9; Oct 97:10; Jul 98:10; Nov 98:34; *CPT Changes* 2002

►(Use 93621 in conjunction with code 93620)◄

+ ▲ **93622** with left ventricular pacing and recording (List separately in addition to code for primary procedure)
  → *CPT Assistant* Summer 94:14; Aug 97:9; Oct 97:10; Jul 98:10; Nov 98:34; *CPT Changes* 2002

►(Use 93622 in conjunction with code 93620)◄

+ **93623** Programmed stimulation and pacing after intravenous drug infusion (List separately in addition to code for primary procedure)
  → *CPT Assistant* Summer 94:14; Aug 97:9

(Use 93623 in conjunction with codes ►93619,◄ 93620)

⊘ **93624** Electrophysiologic follow-up study with pacing and recording to test effectiveness of therapy, including induction or attempted induction of arrhythmia
  → *CPT Assistant* Summer 94:14; Aug 97:9

(93630 has been deleted. To report, use 93631 and 33261)

⊘ **93631** Intra-operative epicardial and endocardial pacing and mapping to localize the site of tachycardia or zone of slow conduction for surgical correction
  → *CPT Assistant* Summer 94:14; Aug 97:9

⊘ **93640** Electrophysiologic evaluation of single or dual chamber pacing cardioverter-defibrillator leads including defibrillation threshold evaluation (induction of arrhythmia, evaluation of sensing and pacing for arrhythmia termination) at time of initial implantation or replacement;
  → *CPT Assistant* Summer 94:14; Aug 97:9; Apr 99:10; Nov 99:50; *CPT Changes* 2000

⊘ **93641** with testing of single or dual chamber pacing cardioverter-defibrillator pulse generator
  → *CPT Assistant* Summer 94:14; Aug 97:9; Apr 99:10; Nov 99:50; Jun 00:5; Jul 00:5; *CPT Changes* 2000

(For subsequent or periodic electronic analysis and/or reprogramming of single or dual chamber pacing cardioverter-defibrillators, see 93642, 93741-93744)

93642 Electrophysiologic evaluation of single or dual chamber pacing cardioverter-defibrillator (includes defibrillation threshold evaluation, induction of arrhythmia, evaluation of sensing and pacing for arrhythmia termination, and programming or reprogramming of sensing or therapeutic parameters)

➲ *CPT Assistant* Summer 94:14; Aug 97:9; Nov 99:50; Jun 00:5; *CPT Changes* 2000

93650 Intracardiac catheter ablation of atrioventricular node function, atrioventricular conduction for creation of complete heart block, with or without temporary pacemaker placement

➲ *CPT Assistant* Summer 94:15; Aug 97:9

93651 Intracardiac catheter ablation of arrhythmogenic focus; for treatment of supraventricular tachycardia by ablation of fast or slow atrioventricular pathways, accessory atrioventricular connections or other atrial foci, singly or in combination

➲ *CPT Assistant* Summer 94:15; Aug 97:9

93652   for treatment of ventricular tachycardia

➲ *CPT Assistant* Summer 94:15; Aug 97:9

93660 Evaluation of cardiovascular function with tilt table evaluation, with continuous ECG monitoring and intermittent blood pressure monitoring, with or without pharmacological intervention

(For testing of autonomic nervous system function, see 95921-95923)

+ 93662 Intracardiac echocardiography during therapeutic/diagnostic intervention, including imaging supervision and interpretation (List separately in addition to code for primary procedure)

➲ *CPT Changes* 2001

(Use 93662 in conjunction with codes 93621, 93622, 93651, or 93652, as appropriate)

(Do not report 92961 in addition to 93662)

Peripheral Arterial Disease Rehabilitation

Peripheral arterial disease (PAD) rehabilitative physical exercise consists of a series of sessions, lasting 45-60 minutes per session, involving use of either a motorized treadmill or a track to permit each patient to achieve symptom-limited claudication. Each session is supervised by an exercise physiologist or nurse. The supervising provider monitors the individual patient's claudication threshold and other cardiovascular limitations for

adjustment of workload. During this supervised rehabilitation program, the development of new arrhythmias, symptoms that might suggest angina or the continued inability of the patient to progress to an adequate level of exercise may require physician review and examination of the patient. These physician services would be separately reported with an appropriate level E/M service code.

93668 Peripheral arterial disease (PAD) rehabilitation, per session

➲ *CPT Changes* 2001

Other Vascular Studies

(For arterial cannulization and recording of direct arterial pressure, use 36620)

(For radiographic injection procedures, see 36000-36299)

(For vascular cannulization for hemodialysis, see 36800-36821)

(For chemotherapy for malignant disease, see 96408-96549)

(For penile plethysmography, use 54240)

(93700 has been deleted)

● 93701 Bioimpedance, thoracic, electrical

➲ *CPT Changes* 2002

(93710 has been deleted)

93720 Plethysmography, total body; with interpretation and report

➲ *CPT Assistant* Mar 99:10

93721   tracing only, without interpretation and report

➲ *CPT Assistant* Mar 99:10

93722   interpretation and report only

➲ *CPT Assistant* Mar 99:10

(For regional plethysmography, see 93875-93931)

93724 Electronic analysis of antitachycardia pacemaker system (includes electrocardiographic recording, programming of device, induction and termination of tachycardia via implanted pacemaker, and interpretation of recordings)

➲ *CPT Assistant* Summer 94:23

(93725-93730 have been deleted. To report, see 93875-93971)

93727 Electronic analysis of implantable loop recorder (ILR) system (includes retrieval of recorded and stored ECG data, physician review and interpretation of retrieved ECG data and reprogramming)

➲ *CPT Assistant* Nov 99:50; Jul 00:5; *CPT Changes* 2000

93731 Electronic analysis of dual-chamber pacemaker system (includes evaluation of programmable parameters at rest and during activity where applicable, using electrocardiographic recording and interpretation of recordings at rest and during exercise, analysis of event markers and device response); without reprogramming
➔ *CPT Assistant* Summer 94:23; Feb 98:11

93732 with reprogramming
➔ *CPT Assistant* Summer 94:23; Feb 98:11; Mar 00:10

93733 Electronic analysis of dual chamber internal pacemaker system (may include rate, pulse amplitude and duration, configuration of wave form, and/or testing of sensory function of pacemaker), telephonic analysis
➔ *CPT Assistant* Summer 94:23

93734 Electronic analysis of single chamber pacemaker system (includes evaluation of programmable parameters at rest and during activity where applicable, using electrocardiographic recording and interpretation of recordings at rest and during exercise, analysis of event markers and device response); without reprogramming
➔ *CPT Assistant* Summer 94:23; Feb 98:11

93735 with reprogramming
➔ *CPT Assistant* Summer 94:23; Feb 98:11

93736 Electronic analysis of single chamber internal pacemaker system (may include rate, pulse amplitude and duration, configuration of wave form, and/or testing of sensory function of pacemaker), telephonic analysis
➔ *CPT Assistant* Summer 94:23

▶(93737 has been deleted. To report, use 93741 or 93743)◀

▶(93738 has been deleted. To report, use 93742 or 93744)◀

93740 Temperature gradient studies

(93750 has been deleted. To report, see 93875-93971)

93741 Electronic analysis of pacing cardioverter-defibrillator (includes interrogation, evaluation of pulse generator status, evaluation of programmable parameters at rest and during activity where applicable, using electrocardiographic recording and interpretation of recordings at rest and during exercise, analysis of event markers and device response); single chamber, without reprogramming
➔ *CPT Assistant* Nov 99:50-51; Jul 00:5; *CPT Changes* 2000

93742 single chamber, with reprogramming
➔ *CPT Assistant* Nov 99:50-51; Jul 00:5; *CPT Changes* 2000

93743 dual chamber, without reprogramming
➔ *CPT Assistant* Nov 99:50-51; Jul 00:5; *CPT Changes* 2000

93744 dual chamber, with reprogramming
➔ *CPT Assistant* Nov 99:50-51; Jul 00:5; *CPT Changes* 2000

93760 Thermogram; cephalic

93762 peripheral

93770 Determination of venous pressure

(For central venous cannulization and pressure measurements, see 36488-36491, 36500)

(93780, 93781 have been deleted)

93784 Ambulatory blood pressure monitoring, utilizing a system such as magnetic tape and/or computer disk, for 24 hours or longer; including recording, scanning analysis, interpretation and report

93786 recording only

93788 scanning analysis with report

93790 physician review with interpretation and report

(93791-93796 have been deleted. To report, see 93731-93736)

Other Procedures

93797 Physician services for outpatient cardiac rehabilitation; without continuous ECG monitoring (per session)

93798 with continuous ECG monitoring (per session)

93799 Unlisted cardiovascular service or procedure
➔ *CPT Assistant* Mar 98:11

Non-Invasive Vascular Diagnostic Studies

Vascular studies include patient care required to perform the studies, supervision of the studies and interpretation of study results with copies for patient records of hard copy output with analysis of all data, including bidirectional vascular flow or imaging when provided.

The use of a simple hand-held or other Doppler device that does not produce hard copy output, or that produces a record that does not permit analysis of bidirectional vascular flow, is considered to be part of the physical examination of the vascular system and is not separately reported.

Duplex scan describes an ultrasonic scanning procedure with display of both two-dimensional structure and motion with time and Doppler ultrasonic signal documentation with spectral analysis and/or color flow velocity mapping or imaging.

⊘ = Modifier '-51' Exempt   ▶ ◀ = New or Revised Text   ✚ = Add-on Code   CPT 2002

Cerebrovascular Arterial Studies

(93850, 93860 have been deleted. To report, see 93875-93882)

(93870 has been deleted. To report, see 93880 and 93882)

93875 Non-invasive physiologic studies of extracranial arteries, complete bilateral study (eg, periorbital flow direction with arterial compression, ocular pneumoplethysmography, Doppler ultrasound spectral analysis)
➔ *CPT Assistant* Jun 96:9; Dec 97:10; Apr 00:1

93880 Duplex scan of extracranial arteries; complete bilateral study
➔ *CPT Assistant* Jun 96:9

93882   unilateral or limited study
➔ *CPT Assistant* Jun 96:9

93886 Transcranial Doppler study of the intracranial arteries; complete study
➔ *CPT Assistant* Jun 96:9

93888   limited study
➔ *CPT Assistant* Jun 96:9

Extremity Arterial Studies (Including Digits)

(93890, 93910 have been deleted. To report, see 93922-93931)

(93920, 93921 have been deleted. To report, see 93922-93924)

93922 Non-invasive physiologic studies of upper or lower extremity arteries, single level, bilateral (eg, ankle/brachial indices, Doppler waveform analysis, volume plethysmography, transcutaneous oxygen tension measurement)
➔ *CPT Assistant* Jun 96:9

93923 Non-invasive physiologic studies of upper or lower extremity arteries, multiple levels or with provocative functional maneuvers, complete bilateral study (eg, segmental blood pressure measurements, segmental Doppler waveform analysis, segmental volume plethysmography, segmental transcutaneous oxygen tension measurements, measurements with postural provocative tests, measurements with reactive hyperemia)
➔ *CPT Assistant* Jun 96:9

93924 Non-invasive physiologic studies of lower extremity arteries, at rest and following treadmill stress testing, complete bilateral study
➔ *CPT Assistant* Jun 96:9

93925 Duplex scan of lower extremity arteries or arterial bypass grafts; complete bilateral study
➔ *CPT Assistant* Jun 96:9

93926   unilateral or limited study
➔ *CPT Assistant* Jun 96:9

93930 Duplex scan of upper extremity arteries or arterial bypass grafts; complete bilateral study
➔ *CPT Assistant* Jun 96:9

93931   unilateral or limited study
➔ *CPT Assistant* Jun 96:9

Extremity Venous Studies (Including Digits)

(93950, 93960 have been deleted. To report, see 93965-93971)

93965 Non-invasive physiologic studies of extremity veins, complete bilateral study (eg, Doppler waveform analysis with responses to compression and other maneuvers, phleborheography, impedance plethysmography)
➔ *CPT Assistant* Jun 96:9

93970 Duplex scan of extremity veins including responses to compression and other maneuvers; complete bilateral study
➔ *CPT Assistant* Jun 96:9

93971   unilateral or limited study
➔ *CPT Assistant* Jun 96:9

Visceral and Penile Vascular Studies

93975 Duplex scan of arterial inflow and venous outflow of abdominal, pelvic, scrotal contents and/or retroperitoneal organs; complete study
➔ *CPT Assistant* Apr 96:11; Jun 96:9

93976   limited study
➔ *CPT Assistant* Apr 96:11; Jun 96:9

93978 Duplex scan of aorta, inferior vena cava, iliac vasculature, or bypass grafts; complete study
➔ *CPT Assistant* Jun 96:9

93979   unilateral or limited study
➔ *CPT Assistant* Jun 96:9

93980 Duplex scan of arterial inflow and venous outflow of penile vessels; complete study
➔ *CPT Assistant* Jun 96:9

93981   follow-up or limited study
➔ *CPT Assistant* Jun 96:9

Extremity Arterial-Venous Studies

93990 Duplex scan of hemodialysis access (including arterial inflow, body of access and venous outflow)
➔ *CPT Assistant* Jun 96:9

(For measurement of hemodialysis access flow using indicator dilution methods, use 90940)

Pulmonary

Items 94010-94799 include laboratory procedure(s) and interpretation of test results. If a separate identifiable Evaluation and Management service is performed, the appropriate E/M service code should be reported in addition to 94010-94799.

➔ *CPT Assistant* Summer 95:4, Feb 96:9, Mar 96:10, Jan 99:8; Feb 99:9

94010 Spirometry, including graphic record, total and timed vital capacity, expiratory flow rate measurement(s), with or without maximal voluntary ventilation

➔ *CPT Assistant* Feb 96:9; Nov 97:45; Nov 98:35; Feb 99:9

94014 Patient-initiated spirometric recording per 30-day period of time; includes reinforced education, transmission of spirometric tracing, data capture, analysis of transmitted data, periodic recalibration and physician review and interpretation

➔ *CPT Assistant* Nov 98:34; Jan 99:8; *CPT Changes* 2000

94015 recording (includes hook-up, reinforced education, data transmission, data capture, trend analysis, and periodic recalibration)

➔ *CPT Assistant* Nov 98:34; Jan 99:8

94016 physician review and interpretation only

➔ *CPT Assistant* Nov 98:34; Jan 99:8

94060 Bronchospasm evaluation: spirometry as in 94010, before and after bronchodilator (aerosol or parenteral)

➔ *CPT Assistant* Feb 96:9; Feb 97:10; Nov 98:34; Jan 99:8; Feb 99:9

(For prolonged exercise test for bronchospasm with pre- and post-spirometry, use 94620)

94070 Prolonged postexposure evaluation of bronchospasm with multiple spirometric determinations after antigen, cold air, methacholine or other chemical agent, with subsequent spirometrics

➔ *CPT Assistant* Feb 96:9; Nov 97:45; Jan 99:8

94150 Vital capacity, total (separate procedure)

➔ *CPT Assistant* Feb 96:9

(94160 has been deleted. For vital capacity measurement only, use 94150. For spirometry with timed expiratory volumes, use 94010)

94200 Maximum breathing capacity, maximal voluntary ventilation

➔ *CPT Assistant* Feb 96:9

94240 Functional residual capacity or residual volume: helium method, nitrogen open circuit method, or other method

➔ *CPT Assistant* Feb 96:9

94250 Expired gas collection, quantitative, single procedure (separate procedure)

➔ *CPT Assistant* Feb 96:9

94260 Thoracic gas volume

➔ *CPT Assistant* Feb 96:9

(For plethysmography, see 93720-93722)

94350 Determination of maldistribution of inspired gas: multiple breath nitrogen washout curve including alveolar nitrogen or helium equilibration time

➔ *CPT Assistant* Feb 96:9

94360 Determination of resistance to airflow, oscillatory or plethysmographic methods

➔ *CPT Assistant* Feb 96:9

94370 Determination of airway closing volume, single breath tests

➔ *CPT Assistant* Feb 96:9

94375 Respiratory flow volume loop

➔ *CPT Assistant* Feb 96:9

94400 Breathing response to CO_2 (CO_2 response curve)

➔ *CPT Assistant* Feb 96:9

94450 Breathing response to hypoxia (hypoxia response curve)

➔ *CPT Assistant* Feb 96:9

94620 Pulmonary stress testing; simple (eg, prolonged exercise test for bronchospasm with pre- and post-spirometry)

➔ *CPT Assistant* Feb 96:9; Nov 98:35; Jan 99:8

94621 complex (including measurements of CO_2 production, O_2 uptake, and electrocardiographic recordings)

➔ *CPT Assistant* Nov 98:35; Jan 99:8

94640 Nonpressurized inhalation treatment for acute airway obstruction

➔ *CPT Assistant* Feb 96:9; May 98:10; Apr 00:11

94642 Aerosol inhalation of pentamidine for pneumocystis carinii pneumonia treatment or prophylaxis

➔ *CPT Assistant* Feb 96:9

94650 Intermittent positive pressure breathing (IPPB) treatment, air or oxygen, with or without nebulized medication; initial demonstration and/or evaluation

➔ *CPT Assistant* Fall 92:30; Feb 96:9; Apr 00:11

94651 subsequent

➔ *CPT Assistant* Fall 92:30; Feb 96:9; Apr 00:11

94652 newborn infants

➔ *CPT Assistant* Fall 92:30; Feb 96:9

94656 Ventilation assist and management, initiation of pressure or volume preset ventilators for assisted or controlled breathing; first day

➔ *CPT Assistant* Fall 92:30; Feb 96:9

94657 subsequent days

➔ *CPT Assistant* Fall 92:30; Feb 96:9

94660 Continuous positive airway pressure ventilation (CPAP), initiation and management

➔ *CPT Assistant* Fall 92:30; Feb 96:9; Jan 99:10

94662 Continuous negative pressure ventilation (CNP), initiation and management

➔ *CPT Assistant* Fall 92:30; Feb 96:9

94664 Aerosol or vapor inhalations for sputum mobilization, bronchodilation, or sputum induction for diagnostic purposes; initial demonstration and/or evaluation

➔ *CPT Assistant* Feb 96:9; May 98:10; Apr 00:11

⊘ =Modifier '-51' Exempt   ▶ ◀ =New or Revised Text   ✚ =Add-on Code   CPT 2002

94665   subsequent
  → *CPT Assistant* Feb 96:9; Apr 00:11

94667   Manipulation chest wall, such as cupping, percussing, and vibration to facilitate lung function; initial demonstration and/or evaluation
  → *CPT Assistant* Feb 96:9

94668   subsequent
  → *CPT Assistant* Feb 96:9

94680   Oxygen uptake, expired gas analysis; rest and exercise, direct, simple
  → *CPT Assistant* Feb 96:9

94681   including CO_2 output, percentage oxygen extracted
  → *CPT Assistant* Feb 96:9

94690   rest, indirect (separate procedure)
  → *CPT Assistant* Feb 96:9

(94700, 94705, 94710 have been deleted. For analysis of arterial blood gas results, see appropriate Evaluation and Management code. For test procedure, see 82800-82810)

(For single arterial puncture, use 36600)

(94715 has been deleted. To report, use 82820)

▲ **94720**   Carbon monoxide diffusing capacity (eg, single breath, steady state)
  → *CPT Assistant* Feb 96:9; *CPT Changes* 2002

94725   Membrane diffusion capacity
  → *CPT Assistant* Feb 96:9

▲ **94750**   Pulmonary compliance study (eg, plethysmography, volume and pressure measurements)
  → *CPT Assistant* Feb 96:9; *CPT Changes* 2002

94760   Noninvasive ear or pulse oximetry for oxygen saturation; single determination
  → *CPT Assistant* Feb 96:9; Feb 97:10; Jul 98:1

(For blood gases, see 82803-82810)

94761   multiple determinations (eg, during exercise)
  → *CPT Assistant* Feb 96:9; Jul 98:1; Jun 99:10

94762   by continuous overnight monitoring (separate procedure)
  → *CPT Assistant* Feb 96:9; Jul 98:1

94770   Carbon dioxide, expired gas determination by infrared analyzer
  → *CPT Assistant* Feb 96:9

(For bronchoscopy, see 31622-31656)

(For placement of flow directed catheter, use 93503)

(For venipuncture, use 36410)

(For central venous catheter placement, see 36488-36491)

(For arterial puncture, use 36600)

(For arterial catheterization, use 36620)

(For thoracentesis, use 32000)

(For phlebotomy, therapeutic, use 99195)

(For lung biopsy, needle, use 32405)

(For intubation, orotracheal or nasotracheal, use 31500)

94772   Circadian respiratory pattern recording (pediatric pneumogram), 12 to 24 hour continuous recording, infant
  → *CPT Assistant* Feb 96:9

(Separate procedure codes for electromyograms, EEG, ECG, and recordings of respiration are excluded when 94772 is reported)

94799   Unlisted pulmonary service or procedure
  → *CPT Assistant* Summer 95:4; Feb 96:9; Mar 96:10

Allergy and Clinical Immunology

Definitions

Allergy sensitivity tests describe the performance and evaluation of selective cutaneous and mucous membrane tests in correlation with the history, physical examination, and other observations of the patient. The number of tests performed should be judicious and dependent upon the history, physical findings, and clinical judgment. All patients should not necessarily receive the same tests nor the same number of sensitivity tests.

Immunotherapy (desensitization, hyposensitization) is the parenteral administration of allergenic extracts as antigens at periodic intervals, usually on an increasing dosage scale to a dosage which is maintained as maintenance therapy. Indications for immunotherapy are determined by appropriate diagnostic procedures coordinated with clinical judgment and knowledge of the natural history of allergic diseases.

Other therapy: for medical conferences on the use of mechanical and electronic devices (precipitators, air conditioners, air filters, humidifiers, dehumidifiers), climatotherapy, physical therapy, occupational and recreational therapy, see **Evaluation and Management** section.

Allergy Testing

(95000-95003 have been deleted. To report, use 95004)

95004   Percutaneous tests (scratch, puncture, prick) with allergenic extracts, immediate type reaction, specify number of tests
  → *CPT Assistant* Summer 91:15

(95005-95007 have been deleted. To report, use 95010)

95010   Percutaneous tests (scratch, puncture, prick) sequential and incremental, with drugs, biologicals or venoms, immediate type reaction, specify number of tests
  → *CPT Assistant* Summer 91:15

(95011 has been deleted. To report, use 95010)

(95014 has been deleted. To report, use 95015)

95015 Intracutaneous (intradermal) tests, sequential and incremental, with drugs, biologicals, or venoms, immediate type reaction, specify number of tests
➔ *CPT Assistant* Summer 91:15

(95016-95018 have been deleted. To report, use 95015)

(95020-95023 have been deleted. To report, use 95024)

95024 Intracutaneous (intradermal) tests with allergenic extracts, immediate type reaction, specify number of tests
➔ *CPT Assistant* Summer 91:15

95027 Skin end point titration
➔ *CPT Assistant* Summer 91:15; Jun 97:10

95028 Intracutaneous (intradermal) tests with allergenic extracts, delayed type reaction, including reading, specify number of tests
➔ *CPT Assistant* Summer 91:14

(95030-95034 have been deleted. To report, use 95028)

(95040-95043 have been deleted. To report, use 95044)

95044 Patch or application test(s) (specify number of tests)
➔ *CPT Assistant* Summer 91:15; Spring 94:31

(95050, 95051 have been deleted. To report, use 95052)

95052 Photo patch test(s) (specify number of tests)
➔ *CPT Assistant* Spring 94:31

95056 Photo tests
➔ *CPT Assistant* Summer 91:16

95060 Ophthalmic mucous membrane tests
➔ *CPT Assistant* Summer 91:16

95065 Direct nasal mucous membrane test
➔ *CPT Assistant* Summer 91:15

95070 Inhalation bronchial challenge testing (not including necessary pulmonary function tests); with histamine, methacholine, or similar compounds
➔ *CPT Assistant* Summer 91:16

95071 with antigens or gases, specify
➔ *CPT Assistant* Summer 91:16

(For pulmonary function tests, see 94060, 94070)

95075 Ingestion challenge test (sequential and incremental ingestion of test items, eg, food, drug or other substance such as metabisulfite)
➔ *CPT Assistant* Summer 91:16

(95077 has been deleted)

95078 Provocative testing (eg, Rinkel test)
➔ *CPT Assistant* Summer 91:16

(95080-95082 have been deleted)

(For allergy laboratory tests, see 86000-86999)

(For intravenous therapy for severe or intractable allergic disease, see 90780, 90781, 90784)

(95105 has been deleted. To report, see appropriate E/M code(s))

Allergen Immunotherapy

Codes 95115-95199 include the professional services necessary for allergen immunotherapy. Office visit codes may be used in addition to allergen immunotherapy if other identifiable services are provided at that time.

95115 Professional services for allergen immunotherapy not including provision of allergenic extracts; single injection
➔ *CPT Assistant* Fall 91:19; Spring 94:30; Summer 95:4; May 96:1; Nov 98:35; Apr 00:4

95117 two or more injections
➔ *CPT Assistant* Fall 91:19; Spring 94:30; May 96:1; Aug 96:10; Nov 98:35; Apr 00:4

95120 Professional services for allergen immunotherapy in prescribing physicians office or institution, including provision of allergenic extract; single injection
➔ *CPT Assistant* Fall 91:19; Spring 94:30; May 96:2; Nov 98:35

95125 two or more injections
➔ *CPT Assistant* Fall 91:19; Spring 94:30; May 96:2; Aug 96:10; Nov 98:35

95130 single stinging insect venom
➔ *CPT Assistant* Fall 91:19; May 96:2; Jun 96:10; Nov 98:35; Sep 99:10

95131 two stinging insect venoms
➔ *CPT Assistant* Fall 91:19; May 96:2; Jun 96:10; Nov 98:35; Sep 99:10

95132 three stinging insect venoms
➔ *CPT Assistant* Fall 91:19; May 96:2; Nov 98:35; Sep 99:11

95133 four stinging insect venoms
➔ *CPT Assistant* Fall 91:19; May 96:2; Nov 98:35; Sep 99:11

95134 five stinging insect venoms
➔ *CPT Assistant* Fall 91:19; May 96:2; Nov 98:35; Sep 99:11

(95135 has been deleted. To report, use 95144)

(95140 has been deleted. To report, use 95144)

▲ **95144** Professional services for the supervision of preparation and provision of antigens for allergen immunotherapy; single dose vial(s) (specify number of vials)
➔ *CPT Assistant* Fall 91:19; Spring 94:30; May 96:10; Nov 98:35; *CPT Changes* 2002

▶(A single dose vial contains a single dose of antigen administered in one injection)◀

▲ **95145** Professional services for the supervision of preparation and provision of antigens for allergen immunotherapy (specify number of doses); single stinging insect venom
➔ *CPT Assistant* Fall 91:19; May 96:1; Nov 98:35; *CPT Changes* 2002

95146 two single stinging insect venoms
➔ *CPT Assistant* Fall 91:19; May 96:11; Nov 98:35

95147 three single stinging insect venoms
➔ *CPT Assistant* Fall 91:19; May 96:11; Nov 98:35

95148 four single stinging insect venoms
➔ *CPT Assistant* Fall 91:19; May 96:11; Nov 98:35

⊘ =Modifier '-51' Exempt   ▶ ◀=New or Revised Text   ✚ =Add-on Code   CPT 2002

95149   five single stinging insect venoms
→ *CPT Assistant* Fall 91:19; May 96:11; Nov 98:35

(95150, 95155 have been deleted. To report, use 95165)

(95160 has been deleted. To report, see 95145-95149)

▲ **95165**   Professional services for the supervision of preparation and provision of antigens for allergen immunotherapy; single or multiple antigens (specify number of doses)
→ *CPT Assistant* Fall 91:19; Spring 94:30; May 96:11; Nov 98:35; Apr 00:4; *CPT Changes* 2002

95170   whole body extract of biting insect or other arthropod (specify number of doses)
→ *CPT Assistant* Fall 91:19; Spring 94:30; May 96:12; Nov 98:35

►(For allergy immunotherapy reporting, a dose is the amount of antigen(s) administered in a single injection from a multiple dose vial)◄

▲ **95180**   Rapid desensitization procedure, each hour (eg, insulin, penicillin, equine serum)
→ *CPT Changes* 2002

95199   Unlisted allergy/clinical immunologic service or procedure
→ *CPT Assistant* Summer 95:4; Nov 98:35

(For skin testing of bacterial, viral, fungal extracts, see 95028, 86485-86586)

(For special reports on allergy patients, use 99080)

(For testing procedures such as radioallergosorbent testing (RAST), rat mast cell technique (RMCT), mast cell degranulation test (MCDT), lymphocytic transformation test (LTT), leukocyte histamine release (LHR), migration inhibitory factor test (MIF), transfer factor test (TFT), nitroblue tetrazolium dye test (NTD), see Immunology section in **Pathology** or use 95199)

►Endocrinology◄

● **95250**   Glucose monitoring for up to 72 hours by continuous recording and storage of glucose values from interstitial tissue fluid via a subcutaneous sensor (includes hook-up, calibration, patient initiation and training, recording, disconnection, downloading with printout of data)
→ *CPT Changes* 2002

►(Do not report 95250 in conjunction with 99091)◄

►(To report physician review, interpretation and written report associated with code 95250, see **Evaluation and Management** services codes)◄

Neurology and Neuromuscular Procedures

Neurologic services are typically consultative, and any of the levels of consultation (99241-99263) may be appropriate.

In addition, services and skills outlined under **Evaluation and Management** levels of service appropriate to neurologic illnesses should be coded similarly.

The EEG, ►autonomic function, and◄ evoked potential services (►95812◄-95829, 95920-►95930◄ and 95950-95962) include ►recording,◄ interpretation ►by a physician,◄ and report. For interpretation only, use modifier '-26'.

►(For repetitive transcranial magnetic stimulation for treatment of clinical depression, use Category III code 0018T)◄

►(Do not report codes 95860-95875 in addition to 96000-96004)◄

Sleep Testing

Sleep studies and polysomnography refer to the continuous and simultaneous monitoring and recording of various physiological and pathophysiological parameters of sleep for 6 or more hours with physician review, interpretation and report. The studies are performed to diagnose a variety of sleep disorders and to evaluate a patient's response to therapies such as nasal continuous positive airway pressure (NCPAP). Polysomnography is distinguished from sleep studies by the inclusion of sleep staging which is defined to include a 1-4 lead electroencephalogram (EEG), an electro-oculogram (EOG), and a submental electromyogram (EMG). Additional parameters of sleep include: 1) ECG; 2) airflow; 3) ventilation and respiratory effort; 4) gas exchange by oximetry, transcutaneous monitoring, or end tidal gas analysis; 5) extremity muscle activity, motor activity-movement; 6) extended EEG monitoring; 7) penile tumescence; 8) gastroesophageal reflux; 9) continuous blood pressure monitoring; 10) snoring; 11) body positions; etc.

►The sleep services (95805-95811) include recording, interpretation and report. For interpretation only, use modifier '-26'.◄

For a study to be reported as polysomnography, sleep must be recorded and staged.

(Report with a '-52' modifier if less than 6 hours of recording or in other cases of reduced services as appropriate)

(For unattended sleep study, use 95806)

95805 Multiple sleep latency or maintenance of wakefulness testing, recording, analysis and interpretation of physiological measurements of sleep during multiple trials to assess sleepiness
➔ *CPT Assistant* Nov 97:45-46; Nov 98:35

95806 Sleep study, simultaneous recording of ventilation, respiratory effort, ECG or heart rate, and oxygen saturation, unattended by a technologist
➔ *CPT Assistant* Aug 98:10; Nov 97:45-46; Nov 98:35

95807 Sleep study, simultaneous recording of ventilation, respiratory effort, ECG or heart rate, and oxygen saturation, attended by a technologist
➔ *CPT Assistant* Nov 97:46; Nov 98:35

95808 Polysomnography; sleep staging with 1-3 additional parameters of sleep, attended by a technologist
➔ *CPT Assistant* Sep 96:11; Nov 97:46; Feb 98:6; Nov 98:35

95810 sleep staging with 4 or more additional parameters of sleep, attended by a technologist
➔ *CPT Assistant* Feb 98:6; Nov 98:35

95811 sleep staging with 4 or more additional parameters of sleep, with initiation of continuous positive airway pressure therapy or bilevel ventilation, attended by a technologist
➔ *CPT Assistant* Nov 97:46; Feb 98:6; Nov 98:35

95812 Electroencephalogram (EEG) extended monitoring; up to one hour
➔ *CPT Assistant* Winter 94:18; Nov 98:35

95813 greater than one hour
➔ *CPT Assistant* Winter 94:18; Nov 98:35

95816 Electroencephalogram (EEG) including recording awake and drowsy (including hyperventilation and/or photic stimulation when appropriate)
➔ *CPT Assistant* Sep 96:11; Nov 98:35; Nov 99:51; Jul 00:1; *CPT Changes* 2000

(For extended EEG monitoring, see 95812, 95813)

(95817 has been deleted. To report, use 95816)

95819 Electroencephalogram (EEG) including recording awake and asleep (including hyperventilation and/or photic stimulation when appropriate)
➔ *CPT Assistant* Nov 98:35; Nov 99:51; Jul 00:1; *CPT Changes* 2000

(For extended EEG monitoring, see 95812, 95813)

(For digital analysis of EEG, use 95957)

(95821 has been deleted. To report, use 95819)

95822 Electroencephalogram (EEG); sleep only
➔ *CPT Assistant* Nov 98:35

(For extended EEG monitoring, see 95812, 95813)

(95823 has been deleted. To report, use 95954)

95824 cerebral death evaluation only
➔ *CPT Assistant* Nov 98:35

(95826 has been deleted. To report, use 95829, 95951 or 95956)

95827 all night sleep only
➔ *CPT Assistant* Nov 98:35

(For ambulatory 24-hour EEG monitoring, use 95950)

(For EEG during nonintracranial surgery, use 95955)

(For Wada activation test, use 95958)

(95828 has been deleted. To report, see 95807-95810)

(For recording of circadian respiratory patterns of infants, use 94772)

95829 Electrocorticogram at surgery (separate procedure)
➔ *CPT Assistant* Nov 98:35

95830 Insertion by physician of sphenoidal electrodes for electroencephalographic (EEG) recording

95831 Muscle testing, manual (separate procedure) with report; extremity (excluding hand) or trunk
➔ *CPT Assistant* Nov 99:51; Dec 99:10; Mar 00:11; Jul 00:1; *CPT Changes* 2000

95832 hand, with or without comparison with normal side
➔ *CPT Assistant* Nov 99:51; Dec 99:10; Mar 00:11; Jul 00:1

95833 total evaluation of body, excluding hands
➔ *CPT Assistant* Nov 99:51; Dec 99:10

95834 total evaluation of body, including hands
➔ *CPT Assistant* Nov 99:51; Dec 99:10; Jul 00:1

(95842 has been deleted. To report, use 95999)

95851 Range of motion measurements and report (separate procedure); each extremity (excluding hand) or each trunk section (spine)
➔ *CPT Assistant* Sep 99:10

95852 hand, with or without comparison with normal side

95857 Tensilon test for myasthenia gravis;

95858 with electromyographic recording

95860 Needle electromyography, one extremity with or without related paraspinal areas
➔ *CPT Assistant* Nov 97:46; Jul 00:1

95861 Needle electromyography, two extremities with or without related paraspinal areas
➔ *CPT Assistant* Nov 97:46; Jul 00:1

▶(For dynamic electromyography performed during motion analysis studies, see 96002-96003)◄

95863 Needle electromyography, three extremities with or without related paraspinal areas
➔ *CPT Assistant* Nov 97:46; Jul 00:1

95864 Needle electromyography, four extremities with or without related paraspinal areas
➔ *CPT Assistant* Nov 97:46; Jul 00:1

95867 Needle electromyography, cranial nerve supplied muscles, unilateral

95868 Needle electromyography, cranial nerve supplied muscles, bilateral

95869 Needle electromyography; thoracic paraspinal muscles
➲ *CPT Assistant* Nov 97:46

95870 limited study of muscles in one extremity or non-limb (axial) muscles (unilateral or bilateral), other than thoracic paraspinal, cranial nerve supplied muscles, or sphincters
➲ *CPT Assistant* Nov 97:46; Nov 99:51; Jul 00:1; *CPT Changes* 2000

(To report a complete study of the extremities, see 95860-95864)

(For needle electromyography of cranial supplied muscles, see 95867, 95868)

(For anal or urethral sphincter, detrusor, urethra, perineum musculature, see 51785-51792)

(For eye muscles, use 92265)

95872 Needle electromyography using single fiber electrode, with quantitative measurement of jitter, blocking and/or fiber density, any/all sites of each muscle studied

▲ **95875** Ischemic limb exercise test with serial specimen(s) acquisition for muscle metabolite(s)
➲ *CPT Changes* 2002

(95880 has been deleted. To report, use 96105)

(95881 has been deleted. To report, use 96111)

(95882 has been deleted. To report, use 96115)

(95883 has been deleted. To report, use 96117)

▶Nerve Conduction Studies◀

⊘ **95900** Nerve conduction, amplitude and latency/velocity study, each nerve; motor, without F-wave study
➲ *CPT Assistant* Jan 96:2; Nov 99:51-52; Jan 00:10; Jul 00:1; *CPT Changes* 2000

⊘ **95903** motor, with F-wave study
➲ *CPT Assistant* Jan 96:2; Nov 99:51-52; Jan 00:10

⊘ ▲ **95904** sensory
➲ *CPT Assistant* Jan 96:2; Sep 99:11; Nov 99:51-52; *CPT Changes* 2002

(Report 95900, 95903, and/or 95904 only once when multiple sites on the same nerve are stimulated or recorded)

+ **95920** Intraoperative neurophysiology testing, per hour (List separately in addition to code for primary procedure)
➲ *CPT Assistant* Nov 98:35-36; Nov 99:52

(Use code 95920 in conjunction with the study performed, 92585, 95822, 95860, 95861, 95867, 95868, 95900, 95904, 95925, 95926, 95927, 95930, 95933, 95934, 95936, 95937)

▶(Code 95920 describes ongoing electrophysiologic testing and monitoring performed during surgical procedures. Code 95920 is reported per hour of service, and includes only the ongoing electrophysiologic monitoring time distinct from performance of specific type(s) of baseline electrophysiologic study(ies) (95860, 95861, 95867, 95868, 95900, 95904, 95933, 95934, 95936, 95937) or interpretation of specific type(s) of baseline electrophysiologic study(ies) (92585, 95822, 95925, 95926, 95927, 95930). The time spent performing or interpreting the baseline electrophysiologic study(ies) should not be counted as intraoperative monitoring, but represents separately reportable procedures. Code 95920 should be used once per hour even if multiple electrophysiologic studies are performed. The baseline electrophysiologic study(ies) should be used once per operative session.)◀

95921 Testing of autonomic nervous system function; cardiovagal innervation (parasympathetic function), including two or more of the following: heart rate response to deep breathing with recorded R-R interval, Valsalva ratio, and 30:15 ratio
➲ *CPT Assistant* Nov 98:35-36

95922 vasomotor adrenergic innervation (sympathetic adrenergic function), including beat-to-beat blood pressure and R-R interval changes during Valsalva maneuver and at least five minutes of passive tilt
➲ *CPT Assistant* Nov 98:35-36

95923 sudomotor, including one or more of the following: quantitative sudomotor axon reflex test (QSART), silastic sweat imprint, thermoregulatory sweat test, and changes in sympathetic skin potential
➲ *CPT Assistant* Nov 98:35-36

95925 Short-latency somatosensory evoked potential study, stimulation of any/all peripheral nerves or skin sites, recording from the central nervous system; in upper limbs
➲ *CPT Assistant* Nov 98:35-36

95926 in lower limbs

95927 in the trunk or head

(To report a unilateral study, use modifier '-52')

(For visual evoked potentials, use 95930)

(For brainstem evoked response recording, use 92585)

(For auditory evoked potentials, use 92585)

95930 Visual evoked potential (VEP) testing central nervous system, checkerboard or flash

95933 Orbicularis oculi (blink) reflex, by electrodiagnostic testing
➲ *CPT Assistant* Nov 98:35-36

95934 H-reflex, amplitude and latency study; record gastrocnemius/soleus muscle
➲ *CPT Assistant* Jan 96:3; Nov 98:35-36

(95935 has been deleted. To report, see 95903, 95934, 95936)
➲ *CPT Assistant* Nov 98:35-36

95936 record muscle other than gastrocnemius/soleus muscle

➲ *CPT Assistant* Jan 96:3

(To report a bilateral study, use modifier '-50')

95937 Neuromuscular junction testing (repetitive stimulation, paired stimuli), each nerve, any one method

➲ *CPT Assistant* Nov 98:35-36

95950 Monitoring for identification and lateralization of cerebral seizure focus, electroencephalographic (eg, 8 channel EEG) recording and interpretation, each 24 hours

➲ *CPT Assistant* Nov 98:35

95951 Monitoring for localization of cerebral seizure focus by cable or radio, 16 or more channel telemetry, combined electroencephalographic (EEG) and video recording and interpretation (eg, for presurgical localization), each 24 hours

➲ *CPT Assistant* Nov 98:35

(95952 has been deleted. To report, use 95950)

95953 Monitoring for localization of cerebral seizure focus by computerized portable 16 or more channel EEG, electroencephalographic (EEG) recording and interpretation, each 24 hours

➲ *CPT Assistant* Nov 98:35

95954 Pharmacological or physical activation requiring physician attendance during EEG recording of activation phase (eg, thiopental activation test)

➲ *CPT Assistant* Winter 94:18; Nov 98:35

(For digital analysis of EEG, use 95957)

95955 Electroencephalogram (EEG) during nonintracranial surgery (eg, carotid surgery)

➲ *CPT Assistant* Nov 98:35

95956 Monitoring for localization of cerebral seizure focus by cable or radio, 16 or more channel telemetry, electroencephalographic (EEG) recording and interpretation, each 24 hours

➲ *CPT Assistant* Nov 98:35

95957 Digital analysis of electroencephalogram (EEG) (eg, for epileptic spike analysis)

➲ *CPT Assistant* Winter 94:18; Nov 98:35

95958 Wada activation test for hemispheric function, including electroencephalographic (EEG) monitoring

➲ *CPT Assistant* Nov 98:35

95961 Functional cortical and subcortical mapping by stimulation and/or recording of electrodes on brain surface, or of depth electrodes, to provoke seizures or identify vital brain structures; initial hour of physician attendance

➲ *CPT Assistant* Winter 94:18; Nov 98:35; Nov 99:52-53; *CPT Changes* 2000

+ 95962 each additional hour of physician attendance (List separately in addition to code for primary procedure)

➲ *CPT Assistant* Winter 94:18; Nov 98:35; Nov 99:52-53

(Use 95962 in conjunction with code 95961)

● **95965** Magnetoencephalography (MEG), recording and analysis; for spontaneous brain magnetic activity (eg, epileptic cerebral cortex localization)

➲ *CPT Changes* 2002

● **95966** for evoked magnetic fields, single modality (eg, sensory, motor, language, or visual cortex localization)

➲ *CPT Changes* 2002

+ ● 95967 for evoked magnetic fields, each additional modality (eg, sensory, motor, language, or visual cortex localization) (List separately in addition to code for primary procedure)

➲ *CPT Changes* 2002

▶(Use 95967 in conjunction with code 95966)◀

▶(For electroencephalography performed in addition to magnetoencephalography, see 95812-95827)◀

▶(For somatosensory evoked potentials, auditory evoked potentials, and visual evoked potentials performed in addition to magnetic evoked field responses, see 92585, 95925, 95926, and/or 95930)◀

▶(For computerized tomography performed in addition to magnetoencephalography, see 70450-70470, 70496)◀

▶(For magnetic resonance imaging performed in addition to magnetoencephalography, see 70551-70553)◀

Neurostimulators, Analysis-Programming

A simple neurostimulator pulse generator/transmitter (95970, 95971) is one capable of affecting 3 or fewer of the following: pulse amplitude, pulse duration, pulse frequency, 8 or more electrode contacts, cycling, stimulation train duration, train spacing, number of programs, number of channels, alternating electrode polarities, ▶dose time (stimulation parameters changing in time periods of minutes including dose lockout times),◀ more than 1 clinical feature (eg, rigidity, dyskinesia, tremor). A complex neurostimulator pulse generator/transmitter (95970, 95972, 95973, 95974, 95975) is one capable of affecting more than 3 of the above.

Code 95970 describes subsequent electronic analysis of a previously-implanted simple or complex brain, spinal cord, or peripheral neurostimulator pulse generator system, without reprogramming. Code 95971 describes intraoperative or subsequent electronic analysis of an implanted simple brain, spinal cord, or peripheral (ie, peripheral nerve, autonomic nerve, neuromuscular) neurostimulator pulse generator system, with programming. Codes 95972 and 95973 describe intraoperative (at initial insertion/revision) or subsequent electronic analysis of an implanted complex brain, spinal cord or peripheral (except cranial nerve) neurostimulator pulse generator system, with programming. Codes 95974 and 95975 describe intraoperative (at initial insertion/

⊘ = Modifier '-51' Exempt   ▶ ◀ = New or Revised Text   ✚ = Add-on Code   CPT 2002

revision) or subsequent electronic analysis of an implanted complex cranial nerve neurostimulator pulse generator system, with programming.

> (For insertion of neurostimulator pulse generator, see 61885, 63685, 63688, 64590)

> (For revision or removal of neurostimulator pulse generator or receiver, see 61888, 63688, 64595)

> (For implantation of neurostimulator electrodes, see 61850-61875, 63650-63655, 64553-64580. For revision or removal of neurostimulator electrodes, see 61880, 63660, 64585)

95970 Electronic analysis of implanted neurostimulator pulse generator system (eg, rate, pulse amplitude and duration, configuration of wave form, battery status, electrode selectability, output modulation, cycling, impedance and patient compliance measurements); simple or complex brain, spinal cord, or peripheral (ie, cranial nerve, peripheral nerve, autonomic nerve, neuromuscular) neurostimulator pulse generator/transmitter, without reprogramming

> *CPT Assistant* Nov 98: 36-37; Sep 99:1; Nov 99:53-54; *CPT Changes* 2000

95971 simple brain, spinal cord, or peripheral (ie, peripheral nerve, autonomic nerve, neuromuscular) neurostimulator pulse generator/transmitter, with intraoperative or subsequent programming

> *CPT Assistant* Nov 98: 36-37; Sep 99:1; Nov 99:53-54; *CPT Changes* 2000

95972 complex brain, spinal cord, or peripheral (except cranial nerve) neurostimulator pulse generator/transmitter, with intraoperative or subsequent programming, first hour

> *CPT Assistant* Nov 98: 36-37; Sep 99:1; Nov 99:53-54; *CPT Changes* 2000

+ 95973 complex brain, spinal cord, or peripheral (except cranial nerve) neurostimulator pulse generator/transmitter, with intraoperative or subsequent programming, each additional 30 minutes after first hour (List separately in addition to code for primary procedure)

> *CPT Assistant* Nov 98: 36-37; Sep 99:1; Nov 99:53-54; *CPT Changes* 2000

(Use 95973 in conjunction with code 95972)

95974 complex cranial nerve neurostimulator pulse generator/transmitter, with intraoperative or subsequent programming, with or without nerve interface testing, first hour

> *CPT Assistant* Nov 98: 36-37; Sep 99:1; Nov 99:53-54

95975 complex cranial nerve neurostimulator pulse generator/transmitter, with intraoperative or subsequent programming, each additional 30 minutes after first hour (List separately in addition to code for primary procedure)

> *CPT Assistant* Nov 98: 36-37; Sep 99:1; Nov 99:53-54

(Use 95975 in conjunction with code 95974)

Other Procedures

95999 Unlisted neurological or neuromuscular diagnostic procedure

> *CPT Assistant* Feb 99:11

▶Motion Analysis◀

▶Codes 96000-96004 describe services performed as part of a major therapeutic or diagnostic decision making process. Motion analysis is performed in a dedicated motion analysis laboratory (ie, a facility capable of performing videotaping from the front, back and both sides, computerized 3-D kinematics, 3-D kinetics, and dynamic electromyography). Code 96000 may include 3-D kinetics and stride characteristics. Codes 96002-96003 describe dynamic electromyography. Do not report codes 95860-95875 in addition to the motion analysis codes.◀

▶Code 96004 should only be reported once regardless of the number of study(ies) reviewed/interpreted.◀

> ▶(For performance of needle electromyography procedures, see 95860-95875)◀

> ▶(For gait training, use 97116)◀

● **96000** Comprehensive computer-based motion analysis by video-taping and 3-D kinematics;

> *CPT Changes* 2002

● **96001** with dynamic plantar pressure measurements during walking

> *CPT Changes* 2002

● **96002** Dynamic surface electromyography, during walking or other functional activities, 1-12 muscles

> *CPT Changes* 2002

● **96003** Dynamic fine wire electromyography, during walking or other functional activities, 1 muscle

> *CPT Changes* 2002

> ▶(Do not report codes 95860-95875 in addition to 96002, 96003)◀

● **96004** Physician review and interpretation of comprehensive computer based motion analysis, dynamic plantar pressure measurements, dynamic surface electromyography during walking or other functional activities, and dynamic fine wire electromyography, with written report

> *CPT Changes* 2002

Central Nervous System Assessments/Tests (eg, Neuro-Cognitive, Mental Status, Speech Testing)

The following codes are used to report the services provided during testing of the cognitive function of the central nervous system. The testing of cognitive processes, visual motor responses, and abstractive abilities is accomplished by the combination of several types of testing procedures. It is expected that the administration of these tests will generate material that will be formulated into a report.

(For development of cognitive skills, see 97532, 97533)

96100 Psychological testing (includes psychodiagnostic assessment of personality, psychopathology, emotionality, intellectual abilities, eg, WAIS-R, Rorschach, MMPI) with interpretation and report, per hour
➔ *CPT Assistant* Jul 96:8

96105 Assessment of aphasia (includes assessment of expressive and receptive speech and language function, language comprehension, speech production ability, reading, spelling, writing, eg, by Boston Diagnostic Aphasia Examination) with interpretation and report, per hour
➔ *CPT Assistant* Jul 96:8

96110 Developmental testing; limited (eg, Developmental Screening Test II, Early Language Milestone Screen), with interpretation and report
➔ *CPT Assistant* Jul 96:9

96111 extended (includes assessment of motor, language, social, adaptive and/or cognitive functioning by standardized developmental instruments, eg, Bayley Scales of Infant Development) with interpretation and report, per hour
➔ *CPT Assistant* Jul 96:9

96115 Neurobehavioral status exam (clinical assessment of thinking, reasoning and judgment, eg, acquired knowledge, attention, memory, visual spatial abilities, language functions, planning) with interpretation and report, per hour
➔ *CPT Assistant* Jul 96:9; Oct 00:7

▶(For mini-mental status examination performed by a physician, see **Evaluation and Management** services codes)◀

96117 Neuropsychological testing battery (eg, Halstead-Reitan, Luria, WAIS-R) with interpretation and report, per hour
➔ *CPT Assistant* Jul 96:9

▶Health and Behavior Assessment/Intervention◀

▶Health and behavior assessment procedures are used to identify the psychological, behavioral, emotional, cognitive, and social factors important to the prevention, treatment, or management of physical health problems. The focus of the assessment is not on mental health but on the biopsychosocial factors important to physical health problems and treatments.◀

▶Health and behavior intervention procedures are used to modify the psychological, behavioral, emotional, cognitive, and social factors identified as important to or directly affecting the patient's physiological functioning, disease status, health, and well being. The focus of the intervention is to improve the patient's health and well being utilizing cognitive, behavioral, social, and/or psychophysiological procedures designed to ameliorate specific disease-related problems.◀

▶Codes 96150-96155 describe services associated with an acute or chronic illness (not meeting criteria for psychiatric diagnosis), prevention of a physical illness or disability, and maintenance of health, not meeting criteria for a psychiatric diagnosis, or representing a preventive medicine service.◀

▶For patients that require psychiatric services (90801-90899) as well as health and behavior assessment/intervention (96150-96155), report the predominant service performed. Do not report codes 96150-96155 in addition to codes 90801-90899 on the same date.◀

▶**Evaluation and Management** services codes should not be reported on the same day.◀

● **96150** Health and behavior assessment (eg, health-focused clinical interview, behavioral observations, psychophysicological monitoring, health-oriented questionnaires), each 15 minutes face-to-face with the patient; initial assessment
➔ *CPT Changes* 2002

● **96151** re-assessment
➔ *CPT Changes* 2002

● **96152** Health and behavior intervention, each 15 minutes, face-to-face; individual
➔ *CPT Changes* 2002

● **96153** group (2 or more patients)
➔ *CPT Changes* 2002

● **96154** family (with the patient present)
➔ *CPT Changes* 2002

● **96155** family (without the patient present)
➔ *CPT Changes* 2002

▶(For health and behavior assessment and/or intervention performed by a physician, see **Evaluation and Management** or **Preventive Medicine** services codes)◀

Chemotherapy Administration

Procedures 96400-96549 are independent of the patient's visit.

If a signficant separately identifiable Evaluation and Management service is performed, the appropriate E/M service code should be reported in addition to 96400-96549.

Either may occur independently on any date of service, or they may occur sequentially on the same day.

Preparation of chemotherapy agent(s) is included in the service for administration of the agent.

Regional (isolation) chemotherapy perfusion should be reported using the codes for arterial infusion ▶(96420-96425).◀ Placement of the intra-arterial catheter should be reported using the appropriate code from the **Cardiovascular Surgery** section. ▶Placement of arterial and venous cannula(s) for extracorporeal circulation via a membrane oxygenator perfusion pump should be reported using code 36823. Code 36823 includes dose calculation and administration of the chemotherapy agent by injection into the perfusate. Do not report code(s) 96408-96425 in conjunction with code 36823.◀

Report separate codes for each parenteral method of administration employed when chemotherapy is administered by different techniques. Medications (eg, antibiotics, steroidal agents, antiemetics, narcotics, analgesics, biological agents) administered independently or sequentially as supportive management of chemotherapy administration, should be separately reported using 90780-90788, as appropriate.

96400   Chemotherapy administration, subcutaneous or intramuscular, with or without local anesthesia
  ➔ *CPT Assistant* Aug 97:19

96405   Chemotherapy administration, intralesional; up to and including 7 lesions
  ➔ *CPT Assistant* Sep 96:5; Aug 97:19

96406   more than 7 lesions
  ➔ *CPT Assistant* Sep 96:5; Aug 97:19

96408   Chemotherapy administration, intravenous; push technique
  ➔ *CPT Assistant* Aug 97:19

96410   infusion technique, up to one hour
  ➔ *CPT Assistant* Dec 96:10; Aug 97:19

+ 96412   infusion technique, one to 8 hours, each additional hour (List separately in addition to code for primary procedure)
  ➔ *CPT Assistant* Dec 96:10; Aug 97:19

  (Use 96412 in conjunction with code 96410)

96414   infusion technique, initiation of prolonged infusion (more than 8 hours), requiring the use of a portable or implantable pump
  ➔ *CPT Assistant* Aug 97:19

  (For pump or reservoir refilling, see 96520, 96530)

96420   Chemotherapy administration, intra-arterial; push technique
  ➔ *CPT Assistant* Aug 97:19; Nov 98:37; Nov 99:54

96422   infusion technique, up to one hour
  ➔ *CPT Assistant* Dec 96:10; Aug 97:19; Nov 98:37

+ 96423   infusion technique, one to 8 hours, each additional hour (List separately in addition to code for primary procedure)
  ➔ *CPT Assistant* Dec 96:10; Nov 98:37

  (Use 96423 in conjunction with code 96422)

  (For regional chemotherapy perfusion ▶via membrane oxygenator perfusion pump◀ to an extremity, use 36823)

96425   infusion technique, initiation of prolonged infusion (more than 8 hours), requiring the use of a portable or implantable pump
  ➔ *CPT Assistant* Nov 99:54

  (For implanted pump or reservoir refilling, see 96520, 96530)

96440   Chemotherapy administration into pleural cavity, requiring and including thoracentesis

96445   Chemotherapy administration into peritoneal cavity, requiring and including peritoneocentesis

▲**96450**   Chemotherapy administration, into CNS (eg, intrathecal), requiring and including spinal puncture
  ➔ *CPT Changes* 2002

  (For intravesical (bladder) chemotherapy administration, use 51720)

  (For insertion of subarachnoid catheter and reservoir for infusion of drug, see 62350, 62351, 62360, 62361, 62362; for insertion of intraventricular catheter and reservoir, see 61210, 61215)

  (96500-96512 have been deleted. To report, see 96408-96414)

96520   Refilling and maintenance of portable pump

  (96524, 96526 have been deleted. To report, see 96420-96425)

96530   Refilling and maintenance of implantable pump or reservoir
  ➔ *CPT Assistant* Spring 93:13; Aug 97:19

  (For collection of blood specimen from a partially or completely implantable venous access device, use 36540)

  (96535 has been deleted. To report, see 96440, 96445)

  (96540 has been deleted. To report, use 96542)

96542   Chemotherapy injection, subarachnoid or intraventricular via subcutaneous reservoir, single or multiple agents
  ➔ *CPT Assistant* Aug 97:19

96545   Provision of chemotherapy agent
  ➔ *CPT Assistant* Aug 97:19; Oct 99:11

  (For radioactive isotope therapy, see 79000-79999)

96549   Unlisted chemotherapy procedure
➔ *CPT Assistant* Aug 97:19

Photodynamic Therapy

● **96567**   Photodynamic therapy by external application of light to destroy premalignant and/or malignant lesions of the skin and adjacent mucosa (eg, lip) by activation of photosensitive drug(s), each phototherapy exposure session
➔ *CPT Changes* 2002

(96570, 96571 are to be used in addition to bronchoscopy, endoscopy codes)

(To report ocular photodynamic therapy, use 67221)

+ **96570**   Photodynamic therapy by endoscopic application of light to ablate abnormal tissue via activation of photosensitive drug(s); first 30 minutes (List separately in addition to code for endoscopy or bronchoscopy procedures of lung and esophagus)
➔ *CPT Assistant* Nov 99:54; Sep 00:5; *CPT Changes* 2000

+ **96571**   each additional 15 minutes (List separately in addition to code for endoscopy or bronchoscopy procedures of lung and esophagus)
➔ *CPT Assistant* Nov 99:54; Sep 00:5; *CPT Changes* 2000

(Use 96570, 96571 in conjunction with codes 31641, 43228 as appropriate)

Special Dermatological Procedures

Dermatologic services are typically consultative, and any of the five levels of consultation (99241-99263) may be appropriate.

In addition, services and skills outlined under **Evaluation and Management** levels of service appropriate to dermatologic illnesses should be coded similarly.

(For intralesional injections, see 11900, 11901)

(For Tzanck smear, use 87207)

96900   Actinotherapy (ultraviolet light)

96902   Microscopic examination of hairs plucked or clipped by the examiner (excluding hair collected by the patient) to determine telogen and anagen counts, or structural hair shaft abnormality
➔ *CPT Assistant* Nov 97:46-47

96910   Photochemotherapy; tar and ultraviolet B (Goeckerman treatment) or petrolatum and ultraviolet B

96912   psoralens and ultraviolet A (PUVA)

96913   Photochemotherapy (Goeckerman and/or PUVA) for severe photoresponsive dermatoses requiring at least four to eight hours of care under direct supervision of the physician (includes application of medication and dressings)

96999   Unlisted special dermatological service or procedure

Physical Medicine and Rehabilitation

(For muscle testing, range of joint motion, electromyography, see 95831 et seq)

(For biofeedback training by EMG, use 90901)

(For transcutaneous nerve stimulation (TNS), use 64550)

(97000 has been deleted. To report, see 97010-97039)

97001   Physical therapy evaluation
➔ *CPT Assistant* Nov 97:47; Feb 00:11

97002   Physical therapy re-evaluation
➔ *CPT Assistant* Nov 97:47; Feb 00:11

97003   Occupational therapy evaluation
➔ *CPT Assistant* Nov 97:47

97004   Occupational therapy re-evaluation
➔ *CPT Assistant* Nov 97:47

● **97005**   Athletic training evaluation
➔ *CPT Changes* 2002

● **97006**   Athletic training re-evaluation
➔ *CPT Changes* 2002

Modalities

Any physical agent applied to produce therapeutic changes to biologic tissue; includes but not limited to thermal, acoustic, light, mechanical, or electric energy.

Supervised

The application of a modality that does not require direct (one-on-one) patient contact by the provider.

97010   Application of a modality to one or more areas; hot or cold packs
➔ *CPT Assistant* Summer 95:5; Apr 96:10; Nov 97:47; Dec 98:1

97012   traction, mechanical
➔ *CPT Assistant* Summer 95:5; Nov 97:47; Dec 98:1

97014   electrical stimulation (unattended)
➔ *CPT Assistant* Summer 95:5; Nov 97:47; May 98:10; Dec 98:1

(For acupuncture with electrical stimulation, use 97781)

97016   vasopneumatic devices
➔ *CPT Assistant* Summer 95:6; Dec 98:1

97018   paraffin bath
➔ *CPT Assistant* Summer 95:6; Dec 98:1

97020   microwave
➔ *CPT Assistant* Summer 95:6; Dec 98:1

97022   whirlpool
➔ *CPT Assistant* Summer 95:6; May 98:10; Dec 98:1

97024   diathermy
➔ *CPT Assistant* Summer 95:6; Dec 98:1

97026   infrared
➔ *CPT Assistant* Summer 95:6; Dec 98:1

97028   ultraviolet
➔ *CPT Assistant* Summer 95:6; Apr 96:11; Dec 98:1

Constant Attendance

The application of a modality that requires direct (one-on-one) patient contact by the provider.

97032   Application of a modality to one or more areas; electrical stimulation (manual), each 15 minutes
➔ *CPT Assistant* Summer 95:6; Dec 98:1

97033   iontophoresis, each 15 minutes
➔ *CPT Assistant* Summer 95:7; Dec 98:1

97034   contrast baths, each 15 minutes
➔ *CPT Assistant* Summer 95:7; Dec 98:1

97035   ultrasound, each 15 minutes
➔ *CPT Assistant* Summer 95:7; Sep 96:10; Dec 98:1

97036   Hubbard tank, each 15 minutes
➔ *CPT Assistant* Summer 95:7; Dec 98:1

97039   Unlisted modality (specify type and time if constant attendance)
➔ *CPT Assistant* Summer 95:7; May 98:10; Dec 98:1; Jan 00:10

Therapeutic Procedures

A manner of effecting change through the application of clinical skills and/or services that attempt to improve function.

Physician or therapist required to have direct (one-on-one) patient contact.

(97100 has been deleted. To report, see 97110-97139)

(97101 has been deleted. To report, see 97110-97139)

97110   Therapeutic procedure, one or more areas, each 15 minutes; therapeutic exercises to develop strength and endurance, range of motion and flexibility
➔ *CPT Assistant* Summer 95:7; Nov 98:37; Dec 99:11

▲ **97112**   neuromuscular reeducation of movement, balance, coordination, kinesthetic sense, posture, and/or proprioception for sitting and/or standing activities
➔ *CPT Assistant* Summer 95:7; *CPT Changes* 2002

97113   aquatic therapy with therapeutic exercises
➔ *CPT Assistant* Summer 95:7

(97114 has been deleted. To report, use 97530)

97116   gait training (includes stair climbing)
➔ *CPT Assistant* Summer 95:8; Sep 96:7

▶(Use 96000-96003 to report comprehensive gait and motion analysis procedures)◀

(97118 has been deleted. To report, use 97032)

(97120 has been deleted. To report, use 97033)

(97122 has been deleted. To report, use 97140)

97124   massage, including effleurage, petrissage and/or tapotement (stroking, compression, percussion)
➔ *CPT Assistant* Summer 95:8; May 96:10; Dec 99:7

(For myofascial release, use 97140)

(97126 has been deleted. To report, use 97034)

(97128 has been deleted. To report, use 97035)

97139   Unlisted therapeutic procedure (specify)
➔ *CPT Assistant* Summer 95:8

97140   Manual therapy techniques (eg, mobilization/manipulation, manual lymphatic drainage, manual traction), one or more regions, each 15 minutes
➔ *CPT Assistant* Nov 98:37; Feb 99:10; Mar 99:1; Jul 99:11; Dec 99:7

(97145 has been deleted. To report, see 97110-97139)

97150   Therapeutic procedure(s), group (2 or more individuals)
➔ *CPT Assistant* Summer 95:8; Dec 96:10; Feb 97:10; Oct 99:10; Nov 99:54-55; Dec 99:11

(Report 97150 for each member of group)

(Group therapy procedures involve constant attendance of the physician or therapist, but by definition do not require one-on-one patient contact by the physician or therapist)

(97200, 97201 have been deleted. To report, see 97010-97039, 97110-97139)

(97220, 97221 have been deleted. To report, use 97036)

(97240, 97241 have been deleted. To report, see 97036, 97113)

(97250 has been deleted. To report, use 97140)

(97260, 97261 have been deleted. To report, use 97140)

(97265 has been deleted. To report, use 97140)

(For manipulation under general anesthesia, see appropriate anatomic section in **Musculoskeletal System**)

(For osteopathic manipulative treatment (OMT), see 98925-98929)

(97500, 97501 have been deleted. To report, use 97504)

▲**97504** Orthotic(s) fitting and training, upper extremity(ies), lower extremity(ies), and/or trunk, each 15 minutes
→ *CPT Changes* 2002

(Code 97504 should not be reported with 97116)

(For casting and strapping of fracture, injury or dislocation, see 29000, 29590)

97520 Prosthetic training, upper and/or lower extremities, each 15 minutes
→ *CPT Assistant* Summer 95:9

(97521 has been deleted. To report, use 97520)

97530 Therapeutic activities, direct (one-on-one) patient contact by the provider (use of dynamic activities to improve functional performance), each 15 minutes
→ *CPT Assistant* Summer 95:9

(97531 has been deleted. To report, use 97530)

97532 Development of cognitive skills to improve attention, memory, problem solving, (includes compensatory training), direct (one-on-one) patient contact by the provider, each 15 minutes
→ *CPT Changes* 2001

97533 Sensory integrative techniques to enhance sensory processing and promote adaptive responses to environmental demands, direct (one-on-one) patient contact by the provider, each 15 minutes
→ *CPT Changes* 2001

▲**97535** Self-care/home management training (eg, activities of daily living (ADL) and compensatory training, meal preparation, safety procedures, and instructions in use of assistive technology devices/adaptive equipment) direct one-on-one contact by provider, each 15 minutes
→ *CPT Assistant* Sep 96:7; Apr 00:11; *CPT Changes* 2002

97537 Community/work reintegration training (eg, shopping, transportation, money management, avocational activities and/or work environment/modification analysis, work task analysis), direct one-on-one contact by provider, each 15 minutes
→ *CPT Assistant* Sep 96:7

(97540 has been deleted. To report, see 97535, 97537)

(97541 has been deleted. To report, see 97535, 97537)

(For wheelchair management/propulsion training, use 97542)

97542 Wheelchair management/propulsion training, each 15 minutes
→ *CPT Assistant* Sep 96:8

97545 Work hardening/conditioning; initial 2 hours

+ **97546** each additional hour (List separately in addition to code for primary procedure)

(Use 97546 in conjunction with code 97545)

Active Wound Care Management

Active wound care procedures are performed to promote healing, and involve selective and non-selective debridement techniques.

(Do not report 97601, 97602 in addition to 11040-11044)

▲**97601** Removal of devitalized tissue from wound(s); selective debridement, without anesthesia (eg, high pressure waterjet, sharp selective debridement with scissors, scalpel and tweezers), including topical application(s), wound assessment, and instruction(s) for ongoing care, per session
→ *CPT Changes* 2001; 2002

97602 non-selective debridement, without anesthesia (eg, wet-to-moist dressings, enzymatic, abrasion), including topical application(s), wound assessment, and instruction(s) for ongoing care, per session
→ *CPT Changes* 2001

Tests and Measurements

(For muscle testing, manual or electrical, joint range of motion, electromyography or nerve velocity determination, see 95831-95904)

(97700, 97701 have been deleted. To report, use 97703)

97703 Checkout for orthotic/prosthetic use, established patient, each 15 minutes
→ *CPT Assistant* Sep 96:7

(97720, 97721 have been deleted. To report, use 97750)

(97740, 97741 have been deleted. To report, use 97530)

97750 Physical performance test or measurement (eg, musculoskeletal, functional capacity), with written report, each 15 minutes
→ *CPT Assistant* Summer 95:5; Feb 97:10; Aug 98:11; Mar 00:11

(97752 has been deleted. To report, use 97750)

Other Procedures

▶(For extracorporeal shock wave musculoskeletal therapy, use Category III code 0019T)◀

(97770 has been deleted. To report, see 97532, 97533)

97780 Acupuncture, one or more needles; without electrical stimulation
→ *CPT Assistant* Nov 97:47

97781 with electrical stimulation
→ *CPT Assistant* Nov 97:47

97799 Unlisted physical medicine/rehabilitation service or procedure
→ *CPT Assistant* Summer 95:5; Oct 99:10

(98900-98902 have been deleted. To report, use appropriate category and level of **Evaluation and Management** codes)

(98910-98912 have been deleted. To report, see 99361-99362)

(98920-98922 have been deleted. To report, see 99371-99373)

Medical Nutrition Therapy

97802 Medical nutrition therapy; initial assessment and intervention, individual, face-to-face with the patient, each 15 minutes
➔ *CPT Changes* 2001

97803 re-assessment and intervention, individual, face-to-face with the patient, each 15 minutes
➔ *CPT Changes* 2001

97804 group (2 or more individual(s)), each 30 minutes
➔ *CPT Changes* 2001

(For medical nutrition therapy assessment and/or intervention performed by a physician, see **Evaluation and Management** or **Preventive Medicine** service codes)

Osteopathic Manipulative Treatment

Osteopathic manipulative treatment is a form of manual treatment applied by a physician to eliminate or alleviate somatic dysfunction and related disorders. This treatment may be accomplished by a variety of techniques.

Evaluation and Management services may be reported separately if, using the modifier '-25,' the patient's condition requires a significant separately identifiable E/M service, above and beyond the usual preservice and postservice work associated with the procedure. The E/M service may be caused or prompted by the same symptoms or condition for which the OMT service was provided. As such, different diagnoses are not required for the reporting of the OMT and E/M service on the same date.

Body regions referred to are: head region; cervical region; thoracic region; lumbar region; sacral region; pelvic region; lower extremities; upper extremities; rib cage region; abdomen and viscera region.
➔ *CPT Assistant* Nov 98:37-38

98925 Osteopathic manipulative treatment (OMT); one to two body regions involved
➔ *CPT Assistant* May 96:10; Jan 97:8, 10; Jul 98:10; Aug 00:11; Dec 00:15

98926 three to four body regions involved
➔ *CPT Assistant* May 96:10; Jan 97:8; Aug 00:11; Dec 00:15

98927 five to six body regions involved
➔ *CPT Assistant* May 96:10; Jan 97:8; Aug 00:11; Dec 00:15

98928 seven to eight body regions involved
➔ *CPT Assistant* May 96:10; Jan 97:8; Aug 00:11; Dec 00:15

98929 nine to ten body regions involved
➔ *CPT Assistant* May 96:10; Jan 97:8, 10; Aug 00:11; Dec 00:15

Chiropractic Manipulative Treatment

Chiropractic manipulative treatment (CMT) is a form of manual treatment to influence joint and neurophysiological function. This treatment may be accomplished using a variety of techniques.

The chiropractic manipulative treatment codes include a pre-manipulation patient assessment. Additional Evaluation and Management services may be reported separately using the modifier '-25', if the patient's condition requires a significant separately identifiable E/M service, above and beyond the usual preservice and postservice work associated with the procedure. The E/M service may be caused or prompted by the same symptoms or condition for which the CMT service was provided. As such, different diagnoses are not required for the reporting of the CMT and E/M service on the same date.

For purposes of CMT, the five spinal regions referred to are: cervical region (includes atlanto-occipital joint); thoracic region (includes costovertebral and costotransverse joints); lumbar region; sacral region; and pelvic (sacro-iliac joint) region. The five extraspinal regions referred to are: head (including temporomandibular joint, excluding atlanto-occipital) region; lower extremities; upper extremities; rib cage (excluding costotransverse and costovertebral joints) and abdomen.
➔ *CPT Assistant* Nov 98:38

98940 Chiropractic manipulative treatment (CMT); spinal, one to two regions
➔ *CPT Assistant* Jan 97:7, 11; Feb 99:10; Dec 00:15

98941 spinal, three to four regions
➔ *CPT Assistant* Jan 97:7, 11; Mar 97:10; Feb 99:10; Dec 00:15

98942 spinal, five regions
➔ *CPT Assistant* Jan 97:7, 11; Feb 99:10; Dec 00:15

98943 extraspinal, one or more regions
➔ *CPT Assistant* Jan 97:7, 11; Mar 97:10; Feb 99:10; Dec 00:15

Special Services, Procedures and Reports

The procedures with code numbers 99000 through ►99091◄ provide the reporting physician with the means of identifying the completion of special reports and services that are an adjunct to the basic services rendered. The specific number assigned indicates the special circumstances under which a basic procedure is performed.

►Code 99091 should be reported no more than once in a 30 day period to include the physician or health care provider time involved with data accession, review and interpretation, modification of care plan as necessary (including communication to patient and/or caregiver), and associated documentation.◄

►If the services described by code 99091 are provided on the same day the patient presents for an E/M service, these services should be considered part of the E/M service and not separately reported.◄

►Do not report 99091 if it occurs within 30 days of care plan oversight services 99374-99380. Do not report 99091 if other more specific CPT codes exist (eg, 93014, 93227, 93233, 93272 for cardiographic services; 95250 for continuous glucose monitoring). Do not report 99091 for transfer and interpretation of data from hospital or clinical laboratory computers.◄

Miscellaneous Services

99000   Handling and/or conveyance of specimen for transfer from the physician's office to a laboratory
➔ *CPT Assistant* Winter 94:26; Feb 99:10; Oct 99:11

99001   Handling and/or conveyance of specimen for transfer from the patient in other than a physician's office to a laboratory (distance may be indicated)
➔ *CPT Assistant* Winter 94:26

99002   Handling, conveyance, and/or any other service in connection with the implementation of an order involving devices (eg, designing, fitting, packaging, handling, delivery or mailing) when devices such as orthotics, protectives, prosthetics are fabricated by an outside laboratory or shop but which items have been designed, and are to be fitted and adjusted by the attending physician
➔ *CPT Assistant* Winter 94:26

(For routine collection of venous blood, use 36415)

(99012, 99013, 99014, 99015 have been deleted. To report, see 99371-99373)

99024   Postoperative follow-up visit, included in global service
➔ *CPT Assistant* Winter 94:26; Sep 97:10

(As a component of a surgical "package," see **Surgery** guidelines)

99025   Initial (new patient) visit when starred (*) surgical procedure constitutes major service at that visit
➔ *CPT Assistant* Winter 94:27

99050   Services requested after office hours in addition to basic service
➔ *CPT Assistant* Winter 94:27

99052   Services requested between 10:00 PM and 8:00 AM in addition to basic service
➔ *CPT Assistant* Winter 94:27; Aug 96:9

99054   Services requested on Sundays and holidays in addition to basic service
➔ *CPT Assistant* Winter 94:27; Aug 96:9

99056   Services provided at request of patient in a location other than physician's office which are normally provided in the office
➔ *CPT Assistant* Winter 94:27

99058   Office services provided on an emergency basis
➔ *CPT Assistant* Winter 94:27

(99062, 99064, 99065 have been deleted. To report, see 99281-99285)

99070   Supplies and materials (except spectacles), provided by the physician over and above those usually included with the office visit or other services rendered (list drugs, trays, supplies, or materials provided)
➔ *CPT Assistant* Winter 94:28; May 98:10; Jun 99:10; Jun 00:11

(For spectacles, see 92390-92395)

99071   Educational supplies, such as books, tapes, and pamphlets, provided by the physician for the patient's education at cost to physician
➔ *CPT Assistant* Winter 94:28

99075   Medical testimony
➔ *CPT Assistant* Winter 94:28

99078   Physician educational services rendered to patients in a group setting (eg, prenatal, obesity, or diabetic instructions)
➔ *CPT Assistant* Winter 94:28; Jan 98:12

99080   Special reports such as insurance forms, more than the information conveyed in the usual medical communications or standard reporting form
➔ *CPT Assistant* Winter 94:28

99082   Unusual travel (eg, transportation and escort of patient)

▲**99090**   Analysis of clinical data stored in computers (eg, ECGs, blood pressures, hematologic data)
➔ *CPT Assistant* Winter 94:28; *CPT Changes* 2002

►(For physician/health care professional collection and interpretation of physiologic data stored/transmitted by patient/caregiver, see 99091)◄

►(Do not report 99090 if other more specific CPT codes exist, eg, 93014, 93227, 93233, 93272 for cardiographic services; 95250 for continuous glucose monitoring, 97750 for musculoskeletal function testing)◄

⊘ =Modifier '-51' Exempt   ► ◄=New or Revised Text   ✚ =Add-on Code   CPT 2002

99091 Collection and interpretation of physiologic data (eg, ECG, blood pressure, glucose monitoring) digitally stored and/or transmitted by the patient and/or caregiver to the physician or other qualified health care professional, requiring a minimum of 30 minutes of time
➔ *CPT Changes* 2002

Qualifying Circumstances for Anesthesia

(For explanation of these services, see **Anesthesia** guidelines)

+ 99100 Anesthesia for patient of extreme age, under one year and over seventy (List separately in addition to code for primary anesthesia procedure)

+ 99116 Anesthesia complicated by utilization of total body hypothermia (List separately in addition to code for primary anesthesia procedure)

+ 99135 Anesthesia complicated by utilization of controlled hypotension (List separately in addition to code for primary anesthesia procedure)

+ 99140 Anesthesia complicated by emergency conditions (specify) (List separately in addition to code for primary anesthesia procedure)

(An emergency is defined as existing when delay in treatment of the patient would lead to a significant increase in the threat to life or body part.)

Sedation With or Without Analgesia (Conscious Sedation)

Sedation with or without analgesia (conscious sedation) is used to achieve a medically controlled state of depressed consciousness while maintaining the patient's airway, protective reflexes and ability to respond to stimulation or verbal commands. Conscious sedation includes performance and documentation of pre- and post-sedation evaluations of the patient, administration of the sedation and/or analgesic agent(s), and monitoring of cardiorespiratory function (ie, pulse oximetry, cardiorespiratory monitor, and blood pressure). The use of these codes requires the presence of an independent trained observer to assist the physician in monitoring the patient's level of consciousness and physiological status.

(If the sedation with or without analgesia (conscious sedation) is administered in support of a procedure provided by another physician, see **Anesthesia** section)

⊘ **99141** Sedation with or without analgesia (conscious sedation); intravenous, intramuscular or inhalation
➔ *CPT Assistant* Nov 97:47-48; Apr 98:1; Jul 98:1; Mar 99:11

(94760-94762 may not be reported in addition to 99141)

⊘ **99142** oral, rectal and/or intranasal
➔ *CPT Assistant* Nov 97:47-48; Apr 98:1; Jul 98:1; Mar 99:11

(94760-94762 may not be reported in addition to 99142)

(99150, 99151 have been deleted. To report, see 99354-99360)

Other Services and Procedures

99170 Anogenital examination with colposcopic magnification in childhood for suspected trauma
➔ *CPT Assistant* Nov 99:55

(For conscious sedation, use 99141, 99142)

99172 Visual function screening, automated or semi-automated bilateral quantitative determination of visual acuity, ocular alignment, color vision by pseudoisochromatic plates, and field of vision (may include all or some screening of the determination(s) for contrast sensitivity, vision under glare)
➔ *CPT Assistant* Feb 01:7; *CPT Changes* 2001

(This service must employ graduated visual acuity stimuli that allow a quantitative determination of visual acuity (eg, Snellen chart). This service may not be used in addition to a general ophthalmological service or an E/M service)

(Do not report 99172 in conjunction with code 99173)

99173 Screening test of visual acuity, quantitative, bilateral
➔ *CPT Assistant* Nov 99:55; *CPT Changes* 2000

(The screening test used must employ graduated visual acuity stimuli that allow a quantitative estimate of visual acuity (eg, Snellen chart). Other identifiable services unrelated to this screening test provided at the same time may be reported separately (eg, preventive medicine services). When acuity is measured as part of a general ophthalmological service or of an E/M service of the eye, it is a diagnostic examination and not a screening test.)

(Do not report 99173 in conjunction with code 99172)

99175 Ipecac or similar administration for individual emesis and continued observation until stomach adequately emptied of poison

(For diagnostic intubation, see 82926-82928, 89130-89141)

(For gastric lavage for diagnostic purposes, see 91055)

(99178 has been deleted. To report, use 96110)

(99180 has been deleted. To report, use 99183)

(99182 has been deleted. To report, use 99183)

99183 Physician attendance and supervision of hyperbaric oxygen therapy, per session

(Evaluation and Management services and/or procedures (eg, wound debridement) provided in a hyperbaric oxygen treatment facility in conjunction with a hyperbaric oxygen therapy session should be reported separately)

99185 Hypothermia; regional

99186 total body

99190 Assembly and operation of pump with oxygenator or heat exchanger (with or without ECG and/or pressure monitoring); each hour

99191 3/4 hour

99192 1/2 hour

99195 Phlebotomy, therapeutic (separate procedure)
➔ *CPT Assistant* Apr 96:3; Jun 96:10

99199 Unlisted special service, procedure or report
➔ *CPT Assistant* Nov 99:55; *CPT Changes* 2000

▶Home Health Procedures/Services◀

▶These codes are used by non-physician health care professionals. Physicians should utilize the home visit codes 99341-99350, and utilize CPT codes other than 99500-99539, for any additional procedure/service provided to a patient living in a residence.◀

▶The following codes are used to report services provided in a patient's residence (including assisted living apartments, group homes, non-traditional private homes, custodial care facilities, or schools).◀

▶Health care professionals who are authorized to use Evaluation and Management Home Visit codes (99341-99350) may report codes 99500-99539 in addition to codes 99341-99350 if both services are performed. Evaluation and Management services may be reported separately, using the modifier '-25', if the patient's condition requires a significant separately identifiable E/M service, above and beyond the home health service(s)/procedure(s) codes 99500-99539.◀

● **99500** Home visit for prenatal monitoring and assessment to include fetal heart rate, non-stress test, uterine monitoring, and gestational diabetes monitoring
➔ *CPT Changes* 2002

● **99501** Home visit for postnatal assessment and follow-up care
➔ *CPT Changes* 2002

● **99502** Home visit for newborn care and assessment
➔ *CPT Changes* 2002

● **99503** Home visit for respiratory therapy care (eg, bronchodilator, oxygen therapy, respiratory assessment, apnea evaluation)
➔ *CPT Changes* 2002

● **99504** Home visit for patients receiving mechanical ventilation
➔ *CPT Changes* 2002

● **99505** Home visit for stoma care and maintenance including colostomy and cystostomy
➔ *CPT Changes* 2002

● **99506** Home visit for intramuscular injections
➔ *CPT Changes* 2002

● **99507** Home visit for care and maintenance of catheter(s) (eg, urinary, drainage, and enteral)
➔ *CPT Changes* 2002

● **99508** Home visit for polysomnography and sleep studies
➔ *CPT Changes* 2002

● **99509** Home visit for assistance with activities of daily living and personal care
➔ *CPT Changes* 2002

▶(To report self-care/home management training, see 97535)◀

▶(To report home medical nutrition assessment and intervention services, see 97802-97804)◀

▶(To report home speech therapy services, see 92507-92508)◀

● **99510** Home visit for individual, family, or marriage counseling
➔ *CPT Changes* 2002

● **99511** Home visit for fecal impaction management and enema administration
➔ *CPT Changes* 2002

● **99512** Home visit for hemodialysis, per diem
➔ *CPT Changes* 2002

▶(For home infusion of peritoneal dialysis, use 99559)◀

● **99539** Unlisted home visit service or procedure
➔ *CPT Changes* 2002

▶Home Infusion Procedures◀

▶Codes 99551-99569 include a home visit by a health care professional and all necessary solutions, equipment, and supplies (except drugs) required to deliver a therapy in a single 24-hour period. All drugs are excluded and should be reported separately. If more than one therapy is given in a 24-hour period, the most complex therapy should be reported first and 99569 should be reported separately for each additional therapy given in that 24-hour period. These codes do not represent self-administration of medications by the patient.◀

● **99551** Home infusion for pain management (intravenous or subcutaneous), per diem
➔ *CPT Changes* 2002

● **99552** Home infusion for pain management (epidural or intrathecal), per diem
➔ *CPT Changes* 2002

⊘ =Modifier '-51' Exempt   ▶ ◀=New or Revised Text   ✚ =Add-on Code

● **99553** Home infusion for tocolytic therapy, per diem
  ➔ *CPT Changes* 2002

● **99554** Home infusion for hematopoietic hormones (eg, erythropoietin, G-CSF, CM-CSF) or platelets, per diem
  ➔ *CPT Changes* 2002

● **99555** Home infusion for chemotherapy, per diem
  ➔ *CPT Changes* 2002

● **99556** Home infusion for antibiotics/antifungals/antivirals, per diem
  ➔ *CPT Changes* 2002

● **99557** Home infusion of continuous anticoagulant therapy (eg, heparin), per diem
  ➔ *CPT Changes* 2002

● **99558** Home infusion of immunotherapy, per diem
  ➔ *CPT Changes* 2002

● **99559** Home infusion of peritoneal dialysis, per diem
  ➔ *CPT Changes* 2002

  ▶(For home visit for hemodialysis, use 99512)◀

● **99560** Home infusion of enteral nutrition, per diem
  ➔ *CPT Changes* 2002

● **99561** Home infusion of hydration therapy, per diem
  ➔ *CPT Changes* 2002

● **99562** Home infusion of total parenteral nutrition, per diem
  ➔ *CPT Changes* 2002

● **99563** Home administration of aerosolized pentamidine, per diem
  ➔ *CPT Changes* 2002

● **99564** Home infusion for anti-hemophilic agents (eg, Factor VIII), per diem
  ➔ *CPT Changes* 2002

● **99565** Home infusion of alpha-1-proteinase inhibitor (eg, Prolastin), per diem
  ➔ *CPT Changes* 2002

● **99566** Home infusion for uninterrupted, long-term intravenous treatment (eg, epoprostenol), per diem
  ➔ *CPT Changes* 2002

● **99567** Home infusion of sympathomimetic agents (eg, dobutamine), per diem
  ➔ *CPT Changes* 2002

● **99568** Home infusion of miscellaneous drugs, per diem
  ➔ *CPT Changes* 2002

+ ● **99569** Home infusion, each additional therapy given on same day (List separately in addition to code for primary visit)
  ➔ *CPT Changes* 2002

Notes

Category III Codes

►The following section contains a set of temporary codes for emerging technology, services, and procedures. Category III codes will allow data collection for these services/procedures. Use of unlisted codes does not offer the opportunity for the collection of specific data. If a Category III code is available, this code must be reported instead of a Category I unlisted code. This is an activity that is critically important in the evaluation of health care delivery and the formation of public and private policy. The use of the codes in this section will allow physicians and other qualified health care professionals, insurers, health services researchers, and health policy experts to identify emerging technology, services, and procedures for clinical efficacy, utilization and outcomes.◄

►The inclusion of a service or procedure in this section neither implies nor endorses clinical efficacy, safety or the applicability to clinical practice. The codes in this section do not conform to the usual requirements for CPT Category I codes established by the Editorial Panel. For Category I codes, the Panel requires that the service/procedure be performed by many health care professionals in clinical practice in multiple locations and that FDA approval, as appropriate, has already been received. The nature of emerging technology, services, and procedures is such that these requirements may not be met. For these reasons, temporary codes for emerging technology, services, and procedures have been placed in a separate section of the CPT book and the codes are differentiated from Category I CPT codes by the use of alphanumeric characters.◄

►Services/procedures described in this section make use of alphanumeric characters. These codes have an alpha character as the 5th character in the string, preceded by four digits. The digits are not intended to reflect the placement of the code in the Category I section of CPT nomenclature. Codes in this section may or may not eventually receive a Category I CPT code. In either case, a given Category III code will be archived after five years of its inception unless it is demonstrated that a temporary code is still needed. New codes in this section are released semi-annually via the AMA/CPT internet site, to expedite dissemination for reporting. The full set of temporary codes for emerging technology, services, and procedures are published annually in the CPT book.◄

● **0001T** Endovascular repair of infrarenal abdominal aortic aneurysm or dissection; modular bifurcated prosthesis (two docking limbs)
➔ *CPT Changes* 2002

● **0002T** aorto-uni-iliac or aorto-unifemoral prosthesis
➔ *CPT Changes* 2002

►(For radiological supervision and interpretation, use 75952 in conjunction with 0001T-0002T)◄

● **0003T** Cervicography
➔ *CPT Changes* 2002

►(0004T has been deleted. To report, use 88380)◄

● **0005T** Transcatheter placement of extracranial cerebrovascular artery stent(s), percutaneous; initial vessel
➔ *CPT Changes* 2002

+ ● **0006T** each additional vessel (List separately in addition to code for primary procedure)
➔ *CPT Changes* 2002

►(Use 0006T in conjunction with code 0005T)◄

►(For radiological supervision and interpretation, use 0007T)◄

● **0007T** Transcatheter placement of extracranial cerebrovascular artery stent(s), percutaneous, radiological supervision and interpretation, each vessel
➔ *CPT Changes* 2002

►(For procedure, see 0005T, 0006T)◄

● **0008T** Upper gastrointestinal endoscopy including esophagus, stomach, and either the duodenum and/or jejunum as appropriate, with suturing of the esophagogastric junction
➔ *CPT Changes* 2002

● **0009T** Endometrial cryoablation with ultrasonic guidance
➔ *CPT Changes* 2002

● **0010T** Tuberculosis test, cell mediated immunity measurement of gamma interferon antigen response
➔ *CPT Changes* 2002

● **0012T** Arthroscopy, knee, surgical, implantation of osteochondral graft(s) for treatment of articular surface defect; autografts
➔ *CPT Changes* 2002

● **0013T** allografts
➔ *CPT Changes* 2002

● **0014T** Meniscal transplantation, medial or lateral, knee (any method)
➔ *CPT Changes* 2002

● **0016T** Destruction of localized lesion of choroid (eg, choroidal neovascularization), transpupillary thermotherapy
➔ *CPT Changes* 2002

● **0017T** Destruction of macular drusen, photocoagulation
➔ *CPT Changes* 2002

● **0018T** Delivery of high power, focal magnetic pulses for direct stimulation to cortical neurons
➔ *CPT Changes* 2002

● **0019T** Extracorporeal shock wave therapy; involving musculoskeletal system
➔ *CPT Changes* 2002

● **0020T**   involving plantar fascia
→ *CPT Changes* 2002

● **0021T**   Insertion of transcervical or transvaginal fetal oximetry sensor
→ *CPT Changes* 2002

● **0023T**   Infectious agent drug susceptibility phenotype prediction using genotypic comparison to known genotypic/phenotypic database, HIV 1
→ *CPT Changes* 2002

● **0024T**   Non-surgical septal reduction therapy (eg, alcohol ablation), for hypertrophic obstructive cardiomyopathy, with coronary arteriograms, with or without temporary pacemaker
→ *CPT Changes* 2002

● **0025T**   Determination of corneal thickness (eg, pachymetry) with interpretation and report, bilateral
→ *CPT Changes* 2002

● **0026T**   Lipoprotein, direct measurement, intermediate density lipoproteins (IDL) (remnant lipoproteins)
→ *CPT Changes* 2002

Appendix A

Modifiers

This list includes all of the modifiers applicable to *CPT* 2002 codes.

-21 **Prolonged Evaluation and Management Services:** When the face-to-face or floor/unit service(s) provided is prolonged or otherwise greater than that usually required for the highest level of evaluation and management service within a given category, it may be identified by adding modifier '-21' to the evaluation and management code number or by use of the separate five digit modifier code 09921. A report may also be appropriate.

-22 **Unusual Procedural Services:** When the service(s) provided is greater than that usually required for the listed procedure, it may be identified by adding modifier '-22' to the usual procedure number or by use of the separate five digit modifier code 09922. A report may also be appropriate.

-23 **Unusual Anesthesia:** Occasionally, a procedure, which usually requires either no anesthesia or local anesthesia, because of unusual circumstances must be done under general anesthesia. This circumstance may be reported by adding the modifier '-23' to the procedure code of the basic service or by use of the separate five digit modifier code 09923.

-24 **Unrelated Evaluation and Management Service by the Same Physician During a Postoperative Period:** The physician may need to indicate that an evaluation and management service was performed during a postoperative period for a reason(s) unrelated to the original procedure. This circumstance may be reported by adding the modifier '-24' to the appropriate level of E/M service, or the separate five digit modifier 09924 may be used.

-25 **Significant, Separately Identifiable Evaluation and Management Service by the Same Physician on the Same Day of the Procedure or Other Service:** The physician may need to indicate that on the day a procedure or service identified by a CPT code was performed, the patient's condition required a significant, separately identifiable E/M service above and beyond the other service provided or beyond the usual preoperative and postoperative care associated with the procedure that was performed. The E/M service may be prompted by the symptom or condition for which the procedure and/or service was provided. As such, different diagnoses are not required for reporting of the E/M services on the same date. This circumstance may be reported by adding the modifier '-25' to the appropriate level of E/M service, or the separate five digit modifier 09925 may be used. **Note:** This modifier is not used to report an E/M service that resulted in a decision to perform surgery. See modifier '-57.'

-26 **Professional Component:** Certain procedures are a combination of a physician component and a technical component. When the physician component is reported separately, the service may be identified by adding the modifier '-26' to the usual procedure number or the service may be reported by use of the five digit modifier code 09926.

-32 **Mandated Services:** Services related to *mandated* consultation and/or related services (eg, PRO, third party payer, governmental, legislative or regulatory requirement) may be identified by adding the modifier '-32' to the basic procedure or the service may be reported by use of the five digit modifier 09932.

-47 **Anesthesia by Surgeon:** Regional or general anesthesia provided by the surgeon may be reported by adding the modifier '-47' to the basic service or by use of the separate five digit modifier code 09947. (This does not include local anesthesia.) **Note:** Modifier '-47' or 09947 would not be used as a modifier for the anesthesia procedures 00100-01999.

-50 **Bilateral Procedure:** Unless otherwise identified in the listings, bilateral procedures that are performed at the same operative session should be identified by adding the modifier '-50' to the appropriate five digit code or by use of the separate five digit modifier code 09950.

-51 **Multiple Procedures:** When multiple procedures, other than E/M services, are performed at the same session by the same provider, the primary procedure or service may be reported as listed. The additional procedure(s) or service(s) may be identified by appending the modifier '-51' to the additional procedure or service code(s) or by the use of the separate five digit modifier 09951. **Note:** This modifier should not be appended to designated "add-on" codes (see Appendix E).

-52 **Reduced Services:** Under certain circumstances a service or procedure is partially reduced or eliminated at the physician's discretion. Under these circumstances the service provided can be identified by its usual procedure number and the addition of the modifier '-52', signifying that the service is reduced. This provides a means of reporting reduced services without disturbing the identification of the basic service. Modifier code 09952 may be used as an alternative to modifier '-52.' **Note:** For hospital outpatient reporting of a previously scheduled procedure/service that is partially reduced or cancelled as a result of extenuating circumstances or those that threaten the well-being of the patient prior to or after administration of anesthesia, see modifiers '-73' and '-74' (see modifiers approved for ASC hospital outpatient use).

-53 **Discontinued Procedure:** Under certain circumstances, the physician may elect to terminate a surgical or diagnostic procedure. Due to extenuating circumstances or those that threaten the well being of the patient, it may be necessary to indicate that a surgical or diagnostic procedure was started but discontinued. This circumstance may be reported by adding the modifier '-53' to the code reported by the physician for the discontinued procedure or by use of the separate five digit modifier code 09953. **Note:** This modifier is not used to report the elective cancellation of a procedure prior to the patient's anesthesia induction and/or surgical preparation in the operating suite. For outpatient hospital/ambulatory surgery center (ASC) reporting of a previously scheduled procedure/service that is partially reduced or cancelled as a result of extenuating circumstances or those that threaten the well being of the patient prior to or after administration of anesthesia, see modifiers '-73' and '-74' (see modifiers approved for ASC hospital outpatient use).

-54   **Surgical Care Only:** When one physician performs a surgical procedure and another provides preoperative and/or postoperative management, surgical services may be identified by adding the modifier '-54' to the usual procedure number or by use of the separate five digit modifier code 09954.

-55   **Postoperative Management Only:** When one physician performed the postoperative management and another physician performed the surgical procedure, the postoperative component may be identified by adding the modifier '-55' to the usual procedure number or by use of the separate five digit modifier code 09955.

-56   **Preoperative Management Only:** When one physician performed the preoperative care and evaluation and another physician performed the surgical procedure, the preoperative component may be identified by adding the modifier '-56' to the usual procedure number or by use of the separate five digit modifier code 09956.

-57   **Decision for Surgery:** An evaluation and management service that resulted in the initial decision to perform the surgery may be identified by adding the modifier '-57' to the appropriate level of E/M service, or the separate five digit modifier 09957 may be used.

-58   **Staged or Related Procedure or Service by the Same Physician During the Postoperative Period:** The physician may need to indicate that the performance of a procedure or service during the postoperative period was: a) planned prospectively at the time of the original procedure (staged); b) more extensive than the original procedure; or c) for therapy following a diagnostic surgical procedure. This circumstance may be reported by adding the modifier '-58' to the staged or related procedure, or the separate five digit modifier 09958 may be used. **Note:** This modifier is not used to report the treatment of a problem that requires a return to the operating room. See modifier '-78.'

-59   **Distinct Procedural Service:** Under certain circumstances, the physician may need to indicate that a procedure or service was distinct or independent from other services performed on the same day. Modifier '-59' is used to identify procedures/services that are not normally reported together, but are appropriate under the circumstances. This may represent a different session or patient encounter, different procedure or surgery, different site or organ system, separate incision/excision, separate lesion, or separate injury (or area of injury in extensive injuries) not ordinarily encountered or performed on the same day by the same physician. However, when another already established modifier is appropriate it should be used rather than modifier '-59.' Only if no more descriptive modifier is available, and the use of modifier '-59' best explains the circumstances, should modifier '-59' be used. Modifier code 09959 may be used as an alternative to modifier '-59.'

-62   **Two Surgeons:** When two surgeons work together as primary surgeons performing distinct part(s) of a procedure, each surgeon should report his/her distinct operative work by adding the modifier '-62' to the procedure code ▶and any associated add-on code(s) for that procedure as long as both surgeons continue to work together as primary surgeons.◀ Each surgeon should report the co-surgery once using the same procedure code. If additional procedure(s) (including add-on procedure(s), are performed during the same surgical session, separate code(s) may ▶also◀ be reported with the modifier '-62' added. Modifier code 09962 may be used as an alternative to modifier '-62'. **Note:** If a co-surgeon acts as an assistant in the performance of additional procedure(s) during the same surgical session, those services may be reported using separate procedure code(s) with the modifier '-80' or modifier ▶'-82'◀ added, as appropriate.

-66   **Surgical Team:** Under some circumstances, highly complex procedures (requiring the concomitant services of several physicians, often of different specialties, plus other highly skilled, specially trained personnel, various types of complex equipment) are carried out under the "surgical team" concept. Such circumstances may be identified by each participating physician with the addition of the modifier '-66' to the basic procedure number used for reporting services. Modifier code 09966 may be used as an alternative to modifier '-66.'

-76   **Repeat Procedure by Same Physician:** The physician may need to indicate that a procedure or service was repeated subsequent to the original procedure or service. This circumstance may be reported by adding the modifier '-76' to the repeated procedure/service or the separate five digit modifier code 09976 may be used.

-77   **Repeat Procedure by Another Physician:** The physician may need to indicate that a basic procedure or service performed by another physician had to be repeated. This situation may be reported by adding modifier '-77' to the repeated procedure/service or the separate five digit modifier code 09977 may be used.

-78   **Return to the Operating Room for a Related Procedure During the Postoperative Period:** The physician may need to indicate that another procedure was performed during the postoperative period of the initial procedure. When this subsequent procedure is related to the first, and requires the use of the operating room, it may be reported by adding the modifier '-78' to the related procedure, or by using the separate five digit modifier 09978. (For repeat procedures on the same day, see '-76'.)

-79 Unrelated Procedure or Service by the Same Physician During the Postoperative Period: The physician may need to indicate that the performance of a procedure or service during the postoperative period was unrelated to the original procedure. This circumstance may be reported by using the modifier '-79' or by using the separate five digit modifier 09979. (For repeat procedures on the same day, see '-76'.)

-80 Assistant Surgeon: Surgical assistant services may be identified by adding the modifier '-80' to the usual procedure number(s) or by use of the separate five digit modifier code 09980.

-81 Minimum Assistant Surgeon: Minimum surgical assistant services are identified by adding the modifier '-81' to the usual procedure number or by use of the separate five digit modifier code 09981.

-82 Assistant Surgeon (when qualified resident surgeon not available): The unavailability of a qualified resident surgeon is a prerequisite for use of modifier '-82' appended to the usual procedure code number(s) or by use of the separate five digit modifier code 09982.

-90 Reference (Outside) Laboratory: When laboratory procedures are performed by a party other than the treating or reporting physician, the procedure may be identified by adding the modifier '-90' to the usual procedure number or by use of the separate five digit modifier code 09990.

-91 Repeat Clinical Diagnostic Laboratory Test: In the course of patient treatment, it may be necessary to repeat the same laboratory test on the same day to obtain subsequent (multiple) test results. Under these circumstances, the laboratory test performed can be identified by its usual procedure number and the addition of the modifier '-91'. **Note:** This modifier may not be used when tests are rerun to confirm initial results; due to testing problems with specimens or equipment; or for any other reason when a normal, one-time, reportable result is all that is required. This modifier may not be used when other code(s) describe a series of test results (eg, glucose tolerance tests, evocative/suppression testing). This modifier may only be used for laboratory test(s) performed more than once on the same day on the same patient.

-99 Multiple Modifiers: Under certain circumstances two or more modifiers may be necessary to completely delineate a service. In such situations modifier '-99' should be added to the basic procedure, and other applicable modifiers may be listed as part of the description of the service. Modifier code 09999 may be used as an alternative to modifier '-99.'

▶Anesthesia Physical Status Modifiers◀

▶The Physical Status modifiers are consistent with the American Society of Anesthesiologists' ranking of patient physical status, and distinguish various levels of complexity of the anesthesia service provided. All anesthesia services are reported by use of the anesthesia five-digit procedure code (00100-03108) with the appropriate physical status modifier appended.◀

▶Example: 00100-P1

Under certain circumstances, when another established modifier(s) is appropriate, it should be used in addition to the physical status modifier.

Example: 00100-P4-53◀

▶**Physical Status Modifier P1:** A normal healthy patient

Physical Status Modifier P2: A patient with mild systemic disease

Physical Status Modifier P3: A patient with severe systemic disease

Physical Status Modifier P4: A patient with severe systemic disease that is a constant threat to life

Physical Status Modifier P5: A moribund patient who is not expected to survive without the operation

Physical Status Modifier P6: A declared brain-dead patient whose organs are being removed for donor purposes◀

Modifiers Approved for Ambulatory Surgery Center (ASC) Hospital Outpatient Use

CPT Level I Modifiers

-25 Significant, Separately Identifiable Evaluation and Management Service by the Same Physician on the Same Day of the Procedure or Other Service: The physician may need to indicate that on the day a procedure or service identified by a CPT code was performed, the patient's condition required a significant, separately identifiable E/M service above and beyond the other service provided or beyond the usual preoperative and postoperative care associated with the procedure that was performed. The E/M service may be prompted by the symptom or condition for which the procedure and/or service was provided. As such, different diagnoses are not required for reporting of the E/M services on the same date. This circumstance may be reported by adding the modifier '-25' to the appropriate level of E/M service, or the separate five digit modifier 09925 may be used. **Note:** This modifier is not used to report an E/M service that resulted in a decision to perform surgery. See modifier '-57.'

-27 Multiple Outpatient Hospital E/M Encounters on the Same Date: For hospital outpatient reporting purposes, utilization of hospital resources related to separate and distinct E/M encounters performed in multiple outpatient hospital settings on the same date may be reported by adding the modifier '-27' to each appropriate level outpatient and/or emergency department E/M code(s). This modifier provides a means of reporting circumstances involving evaluation and management services provided by physician(s) in more than one (multiple) outpatient hospital setting(s) (eg, hospital emergency department, clinic). **Note:** This modifier is not to be used for physician reporting of multiple E/M services performed by the same physician on the same date. For physician reporting of all outpatient evaluation and management services provided by the same physician on the same date and performed in multiple outpatient setting(s) (eg, hospital emergency department, clinic), see **Evaluation and Management, Emergency Department, or Preventive Medicine Services** codes.

-50 **Bilateral Procedure:** Unless otherwise identified in the listings, bilateral procedures that are performed at the same operative session should be identified by adding the modifier '-50' to the appropriate five digit code or by use of the separate five digit modifier code 09950.

-52 **Reduced Services:** Under certain circumstances a service or procedure is partially reduced or eliminated at the physician's discretion. Under these circumstances the service provided can be identified by its usual procedure number and the addition of the modifier '-52', signifying that the service is reduced. This provides a means of reporting reduced services without disturbing the identification of the basic service. Modifier code 09952 may be used as an alternative to modifier '-52.' **Note:** For hospital outpatient reporting of a previously scheduled procedure/service that is partially reduced or cancelled as a result of extenuating circumstances or those that threaten the well-being of the patient prior to or after administration of anesthesia, see modifiers '-73' and '-74' (see modifiers approved for ASC hospital outpatient use).

-58 **Staged or Related Procedure or Service by the Same Physician During the Postoperative Period:** The physician may need to indicate that the performance of a procedure or service during the postoperative period was: a) planned prospectively at the time of the original procedure (staged); b) more extensive than the original procedure; or c) for therapy following a diagnostic surgical procedure. This circumstance may be reported by adding the modifier '-58' to the staged or related procedure, or the separate five digit modifier 09958 may be used. Note: This modifier is not used to report the treatment of a problem that requires a return to the operating room. See modifier '-78.'

-59 **Distinct Procedural Service:** Under certain circumstances, the physician may need to indicate that a procedure or service was distinct or independent from other services performed on the same day. Modifier '-59' is used to identify procedures/services that are not normally reported together, but are appropriate under the circumstances. This may represent a different session or patient encounter, different procedure or surgery, different site or organ system, separate incision/excision, separate lesion, or separate injury (or area of injury in extensive injuries) not ordinarily encountered or performed on the same day by the same physician. However, when another already established modifier is appropriate it should be used rather than modifier '-59.' Only if no more descriptive modifier is available, and the use of modifier '-59' best explains the circumstances, should modifier '-59' be used. Modifier code 09959 may be used as an alternative to modifier '-59.'

-73 **Discontinued Out-Patient Hospital/Ambulatory Surgery Center (ASC) Procedure Prior to the Administration of Anesthesia:** Due to extenuating circumstances or those that threaten the well being of the patient, the physician may cancel a surgical or diagnostic procedure subsequent to the patient's surgical preparation (including sedation when provided, and being taken to the room where the procedure is to be performed), but prior to the administration of anesthesia (local, regional block(s) or general). Under these circumstances, the intended service that is prepared for but cancelled can be reported by its usual procedure number and the addition of the modifier '-73' or by use of the separate five digit modifier code 09973. **Note:** The elective cancellation of a service prior to the administration of anesthesia and/or surgical preparation of the patient should not be reported. For physician reporting of a discontinued procedure, see modifier '-53.'

-74 **Discontinued Out-Patient Hospital/Ambulatory Surgery Center (ASC) Procedure After Administration of Anesthesia:** Due to extenuating circumstances or those that threaten the well being of the patient, the physician may terminate a surgical or diagnostic procedure after the administration of anesthesia (local, regional block(s), general) or after the procedure was started (incision made, intubation started, scope inserted, etc). Under these circumstances, the procedure started but terminated can be reported by its usual procedure number and the addition of the modifier '-74' or by use of the separate five digit modifier code 09974. **Note:** The elective cancellation of a service prior to the administration of anesthesia and/or surgical preparation of the patient should not be reported. For physician reporting of a discontinued procedure, see modifier '-53.'

-76 **Repeat Procedure by Same Physician:** The physician may need to indicate that a procedure or service was repeated subsequent to the original procedure or service. This circumstance may be reported by adding the modifier '-76' to the repeated procedure/service or the separate five digit modifier code 09976 may be used.

-77 **Repeat Procedure by Another Physician:** The physician may need to indicate that a basic procedure or service performed by another physician had to be repeated. This situation may be reported by adding modifier '-77' to the repeated procedure/service or the separate five digit modifier code 09977 may be used.

-78 **Return to the Operating Room for a Related Procedure During the Postoperative Period:** The physician may need to indicate that another procedure was performed during the postoperative period of the initial procedure. When this subsequent procedure is related to the first, and requires the use of the operating room, it may be reported by adding the modifier '-78' to the related procedure, or by using the separate five digit modifier 09978. (For repeat procedures on the same day, see '-76')

-79 **Unrelated Procedure or Service by the Same Physician During the Postoperative Period:** The physician may need to indicate that the performance of a procedure or service during the postoperative period was unrelated to the original procedure. This circumstance may be reported by using the modifier '-79' or by using the separate five digit modifier 09979. (For repeat procedures on the same day, see '-76'.)

-91 **Repeat Clinical Diagnostic Laboratory Test:** In the course of treatment of the patient, it may be necessary to repeat the same laboratory test on the same day to obtain subsequent (multiple) test results. Under these circumstances, the laboratory test performed can be identified by its usual procedure number and the addition of the modifier '-91'. **Note:** This modifier may not be used when tests are rerun to confirm initial results; due to testing problems with specimens or equipment; or for any other reason when a normal, one-time, reportable result is all that is required. This modifier may not be used when other code(s) describe a series of test results (eg, glucose tolerance tests, evocative/suppression testing). This modifier may only be used for laboratory test(s) performed more than once on the same day on the same patient.

Level II (HCPCS/National) Modifiers

-E1 Upper left, eyelid

-E2 Lower left, eyelid

-E3 Upper right, eyelid

-E4 Lower right, eyelid

-F1 Left hand, second digit

-F2 Left hand, third digit

-F3 Left hand, fourth digit

-F4 Left hand, fifth digit

-F5 Right hand, thumb

-F6 Right hand, second digit

-F7 Right hand, third digit

-F8 Right hand, fourth digit

-F9 Right hand, fifth digit

-FA Left hand, thumb

-LC Left circumflex coronary artery (Hospitals use with codes 92980-92984, 92995, 92996)

-LD Left anterior descending coronary artery (Hospitals use with codes 92980-92984, 92995, 92996)

-LT Left side (used to identify procedures performed on the left side of the body)

-QM Ambulance service provided under arrangement by a provider of services

-QN Ambulance service furnished directly by a provider of services

-RC Right coronary artery (Hospitals use with codes 92980-92982, 92995, 92996)

-RT Right side (used to identify procedures performed on the right side of the body)

-T1 Left foot, second digit

-T2 Left foot, third digit

-T3 Left foot, fourth digit

-T4 Left foot, fifth digit

-T5 Right foot, great toe

-T6 Right foot, second digit

-T7 Right foot, third digit

-T8 Right foot, fourth digit

-T9 Right foot, fifth digit

-TA Left foot, great toe

Appendix B

Summary of Additions, Deletions, and Revisions

This listing is a summary of additions, deletions, and revisions applicable to *CPT 2002* codes.

The notes, introductory paragraphs, and cross-references that have been revised or added to *CPT 2002* are not included in Appendix B, but are identified in the main text of *CPT* with "▶ ◀" symbols.

The descriptors of the codes listed as "grammatical change" have not been substantially altered, but involve placement of the semicolon, or other punctuation, or a similar minor change. These codes will not be identified in *CPT* with a ▲ symbol.

'-22'	Modifier revised
'-60'	Modifier deleted
0001T	Endovascular repair of abdominal aortic aneurysm code added
0002T	Endovascular repair of abdominal aortic aneurysm code added
0003T	Cervicography code added
0004T	Code deleted. To report, use 88380
0005T	Percutaneous extracranial cerebrovascular artery stent code added
0006T	Percutaneous extracranial cerebrovascular artery stent code added
0007T	Percutaneous extracranial cerebrovascular artery stent code added
0008T	Upper GI endoscopy with suture of esophagogastric junction code added
0009T	Endometrial cryoablation code added
0010T	Tuberculosis test, cell mediated immunity code added
0012T	Osteochondral knee autograft code added
0013T	Osteochondral knee allograft code added
0014T	Meniscal transplant of knee code added
0016T	Thermotherapy of choroidal eye lesion code added
0017T	Photocoagulation of macular drusen code added
0018T	Transcranial magnetic stimulation code added
0019T	Extracorporeal shock wave therapy code added
0020T	Extracorporeal shock wave therapy code added
0021T	Fetal oximetry code added
0023T	Phenotype drug test for HIV 1 code added
0024T	Transcatheter cardiac reduction code added
0025T	Ultrasonic pachymetry code added
0026T	Remnant lipoproteins code added
00220	Terminology revised
00560	Terminology revised

00797	Anesthesia for surgery for morbid obesity code added
00850	Code deleted. To report, use 01961
00851	Anesthesia for tubal ligation code added
00855	Code deleted. To report, use 01963
00857	Code deleted. To report, see 01968, 01969
00869	Anesthesia for vasectomy code added
00884	Code deleted. To report, use 01930
00942	Terminology revised
00946	Code deleted. To report, use 01960
00955	Code deleted. To report, use 01967
01214	Terminology revised
01402	Terminology revised
01904	Code deleted. To report, use 01905
01905	Anesthesia for spinal injection/repair code added
01906	Code deleted. To report, use 01905
01908	Code deleted. To report, use 01905
01910	Code deleted. To report, use 01905
01912	Code deleted. To report, use 01905
01914	Code deleted. To report, use 01905
01916	Terminology revised
01918	Code deleted. To report, use 01916
01920	Terminology revised
01921	Code deleted. To report, see 01924-01926
01924	Anesthesia for therapeutic interventional radiology arterial procedure code added
01925	Anesthesia for therapeutic interventional radiology arterial procedure code added
01926	Anesthesia for therapeutic interventional radiology arterial procedure code added
01930	Anesthesia for therapeutic interventional radiology venous procedure code added
01931	Anesthesia for therapeutic interventional radiology venous procedure code added
01932	Anesthesia for therapeutic interventional radiology venous procedure code added
01933	Anesthesia for therapeutic interventional radiology venous procedure code added
01951	Terminology revised
01952	Terminology revised
01960	Anesthesia for vaginal delivery code added
01961	Anesthesia for cesarean delivery code added
01962	Anesthesia for urgent hysterectomy following delivery code added
01963	Anesthesia for cesarean hysterectomy code added
01964	Anesthesia for abortion procedures code added
01967	Neuroaxial labor analgesia/anesthesia code added
01968	Neuroaxial labor analgesia/anesthesia add-on procedure code added

01969	Neuroaxial labor analgesia/anesthesia add-on procedure code added
01995	Terminology revised
10021	Fine needle aspiration code added
10022	Fine needle aspiration code added
11755	Terminology revised
11981	Insertion of drug delivery implant device code added
11982	Removal of drug delivery implant device code added
11983	Removal and reinsertion of drug delivery implant device code added
15732	Terminology revised
15860	Terminology revised
17000	Terminology revised
17004	Terminology revised
17110	Terminology revised
17260	Terminology revised
17270	Terminology revised
17280	Terminology revised
20225	Terminology revised
20526	Carpal tunnel therapeutic injection code added
20550	Terminology revised
20551	Injection, tendon origin/insertion code added
20552	Trigger point injection code added
20553	Trigger point injection code added
21182	Terminology revised
21183	Terminology revised
21184	Terminology revised
21750	Terminology revised
23000	Terminology revised
23350	Terminology revised
24075	Terminology revised
24076	Grammatical change
24300	Manipulation, elbow, under anesthesia code added
24332	Tenolysis of triceps code added
24343	Repair of elbow ligament code added
24344	Repair of elbow ligament code added
24345	Repair of elbow ligament code added
24346	Reconstruct elbow ligament code added
25001	Incision of flexor tendon sheath, wrist code added
25020	Terminology revised
25024	Decompression fasciotomy of forearm/wrist code added
25025	Decompression fasciotomy of forearm/wrist code added
25075	Terminology revised
25076	Grammatical change
25259	Manipulation of wrist under anesthesia code added
25274	Terminology revised
25275	Repair of tendon sheath, forearm/wrist code added
25394	Osteoplasty of carpal bone code added
25405	Terminology revised
25420	Terminology revised
25430	Vascular pedicle graft for carpal bone code added
25431	Repair of nonunion carpal bone code added
25440	Terminology revised
25443	Terminology revised
25520	Terminology revised
25526	Terminology revised
25645	Terminology revised
25651	Percutaneous skeletal fixation of ulnar styloid fracture code added
25652	Open treatment of ulnar styloid fracture code added
25671	Percutaneous skeletal fixation of distal radioulnar dislocation code added
26115	Terminology revised
26116	Terminology revised
26160	Terminology revised
26340	Manipulation of finger joint under anesthesia code added
26350	Terminology revised
26356	Terminology revised
26390	Terminology revised
26392	Terminology revised
26415	Terminology revised
26416	Terminology revised
26426	Terminology revised
26428	Terminology revised
26445	Terminology revised
26510	Terminology revised
26585	Code deleted. To report, use 26587
26587	Terminology revised
26590	Terminology revised
26597	Code deleted. To report, see 11041-11042, 14040-14041, or 15120, 15240)
26607	Terminology revised
26670	Terminology revised
26676	Terminology revised
26685	Terminology revised
26843	Terminology revised
27110	Terminology revised
27130	Terminology revised
27132	Terminology revised
27140	Terminology revised
27185	Terminology revised
27447	Terminology revised
27475	Grammatical change

Code	Description	Code	Description
28104	Terminology revised	**35131**	Terminology revised
28238	Terminology revised	**35141**	Terminology revised
28299	Terminology revised	**35151**	Terminology revised
28737	Terminology revised	**35161**	Terminology revised
29049	Terminology revised	**35646**	Terminology revised
29086	Application of finger cast code added	**35647**	Aortofemoral bypass graft code added
29805	Shoulder arthroscopy code added	**35685**	Bypass graft patency/vein patch code added
29806	Shoulder arthroscopy code added	**35686**	Bypass graft patency/AV fistula code added
29807	Shoulder arthroscopy code added	**36002**	Pseudoaneurysm injection code added
29815	Code deleted. To report, use 29805	**36005**	Terminology revised
29819	Grammatical change	**36400**	Terminology revised
29824	Shoulder arthroscopy code added	**36819**	Terminology revised
29900	Metacarpophalangeal joint arthroscopy code added	**36820**	Anastomosis, forearm vein transposition code added
29901	Metacarpophalangeal joint arthroscopy code added	**36823**	Terminology revised
29902	Metacarpophalangeal joint arthroscopy code added	**38220**	Bone marrow aspiration code added
29909	Code deleted. To report, use 29999	**38221**	Bone marrow biopsy code added
29999	Unlisted arthroscopy procedure code added	**42970**	Terminology revised
30117	Terminology revised	**43108**	Terminology revised
30801	Terminology revised	**43113**	Terminology revised
30905	Terminology revised	**43118**	Terminology revised
31238	Terminology revised	**43123**	Terminology revised
31528	Terminology revised	**43227**	Terminology revised
31529	Terminology revised	**43245**	Terminology revised
31641	Terminology revised	**43260**	Grammatical change
32420	Terminology revised	**43264**	Terminology revised
32650	Terminology revised	**43265**	Terminology revised
33250	Terminology revised	**43313**	Esophagoplasty for congenital defect code added
33406	Terminology revised	**43314**	Esophagoplasty for congenital defect code added
33413	Terminology revised	**43361**	Terminology revised
33610	Terminology revised	**43847**	Terminology revised
33967	Percutaneous insertion of intra-aortic balloon code added	**43860**	Terminology revised
33975	Terminology revised	**44020**	Terminology revised
33976	Terminology revised	**44110**	Terminology revised
33977	Terminology revised	**44126**	Enterectomy of small intestine for congenital atresia code added
33978	Terminology revised	**44127**	Enterectomy of small intestine for congenital atresia code added
33979	Insertion of intracorporal ventricular assist device code added	**44128**	Enterectomy of small intestine for congenital atresia code added
33980	Removal of intracorporal ventricular assist device code added	**44160**	Terminology revised
35001	Terminology revised	**44202**	Terminology revised
35005	Terminology revised	**44203**	Laparoscopic resection of small intestine code added
35021	Terminology revised	**44204**	Laparoscopic partial colectomy code added
35045	Terminology revised	**44205**	Laparoscopic partial colectomy code added
35081	Terminology revised	**44322**	Terminology revised
35091	Terminology revised	**44366**	Terminology revised
35102	Terminology revised	**44378**	Terminology revised
35111	Terminology revised	**44391**	Terminology revised
35121	Terminology revised	**44661**	Terminology revised

44700	Terminology revised
45136	Excision of ileoanal reservoir code added
45190	Terminology revised
45303	Terminology revised
45317	Terminology revised
45334	Terminology revised
45382	Terminology revised
46020	Placement of anal seton code added
46604	Terminology revised
46614	Terminology revised
46924	Terminology revised
46940	Terminology revised
47370	Laparoscopic radiofrequency ablation of liver tumor code added
47371	Laparoscopic cryosurgical ablation of liver tumor code added
47380	Open radiofrequency ablation of liver tumor code added
47381	Open cryosurgical ablation of liver tumor code added
47382	Percutaneous radiofrequency ablation of liver tumor code added
47554	Terminology revised
48100	Terminology revised
48160	Terminology revised
48500	Terminology revised
48545	Terminology revised
48547	Terminology revised
49220	Terminology revised
49424	Terminology revised
49491	Inguinal hernia repair on preterm infant code added
49492	Inguinal hernia repair on preterm infant code added
49495	Terminology revised
50220	Terminology revised
50810	Terminology revised
50815	Terminology revised
50820	Terminology revised
50825	Terminology revised
50840	Terminology revised
51065	Terminology revised
51590	Terminology revised
51596	Terminology revised
51940	Terminology revised
51960	Terminology revised
52001	Cystourethroscopy with removal of clots code added
52347	Cystourethroscopy with transurethral resection of ejaculatory ducts code added
52510	Terminology revised
53431	Urethroplasty code added
53443	Code deleted. To report, use 53431
53444	Insertion of tandem cuff code added
53445	Terminology revised
53446	Removal of urethral/bladder neck sphincter code added
53447	Terminology revised
53448	Removal/replacement of urethral/bladder neck sphincter code added
53449	Terminology revised
53853	Prostatic water-induced thermotherapy code added
54065	Terminology revised
54162	Lysis of penile circumcision adhesions code added
54163	Repair of incomplete circumcision code added
54164	Frenulotomy of the penis code added
54402	Code deleted. To report, see 54415, 54416
54405	Terminology revised
54406	Removal of penile prosthesis code added
54407	Code deleted. To report, see 54406, 54408, 54410
54408	Repair of penile prosthesis code added
54409	Code deleted. To report, use 54408
54410	Removal/replacement of penile prosthesis code added
54411	Removal/replacement of penile prosthesis code added
54415	Removal of penile prosthesis code added
54416	Removal/replacement of penile prosthesis code added
54417	Removal/replacement of penile prosthesis code added
54510	Code deleted. To report, use 54512
56501	Terminology revised
56515	Terminology revised
57022	Terminology revised
57061	Terminology revised
57065	Terminology revised
57155	Insertion of uterine tandems/vaginal ovoids for clinical brachytherapy code added
57510	Terminology revised
58140	Terminology revised
58275	Terminology revised
58346	Insertion of Heyman capsules for clinical brachytherapy code added
58563	Terminology revised
58611	Terminology revised
58953	Hysterectomy/removal of tubes/ovaries w/radical dissection code added
58954	Hysterectomy/removal of tubes/ovaries w/radical dissection/lymphadenectomy code added
59000	Terminology revised
59001	Therapeutic amniotic fluid reduction code added
60000	Terminology revised
60270	Terminology revised
61026	Terminology revised
61055	Terminology revised

61618	Terminology revised
62100	Terminology revised
62230	Terminology revised
62252	Terminology revised
62256	Terminology revised
62272	Terminology revised
63707	Terminology revised
63709	Terminology revised
64555	Terminology revised
64561	Percutaneous implantation of neurostimulator electrodes code added
64575	Terminology revised
64581	Incision for neurostimulator electrode implant code added
64755	Terminology revised
64820	Terminology revised
64821	Sympathectomy code added
64822	Sympathectomy code added
64823	Sympathectomy code added
65235	Terminology revised
65900	Terminology revised
65920	Terminology revised
65930	Terminology revised
66020	Terminology revised
66982	Terminology revised
67225	Ocular photodynamic therapy code added
67515	Terminology revised
69310	Terminology revised
69990	Terminology revised
74230	Terminology revised
74245	Terminology revised
74249	Terminology revised
74250	Terminology revised
74305	Terminology revised
74327	Terminology revised
74363	Terminology revised
75898	Terminology revised
75989	Terminology revised
76066	Terminology revised
76070	Terminology revised
76078	Terminology revised
76085	Computerized screening mammography code added
76120	Terminology revised
76125	Terminology revised
76355	Terminology revised
76360	Terminology revised
76362	CAT guidance for tissue ablation code added

76370	Terminology revised
76375	Terminology revised
76380	Terminology revised
76394	MRI guidance for tissue ablation code added
76490	US guidance for tissue ablation code added
76536	Terminology revised
76604	Terminology revised
76645	Terminology revised
76700	Terminology revised
76770	Terminology revised
76778	Terminology revised
76800	Terminology revised
76805	Terminology revised
76819	Terminology revised
76830	Terminology revised
76856	Terminology revised
76870	Terminology revised
76880	Terminology revised
76885	Terminology revised
76886	Terminology revised
76936	Grammatical change
77300	Terminology revised
77301	Intensity modulated radiotherapy plan code added
77418	Intensity modulated treatment delivery code added
78195	Terminology revised
78290	Terminology revised
78615	Terminology revised
78650	Terminology revised
80072	Code deleted. To report, see 84550, 85651, 86255, 86430
82270	Terminology revised
82273	Terminology revised
82274	Fecal hemoglobin immunoassay test code added
82355	Terminology revised
83013	Terminology revised
83873	Terminology revised
83916	Terminology revised
83950	Oncoprotein, HER-2/neu code added
84445	Terminology revised
85095	Code deleted. To report, use 38220
85097	Terminology revised
85102	Code deleted. To report, use 38221
85535	Code deleted. To report, use 85536
86140	Grammatical change
86141	High sensitivity C-reactive protein code added
86325	Terminology revised
86336	Inhibin A code added

87045	Terminology revised
87198	Cytomegalovirus antibody (DFA) code added
87199	Enterovirus antibody (DFA) code added
87802	Strep B detection immunoassay detection with optic code added
87803	Clostridium difficile toxin A immunoassay detection with optic code added
87804	Influenza immunoassay detection with optic code added
87902	Hepatitis C genotype analysis code added
87903	Terminology revised
87904	Terminology revised
88170	Code deleted. To report, use 10021
88171	Code deleted. To report, use 10022
88304	Terminology revised
88305	Terminology revised
88380	Microdissection code added
89050	Terminology revised
90471	Terminology revised
90473	Immunization administration code added
90474	Immunization administration code added
90732	Terminology revised
90780	Terminology revised
90939	Hemodialysis access flow study code added
90940	Grammatical change
91123	Pulsed irrigation of fecal impaction code added
92136	Ophthalmic biometry code added
92532	Terminology revised
92534	Terminology revised
92973	Percutaneous coronary thrombectomy code added
92974	Placement of radiation delivery device for coronary brachytherapy code added
93025	Microvolt T-wave assessment code added
93536	Code deleted. To report, use 33967
93607	Code deleted. To report, use 93622
93609	Terminology revised
93613	3-D intracardiac mapping code added
93619	Terminology revised
93620	Terminology revised
93621	Terminology revised
93622	Terminology revised
93701	Thoracic bioimpedance code added
93737	Code deleted. To report, use 93741 or 93743
93738	Code deleted. To report, use 93742 or 93744
94720	Terminology revised
94750	Terminology revised
95144	Terminology revised
95145	Terminology revised

95165	Terminology revised
95180	Terminology revised
95250	Glucose continuous monitoring code added
95875	Terminology revised
95904	Terminology revised
95965	Magnetoencephalography code added
95966	Magnetoencephalography code added
95967	Magnetoencephalography code added
96000	Motion analysis code added
96001	Motion analysis code added
96002	Motion analysis code added
96003	Motion analysis code added
96004	Motion analysis code added
96150	Health/behavior assessment code added
96151	Health/behavior reassessment code added
96152	Health/behavior intervention code added
96153	Health/behavior intervention code added
96154	Health/behavior intervention code added
96155	Health/behavior intervention code added
96450	Terminology revised
96567	Photodynamic therapy of skin code added
97005	Athletic training evaluation code added
97006	Athletic training re-evaluation code added
97112	Terminology revised
97504	Terminology revised
97535	Terminology revised
97601	Terminology revised
99090	Terminology revised
99091	Collection and interpretation of patient transmitted data code added
99289	Patient transport code added
99290	Patient transport code added
99374	Terminology revised
99377	Terminology revised
99379	Terminology revised
99381	Terminology revised
99391	Terminology revised
99500	Home visit for prenatal assessment code added
99501	Home visit for postnatal assessment code added
99502	Home visit for newborn care assessment code added
99503	Home visit for respiratory therapy care code added
99504	Home visit for patients receiving mechanical ventilation code added
99505	Home visit for stoma care code added
99506	Home visit for intramuscular injections code added
99507	Home visit for catheter maintenance code added

99508   Home visit for sleep studies code added

99509   Home visit for assistance with activities of daily living code added

99510   Home visit for individual, family or marriage counseling code added

99511   Home visit for fecal impaction code added

99512   Home visit for hemodialysis code added

99539   Home visit, NOS code added

99551   Home infusion for pain management code added

99552   Home infusion for pain management code added

99553   Home infusion for tocolytic therapy code added

99554   Home infusion for hematopoietic hormones code added

99555   Home infusion for chemotherapy code added

99556   Home infusion for antibiotics/antifungal/antiviral code added

99557   Home infusion for continuous anticoagulant therapy code added

99558   Home infusion of immunotherapy code added

99559   Home infusion of peritoneal dialysis code added

99560   Home infusion of enteral nutrition code added

99561   Home infusion of hydration therapy code added

99562   Home infusion of total parenteral nutrition code added

99563   Home infusion of aerosolized pentamidine code added

99564   Home infusion for anti-hemophilic agents code added

99565   Home infusion of alpha-1 proteinase inhibitor code added

99566   Home infusion for long-term intravenous treatment code added

99567   Home infusion of sympathomimetic agents code added

99568   Home infusion of miscellaneous drugs code added

99569   Home infusion, each additional therapy code added

Appendix C

Update to Short Descriptors

This listing includes changes necessary to update the short descriptors on the *CPT 2002* data file.

The descriptors have been changed to reflect additions, revisions, or deletions to the *CPT 2002* codes, or to enhance or correct the data file.

The descriptors which have been enhanced, but do not necessarily reflect a change to the *CPT 2002* codes, are indicated with an asterisk.

0001T	Add:ENDOVAS REPR ABDO AO ANEURYS
0002T	Add:ENDOVAS REPR ABDO AO ANEURYS
0003T	Add:CERVICOGRAPHY
0004T	Delete
0005T	Add:PERC CATH STENT/BRAIN CV ART
0006T	Add:PERC CATH STENT/BRAIN CV ART
0007T	Add:PERC CATH STENT/BRAIN CV ART
0008T	Add:UPPER GI ENDOSCOPY W/SUTURE
0009T	Add:ENDOMETRIAL CRYOABLATION
0010T	Add:TB TEST, GAMMA INTERFERON
0012T	Add:OSTEOCHONDRAL KNEE AUTOGRAFT
0013T	Add:OSTEOCHONDRAL KNEE ALLOGRAFT
0014T	Add:MENISCAL TRANSPLANT, KNEE
0016T	Add:THERMOTX CHOROID VASC LESION
0017T	Add:PHOTOCOAGULAT MACULAR DRUSEN
0018T	Add:TRANSCRANIAL MAGNETIC STIMUL
0019T	Add:EXTRACORP SHOCK WAVE TX, MS
0020T	Add:EXTRACORP SHOCK WAVE TX, FT
0021T	Add:FETAL OXIMETRY, TRNSVAG/CERV
0023T	Add:PHENOTYPE DRUG TEST, HIV 1
0024T	Add:TRANSCATH CARDIAC REDUCTION
0025T	Add:ULTRASONIC PACHYMETRY
0026T	Add:MEASURE REMNANT LIPOPROTEINS
00797	Add:ANESTH, SURGERY FOR OBESITY
00850	Delete
00851	Add:ANESTH, TUBAL LIGATION
00855	Delete
00857	Delete
00869	Add:ANESTH, VASECTOMY
00884	Delete
00946	Delete
00955	Delete
01214	Revise:ANESTH, HIP ARTHROPLASTY

01402	Revise:ANESTH, KNEE ARTHROPLASTY
01904	Delete
01905	ANES, SPINE INJECT, X-RAY/REPAIR
01906	Delete
01908	Delete
01910	Delete
01912	Delete
01914	Delete
01916	Revise: ANESTH, DX ARTERIOGRAPHY
01918	Delete
01921	Delete
01924	Add:ANES, THER INTERVEN RAD, ART
01925	Add:ANES, THER INTERVEN RAD, CAR
01926	Add:ANES, TX INTERV RAD HRT/CRAN
01930	Add:ANES, THER INTERVEN RAD, VEIN
01931	Add:ANES, THER INTERVEN RAD, TIPS
01932	Add:ANES, TX INTERV RAD, TH VEIN
01933	Add:ANES, TX INTERV RAD, CRAN V
01951	Revise:ANESTH, BURN, LESS 4 PERCENT
01952	Revise:ANESTH, BURN, 4-9 PERCENT
01960	Add:ANESTH, VAGINAL DELIVERY
01961	Add:ANESTH, CS DELIVERY
01962	Add:ANESTH, EMER HYSTERECTOMY
01963	Add:ANESTH, CS HYSTERECTOMY
01964	Add:ANESTH, ABORTION PROCEDURES
01967	Add:ANESTH/ANALG, VAG DELIVERY
01968	Add:ANES/ANALG CS DELIVER ADD-ON
01969	Add:ANESTH/ANALG CS HYST ADD-ON
01995	Revise: REGIONAL ANESTHESIA LIMB
10021	Add:FNA W/O IMAGE
10022	Add:FNA W/IMAGE
11981	Add:INSERT DRUG IMPLANT DEVICE
11982	Add:REMOVE DRUG IMPLANT DEVICE
11983	Add:REMOVE/INSERT DRUG IMPLANT
20526	Add:THER INJECTION, CARPAL TUNNEL
20551	Add:INJECT TENDON ORIGIN/INSERT
20552	Add:INJECT TRIGGER POINT, 1 OR 2
20553	Add:INJECT TRIGGER POINTS, > 3
24300	Add:MANIPULATE ELBOW W/ANESTH
24332	Add:TENOLYSIS, TRICEPS
24343	Add:REPR ELBOW LAT LIGMNT W/TISS
24344	Add:RECONSTRUCT ELBOW LAT LIGMNT
24345	Add:REPR ELBW MED LIGMNT W/TISSU
24346	Add:RECONSTRUCT ELBOW MED LIGMNT
25001	Add:INCISE FLEXOR CARPI RADIALIS
25020	Revise:DECOMPRESS FOREARM 1 SPACE

* 25023	Revise:DECOMPRESS FOREARM 1 SPACE	38221	Add:BONE MARROW BIOPSY
25024	Add:DECOMPRESS FOREARM 2 SPACES	43313	Add:ESOPHAGOPLASTY CONGENITAL
25025	Add:DECOMPRESS FOREARM 2 SPACES	43314	Add:TRACHEO-ESOPHAGOPLASTY CONG
25075	Revise:REMOVE FOREARM LESION SUBCUT	44020	Revise:EXPLORE SMALL INTESTINE
25076	Revise: REMOVE FOREARM LESION DEEP	44110	Revise:EXCISE INTESTINE LESION(S)
25259	Add:MANIPULATE WRIST W/ANESTHES	44126	Add:ENTERECTOMY W/TAPER, CONG
25275	Add:REPAIR FOREARM TENDON SHEATH	44127	Add:ENTERECTOMY W/O TAPER, CONG
25394	Add:REPAIR CARPAL BONE, SHORTEN	44128	Revise:ENTERECTOMY CONG, ADD-ON
25430	Add:VASC GRAFT INTO CARPAL BONE	44202	Revise:LAP RESECT S/INTESTINE SINGL
25431	Add:REPAIR NONUNION CARPAL BONE	44203	Add:LAP RESECT S/INTESTINE, ADDL
25651	Add:PIN ULNAR STYLOID FRACTURE	44204	Add:LAPARO PARTIAL COLECTOMY
25652	Add:TREAT FRACTURE ULNAR STYLOID	44205	Add:LAP COLECTOMY PART W/ILEUM
25671	Add:PIN RADIOULNAR DISLOCATION	45136	Add:EXCISE ILEOANAL RESERVOIR
26115	Revise: REMOVE HAND LESION SUBCUT	46020	Add:PLACEMENT OF SETON
26116	Revise: REMOVE HAND LESION, DEEP	47370	Add:LAPARO ABLATE LIVER TUMOR RF
26340	Add:MANIPULATE FINGER W/ANESTH	47371	Add:LAPARO ABLATE LIVER CRYOSURG
26585	Delete	47380	Add:OPEN ABLATE LIVER TUMOR RF
26597	Delete	47381	Add:OPEN ABLATE LIVER TUMOR CRYO
27130	Revise:TOTAL HIP ARTHROPLASTY	47382	Add:PERCUT ABLATE LIVER RF
27132	Revise:TOTAL HIP ARTHROPLASTY	48100	Revise: BIOPSY OF PANCREAS, OPEN
27447	Revise:TOTAL KNEE ARTHROPLASTY	48500	Revise: SURGERY OF PANCREATIC CYST
29086	Add:APPLY FINGER CAST	49491	Add:REPAIR ING HERN PREMIE REDUC
29805	Add:SHOULDER ARTHROSCOPY, DX	49492	Add:RPR ING HERN PREMIE, BLOCKED
29806	Add:SHOULDER ARTHROSCOPY/SURGERY	49495	Revise:RPR ING HERNIA BABY, REDUC
29807	Add:SHOULDER ARTHROSCOPY/SURGERY	* 49496	Revise:RPR ING HERNIA BABY, BLOCKED
29815	Delete	* 49500	Revise:RPR ING HERNIA, INIT, REDUCE
29824	Add:SHOULDER ARTHROSCOPY/SURGERY	* 49501	Revise:RPR ING HERNIA, INIT BLOCKED
29900	Add:MCP JOINT ARTHROSCOPY, DX	* 49505	Revise:RPR I/HERN INIT REDUC > 5 YR
29901	Add:MCP JOINT ARTHROSCOPY, SURG	* 49507	Revise:RPR I/HERN INIT BLOCK > 5 YR
29902	Add:MCP JOINT ARTHROSCOPY, SURG	* 49520	Revise:REREPAIR ING HERNIA, REDUCE
29909	Delete	* 49521	Revise:REREPAIR ING HERNIA, BLOCKED
29999	Add:ARTHROSCOPY OF JOINT	* 49525	Revise:REPAIR ING HERNIA, SLIDING
31528	Revise:LARYNGOSCOPY AND DILATION	* 49550	Revise:RPR FEM HERNIA, INIT, REDUCE
31529	Revise:LARYNGOSCOPY AND DILATION	* 49553	Revise:RPR FEM HERNIA, INIT BLOCKED
33967	Add:INSERT IA PERCUT DEVICE	* 49555	Revise:REREPAIR FEM HERNIA, REDUCE
33979	Add:INSERT INTRACORPOREAL DEVICE	* 49557	Revise:REREPAIR FEM HERNIA, BLOCKED
33980	Add:REMOVE INTRACORPOREAL DEVICE	* 49560	Revise:RPR VENTRAL HERN INIT, REDUC
35647	Add:ARTERY BYPASS GRAFT	* 49561	Revise:RPR VENTRAL HERN INIT, BLOCK
35685	Add:BYPASS GRAFT PATENCY/PATCH	* 49565	Revise:REREPAIR VENTRL HERN, REDUCE
35686	Add:BYPASS GRAFT/AV FIST PATENCY	* 49566	Revise:REREPAIR VENTRL HERN, BLOCK
36002	Add:PSEUDOANEURYSM INJECTION TRT	* 49570	Revise:RPR EPIGASTRIC HERN, REDUCE
36005	Revise:INJECTION EXT VENOGRAPHY	* 49572	Revise:RPR EPIGASTRIC HERN, BLOCKED
36819	Revise:AV FUSION/UPPR ARM VEIN	* 49580	Revise:RPR UMBIL HERN, REDUC < 5 YR
36820	Add:AV FUSION/FOREARM VEIN	* 49582	Revise:RPR UMBIL HERN, BLOCK < 5 YR
38220	Add:BONE MARROW ASPIRATION	* 49585	Revise:RPR UMBIL HERN, REDUC > 5 YR
		* 49587	Revise:RPR UMBIL HERN, BLOCK > 5 YR

* **49590** Revise:REPAIR SPIGELIAN HERNIA

50220 Revise:REMOVE KIDNEY, OPEN

* **50225** Revise:REMOVE KIDNEY OPEN, COMPLEX

* **50230** Revise:REMOVE KIDNEY OPEN, RADICAL

50815 Revise:URINE SHUNT TO INTESTINE

51065 Revise:REMOVE URETER CALCULUS

52001 Add:CYSTOSCOPY, REMOVAL OF CLOTS

52347 Add:CYSTOSCOPY, RESECT DUCTS

53431 Add:RECONSTUCT URETHRA/BLADDER

53443 Delete

53444 Add:INSERT TANDEM CUFF

53445 Revise:INSERT URO/VES NCK SPHINCTER

53446 Add:REMOVE URO SPHINCTER

53447 Revise:REMOVE/REPLACE UR SPHINCTER

53448 Add:REMOV/REPLC UR SPHINCTR COMP

53449 Revise:REPAIR URO SPHINCTER

53853 Add:PROSTATIC WATER THERMOTHER

54162 Add:LYSIS PENIL CIRCUMCIS LESION

54163 Add:REPAIR OF CIRCUMCISION

54164 Add:FRENULOTOMY OF PENIS

54402 Delete

54405 Revise:INSERT MULTI-COMP PENIS PROS

54406 Add:REMOVE MULTI-COMP PENIS PROS

54407 Delete

54408 Add:REPAIR MULTI-COMP PENIS PROS

54409 Delete

54410 Add:REMOVE/REPLACE PENIS PROSTH

54411 Add:REMV/REPLC PENIS PROS, COMPL

54415 Add:REMOVE SELF-CONTD PENIS PROS

54416 Add:REMV/REPL PENIS CONTAIN PROS

54417 Add:REMV/REPLC PENIS PROS, COMPL

54510 Delete

56501 Revise:DESTROY, VULVA LESIONS, SIMP

56515 Revise:DESTROY VULVA LESION/S COMPL

57022 Revise:I & D, VAGINAL HEMATOMA, PP

* **57023** Revise:I & D VAG HEMATOMA, NON-OB

57061 Revise:DESTROY VAG LESIONS, SIMPLE

57065 Revise:DESTROY VAG LESIONS, COMPLX

57155 Add:INSERT UTERI TANDEMS/OVOIDS

58346 Add:INSERT HEYMAN UTERI CAPSULE

58953 Add:TAH, RAD DISSECT FOR DEBULK

58954 Add:TAH RAD DEBULK/LYMPH REMOVE

59000 Revise:AMNIOCENTESIS, DIAGNOSTIC

59001 Add:AMNIOCENTESIS, THERAPEUTIC

62272 Revise:DRAIN CEREBRO SPINAL FLUID

64561 Add:IMPLANT NEUROELECTRODES

64581 Add:IMPLANT NEUROELECTRODES

64821 Add: REMOVE SYMPATHETIC NERVES

64822 Add:REMOVE SYMPATHETIC NERVES

64823 Add:REMOVE SYMPATHETIC NERVES

67225 Add:EYE PHOTODYNAMIC THER ADD-ON

74230 Revise: CINE/VIDEO X-RAY, THROAT/ESOPH

75898 Revise: FOLLOW-UP ANGIOGRAPHY

76066 Revise:JOINT SURVEY, SINGLE VIEW

76078 Revise:RADIOGRAPHIC ABSORPTIOMETRY

76085 Add:COMPUTER MAMMOGRAM ADD-ON

76120 Revise: CINE/VIDEO X-RAYS

76125 Revise: CINE/VIDEO X-RAYS ADD-ON

76362 Add:CAT SCAN FOR TISSUE ABLATION

76394 Add:MRI FOR TISSUE ABLATION

76490 Add:US FOR TISSUE ABLATION

76536 Revise:US EXAM OF HEAD AND NECK

76604 Revise:US EXAM, CHEST, B-SCAN

76645 Revise:US EXAM, BREAST(S)

76700 Revise:US EXAM, ABDOM, COMPLETE

* **76705** Revise:US EXAM, ABDOM, LIMITED

76770 Revise:US EXAM ABDO BACK WALL, COMP

* **76775** Revise:US EXAM ABDO BACK WALL, LIM

76778 Revise:US EXAM KIDNEY TRANSPLANT

76800 Revise:US EXAM, SPINAL CANAL

76805 Revise:US EXAM, PG UTERUS, COMPL

* **76810** Revise:US EXAM, PG UTERUS, MULT

* **76815** Revise:US EXAM, PG UTERUS LIMIT

* **76816** Revise:US EXAM PG UTERUS REPEAT

* **76818** Revise:FETAL BIOPHY PROFILE W/NST

76819 Revise:FETAL BIOPHYS PROFIL W/O NST

76830 Revise:US EXAM, TRANSVAGINAL

76856 Revise:US EXAM, PELVIC, COMPLETE

* **76857** Revise:US EXAM, PELVIC, LIMITED

76870 Revise:US EXAM, SCROTUM

76880 Revise:US EXAM, EXTREMITY

76885 Revise:US EXAM INFANT HIPS, DYNAMIC

76886 Revise:US EXAM INFANT HIPS, STATIC

77301 Add:RADIOTHERAPY DOSE PLAN, IMRT

77418 Add:RADIATION TX DELIVERY, IMRT

78615 Revise:CEREBRAL VASCULAR FLOW IMAGE

80072 Delete

82274 Add:ASSAY TEST FOR BLOOD, FECAL

82355 Revise:CALCULUS ANALYSIS, QUAL

* **82360** Revise:CALCULUS ASSAY, QUANT

* **82365** Revise:CALCULUS SPECTROSCOPY

83950	Add:ONCOPROTEIN, HER-2/NEU		96151	Add:ASSESS HLTH/BEHAVE, SUBSEQ
85095	Delete		96152	Add:INTERVENE HLTH/BEHAVE, INDIV
85102	Delete		96153	Add:INTERVENE HLTH/BEHAVE, GROUP
85535	Delete		96154	Add:INTERV HLTH/BEHAV, FAM W/PT
86141	Add:C-REACTIVE PROTEIN, HS		96155	Add:INTERV HLTH/BEHAV FAM NO PT
86336	Add:INHIBIN A		99289	Add:PT TRANSPORT, 30-74 MIN
86683	Delete		99290	Add:PT TRANSPORT, ADDL 30 MIN
87045	Revise:FECES CULTURE, BACTERIA		96567	Add:PHOTODYNAMIC TX, SKIN
87198	Add:CYTOMEGALOVIRUS ANTIBODY DFA		97005	Add:ATHLETIC TRAIN EVAL
87199	Add:ENTEROVIRUS ANTIBODY, DFA		97006	Add:ATHLETIC TRAIN REEVAL
87802	Add:STREP B ASSAY W/OPTIC		97601	Revise:WOUND(S) CARE, SELECTIVE
87803	Add:CLOSTRIDIUM TOXIN A W/OPTIC		* 97602	Revise:WOUND(S) CARE NON-SELECT
87804	Add:INFLUENZA ASSAY W/OPTIC		99091	Add:COLLECT/REVIEW DATA FROM PT
87902	Add:GENOTYPE, DNA, HEPATITIS C		99500	Add:HOME VISIT, PRENATAL
88170	Delete		99501	Add:HOME VISIT, POSTNATAL
88171	Delete		99502	Add:HOME VISIT, NB CARE
88380	Add:MICRODISSECTION		99503	Add:HOME VISIT, RESP THERAPY
90473	Add:IMMUNE ADMIN ORAL/NASAL		99504	Add:HOME VISIT MECH VENTILATOR
90474	Add:IMMUNE ADMIN ORAL/NASAL ADDL		99505	Add:HOME VISIT, STOMA CARE
90732	Revise: PNEUMOCOCCAL VACCINE		99506	Add:HOME VISIT, IM INJECTION
90939	Add:HEMODIALYSIS STUDY, TRANSCUT		99507	Add:HOME VISIT, CATH MAINTAIN
91123	Add:IRRIGATE FECAL IMPACTION		99508	Add:HOME VISIT, SLEEP STUDIES
92136	Add:OPHTHALMIC BIOMETRY		99509	Add:HOME VISIT DAY LIFE ACTIVITY
92532	Revise:POSITIONAL NYSTAGMUS TEST		99510	Add:HOME VISIT, SING/M/FAM COUNS
92534	Revise:OPTOKINETIC NYSTAGMUS TEST		99511	Add:HOME VISIT, FECAL/ENEMA MGMT
92973	Add:PERCUT CORONARY THROMBECTOMY		99512	Add:HOME VISIT, HEMODIALYSIS
92974	Add:CATH PLACE, CARDIO BRACHYTX		99539	Add:HOME VISIT, NOS
93025	Add:MICROVOLT T-WAVE ASSESS		99551	Add:HOME INFUS, PAIN MGMT, IV/SC
93536	Delete		99552	Add:HM INFUS PAIN MGMT, EPID/ITH
93607	Delete		99553	Add:HOME INFUSE, TOCOLYTIC TX
93609	Revise:MAP TACHYCARDIA, ADD-ON		99554	Add:HOME INFUS, HORMONE/PLATELET
93613	Add:ELECTROPHYS MAP, 3D, ADD-ON		99555	Add:HOME INFUSE, CHEMOTHERAPY
93701	Add:BIOIMPEDANCE, THORACIC		99556	Add:HOME INFUS, ANTIBIO/FUNG/VIR
93737	Delete		99557	Add:HOME INFUSE, ANTICOAGULANT
93738	Delete		99558	Add:HOME INFUSE, IMMUNOTHERAPY
95250	Add:GLUCOSE MONITORING, CONT		99559	Add:HOME INFUS, PERITON DIALYSIS
95904	Revise:SENSE NERVE CONDUCTION TEST		99560	Add:HOME INFUS, ENTERO NUTRITION
95965	Add:MEG, SPONTANEOUS		99561	Add:HOME INFUS, HYDRATION TX
95966	Add:MEG, EVOKED, SINGLE		99562	Add:HOME INFUS, PARENT NUTRITION
95967	Add:MEG, EVOKED, EACH ADDL		99563	Add:HOME ADMIN, PENTAMIDINE
96000	Add:MOTION ANALYSIS, VIDEO/3D		99564	Add:HME INFUS, ANTIHEMOPHIL AGNT
96001	Add:MOTION TEST W/FT PRESS MEAS		99565	Add:HOME INFUS, PROTEINASE INHIB
96002	Add:DYNAMIC SURFACE EMG		99566	Add:HOME INFUSE, IV THERAPY
96003	Add:DYNAMIC FINE WIRE EMG		99567	Add:HOME INFUSE, SYMPATH AGENT
96004	Add:PHYS REVIEW OF MOTION TESTS		99568	Add:HOME INFUS, MISC DRUG, DAILY
96150	Add:ASSESS HLTH/BEHAVE, INIT		99569	Add:HOME INFUSE, EACH ADDL TX

Appendix D

Clinical Examples

As described in *CPT 2002*, clinical examples of the CPT codes for Evaluation and Management (E/M) services are intended to be an important element of the coding system. The clinical examples, when used with the E/M descriptors contained in the full text of *CPT*, provide a comprehensive and powerful new tool for physicians to report the services provided to their patients.

The American Medical Association is pleased to provide you with these clinical examples for *CPT 2002*. The clinical examples that are provided in this supplement are limited to Office or Other Outpatient Services, Hospital Inpatient Services, Consultations, Critical Care, Prolonged Services and Care Plan Oversight.

These clinical examples do not encompass the entire scope of medical practice. Inclusion or exclusion of any particular specialty group does not infer any judgment of importance or lack thereof; nor does it limit the applicability of the example to any particular specialty.

Of utmost importance is that these clinical examples are just that: examples. A particular patient encounter, depending on the specific circumstances, must be judged by the services provided by the physician for that particular patient. Simply because the patient's complaints, symptoms, or diagnoses match those of a particular clinical example, does not automatically assign that patient encounter to that particular level of service. The three key components (history, examination, and medical decision making) must be met and documented in the medical record to report a particular level of service.

Office or Other Outpatient Services

New Patient

99201 Initial office visit for a 50-year-old male from out-of-town who needs a prescription refill for a nonsteroidal anti-inflammatory drug. (Anesthesiology)

Initial office visit for a 40-year-old female, new patient, requesting information about local pain clinics. (Anesthesiology/Pain Medicine)

Initial office visit for a 10-year-old girl for determination of visual acuity as part of a summer camp physical (does not include determination of refractive error). (Ophthalmology)

Initial office visit for an out-of-town patient requiring topical refill. (Dermatology)

Initial office visit for a 65-year-old male for reassurance about an isolated seborrheic keratosis on upper back. (Plastic Surgery)

Initial office visit for an out-of-state visitor who needs refill of topical steroid to treat lichen planus. (Dermatology)

Initial office visit for an 86-year-old male, out-of-town visitor, who needs prescription refilled for an anal skin preparation that he forgot. (General Surgery/Colon & Rectal Surgery)

Initial office visit for a transient patient with alveolar osteitis for repacking. (Oral & Maxillofacial Surgery)

Initial office visit for a patient with a pedunculated lesion of the neck which is unsightly. (Dermatology)

Initial office visit for a 10-year-old male, for limited subungual hematoma not requiring drainage. (Internal Medicine)

Initial office visit with an out-of-town visitor who needs a prescription refilled because she forgot her hay fever medication. (Allergy & Immunology/Internal Medicine)

Initial office visit with a 9-month-old female with diaper rash. (Pediatrics)

Initial office visit with a 10-year-old male with severe rash and itching for the past 24 hours, positive history for contact with poison oak 48 hours prior to the visit. (Family Medicine)

Initial office visit with a 5-year-old female to remove sutures from simple wound placed by another physician. (Plastic Surgery)

Initial office visit for a 22-year-old male with a small area of sunburn requiring first aid. (Dermatology/Family Medicine/Internal Medicine)

Initial office visit for the evaluation and management of a contusion of a finger. (Orthopaedic Surgery)

99202 Initial office visit for a 13-year-old patient with comedopapular acne of the face unresponsive to over-the-counter medications. (Family Medicine)

Initial office visit for a patient with a clinically benign lesion or nodule of the lower leg which has been present for many years. (Dermatology)

Initial office visit for a patient with a circumscribed patch of dermatitis of the leg. (Dermatology)

Initial office visit for a patient with papulosquamous eruption of elbows. (Dermatology)

Initial office visit for a 9-year-old patient with erythematous, grouped, vesicular eruption of the lip of three days' duration. (Pediatrics)

Initial office visit for an 18-year-old male referred by an orthodontist for advice regarding removal of four wisdom teeth. (Oral & Maxillofacial Surgery)

Initial office visit for a 14-year-old male, who was referred by his orthodontist, for advice on the exposure of impacted maxillary cuspids. (Oral & Maxillofacial Surgery)

Initial office visit for a patient presenting with itching patches on the wrists and ankles. (Dermatology)

Initial office visit for a 30-year-old male for evaluation and discussion of treatment of rhinophyma. (Plastic Surgery)

Initial office visit for a 16-year-old male with severe cystic acne, new patient. (Dermatology)

Initial office evaluation for gradual hearing loss, 58-year-old male, history and physical examination, with interpretation of complete audiogram, air bone, etc. (Otolaryngology)

Initial evaluation and management of recurrent urinary infection in female. (Internal Medicine)

Initial office visit with a 10-year-old girl with history of chronic otitis media and a draining ear. (Pediatrics)

Initial office visit for a 10-year-old female with acute maxillary sinusitis. (Family Medicine)

Initial office visit for a patient with recurring episodes of herpes simplex who has developed a clustering of vesicles on the upper lip. (Internal Medicine)

Initial office visit for a 25-year-old patient with single season allergic rhinitis. (Allergy & Immunology)

Initial office visit to plan transient dialysis for a 56-year-old stable dialysis patient who has accompanying records. (Nephrology)

99203 Initial office visit for a 76-year-old male with a stasis ulcer of three months' duration. (Dermatology)

Initial office visit for a 30-year-old female with pain in the lateral aspect of the forearm. (Physical Medicine & Rehabilitation)

Initial office visit for a 15-year-old patient with a four-year history of moderate comedopapular acne of the face, chest, and back with early scarring. Discussion of use of systemic medication. (Dermatology)

Initial office visit for a patient with papulosquamous eruption of the elbow with pitting of nails and itchy scalp. (Dermatology)

Initial office visit for a 57-year-old female who complains of painful parotid swelling for one week's duration. (Oral & Maxillofacial Surgery)

Initial office visit for a patient with an ulcerated non-healing lesion or nodule on the tip of the nose. (Dermatology)

Initial office visit for a patient with dermatitis of the antecubital and popliteal fossae. (Dermatology)

Initial office visit for a 22-year-old female with irregular menses. (Family Medicine)

Initial office visit for a 50-year-old female with dyspepsia and nausea. (Family Medicine)

Initial office visit for a 53-year-old laborer with degenerative joint disease of the knee with no prior treatment. (Orthopaedic Surgery)

Initial office visit for a 60-year-old male with Dupuytren's contracture of one hand with multiple digit involvement. (Orthopaedic Surgery)

Initial office visit for a 33-year-old male with painless gross hematuria without cystoscopy. (Internal Medicine)

Initial office visit for a 55-year-old female with chronic blepharitis. There is a history of use of many medications. (Ophthalmology)

Initial office visit for an 18-year-old female with a two-day history of acute conjunctivitis. Extensive history of possible exposures, prior normal ocular history, and medication use is obtained. (Ophthalmology)

Initial office visit for a 14-year-old male with unilateral anterior knee pain. (Physical Medicine & Rehabilitation)

Initial office visit of an adult who presents with symptoms of an upper-respiratory infection that has progressed to unilateral purulent nasal discharge and discomfort in the right maxillary teeth. (Otolaryngology, Head & Neck Surgery)

Initial office visit of a 40-year-old female with symptoms of atopic allergies including eye and sinus congestion, often associated with infections. She would like to be tested for allergies. (Otolaryngology, Head & Neck Surgery)

Initial office visit of a 65-year-old with nasal stuffiness. (Otolaryngology, Head & Neck Surgery)

Initial office visit for initial evaluation of a 48-year-old man with recurrent low back pain radiating to the leg. (General Surgery)

Initial office visit for evaluation, diagnosis and management of painless gross hematuria in a new patient, without cystoscopy. (Internal Medicine)

Initial office visit with couple for counseling concerning voluntary vasectomy for sterility. Spent 30 minutes discussing procedure, risks and benefits, and answering questions. (Urology)

Initial office visit of a 49-year-old male with nasal obstruction. Detailed exam with topical anesthesia. (Plastic Surgery)

Initial office visit for evaluation of a 13-year-old female with progressive scoliosis. (Physical Medicine & Rehabilitation)

Initial office visit for a 21-year-old female desiring counseling and evaluation of initiation of contraception. (Family Practice/Internal Medicine/Obstetrics & Gynecology)

Initial office visit for a 49-year-old male presenting with painless blood per rectum associated with bowel movement. (Colon & Rectal Surgery)

Initial office visit for a 19-year-old football player with three-day-old acute knee injury; now with swelling and pain. (Orthopaedic Surgery)

99204 Initial office visit for a 13-year-old female with progressive scoliosis. (Orthopaedic Surgery)

Initial office visit for a 34-year-old female with primary infertility for evaluation and counseling. (Obstetrics & Gynecology)

Initial office visit for a 6-year-old male with multiple upper respiratory infections. (Allergy & Immunology)

Initial office visit for a patient with generalized dermatitis of 80 percent of the body surface area. (Dermatology)

Initial office visit for an adolescent who was referred by school counselor because of repeated skipping school. (Psychiatry)

Initial office visit for a 50-year-old machinist with a generalized eruption. (Dermatology)

Initial office visit for a 45-year-old female who has been abstinent from alcohol and benzodiazepines for three months but complains of headaches, insomnia, and anxiety. (Psychiatry)

Initial office visit for a 60-year-old maie with recent change in bowel habits, weight loss, and abdominal pain. (Abdominal Surgery/General Surgery)

Initial office visit for a 50-year-old male with an aortic aneurysm who is considering surgery. (General Surgery)

Initial office visit for a 17-year-old female with depression. (Internal Medicine)

Initial office visit of a 40-year-old with chronic draining ear, imbalance, and probable cholesteatoma. (Otolaryngology, Head & Neck Surgery)

Initial office visit for initial evaluation of a 63-year-old male with chest pain on exertion. (Cardiology/Internal Medicine)

Initial office visit for evaluation of a 70-year-old patient with recent onset of episodic confusion. (Internal Medicine)

Initial office visit for a 7-year-old female with juvenile diabetes mellitus, new to area, past history of hospitalization times three. (Pediatrics)

Initial office visit of a 50-year-old female with progressive solid food dysphagia. (Gastroenterology)

Initial office visit for a 34-year-old patient with primary infertility, including counseling. (Obstetrics & Gynecology)

Initial office visit for evaluation of a 70-year-old female with polyarthralgia. (Rheumatology)

Initial office visit for a patient with papulosquamous eruption involving 60 percent of the cutaneous surface with joint pain. Combinations of topical and systemic treatments discussed. (Dermatology)

99205 Initial office visit for a patient with disseminated lupus erythematosus with kidney disease, edema, purpura, and scarring lesions on the extremities plus cardiac symptoms. (Dermatology/General Surgery/Internal Medicine)

Initial office visit for a 25-year-old female with systemic lupus erythematosus, fever, seizures, and profound thrombocytopenia. (Rheumatology/Allergy & Immunology)

Initial office visit for an adult with multiple cutaneous blisters, denuded secondarily infected ulcerations, oral lesions, weight loss, and increasing weakness refractory to high dose corticosteroid. Initiation of new immunosuppressive therapy. (Dermatology)

Initial office visit for a 28-year-old male with systemic vasculitis and compromised circulation to the limbs. (Rheumatology)

Initial office visit for a 41-year-old female new to the area requesting rheumatologic care, on disability due to scleroderma and recent hospitalization for malignant hypertension. (Rheumatology)

Initial office visit for a 52-year-old female with acute four extremity weakness and shortness of breath one week post-flu vaccination. (Physical Medicine & Rehabilitation)

Initial office visit for a 60-year-old male with previous back surgery; now presents with back and pelvic pain, two-month history of bilateral progressive calf and thigh tightness and weakness when walking, causing several falls. (Orthopaedic Surgery)

Initial office visit for an adolescent referred from ER after making suicide gesture. (Psychiatry)

Initial office visit for a 49-year-old female with a history of headaches and dependence on opioids. She reports weight loss, progressive headache, and depression. (Psychiatry)

Initial office visit for a 50-year-old female with symptoms of rash, swellings, recurrent arthritic complaints, and diarrhea and lymphadenopathy. Patient has had a 25 lb. weight loss and was recently camping in the Amazon. (Allergy & Immunology)

Initial office visit for a 34-year-old uremic Type I diabetic patient referred for ESRD modality assessment and planning. (Nephrology)

Initial office visit for a 75-year-old female with neck and bilateral shoulder pain, brisk deep tendon reflexes, and stress incontinence. (Physical Medicine & Rehabilitation)

Initial office visit for an 8-year-old male with cerebral palsy and spastic quadriparesis. (Physical Medicine & Rehabilitation)

Initial office visit for a 73-year-old male with known prostate malignancy, who presents with severe back pain and a recent onset of lower extremity weakness. (Physical Medicine & Rehabilitation)

Initial office visit for a 38-year-old male with paranoid delusions and a history of alcohol abuse. (Psychiatry)

Initial office visit for a 12-week-old with bilateral hip dislocations and bilateral club feet. (Orthopaedic Surgery)

Initial office visit for a 29-year-old female with acute orbital congestion, eyelid retraction, and bilateral visual loss from optic neuropathy. (Ophthalmology)

Initial office visit for a 70-year-old diabetic patient with progressive visual field loss, advanced optic disc cupping and neovascularization of retina. (Ophthalmology)

Initial office visit for a newly diagnosed Type I diabetic patient. (Endocrinology)

Initial office evaluation of a 65-year-old female with exertional chest pain, intermittent claudication, syncope and a murmur of aortic stenosis. (Cardiology)

Initial office visit for a 73-year-old male with an unexplained 20 lb. weight loss. (Hematology/Oncology)

Initial office evaluation, patient with systemic lupus erythematosus, fever, seizures and profound thrombocytopenia. (Allergy & Immunology/Internal Medicine/Rheumatology)

Initial office evaluation and management of patient with systemic vasculitis and compromised circulation to the limbs. (Rheumatology)

Initial office visit for a 24-year-old homosexual male who has a fever, a cough, and shortness of breath. (Infectious Disease)

Initial outpatient evaluation of a 69-year-old male with severe chronic obstructive pulmonary disease, congestive heart failure, and hypertension. (Family Medicine)

Initial office visit for a 17-year-old female, who is having school problems and has told a friend she is considering suicide. The patient and her family are consulted in regard to treatment options. (Psychiatry)

Initial office visit for a female with severe hirsutism, amenorrhea, weight loss and a desire to have children. (Endocrinology/Obstetrics & Gynecology)

Initial office visit for a 42-year-old male on hypertensive medication, newly arrived to the area, with diastolic blood pressure of 110, history of recurrent calculi, episodic headaches, intermittent chest pain and orthopnea. (Internal Medicine)

Established Patient

99211 Office visit for an 82-year-old female, established patient, for a monthly B12 injection with documented Vitamin B12 deficiency. (Geriatrics/Internal Medicine/Family Medicine)

Office visit for a 50-year-old male, established patient, for removal of uncomplicated facial sutures. (Plastic Surgery)

Office visit for an established patient who lost prescription for lichen planus. Returned for new copy. (Dermatology)

Office visit for an established patient undergoing orthodontics who complains of a wire which is irritating his/her cheek and asks you to check it. (Oral & Maxillofacial Surgery)

Office visit for a 50-year-old female, established patient, seen for her gold injection by the nurse. (Rheumatology)

Office visit for a 73-year-old female, established patient, with pernicious anemia for weekly B12 injection. (Gastroenterology)

Office visit for an established patient for dressing change on a skin biopsy. (Dermatology)

Office visit for a 19-year-old, established patient, for removal of sutures from a two cm. laceration of forehead, which you placed four days ago in ER. (Plastic Surgery)

Office visit of a 20-year-old female, established patient, who receives an allergy vaccine injection and is observed for a reaction by the nurse. (Otolaryngology, Head & Neck Surgery)

Office visit for a 45-year-old male, established patient, with chronic renal failure for the administration of erythropoietin. (Nephrology)

Office visit for an established patient, a Peace Corps enlistee, who requests documentation that third molars have been removed. (Oral & Maxillofacial Surgery)

Office visit for a 69-year-old female, established patient, for partial removal of antibiotic gauze from an infected wound site. (Plastic Surgery)

Office visit for a 9-year-old, established patient, successfully treated for impetigo, requiring release to return to school. (Dermatology/Pediatrics)

Office visit for an established patient requesting a return-to-work certificate for resolving contact dermatitis. (Dermatology)

Office visit for an established patient who is performing glucose monitoring and wants to check accuracy of machine with lab blood glucose by technician who checks accuracy and function of patient machine. (Endocrinology)

Follow-up office visit for a 65-year-old female with a chronic indwelling percutaneous nephrostomy catheter seen for routine pericatheter skin care and dressing change. (Interventional Radiology)

Outpatient visit with 19-year-old male, established patient, for supervised drug screen. (Addiction Medicine)

Office visit with 12-year-old male, established patient, for cursory check of hematoma one day after venipuncture. (Internal Medicine)

Office visit with 31-year-old female, established patient, for return to work certificate. (Anesthesiology)

Office visit for a 42-year-old, established patient, to read tuberculin test results. (Allergy & Immunology)

Office visit for 14-year-old, established patient, to re-dress an abrasion. (Orthopaedic Surgery)

Office visit for a 45-year-old female, established patient, for a blood pressure check. (Obstetrics & Gynecology)

Office visit for a 23-year-old, established patient, for instruction in use of peak flow meter. (Allergy & Immunology)

Office visit for prescription refill for a 35-year-old female, established patient, with schizophrenia who is stable but has run out of neuroleptic and is scheduled to be seen in a week. (Psychiatry)

99212 Office visit for an 11-year-old, established patient, seen in follow-up for mild comedonal acne of the cheeks on topical desquamating agents. (Dermatology/Family Medicine/Pediatrics)

Office visit for a 10-year-old female, established patient, who has been swimming in a lake, now presents with a one-day history of left ear pain with purulent drainage. (Family Medicine)

Office visit of a child, established patient, with chronic secretory otitis media. (Otolaryngology, Head & Neck Surgery)

Office visit for an established patient seen in follow-up of clearing patch of localized contact dermatitis. (Family Medicine/Dermatology)

Office visit for an established patient returning for evaluation of response to treatment of lichen planus on wrists and ankles. (Dermatology)

Office visit for an established patient with tinea pedis being treated with topical therapy. (Dermatology)

Office visit for an established patient with localized erythematous plaque of psoriasis with topical hydration. (Dermatology)

Office visit for a 50-year-old male, established patient, recently seen for acute neck pain, diagnosis of spondylosis, responding to physical therapy and intermittent cervical traction. Returns for evaluation for return to work. (Neurology)

Office visit for an established patient with recurring episodes of herpes simplex who has developed a clustering of vesicles on the upper lip. (Oral & Maxillofacial Surgery)

Evaluation for a 50-year-old male, established patient, who has experienced a recurrence of knee pain after he discontinued NSAID. (Anesthesiology/Pain Medicine)

Office visit for an established patient with an irritated skin tag for reassurance. (Dermatology)

Office visit for a 40-year-old, established patient, who has experienced a systemic allergic reaction following administration of immunotherapy. The dose must be readjusted. (Allergy & Immunology)

Office visit for a 33-year-old, established patient, for contusion and abrasion of lower extremity. (Orthopaedic Surgery)

Office visit for a 22-year-old male, established patient, one month after I & D of "wrestler's ear." (Plastic Surgery)

Office visit for a 21-year-old, established patient, who is seen in follow-up after antibiotic therapy for acute bacterial tonsillitis. (Otolaryngology, Head & Neck Surgery)

Office visit for a 4-year-old, established patient, with tympanostomy tubes, check-up. (Otolaryngology, Head & Neck Surgery)

Office visit for an established patient who has had needle aspiration of a peritonsillar abscess. (Otolaryngology, Head & Neck Surgery)

Follow-up office examination for evaluation and treatment of acute draining ear in a 5-year-old with tympanotomy tubes. (Otolaryngology, Head & Neck Surgery)

Office visit, established patient, 6-year-old with sore throat and headache. (Family Medicine/Pediatrics)

Office evaluation for possible purulent bacterial conjunctivitis with one- to two-day history of redness and discharge, 16-year-old female, established patient. (Pediatrics/Internal Medicine/Family Medicine)

Office visit with a 65-year-old female, established patient, returns for three-week follow-up for resolving severe ankle sprain. (Orthopaedic Surgery)

Office visit, sore throat, fever and fatigue in a 19-year-old college student, established patient. (Internal Medicine)

Office visit with a 33-year-old female, established patient, recently started on treatment for hemorrhoidal complaints, for re-evaluation. (Colon & Rectal Surgery)

Office visit with a 36-year-old male, established patient, for follow-up on effectiveness of medicine management of oral candidiasis. (Oral & Maxillofacial Surgery)

Office visit for a 27-year-old female, established patient, with complaints of vaginal itching. (Obstetrics & Gynecology)

Office visit for a 65-year-old male, established patient, with eruptions on both arms from poison oak exposure. (Allergy & Immunology/Internal Medicine)

99213 Office visit for an established patient with new lesions of lichen planus in spite of topical therapies. (Dermatology)

Office visit for the quarterly follow-up of a 45-year-old male with stable chronic asthma requiring regular drug therapy. (Allergy & Immunology)

Office visit for a 13-year-old, established patient, with comedopapular acne of the face which has shown poor response to topical medication. Discussion of use of systemic medication. (Dermatology)

Office visit for a 62-year-old female, established patient, for follow-up for stable cirrhosis of the liver. (Internal Medicine/Family Medicine)

Office visit for a 3-year-old, established patient, with atopic dermatitis and food hypersensitivity for quarterly follow-up evaluation. The patient is on topical lotions and steroid creams as well as oral antihistamines. (Allergy & Immunology)

Office visit for an 80-year-old female, established patient, to evaluate medical management of osteoarthritis of the temporomandibular joint. (Rheumatology)

Office visit for a 70-year-old female, established patient, one year post excision of basal cell carcinoma of nose with nasolabial flap. Now presents with new suspicious recurrent lesion and suspicious lesion of the back. (Plastic Surgery)

Office visit for a 68-year-old female, established patient, with polymyalgia rheumatic, maintained on chronic low-dose corticosteroid, with no new complaints. (Rheumatology)

Office visit for a 3-year-old female, established patient, for earache and dyshidrosis of feet. (Pediatrics/Family Medicine)

Office visit for an established patient for 18 months post-operative follow-up of TMJ repair. (Oral & Maxillofacial Surgery)

Office visit for a 45-year-old male, established patient, being re-evaluated for recurrent acute prostatitis. (Urology)

Office visit for a 43-year-old male, established patient, with known reflex sympathetic dystrophy. (Anesthesiology)

Office visit for an established patient with an evenly pigmented superficial nodule of leg which is symptomatic. (Dermatology)

Office visit for an established patient with psoriasis involvement of the elbows, pitting of the nails, and itchy scalp. (Dermatology)

Office visit for a 27-year-old male, established patient, with deep follicular and perifollicular inflammation unable to tolerate systemic antibiotics due to GI upset, requires change of systemic medication. (Dermatology)

Office visit for a 16-year-old male, established patient, who is on medication for exercise-induced bronchospasm. (Allergy & Immunology)

Office visit for a 60-year-old, established patient, with chronic essential hypertension on multiple drug regimen, for blood pressure check. (Family Medicine)

Office visit for a 20-year-old male, established patient, for removal of sutures in hand. (Family Medicine)

Office visit for a 58-year-old female, established patient, with unilateral painful bunion. (Orthopaedic Surgery)

Office visit for a 45-year-old female, established patient, with known osteoarthritis and painful swollen knees. (Rheumatology)

Office visit for a 25-year-old female, established patient, complaining of bleeding and heavy menses. (Obstetrics & Gynecology)

Office visit for a 55-year-old male, established patient, with hypertension managed by a beta blocker/thiazide regime; now experiencing mild fatigue. (Nephrology)

Office visit for a 65-year-old female, established patient, with primary glaucoma for interval determination of intraocular pressure and possible adjustment of medication. (Ophthalmology)

Office visit for a 56-year-old man, established patient, with stable exertional angina who complains of new onset of calf pain while walking. (Cardiology)

Office visit for a 63-year-old female, established patient, with rheumatoid arthritis on auranofin and ibuprofin, seen for routine follow-up visit. (Rheumatology)

Office visit for an established patient with Graves' disease, three months post I-131 therapy, who presents with lassitude and malaise. (Endocrinology)

Office visit for the quarterly follow-up of a 63-year-old male, established patient, with chronic myofascial pain syndrome, effectively managed by doxepin, who presents with new onset urinary hesitancy. (Pain Medicine)

Office visit for the biannual follow-up of an established patient with migraine variant having infrequent, intermittent, moderate to severe headaches with nausea and vomiting, which are sometimes effectively managed by ergotamine tartrate and an antiemetic, but occasionally requiring visits to an emergency department. (Pain Medicine)

Office visit for an established patient after discharge from a pain rehabilitation program to review and adjust medication dosage. (Pain Medicine)

Office visit with 55-year-old male, established patient, for management of hypertension, mild fatigue, on beta blocker/thiazide regimen. (Family Medicine/Internal Medicine)

Outpatient visit with 37-year-old male, established patient, who is three years post total colectomy for chronic ulcerative colitis, presents for increased irritation at his stoma. (General Surgery)

Office visit for a 70-year-old diabetic hypertensive established patient with recent change in insulin requirement. (Internal Medicine/Nephrology)

Office visit with 80-year-old female, established patient, for follow-up osteoporosis, status-post compression fractures. (Rheumatology)

Office visit for an established patient with stable cirrhosis of the liver. (Gastroenterology)

Routine, follow-up office evaluation at a three-month interval for a 77-year-old female, established patient, with nodular small cleaved-cell lymphoma. (Hematology/Oncology)

Quarterly follow-up office visit for a 45-year-old male, established patient, with stable chronic asthma, on steroid and bronchodilator therapy. (Pulmonary Medicine)

Office visit for a 50-year-old female, established patient, with insulin-dependent diabetes mellitus and stable coronary artery disease, for monitoring. (Family Medicine/Internal Medicine)

99214 Office visit for an established patient now presenting with generalized dermatitis of 80 percent of the body surface area. (Dermatology)

Office visit for a 32-year-old female, established patient, with new onset right lower quadrant pain. (Family Medicine)

Office visit for reassessment and reassurance/counseling of a 40-year-old female, established patient, who is experiencing increased symptoms while on a pain management treatment program. (Pain Medicine)

Office visit for a 30-year-old, established patient, under management for intractable low back pain, who now presents with new onset right posterior thigh pain. (Pain Medicine)

Office visit for an established patient with frequent intermittent, moderate to severe headaches requiring beta blocker or tricyclic antidepressant prophylaxis, as well as four symptomatic treatments, but who is still experiencing headaches at a frequency of several times a month that are unresponsive to treatment. (Pain Medicine)

Office visit for an established patient with psoriasis with extensive involvement of scalp, trunk, palms, and soles with joint pain. Combinations of topical and systemic treatments discussed and instituted. (Dermatology)

Office visit for a 55-year-old male, established patient, with increasing night pain, limp, and progressive varus of both knees. (Orthopaedic Surgery)

Follow-up visit for a 15-year-old withdrawn patient with four-year history of papulocystic acne of the face, chest, and back with early scarring and poor response to past treatment. Discussion of use of systemic medication. (Dermatology)

Office visit for a 28-year-old male, established patient, with regional enteritis, diarrhea, and low-grade fever. (Internal Medicine)

Office visit for a 25-year-old female, established patient, following recent arthrogram and MR imaging for TMJ pain. (Oral & Maxillofacial Surgery)

Office visit for a 32-year-old female, established patient, with large obstructing stone in left mid-ureter, to discuss management options including urethroscopy with extraction or ESWL. (Urology)

Evaluation for a 28-year-old male, established patient, with new onset of low back pain. (Anesthesiology/Pain Medicine)

Office visit for a 28-year-old female, established patient, with right lower quadrant abdominal pain, fever, and anorexia. (Internal Medicine/Family Medicine)

Office visit for a 45-year-old male, established patient, four months follow-up of L4-5 diskectomy, with persistent incapacitating low back and leg pain. (Orthopaedic Surgery)

Outpatient visit for a 77-year-old male, established patient, with hypertension, presenting with a three-month history of episodic substernal chest pain on exertion. (Cardiology)

Office visit for a 25-year-old female, established patient, for evaluation of progressive saddle nose deformity of unknown etiology. (Plastic Surgery)

Office visit for a 65-year-old male, established patient, with BPH and severe bladder outlet obstruction, to discuss management options such as TURP. (Urology)

Office visit for an adult diabetic established patient with a past history of recurrent sinusitis who presents with a one-week history of double vision. (Otolaryngology, Head & Neck Surgery)

Office visit for an established patient with lichen planus and 60 percent of the cutaneous surface involved, not responsive to systemic steroids, as well as developing symptoms of progressive heartburn and paranoid ideation. (Dermatology)

Office visit for a 52-year-old male, established patient, with a 12-year history of bipolar disorder responding to lithium carbonate and brief psychotherapy. Psychotherapy and prescription provided. (Psychiatry)

Office visit for a 63-year-old female, established patient, with a history of familial polyposis, status post-colectomy with sphincter sparing procedure, who now presents with rectal bleeding and increase in stooling frequency. (General Surgery)

Office visit for a 68-year-old male, established patient, with the sudden onset of multiple flashes and floaters in the right eye due to a posterior vitreous detachment. (Ophthalmology)

Office visit for a 55-year-old female, established patient, on cyclosporin for treatment of resistant, small vessel vasculitis. (Rheumatology)

Follow-up office visit for a 55-year-old male, two months after iliac angioplasty with new onset of contralateral extremity claudication. (Interventional Radiology)

Office visit for a 68-year-old male, established patient, with stable angina, two months post myocardial infarction, who is not tolerating one of his medications. (Cardiology)

Weekly office visit for 5FU therapy for an ambulatory established patient with metastatic colon cancer and increasing shortness of breath. (Hematology/Oncology)

Follow-up office visit for a 60-year-old male, established patient, whose post-traumatic seizures have disappeared on medication and who now raises the question of stopping the medication (Neurology)

Office evaluation on new onset RLQ pain in a 32-year-old woman, established patient. (Urology/General Surgery/Internal Medicine/Family Medicine)

Office evaluation of 28-year-old, established patient, with regional enteritis, diarrhea and low-grade fever. (Family Medicine/Internal Medicine)

Office visit with 50-year-old female, established patient, diabetic, blood sugar controlled by diet. She now complains of frequency of urination and weight loss, blood sugar of 320 and negative ketones on dipstick. (Internal Medicine)

Follow-up office visit for a 45-year-old, established patient, with rheumatoid arthritis on gold, methotrexate, or immunosuppressive therapy. (Rheumatology)

Office visit for a 60-year-old male, established patient, two years post-removal of intracranial meningioma, now with new headaches and visual disturbance. (Neurosurgery)

Office visit for a 68-year-old female, established patient, for routine review and follow-up of non-insulin dependent diabetes, obesity, hypertension and congestive heart failure. Complains of vision difficulties and admits dietary noncompliance. Patient is counseled concerning diet and current medications adjusted. (Family Medicine)

99215 Office visit for an established patient who developed persistent cough, rectal bleeding, weakness, and diarrhea plus pustular infection on skin. Patient on immunosuppressive therapy. (Dermatology)

Office visit for an established patient with disseminated lupus erythematosus, extensive edema of extremities kidney disease, and weakness requiring monitored course on azathioprene, corticosteroid and complicated by acute depression. (Dermatology/Internal Medicine/Rheumatology)

Office visit for an established patient with progressive dermatomyositis and recent onset of fever, nasal speech, and regurgitation of fluids through the nose. (Dermatology)

Office visit for a 28-year-old female, established patient, who is abstinent from previous cocaine dependence, but reports progressive panic attacks and chest pains. (Psychiatry)

Office visit for an established adolescent patient with history of bipolar disorder treated with lithium; seen on urgent basis at family's request because of severe depressive symptoms. (Psychiatry)

Office visit for an established patient having acute migraine with new onset neurological symptoms and whose headaches are unresponsive to previous attempts at management with a combination of preventive and abortive medication. (Pain Medicine)

Office visit for an established patient with exfoliative lichen planus with daily fever spikes, disorientation, and shortness of breath. (Dermatology)

Office visit for a 25-year-old, established patient, two years post-burn with bilateral ectropion, hypertrophic facial burn scars, near absence of left breast, and burn syndactyly of both hands. Discussion of treatment options following examination. (Plastic Surgery)

Office visit for a 6-year-old, established patient, to review newly diagnosed immune deficiency with recommendations for therapy including IV immunoglobulin and chronic antibiotics. (Allergy & Immunology)

Office visit for a 36-year-old, established patient, three months status post-transplant, with new onset of peripheral edema, increased blood pressure, and progressive fatigue. (Nephrology)

Office visit for an established patient with Kaposi's sarcoma who presents with fever and widespread vesicles. (Dermatology)

Office visit for a 27-year-old female, established patient, with bipolar disorder who was stable on lithium carbonate and monthly supportive psychotherapy but now has developed symptoms of hypomania. (Psychiatry)

Office visit for a 25-year-old male, established patient with a history of schizophrenia who has been seen bi-monthly but is complaining of auditory hallucinations. (Psychiatry)

Office visit for a 62-year-old male, established patient, three years post-op abdominal perineal resection, now with a rising carcinoembryonic antigen, weight loss, and pelvic pain. (Abdominal Surgery)

Office visit for a 42-year-old male, established patient, nine months post-op emergency vena cava shunt for variceal bleeding, now presents with complaints of one episode of "dark" bowel movement, weight gain, tightness in abdomen, whites of eyes seem "yellow" and occasional drowsiness after eating hamburgers. (Abdominal Surgery)

Office visit for a 68-year-old male, established patient, with biopsy-proven rectal carcinoma, for evaluation and discussion of treatment options. (General Surgery)

Office visit for a 60-year-old, established patient, with diabetic nephropathy with increasing edema and dyspnea. (Endocrinology)

Office visit with 30-year-old male, established patient for three-month history of fatigue, weight loss, intermittent fever, and presenting with diffuse adenopathy and splenomegaly. (Family Medicine)

Office visit for restaging of an established patient with new lymphadenopathy one year post-therapy for lymphoma. (Hematology/Oncology)

Office visit for evaluation of recent onset syncopal attacks in a 70-year-old woman, established patient. (Internal Medicine)

Follow-up visit, 40-year-old mother of three, established patient, with acute rheumatoid arthritis, anatomical Stage 3, ARA function Class 3 rheumatoid arthritis, and deteriorating function. (Rheumatology)

Office evaluation and discussion of treatment options for a 68-year-old male, established patient, with a biopsy-proven rectal carcinoma. (General Surgery)

Follow-up office visit for a 65-year-old male, established patient, with a fever of recent onset while on outpatient antibiotic therapy for endocarditis. (Infectious Disease)

Office visit for a 75-year-old, established patient, with ALS (amyotrophic lateral sclerosis), who is no longer able to swallow. (Neurology)

Office visit for a 70-year-old female, established patient, with diabetes mellitus and hypertension, presenting with a two-month history of increasing confusion, agitation and short-term memory loss. (Family Medicine/Internal Medicine)

Hospital Inpatient Services

Initial Hospital Care

New or Established Patient

99221 Initial hospital visit following admission for a 42-year-old male for observation following an uncomplicated mandible fracture. (Plastic Surgery/Oral & Maxillofacial Surgery)

Initial hospital visit for a 40-year-old patient with a thrombosed synthetic arteriovenous conduit. (Nephrology)

Initial hospital visit for a healthy 24-year-old male with an acute onset of low back pain following a lifting injury. (Internal Medicine/Anesthesiology/Pain Medicine)

Initial hospital visit for a 69-year-old female with controlled hypertension, scheduled for surgery. (Internal Medicine/Cardiology)

Initial hospital visit for a 24-year-old healthy female with benign tumor of palate. (Oral & Maxillofacial Surgery)

Initial hospital visit for a 14-year-old female with infectious mononucleosis and dehydration. (Internal Medicine)

Initial hospital visit for a 62-year-old female with stable rheumatoid arthritis, admitted for total joint replacement. (Rheumatology)

Initial hospital visit for a 12-year-old patient with a laceration of the upper eyelid, involving the lid margin and superior canaliculus, admitted prior to surgery for IV antibiotic therapy. (Plastic Surgery)

Initial hospital visit for a 69-year-old female with controlled hypertension, scheduled for surgery. (Cardiology)

Hospital admission, examination, and initiation of treatment program for a 67-year-old male with uncomplicated pneumonia who requires IV antibiotic therapy. (Internal Medicine)

Hospital admission for an 18-month-old with 10 percent dehydration. (Pediatrics)

Hospital admission for a 12-year-old with a laceration of the upper eyelid involving the lid margin and superior canaliculus, admitted prior to surgery for IV antibiotic therapy. (Ophthalmology)

Hospital admission for a 32-year-old female with severe flank pain, hematuria and presumed diagnosis of ureteral calculus as determined by Emergency Department physician. (Urology)

Initial hospital visit for a patient with several large venous stasis ulcers not responding to outpatient therapy. (Dermatology)

Initial hospital visit for 21-year-old pregnant patient (nine weeks gestation) with hyperemesis gravidarum. (Obstetrics & Gynecology)

Initial hospital visit for a 73-year-old female with acute pyelonephritis who is otherwise generally healthy. (Geriatrics)

Initial hospital visit for 62-year-old patient with cellulitis of the foot requiring bedrest and intravenous antibiotics. (Orthopaedic Surgery)

99222   Initial hospital visit for a 50-year-old patient with lower quadrant abdominal pain and increased temperature, but without septic picture. (General Surgery/Abdominal Surgery/Colon & Rectal Surgery)

Initial hospital visit for airway management, due to a benign laryngeal mass. (Otolaryngology, Head & Neck Surgery)

Initial hospital visit for a 66-year-old female with an L-2 vertebral compression fracture with acute onset of paralytic ileus; seen in the office two days previously. (Orthopaedic Surgery)

Initial hospital visit and evaluation of a 15-year-old male admitted with peritonsillar abscess or cellulitis requiring intravenous antibiotic therapy. (Otolaryngology, Head & Neck Surgery)

Initial hospital visit for a 42-year-old male with vertebral compression fracture following a motor vehicle accident. (Orthopaedic Surgery)

Initial hospital visit for a patient with generalized atopic dermatitis and secondary infection. (Dermatology)

Initial hospital visit for a 3-year-old patient with high temperature, limp, and painful hip motion of 18 hours' duration. (Pediatrics/Orthopaedic Surgery)

Initial hospital visit for a young adult, presenting with an acute asthma attack unresponsive to outpatient therapy. (Allergy & Immunology)

Initial hospital visit for an 18-year-old male who has suppurative sialoadenitis and dehydration. (Oral & Maxillofacial Surgery)

Initial hospital visit for a 65-year-old female for acute onset of thrombotic cerebrovascular accident with contralateral paralysis and aphasia. (Neurology)

Initial hospital visit for a 50-year-old male chronic paraplegic patient with pain and spasm below the lesion. (Anesthesiology)

Partial hospital admission for an adolescent patient from chaotic blended family, transferred from inpatient setting, for continued treatment to control symptomatic expressions of hostility and depression. (Psychiatry)

Initial hospital visit for a 15-year-old male with acute status asthmaticus, unresponsive to outpatient therapy. (Internal Medicine)

Initial hospital visit for a 61-year-old male with history of previous myocardial infarction, who now complains of chest pain. (Internal Medicine)

Initial hospital visit of a 15-year-old on medications for a sore throat over the last two weeks. The sore throat has worsened and now has dysphagia. The exam shows large necrotic tonsils with an adequate airway and small palpable nodes. The initial mono test was negative. (Otolaryngology, Head & Neck Surgery)

Initial hospital evaluation of a 23-year-old allergy patient admitted with eyelid edema and pain on fifth day of oral antibiotic therapy. (Otolaryngology, Head & Neck Surgery)

Hospital admission, young adult patient, failed previous therapy and now presents in acute asthmatic attack. (Family Medicine/Allergy & Immunology)

Hospital admission of a 62-year-old smoker, established patient, with bronchitis in acute respiratory distress. (Internal Medicine/Pulmonary Medicine)

Hospital admission, examination, and initiation of a treatment program for a 65-year-old female with new onset of right-sided paralysis and aphasia. (Neurology)

Hospital admission for a 50-year-old with left lower quadrant abdominal pain and increased temperature, but without septic picture. (General Surgery)

Hospital admission, examination, and initiation of treatment program for a 66-year-old chronic hemodialysis patient with fever and a new pulmonary infiltrate. (Nephrology)

Hospital admission for an 8-year-old febrile patient with chronic sinusitis and severe headache, unresponsive to oral antibiotics. (Allergy & Immunology)

Hospital admission for a 40-year-old male with submaxillary cellulitis and trismus from infected lower molar. (Oral & Maxillofacial Surgery)

99223   Initial hospital visit for a 45-year-old female, who has a history of rheumatic fever as a child and now has anemia, fever, and congestive heart failure. (Cardiology)

Initial hospital visit for a 50-year-old male with acute chest pain and diagnostic electrocardiographic changes of an acute anterior myocardial infarction. (Cardiology/Family Medicine/Internal Medicine)

Initial hospital visit of a 75-year-old with progressive stridor and dysphagia with history of cancer of the larynx treated by radiation therapy in the past. Exam shows a large recurrent tumor of the glottis with a mass in the neck. (Otolaryngology, Head & Neck Surgery)

Initial hospital visit for a 70-year-old male admitted with chest pain, complete heart block, and congestive heart failure. (Cardiology)

Initial hospital visit for an 82-year-old male who presents with syncope, chest pain, and ventricular arrhythmias. (Cardiology)

Initial hospital visit for a 75-year-old male with history of arteriosclerotic coronary vascular disease, who is severely dehydrated, disoriented, and experiencing auditory hallucinations. (Psychiatry)

Initial hospital visit for a 70-year-old male with alcohol and sedative-hypnotic dependence, admitted by family for severe withdrawal, hypertension, and diabetes mellitus. (Psychiatry)

Initial hospital visit for a persistently suicidal latency-aged child whose parents have requested admission to provide safety during evaluation, but are anxious about separation from her. (Psychiatry)

Initial psychiatric visit for an adolescent patient without previous psychiatric history, who was transferred from the medical ICU after a significant overdose. (Psychiatry)

Initial hospital visit for a 35-year-old female with severe systemic lupus erythematosus on corticosteroid and cyclophosphamide, with new onset of fever, chills, rash, and chest pain. (Rheumatology)

Initial hospital visit for a 52-year-old male with known rheumatic heart disease who presents with anasarca, hypertension, and history of alcohol abuse. (Cardiology)

Initial hospital visit for a 55-year-old female with a history of congenital heart disease; now presents with cyanosis. (Cardiology)

Initial hospital visit for a psychotic, hostile, violently combative adolescent, involuntarily committed, for seclusion and restraint in order to provide for safety on unit. (Psychiatry)

Initial hospital visit for a now subdued and sullen teenage male with six-month history of declining school performance, increasing self-endangerment, and resistance of parental expectations, including running away past weekend after physical fight with father. (Psychiatry)

Initial partial hospital admission for a 17-year-old female with history of borderline mental retardation who has developed auditory hallucinations. Parents are known to abuse alcohol, and Child Protective Services is investigating allegations of sexual abuse of a younger sibling. (Psychiatry)

Initial hospital visit of a 67-year old male admitted with a large neck mass, dysphagia, and history of myocardial infarction three months before. (Otolaryngology, Head & Neck Surgery)

Initial hospital visit for a patient with suspected cerebrospinal fluid rhinorrhea which developed two weeks after head injury. (Otolaryngology, Head & Neck Surgery)

Initial hospital visit for a 25-year-old female with history of poly-substance abuse and psychiatric disorder. The patient appears to be psychotic with markedly elevated vital signs. (Psychiatry)

Initial hospital visit for a 70-year-old male with cutaneous T-cell lymphoma who has developed fever and lymphadenopathy. (Internal Medicine)

Initial hospital visit for a 62-year-old female with known coronary artery disease, for evaluation of increasing edema, dyspnea on exertion, confusion, and sudden onset of fever with productive cough. (Internal Medicine)

Initial hospital visit for a 3-year-old female with 36-hour history of sore throat and high fever; now with sudden onset of lethargy, irritability, photophobia, and nuchal rigidity. (Pediatrics)

Initial hospital visit for a 26-year-old female for evaluation of severe facial fractures (LeFort's II/III). (Plastic Surgery)

Initial hospital visit for a 55-year-old female for bilateral mandibular fractures resulting in flail mandible and airway obstruction. (Plastic Surgery)

Initial hospital visit for a 71-year-old patient with a red painful eye four days following uncomplicated cataract surgery due to endophthalmitis. (Ophthalmology)

Initial hospital visit for a 45-year-old patient involved in a motor vehicle accident who suffered a perforating corneoscleral laceration with loss of vision. (Ophthalmology)

Initial hospital visit for a 58-year-old male who has Ludwig's angina and progressive airway compromise. (Oral & Maxillofacial Surgery)

Initial hospital visit for a patient with generalized systemic sclerosis, receiving immunosuppressive therapy because of recent onset of cough, fever, and inability to swallow. (Dermatology)

Initial hospital visit for an 82-year-old male who presents with syncope, chest pain, and ventricular arrhythmias. (Cardiology)

Initial hospital visit for a 62-year-old male with history of previous myocardial infarction, comes in with recurrent, sustained ventricular tachycardia. (Cardiology)

Initial hospital visit for a chronic dialysis patient with infected PTFE fistula, septicemia, and shock. (Nephrology)

Initial hospital visit for a 1-year-old male, victim of child abuse, with central nervous system depression, skull fracture, and retinal hemorrhage. (Family Medicine/Neurology)

Initial hospital visit for a 25-year-old female with recent C4-5 quadriplegia, admitted for rehabilitation. (Physical Medicine & Rehabilitation)

Initial hospital visit for an 18-year-old male, post-traumatic brain injury with multiple impairment. (Physical Medicine & Rehabilitation)

Initial partial hospital admission for 16-year-old male, sullen and subdued, with six-month history of declining school performance, increasing self-endangerment, and resistance to parental expectations. (Psychiatry)

Initial hospital visit for a 16-year-old primigravida at 32 weeks gestation with severe hypertension (200/110), thrombocytopenia, and headache. (Obstetrics & Gynecology)

Initial hospital visit for a 49-year-old male with cirrhosis of liver with hematemesis, hepatic encephalopathy, and fever. (Gastroenterology)

Initial hospital visit for a 55-year-old female in chronic pain who has attempted suicide. (Psychiatry)

Initial hospital visit for a 70-year-old male, with multiple organ system disease, admitted with history of being aneuric and septic for 24 hours prior to admission. (Urology)

Initial hospital visit for a 3-year-old female with 36-hour history of sore throat and high fever, now with sudden onset of lethargy, irritability, photophobia, and nuchal rigidity. (Internal Medicine)

Initial hospital visit for a 78-year-old male, transfers from nursing home with dysuria and pyuria, increasing confusion, and high fever. (Internal Medicine)

Initial hospital visit for a 1-day-old male with cyanosis, respiratory distress, and tachypnea. (Cardiology)

Initial hospital visit for a 3-year-old female with recurrent tachycardia and syncope. (Cardiology)

Initial hospital visit for a thyrotoxic patient who presents with fever, atrial fibrillation, and delirium. (Endocrinology)

Initial hospital visit for a 50-year-old Type I diabetic who presents with diabetic ketoacidosis with fever and obtundation. (Endocrinology)

Initial hospital visit for a 40-year-old female with anatomical stage 3, ARA functional class 3 rheumatoid arthritis on methotrexate, corticosteroid, and nonsteroidal anti-inflammatory drugs. Patient presents with severe arthritis flare, new oral ulcers, abdominal pain, and leukopenia. (Rheumatology)

Initial hospital exam of a pediatric patient with high fever and proptosis. (Otolaryngology, Head & Neck Surgery)

Initial hospital visit for a 25-year-old patient admitted for the first time to the rehab unit, with recent C-4-5 quadriplegia. (Physical Medicine & Rehabilitation)

Hospital admission, examination, and initiation of treatment program for a previously unknown 58-year-old male who presents with acute chest pain (Cardiology)

Hospital admission, examination, and initiation of induction chemotherapy for a 42-year-old patient with newly diagnosed acute myelogenous leukemia. (Hematology/Oncology)

Hospital admission following a motor vehicle accident of a 24-year-old male with fracture dislocation of C5-6; neurologically intact. (Neurosurgery)

Hospital admission for a 78-year-old female with left lower lobe pneumonia and a history of coronary artery disease, congestive heart failure, osteoarthritis and gout. (Family Medicine)

Hospital admission, examination, and initiation of treatment program for a 65-year-old immunosuppressed male with confusion, fever, and a headache. (Infectious Disease)

Hospital admission for a 9-year-old with vomiting, dehydration, fever, tachypnea and an admitting diagnosis of diabetic ketoacidosis. (Pediatrics)

Initial hospital visit for a 65-year-old male who presents with acute myocardial infarction, oliguria, hypotension, and altered state of consciousness. (Cardiology)

Initial hospital visit for a hostile/resistant adolescent patient who is severely depressed and involved in poly-substance abuse. Patient is experiencing significant conflict in his chaotic family situation and was suspended from school following an attack on a teacher with a baseball bat. (Psychiatry)

initial hospital visit for 89-year-old female with fulminant hepatic failure and encephalopathy. (Gastroenterology)

Initial hospital visit for a 42-year-old female with rapidly progressing scleroderma, malignant hypertension, digital infarcts, and oligurea. (Rheumatology)

Subsequent Hospital Care

99231 Subsequent hospital visit for a 65-year-old female, post-open reduction and internal fixation of a fracture. (Physical Medicine & Rehabilitation)

Subsequent hospital visit for a 33-year-old patient with pelvic pain who is responding to pain medication and observation. (Obstetrics & Gynecology)

Subsequent hospital visit for a 21-year-old female with hyperemesis who has responded well to intravenous fluids. (Obstetrics & Gynecology)

Subsequent hospital visit to re-evaluate post-op pain and titrate patient-controlled analgesia for a 27-year-old female. (Anesthesiology)

Follow-up hospital visit for a 35-year-old female, status post-epidural analgesia. (Anesthesiology/Pain Medicine)

Subsequent hospital visit for a 56-year-old male, post-gastrectomy, for maintenance of analgesia using an intravenous dilaudid infusion. (Anesthesiology)

Subsequent hospital visit for a 4-year-old on day three receiving medication for uncomplicated pneumonia. (Allergy & Immunology)

Subsequent hospital visit for a 30-year-old female with urticaria which has stabilized with medication. (Allergy & Immunology)

Subsequent hospital visit for a 76-year-old male with venous stasis ulcers. (Dermatology)

Subsequent hospital visit for a 24-year-old female with otitis externa, seen two days before in consultation, now to have otic wick removal. (Otolaryngology, Head & Neck Surgery)

Subsequent hospital visit for a 27-year-old with acute labyrinthitis. (Otolaryngology, Head & Neck Surgery)

Subsequent hospital visit for a 10-year-old male admitted for lobar pneumonia with vomiting and dehydration; is becoming afebrile and tolerating oral fluids. (Family Medicine/Pediatrics)

Subsequent hospital visit for a 62-year-old patient with resolving cellulitis of the foot. (Orthopaedic Surgery)

Subsequent hospital visit for a 25-year-old male admitted for supra-ventricular tachycardia and converted on medical therapy. (Cardiology)

Subsequent hospital visit for a 27-year-old male two days after open reduction and internal fixation for malar complex fracture. (Plastic Surgery)

Subsequent hospital visit for a 76-year-old male with venous stasis ulcers. (Geriatrics)

Subsequent hospital visit for a 67-year-old female admitted three days ago with bleeding gastric ulcer; now stable. (Gastroenterology)

Subsequent hospital visit for stable 33-year-old male, status post-lower gastrointestinal bleeding. (General Surgery/Gastroenterology)

Subsequent hospital visit for a 29-year-old auto mechanic with effort thrombosis of left upper extremity. (General Surgery)

Subsequent hospital visit for a 14-year-old female in middle phase of inpatient treatment, who is now behaviorally stable and making satisfactory progress in treatment. (Psychiatry)

Subsequent hospital visit for an 18-year-old male with uncomplicated asthma who is clinically stable. (Allergy & Immunology)

Subsequent hospital visit for a 55-year-old male with rheumatoid arthritis, two days following an uncomplicated total joint replacement. (Rheumatology)

Subsequent hospital visit for a 60-year-old dialysis patient with an access infection, now afebrile on antibiotic. (Nephrology)

Subsequent hospital visit for a 36-year-old female with stable post-rhinoplasty epistaxis. (Plastic Surgery)

Subsequent hospital visit for a 66-year-old female with L-2 vertebral compression fracture with resolving ileus. (Orthopaedic Surgery)

Subsequent hospital visit for a patient with peritonsillar abscess. (Otolaryngology, Head & Neck Surgery)

Subsequent hospital visit for an 18-year-old female responding to intravenous antibiotic therapy for ear or sinus infection. (Otolaryngology, Head & Neck Surgery)

Subsequent hospital visit for a 70-year-old male admitted with congestive heart failure who has responded to therapy. (Cardiology)

Follow-up hospital visit for a 32-year-old female with left ureteral calculus; being followed in anticipation of spontaneous passage. (Urology)

Subsequent hospital visit for a 4-year-old female, admitted for acute gastroenteritis and dehydration, requiring IV hydration; now stable. (Family Medicine)

Subsequent hospital visit for a 50-year-old Type II diabetic who is clinically stable and without complications requiring regulation of a single dose of insulin daily. (Endocrinology)

Subsequent hospital visit to reassesses the status of a 65-year-old patient post-open reduction and internal fixation of hip fracture, on the rehab unit. (Physical Medicine & Rehabilitation)

Subsequent hospital visit for a 78-year-old male with cholangiocarcinoma managed by biliary drainage. (Interventional Radiology)

Subsequent hospital visit for a 50-year-old male with uncomplicated myocardial infarction who is clinically stable and without chest pain. (Family Medicine/Cardiology/Internal Medicine)

Subsequent hospital visit for a stable 72-year-old lung cancer patient undergoing a five-day course of infusion chemotherapy. (Hematology/Oncology)

Subsequent hospital visit, two days post admission for a 65-year-old male with a CVA (cerebral vascular accident) and left hemiparesis, who is clinically stable. (Neurology/Physical Medicine and Rehabilitation)

Subsequent hospital visit for now stable, 33-year-old male, status post lower gastrointestinal bleeding. (General Surgery)

Subsequent visit on third day of hospitalization for a 60-year-old female recovering from an uncomplicated pneumonia. (Infectious Disease/Internal Medicine/Pulmonary Medicine)

Subsequent hospital visit for a 3-year-old patient in traction for a congenital dislocation of the hip. (Orthopaedic Surgery)

Subsequent hospital visit for a 4-year-old female, admitted for acute gastroenteritis and dehydration, requiring IV hydration; now stable. (Family Medicine/Internal Medicine)

Subsequent hospital visit for 50-year-old female with resolving uncomplicated acute pancreatitis. (Gastroenterology)

99232 Subsequent hospital visit for a patient with venous stasis ulcers who developed fever and red streaks adjacent to the ulcer. (Dermatology/Internal Medicine/Family Medicine)

Subsequent hospital visit for a 66-year-old male for dressing changes and observation. Patient has had a myocutaneous flap to close a pharyngeal fistula and now has a low-grade fever. (Plastic Surgery)

Subsequent hospital visit for a 54-year-old female admitted for myocardial infarction, but who is now having frequent premature ventricular contractions. (Internal Medicine)

Subsequent hospital visit for an 80-year-old patient with a pelvic rim fracture, inability to walk, and severe pain; now 36 hours post-injury, experiencing urinary retention. (Orthopaedic Surgery)

Subsequent hospital visit for a 17-year-old female with fever, pharyngitis, and airway obstruction, who after 48 hours develops a maculopapular rash. (Pediatrics/Family Medicine)

Follow-up hospital visit for a 32-year-old patient admitted the previous day for corneal ulcer. (Dermatology)

Follow-up visit for a 67-year-old male with congestive heart failure who has responded to antibiotics and diuretics, and has now developed a monoarthropathy. (Internal Medicine)

Follow-up hospital visit for a 58-year-old male receiving continuous opioids who is experiencing severe nausea and vomiting. (Pain Medicine)

Subsequent hospital visit for a patient after an auto accident who is slow to respond to ambulation training. (Physical Medicine & Rehabilitation)

Subsequent hospital visit for a 14-year-old with unstable bronchial asthma complicated by pneumonia. (Allergy & Immunology)

Subsequent hospital visit for a 50-year-old diabetic, hypertensive male with back pain not responding to conservative inpatient management with continued radiation of pain to the lower left extremity. (Orthopaedic Surgery)

Subsequent hospital visit for a 37-year-old female on day five of antibiotics for bacterial endocarditis, who still has low-grade fever.

Subsequent hospital visit for a 54-year-old patient, post MI (myocardial infarction), who is out of the CCU (coronary care unit) but is now having frequent premature ventricular contractions on telemetry. (Cardiology/Internal Medicine)

Subsequent hospital visit for a patient with neutropenia, a fever responding to antibiotics, and continued slow gastrointestinal bleeding on platelet support. (Hematology/Oncology)

Subsequent hospital visit for a 50-year-old male admitted two days ago for sub-acute renal allograft rejection. (Nephrology)

Subsequent hospital visit for a 35-year-old drug addict, not responding to initial antibiotic therapy for pyelonephritis. (Urology)

Subsequent hospital visit of an 81-year-old male with abdominal distention, nausea, and vomiting. (General Surgery)

Subsequent hospital care for a 62-year-old female with congestive heart failure, who remains dyspneic and febrile. (Internal Medicine)

Subsequent hospital visit for a 73-year-old female with recently diagnosed lung cancer, who complains of unsteady gait. (Pulmonary Medicine)

Subsequent hospital visit for a 20-month-old male with bacterial meningitis treated one week with antibiotic therapy; has now developed a temperature of 101.0. (Pediatrics)

Subsequent hospital visit for 13-year-old male admitted with left lower quadrant abdominal pain and fever, not responding to therapy. (General Surgery)

Subsequent hospital visit for a 65-year-old male with hemiplegia and painful paretic shoulder. (Physical Medicine & Rehabilitation)

99233   Subsequent hospital visit for a 38-year-old male, quadriplegic with acute autonomic hyperreflexia, who is not responsive to initial care. (Physical Medicine & Rehabilitation)

Follow-up hospital visit for a teenage female who continues to experience severely disruptive, violent and life-threatening symptoms in a complicated multi-system illness. Family/social circumstances also a contributing factor. (Psychiatry)

Subsequent hospital visit for a 42-year-old female with progressive systemic sclerosis (scleroderma), renal failure on dialysis, congestive heart failure, cardiac arrhythmias, and digital ulcers. (Allergy & Immunology)

Subsequent hospital visit for a 50-year-old diabetic, hypertensive male with nonresponding back pain and radiating pain to the lower left extremity, who develops chest pain, cough, and bloody sputum. (Orthopaedic Surgery)

Subsequent hospital visit for a 64-year-old female, status post-abdominal aortic aneurysm resection, with non-responsive coagulopathy, who has now developed lower GI bleeding. (Abdominal Surgery/Colon & Rectal Surgery/General Surgery)

Follow-up hospital care of a patient with pansinusitis infection complicated by a brain abscess and asthma; no response to current treatment. (Otolaryngology, Head & Neck Surgery)

Subsequent hospital visit for a patient with a laryngeal neoplasm who develops airway compromise, suspected metastasis. (Otolaryngology, Head & Neck Surgery)

Subsequent hospital visit for a 49-year-old male with significant rectal bleeding, etiology undetermined, not responding to treatment. (Abdominal Surgery/General Surgery/Colon & Rectal Surgery)

Subsequent hospital visit for a 50-year-old male, post-aortocoronary bypass surgery; now develops hypotension and oliguria. (Cardiology)

Subsequent hospital visit for an adolescent patient who is violent, unsafe, and noncompliant, with multiple expectations for participation in treatment plan and behavior on the treatment unit. (Psychiatry)

Subsequent hospital visit for an 18-year-old male being treated for presumed PCP psychosis. Patient is still moderately symptomatic with auditory hallucinations and is insisting on signing out against medical advice. (Psychiatry)

Subsequent hospital visit for an 8-year-old female with caustic ingestion, who now has fever, dyspnea, and dropping hemoglobin. (Gastroenterology)

Follow-up hospital visit for a chronic renal failure patient on dialysis who develops chest pain and shortness of breath and a new onset pericardial friction rub. (Nephrology)

Subsequent hospital visit for a 44-year-old patient with electrical burns to the left arm with ascending infection. (Orthopaedic Surgery)

Subsequent hospital visit for a patient with systemic sclerosis who has aspirated and is short of breath. (Dermatology)

Subsequent hospital visit for a 65-year-old female, status post-op resection of abdominal aortic aneurysm, with suspected ischemic bowel. (General Surgery)

Subsequent hospital visit for a 50-year-old male, post-aortocoronary bypass surgery, now develops hypotension and oliguria. (Cardiology)

Subsequent hospital visit for a 65-year-old male, following an acute myocardial infarction, who complains of shortness of breath and new chest pain. (Cardiology)

Subsequent hospital visit for a 65-year-old female with rheumatoid arthritis (stage 3, class 3) admitted for urosepsis. On the third hospital day, chest pain, dyspnea and fever develop. (Rheumatology)

Follow-up hospital care of a pediatric case with stridor, laryngomalcia, established tracheostomy, complicated by multiple medical problems in PICU. (Otolaryngology, Head & Neck Surgery)

Subsequent hospital visit for a 60-year-old female, four days post uncomplicated inferior myocardial infarction who has developed severe chest pain, dyspnea, diaphoresis and nausea. (Family Medicine)

Subsequent hospital visit for a patient with AML (acute myelogenous leukemia), fever, elevated white count and uric acid undergoing induction chemotherapy. (Hematology/Oncology)

Subsequent hospital visit for a 38-year-old quadriplegic male with acute autonomic hyperreflexia, who is not responsive to initial care. (Physical Medicine & Rehabilitation)

Subsequent hospital visit for a 65-year-old female post-op resection of abdominal aortic aneurysm, with suspected ischemic bowel. (General Surgery)

Subsequent hospital visit for a 60-year-old female with persistent leukocytosis and a fever seven days after a sigmoid colon resection for carcinoma. (Infectious Disease)

Subsequent hospital visit for a chronic renal failure patient on dialysis, who develops chest pain, shortness of breath and new onset of pericardial friction rub. (Nephrology)

Subsequent hospital visit for a 65-year-old male with acute myocardial infarction who now demonstrates complete heart block and congestive heart failure. (Cardiology)

Subsequent hospital visit for a 25-year-old female with hypertension and systemic lupus erythmatosus, admitted for fever and respiratory distress. On the third hospital day, the patient presented with purpuric skin lesions and acute renal failure. (Allergy & Immunology)

Subsequent hospital visit for a 55-year-old male with severe chronic obstructive pulmonary disease and bronchospasm; initially admitted for acute respiratory distress requiring ventilatory support in the ICU. The patient was stabilized, extubated and transferred to the floor, but has now developed acute fever, dyspnea, left lower lobe rhonchi and laboratory evidence of carbon dioxide retention and hypoxemia. (Family Medicine/Internal Medicine)

Subsequent hospital visit for 46-year-old female, known liver cirrhosis patient, with recent upper gastrointestinal hemorrhage from varices; now with worsening ascites and encephalopathy. (Gastroenterology)

Subsequent hospital visit for 62-year-old female admitted with acute subarachnoid hemorrhage, negative cerebral arteriogram, increased lethargy and hemiparesis with fever. (Neurosurgery)

Consultations

Office or Other Outpatient Consultations

New or Established Patient

99241 Initial office consultation for a 40-year-old female in pain from blister on lip following a cold. (Oral & Maxillofacial Surgery)

Initial office consultation for a 62-year-old construction worker with olecranon bursitis. (Orthopaedic Surgery)

Office consultation with 25-year-old postpartum female with severe symptomatic hemorrhoids. (Colon & Rectal Surgery)

Office consultation with 58-year-old male, referred for follow-up of creatinine level and evaluation of obstructive uropathy, relieved two months ago. (Nephrology)

Office consultation for 30-year-old female tennis player with sprain or contusion of the forearm. (Orthopaedic Surgery)

Office consultation for a 45-year-old male, requested by his internist, with asymptomatic torus palatinus requiring no further treatment. (Oral & Maxillofacial Surgery)

99242 Initial office consultation for a 20-year-old male with acute upper respiratory tract symptoms. (Allergy & Immunology)

Initial office consultation for a 29-year-old soccer player with painful proximal thigh/groin injury. (Orthopaedic Surgery)

Initial office consultation for a 66-year-old female with wrist and hand pain, numbness of finger tips, suspected median nerve compression by carpal tunnel syndrome. (Plastic Surgery)

Initial office consultation for a patient with a solitary lesion of discoid lupus erythematosus on left cheek to rule out malignancy of self-induced lesion. (Dermatology)

Office consultation for management of systolic hypertension in a 70-year-old male scheduled for elective prostate resection. (Geriatrics)

Office consultation with 27-year-old female, with old amputation, for evaluation of existing above-knee prosthesis. (Physical Medicine & Rehabilitation)

Office consultation with 66-year-old female with wrist and hand pain, and finger numbness, secondary to suspected carpal tunnel syndrome. (Orthopaedic Surgery)

Office consultation for 61-year-old female, recently on antibiotic therapy, now with diarrhea and leukocytosis. (Abdominal Surgery)

Office consultation for a patient with papulosquamous eruption of elbow with pitting of nails and itchy scalp. (Dermatology)

Office consultation for a 30-year-old female with single season allergic rhinitis. (Allergy & Immunology)

99243 Initial office consultation for a 60-year-old male with avascular necrosis of the left femoral head with increasing pain. (Orthopaedic Surgery)

Office consultation for a 31-year-old woman complaining of palpitations and chest pains. Her internist had described a mild systolic click. (Cardiology)

Office consultation for a 65-year-old female with persistent bronchitis. (Infectious Disease)

Office consultation for a 65-year-old man with chronic low-back pain radiating to the leg. (Neurosurgery)

Office consultation for 23-year-old female with Crohn's disease not responding to therapy. (Abdominal Surgery/Colon & Rectal Surgery)

Office consultation for 25-year-old patient with symptomatic knee pain and swelling, with torn anterior cruciate ligament and/or torn meniscus. (Orthopaedic Surgery)

Office consultation for a 67-year-old patient with osteoporosis and mandibular atrophy with regard to reconstructive alternatives. (Oral & Maxillofacial Surgery)

Office consultation for 39-year-old patient referred at a perimenopausal age for irregular menses and menopausal symptoms. (Obstetrics & Gynecology)

99244 Initial office consultation for a 28-year-old male, HIV+, with a recent change in visual acuity. (Ophthalmology)

Initial office consultation for a 15-year-old male with failing grades, suspected drug abuse. (Pediatrics)

Initial office consultation for a 36-year-old factory worker, status four months post-occupational low back injury and requires management of intractable low back pain. (Pain Medicine)

Initial office consultation for a 45-year-old female with a history of chronic arthralgia of TMJ and associated myalgia and sudden progressive symptomatology over last two to three months. (Oral & Maxillofacial Surgery)

Initial office consultation for evaluation of a 70-year-old male with appetite loss and diminished energy. (Psychiatry)

Initial office consultation for an elementary school-aged patient, referred by pediatrician, with multiple systematic complaints and recent onset of behavioral discontrol. (Psychiatry)

Initial office consultation for a 23-year-old female with developmental facial skeletal anomaly and subsequent abnormal relationship of jaw(s) to cranial base. (Oral & Maxillofacial Surgery)

Initial office consultation for a 45-year-old myopic patient with a one-week history of floaters and a partial retinal detachment. (Ophthalmology)

Initial office consultation for a 65-year-old female with moderate dementia, mild unsteadiness, back pain fatigue on ambulation, intermittent urinary incontinence. (Neurosurgery)

Initial office consultation for a 33-year-old female referred by endocrinologist with amenorrhea and galactorrhea, for evaluation of pituitary tumor. (Neurosurgery)

Initial office consultation for a 34-year-old male with new onset nephrotic syndrome. (Nephrology)

Initial office consultation for a 39-year-old female with intractable chest wall pain secondary to metastatic breast cancer. (Anesthesiology/Pain Medicine)

Initial office consultation for a patient with multiple giant tumors of jaws. (Oral & Maxillofacial Surgery)

Initial office consultation for a patient with a failed total hip replacement with loosening and pain upon walking. (Orthopaedic Surgery)

Initial office consultation for a 60-year-old female with three-year history of intermittent tic-like unilateral facial pain; now constant pain for six weeks without relief by adequate carbamazepine dosage. (Neurosurgery)

Initial office consultation for a 45-year-old male heavy construction worker with prior lumbar disk surgery two years earlier; now gradually recurring low back and unilateral leg pain for three months, unable to work for two weeks. (Neurosurgery)

Initial office consultation of a patient who presents with a 30-year history of smoking and right neck mass. (Otolaryngology, Head & Neck Surgery)

Office consultation with 38-year-old female, with inflammatory bowel disease, who now presents with right lower quadrant pain and suspected intra-abdominal abscess. (General Surgery/Colon & Rectal Surgery)

Office consultation with 72-year-old male with esophageal carcinoma, symptoms of dysphagia and reflux. (Thoracic Surgery)

Office consultation for discussion of treatment options for a 40-year-old female with a two-centimeter adenocarcinoma of the breast. (Radiation Oncology)

Office consultation for young patient referred by pediatrician because of patient's short attention span, easy distractibility and hyperactivity. (Psychiatry)

Office consultation for 66-year-old female, history of colon resection for adenocarcinoma six years earlier, now with severe mid-back pain; x-rays showing osteoporosis and multiple vertebral compression fractures. (Neurosurgery)

Office consultation for a patient with chronic pelvic inflammatory disease who now has left lower quadrant pain with a palpable pelvic mass. (Obstetrics & Gynecology)

Office consultation for a patient with long-standing psoriasis with acute onset of erythroderma, pustular lesions, chills and fever. Combinations of topical and systemic treatments discussed and instituted. (Dermatology)

99245 Initial office consultation for a 35-year-old multiple-trauma male patient with complex pelvic fractures, for evaluation and formulation of management plan. (Orthopaedic Surgery)

Initial emergency room consultation for 10-year-old male in status epilepticus, recent closed head injury, information about medication not available. (Neurosurgery)

Initial emergency room consultation for a 23-year-old patient with severe abdominal pain, guarding, febrile, and unstable vital signs. (Obstetrics & Gynecology)

Office consultation for a 67-year-old female longstanding uncontrolled diabetic who presents with retinopathy, nephropathy, and a foot ulcer. (Endocrinology)

Office consultation for a 37-year-old male for initial evaluation and management of Cushing's disease. (Endocrinology)

Office consultation for a 60-year-old male who presents with thyrotoxicosis, exophthalmos, frequent premature ventricular contractions and congestive heart failure. (Endocrinology)

Initial office consultation for a 36-year-old patient, one year status post occupational herniated cervical disk treated by laminectomy, requiring management of multiple sites of intractable pain, depression, and narcotic dependence. (Pain Medicine)

Office consultation for a 58-year-old man with a history of MI and CHF who complains of the recent onset of rest angina and shortness of breath. The patient has a systolic blood pressure of 90mmHG and is in Class IV heart failure. (Cardiology)

Emergency room consultation for a 1-year-old with a three-day history of fever with increasing respiratory distress who is thought to have cardiac tamponade by the ER physician. (Cardiology)

Office consultation in the emergency room for a 25-year-old male with severe, acute, closed head injury. (Neurosurgery)

Office consultation for a 23-year-old female with Stage II A Hodgkins disease with positive supraclavicular and mediastinal nodes. (Radiation Oncology)

Office consultation for a 27-year-old juvenile diabetic patient with severe diabetic retinopathy, gastric atony, nephrotic syndrome and progressive renal failure, now with a serum creatinine of 2.7, and a blood pressure of 170/114. (Nephrology)

Office consultation for independent medical evaluation of a patient with a history of complicated low back and neck problems with previous multiple failed back surgeries. (Orthopaedic Surgery)

Office consultation for an adolescent referred by pediatrician for recent onset of violent and self-injurious behavior. (Psychiatry)

Office consultation for a 6-year-old male for evaluation of severe muscle and joint pain and a diffuse rash. Well until four-six weeks earlier, when he developed arthralgia, myalgias, and a fever of 102 for one week. (Rheumatology)

Initial Inpatient Consultations

New or Established Patient

99251 Initial hospital consultation for a 27-year-old female with fractured incisor post-intubation. (Oral & Maxillofacial Surgery)

Initial hospital consultation for an orthopaedic patient on IV antibiotics who has developed an apparent candida infection of the oral cavity. (Oral & Maxillofacial Surgery)

Initial inpatient consultation for a 30-year-old female complaining of vaginal itching, post orthopaedic surgery. (Obstetrics & Gynecology)

Initial inpatient consultation for a 36-year-old male on orthopaedic service with complaint of localized dental pain. (Oral & Maxillofacial Surgery)

99252 Initial hospital consultation for a 45-year-old male, previously abstinent alcoholic, who relapsed and was admitted for management of gastritis. The patient readily accepts the need for further treatment. (Addiction Medicine)

Initial hospital consultation for a 35-year-old dialysis patient with episodic oral ulcerations. (Oral & Maxillofacial Surgery)

Initial inpatient preoperative consultation for a 43-year-old woman with cholecystitis and well-controlled hypertension. (Cardiology)

Initial inpatient consultation for recommendation of antibiotic prophylaxis for a patient with a synthetic heart valve who will undergo urologic surgery. (Internal Medicine)

Initial inpatient consultation for possible drug induced skin eruption in 50-year-old male. (Dermatology)

Preoperative inpatient consultation for evaluation of hypertension in a 60-year-old male who will undergo a cholecystectomy. Patient had a normal annual check-up in your office four months ago. (Internal Medicine)

Initial inpatient consultation for 66-year-old patient with wrist and hand pain and finger numbness, secondary to carpal tunnel syndrome. (Orthopaedic Surgery/Plastic Surgery)

Initial inpatient consultation for a 66-year-old male smoker referred for pain management immediately status post-biliary tract surgery done via sub-costal incision. (Anesthesiology/Pain Medicine)

99253 Initial hospital consultation for a 50-year-old female with incapacitating knee pain due to generalized rheumatoid arthritis. (Orthopaedic Surgery)

Initial hospital consultation for a 60-year-old male with avascular necrosis of the left femoral heel with increasing pain. (Orthopaedic Surgery)

Initial hospital consultation for a 45-year-old female with compound mandibular fracture and concurrent head, abdominal and/or orthopaedic injuries. (Oral & Maxillofacial Surgery)

Initial hospital consultation for a 22-year-old female, paraplegic, to evaluate wrist and hand pain. (Orthopaedic Surgery)

Initial hospital consultation for a 40-year-old male with 10-day history of incapacitating unilateral sciatica, unable to walk now, not improved by bed rest. (Neurosurgery)

Initial hospital consultation, requested by pediatrician, for treatment recommendations for a patient admitted with persistent inability to walk following soft tissue injury to ankle. (Physiatry)

Initial hospital consultation for a 27-year-old previously healthy male who vomited during IV sedation and may have aspirated gastric contents. (Anesthesiology)

Initial hospital consultation for a 33-year-old female, post-abdominal surgery, who now has a fever. (Internal Medicine)

Initial inpatient consultation for a 57-year-old male, post lower endoscopy, for evaluation of abdominal pain and fever. (General Surgery)

Initial inpatient consultation for rehabilitation of a 73-year-old female one week after surgical management of a hip fracture. (Physical Medicine & Rehabilitation)

Initial inpatient consultation for diagnosis/management of fever following abdominal surgery. (Internal Medicine)

Initial inpatient consultation for a 35-year-old female with a fever and pulmonary infiltrate following cesarean section. (Pulmonary Medicine)

Initial inpatient consultation for a 42-year-old non-diabetic patient, post-op cholecystectomy, now with an acute urinary tract infection. (Nephrology)

Initial inpatient consultation for 53-year-old female with moderate uncomplicated pancreatitis. (Gastroenterology)

Initial inpatient consultation for 45-year-old patient with chronic neck pain with radicular pain of the left arm. (Orthopaedic Surgery)

Initial inpatient consultation for 8-year-old patient with new onset of seizures who has a normal examination and previous history. (Neurology)

99254 Initial hospital consultation for a 15-year-old patient with painless swelling of proximal humerus with lytic lesion by x-ray. (Orthopaedic Surgery)

Initial hospital consultation for evaluation of a 29-year-old female with a diffusely positive medical review of systems and history of multiple surgeries. (Psychiatry)

Initial hospital consultation for a 70-year-old diabetic female with gangrene of the foot. (Orthopaedic Surgery)

Initial inpatient consultation for a 47-year-old female with progressive pulmonary infiltrate, hypoxemia, and diminished urine output. (Anesthesiology)

Initial hospital consultation for a 13-month-old with spasmodic cough, respiratory distress, and fever. (Allergy & Immunology)

Initial hospital consultation for a patient with failed total hip replacement with loosening and pain upon walking. (Orthopaedic Surgery)

Initial hospital consultation for a 62-year-old female with metastatic breast cancer to the femoral neck and thoracic vertebra. (Orthopaedic Surgery)

Initial hospital consultation for a 39-year-old female with nephrolithiasis requiring extensive opioid analgesics, whose vital signs are now elevated. She initially denied any drug use, but today gives history of multiple substance abuse, including opioids and prior treatment for a personality disorder. (Psychiatry)

Initial hospital consultation for a 70-year-old female without previous psychiatric history, who is now experiencing nocturnal confusion and visual hallucinations following hip replacement surgery. (Psychiatry)

Initial inpatient consultation for evaluation of a 63-year-old in the ICU with diabetes and chronic renal failure who develops acute respiratory distress syndrome 36 hours after a mitral valve replacement. (Anesthesiology)

Initial inpatient consultation for a 66-year-old female with enlarged supraclavicular lymph nodes, found on biopsy to be malignant. (Hematology/Oncology)

Initial inpatient consultation for a 43-year-old female for evaluation of sudden painful visual loss, optic neuritis and episodic paresthesia. (Ophthalmology)

Initial inpatient consultation for evaluation of a 71-year-old male with hyponatremia (serum sodium 114) who was admitted to the hospital with pneumonia. (Nephrology)

Initial inpatient consultation for a 72-year-old male with emergency admission for possible bowel obstruction. (Internal Medicine/General Surgery)

Initial inpatient consultation for a 35-year-old female with fever, swollen joints, and rash of one-week duration. (Rheumatology)

99255 Initial inpatient consultation for a 76-year-old female with massive, life-threatening gastrointestinal hemorrhage and chest pain. (Gastroenterology)

Initial inpatient consultation for a 75-year-old female, admitted to intensive care with acute respiratory distress syndrome, who is hypersensitive, has a moderate metabolic acidosis, and a rising serum creatinine. (Nephrology)

Initial hospital consultation for patient with a history of complicated low back pain and neck problems with previous multiple failed back surgeries. (Orthopaedic Surgery/Neurosurgery)

Initial hospital consultation for a 66-year-old female, two days post-abdominal aneurysm repair, with oliguria and hypertension of one-day duration. (Nephrology/Internal Medicine)

Initial hospital consultation for a patient with shotgun wound to face with massive facial trauma and airway obstruction. (Oral & Maxillofacial Surgery)

Initial hospital consultation for patient with severe pancreatitis complicated by respiratory insufficiency, acute renal failure, and abscess formation. (General Surgery/Colon & Rectal Surgery)

Initial hospital consultation for a 35-year-old multiple-trauma male patient with complex pelvic fractures to evaluate and formulate management plan. (Orthopaedic Surgery)

Initial inpatient consultation for adolescent patient with fractured femur and pelvis who pulled out IVs and disconnected traction in attempt to elope from hospital. (Psychiatry)

Initial hospital consultation for a 16-year-old primigravida at 32 weeks gestation requested by a family practitioner for evaluation of severe hypertension, thrombocytopenia, and headache. (Obstetrics & Gynecology)

Initial hospital consultation for a 58-year-old insulin-dependent diabetic with multiple antibiotic allergies, now with multiple fascial plane abscesses and airway obstruction. (Oral & Maxillofacial Surgery)

Initial inpatient consultation for a 55-year-old male with known cirrhosis and ascites, now with jaundice, encephalopathy, and massive hematemesis. (Gastroenterology)

Initial hospital consultation for a 25-year-old male, seen in emergency room with severe, closed head injury. (Neurosurgery)

Initial hospital consultation for a 2-day-old male with single ventricle physiology and subaortic obstruction. Family counseling following evaluation for multiple, staged surgical procedures. (Thoracic Surgery)

Initial hospital consultation for a 45-year-old male admitted with subarachnoid hemorrhage and intracranial aneurysm on angiogram. (Neurosurgery)

Initial inpatient consultation for myxedematous patient who is hypoventilating and obtunded. (Endocrinology)

Initial hospital consultation for a 45-year-old patient with widely metastatic lung carcinoma, intractable back pain, and a history that includes substance dependence, NSAID allergy, and two prior laminectomies with fusion for low back pain. (Pain Medicine)

Initial hospital consultation for evaluation of treatment options in a 50-year-old patient with cirrhosis, known peptic ulcer disease, hypotension, encephalopathy, and massive acute upper gastrointestinal bleeding which cannot be localized by endoscopy. (Interventional Radiology)

Initial inpatient consultation in the ICU for a 70-year-old male who experienced a cardiac arrest during surgery and was resuscitated. (Cardiology)

Initial inpatient consultation for a patient with severe pancreatitis complicated by respiratory insufficiency, acute renal failure and abscess formation. (Gastroenterology)

Initial inpatient consultation for a 70-year-old cirrhotic male admitted with ascites, jaundice, encephalopathy, and massive hematemesis. (Gastroenterology)

Initial inpatient consultation in the ICU for a 51-year-old patient who is on a ventilator and has a fever two weeks after a renal transplantation. (Infectious Disease)

Initial inpatient consultation for evaluation and formulation of plan for management of multiple trauma patient with complex pelvic fracture, 35-year-old male. (General Surgery/Orthopaedic Surgery)

Initial inpatient consultation for a 50-year-old male with a history of previous myocardial infarction, now with acute pulmonary edema and hypotension. (Cardiology)

Initial inpatient consultation for 45-year-old male with recent, acute subarachnoid hemorrhage, hesitant speech, mildly confused, drowsy. High risk group for HIV+ status. (Neurosurgery)

Initial inpatient consultation for 36-year-old female referred by her internist to evaluate a patient being followed for abdominal pain and fever. The patient has developed diffuse abdominal pain, guarding, rigidity and increased fever. (Obstetrics & Gynecology)

Follow-up Inpatient Consultations

Established Patient

99261 Follow-up consultation for a 78-year-old female nursing home resident for evaluation of medical management of pruritus ani. (Colon & Rectal Surgery/Geriatrics/General Surgery)

Follow-up hospital consultation on first post-op day for a 64-year-old male who has undergone uneventful CABG. (Anesthesiology)

Follow-up inpatient consultation for a 67-year-old female admitted several days ago for bleeding ulcer; now stable. (Gastroenterology)

Follow-up hospital consultation for a 35-year-old female with history of mitral valve prolapse. (Cardiology)

Follow-up inpatient consultation to complete initial consultation for dental pain after review of radiographs. (Oral & Maxillofacial Surgery)

Follow-up inpatient consultation for evaluation of response to therapy for moniliasis. (Oral & Maxillofacial Surgery)

Follow-up inpatient consultation for a 22-year-old female with recurrent aphthous ulcers. (Oral & Maxillofacial Surgery)

Follow-up hospital consultation for a 37-year-old female to complete review of previously unavailable studies. (Therapeutic Radiology & Oncology)

Follow-up consultation for a highly functional 75-year-old female with urinary incontinence to review preliminary results of diagnostic evaluation. (Geriatrics)

Follow-up inpatient consultation for a 1-week-old premature female with patent ductus arteriosus. The murmur has disappeared. (Cardiology)

Follow-up hospital consultation to review the results of an audiogram. (Otolaryngology, Head & Neck Surgery)

Follow-up inpatient consultation with 35-year-old female with pulmonary embolism post-op cesarean section, now stable, for assessment of response to anticoagulation and recommended adjustment of heparin dose. (Pulmonary Medicine)

Follow-up inpatient consultation for a 74-year-old male whose postoperative facial paralysis after a cholecystectomy is now resolving. (Neurology)

Follow-up inpatient consultation with 67-year-old female, established patient, for review of diagnostic studies ordered at time of first contact. (Internal Medicine)

Follow-up inpatient consultation for 78-year-old female nursing home resident for evaluation of medical management of pruritis ani. (General Surgery/Colon & Rectal Surgery)

Follow-up inpatient consultation for a 36-year-old female two days after spontaneous passage of 3mm stone. (Urology)

Follow-up inpatient consultation for a 94-year-old male nursing home resident for re-evaluation of hemorrhoids following conservative therapy. (Colon & Rectal Surgery/General Surgery/Geriatrics)

Follow-up inpatient consultation for a 50-year-old male, asymptomatic with borderline ECG abnormality, needs preoperative opinion after a thallium exercise perfusion scan. (Cardiology)

99262   Follow-up inpatient consultation for a 6-year-old female, established patient, with endocarditis and changing heart murmur. (Cardiology)

Follow-up inpatient consultation on a 2-year-old male, one day postoperative ventricular septal defect closure with signs of tachycardia. (Cardiology)

Follow-up inpatient consultation for a 63-year-old man, established patient, with moderately severe pulmonary insufficiency, 10 days postoperative coronary artery bypass for unstable angina. Patient has developed severe dyspnea, fever, and a new exudative right pleural effusion. (Cardiology)

Follow-up inpatient consultation for a 67-year-old woman with lung cancer and syndrome of inappropriate secretion of antidiuretic hormone (SIADH) who has had a seizure following intravenous saline. (Endocrinology)

Follow-up inpatient consultation for a 22-year-old female, established patient, with steroid-dependent systemic lupus erythematosus, arthritis, and glomerulonephritis. Patient is re-evaluated for loss of consciousness and chest pain. (Rheumatology)

Follow-up inpatient consultation for a 75-year-old diabetic with fever, chills, a gangrenous heel ulcer, rhonchi, and dyspnea who appears lethargic and tachypneic. (Endocrinology)

Follow-up inpatient consultation for a 30-year-old, established patient, with intractable neck and low back pain, who is excessively sedated after institution of methadone therapy. (Pain Medicine)

Follow-up inpatient consultation for a 65-year-old man with a history of hypertension and MI who is five days post uncomplicated GI procedure with an unremarkable postoperative recovery. He has just been resuscitated from a cardiopulmonary arrest. (Cardiology)

Follow-up inpatient consultation with 72-year-old female, established patient with bullous pemphigoid on combined oral therapy steroids and immunosuppressive to evaluate progress of cutaneous care orders and adjustment of oral/parenteral therapy dosages. (Dermatology)

Follow-up inpatient consultation for a 71-year-old male who has developed a maculopapular skin rash while on antibiotics recommended for an uncomplicated pneumonia. (Infectious Disease)

Follow-up inpatient consultation with 68-year-old, incapacitated male with spinal stenosis and failure to respond to bedrest, analgesics, and PT. (Neurosurgery)

Follow-up inpatient consultation with 51-year-old male for evaluation and determination of the etiology of postoperative hyponatremia following TURP. (Family Medicine)

Follow-up inpatient consultation for re-evaluation of a stroke patient, and development of plan for initial rehabilitation services. (Neurology)

Follow-up inpatient consultation with 45-year-old male, established patient for discussion of CT scan which demonstrates a cavernous hemangioma. (Ophthalmology)

Follow-up inpatient consultation for an asymptomatic 35-year-old Type I diabetic patient with hyperkalemic, hyperchloremia acidosis, to review lab results. (Nephrology)

Follow-up inpatient consultation for an elderly male with a perioperative myocardial infarction requiring adjustment of vasoactive medications. (Anesthesiology)

99263   Follow-up hospital consultation of an AIDS patient admitted with a sore throat who now has enlarging neck mass. (Otolaryngology, Head & Neck Surgery)

Follow-up hospital consultation of a pansinusitis patient with sudden onset of proptosis. (Otolaryngology, Head & Neck Surgery)

Follow-up inpatient consultation for a 53-year-old man with known angina who develops crescendo angina post cholecystectomy. (Cardiology)

Follow-up inpatient consultation with 72-year-old male established patient admitted for management of alcohol withdrawal, now confused and febrile. (Addiction Medicine)

Follow-up inpatient consultation for an HIV+ patient with an increasing fever following 10 days of antibiotic therapy for pneumocystis carinii pneumonia. (Infectious Disease)

Follow-up inpatient consultation with 58-year-old diabetic female, with bacterial endocarditis, continued fever after two weeks of intravenous antibiotic therapy, and new onset ventricular ectopia. (Cardiology)

Follow-up inpatient consultation for a 90-year-old female with urinary incontinence who has a complicated medical history requiring reassessment of multiple medical problems, recommendations for placement, further recommendation for management of incontinence and reevaluation of cognitive status because of competency issues. (Geriatrics/Psychiatry)

Follow-up inpatient consultation for 42-year-old male with persistent gastrointestinal bleeding, etiology undetermined, not responding to conservative therapy of transfusions. (General Surgery/Colon & Rectal Surgery)

Follow-up inpatient consultation for a 62-year-old female with steroid-dependent asthma, diabetes mellitus, thyrotoxicosis, abdominal pain and possible vasculitis. (Rheumatology)

Follow-up inpatient consultation for a 62-year-old male, status post-op acute small bowel obstruction; now with acute renal failure. (Family Medicine)

Emergency Department Services

New or Established Patient

99281   Emergency department visit for a patient for removal of sutures from a well-healed, uncomplicated laceration. (Emergency Medicine)

Emergency department visit for a patient for tetanus toxoid immunization. (Emergency Medicine)

Emergency department visit for a patient with several uncomplicated insect bites. (Emergency Medicine)

99282   Emergency department visit for a 20-year-old student who presents with a painful sunburn with blister formation on the back. (Emergency Medicine)

Emergency department visit for a child presenting with impetigo localized to the face. (Emergency Medicine)

Emergency department visit for a patient with a minor traumatic injury of an extremity with localized pain, swelling, and bruising. (Emergency Medicine)

Emergency department visit for an otherwise healthy patient whose chief complaint is a red, swollen cystic lesion on his/her back. (Emergency Medicine)

Emergency department visit for a patient presenting with a rash on both legs after exposure to poison ivy. (Emergency Medicine)

Emergency department visit for a young adult patient with infected sclera and purulent discharge from both eyes without pain, visual disturbance or history of foreign body in either eye. (Emergency Medicine)

99283 Emergency department visit for a sexually active female complaining of vaginal discharge who is afebrile and denies experiencing abdominal or back pain. (Emergency Medicine)

Emergency department visit for a well-appearing 8-year-old who has a fever, diarrhea and abdominal cramps, is tolerating oral fluids and is not vomiting. (Emergency Medicine)

Emergency department visit for a patient with an inversion ankle injury, who is unable to bear weight on the injured foot and ankle. (Emergency Medicine)

Emergency department visit for a patient who has a complaint of acute pain associated with a suspected foreign body in the painful eye. (Emergency Medicine)

Emergency department visit for a healthy, young adult patient who sustained a blunt head injury with local swelling and bruising without subsequent confusion, loss of consciousness or memory deficit. (Emergency Medicine)

99284 Emergency department visit for a 4-year-old who fell off a bike sustaining a head injury with brief loss of consciousness. (Emergency Medicine)

Emergency department visit for an elderly female who has fallen and is now complaining of pain in her right hip and is unable to walk. (Emergency Medicine)

Emergency department visit for a patient with flank pain and hematuria. (Emergency Medicine)

Emergency department visit for a female presenting with lower abdominal pain and a vaginal discharge. (Emergency Medicine)

99285 Emergency department visit for a patient with a complicated overdose requiring aggressive management to prevent side effects from the ingested materials. (Emergency Medicine)

Emergency department visit for a patient with a new onset of rapid heart rate requiring IV drugs. (Emergency Medicine)

Emergency department visit for a patient exhibiting active, upper gastrointestinal bleeding. (Emergency Medicine)

Emergency department visit for a previously healthy young adult patient who is injured in an automobile accident and is brought to the emergency department immobilized and has symptoms compatible with intra-abdominal injuries or multiple extremity injuries. (Emergency Medicine)

Emergency department visit for a patient with an acute onset of chest pain compatible with symptoms of cardiac ischemia and/or pulmonary embolism. (Emergency Medicine)

Emergency department visit for a patient who presents with a sudden onset of "the worst headache of her life," and complains of a stiff neck, nausea, and inability to concentrate. (Emergency Medicine)

Emergency department visit for a patient with a new onset of a cerebral vascular accident. (Emergency Medicine)

Emergency department visit for acute febrile illness in an adult, associated with shortness of breath and an altered level of alertness. (Emergency Medicine)

Critical Care Services

99291 First hour of critical care of a 65-year-old man with septic shock following relief of ureteral obstruction caused by a stone.

First hour of critical care of a 15-year-old with acute respiratory failure from asthma.

First hour of critical care of a 45-year-old who sustained a liver laceration, cerebral hematoma, flailed chest, and pulmonary contusion after being struck by an automobile.

First hour of critical care of a 65-year-old woman who, following a hysterectomy, suffered a cardiac arrest associated with a pulmonary embolus.

First hour of critical care of a 6-month-old with hypovolemic shock secondary to diarrhea and dehydration.

First hour of critical care of a 3-year-old with respiratory failure secondary to pneumocystis carinii pneumonia.

Comprehensive Nursing Facility Assessments

New or Established Patient

99301 Annual nursing facility history and physical and MDS/RAI evaluation for a two-year nursing facility resident who is an 84-year-old female with multiple chronic health problems, including: stable controlled hypertension, chronic constipation, osteoarthritis, and moderated stable dementia.

Nursing facility visit for an assessment of a resident with non-insulin dependent diabetes, stable angina, and chronic obstructive pulmonary disease (COPD) one year after previous MDS/RAI.

99302 Nursing facility visit one year after previous MDS/RAI to assess an 80-year-old woman with Parkinson's disease, chronic hypertension, and degenerative arthritis. Visit reveals Stage II decubitus.

Nursing facility assessment of a 28-year-old diabetic, male resident with a new Stage IV pressure ulcer on his left lateral malleolus that is unresponsive to treatment, thus triggering the need for a new MDS/RAI and new medical plan of care.

Nursing facility assessment of an 88-year-old male resident with a permanent change in status following a new cerebral vascular accident (CVA) that has triggered the need for a new MDS/RAI and medical plan of care.

Nursing facility visit and assessment to take over the primary care of a 75-year-old diabetic, previously stable, who was on oral hypoglycemic agents, but who now requires initiation of insulin therapy, a new MDS/RAI, and medical plan of care.

Nursing facility visit and assessment for an 81-year-old female resident with dementia who under structured guidance and intensive nutritional support has regained significant levels of function in three activities of daily living and is now able to feed and dress herself and ambulate with appliance and who now thus requires a new MDS/RAI and medical plan of care.

99303 Initial nursing facility assessment (MDS/RAI and medical plan of care) of a 72-year-old insulin dependent diabetic amputee with hearing and visual impairments and possible dementia seen in the office the day before and judged to require nursing facility care.

Sub-acute nursing facility assessment of a previously independently living 90-year-old male who suffered a recent cerebral vascular accident (CVA) and is transferred to the hospital sub-acute rehabilitation unit for further rehabilitation supportive services.

Initial nursing facility visit to evaluate a 72-year-old woman found confused and wandering, admitted by Adult Protective Services without a qualifying hospital stay or inpatient diagnostic work. The patient lives alone and has no relatives or significant others in the community.

Nursing facility assessment and creation of medical plan of care upon readmission to the nursing facility of an 82-year-old male who was previously discharged. The patient has just been discharged from the hospital where he had been treated for an acute gastric ulcer bleed associated with transient delirium. The patient returns to the nursing facility debilitated, protein depleted, and with a Stage III coccygeal decubitus.

Subsequent Nursing Facility Care

New or Established Patient

99311 Scheduled follow-up visit for a known 70-year-old stable paraplegic with no status change noted during visit.

Scheduled monthly nursing home visit with a patient who has mild senile dementia, Alzheimers' type, with no change in status, stable hypertension, and who is ambulating with a walker one year past stroke.

Follow-up in skilled nursing facility with a 70-year-old patient following a 10-day treatment of a cellulitis of the foot.

99312 Scheduled follow-up visit to a resident with controlled dementia, hypertension, and diabetes. During visit, patient seems to exhibit flu symptoms.

Scheduled nursing facility visit with an afebrile demented resident who also has a mild cough, requiring no change in the medical plan of care.

Subsequent visit in a skilled nursing facility with a patient who is six months post stroke and now has a fever and mild cough.

Scheduled nursing facility visit for an 84-year-old male with chronic renal insufficiency, on digitalis and diuretics, requiring adjustment of medications and revision of medical plan of care.

Nursing facility visit of a resident with multiple chronic health problems who is six months post stroke and now has a fever and mild cough, to evaluate for possible pneumonia. Requires the development of a new medical plan of care, but not a revised MDS/RAI.

99313 Follow-up nursing facility visit to evaluate the reason for frequent falls by a 90-year-old ataxic resident, and to determine possible need for change in medications and medical care plan.

Re-admission of a 75-year-old man with stroke who was hospitalized with pneumonia for his illness and who returns to the nursing facility with no permanent change in status from his condition prior to hospitalization; no new MDS/RAI is required.

Nursing facility visit with a diabetic resident who has developed Stage II decubitus ulcers with cellulitis, requiring a revision in the medical plan of care.

Nursing facility visit to develop a new plan of care for an amputee with atherosclerosis obliterans who has refused to eat for three days and has developed decreased urinary output.

Nursing facility visit for a 78-year-old resident with chronic atrial fibrillation and a history of heart failure to evaluate an acute confusional state and to revise the medical plan of care.

Unscheduled nursing facility visit for evaluation of a patient with fever and obtundation who is determined not to require hospital admission or new MDS, but who does require workup and revision of medical plan of care.

Prolonged Services

Prolonged Physician Service With Direct (Face-to-Face) Patient Contact

Office or Other Outpatient

99354/ 99355 A 20-year-old female with history of asthma presents with acute bronchospasm and moderate respiratory distress. Initial evaluation shows respiratory rate 30, labored breathing and wheezing heard in all lung fields. Office treatment is initiated which includes intermittent bronchial dilation and subcutaneous epinephrine. Requires intermittent physician face-to-face time with patient over a period of two-three hours. (Family Medicine/Internal Medicine)

Inpatient

99356 A 34-year-old primigravida presents to hospital in early labor. Admission history and physical reveals severe preeclampsia. Physician supervises management of preeclampsia, IV magnesium initiation and maintenance, labor augmentation with pitocin, and close maternal-fetal monitoring. Physician face-to-face involvement includes 40 minutes of continuous bedside care until the patient is stable, then is intermittent over several hours until the delivery. (Family Medicine/Internal Medicine/Obstetrics & Gynecology)

Prolonged Physician Service Without Direct Patient (Face-to-Face) Contact

99358/
99359
A 65-year-old new patient with multiple problems is seen and evaluated. After the visit, the physician requires extensive time to talk with the patient's daughter, to review complex, detailed medical records transferred from previous physicians and to complete a comprehensive treatment plan. This plan also requires the physician to personally initiate and coordinate the care plan with a local home health agency and a dietician. (Family Medicine/Internal Medicine)

Physician Standby Services

99360
A 24-year-old patient is admitted to OB unit attempting VBAC. Fetal monitoring shows increasing fetal distress. Patient's blood pressure is rising and labor progressing slowly. A primary care physician is requested by the OB/GYN to standby in the unit for possible cesarean delivery and neonatal resuscitation. (Family Medicine/Internal Medicine)

Care Plan Oversight Services

99375
First month of care plan oversight for terminal care of a 58-year-old woman with advanced intraabdominal ovarian cancer. Care plan includes home oxygen, diuretics IV for edema and ascites control and pain control management involving IV morphine infusion when progressive ileus occurred. Physician phone contacts with nurse, family, and MSW. Discussion with MSW concerning plans to withdraw supportive measures per patient wishes. Documentation includes review and modification of care plan and certifications from nursing, MSW, pharmacy, and DME. (Family Medicine/Internal Medicine)

Appendix E

Summary of CPT Add-on Codes

This listing is a summary of CPT add-on codes for *CPT 2002*. The codes listed below are identified in *CPT 2002* with a ✚ symbol.

0006T	22522	38747	64472	88313	99359
01953	22585	43635	64476	88314	99569
01968	22614	44015	64480	90472	
01969	22632	44121	64484	90474	
11001	26125	44128	64623	90781	
11101	26861	44139	64627	92547	
11201	26863	44203	64727	92973	
11732	27358	44955	64778	92974	
11922	27692	47001	64783	92978	
13102	32501	47550	64787	92979	
13122	33141	48400	64832	92981	
13133	33530	49568	64837	92984	
13153	33572	49905	64859	92996	
15001	33924	56606	64872	92998	
15101	33961	58611	64874	93320	
15121	34808	59525	64876	93321	
15201	34813	60512	64901	93325	
15221	34826	61609	64902	93571	
15241	35390	61610	67225	93572	
15261	35400	61611	67320	93609	
15343	35500	61612	67331	93613	
15351	35681	61795	67332	93621	
15401	35682	63035	67334	93622	
15787	35683	63043	67335	93623	
16036	35685	63044	67340	93662	
17003	35686	63048	69990	95920	
19001	35700	63057	74301	95962	
19126	36218	63066	75774	95967	
19291	36248	63076	75946	95973	
19295	37206	63078	75964	96412	
22103	37208	63082	75968	96423	
22116	37250	63086	75993	96570	
22216	37251	63088	75996	96571	
22226	38102	63091	76085	97546	
22328	38746	63308	76125	99100	
			78020	99116	
			78478	99135	
			78480	99140	
			78496	99290	
			87187	99292	
			87904	99354	
			88141	99355	
			88155	99356	
			88311	99357	
			88312	99358	

Appendix F

Summary of CPT Codes Exempt from Modifier '-51'

This listing is a summary of CPT codes that are exempt from the use of modifier '-51' but have NOT been designated as CPT add-on procedures/services. The codes listed below are identified in *CPT 2002* with a ⊘ symbol.

17004	31500	90385	90702	93533
17304	32000	90386	90703	93539
17305	32002	90389	90704	93540
17306	32020	90393	90705	93541
17307	33517	90396	90706	93542
17310	33518	90399	90707	93543
20660	33519	90476	90708	93544
20690	33521	90477	90709	93545
20692	33522	90581	90710	93555
20900	33523	90585	90712	93556
20902	35600	90586	90713	93600
20910	36488	90632	90716	93602
20912	36489	90633	90717	93603
20920	36490	90634	90718	93610
20922	36491	90636	90719	93612
20924	36620	90645	90720	93615
20926	36660	90646	90721	93616
20930	38792	90647	90723	93618
20931	44500	90648	90725	93619
20936	61107	90657	90727	93620
20937	61210	90658	90732	93624
20938	62284	90659	90733	93631
20974	90281	90660	90735	93640
20975	90283	90665	90740	93641
22840	90287	90669	90743	93642
22841	90288	90675	90744	93650
22842	90291	90676	90746	93651
22843	90296	90680	90747	93652
22844	90371	90690	90748	93660
22845	90375	90691	90749	95900
22846	90376	90692	93501	95903
22847	90378	90693	93503	95904
22848	90379	90700	93505	99141
22851	90384	90701	93508	99142
			93510	
			93511	
			93514	
			93524	
			93526	
			93527	
			93528	
			93529	
			93530	
			93531	
			93532	

Index

Instructions for the Use of the CPT Index

Main Terms

The index is organized by main terms. Each main term can stand alone, or be followed by up to three modifying terms. There are four primary classes of main entries:

1. Procedure or service.
   For example: Endoscopy; Anastomosis; Splint

2. Organ or other anatomic site.
   For example: Tibia; Colon; Salivary Gland

3. Condition.
   For example: Abscess; Entropion; Tetralogy of Fallot

4. Synonyms, Eponyms and Abbreviations.
   For example: EEG; Bricker Operation; Clagett Procedure

Modifying Terms

A main term may be followed by a series of up to three indented terms that modify the main term. When modifying terms appear, one should review the list, as these subterms do have an effect on the selection of the appropriate code for the procedure.

Code Ranges

Whenever more than one code applies to a given index entry, a code range is listed. If several non-sequential codes apply, they will be separated by a comma. For example:

Esophagus
    Reconstruction 43300, 43310, 43113

If two or more sequential codes apply, they will be separated by a hyphen. For example:

Debridement
    Burns 01951-01953, 16010-16030

Conventions

As a space saving convention, certain words infer some meaning. This convention is primarily used when a procedure or service is listed as a subterm. For example:

Knee
    Incision (of)

In this example, the word in parentheses (of) does not appear in the index, but it is inferred. As another example:

Pancreas
    Anesthesia (for procedures on)

In this example, as there is no such entity as pancreas anesthesia, the words in parentheses are inferred. That is, anesthesia for procedures on the pancreas.

The alphabetic index is NOT a substitute for the main text of *CPT*. Even if only one code appears, the user must refer to the main text to ensure that the code selection is accurate.

A

A-II
See Angiotensin II

Abbe-Estlander Procedure
See Reconstruction; Repair, Cleft Lip

Abdomen
Abdominal Wall
Repair
Hernia 49491-49496, 49501, 49507, 49521, 49590
Tumor
Excision 22900
Unlisted Services and Procedures 22999
Abscess
Incision and Drainage 49020, 49040
Open 49040
Percutaneous 49021
Angiography 74175, 75635
Artery
Ligation 37617
Biopsy 49000
Bypass Graft 35907
Cannula/Catheter
Removal 49422
CAT Scan 74150-74175, 75635
Celiotomy
for Staging 49220
Cyst
Destruction/Excision 49200-49201
Drainage
Fluid 49080-49081
Ectopic Pregnancy 59130
Endometrioma
Destruction/Excision 49200-49201
Exploration 49000-49002
Blood Vessel 35840
Staging 58960
Incision 49000
Staging 58960
Incision and Drainage
Pancreatitis 48000
Injection
Air 49400
Contrast Material 49400
Insertion
Catheter 49420-49421
Venous Shunt 49425
Intraperitoneal
Catheter Removal 49422
Shunt
Ligation 49428
Removal 49429
Laparotomy
Staging 49220
Magnetic Resonance Imaging
(MRI) 74181-74183
Needle Biopsy
Mass 49180
Peritoneocentesis 49080-49081
Radical Resection 51597

Repair
Blood Vessel 35221
with Other Graft 35281
with Vein Graft 35251
Hernia 49491-49525, 49560-49587
Suture 49900
Revision
Venous Shunt 49426
Suture 49900
Tumor
Destruction/Excision 49200-49201
Ultrasound 76700-76705
Unlisted Services and Procedures 49999
Wound Exploration
Penetrating 20102
X-Ray 74000-74022

Abdominal Aorta
See Aorta, Abdominal

Abdominal Aortic Aneurysm
See Aorta, Abdominal, Aneurysm

Abdominal Deliveries
See Cesarean Delivery

Abdominal Hysterectomy
See Hysterectomy, Abdominal

Abdominal Lymphangiogram
See Lymphangiography, Abdomen

Abdominal Paracentesis
See Abdomen, Drainage

Abdominal Radiographies
See Abdomen, X-Ray

Abdominal Wall
Surgery 22999
Tumor
Excision 22900

Abdominohysterectomy
See Hysterectomy, Abdominal

Abdominopelvic Amputation
See Amputation, Interpelviabdominal

Abdominoplasty 15831

Ablation
Anal
Polyp 46615
Tumor 46615
CAT Scan Guidance 76362
Colon
Tumor 45339
Endometrial 0009T, 58353, 58563
Endometrium
Ultrasound Guidance 0009T
Heart
Arrhythmogenic Focus 93650-93652
See Cardiology; Diagnostic, Intracardiac
Pacing and Mapping
Liver
Tumor 47380-47383
Laparoscopic 47370-47371
Magnetic Resonance Guidance 76394
Prostate 55873

Renal Cyst 50541
Turbinate Mucosa 30801-30802
Ultrasound Guidance 76490

Abortion
See Obstetrical Care
Incomplete 59812
Induced
by Dilation and Curettage 59840
by Dilation and Evacuation 59841
by Saline 59850-59851
by Vaginal Suppositories 59855-59856
with Hysterectomy 59100, 59852, 59857
Missed
First Trimester 59820
Second Trimester 59821
Septic 59830
Spontaneous 59812
Therapeutic
by Saline 59850
with Dilation and Curettage 59851
with Hysterectomy 59852

Abrasion
Skin
Chemical Peel 15788-15793
Dermabrasion 15780-15783
Lesion 15786-15787
Salabrasion 15810-15811

Abscess
Abdomen 49040-49041
Incision and Drainage
Open 49040
Percutaneous 49021
Anal
Incision and Drainage 46045-46050
Ankle 27603
Appendix
Incision and Drainage 44900
Open 44900
Percutaneous 44901
Arm, Lower 25028
Excision 25145
Incision and Drainage 25035
Arm, Upper
Incision and Drainage 23930-23935
Auditory Canal, External 69020
Bartholin's Gland
Incision and Drainage 56420
Bladder
Incision and Drainage 51080
Brain
Drainage 61150-61151
Excision 61514, 61522
Incision and Drainage 61320-61321
Breast
Incision and Drainage 19020
Carpals
Incision, Deep 25035
Clavicle
Sequestrectomy 23170
Drainage
with X-Ray 75989
Ear, External
Complicated 69005
Simple 69000

Elbow
    Incision and Drainage 23930-23935
Epididymis
    Incision and Drainage 54700
Excision
    Olecranon Process 24138
    Radius 24136
    Ulna 24138
Eyelid
    Incision and Drainage 67700
Facial Bones
    Excision 21026
Finger 26010-26011
    Incision and Drainage 26034
Foot
    Incision 28005
Gums
    Incision and Drainage 41800
Hand
    Incision and Drainage 26034
Hematoma
    Incision and Drainage 27603
Hip
    Incision and Drainage 26990-26992
Humeral Head 23174
Humerus
    Excision 24134
    Incision and Drainage 23935
Kidney
    Incision and Drainage 50020
        Open 50020
        Percutaneous 50021
Leg, Lower
    Incision and Drainage 27603
Liver 47010
    Drainage
        Open 47010
        Injection 47015
        Repair 47300
Localization
    Nuclear Medicine 78806-78807
Lung
    Percutaneous Drainage 32200-32201
Lymphocele Drainage 49062
Lymph Node
    Incision and Drainage 38300-38305
Mandible
    Excision 21025
Mouth
    Incision and Drainage 40800-40801,
           41005-41009, 41015-41018
Nasal Septum
    Incision and Drainage 30020
Neck
    Incision and Drainage 21501-21502
Ovarian
    Incision and Drainage 58820-58822
        Abdominal Approach 58822
        Vaginal Approach 58820
Ovary
    Drainage
        Percutaneous 58823
Palate
    Incision and Drainage 42000
Paraurethral Gland
    Incision and Drainage 53060
Parotid Gland Drainage 42300-42305

Pelvic
    Drainage
        Percutaneous 58823
Pelvis
    Incision and Drainage ...26990-26992, 45000
Pericolic
    Drainage
        Percutaneous 58823
Perineum
    Incision and Drainage 56405
Perirenal or Renal
    Drainage 50020-50021
        Percutaneous 50021
Peritoneum
    Incision and Drainage
        Open 49020
        Percutaneous 49021
Prostate
    Incision and Drainage 55720-55725
    Transurethral Drainage 52700
Radius
    Incision, Deep 25035
Rectum
    Incision and Drainage 45005-45020,
            46040, 46060
Retroperitoneal 49060-49061
    Drainage
        Open 49060
        Percutaneous 49061
Salivary Gland
    Drainage 42300-42320
Scapula
    Sequestrectomy 23172
Scrotum
    Incision and Drainage 54700, 55100
Shoulder
    Drainage 23030
Skene's Gland
    Incision and Drainage 53060
Skin
    Incision and Drainage 10060-10061
    Puncture Aspiration 10160
Soft Tissue
    Incision 20000-20005
    Subdiaphragmatic 49040-49041
Sublingual Gland
    Drainage 42310-42320
Submaxillary Gland
    Drainage 42310-42320
Subphrenic 49040-49041
Testis
    Incision and Drainage 54700
Thoracostomy 32020
Thorax
    Incision and Drainage 21501-21502
Throat
    Incision and Drainage 42700-42725
Tongue
    Incision and Drainage 41000-41006
Tonsil
    Incision and Drainage 42700
Ulna
    Incision, Deep 25035
Urethra
    Incision and Drainage 53040
Uvula
    Incision and Drainage 42000

Vagina
    Incision and Drainage 57010
Vulva
    Incision and Drainage 56405
Wrist
    Excision 25145
    Incision and Drainage 25028, 25035
X-Ray 76080

Abscess, Nasal
See Nose, Abscess

Abscess, Parotid Gland
See Parotid Gland, Abscess

Absorptiometry
Dual Energy
    Bone 76075
        Appendicular 76076
        Axial Skeleton 76075
Dual Photon
    Bone 78351
Radiographic
    Photodensity 76078
Single Photon
    Bone 78350

Absorption Spectrophotometry, Atomic
See Atomic Absorption Spectroscopy

Accessory, Toes
See Polydactyly, Toes

Accessory Nerve, Spinal
See Nerves, Spinal Accessory

ACE
See Angiotensin Converting Enzyme

Acetabuloplasty 27120-27122

Acetabulum
Fracture
    Closed Treatment 27220-27222
    Open Treatment 27226-27228
    without Manipulation 27220
    with Manipulation 27222
Reconstruction 27120
    with Resection, Femoral Head 27122
Tumor
    Excision 27076

Acetaldehyde
Blood 82000

Acetaminophen
Urine 82003

Acetic Anhydrides 84600

Acetone
Blood or Urine 82009-82010

Acetone Body 82009-82010

Acetylcholinesterase
Blood or Urine 82013

AcG
See Clotting Factor

Achilles Tendon
Incision 27605-27606
Lengthening 27612
Repair 27650-27654

Achillotomy
See Tenotomy, Achilles Tendon

Acid
Gastric 82926-82928

Acid, Adenylic
See Adenosine Monophosphate (AMP)

Acid, Aminolevulinic
See Aminolevulinic Acid (ALA)

Acid, Ascorbic
See Ascorbic Acid

Acid, Deoxyribonucleic
See Deoxyribonucleic Acid

Acid, Folic
See Folic Acid

Acid, Glycocholic
See Cholylglycine

Acid, Lactic
See Lactic Acid

Acid, N-Acetylneuraminic
See Sialic Acid

Acid, Phenylethylbarbituric
See Phenobarbital

Acid, Uric
See Uric Acid

Acidity /Alkalinity
See pH

Acids, Amino
See Amino Acids

Acids, Bile
See Bile Acids

Acids, Fatty
See Fatty Acid

Acids, Guanylic
See Guanosine Monophosphate

Acids, N-Acetylneuraminic
See Sialic Acid

Acid Diethylamide, Lysergic
See Lysergic Acid Diethylamide

Acid Fast Bacilli (AFB)
Culture 87116

Acid Fast Bacillus Culture
See Culture, Acid Fast Bacilli

Acid Fast Stain 88312

Acid Perfusion Test
Esophagus 91012, 91030

Acid Phosphatase 84060-84066

Acid Probes, Nucleic
See Nucleic Acid Probe

Acid Reflux Test
Esophagus 91032-91033

Acne Surgery
Incision and Drainage
    Abscess 10060-10061
    Comedones 10040
    Cyst 10040
    Milia, Multiple 10040
    Pustules 10040

Acne Treatment
Abrasion 15786-15787
Chemical Peel 15788-15793
Cryotherapy 17340
Dermabrasion 15780-15783
Exfoliation
    Chemical 17360
Salabrasion 15810-15811

Acoustic Evoked Brain Stem Potential
See Evoked Potential, Auditory Brainstem

Acoustic Neuroma
See Brain, Tumor, Excision; Brainstem; Mesencephalon; Skull Base Surgery

Acromioclavicular Joint
Arthrocentesis 20605
Arthrotomy 23044
    with Biopsy 23101
Dislocation 23540-23552
    Open Treatment 23550-23552
X-Ray 73050

Acromion
Excision
    Shoulder 23130

Acromionectomy
Partial 23130

Acromioplasty 23415-23420
Partial 23130

ACTH
See Adrenocorticotropic Hormone (ACTH)

ACTH Releasing Factor
See Corticotropic Releasing Hormone (CRH)

Actinomyces
Antibody 86602

Actinomycosis 86000

Actinomycotic Infection
See Actinomycosis

Actinotherapy 96900
See Dermatology

Activated Factor X
See Thrombokinase

Activated Partial Thromboplastin Time
See Thromboplastin, Partial, Time

Activation, Lymphocyte
See Blastogenesis

Activities of Daily Living
See Physical Medicine/Therapy/Occupational Therapy

Activity, Glomerular Procoagulant
See Thromboplastin

Acupuncture
One or More Needles
    Electrical Stimulation 97781
    without Electric Stimulation 97780

Acute Poliomyelitis
See Polio

Acylcarnitines 82016-82017

Adamantinoma, Pituitary
See Craniopharyngioma

Addam Operation
See Dupuytren's Contracture

Adductor Tenotomy of Hip
See Tenotomy, Hip, Adductor

Adenoidectomy 42820-42821, 42830-42836

Adenoids
Excision 42830-42836
    with Tonsils 42820-42821
Unlisted Services and Procedures 42999

Adenoma
Pancreas
    Excision 48120
Thyroid Gland Excision 60200

Adenosine 3'5' Monophosphate
See Cyclic AMP

Adenosine Diphosphate
Blood 82030

Adenosine Monophosphate (AMP)
Blood 82030

Adenovirus
Antibody 86603
Antigen Detection
    Enzyme Immunoassay 87301
    Immunofluorescense 87260

Adenovirus Vaccine
See Vaccines

Adenylic Acid
See Adenosine Monophosphate (AMP)

ADH
See Antidiuretic Hormone

Adhesions
Epidural 62263
Eye
    Corneovitreal 65880
    Incision
      Anterior Segment 65860-65870
      Posterior Segment 65875

Intermarginal
    Construction 67880
        Transposition of Tarsal Plate 67882
Intestinal
    Enterolysis 44005
        Laparoscopic 44200
Intrauterine
    Lysis 58559
Labial
    Lysis 56441
Lungs
    Lysis 32124
Pelvic
    Lysis 58660, 58662, 58740
Penile
    Lysis
        Post-circumcision 54162
Preputial
    Lysis 54450

Adipectomy
See Lipectomy

ADL
See Activities of Daily Living

Administration
Immunization
    Each Additional Vaccine/Toxoid 90472, 90474
    One Vaccine/Toxoid 90471, 90473

ADP
See Adenosine Diphosphate

ADP Phosphocreatine Phosphotransferase
See CPK

Adrenalectomy 60540
Anesthesia 00866
Laparoscopic 50545

Adrenalin
See Catecholamines
Blood 82383
Urine 82384

Adrenaline-Noradrenaline
Testing 82382-82384

Adrenal Cortex Hormone
See Corticosteroids

Adrenal Gland
Biopsy 60540-60545
Excision
    Laparoscopy.....................60650
    Retroperitoneal Tumor 60545
Exploration 60540-60545
Nuclear Medicine
    Imaging 78075

Adrenal Medulla
See Medulla

Adrenocorticotropic Hormone (ACTH) 80400-80406, 80412, 80418, 82024
Blood or Urine 82024
Stimulation Panel 80400-80406

Adrenogenital Syndrome .56805, 57335

Adult T Cell Leukemia Lymphoma Virus I
See HTLV I

Advanced Life Support
See Emergency Department Services
Physician Direction 99288

Advancement
Tendon
    Foot 28238

Advancement Flap
See Skin, Adjacent Tissue Transfer

Aerosol Inhalation
See Pulmonology, Therapeutic
Pentamidine 94642, 99563

AFB
See Acid Fast Bacilli (AFB)

Afferent Nerve
See Sensory Nerve

AFP
See Alpha-Fetoprotein

After Hours Medical Services 99050-99054

Agents, Anticoagulant
See Clotting Inhibitors

Agglutinin
Cold 86156-86157
Febrile 86000

Aggregation
Platelet 85576

AHG
See Clotting Factor

AICD (Pacing Cardioverter-Defibrillator)
See Defibrillator, Heart; Pacemaker, Heart

Aid, Hearing
See Hearing Aid

AIDS Antibodies
See Antibody, HIV

AIDS Virus
See HIV-1

Akin Operation
See Bunion Repair

ALA
See Aminolevulinic Acid (ALA)

Alanine 2 Oxoglutarate Aminotransferase
See Transaminase, Glutamic Pyruvic

Alanine Amino (ALT) 84460

Alanine Transaminase
See Transaminase, Glutamic Pyruvic

Albarran Test
See Water Load Test

Albumin
Serum 82040
Urine 82042

Alcohol
Breath 82075
Ethyl
    Blood 82055
    Urine 82055
Ethylene Glycol 82693

Alcohol, Isopropyl
See Isopropyl Alcohol

Alcohol, Methyl
See Methanol

Alcohol Dehydrogenase
See Antidiuretic Hormone

Aldolase
Blood 82085

Aldosterone
Blood 82088
Suppression Evaluation 80408
Urine 82088

Alimentary Canal
See Gastrointestinal Tract

Alkaline Phosphatase 84075-84080
Leukocyte 85540
WBC 85540

Alkaloids
See Specific Drug
Urine 82101

Allergen Bronchial Provocation Tests
See Allergy Tests; Bronchial Challenge Test

Allergen Challenge, Endobronchial
See Bronchial Challenge Test

Allergen Immunotherapy
Allergen
    Prescription/Supply/Injection ..95120-95125
        with Extract Supply 95144
        Injection 95115-95117
Antigens 95144
IgE 86003-86005
IgG 86001
Insect Venom
    Prescription/Supply 95145-95149
    Prescription/Supply/Injection ..95130-95134
Prescription/Supply 95165
    Insect, Whole Body 95170
Rapid Desensitization 95180

Allergy Services/Procedures
See Office and/or Other Outpatient Services; Allergen and Immunotherapy
Education and Counseling 99201-99215
Unlisted Services and Procedures 95199

Anabolic Steroid
See Androstenedione

Analgesia 99141-99142
See Anesthesia; Sedation

Analgesic Cutaneous Electrostimulation
See Application, Neurostimulation

Analysis
Computer Data 99090
Electroencephalogram
    Digital 95957
Electronic
    Drug Infusion Pump 62367-62368
    Pacing Cardioverter-
    Defibrillator 93741-93744
      See Pacemaker, Heart
    Pulse Generator 95970-95971
Physiologic Data, Remote 99091
Protein
    Tissue
      Western Blot 88372
Semen
    Sperm Isolation 89260-89261

Analysis, Spectrum
See Spectrophotometry

Anal Abscess
See Abscess, Anal

Anal Bleeding
See Anus, Hemorrhage

Anal Fistula
See Fistula, Anal

Anal Fistulectomy
See Excision, Fistula, Anal

Anal Fistulotomy
See Fistulotomy, Anal

Anal Sphincter
Dilation 45905
Incision 46080

Anal Ulceration
See Anus, Fissure

Anaspadias
See Epispadias

Anastomosis
Arteriovenous Fistula
    Direct 36821
    with Bypass Graft 35686
    with Graft 36825-36830, 36832
Artery
    to Aorta 33606
    to Artery
      Cranial 61711
Bile Duct
    to Bile Duct 47800
    to Intestines 47760, 47780
Bile Duct to Gastrointestinal 47785
Broncho-Bronchial 32486
Caval to Mesenteric 37160
Colorectal 44620

Epididymis
    to Vas Deferens
      Bilateral 54901
      Unilateral 54900
Excision
    Trachea 31780-31781
Fallopian Tube 58750
Gallbladder to Intestines 47720-47740
Hepatic Duct to Intestines 47765, 47802
Ileo-Anal 45113
Intestines
    Colo-anal 45119
    Cystectomy 51590
    Enterocystoplasty 51960
    Resection
      Laparoscopic 44202-44205
Intestine to Intestine 44130
Jejunum 43825
Microvascular
    Free Transfer
      Jejunum 43496
Nerve
    Facial to Hypoglossal 64868
    Facial to Phrenic 64870
Oviduct 58750
Pancreas to Intestines 48180, 48520-48540
Portocaval 37140
Pulmonary 33606
Renoportal 37145
Splenorenal 37180-37181
Stomach 43825
    to Duodenum 43810, 43855
    Revision 43850
    to Jejunum 43820, 43860-43865
Tubotubal 58750
Ureter
    to Bladder 50780-50785
    to Colon 50810-50815
    Removal 50830
    to Intestine 50800, 50820-50825
    Removal 50830
    to Kidney 50727-50750
    to Ureter 50727, 50760-50770
Vein
    Saphenopopliteal 34530
Vein to Vein 37140-37160

Anastomosis, Aorta-Pulmonary Artery
See Aorta, Anastomosis, to Pulmonary Artery

Anastomosis, Bladder, to Intestine
See Enterocystoplasty

Anastomosis, Hepatic Duct
See Hepatic Duct, Anastomosis

Anastomosis of Lacrimal Sac to Conjunctival Sac
See Conjunctivorhinostomy

Anastomosis of Pancreas
See Pancreas, Anastomosis

Anderson Tibial Lengthening 27715
See Ankle; Tibia, Osteoplasty, Lengthening

Androstanediol Glucuronide ...82154

Androstanolone
See Dihydrotestosterone

Androstenedione
Blood or Urine 82157

Androstenolone
See Dehydroepiandrosterone

Androsterone
Blood or Urine 82160

Anesthesia
See Analgesia
Abbe-Estlander Procedure 00102
Abdomen
    Abdominal Wall 00700-00730,
            00800-00802, 00820-00832
    Halsted Repair 00750-00756
    Blood Vessels 00770, 00880-00882
    Endoscopy 00740, 00810
    Extraperitoneal ..00860-00862, 00866-00870
    Hernia Repair 00830-00832
      Halsted Repair 00750-00756
    Intraperitoneal ..00790-00797, 00840-00842
Abdominoperineal Resection 00844
Abortion
    Induced 01964
Achilles Tendon Repair 01472
Acromioclavicular Joint 01620
Adrenalectomy 00866
Amniocentesis 00842
Aneurysm
    Axillary-Brachial 01652
    Knee 01444
    Popliteal Artery 01444
Angiography 01920
Ankle 00400, 01462-01522
Anorectal Procedure 00902
Anus 00902
Arm
    Lower 00400, 01810-01860
    Upper 00400, 01710-01782
Arrhythmias 00410
Arteriography 01916
Arteriovenous Fistula 01432
Arthroplasty
    Hip 01214-01215
    Knee 01402
Arthroscopic Procedures
    Ankle 01464
    Elbow 01732
    Hip 01202
    Knee 01382
    Shoulder 01622
Auditory Canal, External
    Removal Foreign Body 69205
Axilla 00400, 01610-01682
Back Skin 00300
Batch-Spittler-McFaddin Operation 01404
Biopsy 00100
    Liver 00702
Bladder 00870, 00912
Brain 00210-00218, 00220-00222
Breast 00402-00406
Bronchi 00542
    Intrathoracic Repair of Trauma 00548

Anesthesia Local

See Anesthesia, Local

Aneurysm, Aorta, Abdominal

See Aorta, Abdominal, Aneurysm

Aneurysm, Basilar Artery

See Artery, Basilar, Aneurysm

Aneurysm Artery, Femoral

See Artery, Femoral, Aneurysm

Aneurysm Artery, Radial

See Artery, Radial, Aneurysm

Aneurysm Artery, Renal

See Artery, Renal, Aneurysm

Aneurysm Repair

Balloon 33967, 33970
Catheterization
    Catheter 36200
    Intracatheter/Needle 36160
Circulation Assist 33967, 33970
Conduit to Heart 33404
Excision
    Coarctation 33840-33851
Insertion
    Balloon Device 33967
    Graft .33330-33335
    Intracatheter/Needle 36160
Removal
    Balloon Assist Device 33968, 33971
Repair 33320-33322, 33802-33803
    Coarctation 33840-33851
    Graft .33860-33877
    Hypoplastic or Interrupted Aortic Arch
        without Cardiopulmonary Bypass . . .33852
        with Cardiopulmonary Bypass 33853
    Sinus of Valsalva 33702-33720
Suspension 33800
Suture .33320-33322
Valve
    Incision 33415
    Repair 33400-33403
        Left Ventricle 33414
        Supravalvular Stenosis 33417
    Replacement 33405-33413
X-Ray with Contrast 75600-75630

Aorta-Pulmonary ART Transposition
See Transposition, Great Arteries

Aortic Sinus
See Sinus of Valsalva

Aortic Stenosis
Repair 33415
    Supravalvular 33417

Aortic Valve
See Heart, Aortic Valve

Aortic Valve Replacement
See Replacement, Aortic Valve

Aortocoronary Bypass
See Coronary Artery Bypass Graft (CABG)

Aortocoronary Bypass for Heart Revascularization
See Artery, Coronary, Bypass

Aortography 75600-75605, 75630, 93544
See Angiography
Serial 75625
with Iliofemoral Artery 75630

Aortoiliac
Embolectomy 34151-34201
Thrombectomy 34151-34201

Aortopexy 33800

Aortoplasty
Supravalvular Stenosis 33417

AP
See Voiding Pressure Studies

Apert-Gallais Syndrome
See Adrenogenital Syndrome

Aphasia Testing 96105
See Neurology, Diagnostic

Apheresis
Therapeutic 36520-36521

Apical-Aortic Conduit 33404

Apicectomy
with Mastoidectomy 69605
    Petrous 69530

Apoaminotransferase, Aspartate
See Transaminase, Glutamic Oxaloacetic

Apolipoprotein
Blood or Urine .82172

Appendectomy 44950-44960
Laparoscopic 44970

Appendiceal Abscess
See Abscess, Appendix

Appendico-Vesicostomy
Cutaneous 50845

Appendix
Abscess
    Incision and Drainage
        Open 44900
        Percutaneous 44901
Excision 44950-44960

Application
Allergy Tests 95044
Bone Fixation Device
        Multiplane 20692
        Uniplane .20690
Caliper 20660
Cranial Tongs 20660
Fixation Device
    Shoulder 23700
Halo
    Cranial 20661
        Thin Skull Osteology 20664
    Femoral 20663
    Maxillofacial Fixation 21100
    Pelvic 20662
Interdental Fixation Device 21110
Neurostimulation 64550
Radioelement 77761-77778
    Surface 77789
    with Ultrasound 76965
Stereotactic Frame 20660

Application of External Fixation Device
See Fixation Device, Application, External

APPT
See Thromboplastin, Partial, Time

APTT
See Thromboplastin, Partial, Time

Aquatic Therapy
See Physical Medicine/Therapy/Occupational Therapy

Aqueous Shunt
to Extraocular Reservoir 66180
    Revision 66185

Arch, Zygomatic
See Zygomatic Arch

Arm
See Radius; Ulna; Wrist
Lower
    Abscess 25028
    Amputation 24900-24920, 25900-25905, 25915
        Cineplasty 24940
        Revision 25907-25909
    Angiography 73206
    Artery
        Ligation .37618
    Biopsy 25065-25066
    Bursa
        Incision and Drainage 25031
    Bypass Graft 35903
    Cast 29075
    CAT Scan 73200-73206
    Decompression 25020-25025
    Exploration
        Blood Vessel 35860
    Fasciotomy 24495, 25020-25025
    Hematoma .25028
    Lesion, Tendon Sheath
        Excision 25110
    Magnetic Resonance Imaging
    (MRI) 73218-73220, 73223
    Reconstruction
        Ulna 25337
    Removal
        Foreign Body 25248
    Repair
        Blood Vessel with Other Graft 35266
        Blood Vessel with Vein Graft 35236
        Decompression 24495
        Muscle 25260-25263, 25270
            Secondary 25265
        Secondary
            Muscle 25272-25274
            Tendon 25272-25274
        Tendon 25260-25263, 25270, 25280-25295, 25310-25316
            Secondary 25265
        Tendon Sheath 25275
    Replantation 20805
    Splint 29125-29126
    Tenotomy 25290
    Tumor
        Excision 25075-25077
    Ultrasound .76880
    Unlisted Services and Procedures 25999
    X-Ray 73090
        with Upper Arm 73092
Removal
    Foreign Body
        Forearm or Wrist 25248
Repair
    Muscle 24341
    Tendon 24341

Upper
   Abscess
      Incision and Drainage 23930
        See Elbow; Humerus
   Amputation 23900-23921, 24900-24920
      Cineplasty 24940
      Revision 24925-24930
      with Implant 24931-24935
   Anesthesia 00400, 01710-01782
   Angiography 73206
   Artery
      Ligation 37618
   Biopsy 24065-24066
   Bypass Graft 35903
   Cast 29065
   CAT Scan 73200-73206
   Exploration
      Blood Vessel 35860
   Hematoma
      Incision and Drainage 23930
   Magnetic Resonance Imaging
   (MRI) 73218-73220, 73223
   Muscle Revision 24330-24331
   Removal
      Cast 29705
      Foreign Body 24200-24201
   Repair
      Blood Vessel with Other Graft 35266
      Blood Vessel with Vein Graft 35236
      Muscle Transfer 24301, 24320
      Tendon 24332
      Tendon Lengthening 24305
      Tendon Revision 24320
      Tendon Transfer 24301
      Tenotomy 24310
   Replantation 20802
   Splint 29105
   Tumor
      Excision 24075-24077
   Ultrasound 76880
   Unlisted Services and Procedures 24999
   Wound Exploration
      Penetrating 20103
X-Ray
   with Lower Arm
      Infant 73092

Arnold-Chiari Malformation Repair
See Decompression, Skull

Arrest, Epiphyseal
See Epiphyseal Arrest

Arrhythmogenic Focus
Heart
   Catheter Ablation 93650-93652
   Destruction 33250-33251, 33261

Arsenic 83015
Blood or Urine 82175

ART
See Syphilis Test

Arterial Catheterization
See Cannulation, Arterial

Arterial Dilatation, Transluminal
See Angioplasty, Transluminal

Arterial Grafting for Coronary Artery Bypass
See Bypass Graft, Coronary Artery, Arterial

Arterial Pressure
See Blood Pressure

Arterial Puncture 36600

Arteriography, Aorta
See Aortography

Arteriosus, Ductus
See Ductus Arteriosus

Arteriosus, Truncus
See Truncus Arteriosus

Arteriotomy
See Incision, Artery; Transection, Artery

Arteriovenous Anastomosis 36819-36820

Arteriovenous Fistula
Cannulization
   Vein 36815
Repair
   Abdomen 35182
      Acquired or Traumatic 35189
   Head 35180
      Acquired or Traumatic 35188
   Lower Extremity 35184
      Acquired or Traumatic 35190
   Neck 35180
      Acquired or Traumatic 35188
   Thorax 35182
      Acquired or Traumatic 35189
   Upper Extremity 35184
      Acquired or Traumatic 35190
Revision
   Hemodialysis Graft or Fistula
      without Thrombectomy 36832
      with Thrombectomy 36833
Thrombectomy
   Dialysis Graft
      without Revision 36831
   Graft 36870

Arteriovenous Malformation
Cranial
   Repair 61680-61692, 61705-61708
Spinal
   Excision 63250-63252
   Injection 62294
   Repair 63250-63252

Arteriovenous Shunt
Angiography 75790
Catheterization 36145

Artery
Abdomen
   Angiography 75726
   Catheterization 36245-36248
   Ligation 37617
Adrenal
   Angiography 75731-75733
Anastomosis
   Cranial 61711

Angioplasty 75962-75968
Aorta
   Angioplasty 35452
   Atherectomy 35481, 35491
Aortoiliac
   Embolectomy 34151-34201
   Thrombectomy 34151-34201
Aortoiliofemoral 35363
Arm
   Angiography 75710-75716
   Harvest of Artery for Coronary Artery
      Bypass Graft 35600
Atherectomy
   Open 35480-35485
   Percutaneous 35490-35495
Axillary
   Aneurysm 35011-35013
   Angioplasty 35458
   Bypass Graft 35516-35521, 35533,
         35616-35623, 35650, 35654
   Embolectomy 34101
   Thrombectomy 34101
   Thromboendarterectomy 35321
Basilar
   Aneurysm 61698, 61702
Biopsy
   Transcatheter 75970
Brachial
   Aneurysm 35011-35013
   Angiography 75658
   Catheterization 36120
   Embolectomy 34101
   Exploration 24495
   Thrombectomy 34101
   Thromboendarterectomy 35321
Brachiocephalic
   Angioplasty 35458
   Atherectomy 35484, 35494
   Catheterization 36215-36218
Bypass Graft
   with Composite Graft 35681-35683
Cannulization
   for Extra Corporeal Circulation 36823
   to Vein 36810-36815
Carotid
   Aneurysm 35001-35002, 61697-61705
      Vascular Malformation or Carotid
      Cavernous Fistula 61710
   Angiography 75660-75680
   Bypass Graft 35501-35509, 35526,
         35601-35606, 35626, 35642
   Catheterization 36100
   Decompression ..61590-61591, 61595-61596
   Embolectomy 34001
   Exploration 35701
   Ligation 37600-37606, 61611-61612
   Thrombectomy 34001
   Thromboendarterectomy 35301, 35390
   Transection 61611-61612
Celiac
   Aneurysm 35121-35122
   Bypass Graft 35531, 35631
   Embolectomy 34151
   Thrombectomy 34151
   Thromboendarterectomy 35341

Artery Catheterization, Pulmonary
See Catheterization, Pulmonary Artery

Temporomandibular Joint 21010
with Biopsy
   Acromioclavicular Joint 23101
   Glenohumeral Joint 23100
   Hip Joint 27052
   Knee Joint 27330
   Sacroiliac Joint
     Hip Joint 27050
   Sternoclavicular Joint 23101
with Synovectomy
   Glenohumeral Joint 23105
   Sternoclavicular Joint 23106
Wrist 25040, 25100-25107

Arthrotomy for Removal of Prosthesis of Ankle
See Ankle, Removal, Implant

Arthrotomy for Removal of Prosthesis of Hip
See Hip, Removal, Prosthesis

Arthrotomy for Removal of Prosthesis of Wrist
See Prosthesis, Wrist, Removal

Articular Ligament
See Ligament

Artificial Abortion
See Abortion

Artificial Cardiac Pacemaker
See Heart, Pacemaker

Artificial Eye
See Prosthesis

Artificial Genitourinary Sphincter
See Prosthesis, Urethral Sphincter

Artificial Insemination 58976
See In Vitro Fertilization
Intra-Cervical 58321
Intra-Uterine 58322
Sperm Washing 58323

Artificial Knee Joints
See Prosthesis, Knee

Artificial Penis
See Penile Prosthesis

Artificial Pneumothorax
See Pneumothorax, Therapeutic

Arytenoid
Excision
   Endoscopic 31560-31561

Arytenoidectomy 31400
Endoscopic 31560

Arytenoidopexy 31400

Arytenoid Cartilage
Excision 31400
Repair 31400

Ascorbic Acid
Blood 82180

Aspartate Aminotransferase
See Transaminase, Glutamic Oxaloacetic

Aspergillus
Antibody 86606

Aspiration
See Puncture Aspiration
Bladder 51000-51010
Bone Marrow 38220
Brain Lesion
   Stereotactic 61750-61751
Bronchi
   Endoscopy 31645-31646
Bursa 20600-20610
Catheter
   Nasotracheal 31720
   Tracheobronchial 31725
Cyst
   Bone 20615
   Kidney 50390
   Pelvis 50390
   Spinal Cord 62268
   Thyroid 60001
Duodenal 89100-89105
Ganglion Cyst 20600-20605
Hydrocele
   Tunica Vaginalis 55000
Joint 20600-20610
Laryngoscopy
   Direct 31515
Lens Material 66840
Liver 47015
Lung 32420
Nucleus of Disk
   Lumbar 62287
Orbital Contents 67415
Pelvis
   Endoscopy 49322
Pericardium 33010-33011
Pleural Cavity 32000-32002
Puncture
   Cyst
     Breast 19000-19001
Spinal Cord
   Stereotaxis 63615
Syrinx
   Spinal Cord 62268
Thyroid 60001
Trachea
   Nasotracheal 31720
   Puncture 31612
Tunica Vaginalis
   Hydrocele 55000
Vitreous 67015

Aspiration, Chest
See Thoracentesis

Aspiration, Lung Puncture
See Pneumocentesis

Aspiration, Nail
See Evacuation, Hematoma, Subungual

Aspiration, Spinal Puncture
See Spinal Tap

Aspiration Lipectomies
See Liposuction

Aspiration of Bone Marrow from Donor for Transplant
See Bone Marrow, Harvesting

Assay, Very Long Chain Fatty Acids
See Fatty Acid, Very Long Chain

Assay Tobramycin
See Tobramycin

Assisted Circulation
See Circulation Assist

AST
See Transaminase, Glutamic Oxaloacetic

Astragalectomy 28130

Astragalus
See Talus

Asymmetry, Face
See Hemifacial Microsomia

Ataxia Telangiectasia
Chromosome Analysis 88248

Ataxy, Telangiectasia
See Ataxia Telangiectasia

Atherectomies, Coronary
See Artery, Coronary, Atherectomy

Atherectomy
See X-Ray, Artery
Open
   Aorta 35481
   Brachiocephalic 35484
   Femoral 35483
   Iliac 35482
   Popliteal 35483
   Renal 35480
   Tibioperoneal 35485
   Visceral 35480
Percutaneous
   Aorta 35491
   Brachiocephalic 35494
   Coronary 92995-92996
     See Artery, Coronary
   Femoral 35493
   Iliac 35492
   Popliteal 35493
   Renal 35490
   Tibioperoneal 35495
   Visceral 35490
X-Ray
   Peripheral Artery 75992-75993
   Renal Artery 75994
   Visceral Artery 75995-75996

ATLV
See HTLV I

ATLV Antibodies
See Antibody, HTLV-I

Atomic Absorption Spectroscopy 82190

ATP Creatine Phosphotransferase
See CPK

B-DNA
See Deoxyribonucleic Acid

b-Hexosaminidase 83080

B1 Vitamin
See Thiamine

B6 Vitamin
See Vitamin, B-6

Babcock Operation
See Ligation, Vein, Saphenous

Bacillus Calmette Guerin Vaccine
See BCG Vaccine

Back/Flank
Biopsy 21920-21925
Repair
   Hernia 49540
Strapping 29220
Tumor
   Excision 21930
   Radical Resection 21935
Wound Exploration
   Penetrating .20102

Backbone
See Spine
Bacterial Endotoxins 87176

Bacteria Culture
Additional Methods 87077
Anaerobic 87073-87076
Blood 87040
Feces 87045-87046
Other Source 87070-87073
Screening 87081
Urine 87086-87088

Bactericidal Titer, Serum 87197

Bacterium
Antibody 86609

BAER
See Evoked Potential, Auditory Brainstem

Baker's Cyst 27345

Baker Tube
Intestine Decompression 44021

Balanoplasty
See Penis, Repair

Baldy-Webster Operation
See Uterus, Repair, Suspension

Balkan Grippe
See Q Fever

Balloon Angioplasties, Coronary
See Percutaneous Transluminal Angioplasty

Balloon Angioplasty
See Angioplasty

Balloon Assisted Device
Aorta 33967-33974, 93727

Band, Pulmonary Artery
See Banding, Artery, Pulmonary

Banding
Artery
   Fistula 37607
   Pulmonary .33690

Bank, Blood
See Blood Banking

Bankart Procedure
See Capsulorrhaphy, Anterior

Barany Caloric Test
See Caloric Vestibular Test

Barbiturates
Blood or Urine 82205

Bardenheurer Operation
See Ligation, Artery, Chest

Barium 83015

Barium Enema 74270-74280

Barker Operation
See Talus, Excision

Barr Bodies 88130

Barr Procedure
See Tendon, Transfer, Leg, Lower

Bartholin's Gland
Abscess
   Incision and Drainage 56420
Cyst
   Repair 56440
Excision 56740
Marsupialization 56440

Bartonella
Antibody 86611

Bartonella Detection 87470-87472

Basic Life Services 99450

Basic Proteins, Myelin
See Myelin Basic Protein

Basilar Arteries
See Artery, Basilar

Batch-Spittler-McFaddin Operation
See Disarticulation, Knee

BCG Vaccine
See Vaccines

Bed Sores
See Debridement; Pressure Ulcer (Decubitus);
Skin Graft and Flap

Bekesy Audiometry
See Audiometry, Bekesy

Belsey IV Procedure
See Fundoplasty

Bender-Gestalt Test 96100

Benedict Test for Urea
See Urinalysis, Qualitative

Benign Cystic Mucinous Tumor
See Ganglion

Benign Neoplasm of Cranial Nerves
See Cranial Nerve

Bennett Fracture
See Phalanx; Thumb, Fracture

Bennett Procedure
See Repair, Leg, Upper, Muscle; Revision

Benzidine Test
See Blood, Feces

Benzodiazepine
Assay 80154

Benzoyl Cholinesterase
See Cholinesterase

Bernstein Test
See Acid Perfusion Test, Esophagus

Beryllium .83015

Beta-2-Microglobulin
Blood 82232
Urine 82232

Beta-hydroxydehydrogenase . .80406

Beta 2 Glycoprotein I Antibody . .86146

Beta Glucosidase 82963

Beta Hypophamine
See Antidiuretic Hormone

Beta Lipoproteins
See Lipoprotein, LDL

Beta Test .96100
See Psychiatric Diagnosis

Bethesda System 88164-88167

Be Antigens, Hepatitis
See Hepatitis Antigen, Be

Bicarbonate 82374

Biceps Tendon
Insertion 24342

Bichloride, Methylene
See Dichloromethane

Bicuspid Valve
See Mitral Valve

Bifrontal Craniotomy 61557

Bilaminate Skin Substitute/Neodermis
See Tissue
Repair
   See Tissue, Culture
    Repair; Tissue, Culture, Skin Grafts

Biopsy, Skin
See Skin, Biopsy

Biopsy, Vein
See Vein, Biopsy

Biostatistics
See Biometry

Biosterol
See Vitamin, A

Birthing Room

Bischof Procedure
See Laminectomy, Surgical

Bizzozero's Corpuscle/Cell
See Blood, Platelet

Bladder

Blood Coagulation Factor VII
See Proconvertin

Blood Coagulation Factor VIII
See Clotting Factor

Blood Coagulation Factor X
See Stuart-Prower Factor

Blood Coagulation Factor X, Activated
See Thrombokinase

Blood Coagulation Factor XI
See Plasma Thromboplastin, Antecedent

Blood Coagulation Factor XIII
See Fibrin Stabilizing Factor

Blood Coagulation Test
See Coagulation

Blood Component Removal
See Apheresis

Blood Count, Complete
See Complete Blood Count (CBC)

Blood Flow Check, Graft 15860, 90939-90940

Blood Gases
CO2 82803
HCO3 82803
O2 Saturation 82805-82810
pCO2 82803
pH 82800-82803
pO2 82803

Blood Letting
See Phlebotomy

Blood Lipoprotein
See Lipoprotein

Blood Pool Imaging 78472-78473, 78481-78483, 78494-78496

Blood Pressure
Monitoring, 24 Hour 93784-93790
Venous 93770

Blood Products
Irradiation 86945
Pooling 86965
Splitting 86985

Blood Sample
Fetal 59030

Blood Serum
See Serum

Blood Smear 85060

Blood Syndrome
Chromosome Analysis 88245-88248

Blood Tests
Nuclear Medicine
　Iron, Chelatable 78172
　Iron Absorption 78162
　Iron Utilization 78170
　Plasma Volume 78110-78111

Platelet Survival 78190-78191
Red Cell Volume 78120-78121
Whole Blood Volume 78122
Panels
　Electrolyte 80051
　General Health Panel 80050
　Hepatic Function 80076
　Hepatitis, Acute 80074
　Lipid Panel 80061
　Metabolic
　　Basic 80048
　　Comprehensive 80053
　Obstetric Panel 80055
　Renal Function 80069
Volume Determination 78122

Blood Transfusion, Autologous
See Autotransfusion

Blood Typing
ABO Only 86900
Antigen Screen 86903-86904
Crossmatch 86920-86922
Other RBC Antigens 86905
Paternity Testing 86910-86911
Rh (D) 86901
Rh Phenotype 86906

Blood Urea Nitrogen 84520-84525

Blood Vessels
See Artery; Vein
Angioscopy
　Non-Coronary 35400
Excision
　Arteriovenous Malformation ...63250-63252
Exploration
　Abdomen 35840
　Chest 35820
　Extremity 35860
　Neck 35800
Great
　Suture 33320-33322
Harvest
　Upper Extremity Artery 35600
　Upper Extremity Vein 35500
Kidney
　Repair 50100
Repair
　Abdomen
　　See Aneurysm Repair; Fistula, Repair
　　with Composite Graft 35681-35683
　　with Other Graft 35281
　　with Vein Graft 35251
　Aneurysm 61705-61708
　Arteriovenous Malformation ...61680-61692, 61705-61710, 63250-63252
　Chest
　　with Composite Graft 35681-35683
　　with Other Graft 35271-35276
　　with Vein Graft 35241-35246
　Direct 35201-35226
　Finger 35207
　Graft Defect 35870
　Hand 35207
　Lower Extremity 35226
　　with Composite Graft 35681-35683
　　with Other Graft 35281
　　with Vein Graft 35251

Neck
　with Composite Graft 35681-35683
　with Other Graft 35261
　with Vein Graft 35231
Upper Extremity 35206
　with Composite Graft 35681-35683
　with Other Graft 35266
　with Vein Graft 35236
Shunt Creation
　Direct 36821
　Thomas Shunt 36835
　with Bypass Graft 35686
　with Graft 36825-36830
Shunt Revision
　with Graft 36832

Bloom Syndrome
Chromosome Analysis 88245

Blotting, Western
See Western Blot

Blot Test, Ink
See Inkblot Test

Blow-Out Fracture
Orbital Floor 21385-21395

Blue, Dome Cyst
See Breast, Cyst

BMT
See Bone Marrow, Transplantation

Boarding Home Care 99321-99333

Bodies, Acetone
See Acetone Body

Bodies, Barr
See Barr Bodies

Bodies, Carotid
See Carotid Body

Bodies, Ciliary
See Ciliary Body

Bodies, Heinz
See Heinz Bodies

Bodies, Inclusion
See Inclusion Bodies

Bodies, Ketone
See Ketone Body

Body Cast
Halo 29000
Removal 29700, 29710-29715
Repair 29720
Risser Jacket 29010-29015
Turnbuckle Jacket 29020-29025
Upper Body and Head 29040
Upper Body and Legs 29046
Upper Body and One Leg 29044
Upper Body Only 29035

Body Fluid
Crystal Identification 89060

Body of Vertebra
See Vertebral Body

Body Section
X-Ray 76100
　Motion 76101-76102

Body System, Neurologic
See Nervous System

Boil
See Furuncle

Boil, Vulva
See Abscess, Vulva

Bone
See Specific Bone
Biopsy 20220-20245
CAT Scan
　Density Study 76070
Cyst
　Drainage 20615
　Injection 20615
Dual Energy X-Ray
Absorptiometry 76075-76076
Excision
　Epyphyseal Bar 20150
　Facial Bones 21026
　Mandible 21025
Fixation
　Caliper 20660
　Cranial Tong 20660
　Halo 20661-20663, 21100
　Interdental 21110
　Multiplane 20692
　Pin/Wire 20650
　Skeletal
　　Humeral Epicondyle
　　　Percutaneous 24566
　Stereotactic Frame 20660
　Uniplane 20690
Insertion
　Needle 36680
　Osseointegrated Implant
　　for External Speech Processor/Cochlear
　　Stimulator 69714-69718
Nuclear Medicine
　Density Study 78350-78351
　Imaging 78300-78320
　SPECT 78320
　Unlisted Services and Procedures 78399
Protein 83937
Removal
　Fixation Device 20670-20680
Replacement
　Osseointegrated Implant
　　for External Speech Processor/Cochlear
　　Stimulator 69717-69718
X-Ray
　Age Study 76020
　Dual Energy Absorptiometry ...76075-76076
　Length Study 76040
　Osseous Survey 76061-76065

Bone, Carpal
See Carpal Bone

Bone, Cheek
See Cheekbone

Bone, Facial
See Facial Bone

Bone, Hyoid
See Hyoid Bone

Bone, Metatarsal
See Metatarsal

Bone, Nasal
See Nasal Bone

Bone, Navicular
See Navicular

Bone, Scan
See Bone, Nuclear Medicine; Nuclear Medicine Imaging

Bone, Semilunar
See Lunate

Bone, Sesamoid
See Sesamoid Bone

Bone, Tarsal
See Ankle Bone

Bone, Temporal
See Temporal Bone

Bone 4-Carboxyglutamic Protein
See Osteocalcin

Bone Conduction Hearing Device, Electromagnetic
Implantation/Replacement 69710
Removal/Repair 69711

Bone Density Study
Appendicular Skeleton 76076
Axial Skeleton 76075
Ultrasound 76977

Bone Graft
Augmentation
　Mandibular Body 21127
Femur 27170
Fracture
　Orbit 21408
Harvesting 20900-20902
Malar Area 21210
Mandible 21215
Mandibular Ramus 21194
Maxilla 21210
Microvascular Anastomosis
　Fibula 20955
　Other 20962
Nasal Area 21210
Nasomaxillary Complex Fracture 21348
Open Treatment
　Craniofacial Separation 21436
Osteocutaneous Flap 20969-20973
Reconstruction
　Mandibular Rami 21194
　Midface 21145-21160
Spine Surgery
　Allograft
　　Morselized 20930
　　Structural 20931
　Autograft
　　Local 20936
　　Morselized 20937
　　Structural 20938
Vascular Pedicle 25430

Bone Healing
Electrical Stimulation
　Invasive 20975
　Noninvasive 20974
Ultrasound Stimulation 20979

Bone Infection
See Osteomyelitis

Bone Marrow
Aspiration 38220
Harvesting 38230
Magnetic Resonance Imaging (MRI) 76400
Needle Biopsy 38221
Nuclear Medicine
　Imaging 78102-78104
Smear 85097
T-Cell
　Depletion 86915
Transplantation 38240-38241
Trocar Biopsy 38221

Bone Plate
Mandible 21244

Bone Scan
See Bone, Nuclear Medicine; Nuclear Medicine

Bone Spur
See Exostosis

Bone Wedge Reversal
Osteotomy 21122

Bordetella
Antibody 86615
Antigen Detection
　Direct Fluorescence 87265

Borrelia
Antibody 86618-86619

Borrelia burgdorferi ab
See Antibody, Lyme Disease

Borreliosis, Lyme
See Lyme Disease

Borthen Operation
See Iridotasis

Bost Fusion
See Arthrodesis, Wrist

Bosworth Operation
See Acromioclavicular Joint, Dislocation; Arthrodesis, Vertebrae; Fasciotomy, Elbow

Bottle Type Procedure 55060

Botulinum Toxin
See Chemodenervation

Boutonniere Deformity 26426-26428

Bowel
See Intestine

Bowleg Repair 27455-27457

Boyce Operation
See Nephrotomy

Implants
   Insertion 19340-19342
   Preparation of Moulage 19396
   Removal 19328-19330
   Supply 19396
Incision
   Capsules 19370
Injection
   Radiologic .19030
Magnetic Resonance Imaging
(MRI) 76093-76094
Mammoplasty
   Augmentation 19324-19325
   Reduction 19318
Mastopexy 19316
Metallic Localization Clip Placement 19295
Needle Biopsy .19100
Needle Wire Placement 19290-19291
Periprosthetic Capsulectomy 19371
Periprosthetic Capsulotomy 19370
Reconstruction 19357-19369
   Augmentation 19324-19325
   Mammoplasty 19318-19325
   Nipple 19350-19355
      Areola 19350
   Revision 19380
   with Free Flap 19364
   with Latissimus Dorsi Flap 19361
   with Other Techniques 19366
   with Tissue Expander 19357
   with Transverse Rectus Abdominis
   Myocutaneous Flap 19367-19369
Reduction 19318
Removal
   Capsules 19371
   Modified Radical 19240
   Partial 19140-19162
   Radical 19200-19220
   Simple, Complete 19180
   Subcutaneous 19182
Repair
   Suspension 19316
Stereotactic Localization 76095
Ultrasound 76645
Unlisted Services and Procedures 19499
X-Ray 76090-76092
   Localization Nodule 76096
   with Computer-aided Detection 76085

Breathing, Inspiratory Positive-Pressure
See Intermittent Positive Pressure Breathing (IPPB)

Breath Odor Alcohol
See Alcohol, Breath

Breath Test
Alcohol, Ethyl 82075
Helicobacter Pylori . . .78267-78268, 83013-83014
Hydrogen 91065

Bricker Procedure
Intestines Anastomosis 50820

Bristow Procedure
See Capsulorrhaphy, Anterior

Brock Operation
See Valvotomy, Pulmonary Valve

Broken, Nose
See Fracture, Nasal Bone

Bronchi
Aspiration
   Endoscopic 31645-31646
Biopsy
   Endoscopic 31625-31629
Catheterization
   Insertion 31710
   with Bronchial Brush Biopsy 31717
Endoscopy
   Aspiration 31645-31646
   Biopsy 31625-31629
   Destruction
      Tumor 31641
   Dilation 31630-31631
   Excision
      Lesion 31640
   Exploration .31622
   Foreign Body Removal 31635
   Fracture 31630
   Injection 31656
   Lesion 31640-31641
   Stenosis 31641
   Tumor 31640-31641
Exploration
   Endoscopic .31622
Fracture
   Endoscopy .31630
Injection
   X-Ray 31656, 31715
Instillation
   Contrast Material 31708
Needle Biopsy .31629
Reconstruction .31770
   Graft Repair .31770
   Stenosis 31775
Removal
   Foreign Body 31635
Repair
   Fistula 32815
Stenosis
   Endoscopic Treatment 31641
Tumor
   Excision 31640
Unlisted Services and Procedures 31899
X-Ray
   with Contrast 71040-71060

Bronchial Allergen Challenge
See Bronchial Challenge Test

Bronchial Alveolar Lavage 31624

Bronchial Brushings/Protected Brushing 31623

Bronchial Brush Biopsy
with Catheterization 31717

Bronchial Challenge Test
See Allergy Tests
with Antigens, Gases 95070
with Chemicals .95071

Bronchial Provocation Tests
See Bronchial Challenge Test

Bronchioalveolar Lavage
See Lung, Lavage

Broncho-Bronchial Anastomosis 32486

Bronchoalveolar Lavage
See Lung, Lavage

Bronchography 71040-71060
Catheterization .31710
Injection
   Transtracheal 31715
Instillation
   Contrast Material 31708
Segmental
   Injection 31656

Bronchoplasty 32501
See Reconstruction, Bronchi
Excision Stenosis and Anastomosis 31775
Graft Repair 31770

Bronchopneumonia, Hiberno-Vernal
See Q Fever

Bronchopulmonary Lavage
See Lung, Lavage

Bronchoscopy
Alveolar Lavage .31624
Aspiration 31645-31646
Biopsy .31625-31629
Brushing/Protected Brushing 31623
Catheter Placement
   Intracavitary Radioelement 31643
Dilation 31630-31631
Exploration 31622
Fracture 31630
Injection 31656
Needle Biopsy .31629
Removal
   Foreign Body 31635
   Tumor 31640-31641
Stenosis 31641
Stent Placement 31631
X-Ray Contrast .31656

Bronchospasm Evaluation
See Pulmonology, Diagnostic, Spirometry

Bronkodyl
See Theophylline

Brow Pyrosis
Repair 67900

Brucella 86000
Antibody 86622

Bruise
See Hematoma

Brunschwig Operation 58240
See Hip; Pelvis, Exenteration

Brush Biopsy
See Biopsy; Needle Biopsy
Bronchi 31717

Brush Border ab
See Antibody, Heterophile

Bucca
See Cheek

Buccal Mucosa
See Mouth, Mucosa

Bulbourethral Gland
Excision 53250

Bulla
Incision and Drainage
    Puncture Aspiration 10160
Lung
    Excision-Plication 32141
       Endoscopic 32655

BUN
See Blood Urea Nitrogen; Urea Nitrogen

Bunion Repair 28296-28299
Chevron Procedure 28296
Concentric Procedure 28296
Joplin Procedure 28294
Keller Procedure 28292
Lapidus Procedure 28297
Mayo Procedure 28292
McBride Procedure 28292
Mitchell Procedure 28296
Silver Procedure 28290
with Implant 28293

Burgess Amputation
See Disarticulation, Ankle

Burhenne Procedure
See Bile Duct, Removal, Calculi (Stone);
Gallbladder

Burkitt Herpesvirus
See Epstein-Barr Virus

Burns
Allograft 15350-15351
Debridement 01951-01953,
          15000-15001, 16010-16030
Dressings 16010-16030
Escharotomy 16035-16036
Excision 01951-01953, 15000-15001
Initial Treatment 16000
Tissue Culture Skin Grafts 15100-15121,
               15342-15343
Xenograft 15400-15401

Burrow's Operation
See Skin, Adjacent Tissue Transfer

Burr Hole
Anesthesia 00214
Skull
    Biopsy Brain 61140
    Catheterization 61210

Drainage
    Abscess 61150-61151
    Cyst 61150-61151
    Hematoma 61154-61156
Exploration
    Infratentorial 61253
    Supratentorial 61250
for Implant of Neurostimulator
Array 61862
Injection, Contrast Media 61120
Insertion
    Catheter 61210
    Reservoir 61210

Bursa
Ankle 27604
Arm, Lower 25031
Elbow
    Excision 24105
    Incision and Drainage 23931
Femur
    Excision 27062
Foot
    Incision and Drainage 28001
Hip
    Incision and Drainage 26991
Injection 20600-20610
Ischial
    Excision 27060
Joint
    Aspiration 20600-20610
    Drainage 20600-20610
    Injection 20600-20610
Knee
    Excision 27340
Leg, Lower 27604
Palm
    Incision and Drainage 26025-26030
Pelvis
    Incision and Drainage 26991
Shoulder
    Drainage 23031
Wrist 25031
    Excision 25115-25116

Bursectomy
See Excision, Bursa

Bursitis, Radiohumeral
See Tennis Elbow

Bursocentesis
See Aspiration, Bursa

Button
Nasal Septal Prosthesis
    Insertion 30220

Butyrylcholine Esterase
See Cholinesterase

Bypass, Cardiopulmonary
See Cardiopulmonary Bypass

Bypass Graft
Axillary Artery 35516-35521, 35533,
          35616-35623, 35650, 35654
Carotid Artery 35501-35509, 35526,
          35601-35606, 35626, 35642
Celiac Artery 35531, 35631

Coronary Artery
    Angiography 93556
    Arterial 33533-33536
    Venous Graft 33510-33516
Excision
    Abdomen 35907
    Extremity 35903
    Neck 35901
    Thorax 35905
Femoral Artery 35521, 35533, 35546,
      35551-35558, 35566, 35621, 35646-35647,
          35651-35661, 35666, 35700
Harvest
    Upper Extremity Vein 35500
Iliac Artery 35541, 35563, 35641, 35663
Iliofemoral Artery ..35548-35549, 35565, 35665
Mesenteric Artery 35531, 35631
Peroneal Artery 35566-35571, 35666-35671
Placement
    Vein Patch 35685
Popliteal Artery 35551-35558, 35571, 35623,
         35651, 35656, 35671, 35700
Renal Artery 35536, 35560, 35631-35636
Reoperation 35700
Repair
    Abdomen 35907
    Extremity 35903
    Lower Extremity
      with Composite Graft 35681-35683
    Neck 35901
    Thorax 35905
Revascularization
    Extremity 35903
    Neck 35901
    Thorax 35905
Revision
    Lower Extremity
      with Angioplasty 35879
      with Vein Interposition 35881
Secondary Repair 35870
Splenic Artery 35536, 35636
Subclavian Artery ..35506-35507, 35511-35516,
        35526, 35606-35616, 35626, 35645
Thrombectomy
    Other than Hemodialysis Graft
    or Fistula 35875-35876
Tibial Artery ..35566-35571, 35623, 35666-35671
Vertebral Artery 35508, 35515, 35642-35645
with Composite Graft 35681

Bypass In-Situ
Femoral Artery 35582-35585
Peroneal Artery 35585-35587
Popliteal Artery 35582-35583, 35587
Tibial Artery 35585-35587

B 12, Vitamin
See Cyanocobalamin

B Antibodies, Hepatitis
See Antibody, Hepatitis B

B Antigens, Hepatitis
See Hepatitis Antigen, B

B Complex Vitamins
B-12 Absorption 78270-78272

C-13
Urease Activity 83013-83014
Urea Breath Test 83013-83014

C-14
Urease Activity 83013-83014
Urea Breath Test 78267-78268

C-Peptide 80432, 84681

C-Reactive Protein 86140-86141

C-Section
See Cesarean Delivery

CABG
See Coronary Artery Bypass Graft (CABG)

Cadmium
Urine 82300

Calcaneal Spur
See Heel Spur

Calcaneus
Craterization 28120
Cyst
    Excision 28100-28103
Diaphysectomy .28120
Excision 28118-28120
Fracture
    Open Treatment 28415-28420
    Percutaneous Fixation 28406
    without Manipulation 28400
    with Manipulation 28405-28406
Repair
    Osteotomy 28300
Saucerization 28120
Tumor
    Excision 27647, 28100-28103
X-Ray 73650

Calcareous Deposits
Subdeltoid
    Removal 23000

Calcifediol
Blood or Urine 82306

Calcifediol Assay
See Calciferol

Calciferol
Blood or Urine 82307

Calcification
See Calcium, Deposits

Calciol
See Vitamin, D-3

Calcitonin
Blood or Urine 82308
Stimulation Panel 80410

Calcium
Blood
    Infusion Test .82331
Deposits
    See Removal, Calculi (Stone); Removal,
    Foreign Bodies
Ionized 82330
Total 82310
Urine 82340

Calcium-Binding Protein, Vitamin K-Dependent
See Osteocalcin

Calcium-Pentagastrin Stimulation 80410

Calculus
Analysis 82355-82370
Destruction
    Bile Duct 43265
    Pancreatic Duct 43265
Removal
    Bile Duct 43264, 47554, 74327
    Bladder 51050, 52310-52318, 52352
    Kidney . .50060-50081, 50130, 50561, 50580,
                              52352
    Pancreatic Duct 43264
    Ureter . .50610-50630, 50961, 50980, 51060-
              51065, 52320-52325, 52352
    Urethra 52310-52315, 52352

Calculus of Kidney
See Calculus, Removal, Kidney

Caldwell-Luc Procedure
See Sinus, Maxillary; Sinusotomy; Sternum, Fracture
Orbital Floor Blowout Fracture 21385
Sinusotomy 31030-31032

Caliper
Application/Removal 20660

Callander Knee Disarticulation
See Disarticulation, Knee

Callosum, Corpus
See Corpus Callosum

Calmette Guerin Bacillus Vaccine
See BCG Vaccine

Caloric Vestibular Test 92533

Calycoplasty 50405

Camey Enterocystoplasty 50825

CAMP
See Cyclic AMP

Campbell Procedure 27422

Campylobacter
Antibody 86625

Campylobacter Pylori
See Helicobacter Pylori

Canal, Ear
See Auditory Canal

Canal, Semicircular
See Semicircular Canal

Canaloplasty 69631, 69635

Candida
Antibody 86628
Skin Test 86485

Cannulation 36821
Arterial 36620-36625
Sinus
    Maxillary 31000
    Sphenoid 31002
Thoracic Duct 38794

Cannulation, Renoportal
See Anastomosis, Renoportal

Cannulization
See Catheterization
Arteriovenous 36145, 36810-36815
Declotting 36550, 36860-36861
ECMO 36822
External
    Declotting 36860-36861
Vas Deferens 55200
Vein to Vein 36800

Canthocystostomy
See Conjunctivorhinostomy

Canthopexy
Lateral 21282
Medial 21280

Canthoplasty 67950

Canthorrhaphy 67880-67882

Canthotomy 67715

Canthus
Reconstruction .67950

Cap, Cervical
See Cervical Cap

Capsule
See Capsulodesis
Elbow
    Arthrotomy .24006
    Excision 24006
Foot 28264
Interphalangeal Joint
    Excision 26525
    Incision 26525
Knee 27435
Metacarpophalangeal Joint
    Excision 26520
    Incision 26520
Metatarsophalangeal Joint
    Release 28289
Shoulder
    Incision 23020
Wrist
    Excision 25320

Capsulectomy
Breast
    Periprosthetic 19371

Capsulodesis
Metacarpophalangeal Joint 26516-26518

Capsulorrhaphy
Anterior 23450-23462
Multi-Directional Instability 23466
Posterior 23465
Wrist 25320

Capsulotomy
Breast
    Periprosthetic 19370
Foot 28260-28262
Hip
    with Release, Flexor Muscles 27036
Interphalangeal Joint 28272
Knee 27435
Metacarpophalangeal Joint 26520
Metatarsophalangeal Joint 28270
Toe 28270-28272
Wrist 25085

Captopril 80416-80417

Carbamazepine
Assay 80156-80157

Carbazepin
See Carbamazepine

Carbinol
See Methanol

Carbohydrate Deficient Transferrin 82373

Carbon Dioxide
Blood or Urine 82374

Carbon Monoxide
Blood 82375-82376

Carbon Tetrachloride 84600

Carboxycathepsin
See Angiotensin Converting Enzyme (ACE)

Carboxyhemoglobin 82375-82376

Carbuncle
Incision and Drainage 10060-10061

Carcinoembryonal Antigen
See Antigen, Carcinoembryonic

Carcinoembryonic Antigen 82378

Cardiac
See Coronary

Cardiac Arrhythmia, Tachycardia
See Tachycardia

Cardiac Atria
See Atria

Cardiac Catheterization
Combined Left and Right Heart 93526-93529
Combined Right and Retrograde Left
    Congenital Cardiac Anomalies 93531
Combined Right and Transseptal Left
    Congenital Cardiac Anomalies . .93532-93533
for Biopsy 93505

for Dilution Studies 93561-93562
Imaging 93555-93556
Injection 93539-93545
    See Catheterization, Cardiac
Left Heart .93510-93524
Pacemaker 33210
Right
    Congenital Cardiac Anomalies 93530
Right Heart 93501-93503

Cardiac Electroversion
See Cardioversion

Cardiac Event Recorder
Implantation 33282
Removal 33284

Cardiac Magnetic Resonance Imaging (CMRI)
Complete Study .75554
Limited Study 75555
Morphology 75553
Velocity Flow Mapping 75556

Cardiac Massage
Thoracotomy 32160

Cardiac Muscle
See Myocardium

Cardiac Neoplasm
See Heart, Tumor

Cardiac Output
Indicator Dilution 93561-93562

Cardiac Pacemaker
See Heart, Pacemaker

Cardiac Rehabilitation 93797-93798

Cardiac Septal Defect
See Septal Defect

Cardiac Transplantation
See Heart, Transplantation

Cardiectomy
Donor 33930, 33940

Cardioassist 92970-92971

Cardiolipin Antibody 86147

Cardiology
See Electrocardiography
Diagnostic
    Atrial Electrogram
      Esophageal Recording 93615-93616
    Cardio-Defibrillator
      Evaluation and Testing 93640-93642,
                        93741-93744
    Echocardiography
      Doppler 93303-93321, 93662
      Intracardiac 93662
      Transesophageal 93318
      Transthoracic 93303-93317, 93350
    Electrocardiogram
      Evaluation 93000, 93010, 93014
      Microvolt T-wave Alternans 93025
      Monitoring 93224-93237
      Patient-Demand 93268-93272

      Rhythm 93040-93042
      Tracing 93005
      Transmission 93012
    Ergonovine Provocation Test 93024
    Implantable Loop Recorder System . . .93727
    Intracardiac Pacing and Mapping 93631
      3-D Mapping 93613
      Follow-up Study 93624
      Stimulation and Pacing 93623
    Intracardiac Pacing and Recording
      Arrhythmia Induction 93618-93620
      Bundle of His 93600
      Comprehensive 93619-93622
      Intra-Atrial 93602, 93610
      Right Ventricle 93603
      Tachycardia Sites 93609
      Ventricular .93612
    Intravascular Ultrasound 92978-92979
    Pacemaker Testing 93642
      Antitachycardia System 93724
      Dual Chamber 93731-93733
      Leads 93641
      Single Chamber 93734-93736
    Perfusion Imaging 78460-78461
      See Nuclear Medicine
    Stress Tests
      Cardiovascular 93015-93018
      Drug Induced 93024
      Multiple Gated Acquisition
      (MUGA) 78473
    Tilt Table Evaluation 93660
Therapeutic
    Cardioassist 92970-92971
    Cardioversion 92960-92961
    Intravascular Ultrasound 92978-92979
    Pacing
      Transcutaneous, Temporary 92953
    Thrombolysis 92975-92977
    Thrombolysis, Coronary 92977
    Valvuloplasty
      Percutaneous 92986-92990

Cardiomyotomy
See Esophagomyotomy

Cardioplasty 43320

Cardiopulmonary Bypass
See Heart; Lung, Transplantation

Cardiopulmonary Resuscitation 92950

Cardiotomy 33310-33315

Cardiovascular Stress Test
See Exercise Stress Tests

Cardioversion 92960-92961

Care, Custodial
See Nursing Facility Services

Care, Intensive
See Intensive Care

Care, Neonatal Intensive
See Intensive Care, Neonatal

Care, Self
See Self Care

Pacemaker 33210
Right Heart 36013, 93501
    for Congenital Cardiac Anomalies ... 93530
Cerebral Artery 36215
Cystourethroscopy
    Ejaculatory Duct 52010
    Ureteral 52005
Ear, Middle 69405
Eustachian Tube 69405
Fallopian Tube 58345, 74742
Intracardiac
    Ablation 93650-93652
Jejunum
    for Enteral 44015
Kidney
    Drainage 50392
    with Ureter 50393
Legs 36245-36248
Nasotracheal 31720
Newborn
    Umbilical Vein 36510
Pelvic Artery 36245-36248
Placement
    Arterial Coronary Conduit
       without Concomitant Left Heart
          Catheterization 93508
    Coronary Artery
       without Concomitant Left Heart
          Catheterization 93508
    Venous Coronary Bypass Graft
       without Concomitant Left Heart
          Catheterization 93508
Portal Vein 36481
Pulmonary Artery 36013-36015
Radioelement Application 55859
Removal
    Fractured Catheter 75961
Salivary Duct 42660
Skull 61107
Spinal Cord 62350-62351
Thoracic Artery 36215-36218
Tracheobronchi 31725
Transglottic 31700
Umbilical Artery 36660
Umbilical Vein 36510
Ureter
    Endoscopic 50553, 50572, 50953, 50972,
                       52005
    Injection 50394, 50684
    Manometric Studies 50396, 50686
Urethra 53670-53675
Uterus
    Radiology 58340
Vena Cava 36010
Venous
    Central Line 36488-36491
    First Order 36011
    Intracatheter/Needle 36000
    Organ Blood 36500
    Second Order 36012
    Umbilical Vein 36510
Ventricular 61020-61026, 61210-61215

CAT Scan

Bone
    Density Study 76070
Drainage 75989
Follow-up Study 76380

Guidance
    Localization 76355
    Needle Biopsy 76360
    Radiation Therapy 76370
    Tissue Ablation 76362
    Vertebroplasty 76013
Other Planes 76375
without and with Contrast
    Abdomen 74170-74175, 75635
    Arm 73202-73206
    Brain 70470, 70496
    Chest 71275
    Ear 70482
    Face 70488
    Head 70470, 70496
    Leg 73702-73706, 75635
    Maxilla 70488
    Neck 70492, 70498
    Orbit 70482
    Pelvis 72191, 72194
    Sella Turcica 70482
    Spine
       Cervical 72127
       Lumbar 72133
       Thoracic 72130
    Thorax 71270-71275
without Contrast 70450
    Abdomen 74150
    Arm 73200
    Brain 70450
    Ear 70480
    Face 70486
    Head 70450
    Leg 73700
    Maxilla 70486
    Neck 70490
    Orbit 70480
    Pelvis 72192
    Sella Turcica 70480
    Spine
       Cervical 72125
       Lumbar 72131
       Thoracic 72128
    Thorax 71250
with Contrast 70460
    Abdomen 74160
    Arm 73201
    Brain 70460
    Ear 70481
    Face 70487
    Head 70460
    Leg 73701
    Maxilla 70487
    Neck 70491
    Orbit 70481
    Pelvis 72193
    Sella Turcica 70481
    Spine
       Cervical 72126
       Lumbar 72132
       Thoracic 72129
    Thorax 71260

CAT Scan, Radionuclide

See Emission Computerized Tomography

Cauda Equina

See Spinal Cord
Decompression 63005-63011, 63017,
               63047-63057, 63087-63091
Exploration 63005-63011, 63017

Cauterization

Anal Fissure 46940-46942
Cervix 57522
    Cryocautery 57511
    Electro or Thermal 57510
    Laser Ablation 57513
Chemical
    Granulation Tissue 17250
Everted Punctum 68705
Nasopharyngeal Hemorrhage 42970
Nose
    Hemorrhage 30901-30906
Skin Lesion 11055-11057, 17000-17004
Skin Tags 11200-11201
Turbinate Mucosa 30801-30802

Cavernitides, Fibrous

See Peyronie Disease

Cavernosography

Corpora 54230

Cavernosometry 54231

Cavities, Pleural

See Pleural Cavity

Cavus Foot Correction 28309

CBC

See Blood Cell Count; Complete Blood Count
(CBC)

CCL4

See Carbon Tetrachloride

CCU Visit

See Critical Care Services

CD142 Antigens

See Thromboplastin

CD143 Antigens

See Angiotensin Converting Enzyme (ACE)

CD4 86360

CD8 86360

CEA

See Carcinoembryonic Antigen

Cecil Repair

See Urethroplasty

Cecostomy 44300

Celiac Plexus

Destruction 64680
Injection
    Anesthetic 64530
    Neurolytic 64680

Celiac Trunk Artery

See Artery, Celiac

Celioscopy

See Endoscopy, Peritoneum

Celiotomy 49000
Abdomen
  for Staging 49220

Cell, Blood
See Blood Cell

Cell, Islet
See Islet Cell

Cell, Mother
See Stem Cell

Cell-Stimulating Hormone, Interstitial
See Luteinizing Hormone (LH)

Cellobiase
See Beta Glucosidase

Cellular Inclusion
See Inclusion Bodies

Cell Count
Body Fluid 89050-89051

Central Shunt 33764

Central Venous Catheter Placement
Cutdown
  Child/Adult 36491
  Infant 36490
Percutaneous
  Child/Adult 36489
  Infant 36488
Repositioning 36493

Cephalic Version
of Fetus
  External 59412

Cephalocele
See Encephalocele

Cephalogram, Orthodontic
See Orthodontic Cephalogram

Cerclage
Cervix 57700
  Abdominal 59325
  Removal Under Anesthesia 59871
  Vaginal 59320

Cerebellopontine Angle Tumor
See Brain, Tumor, Excision; Brainstem; Mesencephalon; Skull Base Surgery

Cerebral Cortex Decortication
See Decortication

Cerebral Death
See Brain Death

Cerebral Hernia
See Encephalocele

Cerebral Thermography
See Thermogram, Cephalic

Cerebral Ventriculographies
See Ventriculography

Cerebrose
See Galactose

Cerebrospinal Fluid 86325
Nuclear Imaging 78630-78650

Cerebrospinal Fluid Leak 63744
Brain
  Repair 61618-61619, 62100
Nasal/Sinus Endoscopy
  Repair 31290-31291
Spinal Cord
  Repair 63707-63709

Cerebrospinal Fluid Shunt 63740, 63746
Creation 62180-62192, 62200-62223
Irrigation 62194
Removal 62256-62258
Replacement 62194, 62225-62230
Reprogramming 62252

Ceruloplasmin 82390

Cerumen
Removal 69210

Cervical Cap 57170

Cervical Lymphadenectomy 38720-38724

Cervical Mucus Penetration Test 89330

Cervical Plexus
Injection
  Anesthetic 64413

Cervical Pregnancy 59140

Cervical Puncture 61050-61055

Cervical Smears 88141-88155, 88164-88167
See Cytopathology

Cervical Spine
See Vertebra, Cervical

Cervical Sympathectomy
See Sympathectomy, Cervical

Cervicectomy 57530

Cervicography 0003T

Cervicoplasty 15819

Cervicothoracic Ganglia
See Stellate Ganglion

Cervix
See Cytopathology
Amputation
  Total 57530
Biopsy 57500, 57520
Cauterization 57522
  Cryocautery .57511
  Electro or Thermal 57510
  Laser Ablation 57513
Cerclage 57700
  Abdominal 59325
  Removal Under Anesthesia 59871
  Vaginal 59320
Cervicography .0003T

Conization 57520-57522
Curettage
  Endocervical 57454, 57505
Dilation
  Canal 57800
  Stump 57820
Dilation and Curettage 57820
Ectopic Pregnancy 59140
Excision
  Electrode 57460
  Radical 57531
  Stump
   Abdominal Approach 57540-57545
   Vaginal Approach 57550-57556
  Total 57530
Insertion
  Dilation 59200
  Laminaria 59200
  Prostaglandin 59200
  Sensor, Fetal Oximetry 0021T
Repair
  Cerclage 57700
   Abdominal 59325
   Suture 57720
   Vaginal .59320
Unlisted Services and Procedures 58999

Cesarean Delivery
Antepartum Care 59610, 59618
Delivery
  after Attempted Vaginal Delivery 59618
   Delivery Only 59620
   Postpartum Care 59622
   Routine Care 59610, 59618
Delivery Only 59514
Postpartum Care 59515
Routine Care 59510
Tubal Ligation at Time of 58611
with Hysterectomy 59525

CGMP
See Cyclic GMP

Chalazion
Excision 67805
  Multiple
   Different Lids 67805
   Same Lid .67801
  Single 67800
  Under Anesthesia 67808

Challenge Tests
Bronchial Ingestion 95070-95075

Chambers Procedure 28300

Change
Catheter
  Bile Duct 75984
Fetal Position
  by Manipulation 59412
Tube or Stent
  Endoscopic
   Bile or Pancreatic Duct 43269

Change, Gastrostomy Tube
See Gastrostomy Tube, Change of

Change of, Dressing
See Dressings, Change

Cheek
Bone
    Fracture
        Closed Treatment with
            Manipulation 21355
        Open Treatment 21360-21366
    Reconstruction 21270
Fascia Graft 15840
Muscle Graft 15841-15845
Muscle Transfer .15845

Cheilectomy
Metatarsophalangeal Joint Release 28289

Cheiloplasty
See Lip, Repair

Cheiloschisis
See Cleft Lip

Cheilotomy
See Incision, Lip

Chemical Cauterization
Granulation Tissue 17250

Chemical Exfoliation 17360

Chemical Peel 15788-15793

Chemiluminescent Assay 82397

Chemistry Tests
Clinical
    Unlisted Services and Procedures 84999

Chemocauterization
Corneal Epithelium 65435
    with Chelating Agent 65436

Chemodenervation
Cervical Spinal Muscle 64613
Extraocular Muscle 67345
Extremity Muscle 64614
Facial Muscle 64612
Trunk Muscle 64614

Chemonucleolysis 62292

Chemosurgery
Mohs Technique 17304-17310
Skin Lesion 17004, 17110, 17270, 17280

Chemotaxis Assay 86155

Chemotherapy
Arterial Catheterization 36640
Bladder Instillation 51720
CNS 96450
Extracorporeal Circulation
    Extremity 36823
Home Infusion Procedures 99555
Intra-Arterial 96420-96425
Intralesional 96405-96406
Intramuscular 96400
Intravenous 96408-96414
Peritoneal Cavity 96445
Pleural Cavity 96440
Pump Services
    Implantable .96530
    Portable 96520
Reservoir Filling 96542

    Subcutaneous 96400
    Supply of Agent 96545
    Unlisted Services and Procedures 96549

Chest
See Mediastinum; Thorax
Angiography 71275
Artery
    Ligation 37616
CAT Scan 71250-71275
Exploration
    Blood Vessel 35820
Magnetic Resonance Imaging
(MRI) 71550-71552
Repair
    Blood Vessel 35211-35216
        with Other Graft 35271-35276
        with Vein Graft 35241-35246
Ultrasound 76604
Wound Exploration
    Penetrating 20101
X-Ray 71010-71035
    Complete (four Views)
        with Fluoroscopy 71034
    Insertion Pacemaker 71090
    Partial (Two Views)
        with Fluoroscopy 71023
    Stereo 71015
    with Fluoroscopy 71090

Chest, Funnel
See Pectus Excavatum

Chest Cavity
Bypass Graft 35905
Endoscopy
    Exploration 32601-32606
    Surgical 32650-32665

Chest Wall
See Pulmonology, Therapeutic
Manipulation 94667-94668
Reconstruction .49905
    Trauma 32820
Repair 32905
    Closure 32810
    Fistula 32906
Tumor
    Excision 19260-19272
Unlisted Services and Procedures 32999

Chest Wall Fistula
See Fistula, Chest Wall

Chevron Procedure 28296

Chiari Osteotomy of the Pelvis
See Osteotomy, Pelvis

Chicken Pox Vaccine 90716

Child Procedure
See Excision, Pancreas, Partial

Chin
Repair
    Augmentation 21120
    Osteotomy 21121-21123

Chinidin
See Quinidine

Chiropractic Manipulation
See Manipulation, Chiropractic

Chiropractic Treatment
Spinal
    Extraspinal 98940-98943

Chlamydia
Antibody 86631-86632
Antigen Detection
    Direct Fluorescence 87270
    Enzyme Immunoassay 87320
Culture 87110

Chloramphenicol 82415

Chloride
Blood 82435
Other Source 82438
Spinal Fluid 82438
Urine 82436

Chloride, Methylene
See Dichloromethane

Chlorinated Hydrocarbons 82441

Chlorohydrocarbon
See Chlorinated Hydrocarbons

Chlorpromazine 84022

Choanal Atresia
Repair 30540-30545

Cholangiography
Injection .47500-47505
Intraoperative 74300-74301
Percutaneous 74320
    with Laparoscopy 47560-47561
Postoperative 74305
Repair
    with Bile Duct Exploration 47700
    with Cholecystectomy . .47563, 47605, 47620

Cholangiopancreatography 43260
See Bile Duct; Pancreatic Duct
Repair
    See Bile Duct; Pancreatic Duct
    with Biopsy 43261
    with Surgery 43262-43267, 43269

Cholangiostomy
See Hepaticostomy

Cholangiotomy
See Hepaticostomy

Cholecalciferol
See Vitamin, D-3

Cholecystectomy 47562-47564,
                             47600-47620
Any Method 47562-47564
    with Cholangiography . .47563, 47605, 47620
    with Exploration Common
    Duct .47564, 47610

Cholecystenterostomy 47570,
                             47720-47741

Tumor
　　Excision 23140, 23146, 23200
　　　　with Autograft 23145
　　Radical Resection 23200
X-Ray 73000

Clavicula
See Clavicle

Claviculectomy
Partial 23120
Total 23125

Claw Finger Repair 26499

Cleft, Branchial
See Branchial Cleft

Cleft Cyst, Branchial
See Branchial Cleft, Cyst

Cleft Foot
Reconstruction 28360

Cleft Hand
Repair 26580

Cleft Lip
Repair 40700-40761
Rhinoplasty 30460-30462

Cleft Palate
Repair 42200-42225
Rhinoplasty 30460-30462

Clinical Act of Insertion
See Insertion

Clinical Chemistry Test
See Chemistry Tests, Clinical

Clinical Pathology
See Pathology, Clinical

Clitoroplasty
Intersex State 56805

Closed [Transurethral] Biopsy of Bladder
See Biopsy, Bladder, Cystourethroscopy

Clostridial Tetanus
See Tetanus

Clostridium Botulinum Toxin
See Chemodenervation

Clostridium Difficile
Antigen Detection
　　Enzyme Immunoassay 87324
by Immunoassay
　　with Direct Optical Observation 87803

Clostridium Tetani ab
See Antibody, Tetanus

Closure 12001-13160
Anal Fistula 46288
Atrioventricular Valve 33600
Cystostomy 51880
Enterostomy 44625-44626
Lacrimal Fistula 68770

Lacrimal Punctum
　　Plug 68761
　　Thermocauterization, Ligation or Laser
　　　Surgery 68760
Rectovaginal Fistula 57300-57308
Semilunar Valve 33602
Septal Defect 33615
Sternotomy 21750
Ventricular Tunnel 33722

Closure, Atrial Septal Defect
See Heart, Repair, Atrial Septum

Closure, Cranial Sutures, Premature
See Craniosynostosis

Closure, Fistula, Vesicouterine
See Fistula, Vesicouterine, Closure

Closure, Meningocele Spinal
See Meningocele Repair

Closure, Vagina
See Vagina, Closure

Closure of Esophagostomy
See Esophagostomy, Closure

Closure of Gastrostomy
See Gastrostomy, Closure

Clot 34401-34490, 35875-35876, 50230
See Thrombectomy; Thromboendarterectomy

Clotting Disorder
See Coagulopathy

Clotting Factor 85210-85293

Clotting Inhibitors 85300-85305,
　　　　　　　　　　　　　85307, 99557

Clotting Operation
See Excision, Nail Fold

Clotting Test
Protein C 85303, 85307
Protein S 85306

Clotting Time
See Coagulation Time

Clot Lysis Time 85175

Clot Retraction 85170

Clubfoot Cast 29450
Wedging 29750

CMG
See Cystometrogram

CMRI
See Cardiac Magnetic Resonance Imaging

CMV
See Cytomegalovirus

CNPB
See Continuous Negative Pressure Breathing (CNPB); Pulmonology, Therapeutic

Co-Factor I, Heparin
See Antithrombin III

CO2
See Carbon Dioxide

Coagulation
Unlisted Services and Procedures 85999

Coagulation, Blood
See Blood Clot

Coagulation, Light
See Photocoagulation

Coagulation Defect
See Coagulopathy

Coagulation Factor
See Clotting Factor

Coagulation Factor I
See Fibrinogen

Coagulation Factor II
See Prothrombin

Coagulation Factor III
See Thromboplastin

Coagulation Factor IV
See Calcium

Coagulation Factor IX
See Christmas Factor

Coagulation Factor VII
See Proconvertin

Coagulation Factor VIII
See Clotting Factor

Coagulation Factor X
See Stuart-Prower Factor

Coagulation Factor Xa
See Thrombokinase

Coagulation Factor XI
See Plasma Thromboplastin, Antecedent

Coagulation Factor XII
See Hageman Factor

Coagulation Factor XIII
See Fibrin Stabilizing Factor

Coagulation Time 85345-85348

Coagulin
See Thromboplastin

Coagulopathy 85390
Assay 85130

Cocaine
Blood or Urine 82520
Screen 82486

Coccidioides
Antibody 86635

Coccidioidin Test
See Streptokinase, Antibody

Coccidioidomycosis
Skin Test 86490

Repair
- Volvulus
  - Endoscopy 45337
- Ultrasound
  - Endoscopy 45341-45342

Colonna Procedure
See Acetabulum, Reconstruction

Colonoscopy
- Biopsy 45380
- Collection Specimen 45380
  - via Colotomy 45355
- Destruction
  - Lesion 45383
  - Tumor 45383
- Hemorrhage Control 45382
- Placement
  - Stent 45387
- Removal
  - Foreign Body 45379
  - Polyp 45384-45385
  - Tumor 45384-45385
- via Stoma 44388-44390
  - Biopsy 44389
  - Destruction
    - of Lesion 44393
    - of Tumor 44393
  - Exploration 44388
  - Hemorrhage 44391
  - Placement
    - Stent 44397
  - Removal
    - Foreign Body 44390
    - Polyp 44392, 44394
    - Tumor 44392, 44394

Colorrhaphy
.......................44604

Color Vision Examination
......92283

Colostomy
............44320, 45563
- Abdominal
  - Establishment 50810
- Home Visit 99505
- Intestine, Large
  - with Suture 44605
- Perineal
  - Establishment 50810
- Revision 44340
  - Paracolostomy Hernia 44345-44346

Colotomy
.......................44025

Colpectomy
- Partial 57106
- Total 57110
- with Hysterectomy 58275-58280
  - with Repair of Enterocele 58280

Colpo-Urethrocystopexy
.......58152, 58267
- Marshall-Marchetti-Krantz Procedure ...58152, 58267
- Pereyra Procedure 58267

Colpoceliocentesis
See Colpocentesis

Colpocentesis
.......................57020

Colpocleisis
.....................57120

Colpocleisis Complete
See Vagina, Closure

Colpohysterectomies
See Excision, Uterus, Vaginal

Colpoperineorrhaphy
..........57210

Colpopexy
.....................57280

Colpoplasty
See Repair, Vagina

Colporrhaphy
- Anterior 57240, 57289
- Anteroposterior 57260-57265
  - with Enterocele Repair 57265
- Nonobstetrical 57200
- Posterior 57250

Colposcopy
- Biopsy 57454
- Exploration 57452
- Loop Electrode Excision 57460
- Perineum 99170

Colpotomy
- Drainage
  - Abscess 57010
- Exploration 57000

Colprosterone
See Progesterone

Columna Vertebralis
See Spine

Column Chromatography/Mass Spectrometry
.............82541-82544

Combined Heart-Lung Transplantation
See Transplantation, Heart-Lung

Combined Right and Left Heart Cardiac Catheterization
See Cardiac Catheterization, Combined Left and Right Heart

Comedones
- Removal 10040

Commissurotomy
- Right Ventricle 33476-33478

Common Sensory Nerve
- Repair/Suture 64834

Common Truncus
See Truncus Arteriosus

Community/Work Reintegration
- Training 97537
  - *See* Physical Medicine/Therapy/Occupational Therapy

Compatibility Test
- Blood 86920

Complement
- Antigen 86160
- Fixation Test 86171

Functional Activity 86161
Hemolytic
- Total 86162
Total 86162

Complete Blood Count (CBC)
.......................85022-85025
See Blood Cell Count
- Manual 85031

Complete Colectomy
See Colectomy, Total

Complete Pneumonectomy
See Pneumonectomy, Completion

Complete Transposition of Great Vessels
See Transposition, Great Arteries

Complex, Factor IX
See Christmas Factor

Complex, Vitamin B
See B Complex Vitamins

Component Removal, Blood
See Apheresis

Composite Graft
..........15760-15770, 35681-35683

Compound B
See Corticosterone

Compound F
See Cortisol

Compression, Nerve, Median
See Carpal Tunnel Syndrome

Computed Axial Tomography (CAT)
See CAT Scan; Specific Anatomic Site

Computed Tomographic Scintigraphy
See Emission Computerized Tomography

Computer-aided Detection
- Mammography
  - Screening 76085

Computerized Emission Tomography
See Emission Computerized Tomography

Computer Data Analysis
........99090

Concentration, Hydrogen-Ion
See pH

Concentration, Minimum Inhibitory
See Minimum Inhibitory Concentration

Concentration of Specimen
....87015

Concentric Procedure
..........28296

Conchae Nasale
See Nasal Turbinate

Concha Bullosa Resection
- with Nasal/Sinus Endoscopy 31240

Contrast Aortogram
See Aortography

Contrast Bath Therapy 97034
See Physical Medicine/Therapy/Occupational Therapy

Contrast Material
Injection
    via Peritoneal Catheter 49424
Instillation
    Bronchography 31708
    Laryngography 31708

Contrast Phlebogram
See Venography

Contusion
See Hematoma

Converting Enzyme, Angiotensin
See Angiotensin Converting Enzyme (ACE)

Coombs Test 86880

Copper 82525

Coprobilinogen
Feces 84577

Coproporphyrin 84120

Coracoacromial Ligament Release 23415

Coracoid Process Transfer 23462

Cord, Spermatic
See Spermatic Cord

Cord, Spinal
See Spinal Cord

Cord, Vocal
See Vocal Cords

Cordectomy 31300

Cordocenteses
See Cordocentesis

Cordocentesis 59012

Cordotomy 63194-63199

Corectomy
See Excision, Iris

Coreoplasty 66762

Cornea
Biopsy 65410
Curettage 65435-65436
    with Chelating Agent 65436
Epithelium
    Excision 65435-65436
        with Chelating Agent 65436
Lesion
    Destruction 65450
    Excision 65400
        without Graft 65420
        with Graft 65426
Prosthesis 65770

Pterygium
    Excision 65420
Puncture 65600
Relaxing Incisions 65772-65775
Repair
    Astigmatism 65772-65775
    Wedge Resection 65775
    with Glue 65286
    Wound
        Nonperforating 65275
        Perforating 65280-65285
        Tissue Glue 65286
Reshape
    Epikeratoplasty 65765
    Keratomileusis 65760
    Keratoprosthesis 65767
Scraping
    Smear 65430
Tattoo 65600
Transplantation
    Autograft or Homograft
        Lamellar 65710
        Penetrating 65730-65755
        for Aphakia 65750

Coronary
Atherectomy
    Percutaneous 92995-92996
Thrombectomy
    Percutaneous 92973

Coronary Angioplasty, Transluminal Balloon
See Percutaneous Transluminal Angioplasty

Coronary Artery
Insertion
    Stent 92980-92981
Ligation 33502
Placement
    Radiation Delivery Device 92974
Repair 33500-33506

Coronary Artery Bypass Graft (CABG) 33503-33505, 33510-33516
Arterial 33533-33536
Arterial-Venous 33517-33523
Harvest
    Upper Extremity Artery 35600
Reoperation 33530
Venous 33510-33516

Coronary Endarterectomy 33572

Coroner's Exam 88045

Coronoidectomy
Temporomandibular Joint 21070

Corpora Cavernosa
Corpus Spongiosum Shunt 54430
Glans Penis Fistulization 54435
Injection 54235
Irrigation
    Priapism 54220
Saphenous Vein Shunt 54420
X-Ray with Contrast 74445

Corpora Cavernosa, Plastic Induration
See Peyronie Disease

Corpora Cavernosography 74445

Corpus Callosum
Transection 61541

Corpus Vertebrae (Vertebrale)
See Vertebral Body

Correction of Cleft Palate
See Cleft Palate, Repair

Correction of Lid Retraction
See Repair, Eyelid, Retraction

Correction of Malrotation of Duodenum
See Ladd Procedure

Correction of Syndactyly
See Syndactyly, Repair

Correction of Ureteropelvic Junction
See Pyeloplasty

Cortex Decortication, Cerebral
See Decortication

Cortical Mapping
Transection
    by Electric Stimulation 95961-95962

Corticoids
See Corticosteroids

Corticoliberin
See Corticotropic Releasing Hormone (CRH)

Corticosteroids
Blood 83491
Urine 83491

Corticosteroid Binding Globulin
See Transcortin

Corticosteroid Binding Protein
See Transcortin

Corticosterone
Blood or Urine 82528

Corticotropic Releasing Hormone (CRH) 80412

Cortisol 80400-80406, 80418-80420, 80436, 82530
Stimulation 80412
Total 82533

Cortisol Binding Globulin 84449

Costectomy
See Resection, Ribs

Costen Syndrome
See Temporomandibular Joint (TMJ)

Costotransversectomy 21610

Cothromboplastin
See Proconvertin

Cotte Operation 58400-58410
See Repair, Uterus, Suspension; Revision

Creation

Arteriovenous

Fistula/Autogenous Graft 36825

Colonic Reservoir 45119

Complete Heart Block 93650

Defect 40720

Ileal Reservoir 44153, 45113

Lesion .61790, 63600

Mucofistula 44144

Pericardial Window 32659

Recipient Site 15000

Shunt

Cerebrospinal Fluid 62200

Subarachnoid

Lumbar-Peritoneal 63740

Subarachnoid-Subdural 62190

Ventriculo 62220

Sigmoid Bladder 50810

Speech Prosthesis 31611

Stoma

Bladder 51980

Kidney 50395

Renal Pelvis .50395

Tympanic Membrane 69433-69436

Ureter 50860

Ventral Hernia .39503

CRF

See Corticotropic Releasing Hormone (CRH)

CRH

See Corticotropic Releasing Hormone (CRH)

Cricoid Cartilage Split

Larynx 31587

Cricothyroid Membrane

Incision 31605

Cristobalite

See Silica

Critical Care Services 99289-99292

See Emergency Department Services; Prolonged Attendance

Evaluation and Management 99291-99292

Gastric Intubation 91105

Interfacility Transport 99289-99290

Ipecac Administration for Poison 99175

Neonatal

Initial 99295

Intensive Care 99295-99297

Subsequent 99296-99297

Crossmatch 86920-86922

Crossmatching, Tissue

See Tissue Typing

Cross Finger Flap 15574

Cruciate Ligament

Arthroscopic Repair 29888-29889

Repair .27407-27409

Knee

with Collateral Ligament 27409

Cryoablation

See Cryosurgery

Cryofibrinogen 82585

Cryofixation

See Cryopreservation

Cryoglobulin 82595

Cryopreservation

Cells 88240-88241

Embryo 89258

Freezing and Storage 88240

Sperm 89259

Cryosurgery 17000-17286, 47371, 47381

See Destruction

Labyrinthotomy 69801

Lesion

Mouth 40820

Penis 54056, 54065

Vagina 57061-57065

Vulva 56501-56515

Cryotherapy

Acne 17340

Destruction

Ciliary Body .66720

Lesion

Cornea 65450

Retina 67208, 67227

Retinal Detachment

Prophylaxis .67141

Repair 67101

Trichiasis

Correction 67825

Cryptectomy 46210-46211

Cryptococcus

Antibody 86641

Antigen Detection

Enzyme Immunoassay 87327

Cryptococcus Neoformans

Antigen Detection

Enzyme Immunoassay 87327

Cryptorchism

See Testis, Undescended

Cryptosporidium

Antigen Detection

Direct Fluorescence 87272

Enzyme Immunoassay 87328

Crystal Identification

Any Body Fluid .89060

CSF

See Cerebrospinal Fluid Leak

CT Scan

See CAT Scan

Cuff, Rotator

See Rotator Cuff

Culdocentesis

See Colpocentesis

Culture

Acid Fast Bacilli 87116

Amniotic Fluid

Chromosome Analysis 88235

Bacteria

Additional Methods 87077

Anaerobic 87073-87076

Blood 87040

Feces 87045-87046

Other 87070-87073

Screening 87081

Urine 87086-87088

Bone Marrow

Chromosome Analysis 88237

Chlamydia 87110

Chorionic Villus

Chromosome Analysis 88235

Fertilized Oocyte

for In Vitro Fertilization

Co-Culture of Embryo 89251

Fertilized Oocytes

for In Vitro Fertilization 89250

Fungus

Blood 87103

Identification 87106

Other 87102

Skin 87101

Lymphocyte

Chromosome Analysis 88230

Mold 87107

Mycobacteria 87116-87118

Mycoplasma 87109

Oocyte

Co-Culture of Embryo 89250-89251

Pathogen

by Kit 87084

Skin

Chromosome Analysis 88233

Tissue

Toxin/Antitoxin 87230

Virus 87252-87253

Tubercle Bacilli 87116

Typing .87140-87158

Unlisted Services and Procedures 87999

Yeast 87106

Curettage

See Dilation and Curettage

Cervix

Endocervical 57454, 57505

Cornea .65435-65436

Chelating Agent 65436

Hydatidiform Mole 59870

Postpartum 59160

Curettage, Uterus

See Uterus, Curettage

Curettage and Dilatation

See Dilation and Curettage

Curettement

Skin Lesion 11055-11057, 17004, 17110, 17270, 17280

Curietherapy

See Brachytherapy

Custodial Care

See Domiciliary Services; Nursing Facility Services

Cutaneolipectomy

See Lipectomy

Digestive Tract
See Gastrointestinal Tract

Digit
See Finger; Toe
Replantation 20816-20822

Digital Artery Sympathectomy 64820

Digital Slit-Beam Radiograph
See Scanogram

Digits
Pinch Graft 15050

Digoxin
Assay 80162

Dihydrocodeinone 82646

Dihydrocodeinone Screen 82486

Dihydroepitestosterone
See Dihydrotestosterone

Dihydrohydroxycodeinone
See Oxycodinone

Dihydromorphinone 82486, 82649

Dihydrotestosterone 82651

Dihydroxyethanes
See Ethylene Glycol

Dihydroxyvitamin D 82652

Dilatation, Transluminal Arterial
See Angioplasty, Transluminal

Dilation
See Dilation and Curettage
Anal
　　Endoscopy 46604
　　Sphincter 45905
Bile Duct
　　Endoscopy 43271, 47555-47556
　　Stricture 74363
Bladder
　　Cystourethroscopy 52260-52265
Bronchi
　　Endoscopy 31630
Cervix
　　Canal 57800
　　Stump 57820
Esophagus 43450-43458
　　Balloon 43249
　　Endoscopy 0008T, 43220-43228,
　　　43234-43239, 43241, 43243-43249, 43256
　　Surgical 43510
Intestines, Small
　　Endoscopy 44370
Kidney 50395
　　Intra-Renal Stricture 52343, 52346
Lacrimal Punctum 68801
Larynx
　　Endoscopy 31528-31529
Pancreatic Duct
　　Endoscopy 43271
Rectum
　　Endoscopy 45303
　　Sphincter 45910

Salivary Duct 42650-42660
Trachea
　　Endoscopy 31630-31631
Ureter 50395, 52341-52342, 52344-52345
　　Endoscopy 50553, 50572, 50953, 50972
Urethra .52260-52265
　　General 53665
　　Suppository and/or
　　Instillation 53660-53661
Urethral
　　Stenosis 52281
　　Stricture 52281, 53600-53621
Vagina 57400

Dilation and Curettage 59840
See Curettage; Dilation
Cervix .57800-57820
Corpus Uteri 58120
Hysteroscopy 58558
Postpartum 59160
with Amniotic Injections 59851
with Vaginal Suppositories 59856

Dilation and Evacuation 59841
with Amniotic Injections 59851

Dimethadione 82654

Dioxide, Carbon
See Carbon Dioxide

Dioxide, Silicon
See Silica

Dipeptidyl Peptidase A
See Angiotensin Converting Enzyme (ACE)

Diphenylhydantoin
See Phenytoin

Diphosphate, Adenosine
See Adenosine Diphosphate

Diphtheria
See Vaccines
Antibody 86648

Dipropylacetic Acid
Assay 80164

Direct Pedicle Flap
Formation 15570-15576

Disability Evaluation Services
Basic Life and/or Disability Evaluation 99450
Work-Related or Medical
Disability Evaluation 99455-99456

Disarticulation
Ankle 27889
Hip 27295
Knee 27598
Wrist 25920, 25924
　　Revision 25922

Disarticulation of Shoulder
See Shoulder, Disarticulation

Disc, Intervertebral
See Intervertebral Disk

Discectomies
See Diskectomy

Discectomies, Percutaneous
See Diskectomy, Percutaneous

Discharge, Body Substance
See Drainage

Discharge Services
See Hospital Services
Hospital 99238-99239
Nursing Facility 99315-99316
Observation Care 99234-99236

Discission
Cataract
　　Laser Surgery 66821
　　Stab Incision 66820
Vitreous Strands 67030

Discography
See Diskography

Discolysis
See Chemonucleolysis

Disease
Durand-Nicolas-Favre
　　See Lymphogranuloma Venereum
Erb-Goldflam
　　See Myasthenia Gravis
Heine-Medin
　　See Polio
Hydatid
　　See Echinococcosis
Lyme
　　See Lyme Disease
Ormond
　　See Retroperitoneal Fibrosis
Peyronie
　　See Peyronie Disease
Posada-Wernicke
　　See Coccidioidomycosis

Disease/Organ Panel
See Organ/Disease Panel

Diskectomy 63075-63078
Additional Segment 22226
Arthrodesis
　　Additional Interspace 22585
　　Cervical 22554
　　Lumbar 22558, 22630
　　Thoracic 22556
Cervical 22220
Lumbar 22224, 22630
Percutaneous 62287
Thoracic 22222

Diskography
Cervical Disk 72285
Injection 62290-62291
Lumbar Disk 72295
Thoracic 72285

Disk Chemolyses, Intervertebral
See Chemonucleolysis

Dislocated Elbow
See Dislocation, Elbow

Dislocated Hip
See Dislocation, Hip Joint

Division, Isthmus, Horseshoe Kidney
See Symphysiotomy, Horseshoe Kidney

Division, Scalenus Anticus Muscle
See Muscle Division, Scalenus Anticus

Dl-Amphetamine
See Amphetamine

DMO
See Dimethadione

DNA
Antibody 86225-86226

DNAse
Antibody 86215

DNA Endonuclease
See DNAse

DNA Probe
See Cytogenetics Studies; Nucleic Acid Probe

Domiciliary Services
See Nursing Facility Services
Discharge Services 99315-99316
Established Patient 99331-99333
New Patient 99321-99323

Donor Procedures
Heart/Lung Excision 33930
Heart Excision 33940

Dopamine
See Catecholamines
Blood 82383-82384
Urine 82382, 82384

Doppler Echocardiography 76827-
76828, 93307-93308, 93320-93350
Extracranial 93875
Intracardiac 93662
Transesophageal 93318
Transthoracic 93303-93317

Doppler Scan
Arterial Studies, Extremities 93922-93924
Extremities 93965
Intracranial Arteries 93886-93888

Dorsal Vertebra
See Vertebra, Thoracic

Dose Plan
See Dosimetry

Dosimetry
Radiation Therapy 77300, 77331
Brachytherapy 77326-77328
Intensity Modulation 77301
Teletherapy 77305-77321

Double-Stranded DNA
See Deoxyribonucleic Acid

Doxepin
Assay 80166

DPH
See Phenytoin

Drainage
See Excision; Incision; Incision and Drainage
Abdomen
Abdomen Fluid 49080-49081
Abscess
Appendix 44900-44901
Percutaneous 44901
Brain 61150-61151
Eyelid 67700
Liver 47010-47011
Ovary
Percutaneous 58823
Pelvic
Percutaneous 58823
Pericolic
Percutaneous 58823
Perirenal or Renal 50020-50021
Percutaneous 50021
Prostate .52700
Retroperitoneal 49060-49061
Percutaneous 49061
Subdiaphragmatic or
Subphrenic 49040-49041
Percutaneous 49040-49041
with X-Ray 75989
Bile Duct
Transhepatic 75980
Brain Fluid .61070
Bursa .20600-20610
Cerebrospinal Fluid 61000-61020, 61050,
61070, 62272
Cervical Fluid 61050
Cisternal Fluid 61050
Cyst
Bone 20615
Brain 61150-61151
Breast 19000-19001
Ganglion 20600
Liver 47010-47011
Percutaneous 47011
Salivary Gland 42409
Sublingual Gland 42409
with Fistula 42325-42326
Extraperitoneal Lymphocele
Laparoscopic 49323
Open 49062
Eye
Anterior Chamber Paracentesis
with Diagnostic Aspiration of
Aqueous 65800
with Therapeutic Release of
Aqueous 65805
Removal Blood 65815
Removal of Vitreous and/or Discission
Anterior Hyaloid Membrane 65810
Ganglion Cyst 20600-20605
Hematoma
Brain 61154-61156
Vagina 57022-57023
Hematoma, Subungual 11740
Joint .20600-20610
Liver
Abscess or Cyst 47010-47011
Percutaneous 47011
Lymphocele
Endoscopic 49323
Onychia 10060-10061
Orbit .67405, 67440

Pancreas
See Anastomosis, Pancreas to Intestines
Pseudocyst 48510-48511
Percutaneous 48511
Paronychia 10060-10061
Pericardial Sac 32659
Pericardium
See Aspiration, Pericardium
Pseudocyst
Gastrointestinal, Upper
Transmural Endoscopic 43240
Pancreas 48510
Open .48510
Percutaneous 48511
Puncture
Chest 32000-32002
Skin .10040-10180
Spinal Cord
Cerebrospinal Fluid 62272
Subdural Fluid 61000-61001
Urethra
Extravasation 53080-53085
Ventricular Fluid 61020

Drainage Implant, Glaucoma
See Aqueous Shunt

Dressings
Burns 16010-16030
Change
Anesthesia 15852

DREZ Procedure
See Incision, Spinal Cord; Incision and Drainage

Drill Hole
Skull
Catheter .61107
Drain Hematoma 61108
Exploration 61105
Implant Electrode 61850, 61862

Drinking Test for Glaucoma
See Glaucoma, Provocative Test

Drug
See Drug Assay; Specific Drug
Analysis
Tissue Preparation 80103
Confirmation .80102
Infusion 62360-62362

Drugs, Anticoagulant
See Clotting Inhibitors

Drug Assay
Amikacin 80150
Amitriptyline 80152
Benzodiazepine 80154
Carbamazepine 80156-80157
Cyclosporine .80158
Desipramine .80160
Digoxin 80162
Dipropylacetic Acid 80164
Doxepin 80166
Ethosuximide .80168
Gentamicin 80170
Gold 80172
Haloperidol 80173
Imipramine 80174

Lesion
  Excision 69540
Reconstruction
  Tympanoplasty without
  Mastoidectomy 69631-69633
  Tympanoplasty with Antrotomy or
  Mastoidotomy 69635-69637
  Tympanoplasty with
  Mastoidectomy 69641-69646
Removal
  Ventilating Tube 69424
Repair
  Oval Window 69666
  Round Window 69667
Revision
  Stapes 69662
Tumor
  Excision 69550-69554
  Unlisted Services and Procedures 69799
Outer
  CAT Scan 70480-70482

Ear, Nose, and Throat
See Hearing Aid Services; Otorhinolaryngology, Diagnostic
Audiologic Function Tests
  Acoustic Reflex 92568
  Acoustic Reflex Decay 92569
  Audiometry
    Bekesy 92560-92561
    Comprehensive 92557
    Conditioning Play 92582
    Evoked Response 92585-92586
    Groups 92559
    Pure Tone 92552-92553
    Select Picture 92583
    Speech 92555-92556
  Brainstem Evoked Response ...92585-92586
  Central Auditory Function 92589
  Ear Protector Evaluation 92596
  Electrocochleography 92584
  Filtered Speech 92571
  Hearing Aid Evaluation 92590-92595
  Lombard Test 92573
  Loudness Balance 92562
  Screening Test 92551
  Sensorineural Acuity 92575
  Short Increment Sensitivity
    Index (SISI) 92564
  Staggered Spondaic Word Test ...92572
  Stenger Test 92565, 92577
  Synthetic Sentence Test 92576
  Tone Decay 92563
  Tympanometry 92567
Audiometry
  Evoked Otoacoustic Emissions ..92587-92588
  Visual Reinforcement 92579
Binocular Microscopy 92504
Facial Nerve Function Study 92516
Hearing, Language and Speech
  Evaluation 92506
Laryngeal Function Study 92520
Nasal Function Study 92512
Nasopharyngoscopy 92511
Vestibular Function Tests
  Additional Electrodes 92547
  Caloric Tests 92533, 92543

Nystagmus
  Optokinetic 92534, 92544
  Positional 92532, 92542
  Spontaneous 92531, 92541
Posturography 92548
Torsion Swing Test 92546
Tracking Tests 92545

Ear Canal
See Auditory Canal

Ear Cartilage
Graft
  to Face 21235

Ear Lobes
Pierce 69090

Ear Protector Attenuation 92596
See Hearing Aid Services

Ear Wax
See Cerumen

Ebstein Anomaly Repair 33468

ECG
See Electrocardiogram

Echinococcosis 86171, 86280

Echocardiography
Cardiac 93320-93350
  Intracardiac 93662
  Transesophageal 93318
  Transthoracic 93303-93317
Doppler 93303-93317, 93320-93321, 93662
Fetal Heart 76825-76826
  Doppler
    Complete 76827
    Follow-up or Repeat Study 76828
  for Congenital Anomalies
    Transesophageal 93315-93317
    Transthoracic 93303-93304
Intracardiac 93662
Transesophageal 93318
  for Congenital Anomalies 93315-93317
Transthoracic 93303-93318, 93350
  for Congenital Anomalies 93303-93304

Echoencephalography 76506

Echography
Abdomen 76700-76705
Arm 76880
Breast 76645
Cardiac 93303-93317, 93320-93321,
                              93350, 93662
  Guidance 76932
Chest 76604
Extracranial Arteries 93880-93882
Eyes 76511-76529
Follow-up 76970
Head 76536
Heart
  Imaging Guidance 76932
Hip
  Infant 76885-76886
Intracranial Arteries 93886-93888
Intraoperative 76986

Kidney
  Transplant 76778
Leg 76880
Neck 76536
Pelvis 76856-76857
Placement Therapy Fields 76950
Pregnant Uterus 76805-76816
Prostate 76872-76873
Retroperitoneal 76770-76775
Scrotum 76870
Spine 76800
Transrectal 76872-76873
Transvaginal 76830
Unlisted Services and Procedures 76999
Vagina 76830

Echotomography
See Echography

ECMO
See Extracorporeal Membrane Oxygenation

ECS
See Emission Computerized Tomography

ECSF (Erythrocyte Colony Stimulating Factor)
See Erythropoietin

ECT
See Emission Computerized Tomography

Ectasia
See Dilation

Ectopic Pregnancy
See Obstetrical Care
Abdominal 59130
Cervix 59140
Interstitial
  Partial Resection Uterus 59136
  Total Hysterectomy 59135
Laparoscopy 59150
  with Salpingectomy and/or
  Oophorectomy 59151
Tubal 59121
  with Salpingectomy and/or
  Oophorectomy 59120

Ectropion
Repair
  Blepharoplasty
    Excision Tarsal Wedge 67916
    Extensive 67917
    Suture 67914
    Thermocauterization 67915

Education Services
Group 99078

Education Supplies 99071

EEG
See Electroencephalography (EEG)

Egg
See Ova

Ehrlichia
Antibody 86666

EKG
See Electrocardiogram

Elbow
See Humerus; Radius; Ulna
Abscess
    Incision and Drainage 23930, 23935
Anesthesia 00400, 01710-01782
Arthrectomy 24155
Arthrocentesis 20605
Arthrodesis 24800-24802
Arthroplasty 24360
    Total Replacement 24363
    with Implant 24361-24362
Arthroscopy
    Diagnostic 29830
    Surgical 29834-29838
Arthrotomy 24000
    Capsular Release 24006
    with Joint Exploration 24101
    with Synovectomy 24102
    with Synovial Biopsy 24101
Biopsy 24065-24066, 24101
Bursa
    Incision and Drainage 23931
Dislocation
    Closed Treatment 24600-24605, 24640
    Open Treatment 24615
    Subluxate 24640
Excision 24155
    Bursa 24105
    Synovium 24102
Exploration 24000, 24101
Fracture
    Monteggia 24620-24635
    Open Treatment 24586-24587
Hematoma
    Incision and Drainage 23930
Implant
    Removal 24164
Incision and Drainage 24000
Injection
    Arthrography
      Radiologic 24220
Magnetic Resonance Imaging (MRI) 73221
Manipulation 24300
Radical Resection
    Capsule, Soft Tissue and Bone
      with Contracture Release 24149
Removal
    Foreign Body 24000, 24101, 24200-24201
    Implant.........................24160
    Loose Body 24101
Repair
    Epicondylitis 24350
    Fasciotomy 24350-24356
    Flexorplasty 24330
    Hemiepiphyseal Arrest 24470
    Ligament 24343-24346
    Muscle 24341
    Muscle Transfer 24301
    Tendon 24340-24342
      Lengthening 24305
      Transfer 24301
    Tennis Elbow 24350-24356
Steindler Advancement 24330
Strapping 29260

Tumor
    Excision 24075-24077
Unlisted Services and Procedures 24999
X-Ray 73070-73080
    with Contrast 73085

Elbow, Golfer
See Tennis Elbow

Elbows, Tennis
See Tennis Elbow

Electrical Stimulation
Bone Healing
    Invasive 20975
    Noninvasive 20974
Brain Surface 95961-95962
Physical Therapy
    Attended, Manual 97032
    Unattended 97014

Electric Countershock
See Cardioversion

Electric Stimulation
See Electrical Stimulation

Electric Stimulation, Transcutaneous
See Application, Neurostimulation

Electro-Hydraulic Procedure 52325

Electro-oculography 92270

Electroanalgesia
See Application, Neurostimulation

Electrocardiography
24 Hour Monitoring 93224-93237
Evaluation 93000, 93010, 93014
Patient-Demand Recording
    Transmission and Evaluation 93270
Patient-Demand Transmission and Evaluation
    Interpretation 93272
    Monitoring 93271
Rhythm
    Evaluation 93042
    Microvolt T-wave Alternans 93025
    Tracing 93041
    Tracing and Evaluation 93040
Signal Averaged 93278
Transmission 93012

Electrocautery 17000-17286
See Destruction

Electrochemistry
See Electrolysis

Electroconvulsive Therapy 90870-90871

Electrocorticogram
Intraoperative 95829

Electrode, Depth
See Depth Electrode

Electrodesiccation 17000-17286
Lesion
    Penis 54055

Electroejaculation 55870

Electroencephalography (EEG) 95816
Brain Death 95824
Digital Analysis 95957
Electrode Placement 95830
Intraoperative 95955
Monitoring ...95812-95813, 95950-95953, 95956
    with Drug Activation 95954
    with Physical Activation 95954
    with WADA Activation 95958
Sleep 95822, 95827
Standard 95819

Electrogastrography 91132-91133

Electrogram, Atrial
Esophageal Recording 93615-93616

Electrolysis 17380

Electromyographs
See Electromyography, Needle

Electromyography
Anorectal with Biofeedback 90911
Fine Wire
    Dynamic 96004
Needle
    Extremities 95861-95864
    Extremity 95860
    Face and Neck Muscles 95867-95868
    Limited Study 95869
    Ocular 92265
    Other than Thoracic Paraspinal 95870
    Single Fiber Electrode 95872
    Thoracic Paraspinal Muscles 95869
Sphincter Muscles
    Anus 51784-51785
      Needle 51785
    Urethra 51784-51785
      Needle 51785
Surface
    Dynamic 96002-96004

Electronic Analysis
Drug Infusion Pump 62367-62368
Implantable Loop Recorder System 93727
Neurostimulator Pulse Generator ...95970-95975
Pacing Cardioverter-Defibrillator ...93741-93744

Electron Microscopy 88348-88349

Electrophoresis
Counterimmuno- 86185
Immuno- 86320-86327
Unlisted Services and Procedures 82664

Electrophysiology Procedure 93600-93660

Electroretinogram
See Electroretinography

Electroretinography 92275

Electrostimulation, Analgesic Cutaneous

See Application, Neurostimulation

Electrosurgery

Trichiasis
    Correction 67825

Electroversion, Cardiac

See Cardioversion

Elevation, Scapula, Congenital

See Sprengel's Deformity

Elliot Operation

See Excision, Lesion, Sclera

Eloesser Procedure

See Thoracostomy, Empyema

Eloesser Thoracoplasty

See Thoracoplasty

Embolectomy

Aortoiliac Artery 34151-34201
Axillary Artery 34101
Brachial Artery 34101
Carotid Artery 34001
Celiac Artery .34151
Femoral 34201
Iliac 34151-34201
Innominate Artery 34001-34101
Mesentery Artery 34151
Peroneal Artery 34203
Popliteal Artery 34203
Pulmonary Artery 33910-33916
Radial Artery 34111
Renal Artery 34151
Subclavian Artery 34001-34101
Tibial Artery 34203
Ulnar Artery 34111

Embryo

Cryopreservation 89258
Cryopreserved
    Preparation
        Transfer 89256
Culture
    with Culture
        Fertilized Oocyte 89251
Hatching
    Assisted
        Microtechnique 89253
Preparation
    for Transfer 89255

Embryonated Eggs

Inoculation .87250

Embryo /Fetus Monitoring

See Monitoring, Fetal

Embryo Implantation

See Implantation

Embryo Transfer

In Vitro Fertilization 58974-58976
    Intrafallopian Transfer 58976
    Intrauterine Transfer 58974

Emergency Department Services 99281-99288

See Critical Care; Emergency Department Services
Anesthesia 99140
Physician Direction of Advanced
Life Support .99288

Emesis Induction 99175

EMG

See Electromyography, Needle

Emission-Computed Tomography, Single-Photon

See SPECT

Emission Computerized Tomography 78607

EMI Scan

See CAT Scan

Emmet Operation

See Vagina, Repair, Obstetric

Empyema

Closure
    Chest Wall 32810
Thoracostomy 32020-32036

Empyema, Lung

See Abscess, Thorax

Empyemectomy 32540

Encephalitis

Antibody 86651-86654

Encephalitis Virus Vaccine 90735

Encephalocele

Repair 62120
    Craniotomy 62121

Encephalon

See Brain

End-Expiratory Pressure, Positive

See Pressure Breathing, Positive

Endarterectomy

Coronary Artery 33572
Pulmonary 33916

Endemic Flea-Borne Typhus

See Murine Typhus

Endobronchial Challenge Tests

See Bronchial Challenge Test

Endocavitary Fulguration

See Electrocautery

Endocrine, Pancreas

See Islet Cell

Endocrine System

Unlisted Services and Procedures . .60699, 78099

Endolymphatic Sac

Exploration
    without Shunt 69805
    with Shunt 69806

Endometrial Ablation 0009T, 58353

Exploration
    via Hysteroscopy 58563

Endometrioma

Abdomen
    Destruction/Excision 49200-49201
Retroperitoneal
    Destruction/Excision 49200-49201

Endometriosis, Adhesive

See Adhesions, Intrauterine

Endometrium

Biopsy .58100, 58558

Endonuclease, DNA

See DNAse

Endoscopic Retrograde Cannulation of Pancreatic Duct (ERCP)

See Cholangiopancreatography

Endoscopies, Pleural

See Thoracoscopy

Endoscopy

See Arthroscopy; Thoracoscopy
Adrenal Gland
    Biopsy 60650
    Excision .60650
Anus
    Biopsy 46606
    Dilation .46604
    Exploration 46600
    Hemorrhage 46614
    Removal
        Foreign Body 46608
        Polyp 46610, 46612
        Tumor 46610, 46612
Bile Duct
    Biopsy 47553
    Destruction
        Calculi (Stone) 43265
        Tumor 43272
    Dilation 43271, 47555-47556
    Exploration 47552
    Intraoperative 47550
    Percutaneous 47552-47555
    Removal
        Calculi (Stone) 43264, 47554
        Foreign Body 43269
        Stent .43269
    Specimen Collection 43260
    Sphincterotomy 43262
    Sphincter Pressure 43263
    Tube Placement 43267-43268
Bladder 52000
    Biopsy 52204, 52354
    Catheterization 52005, 52010
    Destruction 52354
        Lesion 52400
    Evacuation
        Clot 52001
    Excision
        Tumor 52355
    Exploration 52351
    Lithotripsy 52353

Manipulation of Ureteral Calculus 52330
Placement
　Stent 50947
Radioactive Substance 50959, 50978
Removal
　Calculus 50961, 50980, 52352
　Foreign Body 50961, 50980
Resection 52355
via Incision 50970-50980
via Stoma 50951-50961
Ureteral
Biopsy 52007
Catheterization 52005
Urethra 52000
Biopsy 52204, 52354
Catheterization 52010
Destruction 52354
　Lesion 52400
Evacuation
　Clot 52001
Excision
　Tumor 52355
Exploration .52351
Incision
　Ejaculatory Duct 52347
Injection of Implant Material 51715
Lithotripsy .52353
Removal
　Calculus .52352
Resection
　Ejaculatory Duct 52347
Vasectomy .52347
Vasotomy 52347
Uterus
Anesthesia .00952
Hysteroscopy
　Diagnostic 58555
　with Division/Resection Intrauterine
　Septum 58560
　with Lysis of Intrauterine
　Adhesions 58559
Removal
　Endometrial 58563
　Impacted Foreign Body 58562
　Leiomyomata 58561
　Surgical with Biopsy 58558
Vagina
Anesthesia .00950
Biopsy 57454
Exploration .57452

Endosteal Implant
Reconstruction
　Mandible 21248-21249
　Maxilla 21248-21249

Endothelioma, Dural
See Meningioma

Endotoxin
Bacteria 87176

Endotracheal Intubation
See Insertion, Endotracheal Tube

Endotracheal Tube
Intubation 31500

Endovascular Repair 0001T-0002T,
　　　　　　　　　　34800-34804, 34825-34826
Angiography 75952-75953

End Stage Renal Disease
Services 90918-90925

Enema
Home Visit for Fecal Impaction 99511
Intussusception 74283
Therapeutic
　for Intussusception 74283

Energies, Electromagnetic
See Irradiation

ENT
See Ear, Nose, and Throat; Otorhinolaryngology,
Diagnostic
Therapeutic
　See Otorhinolaryngology

Entamoeba Histolytica
Antigen Detection
　Enzyme Immunoassay 87336-87337

Enterectomy 44120-44121,
　　　　　　　　　　　44126-44128, 44202
Donor 44132-44133
with Enterostomy 44125

Enterocele
Repair 57556
　Hysterectomy
　　with Colpectomy 58280

Enterocystoplasty 51960
Camey 50825

Enteroenterostomy
See Anastomosis, Intestines

Enterolysis 44005
Laparoscopic 44200

Enteropancreatostomy
See Anastomosis, Pancreas to Intestines

Enterorrhaphy 44602-44603, 44615

Enterostomy 44300
Closure 44625-44626
with Enterectomy
　Intestine, Small 44125

Enterotomy 44615

Enterovirus
Antibody 86658
Antigen Detection
　Direct Fluorescence 87199

Entropion
Repair 67921-67924
　Blepharoplasty
　　Excision Tarsal Wedge 67923
　Suture 67921
　Thermocauterization 67922

Enucleation
Eye
　without Implant 65101
　with Implant 65103
　　Muscles Attached 65105
Pleural 32540

Enucleation, Cyst, Ovarian
See Cystectomy, Ovarian

Environmental Intervention
for Psychiatric Patients 90882

Enzyme, Angiotensin-Forming
See Renin

Enzyme, Angiotensin Converting
See Angiotensin Converting Enzyme (ACE)

Enzyme Activity 82657
Radioactive Substrate 82658

EOG
See Electro-oculography

Eosinocyte
See Eosinophils

Eosinophils
Nasal Smear .89190

Epiandrosterone 82666

Epicondylitides, Lateral Humeral
See Tennis Elbow

Epicondylitis, Radiohumeral
See Tennis Elbow

Epidemic Parotitis
See Mumps

Epididymectomy
Bilateral 54861
Unilateral 54860

Epididymis
Abscess
　Incision and Drainage 54700
Anastomosis
　to Vas Deferens
　　Bilateral 54901
　　Unilateral 54900
Biopsy 54800-54820
Epididymography 74440
Excision
　Bilateral 54861
　Unilateral .54860
Exploration
　Biopsy 54820
Hematoma
　Incision and Drainage 54700
Lesion
　Excision
　　Local 54830
　　Spermatocele 54840
Needle Biopsy 54800
Spermatocele
　Excision 54840
Unlisted Services and Procedures 55899
X-Ray with Contrast 74440

Removal
    Foreign Bodies . .43020, 43045, 43215, 74235
      Lesion 43216
      Polyp 43216-43217, 43228
Repair 43300, 43310, 43313
    Esophagogastric Fundoplasty . .43324-43325
      Laparoscopic 43280
    Esophagogastrostomy 43320
    Esophagojejunostomy 43340-43341
    Fistula . . .43305, 43312, 43314, 43420-43425
    Muscle 43330-43331
    Pre-existing Perforation 43405
    Varices 43401
    Wound 43410-43415
Suture 43405
    Wound 43410-43415
Ultrasound
    Endoscopy 43231-43232
Unlisted Services and Procedures . .43289, 43499
Vein
    Ligation 43205, 43400
Video 74230
X-Ray 74220

Esophagus, Varix
See Esophageal Varices

Esophagus Neoplasm
See Tumor, Esophagus

Established Patient
Confirmatory Consultations 99271-99275
Domiciliary or Rest Home Visit 99331-99333
Emergency Department Services . .99281-99285
Home Services 99347-99350
Hospital Inpatient Services 99221-99239
Hospital Observation Services 99217-99220
Initial Inpatient Consultations 99251-99255
Office and/or Other Outpatient
Consultations 99241-99245
Office Visit 99211-99215
Outpatient Visit 99211-99215

Establishment
Colostomy
    Abdominal .50810
    Perineal 50810

Estes Operation
See Ovary, Transposition

Estlander Procedure 40525

Estradiol 82670
Response 80414

Estriol
Blood or Urine 82677

Estrogen
Blood or Urine 82671-82672
Receptor 84233

Estrone
Blood or Urine 82679

Ethanediols
See Ethylene Glycol

Ethanol
Blood 82055
Breath 82075
Urine 82055

Ethchlorovynol
See Ethchlorvynol

Ethchlorvinol
See Ethchlorvynol

Ethchlorvynol
Blood 82690
Urine 82690

Ethmoid
Fracture
    with Fixation 21340

Ethmoid, Sinus
See Sinus, Ethmoid

Ethmoidectomy 31200-31205
Endoscopic 31254-31255
Skull Base Surgery 61580-61581
with Nasal/Sinus Endoscopy 31254-31255

Ethosuccimid
See Ethosuximide

Ethosuximide 80168
Assay 80168

Ethylene Dichlorides
See Dichloroethane

Ethylene Glycol 82693

Ethylmethylsuccimide
See Ethosuximide

Ethyl Alcohol
See Ethanol

Etiocholanalone Measurement
See Etiocholanolone

Etiocholanolone 82696

ETOH
See Alcohol, Ethyl

Euglobulin Lysis 85360

European Blastomycosis
See Cryptococcus

Eustachian Tube
Catheterization 69405
Inflation
    Myringotomy 69420
      Anesthesia 69421
    without Catheterization 69401
    with Catheterization 69400
Insertion
    Catheter 69405

Eutelegenesis
See Artificial Insemination

Evacuation
Cervical Pregnancy 59140
Hematoma
    Brain .61312-61315
    Subungual .11740
Hydatidiform Mole 59870

Evaluation and Management
Athletic Training
    Evaluation 97005
    Re-evaluation 97006
Basic Life and/or Disability
Evaluation Services 99450
Care Plan Oversight Services 99374-99380
    Home Health Agency Care 99374
    Hospice 99377-99378
    Nursing Facility 99379-99380
Case Management Services 99361-99373
Consultation 99241-99275
Critical Care 99291-99292
    Interfacility Transport 99289-99290
Domiciliary or Rest Home 99321-99333
Emergency Department 99281-99288
Health Behavior
    Assessment .96150
    Family Intervention 96154-96155
    Group Intervention 96153
    Individual Intervention 96152
    Re-assessment 96151
Home Services 99341-99350
Hospital 99221-99233
    Discharge 99238-99239
Hospital Services
    Observation Care 99217-99220
Insurance Exam 99455-99456
Medical
    with Individual Psychotherapy
      Hospital or Residential Care 90817,
        90819, 90822, 90824, 90827, 90829
      Office or Outpatient . .90805, 90807, 90809
    with Individual Psychotherapy, Interactive
      Office or Outpatient . .90811, 90813, 90815
Neonatal Intensive Care 99295-99297
Newborn Care 99431-99440
Nursing Facility 99301-99313
    See Nursing Facility Services
Occupation Therapy Evaluation 97003
    Re-evaluation 97004
Office and Other Outpatient 99201-99215
Physical Therapy Evaluation 97001
    Re-evaluation 97002
Physician Standby Services 99360
Preventive Services 99381-99429
Prolonged Services 99356-99357
Psychiatric
    Records or Reports 90885
Psychiatric Residential Treatment
Facility Care 99301-99313
Unlisted Services and Procedures 99499
Work-Related and/or Medical Disability
Evaluation 99450

Evaluation Studies, Drug, Pre-Clinical
See Drug Screen

Olecranon Process
  with Allograft 24126
  with Autograft 24125
Ovarian 58925
  See Cystectomy, Ovarian
Pericardial 33050
  Endoscopic 32661
Phalanges 26210-26215
  Toe 28108
Pilonidal 11770-11772
Pubis 27066-27067
Radius 24120, 25120-25126
  with Allograft 24126
  with Autograft 24125
Salivary Gland .42408
Scapula 23140
  with Allograft 23146
  with Autograft 23145
Seminal Vesicle 55680
Sublingual Gland 42408
Talus .28100-28103
Tarsal .28104-28107
Thyroglossal Duct 60280-60281
Thyroid Gland 60200
Tibia 27635-27638
Toe 28092
Ulna 24120, 25120-25126
  with Allograft 24126
  with Autograft 24125
Urachal
  Bladder 51500
Vaginal 57135
Destruction of the Vestibule of the Mouth
  See Mouth, Vestibule of, Excision, Destruction
Diverticulum, Meckel's
  See Meckel's Diverticulum, Excision
Ear, External
  Partial 69110
  Total 69120
Elbow Joint 24155
Electrode 57522
Embolectomy/Thrombectomy
  Aortoiliac Artery 34151-34201
  Axillary Artery 34101
  Brachial Artery 34101
  Carotid Artery 34001
  Celiac Artery 34151
  Femoral Artery 34201
  Iliac Artery 34151-34201
  Innominate Artery 34001-34101
  Mesentery Artery 34151
  Peroneal Artery 34203
  Popliteal Artery 34203
  Radial Artery 34111
  Renal Artery 34151
  Subclavian Artery 34001-34101
  Tibial Artery 34203
  Ulnar Artery 34111
Embolism
  Pulmonary Artery 33910-33916
Empyema
  Lung 32540
  Pleural 32540
Epididymis
  Bilateral 54861
  Unilateral .54860
Epiglottis 31420

Esophagus
  Diverticula 43130-43135
  Partial 43116-43124
  Total 43107-43113, 43124
Eye
  See Enucleation, Eye
Fallopian Tube
  Salpingectomy 58700
  Salpingo-Oophorectomy 58720
Fascia
  See Fasciectomy
Femur 27360
  Partial 27070-27071
Fibula 27360, 27455-27457, 27641
Fistula
  Anal 46270-46285
Foot
  Fasciectomy 28060
    Radical 28060-28062
Gallbladder 47600-47620
  Cholecystectomy 47562-47564
    with Cholangiography 47563
    with Exploration Common Duct 47564
Ganglion Cyst
  Knee 27347
  Wrist 25111-25112
Gingiva 41820
Gums 41820
  Alveolus 41830
  Operculum 41821
Heart
  Donor 33940
Heart/Lung
  Donor 33930
Hemangioma 11400-11446
Hemorrhoids 46221, 46250
  Clot 46320
  Complex 46260-46262
  Simple 46255
  with Fissurectomy 46257-46258
Hip
  Partial 27070-27071
Humeral Head
  Resection .23195
  Sequestrectomy 23174
Humerus 23184, 23220-23222, 24134, 24140,
                     24150-24151
Hydrocele
  Spermatic Cord 55500
  Tunica Vaginalis 55040-55041
    Bilateral 55041
    Unilateral 55040
Hygroma, Cystic
  Axillary/Cervical 38550-38555
Hymenotomy 56700
  See Hymen, Excision
Ileum
  Ileoanal Reservoir 45136
  Partial 27070-27071
Inner Ear
  See Ear, Inner, Excision
Interphalangeal Joint
  Toe 28160
Intervertebral Disk
  Decompression 63075-63078
  Hemilaminectomy 63040, 63043-63044
  Herniated 63020-63044, 63055-63066

Intestine
  Laparoscopic
    with Anastomosis 44202-44203
Intestines
  Donor 44132-44133
Intestines, Small 44120-44128
Iris
  Iridectomy
    Optical .66635
    Peripheral 66625
    Sector 66630
    with Corneoscleral or
    Corneal Section 66600
    with Cyclectomy 66605
Kidney
  Donor 50300-50320, 50547
  Partial 50240
  Recipient .50340
  Transplantation 50370
  with Ureters 50220-50236
Kneecap 27350
Labyrinth
  Transcanal 69905
  with Mastoidectomy 69910
Lacrimal Gland
  Partial 68505
  Total 68500
Lacrimal Sac .68520
Larynx
  Partial 31367-31382
  Total 31360-31365
  with Pharynx 31390-31395
Lesion
  Anal 45108, 46922
  Ankle 27630
    Arthroscopic 29891
  Auditory Canal, External
    Exostosis 69140
    Radical without Neck Dissection 69150
    Radical with Neck Dissection 69155
    Soft Tissue 69145
  Bladder 52224
  Brain 61534, 61536
  Brainstem 61575-61576
  Carotid Body 60600-60605
  Colon 44110-44111
  Conjunctiva 68110-68130
    Over 1 cm 68115
    with Adjacent Sclera 68130
  Cornea 65400
    without Graft 65420
  Ear, Middle 69540
  Epididymis
    Local 54830
    Spermatocele 54840
  Esophagus 43100-43101
  Eye 65900
  Eyelid
    Multiple, Different Lids 67805
    Multiple, Same Lid 67801
    Single 67800
    Under Anesthesia 67808
    without Closure 67840
  Femur 27062
  Finger 26160
  Foot 28080, 28090
  Gums 41822-41828
  Hand 26160

Exclusion

Exenteration

Exercise Stress Tests 93015-93018

Exercise Test

Exercise Therapy 97110-97113

Exfoliation

Exocrine, Pancreas

Exomphalos

Exostectomy 28288, 28290

Exostoses

Exostoses, Cartilaginous

Exostosis

Expander, Skin, Inflatable

Expired Gas Analysis 94680-94690, 94770

Exploration

Bronchoscopy 31622
Cauda Equina 63005-63011, 63017
Chest
    Penetrating Wound 20101
Colon
    Endoscopic 44388, 45378
Colon-Sigmoid
    Endoscopic .45330
Common Bile Duct
    with Cholecystectomy 47610
Duodenum 44010
Ear, Inner
    Endolymphatic Sac
        without Shunt 69805
        with Shunt 69806
Ear, Middle 69440
Elbow 24000, 24101
Epididymis 54820
Esophagus
    Endoscopy 43200
Extremity
    Penetrating Wound 20103
Finger Joint 26075-26080
Flank
    Penetrating Wound 20102
Gallbladder 47480
Gastrointestinal Tract, Upper
    Endoscopy 43234-43235
Hand Joint 26070
Heart 33310-33315
Hepatic Duct 47400
Hip 27033
Interphalangeal Joint
    Toe 28024
Intertarsal Joint 28020
Intestines, Small
    Endoscopy 44360
    Enterotomy 44020
Kidney 50010, 50045, 50120
Knee 27310, 27331
Lacrimal Duct 68810
    Canaliculi 68840
    with Anesthesia 68811
    with Insertion Tube or Stent 68815
Larynx 31320
    Endoscopy 31505, 31520-31526, 31575
Liver
    Wound 47361-47362
Mediastinum 39000-39010
Metatarsophalangeal Joint 28022
Nasolacrimal Duct 68810
    with Anesthesia 68811
    with Insertion Tube or Stent 68815
Neck
    Lymph Nodes 38542
    Penetrating Wound 20100
Nipple 19110
Nose
    Endoscopy 31231-31235
Orbit 61332-61334
    with/without Biopsy 67450
    without Bone Flap 67400
Parathyroid Gland 60500-60505
Pelvis 49320
Prostate 55860
    with Nodes 55862-55865

Rectum
    Endoscopic .45300
    Injury .45562-45563
Retroperitoneal Area 49010
Scrotum 55110
Shoulder Joint 23040-23044, 23107
Sinus
    Frontal 31070-31075
    Maxillary 31020-31030
Skull 61105
Spinal Cord 63001-63011,
            63015-63017, 63040-63044
Spine Fusion 22830
Stomach 43500
Tarsometatarsal Joint 28020
Testis
    Undescended 54550-54560
Toe Joint 28024
Ureter 50600
Vagina 57000
    Endocervical 57452
Wrist 25101, 25248
    Joint 25040

Exploration, Larynx by Incision
See Laryngotomy, Diagnostic

Exploratory Laparotomy
See Abdomen, Exploration

Expression
Lesion
    Conjunctiva .68040

Exteriorization, Small Intestine
See Enterostomy

External Auditory Canal
See Auditory Canal

External Cephalic Version 59412

External Ear
See Ear, External

External Extoses
See Exostosis

External Fixation
Adjustment/Revision 20693
Application 20690-20692
Mandibular Fracture
    Open Treatment 21454
    Percutaneous Treatment 21452
Removal 20694

Extirpation, Lacrimal Sac
See Dacryocystectomy

Extracorporeal Circulation 33960-33961
for Regional Chemotherapy
    Extremity 36823

Extracorporeal Dialyses
See Hemodialysis

Extracorporeal Membrane Oxygenation
Cannulization 36822

Extracorporeal Photochemotherapies
See Photopheresis

Extracorporeal Shock Wave Therapy
See Lithotripsy
Musculoskeletal .0019T
Plantar Fascia 0020T

Extraction
Lens
    Extracapsular 66940
    Intracapsular 66920
        for Dislocated Lens 66930

Extraction, Cataract
See Cataract, Excision

Extradural Anesthesia
See Anesthesia, Epidural

Extradural Injection
See Epidural, Injection

Extraocular Muscle
See Eye Muscles

Extrauterine Pregnancy
See Ectopic Pregnancy

Extravasation Blood
See Hemorrhage

Extremity
Lower
    Harvest of Vein for Bypass Graft 35500
    Revision 35879-35881
Upper
    Harvest of Artery for Coronary Artery
        Bypass Graft 35600
    Harvest of Vein for Bypass Graft 35500
    Repair
        Blood Vessel 35206
Wound Exploration
    Penetrating Wound 20103

Eye
See Ciliary Body; Cornea; Iris; Lens; Retina;
Sclera; Vitreous
Biometry 76516-76519, 92136
Drainage
    Anterior Chamber
        Discission of Anterior Hyaloid
        Membrane 65810
        with Diagnostic Aspiration of
        Aqueous .65800
        with Removal of Blood 65815
        with Removal of Vitreous and/or with
        Therapeutic Release of Aqueous 65805
Goniotomy 65820
Incision
    Adhesions
        Anterior Synechiae 65860, 65870
        Corneovitreal Adhesions 65880
        Goniosynechiae 65865
        Posterior Synechiae 65875
        Anterior Chamber 65820
        Trabeculae 65850

F

E B Virus
See Epstein-Barr Virus

E Vitamin
See Tocopherol

Face
CAT Scan 70486-70488
Lesion
Destruction 17000-17004, 17280-17286
Magnetic Resonance Imaging
(MRI) 70540-70543
Tumor Resection 21015

Face Lift 15824-15828

Facial Asymmetries
See Hemifacial Microsomia

Facial Bone
See Mandible; Maxilla
Tumor
Excision 21034

Facial Bones
Abscess
Excision 21026
Reconstruction
Secondary 21275
Repair 21208-21209
Tumor
Excision 21029-21030
Resection
Radical 21015
X-Ray 70140-70150

Facial Nerve
Anastomosis
to Hypoglossal 64868
to Phrenic Nerve 64870
to Spinal Accessory 64866
Avulsion 64742
Decompression 61590, 61596
Intratemporal
Lateral to Geniculate
Ganglion 69720, 69740
Medial to Geniculate
Ganglion 69725, 69745
Total 69955
Function Study 92516
Incision 64742
Injection
Anesthetic 64402
Mobilization 61590
Repair
Lateral to Geniculate Ganglion 69740
Medial to Geniculate Ganglion 69745
Repair/Suture
with or without Graft 64864-64865
Suture
Lateral to Geniculate Ganglion 69740
Medial to Geniculate Ganglion 69745
Transection 64742

Facial Nerve Paralysis
Graft 15840-15845
Repair 15840-15845

Facial Prosthesis
Impression 21088

Facial Rhytidectomy
See Face Lift

Factor, ACTH-Releasing
See Corticotropic Releasing Hormone (CRH)

Factor, Antinuclear
See Antinuclear Antibodies (ANA)

Factor, Blood Coagulation
See Clotting Factor

Factor, Fitzgerald
See Fitzgerald Factor

Factor, Fletcher
See Fletcher Factor

Factor, Hyperglycemic-Glycogenolytic
See Glucagon

Factor, Intrinsic
See Intrinsic Factor

Factor, Sulfation
See Somatomedin

Factor I
See Fibrinogen

Factor II
See Prothrombin

Factor III
See Thromboplastin

Factor Inhibitor Test 85335

Factor IV
See Calcium

Factor IX
See Christmas Factor

Factor Rheumatoid
See Rheumatoid Factor

Factor VII
See Proconvertin

Factor VIII
See Clotting Factor

Factor X
See Stuart-Prower Factor

Factor X, Activated
See Thrombokinase

Factor Xa Inhibitor
See Antithrombin III

Factor XI
See Plasma Thromboplastin, Antecedent

Factor XII
See Hageman Factor

Factor XIII
See Fibrin Stabilizing Factor

Fallopian Tube
Anastomosis 58750
Catheterization 58345, 74742
Destruction
Endoscopy 58670
Ectopic Pregnancy 59121
with Salpingectomy and/or
Oophorectomy 59120
Excision 58700-58720
Ligation 58600-58611
Lysis
Adhesions 58740
Occlusion 58615
Endoscopy 58671
Repair 58752
Anastomosis 58750
Create Stoma 58770
Tumor
Resection 58950, 58952-58954
Unlisted Services and Procedures 58999
X-Ray 74742

Fallopian Tube Pregnancy
See Ectopic Pregnancy, Tubal

Fallot, Tetralogy of
See Tetralogy of Fallot

Family Psychotherapy
See Psychotherapy, Family

Fanconi Anemia
Chromosome Analysis 88248

Farnsworth-Munsell Color Test
See Color Vision Examination

Farr Test
See Gammaglobulin, Blood

Fasanella-Servat Procedure . . .67908

Fascial Defect
Repair 50728

Fascial Graft
Free
Microvascular Anastomosis 15758
Open Treatment
Sternoclavicular Dislocation 23532

Fascia Graft .15840

Fascia Lata Graft
Harvesting .20920-20922

Fasciectomy
Foot 28060
Radical .28060-28062
Palm 26121-26125

Fasciocutaneous Flaps . . .15732-15738

Fasciotomy
Arm, Lower 24495, 25020-25025
Elbow .24350-24356
Foot 28008
Hand Decompression 26037
Hip 27025

FAST
See Allergen Immunotherapy

Fat

Fatty Acid

Fat Stain

Favre-Durand Disease
See Lymphogranuloma Venereum

FC Receptor 86243

FDP
See Fibrin Degradation Products

Feedback, Psychophysiologic
See Biofeedback; Training, Biofeedback

Female Castration
See Oophorectomy

Female Gonad
See Ovary

Femoral Arteries
See Artery, Femoral

Femoral Stem Prosthesis
See Arthroplasty, Hip

Femoral Vein
See Vein, Femoral

Femur
See Hip; Knee; Leg, Upper

Fenestration, Pericardium
See Pericardiostomy

Fenestration Procedure

Fern Test 87210
See Smear and Stain, Wet Mount

Ferric Chloride

Ferrihemoglobin
See Methemoglobin

Ferritin

Ferroxidase
See Ceruloplasmin

Fertility Control
See Contraception

Fertility Test

Fertilization

Fertilization in Vitro
See In Vitro Fertilization

Fetal Biophysical Profile .76818-76819

Fetal Contraction Stress Test . .59020

Fetal Hemoglobin 85461

Fetal Lung Maturity Assessment; Lecithin Sphingomyelin Ratio . .83661

Fetal Monitoring
See Monitoring, Fetal

Fetal Non-Stress Test 59025

Fetal Testing

Fetuin
See Alpha-Fetoprotein

Fever, Australian Q
See Q Fever

Fever, Japanese River
See Scrub Typhus

Fibrillation

Fibrillation, Heart
See Heart, Fibrillation

Fibrinase
See Plasmin

Fibrinogen 85384-85385

Fibrinolysin
See Plasmin

Fibrinolysins 85390

Fibrinolysis
Alpha-2 Antiplasmin 85410
Plasmin 85400
Plasminogen 85420-85421
Plasminogen Activator 85415

Fibrin Degradation Products 85362-85379

Fibrin Deposit
Removal 32150

Fibrin Stabilizing Factor 85290-85291

Fibroadenoma
Excision 19120-19126

Fibroblastoma, Arachnoidal
See Meningioma

Fibrocutaneous Tags 11200-11201

Fibromatosis, Dupuytren's
See Dupuytren's Contracture

Fibromatosis, Penile
See Peyronie Disease

Fibromyoma
See Leiomyomata

Fibronectin, Fetal 82731

Fibrosis, Penile
See Peyronie Disease

Fibrosis, Retroperitoneal
See Retroperitoneal Fibrosis

Fibrous Cavernitides
See Peyronie Disease

Fibrous Dysplasia 21029,
　　　　　　　　　　　　　　　　　21181-21184

Fibula
See Ankle; Knee; Tibia
Bone Graft with Microvascular
Anastomosis 20955
Craterization 27360, 27641
Cyst
　　Excision 27635-27638
Diaphysectomy 27360, 27641
Excision 27360, 27641
　　Epiphyseal Bar 20150
Fracture
　　Malleolus 27786-27814
　　Shaft 27780-27784
Incision 27607
Osteoplasty
　　Lengthening 27715

Repair
　　Epiphysis 27477-27485, 27730-27742
　　Osteotomy 27707-27712
Saucerization 27360, 27641
Tumor
　　Excision 27635-27638, 27646
X-Ray 73590

Figure of Eight Cast 29049

Filariasis .86280

Filtering Operation
See Incision, Sclera, Fistulization; Incision and
Drainage

Filtration Implant, Glaucoma
See Aqueous Shunt

Fimbrioplasty 58760
Laparoscopic .58672

Fine Needle Aspiration . . .10021-10022
Evaluation 88172-88173

Finger
See Phalanx, Finger
Abscess
　　Bone
　　　　Incision and Drainage 26034
　　Incision and Drainage 26010-26011
Amputation 26951-26952
　　with Exploration or Removal 26910
Arthrocentesis 20600
Arthrodesis
　　Interphalangeal Joint 26860-26863
　　Metacarpophalangeal Joint 26850-26852
Bone
　　Incision and Drainage 26034
Cast 29086
Collection of Blood 36415
Decompression .26035
Excision
　　Constricting Ring 26596
　　Tendon 26180, 26390, 26415
Insertion
　　Tendon Graft 26392
Magnetic Resonance Imaging (MRI) 73221
Reconstruction
　　Extra Digit .26587
　　Toe to Hand Transfer 26551-26556
Removal
　　Implantation 26320
　　Tube 26392, 26416
Repair
　　Blood Vessel 35207
　　Claw Finger 26499
　　Extra Digit 26587
　　Macrodactylia 26590
　　Tendon
　　　　Extensor 26415-26434,
　　　　　　　　　　　　26445-26449, 26460
　　　　Flexor 26356-26358,
　　　　　　　　　　　　26440-26442, 26455
　　Volar Plate 26548
　　Web Finger 26560-26562
Replantation 20816-20822
Reposition 26555
Sesamoidectomy 26185

Splint 29130-29131
Strapping 29280
Tendon Sheath
　　Excision 26145
　　Incision 26055
　　Incision and Drainage 26020
Tenotomy 26060, 26460
　　Flexor 26455
Tumor
　　Excision 26115-26117
Unlisted Services and Procedures 26989
X-Ray 73140

Finger Flap
Tissue Transfer 14350

Finger Joint
See Intercarpal Joint

Finney Operation
See Gastroduodenostomy

Fishberg Concentration Test
See Water Load Test

Fissurectomy 46200

Fissurectomy, Anal
See Anus, Fissure, Excision

Fissure in Ano
See Anus, Fissure

Fistula
Anal
　　Repair 46288
Autogenous Graft 36825
Bronchi
　　Repair 32815
Carotid-Cavernous
　　Repair 61710
Chest Wall
　　Repair 32906
Conjunctiva
　　without Tube 68745
　　with Tube or Stent 68750
Enterovesical
　　Closure 44660-44661
Kidney 50520-50526
Lacrimal Gland Closure 68770
　　Dacryocystorhinostomy 68720
Nose
　　Repair 30580-30600
Oval Window .69666
Postauricular .69700
Rectovaginal
　　Abdominal Approach 57305
　　Transperineal Approach 57308
　　with Concomitant Colostomy 57307
Round Window 69667
Sclera
　　Iridencleisis or Iridotasis 66165
　　Sclerectomy with Punch or Scissors
　　　with Iridectomy 66160
　　Thermocauterization with Iridectomy . .66155
　　Trabeculectomy ab Externo in
　　　Absence Previous Surgery 66170
　　Trabeculectomy ab Externo with
　　　Scarring .66172
　　Trephination with Iridectomy 66150

without Manipulation	.......25560, 25600
with Manipulation	.........25565, 25605
with Ulna	25560-25565
Open Treatment	25575

Rib
Closed Treatment	21800
External Fixation	21810
Open Treatment	21805

Scaphoid
Closed Treatment	25622
Open Treatment	25628

with Dislocation
Closed Treatment	25680
Open Treatment	25685
with Manipulation	25624

Scapula
Closed Treatment
without Manipulation	23570
with Manipulation	23575
Open Treatment	23585

Sesamoid
Closed Treatment	28530
Foot	28530-28531
Open Treatment	28531

Skin
Debridement	11010-11012

Skull
	62000-62010
Closed Treatment	21300

Sternum
Closed Treatment	21820
Open Treatment	21825

Talus
Closed Treatment	28430-28435
Open Treatment	28445
without Manipulation	28430
with Manipulation	28435-28436

Tarsal
Open Treatment	28465
Percutaneous Fixation	28456
with Manipulation	28455-28456

Thumb
with Dislocation	26645-26650
Open Treatment	26665

Tibia
Arthroscopic Treatment	29855-29856
Closed Treatment	.....27530-27532, 27538,
	27750-27752, 27760-27762,
	27808-27810, 27824-27825
Distal	27824-27828
Intercondylar	27538-27540
Malleolus	......27760-27766, 27808-27814
Open Treatment	.......27535-27536, 27540,
	27758-27759, 27766, 27814, 27826-27828
Percutaneous Fixation	27756
Plateau	........27530-27536, 29855-29856
Shaft	27750-27759
without Manipulation	........27530, 27750,
	27760-27762, 27808, 27825
with Manipulation	.....27752, 27760-27762,
	27810

Trachea
Endoscopy	31630

Ulna
See Elbow; Humerus; Radius
Closed Treatment	25560-25565

Olecranon
Closed Treatment	24670-24675
Open Treatment	24685

Open Treatment	25574-25575

Shaft
Closed Treatment
	25530-25535
Open Treatment	.........25545, 25574

Styloid Process
Closed Treatment	25650
Open Treatment	25652
Percutaneous Fixation	25651
without Manipulation	.....25530, 25560

with Dislocation
Closed Treatment	24620
Monteggia	24620-24635
Open Treatment	24635
with Manipulation	..........25535, 25565
with Radius	25560-25565
Open Treatment	25575

Vertebra
Additional Segment
Open Treatment	22328

Cervical
Open Treatment	22326

Closed Treatment
without Manipulation	22310
with Manipulation, Casting and/or Bracing	22315

Lumbar
Open Treatment	22325

Posterior
Open Treatment	22325-22327

Thoracic
Open Treatment	22327

with Shoulder Dislocation
Closed Treatment	23675
Open Treatment	23680

Vertebral Process
Closed Treatment	22305

Wrist
with Dislocation
Closed Treatment	25680
Open Treatment	25685

Zygomatic Arch
Open Treatment	21356-21366
with Manipulation	21355

Fragile-X
Chromosome Analysis	88248

Fragility
Red Blood Cell
Mechanical	85547
Osmotic	85555-85557

Frames, Stereotactic
See Stereotactic Frame

Francisella 86000
Antibody	86668

Fredet-Ramstedt Procedure 43520

Free E3
See Estriol

Free Skin Graft
See Skin, Grafts, Free

Free T4
See Thyroxine, Free

Frei Disease
See Lymphogranuloma Venereum

Frenectomy 40819, 41115

Frenectomy, Lingual
See Excision, Tongue, Frenum

Frenotomy 40806, 41010

Frenulectomy 40819

Frenuloplasty 41520

Frenum
Lip
Incision	40806
See Lip	

Frenumectomy 40819

Frickman Operation
See Proctopexy

Frontal Craniotomy 61556

Frontal Sinus
See Sinus, Frontal

Frontal Sinusotomy
See Exploration, Sinus, Frontal

Frost Suture 67875

Frozen Blood Preparation 86930-86932

Fructose 84375
Semen	82757

Fruit Sugar
See Fructose

FSF 85290-85291

FSH
See Follicle Stimulating Hormone (FSH)

FSP
See Fibrin Degradation Products

FT-4 84439

Fulguration
See Destruction
Bladder	51020
Cystourethroscopy with	52214
Lesion	52224
Tumor	52234-52240
Ureter	..........50957-50959, 50976-50978

Ureterocele
Ectopic	52301
Orthotopic	52300

Fulguration, Endocavitary
See Electrocautery

Full Thickness Graft 15200-15261

Function, Study, Nasal
See Nasal Function Study

Functional Ability
See Activities of Daily Living

Function Test, Lung
See Pulmonology, Diagnostic

H

Hemoglobin F
Fetal
    Chemical 83030
    Qualitative 83033

Hemogram
Added Indices 85021-85027
Automated 85021-85027
Manual 85031

Hemolysins 85475
with Agglutinins 86940-86941

Hemolytic Complement
See Complement, Hemolytic

Hemolytic Complement, Total
See Complement, Hemolytic, Total

Hemoperfusion 90997

Hemophil
See Clotting Factor

Hemophilus Influenza
Antibody 86684

Hemorrhage
Abdomen 49002
Anal
    Endoscopic Control 46614
Bladder
    Postoperative 52606
Chest Cavity
    Endoscopic Control 32654
Colon
    Endoscopic Control 44391, 45382
Colon-Sigmoid
    Endoscopic Control 45334
Esophagus
    Endoscopic Control 43227
Gastrointestinal, Upper
    Endoscopic Control 43255
Intestines, Small
    Endoscopic Control 44366, 44378
Liver
    Control 47350
Lung 32110
Nasal
    Cauterization 30901-30906
    Endoscopic Control 31238
Nasopharynx 42970-42972
Oropharynx 42960-42962
Rectum
    Endoscopic Control 45317
Throat .42960-42962
Uterus
    Postpartum 59160
Vagina 57180

Hemorrhoidectomy
Complex 46260
    with Fissurectomy 46261-46262
External Complete 46250
Ligature 46221
Simple 46255
    with Fissurectomy 46257-46258

Hemorrhoids
Destruction 46934-46936
Incision
    External 46083
Injection
    Sclerosing Solution 46500
Ligation 46945-46946
Suture 46945-46946

Hemosiderin 83070-83071

Hemothorax
Thoracostomy 32020

Heparin 85520
See Clotting Inhibitors
Neutralization 85525
Protamine Tolerance Test 85530

Heparin Cofactor I
See Antithrombin III

Hepatectomy
Extensive 47122
Left Lobe 47125
Partial
    Donor 47134
    Lobe 47120
Right Lobe 47130
Total
    Donor 47133

Hepaticodochotomy
See Hepaticostomy

Hepaticoenterostomy 47802

Hepaticostomy 47400

Hepaticotomy 47400

Hepatic Abscess
See Abscess, Liver

Hepatic Arteries
See Artery, Hepatic

Hepatic Artery Aneurysm
See Artery, Hepatic, Aneurysm

Hepatic Duct
Anastomosis
    with Intestines 47765, 47802
Exploration .47400
Incision and Drainage 47400
Nuclear Medicine
    Imaging 78223
Removal
    Calculi (Stone) 47400
Repair
    with Intestines 47765, 47802
Unlisted Services and Procedures 47999

Hepatic Haemorrhage
See Hemorrhage, Liver

Hepatic Portal Vein
See Vein, Hepatic Portal

Hepatic Portoenterostomies
See Hepaticoenterostomy

Hepatic Transplantation
See Liver, Transplantation

Hepatitis Antibody
A 86708-86709
B
    Be 86707
    B Core 86704-86705
    B Surface .86706
C 86803-86804
Delta Agent .86692
IgG 86704, 86708
IgM 86704-86705, 86708-86709

Hepatitis Antigen
B 87515-87517
Be 87350
B Surface 87340-87341
C 87520-87522
Delta Agent .87380
G 87525-87527

Hepatitis A and Hepatitis B 90636

Hepatitis A Vaccine
Adolescent/Pediatric
    2 Dose Schedule 90633
    3 Dose Schedule 90634
Adult Dosage 90632

Hepatitis B and Hib 90748

Hepatitis B Vaccine
Dosage
    Adolescent 90743
    Adult 90746
    Immunosuppressed 90740, 90747
    Pediatric/Adolescent 90744

Hepatitis B Virus E Antibody
See Antibody, Hepatitis

Hepatitis B Virus Surface ab
See Antibody, Hepatitis B, Surface

Hepatorrhaphy
See Liver, Repair

Hepatotomy
Abscess 47010-47011
    Percutaneous 47011
Cyst 47010-47011
    Percutaneous 47011

Hernia
Repair
    Abdominal .49590
        Incisional 49560
        Recurrent 49565
    Diaphragmatic 39502-39541
    Epigastric .49570
        Incarcerated 49572
    Femoral 49550
        Incarcerated 49553
        Recurrent 49555
        Recurrent Incarcerated 49557
    Incisional
        Incarcerated 49561

Hip Stem Prostheses
See Arthroplasty, Hip

Histamine 83088

Histamine Release Test 86343

Histochemistry 88318-88319

Histocompatibility Testing
See Tissue Typing

Histoplasma
Antibody 86698
Antigen 87385

Histoplasma capsulatum
Antigen Detection
    Enzyme Immunoassay 87385

Histoplasmin Test
See Histoplasmosis, Skin Test

Histoplasmoses
See Histoplasmosis

Histoplasmosis
Skin Test 86510

History and Physical
See Evaluation and Management, Office and/or Other Outpatient Services
Pelvic Exam 57410

HIV
Antibody 86701-86703
    Confirmation Test 86689

HIV-1
Antigen Detection
    Enzyme Immunoassay 87390

HIV-2
Antigen Detection
    Enzyme Immunoassay 87391

HK3 Kallikrein
See Antigen, Prostate Specific

HLA Typing 86812-86817

HMRK
See Fitzgerald Factor

HMW Kininogen
See Fitzgerald Factor

Hoffman Apparatus 20690

Hofmeister Operation
See Gastrectomy, Total

Holographic Imaging 76375

Holten Test
See Creatinine, Urine, Clearance

Home Services
Activities of Daily Living 99509
Catheter Care 99507
Enema Administration 99511
Established Patient 99347-99350
Hemodialysis 99512

Home Infusion Procedures 99550-99560, 99562, 99564-99569
Individual or Family Counseling 99510
Inhalation Therapy 99563
Intramuscular Injections 99506
Mechanical Ventilation 99504
Newborn Care 99502
New Patient 99341-99345
Postnatal Assessment 99501
Prenatal Monitoring 99500
Respiratory Therapy 99503
Sleep Studies 99508
Stoma Care 99505
Unlisted Services and Procedures 99539

Home Visit
See House Calls

Homocystine 83090
Urine 82615

Homogenization, Tissue 87176

Homograft
Skin 15350

Homologous Grafts
See Graft

Homologous Transplantation
See Homograft

Homovanillic Acid
Urine 83150

Hormone, Adrenocorticotrophic
See Adrenocorticotropic Hormone (ACTH)

Hormone, Corticotropin-Releasing
See Corticotropic Releasing Hormone (CRH)

Hormone, Growth
See Growth Hormone

Hormone, Human Growth
See Growth Hormone, Human

Hormone, Interstitial Cell-Stimulating
See Luteinizing Hormone (LH)

Hormone, Parathyroid
See Parathormone

Hormone, Pituitary Lactogenic
See Prolactin

Hormone, Placental Lactogen
See Lactogen, Human Placental

Hormone, Somatotropin Release-Inhibiting
See Somatostatin

Hormone, Thyroid-Stimulating
See Thyroid Stimulating Hormone (TSH)

Hormone-Binding Globulin, Sex
See Globulin, Sex Hormone Binding

Hormones, Adrenal Cortex
See Corticosteroids

Hormones, Antidiuretic
See Antidiuretic Hormone

Hormone Assay
ACTH 82024
Aldosterone
    Blood or Urine 82088
Androstenedione
    Blood or Urine 82157
Androsterone
    Blood or Urine 82160
Angiotensin II 82163
Corticosterone 82528
Cortisol
    Total 82533
Dehydroepiandrosterone 82626
Dihydroelestosterone 82651
Dihydrotestosterone 82651
Epiandrosterone 82666
Estradiol 82670
Estriol 82677
Estrogen 82671-82672
Estrone 82679
Follicle Stimulating Hormone 83001
Growth Hormone 83003
Hydroxyprogesterone 83498-83499
Luteinizing Hormone 83002
Somatotropin 83003
Testosterone 84403
Vasopressin 84588

Hormone Pellet Implantation 11980

Hospital Discharge Services
See Discharge Services, Hospital

Hospital Services
Inpatient Services 99238-99239
    Discharge Services 99238-99239
    Initial Care
        New or Established Patient ..99221-99233
    Initial Hospital Care 99221-99223
    Newborn 99431-99433
    Prolonged Services 99356-99357
    Subsequent Hospital Care 99231-99233
Observation
    Discharge Services 99234-99236
    Initial Care 99218-99220
        New or Established Patient ..99218-99220
Same Day Admission
    Discharge Services 99234-99236
Subsequent Newborn Care 99433

Hot Pack Treatment 97010
See Physical Medicine and Rehabilitation

House Calls 99341-99350

Howard Test
See Cystourethroscopy, Catheterization, Ureter

HPL
See Lactogen, Human Placental

HTLV-IV
See HIV-2

Iliac Crest
Free Osteocutaneous Flap with Microvascular
Anastomosis 20970

Iliohypogastric Nerve
Injection
    Anesthetic 64425

Ilioinguinal Nerve
Injection
    Anesthetic 64425

Ilium
Craterization 27070
Cyst
    Excision 27065-27067
Excision 27070
Fracture
    Open Treatment 27215, 27218
Saucerization 27070
Tumor
    Excision 27065-27067

Ilizarov Procedure
Monticelli Type 20692
    See Application, Bone Fixation Device

Imaging
See Vascular Studies

Imaging, Gamma Camera
See Nuclear Medicine

Imaging, Magnetic Resonance
See Magnetic Resonance Imaging (MRI)

Imaging, Ultrasonic
See Echography

Imbrication
Diaphragm 39545

Imidobenzyle
See Imipramine

Imipramine
Assay 80174

Immune Complex Assay 86332

Immune Globulins
Antitoxin
    Botulinum .90287
    Diphtheria .90296
Botulism 90288
Cytomegalovirus .90291
Hepatitis B 90371
Human 90281-90283
Rabies 90375-90376
Respiratory Syncytial Virus 90378-90379
Rho (D) 90384-90386
Tetanus 90389
Unlisted Immune Globulin 90399
Vaccinia 90393
Varicella-Zoster .90396

Immune Globulin Administration 90780-90784

Immune Globulin E
See IgE

Immunization, Mumps
See Mumps, Immunization

Immunization Administration
Each Additional Vaccine/Toxoid 90472, 90474
One Vaccine/Toxoid 90471, 90473

Immunoassay
Analyte 83519-83520
Infectious Agent 86317-86318, 87449-87451
Nonantibody 83516-83519
Tumor Antigen 86294, 86316
    CA 125 86304
    CA 15-3 86300
    CA 19-9 86301

Immunoblotting, Western
See Western Blot

Immunochemical, Lysozyme (Muramidase)
See Lysozyme

Immunocytochemistry 88342

Immunodeficiency Virus, Human
See HIV

Immunodeficiency Virus Type 1, Human
See HIV-1

Immunodeficiency Virus Type 2, Human
See HIV-2

Immunodiffusion 86329-86331

Immunoelectrophoresis 86320-86327, 86334

Immunofixation Electrophoresis 86334

Immunofluorescent Study .88346-88347

Immunogen
See Antigen

Immunoglobulin 82787
Platelet Associated 86023
Thyroid Stimulating 84445

Immunoglobulin E
See IgE

Immunoglobulin Receptor Assay 86243

Immunologic Skin Test
See Skin, Tests

Immunology
Unlisted Services and Procedures . .86849, 99558

Immunotherapies, Allergen
See Allergen Immunotherapy

Impedance Testing 92567
See Audiologic Function Tests

Imperfectly Descended Testis
See Testis, Undescended

Implant, Breast
See Breast, Implants

Implant, Glaucoma Drainage
See Aqueous Shunt

Implant, Orbital
See Orbital Implant

Implant, Penile
See Penile Prosthesis

Implant, Penile Prosthesis, Inflatable
See Penile Prosthesis, Insertion, Inflatable

Implant, Subperiosteal
See Subperiosteal Implant

Implant, Ureters into, Bladder
See Anastomosis, Ureter, to Bladder

Implantation
Bone
    for External Speech Processor/Cochlear
      Stimulator 69714-69718
Cardiac Event Recorder 33282
Contraceptive Capsules 11975, 11977
Drug Delivery Device 11981, 11983
Electrode
    Brain 61850-61875
    Nerve 64553-64581
    Spinal Cord 63650-63655
Eye
    Anterior Segment 65920
    Aqueous Shunt to Extraocular Placement or
      Replacement of Pegs 65125
    Posterior Segment
      Extraocular 67120
      Intraocular 67121
    Reservoir 66180
    Vitreous
      Drug Delivery System 67027
Hearing Aid Hormone Pellet(s)
    Bone Conduction 69710
Hip Prosthesis
    See Arthroplasty, Hip
Hormone Pellet 11980
Intraocular Lens
    See Insertion, Intraocular Lens
Joint
    See Arthroplasty
Mesh
    Hernia Repair 49568
Nerve
    into Bone 64787
    into Muscle .64787
Neurostimulators
    Pulse Generator 61885
    Receiver 61886
Pulse Generator
    Brain 61885-61886
    Spinal Cord Electrode Array 63685
Receiver
    Brain 61885-61886
    Spinal Cord .63685
Removal 20670-20680
    Elbow 24164
    Radius 24164

Incisional Hernia Repair

Incision and Drainage

Carbuncle
  Skin 10060-10061
Carpals 25035, 26034
Comedones
  Skin 10040
Cyst
  Conjunctiva 68020
  Gums 41800
  Liver
    Open 47010
    Percutaneous 47011
  Lung 32200
    Percutaneous 32201
  Mouth 40800-40801, 41005-41009,
                                41015-41018
  Ovarian 58800-58805
  Skin .10040-10061
    Pilonidal 10080-10081
    Puncture Aspiration 10160
  Spinal Cord 63172-63173
  Thyroid Gland 60000
  Tongue 41000-41006, 41015, 60000
Elbow
  Abscess 23935
  Arthrotomy .24000
Femur 27303
Fluid Collection
  Skin 10140
Foreign Body
  Skin .10120-10121
Furuncle 10060-10061
Gallbladder .47480
Hematoma
  Ankle 27603
  Arm, Lower 25028
  Arm, Upper 23930
  Brain 61312-61315
  Ear, External
    Complicated 69005
    Simple 69000
  Elbow 23930
  Epididymis .54700
  Gums 41800
  Hip 26990
  Knee 27301
  Leg, Lower 27603
  Leg, Upper 27301
  Mouth 40800-40801, 41005-41009,
                                41015-41018
  Nasal Septum 30020
  Neck 21501-21502
  Nose 30000-30020
  Pelvis 26990
  Scrotum 54700
  Skin 10140
    Puncture Aspiration 10160
  Skull 61312-61315
  Testis 54700
  Thorax 21501-21502
  Tongue 41000-41006, 41015
  Vagina 57022-57023
  Wrist 25028
Hepatic Duct 47400
Hip
  Bone 26992, 27030
Humerus
  Abscess 23935

Interphalangeal Joint
  Toe 28024
Intertarsal Joint 28020
Kidney 50040, 50125
Knee .27303, 27310
Lacrimal Gland 68400
Lacrimal Sac 68420
Liver
  Abscess or Cyst 47010-47011
    Percutaneous 47011
Mediastinum 39000-39010
Metatarsophalangeal Joint 28022
Milia, Multiple 10040
Onychia 10060-10061
Orbit .67405, 67440
Paronychia 10060-10061
Pelvic
  Bone 26992
Penis 54015
Pericardium .33025
Phalanges
  Finger 26034
Pilonidal Cyst 10080-10081
Pustules
  Skin 10040
Radius 25035
Seroma
  Skin 10140
Shoulder
  Abscess 23030
  Arthrotomy
    Acromioclavicular Joint 23044
    Sternoclavicular Joint 23044
  Bursa 23031
  Hematoma .23030
Shoulder Joint
  Arthrotomy
    Glenohumeral Joint 23040
Tarsometatarsal Joint 28020
Tendon Sheath
  Finger 26020
  Palm 26020
Thorax
  Deep 21510
Toe 28024
Ulna 25035
Ureter 50600
Vagina 57020
Wound Infection
  Skin 10180
Wrist .25028, 25040

Inclusion Bodies
Fluid 88106
Smear 87207-87210

Incomplete Abortion
See Abortion, Incomplete

Indicator Dilution Studies 93561-93562

Induced Abortion
See Abortion

Induced Hyperthermia
See Thermotherapy

Induced Hypothermia
See Hypothermia

Induratio Penis Plastica
See Peyronie Disease

Infant, Newborn, Intensive Care
See Intensive Care, Neonatal

Infantile Paralysis
See Polio

Infection
Immunoassay 86317-86318
Rapid Test 86403-86406

Infection, Actinomyces
See Actinomycosis

Infection, Bone
See Osteomyelitis

Infection, Filarioidea
See Filariasis

Infection, Postoperative Wound
See Postoperative Wound Infection

Infection, Wound
See Wound, Infection

Infectious Agent
Antigen Detection
  Direct Fluorescence . . .87198-87199, 87265-
     87272, 87276, 87278, 87280, 87285-87290
    Bordetella 87265
    Chlamydia Trachomatis 87270
    Cryptosporidium/Giardia 87272
    Cytomegalovirus 87198
    Enterovirus 87199
    Influenza A 87276
    Legionella Pneumophila 87278
    Respiratory Syncytial Virus 87280
    Treponema Pallidum 87285
    Varicella-Zoster 87290
  Enzyme Immunoassay
    Adenovirus 87301
    Chlamydia Trachomatis 87320
    Clostridium Difficile 87324
    Cryptococcus Neoformans 87327
    Cryptosporidium/Giardia 87328
    Cytomegalovirus 87332
    Entamoeba Histolytica Dispar
    Group 87336
    Entamoeba Histolytica Group 87337
    Escherichia coli 0157 87335
    Helicobacter Pylori 87338-87339
    Hepatitis, Delta Agent 87380
    Hepatitis Be Antigen (HBeAg) 87350
    Hepatitis B Surface Antigen
    (HBsAg) .87340
    Hepatitis B Surface Antigen (HBsAg)
    Neutralization 87341
    Histoplasma capsulatum 87385
    HIV-1 87390
    HIV-2 87391
    Influenza A 87400
    Influenza B 87400
    Multiple Step Method 87301-87449,
                                87451
    See specific agent
    Not Otherwise Specified 87449, 87451
    Respiratory Syncytial Virus 87420
    Rotavirus 87425

Carpal Tunnel
    Therapeutic 20526
Chemotherapy 96400-96450, 96542
Cistern
    Medication or Other 61055
Contrast
    via Catheter 49424
Corpora Cavernosa 54235
Cyst
    Bone 20615
    Kidney 50390
    Pelvis 50390
    Thyroid 60001
Elbow
    Arthrography
       Radiologic 24220
Epidural
    See Epidural, Injection
Esophageal Varices
    Endoscopy 43243
Esophagus
    Sclerosing Agent 43204
Extremity
    Pseudoaneurysm 36002
Eye
    Air 66020
    Medication 66030
Eyelid
    Subconjunctival 68200
Ganglion
    Anesthetic 64505, 64510
Ganglion Cyst 20550, 20600-20605
Gastric Secretion Stimulant 91052
Gastric Varices
    Endoscopy 43243
Heart Vessels
    Cardiac Catheterization 93539-93545
       See Catheterization, Cardiac
    Radiologic 93545
Hemorrhoids
    Sclerosing Solution 46500
Hip
    Radiologic 27093-27095
Insect Venom 95130-95134
Intervertebral Disk
    Chemonucleolysis Agent 62292
    Radiological 62290-62291
Intraamniotic 59852
Intraarterial
    Diagnostic 90783
    Therapeutic 90783
Intradermal
    for Tattooing 11920-11922
Intralesional
    Skin 11900-11901
Intramuscular
    Antibiotic 90788
    Diagnostic 90782
    Therapeutic 90782, 99506
Intravenous
    Diagnostic 90784
    Therapeutic 90784
    Vascular Flow Check, Graft 15860
Joint 20600-20610
Kidney
    Radiologic 50394
Knee
    Radiologic 27370

Lacrimal Gland
    Radiologic 68850
Left Heart
    Radiologic 93543
Lesion
    Skin 11900-11901
Ligament 20550
Liver 47015
    Radiologic 47500-47505
Mammary Ductogram/Galactogram 19030
Muscle Endplate
    Cervical Spine 64613
    Extremity 64614
    Facial 64612
    Trunk 64614
Nerve
    Anesthetic 64400-64530
Neurolytic Agent 64600-64680
Orbit
    Retrobulbar
       Alcohol 67505
       Medication 67500
    Tenon's Capsule 67515
Pancreatography 48400
Paravertebral Facet Joint/Nerve . .64470-64476
Penis
    for Erection .54235
    Peyronie Disease 54200
      with Surgical Exposure of Plaque . .54205
    Radiology 54230
    Vasoactive Drugs 54231
Peritoneal Cavity Air
    See Pneumoperitoneum
Radiologic
    Breast 19030
Rectum
    Sclerosing Solution 45520
Right Heart
    See Cardiac Catheterization, Injection
    Radiologic 93542
Sacroiliac Joint
    for Arthrography 27096
Salivary Duct 42660
Salivary Gland
    Radiologic 42550
Sclerosing Agent
    Esophagus 43204
    Intravenous 36470-36471
Sentinel Node Identification 38792
Shoulder
    Arthrography
       Radiologic 23350
Shunt
    Peritoneal
       Venous 49427
Sinus Tract 20500
    Diagnostic 20501
Spider Veins
    Telangiectasia 36468-36469
Spinal Artery 62294
Spinal Cord
    Anesthetic 62310-62319
    Blood 62273
    Neurolytic Agent 62280-62282
    Other .62310-62311
    Radiological .62284

Steroids
    Urethral Stricture 52283
Subcutaneous
    Diagnostic 90782
    Silicone 11950-11954
    Therapeutic 90782
Temporomandibular Joint
    Arthrography .21116
Tendon Origin, Insertion 20551
Tendon Sheath .20550
Therapeutic
    Extremity Pseudoaneurysm 36002
    Lung 32960
    Thyroid 60001
    Turbinate 30200
Thoracic Cavity
    See Pleurodesis, Chemical
Trachea 31612
    Puncture 31612
Transtracheal
    Bronchography 31715
Trigger Point(s)
    One or Two Muscle Groups 20552
    Two or More Muscle Groups 20553
Turbinate 30200
Unlisted Services and Procedures 90799
Ureter
    Radiologic 50684
Venography 36005
Ventricle
    Dye 61120
    Medication or Other 61026
Vitreous 67028
    Fluid Substitute 67025
Vocal Cords
    Therapeutic 31513, 31570-31571
Wrist
    Carpal Tunnel
       Therapeutic 20526
    Radiologic 25246

Inkblot Test .96100

Inner Ear
See Ear, Inner

Innominate
Tumor
    Excision 27077

Innominate Arteries
See Artery, Brachiocephalic

Inorganic Sulfates
See Sulfate

Insemination
Artificial .58321-58322

Insertion
See Implantation; Intubation; Transplantation
Baffle
    Ear, Middle .69410
Balloon
    Intra-Aortic 33967, 33973
Breast
    Implants 19340-19342

Coronary 92980-92981
Esophagus 43219
Gastrointestinal, Upper 43256
Ileum 44383
Indwelling 50605
Lacrimal Duct 68815
Pancreatic Duct 43268
Small Intestines 44370, 44379
Ureteral 50947, 52332
Ureter via Kidney 50393
Urethral .52282
Tamponade
Esophagus 43460
Tandem
Uterus
for Brachytherapy 57155
Tendon Graft
Finger 26392
Hand 26392
Testicular Prosthesis
See Prosthesis, Testicular, Insertion
Tissue Expanders
Skin 11960-11971
Tube
Bile Duct 43268
Esophagus 43510
Gastrointestinal, Upper 43241
Ileum 44383
Kidney .50398
Pancreatic Duct 43268
Small Intestines 44379
Trachea 31730
Ureter 50688
Ureteral Guide Wire 52334
Vascular Pedicle
Carpal Bone 25430
Venous Access Device 36533
Ventilating Tube 69433
Ventricular Assist Device 33975
Wire
Skeletal Traction 20650

Inspiratory Positive Pressure Breathing
See Intermittent Positive Pressure Breathing (IPPB)

Instillation
Contrast Material
Bronchography 31708
Laryngography 31708
Drugs
Bladder 51720

Instillation, Bladder
See Bladder, Instillation

Instrumentation
See Application; Bone, Fixation; Spinal Instrumentation
Spinal
Insertion 22840-22848, 22851
Reinsertion 22849
Removal 22850, 22852-22855

Insufflation, Eustachian Tube
See Eustachian Tube, Inflation

Insulin 80422, 80432-80435
Antibody .86337
Blood 83525
Free 83527

Insulin C-Peptide Measurement
See C-Peptide

Insulin Like Growth Factors
See Somatomedin

Insurance
Basic Life and/or Disability
Evaluation Services 99450
Examination 99450-99456

Integumentary System
Biopsy .11100-11101
Breast
Excision 19100-19272
Incision 19000-19030
Metallic Localization Clip Placement . .19295
Preoperative Placement of Needle
Localization 19290-19291
Reconstruction 19316-19396
Repair 19316-19396
Unlisted Services and Procedures 19499
Burns . .15000-15001, 15100-15121, 15342-15401
Debridement 11000-11044
Destruction
See Dermatology
Actinotherapy 96900
Benign or Premalignant Lesion 17000-17250
by Photodynamic Therapy 96567
Chemical Exfoliation 17360
Cryotherapy 17340
Electrolysis Epilation 17380
Malignant Lesion 17260-17286
by Photodynamic Therapy 96567
Mohs Micrographic Surgery . . .17304-17310
Unlisted Services and Procedures 17999
Drainage 10040-10180
Excision
Benign Lesion 11400-11471
Debridement 11000-11044
Malignant Lesion 11600-11646
Incision 10040-10180
Introduction 11900-11977
Drug Delivery Implant 11981, 11983
Nails .11720-11765
Paring 11055-11057
Pressure Ulcers 15920-15999
Removal
Drug Delivery Implant 11982-11983
Repair
Adjacent Tissue
Transfer/Rearrangement 14000-14350
Complex 13100-13160
Flaps
Other 15740-15776
Free Skin Grafts 15000-15400
Intermediate 12031-12057
Other Procedures 15780-15879
Simple 12001-12021
Skin and/or Deep Tissue 15570-15738
Shaving of Epidermal or
Dermal Lesion 11300-11313
Skin Tags
Removal 11200-11201

Integumentum Commune
See Integumentary System

Intelligence Test 96100

Intensive Care
Neonatal
Initial Care 99295
Subsequent Care 99296-99297

Intercarpal Joint
Arthrodesis 25820-25825
Dislocation
Closed Treatment 25660
Repair 25447

Intercostal Nerve
Destruction 64620
Injection
Anesthetic 64420-64421
Neurolytic 64620

Interdental Fixation
Device
Application 21110
Mandibular Fracture
Closed Treatment 21453
Open Treatment 21462
without Fracture 21497

Interdental Papilla
See Gums

Interdental Wire Fixation
Closed Treatment
Craniofacial Separation 21431

Interferometry
Eye
Biometry 92136

Intermediate Care Facilities (ICFs)
See Nursing Facility Services

Intermediate Care Facility
Visits .99301-99313

Intermittent Positive Pressure
Breathing (IPPB) 94650-94652
See Continuous Negative Pressure Breathing (CNPB); Continuous Positive Airway Pressure (CPAP)

Internal Breast Prostheses
See Breast, Implants

Internal Ear
See Ear, Inner

Internal Rigid Fixation
Reconstruction
Mandibular Rami 21196

Interphalangeal Joint
Arthrodesis 26860-26863
Arthroplasty 26535-26536
Arthrotomy 26080, 28054
Biopsy
Synovium 26110
Capsule
Excision 26525
Incision 26525

Intestinovesical Fistula
See Fistula, Enterovesical

Intimectomy
See Endarterectomy

Intra-Abdominal Voiding Pressure Studies

Intra-Osseous Infusion
See Infusion, Intraosseous

Intracapsular Extraction of Lens
See Extraction, Lens, Intracapsular

Intracardiac Echocardiography

Intracranial

Intracranial Arterial Perfusion

Intracranial Neoplasm, Acoustic Neuroma
See Brain, Tumor, Excision

Intracranial Neoplasm, Craniopharyngioma
See Craniopharyngioma

Intracranial Neoplasm, Meningioma
See Meningioma

Intrafallopian Transfer, Gamete
See GIFT

Intraluminal Angioplasty
See Angioplasty

Intramuscular Injection
See Injection, Intramuscular

Intraocular Lens

Intratracheal Intubation
See Insertion, Endotracheal Tube

Intrauterine Contraceptive Device
See Intrauterine Device (IUD)

Intrauterine Device (IUD)

Intrauterine Synechiae
See Adhesions, Intrauterine

Intravascular Stent
See Transcatheter, Placement, Intravascular Stents

Intravascular Ultrasound

Intravenous Injection
See Injection, Intravenous

Intravenous Pyelogram
See Urography, Intravenous

Intravenous Therapy

Intravesical Instillation
See Bladder, Instillation

Intravitreal Injection

Intra Arterial Injections
See Injection, Intraarterial

Intrinsic Factor

Introduction

Intubation

Intubation Tube
See Endotracheal Tube

Intussusception

Invagination, Intestinal
See Intussusception

Inversion, Nipple
See Nipples, Inverted

In Vivo NMR Spectroscopy
See Magnetic Resonance Spectroscopy

Iodide Test
See Nuclear Medicine, Thyroid, Uptake

Iodine Test
See Starch Granules, Feces

Ionization, Medical
See Iontophoresis

Iontophoreses
See Iontophoresis

Iontophoresis
See Physical Medicine and Rehabilitation

IP
See Allergen Immunotherapy

Ipecac Administration

IPPB
See Intermittent Positive Pressure Breathing; Pulmonology, Therapeutic

Iridectomy

Iridencleisis

Iridodialysis

Iridoplasty

Iridotasis

Iridotomy

Iris

K

Lactic Acid 83605

Lactic Acid Measurement
See Lactate

Lactic Cytochrome Reductase
See Lactic Dehydrogenase

Lactic Dehydrogenase 83615-83625

Lactiferous Duct
Excision 19112
Exploration 19110

Lactogen, Human Placental 83632

Lactogenic Hormone
See Prolactin

Lactose
Urine 83633-83634

Ladd Procedure 44055

Laki Lorand Factor
See Fibrin Stabilizing Factor

Lamblia Intestinalis
See Giardia Lamblia

Lambrinudi Operation
See Arthrodesis, Foot Joint

Lamellar Keratoplasties
See Keratoplasty, Lamellar

Laminaria
Insertion 59200

Laminectomy ..62351, 63001, 63005-63011,
63015-63044, 63180-63200, 63265-63655
Lumbar 22630, 63012
Surgical 63170-63172
with Facetectomy 63045-63048

Langerhans Islands
See Islet Cell

Language Evaluation 92506

Language Therapy 92507-92508

LAP
See Leucine Aminopeptidase

Laparoscopic Appendectomy
See Appendectomy, Laparoscopic

Laparoscopic Biopsy of Ovary
See Biopsy, Ovary, Laparoscopic

Laparoscopy
Adrenalectomy 50545
Adrenal Gland
Biopsy 60650
Excision 60650
Appendectomy 44970
Aspiration 49322
Biopsy 47561, 49321
Lymph Nodes 38570
Cholangiography 47560-47561
Cholecystectomy 47562-47564
Cholecystenterostomy 47570

Destruction
Lesion 58662
Diagnostic 49320
Drainage
Extraperitoneal Lymphocele 49323
Ectopic Pregnancy 59150
with Salpingectomy and/or
Oophorectomy 59151
Enterolysis 44200
Esophagogastric Fundoplasty 43280
Fimbrioplasty 58672
Gastrostomy
Temporary 43653
Hernia Repair
Initial 49650
Recurrent 49651
Incontinence Repair 51990-51992
In Vitro Fertilization 58976
Retrieve Oocyte 58970
Transfer Embryo 58974
Transfer Gamete 58976
Jejunostomy 44201
Ligation
Veins, Spermatic 55550
Liver
Ablation
Tumor 47370-47371
Lymphadenectomy 38571-38589
Lysis of Adhesions 58660
Lysis of Intestinal Adhesions 44200
Nephrectomy 50545-50548
Orchiectomy 54690
Orchiopexy 54692
Oviduct Surgery 58670-58671, 58679
Pelvis 49320
Pyeloplasty 50544
Removal
Fallopian Tube 58661
Leiomyomata 58551
Ovaries 58661
Spleen 38120
Testis 54690
Resection
Intestines
with Anastomosis 44202-44203
Salpingostomy 58673
Splenectomy 38120-38129
Surgical 38570-38572, 43651-43653, 44200-
44205, 44970, 47370-47371, 49321-49323,
49650-49651, 50541, 50545, 50945-50948,
51990-51992, 54690-54692, 55550
with Guided Transhepatic
Cholangiography 47560-47561
Unlisted Services and Procedures 38129,
38589, 43289, 43659, 44209,
44979, 47379, 47579, 49329, 49659,
50549, 50949, 54699, 55559,
58578-58579, 58679, 59898
Ureterolithotomy 50945
Ureteroneocystostomy 50947-50948
Urethral Suspension 51990
Vaginal Hysterectomy 58550
Vagus Nerves
Transection 43651-43652
with X-Ray 47560

Laparotomy
Exploration 47015, 49000-49002, 58960
for Staging 49220
Hemorrhage Control 49002
Second Look 58960
Staging 58960
with Biopsy 49000

Laparotomy, Exploratory
See Abdomen, Exploration

Lapidus Procedure 28297

Large Bowel
See Anus; Cecum; Rectum

Laroyenne Operation
See Vagina, Abscess, Incision and Drainage

Laryngeal Function Study 92520

Laryngectomy 31360-31382
Partial 31367-31382
Subtotal 31367-31368

Laryngocele
Removal 31300

Laryngofissure 31300

Laryngography 70373
Instillation
Contrast Material 31708

Laryngopharyngectomy
See Excision, Larynx, with Pharynx

Laryngopharynx
See Hypopharynx

Laryngoplasty
Burns 31588
Cricoid Split 31587
Laryngeal Stenosis 31582
Laryngeal Web 31580
Open Reduction of Fracture 31584

Laryngoscopy
Diagnostic 31505
Direct 31515-31571
Exploration 31505, 31520-31526, 31575
Fiberoptic 31575-31579
with Stroboscopy 31579
Indirect 31505-31513
Newborn 31520
Operative 31530-31561

Laryngotomy 31300
Diagnostic 31320
Total 31360-31368

Larynx
Aspiration
Endoscopy 31515
Biopsy
Endoscopy 31510, 31535-31536, 31576
Dilation
Endoscopic 31528-31529
Endoscopy
Direct 31515-31571
Exploration 31505, 31520-31526, 31575

Unna Boot 29580
X-Ray 73592
Wound Exploration
    Penetrating 20103

Legionella
Antibody 86713
Antigen 87277-87278, 87540-87542

Legionella Micdadei
Antigen Detection
    Immunofluorescence 87277

Legionella Pneumophila
Antigen Detection
    Direct Fluorescence 87278

Leg Length Measurement X-Ray
See Scanogram

Leiomyomata
Removal 58140, 58551, 58561

Leishmania
Antibody 86717

Lengthening, Tendon
See Tendon, Lengthening

Lens
Extracapsular 66940
Intracapsular 66920
    Dislocated 66930
Intraocular
    Exchange 66986
    Reposition 66825
Prosthesis
    Insertion......................66983
      Manual or Mechanical
      Technique 66982, 66984
      Not Associated with Concurrent Cataract
      Removal 66985
Removal
    Lens Material
      Aspiration Technique 66840
      Extracapsular 66940
      Intracapsular 66920-66930
      Pars Plana Approach 66852
      Phacofragmentation Technique 66850

Lens Material
Aspiration Technique 66840
Pars Plana Approach 66852
Phacofragmentation Technique 66850

Leptomeningioma
See Meningioma

Leptospira
Antibody 86720

Leriche Operation 64809
See Sympathectomy, Thoracolumbar

Lesion
See Tumor
Anal
    Destruction 46900-46917, 46924
    Excision 45108, 46922
Ankle
    Tendon Sheath 27630

Arm, Lower
    Tendon Sheath
      Excision 25110
Auditory Canal, External
    Excision
      Exostosis 69140
      Radical without Neck Dissection 69150
      Radical with Neck Dissection 69155
      Soft Tissue 69145
Bladder
    Destruction 51030
Brain
    Excision 61534, 61536,
          61600-61608, 61615-61616
    Radiation Treatment 77432
Brainstem
    Excision 61575-61576
Breast
    Excision 19120-19126
Carotid Body
    Excision 60600-60605
Chemotherapy 96405-96406
    Destruction 67220-67225
Choroid
    Destruction 0016T
Ciliary Body
    Destruction 66770
Colon
    Destruction 44393, 45383
    Excision 44110-44111
Conjunctiva
    Destruction 68135
    Excision 68110-68130
      Over 1 cm 68115
      with Adjacent Sclera 68130
    Expression 68040
Cornea
    Destruction 65450
    Excision 65400
    of Pterygium 65420-65426
Destruction
    Ureter 52341-52342, 52344-52345
Ear, Middle
    Excision 69540
Epididymis
    Excision 54830
Esophagus
    Ablation 43228
    Excision 43100-43101
    Removal 43216
Excision 59100
    Bladder 52224
    Urethra 52224, 53265
Eye
    Excision 65900
Eyelid
    Destruction 67850
    Excision
      Multiple, Different Lids 67805
      Multiple, Same Lid 67801
      Single 67800
      Under Anesthesia 67808
      without Closure 67840
Facial
    Destruction 17000-17004, 17280-17286
Femur
    Excision 27062

Finger
    Tendon Sheath 26160
Foot
    Excision 28080, 28090
Gums
    Destruction 41850
    Excision 41822-41828
Hand Tendon Sheath 26160
Intestines
    Excision 44110
Intestines, Small
    Destruction 44369
    Excision 44111
Iris
    Destruction 66770
Leg, Lower
    Tendon Sheath 27630
Lymph Node
    Incision and Drainage 38300-38305
Mesentery
    Excision 44820
Mouth
    Destruction 40820
    Excision 40810-40816, 41116
    Vestibule
      Destruction 40820
      Repair 40830
Nerve
    Excision 64774-64792
Nose
    Intranasal
      External Approach 30118
      Internal Approach 30117
Orbit
    Excision 61333, 67412
Palate
    Destruction 42160
    Excision 42104-42120
Pancreas
    Excision 48120
Pelvis
    Destruction 58662
Penis
    Destruction
      Cryosurgery 54056
      Electrodesiccation 54055
      Extensive 54065
      Laser Surgery 54057
      Simple 54050-54060
      Surgical Excision 54060
      Excision 54060
      Penile Plaque 54110-54112
Pharynx
    Destruction 42808
    Excision 42808
Rectum
    Excision 45108
Removal
    Larynx 31512, 31578
Resection 52354
Retina
    Destruction
      Extensive 67227-67228
      Localized 0017T, 67208-67210
    Radiation by Implantation of Source ...67218
Sclera
    Excision 66130

Lip
Biopsy 40490
Excision .40500-40530
   Frenum 40819
Incision
   Frenum 40806
Reconstruction 40525-40527
Repair 40650-40654
   Cleft Lip 40700-40761
   Fistula 42260
Unlisted Services and Procedures 40799

Lip, Cleft
See Cleft Lip

Lipase 83690

Lipectomies, Aspiration
See Liposuction

Lipectomy 15831-15839
Suction Assisted 15876-15879

Lipids
Feces 82705-82710

Lipo-Lutin
See Progesterone

Lipolysis, Aspiration
See Liposuction

Lipophosphodiesterase I
See Tissue Typing

Lipoprotein
Blood 83715-83719
LDL 83716, 83721

Lipoprotein, Alpha
See Lipoprotein

Lipoprotein, Pre-Beta
See Lipoprotein, Blood

Liposuction 15876-15879

Lisfranc Operation
See Amputation, Foot; Radical Resection;
Replantation

Listeria Monocytogenes
Antibody 86723

Lithium
Assay 80178

Litholapaxy 52317-52318

Lithotripsy
See Extracorporeal Shock Wave Therapy
Bile Duct Calculi (Stone)
   Endoscopy .43265
Bladder 52353
Kidney 50590, 52353
Pancreatic Duct Calculi (Stone)
   Endoscopy .43265
Ureter 52353
Urethra 52353
with Cystourethroscopy 52353

Lithotrity
See Litholapaxy

Liver
See Hepatic Duct
Ablation
   Tumor .47380-47383
     Laparoscopic 47370-47371
Abscess
   Aspiration .47015
   Incision and Drainage
     Open 47010
     Percutaneous 47011
   Injection .47015
Aspiration 47015
Biopsy 47100
Cyst
   Aspiration .47015
   Incision and Drainage
     Open 47010
     Percutaneous 47011
Excision
   Extensive .47122
   Partial 47120, 47125-47130, 47134
   Total 47133
Injection 47015
   Radiologic .47505
   X-Ray 47500
Lobectomy 47125-47130
   Partial 47120
Needle Biopsy 47000-47001
Nuclear Medicine
   Function Study 78220
   Imaging 78201-78216
   Vascular Flow 78206
Repair
   Abscess 47300
   Cyst 47300
   Wound 47350-47362
Suture
   Wound 47350-47362
Transplantation 47135-47136
Trisegmentectomy 47122
Unlisted Services and Procedures . .47379, 47399

Living Activities, Daily
See Activities of Daily Living

Lobectomy
Brain 61539
Contralateral Subtotal
   Thyroid Gland 60212, 60225
Liver 47120-47130
Lung 32480-32482
   Sleeve 32486
Parotid Gland 42410-42415
Segmental 32663
Sleeve 32486
Temporal Lobe 61538
Thyroid Gland Partial 60210-60212
   Total 60220-60225
Total 32663

Lobotomy
Frontal 61490

Localization of Nodule
Radiographic
   Breast 76096

Local Excision Mastectomies
See Breast, Excision, Lesion

Local Excision of Lesion or Tissue of Femur
See Excision, Lesion, Femur

Log Hydrogen Ion Concentration
See pH

Lombard Test
See Audiologic Function Test

Longmire Operation
See Anastomosis, Hepatic Duct to Intestines

Long Acting Thyroid Stimulator
See Thyrotropin Releasing Hormone (TRH)

Long Term Care Facility Visits
See Nursing Facility Services

Loopogram
See Urography, Antegrade

Loose Body
Removal
   Ankle 27620
   Carpometacarpal Joint 26070
   Elbow 24101
   Interphalangeal Joint 28020
     Toe 28024
   Knee Joint 27331
   Metatarsophalangeal Joint 28022
   Tarsometatarsal Joint 28020
   Toe 28022
   Wrist 25101

Lord Procedure
See Anal Sphincter, Dilation

Louis Bar Syndrome
See Ataxia Telangiectasia

Lower Extremities
See Extremity, Lower

Lower GI Series
See Barium Enema

Low Density Lipoprotein
See Lipoprotein, LDL

Low Vision Aids
See Spectacle Services
Fitting .92354-92355
Supply 92392

LRH
See Luteinizing Releasing Factor

LSD
See Lysergic Acid Diethylamide

LTH
See Prolactin

Lumbar
See Spine
Aspiration, Disk
   Percutaneous 62287

Lumbar Plexus
Decompression 64714
Neuroplasty .64714
Release 64714
Repair/Suture 64862

Peripancreatic 38747
Portal 38747
Radical
    Axillary 38740-38745
    Cervical 38720-38724
    Pelvic 54135, 55845
    Suprahyoid 38700
Regional 50230
Retroperitoneal Transabdominal 38780
Thoracic 38746
Unilateral Inguinofemoral 56631, 56634

Lymphadenitis
Incision and Drainage 38300-38305

Lymphadenopathy Associated Antibodies
See Antibody, HIV

Lymphadenopathy Associated Virus
See HIV

Lymphangiogram, Abdominal
See Lymphangiography, Abdomen

Lymphangiography
Abdomen 75805-75807
Arm 75801-75803
Injection 38790
Leg 75801-75803
Pelvis 75805-75807

Lymphangioma, Cystic
See Hygroma

Lymphangiotomy 38308

Lymphatics
See Specific Procedure

Lymphatic Channels
Incision 38308

Lymphatic Cyst
See Lymphocele

Lymphatic System
Unlisted Procedure 38999

Lymphoblast Transformation
See Blastogenesis

Lymphocele
Drainage
    Laparoscopic 49323
Extraperitoneal
    Open Drainage 49062

Lymphocoele
See Lymphocele

Lymphocyte
Culture 86821-86822
Toxicity Assay 86805-86806
Transformation 86353

Lymphocyte, Thymus-Dependent
See T-Cells

Lymphocytes, CD4
See CD4

Lymphocytes, CD8
See CD8

Lymphocytic Choriomeningitis
Antibody 86727

Lymphocytotoxicity 86805-86806

Lymphogranuloma Venereum
Antibody 86729

Lymphoma Virus, Burkitt
See Epstein-Barr Virus

Lynch Procedure 31075

Lysergic Acid Diethylamide ...80102-
                         80103, 80299

Lysergide
See Lysergic Acid Diethylamide

Lysis
Adhesions
    Epidural 62263
    Fallopian Tube 58740
    Foreskin 54450
    Intestinal 44005
    Labial 56441
    Lung 32124
    Nose 30560
    Ovary 58740
    Oviduct 58740
    Penile
        Post-circumcision 54162
    Ureter 50715-50725
    Uterus 58559
Euglobulin 85360
Labial
    Adhesions 56441
Nose
    Intranasal Synechia 30560

Lysozyme 85549

L Ascorbic Acid
See Ascorbic Acid

L Aspartate 2 Oxoglutarate Aminotransferase
See Transaminase, Glutamic Oxaloacetic

L Glutamine
See Glutamine

M

MacEwen Operation
See Hernia, Repair, Inguinal

Machado Test
See Complement, Fixation Test

MacLean-De Wesselow Test
See Blood Urea Nitrogen; Urea Nitrogen, Clearance

Macrodactylia
Repair 26590

Madlener Operation
See Tubal Ligation

Magnesium 83735

Magnetic Resonance Angiography (MRA)
Abdomen 74185
Arm 73225
Chest 71555
Head 70544-70546
Leg 73725
Neck 70547-70549
Pelvis 72198
Spine 72159

Magnetic Resonance Imaging (MRI)
Abdomen 74181-74183
Ankle 73721-73723
Arm 73218-73220, 73223
Bone Marrow Study 76400
Brain 70551-70553
Breast 76093-76094
Chest 71550-71552
Elbow 73221
Face 70540-70543
Finger Joint 73221
Foot 73718-73719
Foot Joints 73721-73723
Guidance
    Needle Placement 76393
    Tissue Ablation 76394
Hand 73218-73220, 73223
Heart 75552
    Complete Study 75554
    Flow Mapping 75556
    Limited Study 75555
    Morphology 75553
Joint
    Lower Extremity 73721-73723
    Upper Extremity 73221-73223
Knee 73721-73723
Leg 73718-73720
Neck 70540-70543
Orbit 70540-70543
Pelvis 72195-72197
Radiology
    Diagnostic
        Procedures 76499
Spectroscopy 76390
Spine
    Cervical 72141-72142, 72156-72158
    Lumbar 72148-72158
    Thoracic 72146-72147, 72156-72158
Temporomandibular Joint (TMJ) 70336
Toe 73721-73723
Wrist 73221

Magnetic Resonance Spectroscopy 76390

Magnetic Stimulation
Brain Cortex 0018T

Great Toe 28495-28496
Toes 28515
Radial 24655, 25565
Radial Shaft 25505
Radiocarpal 25660
Radioulnar 25675
Scapular 23575
Shoulder 23650-23655
with Greater Tuberosity 23665
Shoulder Dislocation
Sternoclavicular 23525
with Surgical or Anatomical Neck . . .23675
Talus 28435-28436
Tarsal 28455-28456
Thumb 26641-26650
Tibial 27532, 27752
Trans-Scaphoperilunar 25680
Ulnar 24675, 25535, 25565
Vertebral 22315
Wrist . . .25259, 25624, 25635, 25660, 25675,
25680, 25690
Foreskin 54450
Globe 92018-92019
Hip 27275
Interphalangeal Joint, Proximal 26742
Knee .27570
Osteopathic 98925-98929
Shoulder
Application of Fixation Apparatus 23700
Spine
Anesthesia 22505
Tibial, Distal 27762

Manometric Studies
Kidney
Pressure 50396
Rectum/Anus 91122
Ureter
Pressure 50686
Ureterostomy 50686

Manometry
Rectum 90911

Mantoux Test
See TB Test, Skin Test

Manual Therapy 97140

Maquet Procedure 27418

Marcellation Operation
See Hysterectomy, Vaginal

Marrow, Bone
See Bone Marrow

Marshall-Marchetti-Krantz
Procedure 51840-51841, 58152, 58267

Marsupialization 10040
Bartholin's Gland Cyst 56440
Cyst
Sublingual Salivary 42409
Liver
Cyst or Abscess 47300
Pancreatic Cyst 48500
Urethral Diverticulum 53240

Massage
Cardiac 32160
Therapy 97124
See Physical Medicine/Therapy/Occupational
Therapy

Masseter Muscle/Bone
Reduction 21295-21296

Mass Spectrometry and Tandem Mass Spectrometry
Analyte
Qualitative 83788
Quantitative 83789

Mastectomy
Gynecomastia 19140
Modified Radical 19240
Partial 19160-19162
Radical 19200-19220
Simple, Complete 19180
Subcutaneous 19182

Mastectomy, Halsted
See Mastectomy, Radical

Mastoid
Excision
Complete 69502
Radical 69511
Modified 69505
Petrous Apicectomy 69530
Simple 69501
Obliteration 69670
Repair
by Excision 69601-69603
Fistula 69700
with Apicectomy 69605
with Tympanoplasty 69604

Mastoidectomy
Osseointegrated Implant
for External Speech Processor/Cochlear
Stimulator 69715, 69718
with Apicectomy 69605
with Skull Base Surgery 61590, 61597
Decompression 61595
Facial Nerve 61595
with Tympanoplasty 69604, 69641-69646
Cochlear Device Implantation 69930
Complete 69502
Revision 69601
Ossicular Chain Reconstruction 69605
Radical 69511
Modified 69505
Revision 69602-69603
Simple 69501
with Labyrinthectomy 69910
with Labyrinthotomy 69802
with Petrous Apicectomy 69530

Mastoidotomy 69635-69637
with Tympanoplasty 69635
Ossicular Chain Reconstruction 69636
and Synthetic Prosthesis 69636

Mastoids
Polytomography 76101-76102
X-Ray 70120-70130

Mastoid Cavity
Debridement 69220-69222

Mastopexy 19316

Mastotomy 19020

Maternity Care
See Abortion; Cesarean Delivery; Ectopic
Pregnancy; Obstetrical Care

Maternity Care and Delivery 59612-59622, 59898

Maxilla
See Facial Bones; Mandible
Bone Graft 21210
CAT Scan 70486-70488
Excision 21032
Fracture
Closed Treatment 21345, 21421
Open Treatment .21346-21348, 21422-21423
with Fixation 21345-21347
Osteotomy 21206
Reconstruction
with Implant 21245-21246, 21248-21249

Maxillary Arteries
See Artery, Maxillary

Maxillary Sinus
See Sinus, Maxillary

Maxillary Torus Palatinus
Tumor Excision 21032

Maxillectomy 31225-31230

Maxillofacial Fixation
Application
Halo Type Appliance 21100

Maxillofacial Impressions
Auricular Prosthesis 21086
Definitive Obturator Prosthesis 21080
Facial Prosthesis 21088
Interim Obturator Prosthesis 21079
Mandibular Resection Prosthesis 21081
Nasal Prosthesis 21087
Oral Surgical Splint 21085
Orbital Prosthesis 21077
Palatal Augmentation Prosthesis 21082
Palatal Lift Prosthesis 21083
Speech Aid Prosthesis 21084
Surgical Obturator Prosthesis 21076

Maxillofacial Procedures
Unlisted Services and Procedures 21299

Maxillofacial Prosthetics 21076-21089
Unlisted Services and Procedures 21089

Maydl Operation 45563, 50810
See Colostomy

Mayo Hernia Repair
See Hernia, Repair, Umbilicus

Mayo Operation
See Varicose Vein, Removal

Metacarpophalangeal Joint
Arthrodesis 26850-26852
Arthroplasty 26530-26531
Arthroscopy
  Diagnostic 29900
  Surgical 29901-29902
Arthrotomy 26075
Biopsy
  Synovium 26105
Capsule
  Excision 26520
  Incision 26520
Capsulodesis 26516-26518
Dislocation
  Closed Treatment 26700
  Open Treatment 26715
  Percutaneous Fixation 26705-26706
  with Manipulation 26340
Exploration 26075
Fracture
  Closed Treatment 26740
  Open Treatment 26746
  with Manipulation 26742
Fusion 26516-26518, 26850-26852
Removal of Foreign Body 26075
Repair
  Collateral Ligament 26540-26542
Synovectomy 26135

Metadrenaline
See Metanephrines

Metals, Heavy
See Heavy Metal

Metamfetamine
See Methamphetamine

Metanephrines 83835

Metatarsal
See Foot
Amputation 28810
Condyle
  Excision 28288
Craterization 28122
Cyst
  Excision 28104-28107
Diaphysectomy 28122
Excision 28110-28114, 28122, 28140
Fracture
  Closed Treatment
    without Manipulation 28470
    with Manipulation 28475-28476
  Open Treatment 28485
  Percutaneous Fixation 28476
Free Osteocutaneous Flap with Microvascular
Anastomosis 20972
Repair 28322
  Lengthening 28306-28307
  Osteotomy 28306-28309
Saucerization 28122
Tumor
  Excision 28104-28107, 28173

Metatarsectomy 28140

Metatarsophalangeal Joint
Arthrotomy 28022, 28052
Cheilectomy 28289
Dislocation 28630-28635, 28645
  Percutaneous Fixation 28636
Exploration 28022
Great Toe
  Arthrodesis 28750
  Fusion 28750
Removal
  of Foreign Body 28022
  of Loose Body 28022
Repair
  Hallux Rigidus 28289
Synovial
  Biopsy 28052
  Excision 28072
Toe 28270

Methadone 83840

Methaemoglobin
See Methemoglobin

Methamphetamine
Blood or Urine 82145

Methanol 84600

Methbipyranone
See Metyrapone

Methemalbumin 83857

Methemoglobin 83045-83050

Methenamine Silver Stain 88312

Methopyrapone
See Metyrapone

Methoxyhydroxymandelic Acid
See Vanillylmandelic Acid

Methsuximide 83858

Methylamphetamine
See Methamphetamine

Methylene Bichloride
See Dichloromethane

Methylfluorprednisolone
See Dexamethasone

Methylmorphine
See Codeine

Methyl Alcohol
See Methanol

Metroplasty
See Hysteroplasty

Metyrapone 80436

MIC
See Minimum Inhibitory Concentration

Micro-Ophthalmia
Orbit Reconstruction 21256

Microalbumin
Urine 82043-82044

Microbiology 0023T, 87001-87999

Microdissection 88380

Microfluorometries, Flow
See Flow Cytometry

Microglobulin, Beta 2
Blood 82232
Urine 82232

Micrographic Surgery
Mohs Technique 17304-17310

Micrographic Surgery, Moh
See Mohs Micrographic Surgery

Micropigmentation
Correction 11920-11922

Microscope, Surgical
See Operating Microscope

Microscopic Evaluation
Hair 96902

Microscopies, Electron
See Electron Microscopy

Microscopy
Ear Exam 92504

Microsomal Antibody 86376

Microsomia, Hemifacial
See Hemifacial Microsomia

Microsurgery
Operating Microscope 69990

Microvascular Anastomosis
Bone Graft
  Fibula 20955
  Other 20962
Fascial Flap, Free 15758
Muscle Flap, Free 15756
Osteocutaneous Flap with 20969-20973
Skin Flap, Free 15757

Microvite A
See Vitamin, A

Microwave Therapy 97020
See Physical Medicine/Therapy/Occupational
Therapy

Midbrain
See Brain; Brainstem; Mesencephalon; Skull
Base Surgery

Midcarpal Medioccipital Joint
Arthrotomy 25040

Middle Ear
See Ear, Middle

Midface
Reconstruction
  Forehead Advancement 21159-21160
  without Bone Graft 21141-21143
  with Bone Graft 21145-21160, 21188

Myelography
Brain 70010
Spine
    Cervical 72240
    Lumbosacral 72265
    Thoracic 72255
    Total 72270

Myelomeningocele
Repair 63704-63706

Myelotomy
. 63170

Myocardial
Perfusion Imaging . . .78460-78465, 78478-78480
    See Nuclear Medicine
Positron Emission Tomography (PET) 78459

Myocardial Imaging 78466-78469
Positron Emission Tomography
    Perfusion Study 78491-78492
Repair
    Postinfarction .33542

Myocutaneous Flaps 15732-15738

Myofascial Pain Dysfunction Syndrome
See Temporomandibular Joint (TMJ)

Myofibroma
See Leiomyomata

Myoglobin 83874

Myomectomy
Anorectal 45108
Uterus 58140-58145

Myoplasty
See Muscle, Repair

Myotomy
Esophagus 43030

Myringoplasty 69620

Myringostomy
See Myringotomy

Myringotomy 69420-69421

Myxoid Cyst
See Ganglion

N

N. Meningitidis
See Neisseria Meningitidis

Naffziger Operation
See Decompression, Orbit; Section

Nagel Test
See Color Vision Examination

Nails
Avulsion 11730-11732
Biopsy 11755
Debridement 11720-11721
Evacuation
    Hematoma, Subungual 11740
Excision .11750-11752
    Cyst
      Pilonidal 11770-11772
KOH Examination 87220
Removal 11730-11732, 11750-11752
Trimming 11719

Nail Bed
Reconstruction 11762
Repair 11760

Nail Fold
Excision
    Wedge 11765

Nail Plate Separation
See Onychia

Narcosynthesis
Diagnostic and Therapeutic 90865

Nasal Abscess
See Nose, Abscess

Nasal Area
Bone Graft 21210

Nasal Bleeding
See Epistaxis

Nasal Bone
Fracture
    Closed Treatment 21310-21320
    Open Treatment 21325-21335
    without Manipulation 21310
    with Manipulation 21315-21320
X-Ray 70160

Nasal Deformity
Repair 40700-40761

Nasal Function Study 92512

Nasal Polyp
See Nose, Polyp

Nasal Prosthesis
Impression 21087

Nasal Septum
Abscess
    Incision and Drainage 30020
Fracture
    Closed Treatment 21337
    Open Treatment 21336
Hematoma
    Incision and Drainage 30020
Repair 30630
Submucous Resection 30520

Nasal Sinuses
See Sinus; Sinuses

Nasal Smear
Eosinophils 89190

Nasal Turbinate
Fracture
    Therapeutic .30930

Nasoethmoid Complex
Fracture
    Open Treatment 21338-21339
    Percutaneous Treatment 21340
Reconstruction 21182-21184

Nasogastric Tube
Placement 43752

Nasolacrimal Duct
Exploration 68810
    with Anesthesia 68811
Insertion
    Stent 68815
X-Ray
    with Contrast 70170

Nasomaxillary
Fracture
    Closed Treatment 21345
    Open Treatment 21346-21348
    with Bone Grafting 21348

Nasopharynges
See Nasopharynx

Nasopharyngoscopy 92511

Nasopharynx
See Pharynx
Biopsy .42804-42806
Hemorrhage 42970-42972
Unlisted Services and Procedures 42999

Natural Ostium
Sinus
    Maxillary 31000
    Sphenoid 31002

Navicular
Arthroplasty
    with Implant .25443
Fracture
    Closed Treatment 25622
    Open Treatment 25628
    with Manipulation 25624
Repair 25440

Neck
Angiography 70498, 70547-70549
Artery
    Ligation 37615
Biopsy 21550
Bypass Graft 35901
CAT Scan 70490-70492, 70498
Dissection, Radical
    See Radical Neck Dissection
Exploration
    Blood Vessel .35800
    Lymph Nodes 38542
Incision and Drainage
    Abscess 21501-21502
    Hematoma 21501-21502
Lipectomy, Suction Assisted 15876
Magnetic Resonance Angiography
(MRA) .70547-70549

Magnetic Resonance Imaging
(MRI) 70540-70543
Nerve
    Graft 64885-64886
Repair
    Blood Vessel .35201
      with Other Graft 35261
      with Vein Graft 35231
Skin
    Revision 15819
Tumor
    Excision 21555-21556
    Excision/Resection 21557
Ultrasound Exam 76536
Unlisted Services and Procedures,
Surgery 21899
Urinary Bladder
    See Bladder, Neck
Wound Exploration
    Penetrating .20100
X-Ray 70360

Neck Muscle
Division
    Scalenus Anticus 21700-21705
    Sternocleidomastoid 21720-21725

Necropsy
Coroner's Exam .88045
Forensic Exam .88040
Gross and Micro Exam 88020-88029
Gross Exam 88000-88016
Organ 88037
Regional 88036
Unlisted Services and Procedures 88099

Needle Biopsy
See Biopsy
Abdomen Mass .49180
Bone 20220-20225
Bone Marrow 38221
Breast 19100
CAT Scan Guidance 76360
Colon-Sigmoid
    Endoscopy 45342
Epididymis 54800
Esophagus
    Endoscopy 43232
Fluoroscopic Guidance 76003
Gastrointestinal, Upper
    Endoscopy 43242
Kidney 50200
Liver 47000-47001
Lung 32405
Lymph Nodes 38505
Mediastinum 32405
Muscle 20206
Pancreas 48102
Pleura 32400
Prostate 55700
Retroperitoneal Mass 49180
Salivary Gland .42400
Spinal Cord 62269
Testis 54500
Thyroid Gland 60100
Transbronchial .31629

Needle Localization
Breast
    Placement 19290-19291
    with Lesion Excision 19125-19126
Magnetic Resonance Guidance 76393

Needle Manometer Technique 20950

Needle Wire
Introduction
    Trachea 31730
Placement
    Breast 19290-19291

Neer Procedure 23470

Neisseria gonorrheae 87590-87592, 87850

Neisseria Meningitidis
Antibody 86741

Neobladder
Construction 51596

Neonatal Intensive Care
See Newborn Care
Initial 99295
Subsequent 99296-99298

Neoplasm
Cancer Photoradiation Therapy
    See Photochemotherapy
Cardiac
    See Heart, Tumor
Colon
    See Colon, Tumor
Esophageal
    See Tumor, Esophagus
Spinal Cord
    See Spinal Cord, Neoplasm
Unspecified Nature of Brain
    See Brain, Tumor

Neoplastic Growth
See Tumor

Nephelometry 83883

Nephrectomy
Donor 50300-50320, 50547
Laparoscopic 50545-50548
Partial 50240
Recipient 50340
with Ureters 50220-50236, 50546, 50548

Nephrolith
See Calculus, Removal, Kidney

Nephrolithotomy 50060-50075

Nephropexy 50400-50405

Nephroplasty
See Kidney, Repair

Nephropyeloplasty
See Pyeloplasty

Nephrorrhaphy 50500

Nephroscopy
See Endoscopy, Kidney

Nephrostogram 50394

Nephrostolithotomy
Percutaneous 50080-50081

Nephrostomy 50040
Change Tube 50398
Endoscopic 50570
Percutaneous 52334
with Drainage .50040
X-Ray with Contrast
    Guide Dilation 74485

Nephrostomy Tract
Establishment 50395

Nephrotomogram
See Nephrotomography

Nephrotomography 74415

Nephrotomy 50040-50045
with Exploration 50045

Nerve
Cranial
    See Cranial Nerve
Facial
    See Facial Nerve
Intercostal
    See Intercostal Nerve
Lingual
    See Lingual Nerve
Median
    See Median Nerve
Obturator
    See Obturator Nerve
Peripheral
    See Peripheral Nerve
Phrenic
    See Phrenic Nerve
Sciatic
    See Sciatic Nerve
Spinal
    See Spinal Nerve
Tibial
    See Tibial Nerve
Ulnar
    See Ulnar Nerve
Vestibular
    See Vestibular Nerve

Nerves
Anastomosis
    Facial to Hypoglossal 64868
    Facial to Phrenic 64870
    Facial to Spinal Accessory 64866
Avulsion .64732-64772
Biopsy 64795
Decompression 64702-64727
Destruction 64600-64680
    Laryngeal, Recurrent 31595
Foot
    Excision 28030
    Incision 28035
Graft 64885-64907

Direct Probe Detection
  Infectious Agent
    Bartonella henselae 87470
    Bartonella quintana 87470
    Borrelia burgdorferi 87475
    Candida species 87480
    Chlamydia pneumoniae 87485
    Chlamydia Trachomatis 87490
    Cytomegalovirus 87495
    Gardnerella Vaginalis 87510
    Hepatitis B Virus 87515
    Hepatitis C 87520
    Hepatitis G 87525
    Herpes Simplex Virus 87528
    Herpes Virus-6 87531
    HIV-1 87534
    HIV-2 87537
    Legionella Pneumophila 87540
    Multiple Organisms 87800
    Mycobacteria avium-intracellulare . .87560
    Mycobacteria species 87550
    Mycobacteria tuberculosis 87555
    Mycoplasma pneumoniae 87580
    Neisseria gonorrheae 87590
    Not Otherwise Specified 87797
    Papillomavirus, Human 87620
    Streptococcus, Group A 87650
Genotype Analysis
  Infectious Agent
    Hepatitis C Virus 87902
    HIV-1 87901
In Situ Hybridization 88365
Phenotype Analysis
  Infectious Agent
    HIV-1 Drug Resistance 87903-87904
Quantification
  Infectious Agent
    Bartonella henselae 87472
    Bartonella quintana 87472
    Borrelia burgdorferi 87477
    Candida species 87482
    Chlamydia pneumoniae 87487
    Chlamydia Trachomatis 87492
    Cytomegalovirus 87497
    Gardnerella Vaginalis 87512
    Hepatitis B Virus 87517
    Hepatitis C 87522
    Hepatitis G 87527
    Herpes Simplex Virus 87530
    Herpes Virus-6 87533
    HIV-1 87536
    HIV-2 87539
    Legionella Pneumophila 87542
    Mycobacteria avium-intracellulare . .87562
    Mycobacteria species 87552
    Mycobacteria tuberculosis 87557
    Mycoplasma pneumoniae 87582
    Neisseria gonorrheae 87592
    Not Otherwise Specified 87799
    Papillomavirus, Human 87622
    Streptococcus, Group A 87652

Nucleolysis, Intervertebral Disk
See Chemonucleolysis

Nucleotidase 83915

Nursemaid Elbow 24640

Nursing Facility Discharge Services
See Discharge Services, Nursing Facility

Nursing Facility Services
Care Plan Oversight Services 99379-99380
Comprehensive Assessments
  New or Established Patient 99301-99303
Discharge Services 99315-99316
Subsequent Care
  New or Established Patient 99311-99313
    See Domiciliary Services

Nutrition Therapy
Enteral 99560-99561
Group 97804
Initial Assessment 97802
Reassessment 97803
Total Parenteral 99562

Nystagmus Tests
See Vestibular Function Tests
Optokinetic 92534, 92544
Positional 92532, 92542
Spontaneous 92531, 92541

O

O2 Saturation
See Oxygen Saturation

Ober-Yount Procedure 27025
See Fasciotomy, Hip

Obliteration
Mastoid 69670

Obliteration, Total Excision of Vagina
See Excision, Vagina, Complete

Obliteration, Vaginal Vault
See Vagina, Closure

Oblongata, Medulla
See Medulla

Observation 99234-99236
See Evaluation and Management; Hospital Services

Obstetrical Care
Abortion
  Induced
    by Amniocentesis Injection . .59850-59852
      See Abortion; Cesarean Delivery;
      Ectopic Pregnancy
    by Dilation and Curettage 59840
    by Dilation and Evaluation 59841
  Missed
    First Trimester 59820
    Second Trimester 59821
  Spontaneous 59812
  Therapeutic 59840-59852
Antepartum Care 59425-59426

Cesarean Delivery 59618-59622
  Only 59514
  Postpartum Care 59515
  Routine 59510
  with Hysterectomy 59525
Curettage
  Hydatidiform Mole 59870
Evacuation
  Hydatidiform Mole 59870
External Cephalic Version 59412
Miscarriage
  Surgical Completion 59812-59821
Placenta Delivery 59414
Postpartum Care 59430, 59514
Septic Abortion 59830
Total (Global) 59400, 59610, 59618
Unlisted Services and Procedures . .59898-59899
Vaginal
  after Cesarean 59610-59614
Vaginal Delivery 59409-59410
  Delivery after Cesarean 59610-59614

Obstruction
See Occlusion

Obstruction Colon
See Colon, Obstruction

Obturator Nerve
Avulsion 64763-64766
Incision 64763-64766
Transection 64763-64766

Obturator Prosthesis 21076
Definitive 21080
Insertion
  Larynx 31527
Interim 21079

Occipital Nerve, Greater
Avulsion 64744
Incision 64744
Injection
  Anesthetic 64405
Transection .64744

Occlusion
Fallopian Tube
  Oviduct 58615
Penis
  Vein 37790

Occlusive Disease of Artery
See Repair, Artery; Revision

Occult Blood 82270
  by Hemoglobin Immunoassay 82274

Occupational Therapy
Evaluation 97003-97004

Ocular Implant 65175
See Orbital Implant
Insertion
  in Scleral Shell 65130
  Muscles, Not Attached 65135
  Muscles Attached 65140
Modification 65125
Reinsertion .65150
  with Foreign Material 65155
Removal 65175

Schlatter Total Gastrectomy
See Excision, Stomach, Total
Smithwick
See Excision, Nerve, Sympathetic
Winiwarter Cholecystoenterostomy
See Anastomosis, Gallbladder to Intestines

Operation Microscopes
See Operating Microscope

Operculectomy 41821

Operculum
See Gums

Ophthalmic Mucous Membrane Test 95060
See Allergy Tests

Ophthalmology
Unlisted Services and Procedures 92499
   See Ophthalmology, Diagnostic

Ophthalmology, Diagnostic
Color Vision Exam 92283
Computerized Scanning 92135
Computerized Screening 99172
Dark Adaptation 92284
Electro-oculography 92270
Electromyography, Needle 92265
Electroretinography 92275
Eye Exam
   Established Patient 92012-92014
   New Patient 92002-92004
   with Anesthesia 92018-92019
Glaucoma Provocative Test 92140
Gonioscopy 92020
Ocular Photography
   External 92285
   Internal 92286-92287
Ophthalmoscopy 92225-92226
   with Dynamometry 92260
   with Fluorescein Angiography 92235
   with Fluorescein Angioscopy 92230
   with Fundus Photography 92250
   with Indocyanine-green Angiography ..92240
Refractive Determination 92015
Sensorimotor Exam 92060
Tonography 92120
   with Provocation 92130
Tonometry
   Serial 92100
Visual Acuity Screen 99172-99173
Visual Field Exam 92081-92083
Visual Function Screen 99172

Ophthalmoscopy 92225-92226
See Ophthalmology, Diagnostic

Opiates 83925

Opinion, Second
See Confirmatory Consultations

Optic Nerve
Decompression.....................67570
   with Nasal/Sinus Endoscopy 31294

Optokinetic Nystagmus Test
See Nystagmus Tests, Optokinetic

Oral Lactose Tolerance Test 82951-82953
See Glucose, Tolerance Test

Oral Mucosa
See Mouth, Mucosa

Oral Surgical Splint 21085

Orbit
See Orbital Contents; Orbital Floor; Periorbital Region
Biopsy 61332
   Exploration 67450
   Fine Needle Aspiration or Orbital
   Contents 67415
   Orbitotomy without Bone Flap 67400
CAT Scan 70480-70482
Decompression.....................61330
   Bone Removal 67414, 67445
Exploration 61332, 67400, 67450
   Lesion
      Excision 61333
Fracture
   Closed Treatment
      without Manipulation 21400
      with Manipulation 21401
   Open Treatment 21406-21408
      Blowout Fracture 21385-21395
Incision and Drainage 67405, 67440
Injection
   Retrobulbar 67500-67505
   Tenon's Capsule 67515
Insertion
   Implant 67550
Lesion
   Excision 67412, 67420
Magnetic Resonance Imaging
(MRI) 70540-70543
Removal
   Decompression 67445
   Exploration 61334
   Foreign Body 61334, 67413, 67430
   Implant 67560
Sella Turcica 70482
Unlisted Services and Procedures 67599
X-Ray 70190-70200

Orbital Contents
Aspiration 67415

Orbital Floor
See Orbit; Periorbital Region
Fracture
   Blow Out 21385-21395

Orbital Hypertelorism
Osteotomy
   Periorbital 21260-21263

Orbital Implant
See Ocular Implant
Insertion 67550
Removal 67560

Orbital Prosthesis 21077

Orbital Rims
Reconstruction 21182-21184

Orbital Rim and Forehead
Reconstruction 21172-21180

Orbital Transplant...............67560

Orbital Walls
Reconstruction 21182-21184

Orbitocraniofacial Reconstruction
Secondary 21275

Orbitotomy
without Bone Flap
   for Exploration 67400
   with Drainage Only 67405
   with Removal Lesion 67412
with Bone Flap
   for Exploration 67450
   Lateral Approach 67420
   with Drainage 67440
   with Removal Foreign Body 67430
   with Removal of Bone for
   Decompression 67445
with Removal Foreign Body 67413
with Removal of Bone for Decompression .67414

Orbit Area
Reconstruction
   Secondary 21275

Orbit Wall
Decompression
   with Nasal/Sinus Endoscopy ...31292-31293

Orchidectomies
See Excision, Testis

Orchidopexy
See Orchiopexy

Orchidoplasty
See Repair, Testis

Orchiectomy
Laparoscopic 54690
Partial 54522
Radical
   Abdominal Exploration 54535
   Inguinal Approach 54530
Simple 54520

Orchiopexy
Abdominal Approach 54650
Inguinal Approach 54640
Intra-Abdominal Testis 54692

Orchioplasty
See Repair, Testis

Organic Acids 83918-83921

Organ Grafting
See Transplantation

Organ or Disease-Oriented Panel
Electrolyte 80051
General Health Panel 80050
Hepatic Function Panel 80076
Hepatitis Panel 80074
Lipid Panel 80061
Metabolic
   Basic 80048
   Comprehensive 80053

Thoracic
    Anterior Approach 22222
    Posterior/Posterolateral Approach ..22212
with Graft
    Reconstruction
      Periorbital Region 21267-21268

Os Calcis Fracture
See Calcaneus, Fracture

Otolaryngology
Diagnostic
    Exam Under Anesthesia 92502

Otomy
See Incision

Otoplasty 69300

Otorhinolaryngology
Unlisted Services and Procedures 92599

Ouchterlony
Immunodiffusion 86331

Outer Ear
See Ear, Outer

Outpatient Visit
See History and Physical; Office and/or Other
Outpatient Services

Output, Cardiac
See Cardiac Output

Ova
Smear 87177

Oval Window
Repair Fistula 69666

Oval Window Fistula
See Fistula, Oval Window

Ovarian Cyst
See Cyst, Ovarian; Ovary, Cyst

Ovarian Vein Syndrome
Ureterolysis 50722

Ovariectomies
See Oophorectomy

Ovariolysis 58740

Ovary
Abscess
    Incision and Drainage 58820-58822
      Abdominal Approach 58822
Biopsy 58900
Cyst
    Incision and Drainage 58800-58805
Excision 58662, 58720
    Cyst 58925
    Partial
      Ouphorectomy 58661, 58940
      Ovarian Malignancy 58943
      Peritoneal Malignancy 58943
      Tubal Malignancy 58943
      Wedge Resection 58920
    Total 58940-58943
Laparoscopy 58660-58662, 58679

Lysis
    Adhesions 58660, 58740
Radical Resection 58950-58952
Transposition 58825
Tumor
    Resection 58950-58954
Unlisted Services and Procedures ..58679, 58999
Wedge Resection 58920

Oviduct
Anastomosis 58750
Chromotubation 58350
Ectopic Pregnancy 59120-59121
Excision 58700-58720
Fulguration
    Laparoscopic 58670
Hysterosalpingography 74740
Laparoscopy 58679
Ligation 58600-58611
Lysis
    Adhesions 58740
Occlusion 58615
    Laparoscopic 58671
Repair 58752
    Anastomosis 58750
    Create Stoma 58770
Unlisted Services and Procedures ..58679, 58999
X-Ray with Contrast 74740

Ovocyte
See Oocyte

Ovulation Tests 84830

Ovum Implantation
See Implantation

Ovum Transfer Surgery
See GIFT

Oxalate 83945

Oxidase, Ceruloplasmin
See Ceruloplasmin

Oxidoreductase, Alcohol-Nad+
See Antidiuretic Hormone

Oximetry (Noninvasive)
See Pulmonology, Diagnostic
Blood O2 Saturation
    Ear or Pulse 94760-94762

Oxoisomerase
See Phosphohexose Isomerase

Oxosteroids
See Ketosteroids

Oxycodinone 80102-80103, 83925

Oxygenation, Extracorporeal
Membrane
See Extracorporeal Membrane Oxygenation

Oxygen Saturation 82805-82810

Oxyproline
See Hydroxyproline

Oxytocin Stress Test, Fetal 59020

P-Acetamidophenol
See Acetaminophen

Pacemaker, Heart
See Defibrillator, Heart
Conversion 33214
Electronic Analysis 93641-93642
    Antitachycardia System 93724
    Dual Chamber 93731-93732
    Single Chamber 93734-93735
Insertion 33200-33208
    Electrode 33210-33211, 33216-33217
    Pulse Generator Only 33212-33213
Removal 33233-33237
    via Thoracotomy 33236-33237
Repair
    Electrode 33218-33220
Replacement
    Catheter 33210
    Electrode 33210-33211, 33217
    Insertion 33200-33208
    Pulse Generator 33212-33213
Revise Pocket
    Chest 33222
Telephonic Analysis 93733, 93736
Upgrade 33214

Packing
Nasal Hemorrhage 30901-30906

Pain Management 99551
See Injection, Chemotherapy
Epidural/Intrathecal 62351, 62360-62362,
                        99552
Intravenous Therapy 90783-90784

Palatal Augmentation
Prosthesis 21082

Palatal Lift Prosthesis 21083

Palate
Abscess
    Incision and Drainage 42000
Biopsy 42100
Excision 42120, 42145
Fracture
    Closed Treatment 21421
    Open Treatment 21422-21423
Lesion
    Destruction 42160
    Excision 42104-42120
Prosthesis 42280-42281
Reconstruction
    Lengthening 42226-42227
Repair
    Cleft Palate 42200-42225
    Laceration 42180-42182
    Vomer Flap 42235
Unlisted Services and Procedures 42299

Palate, Cleft
See Cleft Palate

Percutaneous Lysis 62263

Percutaneous Nephrostomies
See Nephrostomy, Percutaneous

Percutaneous Transluminal Angioplasty
Artery
  Aortic 35472
  Brachiocephalic 35475
  Coronary 92982-92984
  Femoral-Popliteal 35474
  Iliac 35473
  Pulmonary 92997-92998
  Renal 35471
  Tibioperoneal 35470
  Visceral 35471
Venous 35476

Percutaneous Transluminal Coronary Angioplasty
See Percutaneous Transluminal Angioplasty

Pereyra Procedure 51845, 57289, 58267

Performance Test 96100
See Physical Medicine/Therapy/Occupational Therapy
Physical Therapy 97750

Perfusion
Myocardial 78460-78465, 78478-78480
  Imaging 78466-78469
Positron Emission Tomography (PET)
  Myocardial Imaging 78491-78492

Perfusion, Intracranial Arterial
Thrombolysis 61624

Perfusion Pump
See Infusion Pump

Pericardectomies
See Excision, Pericardium

Pericardial Cyst
See Cyst, Pericardial

Pericardial Sac
Drainage 32659

Pericardial Window
for Drainage 33025

Pericardial Window Technic
See Pericardiostomy

Pericardiectomy
Complete 33030-33031
Subtotal 33030-33031
Total
  Endoscopic 32660

Pericardiocentesis 33010-33011
Ultrasound Guidance 76930

Pericardiostomy
Tube 33015

Pericardiotomy
Removal
  Clot 33020
  Foreign Body 33020

Pericardium
Cyst
  Excision 32661, 33050
Excision 32659, 33030-33031
Incision
  Removal
    Clot 33020
    Foreign Body 33020
  with Tube 33015
Incision and Drainage 33025
Puncture Aspiration 33010-33011
Removal
  Clot
    Endoscopic 32658
  Foreign Body
    Endoscopic 32658
Tumor
  Excision 32661, 33050

Peridural Anesthesia
See Anesthesia, Epidural

Peridural Injection
See Epidural, Injection

Perineal Prostatectomy
See Prostatectomy, Perineal

Perineoplasty 56810

Perineorrhaphy
Repair
  Rectocele 57250

Perineum
Abscess
  Incision and Drainage 56405
Colposcopy 99170
Removal
  Prosthesis 53442
Repair 56810
X-Ray with Contrast 74775

Perionychia
See Paronychia

Periorbital Region
Reconstruction
  Osteotomy with Graft 21267-21268
Repair-Osteotomy 21260-21263

Peripheral Artery Disease (PAD) Rehabilitation 93668

Peripheral Nerve
Repair/Suture
  Major 64856, 64859

Periprosthetic Capsulectomy
Breast 19371

Peristaltic Pumps
See Infusion Pump

Peritoneal Dialysis 90945-90947

Peritoneal Free Air
See Pneumoperitoneum

Peritoneal Lavage 49080

Peritoneocentesis 49080-49081

Peritoneoscopy
See Endoscopy, Peritoneum

Peritoneum
Abscess
  Incision and Drainage 49020
    Percutaneous 49021
Chemotherapy Administration 96445
  See Chemotherapy
Endoscopy
  Biopsy 47561
  Drainage
    Lymphocele 49323
    X-Ray 47560
Exchange
  Drainage Catheter 49423
Injection
  Contrast
    via Catheter 49424
Ligation
  Shunt 49428
Removal
  Cannula/Catheter 49422
  Foreign Body 49085
  Shunt 49429
Tumor
  Resection 58950-58954
Unlisted Services and Procedures 49999
Venous Shunt
  Injection 49427
X-Ray 74190

Persistent, Omphalomesenteric Duct
See Diverticulum, Meckel's

Persistent Truncus Arteriosus
See Truncus Arteriosus

Personal Care
See Self Care

Pessary
Insertion 57160

Pesticides
Chlorinated Hydrocarbons 82441

PET
See Positron Emission Tomography

Petrous Temporal
Excision
  Apex 69530

Peyronie Disease
Injection 54200
Surgical Exposure 54205
with Graft 54110-54112

pH
See Blood
Other Fluid 83986
Urine 83986

Phosphokinase, Creatine
See CPK

Phospholipase C
See Tissue Typing

Phospholipid Antibody 86147

Phosphomonoesterase
See Phosphatase

Phosphoric Monoester Hydrolases
See Phosphatase

Phosphorus 84100
Urine 84105

Phosphotransferase, ADP Phosphocreatine
See CPK

Photochemotherapies, Extracorporeal
See Photopheresis

Photochemotherapy 96910-96913
See Dermatology
Endoscopic Light 96570-96571

Photocoagulation
Endolaser Panretinal
    Vitrectomy 67040
Focal Endolaser
    Vitrectomy 67040
Iridoplasty 66762
Lesion
    Cornea 65450
    Retina 0017T, 67210, 67227-67228
Retinal Detachment
    Prophylaxis 67145
    Repair 67105

Photodensity
Radiographic
    Absorptiometry 76078

Photodynamic Therapy
External 96567

Photography, Ocular
See Ophthalmosocpy, Diagnostic

Photopheresis
Extracorporeal 36522

Photophoresis
See Actinotherapy; Photochemotherapy

Photoradiation Therapies
See Actinotherapy

Photosensitivity Testing 95056
See Allergy Tests

Phototherapies
See Actinotherapy

Phototherapy, Ultraviolet
See Actinotherapy

Photo Patch
Allergy Test 95052
    See Allergy Tests

Phrenic Nerve
Anastomosis
    to Facial Nerve 64870
Avulsion 64746
Incision 64746
Injection
    Anesthetic 64410
Transection 64746

Physical Medicine/Therapy/Occupational Therapy
See Neurology, Diagnostic
Activities of Daily Living 97535, 99509
Aquatic Therapy
    with Exercises 97113
Athletic Training
    Evaluation 97005
    Re-evaluation 97006
Check-Out
    Orthotic/Prosthetic 97703
Cognitive Skills Development 97532
Community/Work Reintegration 97537
Evaluation 97001-97002
Kinetic Therapy 97530
Manual Therapy 97140
Modalities
    Contrast Baths 97034
    Diathermy Treatment 97024
    Electric Simulation
      Unattended 97014
    Electric Stimulation
      Attended, Manual 97032
    Hot or Cold Pack 97010
    Hydrotherapy (Hubbard Tank) 97036
    Infrared Light Treatment 97026
    Iontophoresis 97033
    Microwave Therapy 97020
    Paraffin Bath 97018
    Traction 97012
    Ultrasound 97035
    Ultraviolet Light 97028
    Unlisted Services and Procedures 97039
    Vasopneumatic Device 97016
    Whirlpool Therapy 97022
Orthotics Training 97504
Osteopathic Manipulation 98925-98929
Procedures
    Aquatic Therapy 97113
    Gait Training 97116
    Group Therapeutic 97150
    Massage Therapy 97124
    Neuromuscular Reeducation 97112
    Physical Performance Test 97750
    Therapeutic Exercises 97110
    Traction Therapy 97140
    Work Hardening 97545-97546
Prosthetic Training 97520
Sensory Integration 97533
Therapeutic Activities 97530
Unlisted Services and Procedures ..97139, 97799
Wheelchair Management/Propulsion 97542
Work Reintegration 97537

Physical Therapy
See Physical Medicine/Therapy/Occupational Therapy

Physician Services
Care Plan Oversight Services 99374-99380
    Home Health Agency Care 99374
    Hospice 99377-99378
    Nursing Facility 99379-99380
Direction, Advanced Life Support 99288
Prolonged
    without Direct Patient Contact .99358-99359
    with Direct Patient Contact 99354-99357
      Outpatient/Office 99354-99355
    with Direct Patient Services
      Inpatient 99356-99357
Standby 99360
Supervision, Care Plan Oversight
    Services 99374-99380

Pierce Ears 69090

Piercing of Ear Lobe
See Ear Lobes, Pierce

Piles
See Hemorrhoids

Pilonidal Cyst
Excision 11770-11772
Incision and Drainage 10080-10081

Pin
See Wire
Insertion/Removal
    Skeletal Traction 20650
Prophylactic Treatment
    Femur 27187
    Humerus 24498
    Shoulder 23490-23491

Pinch Graft 15050

Pinna
See Ear, External

Pinworms
Examination 87172

Pirogoff Procedure 27888

Pituitary Epidermoid Tumor
See Craniopharyngioma

Pituitary Gland
Excision 61546-61548
Tumor
    Excision 61546-61548

Pituitary Growth Hormone
See Growth Hormone

Pituitary Lactogenic Hormone
See Prolactin

Pituitectomy
See Excision, Pituitary Gland

PKU
See Phenylalanine

Pneumonology
See Pulmonology

Pneumonolysis 32940
Intrapleural 32652
Open Intrapleural 32124

Pneumonostomy 32200-32201

Pneumonotomy
See Incision, Lung

Pneumoperitoneum 49400

Pneumoplethysmography
Ocular 93875

Pneumothorax
Chemical Pleurodesis 32005
Pleural Scarification for Repeat 32215
Therapeutic
    Injection Intrapleural Air 32960
Thoracentesis with Tube Insertion 32002

Polio
Antibody 86658
Vaccine 90712-90713

Poliovirus Vaccine, Inactivated
See Vaccines

Pollicization
Digit 26550

Polya Gastrectomy
See Gastrectomy, Partial

Polydactylism
See Supernumerary Digit

Polydactylous Digit
Reconstruction 26587
Repair 26587

Polydactyly, Toes 28344

Polymerase Chain Reaction 83898

Polyp
Antrochoanal
    Removal 31032
Esophagus
    Ablation 43228
Nose
    Excision
        Endoscopic 31237-31240
        Extensive 30115
        Simple 30110
Sphenoid Sinus
    Removal 31051
Urethra
    Excision 53260

Polypectomy
Nose
    Endoscopic......................31237
Uterus 58558

Polypeptide, Vasoactive Intestinal
See Vasoactive Intestinal Peptide

Polysomnography ...95808-95811, 99508

Polyuria Test
See Water Load Test

Pomeroy's Operation
See Tubal Ligation

Pooling
Blood Products 86965

Popliteal Arteries
See Artery, Popliteal

Popliteal Synovial Cyst
See Baker's Cyst

Poradenitistras
See Lymphogranuloma Venereum

Porphobilinogen
Urine 84106-84110

Porphyrins
Feces 84126-84127
Urine 84119-84120

Porphyrin Precursors 82135

PORP (Partial Ossicular Replacement Prosthesis) 69633, 69637

Portal Vein
See Vein, Hepatic Portal

Porter-Silber Test
See Corticosteroid, Blood

Portoenterostomies, Hepatic
See Hepaticoenterostomy

Portoenterostomy 47701

Port Film 77417

Posadas-Wernicke Disease
See Coccidioidomycosis

Positional Nystagmus Test
See Nystagmus Tests, Positional

Positive-Pressure Breathing, Inspiratory
See Intermittent Positive Pressure Breathing (IPPB)

Positive End Expiratory Pressure
See Pressure Breathing, Positive

Positron Emission Tomography (PET)
Brain 78608-78609
Heart 78459
Myocardial Imaging
    Perfusion Study 78491-78492
Tumor 78810

Post-Op Visit 99024

Postauricular Fistula
See Fistula, Postauricular

Postcaval Ureter
See Retrocaval Ureter

Postmortem
See Autopsy

Postoperative Wound Infection
Incision and Drainage 10180

Postop Vas Reconstruction
See Vasovasorrhaphy

Postpartum Care
Cesarean Delivery 59515
    after Attempted Vaginal Delivery 59622
    Previous 59610, 59614-59618, 59622
Vaginal Delivery 59430
    after Previous Cesarean Delivery 59614

Potassium 84132
Urine 84133

Potential, Auditory Evoked
See Auditory Evoked Potentials

Potential, Evoked
See Evoked Potential

Potts-Smith Procedure 33762

Pouch, Kock
See Kock Pouch

PPP
See Fibrin Degradation Products

PRA
See Cytotoxic Screen

Prealbumin 84134

Prebeta Lipoproteins
See Lipoprotein, Blood

Pregl's Test
See Cystourethroscopy, Catheterization, Urethral

Pregnancy
Abortion
    Induced 59855-59857
        by Amniocentesis Injection ..59850-59852
        by Dilation and Curettage 59840
        by Dilation and Evaluation 59841
    Septic 59830
    Therapeutic
        by Dilation and Curettage 59851
        by Hysterectomy 59852
        by Saline 59850
Cesarean Delivery 59618-59622
    Only 59514
    Postpartum Care 59514-59515
    Routine Care 59510
    Vaginal Birth After 59610-59614
    with Hysterectomy 59525
Ectopic
    Abdominal 59130
    Cervix 59140
    Interstitial
        Partial Resection Uterus 59136
        Total Hysterectomy 59135
    Laparoscopy
        without Salpingectomy and/or
        Oophorectomy 59150
        with Salpingectomy and/or
        Oophorectomy 59151

Protein
C-Reactive 86140-86141
Glycated 82985
Myelin Basic 83873
Osteocalcin 83937
Prealbumin 84134
Serum .84160-84165
Total 84155
Western Blot 84181-84182, 88372

Protein Analysis, Tissue
Western Blot 88371

Protein Blotting
See Western Blot

Protein C Activator 85337

Protein C Antigen 85302

Protein C Assay 85303

Protein C Resistance Assay 85307

Protein S
Assay 85306
Total 85305

Prothrombase
See Thrombokinase

Prothrombin .85210

Prothrombinase
See Thromboplastin

Prothrombin Time 85610-85611

Prothrombokinase 85230

Protime
See Prothrombin Time

Proton Treatment Delivery
Complex 77525
Intermediate 77523
Simple 77520-77522

Protoporphyrin 84202-84203

Protozoa
Antibody 86753

Provitamin A
See Vitamin, A

Provocation Test
for Allergies 95078
    See Allergy Tests
for Glaucoma 92140

Provocation Tonography 92130

Prower Factor
See Stuart-Prower Factor

PSA
See Prostate Specific Antigen

Pseudocyst, Pancreas
See Pancreas, Pseudocyst

PSG
See Polysomnography

Psoriasis Treatment 96910-96913
See Dermatology; Photochemotherapy

Psychiatric Diagnosis
Evaluation of Records or Reports 90885
Interventional Evaluation
    Interactive 90802
Interview and Evaluation 90801-90802
Psychological Testing 96100
Unlisted Services and Procedures 90899

Psychiatric Treatment
See Psychotherapy
Biofeedback Training 90875-90876
Consultation with Family 90887
Drug Management 90862
Electroconvulsive Therapy 90870-90871
Environmental Intervention 90882
Family 90846-90849, 99510
Group 90853-90857
Hypnotherapy .90880
Individual
    Insight-Oriented
        Home Visit 99510
        Hospital or Residential Care . .90816-90822
        Office or Outpatient 90804-90809
    Interactive
        Home Visit 99510
        Hospital or Residential Care . .90823-90829
        Office or Outpatient 90810-90815
Narcosynthesis Analysis 90865
Psychoanalysis 90845
Report Preparation 90889
Residential
    Facility Care 90816-90829
Unlisted Services and Procedures 90899

Psychoanalysis 90845

Psychophysiologic Feedback
See Biofeedback

Psychotherapy
Family 90846-90849, 99510
Group 90853-90857
    Insight-Oriented
        Hospital or Residential Care . .90816-90822
        Office or Outpatient 90804-90809
    Interactive
        Hospital or Residential Care . .90823-90829
        Office or Outpatient 90810-90815

PTA 85270

PTA (Factor XI)
See Clotting Factor

PTC Factor 85250

PTCA
See Percutaneous Transluminal Angioplasty

Pteroylglutamic Acid
See Folic Acid

Pterygium
Excision 65420
    with Graft 65426

Pterygomaxillary Fossa
Incision 31040

Pterygopalatine Ganglion
See Sphenopalatine Ganglion

PTH
See Parathormone

Ptosis
See Blepharoptosis; Procidentia

PTT
See Thromboplastin, Partial, Time

Ptyalectasis
See Dilation, Salivary Duct

Pubic Symphysis 27282

Pubis
Craterization 27070
Cyst
    Excision 27065-27067
Excision 27070
Saucerization .27070
Tumor
    Excision 27065-27067

Pudendal Nerve
Avulsion 64761
Destruction 64630
Incision 64761
Injection
    Anesthetic .64430
    Neurolytic .64630
Transection 64761

Puestow Procedure 48180

Pulled Elbow
See Nursemaid Elbow

Pulmonary Artery 33690
Catheterization
    See Catheterization, Pulmonary Artery
Embolism 33910-33916
    Excision 33910-33916
Percutaneous Transluminal
Angioplasty 92997-92998
Reimplantation 33788
Repair 33690, 33917-33920
    Reimplantation 33788
Shunt
    from Aorta 33755-33762, 33924
    from Vena Cava 33766-33767
    Subclavian .33750
Transection 33922

Pulmonary Function Test
See Pulmonology, Diagnostic

Pulmonary Haemorrhage
See Hemorrhage, Lung

Pulmonary Perfusion Imaging
Nuclear Medicine 78588

Pulmonary Valve
Incision .33470-33474
Repair 33470-33474
Replacement 33475

Pulmonary Vein
Repair 33730

Pulmonology
Diagnostic
   Airway Closing Volume 94370
   Bronchodilation 94664-94665
   Carbon Dioxide Response Curve 94400
   Carbon Monoxide Diffusion Capacity . .94720
   Expired Gas Analysis 94250
      CO2 94770
      O2 and CO2 94681
      O2 Update, Direct 94680
      O2 Uptake, Indirect 94690
   Flow-Volume Loop 94375
   Functional Residual Capacity 94240
   Function Study 78596
   Hemoglobin O2 Affinity 82820
   Hypoxia Response Curve 94450
   Maldistribution of Inspired Air 94350
   Maximum Breathing Capacity 94200
   Maximum Voluntary Ventilation 94200
   Membrane Compliance 94750
   Membrane Diffusion Capacity 94725
   Nitrogen Washout Curve 94350
   Oximetry
      Ear or Pulse 94760-94762
   Resistance to Airflow 94360
   Spirometry 94010-94070
      Evaluation 94010-94070
      Patient Initiated with
      Bronchospasm 94014-94016
   Sputum Mobilization with
   Inhalants 94664-94665
   Stress Test 94621
   Stress Test, Pulmonary 94620
   Thoracic Gas Volume 94260
Therapeutic
   Expired Gas Analysis 94250
   Inhalation
      Pentamidine 94642, 99563
   Inhalation Treatment . . .94640, 94664-94665,
                         99503
   Manipulation of Chest Wall 94667-94668
   Pressure Ventilation
      Negative CNPB 94662
      Positive CPAP 94660
      Positive IPPB 94650-94652
   Unlisted Services and Procedures 94799
   Ventilation Assist 94656-94657, 99504
Unlisted Services and Procedures 94799

Pulse Generator
Electronic Analysis 95970-95971
Heart
   Insertion/Replacement 33212-33213

Pulse Rate Increased
See Tachycardia

Pump
See Chemotherapy, Pump Services; Infusion
Pump

Pump, Infusion
See Infusion Pump

Pump Services
Oxygenator/Heat Exchanger 99190-99192

Pump Stomach for Poison 91105

Punch Graft 15775-15776

Puncture
Artery 36600
Chest
   Drainage 32000-32002
Cisternal
   See Cisternal Puncture
Lumbar
   See Spinal Tap
Lung 32420
Pericardium 33010-33011
Pleural Cavity
   Drainage 32000-32002
Skull
   Drain Fluid 61000-61020
      Cistern 61050
   Inject Cistern 61055
   Inject Ventricle 61026
   Shunt
      Drain Fluid 61070
      Injection 61070
Spinal Cord
   Diagnostic .62270
   Drain Fluid .62272
   Lumbar 62270
Tracheal
   Aspiration and/or Injection 31612

Puncture Aspiration
Abscess
   Skin 10160
Bulla 10160
Cyst
   Breast 19000-19001
   Skin 10160
Hematoma 10160

Puncturing
See Puncture

Pure-Tone Audiometry
See Audiometry, Pure Tone

Pustules
Removal 10040

Putti-Platt Procedure 23450

PUVA
See Dermatology; Photochemotherapy;
Ultraviolet Light Therapy

Pyelogram
See Urography, Intravenous; Urography,
Retrograde

Pyelography 74400, 74425
Injection 50394

Pyelolithotomy 50130
Anatrophic 50075
Coagulum 50130

Pyeloplasty 50400-50405, 50544
Repair
   Horseshoe Kidney 50540
Secondary 50405

Pyeloscopy
with Cystourethroscopy 52351
   Biopsy 52354
   Destruction 52354
   Lithotripsy 52353
   Removal
      Calculus 52352
   Tumor Excision 52355

Pyelostogram 50394

Pyelostolithotomy
Percutaneous 50080-50081

Pyelostomy 50125, 50400-50405
Change Tube .50398

Pyelotomy
Complicated .50135
Endoscopic 50570
Exploration 50120
with Drainage 50125
with Removal Calculus 50130

Pyeloureterogram
Antegrade 50394

Pyeloureteroplasty
See Pyeloplasty

Pyloric Sphincter
Incision 43520
Reconstruction 43800

Pyloromyotomy 43520
with Gastrectomy 43639

Pyloroplasty 43800
with Gastrectomy 43639
with Vagotomy 43640

Pyothorax
See Abscess, Thorax

Pyridoxal Phosphate 84207

Pyrophosphate, Adenosine
See Adenosine Diphosphate

Pyrophosphorylase, Udp Galactose
See Galactose-1-Phosphate, Uridyl Transferase

Pyruvate 84210-84220

P & P
See Proconvertin

P B Antibodies
See Antibody, Heterophile

Q

Quadriceps Repair 27430

Quick Test
See Prothrombin Time

Quinidine
Assay 80194

Quinine 84228

Q Fever 86000, 86638

Q Fever ab
See Antibody, Coxiella Burnetii

R

Rabies Vaccine
See Vaccines

Rachicentesis
See Spinal Tap

Radial Arteries
See Artery, Radial

Radial Head, Subluxation
See Nursemaid Elbow

Radial Keratotomy 65771

Radiation
See Irradiation

Radiation, X
See X-Ray

Radiation Physics
Consultation 77336-77370
Unlisted Services and Procedures 77399

Radiation Therapy 77280-77295
CAT Scan Guidance 76370
Consultation
   Radiation Physics 77336-77370
Dose Plan 77300, 77305-77331
   Brachytherapy 77326-77328
   Intensity Modulation 77301
   Teletherapy 77305-77321
Field Set-up 77280-77295
Planning 77261-77263, 77299
Special 77470
Stereotactic 77432
Treatment Delivery
   Intensity Modulation 77418
   Proton Beam 77520-77525
   Single 77402-77406
   Superficial 77401
   Three or More Areas 77412-77416
   Two Areas 77407-77411
   Weekly 77427

Treatment Device 77332-77334
Treatment Management
   One or Two Fractions Only 77431
   Unlisted Services and Procedures 77499
   Weekly 77427

Radical Excision of Lymph Nodes
See Excision, Lymph Nodes, Radical

Radical Mastectomies, Modified
See Mastectomy, Modified Radical

Radical Neck Dissection
Laryngectomy 31365-31368
Pharyngolaryngectomy 31390-31395
with Auditory Canal Surgery 69155
with Thyroidectomy 60254
with Tongue Excision 41135, 41145,
                                   41153-41155

Radical Resection
See Resection, Radical
Abdomen 51597
Acetabulum 27076
Ankle 27615
Arm, Lower 25077
Calcaneus 27647
Elbow
   Capsule, Soft Tissue, Bone
     with Contracture Release 24149
Face 21015
Fibula 27646
Finger 26117
Foot 28046
Forearm 25077
Hand 26115
Hip
   Soft Tissue 27049
   Tumor or Infection 27075-27076
Humerus 23220-23222
Innominate 27077
Ischial 27078-27079
Knee 27329
Leg
   Lower 27615
   Upper 27329
Metacarpal 26250-26255
Metatarsal 28173
Mouth
   with Tongue Excision 41150, 41155
Ovarian Tumor
   Bilateral Salpingo-Oophorectomy-
   Omentectomy 58950-58954
   with Radical Dissection for
   Debulking 58952-58954
   with Total Abdominal Hysterectomy . .58951,
                             58953-58954
Pelvis
   Soft Tissue 27049
Peritoneal Tumor
   Bilateral Salpingo-Oophorectomy-
   Omentectomy 58952-58954
   with Radical Dissection for
   Debulking 58952-58954
Phalanges
   Finger 26260-26262
   Toe 28175
Radius 25170
Scalp 21015

Scapula 23210
Shoulder 23077
Sternum 21630-21632
Talus
   Tumor 27647
Tarsal 28171
Tibia 27645
Tonsil 42842-42845
Tumor
   Back/Flank 21935
   Femur 27365
   Knee 27329, 27365
   Leg, Upper 27329
   Neck 21557
   Thorax 21557
Ulna 25170
Wrist 25077

Radical Vaginal Hysterectomy
See Hysterectomy, Vaginal, Radical

Radical Vulvectomy
See Vulvectomy, Radical

Radio-Cobalt B12 Schilling Test
See Vitamin, B12, Absorption Study

**Radioactive Colloid
Therapy** 79200-79300

Radioactive Substance
Insertion
   Kidney 50578
   Prostate 55860
   Ureteral Endoscopic 50978
   Urethral Endoscopic 50959

Radiocarpal Joint
Arthrotomy 25040
Dislocation
   Closed Treatment 25660

Radiocinematographies
See Cineradiography

Radioelement
Application 77761-77778
   Surface 77789
   with Ultrasound 76965
Handling 77790
Infusion 77750

Radioelement Substance
Catheterization 55859
Catheter Placement
   Bronchus 31643

Radiography
See Radiology, Diagnostic; X-Ray

Radioimmunosorbent Test
See Gammaglobulin, Blood

Radioisotope Brachytherapy
See Brachytherapy

Radioisotope Scan
See Nuclear Medicine

Radiological Marker
Preoperative Placement
   Excision of Breast Lesion 19125-19126

Radiology

Diagnostic
　Unlisted Services and Procedures 76499
Examination 70030
　Stress Views 76006
Therapeutic
　See Specific Procedure
　　Field Set-up 77280-77290
　　Planning 77261-77263, 77299
　　Port Film 77417

Radionuclide CAT Scan

See Emission Computerized Tomography

Radionuclide Imaging

See Nuclear Medicine

Radionuclide Therapy

Intra-articular 79440
Intravascular 79420
Leukemia 79100
Other 79400
Polycythemia Vera 79100
Thyroid Gland 79000-79035
Unlisted Services and Procedures 79999

Radionuclide Tomography, Single-Photon Emission-Computed

See SPECT

Radiopharmaceutical Therapy

Heart 79440
Intravascular 79420
Leukemia 79100
Other 79400
Polycythemia Vera 79100
Thyroid Gland 79020-79035
Unlisted Services and Procedures 79999

Radiotherapeutic

See Radiation Therapy

Radiotherapies

See Irradiation

Radiotherapy, Surface

See Application, Radioelement, Surface

Radioulnar Joint

Arthrodesis
　with Resection of Ulna 25830
Dislocation
　Closed Treatment 25675
　Open Treatment 25676
　Percutaneous Fixation 25671

Radius

See Arm, Lower; Elbow; Ulna
Arthroplasty 24365
　with Implant 24366, 25441
Craterization 24145, 25151
Cyst
　Excision 24125-24126, 25120-25126
Diaphysectomy 24145, 25151
Dislocation
　Partial 24640
　Subluxate 24640
　with Fracture
　　Closed Treatment 24620
　　Open Treatment 24635

Excision 24130, 24136, 24145, 24152-24153
　Epiphyseal Bar 20150
　Partial 25145
　Styloid Process 25230
Fracture 25605
　Closed Treatment 25500-25505, 25520,
　　　　　　　　　　　　　　　25600-25605
　　without Manipulation 25600
　　with Manipulation 25605
　Distal 25600-25611
　　Open Treatment 25620
　Head/Neck
　　Closed Treatment 24650-24655
　　Open Treatment 24665-24666
　Open Treatment 25515, 25525-25526,
　　　　　　　　　　　　　　　25574
　　Percutaneous Fixation 25611
　Shaft 25500-25526
　　Open Treatment 25574
　　with Ulna 25560-25565
　　　Open Treatment 25575
Implant
　Removal 24164
Incision and Drainage 25035
Osteomyelitis 24136, 24145
Osteoplasty 25390-25393
Prophylactic Treatment 25490, 25492
Repair
　Epiphyseal Arrest 25450-25455
　Epiphyseal Separation
　　Closed 25600
　　Closed with Manipulation 25605
　　Open Treatment 25620
　　Percutaneous Fixation 25611
　Malunion or Nonunion 25400, 25415
　Osteotomy 25350-25355, 25370-25375
　　and Ulna 25365
　　with Graft 25405, 25420-25426
Saucerization 24145, 25151
Sequestrectomy 24136, 25145
Tumor
　Cyst 24120
　Excision . .24125-24126, 25120-25126, 25170

Ramstedt Operation

See Pyloromyotomy

Ramus Anterior, Nervus Thoracicus

See Intercostal Nerve

Range of Motion Test

Extremities or Trunk 95851
Eye 92018-92019
Hand 95852

Rapid Heart Rate

See Tachycardia

Rapid Plasma Reagin Test 86592-86593

Rapid Test for Infection 86308, 86403-86406

Monospot Test 86308

Rapoport Test 52005

Raskind Procedure 33735-33737

Rathke Pouch Tumor

See Craniopharyngioma

Rat Typhus

See Murine Typhus

Rays, Roentgen

See X-Ray

Raz Procedure 51845

See Repair, Bladder, Neck

RBC

See Red Blood Cell (RBC)

RBC ab

See Antibody, Red Blood Cell

Reaction

Lip
　without Reconstruction 40530

Reaction, Polymerase Chain

See Polymerase Chain Reaction

Realignment

Femur
　with Osteotomy 27454
Knee
　Extensor 27422

Receptor

See CD4; Estrogen, Receptor; FC Receptor; Progesterone Receptors

Receptor Assay

Hormone 84233-84235
Non Hormone 84238

Recession

Gastrocnemius
　Leg, Lower 27687

Reconstruction

See Revision
Acetabulum 27120-27122
Anal
　Congenital Absence 46730-46740
　Fistula 46742
　Graft 46753
　Sphincter 46750-46751, 46760-46762
　with Implant .46762
Ankle 27700-27703
Apical-Aortic Conduit 33404
Atrial 33253
Auditory Canal, External 69310-69320
Bile Duct
　Anastomosis 47800
Bladder
　and Urethra 51800-51820
　from Colon 50810
　from Intestines 50820, 51960
Breast 19357-19369
　Augmentation 19324-19325
　Mammoplasty 19318-19325
　Nipple .19350-19355
　Revision 19380
　Transverse Rectus Abdominis Myocutaneous
　Flap 19367-19369
　with Free Flap 19364
　with Latissimus Dorsi Flap 19361
　with Other Techniques 19366
　with Tissue Expander 19357

Trachea
- Carina 31766
- Cervical 31750
- Fistula 31755
- Intrathoracic 31760

Trapezium 25445

Tympanic Membrane 69620

Ulna 25390-25393, 25442
- Radioulnar 25337

Ureter 50700
- with Intestines 50840

Urethra 53410-53440, 53445
- Complications 54340-54348
- Hypospadias
  - One Stage Distal with Meatal
    Advancement 54322
  - One Stage Distal with
    Urethroplasty 54324-54328
  - Suture to Bladder 51840-51841
  - Urethroplasty for Second
    Stage 54308-54316
  - Urethroplasty for Third Stage 54318

Uterus 58540

Vas Deferens
- *See* Vasovasorrhaphy

Vena Cava 34502
- with Resection 37799

Wound Repair 13100-13160

Wrist 25332
- Capsulectomy 25320
- Capsulorrhaphy 25320
- Realign 25335

Zygomatic Arch 21255

Rectal Bleeding
See Hemorrhage, Rectum

Rectal Prolapse
See Procidentia, Rectum

Rectal Sphincter
Dilation 45910

Rectocele
Repair 45560

Rectopexy
See Proctopexy

Rectoplasty
See Proctoplasty

Rectorrhaphy
See Rectum, Suture

Rectovaginal Fistula
See Fistula, Rectovaginal

Rectovaginal Hernia
See Rectocele

Rectum
See Anus

Abscess
- Incision and Drainage 45005-45020,
  46040, 46060

Biopsy 45100

Dilation
- Endoscopy 45303

Endoscopy
- Destruction
  - Tumor 45320
- Dilation 45303
- Exploration 45300
- Hemorrhage 45317
- Removal
  - Foreign Body 45307
  - Polyp 45308-45315
  - Tumor 45308-45315
- Volvulus 45321

Excision
- Partial 45111, 45113-45116, 45123
- Total 45110, 45112, 45119-45120
- with Colon 45121

Exploration
- Endoscopic 45300

Hemorrhage
- Endoscopic 45317

Injection
- Sclerosing Solution 45520

Lesion
- Excision 45108

Manometry 91122

Prolapse
- Excision 45130-45135

Pulsed Irrigation
- Fecal Impaction 91123

Removal
- Fecal Impaction 45915
  - by Pulsed Irrigation 91123
- Foreign Body 45307, 45915

Repair
- Fistula 45800-45825
- Injury 45562-45563
- Prolapse 45505-45541, 45900
- Rectocele 45560
- Stenosis 45500
- with Sigmoid Excision 45550

Stricture
- Excision 45150

Suture
- Fistula 45800-45825
- Prolapse 45540-45541

Tumor
- Destruction 45190, 45320, 46937-46938
- Excision 45160-45170

Unlisted Services and Procedures 45999

Reductase, Glutathione
See Glutathione Reductase

Reductase, Lactic Cytochrome
See Lactic Dehydrogenase

Reduction
Forehead 21137-21139
Lung Volume 32491
Mammoplasty 19318
Masseter Muscle/Bone 21295-21296
Osteoplasty
- Facial Bones 21209
Pregnancy
- Multifetal 59866
Skull
- Craniomegalic 62115-62117
Ventricular Septum
- Non-surgical 0024T

Red Blood Cell (RBC)
Antibody 86850-86870
- Pretreatment 86970-86972
Count 85041
Fragility
- Mechanical 85547
- Osmotic 85555-85557
Hematocrit 85014
Iron Utilization 78170
Morphology 85007
Platelet Estimation 85007
Sedimentation Rate
- Automated 85652
- Manual 85651
Sequestration 78140
Sickling 85660
Survival Test 78130-78135
Volume Determination 78120-78121

Red Blood Cell ab
See Antibody, Red Blood Cell

Reflex Test
Blink Reflex 95933
H-Reflex 95934-95936

Reflux Study 78262

Refraction 92015

Rehabilitation
Artery
- Occlusive Disease 93668
Aural 92510
Cardiac 93797-93798

Rehabilitative
See Rehabilitation

Rehfuss Test
See Gastroenterology, Diagnostic, Stomach

Reichstein's Substance S
See Deoxycortisol

Reimplantation
Arteries
- Carotid 35691, 35694-35695
- Subclavian 35693-35695
- Vertebral 35691-35693
Kidney 50380
Ovary 58825
Pulmonary Artery 33788
Ureter, to Bladder 50780-50785
Ureters 51565

Reinnervation
Larynx
- Neuromuscular Pedicle 31590

Reinsch Test 83015

Reinsertion
Drug Delivery Implant 11983
Implantable Contraceptive Capsules 11977
Spinal Fixation Device 22849

Relative Density
See Specific Gravity

Release

Carpal Tunnel 64721
Elbow Contracture
    with Radical Release of Capsule 24149
Flexor Muscles
    Hip 27036
Muscle
    Knee 27422
Nerve 64702-64726
    Neurolytic 64727
Retina
    Encircling Material 67115
Spinal Cord 63200
Stapes 69650
Tarsal Tunnel 28035
Tendon .24332, 25295

Release-Inhibiting Hormone, Somatotropin

See Somatostatin

Removal

Balloon
    Intra-Aortic .33974
Balloon Assist Device
    Intra-Aortic 33968, 33971
Blood Clot
    Eye 65930
Blood Component
    Apheresis 36520-36521
Breast
    Capsules 19371
    Implants 19328-19330
    Modified Radical 19240
    Partial 19140-19162
    Radical 19200-19220
    Simple, Complete 19180
    Subcutaneous 19182
Calcareous Deposits
    Subdeltoid 23000
Calculi (Stone)
    Bile Duct 43264, 47420-47425
      Percutaneous 47554, 47630
    Bladder 51050, 52310-52318, 52352
    Gallbladder .47480
    Hepatic Duct 47400
    Kidney 50060-50081, 50130, 50561,
                     50580, 52352
    Pancreas 48020
    Pancreatic Duct 43264
    Salivary Gland 42330-42340
    Ureter 50610-50630, 50961, 50980,
        51060-51065, 52320-52330, 52352
    Urethra 52310-52315, 52352
Cardiac Event Recorder 33284
Cast 29700-29715
Cataract
    with Replacement
      Extracapsular 66982, 66984
      Intracapsular 66983
      Not Associated with Concurrent . . .66983
Catheter
    Fractured 75961
    Peritoneum .49422
    Spinal Cord .62355
Cerclage
    Cervix 59871

Cerumen
    Auditory Canal, External 69210
Clot
    Pericardium .33020
      Endoscopic 32658
Comedones 10040
Contraceptive Capsules 11976-11977
Cranial Tongs 20665
Cyst 10040
Dacryolith
    Lacrimal Duct 68530
    Lacrimal Gland 68530
Defibrillator
    Heart 33244
      Pulse Generator Only 33241
      via Thoracotomy 33243
Drug Delivery Implant 11982-11983
Ear Wax
    Auditory Canal, External 69210
Electrode
    Brain 61535, 61880
    Heart 33238
    Nerve 64585
    Spinal Cord .63660
Embolus
    See Embolectomy
External Fixation System 20694
Eye
    Bone 67414, 67445
    Ocular Contents
      without Implant 65091
      with Implant 65093
    Orbital Contents Only 65110
    without Implant 65101
    with Bone 65112
    with Implant
      Muscles, Not Attached 65103
      Muscles Attached 65105
    with Muscle or Myocutaneous Flap . . .65114
Fallopian Tube
    Laparoscopy 58661
Fat
    Lipectomy 15876-15879
Fecal Impaction
    Rectum 45915
Fibrin Deposit 32150
Fixation Device 20670-20680
Foreign Bodies 65205-65265
    Anal 46608
    Ankle Joint 27610, 27620
    Arm
      Lower 25248
      Upper 24200-24201
    Auditory Canal, External 69200
      with Anesthesia 69205
    Bile Duct 43269
    Bladder 52310-52315
    Brain 61570
    Bronchi 31635
    Colon 44025, 44390, 45379
    Colon-Sigmoid 45332
    Conjunctival Embedded 65210
    Cornea
      without Slit Lamp 65220
      with Slit Lamp 65222
    Duodenum .44010
    Elbow 24000, 24101, 24200-24201

Esophagus 43020, 43045, 43215, 74235
External Eye 65205
Eyelid 67938
Finger 26075-26080
Foot 28190-28193
Gastrointestinal, Upper 43247
Gum 41805
Hand 26070
Hip 27033, 27086-27087
Hysteroscopy .58562
Interphalangeal Joint
    Toe 28024
Intertarsal Joint 28020
Intestines, Small 44020, 44363
Intraocular 65235
Kidney 50561, 50580
Knee Joint 27310, 27331, 27372
Lacrimal Duct .68530
Lacrimal Gland 68530
Larynx 31511, 31530-31531, 31577
Leg, Upper 27372
Lung 32151
Mandible 41806
Mediastinum 39000-39010
Metatarsophalangeal Joint 28022
Mouth 40804-40805
Muscle 20520-20525
Nose 30300
    Anesthesia 30310
    Lateral Rhinotomy 30320
Orbit 61334, 67413, 67430
    without Bone Flap 67413
    with Bone Flap 67430
Pancreatic Duct 43269
Patella
    See Patellectomy
Pelvis 27086-27087
Penile Tissue .54115
Penis 54115
Pericardium 33020
    Endoscopic 32658
Peritoneum 49085
Pharynx 42809
Pleura 32150-32151
    Endoscopic 32653
Posterior Segment
    Magnetic Extraction 65260
    Nonmagnetic Extraction 65265
Rectum 45307, 45915
Scrotum 55120
Shoulder 23040-23044
    Complicated 23332
    Deep 23331
    Subcutaneous 23330
Skin
    with Debridement 11010-11012
Stomach 43500
Subcutaneous Tissue 10120-10121
    with Debridement 11010-11012
Tarsometatarsal Joint 28020
Tendon Sheath 20520-20525
Toe 28022
Ureter 50961, 50980
Urethra 52310-52315
Uterus 58562
Vagina 57415
Wrist 25040, 25101, 25248

Foreign Body
    Elbow 24101
Hair
    Electrolysis 17380
Halo 20665
Hearing Aid
    Bone Conduction 69711
Hematoma
    Brain 61312-61315
Implantation 20670-20680
    Ankle 27704
    Contraceptive Capsules 11976-11977
    Elbow 24160
    Eye 67120-67121
    Finger 26320
    Hand 26320
    Radius 24164
    Wrist 25449
Infusion Pump
    Intraarterial 36262
    Intravenous 36532
    Spinal Cord 62365
Intra-Aortic Balloon 33974
    Assist Device 33968, 33971
Intrauterine Device (IUD) 58301
Keel
    Laryngoplasty .31580
Lacrimal Gland
    Partial 68505
    Total 68500
Lacrimal Sac
    Excision/(Optional) 68520
Laryngocele 31300
Leiomyomata 58551, 58561
Lens 66920-66940
Lens Material 66840-66852
Lesion
    Conjunctiva 68040
    Larynx 31512, 31578
Loose Body
    Ankle 27620
    Carpometacarpal Joint 26070
    Elbow 24101
    Interphalangeal Joint
        Toe 28024
    Intertarsal Joint 28020
    Knee Joint 27331
    Metatarsophalangeal Joint 28022
    Tarsometatarsal Joint 28020
    Toe 28022
    Wrist 25101
Lung
    Bronchoplasty 32501
    Completion Pneumonectomy 32488
    Cyst 32140
    Extrapleural 32445
    Single Lobe 32480
    Single Segment 32484
    Sleeve Lobectomy 32486
    Sleeve Pneumonectomy 32442
    Total Pneumonectomy 32440-32445
    Two Lobes 32482
    Volume Reduction 32491
    Wedge Resection 32500
Lymph Nodes
    Abdominal 38747
    Inguinofemoral 38760-38765
    Pelvic 38770

Retroperitoneal
    Transabdominal 38780
    Thoracic 38746
Mammary Implant 19328-19330
Mastoid
    Air Cells 69670
Milia, Multiple 10040
Nails 11730-11732, 11750-11752
Neurostimulators
    Pulse Generator 64595
    Receiver 64595
Ocular Implant 65175, 65920
Orbital Implant 67560
Ovaries
    Laparoscopy .58661
Pacemaker
    Heart .33233-33237
Patella, Complete 27424
Plate
    Skull 62142
Polyp
    Anal .46610, 46612
    Antrochoanal .31032
    Colon 44392, 45385
    Colon-Sigmoid 45333
    Endoscopy 44364-44365, 44394
    Esophagus 43217, 43250
    Gastrointestinal, Upper 43250-43251
    Rectum 45315
    Sphenoid Sinus 31051
Prosthesis
    Abdomen 49606
    Hip 27090-27091
    Knee 27488
    Penis 54406, 54410-54417
    Perineum 53442
    Skull 62142
    Urethral Sphincter 53446-53447
    Wrist .25250-25251
Pulse Generator
    Brain 61888
    Spinal Cord 63688
Pustules 10040
Receiver
    Brain 61888
    Spinal Cord 63688
Reservoir
    Spinal Cord 62365
Seton
    Anal 46030
Shoulder Joint
    Foreign or Loose Body 23107
Shunt
    Brain .62256-62258
    Heart 33924
    Peritoneum 49429
    Spinal Cord 63746
Skin Tags 11200-11201
Sling
    Vagina 57287
Spinal Instrumentation
    Anterior 22855
    Posterior Nonsegmental
        Harrington Rod 22850
    Posterior Segmental 22852
Stent
    Bile Duct 43269
    Pancreatic Duct 43269

Suture
    Anal 46754
    Anesthesia 15850-15851
Thrombus
    See Thrombectomy
Tissue Expanders
    Skin 11971
Transplant Kidney 50370
Tube
    Ear, Middle 69424
    Finger 26392, 26416
    Hand 26392, 26416
Tumor
    Temporal Bone 69970
Ureter
    Ligature 50940
Urethral Stent
    Bladder 52310-52315
    Urethra 52310-52315
Vein
    Perforation 37760
    Saphenous 37720-37735, 37780
    Secondary 37785
Venous Access Device 36535
Ventilating Tube
    Ear, Middle 69424
Ventricular Assist Device 33977-33978
    Intracorporeal 33980
Vitreous
    Anterior Approach 67005-67010
Wire
    Anal 46754

Renal Abscess
See Abscess, Kidney

Renal Arteries
See Artery, Renal

Renal Autotransplantation
See Autotransplantation, Renal

Renal Calculus
See Calculus, Removal, Kidney

Renal Cyst
See Cyst, Kidney

Renal Dialyses
See Hemodialysis

Renal Disease Services
See Dialysis

Renal Transplantation
See Kidney, Transplantation

Renin 80408, 80416, 84244
Peripheral Vein .80417

Renin-Converting Enzyme 82164

Reoperation
Carotid
    Thromboendarterectomy 35390
Coronary Artery Bypass
    Valve Procedure 33530
Distal Vessel Bypass 35700

Retinopathy
  Destruction
    Cryotherapy, Diathermy 67227
    Photocoagulation 67228

Retinacular
Knee
  Release 27425

Retinopathy
Destruction
  Cryotherapy, Diathermy 67227
  Photocoagulation 67228

Retraction, Clot
See Clot Retraction

Retrieval
Transcatheter Foreign Body 37203

Retrocaval Ureter
Ureterolysis 50725

Retrograde Cholangiopancreatographies, Endoscopic
See Cholangiopancreatography

Retrograde Cystourethrogram
See Urethrocystography, Retrograde

Retrograde Pyelogram
See Urography, Retrograde

Retroperitoneal Area
Abscess
  Incision and Drainage
    Open 49060
    Percutaneous 49061
Biopsy 49010
Cyst
  Destruction/Excision 49200-49201
Endometriomas
  Destruction/Excision 49200-49201
Exploration 49010
Needle Biopsy
  Mass 49180
Tumor
  Destruction/Excision 49200-49201

Retroperitoneal Fibrosis
Ureterolysis 50715

Retropubic Prostatectomies
See Prostatectomy, Retropubic

Revascularization
Penis 37788
Transmyocardial 33140-33141

Reversal, Vasectomy
See Vasovasorrhaphy

Reverse T3
See Triiodothyronine, Reverse

Reverse Triiodothyronine
See Triiodothyronine, Reverse

Revision
See Reconstruction
Aorta 33404
Atrial 33253

Blepharoplasty 15820-15823
Bronchus 32501
Bypass Graft
  Vein Patch .35685
Cervicoplasty .15819
Colostomy
  See Colostomy, Revision
Cornea
  Prosthesis .65770
  Reshaping
    Epikeratoplasty 65767
    Keratomileusis 65760
    Keratophakia 65765
Defibrillator Site
  Chest 33223
Ear, Middle 69662
External Fixation System 20693
Eye
  Aqueous Shunt 66185
Gastrostomy Tube 44373
Hip Replacement
  See Replacement, Hip, Revision
Hymenal Ring .56700
Ileostomy
  See Ileostomy, Revision
Infusion Pump
  Intraarterial 36261
  Intravenous 36531
Iris
  Iridoplasty .66762
  Iridotomy 66761
Jejunostomy Tube 44373
Lower Extremity Arterial Bypass . . .35879-35881
Pacemaker Site
  Chest 33222
Rhytidectomy 15824-15829
Semicircular Canal
  Fenestration 69840
Stapedectomy
  See Stapedectomy, Revsion
Stomach
  for Obesity 43848
Tracheostomy
  Scar 31830
Urinary-Cutaneous Anastomosis . . .50727-50728
Vagina
  Sling
    Stress Incontinence 57287
Venous Access Device 36534
Ventricle
  Ventriculomyectomy 33416
  Ventriculomyotomy 33416

Rh (D)
See Blood Typing

Rh Immune Globulin
See Immune Globulins, Rho (D)

Rheumatoid Factor 86430-86431

Rhinectomy
Partial 30150
Total 30160

Rhinomanometry 92512

Rhinopharynx
See Nasopharynx

Rhinophyma
Repair 30120

Rhinoplasty
Cleft Lip/Cleft Palate 30460-30462
Primary .30400-30420
Secondary 30430-30450

Rhinoscopy
See Endoscopy, Nose

Rhinotomy
Lateral 30118, 30320

Rhizotomy 63185-63190

Rho Variant Du 86905

Rhytidectomy 15824-15829

Rhytidoplasties
See Face Lift

Rib
Excision 21600-21616, 32900
Fracture
  Closed Treatment 21800
  External Fixation 21810
  Open Treatment 21805
Graft
  to Face 21230
Resection 32900
X-Ray .71100-71111

Riboflavin 84252

Richardson Operation Hysterectomy
See Hysterectomy, Abdominal, Total

Richardson Procedure 53460

Rickettsia
Antibody 86757

Ridell Operation
See Sinusotomy, Frontal

Ridge, Alveolar
See Alveolar Ridge

Right Atrioventricular Valve
See Tricuspid Valve

Right Heart Cardiac Catheterization
See Cardiac Catheterization, Right Heart

Ripstein Operation
See Proctopexy

Risk Factor Reduction Intervention
See Preventive Medicine

Risser Jacket 29010-29015
Removal 29710

Rocky Mountain Spotted Fever 86000

Roentgenographic
See X-Ray

S

Scabies
See Tissue, Examination for Ectoparasites

Scalenotomy
See Muscle Division, Scalenus Anticus

Scalenus Anticus
Division 21700-21705

Scaling
See Exfoliation

Scalp
Tumor Resection
    Radical 21015

Scalp Blood Sampling 59030

Scan
See Specific Site, Nuclear Medicine
Abdomen
    See Abdomen, C.A.T. Scan
C.A.T.
    See C.A.T. Scan
MRI
    See Magnetic Resonance Imaging
PET
    See Positron Emission Tomography
Radionuclide
    See Emission Computerized Tomography

Scanning, Radioisotope
See Nuclear Medicine

Scanogram 76040

Scaphoid
Fracture
    Closed Treatment 25622
    Open Treatment 25628
    with Manipulation 25624

Scapula
Craterization 23182
Cyst
    Excision 23140
        with Allograft 23146
        with Autograft 23145
Diaphysectomy 23182
Excision 23172, 23190
    Partial 23182
Fracture
    Closed Treatment
        without Manipulation 23570
        with Manipulation 23575
    Open Treatment 23585
Ostectomy 23190
Repair
    Fixation 23400
    Scapulopexy 23400
Saucerization 23182
Sequestrectomy 23172
Tumor
    Excision 23140, 23210
        with Allograft 23146
        with Autograft 23145
    Radical Resection 23210
X-Ray 73010

Scapulopexy 23400

Scarification
Pleural 32215

Scarification of Pleura
See Pleurodesis

Schanz Operation
See Femur, Osteotomy

Schauta Operation
See Hysterectomy, Vaginal, Radical

Schede Procedure 32905-32906

Scheie Procedure
See Iridectomy

Schilling Test 78270
See Vitamin B-12 Absorption Study

**Schlatter Operation Total
Gastrectomy**
See Excision, Stomach, Total

Schlicter Test 87197
See Bactericidal Titer, Serum

Schocket Procedure 66180
See Aqueous Shunt

Schonbein Test
See Blood, Feces

Schuchard Procedure
Osteotomy
    Maxilla 21206

Schwannoma, Acoustic
See Brain, Tumor, Excision

Sciatic Nerve
Decompression 64712
Injection
    Anesthetic 64445
Lesion
    Excision 64786
Neuroma
    Excision 64786
Neuroplasty 64712
Release 64712
Repair/Suture 64858

Scintigraphy
See Nuclear Medicine
Computed Tomographic
    See Emission Computerized Tomography

Scissoring
Skin Tags 11200-11201

Sclera
Excision
    Sclerectomy with Punch or Scissors ...66160
Fistulization
    Iridencleisis or Iridotasis 66165
    Sclerectomy with Punch or Scissors with
    Iridectomy 66160
    Thermocauterization with Iridectomy ..66155

Trabeculectomy ab Externo in Absence of
    Previous Surgery 66170
    Trephination with Iridectomy 66150
Incision
    Fistulization
        Iridencleisis or Iridotasis 66165
        Sclerectomy with Punch or Scissors with
        Iridectomy 66160
        Thermocauterization
        with Iridectomy 66155
        Trabeculectomy ab Externo in Absence of
        Previous Surgery 66170
        Trephination with Iridectomy ...66150
Lesion
    Excision 66130
Repair
    Reinforcement
        without Graft 67250
        with Graft 67255
    Staphyloma
        without Graft 66220
        with Graft 66225
    with Glue 65286
    Wound
        Operative 66250
        Tissue Glue 65286

Scleral Buckling Operation
See Retina, Repair, Detachment

Scleral Ectasia
See Staphyloma, Sclera

Sclerectomy 66160

Sclerotherapy
Venous 36468-36471

Sclerotomy
See Incision, Sclera

Screening, Drug
See Drug Screen

Scribner Cannulization 36810

Scrotal Varices
See Varicocele

Scrotoplasty 55175-55180

Scrotum
Abscess
    Incision and Drainage 54700, 55100
Excision 55150
Exploration 55110
Hematoma
    Incision and Drainage 54700
Removal
    Foreign Body 55120
Repair 55175-55180
Ultrasound 76870
Unlisted Services and Procedures 55899

Scrub Typhus 86000

Second Look Surgery
See Reoperation

Second Opinion
See Confirmatory Consultations

Splanchnicectomy
See Nerves, Sympathectomy, Excision

Spleen
Excision 38100-38102
     Laparoscopic 38120
Injection
     Radiologic 38200
Nuclear Medicine
     Imaging 78185, 78215-78216
Repair 38115

Splenectomy
Laparoscopic 38120
Partial 38101
Partial with Repair, Ruptured Spleen 38115
Total 38100
     En bloc 38102

Splenoplasty
See Repair, Spleen

Splenoportography 75810
Injection Procedures 38200

Splenorrhaphy 38115

Splint
See Casting; Strapping
Arm
     Long 29105
     Short 29125-29126
Finger 29130-29131
Foot 29590
Leg
     Long 29505
     Short 29515
Oral Surgical 21085
Ureteral
     See Ureteral Splinting

Splitting
Blood Products 86985

Split Grafts 15100-15121

Split Renal Function Test
See Cystourethroscopy, Catheterization, Ureteral

Spontaneous Abortion
See Abortion

Sprengel's Deformity 23400

Spring Water Cyst
See Cyst, Pericardial

Spur, Bone
See Exostosis
Calcaneal
     See Heel Spur

Sputum Analysis 89350

SRIH
See Somatostatin

Ssabanejew-Frank Operation
See Incision, Stomach, Creation, Stoma; Incision and Drainage

Stabilizing Factor, Fibrin
See Fibrin Stabilizing Factor

Stable Factor 85230

Stallard Procedure
See Conjunctivorhinostomy

Stamey Procedure 51845
See Repair, Bladder, Neck

Standby Services
Physician 99360

Stanford-Binet Test
See Psychiatric Diagnosis

Stanftan
See Binet Test

Stapedectomy
Revision 69662
without Foreign Material 69660
with Footplate Drill Out 69661

Stapedotomy
Revision 69662
without Foreign Material 69660
with Footplate Drill Out 69661

Stapes
Excision
     without Foreign Material 69660
     with Footplate Drill Out 69661
Mobilization
     See Mobilization, Stapes
Release 69650
Revision 69662

Staphyloma
Sclera
     Repair
         without Graft 66220
         with Graft 66225

Starch Granules
Feces 89355

State Operation
See Proctectomy

Statistics /Biometry
See Biometry

Steindler Stripping 28250

Stellate Ganglion
Injection
     Anesthetic 64510

Stem, Brain
See Brainstem

Stem Cell
Cryopreservation 88240
Harvesting 38231
Modification or Treatment 86915
Thawing 88241
Transplantation 38240-38241

Stenger Test 92565, 92577
See Audiologic Function Test; Ear, Nose and Throat

Stenosis
Aortic
     See Aortic Stenosis
Bronchi 31641
     Reconstruction 31775
Excision
     Trachea 31780-31781
Laryngoplasty 31582
Reconstruction
     Auditory Canal, External 69310
Repair
     Trachea 31780-31781
Tracheal
     See Trachea Stenosis
Urethral
     See Urethral Stenosis

Stensen Duct
See Parotid Duct

Stent
Indwelling
     Insertion
         Ureter 50605
Placement
     Bronchoscopy 31631
     Colonoscopy 45387
     via Stoma 44397
     Endoscopy
         Gastrointestinal, Upper 43256
     Enteroscopy 44370
     Proctosigmoidoscopy 45327
     Sigmoidoscopy 45345
     Ureteroneocystomy 50947-50948
Urethra
     Insertion 52282

Stent, Intravascular
See Transcatheter, Placement, Intravascular Stents

Stents, Tracheal
See Tracheal Stent

Stereotactic Frame
Application/Removal 20660

Stereotaxis
Aspiration
     Brain Lesion .61750
     with CAT Scan and/or MRI 61751
     Spinal Cord .63615
Biopsy
     Aspiration
         Brain Lesion 61750
     Brain 61750
     with CAT Scan and/or MRI 61751
     Breast 76095
     Spinal Cord .63615
CAT Scan
     Aspiration 61751
     Biopsy 61751
Computer Assisted
     Brain Surgery 61795
Creation Lesion
     Brain
         Deep 61720-61735
         Percutaneous 61790

Gasserian Ganglion 61790
Spinal Cord 63600
Trigeminal Tract 61791
Excision Lesion
Brain .61750
Spinal Cord 63615
Focus Beam
Radiosurgery 61793
Localization
Brain 61770
Radiation Therapy 77432
Stimulation
Spinal Cord 63610

Sterile Coverings
See Dressings

Sternal Fracture
See Fracture, Sternum

Sternoclavicular Joint
Arthrotomy 23044
with Biopsy 23101
with Synovectomy 23106
Dislocation
Closed Treatment
without Manipulation 23520
with Manipulation 23525
Open Treatment 23530-23532
with Fascial Graft 23532

Sternocleidomastoid
Division 21720-21725

Sternotomy
Closure 21750

Sternum
Debridement 21627
Excision 21620, 21630-21632
Fracture
Closed Treatment 21820
Open Treatment 21825
Ostectomy 21620
Radical Resection 21630-21632
Reconstruction 21740-21750
X-Ray 71120-71130

Steroid-Binding Protein, Sex
See Globulin, Sex Hormone Binding

Steroids
Anabolic
See Androstenedione
Injection
Urethral Stricture 52283
Ketogenic
Urine 83582

STH (Somatotropic Hormone)
See Growth Hormone

Stimulating Antibody, Thyroid
See Immunoglobulin, Thyroid Stimulating

Stimulation
Electric
See Electrical Stimulation
Lymphocyte
See Blastogenesis

Spinal Cord
Stereotaxis 63610
Transcutaneous Electric
See Application, Neurostimulation

Stimulator, Long-Acting Thyroid
See Thyrotropin Releasing Hormone (TRH)

Stimulators, Cardiac
See Heart, Pacemaker

Stimulus Evoked Response 51792

Stoffel Operation
See Rhizotomy

Stoma
Creation
Bladder 51980
Kidney 50551-50561
Stomach
Neonatal 43831
Temporary 43830-43831
Ureter 50860
Ureter
Endoscopy via 50951-50961

Stomach
Anastomosis
with Duodenum 43810, 43850-43855
with Jejunum . . .43820-43825, 43860-43865
Biopsy .43600-43605
Creation
Stoma
Temporary 43830-43831
Temporary Stoma
Laparoscopic 43653
Electrogastrography 91132-91133
Excision
Partial 43631-43639
Total 43620-43622
Exploration .43500
Gastric Bypass 43846
Revision 43848
Incision 43830-43832
Exploration 43500
Pyloric Sphincter 43520
Removal
Foreign Body 43500
Intubation with Specimen Prep 91055
Nuclear Medicine
Blood Loss Study 78278
Emptying Study 78264
Imaging 78261
Protein Loss Study 78282
Reflux Study 78262
Vitamin B-12 Absorption 78270-78272
Reconstruction
for Obesity 43842-43847
Roux-En-Y 43846
Removal
Foreign Body 43500
Repair 48547
Fistula .43880
Fundoplasty 43324-43325
Laparoscopic 43280
Laceration 43501-43502
Stoma .43870
Ulcer 43501

Saline Load Test 91060
Specimen Collection 89130-89141
Stimulation of Secretion 91052
Suture
Fistula 43880
for Obesity 43842-43843
Stoma .43870
Ulcer 43840
Wound .43840
Tumor
Excision 43610-43611
Ulcer
Excision 43610
Unlisted Services and Procedures . .43659, 43999

Stomatoplasty
See Mouth, Repair

Stone, Kidney
See Calculus, Removal, Kidney

Stookey-Scarff Procedure
See Ventriculocisternostomy

Stool Blood
See Blood, Feces

Strabismus
Chemodenervation 67345
Repair
Adjustable Sutures 67335
Extraocular Muscles 67340
One Horizontal Muscle 67311
One Vertical Muscle 67314
Posterior Fixation Suture
Technique 67334-67335
Previous Surgery, Not Involving Extraocular
Muscles 67331
Release Extensive Scar Tissue 67343
Superior Oblique Muscle 67318
Transposition 67320
Two Horizontal Muscles 67312
Two or More Vertical Muscles 67316

Strapping
See Cast; Splint
Ankle 29540
Back 29220
Chest 29200
Elbow 29260
Finger 29280
Foot 29590
Hand 29280
Hip 29520
Knee 29530
Shoulder 29240
Thorax 29200
Toes 29550
Unlisted Services and Procedures 29799
Unna Boot 29580
Wrist 29260

Strassman Procedure 58540

Strayer Procedure
Leg, Lower 27687

Streptococcus, Group A
Antigen Detection
    Enzyme Immunoassay 87430
    Nucleic Acid 87650-87652
Direct Optical Observation 87880

Streptococcus, Group B
by Immunoassay
    with Direct Optical Observation 87802

Streptococcus pneumoniae Vaccine
See Vaccines

Streptokinase, Antibody 86590

Stress Tests
Cardiovascular 93015-93024
Multiple Gated Acquisition
(MUGA) .78472-78473
Myocardial Perfusion Imaging 78460-78465
Pulmonary 94620-94621
    See Pulmonology, Diagnostic

Stricture
Repair
    Urethra 53400-53405
Urethra
    See Urethral Stenosis

Stricturoplasty
Intestines 44615

Stroboscopy
Larynx 31579

STS 86592-86593
See Syphilis Test

Stuart-Prower Factor 85260

Study, Color Vision
See Color Vision Examination

Sturmdorf Procedure 57520

Styloidectomy
Radial 25230

Styloid Process
Radial
    Excision 25230

Stypven Time
See Russell Viper Venom Time

Subacromial Bursa
Arthrocentesis .20610

Subclavian Arteries
See Artery, Subclavian

Subcutaneous Injection
See Injection, Subcutaneous

Subcutaneous Mastectomies
See Mastectomy, Subcutaneous

Subcutaneous Tissue
Excision .15831-15839

Subdiaphragmatic Abscess
See Abscess, Subdiaphragmatic

Subdural Electrode
Insertion 61531-61533
Removal 61535

Subdural Hematonia
See Hematoma, Subdural

Subdural Puncture 61105-61108

Subdural Tap 61000-61001

Sublingual Gland
Abscess
    Incision and Drainage 42310-42320
Calculi (Stone)
    Excision 42330
Cyst
    Drainage 42409
    Excision 42408
Excision 42450

Subluxation
Elbow 24640

Submandibular Gland
Calculi (Stone)
    Excision 42330-42335
Excision 42440

Submaxillary Gland
Abscess
    Incision and Drainage 42310-42320

Submucous Resection of Nasal Septum
See Nasal Septum, Submucous Resection

Subperiosteal Implant
Reconstruction
    Mandible 21245-21246
    Maxilla 21245-21246

Subphrenic Abscess
See Abscess, Subdiaphragmatic

Substance S, Reichstein's
See Deoxycortisol

Subtrochanteric Fracture
See Femur, Fracture, Subtrochanteric

Sucrose Hemolysis Test
See Red Blood Cell (RBC), Fragility, Osmotic

Suction Lipectomies
See Liposuction

Sudiferous Gland
See Sweat Glands

Sugars 84375-84379

Sugar Water Test
See Red Blood Cell (RBC), Fragility, Osmotic

Sugiura Procedure
See Esophagus, Repair, Varices

Sulfate
Chondroitin
    See Chondroitin Sulfate

DHA
    See Dehydroepiandrosterone Sulfate
Urine 84392

Sulfation Factor
See Somatomedin

Sulphates
See Sulfate

Sumatran Mite Fever
See Scrub Typhus

Superficial Musculoaponeurotic System (SMAS) Flap
Rhytidectomy .15829

Supernumerary Digit
Reconstruction 26587
Repair 26587

Supply
Chemotherapeutic Agent 96545
    See Chemotherapy
Contact Lenses 92391, 92396
Educational Materials 99071
Low Vision Aids 92392
    See Spectacle Services
Materials 99070
Ocular Prosthesis 92393
Prosthesis
    Breast 19396
Radionuclide 78990
Radionuclide Therapy 79900
Radiopharmaceutical 78990
Radiopharmaceutical Therapy 79900
Spectacles 92390
Spectacle Prosthesis 92395

Suppositories, Vaginal
See Pessary

Suppression 80400-80408

Suppression/Testing
See Evocative/Suppression Test

Suppressor T Lymphocyte Marker
See CD8

Suppurative Hidradenitides
See Hidradenitis, Suppurative

Suprahyoid
Lymphadenectomy 38700

Supraorbital Nerve
Avulsion 64732
Incision 64732
Transection 64732

Supraorbital Rim and Forehead
Reconstruction 21179-21180

Suprapubic Prostatectomies
See Prostatectomy, Suprapubic

Suprarenal
Gland
    See Adrenal Gland

Vein
　See Vein, Adrenal

Suprascapular Nerve
Injection
　Anesthetic 64418

Suprasellar Cyst
See Craniopharyngioma

Surface CD4 Receptor
See CD4

Surface Radiotherapy
See Application, Radioelement, Surface

Surgeries
Breast-Conserving
　See Breast, Excision, Lesion
Conventional
　See Celiotomy
Laser
　See Laser Surgery
Mohs
　See Mohs Micrographic Surgery
Repeat
　See Reoperation

Surgical
Avulsion
　See Avulsion
Cataract Removal
　See Cataract, Excision
Collapse Therapy; Thoracoplasty
　See Thoracoplasty
Diathermy
　See Electrocautery
Galvanism
　See Electrolysis
Incision
　See Incision
Microscopes
　See Operating Microscope
Pathology
　See Pathology, Surgical
Planing
　Nose
　　Skin 30120
Pneumoperitoneum
　See Pneumoperitoneum
Removal, Eye
　See Enucleation, Eye
Revision
　See Reoperation
Services
　Post-Op Visit .99024

Surveillance
See Monitoring

Suspension
Aorta 33800
Kidney
　See Nephropexy
Vagina
　See Colpopexy

Suture
See Repair
Abdomen 49900

Aorta 33320-33322
Bile Duct
　Wound 47900
Bladder
　Fistulization 44660-44661, 45800-45805,
　　　　　　　　　　　　　　　51880-51925
　　Vesicouterine 51920-51925
　　Vesicovaginal 51900
　　Wound 51860-51865
Cervix 57720
Colon
　Diverticula 44604-44605
　Fistula 44650-44661
　Plication 44680
　Stoma 44620-44625
　Ulcer .44604-44605
　Wound 44604-44605
Esophagus
　Wound 43410-43415
Eyelid 67880
　Closure of .67875
　with Transposition of Tarsal Plate 67882
　Wound
　　Full Thickness 67935
　　Partial Thickness 67930
Facial Nerve
　Intratemporal
　　Lateral to Geniculate Ganglion 69740
　　Medial to Geniculate Ganglion 69745
Foot
　Tendon 28200-28210
Gastroesophageal 0008T, 43405
Great Vessel 33320-33322
Hemorrhoids 46945-46946
Hepatic Duct
　See Hepatic Duct, Repair
Intestine
　Large
　　Diverticula 44605
　　Ulcer 44605
　　Wound 44605
Intestines
　Large
　　Diverticula 44604
　　Ulcer 44604
　　Wound 44604
　Small
　　Diverticula 44602-44603
　　Fistula 44640-44661
　　Plication 44680
　　Ulcer 44602-44603
　　Wound 44602-44603
　　Stoma 44620-44625
Iris
　with Ciliary Body 66682
Kidney
　Fistula 50520-50526
　Horseshoe .50540
　Wound 50500
Leg, Lower
　Tendon 27658-27665
Leg, Upper
　Muscle 27385-27386
Liver
　Wound 47350-47361
Mesentery 44850
Nerve 64831-64876

Pancreas 48545
Pharynx
　Wound 42900
Rectum
　Fistula 45800-45825
　Prolapse 45540-45541
Removal
　Anesthesia 15850-15851
Spleen
　See Splenorrhaphy
Stomach
　Fistula 43880
　Laceration 43501-43502
　Stoma 43870
　Ulcer 43501, 43840
　Wound 43840
Tendon
　Foot 28200-28210
　Knee 27380-27381
Testis
　Injury 54670
　Suspension 54620-54640
Thoracic Duct
　Abdominal Approach 38382
　Cervical Approach 38380
　Thoracic Approach 38381
Throat
　Wound 42900
Tongue
　to Lip 41510
Trachea
　Fistula
　　without Plastic Repair 31820
　　with Plastic Repair 31825
　Stoma
　　without Plastic Repair 31820
　　with Plastic Repair 31825
　Wound
　　Cervical 31800
　　Intrathoracic 31805
Ulcer .44604-44605
Ureter 50900
　Deligation 50940
　Fistula 50920-50930
Urethra
　Fistula 45820-45825, 53520
　Stoma 53520
　to Bladder 51840-51841
　Wound 53502-53515
Uterus
　Fistula 51920-51925
　Rupture 58520, 59350
　Suspension 58400-58410
Vagina
　Cystocele 57240, 57260
　Enterocele 57265
　Fistula
　　Rectovaginal 57300-57307
　　Transvesical and Vaginal Approach . .57330
　　Urethrovaginal 57310-57311
　　Vesicovaginal 51900, 57320-57330
　Rectocele 57250-57260
　Suspension 57280
　Wound 57200-57210
Vas Deferens .55400

Talectomy
See Astragalectomy

Talotarsal Joint
Dislocation 28570-28575, 28585
　　　Percutaneous Fixation 28576

Talus
Arthrodesis
　　　Pantalar 28705
　　　Subtalar 28725
　　　Triple 28715
Arthroscopy
　　　Surgical 29891-29892
Craterization 28120
Cyst
　　　Excision 28100-28103
Diaphysectomy 28120
Excision 28120, 28130
Fracture
　　　Open Treatment 28445
　　　Percutaneous Fixation 28436
　　　without Manipulation 28430
　　　with Manipulation 28435-28436
Repair
　　　Osteochondritis Dissecans 29892
　　　Osteotomy 28302
Saucerization 28120
Tumor
　　　Excision 27647, 28100-28103

Tap
Cisternal
　　　See Cisternal Puncture
Lumbar Diagnostic
　　　See Spinal Tap

Tarsal
Fracture
　　　Percutaneous Fixation 28456

Tarsal Bone
See Ankle Bone

Tarsal Joint
See Foot
Arthrodesis 28730-28735, 28740
　　　with Advancement 28737
　　　with Lengthening 28737
Craterization 28122
Cyst
　　　Excision 28104-28107
Diaphysectomy 28122
Dislocation 28540-28545, 28555
　　　Percutaneous Fixation 28545-28546
Excision 28116, 28122
Fracture
　　　Open Treatment 28465
　　　without Manipulation 28450
　　　with Manipulation 28455-28456
Fusion 28730-28735, 28740
　　　with Advancement 28737
　　　with Lengthening 28737
Repair 28320
　　　Osteotomy 28304-28305
Saucerization 28122
Tumor
　　　Excision 28104-28107, 28171

Tarsal Strip Procedure 67917

Tarsal Tunnel Release 28035

Tarsometatarsal Joint
Arthrodesis 28730-28735, 28740
Arthrotomy 28020, 28050
Dislocation 28600-28605, 28615
　　　Percutaneous Fixation 28606
Exploration 28020
Fusion 28730-28735, 28740
Removal
　　　Foreign Body 28020
　　　Loose Body .28020
Synovial
　　　Biopsy 28050
　　　Excision 28070

Tarsorrhaphy 67875
Median 67880
Severing 67710
　　　with Transposition of Tarsal Plate 67882

Tattoo
Cornea 65600
Skin 11920-11922

TBG
See Thyroxine Binding Globulin

TBS
See Bethesda System

TB Test
Antigen Response .0010T
Skin Test 86580-86585

TCT
See Thrombin Time

Td Shots
See Tetanus Immunization; Vaccines

Team Conference
Case Management Services 99361-99373

Tear Duct
See Lacrimal Duct

Tear Gland
See Lacrimal Gland

Technique
Pericardial Window
　　　See Pericardiostomy
Projective
　　　See Projective Test

Teeth
X-Ray 70300-70320

Telangiectasia
Chromosome Analysis 88248
Injection 36468

Telangiectasia, Cerebello-Oculocutaneous
See Ataxia Telangiectasia

Telephone
Case Management Services 99361-99373
Pacemaker Analysis 93733, 93736
Transmission of ECG 93012

Teletherapy
Dose Plan 77305-77321

Temperature Gradient Studies 93740

Temporal, Petrous
Excision
　　　Apex 69530

Temporal Arteries
See Artery, Temporal

Temporal Bone
Electromagnetic Bone Conduction Hearing Device
　　　Implantation/Replacement 69710
　　　Removal/Repair 69711
Excision 69535
Resection 69535
Tumor
　　　Removal 69970
Unlisted Services and Procedures 69979

Temporomandibular Joint (TMJ)
Arthrocentesis 20605
Arthrography 70328-70332
　　　Injection 21116
Arthroplasty 21240-21243
Arthroscopy
　　　Diagnostic 29800
　　　Surgical 29804
Arthrotomy 21010
Cartilage
　　　Excision 21060
Condylectomy 21050
Coronoidectomy .21070
Dislocation
　　　Closed Treatment 21480-21485
　　　Open Treatment 21490
Injection
　　　Radiologic 21116
Magnetic Resonance Imaging (MRI) 70336
Meniscectomy 21060
Prostheses
　　　See Prosthesis, Temporomandibular Joint
Reconstruction
　　　See Reconstruction, Temporomandibular Joint
X-Ray with Contrast 70328-70332

Tenago Procedure 53431

Tendinosuture
See Suture, Tendon

Tendon
Achilles
　　　See Achilles Tendon
Arm, Upper
　　　Revision 24320
Finger
　　　Excision 26180
Forearm
　　　Repair .25260-25274
Graft
　　　Harvesting 20924
Insertion
　　　Biceps Tendon 24342

Lengthening

Ankle 27685-27686
Arm, Upper 24305
Elbow 24305
Finger 26476, 26478
Forearm 25280
Hand 26476, 26478
Leg, Lower 27685-27686
Leg, Upper 27393-27395
Toe 28240
Wrist 25280

Palm
Excision 26170

Release
Arm, Lower 25295
Arm, Upper 24332
Wrist 25295

Shortening
Ankle 27685-27686
Finger 26477, 26479
Hand 26477, 26479
Leg, Lower 27685-27686

Transfer
Arm, Lower 25310-25312, 25316
Arm, Upper 24301
Elbow 24301
Finger 26497-26498
Hand 26480-26489
Leg, Lower 27690-27692
Leg, Upper 27400
Pelvis 27098
Thumb 26490-26492, 26510
Wrist 25310-25312, 25316

Transplant
Leg, Upper 27396-27397

Wrist
Repair 25260-25274

Tendon Origin

Insertion
Injection 20551

Tendon Pulley Reconstruction of Hand

See Hand, Reconstruction, Tendon Pulley

Tendon Sheath

Arm
Lower
Repair 25275
Finger
Incision 26055
Incision and Drainage 26020
Lesion 26160
Foot
Excision 28086-28088
Hand Lesion 26160
Injection 20550
Palm
Incision and Drainage 26020
Removal
Foreign Body 20520-20525
Wrist
Excision, Radical 25115-25116
Incision 25000-25001
Repair 25275

Tenectomy, Tendon Sheath

See Excision, Lesion, Tendon Sheath

Tennis Elbow

Repair 24350-24356

Tenodesis

Biceps Tendon
at Elbow 24340
Shoulder 23430
Finger 26471-26474
Wrist 25300-25301

Tenolysis

Ankle 27680-27681
Arm, Lower 25295
Arm, Upper 24332
Finger
Extensor 26445-26449
Flexor 26440-26442
Foot 28220-28226
Hand Extensor 26445-26449
Flexor 26440-26442
Leg, Lower 27680-27681
Wrist 25295

Tenomyotomy

Shoulder 23405-23406

Tenon's Capsule

Injection 67515

Tenoplasty

Anesthesia 01714

Tenorrhaphy

See Suture, Tendon

Tenosuspension

See Tenodesis

Tenosuture

See Suture, Tendon

Tenotomy

Achilles Tendon 27605-27606
Ankle 27605-27606
Arm, Lower 25290
Arm, Upper 24310
Finger 26060, 26455-26460
Foot 28230, 28234
Hand 26450, 26460
Hip
Iliopsoas Tendon 27005
Hip, Abductor 27006
Hip, Adductor 27000-27003
Leg, Upper 27306-27307, 27390-27392
Toe 28010-28011, 28232-28234, 28240
Wrist 25290

TENS

See Application, Neurostimulation; Physical Medicine/Therapy/Occupational Therapy

Tensilon Test 95857-95858

Tension, Ocular

See Glaucoma

Tentorium Cerebelli

Section 61440

Terman-Merrill Test 96100

Termination, Pregnancy

See Abortion

Test

Antiglobulin
See Coombs Test
Aphasia
See Aphasia Testing
Bender Visual-Motor Gestalt
See Bender-Gestalt Test
Binet
See Binet Test
Blood
See Blood Tests
Blood Coagulation
See Coagulation
Breath
See Breath Test
Cervical Mucus Penetration
See Cervical Mucus Penetration Test
Clinical Chemistry
See Chemistry Tests, Clinical
Complement Fixation
See Complement, Fixation Test
Exercise
See Exercise Stress Tests
Fern
See Smear and Stain, Wet Mount
Fetal, Nonstress
See Fetal Non-Stress Test
Function, Vestibular
See Vestibular Function Tests
Gel Diffusion
See Immunodiffusion
Glucose Tolerance
See Glucose, Tolerance Test
Hearing
See Audiologic Function Tests
Hemagglutination Inhibition
See Hemagglutination Inhibition Test
Ink Blot
See Inkblot Test
Intelligence
See Intelligence Test
Lung Function
See Pulmonology, Diagnostic
Neutralization
See Neutralization Test
Papanicolaou
See Pap Smears
Pregnancy
See Pregnancy Test
Quick
See Prothrombin Time
Radioimmunosorbent
See Gammaglobulin, Blood
Rorschach
See Rorschach Test
Schilling
See Schilling Test
Skin
See Skin, Tests
Stanford-Binet
See Psychiatric Diagnosis
Tuberculin
See Skin, Tests, Tuberculosis

Empyema
    See Abscess, Thorax
Surgery
    Video-Assisted
        See Thoracoscopy
Vertebra
    See Vertebra, Thoracic
Wall
    See Chest Wall

Thoracocentesis
See Thoracentesis

Thoracoplasty 32905
with Closure Bronchopleural Fistula 32906

Thoracoscopy
Diagnostic 32601-32606
    without Biopsy 32601, 32603, 32605
    with Biopsy 32602, 32604, 32606
Surgical 32650-32665
    with Control Traumatic Hemorrhage ...32654
    with Creation Pericardial Window 32659
    with Esophagomyotomy 32665
    with Excision-Plication of Bullae 32655
    with Excision Mediastinal Cyst, Tumor
    and/or Mass 32662
    with Excision Pericardial Cyst, Tumor
    and/or Mass 32661
    with Lobectomy 32663
    with Parietal Pleurectomy 32656
    with Partial Pulmonary Decortication ..32651
    with Pleurodesis 32650
    with Removal Intrapleural Foreign
    Body 32653
    with Removal of Clot/Foreign Body ...32658
    with Thoracic Sympathectomy 32664
    with Total Pericardiectomy 32660
    with Total Pulmonary Decortication ...32652
    with Wedge Resection of Lung 32657

Thoracostomy
Empyema 32035-32036
Tube, with/without Water Seal 32020

Thoracotomy
Cardiac Massage 32160
for Pacing Cardioverter-Defibrillator
    Pads 33245-33246
for Post-Op Complications 32120
Hemorrhage 32110
Removal
    Bullae 32141
    Cyst 32140
    Defibrillator 33243
    Electrodes 33238
    Foreign Body
        Intrapleural 32150
        Intrapulmonary 32151
    Pacemaker 33236-33237
        with Biopsy 32095-32100
        with Excision-Plication of Bullae 32141
        with Lung Repair 32110
        with Open Intrapleural
        Pneumolysis 32124
Transmyocardial Laser
Revascularization 33140-33141

Thorax
See Chest; Chest Cavity; Mediastinum
Angiography 71275
Bioimpedance 93701
Biopsy 21550
CAT Scan 71250-71275
Incision
    Empyema 32035-32036
    Pneumothorax 32020
Incision and Drainage
    Abscess 21501-21502
    Deep 21510
    Hematoma 21501-21502
Strapping 29200
Tumor
    Excision 21555-21556
    Excision/Resection 21557
Unlisted Services and Procedures,
Surgery 21899

Three-Day Measles
See Rubella

Three Glass Test
See Urinalysis, Glass Test

Throat
See Pharynx
Abscess
    Incision and Drainage 42700-42725
Biopsy 42800-42806
Hemorrhage 42960-42962
Reconstruction 42950
Removal
    Foreign Body 42809
Repair
    Pharyngoesophageal 42953
    Wound 42900
Suture
    Wound 42900
Unlisted Services and Procedures 42999

Thrombectomy
See Thromboendarterectomy
Aortoiliac Artery 34151-34201
Arteriovenous Fistula
    Graft 36870
Axillary Artery 34101
Axillary Vein 34490
Brachial Artery 34101
Bypass Graft
    Other than Hemodialysis Graft or
    Fistula 35875-35876
Carotid Artery 34001
Celiac Artery 34151
Dialysis Graft
    without Revision 36831
Femoral 34201
Femoropopliteal Vein 34421-34451
Iliac 34151-34201
Iliac Vein 34401-34451
Innominate Artery 34001-34101
Mesentery Artery 34151
Percutaneous
    Coronary Artery 92973
Peroneal Artery 34203
Popliteal Artery 34203
Radial Artery 34111
Renal Artery 34151

Subclavian Artery 34001-34101
Subclavian Vein 34471-34490
Tibial Artery 34203
Ulnar Artery 34111
Vena Cava 34401-34451
Vena Caval 50230

Thrombin Inhibitor I
See Antithrombin III

Thrombin Time 85670-85675

Thrombocyte (Platelet)
See Blood, Platelet

Thrombocyte ab
See Antibody, Platelet

Thromboendarterectomy
See Thrombectomy
Aorta, Abdominal 35331
Aortoiliofemoral Artery 35363
Axillary Artery 35321
Brachial Artery 35321
Carotid Artery 35301, 35390
Celiac Artery 35341
Femoral Artery 35371-35381
Iliac Artery 35351, 35361-35363
Iliofemoral Artery 35355, 35363
Innominate Artery 35311
Mesenteric Artery 35341
Peroneal Artery 35381
Popliteal Artery 35381
Renal Artery 35341
Subclavian Artery 35301-35311
Tibial Artery 35381
Vertebral Artery 35301

Thrombokinase 85260

Thrombolysin
See Plasmin

Thrombolysis
Catheter Exchange
    Arterial 37209, 75900
Cerebral
    Intravenous Infusion 37195
Coronary Vessels 92975-92977
Cranial Vessels 37195

Thrombolysis Biopsy Intracranial
Arterial Perfusion 61624

Thrombolysis Intracranial 65205
See Ciliary Body; Cornea; Eye, Removal, Foreign
Body; Iris; Lens; Retina; Sclera; Vitreous

Thrombomodulin 85337

Thromboplastin
Inhibition 85705
Inhibition Test 85347
Partial Time 85730-85732

Thromboplastinogen
See Clotting Factor

Thromboplastinogen B
See Christmas Factor

Thromboplastin Antecedent, Plasma
See Plasma Thromboplastin, Antecedent

Thumb
See Phalanx
Amputation 26910-26952
Arthrodesis
    Carpometacarpal Joint 26841-26842
Dislocation
    with Fracture 26645-26650
        Open Treatment 26665
    with Manipulation 26641
Fracture
    with Dislocation 26645-26650
        Open Treatment 26665
Fusion
    in Opposition 26820
Reconstruction
    from Finger 26550
    Opponensplasty 26490-26496
Repair
    Muscle 26508
    Muscle Transfer 26494
    Tendon Transfer 26510
Replantation 20824-20827
Sesamoidectomy 26185
Unlisted Services and Procedures 26989

Thymectomy 60520-60521
Sternal Split/Transthoracic
Approach 60521-60522
Transcervical Approach 60520

Thymotaxin
See Beta-2-Microglobulin

Thymus Gland 60520
Excision 60520-60521

Thyramine
See Amphetamine

Thyrocalcitonin
See Calcitonin

Thyroglobulin 84432
Antibody 86800

Thyroglossal Duct
Cyst
    Excision 60280-60281

Thyroidectomy
Partial 60210-60225
Secondary..........................60260
Total 60240, 60271
    Cervical Approach 60271
    for Malignancy
        Limited Neck Dissection 60252
        Radical Neck Dissection 60254
    Removal All Thyroid Tissue 60260
    Sternal Split/Transthoracic Approach ..60270

Thyroid Gland
Cyst
    Aspiration 60001
    Excision 60200
    Incision and Drainage 60000
    Injection 60001

Excision
    for Malignancy
        Limited Neck Dissection 60252
        Radical Neck Dissection 60254
    Partial 60210-60225
    Secondary 60260
    Total 60240, 60271
        Cervical Approach 60271
        Removal All Thyroid Tissue 60260
        Sternal Split/Transthoracic
        Approach 60270
        Transcervical Approach 60520
Metastatic Cancer
    Nuclear Imaging 78015-78018
Needle Biopsy 60100
Nuclear Medicine
    Imaging 78010
    Imaging for Metastases 78015-78018
    Imaging with Flow 78011
    Imaging with Uptake 78006-78007
    Metastases Uptake 78020
    Uptake 78000-78003
Radionuclide Therapy
    Ablation 79030
    Hyperthyroidism 79000-79001
    Metastases 79035
    Suppression 79020
Radiopharmaceutical Therapy
    Ablation 79030
    Metastases 79035
    Suppression 79020
Tumor
    Excision 60200

Thyroid Hormone Binding Ratio 84479

Thyroid Hormone Uptake 84479

Thyroid Stimulating Hormone (TSH) 80418, 80438-80440, 84443

Thyroid Stimulating Hormone Receptor ab
See Thyrotropin Releasing Hormone (TRH)

Thyroid Stimulating Immune Globulins 84445

Thyroid Stimulator, Long Acting
See Thyrotropin Releasing Hormone (TRH)

Thyroid Suppression Test
See Nuclear Medicine, Thyroid, Uptake

Thyrolingual Cyst
See Cyst, Thyroglossal Duct

Thyrotomy 31300

Thyrotropin Receptor ab
See Thyrotropin Releasing Hormone (TRH)

Thyrotropin Releasing Hormone (TRH) 80438-80439

Thyroxine
Free 84439
Neonatal 84437
Total 84436
True 84436

Thyroxine Binding Globulin 84442

Tibia
See Ankle
Arthroscopy Surgical 29891-29892
Craterization 27360, 27640
Cyst
    Excision 27635-27638
Diaphysectomy 27360, 27640
Excision 27360, 27640
    Epiphyseal Bar 20150
Fracture
    Arthroscopic Treatment 29855-29856
        Plafond 29892
    Closed Treatment 27824-27825
    Distal 27824-27828
    Intercondylar 27538-27540
    Malleolus 27760-27766, 27808-27814
    Open Treatment 27535-27536,
            27758-27759, 27826-27828
    Plateau 29855-29856
        Closed Treatment 27530-27536
    Shaft 27752-27759
    without Manipulation 27824
    with Manipulation 27825
Incision 27607
Osteoplasty
    Lengthening 27715
Prophylactic Treatment 27745
Reconstruction 27418
    at Knee 27440-27443, 27446
Repair 27720-27725
    Epiphysis 27477-27485, 27730-27742
    Osteochondritis Dissecans
        Arthroscopy 29892
    Osteotomy 27455-27457, 27705,
               27709-27712
    Pseudoarthrosis 27727
Saucerization 27360, 27640
Tumor
    Excision 27635-27638, 27645
X-Ray 73590

Tibial
Arteries
    See Artery, Tibial
Nerve
    Repair/Suture
        Posterior 64840

Tibiofibular Joint
Arthrodesis 27871
Dislocation 27830-27832
Disruption
    Open Treatment 27829
Fusion 27871

TIG
See Immune Globulins, Tetanus

Time
Bleeding
    See Bleeding Time
Prothrombin
    See Prothrombin Time
Reptilase
    See Thrombin Time

TORP (Total Ossicular Replacement Prosthesis) 69633, 69637

Torsion Swing Test 92546

Torula
See Cryptococcus

Torus Mandibularis
Tumor Excision 21031

Total
Abdominal Hysterectomy
   See Hysterectomy, Abdominal, Total
Bilirubin Level
   See Bilirubin, Total
Catecholamines
   See Catecholamines, Urine
Cystectomy
   See Bladder, Excision, Total
Dacryoadenectomy
   See Dacryoadenectomy, Total
Elbow Replacement
   See Replacement, Elbow, Total
Esophagectomy
   See Esophagectomy, Total
Gastrectomy
   See Excision, Stomach, Total
Hemolytic Complement
   See Complement, Hemolytic, Total
Hip Arthroplasty
   See Hip, Total Replacement
Knee Arthroplasty
   See Prosthesis, Knee
Mastectomies
   See Mastectomy
Ostectomy of Patella
   See Patellectomy
Splenectomy
   See Splenectomy, Total

Touroff Operation 37615
See Ligation, Artery, Neck

Toxicology Screen 80100-80103

Toxin, Botulinum
See Chemodenervation

Toxin Assay 87230

Toxoplasma
Antibody 86777-86778

Trabeculectomies
See Trabeculoplasty

Trabeculectomy ab Externo
in Absence of Previous Surgery 66170
with Scarring Previous Surgery 66172

Trabeculoplasty
by Laser Surgery.....................65855

Trabeculotomy ab Externo
Eye 65850

Trachea
Aspiration 31720
   Catheter 31720-31725
Catheterization 31700
Dilation 31630-31631

Endoscopy
   via Tracheostomy 31615
Excision
   Stenosis 31780-31781
Fistula
   without Plastic Repair 31820
   with Plastic Repair 31825
Fracture
   Endoscopy 31630
Incision
   Emergency 31603-31605
   Planned 31600-31601
   with Flaps 31610
Instillation
   Contrast Material 31708
Introduction
   Needle Wire 31730
Puncture
   Aspiration and/or Injection 31612
Reconstruction
   Carina 31766
   Cervical 31750
   Fistula 31755
   Intrathoracic 31760
Repair
   Cervical 31750
   Fistula 31755
   Intrathoracic 31760
   Stoma 31613-31614
Revision
   Stoma
      Scars 31830
Scar
   Revision 31830
Stenosis
   Excision 31780-31781
   Repair 31780-31781
Stoma
   Repair
      without Plastic Repair 31820
      with Plastic Repair 31825
   Revision
      Scars 31830
Tumor
   Excision
      Cervical 31785
      Thoracic 31786
Unlisted Services and Procedures
   Bronchi.........................31899
Wound
   Suture
      Cervical 31800
      Intrathoracic 31805

Tracheal
Stent
   Placement 31631
Tubes
   See Endotracheal Tube

Trachelectomy 57530
Radical 57531

Tracheloplasty
See Cervicoplasty

Trachelorrhaphy 57720

Tracheo-Esophageal Fistula
See Fistula, Tracheoesophageal

Tracheobronchoscopy
through Tracheostomy 31615

Tracheoplasty
Cervical 31750
Intrathoracic 31760
Tracheopharyngeal Fistulization 31755

Tracheostoma
Revision 31613-31614

Tracheostomy
Emergency 31603-31605
Planned 31600-31601
Revision
   Scar 31830
Surgical Closure
   without Plastic Repair 31820
   with Plastic Repair 31825
Tracheobronchoscopy through 31615
with Flaps 31610

Tracheotomy
Tube Change 31502

Tracking Tests (Ocular) 92545
See Ear, Nose and Throat

Tract, Urinary
See Urinary Tract

Traction Therapy
See Physical Medicine/Therapy/Occupational
Therapy
Manual 97140
Mechanical 97012

Tractotomy
Medulla 61470
Mesencephalon 61480

Training
Activities of Daily Living 97535, 99509
Biofeedback 90901-90911
Cognitive Skills 97532
Community/Work Reintegration 97537
Home Management 97535, 99509
Orthoptic/Pleoptic 92065
Orthotics 97504
Prosthetics 97520
Self Care 97535, 99509
Sensory Integration 97533
Walking (Physical Therapy) 97116
Wheelchair Management/Propulsion 97542

TRAM Flap
Breast Reconstruction 19367-19369

Trans-Scaphoperilunar
Fracture/Dislocation
   Closed Treatment 25680
   Open Treatment 25685

Transaminase
Glutamic Oxaloacetic 84450
Glutamic Pyruvic 84460

Transcatheter
Biopsy 37200
Embolization
   Percutaneous....................37204
      Cranial 61624-61626

Treacher-Collins Syndrome
Midface Reconstruction 21150-21151

Treatment, Tocolytic
See Tocolysis

Trendelenburg Operation
See Varicose Vein, Removal, Secondary Varicosity

Trephine Procedure
Sinusotomy
    Frontal 31070

Treponema Pallidum
Antibody
    Confirmation Test 86781
Antigen Detection
    Direct Fluorescence 87285

TRH
See Thyrotropin Releasing Hormone (TRH)

Triacylglycerol
See Triglycerides

Triacylglycerol Hydrolase
See Lipase

Tributyrinase
See Lipase

Trichiasis
Repair 67825
    Epilation, by Forceps 67820
    Epilation, by Other than Forceps 67825
    Incision of Lid Margin 67830
        with Free Mucous Membrane Graft .67835

Trichina
See Trichinella

Trichinella
Antibody 86784
Trichogram 96902

Trichrome Stain 88313

Tricuspid Valve
Excision 33460
Repair 33463-33465
Replacement 33465
Repositioning 33468

Tridymite
See Silica

Trigeminal Ganglia
See Gasserian Ganglion

Trigeminal Nerve
Destruction 64600-64610
Injection
    Anesthetic 64400
    Neurolytic 64600-64610

Trigeminal Tract
Stereotactic
    Create Lesion 61791

Trigger Finger Repair 26055

Trigger Point
Injection
    One or Two Muscle Groups 20552
    Two or More Muscle Groups 20553

Triglyceridase
See Lipase

Triglycerides 84478

Triglyceride Lipase
See Lipase

Trigonocephaly 21175

Triiodothyronine
Free 84481
Reverse 84482
Total 84480
True 84480

Triolean Hydrolase
See Lipase

Trioxopurine
See Uric Acid

Tripcellim
See Trypsin

Trisegmentectomy 47122

Trocar Biopsy
Bone Marrow 38221

Trochanteric Femur Fracture
See Femur, Fracture, Trochanteric

Trophoblastic Tumor GTT
See Hydatidiform Mole

Troponin .84484
Qualitative 84512
Quantitative 84484

Truncal Vagotomies
See Vagotomy, Truncal

Truncus Arteriosus
Repair 33786

Truncus Brachiocephalicus
See Artery, Brachiocephalic

Trunk, Brachiocephalic
See Artery, Brachiocephalic

Trypanosomiases
See Trypanosomiasis

Trypanosomiasis 86171, 86280

Trypsin
Duodenum 84485
Feces 84488-84490

Trypsin Inhibitor, Alpha 1-Antitrypsin
See Alpha-1 Antitrypsin

Trypure
See Trypsin

Tsalicylate Intoxication
See Salicylate

TSH
See Thyroid Stimulating Hormone

TSI
See Thyroid Stimulating Immunoglobulin

Tsutsugamushi Disease
See Scrub Typhus

TT
See Thrombin Time

TT-3
See Triiodothyronine, True

TT-4
See Thyroxine, True

Tubal Embryo Stage Transfer
See Embryo Transfer

Tubal Ligation 58600
Laparoscopic 58670
with Cesarean Delivery 58611

Tubal Occlusion
See Fallopian Tube
with Cesarean Delivery
    See Fallopian Tube, Occlusion; Occlusion
    Create Lesion
        See Fallopian Tube, Occlusion; Occlusion,
        Fallopian Tube

Tubal Pregnancy 59121
with Salpingectomy and/or
Oophorectomy .59120

Tuba Auditoria (Auditiva)
See Eustachian Tube

Tube Change
Tracheotomy 31502

Tube, Fallopian
See Fallopian Tube

Tube Placement
Endoscopic
    Bile Duct, Pancreatic Duct 43268
    Nasobiliary, Nasopancreatic
        for Drainage 43267
Gastrostomy Tube 43750
Nasogastric Tube 43752
Orogastric Tube 43752

Tubectomy
See Excision, Fallopian Tube

Tubed Pedicle Flap
Formation .15570-15576

Tubercleplasty
Tibia
    Anterior 27418

Tubercle Bacilli
Culture 87116

Tuberculin Test
See Skin, Tests, Tuberculosis

Wrist
    Excision 25075
    Radical Resection 25077
Spinal Cord
    Excision 63275-63290
Stomach
    Excision 43610-43611
Talus 28100-28103
    Excision 27647
Tarsal 28104-28107
    Excision 28171
Temporal Bone
    Removal 69970
Testis
    Excision 54530-54535
Thorax
    Excision 21555-21556
    Radical Resection 21557
Thyroid
    Excision 60200
Tibia 27365-27638
    Excision 27645
Torus Mandibularis 21031
Trachea
    Excision
        Cervical 31785
        Thoracic 31786
Ulna 25120-25126, 25170
    Excision 24120
    with Allograft
        Excision 24126
    with Autograft
        Excision 24125
Ureter
    Excision 52355
Urethra 52234-52240, 53220
    Excision 52355
Uterus
    Excision 58140-58145
Vagina
    Excision 57135
Vertebra
    Additional Segment
        Excision 22116
    Cervical
        Excision 22100
    Lumbar 22102
    Thoracic
        Excision 22101
Wrist 25075-25077, 25135-25136
    Radical Resection 25077

Tunica Vaginalis

Hydrocele
    Aspiration 55000
    Excision 55040-55041
    Repair 55060

Turbinate

Excision 30130-30140
Fracture
    Therapeutic 30930
Injection 30200
Submucous Resection
    Nose Excision 30140

Turbinate Mucosa

Cauterization 30801-30802

Turcica, Sella

See Sella Turcica

Turnbuckle Jacket 29020-29025

Removal 29715

TURP

See Prostatectomy, Transurethral

Tylectomy

See Breast, Excision, Lesion

Tylenol

Urine 82003

Tympanic Membrane

Create Stoma 69433-69436
Incision 69420-69421
Reconstruction 69620
Repair 69450, 69610

Tympanic Nerve

Excision 69676

Tympanolysis 69450

Tympanometry 92567

See Audiologic Function Tests

Tympanoplasty

See Myringoplasty
Radical or Complete 69645
    with Ossicular Chain Reconstruction ..69646
without Mastoidectomy 69631
    with Ossicular Chain Reconstruction ..69632
    and Synthetic Prosthesis 69633
with Antrotomy or Mastoidotomy 69635
    with Ossicular Chain Reconstruction ..69636
    and Synthetic Prosthesis 69637
with Mastoidectomy 69641
    with Intact or Reconstructed Wall ...69643
    and Ossicular Chain Reconstruction .69644
    with Ossicular Chain Reconstruction ..69642

Tympanostomy 69433-69436

Tympanotomy

See Myringotomy

Typhoid Vaccine 90690-90693

AKD 90693
Oral 90690
Polysaccharide 90691

Typhus

Endemic
    See Murine Typhus
Mite-Borne
    See Scrub Typhus
Sao Paulo
    See Rocky Mountain Spotted Fever
Tropical
    See Scrub Typhus

Typing, Blood

See Blood Typing

Typing, HLA

See HLA Typing

Typing, Tissue

See Tissue Typing

Tyrosine 84510

Tzank Smear 87207

T Cell Leukemia Virus I, Human

See HTLV I

T Cell Leukemia Virus II, Human

See HTLV II

T Cell Leukemia Virus II Antibodies, Human

See Antibody, HTLV-II

T Cell Leukemia Virus I Antibodies, Adult

See Antibody, HTLV-I

T Lymphotropic Virus Type III Antibodies, Human

See Antibody, HIV

U

Uchida Procedure

See Tubal Ligation

UDP Galactose Pyrophosphorylase

See Galactose-1-Phosphate, Uridyl Transferase

UFR

See Uroflowmetry

Ulcer

Anal
    See Anus, Fissure
Decubitus
    See Debridement; Pressure Ulcer (Decubitus);
    Skin Graft and Flap
Pinch Graft 15050
Pressure 15920-15999
Stomach
    Excision 43610

Ulcerative, Cystitis

See Cystitis, Interstitial

Ulna

See Arm, Lower; Elbow; Humerus; Radius
Arthrodesis
    Radioulnar Joint
        with Resection 25830
Arthroplasty
    with Implant 25442
Centralization or Wrist 25335
Craterization 24147, 25150-25151
Cyst
    Excision 24125-24126, 25120-25126
Diaphysectomy 24147, 25150-25151
Excision 24147
    Abscess 24138
    Complete 25240
    Epiphyseal Bar 20150
    Partial 25145-25151, 25240

Injection
   Radiologic 50684, 50690
Insertion
   Catheter 50393
   Stent 50393, 50947, 52332-52334
   Tube 50688
Lesion
   Destruction 52354
Lithotripsy 52353
Lysis
   Adhesions 50715-50725
Manometric Studies
   Pressure 50686
Meatotomy 52290
Nuclear Medicine
   Reflux Study 78740
Postcaval
   See Retrocaval Ureter
Reconstruction 50700
   with Intestines 50840
Reflux Study 78740
Reimplantation 51565
Removal
   Anastomosis 50830
   Calculus 50610-50630, 50961,
          51060-51065, 52320-52325
   Foreign Body 50961
Repair 50900
   Anastomosis 50740-50825
   Continent Diversion 50825
   Deligation 50940
   Fistula 50920-50930
   Lysis Adhesions 50715-50725
   Ureterocele 51535
      Ectopic 52301
      Orthotopic 52300
   Urinary Undiversion 50830
Replacement
   with Intestines 50840
Resection 52355
Revision
   Anastomosis 50727-50728
Suture 50900
   Deligation 50940
   Fistula 50920-50930
Tube
   Change 50688
   Insertion 50688
Tumor Resection 52355
Unlisted Services and Procedures ..50949, 53899
X-Ray with Contrast
   Guide Catheter 74480
   Guide Dilation 74485

Ureteral

Catheterization
   See Catheterization, Ureter
Guide Wire Insertion 52334
Meatotomy
   See Meatotomy, Ureteral
Splinting 50400-50405
Stent Insertion 52332

Ureterectomy 50650-50660
Partial 50220, 50546
Total 50548

Ureterocalycostomy 50750

Ureterocele
Excision 51535
Fulguration
      Ectopic 52301
      Orthotopic 52300
Incision 51535
Repair 51535
Resection
      Ectopic 52301
      Orthotopic 52300

Ureterocolon Conduit 50815

Ureteroenterostomy 50800
Revision 50830

Ureterography
Injection Procedure 50684

Ureteroileal Conduit 50820
Cystectomy 51590
Removal 50830

Ureterolithotomy 50610-50630
Laparoscopy 50945
Transvesical 51060

Ureterolysis
for Ovarian Vein Syndrome 50722
for Retrocaval Ureter 50725
for Retroperitoneal Fibrosis 50715

Ureteroneocystostomy ...50780-50785,
            50830, 51565
Laparoscopic 50947-50948

Ureteroplasty 50700

Ureteropyelography 50951, 52005
Injection Procedure 50684, 50690

Ureteropyelostomy 50740

Ureteroscopy
Dilation
   Intra-Renal Stricture 52346
   Ureter 52344-52345
Third Stage with Cystourethroscopy 52351
   Biopsy 52354
   Destruction 52354
   Lithotripsy 52353
   Removal
     Calculus 52352
   Tumor Excision 52355

Ureterosigmoidostomy 50810
Revision 50830

Ureterostomy 50860, 50951
Injection Procedure 50684
Manometric Studies 50686

Ureterostomy Tube
Change 50688

Ureterotomy 50600
Insertion Indwelling Stent 50605

Ureteroureterostomy 50760-50770,
            50830

Urethra
Abscess
   Incision and Drainage 53040
Artificial Sphincter
   Repair 53449
Biopsy 52204, 53200
Destruction 52214-52224
Dilation 52260-52265, 53600-53621
   General 53665
   Suppository and/or
     Instillation 53660-53661
Diverticulum
   See Urethral Diverticulum
Drainage
   Extravasation 53080-53085
Endoscopy 52000
   Biopsy 52204, 52354
   Catheterization 52010
   Destruction 52354, 52400
   Evacuation
     Clot 52001
   Excision
     Tumor 52355
   Exploration 52351
   Incision
     Ejaculatory Duct 52347
     Injection of Implant Material 51715
     Lithotripsy 52353
   Removal
     Calculus 52352
   Resection
     Ejaculatory Duct 52347
     Vasectomy 52347
     Vasotomy 52347
Excision
   Diverticulum 53230-53235
   Total
     Female 53210
     Male 53215
Incision 53000-53010
   Meatus 53020-53025
Incision and Drainage 53060
Insertion
   Catheter 53670-53675
   Stent 52282
Lesion
   Destruction 53265
   Excision 53260
Paraurethral Gland
   Incision and Drainage 53060
Polyp
   Destruction 53260
   Excision 53260
Pressure Profile 51772
Prolapse
   Destruction 53275
   Excision 53275
   Repair 53275
Prostate
   Transurethral Balloon Dilation 52510
Radiotracer 52250
Reconstruction 53410-53440, 53445
   and Bladder 51800-51820
   Complications 54340-54348

Hypospadias
 One Stage 54322-54328
 Second Stage 54308-54316
 Third Stage 54318
Meatus 53450-53460
Removal
 Calculus 52310-52315
 Foreign Body 52310-52315
 Urethral Stent 52310-52315
Repair
 Diverticulum 53240, 53400-53405
 Fistula . . .45820-45825, 53400-53405, 53520
 Sphincter 57220
 Stricture 53400-53405
 Urethrocele 57230
 Wound 53502-53515
Skene's Gland
 Incision and Drainage 53060
Sphincter .52277
 Electromyography 51784-51785
  Needle 51785
 Insertion
  Prosthesis 53444
 Reconstruction 53445
 Removal
  Prosthesis 53446-53447
 Repair
  Prosthesis 53449
 Replacement
  Prosthesis 53448
Suture
 Fistula 45820-45825, 53520
 to Bladder 51840-51841
 Wound 53502-53515
Tumor
 Destruction 53220
 Excision 53220
Unlisted Services and Procedures 53899
Urethrocystography 74450-74455
Urethrotomy 52270-52276
X-Ray with Contrast 74450-74455

Urethral

Diverticulum
 Marsupialization 53240
Meatus, Dorsal
 See Epispadias
Sphincter
 Biofeedback Training 90911
 Insertion
  Prosthesis 53444
 Removal
  Prosthesis 53446-53447
 Replacement
  Prosthesis 53448
Stenosis
 Dilation .52281
Stent
 Insertion .52282
 Removal
  Bladder 52310-52315
  Urethra 52310-52315
Stricture
 Dilation 52281, 53600-53621
 Injection
  Steroids 52283
Syndrome
 Cystourethroscopy 52285

Urethrectomy

Total
 Female 53210
 Male 53215

Urethrocele

See Urethra, Prolapse

Urethrocystography 74450-74455

Contrast and/or Chain 51605
Retrograde 51610
Voiding 51600

Urethrocystopexy

See Vesicourethropexy

Urethromeatoplasty 53450-53460

Urethropexy 51840-51841

Urethroplasty 46744-46746

First Stage .53400
One Stage
 Hypospadias 54322-54328
Reconstruction
 Female Urethra 53430
 Male Anterior Urethra 53410
 Prostatic/Membranous Urethra
  First Stage 53420
  One Stage 53415
  Second Stage 53425
Second Stage 53405
 Hypospadias 54308-54316
Third Stage
 Hypospadias 54318

Urethrorrhaphy 53502-53515

Urethroscopy

See Endoscopy, Urethra

Urethrostomy 53000-53010

Urethrotomy 53000-53010

Direct Vision
 with Cystourethroscopy 52276
Internal 52601, 52647-52648
with Cystourethroscopy
 Female .52270
 Male 52275

Uric Acid

Blood 84550
Other Source 84560
Urine 84560

Uridyltransferase, Galactose-1-Phosphate

See Galactose-1-Phosphate, Uridyl Transferase

Uridylyltransferase, Galactosephosphate

See Galactose-1-Phosphate, Uridyl Transferase

Urinalysis 81000-81099

Automated 81001, 81003
Glass Test 81020
Microalbumin 82043-82044
Microscopic .81015
Pregnancy Test 81025

Qualitative .81005
Routine 81002
Screen 81007
Semiquantitative 81005
Unlisted Services and Procedures 81099
Volume Measurement 81050
without Microscopy 81002

Urinary Bladder

See Bladder

Urinary Catheter Irrigation

See Irrigation, Catheter

Urinary Concentration Test

See Water Load Test

Urinary Sphincter, Artificial

See Prosthesis, Urethral Sphincter

Urinary Tract

X-Ray with Contrast 74400-74425

Urine

Albumin
 See Albumin, Urine
Blood
 See Blood, Urine
Colony Count 87086
Pregnancy Test 81025
Tests 81001

Urobilinogen

Feces 84577
Urine .84578-84583

Urodynamic Tests

Cystometrogram 51725-51726
Electromyography Studies
 Needle .51785
Stimulus Evoked Response 51792
Urethra Pressure Profile 51772
Uroflowmetry 51736-51741
Voiding Pressure Studies
 Bladder .51795
 Intra-Abdominal 51797

Uroflowmetry 51736-51741

Urography

Antegrade .74425
Infusion 74410-74415
Intravenous 74400-74415
Retrograde .74420

Uroporphyrin 84120

Urothromboplastin

See Thromboplastin

Uterine

Adhesion
 See Adhesions, Intrauterine
Cervix
 See Cervix
Endoscopies
 See Endoscopy, Uterus
Haemorrhage
 See Hemorrhage, Uterus

Strands
Discission 67030
Severing 67031
Subtotal 67010

VLDL
See Lipoprotein, Blood

VMA
See Vanillylmandelic Acid

Vocal Cords
Injection
Endoscopy .31513
Therapeutic 31570-31571

Voice Box
See Larynx

Voice Button 31611

Voiding Pressure Studies
Abdominal 51797
Bladder 51795

Volatiles 84600

Volhard's Test
See Water Load Test

Volkman Contracture 25315-25316

Volume Reduction, Lung
See Lung Volume Reduction

Von Kraske Proctectomy
See Proctectomy, Partial

VP
See Voiding Pressure Studies

Vulva
Abscess
Incision and Drainage 56405
Excision
Complete 56625, 56633-56640
Partial 56620, 56630-56632
Radical 56630-56631, 56633-56640
Complete 56633-56640
Partial 56630-56632
Simple
Complete 56625
Partial .56620
Lesion
Destruction 56501-56515
Perineum
Biopsy 56605-56606
Incision and Drainage 56405
Repair
Obstetric 59300

Vulvectomy
Complete 56625, 56633-56640
Partial 56620, 56630-56632
Radical 56630-56631, 56633-56640
Complete
with Bilateral Inguinofemoral
Lymphadenectomy 56637
with Inguinofemoral, Iliac, and Pelvic
Lymphadenectomy 56640
with Unilateral Inguinofemoral
Lymphadenectomy 56634

Partial
with Bilateral Inguinofemoral
Lymphadenectomy 56632
with Unilateral Inguinofemoral
Lymphadenectomy 56631
Simple
Complete .56625
Partial 56620

VZIG
See Immune Globulins, Varicella-Zoster

V Flap Procedure
One Stage Distal Hypospadias Repair 54322

W

W-Plasty
See Skin, Adjacent Tissue Transfer

WADA Activation Test 95958
See Electroencephalography

WAIS-R 96100

Waldius Procedure 27445

Wall, Abdominal
See Abdominal Wall

Walsh Modified Radical Prostatectomy
See Prostatectomy

Warts
Flat
Destruction 17110-17111

Washing
Sperm 58323

Wasserman Test
See Syphilis Test

Wassmund Procedure
Osteotomy
Maxilla 21206

Waterston Procedure 33755

Water Load Test 89365

Water Wart
See Molluscum Contagiosum

Watson-Jones Procedure 27695-27698

Wave, Ultrasonic Shock
See Ultrasound

WBC
See White Blood Cell

Webbed
Toe
Repair 28280

Wedge Excision
Osteotomy 21122

Wedge Resection
Ovary 58920

Well-Baby Care 99381, 99391, 99432

Wellness Behavior
See Evaluation and Management, Health
Behavior

Wernicke-Posadas Disease
See Coccidioidomycosis

Westergren Test
See Sedimentation Rate, Blood Cell

Western Blot
HIV 86689
Protein 84181-84182
Tissue Analysis 88371-88372

Wheelchair Management/Propulsion
See Physical Medicine/Therapy/Occupational
Therapy
Training 97542

Wheeler Knife Procedure
See Discission, Cataract

Wheeler Procedure
See Blepharoplasty, Entropion
Blepharoplasty 67924
Discission Secondary Membranous
Cataract 66820

Whipple Procedure 48150

Whirlpool Therapy 97022
See Physical Medicine/Therapy/Occupational
Therapy

Whitemead Operation
See Hemorrhoidectomy, Complex

White Blood Cell
Alkaline Phosphatase 85540
Antibody 86021
Count 85048
Differential 85007, 85009
Histamine Release Test 86343
Phagocytosis .86344
Transfusion
See Leukocyte, Transfusion

Whitman Astragalectomy
See Talus, Excision

Whitman Procedure 27120

Wick Catheter Technique 20950

Widal Serum Test
See Agglutinin, Febrile

Window
Oval
See Oval Window
Round
See Round Window

X-Ray Tomography, Computed

See CAT Scan

Xa, Coagulation Factor

See Thrombokinase

Y

Z

CPT Assistant . . .
your monthly coding advisor

You know how critical it is to have the "hot" coding information first . . . to receive coding commentaries that give you insight behind confusing coding issues . . . obtain tips and interpretations that are accurate and reliable and save you time and unnecessary errors in determining the right codes.

CPT Assistant is the only coding newsletter that can offer you the rationale behind the codes.
And, only *CPT Assistant* is published by the source of CPT codes – The American Medical Association.

▼ ***Practical advice you can use.***
Find articles written by the industry's top coding specialists and the latest information on new codes and how to interpret them.

▼ ***Timely articles keep you current.***
Every issue features articles designed to demystify certain codes and give you the latest trends and developments in coding.

▼ ***Clinical vignettes.***
Through detailed case studies we'll demonstrate the practical application of codes.

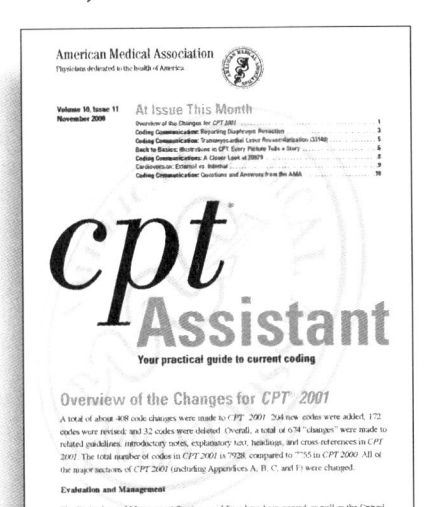

▼ ***Coding communication.***
Discover timely information on codes and trends in the industry.

▼ ***Questions and answers.*** Your direct link to the coding experts at the AMA. Find the answers to the questions professional coders ask most often.

▼ ***Anatomical illustrations, charts, and graphs for quick reference.***

CPT Assistant is a must for users of *CPT Professional*. The arrow symbol " ⊃ " found next to various codes in *CPT Professional*, directs you to the exact issue of *CPT Assistant* that contains further information on that code.

Subscribe today and save 15% off your newsletter subscription.

Order #: CA500900BMP

SAVE $44.85 – Price: $254.15/two-years
SAVE $25.35 – Price: $143.65/one-year

SAVE $30.75 – AMA Member Price: $174.25/two-year
SAVE $17.25 – AMA Member Price: $97.75/one-year

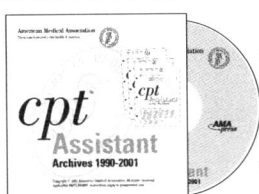

A complete digital library of *CPT Assistant* is available on CD-ROM – from its inception in 1990 through 2001. Just point and click and you're instantly in touch with the actual *CPT Assistant* articles referenced in *CPT Professional*. Coming March 2002.

Order # OP511302BMP (single user) Price: $235.00 AMA Member Price: $185.00

Call 800-621-8335 *Today to Order or Order Online at www.amapress.org*

Prices do not include shipping & handling, or state sales tax if applicable. Visa, MasterCard, and Amex/Optima accepted.
CPT is a registered trademark of the American Medical Association.

American Medical Association
Physicians dedicated to the health of America

Comprehensive Coding Resources . . .
From the Publisher of CPT®

The American Medical Association, the source of CPT codes, offers so many ways to help health care professionals code more accurately and efficiently. Whether you are new to CPT coding or are a veteran coder, stay up-to-date with the CPT references that simplify the coding process.

CPT 2002 Professional Edition – The code book designed for the professional coder! The AMA's most comprehensive coding resource in spiral-bound format. Contains more than 700 code changes and the new Category III "Emerging Technology" subsection. Includes illustrations, color-coded keys, and references to the *CPT Assistant* newsletter and *CPT Changes*.
EP054102BMP Price: $74.95 AMA Member Price: $64.95

CPT Changes 2002: An Insider's View – A reference tool for understanding each of the more than 700 code changes found in CPT 2002. Every new, revised, or deleted code is listed along with a detailed rationale for the change.
OP512902BMP Price: $49.95 AMA Member Price: $39.95

CPT Assistant – A monthly newsletter that brings you the kind of coding information you need to keep your claims running smoothly. Articles include timely coding information, case studies, clinical vignettes, coding scenarios, and answers to tough coding questions.
CA500900BMP Price: $169.00 (One-Year) AMA Member Price: $115.00 (One-Year)

CPT Assistant Archives 1990-2001 – A complete digital library of the AMA's CPT coding newsletter from 1990 through 2001 on one easy-to-use fully searchable CD-ROM. Annual updates are available. *Coming April 2002*
OP511302BMP Price: $235.00 (Single User) AMA Member Price: $185.00 (Single User)

CPT 2002 for Hospital Outpatient Services – A specially annotated version of CPT containing the most recent instructional information released by HCFA regarding hospital use of CPT in Medicare. *Coming February 2002*
OP055002BMP Price: $56.95

CPT Companion – The most comprehensive source of frequently asked questions and answers regarding CPT codes. An excellent source of examples, discussion points, and exam questions for the classroom! *Available Now*
OP083101BMP Price: $49.95 AMA Member Price: $39.95

CodeManager 2002 – The ultimate coders' resource, providing eight essential coding tools on one CD-ROM. This easy-to-learn software package puts the most up-to-date versions of the most widely used medical coding references at your fingertips. Three updates per year are included to keep you current. *Coming December 2001*
OP081702BMP Price: $449.00 (Single User) AMA Member Price: $349.00 (Single User)

Call **800 621-8335** to order or to request a catalog of all our coding and reimbursement, practice management, and reference products.
Or visit us online at **www.amapress.org**.

Prices do not include shipping & handling, or state sales tax if applicable. Visa, MasterCard, and Amex/Optima accepted. CPT is a registered trademark of the American Medical Association.

American Medical Association
Physicians dedicated to the health of America

Order Your *ICD-9-CM 2002* and
HCPCS 2002 main books from the AMA

AMA Physician ICD-9-CM 2002 Volumes 1 & 2

This best-selling code book provides the most up-to-date information on medical diagnosis coding. Stay current on the new ICD-9-CM code changes that will impact code accuracy and claims submission. Provide your email address when ordering to receive Email Delivered Code Change Special reports. These reports will help you stay current on important code developments and changes.

Spiral Bound Edition

Order #: OP065102BMP
Price: $79.95
AMA Member Price: $69.95

Softbound Edition

Order #: OP065302BMP
Price: $79.95
AMA Member Price: $69.95

New symbols, just like the symbols in CPT, alert the coder of new and revised codes and text

Clinically oriented illustrations and definitions enhance clarity and aid in code selection

Color-coded bars highlight unspecified, nonspecific, and manifestation coding situtations

New intuitive color-coded symbol alerts the coder to whether a 4th or 5th digit is required

Dictionary–style headers and QuickFlip Color Tabs help you find the right code or section

Each page has a key to common symbols; saves time searching

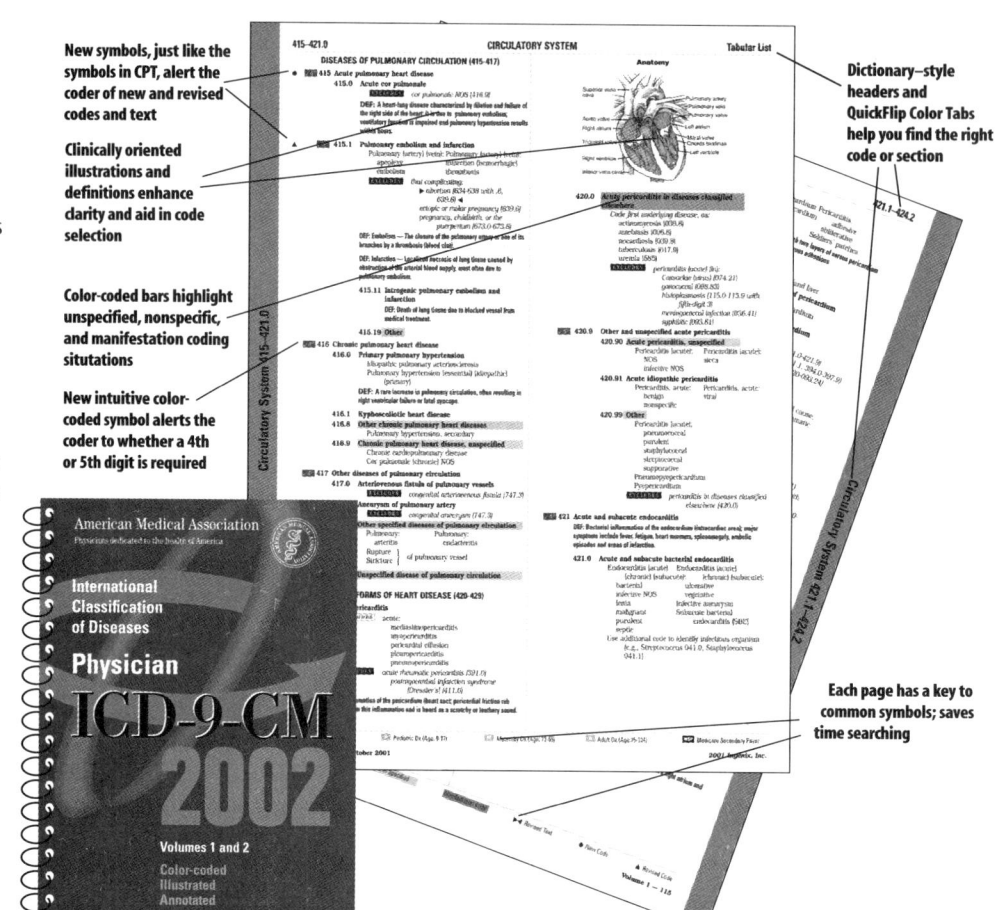

AMA HCPCS 2002

Everything You Need From a Single Source.

The AMA's guide to Medicare's National Level II Codes for DME, medical supplies, and drugs. Contains the mandated changes and new codes for 2002.

- Detailed Annotations and Coding Advice make code selection easier and more accurate.
- Enhanced color-coded icons flag codes with special Medicare instructions and coverage issues.
- Modifier Information.
- Improved Medicare Carriers Manual and Coverage Issues Manual Reference.
- Expanded Front Index.
- Payor Appendix.

Softbound

Order #: OP095102BMP Price: $79.95 AMA Member Price: $69.95

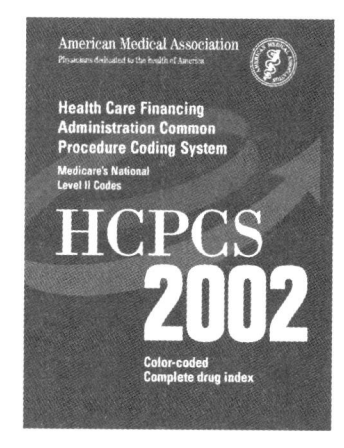

Call *800-621-8335* Today to Order or Order Online at *www.amapress.org*

Prices do not include shipping & handling, or state sales tax if applicable. Visa, MasterCard, and Amex/Optima accepted.
CPT is a registered trademark of the American Medical Association.

American Medical Association
Physicians dedicated to the health of America

Teach Coding with Confidence
with the AMA's Coding Educational Resources

The ***Coding Trainer's Package***, a unique collection of five educational coding resources, is perfect for trainers, coding supervisors, instructors, new coders and veteran coders alike.

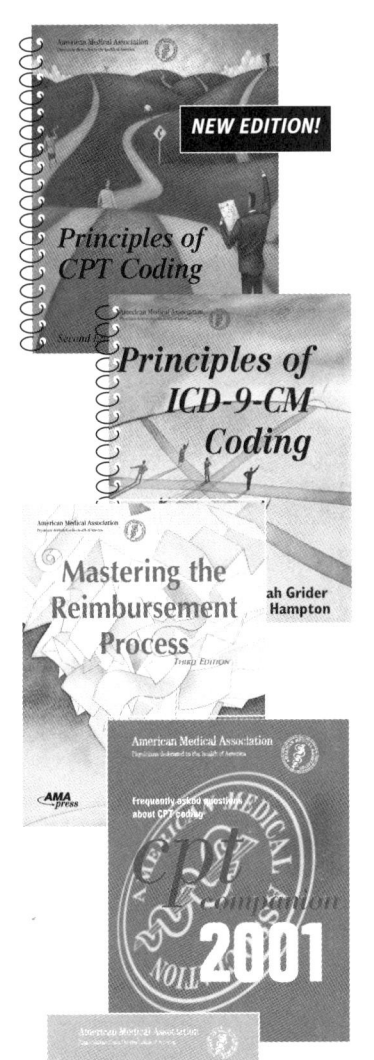

Principles of CPT Coding, Second Edition is a newly revised training and educational tool that covers the basic to intermediate concepts of CPT coding. Chapters include all areas of CPT – from the history and basic coding concepts, to E/M guidelines and medical specialties, to chapters on hospital outpatient reporting and CPT-5. Ample use is made of illustrations, charts and diagrams, coding tips, practical examples and chapter quizzes, all to help facilitate faster learning.
OP501001BMP   *Price: $54.95*   ***AMA Member Price: $44.95***

Principles of ICD-9-CM Coding is an essential coding textbook designed to help students and professional coders gain a better understanding of ICD-9-CM coding and its relationship to the reimbursement process. *Principles* will help beginning and veteran coders learn how to apply coding conventions, interpret basic coding guidelines for outpatient care, and assign ICD-9-CM codes to the highest level of specificity. Includes chapter learning objectives and section checkpoint exercises, history, coding trivia, tips and clinical examples.
OP065800BMP   *Price: $54.00*   ***AMA Member Price: $45.00***

Mastering the Reimbursement Process, Third Edition leads the reader to a comprehensive understanding of health insurance, claims submission, and the follow-up necessary to get paid by third-party payers. Revised and updated with 200 new pages, this outstanding text contains significant new material about Medicare program changes, patient confidentiality, sample position descriptions and tips on appeals. Also includes entirely new chapters covering Electronic Data Interchange (EDI), compliance programs and OIG, and privacy, confidentiality and HIPPA.
OP080000BMP   *Price: $54.95*   ***AMA Member Price: $44.95***

CPT Companion is the most comprehensive source of frequently asked questions and answers regarding CPT codes. Questions are drawn from the volumes of correspondence answered by the AMA each year and the answers have been subjected to careful medical review. An excellent source of examples, discussion points, and exam questions for the classroom!
OP083101BMP   *Price: $49.95*   ***AMA Member Price: $39.95***

CPT Changes 2002 serves as a reference tool to understanding each of the more than 700 code changes found in *CPT 2002*. Every new, revised and deleted code is listed along with a detailed rationale for the change. References to new, revised and deleted CPT codes, cited in *CPT Changes*, are now included in *CPT Professional*.
OP512902BMP   *Price: $49.95*   ***AMA Member Price: $39.95***

Order all five with the *Coding Trainer's Package* today and save 15%!
Order #: OP506702BMP   *Price $224.23*   ***AMA Member Price: $182.58***

Call 800 621-8335 or order online at www.amapress.org

Prices do not include shipping & handling, or state sales tax if applicable. Visa, MasterCard, and Amex/Optima accepted. CPT is a registered trademark of the American Medical Association.

American Medical Association
Physicians dedicated to the health of America

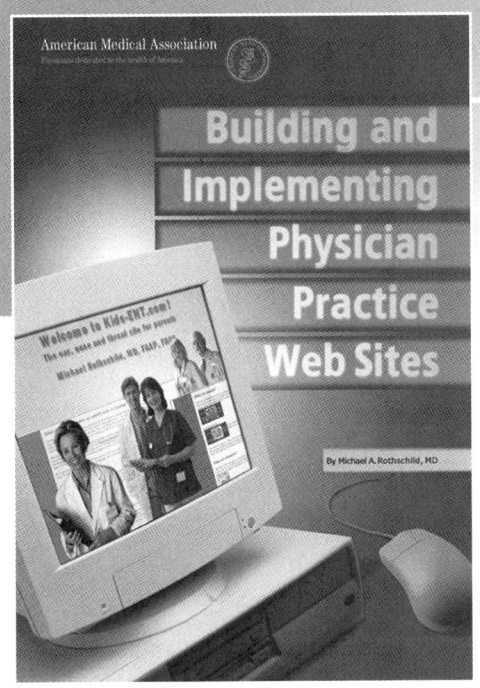

How to Build Physician Practice Web Sites

The internet presents incredible opportunities to promote and expand your medical practice. To stay competitive, building a successful web site has become more a necessity than an option. AMA Press now offers all the information you need to create a dynamic, vibrant web site in one valuable resource: *Building and Implementing Physician Practice Web Sites.*

Written by Michael A. Rothschild, MD, an expert in the online marketing of medical practices, this book provides a comprehensive understanding of web site development, including how to:

- Create, design, and post the site
- Avoid common errors in web site creation
- Include the web site as part of an integrated marketing strategy
- Register a domain, and host/promote the site
- Understand the ethical and legal issues regarding "cybermedicine"

To Order:

Call AMA Press at: 800 621-8335

Visit our secure Web site at: www.amapress.com

Order #: OP318200BMA
Price: $50.00
AMA member price: $45.00

VISA, MasterCard, American Express and Optima accepted. State sales tax and shipping/ handling charges apply. Satisfaction guaranteed or return within 30 days for full refund.

American Medical Association
Physicians dedicated to the health of America